Retail MARKETING
Second Edition

ROBERT F. LUSCH
University of Oklahoma

PATRICK DUNNE
Texas Tech University

RANDALL GEBHARDT
Fitch Inc.

COLLEGE DIVISION South-Western Publishing Co.
Cincinnati Ohio

Sponsoring Editor: Randy G. Haubner
Production Editor: Rebecca Roby
Production House: WordCrafters Editorial Services, Inc.
Cover and Internal Design: Joseph M. Devine
Cover Photo: © Ken Glaser, New Orleans
Photo Editor: Kathryn A. Russell
Marketing Manager: Scott D. Person

SF62BA

Copyright © 1993

by SOUTH-WESTERN PUBLISHING CO.

Cincinnati, Ohio

ALL RIGHTS RESERVED

The text of this publication, or any part thereof, may not be reproduced or transmitted in any form or by any means, electronic or mechanical, including photocopying, recording, storage in an information retrieval system, or otherwise, without the prior written permission of the publisher.

ISBN: 0-538-82697-5

1 2 3 4 5 6 7 8 9 0 D 10 9 8 7 6 5 4 3 2

Printed in the United States of America

Library of Congress Cataloging-in-Publication Data

Lusch, Robert F.
    Retail marketing / Robert Lusch, Patrick Dunne, Randall Gebhardt. —2nd ed.
      p. cm.
    Rev. ed. of: Retail management. 1990.
    Includes index.
    ISBN 0-538-82697-5
    1. Retail trade—Management. 2. Marketing. I. Dunne, Patrick M. II. Gebhardt, Randall. III. Lusch, Robert F. Retail management. IV. Title.
HF5429.L785 1993
658.8'7—dc20   92-2394
                                                                                    CIP

 This book is printed on acid-free paper that meets Environmental Protection Agency standards for recycled paper.

*This text is dedicated to the
family and associates of
SAM WALTON.
May they be able to continue
the many contributions
he made to the field
of Retailing.*

PHOTO CREDITS

The authors would like to acknowledge and thank the following persons and organizations for providing photos in this book:

Retail Planning Associates (RPA) for photos on pages 8, 12, 19, 48, 55 (right), 74, 88, 95, 112 (right), 133, 144, 147, 191, 242, 253, 265 (left), 292, 330, 363, 374, 407, 493, 535, 630, and 633.
Billy E. Barnes (© Billy E. Barnes/Stock, Boston), for photo on page 225.
Gabor Demjen (© Gabor Demjen/Stock, Boston) for photo on page 217.
Steve Elmore (© Steve Elmore/Stock Market) for part operner photos on pages 68 and 338.
McDonald's Restaurants of Canada Limited for photo on page 162.
Northland Volkswagen for location photo on page 34.
Kunio Owaki (© Kunio Owaki/Stock Market) for part opener photo on page 546.
H. Armstrong Roberts for photos on pages 320 and 549.
John M. Roberts (© John M. Roberts/Stock Market) for part opener photo on page 478.
Pete Steiner (© Pete Steiner/Stock Market) for part opener photo on page 214.
Steve Steiner (©Steve Steiner/Stock Market) for part opener photo on page xv.

CONTENTS

PART 1 INTRODUCTION TO RETAIL MARKETING

1 PERSPECTIVES ON RETAILING   1

What is Retailing? 5   Retailing in Action 1.1: International Trends: Russian Retail System Falters 6   Categorizing Retailers 7   Entry Barriers 13   Retail Marketing Management 14   A Retail Career 16   Retailing in Action 1.2: Careers in Retailing: The Women Who Lead The Limited, Inc. 19   Methods of Retail Management 22   The Orientations of This Book 23   The Book Outline 25   Summary 27

2 STRATEGIC PLANNING IN RETAILING   30

The Need for Planning 31   The Strategic Planning Process 32   Statement of Mission 32   Statement of Objectives 34   Retailing in Action 2.1: Sears, Roebuck and Company's Mission Statement in Its Early Years 35   Statement of Market Position 47   Analysis of Opportunities in the Retail Marketplace 51   Retailing in Action 2.2: Quality Japanese Service 53   Strategies 54   Control System 59   Strategic Planning in Large Retailing Firms 62   Key Mistakes in Strategic Planning 63   Summary 64

PART 2 THE RETAILING MARKETPLACE

3 UNDERSTANDING RETAIL CUSTOMERS   69

The Importance of Understanding the Retail Customer 71   Socioeconomic Environment 75   Demographic Characteristics 78   Retailing in Action 3.1: Worldwide Changes in Household Structure 84   Psychographic Characteristics 86   Behavioral Characteristics 89   Retailing in Action 3.2: What Motivates Shopping Trips? 94   Retail Patronage Model 100   Summary 107

4 COMPETITION IN RETAILING   110

Evolution of Retail Competition 111   Competition from Nonstore Retailers 118   A Model of Retail Competition 120   Types of Competition 131   Retailing in Action 4.1: Competing with Nonprice Variables 132   Trends in International Retailing 135   Retailing in Action 4.2: Changing Competitive Structure in Food Retailing in the Reunified Germany 137   Summary 138

5 UNDERSTANDING RETAILING'S ROLE IN THE CHANNEL   142

The System Is the Solution 143   The Marketing System 145   Conventional Marketing Channels 154   Vertical Marketing Systems 155   Retailing in Action 5.1: Using Cooperation to Strengthen Vertical Marketing Systems 156   Retailing in Action 5.2: International Expansion in Franchising 161   Managing Retailer/Supplier Relations 166   Summary 175

6 UNDERSTANDING THE LEGAL ENVIRONMENT   180

Pricing Constraints 182   Promotion Constraints 192   Retailing in Action 6.1: You Be the Judge 195   Product Constraints 196   Channel Constraints 201   Mergers and Acquisitions 206   Other Federal Laws 208   Retailing in Action 6.2: States Expand Their Legal Role in Mergers 208   State and Local Laws 209   Summary 210

PART 3   MERCHANDISING AND PRICING

7 INTRODUCTION TO MERCHANDISING CONTROL   215

The Merchandise Budget 216   Inventory Valuation 227   Retail Accounting Statements 235   Retailing in Action 7.1: Dressing up the Balance Sheet 238   Retailing in Action 7.2: International Retailers Use Different Accounting Rules 244   Summary 247

8 THE MERCHANDISE BUYING AND HANDLING PROCESS   251

Planning and Control 254   Dollar Merchandise Planning 254   Dollar Merchandise Control 261   Unit Stock Planning 263   Selection of Merchandising Sources 273   Retailing in Action 8.1: More Than License Plates Are Made in Some Prisons 274   Vendor Negotiations 278   Retailing in Action 8.2: Can Manufacturers Stop Diverters? 282   In-Store Merchandise Handling 285   Evaluating Merchandise Performance 286   Summary 295

9 PRICING IN THE RETAIL OPERATION   299

Interactive Price Decisions 302   Demand-Oriented Pricing 305   Supply-Oriented Pricing 310   Using Markups and Markdowns 311   Planning Initial Markups 315   Maintained Markup Percentage 317   Markdown Management 318   Markdown Policy 321   Pricing Objectives 323   Pricing Policies and Strategies 324   Retailing in Action 9.1: Off-Price Retailers: Are Their Days Numbered? 327   Specific Pricing Strategies 327   Retailing in Action 9.2: The Origin of Odd Pricing 331   Summary 332

PART 4 THE SELLING ENVIRONMENT

10 IDENTIFYING ATTRACTIVE MARKETS FOR RETAIL STORES 339

Steps in the Retail Location Decision 341 Theories of Market Identification 343 Demand Factors 354 Retailing in Action 10.1: CACI Marketing Systems Paves the Way for Easy Use of 1990 U.S. Census Data 356 Supply Factors 360 Retailing in Action 10.2: How the Great Atlantic & Pacific Tea Company, Inc. Tailors Its Strategy to Community Characteristics 362 Secondary Sources of Information 363 A Simple Example 364 Summary 365

11 STORE SITE ANALYSIS 368

Types of Location 369 Retailing in Action 11.1: Ghetto Retailing: Ethics and Profits 371 Evaluation of Demand and Supply Within the Market 379 Retailing in Action 11.2: Using Demand Factors in Location 387 Site Selection Decision Process 392 Measuring Performance 399 Summary 399

12 STORE PLANNING, DESIGN, AND MERCHANDISING 403

Introduction 405 Retailing in Action 12.1: Image Repositioning in Mexico City 408 Store Planning 412 Fixture Selection and Merchandise Presentation Planning 423 Retailing in Action 12.2: Will the Real Retailer Please Stand Up 430 Store Design 433 Visual Communications 436 Summary 440

13 RETAILING OF SERVICES 444

The Retailing of Services 445 Retailing in Action 13.1: Funeral Homes Learn to Merchandise Their Services 446 The Nature of Services and the Retailing of Services 450 Service Quality in the Retail Environment 457 Strategies for Enhancing Retailing of Services 468 Retailing in Action 13.2: Deregulation Prompts Banks to Become Retailers 471 Summary 474

PART 5 PROMOTION AND SELLING

14 RETAIL ADVERTISING AND PROMOTION 479

The Retail Promotion Mix 481 Integrated Effort 482 Promotion and the Marketing Channel 483 Law, Ethics, and Promotion 484 Promotion and Creativity 484 Retailing in Action 14.1: Some Vendors Don't Want Their "Specials" Promoted 485 Promotion Strategy 486 Promotion Objectives 487 Retail Advertising Management 489 Retailing in Action 14.2: International Promotion Isn't Just Translating an Ad 508 Sales Promotion Management 509 Publicity Management 510 Summary 512

15 PERSONAL SELLING 516

Determining the Level and Types of Sales Personnel 517 Retailing in Action 15.1: This Store's Return Policy Is Unbeatable 521 Retail Selling 522 Retailing in

Action 15.2: Close That Sale: Tips that Work! 535   The Customer Service and Sales Enhancement Audit 541   Summary 543

PART 6   RETAIL OPERATIONS AND ADMINISTRATION

16 MANAGEMENT OF HUMAN RESOURCES   547

Human Resource Management 549   Planning for Human Resources 550   Retailing in Action 16.1: Labor: The Number 1 Issue Facing Retailers Around the World 551   Hiring the Right Person for the Job 554   Training and Development 559   Retailing in Action 16.2: Wal-Mart's People Approach 561   Performance Appraisal 561   Employee Motivation 564   Human Resource Compensation 567   Job Enrichment 573   Organizing Human Resources 574   Summary 586

17 RETAIL INFORMATION SYSTEMS   589

Introducing the Retail Information System 591   Sources of Retail Information 594   The Scope of a Retail Information System 598   The Problem Idenfication Subsystem 600   Retailing in Action 17.1: Retailers Should Make Use of Newspaper Research Staffs 609   The Problem Solution Subsystem 624   Organizing the RIS 628   Future Developments in RIS 629   Retailing in Action 17.2: Developments in Information Technology Lead Retail Technology 631   Summary 632

CASES

1 Tom Borch Traditional Clothier, 636;   **2** City Drugstores, Inc., 646;   **3** Competitech Learns to Use Telemarketing, 649;   **4** Frey's Floorcovering, 651;   **5** HealthMore Pharmacies, Inc., 656;   **6** A. B. King's, 659;   **7** Oakland Department Store, 663;   **8** Taylor's Furniture, 666;   **9** East Towne Mall, 669;   **10** Zig Zag, 672;   **11** Homeworld-America, 678;   **12** Competitech-B, 682;   **13** Porsche AG, 683;   **14** Smith's IGA: Part A, 688;   **15** Smith's IGA: Part B, 691;   **16** Central City Savings Bank, 693;   **17** Toys "R" Us International, 699;   **18** Higby's Hardware, 703;   **19** Quality Markets, 707;   **20** Wal-Mart: Strategies for Market Dominance, 714;   **21** A New Mall for Mankato, 731;   **22** Sonic Corp., 736;   **23** Circle K Corporation, 756;   **24** IKEA North America: The Vikings Rediscover America, 772;   **25** Sears: A Giant in Transition, 782;   **26** Food4Less Stores, Inc., 797;   **27** Rich's Department Store, 811

GLOSSARY   836

SUBJECT INDEX   849

NAME INDEX   856

COMPANY INDEX   861

PREFACE
Why *Retail Marketing* is Different

Retail Marketing is different and, we think, better. As we reviewed the first edition of this textbook (called *Retail Management*), as well as many competitive books, we realized that while the world of retailing has changed drastically in the past 10 years, textbooks on the subject have remained essentially the same for the past 30 years. We committed ourselves to creating a new retail textbook that not only reflects retailing today, but suggests trends and directions for tomorrow. Along the way, it became clear the textbook should be renamed *Retail Marketing,* to reflect the coming era of retailing in which marketing, rather than real estate and operations, will dominate as the key tool for differentiation and success.

The most obvious change in this textbook is its organization. While many of the same subjects are covered, they have been reorganized around the basic premises of marketing that you have learned in your basic marketing courses. Marketing, in retailing and elsewhere, is the process of satisfying unfulfilled customer needs by understanding the marketplace and aligning the four key marketing variables—product, price, place, and promotion—in response to expressed needs. This book is organized simply to correspond to the elements. We begin with an overview of retailing and the importance of strategic planning. Next, we explore the retail marketplace and methods for understanding it and identifying unsatisfied marketplace needs. Then we discuss, in turn, the retail equivalents of the four marketing variables: merchandise (product), price, the selling environment (place) and, finally, promotion.

Some might argue this is an oversimplification of retailing, which is, after all, a very complicated business. But we think retailing is easier learned—and, indeed, practiced by retailers—when its complexities are mentally organized in this simple yet powerful framework that is rooted in the pursuit of serving the customer. Retailers lose their way when they forget this basic mission and become focused on the necessary thousands of operational details as an end in themselves. That's why this book is appropriately dedicated to the family and associates of Sam Walton, who said in his autobiography, *Sam Walton: Made in America*, "The secret of successful retailing is to give your customers what they want." More than any retailer in this half-century, Mr. Sam maintained a steadfast devotion to serving the customer's unsatisfied needs, believing all else would fall into place. And, of course, it did. It is our hope that this textbook not only introduces you to the complex functions retailers must undertake, but does so in a fashion that is easy to understand and that can be put into practice every day.

ACKNOWLEDGMENTS

The completion of any text is never the work of only the authors. In our case many outstanding individuals made important contributions to this project.

First, we would be remiss if we failed to note the contributions of our co-author on our *Retailing* textbook and the person who served as both our consulting and case editor on the first edition: Dr. Myron (Mike) Gable. Mike, it should be noted, is also a recent inductee in the Retailing Educators Hall of Fame.

Case studies are an important strength of Retail Marketing, and the high quality cases included in this book would not have been possible without the following contributors:

Kenneth L. Bernhardt Georgia State University	Myron Gable Shippensburg University
James W. Camerius Northern Michigan University	Jack Gifford Miami University
John Coppett University of Houston	Pat Gifford Elder-Beerman Stores
G. Peter Dapiran David J. Frayer	Carolyn J. Hanka Mankato State University

Roger Kerin
Southern Methodist University

Ray Serpkenci
Consultant

Michael Little
Virginia Commonwealth University

William Staples
University of Houston

Virginia Newell Lusch
Consultant

Heiko de B. Wijnholds
Virginia Commonwealth University

Richard M. Petreycik
Progressive Grocer

Deborah Zizzo
University of Oklahoma

We would also like to acknowledge and thank the following professors for their review of the first edition of this text:

Charles Ingene
University of Washington

Bruce Kellam
Eastern Washington University

Frederick Langrehr
Valparaiso University

George Lucas
Memphis State University

Antigone Kotsiopulos
Colorado State University

Louise Luchsinger
Texas Tech University

Dale Achabal
Santa Clara University

Donald McBane
Clemson University

Edward Blair
University of Houston-
University Park

Lewis Neisner
University of Maryland—Baltimore
County

Terri Coons
University of Southern California

Charles Patton
Pam American University

Jack Gifford
Miami University

Michael Pearson
Bowling Green State University

Donald Granbois
Indiana University

Rodger Singley
Illinois State University

Shelley Harp
Texas Tech University

Terrell Williams
Western Washington University

Marvin Jolson
University of Maryland

Julian Yudelson
Rochester Institute of Technology

For this edition, we were again provided with excellent reviewers, whom we thank:

Barbara Bart
Savannah State College

Elaine M. Notarantonio
Bryant College

Ed Cerny
University of South Carolina
Coastal Carolina College

Robert H. Solomon
Stephen F. Austin State University

Dorothy H. Goins
University of Kentucky

Robert Stassen
University of Arkansas

L. W. Turley
Western Kentucky University

In addition to the seven academics named above, Marvin Rothenberg, of Marvin J. Rothenberg Retail Marketing Consultants, Inc., provided detailed reviews and comments, as well as insights and direction, on this project. As a result, this text is not only structured for the academic, but is full of current practical examples. To Marv, a friend and colleague for over twenty years, we are ever so grateful.

To the people at South-Western, we can only say thanks for letting us play on the winning team. These individuals include: James R. Sitlington, Jr., Vice President, Acquisitions; our three Acquisitions Editors: Dave Shaut, who got us started, Jeanne Busemeyer, who was there as we finished our final draft; and Randy Haubner, who saw us through production; Scott Person, Marketing Manager; and Rebecca Roby, Production Editor.

Predictably, we could not have completed this edition without the constant encouragement, support, and understanding of our wives: Virginia, Judy, and Kara.

Robert F. Lusch
Norman, OK

Patrick M. Dunne
Lubbock, TX

Randall E. Gebhardt
Columbus, OH

FOREWORD

From the President of Wal-Mart Stores, Inc.

Many people think of Sam Walton as the man who revolutionized retailing over the past three decades. What he really did was put marketing into retailing, which is what this text is seeking to do. In fact, the very success of Wal-Mart can be attributed to Sam Walton's ability to follow the dictates of the customer. It was no accident that Mr. Sam, as he preferred to be called, spent so much time visiting the 1,800 Wal-Marts and its customers and "associates" across the country, as Wal-Mart's top executives do today. Wal-Mart is built on the very premise of the marketing concept—customer satisfaction.

All of the things Mr. Sam did with Wal-Mart—popularize discounting brand name products with "low prices always," introduce high quality private labels, recognize the profitability of serving small towns in the midwestern and southern states, and devise new and better means of distributing the merchandise—were the result of his being aware of the consumer's needs and wants. Sam Walton also realized that the old system of having local stores cater to local needs still works with a modern retailer. Each Wal-Mart store today, with its 80,000 to 100,000 square feet of merchandise including apparel, appliances and furniture, prescription drugs, and photo service, is built around a national merchandise offering, but tailored to fit the community. Sam Walton, with his bare-bones corporate culture, was focused on not making the mistakes of past retailers and keeping Wal-Mart lean and mean enough to react to the slightest change in the consumers' wants and needs.

That's why I believe that Mr. Sam would have been extremely happy to see the dedication of *Retail Marketing*. He knew and respected the authors and would have been pleased that his message is being carried on, not only at Wal-Mart, but in the academic community as well.

David Glass, President
Wal-Mart Stores, Inc.

Retail MARKETING

Part 1

INTRODUCTION TO RETAIL MARKETING

CHAPTER 1

PERSPECTIVES ON RETAILING

OVERVIEW

This chapter acquaints you with the nature and scope of retailing. We look at retailing as a major economic force and as a significant and exciting area for career opportunities. Next, we introduce the approach used throughout the text to study and learn about the marketing and management of retail enterprises.

PERSPECTIVES ON RETAILING

I. What Is Retailing?
II. Categorizing Retailers
    A. Census Bureau
    B. Number of Outlets
    C. Margin versus Turnover
    D. Location
    E. Size
III. Entry Barriers
IV. Retail Marketing Management
V. A Retail Career
    A. Aspects of a Career in Retailing
        1. College Education
        2. Salary
        3. Career Progression
        4. Geographic Mobility

             5. Women in Retailing
             6. Societal Perspective
        B. Prerequisites for Success
             1. Analytical Skills
             2. Creativity
             3. Decisiveness
             4. Flexibility
             5. Initiative
             6. Leadership
             7. Organization
             8. Risk Taking
             9. Stress Tolerance
            10. Perseverance
   VI. Methods of Retail Management
        A. Analytical Method
        B. Creative Method
        C. Two-Pronged Approach
  VII. The Orientations of This Book
 VIII. The Book Outline
        A. Introduction to Retail Marketing
        B. The Retailing Marketplace
        C. Merchandising and Pricing
        D. The Selling Environment
        E. Promotion and Selling
        F. Retail Operations and Administration
   IX. Summary

"Give me a T!" Vince Orza shouted as he flung his jubilant fist in the air in full view of the video cameras. "What's that spell? All right! Let's get out there and have some fun and serve those customers!"

Orza, chairman and chief executive officer of a leading discount department store chain, was concluding a national teleconference via satellite to over 2,000 management employees of the firm. The conference originated at corporate headquarters and was broadcast over the company's new satellite communication system to over 500 stores and distribution centers. Mr. Orza wanted to get all managers excited about the firm's new information system. He used the occasion to challenge them to immediately turn on their personal computers, which were all linked to the new information/communication system, and experience first-hand the new management tool they would have available to improve their decision-making and, consequently, store performance. The session ended with Mr. Orza leading a cheer in which the name of the company was chanted over and over. Sharon Williams, Vice President of Merchandising, and Henry Castillo, Assistant Merchandise Manager, could not wait to get back to their offices and try the new system. Earlier in the day Henry had begun to experiment with the system, and he invited Sharon to join him.

Sharon looked over Henry's shoulders as he leaned back in his chair. Both were amazed at what they saw. The new information system the company had worked so hard to develop was up and running. Even more astonishing was the speed with which they were able to monitor the performance of the more than 500 stores in the organization. The satellite communication system that linked all stores and the electronic scanning of merchandise at the point-of-sale terminals in each of the stores had created a formidable data base. Sharon reflected back to only 15 years earlier when she had joined the company as an assistant merchandise manager. She recalled how monotonous and laborious it was to develop merchandise reports. She also recalled that the reports were outdated by the time they were complete.

Sharon asked Henry to key into the computer merchandise item #1241, a newly released compact disc. Instantly they were informed that sales of this item were 654 units on the preceding day, with a total sales of $11,413 and a gross profit of $2,229. Next Sharon asked to see the sales of this item in store #79, located in Tyler, Texas. Instantly the answer came up on the screen.

Sharon exclaimed that this was the greatest merchandising tool she could imagine. Henry said she hadn't seen anything yet. "What do you mean?" she inquired. Henry proceeded to show her how he could instantly answer the following questions:

1. Who are our major competitors within the trade area of each store?

2. How much inventory do we have on hand for the more than 80,000 items in inventory, and in what distribution centers is this inventory located?

3. What are the demographics of the trade areas of each of the stores?

4. What markdowns have been taken recently on each of the more than 80,000 items?

And Henry emphasized that this was just the beginning. But Sharon had to interrupt the demonstration because of a meeting she had to attend with a leading store design firm.

The meeting was with Charles Ryan, Director of Market Research. Charles was 32, held a master's degree in marketing research, and had designed a new model of shopping behavior at discount department stores. His model showed retailers how to design their store layouts to help increase the average transaction size of the store. Henry himself had to prepare for a meeting with a vendor of in-store advertising programs—programs that place video and computer terminals on shopping carts. As shoppers travel through the store they can be sent messages about items on sale in areas of the store they are shopping, such as "Soup in aisle 3 is on sale, and crackers to go with the soup are on sale in aisle 5." These site-based promotion programs can also be used to send advertisements to shoppers while they wait in line to pay for their purchases, during which time they are receptive to viewing commercials. This can be an added source of profit to the store because the store can sell advertising time to firms such as Chevrolet or American Airlines.

Retailing has changed dramatically over the last decade—and it will continue to change. What was once a relatively low-technology industry has become dominated by high-technology systems offering almost instantaneous flow of information and precision movement of merchandise. And yet—perhaps because it is closer to consumers than any other industry—retailing will always be a people business, and the successful retail executives of tomorrow will be those people with the elusive ability to marry technology and people. With these greater challenges, the attractiveness of retailing as a career has increased dramatically, and more and more retailers are recruiting college graduates to be tomorrow's retail leaders.

Retailing not only promises to be an exciting career opportunity, but it also plays an important role in our economy. Throughout history the nations that have enjoyed the greatest economic growth have been those with strong economic and retail sectors. Because strong retail performance is such an important factor in economic growth, this text will focus on how to manage and plan retail enterprises to achieve high levels of performance, using a micro, rather than a macro, approach. That is, we will concentrate on how individuals in retail enterprises should manage and plan, rather than how the retail sector of the economy, in aggregate, should be structured, managed, or planned through government policies.[1] In order to put in proper perspective how retail organizations should plan and manage operations, we will frequently review the practices of many retailers with which you are familiar. These frequent examples often reflect good practices and thus reflect how others should manage in retailing. However, we also highlight poor retail practices in order to better instruct you about how not to manage a retail organization.

Although progressive societies have always had strong retail sectors, the retail trades have not always been recognized. Consider Aristotle's ranking of occupations:

Now in the course of nature, the art of agriculture is prior, and next comes those arts which extract the products of the earth, mining and the like.

Agriculture ranks first because of its justice: for it does not take anything away from men, either with their consent, as does retail trade and mercenary arts, or against their will, as do the warlike arts. Further agriculture is natural, for by nature all derive their sustenance from the earth.[2]

Thousands of years of commerce have now made retailers valued members of society. For example, when a McDonald's or a Wal-Mart decides to locate in a small town, there is a great deal of excitement in the community due to the increased merchandise and service assortments. People love choices and retailing provides that. Perhaps the critical role of retailing in society can be illustrated when retailing doesn't perform as it should. Retailing in Action 1.1 reveals the state of retailing in Russia in the 1990s. Interestingly, when Pizza Hut and McDonald's opened for business in Moscow, they became instant successes. The excitement of the Russian citizens was amazing, which illustrates very well the value people of all cultures place on retailing that is responsive to the needs and wants of the consumer.

WHAT IS RETAILING?

Retailing consists of the final activities and steps needed to place merchandise in the hands of the consumer or to provide services to the consumer. Quite simply, any firm that sells merchandise or provides services to the final consumer is performing the retailing function. Retailers provide utility to the consumer and the types of utility provided are time, place, and possession utility. Retailers are not involved in providing "form" utility but rather this is done by manufacturers and processors.

Regardless of whether a firm sells to the consumer in a store, through the mail, over the telephone, through a television shopping network, door to door, or through a vending machine, it is retailing. In fact, another definition of retailing is any time the consumer spends money.

Retailing is not a static or homogeneous business function. Retailing is continuously changing in exciting ways. Consider, for example, some major developments over the past century: the development of department stores in the 1870s, of mail-order houses in the 1880s, of chain stores in the early part of this century, of supermarkets in the 1930s, of discount stores in the 1940s, of shopping centers in the 1950s, of commodity-specialized mass merchandisers in the 1970s, of warehouse clubs in the 1980s. In the 1990s the change will continue and some experts believe it will accelerate.

Retailing is a business of managing change. The declining birthrate, the redistribution of income levels, and the increased participation of women in the work force have had profound effects on our society. Computer technology is producing data faster than ever and retailers must use these data to make better decisions. Entrepreneurs capitalize on emerging retail opportunities. Fashion trends that in the past would have lasted for years now last a

RETAILING IN ACTION

1.1 International Trends: Russian Retail System Falters

Retailing in Russia has never been a model of high performance. The system has for years been a standard for mediocre service and inefficiency. But now, things are getting worse. With the breakup of the Soviet Union, retailing in Russia began to break down, in large part, due to a severe shortage of goods and special deals for a few. Perhaps this is best illustrated by the plight of Olga Avilova who attempted to locate a simple pair of shoes for summer camp for her daughter, Liza. After four months of visits to dozens of stores (one store was visited a dozen times), Olga located a pair of vinyl sandals with poorly glued thin soles for six rubles (about $10 at the official exchange rate).

Shopping often occurs by invitation or under the counter. Shopping by invitation has grown 20-fold since the mid-1980s. Under this system, employees who work for large organizations (frequently factories) apply to their union official to receive a special invitation to purchase a product, such as a television. When merchandise arrives in the store, the officials hand out invitations, and only those with invitations can shop. Not surprisingly, some union officials keep a supply of coupons for themselves and friends or to market for extra income. For example, an invitation to purchase a television at 600 rubles may trade for 200 rubles and upward. Thus, there is a price not only on the merchandise, but on the right to purchase it.

A variation on the invitation to shop is the store for newlyweds. Shopping there is allowed only if one shows documents of registration to be married. The problem is that a lot of people are registering to get married just for the privilege to shop. In 1989, 31,500 couples in Moscow did not show up to be married—25 percent of those registered.

Another phenomenon that has developed is underground stores. These stores develop as a result of black marketers working closely with corrupt factory union and retail officials. They can divert truckloads of shoes, coats, and so on. This phenomenon is so big that entire underground department stores have developed.

Sources: Based on Esther B. Fein, "Daily Routine in Moscow: Waiting, Always Waiting," *New York Times*, 17 June 1990, 1, 6; Esther B. Fein, "A Child's Invitation to Summer Camp Provokes a Crisis," *New York Times*, 17 June 1990, 6; Peter Gumbel, "Soviet Retail System Gets Strikingly Worse in Era of Perestroika," *Wall Street Journal*, 23 July 1990, A1, A6.

---

season. Furthermore, recent industry studies have shown that the country already has more than sufficient retail space to meet the needs of the next decade: there are 17 square feet of shopping center space for every person in the United States.[3] Coupled with these trends is the maturing of the U.S. economy where low to no economic growth is the consensus of economists.

Thus, with market growth slowing, retailers will find it more difficult to sustain long-term growth by adding new stores. Instead, most growth will come at the expense of a competitor's market share. Retailers today must be able to analyze these changes, understand these changes, anticipate other changes, and adapt to changes made by others. Successful retailers can look at the changing environment and see opportunities. Ray Kroc, the entrepreneur behind McDonald's, saw the post–World War II baby boom and the resulting demand for reasonably priced fast food as an opportunity. Unsuccessful retailers such as Circle K Corporation, a convenience food chain which grew from 1,221 stores in 1983 to 4,685 stores in 1988, failed because it did not foresee the changing nature of competition. Circle K didn't foresee how the major oil companies would enter the convenience food store business. With Circle K's explosive growth and high debt, it was unable to maintain a positive cash flow and was forced into bankruptcy in 1990. As the environment changes, retailers must change to survive and prosper. Success in retailing is dependent on being able to interpret properly what changes are occurring and building a strategy to respond to these changes. Therein lies the excitement and challenge of a career in retailing.

Retail analysts and experts often project what the future will be like. One of the most respected consulting firms in the field of retailing is Management Horizons (a division of Price Waterhouse). Management Horizons makes the following projections for retailing during the decade of the 1990s.[4]

1. By the end of the 1990s, more than half of the retailers operating in 1990 will be out of business.
2. The gross excess in retail space will be converted to nonretail facilities and shopping mall space will decline.
3. Nonstore retailing will command a much larger share of almost all consumer markets because it offers more convenience and often greater selection.
4. The mass market will decline in importance as retailing becomes more intensely localized with more emphasis on neighborhood shopping alternatives.
5. The structure of retail organizations will become more flat, lean, and decentralized and thus middle-management positions will decline.
6. Retailers and suppliers will work more closely together in a cooperative fashion.

CATEGORIZING RETAILERS

One way to better understand the scope of retailing is to study methods used to classify retailers. There is no single, accepted method of classifying retailers, although many classification schemes have been proposed. The five most popular schemes will follow.

CENSUS BUREAU

The U.S. Bureau of the Census, for purposes of conducting the census of retail trade, classifies all retailers using two-digit standard industrial classification (SIC) codes, given as follows:

1. Building materials, hardware, garden supply, and mobile home dealers (SIC 52)—there are approximately 107,000 of these retailers.

2. General-merchandise group stores (SIC 53)—there are approximately 57,000 of these retailers.
3. Food stores (SIC 54)—these stores number over 290,000.
4. Automotive dealers and gasoline service stations (SIC 55)—there are roughly 331,000 of these retailers.
5. Apparel and accessory stores (SIC 56)—there are approximately 197,000 of these stores.
6. Furniture, home furnishings, and equipment stores (SIC 57)—there are roughly 180,000 of these retailers.
7. Eating and drinking places (SIC 58)—over 490,000 of these establishments exist.
8. Miscellaneous retail stores (SIC 59)—there are approximately 766,000 miscellaneous retail establishments.

Typically, when we think of retailers we envision stores. In SIC 59 is SIC 596—nonstore retailers. There are approximately 66,000 nonstore retailers in the United States. Within this number are 31,000 catalog and mail-order houses (Lands End and Eddie Bauer, for example), 24,000 merchandising machine operators that sell everything from snack food to toiletries, and 11,000 direct-selling establishments such as Mary Kay Cosmetics and AMWAY.

In almost all instances, the SIC code reflects the type of merchandise the retailer sells. The major portion of a retailer's competition comes from other retailers in its SIC category. General-merchandise stores (SIC 53) are the exception to this rule. General-merchandise stores, due to the breadth of merchandise carried, compete with retailers in most other SIC categories. Likewise, most retailers must compete to a considerable extent with general-

ILLUSTRATION 1.1

Eddie Bauer is one of the 31,000 catalog and mail order houses in the United States. In addition to its mail order business, it offers its merchandise through its own chain of stores.

merchandise stores, because those larger stores probably handle many of the same types of merchandise that smaller, more limited retailers sell. Of course, in a very broad sense, all retailers compete with each other since they are all vying for the same limited consumer dollars.

The SIC codes do not reflect all retailing activity. The Census Bureau definition equates retailing only with the sale of "tangible" goods or merchandise. However, by our definition, selling services to the final consumer is also retailing. And this suggests that the principles of retail marketing management you are studying can also be applied to businesses such as barber/beauty shops, dry cleaners, movie theaters, amusement parks, dental clinics, one-hour photo labs, and so on. Remember, any time the consumer spends money—either on tangibles (merchandise) or on intangibles (services)—retailing has occurred.

NUMBER OF OUTLETS

Another method of classifying retailers is by the number of outlets each operates. Generally, retailers with several units are a stronger competitive threat because they can spread many fixed costs, such as advertising and top management salaries, over a larger volume of sales and can achieve economies in purchasing. However, single-unit retailers do have advantages. They are generally owner- and family-operated and tend to have harder working, more motivated employees. Also, they can focus all their efforts on one trade area and tailor their merchandise to that area.

Any retail organization that operates more than one unit is technically a chain, but this is really not a very practical definition. The Census Bureau breaks down chain stores into two size categories: two to ten stores and eleven or more.

Over 36 percent of all retail sales are accounted for by large chain store organizations (those operating 11 or more units). However, in some lines of retail trade, large chains are more dominant. Over 96 percent of department store sales come from large chains, and over 63 percent of shoe store sales come from large chains.[5] In Exhibit 1.1 we profile nine successful chain store retailers. These retail organizations have experienced solid growth over the last five years and have been able to engineer their businesses to achieve a return on equity in excess of 20 percent. There are many career opportunities with the retailers listed in Exhibit 1.1 so you may wish to study the list carefully.

Not all chain operations enjoy the same advantages. Small chains are local in nature and may enjoy some economies in buying and in having the merchandise tailored to their market needs. Large chains are generally regional or national and can take full advantage of the economies of scale that centralized buying and a **standard stock list** can achieve. Other national chains, recognizing the variations of regional tastes, give each store the necessary flexibility to adjust merchandise to local demands. This flexibility,

EXHIBIT 1.1

Selected High-Performance Chain Store Retailers

Company[b]	1990 Fiscal Year Sales (000)	Five-Year Sales Growth	Number of Stores	Return on Equity[a]
Claire's Stores, Inc.	$ 190,246	155%	831	57.9%
Costco Wholesale Corp.	4,059,600	443	69	20.3
Dayton Hudson Corp.	14,739,000	59	708	23.5
The Gap, Inc.	1,933,780	128	1,092	42.8
The Home Depot	3,815,356	277	145	31.9
The Limited Stores, Inc.	5,253,509	14	3,864	25.5
Melville Corporation	8,686,765	62	7,754	23.8
The TJX Companies, Inc.	2,446,279	90	967	32.4
Wal-Mart Stores, Inc.	32,601,594	174	1,721	32.6

[a]After-tax return on beginning-of-year stockholder's equity.
[b]These companies operate stores under a variety of tradenames which are identified below.
1. Claire's Stores, Inc. operates stores under the names of Claire's Boutiques, Topkapi, and Dara Michelle.
2. Costco Wholesale Corp. operates warehouse stores under the name of Costco.
3. Dayton Hudson Corp. operates stores under the names of Target, Mervyn's, Dayton's, Hudson's, Marshall Field's.
4. The Gap, Inc. operates stores under the names of Gap, GapKids, BABYGap, and Banana Republic.
5. The Home Depot operates stores under the name of Home Depot.
6. The Limited Stores, Inc. operates stores under the names of Limited, Limited Express, Victoria's Secret, Lerner, Lane Bryant, Henri Bendel, Abercrombie & Fitch, Structure, Limited Too, Victoria's Secret Bath, and nonstore operations that include Victoria's Secret Catalog and Brylane Catalog.
7. Melville Corporation operates stores under the names of Marshalls, Wilsons, Chess King, Bob's, Accessory Lady, CVS, Freddy's, Meldisco, Thom McAn, Fan Club, Kay-Bee, Linens 'n Things, This End Up, Prints Plus.
8. The TJX Companies, Inc. operates stores under the names of T.J. Maxx, Hit or Miss, Chadwick's of Boston, Winners Apparel Ltd.
9. Wal-Mart Stores, Inc. operates stores under the names of Wal-Mart, Sam's Club, Hypermart* USA.

which is used by national retailers such as JCPenney, is called the **optional stock list approach.** Both merchandising methods provide scale advantages in other retailing activities; for example, promotion savings when more than one store operates in an area. Finally, chain stores have long been aware of the benefits of vertically integrating their channels of distribution, as we will discuss in Chapter 5.

MARGIN VERSUS TURNOVER

Retailers can be classified according to their average gross margin percentage and rate of inventory turnover. The gross margin percentage shows how much gross profit (sales less cost of goods sold) the retailer makes as a percentage of sales. A 40 percent gross margin indicates that on each dollar of sales, the retailer generates 40 cents in gross margin dollars. Inventory turnover refers to the number of times per year, on average, that a retailer sells its inventory. Thus, an inventory turnover of 12 indicates that, on average, the retailer turns its inventory 12 times each year or once a month. An average inventory of $40,000 (retail) and annual sales of $240,000 mean the retailer turns over its inventory six times a year ($240,000 ÷ $40,000).

High-performance retailers have long recognized the relationship between gross margin, turnover, and gross profit. Gross profit (the amount of money a firm has left after paying for the merchandise) is gross margin per unit times units sold. As shown in Exhibit 1.2, retailers can be classified into four basic types using the concepts of margin and turnover.

Typically, a *low-margin/low-turnover* retailer will not be able to generate sufficient profits to remain competitive and survive. There are few good examples of this type of retailer. On the other hand, *low-margin/high-turnover* retailers are common in the United States. Examples are discount department stores such as Kmart and Target and full-line supermarkets such as Safeway, Kroger, or Food Giant. *High-margin/low-turnover* retailers are also common in the United States. Furniture stores, television and appliance stores, jewelry stores, and hardware stores are examples of high-margin/low-turnover operations. Finally, some retailers find it possible to operate on both *high margins and high turnover*. As you might expect, this strategy can be very profitable. Fast-food restaurants such as McDonald's and Taco Bell have used this strategy. Other types of retailers can also achieve high-margin and high-turnover status. An excellent example occurred when Dillard's Department Stores acquired St. Louis–based Stix, Baer, & Fuller from Associated Dry Goods. Dillard's added more costly name-brand merchandise to appeal to affluent shoppers, doubled advertising, increased the sales force by 50 percent, and installed a computer system to manage inventory levels more effectively. The

EXHIBIT 1.2

Retailers Classified by Margin and Turnover

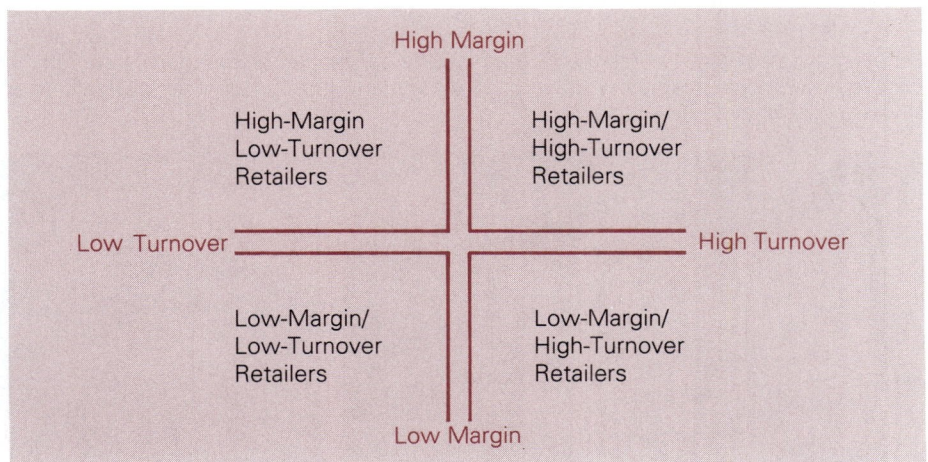

results were a high-performance gross margin and an improvement in turnover.

The low-margin/low-turnover retailer is the least able of the four to withstand a competitive attack because this retailer is barely profitable, and when competitive intensity increases, profits are driven even lower. On the other hand, the high-margin/high-turnover retailer is in an excellent position to withstand and counter competitive threats because profit margins enable it to finance competitive wars.

LOCATION

Retailers have long been classified according to their location within a metropolitan area, be it the central business district, a shopping center, or as a freestanding unit. These traditional locations will be discussed in greater detail in Chapters 10 and 11. However, the 1980s have witnessed a major change in retail locations. Retailers in this decade have become aware that opportunities to improve financial performances can be achieved by either improving the productivity of existing traditional stores or operating in nontraditional retail areas. Furthermore, retailers face a 1990s in which retail market growth will slow considerably. Retailers realize that most metropolitan areas have all the stores they can support. Therefore, rather than expand into unprofitable territories, retailers are renovating existing stores. Even when a retailer finds an ideal location for expansion, competitors are sure to follow. One retailer spent two years studying market conditions before deciding to open the first frozen-yogurt store in Albuquerque, New Mexico. Within a year, four other yogurt stores were competing for his business on the northeast edge of town.

Other retailers are reaching out for nontraditional or alternative retail

ILLUSTRATION 1.2

Different types of retail stores are located in different market areas. Macy's on 34th Street in New York City (*left*) is a traditional multi-story downtown department store, while Target Greatland (*right*) is a suburban single-story discount store.

locations. Baskin-Robbins has ice cream shops on board U.S. Navy ships. Burger King is now on military bases as well as in Woolworth stores, Greyhound bus terminals, airports, and even has 20 roving buses in Miami. McDonald's is on military bases and college campuses as well as in hospitals and museums. Furthermore, Dunkin' Donuts is opening outlets in conjunction with gasoline service stations.

SIZE

Many retail trade associations classify retailers by sales volume or number of employees. The reason for classifying by size is that the operating performance of retailers tends to vary according to size. For example, the American Floorcovering Association reports operating performance data by five sales volume categories (under $499,000; $500,000 to $999,999; $1 million to $1.9 million; $2 million to $4.9 million; and $5 million or more). The National Retail Hardware Association classifies lumber and building materials stores into three categories by annual sales (under $500,000, $500,000 to $1 million, and over $1 million). The National Retail Federation categorizes department stores into seven volume groups ($1–$2 million; $2–$5 million; $5–$10 million; $10–$20 million; $20–$50 million; $50–$100 million; and over $100 million). Other retail trade associations provide similar breakdowns. Generally, retailers should compare their results only against competitors of a similar size.

ENTRY BARRIERS

The preceding review of ways to classify retailers suggests that retailing is large and complex.[6] In addition, retail management decision making is becoming increasingly sophisticated. Once it was considered an easy industry to enter, but now substantial entry barriers are rising, especially if one desires to locate in large regional malls or other prime locations. Competition is intense for high-traffic locations, and construction costs and lease payments have risen drastically over the last decade. The average new supermarket is over 50,000 square feet, and construction costs are over $3 million. This does not include the cost of land, which is probably $500,000 to $1,000,000, or inventory to stock the store, which is probably another $2,000,000. Thus, to enter the supermarket business with a single new store in a good location with adequate inventory, approximately $6 million in investment capital is required. Of course, if the retailer decided to lease space rather than buy, the initial investment would be considerably less. In fact, sometimes with a lease a retailer can obtain fixturing allowances that go a long way toward covering the costs of fixtures. If the retailer has good credit, it could also attract suppliers to finance most of its opening inventory. All of this goes to suggest that some retailers can open a new store by getting others (leasors, suppliers, and banks) to furnish the capital.

In light of the rising entry barriers in retailing, the number of new retail enterprises that have been developed in the last two decades is truly amazing. The driving force behind retailing today is the development of new forms of retailing. Most of these new businesses have been new kinds of retailers; for example, warehouse retailing, home shopping using the television, discount drugs, or home-delivery fast foods. Exhibit 1.3 profiles the rapid growth of four warehouse club chains.

RETAIL MARKETING MANAGEMENT

In Exhibit 1.4 we present the three concentric circle model of retail marketing management. The outermost circle of this model is the retail marketplace. A marketplace is where supply and demand factors meet. It consists of the consumer, who is the fountainhead of all demand (i.e., revenue), the competing retail organizations that are battling for consumer patronage, the members of the marketing channel that create and deliver the supply of merchandise and services the consumer demands, and the legal or regulatory environment. Although the United States is a free-enterprise economy, the behavior of retailers is constrained by many laws and regulations and thus the regulatory system is a critical part of the retail marketplace.

The middle circle of the retail marketing management model presents the major types of retail decisions. First, the retailer must select and price the merchandise that it will offer to the retail marketplace. Second, the retailer must establish its selling environment which consists of its geographic location and place of business or its store building. Third, the merchandise and services must be properly promoted and sold. Importantly, decisions related to these three areas must be made with the retail marketplace in mind—the consumer, competitors, channel and regulatory environment (i.e., the outermost circle of the model).

Finally, the innermost circle of the model is divided into two parts—

EXHIBIT 1.3

Growth of Leading Warehouse Clubs

	1986		1990	
Club	Sales (millions)	Warehouse Units	Sales (millions)	Warehouse Units
Sam's Club	$1,678	49	$9,280	211
Price Company	$2,806	25	$6,598	65
Costco Wholesale Club	$ 843	37	$4,725	75
Pace Membership Warehouse	$ 595	25	$3,900	88

Source: "Keeping up with the Wholesale Club," *Discount Merchandiser* (November 1988): 30, 32 and "Wholesale Club Update," *Discount Merchandiser* (November 1991): 33-35.

human resources and information resources. These are the two sets of resources that are most critical to the administration and operations of a retail enterprise. Retailing is a people business and people get things done. The retailer needs to attract, motivate, and retain the best people possible. Retailing is also an information business. In fact, retail decisions made without information are decisions for disaster. Superior retail decisions cannot be made without quality information on all aspects of the business and the retail marketplace. Consequently, it is not surprising that the number-one retailer in the United States, Wal-Mart, achieved its dominance by emphasizing its people and information resources. Suzanne Allford, vice-president of the people division, has stated that people development is not just a good "program" for any growing company but a must to secure its future. Wal-Mart invests heavily in continuing education and training for its employees. Wal-Mart also invests heavily in information resources by having its own

EXHIBIT 1.4

Three Concentric Circle Model of Retail Marketing Management

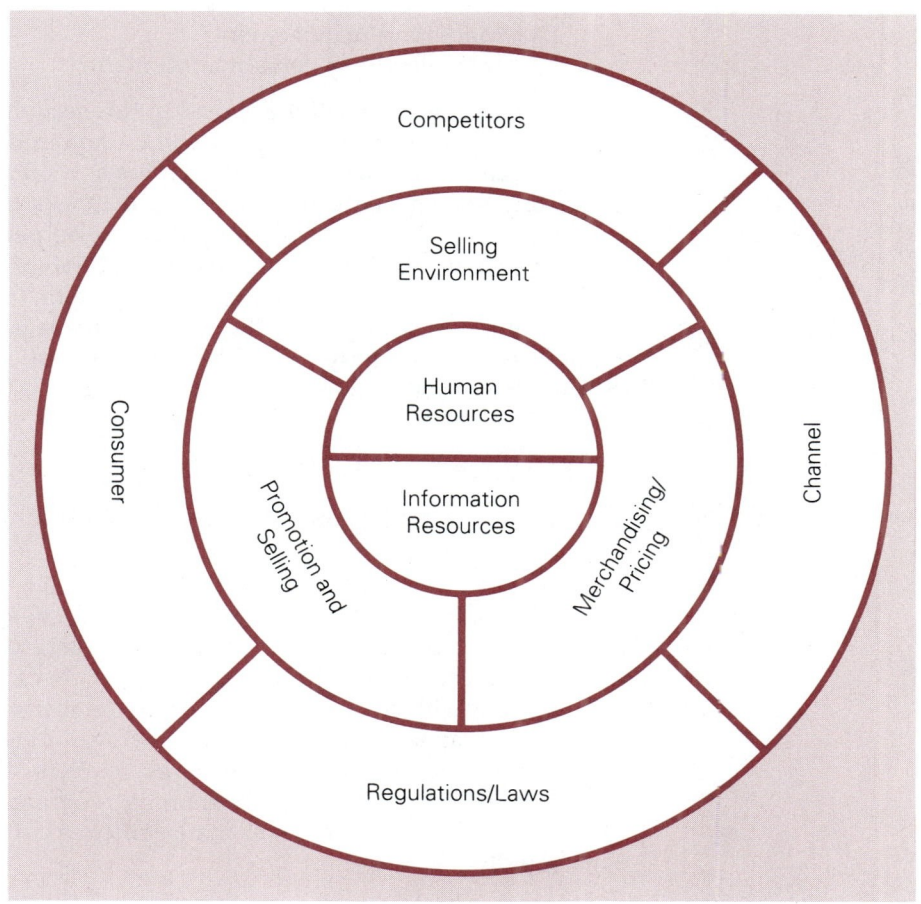

satellite communication system that allows it to send and receive information from all its stores and distribution centers. Wal-Mart also shares information with its suppliers through a program called Retail-Link.[7] The information system capitalizes on bar code and satellite communications capacities to bring suppliers information concerning sales trends and inventory levels at individual stores. This sharing of information helps to bring Wal-Mart closer to its channel partners.

A RETAIL CAREER

Do you think a successful retail store manager needs to be capable in:

Economics?	Yes	No
Transportation management?	Yes	No
Financial management?	Yes	No
Personnel management?	Yes	No
Marketing management?	Yes	No
Information systems management?	Yes	No

The answer is yes to all the above! In this section we will demonstrate the validity of this statement. Retailing will train you to become an expert not in just one field, but in all business disciplines. It offers the economist's job of forecasting sales growth, the marketing manager's job of determining what will be popular during the coming season, the personnel manager's job of hiring the right people, the traffic manager's job of arranging deliveries, the information system manager's job of obtaining the right information to make good retailing decisions, and the financial manager's job of arriving at the bottom line. In summary, no other occupation offers the immediate opportunities that retailing does.

ASPECTS OF A CAREER IN RETAILING

In the following discussion we hope to help you construct an accurate picture of a career in retailing.

College Education. Is college a prerequisite to a career in retailing? It depends. To be an assistant buyer or department manager, the answer is probably no. A college degree would be helpful but not required. However, for career advancement with a fast-track progressive retailer or a career in top management (store manager, vice-president, chief executive officer), college training is generally a prerequisite. Many large retailers will not consider anyone without a college degree for their training programs. Some retail firms even recruit MBAs to fill entry-level management positions, and then advance them rapidly.

Salary. Is retailing competitive in terms of compensation? A recent graduate with a bachelor's degree seeking an entry-level position can probably obtain a higher salary in other fields. In general, retailers offer 10 to 15 percent below what college graduates can earn from manufacturers, insurance companies, and many other campus recruiters. Starting salaries in executive training programs approximate $22,000 to $28,000 a year. That is only the short-run perspective, however. In the long run, a retail manager or buyer is directly rewarded on performance. An entry-level retail manager or buyer who does exceptionally well can double or triple his or her income in three to five years and often be ahead of classmates who chose other career fields. High-level retail managers receive salaries comparable to their counterparts in other industries.

Career Progression. Can you advance rapidly in retailing? The answer depends on both the retail organization and the individual. A person capable of handling more responsibility than he or she is given can move up quickly; even if that person works for a firm too small or growing too slowly to promote, he or she can easily advance by joining another retail organization. There is no standard career progression, but a typical example may be useful. A college graduate starting a career with a department store chain might first work as a management trainee and then progress as shown in Exhibit 1.5.

Geographic Mobility. Will retailing allow you to live in the area of the country where you desire? Perhaps. Retailing exists in all geographic areas of the United States. In the largest 300 cities in the United States, there are sufficient employment and advancement opportunities in retailing. However, in order to progress rapidly, a person must often be willing and able to make several geographic moves, all of which may not be attractive. Rapidly growing chain stores almost always transfer individuals in order to open stores in new areas. These transfers are generally coupled with promotions and salary increases. A person may stay in one area if he or she wants to, but it may cost that person opportunities for advancement.

Women in Retailing. Retailing has been viewed as a good career for women, but their role was most often restricted to the sales floor, the buying office, or middle management. Women typically found the door shut when it was time to move into the executive suite. However, statistics compiled by Gable, Gillespie, and Topol showed that females constitute close to 44 percent of all department store executives, making it the profession where women have achieved the highest level of attainment.[8] Retailing in Action 1.2 presents a sketch of the highly successful women executives who lead The Limited.

Societal Perspective. Most retail executives are well-rounded individuals with a high social consciousness. Many of them serve on the boards of nonprofit

EXHIBIT 1.5
JCPenney Career Progression Chart

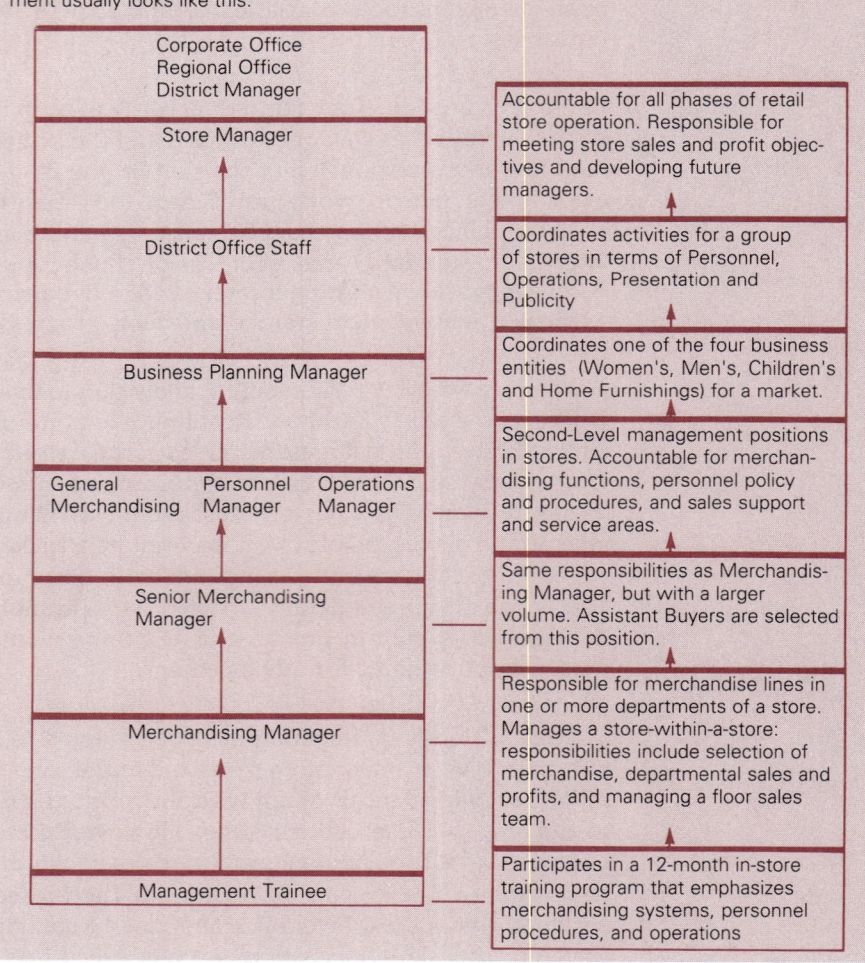

Source: Reprinted with permission of JCPenney.

RETAILING IN ACTION

1.2 Careers in Retailing: The Women Who Lead The Limited, Inc.

Retailing is an industry in which women have good opportunities for promotion to the executive ranks. However, few, if any retailers have made the executive suite more accessible than The Limited, Inc. Women preside over five of the divisions of The Limited.

Susan Falk is president of Bendel's and previously was executive vice-president of The Limited's Express division. Susan was born in Chicago and began her career in retailing during college as a part-time employee at The Broadway in the juniors area and later went through the Bullocks training program. She is in her early 40s.

Cynthia Fedus is president of Victoria's Secret Catalogue. Cynthia was born in Oxford, Ohio, and began her career in retailing after college in 1971 in the swimwear department at Rike's (a department store chain in Ohio). Cynthia is in her mid-40s.

ILLUSTRATION 1.3

Retailing offers many career opportunities and has one of the highest percentages of female executives of all industries. Many divisions of The Limited, Inc., are headed by women.

> Cheryl Nido Turpin is president of Lane Bryant and was previously president and chief executive of Weinstock's, a Carter Hawley Hale department store based in Sacramento, California. Cheryl grew up in Michigan where she was a student at the University of Michigan.
>
> Grace Nichols is president of Victoria's Secret Stores. She was born in Alameda, California, and began her retailing career selling junior sportswear at Emporium Capwell. She has a master's degree in U.S. history.
>
> Sources: Based on David Moin, "The Women Who Lead The Limited," *Women's Wear Daily*, 9 January 1991, 6-7 and 10 January 1991, 4-5.

arts organizations, as regents or trustees of universities, on local chambers of commerce, on school boards, and in other service-related activities. Retailers serve society not only outside their retailing career, but also within it. Take a moment to envision a world without merchants or retailers. How could any advanced industrial society survive in their absence? It couldn't. It is not the profession that determines one's contribution to society but the soundness of one's ethical principles. You need to develop a firm set of ethical principles to guide you throughout any career.

PREREQUISITES FOR SUCCESS

What is required for success as a retail executive? Hard work. The hours almost always exceed 40 per week, and a six-day week is not unusual for a retail executive. However, work is not the only prerequisite. Let us look at some others.

Analytical Skills. The successful retail executive analyzes facts and data in order to plan, manage, and control. An understanding of the past and present performance of the store, its merchandise lines, and its departments is also necessary and forms the basis for future actions. Thus, good analytical skills are a must.

Creativity. The ability to generate novel ideas and solutions is known as creativity. Retail executives cannot operate a store by a set of preprogrammed equations and formulas; they need to be idea people as well as analysts. Success in retailing is the result of sensitive, perceptive decisions and imaginative, innovative techniques. For example, a buyer must be able to detect changes in the retail marketplace and relate these changes to new merchandise and service needs.

Decisiveness. Decisiveness is the ability to render judgments, take action, and commit oneself to a course of action until the desired results are achieved. A retail executive must be decisive. Sometimes better decisions could be made if more time were available, but variables such as fashion trends and consumer desires change quickly. In order to be successful, an executive must make decisions quickly, confidently, and correctly, even if complete information is not available.

Flexibility. Flexibility is the ability to adjust to ever-changing situations. The retail executive must have the willingness and enthusiasm to do whatever is necessary to get the job done, even if it means changing plans. In retailing, surprises never cease. Because plans must be altered quickly to accommodate changes in trends, styles, and attitudes, successful retail executives must be flexible.

Initiative. Retail executives must have the ability to originate action rather than wait to be told what to do. This ability is called initiative. To be a success, the retail executive must seize opportunities for improving the store's performance.

Leadership. Leadership is the ability to inspire others to trust and respect your judgment and to do what you ask. In any large-scale retail enterprise, the executive must depend on others to get the work done. Retail executives therefore must be managers that can lead.

Organization. Organization is the ability to establish priorities and courses of action for yourself and others, and to plan and follow up to achieve results. Retail executives often coordinate many different factors, issues, functions, and projects at the same time. The successful ones set the right priorities and skillfully organize personnel and resources.

Risk Taking. Retail executives must be willing to take risks based on thorough analysis and sound judgment; they must also be willing to accept responsibility for the results. Success in retailing often comes from taking calculated risks and having the confidence to try something new before someone else does. A study of the history of retailing, its successes and failures, can help one to lower significantly the risks in retailing.

Stress Tolerance. As the other prerequisites to success in retailing suggest, retailing is fast-paced and demanding. Retail executives must be able to perform consistently under pressure and to thrive on constant change and challenge. They must be resilient.

Perseverance. Because of the difficult challenges that a retail career presents, it is important to have perseverance. Often the person pursuing a retail career will become frustrated due to many things occurring that he or she does not control. Retailing occurs in an open and unpredictable environment and the best laid plans may not lead to high-performance results. Furthermore, one might become frustrated with fellow employees and/or superiors, long hours, and the demanding pace of a retail career. The person that finds in him- or herself the ability to persevere and take all of this in stride will find an increasing number of promotion opportunities because many of his or her fellow colleagues did not persevere. Retailing is truly the survival of the fittest.

These 10 prerequisites to success in retailing are not intended to scare you off. You probably do not yet possess all of them. The important thing is that a person beginning a retail career should have the desire to acquire them. If you desire these abilities, this book will help you move toward a career in retailing.

METHODS OF RETAIL MANAGEMENT

As we have seen, the first two prerequisites to success as a retail executive are analytical skills and creativity. These attributes also represent common approaches to retail management.

ANALYTICAL METHOD

The analytical retail executive is a finder and investigator of facts: reducing, synthesizing, and dissecting facts in order to make decisions systematically. To make these decisions, the executive uses models and theories of retail phenomena that enable her or him to structure all dimensions of retailing.[9] Thus, the theories and concepts developed in this book will help you develop an analytical approach to retailing. An analytical perspective usually results in a standardized set of procedures, success formulas, and guidelines.

Consider, for example, the manager of a McDonald's restaurant, where everything is preprogrammed, including the menu, decor, location, hours of operation, cleanliness standards, customer service policies, and advertising. The store manager needs only to gather and analyze facts to determine whether the preestablished guidelines are being met and to take appropriate corrective actions if necessary.

CREATIVE METHOD

The creative retail executive is a producer of ideas. This executive tends to be a conceptualizer and is very imaginative. She or he uses insight and intuition more often than facts, and the result is usually a novel way to look at or solve a retail problem. This book has 27 case studies and when they are assigned for study you should attempt to develop some creative solutions to the problems confronting the retailers in the case studies. It is possible to operate a retail establishment with creativity, but in the long run, using creativity alone will be inadequate. Analytical decision making must be used to respond profitably to unforeseen events in the environment.

In grocery retailing, for example, creative retail management can help set one grocery store apart from the competition. Burton Hubbard, store manager of a Tom Thumb-Page in Plano, Texas, knows the role of creativity.[10] The displays and promotions he designs are full of excitement and style. During spring 1990, the store featured a complete wedding scene with mannequins as the bride, groom, and guests and included an eight-tier cake from the bakery department. Burton Hubbard also recognizes the role of analysis and profit planning. A display that doesn't create sales or generate store traffic may be creative but not analytically prudent. Incidentally, the wedding scene generated sales of 400 cases of champagne.

TWO-PRONGED APPROACH

As shown through the McDonald's and Tom Thumb-Page examples, retailing can be practiced using analytical and creative approaches. The retailer that employs both approaches is most successful in the long run. The McDonald's store manager can operate quite successfully in a purely analytical mode. However, behind the manager is a corporation that is creative as well as analytical. Examples of the corporation's creative dimensions are the development of McDonald's characters (Ronald McDonald, Grimace, and Hamburglar) and selected menu items (Egg McMuffin, Big Mac, and Happy Meals). It is the combination of the creative with the analytical that has made McDonald's what it is today.

Indeed, the synthesis of creativity and analysis is necessary. Roger Dickinson, a former retail executive and now professor of marketing, has stated that "many successful merchandisers are fast duplicators rather than originators."[11] To decide who or what to duplicate requires not only creativity but an analysis of the strategies that competitors are pursuing. Dickinson further states that "creativity in retailing is for the sake of increasing the sales and profits of the firm."[12] If creativity is tied to sales and profits, then analysis cannot be avoided.

Retailers in the 1990s and beyond cannot do without either creativity or analytical skills. This book will develop your skills in both areas. At the outset, however, you should note that whether you use creativity or analytical skills, you will always be solving problems. Similarities between the creative and analytical methods of solving problems are presented in Exhibit 1.6.

THE ORIENTATIONS OF THIS BOOK

The approach to the study of retailing we use in this book has four major orientations: (1) a marketplace orientation, (2) a strategic planning orientation, (3) a profit orientation, and (4) a decision-making orientation. Retailers

EXHIBIT 1.6

Problem Solving from Two Perspectives

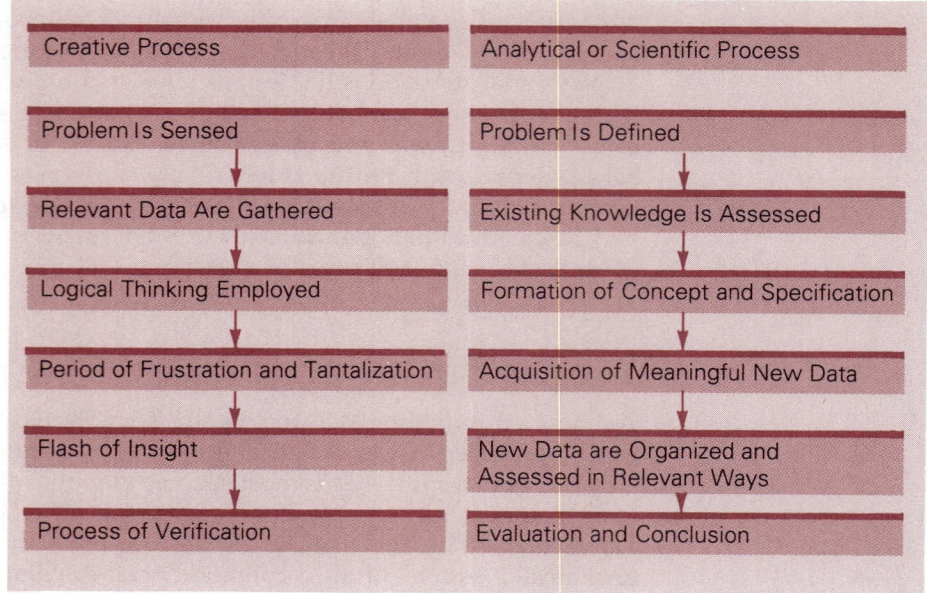

Sources: Lewis E. Walkup, "Creativity in Science Through Visualization," *Journal of Creative Behavior,* 1 (Summer 1967):283-84 and Gerald Zaltman, Christian R. A. Pinson, and Reinhard Angelmar, *Meta theory and Consumer Research* (New York: Holt, Rinehart and Winston, 1973), 13-15.

should have an orientation to the marketplace, which will allow them to adapt continuously to the consumer, competitor, channel, and regulatory system. Retailing is not static. With the retail marketplace always in flux, the retailer finds it necessary to study these changes.

Retailers should have a strategic planning orientation, which will help them to adapt systematically to a changing retail marketplace. After studying the changes in the retail marketplace, retailers must plan and *planning* is deciding today what to do tomorrow. A retailer that wants to have a competitive edge must plan.

Retailers should have a profit orientation, since all retail decisions have an effect on the income statement, the balance sheet, or both. This text will therefore focus on management of the balance sheet and income statement. Tools that show how to evaluate the profit impact of retail decisions will be discussed.

Retailers should have a decision-making orientation, which allows them to focus on collecting and analyzing data in order to make intelligent retail decisions. A retail information system is needed to help retail executives program their operations for profitable results.

THE BOOK OUTLINE

This book consists of 17 chapters and 27 case studies. The material in the text and the case studies are intended to reinforce each other. The cases bring the real world into your studies, and give you insight into the kind of situation you might face some years from now as a retail executive. Through careful analysis of the cases and discussion with fellow students, you will discover retailing concepts. The concepts will be vividly retained because of the concrete context in which they were learned. Furthermore, the cases require you to think of yourself as a retail decision maker who must work with less-than-perfect information.

INTRODUCTION TO RETAIL MARKETING

This book is divided into six parts. The first part, Introduction to Retail Marketing, has two chapters. You have already learned something about the nature and scope of retailing in this chapter. In Chapter 2, Strategic Planning in Retailing, you will learn about a framework that can be used for retail strategy development.

THE RETAILING MARKETPLACE

Part 2 focuses on understanding the retail marketplace. The four chapters examine the four factors shown in the outer circle of Exhibit 1.4 in greater detail and thus will help you to appreciate the market orientation that retailers should develop.

- Chapter 3, Understanding Retail Customers, will look at the behavior of the retail consumer and the socioeconomic environment.
- Chapter 4, Competition in Retailing, will examine the behavior of competitors.
- Chapter 5, Understanding Retailing's Role in the Channel, will focus on the behavior of the various members of the channel of distribution and their effect on the retailer.
- Chapter 6, Understanding the Legal Environment, will analyze the effect of legal constraints on today's retailer.

MERCHANDISING AND PRICING

Retailers with a marketing orientation view merchandising and pricing strategy as the pivotal elements around which their total marketing strategy is developed. That is because they are customer focused and customers seek merchandise within their budget constraints which influences pricing. Three chapters compose Part 3.

- Chapter 7, Introduction to Merchandising Control, will introduce the

types of financial statements used in retailing planning and their use. It is important to become acquainted with financial planning before merchandising and pricing are discussed since merchandise is a major investment and its pricing helps to determine profitability.
- Chapter 8, The Merchandise Buying and Handling Process, will discuss merchandise management personnel and the planning and control of merchandise.
- Chapter 9, Pricing in the Retail Operation, will present concepts and methods for considering demand and supply factors in making pricing decisions.

THE SELLING ENVIRONMENT

Four chapters compose Part 4 and each of these deals with the selling environment. The **selling environment** represents the place where interaction with the customer occurs and typically comprises a physical facility (store) at a geographic location (store site). Location is one of the most critical determinants of the selling environment for the retail firm.

- Chapter 10, Identifying Attractive Markets for Retail Stores, will discuss which geographic markets to enter.
- Chapter 11, Store Site Analysis, will focus on the specific site location within a geographic market. The store itself is also an important determinant of the selling environment.
- Chapter 12, Store Planning, Design, and Merchandising, will show how to create an exciting and high-impact store.
- Chapter 13, Retailing of Services, will discuss the retailing of services, which require specialized in-store selling strategies due to their intangibility.

PROMOTION AND SELLING

Having made merchandising, pricing, and selling environment decisions, one can turn to demand generation decisions. Part 5 comprises two chapters:

- Chapter 14, Retail Advertising and Promotion, will examine the role of advertising, sales promotion, and publicity in generating demand for a retail business.
- Chapter 15, Personal Selling, will explain how to use personal selling to generate demand and how to manage the retail sales force.

RETAIL OPERATIONS AND ADMINISTRATION

We conclude with Part 6 which deals with retail operations and administration. Two critical resources come into play in retail operations and administration and these are human resources and information resources. The role of both human and information resources is to assist in the implementation and control of the retail marketing strategy that was developed in Parts 3 through 5.

- Chapter 16, Management of Human Resources, will examine the role of human resources in a retail firm.
- Chapter 17, Retail Information Systems, will develop a framework for collecting information that is needed for achieving optimal performance in retailing.

SUMMARY

Retailing consists of the final activities and steps needed to place merchandise in the hands of the consumer or to provide services to the consumer. Retailing concentrates on delivering time, place, and possession utilities to the final consumer. There are over 1.9 million retail establishments in the United States and they can be categorized based on SIC codes, number of outlets, profit margins and inventory turnover, location, and size.

Retailing involves effectively combining creative and analytical skills to make a profit in an ever-changing environment. A framework for managing retail enterprises is the three concentric circle model of retail marketing management. This model suggests that a retail manager consider the retail marketplace when making a host of decisions which can be categorized as selling environment decisions, merchandising and pricing decisions, and selling and promotion decisions. Importantly, the retailer must use both human and information resources to make these decisions and administer and operate a retail enterprise.

What possibilities does a retailing career offer to the student? In the long run, a retail career can offer salary comparable to other careers, opportunities for career advancement, and geographic mobility. What are the prerequisites for success as a retailing executive? Besides hard work, the 10 prerequisites for success are analytical skills, creativity, decisiveness, flexibility, initiative, leadership, organization, risk taking, stress tolerance, and perseverance. All are important, but it is most important for the retail executive to have an attitude of openness to new ideas and a willingness to learn.

From what perspective should retailing be studied? In this book, we utilize four orientations to the study and practice of retailing: a marketplace orientation, a strategic planning orientation, a profit orientation, and a decision-making orientation.

QUESTIONS FOR DISCUSSION

1. What do you see as the relationship between retail management and marketing management?
2. What concepts and techniques from economics and/or finance do you believe would be most helpful in retail decision making? Why?
3. A retail manager who is both creative and analytical will definitely succeed. Agree or disagree with this statement and defend your position.
4. Management Horizons has stated that during the 1990s retailers and suppliers will work more closely together in a cooperative fashion. If this is the case, then why are more "factory outlet" malls being opened? Do you agree with the five other trends that Management Horizons projects for the 1990s? Why or why not?
5. Is managing a store of a large retail chain with 100 employees any different from managing your own store with only two employees? Why?
6. Regardless of what they sell, many retail enterprises have identical problems. Agree or disagree with this statement and defend your position.

7. If you were on the board of directors of one of the largest retail chains in the United States and had to head a committee to select a new president for the retail chain, what criteria would you use to evaluate the potential candidates? Why?
8. Many of today's retail marketplace trends will have an impact on retailing operations over the next decade. Discuss three such trends and their potential effects on retailing.
9. Ask some local retailers how they view the outlook for opportunities in retailing. Do they believe a college education is necessary for success in retailing?

MANAGEMENT MEMO

You are a district manager supervising 42 stores in a 300+ retail store chain. Sharon Womack, vice-president of human resources, has appointed you and four others to a "college recruiting task force." This task force is charged with assisting the retail chain in recruiting 100 college graduates per year for each of the next five years. Ninety percent of the positions filled will be in retail buying and store management. Fifteen college campuses have been targeted for recruiting and Sharon Womack wants the screening and interviewing of these candidates to be uniform across the campuses. She has asked you to prepare a memo outlining the three criteria to be used to screen students who desire an interview with the firm and to develop three questions that should be asked of all students who are interviewed.

BOARDROOM REPORT

You are the executive assistant to the chairperson of the board of a retail grocery chain with $900 million in annual sales. All the stores are in middle- to high-income neighborhoods. The chain is regional and has been under the same corporate ownership for 50 years. The firm gives away $500,000 annually to charitable causes. The breakdown is: higher education scholarships $75,000, local cultural events $50,000, community United Way campaigns $150,000, local child athletic events/programs $150,000, miscellaneous $75,000. The chairperson of the board would like to propose allocating $100,000 to college scholarships for underprivileged students from low-income neighborhoods. Prepare a two-page report or a five-to-seven-minute oral presentation to the board recommending this action and highlighting the benefit to the supermarket. Indicate from which current use the $100,000 should be reallocated.

SUGGESTED READINGS

Bruner, Robert F., and Kenneth M. Eades. "The Crash of the Revco Leveraged Buyout: The Hypothesis of Inadequate Capital." *Financial Management* (Spring 1992): 35-49.

Ozment, John, and Greg Martin. "Effects of Discount Chain Stores on the Competitive Environments of Rural Trade Areas: Some Preliminary Findings." In *Proceedings of the Symposium on Patronage Behavior and Retail Strategy,* edited by William R. Darden, 97-108. Baton Rouge: Louisiana State University, 1989.

Peters, Tom. "Prometheus Barely Unbound." *Academy of Management Executive* no. 4 (1990): 70-84.

Schwartz, Joe. "The Evolution of Retailing." *American Demographics* (December 1986): 30-37.

Swineyard, William R. "The Appeal of Retailing as a Career." *Journal of Retailing* (Winter 1981): 86-97.

ENDNOTES

1. Some examples of the macro approach to retailing are Elizabeth C. Hirschman, "A Descriptive Theory of Retail Market Structure," *Journal of Retailing* (Winter 1978): 29-48; Louis P. Bucklin, *Competition and Evolution in the Distributive Trades* (Englewood Cliffs, N.J.: Prentice-Hall, Inc., 1972); Madhav Kacker, "International Flow of Retailing Know-How: Bridging the Technol-

ogy Gap in Distribution," *Journal of Retailing* (Spring 1988): 41-67; Stanley C. Hollander and Glenn S. Omura, "Chain Store Developments and Their Political, Strategic, and Social Interdependencies," *Journal of Retailing* (Fall 1989): 299-325; and Rodger R. Singley and Roy D. Howell, "Information as a Public Good: The Case of Consumer Free Riding," in William R. Darden, ed., *Proceedings of the Symposium on Patronage Behavior and Retail Strategy* (Baton Rouge: Louisiana State University, 1989), 85-95.

2. E. E. Foster, trans., "The Works of Aristotle," *The Oeconomica* Oxford 10 (1920): 1343a-43b.
3. *The Scope of the Shopping Center Industry in the United States* (New York: International Council of Shopping Centers, 1990).
4. Linda Hyde, Carl E. Steidtmann, and Daniel J. Sweeney, *Retailing 2000* (Dublin, Ohio: Management Horizons, 1990). For a further discussion of changes that have occurred in retailing, see William R. Davidson, Albert Bates, and Stephen Bass, "The Retail Life Cycle," *Harvard Business Review* (November-December 1976): 89-96; Delbert J. Duncan, "Responses of Selected Retail Institutions to Their Changing Environment," in Peter Bennett, ed., *Marketing and Economic Development* (Chicago: American Marketing Association, 1965), 483-602; William J. Regan, "The Stages of Retail Development," in Reavis Cox, Wroe Alderson, and Stanley Shapiro, eds., *Theory in Marketing* (Homewood, Ill: Richard D. Irwin, 1964), 139-53; Stanley Marcus, "Merchandising for the 1990s," *Retailing Issues Letter* (July 1990): 1-4; Robert A. Peterson and Richard C. Bartlett, *A Retailing Agenda for the Year 2000* (Washington, D.C.: Direct Selling Foundation, 1990); and Roger Selbert, "Retailing's Five Most Important Trends," *Retailing Issues Letter* (March 1991):1-4.
5. U.S. Bureau of the Census, *Statistical Abstract of the United States: 1991,* 111th ed. (Washington, D.C.: Government Printing Office, 1991), 771, Table 1357.
6. For additional insights on the magnitude of retailing, see U.S. Department of Commerce, Bureau of the Census, *1987 Census of Retail Trade* (Washington, D.C.: Government Printing Office).
7. "Wal-Mart: Beyond Regional Merchandising," *Discount Merchandiser* (April 1992): 44-45.
8. Myron Gable, Karen R. Gillespie, and Martin Topol, "The Current Status of Women in Department Store Retailing: An Update," *Journal of Retailing* (Summer 1984): 92 and Myron Gable and B. J. Read, "The Current Status of Women in Professional Selling," *Journal of Personal Selling and Sales Management* (May 1987):33-39.
9. The analytical approach to retailing has been espoused for over 75 years. See Walter Hoving, "More Science in Merchandising," *Journal of Retailing* (October 1929):3-9 and Paul H. Nystrom, *The Economics of Retailing* (New York: Ronald Press, 1915).
10. "Creative Merchandising," *Progressive Grocer* (April 1991): 50-51.
11. Roger Dickinson, "Creativity in Retailing," *Journal of Retailing* (Winter 1969-1970): 4; also see William C. Miller, *The Creative Edge* (Reading, Mass.: Addison-Wesley Publishing Co., Inc., 1987).
12. Dickinson, 4.

CHAPTER 2

STRATEGIC PLANNING IN RETAILING

Retail MARKETING

OVERVIEW

The purpose of this chapter is to outline, in detail, the strategic planning process. The retail strategic planning process consists of five interrelated steps: definition of a firm's mission, definition of the firm's objectives and market position, analysis of opportunities in the retail marketplace, generation of strategy, and control of the strategic plan which is in large part done with human and information resources. We will discuss the extent to which strategic planning is used by retailers. The chapter will be concluded with a look at some of the key mistakes that retailers have made in strategic planning.

STRATEGIC PLANNING IN RETAILING

I. The Need for Planning
II. The Strategic Planning Process
III. Statement of Mission
IV. Statement of Objectives
    A. Market Performance Objectives
    B. Financial Performance Objectives
        1. Profitability Objectives
        2. Productivity Objectives
        3. Strategic Resource Management Model
    C. Societal Objectives
        1. Employment

2. Payment of Taxes
3. Consumer Choice
4. Equity
5. Benefactor
D. Personal Objectives
1. Self-Gratification
2. Status and Respect
3. Power and Authority
E. Three Recommendations
1. Realistic
2. Quantitative
3. Consistent
V. Statement of Market Position
A. Demographic Segmentation
B. Effective Segmentation
VI. Analysis of Opportunities in the Retail Marketplace
VII. Strategies
A. S.S. Kresge (Kmart)
B. Wal-Mart
C. Home Depot
D. Campeau
E. A Recap
VIII. Control System
A. Informal Control
B. Formal Control
1. Who Should Perform the Review
2. When and How Often to Review
3. What Areas Should Be Reviewed
4. Conducting the Review
5. Management Reactions
C. Review Process Problems
IX. Strategic Planning in Large Retail Firms
X. Key Mistakes in Strategic Planning
XI. Summary

THE NEED FOR PLANNING

People not familiar with retailing often wonder how retailers can anticipate what consumers are going to want the next Summer or Winter season. They may assume that retailers do it with some sort of magic. However, success for all retailers, large and small, is generally a matter of planning and its implementation. **Planning** is the anticipation and organization of what needs to be done to reach an objective. This sounds simple enough, but it is difficult to know in advance of an upcoming merchandising season what styles, quantities, and sizes customers will want, and how these wants will change during the season. Superior planning can offset some of the advantages the competition may have. Many small specialty stores have taken significant market share away from larger department stores by studying changes in the retail marketplace, anticipating future changes, and planning accordingly.

Strategic planning is a type of planning that involves adapting the firm to the opportunities and constraints of an ever-changing marketplace. Let's take a closer look at the components of the strategic planning process.

THE STRATEGIC PLANNING PROCESS

Strategic planning consists of six components:

1. Development of a statement of purpose or mission for the firm
2. Definition of specific objectives
3. Statement of desired market position for the firm
4. Analysis of opportunities in the retail marketplace
5. Development of basic strategies that will enable the firm to reach its objectives and fulfill its mission
6. Control of the plan

Exhibit 2.1 illustrates the process of strategic planning in a retail enterprise. At the top of this exhibit, we see that the retailer must develop a retail mission which must be in tune with the retail marketplace. Recall from Chapter 1 that the retail marketplace comprises the consumer, competitor, channel, and regulations or laws. After the mission is developed the retailer must establish objectives and a desired market position that identifies the market it wishes to target. Once again, these must be consistent with trends in the retail marketplace. Next, basic strategies are developed in three areas: merchandising and pricing strategy, selling environment strategy, and promotion and selling strategy. In the model you will note that human and information resources are used to develop and implement each of these strategies. In brief, the human and information resources are used to control the strategic plan. The result of this type of strategic planning should be high-performance financial results.

STATEMENT OF MISSION

The retailer's **statement of mission** is its overall justification for existing. A retailer with a mission will find it much easier to survive and prosper than one without. A retailer's mission statement should not be time- or merchandise-dependent but rather should be generic. That is, it should be stated so that it will be just as applicable in five, ten, or twenty years as it is today and should

EXHIBIT 2.1

Strategic Planning in Retailing

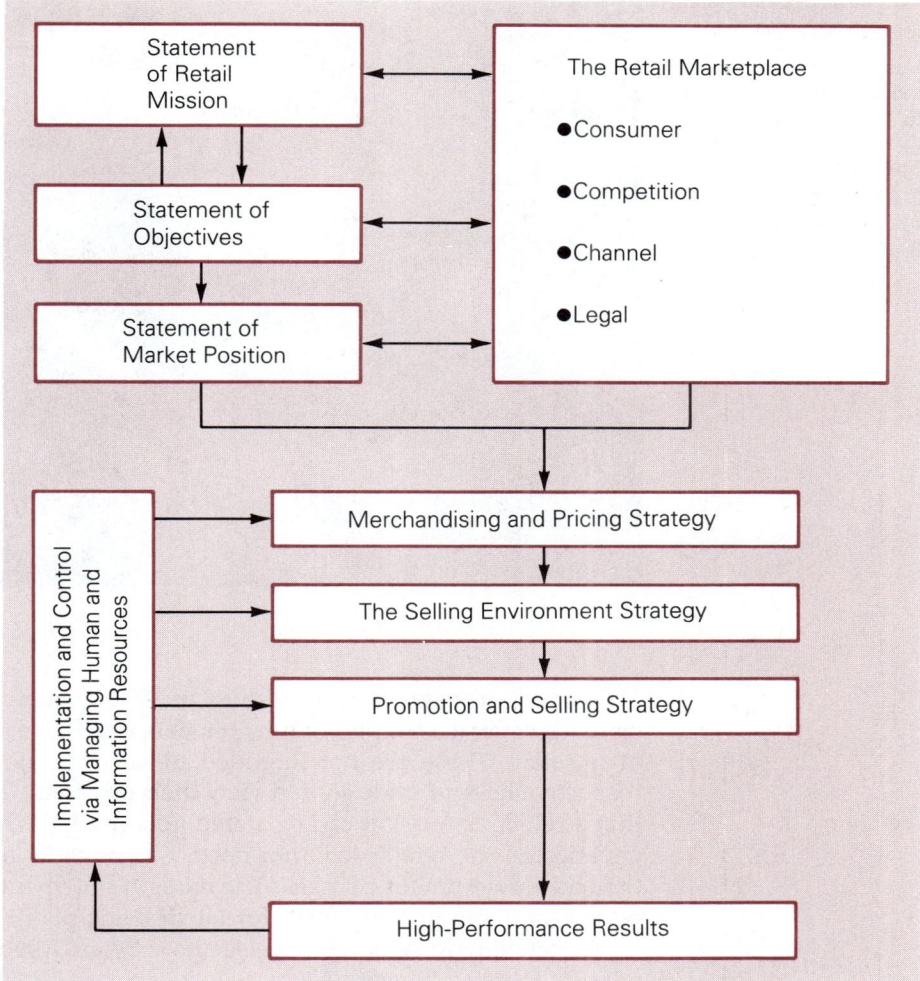

not be stated in terms of specific merchandise lines, brands, or other specific factors that reduce a retailer's flexibility to respond to changing market conditions.

The retail customer does not patronize a retail establishment to purchase merchandise or services, but to buy need fulfillment. The automobile dealer's mission is not to sell Chevrolets or even necessarily to sell automobiles. Rather, it is to help fulfill some basic needs of the customer—probably a need for personal transportation. Most beauty shops are patronized not to get one's hair cut, but to acquire a feeling of beauty. The supermarket is patronized not to purchase food but to provide substance to satisfy physiological and often psychological needs.

ILLUSTRATION 2.1

People purchase merchandise or services to fulfill needs—such as the need for personal transportation. Often the need is psychological as well as physiological.

A mission statement can be short and very general in meaning. Exhibit 2.2 contains several examples of how retailers might use a very general statement of mission. These are not intended to illustrate how all retailers in these respective lines of trade should view their missions, they only help to convey that a retailer's mission can be stated generically. When its mission is stated generically, the retailer will not need to change its mission statement every time the environment changes. The mission statement will provide a long-run perspective and guiding force for all strategic plans.

In Retailing in Action 2.1 we see how Sears, Roebuck and Co. viewed its mission in its early years. Do you believe Sears is still following this mission today?

STATEMENT OF OBJECTIVES

The second stage in our planning process is to define specific *objectives*. These objectives should derive from and give precision and direction to the retailer's mission statement. They identify the results that the retailer intends to bring about through the execution and control of its major strategies.

The statement of objectives serves two purposes. First, it provides direction and guidance to the firm in the formulation of its strategy. Second, it provides a standard against which the firm can measure and evaluate its

EXHIBIT 2.2

Examples of Mission Statements

> Our mission is to help make ordinary women feel beautiful.
>
> —Retail apparel chain
>
> Our primary mission is to help people of all ages experience and enjoy literature.
>
> —Retail book chain
>
> Our primary mission is to help people better express their feelings toward others.
>
> —Retail card and gift store
>
> Our primary objective is to help households protect their investments in transportation.
>
> —Automotive repair shop

RETAILING IN ACTION

2.1 Sears, Roebuck and Company's Mission Statement in Its Early Years

Covering a short period of about 12 years, we have grown, from a very small beginning, to a position where our volume of sales is larger than any other house in the world selling general merchandise, a position where we probably sell more merchandise directly to the user than all other mail-order catalog houses in the world. In making these rapid strides, we have had much to do in bringing about a great change in the system of merchandising, in the economies of manufacturing, wholesaling, retailing, etc., much to do with lessening cost from everyone to everyone, much to do with bettering qualities, and while this great work of manufacturing, assembling, controlling, bringing together and distributing in a single year over Fifty Million Dollars' worth of merchandise to users all over the United States has made us millions of friends (for our customers are our friends), unfortunately for us, and not that we would have it so, nor because we bear any ill will toward any of our competitors, great or small, this wonderfully rapid growth and development has created for us a good many enemies, especially among the smaller retail dealers, storekeepers in country towns, and among manufacturers, especially those manufacturers from whom we decline to buy goods, either because they cannot furnish us satisfactorily high qualities or satisfactorily low prices.

If our prices were not so much lower than people can buy elsewhere, if our qualities were not uniformly high, if our policy was not such that says, you must save money on every purchase you make from us or return the goods to us at our expense, if our financial strength and standing was not such that everyone can feel perfectly safe in sending their money and orders to us, if we did not give you all these advantages and our competitors did not know it, if the retail dealers and the storekeepers of the country and the small manufacturers of the country did not know all this to be true, there would be no jealousy on their part, there would be no occasion for them to attack us with their thousand and one misrepresentations.

If all this were not true, we would have no enemies, but, unfortunately, neither would we have the friends, the millions of customers.

If all this were not true, we could not say, as we can today, that nearly one-half of all the families in the United States, outside of the larger cities, have sent to us for goods. They are our customers, and, being our customers, they are our friends. They have tried us and in trying they have found us out and they know.

No friend or enemy, competitor or customer, can honestly accuse us of ever doing other than giving the greatest possible value for the money, making or buying goods at the lowest possible cost, and then selling them at this cost, plus only one small percentage of profit, giving the highest possible standard of quality, maintaining the most strict system of inspection to insure a high standard of quality, asking every customer with every shipment to return the goods to us at our expense and get their money back if they are not satisfied, treating every customer exactly as we would like to be treated if we were in the customer's place.

Anyone who is honest can only say we do simply this, nothing more, nothing less, and it's a policy that has won, is winning and will continue to win in spite of any and all kinds of competition.

Never once deviating from this policy, our growth has been continuous and rapid until today we are, in point of capital, of money actually invested in the business, in volume of sales, manufacturing, buying, selling and financial strength, by far the largest and strongest institution of the kind in the world. Today we have millions of dollars invested in our own real estate, free of encumbrance, millions of dollars invested in merchandise here in Chicago and in factories all over the country; today we have a capital stock of Forty Million Dollars, fully paid, an enviable credit thoroughly established all over the world, and the fullest confidence of our millions of customers, the highest reward we could ask for a policy that has ever guided us in the past and shall ever guide us in the future.

Source: Historical/corporate document.

performance results. In addition to the market performance and financial performance objectives that retailers may set for themselves, retailers may also establish societal objectives and personal objectives. Retail objectives can be categorized into four groups:

1. **Market performance objectives** are those that compare the retailer's dominance in the marketplace to that of the competition.
2. **Financial performance objectives** are those that can be stated in monetary or economic terms. These are objectives that directly relate to the dollars and cents of retailing.

3. **Societal objectives** are phrased in terms of helping society fulfill some of its needs.
4. **Personal objectives** relate to helping people employed in retailing fulfill some of their needs.

Let us examine each type of objective in more detail.

MARKET PERFORMANCE OBJECTIVES

Market performance objectives establish the amount of dominance the retailer has in the marketplace. The most popular measures of market performance in retailing are sales volume and market share. **Market share** is the proportion of total sales in a particular market that the retailer has been able to capture. It is calculated by dividing the retailer's total sales by total market sales. In measuring market share, it is important to pay particular attention to delineation of the geographic and line-of-trade markets. For instance, if we desire to compute the market share of a supermarket chain in Cincinnati, Ohio, we would state the total sales of that chain in the Cincinnati area not in relation to total retail sales in the state of Ohio, but in relation to total food store sales in the Cincinnati area.

Some aggressive retailers saw the slow retail market of 1990–1992 as an opportunity to expand in order to increase market share. For example, Merry-Go-Round added over 120 stores in 1990 and 1991. Other retailers, such as The Limited, Wal-Mart, and Home Depot, also sought growth during this period.[1]

FINANCIAL PERFORMANCE OBJECTIVES

Retailers can establish many financial performance objectives, but they can all be conveniently fitted into categories of profitability and productivity.

Profitability Objectives. Profit-based objectives deal directly with the monetary return a retailer desires from its business. The most frequently encountered profit objectives in a retail enterprise are:

1. **Gross margin return on sales.** Gross margin return on sales is defined as gross margin divided by net sales. A retailer's gross margin return on sales depicts what percentage of the average dollar of sales is available to pay fixed and operating expenses and produce a profit.
2. **Return on assets.** A retailer's return on assets is defined as net profit divided by total assets. This ratio depicts what percentage of the average dollar invested in assets is returned in profit.
3. **Financial leverage.** A retailer's financial leverage is defined as total assets divided by net worth or owner's equity. This ratio depicts the extent to

which the retailer is using debt to finance its business. For example, a ratio of 2.0 means that for each dollar of equity the retailer has two dollars in assets. This would suggest that one dollar of debt is being used to finance each two dollars in assets.

4. **Return on net worth.** Return on net worth (also called return on equity) is net profit divided by owner's or stockholder's equity. It shows the percentage profit return on each dollar invested in equity. Return on net worth can be obtained by multiplying return on assets by financial leverage.
5. **Earnings per share.** This ratio is defined as total earnings available to common stockholders divided by shares of common stock outstanding. It shows the profit that each share of common stock has earned.
6. **Operating profit margin.** Operating profit margin is the retailer's operating profit divided by net sales.

All retail enterprises establish some form of profit objective. These objectives play an important role in evaluating potential strategic opportunities.

Productivity Objectives. Productivity objectives state how much output the retailer desires for each unit of resource input. The major resources at the retailer's disposal are space, labor, and merchandise; productivity objectives for each may be established.

1. **Space productivity.** Space productivity is defined as net sales divided by the total square feet of retail floor space. (In this discussion, whenever we refer to net sales we are talking about annual net sales.) A space productivity objective states how many dollars in sales the retailer wants to generate for each square foot of store space.
2. **Labor productivity.** Labor productivity is defined as net sales divided by the number of full-time-equivalent employees. A full-time-equivalent employee is one who works 40 hours per week; typically two part-time workers equal one full-time employee. A labor productivity objective reflects how many dollars in sales the retailer desires to generate for each full-time-equivalent employee.
3. **Merchandise productivity.** Merchandise productivity is net sales divided by the average dollar investment in inventory. This measure is also known as the sales-to-stock ratio. Specifically, this objective states the dollar sales the retailer desires to generate for each dollar invested in inventory.

Productivity objectives are vehicles by which a retailer can program its business for high-profit results. For instance, it would be impossible for a supermarket chain to achieve a respectable return on assets while experiencing dismal space, labor, and merchandise productivity. In short, productivity is a key determinant of profit in retailing.

This might be a good time to examine the basic return on investment model, which is also often referred to as the *strategic profit model* (Exhibit 2.3a and b) to see how the profitability and productivity objectives are interrelated. Space productivity is reflected in boxes 13, 14, 15, 16, and 19 of this exhibit. If

EXHIBIT 2.3a
Basic Return on Investment Model

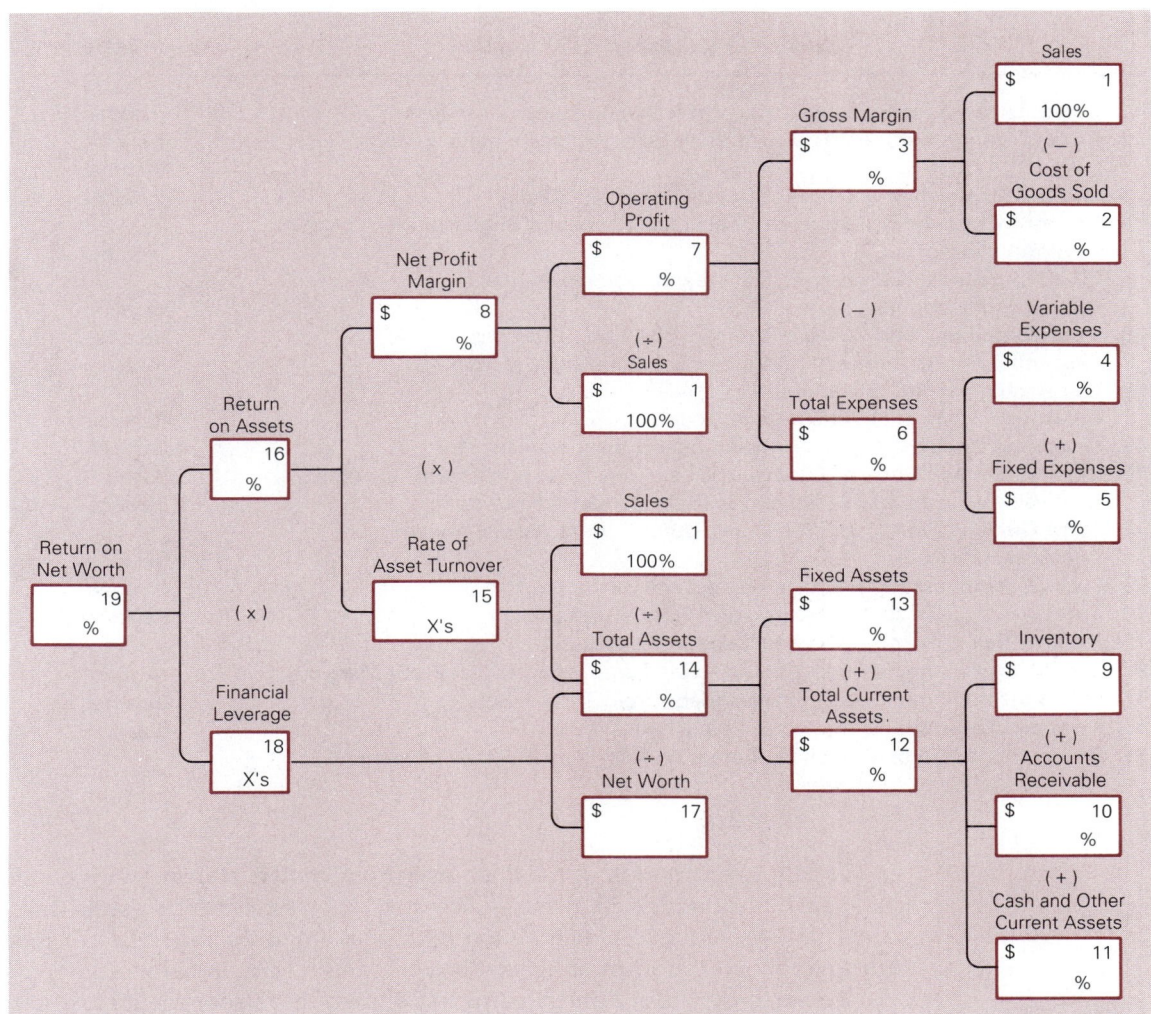

retailers fail to utilize fully their space, the amount in box 13 will be overstated. This in turn will overstate total assets (box 14), causing the rate of asset turnover to be lower or unproductive (box 15) and lowering both the return on assets (box 16) and return on net worth (box 19).

Labor productivity is reflected in boxes 4 and 5, the cost of labor plus other expenses. If retailers pay too much for labor, total expenses (box 6) will be too high, thus lowering operating profit (box 7), net profit margin (box 8), return on assets (box 16), and return on net worth (box 19).

EXHIBIT 2.3b
Definition of Terms in the Basic ROI Model

Item and Calculation	Source Statement
1. **Sales**: all revenues from exchange of merchandise and/or services	Income
2. **Cost of goods sold**: cost value of those sales which are made during a period.	Income
3. **Gross Margin**: subtract Cost of Goods Sold from Sales.	Income
4. **Variable Expenses**: all expenses which change with changes in sales volume; short run concept.	Income
5. **Fixed Expenses**: All expenses that stay the same over a wide range of sales volume and a long time period.	Income
6. **Total Expenses**: add Variable Expenses and Fixed Expenses.	Income
7. **Operating Profit**: subtract Total Expenses from Gross Margin.	Income
8. **Net Profit Margin**: operating profit divided by sales.	Income
9. **Inventory**: value of merchandise in stock	Balance
10. **Accounts Receivable**: money owed retailer by customers.	Balance
11. **Cash and other Current Assets**: cash and any asset other than Accounts Receivable or Inventory which can easily be converted into cash.	Balance
12. **Total Current Assets**: add Cash and Other Current Assets, Inventory, Accounts Receivable.	Balance
13. **Fixed Assets**: assets which are depreciated over time.	Balance
14. **Total Assets**: add Current Assets and Fixed Assets.	Balance
15. **Rate of Asset Turnover**: divide Sales by Total Assets.	
16. **Return on Assets**: multiply Rate of Asset Turnover times Net Profit Margin.	
17. **Net Worth**: subtract total Liabilities (debt) from Total Assets.	Balance
18. **Financial Leverage**: divide Total Assets by Net Worth.	Balance
19. **Return on Net Worth**: multiply Return on Assets by Financial Leverage.	

Finally, we can look at merchandise productivity, starting with box 9. If retailers have too high an average inventory, then total current assets (box 12) and total assets (box 14) will be too high, thereby reducing the rate of asset turnover (box 15), return on assets (box 16), and return on net worth (box 19).

Research by Gifford and Stearns has shown that department store executives rank operating profit margin, gross margin return on sales, and space productivity as the three most important indicators of financial performance. Specialty store executives ranked, in order of importance, operating profit margin, merchandise productivity, and gross margin return on sales. Retailing faculty members ranked merchandise productivity, operating profit margin, and gross margin return on sales in that order.[2]

Strategic Resource Management Model. In Exhibit 2.4a we present the strategic resource management model, which provides a framework for strategically managing space, labor, and merchandise resources.[3] In examining this

EXHIBIT 2.4a

The Strategic Resource Management Model

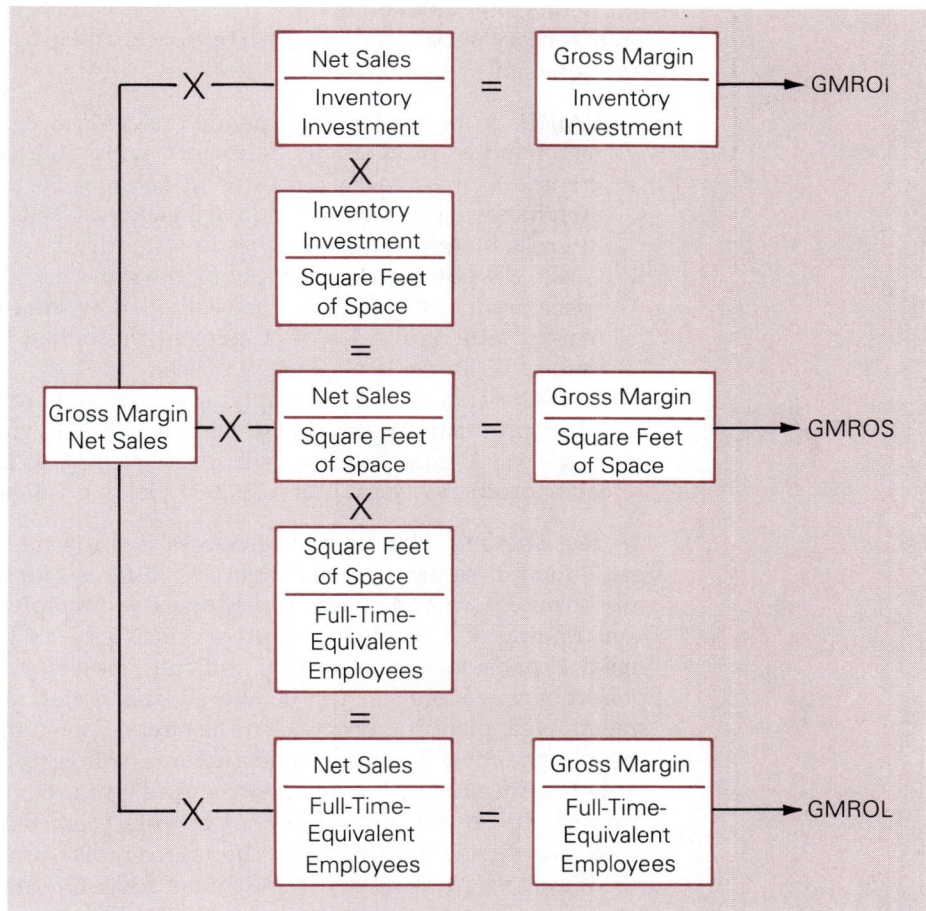

model, we should keep in mind that retailers use their financial resources to acquire three critical resources—space, inventory or merchandise, and labor. Essentially, inventory is acquired and displayed on floor space and labor is used to handle and sell the merchandise. All major innovations in retailing originated from some reorganization and recombination of these resources. For example, self-service stores used less labor, warehouse retailing put more inventory in a limited space and used less labor, full-service department stores used more labor, merchandise and space, and so on.

The strategic resource management model underscores the importance of gross margin return on sales. This is the first financial ratio in the model and it has a cumulative effect. As the retail operation is strategically planned to generate a higher gross margin return on sales, then all else remaining equal, investments in inventory, space, and employees will be more profitable. Let's study this phenomenon in more detail by explaining how gross margin return on inventory, gross margin return on space, and gross margin return on labor are obtained.

1. *GMROI* is obtained by multiplying the gross margin return on sales by the merchandise productivity ratio (net sales divided by inventory investment). A gross margin return on sales of 30 percent multiplied by a merchandise productivity ratio of 5 yields a GMROI of 150 percent or $150 in gross margin for each dollar invested in inventory.
2. *GMROS* is obtained by multiplying the gross margin return on sales by the space productivity ratio (net sales divided by square feet of space). A gross margin return on sales of 30 percent multiplied by a space productivity ratio of $300 yields a GMROS of $90.
3. *GMROL* is obtained by multiplying the gross margin return on sales by the labor productivity ratio (net sales divided by full-time-equivalent employees). A gross margin return on sales of 30 percent multiplied by a labor productivity ratio of $120,000 yields a GMROL of $36,000.

The strategic planning of resources is important not only for setting a gross margin return on sales objective, but also for establishing the proper mix of inventory and space, and of space and employees. Space is the most constraining of a retailer's resources, since lease or building constraints can make expansion or contraction difficult. However, since over the longer period of time store size can be altered, this option should not be ignored in the strategic planning process. In the strategic resource management model, the merchandise intensity ratio (inventory investment per square feet of space) is multiplied by the merchandise productivity ratio to yield space productivity. If the firm has $60 of inventory investment per square foot of space and this is multiplied by the merchandise productivity ratio of 5, the result is space productivity (GMROS) of $300. On the other hand, if the firm has an employee intensity ratio of 400 (which means each employee has an average 400 square feet of space to handle) and this is multiplied by the space productivity ratio of $300, the result is labor productivity (GMROL) of $120,000 (net sales per full-time-equivalent employee).

Now that we have developed the strategic resource management model, you might wish to review Exhibit 2.4a, which outlines the algebra of the model, Exhibit 2.4b, which provides the proper labels for all the financial ratios, and Exhibit 2.4c, which shows the values of the ratios for a discount department store versus a traditional department store.

SOCIETAL OBJECTIVES

Sometime in the early 1970s, a significant number of retailers began to establish societal objectives. Societal objectives are generally not as specific or as quantitative as market or financial objectives, but they do highlight the retailer's concern with broader issues in our world. There is no agreed-upon

Chapter 2 Strategic Planning in Retailing   43

EXHIBIT 2.4b
The Strategic Resource Model Concept Description

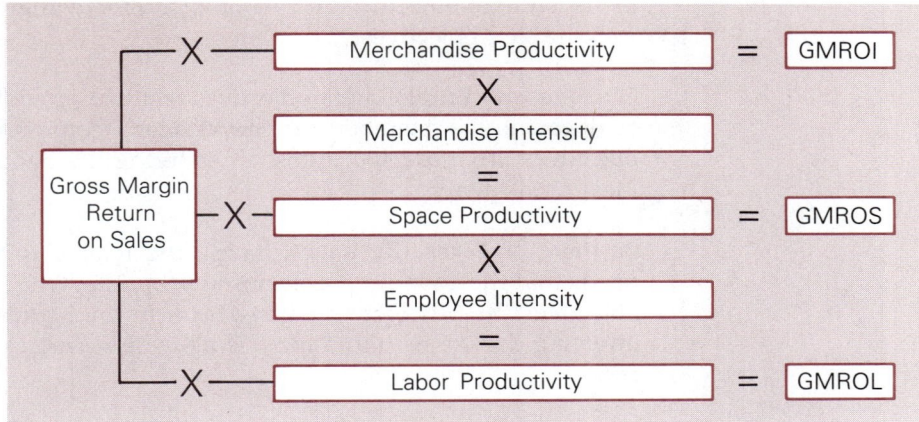

EXHIBIT 2.4c
The Strategic Resource Model: Discount Department Store versus Conventional Department Store

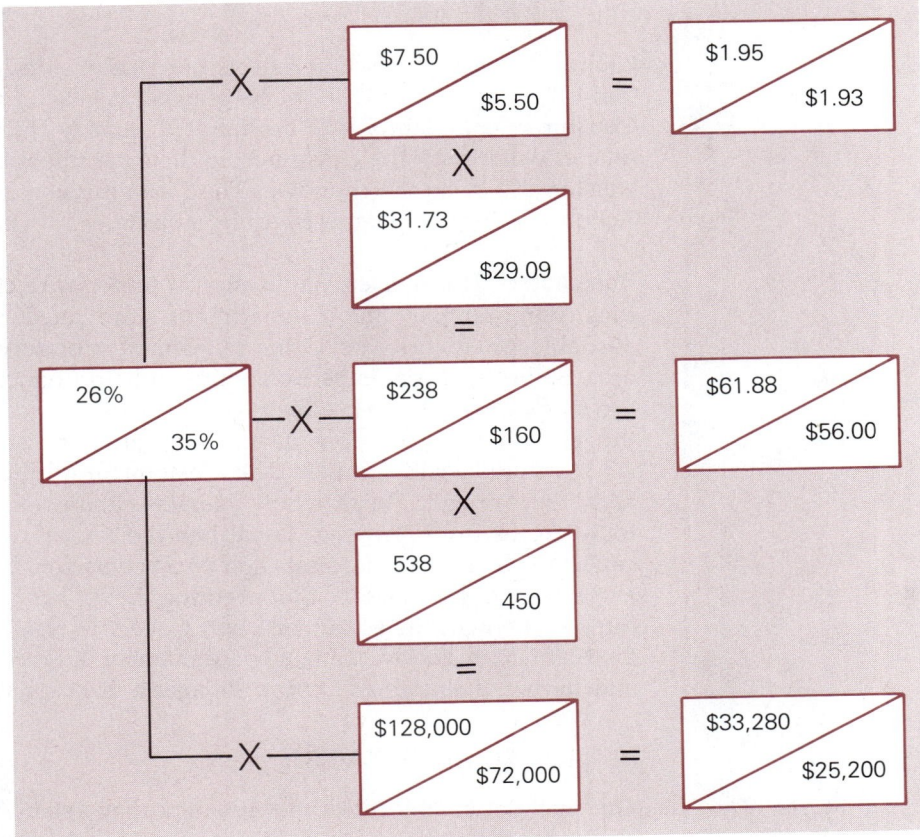

list of societal objectives in retailing; the following are the most frequently encountered objectives.

Employment. Employment objectives relate to providing employment opportunities for the members of the retailer's community. Many times these objectives are more specific, such as hiring the handicapped, ethnic minorities, or students.

Payment of Taxes. By paying taxes, the retailer is helping finance societal needs that the government deems appropriate. One retailer had as his stated objective "the privilege of paying taxes in the highest possible tax bracket," implying that he wouldn't mind if he were so successful he had to pay high taxes.

Consumer Choice. A retailer may have as a societal objective to compete in such a fashion that the consumer will be given a real alternative. A retailer with such an objective desires to be a leader and innovator in merchandising and provide the consumer with choices that were not previously available in the trading area.

Equity. An equity objective reflects the retailer's desire to treat the consumer fairly. The consumer will not be gouged in case of merchandise shortages. Consumer complaints will be handled quickly, fairly, and equitably. The retailer will inform the consumer, to the extent possible, of the strengths and weaknesses of its merchandise. The Sears mission statement in Retailing in Action 2.1 strongly suggests equity objectives.

Benefactor. The retailer may desire to underwrite certain community activities. For example, many department store retailers make meeting rooms available for civic groups. Other retailers help underwrite various performing arts. Still others provide scholarships to help finance education. Centers for the study of retailing at colleges and universities are all supported in part by the generous contributions of retailers, large and small.

Mortimer Levitt founded The Custom Shop Shirtmakers in 1937 with a $2,000 investment. The firm now operates nationwide with 81 stores. When he founded the firm, however, Levitt had the goal of retiring in five years so he could pursue his own interests and be a benefactor. He actually retired in 1941 and now is in his mid-80s. Since retiring, Levitt has devoted time to charitable causes. He owns the Mortimer Levitt Gallery in New York and is a founder of the Manhattan Theatre Club, a board member of Lincoln Center's Film Society, and former chairman of Daytop Village, a drug rehabilitation center.[4]

PERSONAL OBJECTIVES

The final set of objectives that retailers may establish is personal. Personal objectives may relate only to the owners or top-level executives in the firm, or they may apply to all employees of the retail establishment. No standard list of personal objectives exists, but retailers tend to pursue three types of personal objectives.

Self-Gratification. Self-gratification has as its focus the needs and desires of the owners, managers, or employees of the firm to pursue what they truly want out of life. This was a large factor in Shirley Link's motivation to open Turner's Outdoorsman in Southern California. Turner's Outdoorsman specializes in hunting and fishing equipment, with eight stores and annual sales of $34 million. Link grew up in the Ozarks and her parents operated a country store and gas station. At an early age, she became an avid hunting and fishing enthusiast. She always wanted to own her own business and when she decided to do so it made sense to also fulfill her personal interests in hunting and fishing.[5]

Status and Respect. All humans strive for status and respect. In stating this type of objective, the retailer recognizes that the owners, managers, or employees need status and respect in their community or within their circle of friends. The retailer may, for example, give annual awards to outstanding employees. Or when promotions occur, press releases may be sent to local newspapers or trade journals such as *Stores* or *Chain Store Age*.

Power and Authority. Objectives based on power and authority reflect the need of managers and other employees to be in positions of influence. Retailers may establish objectives that give buyers and department managers maximum flexibility to determine their own destiny, including power and authority to allocate scarce resources such as space, dollars, and labor to achieve a profit objective. Having the power and authority to allocate resources makes managers feel important and gives them a sense of pride when they excel.

Exhibit 2.5 is a synopsis of the market performance, financial performance, and societal and personal objectives that retailers can establish in the strategic planning process. All retail objectives, of whatever type, must be consistent with the overall mission of the retailer. The retailer's objectives must reinforce its mission.

THREE RECOMMENDATIONS

Philip Kotler has stated that, as a general rule, an organization's objectives should be realistic, quantitative, and consistent.[6] Retail organization objectives are no exception.

Realistic. Objectives should be developed so that they are within the realm of reason. To state during a recessionary year that a moderately successful supermarket chain in Detroit, Michigan, is going to increase sales by 50 percent is unrealistic. Some overstatement may help stimulate managers and employees, but an unrealistic objective will tend to frighten them off rather

EXHIBIT 2.5

Retail Objectives

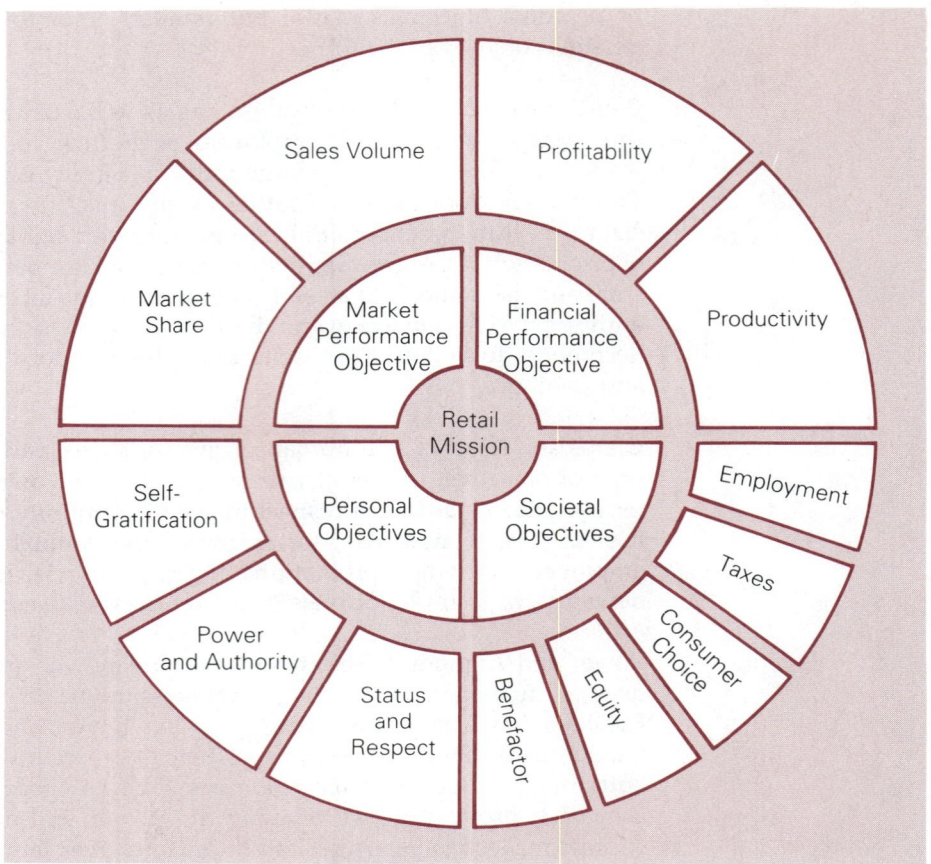

than motivate them. Furthermore, if the retailer continually states unrealistic objectives, employees will quickly begin to discount *any* objectives that are established for them. Objectives that are established should have a reasonable chance of being achieved as long as the environment does not change significantly.

Quantitative. Objectives that are quantitative are better than those that are nonquantitative. Performance can be more accurately measured if specific quantities are stated as part of the objectives.

Assume a retailer stated that one of its primary objectives was to increase return on net worth over the next three years. At the close of the three-year period, financial statements show that return on net worth increased from 10 percent in the first year to 10.4 percent in the third year. Did this retailer attain its objective? Mathematically, it did, because 10.4 percent is greater than 10 percent. But what if the retailer really had in mind a much more significant increase—say, an increase of 14 to 16 percent? Then the objective was not achieved. Unless a precise quantitative goal to be achieved within a given period of time is established, the degree of achievement of that objective will be difficult to assess.

Of the four types of retail objectives, market performance and financial performance objectives are the easiest to state in quantitative terms. Societal and personal objectives are much more difficult, but not impossible, to state quantitatively. See whether you can develop quantitative measures of some of the personal and societal objectives that were discussed earlier in this chapter.

Consistent. A third criterion of good retail objectives is consistency. A retailer will state not one, but many, objectives. The potential exists for some of these objectives to be internally inconsistent. Early in the strategic planning process, the retailer must ensure consistency.

For example, the retailer that states a financial objective of maximizing return on assets and a societal objective of maximizing consumer choice introduces a glaring inconsistency. If the retailer truly wanted to maximize consumer choice, it would need to offer many brands or product lines, and these would not generate high enough margins or rates of inventory turnover to aid the retailer in maximizing its return on assets. Clearly, these two objectives, like many others, can exist only in trade-off relationships. Maximizing both is not possible.

Eight basic trade-offs confronting any company are[7]:

1. Short-term profits versus long-term growth
2. Profit margin versus competitive position
3. Direct sales effort versus market development
4. Penetration of existing markets versus the development of new markets
5. Related versus nonrelated new opportunities as a source of long-term growth
6. Profit versus nonprofit goals (i.e., social responsibilities and personal goals)
7. Growth versus stability
8. Riskless environment versus high-risk environment

Each of these trade-offs needs to be explicitly considered in the retailer's attempt to develop strategic plans. The relative emphasis to be placed on each should be selected early in the strategic planning process to avoid problems in implementation and execution of retail plans.

STATEMENT OF MARKET POSITION

The third stage of the strategic planning process (see Exhibit 2.1) is to state the market position desired. This is also often referred to as selecting the target market. A **market position** is the segment of the market that the retailer desires to attract with its strategy. It is the "niche" in the market that is being

ILLUSTRATION 2.2

Wendy's attempts to create a market position distinct from its competitors by appealing to the over-25, childless fast-food consumer.

sought. Whatever strategy the retailer develops, it will need to decide which market position or group of consumers to focus its efforts on. Consumers are not homogeneous in their wants and preferences. The retailer needs to focus its efforts in order to use its resources more efficiently and better achieve its financial objectives. Wendy's, McDonald's, and Steak and Ale seek different market positions. Wendy's seeks the over-25, childless, fast-food consumer. McDonald's seeks the couples with children, as well as the under-19 crowd, and Steak and Ale targets the upper- and upper-middle-income groups desiring non-fast-food dining. These retailers have realized that marketplaces are becoming more heterogeneous, with great diversity in lifestyles and values.[8] Eleanor May, a leading retail academician, states, "A long-established goal of being 'all things to all people' is not possible in today's consumer market. A store must decide which segments of the market it is serving, or wants to serve, and then attempt to match the store to the need of these consumers."[9] The retail manager must develop an effective market positioning that will complement its overall retail strategy and allow it to compete effectively in the geographic markets it serves.[10]

Proper market positioning requires the retailer to segment the market. **Market segmentation** is the process of dividing a heterogeneous group of consumers into smaller, more homogeneous groups. The smaller groups will be quite different from one another and respond differently to a retailer's merchandise and service offering, but ideally members within any given group will be quite similar. How consumers respond to different retail marketing variables will differ from one segment to the next. For example, the retailer might find that respective segments vary in how responsive they are to lower prices, increased advertising, or higher levels of customer services.

DEMOGRAPHIC SEGMENTATION

Retailers can segment their market by using **demographic characteristics,** which describe the population characteristics of the market. Common demographic variables used to segment retail markets are age, ethnic group, income, education, sex, geography, family life cycle, and social class.

Age is a good variable to segment many retail markets. For instance, most music tapes and compact discs are purchased by people between ages 12 and 24. Stereo retailers receive a disproportionate amount of their business from people in the 18-to-30-year-old bracket. The Limited has created a new chain of stores called "Limited Too" that cater to young girls. The target customer is the size 4–14 girl who seeks high-fashion, high-quality, moderate-priced clothing.

Ethnic group is another useful segmentation variable. Grocery stores, especially, may cater to local ethnic groups, designing their merchandise assortment to support the ethnic dishes these groups frequently prepare. Occasionally, clothing stores or restaurants will focus their efforts on certain ethnic groups. For example, in El Paso and San Diego, there are clothing stores that appeal primarily to Mexican-Americans, while many restaurants in the Midwest and East Coast cater to the Catholic market by offering nonmeat specials on Fridays during Lent.

Income can also be used as a segmentation variable. Exclusive restaurants often cater to high-income households. However, not all retailers should aim at the higher income segments. Retailers like Dollar General and Family Dollar Stores, Inc., primarily target lower-income shoppers. Another example of an income segment is the professional woman who, with her higher income level, has different shopping habits than her nonprofessional counterpart.

Education level is occasionally used to partition the retailer's market. Consumption of most products or retail services is not a function of educational attainment, but there are notable exceptions. For example, book stores generally cater to more educated individuals, and consumers with lower levels of education represent the largest market for fishing and camping equipment. Also, college graduates or those with some post–high school education are more likely to purchase computers.

Sex, when used to segment a retailer's market, can be approached from two perspectives. First, merchandise appeal can be based on sales to only one sex. This would be applicable to bridal stores, for example. Second, regardless of the product's appeal, the market could be segmented on the basis of whether women or men make the most purchase decisions. Thus, a menswear store might try to appeal to females if a significant number of wives made clothing decisions for their husbands. Or, a retailer like Victoria's

Secret, which sells intimate female apparel, might try to cater to male shoppers buying gifts through both its stores and catalog mail division.

Geography can also be approached from two perspectives. First, the retailer must decide which area of the country to focus its efforts on. Major geographic areas include Pacific, Mountain, West North Central, West South Central, East North Central, East South Central, South Atlantic, Middle Atlantic, and New England. Second, the retailer must decide where to concentrate its efforts within an area. Options include the central business district (CBD), the non-CBD central city, and the suburbs. All retailers must explicitly or implicitly focus on some geographic segment. Every time a store location decision is made, the retailer is making a decision to cater to a geographic market. It is also important to recognize that each geographic market has its unique population composition, consisting of different proportions of age groups, ethnic groups, educational levels, and so on.

Family life cycle refers to the changes in family composition that, over time, substantially alter family needs, decision making, and market behavior. The three stages of the family life cycle are[11]:

1. Young
    a. Single without children
    b. Married without children
    c. Single with children
    d. Married with children
2. Middle-aged
    a. Single without children
    b. Married without children
    c. Single with children
    d. Married with children
    e. Single without dependent children
    f. Married without dependent children
3. Older
    a. Single
    b. Married

Households in each of these stages exhibit different wants and preferences for such basic items as housing, home furnishings, food, automobiles, and recreational equipment. The family life cycle idea enables retailers to identify which groups are the heaviest users, and thus the best customers, for specific merchandise and services.

Social class refers to relatively permanent and homogeneous divisions in a society, in which individuals or families share similar values, lifestyles, interests, and behavior.[12] In the United States, six social classes (based on income source, wealth, education, and occupational prestige) are typically identified: upper-upper, lower-upper, upper-middle, lower-middle, upper-lower, and lower-lower. Retailers can direct their overall retail strategy to a particular social class. For instance, Kmart and other discount department stores tend to target efforts on the lower-middle and upper-lower social classes. Bergdorf Goodman and Neiman-Marcus focus on the lower-upper and upper-middle classes.

EFFECTIVE SEGMENTATION

Philip Kotler notes that, regardless of the variables used to segment the market, there are three requirements for effective segmentation:

1. **Measurability,** or the "degree to which the size and purchasing power of the resulting segments can be measured."
2. **Accessibility,** or the "degree to which the resulting segments can be effectively reached and served."
3. **Substantiality,** or the "degree to which the resulting segments are large and/or profitable enough to be worth considering for separate marketing attention."[13]

Some of these variables produce segments that are much easier to measure than others. Consider age versus lifestyle. Using census data, the retailer can easily determine how many people within its trading area are in various age brackets. But if the retailer wanted to know how many people in its trading area pursued a "casual" lifestyle, no ready source of data would be available. There is not even an agreed-upon definition of what a "casual" lifestyle is. Therefore, segmenting on this variable would be more difficult than segmenting according to age. It is encouraging to note, however, that more data are becoming readily available on lifestyles. National Planning Data Corporation offers retailers data on 40 lifestyle groupings as related to neighborhoods and other small geographic areas. This helps to provide measurable data on useful segmentation variables.

Some segmentation variables produce segments that are easier to gain access to than others. For example, teenagers can be reached by advertising on popular radio stations. But how does a store manager direct advertising at upper-middle-class households? Do these households tend to watch different television programs or read different parts of the newspaper? Unless the retailer can readily obtain access to a market segment, the segmentation strategy will not be totally effective.

Finally, the retailer needs to be concerned with the substantiality or size of the segment. Does it offer sufficient profit potential? A menswear retailer could decide to focus its retailing efforts on extra-large or tall men, but the number of these men in its trading area might not justify such a segmentation strategy.

ANALYSIS OF OPPORTUNITIES IN THE RETAIL MARKETPLACE

Once retailers have firmly established their mission, objectives, and market position, they must attempt to identify and analyze opportunities for which they can develop strategy. This is the fourth stage in the strategic planning process. The key to identifying opportunities is analysis of the retail marketplace. It should be pointed out, however, that the mission, objectives, market position, and retail marketplace are all interrelated. In fact, it may be necessary to begin the strategic planning process with an analysis of the retail marketplace. This would be especially true when a new retail enterprise is being established. An examination of Exhibit 2.1 will show that the arrows between the mission, objectives, market position, and retail marketplace point in two directions. This communicates the interrelationship between these steps of the strategic planning process.

The forces in the retail marketplace that need to be carefully examined will be discussed in Chapters 3 through 6. These forces, which retailers have little control over, are the behavior of consumers, the behavior of competitors, the behavior of members of the marketing channel, and the regulatory environment. Let's briefly see why each is important:

1. *Consumer behavior.* The behavior of consumers will obviously have a significant impact on the retailer's future. Specifically, the retailer will need to understand the determinants of shopping behavior so that likely changes in that behavior can be identified and appropriate strategies developed. The senior management at Pier 1 know all too well the importance of keeping an eye on the changing consumer. Pier 1 stores originally appealed to the hippie movement of the 1960s and offered incense, soap, beaded curtains, tie-dyed bedspreads, peacock feathers, and other hallmarks of the antiestablishment. During the 1970s, Pier 1 drifted unfocused and failed to move from the age of Aquarius to the age of disco. However, after major marketplace research in the 1980s, the company is now back in focus; it has decided to target middle-aged Americans who are interested in the home and home furnishings.[14] This is only one example of the importance of monitoring the changing consumer. Chapter 3 will be devoted to helping you understand the retail consumer.

2. *Competitor behavior.* How competing retailers behave will have a major impact on which strategy will be most appropriate. Retailers must develop a competitive strategy that is not easily imitated in a highly competitive arena. One of the trends in the retail marketplace that many U.S. retailers are watching is the entry of Japanese firms into retail service industries in the United States. Retailing in Action 2.2 addresses this issue. Chapter 4 will be devoted to helping you understand the behavior of competitive forces in retailing.

3. *Channel behavior.* The behavior of members of the retailer's marketing channel, the flow from manufacturer to consumer, can have a significant impact on the retailer's future. For example, are certain channel members, such as manufacturers or wholesalers, establishing their own retail outlets? Are wholesalers requiring larger minimum orders and offering less attractive credit terms? Behaviors such as these have implications for the retailer's strategy.

4. *Regulatory behavior.* The retailer should be familiar with local, state, fed-

RETAILING IN ACTION

2.2 Quality Japanese Service

Over the last three decades, the Japanese have made major inroads into manufacturing, creating formidable competition for U.S. manufacturers in the automobile, motorcycle, and consumer electronics industries. How will the Japanese fare if they enter the retail services industries in the United States? Certainly if they export their high levels of quality service, U.S. retailers will face a tough challenge.

What is customer service like in Japan? Let's take a brief glimpse.

- Salesclerks and executives line up to bow to the first customers that enter department stores each day.
- Japanese auto dealers will often provide pickup and delivery for customers getting their cars serviced.
- Japanese banks may offer customers tax advice or assistance in selling or buying a home.
- Service departments in many Japanese auto dealerships are open seven days a week.

What are some of the techniques Japanese firms use to constantly improve service?

- Intensive training is provided in customer service and how to treat the customers, handle complaints, and keep customers satisfied.
- Quality circles are used where employees meet regularly to develop ways to improve customer service.
- Customer satisfaction levels are regularly measured and become a central part of compensation systems and the development of employees.

Professor David Aaker believes that Japanese firms will not export a high level of service quality to the United States. He believes that this will be hindered by the lack of employee loyalty and work habits in the United States, heterogeneity of the U.S. work force, the reduced role of personal service in the United States, and the consensus among Japanese firms that service levels in Japan are excessive and they have no desire to create this level of service in the United States.

Sources: Authors' background and David A. Aaker, "How Will the Japanese Compete in Retail Services?" *California Management Review* (Fall 1990): 54-67.

---

eral, and possibly foreign regulations of the retail system, as well as evolving legal patterns, in order to design retail strategies that are legally defensible.

Retailers need to analyze all these forces for two reasons. First, because they are largely uncontrollable, retailers will have to be able to adapt to them. Second, retailers need to translate threats emanating from changing external forces into opportunities and subsequently into strategies. For example, when Macy's witnessed the demographics of its trade area change in New York City, it in turn changed its market position from one catering to the working classes to a trendy boutique store catering to the upper-middle classes. This strategy went well until Macy's lured investors to put up $3.7 billion for a leveraged buyout in 1986, which subsequently created such a large debt burden that the company entered bankruptcy in January 1992. Its problems are now mainly financial and not merchandising.[15]

The notion that threats can be translated into opportunities is highlighted in Exhibit 2.6, which shows how specific marketplace trends were changed from threats to specific lines of retail trade into opportunities. For example, one trend was the increasing proportion of households eating food outside the home. Most grocery store managers perceived this as a threat to their livelihood. But astute and adaptive managers viewed this trend as an opportunity to develop in-store delicatessens, expand frozen-food departments, and increase the assortment of food items that are easy and quick to prepare.

Another example of a retailer responding positively to a change in the marketplace and translating this change into an opportunity involves Von's, a major California grocery chain.[16] Von's recognized the American consumer was finding time increasingly scarce. Consequently, it developed no-stop (or drive-through) shopping. Without leaving their cars, motorists can now order, via a microphone, any of the store's 1,400 food, HBA (health and beauty aids), or deli products, pay the cashier, and drive off—within three minutes. This is especially popular with the elderly who find it difficult to walk around a supermarket. To keep the line of motorists moving, no more than 10 items can be ordered at a time. The store is limited to the number-one brand in each category to reduce the need to make brand selections. And, to compete with convenience stores, these stores never close.

Retailers should be able to generate many attractive opportunities. The difficult task is deciding which to pursue. The opportunities must be narrowed down, since all retailers have limited resources and cannot pursue all opportunities. Retailers must select the opportunities that offer the best prospects for fulfilling their mission and accomplishing their objectives.

STRATEGIES

After stating the firm's mission, establishing goals and objectives, and stating a desired market position, a retailer must develop a marketing strategy, that is, a course of action to accomplish the goals. This is the fifth stage in the strategic planning process. The strategy is a plan that, when executed, will produce the desired levels of performance.

Notice the close relationship between a retailer's objectives and its strategies. Objectives indicate what the retailer wants to accomplish. Strategies indicate how the retailer will attempt to accomplish those goals with the resources available. The major marketing variables in retailing are addressed in Parts 3 through 5 of this book which involve Chapters 7 through 15. The most pivotal strategic decisions concern merchandise and pricing because

ILLUSTRATION 2.3

Supermarkets have developed more appetizing salad bars and delicatessens with larger selections in reaction to the consumer trend to eat more food outside the home.

they are the ones that will need to be adjusted most to satisfy the retailer's desired market position. These decisions are reviewed in Chapters 7 through 9. The selling environment strategy involves the location of the store and the design of the physical store itself. These strategy areas are discussed in Chapters 10 through 13. Finally, promotion and selling strategies are the focus of Chapters 14 and 15.

In this chapter we will not discuss how to develop the merchandising, pricing, selling environment, and promotion and selling strategies. Instead, we will present three case histories that depict the payoff of good strategic planning in retailing and a fourth case study that represents what happens as a result of poor strategic planning.

S.S. KRESGE (KMART)

S.S. Kresge was a declining old-line variety store chain muddling through the post–World War II era. With astute planning, however, it earned the rank of the second-largest U.S. retailer by 1991.[17] How was this accomplished?

In 1957, Harry B. Cunningham, a general vice-president of the firm, was assigned to travel the country to study retail trends first hand. Cunningham traveled for two years and finally confirmed that variety stores—like the earlier five-and-dime stores—had somehow drifted away from their original formula for success: low margins and high turnover. Instead of pricing merchandise to stimulate sales, they were pricing it on the basis of current costs. Variety stores were extremely vulnerable; supermarkets, discount houses, and other new mass merchandisers were beating them at their own game and many wanted to enter a new form of retailing.

EXHIBIT 2.6
Threats Can Be Retail Opportunities

Trend	Threatened Retailer	Opportunity
Increasing proportion of households eating food out of the home (social-environmental trend)	Grocery stores	Grocery store managers should view this as an opportunity to develop in-store delis, expanded frozen food departments, and an increased assortment of food items that are easy and quick to prepare but that compare favorably to food sold at fast-food restaurants.
Decline in birth rate (social-environmental trend)	Toy stores	Toy store managers should view this as an opportunity to broaden their market base to appeal to adults by adding sophisticated toys and games.
Casual wear for wide variety of occasions (social-environmental trend)	Formal wear store	The manager of the retail formal wear store should view this as an opportunity to put increased emphasis on rental vs. purchase of formal wear.
Increasing costs of personal transportation (economic-environmental trend)	Regional shopping centers	This presents the manager of a regional shopping center with the opportunity to use the shopping center as a regional recreational area in order to attract people for social motives; for instance, having an art show or boat show in the mall.
Increasing minimum wage (legal-environmental trend)	All retail stores	Presents the retail manager with increased incentive to explore new methods and techniques for improving labor productivity.

In-home ordering of merchandise via computer (trend in technological environment)	General merchandise retailers	Presents the traditional general merchandise retailer with the opportunity to offer both in-home and in-store shopping services and therefore obtain a significant advantage over the new retail firms that offer only in-home purchasing services.
Growth of low-cost warehouse food stores	Grocery stores	Offers the manager of a traditional grocery store the opportunity to strongly differentiate itself on nonprice variables such as friendliness of employees, store decor, and customer service.

In 1959, Cunningham was named president and chief executive officer and ordered another two-year study to focus exclusively on trends in discount retailing in the United States. When the results were in, Cunningham made the decision to transform S.S. Kresge into a discount retailer. He was determined to avoid the merchandising mistakes of the other discounters flooding the market. The result was Kmart, a conveniently located, large-scale, one-stop shopping unit, where customers could buy quality merchandise at discount prices. In March 1962, Kresge opened its first Kmart in Garden City, Michigan, and by 1991 Kmart was the second-largest retailer in the United States, with annual sales in excess of $32 billion.

WAL-MART

Wal-Mart entered the discount department store business in 1962, at about the same time as S.S. Kresge. Although Wal-Mart got off to a slower start than Kmart, today it is the number-one retailer in the United States. Whereas the Kmart chain concentrated its expansion in major metropolitan markets, Wal-Mart's Sam Walton and his brother Bud saw a great opportunity for discount department store merchandising in small rural towns of less than 20,000 in population. In these smaller towns there were four principal strategic advantages: (1) competitive intensity was low, (2) labor costs were low and workers plentiful, (3) land costs were low and zoning regulations tended to be fewer, and (4) a lot of households were forced to shop outside the immediate community to get attractive prices. When Wal-Mart built 40,000–

50,000-square-foot stores in these small towns, they rapidly gained the dominant market share. With their low operating costs, profits expanded quickly. By 1980, the firm reached $1 billion in sales and began to expand into larger metropolitan markets. Shortly after, they entered the warehouse club market with Sam's Clubs (100,000-square-foot grocery and hard-good warehouses selling wholesale and direct to the consumer market). In 1991, Wal-Mart was the number-one retailer in the United States with sales in excess of $40 billion. The company projects sales to be $120 billion by the year 2000 and employees to number over one million.

HOME DEPOT

Home Depot was started in 1979 and by 1991 had achieved sales of close to $4 billion. Home Depot used a very well thought out but simple strategy: to apply warehouse retailing concepts to the hardware/home-improvement market.

Home Depot offers high levels of customer service, excellent merchandise selection, and everyday low prices. CEO Bernard Marcus wants the public to think of Home Depot when they think of a do-it-yourself project. The vehicle for accomplishing this is high customer service. If a customer is thinking of building a patio deck, a Home Depot salesperson can explain how many of each size boards to purchase, the correct type of nails, and the accessories needed and even offer assembly tips.

Because the firm wants to emphasize excellent selection, Home Depot has also learned when to stop selling. For example, from the outset, Home Depot was a big seller of unfinished furniture—about $80 million annually. But, it stopped selling unfinished furniture because Home Depot was not able to be a power retailer in this category. Bernard Marcus saw that Home Depot would increasingly have to go head to head with retailers like IKEA, the Swedish retailer which dedicates most of its 200,000 square feet of store space to furniture—whereas Home Depot could only commit 2,000 to 7,000 square feet to furniture. Home Depot has instead taken this space to expand its selection of floor tiles and wallpaper.

The final part of Home Depot's strategy is everyday low prices. It accomplishes this by aggressive volume buying and by increasing its sales per square foot of selling space. When space productivity (sales per square foot) rises, operating costs as a percentage of sales decline, allowing Home Depot to lower its prices to customers.[18]

CAMPEAU

Robert Campeau, a Canadian entrepreneur successful in real estate but inexperienced in retailing, invaded U.S. retailing in the mid-to-late 1980s. During October 1986, Campeau acquired Allied Stores, a diversified retail chain, in a highly debt-structured $3.6 billion purchase. Allied Stores operated stores under more than 20 names including Ann Taylor, Bonwit Teller, Brooks Brothers, Joske's, Jordan Marsh, and Bon Marché. In April 1988, Campeau acquired Federated Department Stores in another highly debt-structured $6.5 billion buyout. Federated operated stores under a variety of names including Abraham & Strauss, Bloomingdale's, Burdines, Lazarus, Rich's, Bullocks, Foley's, and other names. By early 1990, both Federated and Allied were in bankruptcy.

Campeau was a real estate developer who was attracted to the free and open culture in the United States. He believed that by acquiring retail giants, he would have a series of built-in tenants for shopping centers he planned to develop in the United States. However, retailers operate on very thin profit margins and most of their cash flow is needed to purchase inventory and to remodel stores regularly to keep their atmospheres attractive and appealing to changing consumer tastes. Consequently, the highly debt-laden Campeau empire could not make its payments on its debt despite selling 17 of the Allied divisions for $2.2 billion and 9 Federated divisions for $4.1 billion.[19]

A RECAP

Note that the first three retail firms we discussed designed their strategies around merchandise and pricing, a selling environment, or promotion and selling. For example:

- Kmart developed conveniently located, large-scale stores (selling environment), and stocked them with quality merchandise at low prices.
- Wal-Mart focused on secondary-market locations (selling environment), and as did Kmart offered quality merchandise at low prices.
- Home Depot focused on high levels of customer service, excellent merchandise selection, and low everyday prices.

On the other hand, what did Campeau focus on that was retailing in nature? Nothing. Campeau had no sense of bringing to the retail enterprises he acquired any type of unique selling environment, merchandising, pricing, promotion, or selling strategy. His strategy of trying to ensure built-in tenants for shopping centers he would build was not tuned to the retail marketplace but was tuned to his own desire to build shopping centers and continue to be a real estate developer.

CONTROL SYSTEM

The sixth and last stage in the strategic planning process is the development of a control system. Strategic planning is useless unless the retailer has a systematic process in place for monitoring the retail marketplace and performance of the firm. Two resources that are used to monitor the strategic plan are human resources and information resources. These are discussed in Chapters 16 and 17, where we show their critical role in administration and operation of the retail enterprise.

If the retailer develops and implements a strategy in tune with the contemporary retail marketplace and implements that strategy, but then fails to monitor the retail marketplace, the strategy will, over time, become inappropriate. As the marketplace slowly changes, retailers occasionally need to alter their strategy so that it stays current and relevant. McDonald's initially focused its strategy on providing low-cost, quick, and tasty lunches for workers and low-cost dinners for families. Over time, more households had two working spouses and McDonald's realized that it had some excess capacity available—its restaurants were not open in the morning. Thus, McDonald's expanded its strategy to appeal to working families that need quick, low-cost, nutritious breakfasts.

INFORMAL CONTROL

The execution of any retail strategy is also dependent on people, the firm's human resources. A retail strategy suggests a certain type of behavior by employees. Quite often, this relates to courteous treatment of customers, neat appearance and dress, use of certain selling techniques or approaches, team-oriented behavior, and so on. The best way to control employee behavior is through informal controls.[20]

Three types of informal controls are self-control, social control, and cultural control. With **self-control,** the employee sets personal objectives, monitors attainment, and appropriately adjusts behavior if off course. Retailers that hire highly motivated individuals will go farther toward obtaining good self-control in the organization. **Social control** is a second form of informal control. With social control, the work unit (e.g., employees in the shoe department of a department store) sets standards or norms, monitors conformity, and takes actions when behavior is inconsistent with norms. Social controls come from internalization of values and mutual commitment toward a common goal. Finally, **cultural control** is a broader type of social control wherein a wider set of norms guide employee actions in the entire organization. These informal controls have been shown to have a significant influence on retail store performance. A good example of informal controls is the practice at Von's Supermarkets whereby each store and department manager starts the day by placing 10 pennies in a left-hand pocket. When a manager recognizes an employee for doing something right, he or she moves a penny from the left pocket to the right pocket. The result has been that employees are better recognized for their good performance; trust of management has increased and so has self-esteem. More self-control and social control are exercised because appropriate employee behavior has been reinforced.[21]

FORMAL CONTROL

Although informal controls are important, it is also wise to have a formal control review process. Several steps must be performed by retail executives when implementing a control process review of the firm's strategic plans. They are:

1. Determining who should perform the review
2. Determining when and how often the review should take place
3. Determining what areas of the strategic plan should be reviewed
4. Conducting the review
5. Reacting to the review's findings

Who Should Perform the Review. Any one of three different groups can perform the review: a special group of internal staff, outside consultants, or department or store managers.

The special internal staff group has the advantage of being an ongoing operation that is able to make use of the data provided by the retail information system (RIS) we will discuss in Chapter 17. In addition, its members will be knowledgeable about the retailer's operations. The disadvantage of this source is that many small retailers cannot afford to have a full-time review staff, and some large retailers question the independence of an internal staff.

Outside consultants have independence but are expensive, and while they have broad experience, they lack familiarity with the firm.

The third group—department and store heads—is the source most commonly used. The process is inexpensive and the members are familiar with the firm's operations. However, it takes managers away from their main duties and sometimes results in a lack of objectivity.

When and How Often to Review. The most logical time for conducting a review is at the end of a retailer's fiscal year when a physical inventory is taken. The date can vary, but the review should be conducted at least once a year. Some firms may want to review even more frequently. However, for meaningful comparisons, the same dates should be used each year.

What Areas Should Be Reviewed. A review of the strategic plan is more than an audit of the firm's financial affairs by a certified public accountant. It should be used to examine all aspects of a firm's strategy and operations. However, circumstances may prevent retail executives from examining more than one or two areas of operations in depth. An **overall review** is an analysis of the overall performance of the retailer to determine whether the objectives are reasonable and the strategy workable. A **segmental review** is an in-depth analysis of only one area's performance (e.g., credit or promotion).

Conducting the Review. Some questions should be answered when conducting the review itself. Should the firm's employees be made aware that the review is being conducted? It is always desirable to have complete employee cooperation when doing a review. However, if a particular area such as credit or sales personnel is being examined, it might be better not to inform personnel of the review. This will help guarantee that their normal behavior is not altered as a part of the review.

Management Reactions. The most important element of any review process is management's reactions to the findings. If the firm's objectives are unobtainable or the strategy is ill-conceived, it would be unwise to continue with the current strategy. High-performance results can be attained only if management uses the review process to control operations. This is why a retailer must have some type of retail information system. A serious error could be made if the findings of the review are downplayed by management. Long-term success comes from control, which is based on evaluating the present and adapting to the future.

REVIEW PROCESS PROBLEMS

There are several potential pitfalls in performing a review. They are:

1. The process involves a considerable amount of expense, especially if outside consultants are used.
2. The process ties up top management's time.
3. Management might choose the wrong source to conduct the review.
4. Incorrect data and information might be obtained.
5. The wrong conclusions may be drawn from the review.
6. A reluctant management may ignore the findings.[22]

In spite of its problems, the review process is worthwhile and it is a major contributor to high-performance results.

STRATEGIC PLANNING IN LARGE RETAILING FIRMS

Earlier in this chapter we mentioned that even though other industries were adopting the strategic planning process, retailers were slow to endorse it. Retailers claimed that flexibility and focus hindered their use of strategic planning. This is not true today. Since the beginning of the 1980s, many large retailers have adopted the strategic planning process as wholeheartedly as their counterparts in other businesses. William A. Andres, former chairman and CEO of Dayton Hudson Corporation, states:

> *We manage change at Dayton Hudson through our comprehensive strategic planning process. That process, which, incidentally, is a continuous one (rather than a once-a-year exercise), forces us to examine, and reexamine, our "niche" in the marketplace. It causes us to reexamine our "reason for being."*

> *Strategic planning helps us identify and respond to how the world is changing: how the customer is changing, how the market and the competition are changing, and, most of all, how we must change to capitalize on these opportunities.*
>
> *Our five-year strategic plan becomes the blueprint for how we change the business to respond to the trends we foresee continuing and becoming more important. After all, it does little good to analyze trends if we're not willing to **act** on the basis of that analysis.*[23]

A study of retailers with annual sales over $100 million[24] found that more than 90 percent of these retailers have, at least occasionally, engaged in strategic planning and more than half have done so frequently. Top management devoted 5 to 10 percent of its time to strategic planning. The functional areas with the highest participation level were, in order, finance, merchandising, operations, promotion, and personnel. The major external environmental factors considered were, in order, competition, consumer behavior, economy, technology, and government regulations. Finally, Rosenbloom and Tripuraneni found that only 23 percent of the large retailing chains used a time frame of one year or less and that more than half used a time frame of two or more years.

Research conducted on smaller retailers found that while smaller retailers generally don't commit their plans to writing, 30 percent of them claim to plan and include the firm's goals and strengths and weaknesses in their plans.[25] However, it may be assumed that because of the smaller retailers' lack of expertise in this area, lack of necessary resources, or failure to realize the need for strategic planning, they have not yet advanced to the level of their large-scale counterparts. Nevertheless, that day is drawing near.

KEY MISTAKES IN STRATEGIC PLANNING

Of course, mistakes can be made in strategic planning. Most retailers that have failed at strategic planning focused on the trappings of strategic planning rather than its substance. This is the conclusion of Allan Pennington, the former vice-president of corporate development at Dayton Hudson Corporation, who has identified seven key mistakes that retail executives make in strategic planning[26]:

1. *Thinking that strategic plans are an extension of financial plans. . . . Strategic plans and financial plans must be linked, but in the right sequence. Financial plans should follow the strategic plans and be merely the quantitative expression of the overall strategy.*

2. *Confusing strategy and objective. What we want to accomplish is not the strategy. The statement that "our strategy is to operate on a 20 percent gross margin" is not a strategy, but an objective. The strategy tells how to accomplish what we want to accomplish.*

3. *Expecting consultants to plan. . . . Consultants can play a very important role. They can help define the process of planning, interpret the external environment, serve as a devil's advocate, and provide research and perspective. But they cannot assume the responsibility for the content of a company's strategy. This must fall upon the shoulders of those accountable for the execution of the plan—top management.*

4. *Reliance on staff experts. . . . Staff experts can't provide any better plans than outside consultants, and for the same reasons.*

5. *Reliance on quantitative tools. . . . Just as financial plans can obscure the quality of strategic plans, so can formulas, models, and other mechanistic devices which take the focus off direction, commitment, and execution. These tools, if they are used at all, should be employed as an adjunct to the effective planning process, not as the core of it.*

6. *Too many retailers focus too sharply on expansion and diversification and ignore their base business in the strategic planning process.*

7. *Taking too narrow a perspective. . . . Placing planning in too narrow a perspective results in strategic inconsistencies that are difficult or expensive to correct. A common example is the development of a rapid expansion program that is inconsistent with the financial structure of the company.*

These mistakes are the central causes of strategic failure in retailing.

SUMMARY

While other industries adopted the strategic planning process a couple of decades ago, it has only recently been implemented by retailers. Retailers lagged because they wanted a process that would enable them to become more flexible in responding to their retail marketplace.

The strategic planning process begins with the retailer's statement of mission, which is its overall justification for existing. Next, the retailer should state specific objectives. These objectives can relate to market performance, financial performance, societal goals, or personal goals. The financial performance objectives are especially important because survival is not possible without profit. Financial performance objectives were discussed in terms of a return on investment model, often referred to as the strategic profit model, and the strategic resource management model. This latter model outlines the interrelationships between merchandise, space, and labor productivity and the way they can contribute to a retailer's financial performance.

After the objectives have been defined, the desired market position must be stated. The retailer must focus on a well-defined market position. For this reason, we discussed market segmentation as it applies in a retail setting.

The third stage in the strategic planning process is the study and analysis of the retail marketplace. This marketplace consists of the consumer, competitor rivalry for that consumer, the marketing channel to deliver the merchandise and/or service, and the regulations and laws that constrain the marketplace. The marketplace is constantly changing and is the source of many opportunities.

Strategy development is the fourth stage of the process. Here the retailer develops a merchandising and pricing strategy, a selling environment strategy, and a promotion and selling strategy.

Chapter 2 Strategic Planning in Retailing

A strategy that is in tune with the retail marketplace and the retailer's mission and objectives and market position should provide high-performance results. However, implementation and control is done largely through human and information resources. Informal control systems are important for fostering the right types of behavior among employees. In addition, formal control procedures are necessary to make certain the strategic plan is on track.

We concluded this chapter with a discussion of the increasing use of strategic planning that has occurred since the 1980s. However, this rapid growth is mainly among large retail enterprises. We also discussed seven major mistakes that retailers make in using strategic planning.

QUESTIONS FOR DISCUSSION

1. Does strategic planning become more or less important as uncertainty in the external environment increases?
2. The retailer could simplify the strategic planning process if it stated only profit objectives. Agree or disagree and explain why.
3. Return on assets is a better measure than return on net worth (or return on investment) for assessing a retailer's financial performance. Agree or disagree and explain why.
4. Given today's economic conditions, which retail firm would you most like to own and which one would you find least desirable? Explain your position.

Retailer	Asset Turnover	Profit Margin (Before Tax)	Financial Leverage
A	3.8×	7.0	2.4
B	5.0×	6.0	1.9
C	3.3×	6.3	3.2

5. Is planning in a high-inflation environment more or less difficult for a retailer than planning in a low-inflation environment? Why?
6. In analyzing opportunities, the retailer should develop a strategy for the opportunity that offers the highest expected return on investment. Agree or disagree and explain why.
7. You are in charge of developing a strategic plan for a chain of three children's apparel/gift/toy stores. Your first step is to try to summarize the financial performance of the three stores using the following data:

	Store A	Store B	Store C
Annual sales	$840,809	$1,210,990	$2,080,907
Gross margin percentage	38%	37%	35%
Full-time-equivalent employees	14	14	17
Retail space (square feet)	7,018	8,042	12,340
Average inventory investment	$214,701	$265,171	$604,334

8. Identify the major trends occurring in the 21st century that retailers should strongly consider when developing their strategic plans for the late 1990s. Briefly discuss each trend.
9. Strategic planning is an exercise in creative thinking versus analytical problem solving. Agree or disagree and explain why.

10. Identify and briefly discuss the steps in the strategic planning process.
11. Why are quantitative objectives preferable to qualitative objectives? Should a retailer have no qualitative objectives?

MANAGEMENT MEMO

You are the retail controller for a small chain of 10 drugstores operating in seven small southern Arizona towns of 10,000 people or less. Last year, the chain had sales of $9,400,000 and a net profit margin of 2.1 percent. This year, the president of the firm and majority stockholder, Frank Hernandez, has set a net profit margin goal of 2.5 percent on sales of $10,000,000. The company does not establish goals for return on assets, asset turnover, financial leverage, or return on net worth. Mr. Hernandez believes the critical thing is "how much profit we make on each dollar of sales." He argues that sales drive the business and thus the annual profit goals should be related to sales dollars. Because you disagree, you have decided to write a memo to the president stating why annual profit goals should be stated differently.

BOARDROOM REPORT

You serve on the board of directors of a regional chain of home appliance and electronics stores. The 23 stores have an annual volume of $61 million and net profits (after taxes) for the most recent fiscal year were $1,279,000. During the annual budgeting process and five-year strategic plan development, the firm only states financial objectives. You believe it should begin to state some well-defined societal objectives as well. You have been given five minutes on the agenda of the next board meeting to make your recommendation.

SUGGESTED READINGS

Bates, Albert D. "The Extended Specialty Store: A Strategic Opportunity for the 1990s." *Journal of Retailing* (Fall 1989): 379-88.
Dodge, H. Robert, and E. Terry Deiderick. "Retail Metamorphosis: A Fundamental Change in Strategic Orientation." *Retailing: Its Present and Future*. Proceedings of 1988 AMS/ACRA Conference, 12-16.
Ellis, Joseph. "New Opportunities in the Retail Marketplace." *Retail Control* (March 1990): 3-8.
"Information on Demographics and Psychographics Serves as Guidepost to Help Retailers Prepare for Turn of the Century." *Chain Store Age Executive* (May 1987): 19-25.
Johnson, Gerry, ed. *Business Strategy and Retailing*. Chichester: John Wiley and Sons, 1987.
Langer, Judith, John E. Merriam, and Geoffrey Greene. "Secrets of the Trend Spotters." *American Demographics* (February 1991): 36-42.
Meloche, Martin S., C. Anthony di Benedetto, and Julian E. Yudelson. "A Framework for the Analysis of the Growth and Development of Retail Institutions." *Retailing: Its Present and Future*. Proceedings of 1988 AMS/ACRA Conference, 6-11.
Robinson, R. B., Jr., J. E. Logan, and M. Y. Salem. "Strategic Versus Operational Planning in Small Retail Firms." *American Journal of Small Business* (Winter 1986): 7-16.
Scarborough, Norman M., and Thomas W. Zimmerer. "Strategic Planning for the Small Business." *Business* (April-June 1987): 11-19.
Schwartz, Joe. "Will Baby Boomers Dump Department Stores?" *American Demographics* (December 1990): 42.
Selbert, Roger. "Retailing's Five Most Important Trends." *Retailing Issues Letter* (March 1991): 1-4.

ENDNOTES

1. "Is Now the Right Time to Expand," *Chain Store Age Executive* (February 1991): 33-35.
2. John B. Gifford and James M. Stearns, "Perceived Importance of Financial Ratios as Indicators of Corporate Health and Vitality in the Retail Industry" (Paper presented at 1985 ACRA Spring Conference).

3. Robert F. Lusch, "The New Algebra of High Performance Retail Management," *Retail Control* (September 1986): 15-35.
4. "Retail Entrepreneurs of the Year," *Chain Store Age Executive* (December 1990): 34-48, 57-62.
5. Ibid.
6. Philip Kotler, *Marketing Management: Analysis, Planning and Control,* 4th ed. (Englewood Cliffs, N.J.: Prentice-Hall, Inc., 1980), 69-70.
7. Robert Weinberg, "Development Management Strategies for Short-Term Profits and Long-Term Growth" (Presented in a seminar sponsored by Advanced Management Research, Inc., New York City, September 29, 1969).
8. Roger D. Blackwell and W. Wayne Talarzyk, "Lifestyle Retailing: Competitive Strategies for the 1980s," *Journal of Retailing* (Winter 1983): 10, 13.
9. Eleanor G. May, "Practical Applications of Recent Retail Image Research," *Journal of Retailing* (Winter 1974-1975): 19.
10. For examples of sophisticated segmentation research, see Robert J. Kopp, Robert J. Eng, and Douglas Tigert, "A Competitive Structure and Segmentation Analysis of the Chicago Fashion Market," *Journal of Retailing* (Winter 1989): 496-515 and Sandra McCurley Hartman, Arthur W. Allaway, J. Barry Mason, and John Rasp, "Multi-Segment Analysis of Supermarket Patronage," in William R. Darden, ed., *Proceedings of the Symposium on Patronage Behavior and Retail Strategy* (Baton Rouge: Louisiana State University, 1989), 49-62.
11. Adapted from Patrick E. Murphy and William A. Staples, "A Modernized Family Life Cycle," *Journal of Consumer Research* (June 1979): 16.
12. For a discussion on using social class or income to segment retail markets, see Robert F. Lusch and Humayun Akhter, "Social Class and Income: Not Social Class vs. Income," in William R. Dorden et al., eds., *The Cutting Edge: Proceedings of the 1991 Symposium on Patronage Behavior and Retail Strategy.* (Baton Rouge: Louisiana State University), 271-282.
13. Kotler, *Marketing Management,* 205-6.
14. "Bringing It All Back Home," *Texas Monthly* (January 1989): 122-25 and Pier 1 Imports 1988-1990 Annual Reports; "Wall Street Is Touting Pier 1 Imports as a Bet on Baby Boomers' Resurgent Urge to Splurge," *Wall Street Journal* (June 3, 1992): C2.
15. "Macy's Is Counting on a Number-Cruncher," *Business Week* (June 22, 1992): 72-73.
16. "Winning Over the New Consumer," *Fortune,* 29 June 1991, 113-25.
17. For a more detailed discussion of Kresge and Kmart's early development, see "How Kresge Became the Top Discounter," *Business Week,* 24 October 1970, 62-63ff; "Retailing: K is for Krunch," *Sales Management,* 29 November 1971, 3; "Kmart: The Tail That Wags the Kresge Dog," *Merchandising Week,* 9 July 1973, 8ff; and "What Woolworth Didn't Know Apparently Kresge Did," *Financial World,* 22 May 1974, 18-19. For a more recent discussion, see "Kmart's Antonini Moves Far Beyond Retail 'Junk' Image," *Advertising Age,* 25 July 1988, 1.67; "Attention non-Kmart Shoppers: A Blue-Light Special Just for You," *Wall Street Journal,* 6 October 1987, 40; and "Attention Shoppers: Kmart is Fighting Back," *Business Week,* 7 October 1991, 118, 120.
18. Susan Caminiti, "The New Champs of Retailing," *Fortune,* 24 September 1990, 85, 86, 90, 94, 96, 100.
19. Carol J. Loomis, "The Biggest Looniest Deal Ever," *Fortune,* 18 June 1990, 48-51, 54, 58, 62, 66, 68, 70, 72; "The 'How' in Home Improvement," *The New York Times* (June 14, 1992): F5.
20. Bernard J. Jaworski, "Toward a Theory of Marketing Control: Environmental Context Control Type and Consequences," *Journal of Marketing* (July 1988): 23-39 and Robert F. Lusch and Bernard Jaworski, "Retail Control Systems for the 1990s," *Retailing Issues Letter* (January 1990): 1-3.
21. Richard M. Petreycik, "Critical Steps to More Effective Management," *Progressive Grocer* (June 1991): 24-27.
22. Adapted from Martin J. Bell, *Marketing Concepts and Strategy* (Boston: Houghton Mifflin Co., 1979), 474.
23. William A. Andres, "Managing Change: A Challenge for Retailers" (Texas A&M Center for Retailing Studies Lecture Series, April 21, 1983).
24. Bert Rosenbloom and Ravi V. Tripuraneni, "Strategic Planning in the One Hundred Million Club" (Proceedings of the Research and Teaching in Retailing Conference, San Antonio, February and March 1984), 18-23.
25. Myron Gable and Martin T. Topol, "Planning Practices of Small-Scale Retailers," *American Journal of Small Business* (Fall 1987): 19-32.
26. Allan L. Pennington, "Do's and Don'ts of Retail Strategic Plans," *Marketing News,* 7 March 1980, 5. Reprinted with permission.

Part 2

THE RETAILING MARKETPLACE

CHAPTER 3

UNDERSTANDING RETAIL CUSTOMERS

OVERVIEW

In this chapter we focus on the market that retailers exist to serve—the retail customer. We shall adopt a marketing perspective of retailing, which proposes that to be successful, retailers must identify existing consumer needs that are currently unsatisfied, then position themselves to serve these needs. This can only be accomplished by understanding retail customers, as well as other elements of the retail marketplace. The retailer can then adjust the key marketing variables—merchandise mix and price, the selling environment, and the promotion and selling strategy—to achieve the desired market positioning. In analyzing retail customers, we first review the socioeconomic environment in which consumers live, and then the demographic, psychographic, and behavioral characteristics that describe consumers. We conclude with the development of a retail patronage model incorporating all these factors to describe overall shopping and buying practices.

UNDERSTANDING RETAIL CUSTOMERS

I. The Importance of Understanding the Retail Customer
   A. A Marketing Perspective of Retailing
   B. The Concept of Market Positioning
   C. Constraints on Market Positioning
   D. Market Position Image
   E. Market Segmentation Schemes
II. Socioeconomic Environment
   A. Gross Domestic Product

B. Interest Rates
C. Economic Turbulence
D. National Debt
E. Unemployment
III. Demographic Characteristics
  A. Population Trends
    1. Population Growth
    2. Age Distribution
  B. Geographic Shifts
    1. Shifting Geographic Centers
    2. Urban Centers
    3. Mobility
  C. Social Trends
    1. Education
    2. Changing Makeup of U.S. Households
  D. Economic Trends
    1. Income Growth
    2. Personal Savings
    3. Women in the Labor Force
IV. Psychographic Characteristics
  A. Male and Female Role Flexibility
  B. Deterioration of Institutional Confidence
  C. Management of Time Versus Money
  D. Value and Lifestyle Fragmentation
V. Behavioral Characteristics
  A. Behavior Versus Attitude
  B. Dimensions of Buying Behavior
    1. Extensive, Simplified, and Routine Purchasing
    2. Destination Versus Intercept Merchandise
    3. Destination Versus Intercept Stores
    4. Store Choice
      a. Multi-Attribute Decision Model
    5. Other Reasons for Shopping
VI. Retail Patronage Model
  A. Nature of a Conceptual Model
  B. Steps in the Buying Process
    1. Passive Information Gathering
    2. Need Recognition
      a. Ideal State Versus Actual State
      b. Shop Trigger Event: Need Versus Barrier Quotient
      c. Retailer-Induced Need and Barrier Recognition
    3. Active Information Gathering
    4. Decision Making
      a. Deciding Not to Buy
      b. Buy Trigger Event
    5. Transaction

6. Use and Evaluation
   a. Post-Purchase Resentment
   b. Customer Satisfaction Programs
   C. Dynamic Nature of Retail Patronage Model
VII. Summary

THE IMPORTANCE OF UNDERSTANDING THE RETAIL CUSTOMER

A MARKETING PERSPECTIVE OF RETAILING

In Chapter 1 we said retailing was any transaction in which the final consumer spends money for goods or services. Thus, retailing is defined in terms of the person doing the action—the customer—rather than in terms of the merchandise or stores on which retailing studies have historically focused. Exhibit 3.1 shows this contemporary marketing view of retailing. The merchandise mix, pricing strategy, selling environment, and promotion and selling practices are all elements of the retailer's marketing mix. Operational and administrative practices, such as how store personnel are deployed and what sales information is tracked, support and make possible execution of the marketing variables. The retail manager adjusts these variables in response to and in interaction with the retail marketplace, which is composed of the consumer, the competition, other members of the distribution channel, and the legal/regulatory environment. You should note the similarity between Exhibits 3.1 and 1.4 (page 15). Both exhibits communicate essentially the same message: Retailers must use operational and administrative practices or resources to adjust their controllable marketing variables to ever-changing external forces (consumer, channel, competition, legal/regulatory).

THE CONCEPT OF MARKET POSITIONING

The goal of effective retail marketing, like that of all marketing, is to find and occupy a position or niche in this retail marketplace, by identifying consumer needs that are currently unserved and adjusting the elements of the marketing mix to serve them. The process of identifying such niches, determining which niches a retailer should occupy, and coordinating the various marketing variables to occupy these niches, is called **market positioning,** and it is the cornerstone of every successful retailer's strategy. Conversely, ineffective market positioning—whether through lack of positioning, incorrect positioning, or positioning too broadly—has been the downfall of many unsuccessful retailers.

The first step in effective retail marketing is to understand the consumer's unsatisfied needs. Effective retail marketers fill these unsatisfied needs better than the competition, rather than offering goods or services which are unneeded or currently satisfied by competitors. To put it bluntly, contemporary

EXHIBIT 3.1

A Marketing Perspective of Retailing

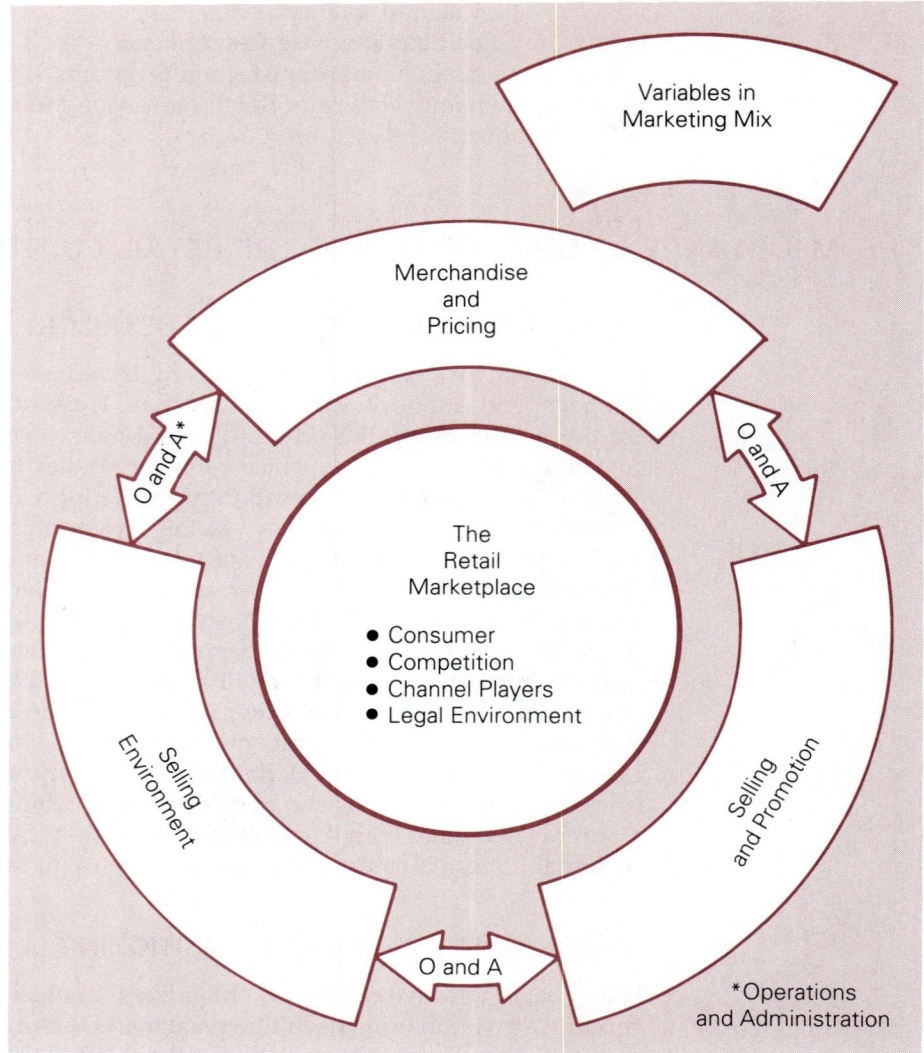

marketing theory suggests that unless a retailer has identified and can serve an available niche in the marketplace, it should not be in business.

CONSTRAINTS ON MARKET POSITIONING

Of course, positioning doesn't happen in a vacuum, so simply identifying a niche doesn't guarantee success. Effective market positioning must also account for constraints on the firm's ability to serve the available niche, most notably the competition. If other retailers are serving the niche, or are moving in that strategic direction, perhaps it is wisest for the retailer to seek a less crowded or more realistic market position. Many general-merchandise retailers have found, for instance, that the entry of Wal-Mart into their market means they must either reposition or perish.[1] Accordingly, market positioning requires a keen understanding of the competition, which is the topic of the next chapter.

Competition may be the most obvious constraint on a retailer's ability to achieve a certain market position, but it is not alone. Retailers rely on other members of the distribution channel, including manufacturers, shippers, distributors, and wholesalers, and are subject to regulations imposed by governmental bodies. Positioning constraints presented by these factors are discussed in Chapters 4 through 6.

Finally, the retail organization itself may pose constraints, such as the expertise and availability of its management staff. A senior management group that has spent its entire career in the supermarket business, for instance, may find it difficult to successfully operate shoe stores, despite consumer research suggesting such an opportunity. The number, size, and location of existing stores may also present barriers to certain repositioning moves, or the nature of a retailer's distribution centers and systems may make it financially impractical to distribute different types of merchandise.

MARKET POSITION IMAGE

One of the most frustrating constraints faced by retailers is the fact that a firm's market position is not an absolute characteristic, but rather an "amalgam" or accumulation of intangible perceptions which live in the minds of consumers.[2] Marketing managers must therefore be as concerned with **market position image** as with actual market position. Since these perceptions are made by millions of consumers whose needs and expectations change frequently, creating the desired market position image can be difficult, and once established, it can be even more difficult to change.

Therefore, a retailer is limited in the speed with which it can alter its market position image, and this imposes a significant constraint on both short-term and long-term positioning strategies. Kmart has spent many years building a strong reputation as one of the leading providers of name-brand goods at discount prices. But if market conditions changed, and Kmart felt a need to reposition to become a retailer of high-priced designer-label fashions, its long-standing image as a discounter could hamper the repositioning. Similarly, in the 1980s, Sears and JCPenney, which for generations enjoyed the market positioning image as national general merchandisers, found it necessary to reposition due to the competitive squeeze of specialty stores on the one hand and discounters on the other. JCPenney embarked on a long-range repositioning program in the mid-1980s, and by 1990 was slowly gaining acceptance by customers as a legitimate specialty department store, offer-

ILLUSTRATION 3.1
JCPenney began a long-term repositioning program in the mid-1980s to move from a value-oriented general merchandise chain (*left*) to a market position of higher fashion appeal (*right*).

ing fashion apparel and home fashions at reasonable prices.[3] Sears, on the other hand, struggled to find a profitable niche in which customers would accept it.[4]

MARKET SEGMENTATION SCHEMES

To manage market position image, retailers must first understand current consumer perceptions, and measuring the changing perceptions of millions of consumers can be frustrating at best. Imagine listening to a radio with no tuning knob. The receiver picks up so many different signals, some in harmony, some in conflict, that the result coming through the speaker is noise. You're getting something, but you can't understand it. To make sense of the confusing array of information, marketers use market segmentation techniques to "tune in" small segments of the consumer population, hoping to hear a series of clear messages which can then be constructed into some overall meaning.

In the remainder of this chapter, we will examine ways to segment the heterogeneous consumer population into smaller, more homogeneous groups based on demographic, psychographic, and behavioral characteristics. These segmentation schemes help us understand who customers are, how they think, and what they do, respectively, and can help us build a meaningful picture of consumer needs, desires, perceptions, shopping behaviors, and the current market position image of a retailer and its competitors.

Demographic characteristics are essentially descriptors, or defining characteristics that help us know who customers are. Examples are age, gender, household size, income, and marital status. They do little to tell us how consumers think or what they actually do. Often, however, demographic characteristics give us labels for certain customer groups, which help us track and analyze the same customers through different segmentation schemes.

Psychographic characteristics are measures of attitudes, interests, and opinions of the population, such as how consumers feel about various issues and how these feelings affect their perceptions of marketing strategies. Psychographic characteristics help us understand trends and differences between consumer segments, identify unserved market needs, and understand market position image.

Behavioral characteristics describe actual shopping behaviors such as recognizing a need for merchandise, selecting a store, comparing prices, and purchasing. While such behaviors tell us much about the buying process, helping retailers to enhance their sales productivity, alone they don't tell us much about who certain consumers are and why they do what they do.

Together, demographic, psychographic, and behavioral characteristics provide a rich mosaic of information which talented strategists can understand and use in the development of long-term market positioning objectives and strategies. Before exploring these characteristics, however, we must understand the socioeconomic backdrop in which consumers exist.

SOCIOECONOMIC ENVIRONMENT

The social and economic environment in which consumers live and retailers operate is complex. Consider all the conflicting economic predictions you have heard during the past several months. Our brief overview will not pretend to explain the complexities of this environment, but rather will focus on five important factors the retail manager should regularly monitor: gross domestic product, interest rates, economic turbulence, national debt, and unemployment.

GROSS DOMESTIC PRODUCT

The most important long-range economic indicator is the **gross domestic product,** or GDP. GDP, which in 1991 replaced the gross national product as the government's leading indicator of economic output,[5] is the total value of all the goods and services produced in the United States during one year. Retailers want the GDP to grow at a moderate and steady rate. Too-rapid growth in the GDP will produce inflation (a decline in buying power due to prices rising faster than income) and too-slow growth or no growth will result in reduced consumer spending. GDP figures are useful for projecting future national disposable income levels (the total amount of personal income that all U.S. consumers have left after taxes and social security levies), which in turn can be used to project future retail sales figures. An ideal growth rate is between 3 and 5 percent annually. Over the past quarter-century, the country's real GDP (after subtracting the effect of inflation) has grown at an annual rate of 3.3 percent.

Implications for Retailers. GDP growth translates into increased retail sales. However, while the overall average has been up for the last three decades, GDP has had its ups and downs. That is why it is important for retailers to keep an eye on this indicator in predicting future sales performance. In 1991, for instance, GDP dropped for three consecutive quarters (the technical definition of a recession), and retail sales were lackluster throughout the year.

INTEREST RATES

An **interest rate** is the price paid for the use of money. Both consumers and retailers use other people's money to purchase merchandise and must pay interest for this privilege. Consumers use credit cards or installment plans to purchase a large number of goods—especially durables such as household appliances, furniture, and automobiles. Retailers use bank credit to help finance their heavy investment in inventory. For example, the typical new car dealer with a modest inventory of 200 cars has to finance between $1.5 and $3 million in inventory investment. At an interest rate of 10 percent, the daily interest expense to carry this inventory would be over $600.

Interest rates affect consumer spending as well as retailers' costs. Because the interest rate is the price of money, and because the consumer needs money to buy merchandise, each time the interest rate rises potential customers are eliminated from the market because they cannot afford the purchase. Just as rising rates slash the size of the market, declining rates expand it.

Implications for Retailers. Retailers must purchase merchandise on credit. As the cost of credit increases it becomes more expensive to finance and hold inventory. The net result of this higher cost of carrying inventory is that less of the proceeds from sales to customers can be used to pay for the merchandise and make a profit. Consequently, retailers need to be aware of interest rate fluctuations and their resulting impact not only on their financial performance, but also on the consumer's behavior.

ECONOMIC TURBULENCE

The U.S. economy is beginning to be characterized by economic turbulence, or frequent swings in the business cycle. A business cycle consists of three stages: prosperity, recession, and recovery. Economic turbulence has become one of the realities of retail planning. Today's consumers are confused—they don't know whether they should purchase today because prices might increase, or postpone the purchase in hopes of a price decrease. Because the economy is so volatile, consumers have become more conservative in their purchasing activities.

Implications for Retailers. Swings in the business cycle make the retailer's job more difficult. Does the retailer increase inventory in hopes of a good season or keep inventory stable? Since it takes time to order and receive merchandise (usually several weeks to months), the retailer can easily over- or undercommit inventory stock. In January 1991, for example, after several quarters of weak retail sales, experts projected an upturn in the economy during 1991, and retailers were faced with the difficult quandary of whether to order aggressively or conservatively. One year later, the recession had still not lifted, and experts were again predicting an upturn in the economy for 1992.

NATIONAL DEBT

Retailers in the 1990s are affected by another economic condition: high national debt as a result of deficits in the national budget through the 1980s. National debt is a composite of the nation's annual budget deficit (when the government spends more than it receives in taxes, fees, tariffs, etc.) and negative balance of trade (when imports exceed exports). As the debt level increases, the Federal Reserve is forced to raise interest rates on the money it lends to financial institutions to fund this debt. As interest rates rise, the cost of money for retailers increases. Consumers, fearful of even higher rates, generally reduce their spending, thus reducing retail sales.

Implications for Retailers. An increase or decrease in interest rates triggered by the need to finance the national debt especially affects retailers selling higher-priced durable goods, which are typically bought on credit. For instance, automobile dealers often respond to higher interest rates by offering below-market interest rates. While this results in higher sales, dealer profits are hurt by subsidizing the interest rate.

UNEMPLOYMENT

In the past, unemployment data were rather simple to analyze. Retailers wanted to see unemployment rates decrease because that meant more people had jobs, jobs produced income, and this income led to increased retail sales. When unemployment increases, consumer demand decreases. When unemployment falls below 5 percent, however, many experts feel the economy is nearing a level of full employment, and the shortage in the supply of labor forces wages upwards, causing increases in prices and higher inflation.

Implications for Retailers. In the most recent period of full employment, fast-food retailers in the Northeast, where unemployment was only 4.5 percent at the beginning of 1990, found it necessary to pay starting wages of over $7 an hour, while similar employees in other geographic locations earned only $4.50 an hour. Many firms also offered free transportation to and from work and other extraordinary benefits to entice workers. Just two years later, 1992 presidential candidates appealed to tens of thousands of unemployed New Englanders—as well as all Americans—with their remedies for an ailing economy.[6]

The unemployment issue is complicated by the fact that as unemployment falls and wages increase, the Federal Reserve may raise interest rates in an attempt to halt inflation.

DEMOGRAPHIC CHARACTERISTICS

Now that we have a better understanding of the socioeconomic environment, we can begin to understand consumers themselves. The first step in this process is to understand who consumers are and how they live, as described by **demographic characteristics.** Retailers often find it useful to group consumers according to demographic variables such as population trends, geographic shifts, social trends, and economic trends. This is useful for two reasons. First, demographic trends often reflect marketplace needs. Second, demographic data are readily available and easily applied in analyzing markets.

POPULATION TRENDS

In this section we will discuss the various population trends that affect retailing. We will examine how changes in population growth and the gradual aging of the American population affect the retailer's ability to achieve high-performance results.

Population Growth. Retailers have long viewed an expanding population base as synonymous with growth in retail markets. Unfortunately, this natural growth in market size has been declining during the past three decades as families have fewer children. From a historical viewpoint, the fertility rate in the United States—the average number of births per woman—has never been as low as its current level. The fertility rate was 2.2 children per woman in the 1930s, rose to 3.6 in the 1950s—the "baby boom era"—and dropped to 1.85 in 1990. It is expected to remain stable for the next 15 years. Despite this decreased birthrate, the total number of births has increased in recent years, as the baby boom generation reached childbearing years. Though each woman may be having fewer children, there are more baby boom women in childbearing years, and the increase in births has therefore been dubbed the "baby boomlet." As baby boomers move beyond childbearing years, however, total childbirths are expected to drop off significantly.

Two other important influences on population growth are life-expectancy rates and net immigration totals. As Americans live longer the population base becomes larger. In 1970, the average life expectancies for a male and female at birth were 67 and 75 years, respectively; by 2000, these figures are projected to increase to 74 and 81 years. Since immigration laws are under the control of Congress and difficult to predict, we will not project their impact on future population other than to report estimates on annual future net immigrations, both legal and illegal, range from 250,000 to 750,000 persons annually. Of course, the economic conditions existing in this and other countries could greatly influence this figure.

Implications for Retailers. Overall, population growth is slowing, and if current projections for fertility rate, immigration, and death rate are correct, the United States could begin to experience zero (or negative) population growth by 2025. A decline in population growth will mean a decreased demand for goods and services domestically. The key to high retail performance is shifting from new store openings and expansion to strategies built upon increasing productivity of existing stores, stealing market share from competitors, and managing gross margin through selling price and cost control.

Age Distribution. The age distribution of the U.S. population is changing significantly. As seen in Exhibit 3.2, the most significant change is the bulge of baby boomers moving into their 30s and 40s. During the 1980s, the number of people aged 40 to 44 grew by nearly 50 percent. At the same time, the total number of Americans aged 55 and older—a demographic group known as the "gray market"—was also growing rapidly. Based on the aging baby boomers and the growing gray market, the median age of the U.S. population has risen steadily from 29.4 in 1960 to 32.6 in 1991.

Implications for Retailers. Since different retailers tend to serve different age groups, the changing distribution of the U.S. population poses many challenges and opportunities. Retailers should be aware that consumers over 40, the first wave of baby boomers, tend to focus more on their families and finances than those in other age groups, and that the products and services that appealed to them as free-spending younger consumers will not necessarily be the ones that appeal to them now as parents, managers, and home owners. This age group also consumes more reading material than any other. Thus, bookstores, for example, should do well in the 1990s.

The "graying of America" is going to have enormous consequences for business in general, not just retailing.[7] Besides the increase in health care services, restaurants (where the over-60 category accounts for more than 30 percent of the breakfast and dinner trade) will have to consider such items as

EXHIBIT 3.2

Aging U.S. Population Distribution

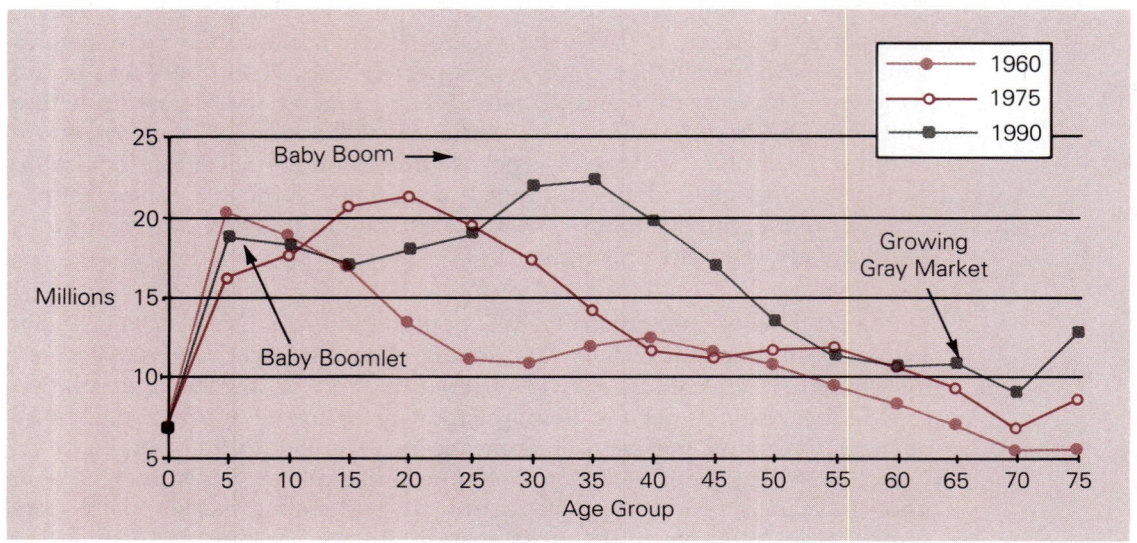

Source: Based on information from *Statistical Abstract of the United States 1991*, Table #13,22,30, p. 80. U.S. Department of Commerce.

the design of their tables and seats; financial service firms will have to reconsider their product offerings to this fixed-income category of consumers; and retailers in general will have to rethink the way they portray and target senior citizens in their advertising. Exhibit 3.3 shows how one retailer targets this market during the Christmas season by letting the seniors have the run of the store for several hours, free from noisy kids and impatient shoppers.

GEOGRAPHIC SHIFTS

The location of consumers in relation to the retailer often affects how they buy. In this section we take a closer look at the geographic patterns of consumers.

Shifting Geographic Centers. Retailers should be concerned not only with the numbers of people and their ages, but also with where they reside. As we will discuss in Chapter 10, consumers will not travel great distances to make retail purchases. They want convenience and will therefore patronize local retail outlets, even though the local outlet may be part of a national chain. Because the U.S. population for the past 200 years has been moving toward the West and the South, as seen in Exhibit 3.4, growth opportunities in retailing should be greatest in these areas.

EXHIBIT 3.3
Marketing Efforts Directed at Senior Citizens

October 15, 1992

Dear Nursing Home Administrator:

JCPenney applauds your service to the Nursing Home Community. We understand that during the Holiday season many of your residents have special requests and need personalized service without the shopping crowds. Therefore, JCPenney will open the doors early at our Prestonwood store from 8:00 to 10:00 a.m. on Monday, November 30.

We invite you to bring your residents and staff to shop hassle free without the crowds. We will offer personalized shopping service, a complimentary continental breakfast, a free goody bag filled with cosmetic samples and a photo with Santa Mouse.

To accommodate your needs, please RSVP (to 387–6969) by Tuesday, November 24, 1992. You may enter through the South side (Beltline Rd.) door with a sign that says **"Happy Holidays"** where your breakfast and goody bag will be waiting and our JCPenney staff will welcome you with **Merry Christmas.**

Cordially,

Denise Tickner
Publicist

DT:sm

JCPENNEY
PRESTONWOOD TOWN CENTER
5301 BELTLINE RD.
DALLAS, TX 75240
214-386-8900

12700 Park Central Place, P.O. Box 2405, Dallas, TX 75221

EXHIBIT 3.4
Center of United States Population

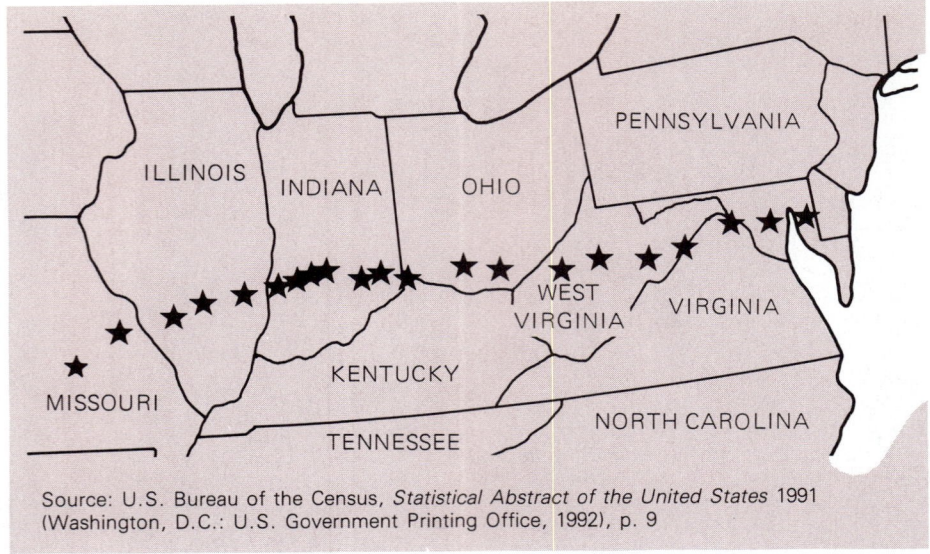

Source: U.S. Bureau of the Census, *Statistical Abstract of the United States* 1991 (Washington, D.C.: U.S. Government Printing Office, 1992), p. 9

Urban Centers. Most of the U.S. population resides in metropolitan areas with populations greater than 50,000, which the Census Bureau calls **metropolitan statistical areas (MSAs).** The proportion of the population residing in these cities has increased dramatically, from 56 percent in 1950 to over 77 percent today. The 1990 census showed that three-fourths of the U.S. population was concentrated into 3 percent of the land. This migration to MSAs, however, is directed more to suburban than central city areas.

Implications for Retailers. Every shift in population patterns affects where expenditures are made for household products. While recent shifts have resulted in a decline in downtown retail sales, sales increases in large regional malls have more than made up for any decline. Retail analysts have cited this as a major contributing factor to the recent merger mania in the supermarket industry. Suburban locations attracted American Stores to acquire Lucky Stores and A & P to acquire Shopwell, Food Emporium, and Waldbaums Supermarkets.

However, there are opportunities for retailers in the smaller markets. During the past decade, retailers have witnessed a rapid growth in secondary markets, areas with a population of less than 50,000. Historically, most chain retailers have ignored these markets. Secondary markets are also attractive because of the low level of retail competition, lower building costs, cheaper labor, and fewer building and zoning regulations. As MSAs began to stabilize and secondary markets continued to grow, retailers have begun to notice the success of retailers such as Wal-Mart and Family Dollar Stores in satisfying these secondary markets.

Mobility. In many countries, people are born, raised, married, raise families, and die in the same city or immediate geographic area. While this was historically true in the United States, it certainly is not true now. Today's population is extremely mobile. In fact, half of the nation's population moved between 1985 and 1989. However, while Americans move nearly twice as often as the Japanese, French, and British, overall mobility has been slowly decreasing over the past four decades, a trend expected to continue as baby boomers reach older, more stable stages in their lives.

Implications for Retailers. Mobility is important to retailers because they tend to serve local markets and cater to well-defined demographic groups. If the population moves, the retailer may find that its target market no longer resides in its trading area. Likewise, retailers in areas undergoing population growth will want to be prepared to serve these new consumers. After a move, consumers must locate new sources for food, clothing, household goods, and recreation. This presents an advantage for chain operations, in that a consumer moving from Des Moines to New Orleans knows what to expect at a Target, Casual Corner, Kroger, or other familiar retailer.

SOCIAL TRENDS

In this section we continue our examination of the external forces affecting the modern retailer by looking at several social trends: the increasing level of educational attainment, the state of marriage and divorce, and the makeup of the American household.

Education. The education level of the average American is increasing. In 1990, nearly 19 percent of the population had at least a bachelor's degree. The leading edge of the "baby boomers," those between 35 and 45 in 1990, is the most educated generation ever. One in four has completed four years of college.

Implications for Retailers. There is a close correlation between formal education and consumer taste levels and expectations. Thus, college-educated consumers differ in buying behavior from other workers of the same age and income level in that they are more alert to price, quality, and advertised claims. Since education levels for the overall population are expected to continue to rise, retailers can expect consumers to become increasingly sophisticated and discriminating and more independent in their search for consumer products. They will also demand a sales force capable of intelligently dealing with their needs.

Changing Makeup of U.S. Households. A relatively new social phenomenon has occurred during the past quarter-century as the makeup of households became less predictable due to several factors. First, more people are waiting longer before getting married. In fact, married couples were one of the slowest-growing household types, not just in this country but worldwide.[8] Even those who have been married once are delaying later marriages longer than ever.[9] Second, the divorce rate has increased by 227 percent since 1960. Because more people are remaining single and the divorce rate is increasing, the number of single-person households grew 26 percent in the 1980s. Nontraditional households, such as cohabitating couples, are also growing rapidly. As you can see in Retailing in Action 3.1, this changing structure in the makeup of households is a worldwide trend.

Implications for Retailers. For the retailer the trend toward single individual households presents many opportunities, because it creates a larger number of smaller-sized houses requiring home furnishings. This is especially true for the young adult market. Store hours may require an adjustment to accommodate the needs of this market. Divorces are not happy occasions, of course, but they do stimulate retail purchases by creating a new household.

RETAILING IN ACTION

3.1 Worldwide Changes in Household Structure

The United States isn't the only country in which nontraditional households are becoming mainstream. Retailers in other developed countries are facing similar trends.

For example, the rise in the numbers of single parents, unmarried couples, and people living alone is common to most countries in the developed world. The difference is in the pace at which these trends are progressing.

Four main factors have changed the makeup of households and families in the past two decades: Women are having fewer children, more women are having children out of wedlock, populations are aging, and marriage is down while divorce is up.

Japan remains the most traditional of the developed nations, with low rates of divorce and low rates of out-of-wedlock births. It also has the largest share of married couples. Sweden and Germany have the largest shares of single-person households, in part because they have older populations.

Scandinavia has been setting the pace for out-of-wedlock births and cohabitation. Sweden and Denmark have the largest shares of births to unmarried women, yet they don't have the highest shares of single parents, because many unmarried mothers in these countries live with partners.

It's not clear which country has the highest shares of "mingles" or cohabitating couples because some countries now include them with married couples in official household statistics. One estimate shows that virtually all young Swedes cohabitate before they marry.

The United States tops the list for single parents, partly because of high divorce rates, but also because American single parents are more likely to be young, never-married women on their own, rather than cohabitators.

Today, the combination of "mingles," "singles," and "dinks" (Dual Income, No Kids households) accounts for over 50 percent of all U.S. households. This market is not concerned about "Back-to-School" sales and other traditional, family-oriented retail activities, but rather in CD players, high image, and gourmet foods.

ECONOMIC TRENDS

In this section we look at the effect of income growth, the declining rate of personal savings, and the increase in the number of working women.

Income Growth. In 1990, the median household income was nearly $30,000 — 2.7 percent greater than 10 years earlier, after adjusting for inflation. But this income gain has not been shared equally by all age groups.

While income for households headed by someone under age 25 fell by 30 percent during the 1980s, it grew 15 percent in households headed by people age 25 to 34, just keeping pace with inflation. But income grew rapidly for middle-age households nearing their peak earning years. Income in households headed by 35 to 44 year olds grew by 51 percent, and just as impressively in households headed by people age 44 to 54. Households headed by 55 to 64 year olds, however, experienced a 2 percent decline over the past decade, a result of the trend toward early retirement.

Implications for Retailers. The imbalanced growth in income across age groups has created increased demand for value-oriented retailers such as discounters and manufacturers' outlets, and explains why many of the upscale retailers (such as Macy's, Nordstrom, and Neiman Marcus) have added discount outlets in recent years. One of the fastest-growing retail formats is warehouse clubs, which cater to small businesses and value-conscious shoppers, and most retail experts expect this trend to continue.

Personal Savings. A major criticism of this nation's economic system is that it does not reward personal savings. Changes in tax laws during the mid-1980s sought to rectify this, encouraging increased savings that could be used to finance capital growth in the economy. As a result, the percentage of after-tax income that U.S. citizens saved, which had dwindled from 8.1 percent in 1970 to 2.9 percent in 1987, grew again to 4.2 percent in 1988 and 4.6 percent in 1989. With a continually aging population, experts predict that the 1990s will be a period of increased savings.

Implications for Retailers. Retailers have enjoyed continued sales growth over this period because even though median household income has basically remained stable, spending percentages have increased. However, retailers must be prepared for the 1990s as the baby boomers plan for retirement by reducing spending and increasing savings.

Women in the Labor Force. Over the past three decades women have become a dominant factor in the labor force. In 1960, 38 percent of all women over the age of 16 were in the labor force; by 1990, the participation had risen to 58 percent. This trend is true of all age groups, even women age 25 to 34, who might be expected to be raising families. Seventy-five percent of all women age 25 to 34 were in the labor force compared to only 36 percent in 1960. The percentage of all married women with preschoolers in the labor force increased from 45 to 59 percent in the last decade.

This significant rise in the number of working women has protected many households from inflation and recession. In fact, many economists suggest that the working woman has been the nation's secret weapon against economic hardships.

Implications for Retailers. The rise in the number of working women has many retail implications. Many consumers have less time for shopping, whether they are female heads of households or males and females sharing household chores in dual-income families. Working men and women are often unable to shop during regular retailing hours and prefer that retailers hold sales and special events in the evening. Time-pressed shoppers find that price is sometimes less important than convenience, availability, and service. One study found that part-time working mothers of preschoolers tend to do more in-home shopping.[10] Retailers must develop strategies, such as using direct mail, adjustment of store hours, and even baby-sitting services, for their working customers. These special services will go a long way in capturing the time-pressed shopper's store loyalty.

PSYCHOGRAPHIC CHARACTERISTICS

Changing demographic and economic factors alone do not explain changing consumption patterns in the United States. We must also understand **psychographics,** which is the examination of the attitudes, interests, and opinions of the population or of a meaningful segment of the population.[11] Closely related to psychographics is lifestyle analysis. Lifestyle can be defined as "the patterns in which people live and spend time and money."[12] Several of the major changes in lifestyles that have or will impact retailing in the remaining years of this century are outlined in the sections that follow.

MALE AND FEMALE ROLE FLEXIBILITY

The distinction between male and female roles in society is becoming blurred. Women are entering traditionally male jobs: bus drivers, telephone repair persons, police officers, and business executives. Males are taking traditionally female jobs. The number of male nurses, telephone operators, and airline attendants are all increasing dramatically. More men are deciding to stay home and take care of households as their wives become the major breadwinners, and technology permits "electronic commuting" from home offices.

Implications for Retailers. With more men at home, supermarkets will have to direct promotions toward their needs and make them feel comfortable in this new environment. Likewise, as we pointed out in our section on women in the labor force, retailers must make specific adjustments to this market by adjusting store hours, providing more consumer information, and changing the product assortment.

DETERIORATION OF INSTITUTIONAL CONFIDENCE

Recently, the American public has shown an increasing distrust of government and other institutions (e.g., Wall Street, television religion, and business in general). Much of this distrust is latent, but it became overt after the various religious scandals, insider-trading scandals on Wall Street, the Iran-Contra arms-for-hostages controversy, the savings and loans problems, and the House banking scandal, with their subsequent convictions of public officials. This skepticism regarding business, religious, and governmental institutions is perhaps based on feelings that these institutions are more interested in satisfying their goals rather than meeting the public's needs.

Implications for Retailers. Many established retailers no longer enjoy the customer loyalty they once had. These retailers still have a loyal following among older adults, but the "baby boomers" are a different story. With so many competing stores available today, the successful retailer of the next decade will be the one that does the best job of getting its message out. The deliverance of the "best value for the money" will help retailers reestablish the consumer loyalty they so long enjoyed. Finally, retailers should exemplify the highest ethical and moral conduct in all their dealings with consumers, employees, suppliers, and other retailers. This type of behavior will go a long way toward resolving this deterioration in confidence.

MANAGEMENT OF TIME VERSUS MONEY

Many households, especially multiple-income households, are becoming more concerned with the management of time versus money. In fact, Americans in 1990 had more free time at their disposal than they had in 1970, yet an increasing number felt that they had less free time.[13] Money management obviously cannot be ignored, but households frequently realize that it is time, not money, that determines whether they participate. Consumers who fit this description of having "time poverty" want to reduce the amount of time spent in retail stores. They don't want to wander around for hours or even minutes in search of a particular product. They have too many other things to do.

Implications for Retailers. In view of this new time management crisis, it is not surprising to find mail-order and home television shopping have increased dramatically.[14] In addition, any store manager who can ease this time crunch by means of express checkouts, phone-ahead orders, or free delivery can turn a problem into an opportunity for success.

Supermarkets, probably more than any other retailers, have been dramatically affected by symptoms of "time poverty." In addition to stocking more microwavable and ready-to-eat foods, supermarket managers are adapting to one-stop shopping by offering goods and services such as postage stamps and video rentals. Supermarkets, in an effort to speed customers through their stores, are improving aisle signs, opening more checkout stations, and offering specialized express checkouts. But most supermarkets still have a lot to do to streamline food shopping. Although they are investing in salad bars, delis, and other takeout-food departments, many put these services deep in the store, forcing customers to make a longer stop than they want to. A recent Food Marketing Institute study found that half of all food shoppers would buy takeout food from supermarkets more often if they could get in and out of the store faster (this includes parking). Supermarket operators would do better by putting takeout sections in the front of the store, possibly with a separate entrance, checkout, or a drive-through window.

The combination of technology (like the fax machine), new distribution systems (like Domino's Pizza), and the perception of time scarcity is changing people's concept of convenience. In just a few years, the standards for photoprocessing have shifted from seven days to overnight to one hour. The

ILLUSTRATION 3.2

As dual-career families have become more pressed for time, retailers such as CPI photo finish have responded by offering in-store photo processing in just one hour.

same thing is occurring with mail delivery, eyeglass service, furniture delivery, automobile maintenance, and other categories. Convenience is not just a state of mind, it is a dynamic state of mind. It is a "moving target" that savvy retailers should monitor closely.[15]

VALUE AND LIFESTYLE FRAGMENTATION

In what is considered the most advanced study of this nation's lifestyle patterns, SRI International, a west-coast marketing research operation, developed its *Values and Lifestyle (VALS) Program*. VALS, first introduced in 1978, helped marketers predict patterns of consumption based on consumers' attitudes regarding values and lifestyles. However, significant changes in the consumer and market have led to diversity in the consumer population and *value and lifestyle fragmentation,* making it increasingly difficult for marketers to predict consumer behavior based on attitudes. SRI developed *VALS 2*, which is based on more permanent psychological states.[16] Consumers are organized into eight classifications which vary on two dimensions: resources such as money and education available to the consumer; and whether the consumer is oriented toward principles, status, or action. The basic orientations to consumption are:

1. Principle-Oriented—people guided by how they believe the world is or should be.
2. Status-Oriented—people driven by the opinions of others.
3. Action-Oriented—people driven by a need for diverse social and physical activity, as well as experimentation.

As consumers obtain more resources (money, education, etc.), they are able to achieve more of their goals—or become actualized—within each of these consumption orientations.

Implications for Retailers. The population is getting older, and financial and other resources tend to accumulate with age. As baby boomers age, obtain greater resources, and consume more goods and services, retailers must understand how to satisfy principle-, status-, or action-oriented goals, as appropriate for their target market.

BEHAVIORAL CHARACTERISTICS

Now that we understand not only who customers are (demographics) and how they think (psychographics), we can explore what they do, or their **behavioral characteristics.** Our quest in this chapter is to understand complex shopping behaviors such as how shoppers determine a need for merchandise, choose stores, gather and evaluate information, and complete transactions.

BEHAVIOR VERSUS ATTITUDE

The examination of actual shopping behavior is important for several reasons. For one thing, attitudes—being intangible, ephemeral, even fleeting states of mind—have proven elusive to measure. Behaviors, by their very nature tangible and observable, can be much more reliably measured. Consumers don't always do what they say they're going to do, but they always do what they do. Most importantly, shopping behaviors are the activities through which purchasing actually takes place, whereas attitudes are simply states of mind which, while they motivate behavior, are one step removed from actual purchasing.

As an example, think for a moment of the best store in which to buy toothpaste. Many consumers suggest a deep-discount drugstore, perhaps, or some other source of very low priced toiletries. Now think of where you purchased your last tube of toothpaste. For many consumers, the answer is a convenience store or moderately priced supermarket. Despite good intentions to shop wisely—intentions which are measured as attitudes—situational factors such as convenience and lifestyle often intervene between intention and behavior. To paraphrase the old adage, something seems to happen on the way to the market.

DIMENSIONS OF BUYING BEHAVIOR

There are a number of key dimensions which drive shopping behavior, and successful retailers must understand how they sometimes intervene between intention and behavior.

Extensive, Simplified, and Routine Purchasing. Not all purchases are equally important, and therefore not all items are purchased in the same manner. For instance, few consumers occupy themselves with deciding where to buy toothpaste, but the purchase of a car or house often requires considerable research and consideration. (There are, surprisingly, consumers whose purchase process for a car is nearly as short and uninvolved as that for toothpaste.[17])

We can describe the purchasing process for various goods and services on a continuum from extensive to simplified to routine purchasing. This continuum, shown in Exhibit 3.5, describes the effort consumers will exert in shopping for an item. More expensive, long-lasting, and infrequently purchased items often evoke an *extensive* shopping process, in which the consumer takes a relatively long time to evaluate options, gathers information, and carefully considers a variety of options before making a purchase decision. Examples of extensive shopping processes are those for homes, cars, and large appliances. Since these items are not purchased frequently, consumers feel they must make the right choice, or long suffer the consequences.

Generally, goods that are purchased more frequently, are less expensive, or perform simple functional roles in the consumer's life are purchased in a

EXHIBIT 3.5

Continuum of Shopping Processes

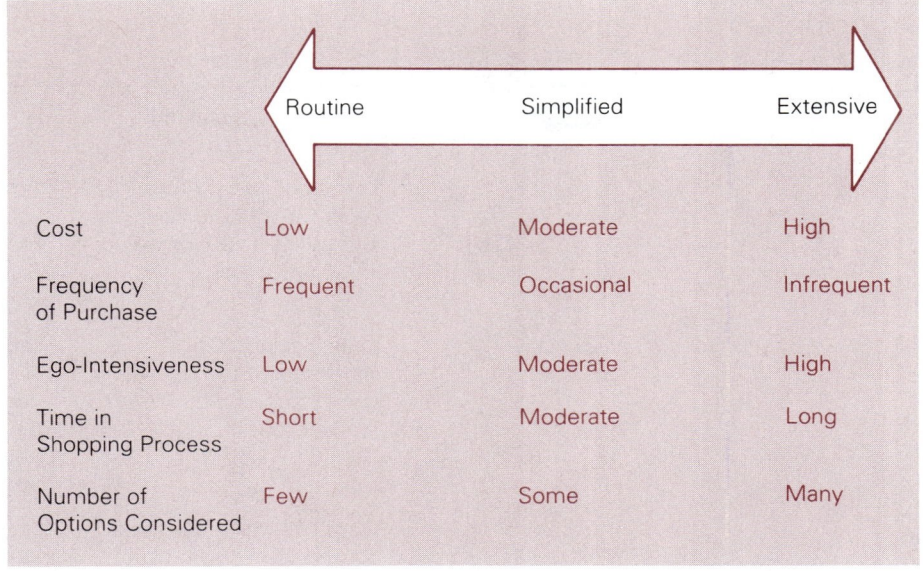

	Routine	Simplified	Extensive
Cost	Low	Moderate	High
Frequency of Purchase	Frequent	Occasional	Infrequent
Ego-Intensiveness	Low	Moderate	High
Time in Shopping Process	Short	Moderate	Long
Number of Options Considered	Few	Some	Many

simplified process, in which the consumer will exert some effort to identify and evaluate options, perhaps searching for the best price, but will not get into a belabored, protracted shopping process. Items such as fashion apparel, home decorations, and books fall into this category. It's worth shopping a little for these items, but not a lot.

Frequently purchased items such as consumables, household supplies, health and beauty aids, paper products, and groceries are considered *routine* purchase items, because the consumer forms a habit of purchasing them in a certain way or at a certain store. Often, opinions regarding such items—and the stores in which they are purchased—are formed over time through trial and error, and the purchase process becomes habitualized.

It may be helpful to think of these different shopping *processes* in relation to the different types of *products* often discussed in basic marketing texts: convenience, shopping, specialty, and unsought. Exhibit 3.6 describes each of these types of products and the process consumers often follow in purchasing them.

Naturally, many of the differences in the shopping processes have to do with consumer attitudes regarding the importance of the merchandise, but recent research has suggested that it has as much to do with behavioral patterns in shoppers' lives. In 1989, the authors conducted an extensive analysis of the process by which car buyers purchase cars.[18] The goal of this research was to identify the actual behaviors undertaken by consumers in the identification, evaluation, and selection of car models, in hopes that this behavioral understanding would provide insight into how to sell cars more effectively. The results indicated that most consumers shop for cars in one of six distinct behavioral patterns, and that a limited number of basic shopping

EXHIBIT 3.6

Types of Products and the Shopping Process

Type of Product	Description	Type(s) of Shopping Process
Convenience	Inexpensive, frequently purchased items.	Usually purchased in routine process.
Shopping	Less frequently purchased items for which consumers are willing to search, shop, and compare.	Purchased either in a simplified or extensive process, depending on the consumer's attitudes toward the product and the cost.
Specialty	Items having unique characteristics (e.g., brand name) that evoke absolute product loyalty.	Purchased in either routine process, if shopper is accustomed to purchasing item, or in simplified manner if consumer needs to locate item or best price.
Unsought	Items for which consumer does not anticipate need, but purchases due to emergency (like car repair) or impulse.	Purchase process can be extensive, simplified, or routine. A failed central air conditioner might evoke an extensive process, while a candy bar bought on impulse would obviously be a routine process.

activities could be used to classify these shoppers. A sampling of these specific behaviors is contained in the following research questions:

1. How often do you read consumer advisory and product description magazines?
2. Do you sometimes visit car dealerships when you are not serious about buying a car, just to see what's new?
3. During your last car purchase, did you read comparisons of different brands and models to determine what to consider?
4. Was your decision about which model to buy made at the dealership or somewhere else, such as your home?
5. Was your previous car the same brand?

This behavioral analysis allowed the researchers to segment the broad consumer population into six categories according to their actual buying behavior, and then learn more about these consumer segments' shopping patterns. The six car-buyer segments cut across all demographic and lifestyle characteristics, countering the notion that such purchase patterns are a factor of income, education, or some other demographic variable. Through extensive analysis, the researchers determined that three of the buying segments, representing 54 percent of the buying population, purchase cars in an extensive manner, taking a relatively long time to shop, test driving several brands of cars several times each, collecting and evaluating extensive amounts of information, and usually making a rational decision in their homes before proceeding to make the purchase. The other 46 percent of the car-buying population purchased cars in a simplified manner, often considering only one make or model, relying heavily on the dealer or a trusted salesperson rather than their own research, and usually making an on-the-spot purchase decision rather than carefully considering the options at home. By understanding the preferred shopping behaviors of these two dramatically different consumer segments, marketers can refine selling practices to cater to individual shopping preferences.

Destination Versus Intercept Merchandise. Closely related to the extensiveness of the shopping process is whether the merchandise is considered a destination or intercept item. **Destination merchandise** is that which motivates or triggers a trip to a specific store. Intercept merchandise is that which the customer does not specifically go to a store to buy, but buys because the retailer "intercepts" them in the course of their lives. **Intercept merchandise** falls into two categories, sought-intercept merchandise and impulse-intercept merchandise. **Sought-intercept merchandise** is that for which consumers recognize a need, but is not seen as important enough to trigger a special trip. Often, consumers develop a mental shopping list of items, and an accumulation of items rather than any specific item triggers the shopping trip. **Impulse-intercept merchandise,** on the other hand, is merchandise purchased purely on impulse, when the customer happens to see it in the store. The customer has not previously recognized a need for the item.

While it may seem obvious that destination items are purchased in an extensive shopping process, and intercept items tend to be purchased in a routine process, this is not always the case. For instance, a light bulb is an inexpensive, frequently purchased item which is usually bought in a routine process. However, the failure of certain light bulbs in the home—perhaps the 100-watt clear bulb in the kitchen ceiling light, or the flood light that provides security lighting for the front yard at night—can motivate an immediate trip to a store and therefore serves as a destination item. Conversely, an expensive item that requires considerable research and consideration, such as a mattress, may evoke an extensive purchase process but may not trigger an immediate trip to a store. Rather, the consumer may put the item on a "mental shopping list" and remember to inquire about it when next in a department store. Retailing in Action 3.2 details some exciting research on the effect of destination and intercept merchandise on shopping behavior.

Destination Versus Intercept Stores. Now that we understand destination and intercept merchandise, and their influence on shopping behavior, we can expand the concept from merchandise categories to entire stores. Just as certain merchandise is destination merchandise, certain stores are considered **destination stores.** By virtue of the type of merchandise they carry, the

RETAILING IN ACTION

3.2 What Motivates Shopping Trips?

In 1989, the International Mass Retail Association (IMRA) asked the Ambassador Cards division of Hallmark to help answer the question, "What motivates consumers to patronize certain stores?" IMRA, whose membership includes most of the nation's discount, variety, and general-merchandise stores, commissioned the research in order to help its member retailers understand determinants of store choice and shopping behavior, which in turn would help them become more competitive in the marketplace. The study was based on interviews with more than 2000 customers of discount stores and probed what motivated their trips to discount and competitive stores.

The findings indicated that certain items carried in discount stores were considered by consumers to be "destination" items, because recognition of a need for these items was in itself enough to trigger a trip to a discount store. Destination items for discount stores included housewares, drugs and toiletries, and hardware. In addition, the study revealed that there is at least one other mechanism that could trigger store visits. Certain items are considered by consumers as "intercept" items, which consumers recognize a need for but don't consider important enough to warrant a special shopping trip. The consumer builds a mental shopping list for these items, and once the list reaches four to seven items, a shopping trip is triggered.

The study further broke intercept items into three categories: planned-look for, unplanned-look for, and impulse. Planned-look-for items are those which customers recognize they need and plan to look for the next time they are in the right type of store, although they will not make a special trip to purchase them. Unplanned-look-for items are those customers don't plan to look for until after they enter the store. As the name implies, impulse items are those which customers never look for, but rather purchase purely on impulse because they happen to see them. If shoppers aren't exposed to impulse items, they don't think to purchase them.

The study concluded it would be difficult for discounters to prompt store visits through intercept items, but that being top-of-mind for the destination items could ensure the retailer a portion of the consumer's shopping trips. Stores could then identify the key destination merchandise for their target customers and communicate their position as a dominant provider for these goods. The next time consumers recognize a need for these items, they theoretically will first visit the retailer that has most successfully communicated this dominance.

breadth of their assortment, pricing, and the convenience with which shoppers can access and shop the store, destination stores are those to which consumers generally make a special trip with the intent of shopping. Historically, the most obvious example of a destination store is a department store. Traditional thinking has held that department stores, considered to be the "anchors" of shopping malls, are responsible for attracting customer traffic to the mall. A mall typically consists of two to four anchor stores, with concourses connecting them. The small specialty shops lining the concourses are considered **intercept stores,** because they intercept customers passing by in the concourse. For this reason, the first 10 feet of a mall specialty store is often considered the most important space, because this area entices shoppers off the concourse into the store. However, recent consumer trends have suggested that this pattern may be shifting, since more shoppers are driving to malls specifically to visit the specialty stores, often entering via the mall's main entrance.[19]

Other examples of destination stores are stores that are called category killers and power formats. **Category killers,** such as Toys "R" Us, are usually large stores concentrating on one category (like toys), which allows them to carry both a broad assortment and deep selection of merchandise, usually coupled with low price and moderate service. A successful category killer is so dominant in its specific category that it is the only store consumers seriously consider when in need of that merchandise, which is precisely how it functions as a motivator of shopping trips and a destination store.

A **power format** operates in a broader niche by carrying a wider variety of merchandise, but offering a narrower assortment within each category. A good example is Drug Emporium, a deep-discount drugstore that offers a wide variety of health and beauty aids, household goods, and candy and snacks.[20] Within each category, though, the assortment may be limited. There will be some type of rubbing alcohol, for instance, but not a choice of several brands in multiple sizes. By limiting the number of items carried, the power format sells larger quantities of each item, therefore reducing its costs by purchasing in large quantities. This savings is usually passed on to consumers, which increases sales and allows even better quantity discounts. The power format is a strong traffic draw and therefore serves as a destination store.

Examples of intercept stores are convenience stores and fast-food restaurants, which draw much of their traffic through "curb appeal" and intercepting passing motorists. These stores rely on highly visible sites, preferably on

ILLUSTRATION 3.3

"Category killers" such as Circuit City pre-empt the competition by offering tremendous selections within a single product category (such as consumer electronics) along with moderate service and good values.

street corners, and utilize large, colorful signs that are easily noticed. Of course, these stores also function as destination stores in some shopping trips, just as destination stores sometimes serve as intercept stores. The fundamental mission of a store, however, should be defined as a destination or intercept store, and all marketing variables such as merchandise mix, pricing strategy, site selection, store name and signage, and promotion strategies should be coordinated toward conveying this image.

Store Choice. We have discussed consumer attitudes and behaviors extensively, so let's look more closely at some of the attributes that often influence store choice decisions. Eight of the most frequently cited attributes are as follows[21]:

1. Price
2. Merchandise (including quality, style and fashion, assortment, national versus private labels)
3. Physical characteristics (including decor, layout, and floor space)
4. Sales promotions
5. Advertising
6. Convenience (including hours, location, ease of entrance and parking, ease of finding items)
7. Services (including credit, delivery, return policy, and guarantees)
8. Store personnel (including helpfulness, friendliness, and courtesy)

This list of attributes is not exhaustive, and not all attributes apply to all stores and shopping trips.[22] For example, when evaluating grocery stores, the style or fashion of merchandise is not usually relevant. In a cross-cultural study, retail researchers Arnold, Oum, and Tigert found locational convenience and lower prices were clearly the most important attributes in choosing a retail grocer. While the importance of these attributes did not change from season to season, significant changes were seen over a seven-year period.[23]

Multi-Attribute Decision Model. In theory, consumers evaluate alternative stores on all applicable store attributes, weighing in their perception of the relative importance of each attribute. It would be useful to combine all of these attributes in a model that shows how they interact to influence store choice. Psychologists Fishbein and Rosenberg have developed models for relating attitudes, beliefs, and behaviors,[24] frequently referred to as multi-attribute models, and market researchers have adapted them for business applications. A useful multi-attribute model is the one developed by Talarzyk and Moinpour,[25] which we will formulate in terms of an attitude toward a retail outlet:

$$A_b = \sum_{i=1}^{n} W_i B_{ib}$$

where: A_b = attitude toward retail outlet b

W_i = weight or importance of store attribute i

B_{ib} = evaluation or belief regarding outlet b on attribute i

$\sum_{i=1}^{n}$ = summation of the number (n) of attributes important in selecting retail outlet

This mathematical equation is a helpful tool for understanding how consumers relate the dozens of pieces of information regarding stores as they decide where to shop. It is not, however, an absolute predictive formula, and retailers cannot simply calculate market share by measuring the variables and running them through the formula. The multi-attribute model's predictive capability is limited by three factors:

1. First, the model by definition produces a measure of *attitude* toward a store relative to purchasing a specific item. As we have said throughout this section, attitudes are not necessarily direct predictors of shopping behavior, because lifestyle and other behavioral factors often intervene.
2. Second, the key variables W (relative importance of attribute) and B (evaluation or belief about the store on a certain attribute) are shown as first-order, or relatively stable, factors. In reality, both factors vary greatly with the type of merchandise being considered, time, and circumstance. At any given time, a consumer might rate price as the most important attribute and Store A as the lowest-priced store, but 10 minutes later decide that convenience is more important than price, and so visit Store B. So to have any real meaning, this model would have to be calculated for every combination of merchandise, moment in time, and point in the consumer's life, resulting in a highly complex differential equation requiring a supercomputer to solve.
3. Finally, this model is presented as a *compensatory model*, meaning that strength in one attribute can offset a weakness in another. While this is generally true, it is not always true. Depending on the merchandise being considered and the consumer's attitudes and behavioral patterns, one or more attributes can be absolute store choice criterion. For instance, a store or restaurant can rate highly on all attributes except one, such as the acceptance of credit cards, and a particular consumer may never eat there for that one reason.

While multi-attribute decision models are not absolute predictive tools, they can be helpful to the retail marketer. For instance, a continuing survey can track the movement in time of both the attributes consumers consider important in store choice, and consumers' evaluations of the retailer and its competitors on these attributes. This information can be critical to a retailer's ability to maintain and evolve its market positioning image in response to changing consumer needs and desires.

To illustrate this point, consider Exhibit 3.7, which shows attitude ratings of two retail outlets over three years, in terms of the multi-attribute model

EXHIBIT 3.7

Attributes Ratings of Three Stores over Time

	Attribute Importance W	1983 Store:		1988 Store:		1993 Store:	
		A	B	A	B	A	B
Competitive Prices	5	3	2	4	2	5	3
Convenient Location	3	3	4	3	4	2	4
Helpful Store Personnel	4	3	3	3	3	3	3
Wide Merchandise Assortment	4	4	2	3	3	3	4
Attractive Store Decor	2	3	4	4	4	4	3
Total Score from 4 Multi-Attribute Model	—	58	50	61	57	63	61

discussed previously. Consumers are increasingly seeking retail outlets that have more competitive prices and more convenient locations. The importance of helpful store personnel, wide merchandise assortments, attractive store decor, and informative advertising have remained relatively constant over the three-year period. If we were to compute the composite attitude score for Retailer A and Retailer B over the three-year period (using the equation on pages 96 and 97), we would see that consumers overall still have a more favorable attitude toward Retailer A. However, this situation is changing. Exhibit 3.8 dramatically reveals that Retailer A is quickly losing its favorable position. Since a change in attitude is a leading indicator of a change in sales or market share, all other factors being equal, we would predict that the market share of Retailer B will increase in coming years unless Retailer A is effective in reversing its decline in relative ratings on attributes consumers consider important.

Another use of attitude data is fine-tuning strategy. It is clear that Retailer A needs to do something—but what? The retailer should do something that is important to the consumer and that will give it a unique advantage. Retailer B stands out in terms of having competitive prices, and consumers are placing heavier emphasis on this attribute. If Retailer A decided to offer more competitive prices, that would not create a differential competitive advantage. Retailer A would be better off trying to offset this disadvantage by improving service, informative advertising, or other highly weighted attributes. However, Retailer A must be aware that if price is an absolute store choice criterion, it must at least match Retailer B's prices to establish an even playing field.

Other Reasons for Shopping. Up to this point, we have assumed that consumers shop because they recognize a need to buy a particular item. However, shopping behavior may be triggered by the recognition of needs other than buying, such as the need for social interaction or personal fulfillment.

EXHIBIT 3.8

Changing Attribute Ratings of Competing Stores

These nonbuying needs have been described by Edward Tauber,[26] who suggests that social motives for shopping include the following:

1. Social experience outside the home
2. Communication with others having a similar interest
3. Association with peer groups
4. Status and authority
5. Pleasure of bargaining

Similarly, Tauber suggests that shopping trips may be triggered by the following personal motives:

1. Role playing
2. Diversion
3. Self-gratification
4. Learning about new trends
5. Physical activity
6. Sensory stimulation

Some of these social and personal motives can be combined with buying and information motives. Shopping does not necessarily arise from any single motive.

RETAIL PATRONAGE MODEL

Now that we have examined socioeconomic, demographic, psychographic, and behavioral characteristics of consumers, we can develop a comprehensive model that describes, and to some degree predicts, how these factors come together to affect consumer buying patterns. We call this the **retail patronage model.**

NATURE OF A CONCEPTUAL MODEL

Before presenting and discussing the retail patronage model, we should clarify the objectives and uses of such conceptual models. We develop models as a framework or organization for understanding complex phenomena which defy understanding through simple observation. Such phenomena are usually dependent on many input factors, which interact in a complex manner to "cause" certain outcomes. Consumer behavior is so incredibly complex, and the input factors so variable and difficult to measure, that it is virtually impossible to trace the routes of causation. Nonetheless, the retail patronage model serves as a representation of a *typical* buying process.

Examine the retail patronage model in Exhibit 3.9. This model suggests that patronage is a process, with a series of steps occurring against a backdrop of individual, social, and situational factors. Furthermore, the process is cyclic, with the steps of need recognition, active information gathering, decision, transaction, and evaluation cycling around the central element of passive information gathering, all feeding back into formation of long-term beliefs about certain shopping alternatives.

We can simplify this model by considering the purchase of a specific item, beginning with need recognition and ending with use and evaluation. This is a highly rationalized, stepwise shopping process, but as we have suggested, human beings often don't behave quite that rationally. The very first step of need recognition, along with all subsequent steps, is dependent on beliefs formed from all previous purchases and the long-term use of the goods or services purchased, and these beliefs strongly influence future shopping behavior. After a consumer's first purchase, then, it is difficult to determine which step in the process is the initial step. The patronage model is therefore made somewhat more complex, though more representative of reality, by viewing it as a cyclic process.

STEPS IN THE BUYING PROCESS

Passive Information Gathering. We begin with **passive information gathering,** which is the ongoing receipt and processing of information regarding the existence and quality of merchandise, stores, shopping convenience, pricing, and other factors. As we move through our daily routine, we are constantly

Chapter 3 Understanding Retail Customers

EXHIBIT 3.9

Dynamic Retail Patronage Model

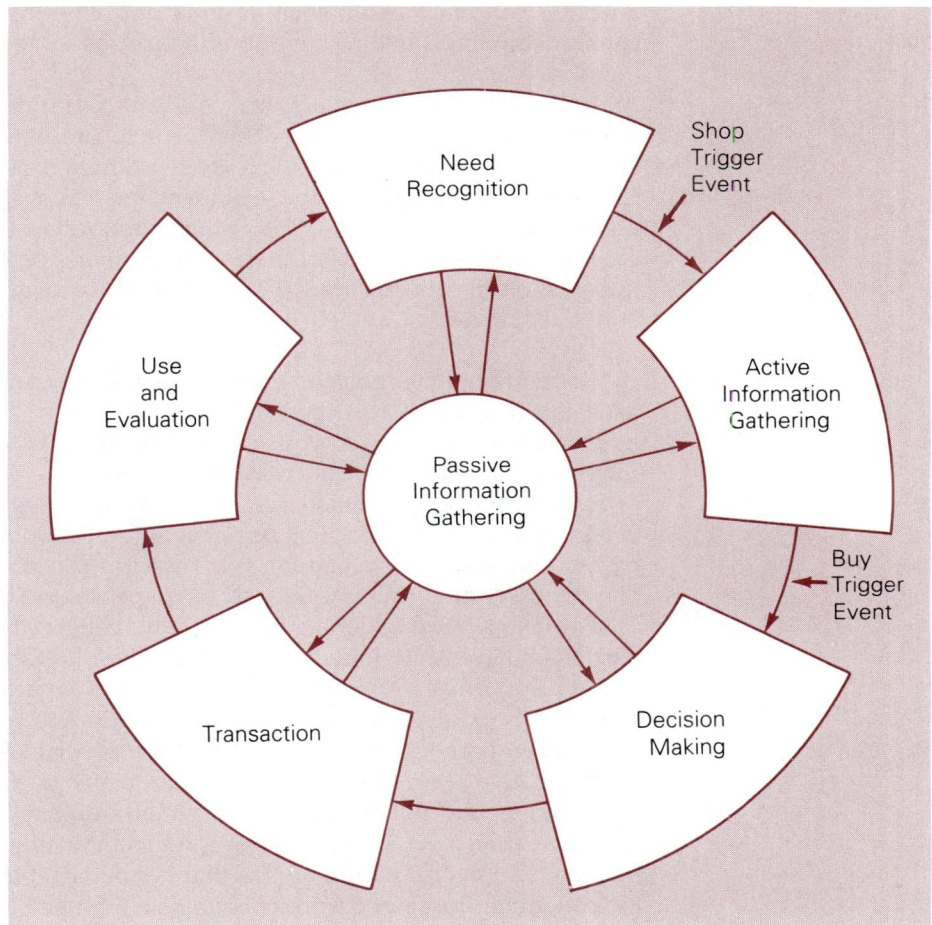

exposed to messages regarding merchandise, services, and the retailers that sell them to us. Virtually all advertising is intended to convey these messages. We talk with friends who report on their recent shopping visit to a new or familiar store, or their use of a new product or service. All of this information is registered, though perhaps not consciously, through passive information gathering, and this *learning* subsequently influences all other steps in the buying process.

Need Recognition. **Need recognition,** often called "problem recognition," has traditionally been considered the beginning of the shopping process, and indeed, if every consumer behaved perfectly rationally, every buying process would begin here. Need recognition occurs when the consumer recognizes a need or desire for an item or service. The term "need" here is inclusive of both absolute survival needs, such as food and clothing, and desires, or items consumers would like to have to enhance the quality of their lives.

Ideal State Versus Actual State. A formal definition of need recognition is when consumers perceive that their actual state differs greatly enough from their ideal state that they decide to do something to resolve the discrepancy.[27] Of course, the consumer's sense of ideal and actual states is highly subjective and constantly changing, so it is virtually impossible to measure and often not even conscious to the consumer. A consumer's ongoing learning and new information inputs can dramatically affect the consumer's perception of ideal and actual states.

Shop Trigger Event: Need Versus Barrier Quotient. Recognition of need in itself is not enough to trigger consumers to begin shopping, for there are many needs and desires you and I have for which we have not made a purchase. To move beyond need recognition, the consumer must perceive some type of event or set of circumstances which suggests the degree of need is high relative to the barriers to resolving it. The point at which this "need/barrier quotient" is high enough is known as the **shop trigger event,** though it may be a set of conditions as well as a specific event.

For instance, consider a consumer who believes her mattress is becoming a bit saggy and isn't giving her as good a night's sleep as before. Clearly, she has recognized a problem, but she wonders whether it is yet time to do something about it. That can only be determined relative to the cost—in financial and other terms—of correcting the problem. Perhaps she remembers what a hassle it was to shop for her last mattress. She knows from talking with friends and noticing advertising that a quality king-sized mattress can cost more than $1,000 today, so she is reluctant to enter the shopping process. She may rationalize within herself that her bed isn't that bad yet. Simply put, the consumer does not currently recognize her need as being acute enough to overcome certain barriers, such as convenience and cost.

Retailer-Induced Need and Barrier Recognition. Can retailers induce need recognition in consumers? This is a highly debated question, since influencing need recognition theoretically requires changing a consumer's ideal and actual states, a seemingly impossible challenge. However, ideal and actual states are perceptions made by consumers rather than absolute realities. A critical factor in the formation of these perceptions is information consumers receive through many sources, and retailers can be one of the richest sources of this information. For customers who have not yet entered the store, retailers can provide information through advertising that alerts customers to the availability of certain merchandise, the convenience of shopping, or the price or savings available.

Recall our consumer whose mattress is becoming worn, who has for now decided her need is not great relative to the costs of solving it. New information, perhaps provided by the retailer, can change her perception of either the degree of her problem, or the barriers to correcting it. Watching the local news, for instance, our shopper might see a commercial for a local bedding retailer that demonstrates a test for determining how worn a mattress is. Based on this test, the customer might conclude that her need is greater than she thought. One of the most famous of these "test" programs is the Special K pinch, in which Kellogg's showed consumers a quick, painless, and private test for whether they should lose weight, and by inference, if they could pinch more than an inch of skin around their waistline, perhaps they better start eating Special K cereal. Such communications influence consumers' perceptions of their ideal or actual state, and therefore their degree of need.

Alternatively, retailers can send messages that influence consumers' perceptions of the barriers to solving needs. Our consumer might read in a newspaper advertisement that a local mattress retailer is holding a 50 percent off sale, with free delivery of the new mattress and free disposal of the old mattress. With this new information, the consumer might conclude that while the degree of her problem has not increased, the barriers to correcting it have decreased, and therefore she is triggered into the shopping process.

Remember, retailers can influence consumer perceptions in the store as well. We stated earlier that many purchases are intercept purchases, for which the shopping process is triggered after the shopper has arrived at a store. In fact, the Point-of-Purchase Advertising Institute (POPAI) now reports that nearly 60 percent of all purchases are decided upon after the customer has entered the store.[28] This means retailers can influence consumer perceptions regarding the need/barrier quotient through sales associates, visual communications, and, most importantly, the presentation of the merchandise itself.

Remember, however, that our marketing orientation to retailing means we can never create consumer needs, only identify them, and possibly influence consumers' perceptions regarding their severity and the barriers to solving them.

Active Information Gathering. Once consumers reach the shopping trigger event, they move from need recognition into **active information gathering.** In this phase, consumers gather and evaluate information that will eventually lead to a decision either to not purchase or which item to purchase and where to purchase it. Active information gathering typically involves three stages:

1. Development of an **initial consideration set,** or the set of possibilities that should be considered, as well as the key attributes on which the purchase decision will be based. The initial consideration set and evaluation attributes are often based on general information sources such as preexisting knowledge, advertising, discussions with friends and relatives, and reading of magazines such as *Consumer Reports*. For more extensive purchases, consumers often also utilize visits to stores to build their initial consideration set. In the highest-expenditure categories, such as cars and large appliances, salespeople must be careful to ascertain whether a customer is

in this process of building the initial consideration set, or in the buying stage, and adjust their sales approach in response. While in some cases sales pressure or just the right product or price can move customers directly into the buying stage, too much pressure can intimidate or irritate consumers, causing them not only to leave without purchasing, but also to not return once they reach the buying stage.

To gauge the state customers are in, automotive salespeople often use certain tests such as, "What kind of deal would it take to get you into this car today," or asking for a refundable "earnest check" before they will begin negotiating sales figures. Unfortunately, when salespeople determine a shopper is unlikely to be moved beyond active information gathering into the buying stage, they all too often ignore or anger the shopper. A better approach would be to courteously provide shoppers with the information they seek, then follow up with later calls. More progressive automotive manufacturers, such as the Lexus division of Toyota, are encouraging their retailers to employ this consumer-responsive sales practice today.[29]

2. In the second stage, consumers narrow the consideration set to a more manageable number of possibilities. While consumers want to feel that they have considered a wide range of options so as to not miss a golden opportunity, they do not want to be confused by a myriad of options. In the second stage, consumers might visit stores to gather more specific information, including rough price ranges, in order to narrow their list.
3. In the final stage, consumers directly compare the key attributes of the alternatives remaining on the "short list." Here consumers are very active in their search for specific information and often begin ascertaining actual prices through store visits or preliminary negotiating where appropriate.

One of the most important variables of active information gathering is the information resources used by consumers. A useful market research technique is for retailers to understand what information resources their consumers prefer to use, then match their communications programs to these vehicles. Just as importantly, retailers should understand the information resources used by noncustomers, to identify new communication strategies which can reach new consumers.

Decision Making. Based on information gathered in the previous phase, consumers decide whether they intend to purchase, and which product and store they intend to choose. We stress that these are "intent" decisions, because other factors can intervene before the transaction is completed.

Deciding Not to Buy. Of course, a possible outcome of the active information-gathering stage is a decision not to buy, or to delay the purchase. A shopper might conclude that an adequate product or service isn't available, or that the cost (financial or otherwise) is greater than previously thought. Though a purchase is not made, the information gathered is often mentally recorded and influences future shopping processes.

Buy Trigger Event. When active information gathering yields a combination of elements that works for the consumer, he or she reaches the **buy trigger event.** At this point, the consumer has decided to purchase a good or service and often where to buy it. In some cases the consumer decides on an item but retains more than one store in the consideration set, leaving the final purchase decision to be made in the transaction stage based on the results of negotiation. Of course, prices for most consumer goods are not negotiable, so in most cases a final decision is made prior to the transaction stage.

Transaction. The consumer is now ready to enter into the transaction stage, in which the actual purchase is made. The transaction may include final negotiation, application for credit if necessary, and determination of the terms of purchase (cash, credit card, etc.). As we mentioned earlier, situational factors can sometimes intervene during the transaction phase to preempt the purchase. For instance, the consumer can become aware of unanticipated costs, such as taxes, delivery charges, or other items, and decide not to buy.

The transaction is often used by retailers as an opportunity to sell add-on or related purchases, such as extended service warranties, batteries for toys, and other impulse merchandise. If handled properly, consumers can view this selling practice as a customer service, as if the retailer were "looking out" for the customer's long-term satisfaction. If handled poorly, the customer can view this as an attempt to gouge the unsuspecting consumer. In extreme cases, the consumer may even decide to cancel the initial transaction.

Use and Evaluation. The consumer patronage process does not end with the transaction. In fact, according to our model, the process continually cycles on itself. Therefore, successful retailers must concern themselves not just with the activities leading to the transaction, but also with what happens after the transaction. Ultimately, consumers are buying solutions to their perceived needs, and successful retailers take an active interest in ensuring that customers feel satisfied over the long term that their need has been resolved. The consumer's use and evaluation is therefore a critical, though sometimes overlooked, stage in the consumer patronage process.

Post-Purchase Resentment. The first important moment in the use and evaluation is immediately after the transaction, in the first hours and days in which the consumer uses the product or service. During this critical time, consumers form lasting impressions regarding the soundness of their purchase decision which feed directly into passive information gathering and influence all future purchases. If the consumer is dissatisfied, a condition can emerge known as **post-purchase resentment,** in which the consumer's dissatisfaction results in resentment toward the retailer.

If post-purchase resentment is not identified and rectified by the retailer, it can have a long-term negative influence on the retailer's ability to recapture the consumer as a satisfied customer. Post-purchase resentment is like concrete around the retailer's ankles; it takes time to set, but once established, it can be virtually impossible to dislodge. Even worse, post-purchase resentment spreads beyond the affected customer. It is wise to remember the old marketing adage: A satisfied customer tells four friends, while a dissatisfied customer tells eleven.

Customer Satisfaction Programs. Fortunately, if the retailer is proactive in its customer satisfaction program and responds quickly to budding resentment, it can be overcome. The problem is that many unhappy consumers do not report their dissatisfaction, so retailers must be vigilant in their monitoring of customer satisfaction. This process begins with the establishment of proactive policies such as full-satisfaction guarantees, which should be boldly communicated to the shopper. This tells consumers that if they do have a problem, the retailer wants to hear about and rectify it. Beyond this, many retailers have started customer follow-up programs, such as customer satisfaction reply cards given out at the time of purchase or mailed to the customer several days later. Electronic cash registers have aided in this process by efficiently gathering the names and addresses of customers, recording the merchandise purchased, and automatically mailing the customer satisfaction surveys.

Many large retailers—especially chains in which individual stores are not under central control such as in cooperatives, franchises, and dealerships—have taken this customer satisfaction process one step further. They have instituted programs that measure customer satisfaction on an ongoing basis and compare customer service ratings of individual retail locations against preestablished benchmarks or a chainwide average.

Ford Motor Company has been a leader in this program with its Customer Satisfaction Rating (CSR) program, which rates dealers across the country. Dealers feed customer purchase information to Ford, which sends out customer satisfaction surveys at various times after the purchase, asking questions not only about the product but also the dealership, sales practices, and quality of its service department. Awards are given each year at Ford's national dealer show to those with the highest CSR ratings, providing dealers with incentives for enhancing their quality and service. By instilling this focus on customer satisfaction throughout its entire distribution network, Ford has instilled a culture of customer satisfaction throughout the company, including its suppliers, manufacturing operations, and dealers.[30]

DYNAMIC NATURE OF RETAIL PATRONAGE MODEL

It should be apparent from the preceding discussion that the retail patronage model is not a linear series of steps, but rather a dynamic, interactive process of shopping, learning, purchasing, evaluating, and shopping again. We have placed passive information gathering at the center of this dynamic model because the consumer can jump to and from this point from virtually every other stage in the process. Consumers who reach a decision but fail to purchase in the transaction stage because of new information do not necessarily return to the need recognition stage. Instead, information they have gathered feeds into subsequent purchasing processes. At some later time, perhaps when the customer is approved for a credit card, he or she may jump directly from passive information gathering to transaction, for an item previously considered. One of the richest sources of passive information gathering is the browsing done while shoppers are in the active information-gathering stage for other items. Shopping processes are ongoing, so successful retailers must be constantly attentive to providing information, presenting goods and services which solve perceived needs, and satisfying the customer.

SUMMARY

This chapter has concentrated on understanding the retail customer. To be successful, retailers must identify and attempt to serve unsatisfied consumer needs, through a process of market positioning in which the retailer adjusts the marketing variables discussed throughout the remainder of this book. Successful market positioning begins with an understanding of consumers and identification of unserved consumer needs.

Five socioeconomic factors significantly influence both the retailer and the consumer: gross domestic product, interest rates, economic turbulence, national debt, and unemployment. Demographic trends which affect retailers include a slowing of population growth, changing age distribution as America ages, geographic shifting of the population, and changes in the structure of U.S. households. Retailers must also understand psychographic or attitudinal characteristics of the consumer, such as male and female role flexibility, a deterioration of institutional confidence, the management of time versus money, and a movement toward value and lifestyle fragmentation. It is as important to observe actual buying behavior as it is to understand consumer attitudes. Some behavioral characteristics include extensive, simplified, and routine purchasing; destination versus intercept shopping; and attribute evaluation and store choice.

The retail patronage model incorporates all these consumer characteristics to describe the overall shopping process. We presented this model as a cyclic process, which helps us to understand shopping behavior rather than absolutely predicting shopping behavior. The steps in this process are need recognition, active information gathering, decision making, transaction, and use and evaluation, all of which revolve around and interact with passive information gathering. The entire patronage model is set against the backdrop of individual, social, and situational influences.

QUESTIONS FOR DISCUSSION

1. Why is it so difficult for retailers to control their market position image?
2. What are the major trends in the age distribution of the U.S. population? What types of retailers will benefit and/or be disadvantaged by these trends?
3. Why is it more difficult for retailers to manage their businesses in a roller-coaster economy?
4. How does a demographic trend, such as more women in the labor force, affect different types of retailers?
5. What is the graying of America and what opportunities does it present for retailers?
6. What strategies should retailers adopt in the face of slowing population growth?
7. Describe how a bookstore can use the demographic trends discussed in this chapter.
8. Compare your lifestyle with that of your parents. What opportunities do any differences present for different types of retailers?
9. Do consumers shop in a rational manner? Defend your answer and discuss its implications for retailers.

10. Discuss the concept of post-purchase resentment. How can the retailer overcome it?
11. Why is it important for retailers to understand consumer behaviors as well as attitudes?
12. Explain the concept of destination and intercept stores and merchandise.
13. How should retailers use multi-attribute models such as the one presented in this chapter?
14. Is the retail patronage model linear or cyclic? Explain the implications of your answer to retailers.

MANAGEMENT MEMO

You have recently been hired as the assistant manager for a large regional mall in Phoenix. One of the first things you notice on an early inspection tour of the mall is a lack of benches in the common areas for the elderly and mothers with babies to sit and rest while shopping. This is said to reduce the selling area that the mall can rent to various temporary vendors, such as arts-and-crafts shows. You also find a memo from your predecessor banning the early opening of the mall commons so that elderly physical fitness groups can use the mall for walking and exercise classes. Prepare a one-page memo agreeing or disagreeing with the current mall policy and explaining your reasoning.

BOARDROOM REPORT

You are the director of strategic planning for Frey Stores, a chain of 18 regional department stores in Cleveland, Detroit, and Pittsburgh. As the company is putting together its five-year strategic plan, including plans for more than $50 million in capital expenditures, a controversy has developed among the senior management group. One group of managers, headed by the vice-president of real estate, believes the company should invest the capital in building new stores. Another group, with the vice-president of store operations as its spokesperson, believes the money should be used to remodel and expand existing stores. You have been asked to make a presentation at Friday's meeting of the board of directors regarding your evaluation of both options, and your final recommendation on how to proceed. Prepare a two-page executive summary of your presentation, including any demographic, economic, or lifestyle trends which support your comments.

SUGGESTED READINGS

Darden, William R., Robert F. Lusch, and J. Barry Mason. *The Cutting Edge II: Proceedings of the 1991 Symposium on Patronage Behavior and Retail Strategy* (Baton Rouge: Louisiana State University).

Jan-Benedict, E.M., and Michel Wedel. "Segmenting Retail Markets on Store Image Using a Consumer-Based Methodology." *Journal of Retailing* (Fall 1991): 300-320.

McNeal, James V. "The Littlest Shoppers." *American Demographics* (February 1992): 48-53.

Robinson, John P. "Your Money or Your Time." *American Demographics* (November 1991): 22-26.

E.M. Steenkamp. "Male Grocery Shoppers: A Different and Growing Breed." *Retail Market Analysis* (Vol. 1, No. 4, 1992).

ENDNOTES

1. "Merchants Mobilize to Battle Wal-Mart in a Small Community," *Wall Street Journal,* 5 June 1991.
2. Edward M. Tauber, "Why Do People Shop?" *Journal of Marketing* 36 (October 1972): 46-59.
3. "JCPenney Struggles to Maintain Upscale Image," *Discount Store News,* 7 October 1991, 34.
4. "Sears out of Touch—and Time," *Mass Market Retailer,* 25 November 1991, 9.
5. The U.S. government changed its focus from gross national product to gross domestic product (GDP) in December 1991, feeling GDP is a more precise measure of domestic economic output.

GNP, which prevailed as the nation's primary economic output indicator for more than 40 years, measures economic output of all U.S. firms, both ignoring domestic activity of foreign-owned firms and including overseas revenues of U.S. firms. The GDP measures all economic activity on U.S. territory, regardless of ownership. "Numbers games," *Forbes,* 25 November 1991, 35.
6. "Northern Exposure," *Newsweek,* 17 February 1992, 20-22.
7. For a more detailed discussion, see Charles D. Schewe and Anne L. Balazs, "Playing the Part," *American Demographics* (April 1990): 24-27, 30.
8. "Traditional Households Are Fading World-Wide," *Wall Street Journal,* 4 April 1990, B1.
9. "Delaying Marriage, Time and Again," *Wall Street Journal,* 31 May 1990, B1.
10. Jean C. Darian, "In-Home Shopping: Are There Consumer Segments?" *Journal of Retailing* (Summer 1987): 163-86.
11. For a detailed discussion of the general use of psychographics in business, the reader is referred to "Psychographics Still an Issue on Madison Avenue," *Fortune,* 16 January 1978, 78-84.
12. James F. Engel and Roger D. Blackwell, *Consumer Behavior,* 4th ed. (Chicago: Dryden Press, 1982), 188.
13. "The Time Squeeze," *American Demographics* (February 1990): 30-33. "Trading Fat Paychecks for Free Time," *Wall Street Journal* (August 5, 1991): B1.
14. "Electronic Sales," *Chain Store Age Executive* (August 1988): 15.
15. The above was based on Leonard L. Berry, "Market to the Perception," *American Demographics* (February 1990): 32.
16. Martha Farnsworth Richie, "Psychographics for the 1990s," *American Demographics* (July 1989) 11: 24-26.
17. Proprietary research by the authors, Columbus, Ohio, 1989.
18. Proprietary research by the authors, Columbus, Ohio, 1989.
19. "Off with Their Heads," *Forbes,* 9 February 1987, 34-35.
20. "Drug Emporium's Sales to Top $1B," *Drug Store News* (9 April 1990): 90.
21. Many of these studies fall under the guise of store image studies. A review of more than 20 of these studies is provided in Douglas J. Lincoln and A. Coskun Samli, "Definitions, Dimensions and Measurement of Store Image: A Literature Summary and Syntheses, " in Robert S. Franz et al., eds., *Proceedings, Southern Marketing Association* (Southern Marketing Association, 1979), 430-33.
22. For an approach to designing and analyzing complex multi-attribute consumer judgment and decision making in supermarket choices, see Jordan J. Louviere and Gary J. Gaeth, "Decomposing the Determinants of Retail Facility Choice Using the Method of Hierarchical Information Integration: A Supermarket Illustration," *Journal of Retailing* (Spring 1987): 25-48.
23. Stephen J. Arnold, Tac H. Oum, and Douglas J. Tigert, "Determination Attributes in Retail Patronage: Seasonal, Temporal, Regional and International Comparisons," *Journal of Marketing Research* (May 1983): 149-57.
24. Martin Fishbein, "The Relationship Between Beliefs, Attitudes and Behavior," in Shel Feldman, ed., *Cognitive Consistency* (New York: Academic Press, 1966), 199-223 and Milton J. Rosenberg, "Cognitive Structure and Attitudinal Effect," *Journal of Abnormal and Social Psychology* (1956): 367-72.
25. W. W. Talarzyk and Reza Moinpour, "Comparison of an Attitude Model and Unfolding Analysis for the Prediction of Individual Brand Preference" (Paper presented at the Workshop on Attitude Research and Consumer Behavior, University of Illinois, 1970).
26. Reprinted with permission from Edward M. Tauber, "Marketing Notes and Communications—Why Do People Shop?" *Journal of Marketing* (October 1972): 47-48.
27. Gordon C. Bruner II and Richard J. Pomazal, "Problem Recognition: The Crucial First Stage of the Consumer Decision Process," *Journal of Consumer Marketing* (Winter 1988): 53-63.
28. "Supermarket Sweepstakes," *Marketing and Media Decisions* (November 1988): 33-38.
29. Proprietary research by Retail Planning Associates, Columbus, Ohio, 1989.
30. "Ford Dealer Service Employees Get Perks for Better Customer Satisfaction Ratings," *Automotive News,* 7 May 1990, 18 and "Lincoln: 80s Were Great; CSI [Customer Satisfaction Index] Is Theme Until New Lines for '93," *Automotive News,* 25 February 1991.

CHAPTER 4

COMPETITION IN RETAILING

OVERVIEW

The behavior of competitors is so important and dynamic an aspect of the retail marketplace that effective planning and management in a retail enterprise cannot be accomplished without proper analysis of competitors. In this chapter we discuss the evolution of retail competition and look at the upcoming revolution in nonstore retailing. Next we develop a model of retail competition that includes both supply and demand factors. Finally, we study some trends in international retailing.

COMPETITION IN RETAILING

I. Evolution of Retail Competition
   A. The Wheel of Retailing
   B. The Retail Accordion
   C. Natural Selection
   D. The Dialectic Process
   E. The Retail Life Cycle
      1. Innovation
      2. Accelerated Development
      3. Maturity
      4. Decline
II. Competition from Nonstore Retailers
   A. Nature and Scope

  B. Nonstore Growth
III. A Model of Retail Competition
  A. The Competitive Marketplace
  B. Market Structure
  C. The Demand Side of Retailing
  D. The Supply Side of Retailing
  E. The Profit-Maximizing Price
  F. Nonprice Decisions
  G. Competitive Actions
IV. Types of Competition
  A. Intratype and Intertype Competition
  B. Intercept Competition
  C. Competition for Market Share
  D. Developing a Protected Niche
V. Trends in International Retailing
VI. Summary

So far in Part 2, we have looked at consumer behavior in the retail marketplace. We will now discuss how the retailer can become an effective competitor. A high-performance retailer must always be on the offensive and set the trend for others to follow. A retailer forced to compromise or follow the path of others will have substandard performance.

  No retailer can design a strategy that will totally insulate it from the competitive actions of others. Merchandising innovations can easily be copied and cannot be patented. Furthermore, the relatively low entry barriers in retailing mean that the successful retailer can count on being copied by others when it unveils a profitable strategy. The rapid growth of fast-food restaurants, mail-order pharmacies, discount department stores, quick auto lube centers, and supermarkets offering prepared foods for either take-out or eating in the supermarket attest to that.

  If you plan to become a retail executive, you must develop a talent for designing and implementing innovative competitive strategies. Furthermore, you need to recognize that in retailing competition is a fact of life.

EVOLUTION OF RETAIL COMPETITION

The retail marketplace is dynamic, and one of the reasons for this dynamism is the constantly changing nature and scope of retailing. We refer to this process of change as the "evolution of retail competition." Several theories explain and describe the evolution of competition in retailing; we will briefly review five of them.

THE WHEEL OF RETAILING

Professor Malcolm P. McNair developed the **wheel of retailing hypothesis** to describe patterns of competitive development in retailing.[1] McNair contends that new types of retailers enter the market as low-status, low-margin, low-price operators. This modest strategy allows them to compete effectively and take market share away from the more traditional retailers. However, as they meet with success, these new retailers gradually acquire more sophisticated and elaborate facilities. This creates both a higher investment and a subsequent rise in operating costs. Predictably, these retailers must raise prices and margins, thus becoming vulnerable to new types of low-margin retail competitors which progress through the same pattern. This appears to be the case today in the fast-food hamburger business. Burger King, Wendy's, and McDonald's have all upgraded their restaurants, promotions, and food selections leaving the door open for a number of very small regional chains. These chains have developed a back-to-basics approach, selling burger-only menus from buildings limited to drive-through and walk-up service. Their competitive advantage is size, speed, location, and price (40 percent less than their big-name competitors). Their strategy is to eliminate the frills, undercut the giants, and grow quickly.

Not all retailing scholars agree with the wheel of retailing theory. Hollander, a leading retailing educator at Michigan State University, notes that,

ILLUSTRATION 4.1

As the wheel of retailing evolves, pioneers such as McDonald's enter the cycle with low margins and eventually expand their offering and enhance their store atmosphere, thus increasing their margin (*left*); and then new entrants such as Rally's (*right*) come in with no-frill, simplified product offerings and lower margins.

in both the United States and foreign retail environments, there are nonconforming examples. In reference to retailing in the United States, he states, "The department-store branch movement and the concomitant rise of planned shopping centers also has progressed directly contrary to the wheel pattern. The early department-store branches consisted of a few stores in exclusive suburbs and some equally high-fashion college and resort shops."[2]

Furthermore, Hollander states in regard to retailing in underdeveloped countries that "the relatively small middle- and upper-income groups have formed the major markets for 'modern' types of retailing. Supermarkets and other modern stores have been introduced in those countries largely at the top of the social and price scales, contrary to the wheel pattern."[3] Other experts have also taken issue with the wheel model, contending that changes in the retail environment increase the likelihood that retailers will seek to remain where they are, rather than move up the wheel.[4] Wal-Mart is an example of avoiding the temptation to move up the wheel. It has, for over 20 years, maintained its image as a low-price, low-cost merchant.

THE RETAIL ACCORDION

Several other theorists have noted that retail institutions evolve from outlets that offer wide assortments to specialized stores that offer narrow assortments, and then return to the wide-assortment stores to continue through the pattern once more. This contraction and expansion suggests the term **retail accordion theory**.[5] Ralph Hower writes:

> *Throughout the history of retail trade (as, indeed, in all business evolution) there appears to be an alternating movement in the dominant method of conducting operations. One swing is toward the specialization of the function performed on the merchandise handled by the individual firm. The other is away from such specialization toward the integration of related activities under one management or the diversification of products handled by a single firm.*[6]

Retail historians have observed that, in the United States, retail trade was dominated by the general store until 1860. The general store carried a broad assortment of merchandise ranging from farm implements to textiles to food. After 1860, due to the growth of cities and roads, retail trade became more specialized and was concentrated in the central business districts of cities. Here department and specialty stores were the dominant competitive force. Both carried more specialized assortments than the general store. In the 1950s, retailing began to move again to wider merchandise lines. Typical was the grocery store, which added produce and dairy products; nonfood items such as kitchen utensils and health and beauty aids; and small household appliances. By the mid-1980s, specialization in merchandise lines once again became a dominant competitive strategy. Witness the recent success of such companies as Athlete's Foot, The Limited, Hickory Farms, Charming

Shoppes, Benetton, Casual Corner, Pants West, and Walden Books. Retailers that offer a narrow variety but deep assortment of merchandise are **category specialists.** The category specialists that operate in large-scale facilities, offer a broad assortment and deep selection of merchandise, moderate service, and offer discount prices are referred to as category killers. They are called this because they can "kill" a merchandise category for other retailers operating in the trade area. Some popular category killers are Toys "R" Us, Circuit City, IKEA, and Herman's.

Furthermore, we can witness the retail accordion in operation in a particular line of retail trade if we study the evolution of computer stores. These stores emerged in the late 1970s and early 1980s as limited-assortment mom-and-pop operations or highly focused retail chains such as Computer Land. By the late 1980s and early 1990s, the accordion began to expand as warehouse-style stores emerged such as Comp USA. Comp USA stocks 5,000 items and covers 30,000 square feet of floor space. In 1989, computer superstores had a 6 percent market share, and by the mid-1990s they are expected to have a 45 percent market share.[7]

NATURAL SELECTION

The theory of natural selection in retailing is a direct adaptation of Charles Darwin's theory of natural selection, which has been captured in the phrase, "survival of the fittest." Basically, Darwin's theory states that the species that most effectively adapts to its environment is most likely to survive and perpetuate its kind. The environment of a retail enterprise is the retail marketplace (consumer, competitor, channel, and regulatory elements). In retailing, management is continually monitoring environmental changes that can affect retail survival. While all retailing institutions have felt the effects of environmental changes, department stores have had the most trouble adapting to change. For example, after World War II the conventional downtown department store dragged its feet, while growth in the suburbs was explosive.

It has been observed:

> *Those firms whose management did recognize the challenge of the changing social and economic forces, however, and established branches of various sizes and types to serve these new markets, made the necessary shift in organization structure to accommodate multi-unit operation, and adopted other innovations, have been richly rewarded. Moreover, in doing so, they helped to pioneer the development of the regional shopping center, one of the most important developments of the past two decades. Yet the measures adopted by the traditional department stores to meet the changing social and economic scene brought them face to face with problems not wholly anticipated. Moving from their long-established fortresses in downtown areas, they became vulnerable to the sharply increasing competition of other retailers quick to make innovations in policies and practices.*[8]

During the past two decades, consumer markets became more segmented. Department stores were slow to respond in a positive fashion.

Consequently, many specialty stores experienced rapid growth because they developed very viable market positions by designing their total store offerings to appeal to a select demographic or lifestyle group. For example, The Limited Inc. has tailored stores to many different women's markets with its Limited, Limited Express, Victoria's Secret, Lerner, Lane Bryant, Lerner Woman, and Henri Bendel retail outlets. Recently, The Limited Inc. has begun to seek male-oriented market positions and to develop new stores such as Structures. It was not until the late 1980s and early 1990s that department stores began to recognize the magnitude of this challenge. Many responded by tailoring more than 20 departments within their stores to distinct groups, becoming, in effect, a group of specialty stores under one roof. Nonetheless, even this competitive response has been questioned by some retail analysts. Too many disparate departments under one roof can be nothing more than an uncoordinated effort to use up space, and not to use it to full advantage. A department store must be able to move the customers around the store in order to increase the rate of purchasing. Marvin Rothenberg, a leading retail consultant, has stated to have space used as a series of individual specialty stores is to defeat one of the major advantages of a department store which is to create store traffic and multiple purchases across departments within the store.[9]

THE DIALECTIC PROCESS

The **dialectic process theory** of retailing, sometimes called the melting-pot theory, was first proposed by Gist[10] and later validated.[11] The dialectic process theory is based on Hegel's dialectic. According to Hegel, "Any idea, by the very nature of things, begets a negation of itself; the combination of the original idea, called the 'thesis,' with its negation called the 'antithesis,' results in a 'synthesis'—which in turn, serves as the thesis when the process begins all over."[12]

A concise application of Hegel's dialectic to competitive behavior in retailing has been made by Thomas Maronick and Bruce Walker:

In terms of retail institutions, the dialectic model implies that retailers mutually adapt in the face of competition from "opposites." Thus, when challenged by a competitor with a differential advantage, an established institution will adopt strategies and tactics in the direction of that advantage, thereby negating some of the innovator's attraction. The innovator, meanwhile, does not remain unchanged. Rather, as McNair noted, the innovator over time tends to upgrade or otherwise modify products and facilities. In doing so, he moves toward the "negated" institution. As a result of these mutual adaptations, the two retailers gradually move together in terms of offerings, facilities, supplementary services, and prices. They thus become indistinguishable or at least quite similar and constitute a new retail institution, termed the synthesis. This new institution is then vulnerable to "negation" by new competitors as the dialectic process begins anew.[13]

To illustrate the dialectic process in retailing, let us examine the evolution of competition in general-merchandise retailing. First were department stores, with high margins, low turnover, high prices, full service, downtown locations, and plush facilities. These department stores were the thesis. The antithesis was the discount store, the post–World War II innovation that was able to offer lower prices due to lower margins, higher turnover, self-service operations, low-rent locations, and spartan facilities with narrow aisles to maximize use of space. The synthesis is the more contemporary discount department store, such as Kmart and Target, generally located in suburban areas and having pleasing store decors that are brightly decorated with wider aisles for easier shopping and browsing than the original discounter.

THE RETAIL LIFE CYCLE

The final framework we will examine for the evolution of retail competition is the **retail life cycle.** William R. Davidson, a retail consultant and educator, and his colleagues argue that "retailing institutions, like the products they distribute, pass through an identifiable cycle."[14] This cycle can be partitioned into four distinct stages: (1) innovation, (2) accelerated development, (3) maturity, and (4) decline.

Innovation. The cycle begins with an aggressive, bold entrepreneur who is willing and able to develop an approach to retailing that departs sharply from conventional approaches. Many times the approach is oriented to reducing costs and passing the resulting savings on to the customer, for example, the supermarket in the early 1930s was able to operate on a gross margin of 12 percent, whereas conventional food outlets required 20 percent. Innovation can also center on a distinctive product assortment, shopping ease, locational convenience, advertising, or promotion. For example, self-service gasoline stations with convenience-oriented food and nonfood items offer more convenient shopping and lower prices than conventional service stations.

If the new advantage being offered is significant enough in the minds of consumers, sales will grow in the innovative stage. Profits, however, will not be attractive and may even be nonexistent. In any new business there are operating problems that need to be solved. High start-up costs and the absence of scale economies due to relatively low sales put a damper on profits. But at the end of the innovation stage, sales begin to grow more rapidly and operating problems are overcome, stimulating profit levels.

Accelerated Development. During development, sales and profit growth are explosive. Many new entrants arrive to share in the success of the new form of retailing. The market share of the innovators increases at the expense of conventional outlets. Firms that were astute enough to take part in the innovation stage expand their number of outlets by entering new geographic markets:

However, toward the end of the period these favorable factors tend to be counter-balanced by cost pressures that arise from the need for a larger staff,

ILLUSTRATION 4.2

Warehouse clubs such as Sam's Wholesale Club are in the accelerated growth stage of the retail life cycle in the 1990s. Sam's, founded just five years ago, is now one of the 20 largest retail chains.

more complex internal systems, increased management controls, and other requirements of operating large, multi-unit organizations. Consequently, near the end of the accelerated development period both market share and profitability tend to approach their maximum level.[15]

Maturity. In maturity, market share stabilizes and severe profit declines are experienced for several reasons. First, managers have become accustomed to a high-growth firm that was simple and small, but now they must manage a large, complex firm in a stable market. Second, the industry has typically overexpanded. Selecting markets and building new stores takes a long planning horizon (12 to 36 months), and it is inevitable that many stores planned in the accelerated development stage will open in the maturity state. Third, competitive assaults will be made on these firms by new forms of retailing (a bold entrepreneur starting a new retail life cycle).

Decline. Although decline is inevitable, retail managers try to postpone it by serious attempts to reposition, modify, or adapt the firm. These attempts can postpone the decline stage, but a return to earlier, attractive levels of operating performance is not likely. Sooner or later decline will occur, and "the consequences are traumatic. Major losses of market share occur, profits are marginal at best, and a fatal inability to compete in the market becomes apparent to investors and competitors."[16]

The implications for retail managers of the retail life cycle theory are:

1. Retailers should remain flexible so that they are able to adapt their strategies to various stages in the life cycle.

2. Since profits vary by stage in the retail life cycle, retail managers need to analyze carefully the risks and profits of entering the market or expanding their outlets at various stages in the life cycle.
3. Retailers need to extend the maturity stage. Since retailers have substantial investments in a particular form of retailing by the time of the maturity stage, they should try to work that investment as long as possible.

These three points are reinforced by the fact that the retail life cycle is growing shorter. The downtown department store took 80 years to reach maturity, the variety store 45 years, the supermarket 35 years, the discount department store 20 years, home-improvement centers 15 years, and video stores a short 5 years. Retail managers must recognize that high-performance results can only be regularly achieved, by programming the firm to enter new lines of retail trade or to develop new retail formats at appropriate points in time.

COMPETITION FROM NONSTORE RETAILERS

Several industry analysts contend that nonstore retailing, sometimes called direct retailing, or direct marketing, will be the next revolution in retailing. The mechanics for such a revolution are already in place, as a variety of established selling techniques permit consumers to purchase goods and services without having to leave home. With accelerated communications technology and changing consumer lifestyles, the growth potential for nonstore retailing is explosive. Traditional retailers need to monitor continuously developments in nonstore retailing.

NATURE AND SCOPE

The Census of Retailing classifies nonstore retailers into three major types:

1. **Mail-order houses.** Establishments primarily engaged in the retail sale of products by catalog and mail order. Included are book and record clubs, jewelry firms, novelty merchandise firms, specialty merchandisers (such as sporting goods retailers), and the catalog divisions of large general merchandisers (such as Sears). Not included, however, are seasonal and special promotional catalog houses, which do three-fourths of their annual volume during the Christmas season. The number of catalogs distributed annually has tripled over the last decade and is now in excess of 15 billion.
2. **Automatic merchandising machine operators.** Establishments primarily engaged in the retail sale of products by means of automatic merchandising units, also referred to as vending machines. This industry does not include coin-operated service machines, such as music machines, amusement and game machines, lockers, or scales.

3. **Direct-selling establishments.** Establishments primarily engaged in the retail sale of merchandise by telephone or house-to-house canvass or in the workplace. In the United States direct-selling sales total about $9 billion annually and are made by over four million individuals who are not employed by the organization they represent but are independent contractors. Worldwide direct-selling sales are $39 billion, with Japan being the largest direct-selling country. Major products sold include personal care items (Mary Kay Cosmetics), decorative home products (Princess House, Home Interiors and Gifts), cookware (West Bend, CUTCO), and encyclopedias (World Book, Encyclopedia Britannica). Today, with women increasingly employed outside the home, little "cold canvassing" is done, with many companies telephoning to make appointments to show their merchandise. In addition, traditional direct-selling techniques are being merged with newer marketing channels, such as mail order. Catalogs and merchandise are being shown and sold anywhere people gather, such as at state fairs, in shopping malls, and at airports. The major attributes of direct selling remain the same: support for the independent contractor, knowledge and demonstration of the product by the salesperson, excellent warranties and guarantees, and the person-to-person component.

It should be noted that the preceding classification, which was developed by the Department of Commerce prior to 1930, is quite archaic.[17] Nevertheless, the Census Bureau persists in its use, despite the fact that such nonstore retailers as television shopping networks are not included.

NONSTORE GROWTH

Many retail analysts predict that, as a result of several key forces at work today, nonstore sales will continue to grow in the 1990s. Some of these forces are:

- Consumers' need to save time
- The erosion of fun in the shopping experience
- The lack of qualified sales help in stores to provide information
- The explosive increase in the use of the telephone, the computer, and telecommunications
- Consumer desire to eliminate the intermediary's profit

Not everyone is convinced that nonstore retailing's prospects for growth are unlimited. Critics contend that the consumers' loss of discretionary income, the lack of personal touch in nonstore shopping, the limited number of products that are appropriate for nonstore sale, failure by manufacturers to take control of this channel of distribution, and the reactions of store retailers threatened by it will limit nonstore growth. These critics believe that the nonstore revolution *will* take place, but that due to the factors cited previously, it will be slower than expected. In either case, high-performance retail managers must continue to monitor developments in nonstore retailing.

A MODEL OF RETAIL COMPETITION

Competition in retailing, as in any other industry, involves the interplay of supply and demand. We cannot appreciate the nature and scope of competition in retailing by studying only the supply factors, that is, the type and number of retailers that exist. We must also examine consumer demand factors. Let's examine a formal framework for describing and explaining competition in retailing.[18]

THE COMPETITIVE MARKETPLACE

When retailers compete for customers, they generally compete on a local level unless they are nonstore mail-order retailers. Retailers may compete nationally for financial capital, top executives, and employees who are college graduates, but for customers they compete locally. Why? Because households will not typically travel beyond local markets to purchase the goods they desire. When they do travel beyond local markets, it is usually because their city or town is too small to support retailers with the selection of merchandise they desire. But most cities of over 50,000 can provide the consumer with sufficient selection in almost all lines of merchandise. And in cities of less than 50,000, the household may need to travel to another town or city only for large purchases such as a new automobile, television, or furniture.

MARKET STRUCTURE

Economists generally discuss four types of competitive market structures. **Pure competition** is a type of competitive market structure in which there are no or few entry barriers to competition. Thus, there are many sellers, products are homogeneous, and price cannot be controlled by individual buyers or sellers. **Monopolistic competition** is a type of competitive market structure in which there is a large number of sellers and some product differentiation exists. In **oligopolistic competition** the industry is controlled by a few larger sellers that establish entry barriers and do not take competitive actions without strong consideration of how competitors will react. Finally, **pure monopoly** means there is only one producer or seller of the product. Retailing can be characterized as monopolistic or sometimes oligopolistic competition. The distinction between monopolistic competition and oligopolistic competition lies in the number of sellers. An oligopoly means there are few sellers, so any action by one is noticed and reacted to by the others. Conventional economic thought suggests that for oligopoly to occur, the top four firms have to account for over 60 to 80 percent of the market. For retailing in the United States this does not occur on a national level. However, it is not uncommon at a local level for food stores and department or discount department stores. Furthermore, in smaller communities of less than 50,000 population, retailing is often oligopolistic. However, if prices become too high, residents of these smaller communities will travel to larger communities to shop—this is known as **outshopping.**

Leonard Weiss, a leading industrial economist, notes that even where retailing becomes concentrated at the local level, there are several checks on the retailers' power:

The country is full of automobiles, so most customers have large numbers of alternatives. Moreover, many modern retailers are becoming less specialized. The supermarket that sells nylons and the drugstore where you cannot find the drug counter are famous. Any seller who tries to maintain high prices is apt to find the grocers or the gas stations or someone equally far removed trying to take over his profitable lines. At any rate, there seems to be a continuous supply of new shopkeepers, ready to appear whenever prospects are good, and often even when they are not. It takes a good deal more to break into such fields as food retailing than it once did, but the cost of entry is still much lower than in most concentrated segments of manufacturing.[19]

THE DEMAND SIDE OF RETAILING

Most retailers face monopolistic competition and we assume that market structure in our model, but our model would generally apply in oligopolistic competition as well.

In a monopolistically competitive market, the retailer is confronted with a negatively sloping demand curve. That is, as price is lowered the consumer demands a higher quantity. You may conclude that a typical retailer faces a demand function like the one shown in Exhibit 4.1. However, a more appropriate model would incorporate the retailer's location, providing a **three-dimensional demand function** (see Exhibit 4.2).[20] The three dimensions are: (1) quantity demanded per household, (2) price at the retail store, and (3) distance from the household's place of residence or work to the store. The quantity demanded by a household is inversely related to the prices charged and the distance to the store.

Higher prices result in less quantity demanded, because households have limited incomes and many alternatives for allocating their dollars. If a retailer raises prices and all else remains unchanged, then households will try to shift some of their purchasing power to other retailers. (If other retailers also raise their prices or consumer incomes are rising, this may not be the net effect.)

Because it costs the consumer dollars and time to travel to a store, the farther the consumer lives from the retailer, the more quantity demanded will drop. The consumer's costs consist of three components: (1) the *actual dollar costs* of transporting oneself to the store and back; (2) the time involved, which is related to *opportunity costs* (i.e., what else could you be doing with your time and what value do you attach to those alternative activities?); and (3) the *psychic costs* of traveling to the store and back (i.e., if traffic arteries or public transportation are very congested, then you may become frustrated

EXHIBIT 4.1

Monopolistic Competitive Industry

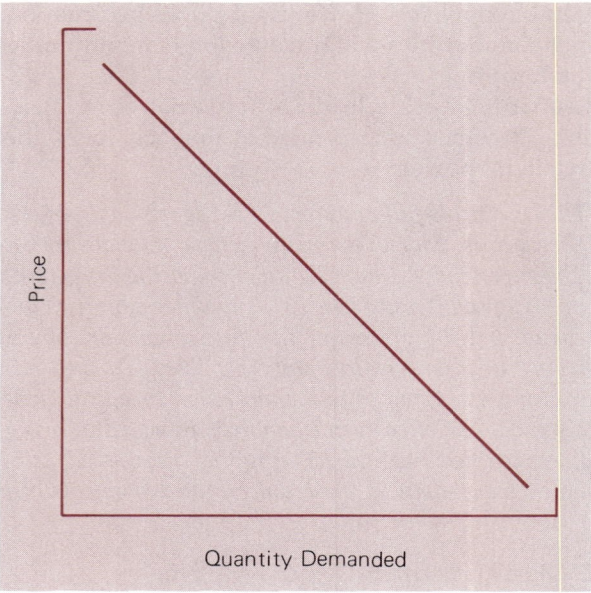

and upset). Spend a few moments studying Exhibit 4.2 and the accompanying numerical example.

From the three-dimensional demand model, we can derive several key concepts that the retail manager needs to understand.

1. There is a *maximum demand price* the retailer can obtain for the goods or services it offers the consumer. Refer to Exhibit 4.2 to find this maximum demand price—note that it is (a/b). Notice that the maximum demand price occurs only when the consumer's residence coincides with that of the store (an obviously unlikely occurrence) and when the retailer is willing to sell only a very small quantity of goods or services. Obviously, if the retailer desires to sell in large quantities to households located at increasing distances from the retailer's place of business, it must set its price below the maximum price it could theoretically establish.

2. There is a *maximum quantity* a consumer will demand from the retailer. This maximum quantity is obtained when the consumer lives very close to the store and the retailer's price on the good or service approaches zero. Find the maximum demand quantity on the three-dimensional demand model in Exhibit 4.2—it is denoted as (a). Predictably, the retailer cannot operate profitably by selling at the maximum quantity price, since the revenues generated would not cover the retailer's expenses.

3. There is a *maximum distance* the consumer will travel to shop at a retail store. This distance is obtained by allowing price and quantity to approach zero. Refer to Exhibit 4.2 to locate this point—it is (a/b)/t. The retailer will not typically attract customers from the maximum distance, since to do so would necessitate having to give merchandise or services away.

EXHIBIT 4.2

The Three-Dimensional Demand Model

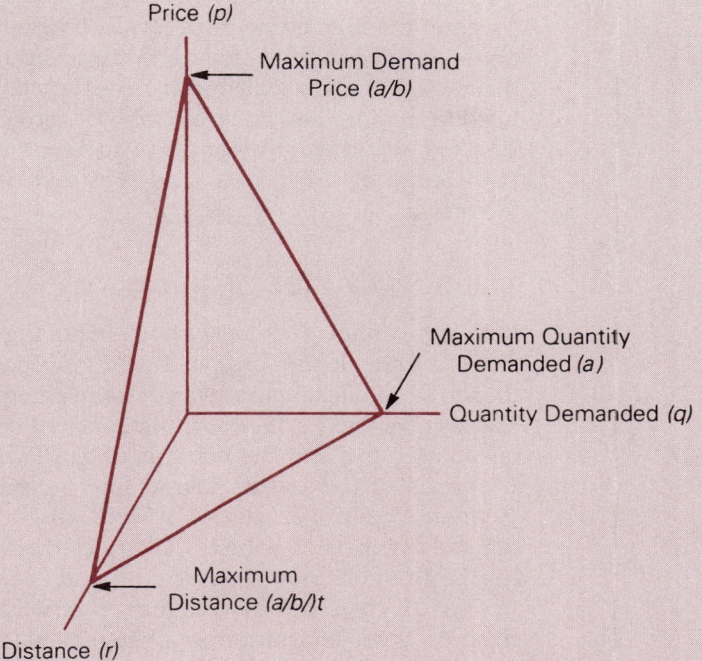

In functional form the three-dimensional demand model can be stated as follows:
$$q = a - bp - btr$$
where q = quantity demanded
  p = price per unit
  t = round trip transportation costs per mile, which includes actual transport costs and time and psychic costs
  r = the radius or distance from the consumer's home or work to the store
  a,b = parameters that describe shape of the demand function

Illustrating the three-dimensional demand model with a specific example:
$$q = 10 - 2p - 2(.25)r$$
Then we can determine (1) the maximum demand price, by setting q and r equal to zero
$$0 = 10 - 2p - 2(.25)0$$
$$2p = 10$$
$$p = 5,$$
note that this is equivalent to (a/b), or $(10/2) = 5$; (2) the maximum distance by setting p or q equal to zero,
$$0 = 10 - 2(0) - 2(.25)r$$
$$0 = 10 - 2(.25)r$$
$$r = 20$$
note that this is $(a/b)t$ or $(10/2)/(.25) = 20$; and (3) the maximum quantity demanded, by setting p and r equal to zero,
$$q = 10 - 2(0) - 2(.25)0$$
$$q = 10$$
note that this is a, or 10 in the model

These three concepts suggest that retailers cannot be profitable by setting prices at the highest possible levels, trying to sell the largest possible quantity of goods or services, or trying to attract households from the greatest possible distance. Retailers will find it necessary to set prices somewhere below the maximum possible price but above zero. But where? It seems reasonable retailers would want to set prices to maximize profits. To do so, retailers need knowledge of their costs, and that involves an examination of the supply factors.

THE SUPPLY SIDE OF RETAILING

Retailers cannot operate without incurring costs, which can be classified as fixed or variable and are portrayed graphically in Exhibit 4.3. **Fixed costs** are those the retailer incurs regardless of the quantity of goods or services sold. These costs are, for the most part, related to the size of the store and the costs of maintaining and financing it, regardless of whether it is open or closed. Examples of fixed costs in retailing include insurance, taxes, rent or lease payments, and security. **Variable costs** are those that increase proportionately with sales volume. The two largest variable costs in retailing are the cost of the goods or services sold and salaries and wages.

Not all costs can be categorized strictly as fixed or variable costs. **Semifixed costs** are constant over a range of sales volume, but past a crucial point they increase and then again remain constant at another, higher, sales volume range. For example, labor can be viewed as semifixed (see Exhibit 4.4). Before the doors of the store can be opened each day, a staff of employees must be on hand, but when store traffic volume rises past a crucial point, more employees need to be added, since the existing staff would be inadequate.

Regardless of the exact form of the retailer's cost functions, the retailer

EXHIBIT 4.3

Cost Functions in Retailing

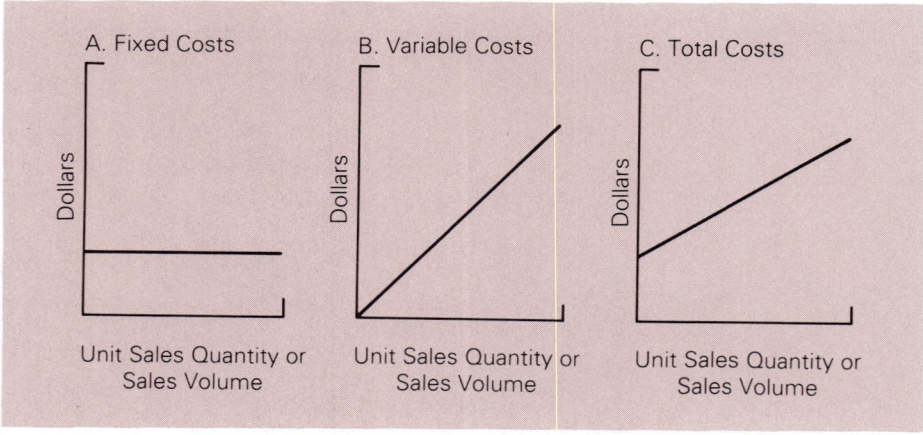

must examine the supply side of retailing in order to set a profit-maximizing price. The principles of microeconomic price theory cannot be ignored.

THE PROFIT-MAXIMIZING PRICE

Assume that a retailer has established the price level at which to sell its goods or services. Having established a price and knowing its costs, the retailer could determine its break-even quantity (that quantity at which total revenue equals total cost) as shown in Exhibit 4.5. The cost function is borrowed directly from Exhibit 4.3c, and the total revenue function is obtained by multiplying the price the retailer has established by the quantity Q. Note that Q is the total quantity the retailer sells and not the quantity any individual household demands (q) as portrayed in Exhibit 4.2. Let us examine how one might go about obtaining Q.

The retailer will sell to more than one household. Q is simply the summation of the individual household demand curves (q) shown in the three-dimensional demand model in Exhibit 4.2. As the retailer sets a lower price, it will be able to attract customers from a greater distance. And the greater the density of households (households per square mile), the more households the retailer can attract to its store.

With an established price, the greatest distance a household will travel to a particular retail outlet can be defined as $(a/b - p)/t$, where a/b is the maximum demand price, p is the price the retailer has established, and t is the transport cost (round-trip cost per mile). Let us construct a numerical example

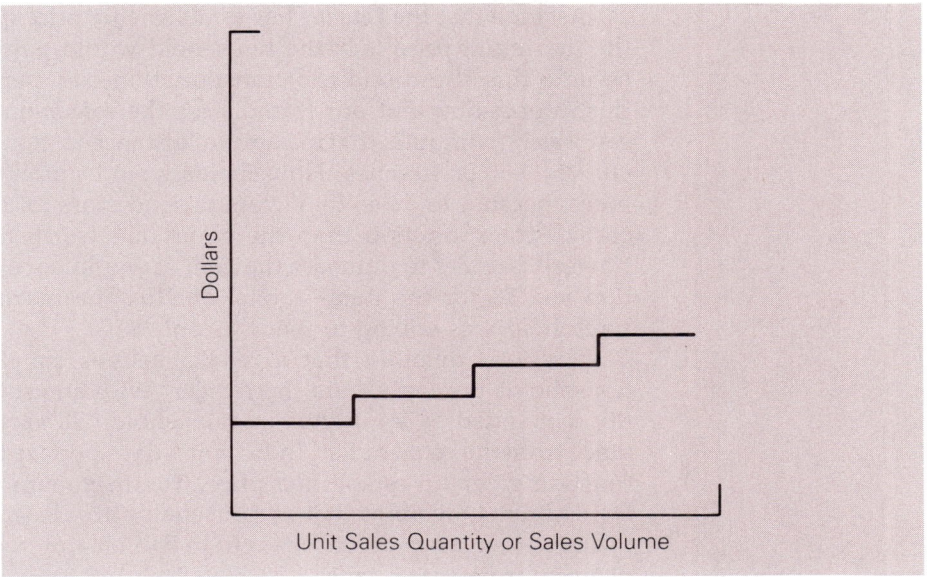

EXHIBIT 4.4
Labor Cost in Retailing

EXHIBIT 4.5

A Retailer's Break-Even Chart

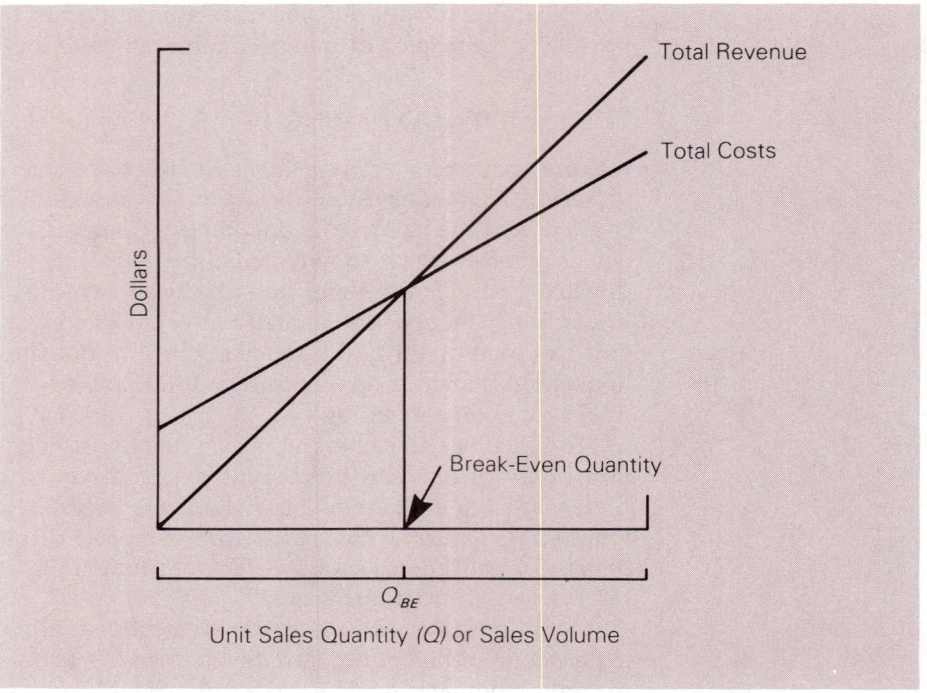

of the greatest distance a household would travel to purchase a particular item at a particular retail outlet.

Assume that the retailer has established a price (p) of $5 per unit and that the maximum price (a/b) the household would pay is $10 per unit. Further assume that the round-trip transportation cost per mile (t) is $0.50. From this information and our formula for the maximum distance $(ab - p)/t$, we can easily compute the maximum distance a household would travel as $(10 - 5)/0.50$ or 10 miles. Households would simply not travel more than 10 miles, because to do so they would spend more for the merchandise and the cost of transportation than the goods are worth to them. If a household traveled 20 miles to purchase the item, it would have spent $10 for transportation and $5 for the item—a total of $15. The maximum demand price the household was willing to pay was only $10.

The total quantity that a retailer sells is simply the sum of what all households purchase from the retailer. With an established price, the quantity demanded by an individual household will vary inversely with the distance from the retail outlet. In Exhibit 4.6 we portray the household's demand function given an established price. The maximum quantity demand is ($a - bp$). Exhibit 4.6 verifies that as households are closer to the retailer's place of business (i.e., as r approaches zero in Exhibit 4.6), they will purchase a larger quantity from that retailer.

EXHIBIT 4.6

A Household's Demand Curve at a Given Retail Price

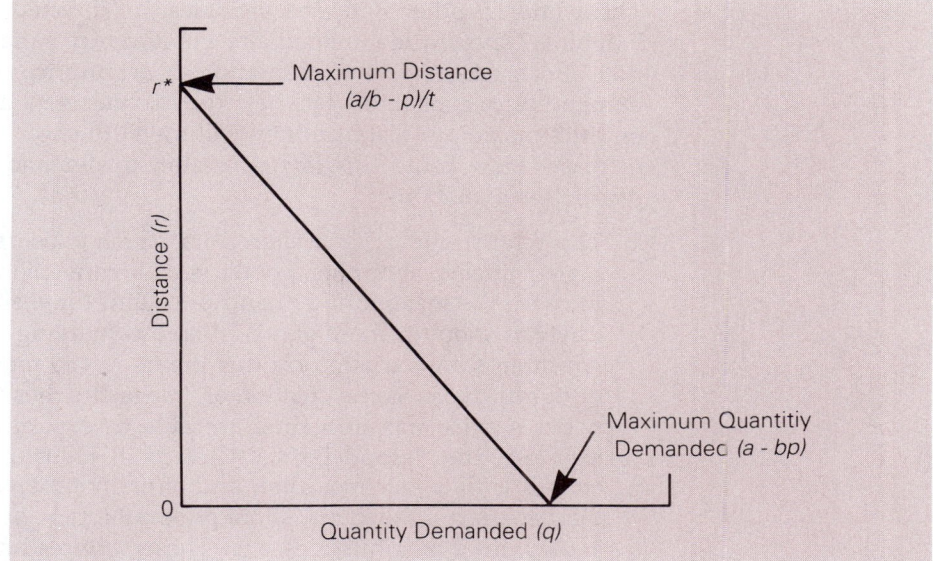

If we now sum up the demand functions for all households located at a distance of up to (r^*) from the store, we will obtain Q, the total unit volume the retailer will sell. We can now compare Q to the retailer's break-even quantity (Q_{BE}) in Exhibit 4.5. If Q exceeds Q_{BE}, the price the retailer established was profitable; but if Q fell short of Q_{BE}, the established price was unprofitable. What this all simply says is that if the total sales to all households is less than the retailer's total costs, then the pricing level is unprofitable.

In theory, it is possible for a retailer to establish a profit-maximizing price with knowledge of its own cost functions and the demand functions of households in its trading area. The procedure would be similar to that used in microeconomics when a manufacturer equates marginal cost (the additional cost that results from the sale of one more unit) with marginal revenue (the additional revenue that results from the sale of one more unit). When the profit-maximizing price is established, retailers will attract customers from a well-defined distance, obtained by inserting the profit-maximizing price into the formula $(a/b - p)/t$. To attract customers from a greater distance by cutting price would be unprofitable, since the marginal cost of doing so would exceed the marginal revenue generated.

NONPRICE DECISIONS

The retailer has more tools than just price to influence the quantity it will sell and its profit level. Some important nonprice variables are merchandise mix, advertising, special promotions, personal selling, and store atmosphere.

These and all other nonprice variables are directed at increasing demand. Exhibit 4.7 shows the intended effect of nonprice variables in retailing. Notice that after successful implementation of a nonprice strategy, the maximum demand price consumers will pay, the maximum quantity they will demand, and the maximum distance they will travel to shop at the retailer's store all increase. How could this favorable shift in demand occur? Here are some possible explanations:

1. The retailer could have altered its merchandise mix in the direction of higher-quality shopping goods versus convenience goods. This would increase the maximum demand price and the distance consumers would travel to shop for these goods, thereby enlarging the retailer's trade area. An interesting variation on this theme in the retailing of services in the nonprofit sector is the creation of "megachurches." Megachurches have a wider service mix and thus are able to expand their trade areas. For example, the Second Baptist Church in Houston operates a 6,000-seat church with a 400-voice choir and offers not merely a place to pray but a place to play, lift weights, shoot pool, eat lunch, or catch a Broadway-style show with a religious message. These services have shifted the demand curve so that the church can attract 12,000 visitors a week.[21]

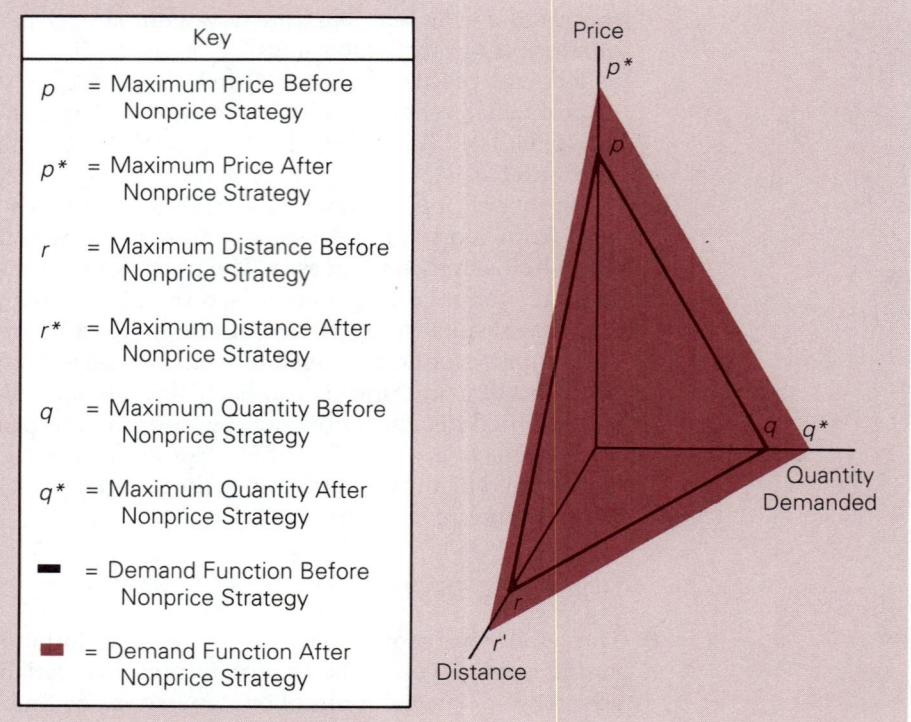

EXHIBIT 4.7

The Impact of Nonprice Strategies

2. The retailer could have provided customers with free "park and shop" or "ride and shop" coupons, which would effectively lower transportation costs for customers. The lower transportation costs would increase the maximum distance the customer would be willing to travel, thereby increasing the retailer's trade area.
3. The retailer could have engaged in an extensive advertising campaign directed at persuading consumers to purchase more of the goods it sells.

All retail decision variables, whether price or nonprice, are directed at influencing demand. Of course, the profitability of the decisions depends on the marginal cost of the action versus the marginal revenue it generates.

COMPETITIVE ACTIONS

In the retail competition model, we saw that retailers attract customers from a limited geographic area, and that as prices are lowered, this area expands. We also noted that nonprice variables can be used to expand the trade area. But even at a zero price and the most attractive set of nonprice variables, households can only afford to travel a certain distance to obtain the goods and services retailers offer. Therefore, in most cities there are several, if not many, retailers in each line of retail trade.

When there are too many retail establishments competing in a particular city, the profitability of all the retailers will suffer. Eventually, some retailers may even leave the market. If there are too few retailers, profits will be high enough to attract new competitors, or existing retailers will be enticed to expand. A market is in equilibrium in terms of number of retail establishments if the return on investment is high enough to justify keeping capital invested in retailing, but not so high as to invite more competition.

A good measure of competitive activity in a market is the number of retail establishments per thousand households ($N/1,000H$). If the stores are of the same approximate size, then as the number of stores per thousand households increases, the degree of competition intensifies. This intensified competition will tend to decrease the return on investment as illustrated in Exhibit 4.8. If $N/1,000H$ is at the level where the resulting return on investment is just enough to keep the capital employed in retailing, then the market is in equilibrium. This is at the point where $(N/1,000H)^*$ and *Return on Investment** intersect in Exhibit 4.8. When the number of stores per thousand households is below $(N/1,000H)^*$, the return on investment will exceed Return on Investment* and the market can be characterized as **understored.** A market is understored when there are attractive profit opportunities and thus more stores are attracted to the community. In the early 1990s, this is how the Dallas and Houston markets were viewed by firms that operated warehouse clubs.[22] The biggest market for Sam's Clubs was Texas, but due to the market's large and growing size, other firms such as Kmart's Pace Membership Warehouse Clubs and Costco Wholesale Corp. decided to enter it. At the same time Sam's decided to expand in Texas. Texas was clearly understored with warehouse clubs, which invited new competition. On the other hand, if

EXHIBIT 4.8

The Profitability of Under- and Overstoring

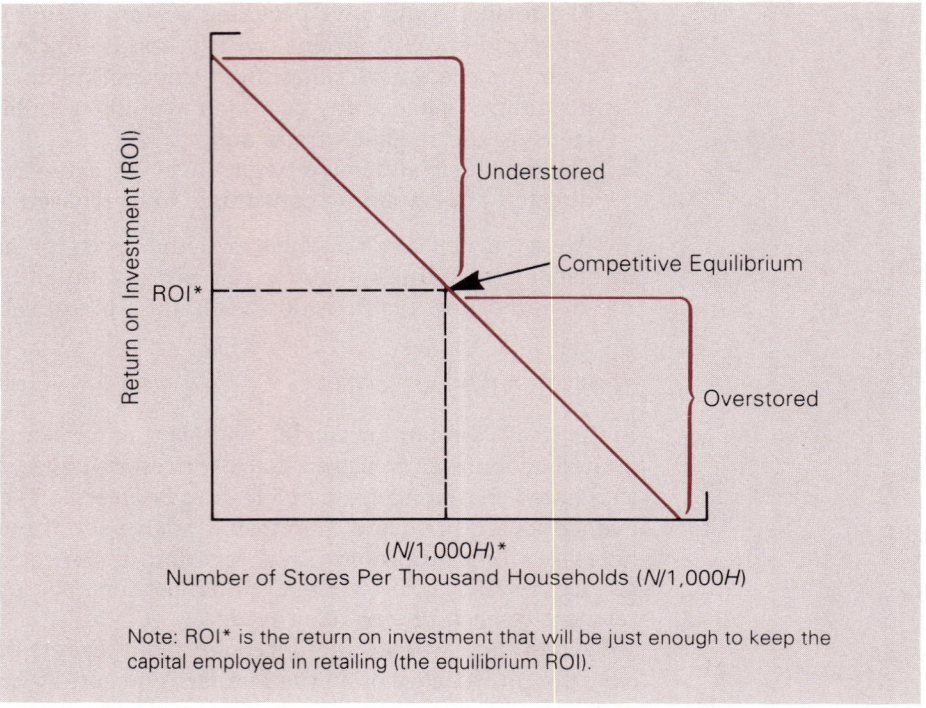

$(N/1,000H)^*$ is exceeded, the return on investment will fall below *Return on Investment** and the market will be characterized as **overstored**. This is precisely what characterized the Chicago downtown shopping environment along North Michigan Avenue in the early 1990s. Within one mile along this avenue, there were three vertical malls: Water Tower Place was the home of Lord & Taylor and Marshall Field's, Chicago Place Mall was the home of Saks Fifth Avenue, and the North Michigan Mall housed Bloomingdale's. Other large retailers along the "magnificent mile" were Mark Shale, I. Magnin, Neiman Marcus, and hundreds of specialty stores. This mile of shopping became one of the densest and most overstored in the United States.[23] Although overstored markets are often viewed as unattractive, some retail analysts believe there is no such thing as an overstored market but only *undermanaged* markets. In brief, they believe that well-managed stores that are in tune with the needs of the retail marketplace can prosper in overstored markets, and such was the case when Nordstrom moved into the relatively overstored East Coast market in the late 1980s.

Competition is most intense in overstored markets, since many retailers are achieving an inadequate return on investment. These retailers face a major performance imperative and will implement both price and nonprice actions in an all-out attempt to increase sales and profit levels. Since retailers operate in a relatively closed geographic market, with a fixed number of households and a limited number of dollars to compete for, any action by one retailer to increase its sales or profit level will warrant an action from competitors.

The easiest and quickest actions to copy are price based. If a retailer cuts price, many competitors will respond with a similar price cut. This is what began to occur in the early 1990s in the restaurant field. As the field became overstored, chains such as McDonald's, Wendy's, Taco Bell, and Pizza Hut began to cut price. At the same time, mid-priced casual restaurants such as Perkins, Denny's, and Golden Corral began to emphasize price and how near they were in cost to the fast-food restaurants. As a result, a wave of price cutting spread throughout the industry.[24]

Retailing in Action 4.1 shows how by using creativity, IKEA (an international retailing chain) developed an innovative promotion rather than an easy-to-duplicate price-cutting promotion. And this is not the only example of IKEA using creativity and nonprice variables to influence demand. At IKEA customers wait in long lines to pay for their merchandise and the unpleasant task of waiting in line can weaken future demand; IKEA makes this experience more enjoyable because it incorporates playrooms in its stores where parents can leave their children to play while they shop and wait in those long lines.[25]

TYPES OF COMPETITION

INTRATYPE AND INTERTYPE COMPETITION

It is possible to merge the preceding discussion of competition in retailing with the classification schemes used by the Department of Commerce in conducting the Census of Retail Trade. **Intratype competition** occurs when any two or more retailers of the same type (as defined in the Census of Retail Trade) compete with each other for the same households. This is the most common type of retail competition. Firestone competes with Goodyear and Kmart competes with Wal-Mart and Target. Historically, most competition in retailing has been of this form.

Recently, many retailers have been moving toward **scrambled merchandising,** carrying any merchandise line that can be sold profitably. Some examples include:

- Discount department stores (such as Kmart, Target, and Wal-Mart) handling more cosmetics and fragrances which were traditionally the province of the traditional department stores.[26]
- Supermarkets (such as Albertsons, Kroger, and Food Giant) handling video-cassette rentals. In 1990, supermarkets were estimated to have 11 percent of this market.[27]

RETAILING IN ACTION

4.1 Competing with Nonprice Variables

In recent years, U.S. retailers have gotten into the habit of only running promotions featuring BIG SAVINGS for the consumers. These types of promotions, while important, should not be the retailer's only focus. After all, these promotions train the consumer to wait for sales, which means that the retailer will end up giving away the store. Another reason to avoid such panic tactics is that such promotions are among the easiest technique for competitors to copy.

During the 1990 and 1991 Christmas season, a foreign-owned retailer, IKEA, showed U.S. retailers how to run a promotion without giving away the store. The Swedish furniture chain found a different way to build store traffic, which in retailing means increased sales. IKEA, which is already perceived as having the lowest prices, built traffic not by lowering prices even more but by *renting* Christmas trees.

IKEA ran newspaper advertisements stating, "The spirit of Christmas can't be bought, but for $10 you can rent it." The fine print explained that for $20 ($10 for the rental and a $10 deposit), IKEA would rent you a beautiful Douglas fir. (The going purchase price for similar trees in New York City was $50 and up.) "After the holidays, just return the tree, pick up your deposit and IKEA will mulch the tree for your garden or donate the mulch to the community. You will also receive a coupon for a free four-year-old Blue Spruce sapling to help save the environment. You can pick up your free tree the first week in April."

While its U.S. counterparts were running price special after price special, IKEA was fighting off the crowds. IKEA made it worthwhile to visit the store three separate times. (Remember, to keep overhead low, IKEA stores are usually in out-of-the-way locations.) Without resorting to discounts, IKEA, which began using this promotion even before it entered the U.S. market in 1985, had the customers lined up, while other furniture stores were empty or selling merchandise below cost. No wonder in 1991, right smack in the middle of a recession, IKEA opened its seventh U.S. category-killer store to great fanfare and hordes of customers.

Could their sales campaigns have had anything to do with IKEA's success? IKEA sold the idea of visiting its stores and retail sales increased.

Sources: Based on the authors' personal observation of the huge lines waiting to get in IKEA the day after the ad broke, and an article by Jack Falvey, "How to Sell Your Way out of the Recession," *Wall Street Journal*, 1 April 1991, A10.

- Convenience food stores (such as 7-Eleven) selling motor oil and related auto care products.
- Department stores, discount department stores, and warehouse clubs handling computers and computer equipment.[28]

Every time different types of retail outlets sell the same lines of merchandise and compete for the same limited consumer dollars, **intertype competition** occurs. In each of the preceding examples, as intertype competition expanded, gross margins on the respective merchandise lines declined. For example, starting in the late 1980s and exploding in growth in the early 1990s,

ILLUSTRATION 4.3

Scrambled merchandising occurs when stores carry merchandise not traditionally within their line of trade, such as supermarkets' introduction of videocassette rental services.

mail-order pharmacies cornered a growing share of prescription drugs. Their market share is now close to 20 percent, and the impact on the locally operated or chain-operated retail drugstore has been dramatic.[29] Consequently, the average gross margin on drugs has declined due to this increased competition.

INTERCEPT COMPETITION

In Chapter 3 we discussed destination merchandise and intercept merchandise. We saw that with intercept merchandise the customer does not have a strong enough need to warrant a special trip to purchase the merchandise. For this type of merchandise the competition is often divertive. **Divertive competition** occurs when a retailer intercepts a customer to purchase merchandise that normally would have been purchased at another retail store. For example, an individual may recognize that she needs to get a birthday card for a relative and will probably do this the next time she visits the local shopping mall which has a very well stocked Hallmark Card Store. However, one day while picking up a prescription at the drugstore she walks by the card stand and decides to purchase the greeting card at the drugstore. The drugstore retailer has intercepted this customer from the Hallmark store. The growth of scrambled merchandising has resulted in more intercept competition as customers are diverted from their normal patronage habits.

To comprehend the significance of intercept competition, one needs to recognize that most retailers operate very close to their break-even point. For instance, supermarkets, with their extremely low gross margins, tend to have a break-even point of 94 to 96 percent of current sales. Even general-merchandise retailers, with relatively large gross margins, face a break-even point of 85 to 92 percent of their current sales. A modest drop in sales volume could put these retailers in the red. The precise drop in sales volume needed to fall below break-even would depend on such factors as the retailer's cost structure, gross margin, current profit level, and a host of other factors.

COMPETITION FOR MARKET SHARE

Historically, retailers in the United States have been confronted with an ever-expanding market. The population was growing, real per capita incomes were climbing, and the suburbs awaited new retail stores. The 1990s, however, will be characterized by flat, or at best moderate, growth curves. Faced with a constant market, retailers will achieve growth only by aggressive expansion of market share. This is important because a large and growing market share has been shown to lead to improved profitability. It is also important to recognize that costs in retailing can only be reduced to a fixed point, and generally these fixed costs are rather large. Consequently, growth in sales volume is a key to covering not only fixed costs and variable costs but also to returning a profit.

Management Horizons, a division of Price Waterhouse, has developed a management model referred to as IMPACT that can help the retailer identify critical variables to focus in on for increased sales and market share during the 1990s.[30]

The IMPACT model tells us that the key to increasing sales is to first work on the determinants of store traffic. Store traffic is a function of the retailer's strategy and specifically the effectiveness of its merchandise and pricing strategy (Chapters 7 through 9); its selling environment strategy (Chapters 10 through 13); and its promotion and selling strategy (Chapters 14 and 15). Thus, the first key to competing for market share is to compete for store traffic, that is, get a lot of people to visit your store. Store traffic is multiplied by the closure rate, which is the share of visitors to the store who leave with a purchase. The result of this multiplication is the number of transactions. Thus, the second key to increasing market share is to increase the closure rate and thus the number of transactions. Finally, the number of transactions is multiplied by average transaction size, which indicates how large the average purchase is in dollar terms. Therefore, the third key to increasing market share is to increase the average amount each customer purchases on each visit to the store. The IMPACT model states that dollar sales is equal to $T \times C \times A$, where T is the traffic or the number of store visitors, C is the percentage of store visitors who make a purchase and is also called closure, and *A* is average transaction size.

Let us look at an example. An independent supermarket is able to develop a strategy to generate an average of 1,200 store visits a day. Of the visitors to the store, 97 percent purchase, and when this closure rate is multiplied by the 1,200 visits, one obtains 1,164 transactions a day. The average transaction size is $23.64, and when this is multiplied by the 1,164 transactions, one obtains average daily sales of $27,517.

DEVELOPING A PROTECTED NICHE

As competition intensifies in retailing, the retail manager will find it harder to be protected from competitive threats on the basis of the merchandise offered. Why? Because all retailers have access to the same merchandise. Therefore, retailers in the future will find it more rewarding to develop a protected niche in the marketplace. As we pointed out in Chapter 3, careful market positioning can be used to accomplish this. Retailers that have done an especially good job at market positioning include Ann Taylor, Talbot's, and Gantos which all appeal to the upscale, over-30, high-fashion women's market. The merchandising, store atmosphere, price points, customer services, and retail personnel are all positioned to appeal to this segment. Since it is difficult to find unique merchandise, many retailers (to include Ann Taylor, Talbot's, and Gantos) have developed their own store brands to help set them apart from the competition and develop a protected niche. Wal-Mart, to further distinguish itself from other discount retailers, recently developed its own private label. The label "Sam's American Choice" includes colas, chocolate chip cookies, and fruit drinks and other merchandise lines are expected to be added.[31]

TRENDS IN INTERNATIONAL RETAILING

Retailing in other countries exhibits even greater diversity in its structure than retailing in the United States. In some countries, such as Italy, retailing is composed largely of specialty houses carrying narrow lines. Finnish retailers generally carry a more general line of merchandise. The size of the average retailer is also diverse, from Harrod's in London and Mitsukoshi Ltd. in Japan, which serve over ten thousand customers a day, to the small one- or two-person stalls in developing African and Latin American nations.

The rate of change in retailing appears to be directly related to the stage and speed of economic development in the countries concerned, but even the least-developed countries are experiencing dramatic changes. Self-service, a retailing innovation developed in California in 1912, has grown at an overwhelming pace throughout the world. Supermarkets, a development of the United States 1930s depression, are now standard in both developed and developing nations, although over 80 percent of European food sales are still in the hands of small retailers. Discount houses, a product of the post–World War II era, have gained market share in countries where such activity is legal. Electronic retailing spread to other countries from U.S. merchants.

However, as has been pointed out, new retail formats have emerged in countries other than the United States.[32] This development can be attributed to a variety of economic and social factors: a widespread concern for health, a steady increase in the number of working women and two-income families, long and persistent energy shortages and the consequent upsurge in price levels, consumerism, and so forth. These factors, and their effects on con-

EXHIBIT 4.9

Retailing Concepts of Three European Specialty Stores

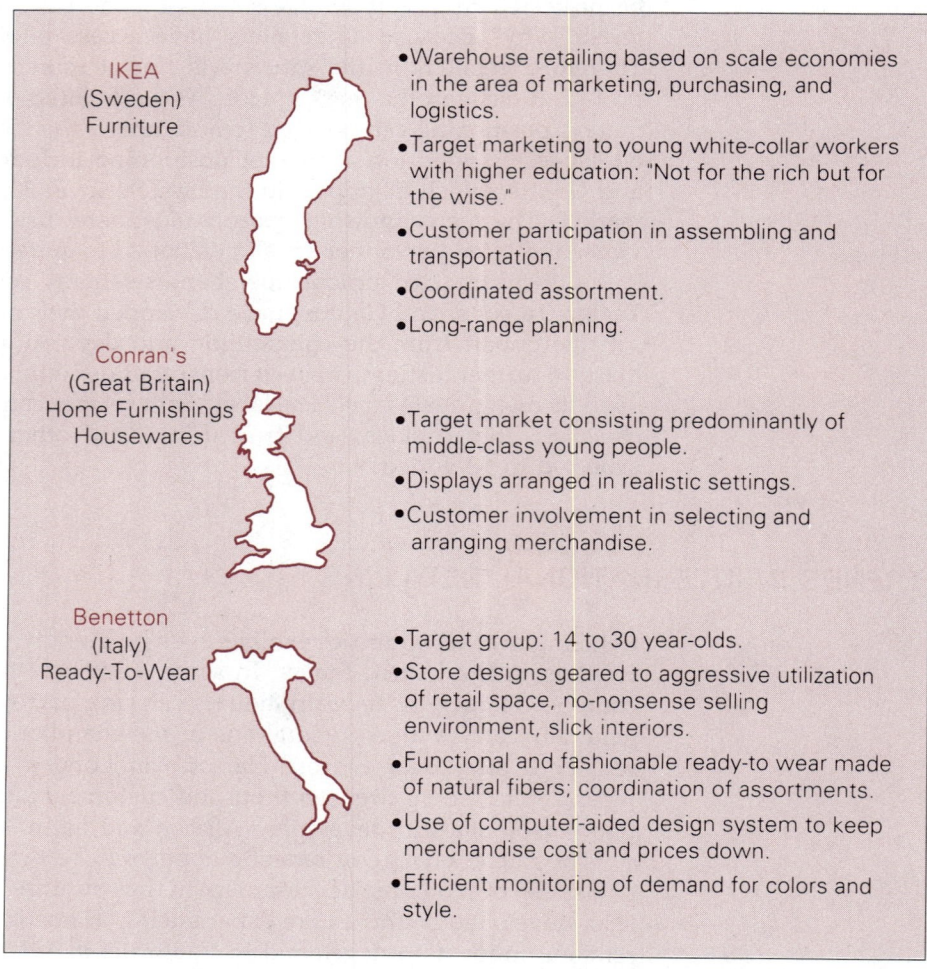

IKEA (Sweden) Furniture
- Warehouse retailing based on scale economies in the area of marketing, purchasing, and logistics.
- Target marketing to young white-collar workers with higher education: "Not for the rich but for the wise."
- Customer participation in assembling and transportation.
- Coordinated assortment.
- Long-range planning.

Conran's (Great Britain) Home Furnishings Housewares
- Target market consisting predominantly of middle-class young people.
- Displays arranged in realistic settings.
- Customer involvement in selecting and arranging merchandise.

Benetton (Italy) Ready-To-Wear
- Target group: 14 to 30 year-olds.
- Store designs geared to aggressive utilization of retail space, no-nonsense selling environment, slick interiors.
- Functional and fashionable ready-to wear made of natural fibers; coordination of assortments.
- Use of computer-aided design system to keep merchandise cost and prices down.
- Efficient monitoring of demand for colors and style.

Source: Madhau Kacker, "International Flow of Retailing Know-How: Bridging the Technology Gap in Distribution, *Journal of Retailing* (Spring 1988): 41-67.

RETAILING IN ACTION

4.2 Changing Competitive Structure in Food Retailing in the Reunified Germany

The reunification of East and West Germany on October 3, 1990, set in place the stimulus for a major restructuring of food retailing. For several decades food retailing in West Germany had been undergoing major changes as small mom-and-pop food markets began to decline in numbers. This was part of the natural evolution of retailing in a free-enterprise economy. In 1970, there were 127,000 food stores in West Germany; by 1980, that number had declined to 76,000; and in 1990, it reached 60,000. German retail analysts project that by 1995 there will be only 50,000 retail food stores in West Germany. This precipitous decline was due to the rapid rise of hypermarkets and price-aggressive discount food stores. The result was better prices and broader assortments. In short, in the early 1990s, West Germany had a very sophisticated retail food system with very good value delivered to the consumer. This, combined with the high standard of living in West Germany, resulted in the typical household spending only 19 percent of net income on food in 1988.

On the other hand, the structure of food retailing in East Germany was very small in scale and the generally low standard of living resulted in the typical East German spending 31 percent of net income on food. Also, prior to reunification all East German retailing was controlled by the central planning office of the government, which allocated merchandise to stores. Thus, retailers did not influence assortment or other marketing methods. Merchandise was primarily bulk goods that had no branding and quality and active selling were nonexistent. Advertising and customer service were unimportant and prices were set by the planning office. In East Germany there is only 157 square meters of retail food floor space per 1,000 people less than half the 368 square meters per 1,000 people in West Germany.

Now that the two German nations are one free-enterprise country we can expect to see the two retailing structures become more parallel and of course the major changes will occur in the former East Germany. A continued consolidation of food retailing and the emergence of discount supermarkets and hypermarkets may become the dominant forms of food retailing in Germany. Nonetheless, free enterprise will allow small independent merchants to create specialty bakery, meat, and produce stores to cater to special niches. In addition, prices will come down, quality will rise, and customer service will become widespread.

Source: Based on a variety of sources, including Georg Virnich and Martin Muser, "Analysis of Retailing in Germany," *International Trends in Retailing* (Spring 1991): 5-29.

sumer lifestyles, encouraged high-performance retailers around the world to seek new market segments, make adjustments in the retail mix, alter location patterns, and adopt new multisegment strategies. In the process, many new retail concepts and formats have emerged and spread, not only from firm to firm but from country to country. Exhibit 4.9 presents unique retailing concepts applied by three European specialty chains operating in the United States. As large retailers become more global in their operations, it can be expected that new retail formats will spread much more quickly worldwide.

Retailing is changing rapidly throughout the world, but one place where change is very evident is Germany. With the recent reunification of East and West Germany, the stimulus for change in retailing became strong. Retailing in Action 4.2 explores the changing structure of retail food store competition in the reunified Germany.

SUMMARY

Retail competition is dynamic and it is important to understand how it evolves over time. Five ways of viewing changing competitive patterns in retailing are reviewed. The wheel of retailing proposes that new types of retailers enter the market as low-status, low-margin, low-price operators; as they succeed, they become more complex, increasing their margins and prices and becoming vulnerable to new types of low-margin competitors, which, in turn, follow the same pattern. The retail accordion theory suggests that retail institutions evolve from outlets offering wide assortments to specialized narrow-assortment stores and then return to wide assortments to repeat the pattern. The theory of natural selection argues that those retail institutions that most readily adapt to a changing environment will prosper and others will not. The dialectic process of retailing suggests that each new form of retailing (called the thesis) begets a negation of itself (called the antithesis), which results in a blending of the two called a synthesis. The synthesis ultimately becomes the thesis and the process begins again. Finally, the retail life cycle theory argues that retail institutions, like the products they distribute, pass through identifiable cycles during which the basis of strategy and competition change.

Industry analysts contend that nonstore retailing will be a major competitive force in the future. Types of nonstore retailers are: mail-order firms, automatic merchandising machine operators, and direct-selling establishments such as party plan sellers.

We developed a model of retail competition to serve as an aid in illustrating certain principles of retail competition. This model suggests that retail competition is typically local; the retail industry is monopolistically competitive or oligopolistic; the demand side of retailing must consider the distance of the consumer from the store; both supply and demand factors must be examined in developing price and nonprice strategies; and an action by a retailer to increase its trade area is likely to elicit a response from competitors.

The economics of intratype and intertype competition, intercept competition, and the struggle for market share in retailing can affect retail profits. Therefore, retailers need to develop a protected market niche. One increasingly popular way to do this is by developing a market positioning strategy.

We concluded our discussion of retail competition by looking at how retailing concepts and formats differ between countries as a result of differences in their economic and social environments. It was learned that new retail formats are spreading much more quickly across countries as retailers become involved in global retailing.

QUESTIONS FOR DISCUSSION

1. Describe the wheel of retailing theory of retail competition. What are the theory's major strength and weakness?
2. Describe the retail accordion theory of competition. What are this theory's major strengths and weaknesses?
3. What is the dialectic process of competition? How can it be used to describe the evolution in gasoline retailing?
4. What trends do you see taking place in retail competition over the next decade?

5. In terms of the retail life cycle, what is likely to happen to the innovative retail firms of today?
6. What type of competitive market structure do most retailers face?
7. Which of the following retailers would you expect to face the strongest competition: gas station, flower shop, women's apparel store, pet shop, discount department store? Why?
8. Why are furniture stores able to attract customers from a greater distance than food stores?
9. Explain in your own words why retailers face a three-dimensional demand function. Do *all* retailers face a three-dimensional demand model?
10. The 1990s are expected to be a period of slow or no growth in retail sales (adjusted for inflation). Explain how a retailer could go about developing a strategy to significantly increase sales at a greater rate than inflation and thus increase its market share.
11. Develop a list of expenses or costs for a department store and categorize them as fixed, variable, or semifixed.
12. Assume that you are in the market for a new Nissan. The local Nissan dealer will sell you the model you want for $14,850. However, you notice an advertisement by a Nissan dealer located in a city 180 miles away. The ad prices the car you want at $13,995. Should you travel to the distant city to purchase the Nissan?
13. A small hardware store of 7,000 square feet in a community of 114,000 people is able to attract 715 visitors per week. On average 68 percent of the visitors make a purchase and the average purchase is $24. What is the average sales per week of the hardware store? What are the different methods the retailer could use to increase its sales?

MANAGEMENT MEMO

You are the service manager of a locally owned Ford dealership in a city of 220,000 population. Within the last 18 months, Firestone has opened two new stores, and Pep Boy has opened a 23,000-square-foot automotive parts supermarket that appeals to both the do-it-yourself auto enthusiast and the person who wants auto service done by others. This latter person can purchase parts and accessories at a Pep Boy at discount prices and have them installed by Pep Boy technicians. During this time period, service sales at the Ford dealership declined 8 percent. Previously, sales had been growing at 10 percent annually. Fred Morgan, the owner of the dealership, has asked you what strategies can be implemented to combat this increased competition and put the dealership back on a sales growth curve in service sales. Write a one-page memo outlining your suggestions.

BOARDROOM REPORT

H. Wayne Huizengo, the chairman of Blockbuster Video, has hired you as a consultant. Your assignment is to develop for Blockbuster an outline of the competitive factors the firm should consider as it develops its five-year strategic growth plan. Mr. Huizengo is especially concerned about the increased level of intertype competition in video rentals as more supermarkets enter the rental business. At the same time, he wonders whether the growth of cable television and the rental of films over cable lines will soften future growth. He wants you to identify four or five broad competitive issues that should be addressed in the firm's planning efforts. He wants you to keep your presentation to five minutes and thus each issue should be described in a few sentences (or one minute).

SUGGESTED READINGS

Nishimura, Shunroku, and Masaru Yokawa. "Analysis of Retailing in Japan." *International Trends in Retailing* (Fall 1991): 3-16.

Siegel, Joseph B. "Retailing: Back to Fundamentals." *Retail Control* (February 1990): 20-25.

Stone, Donald. "Mergers and Acquisitions in Retailing—Good and Bad News." *Retailing Issues Letter* (May 1990): 1-5.

Varadarajon, R. Rajan. "Perspectives on Corporate Excellence in Retailing." In *Proceedings of the Symposium on Patronage Behavior and Retail Strategy,* edited by William R. Darden, 251-67. Baton Rouge: Louisiana State University, 1989.

ENDNOTES

1. Malcolm P. McNair, "Significant Trends and Developments in the Postwar Period," in A. B. Smith, ed., *Competitive Distribution in a Free High-Level Economy and Its Implications for the University* (Pittsburgh: University of Pittsburgh Press, 1958).
2. Stanley C. Hollander, "The Wheel of Retailing," *Journal of Marketing* (July 1960):41.
3. Hollander, 40.
4. Dillard B. Tinsley, John R. Brooks, Jr., and Michael d'Amico, "Will the Wheel of Retailing Stop Turning?" *Akron Business and Economic Review* (Summer 1978): 26-29.
5. Stanley C. Hollander, "Notes on the Retail Accordion," *Journal of Retailing* (Summer 1966): 29-40, 54.
6. Ralph Hower, *History of Macy's of New York 1858-1919* (Cambridge, Mass: Harvard University Press, 1943), 73.
7. For a further discussion of these trends, see "Superstores Force PC Chains to Reinvent Themselves," *New York Times,* 12 May 1991, sec. F, p. 4 and "Whatever Happened to the Corner Computer Store?" *Business Week,* 20 May 1991, 131, 132, 137.
8. Reprinted from Delbert J. Duncan, "Responses of Selected Retail Institutions to Their Changing Environment," in Peter D. Bennett, *Marketing and Economic Development* (Chicago: American Marketing Association, 1965), 593.
9. Marvin Rothenberg, "New Methods in Increasing Market Share," National Retail Merchants Association presentation (New York, 1988).
10. Ronald R. Gist, *Retailing: Concepts and Decisions* (New York: John Wiley and Sons, 1968), 106-9.
11. Thomas J. Maronick and Bruce J. Walker, "The Dialectic Evolution of Retailing," in Barnett Greenberg, ed., *Proceedings, Southern Marketing Association* (Atlanta: Georgia State University, 1975), 147-51.
12. Thomas P. Neill, *Makers of the Modern Mind* (Milwaukee: Bruce Publishing Co., 1985), 298.
13. Maronick and Walker, "Dialectic Evolution," 147.
14. Reprinted by permission of the *Harvard Business Review*. From William R. Davidson, Albert D. Bates, and Stephen J. Bass, "The Retail Life Cycle," *Harvard Business Review* (November-December 1976): 89. Copyright 1976 by President and Fellows of Harvard College; all rights reserved.
15. Davidson, Bates, and Bass, 92. Reprinted by permission of the *Harvard Business Review*.
16. Davidson, Bates, and Bass, "Retail Life Cycle," 93.
17. William R. Davidson and Alice Rogers, "Non-Store Retailing: Its Importance to and Impact on Merchandise Suppliers and Competitive Channels," in Marcia Bielfield and Linda Nagel, eds., *The Growth of Non-Store Retailing: Implications for Retailers, Manufacturers, and Public Policy Makers* (New York: Institute of Retail Management, New York University, 1978), 22-29.
18. The framework is developed in elaborate detail by Charles A. Ingene and Robert F. Lusch, "A Model of Retail Structure, in Jagdish Sheth, ed., *Research in Marketing,* 101-64 and Jagdish Sheth, "An Integrative Theory of Patronage Preference and Behavior," in William Darden and Robert Lusch, eds., *Patronage Behavior and Retail Management* (New York: North-Holland, 1983), 9-28.
19. Leonard W. Weiss, *Case Studies in American Industry* (New York: John Wiley and Sons, 1971), 222-23.
20. In the simple model to be developed, we assume the retailer sells a single item. This need not be the case for the validity of the model to hold up; it is done only to reduce the amount of mathematics in our discussions.
21. "Megachurches Strive to Be All Things to All Parishioners," *Wall Street Journal,* 13 May 1991, A1, A6.
22. "Shopping Clubs Ready for Battle in Texas Market," *Wall Street Journal,* 24 October 1991, B1, B5.

23. "Tony Chicago Shopping Area's Struggles Reflect Nationwide Glut of Store Space," *Wall Street Journal,* 19 December 1990, B1, B6.
24. "Super-Cheap and Midpriced Eateries Bite Fast-Food Chains from Both Sides," *Wall Street Journal,* 22 June 1990, B1, B4 and "Firms Change Pitch as Economy Falters," *Wall Street Journal,* 9 November 1990, B1, B5.
25. "IKEA Furniture Chain Pleases with Its Prices, Not with Its Service," *Wall Street Journal,* 17 September 1991, A1, A5.
26. "Department Stores in Fight of Their Lives," *Advertising Age,* 4 March 1991, 29.
27. "Video Rental: Supermarkets Meet the Blockbusters," *Progressive Grocer* (November 1990): 75-80.
28. "Whatever Happened to the Corner Computer Store?" *Business Week,* 20 May 1991, 131.
29. "Pharmacies Fight off New Competition," *New York Times,* 5 November 1989, sec. 3, p. 17; and "Drugs by Mail," *Forbes,* 15 April 1991, 60-63.
30. For a further discussion of the IMPACT model, see Thomas Rubel, "Retail Marketing with IMPACT: Profit Engineering for the 90s," *Retail Control* (May-June 1990): 17-21.
31. "Wal-Mart Puts Its Own Spin on Private Label," *Advertising Age,* 16 December 1991, 26.
32. Madhau Kacker, "International Flow of Retailing Know-How: Bridging the Technology Gap in Distribution," *Journal of Retailing* (Spring 1988): 41-67.

CHAPTER 5

UNDERSTANDING RETAILING'S ROLE IN THE CHANNEL

OVERVIEW

This chapter addresses the retailer's need to analyze and understand the marketing channel to which it belongs. We begin by discussing how all the activities in the marketing system must be performed by either the retailer or another channel member. Next we review the various types of marketing channels and their benefits to the retailer. We conclude with some practical suggestions to improve channel relationships.

At the outset of this text, we stated that retailing is the final movement in the progression of merchandise from producer to consumer. Many other movements occur over time and geographical space, and all of them need to be executed properly for the retailer to achieve its best performance. In this chapter we discuss how those movements fit into the larger marketing system.

UNDERSTANDING RETAILING'S ROLE IN THE CHANNEL

I. The System Is the Solution
II. The Marketing System
    A. The Marketing Functions
        1. Buying
        2. Selling
        3. Storing
        4. Transporting
        5. Sorting

            6. Financing
            7. Information Gathering
            8. Risk Taking
        B. Pervasiveness of the Functions
        C. Marketing Institutions
            1. Primary Marketing Institutions
            2. Facilitating Institutions
    III. Conventional Marketing Channels
    IV. Vertical Marketing Systems
        A. Corporate Systems
        B. Contractual Systems
            1. Wholesaler-Sponsored Voluntary Groups
            2. Retailer-Owned Cooperatives
            3. Franchise
        C. Administered Systems
    V. Managing Retailer/Supplier Relations
        A. Dependency
        B. Power
        C. Conflict
            1. Interdependency and Conflict Potential
            2. Perceived Conflict
            3. Felt Conflict
            4. Manifest Conflict
            5. Conflict Resolution
            6. Feedback
    VI. Summary

THE SYSTEM IS THE SOLUTION

Consider the following example. The final movement of a retail item occurs on November 17 at 10:47 a.m., when the customer of a specialty store in a suburban Chicago mall purchases a new coat for the winter season. At some prior time (probably three to six months to a year earlier), that coat was manufactured. Later, it was warehoused and placed on display in the manufacturer's showroom. Next, a quantity of these coats was purchased by the specialty retailer. Goods were shipped by the manufacturer to the retailer to be placed on display in the store in the Chicago mall. Manufacturing occurred in Taiwan, a Japanese freighter was used to transport the coats to the United States, and the coats were warehoused in Los Angeles prior to being shipped to Chicago. Thus, before the final retail transaction could take place, many physical movements were needed, involving many firms other than the retailer.

Retailers cannot properly perform their roles without these other firms. They are part of a complex marketing system—an important part, but not the only one. Retailers that understand this complex system will be able to gain competitive advantage. For instance, The Limited Stores have been able to design their distribution system so that they can go from the design of an item of apparel to merchandising the item in their over 1,000 stores within six weeks, not the typical six months in our example.

To understand the retailer's part in the marketing system, we view it as a member of one, or even several, marketing channels. A **marketing channel** is a set of institutions involved in the movement of goods from the point of production to the point of consumption and, as such, consists of all the institutions and all the marketing activities in the marketing process. Each member of the marketing channel that does the best job will achieve dramatically higher levels of performance.

Entire marketing channels compete with each other. Firestone doesn't compete with Goodyear at just the local dealer level; rather, the marketing channel for Firestone tires competes with the marketing channel for Goodyear tires. Similarly, Kmart doesn't only compete with Target or Wal-Mart; rather the marketing channels that Kmart utilizes are in competition with the marketing channels that Target and Wal-Mart have structured.

Why should the retailer view itself as part of a larger marketing system? Why can't it simply seek out the best assortment of goods for its customers, sell the goods, make a profit, go to the bank, and forget about the system? The answer is straightforward. The retailer could forget about the system and make a short-run profit, but in the long run, the system will forget about the retailer. If that happens, profits sufficient for survival and growth will be

ILLUSTRATION 5.1

By operating its own MasterCare Service Centers, Firestone competes with competitors not just at the local store level, but throughout the marketing channel, for tires.

difficult, if not impossible, to achieve. This doesn't mean that the system should not, or cannot, be changed. Sometimes an innovative retailer might see that the entire system needs changing as a result of other changes in the retail marketplace. Here an innovative channel member, like a retailer, might solve the problem by breaking out of the existing system and replacing it with a new one. For example, retail mail-order druggists such as Medco have established themselves firmly in the drug distribution channel because they are able to deliver large purchases to drug manufacturers and pass significant savings onto customers.[1] Today, companies like General Motors and Aetna pay Medco to fill prescriptions sent in by employees since the benefit managers of these firms have discovered that drugs account for 9 to 12 percent of total benefit bills for employees. In 1991, Medco had sales in excess of $1.3 billion.

THE MARKETING SYSTEM

The marketing system can be defined in a variety of ways. For our purposes, we will define the **marketing system** as that set of institutions performing marketing functions, the relationships among these institutions, and the functions that are necessary to create transactions with target populations. We will view the marketing system as largely synonymous with the marketing channel.

Exhibit 5.1 is a graphic representation of the marketing system that portrays many of the links between institutions and functions that are necessary to bring about final exchange with some target populations. Note that the marketing system is affected by five external forces: consumer behavior, competitor behavior, the socioeconomic environment, the technological environment, and the legal environment. These external forces cannot be completely controlled by the retailer or any other institution in the marketing system, but they need to be taken into account when retailers make decisions.

THE MARKETING FUNCTIONS

What marketing functions need to be performed in the marketing system? Eight functions are necessary: buying, selling, storing, transporting, sorting, financing, information gathering, and risk taking.[2]

Buying. Before a retailer can sell merchandise to the final consumer, the retailer must purchase the merchandise from either the manufacturer or a wholesaler who buys it from the manufacturer. The manufacturer of the merchandise also needs to purchase many items (raw materials, subcomponents, supplies, etc.) before it can sell merchandise to the retailer or wholesaler. Buying is as important to a retailer as selling, and in some cases more important. Tuesday Morning, a Dallas-based chain of stores, specializes in

EXHIBIT 5.1

The Marketing System

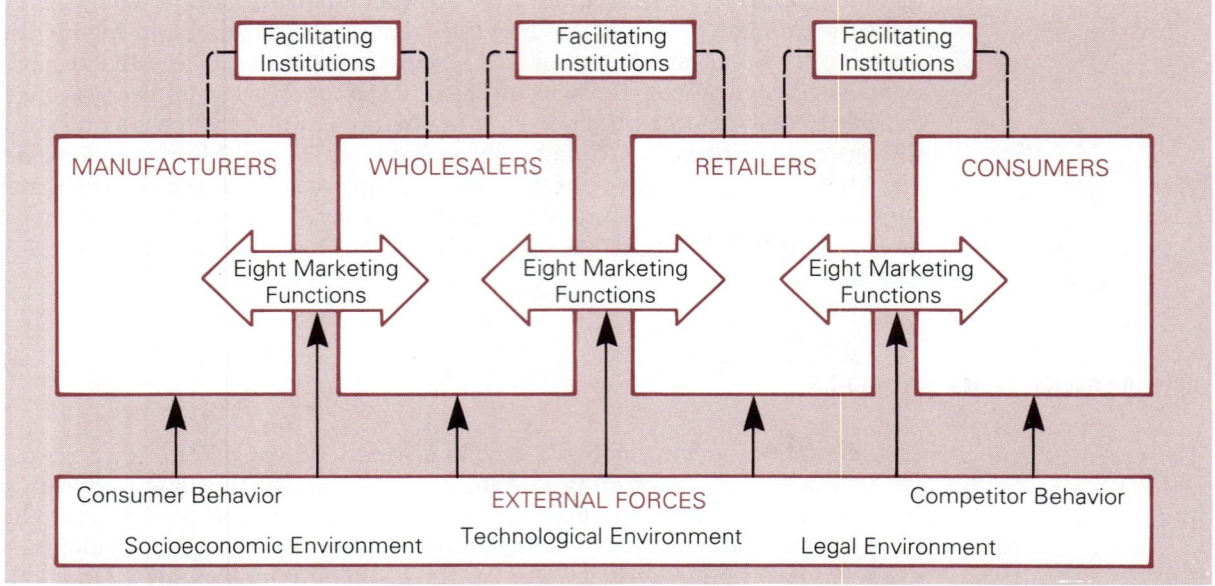

selling top-quality brands of giftware at deep discounts. This strategy revolves around the buying function. The company typically purchases manufacturers' goods at 25 cents or less on the dollar. This allows Tuesday Morning to buy a $10 item for $2.50 and sell it for $5, which is a 50 percent savings to the customer. All Tuesday Morning's literature says "Gifts, 50% to 80% Off Everything." Since special buying opportunities are concentrated during selected times of the year, the stores are only open 185 days per year during February, March, May, June, August, September, November, and December.[3]

Selling. Selling is the function that most consumers associate with retailing, and it obviously is important. It involves all activities that are necessary and incidental to contacting customers and persuading them to purchase. Selling activities include advertising, personal selling, and sales promotions. One controversial practice that occurs in retail marketing channels is some retailers selling their merchandise not to the final consumer but to **diverters** or off-price discount operations.[4] A diverter is an unauthorized member of a channel who buys and sells excess merchandise from authorized channel members. For instance, suppose a retailer could buy a name-brand appliance intended to retail for $389 at $185 if it purchases 100 units. However, if the retailer orders 500 units it can purchase the item at $158. What does the retailer do? Some retailers will purchase 500 units even though they only need 100. They in turn sell the 400 extra units at a slight loss, for example at $155, to an off-price discount store which may retail the item for $219. The net result is that the retailer loses $3 a unit on 400 units or $1,200; however, it has the remaining 100 units at $27 a unit less, for a savings of $2,700. The retailer is $1,500 ahead on the transaction; however, the manufacturer is upset because the appliance has been diverted into a retail channel it did not intend.

Storing. Storage is necessary whenever there is a discrepancy between the time at which supplies are created and the time at which demand occurs. For example, an apparel manufacturer may have a production run of 1,000 blue dresses within two days, but since the demand for those dresses will not occur immediately, storage becomes necessary. Since the storage function involves expenses (rent for the warehouse, insurance, fixtures, wages, etc.), members of marketing systems often try to shift this function onto other members. For example, a manufacturer might offer the wholesaler or retailer a discount for accepting early delivery.

Transporting. Transportation is necessary when the place of supply is removed from the place of demand. Production occurs in geographical pockets (such as apparel in the Far East). But demand occurs throughout the United States and as a result, merchandise needs to be transported. The only alternative would be to produce all products in all locations where people reside

ILLUSTRATION 5.2

Storing is one of the eight functions of the marketing system. This retail distribution center holds supplies between the time they are purchased by the retailer and the time at which demand occurs.

—which would obviously be extremely expensive. Transportation of merchandise from the store to the customer is also considered part of the transportation function. In fact, increasingly retail stores such as supermarkets and restaurants are providing home delivery.

Sorting. Sorting needs to occur because both demand and supply are heterogeneous.[5] Matching heterogeneous demands with heterogeneous supplies involves four sorting processes.

Accumulation means building up larger homogeneous supplies. For example, a number of small manufacturers or producers of a homogeneous product like corn might gather together so the larger quantity can be handled more economically.

Allocation is the breaking down of those homogeneous supplies into smaller lots. For example, a grain elevator that has accumulated large supplies of Grade 2 corn will sell it off in smaller quantities. Or a manufacturer of baseballs will divide its inventory into the smaller quantities needed by wholesalers and retailers.

Sorting out refers to the breaking down of heterogeneous supplies into more homogeneous groups. Here the baseballs might be further subdivided into big-league, high school, and Little League categories.

Finally, **assorting** is the building up of assortments of products for use in association with each other. Consumers typically seek an assortment of goods, and retailers serve the consumer by building these assortments. In the previous example, the retailer carrying the baseballs would also carry other baseball equipment such as gloves, bats, uniforms, and caps.

Financing. If we recognize that there are discrepancies between the time demand occurs and the time supplies are created, and also between points of production (supply) and points of consumption (demand), then it becomes clear that someone needs to finance these discrepancies. Ideally, the final consumer pays the retailer for the merchandise before the retailer must pay its supplier, but this generally doesn't happen. For example, most retailers have to pay for their Christmas merchandise before the Christmas selling season is over. Retailers find it difficult to operate without credit from suppliers. This is why retail suppliers were urged by several credit rating agencies to show caution in shipping new merchandise on credit to Macy's in 1992. The store was accused of being slow in paying because of the very high debt it had taken on in a leveraged buyout. Often manufacturers that sell to retailers cannot afford or do not care to finance the inventory, and in these cases they sell their receivables (what the retailers owe the manufacturer) to what are referred to as "factors." Factors buy receivables at a discount and then assume the risk of collecting from the retailers. One of the largest factors is Heller Financial Inc., which in July 1991 decided it did not want to buy the receivables of Saks Fifth Avenue because it thought the risk was too high that Saks may not be able to pay its bills.[6]

Information Gathering. Sellers know what their supplies are and buyers know what their demands are, but without an exchange of information, the seller doesn't know what the buyer wants and the buyer doesn't know what the seller has. Information is essential to match suppliers properly with the demands of the retailer's market. It will not do any good to have suppliers producing tight jeans when the marketplace wants loose-fitting jeans.

Risk Taking. It is obvious that demands cannot be forecast precisely. Products will be produced or purchased for resale for which a demand might not materialize. In that case, the retailer can incur a loss. Consider toy retailers, for example if they incorrectly assess the demand for certain toys at the Christmas toy shows in June and July, they may under- or overstock. Either way, a loss will occur. No wonder retailers say, "Risk taking's reward is profit." Remember how unexpectedly popular the hypercolor shirt, which changed color as your body heat changed, and Pet Rocks were a decade ago, only to be duds for retailers a few years later.

PERVASIVENESS OF THE FUNCTIONS

Regardless of the type of economic system a country has, these eight marketing functions will exist. They cannot be eliminated. They can, however, be shifted or divided among the institutions and consumers in the marketing system.

All forms of retailing were created by rearranging the marketing functions among institutions and consumers. For example, department stores were created specifically to build a larger and better assortment of goods. They capitalized on the opportunity to perform more of the sorting process. No longer was it necessary to travel to one store for a shirt, another for slacks, and yet another for shoes; the necessary assortment was available in a single store. Supermarkets increased consumers' workload by shifting more of the information gathering, buying, and transporting functions to them. Before supermarkets, consumers could have the corner grocer select items and deliver them. But with the supermarket came self-service. Consumers had to locate the goods within the store, select them from an array of products, and transport them home. For performing more of these marketing functions, the consumer was compensated by lower prices.

A marketing function does not have to be shifted in its entirety to another institution or to the consumer. It can be divided among several entities. For example, the manufacturer that does not want to perform the entire selling function could have the retailer perform part of the job through in-store promotions and local advertising. At the same time, the manufacturer could assume some of the task through national advertising.

No member of the marketing channel would want, or be able, to perform all eight marketing functions. For this reason, the retailer must view itself as being dependent on others in the marketing system.

MARKETING INSTITUTIONS

What institutions perform the eight marketing functions? There are many more than you might think. These institutions can be broken into two categories: **primary marketing institutions,** those that take title to the goods, and **facilitating institutions,** those that do not actually take title but facilitate the marketing process by specializing in the performance of certain functions. Exhibit 5.2 is a classification of the major institutions participating in the marketing system.

Primary Marketing Institutions. There are three types of primary marketing institutions: manufacturers, wholesalers, and retailers. Each takes legal title to the goods as they flow through the marketing channel.

Often, we don't think of manufacturers as marketing institutions, since they produce goods. But manufacturers cannot exist by only producing goods; they must also market the goods produced. They often need the assistance of other institutions in performing the eight marketing functions. There are over 369,000 manufacturers in the United States.

A second type of primary marketing institution is the wholesaler. Wholesalers buy and resell merchandise to retailers, other merchants, industrial institutions, and commercial users. There are nearly 467,000 wholesalers in the United States, each performing some of the eight marketing functions.

EXHIBIT 5.2

Institutions Participating in the Marketing System

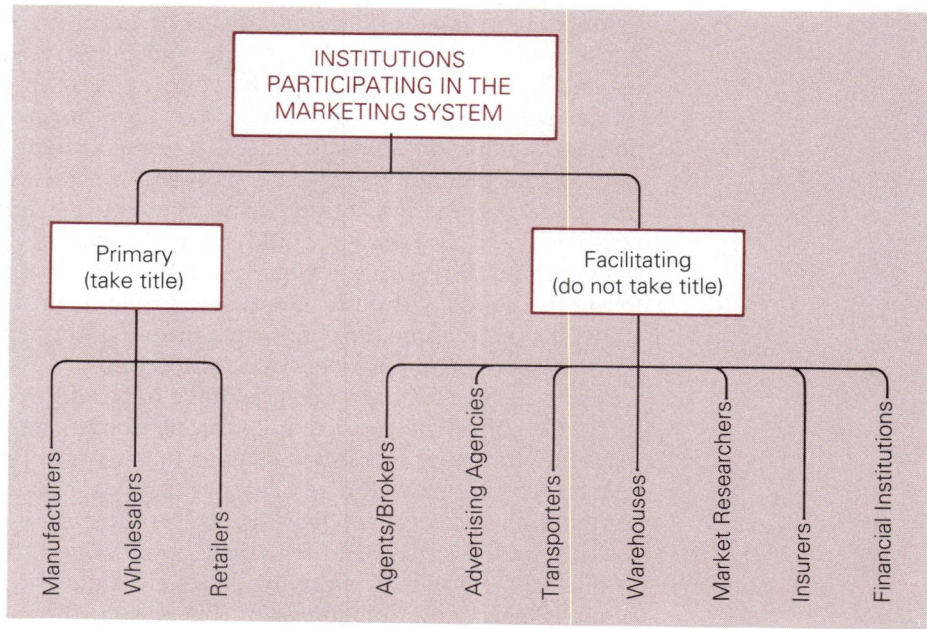

The third type of primary institution is the retailer. There are 2.4 million retail stores and 6.2 million service establishments in the United States.[7] Retailers can perform portions of all eight marketing functions. Since the focus of this text is on retailing, let us examine how a typical retailer can contribute to the performance of these eight functions.

Buying is a side of retailing that the consumer rarely notices. When you next walk into a department store, try to think about how much effort went into buying the assortment of merchandise you see. The merchandise comes from all over the world. Many top retail executives started their careers as assistant buyers, just as you might.

Selling is the function consumers identify most with retailing. Retailers need to sell, not just have merchandise available. To do this, they must advertise, use sales promotions, and frequently use personal selling to ensure that merchandise is moved in adequate quantities.

The retail storage function operates in the inventory and floor space necessary to make merchandise available at the time and place it is demanded.

Retailers also help perform the transportation function. Often retailers have to transport goods from the point of purchase (the manufacturer or wholesaler) to the retail store. At other times the retailer needs to deliver merchandise to the customer's residence. Retailers may need to be concerned with both inbound and outbound transportation. Thus, the location of retailers and their warehouses is extremely important.

Retailers do a considerable amount of sorting, especially assorting. Retailers build assortments of merchandise that match consumer demand patterns.

The retailer cannot operate on a profitable basis without information about consumer wants and needs, changing economic conditions, and competitive trends. A lack of such information will cause error in the retail planning and management process. The retailer needs timely and relevant information to make intelligent decisions.

The retailer cannot avoid risk taking. The consumer may reject the merchandise the retailer has selected. There may be a recession, or households may leave the retailer's trading area and new households may not move in. The merchandise may not arrive on time, it may arrive damaged, or it may not be what was ordered. The store may burn down, or customers may injure themselves in the store. The management of these risks is becoming an increasingly important function in retailing. Some risk can be decreased through insurance and by securing "return privileges" in case the merchandise is a flop or the season is over before the merchandise arrives.

Finally, the retailer must perform part of the financing function. Retailers need to finance the preceding functions with either debt or equity capital.

Facilitating Institutions. A variety of institutions facilitate the performance of the marketing functions. Most of these specialize in one or two functions;

none of them takes title to the goods. Institutions that facilitate buying and selling in the marketing system include:

1. The **free-lance broker** has no permanent ties with any manufacturer and may negotiate sales for a large number of manufacturers over time. No limit is placed on the territory in which sales may occur, but the broker is strictly bound by the manufacturer regarding prices, terms, and conditions of sale. An example of a free-lance broker is someone who contracts with a manufacturer to sell the manufacturer's excess output. Once the products are sold, the free-lance broker is free to obtain the output of any other manufacturer and perform his or her duties again.
2. The **manufacturer's agent** acts as the sales force for several manufacturers at the same time within a prescribed market area. The manufacturer's agent has a rather loose arrangement with the manufacturer that is seldom permanent beyond a year; it is usually renewed but it can also be terminated on notice. The manufacturer's agent, like the free-lance broker, is strictly bound by the manufacturer for the prices, terms, and conditions of sale but is additionally bound by geographic territory. Manufacturer's agents usually have jurisdiction over only a part of the manufacturer's total output. Manufacturer's agents are extremely important in product lines like furniture, dry goods, apparel, and accessories.
3. The **sales agent** has long-term arrangements with one or a very few manufacturers. This agent sells the entire output for the manufacturer and has no limitation on the territory, prices, terms, or conditions of sale. The sales agent also frequently finances the manufacturer and is generally used in such product lines as home furnishings, textiles, and canned foods.
4. **Purchasing agents** specialize in seeking out sources of supply for some members of the channel. They operate on a contractual basis for a limited number of customers and receive a commission just as sales agents do. Purchasing agents, who are sometimes known as **resident buyers,** usually operate in the central market headquarters for a particular type of product. They are specialists on the availability of products; the reliability of suppliers; present and future market trends; and special deals, prices, shipping, and other considerations. Retailers make considerable use of two different types of resident buyers: store-owned and independent buyers.

These facilitating agents and brokers are independent businesspeople who receive a commission when they are able to bring buyer and seller together to negotiate a transaction. The purchasing agent aids in buying and the others assist in selling. Wal-Mart, the nation's largest retailer, refuses to deal with brokers or agents who represent smaller manufacturers. Wal-Mart wants to deal with principal employees of manufacturers and not their agents or brokers because Wal-Mart believes it can better coordinate deliveries and inventory levels when it deals direct unless a manufacturer is so small it cannot afford a direct sales force.[8]

Advertising agencies also facilitate the selling process by designing effective advertisements and advising management on where and when to place them. Institutions that facilitate the transportation function are motor, rail, and air carriers and pipeline and shipping companies. These firms offer differing advantages in terms of delivery, service, and cost; generally, the quicker the delivery, the more costly it is. Transporters can have a significant effect on how efficiently goods move through the marketing system and can be a major source of conflict when they fail to perform their jobs properly.

Imagine you are the lawn and garden department manager for a local discount store. You are waiting for a shipment of three hundred 50-pound bags of lawn food for a special national promotion. You placed your order in time and should have received the product two days ago. Upon calling the manufacturer, you discover that the product was sent out last week by truck for delivery to you two days ago. You try to trace the shipment through the trucking company, only to find that nobody seems to know where your shipment is or when it is expected to arrive. This type of incident is often a cause for considerable conflict between the retailer and the transporter, the manufacturer and the transporter, the retailer and the manufacturer, and even the retailer and the customer—when the goods don't arrive on schedule after they have been advertised, customers become irritated with the retailer.

The major facilitating institution involved in storage is the public warehouse. A **public warehouse** will store goods for safekeeping in return for a fee. Fees are usually based on cubic feet used per month, but some warehouses charge daily fees. Frequently, retailers take advantage of special buys but have no space for the goods in their store or warehouse and find it necessary to use a public warehouse.

A variety of facilitating institutions assist in providing information in the marketing system. For example, the role of the mail and phone in transmitting information is pervasive. In addition, computers are playing an increasing role in information transmission. Retailers can now order many types of merchandise using an on-line computer. An order is keyed into a computer at the retail firm and fed directly into the wholesaler's or manufacturer's computer. That computer will print out a purchase order and a warehouse routing slip to show what items are to be pulled from the warehouse and shipped to the retailer. Also assisting in the information function are market research firms, which provide problem-solving information in specialized areas.

There are also facilitating institutions that aid in financing, such as commercial banks, savings and loan associations, and stock exchanges. These institutions can provide, or help the retailer obtain, funds to finance marketing functions. Retailers frequently need short-term loans of working capital (to handle increased inventory and accounts receivables) and long-term loans for continued growth and expansion (adding new stores or remodeling).

Finally, insurance firms facilitate by assuming some of the risks in the marketing system. They can insure against theft, fire, and other damages, inventories, trucks, equipment, buildings and fixtures, and other assets for the retailer and other primary marketing institutions. They can also insure against employee and customer injuries.

Let us now examine how the primary marketing institutions are arranged into a marketing channel.

CONVENTIONAL MARKETING CHANNELS

A large part of the marketing system consists of the marketing functions and the primary marketing institutions that perform them—but how are these functions and institutions arranged into a marketing channel? There are two basic channel patterns: the conventional marketing channel and the vertical marketing system. Exhibit 5.3 provides an illustration of these major channel patterns.

A **conventional marketing channel** is one in which each member of the channel is loosely aligned with the others. Predictably, each member's orientation is toward the next institution in the channel. Thus, the manufacturer interacts with and focuses efforts on the wholesaler, the wholesaler focuses efforts on the retailer, and the retailer focuses efforts on the final consumer. In

EXHIBIT 5.3

Marketing Channel Patterns

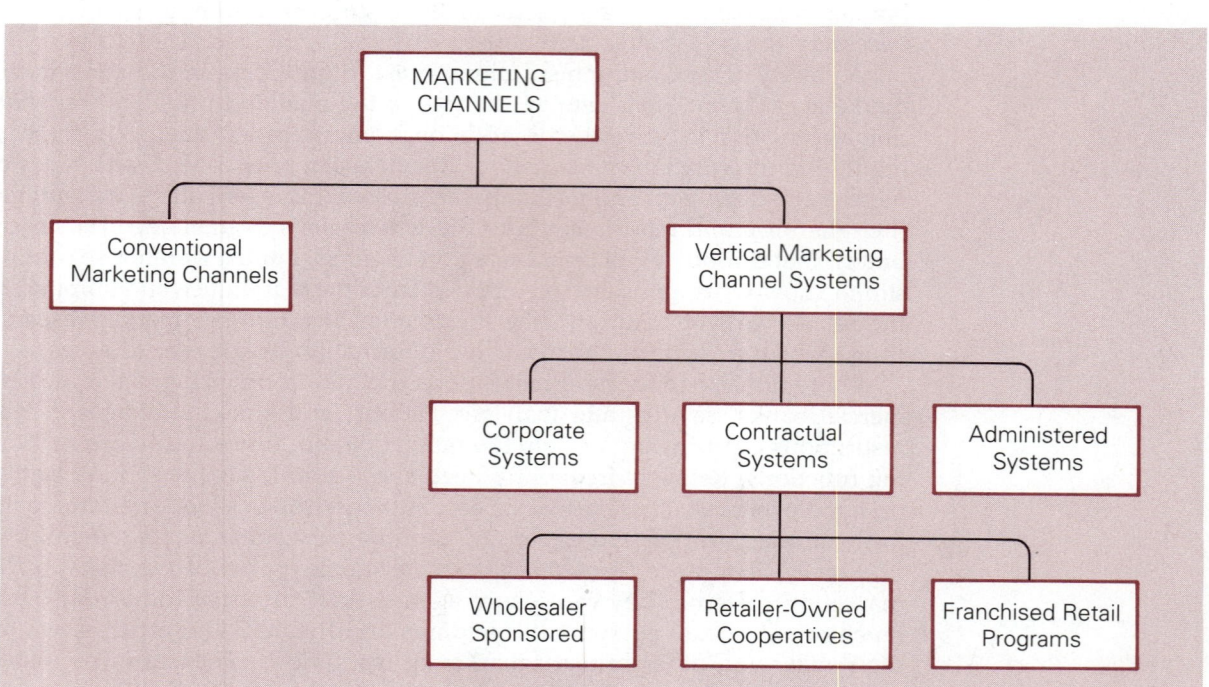

short, the conventional marketing channel consists of a series of dyads in which the members recognize each other but not those outside.

The conventional marketing channel, although historically predominant in the United States, is a sloppy and inefficient method of conducting business. It fosters intense negotiations in each dyad in the channel, and the channel members do not see the possibility of shifting or dividing the marketing functions among *all* channel participants. It is an unproductive mode for marketing goods and has been on the decline in the United States since the early 1950s.

VERTICAL MARKETING SYSTEMS

Vertical marketing systems are rationalized, capital-intensive networks of several levels that are professionally managed and centrally programmed to realize technological, managerial, and promotional economies. There are three types of vertical marketing systems—corporate, contractual, and administered—each of which has grown explosively since the early 1950s.[9] In Retailing in Action 5.1 we discuss how some leading retailers have developed cooperative strategies with suppliers to create stronger vertical marketing systems.

CORPORATE SYSTEMS

Corporate vertical marketing systems typically consist of either a manufacturer that has integrated vertically to reach the consumer, or a retailer that has integrated vertically to create a self-supply network. The first type includes manufacturers such as Singer (sewing machines), Radio Shack (electronic products), Sherwin Williams (paint), Hart, Schaffner and Marx (men's apparel), Famolare (shoes), and Xerox (office equipment), which have created their own warehousing and retail outlets. The second type includes retailers such as Holiday Inns and Sears. For example, Holiday Inns has vertically integrated to control a carpet mill, furniture manufacturer, and numerous other suppliers needed to build and operate its motels.

A recent example of a trend toward corporate systems is the automobile business, where manufacturers are capturing many of their customers by purchasing car-rental firms. For instance, Chrysler Corp. owns Dollar Rent A Car Systems, Inc., Thrifty Rent-A-Car Systems, Inc., and Snappy Rental, Inc. Ford Motor Co. has put money into Hertz Corp. and Budget Rent A Car Corp. General Motors Corp. has invested in Avis, Inc., and National Car Rental System.[10] Another example is in the trend of such manufacturers as Liz Claiborne, London Fog, Van Heusen, Guess, and Esprit to open factory outlet stores that sell direct to the public at 50 to 70 percent off regular retail prices. These outlets traditionally were located near a manufacturer's factory, but in the 1990s the trend is to open these stores in factory outlet malls. This

RETAILING IN ACTION

5.1 Using Cooperation to Strengthen Vertical Marketing Systems

Increasingly, retailers and their suppliers are developing cooperative partnerships that create strong vertical marketing systems. Much of the progress has occurred in distribution and logistics systems where cooperative programs have been developed to create quick response/just-in-time inventory systems that improve systemwide inventory productivity.

Fundamentally, quick response/just-in-time inventory systems change the strategy of operating the marketing channel from a "push" strategy, which has traditionally built up a great amount of undesirable inventory at the endpoint in the supply chain, to a "pull" strategy. With a "pull" strategy, inventory is based on the consumer and actual demand patterns that pull the merchandise through the channel. The marketing channel becomes a continuous replenishment system triggered by customer demand and supported by timely and accurate information generated by the use of universal product code (UPC) scanning, point-of-sale (POS) terminals, and electronic data interchange (EDI).

One retail chain that has moved rapidly in developing vertical partnerships is Target, which has developed a quick response program with over a dozen key vendors. Gains have been recorded in terms of shorter lead time in placing and receiving orders, increased fill rates (i.e., fewer backorders), fewer retail out of stocks, increased sales, and improved inventory turnovers due to lower average inventory and higher sales. Retail chains experiencing similar gains are Wal-Mart and Dillards. In fact, Dillards now has its quick response program installed with over 180 of its suppliers and is able to restock its stores in less than 12 days.

Sources: Based on Renee Covino Rouland, "TARGET: Partnerships in Progress," *Discount Merchandiser* (January 1991): 37-39; Renee Covino Rouland, "Distribution Technology: The Seamless Pipeline Dream," *Discount Merchandiser* (April 1991): 48-50, 74; Jay L. Johnson, "Partnership via Technology: Improving Operations, *Discount Merchandiser* (May 1991): 72, 74, 94; "Two Disparate Firms Find Keys to Success in Troubled Industries," *Wall Street Journal*, 29 May 1991, A1, A9.

practice has angered traditional retailers that buy from these manufacturers and has created considerable conflict.[11]

An international example of a corporate marketing channel system is the Italian sportswear company, Benetton. Located in Ponzano, Italy, Benetton annually makes and distributes 50 million pieces of clothing worldwide. The firm has 5,000 stores in 60 countries. Distribution is accomplished through one massive distribution center which is fully automated—it is run by eight people and moves 230,000 pieces of clothing a day. The warehouse has 300,000 slots and merchandise is placed and retrieved by robots. In addition, manufacturing is computer controlled. The result is that a Benetton store anywhere in the world can get an order filled in one week. Furthermore, if the item is not in stock, it can be manufactured and delivered within a month.[12]

In corporate systems it is much easier to program the channel for productivity and profit goals, since a well-established authority structure already exists. Independent retailers that have aligned themselves in a conventional marketing channel are at a significant disadvantage when competing against a corporate vertical marketing system.

CONTRACTUAL SYSTEMS

Contractual vertical marketing systems include wholesaler-sponsored voluntary groups, retailer-owned cooperatives, and franchised retail programs. Each of these channel types allows for a more coordinated and systemwide perspective than conventional marketing channels; however, they are more difficult to manage than corporate vertical marketing systems because the authority and power structures are not as well defined. Channel members must give up some autonomy to gain system economies and greater market impact.

Wholesaler-Sponsored Voluntary Groups. Wholesaler-sponsored voluntary groups are created when a wholesaler brings together a group of independently owned retailers (*independent retailers* is a term embracing anything from a single mom-and-pop store to a small local chain), grocers for example, and offers them a coordinated merchandising and buying program that will provide them with economies like those their chain store rivals are able to obtain. In return, the independent grocers agree to concentrate their purchases with that wholesaler. It is a voluntary relationship; that is, there are no membership or franchise fees. The independent grocers may terminate the relationship whenever they desire, so it is to the wholesaler's advantage to build competitive merchandise assortments and offer other services that will keep the voluntary group satisfied. Nonetheless, some retailers will reach a level of sophistication and sales volume at which they believe they can handle their own distribution. In the early 1990s, Fleming Companies (the nation's second largest food wholesaler with annual sales in excess of $12 billion) lost many customers such as Smith Food & Drug and Raley's (a California customer) who decided to cut out the intermediaries.[13]

It is common for the voluntary group wholesaler to offer the retailer the following services: store design and layout, store site and location analysis, inventory management systems, accounting and bookkeeping systems, insurance services, pension plans, trade area studies, advertising and promotion assistance, and employee training programs. The better the services and merchandising programs offered by the wholesaler, the more loyal is the retailer. In such a situation, the wholesaler can become the channel leader and program the channel for high-performance results. Exhibit 5.4 profiles some of the retail support services a voluntary group wholesaler generally provides to its retailers.

In the past, local food wholesalers obtained practically all their business from independent grocers. Recently, however, as transportation costs have risen, major chains operating over a wide geographic area have started using local wholesalers, too.

EXHIBIT 5.4

Support Services A Voluntary Group Wholesaler Offers to Its Retailers

Support Service	Description
Financial counsel	Qualified personnel answer retailers' financial questions. Upon request, a retailer may receive advice on financing store expansion, cash-flow problems, loans, and other related financial concerns.
Engineering	The store engineering and development department offers retailers designs for new stores, additions, and remodelings. Expert advice on equipment and its procurement is offered. Market analysis services are provided, which prove invaluable to a retailer planning a new store or moving to a new location. Professional consumer research is offered to help retailers appraise customer acceptance. Energy saving advice is given directly, and tips are published in a weekly merchandiser.
Computer service	Wholesalers' data processing facilities provide case labels as a pricing aid to retailers; electronic ordering for speed, accuracy, and backroom space saving; commodity purchase analysis reports on a scheduled basis; and many other benefits.
Advertising	The emphasis of the advertising program is built around private brands, and by continuous use of banners and themes gives the impression of a large chain-like advertising campaign rather than a small one-store effort. In addition to placing newspaper, handbills, radio, and TV ads, the department lends assistance in planning special sales, promotions, anniversary sales, and grand openings.
Retail accounting	The accounting department handles bookkeeping, tax preparation, bill-out service, computerized payrolls, and many other accounting-oriented functions. Assistance is communicated by standardized forms, computer printouts, telephone calls, and visits by wholesaler's accountants for special problems.
Retail training	The training department provides retailers with a comprehensive training program for management and employees which includes all facets of merchandising, marketing, in-store security, and other appropriate functions.
Printing	The printing department continually provides printed material including letterheads, cash register refund forms, bag stuffers, envelopes, store directories, etc.

Wholesaler-sponsored voluntary groups have been a major force in marketing channels since the mid-1960s. They are now prevalent in many lines of trade. Independent Grocers Alliance (IGA), Ace Hardware, Western Auto, Ben Franklin, and Economost are all examples of wholesaler-sponsored voluntary groups.

Retailer-Owned Cooperatives. Another common type of contractual vertical marketing system is retailer-owned cooperatives. These systems are organized and owned by retailers and are most common in the grocery field (e.g., Associated Grocers and Certified Grocers). They offer scale economies and service to member retailers, allowing their members to compete with larger chain-buying organizations.

Wholesaler-sponsored voluntary groups and retailer-owned cooperatives have very different leadership patterns, and these differences affect their competitive intensity. Generally, wholesaler-sponsored voluntary groups are more effective competitors, but both types of groups have advantages and disadvantages. For example, a wholesaler can provide more leadership to its voluntary group because it represents the locus of power within the system. In retailer-owned cooperatives, power is diffused throughout the retail membership, making it difficult to define roles and allocate resources and thus creating more bureaucracy. Nonetheless, Wakefern Food Corp. of Elizabeth, New Jersey, is a co-op (with 30 members operating 181 stores in six New England and mid-Atlantic states) that has been able to overcome this common problem.[14] The secret to its success is largely its committee system of decision making and the heavy involvement of all members in the management of the co-op. Wakefern has been able to turn the diffuse power of its members into an asset by viewing this diffuse power as individual expertise. On the other hand, members of wholesaler-sponsored voluntary groups have relinquished some of their autonomy by making themselves highly dependent on specific wholesalers for expertise. In retailer-owned cooperatives, members retain more autonomy and thus tend to depend much less on the supply unit for assistance and direction.[15]

Franchise. The third type of contractual vertical marketing system is the franchise.[16] The term originally came from the French word meaning *to be free from servitude*. Today, franchising gives individuals the opportunity to own their own business, even if they are inexperienced and lacking adequate capital. **Franchising** is a form of licensing by which the owner of a product, service, or method, the franchisor, obtains distribution through affiliated dealers, franchisees. The franchisee or holder of the franchise right is often given exclusive access to a defined geographical area. The product, method, or service being marketed is identified by a brand name, and the franchisor maintains control over the marketing methods employed.

During recent years, franchising has been expanding rapidly and entering new areas of application. This growth is the result of individuals trying to overcome two of the most common causes of retail failure: lack of management know-how and inadequate financial resources. Statistical evidence of such expansion is contained in the study entitled *Franchising in the Economy*, published regularly by the International Franchise Association Educational Foundation, Inc. The latest study revealed that franchised businesses accounted for $716 billion in sales in 1990. In Exhibit 5.5 we show the growth in franchising over the last decade in six lines of trade.

In many cases the franchise operation resembles a large chain with trademarks, uniform symbols, equipment, and storefronts, and standardized services, products, and practices as outlined in the franchise agreement. The ability to look like and compete as a big retail chain is especially important when a line of retail trade begins to be dominated by large chains. Small independent retailers are almost always unable to compete effectively against

EXHIBIT 5.5

Franchise Sales Volume and Number of Establishments: 1980–1990[a]

	1980		1990	
	Number of Establishments (1,000)	Sales (billions)	Number of Establishments (1,000)	Sales (billions)
Auto and truck dealers	29.4	$143.9	27.6	$362.3
Restaurants	60.0	27.9	102.1	76.5
Gasoline service stations	158.5	94.5	111.7	115.1
Convenience stores	15.6	7.8	17.5	14.4
Hotels/Motels	6.4	9.5	11.1	23.9
Laundry/drycleaning	3.4	0.3	2.6	0.3

[a]This listing of franchise establishments does not cover all lines of retail trade.

Source: U.S. Department of Commerce, International Trade Administration, *Franchising in the Economy: 1986–1988*. Beginning 1988, International Franchise Association Educational Foundation, Inc., Washington D.C. and Horwath International, New York, N.Y., *Franchising in the Economy, 1986–1990, 1990*. Also, reported in U.S. Bureau of the Census, *Statistical Abstract of the United States: 1991*, 111th ed. (Washington, D.C., 1991), Table 1369.

chains. For example, with the rapid growth of chain drugstores such as Dart Drug, Drug Emporium, and Walgreens, the independent pharmacist needs to find a way to be a strong competitor. Medicine Shoppe International (MSI) is a St. Louis–based franchise company that ranks as the nation's seventh-largest drugstore operator with over 800 stores and offers an alternative to the independent pharmacist. MSI will offer to convert an independent pharmacy to a Medicine Shoppe franchise. The franchisee will be provided with accounting, store operations, marketing, and general business support services. MSI will provide significant buying economies along with monthly in-depth financial statements that track expenses, gross profits, and sales.[17]

The International Franchise Association defines franchising as "a continuing relationship in which the franchisor provides a licensee privilege to do business, plus assistance in organizing, training, merchandising, and management in return for a consideration from the franchisee." Franchising continues to be a rapid growth industry, and some of the international trends are discussed in Retailing in Action 5.2.

Franchising has also been described as a convenient and economic means of fulfilling the desire for independence with a minimum of risk and investment and maximum opportunities for success, through the utilization of a proven product or service and marketing method. However, the owner of a franchise gives up some freedom in business decisions that the owner of a nonfranchised business would have.

In a way, franchisees are not their own bosses. In order to maintain uniformity of service and to ensure that the operations of each outlet will reflect favorably on the organization as a whole, the franchisor usually exercises some degree of control over the operations of franchisees, requiring them to meet stipulated standards of quality. The extent of such control varies. In some cases, franchisees are required to conduct every step of their operation in strict conformity with a manual furnished by the franchisor—and this may be desirable. In return for this surrender of freedom, the individual franchisee can share in the goodwill built up by all other outlets that bear the same name.

Since the last years of the 1980s, change has been occurring in franchising. Mom-and-pop franchisees are being replaced by a new breed of franchise owners. For years, most franchisors sought to sell their operations almost exclusively to would-be entrepreneurs with little or no business experience. Now a growing number of cash-rich investors and companies are sinking money into franchises or buying rights to an entire state or foreign country. Business executives who lost their jobs in the mergers of the late 1980s are turning to franchise ownership, and an increasing number of franchisees are women.[18] Independent store owners are converting to franchises to gain advertising clout. And franchisees experienced in one field are snapping up franchises in other fields. While the mom-and-pops are still important to the growth of the franchise operation, there has been a marked shift recently toward more sophisticated buyers with proven business skills and deep

RETAILING IN ACTION

5.2 International Expansion in Franchising

"A growing number of franchisors based in the US are entering foreign markets. According to *Franchising in the Economy: 1988–1990*, one-sixth of all business-format franchisers had units outside the US in 1988. The number of foreign units operated by US franchisers jumped more than 10 percent between 1986 and 1988. Furthermore, according to my own recent survey of US franchise systems, almost one-half of the responding franchisers without foreign units plan to initiate such expansion, and more than 90 percent of the systems with foreign units intend to increase their presence in foreign countries.

"The most common location of franchises outside the US is Canada. However, with the upcoming reduction of trade barriers, a growing number of US franchisers will expand their activities in Western European countries. Although the entry of Alphagraphics and Pizza Hut into Russia has been widely publicized, widespread expansion by US franchisers into Eastern European countries will be very, very slow. In fact, early initiatives in Russia and other Eastern European countries have involved joint ventures rather than traditional franchises. The busiest McDonald's restaurant in the world, which is located in Moscow, is a joint venture between McDonald's Canada and the city of Moscow."

ILLUSTRATION 5.3

Many franchisors, such as this McDonald's in Moscow, are expanding overseas and pursuing footholds in the newly opened Eastern European countries.

"Besides the movement of US franchisers into foreign countries, other forms of international expansion merit brief mention. Non-US franchisers that have found success in their home markets will expand into foreign countries in much the same way that US franchisers have expanded into foreign countries. However, few non-US franchisers have penetrated the US market. Why? Stiff competition and government regulations covering franchise sales are likely explanations. Still, one wonders how long the US market can—and will—remain insulated from the activities of successful franchise systems from other countries."

Source: Bruce J. Walker, "Retail Franchising in the 1990s," *Retailing Issues Letter* (January 1991): 3.

pockets. A survey of franchisors revealed that the most common reason for franchise failure was that the buyer had little or no previous business experience. On the other hand, most successful franchisees had previously owned businesses or franchises.[19]

Franchisors participate in many aspects of the marketing channel. They can be manufacturers, such as Chevrolet or Midas Mufflers; service specialists, such as H & R Block, Kelly Girl, Century 21 Real Estate, or Manpower; or retailers, such as McDonald's, Kentucky Fried Chicken (KFC), or Dunkin' Donuts. Franchisors depend on the successful operation of franchise outlets for continued growth and need individuals who are willing to learn the business and have the energy for a considerable amount of effort. The franchisor can supply the other essentials for successful operation of the outlet.

Among the services franchisors might provide to franchise operators are: (1) reduced uncertainty, since the approach to doing business has been proven successful by the franchisor; (2) location analysis and counsel; (3) store design and equipment purchasing; (4) initial employee and management training and continuing management counseling; (5) advertising and merchandising counsel and assistance; (6) standardized procedures and operations; (7) centralized purchasing with consequent savings; (8) financial assistance in the establishment of the business; and (9) store development aid, including lease negotiation.

To the franchisor, franchising offers these advantages:

1. Capital advantages, since franchisees are typically charged a franchise fee. The franchisor can use these fees as a major source of working capital, allowing the franchise to grow at a rapid pace without diluting its equity in the business.
2. Reduction in fixed overhead expenses, since the high cost of maintaining company-owned outlets will be eliminated.
3. More motivated managers, because the franchisees, as independent businesspeople, will be more committed to developing markets than salaried employees would be.[20]

Although franchises offer significant advantages to both franchisor and franchisee, conflict between them is common, and usually occurs over the following issues:

1. How should the direct channel profits be divided? The establishment of fees and margins, specification of investment requirements, and location of expense-incurring activities are involved.
2. When should franchisee investment in new or upgraded facilities be required, and who should participate in this decision?
3. How far should the franchisor go in saturating a single market area with franchise outlets?[21]
4. What amount of capital reserves and expertise are needed by the franchisee?

The most important determinant in avoiding conflict in a franchise system is the contract. The contract should not be one-sided in favor of the franchisor. Several principles to guide franchise contract development have been suggested:

1. The contract should be frank, completely disclosing the relationship between franchisor and franchisee. The objective is to make explicit all mutual rights and obligations with performance standards to ensure that neither party may reasonably claim it was deceived by the other.
2. The provisions should be fair so that neither party may claim unreasonable dominance by the other.
3. The contract should be tailored to the specific situation, recognizing the uniqueness of individual franchise systems and the difficulty of designing a generalized franchise contract.

4. Contract provisions should be enforceable so that no party can use economic strength for cavalier violation of agreed-on covenants.[22]

Ambiguity, a major source of conflict, can be removed by:

1. Specifying the unique roles of the contracting parties
2. Making operating procedures as specific as possible within the confines of antitrust regulations and local market differences
3. Specifying in substantial detail the performance obligations of both parties
4. Specifying how performance standards will be established and revised
5. Specifying criteria for new outlet penetration of given markets
6. Specifying reasonable causes leading to termination[23]

The franchise contract gives the franchisor legitimate power to control the marketing channel. The franchisor obtains additional power by providing services and assistance that increase franchisee dependence. These are provided both when the franchisor helps the franchisee establish the business and after the franchise has been established. Ongoing assistance typically includes: field supervision, merchandising and promotional materials, management and employee training, quality inspection, national advertising, centralized purchasing, market data and guidance, auditing and record keeping, management reports, and group insurance plans.

Many legal problems arise in controlling a franchise system. These legal problems are discussed in considerable detail in Chapter 6.

ADMINISTERED SYSTEMS

The final type of vertical marketing system is the administered system. **Administered vertical marketing systems** are similar to conventional marketing channels, but one of the channel members takes the initiative to lead the channel by applying the principles of effective interorganizational management. Administered systems, although not new in concept, have grown substantially since the 1960s.

Frequently, administered systems are initiated by manufacturers. As has been observed:

> *Manufacturing organizations have historically relied on administrative expertise to coordinate reseller marketing efforts. Suppliers with dominant brands have predictably experienced the least difficulty in securing strong trade support, but many manufacturers with "fringe" items have been able to elicit reseller cooperation through the use of liberal distribution policies that take the form of attractive discounts (or discount substitutes), financial assistance, and various types of concessions that protect resellers from one or more of the risks of doing business.*[24]

Exhibit 5.6 provides a list of some common concessions that manufacturers might use to obtain retailer support of their marketing programs.

Manufacturers can also develop an administered system through **pro-**

EXHIBIT 5.6

Common Concessions Manufacturers Offer to Gain Retailer Support

Price Concessions

Discount Structure	*Discount Substitutes*
Trade (functional) discounts	Display materials
Quantity discounts	Premarked merchandise
Cash discounts	Inventory control programs
Anticipation allowances	Catalogs and sales promotion literature
Free goods	Training programs
Prepaid freight	Shelf-stocking programs
New product, display, and advertising allowances (without performance requirements)	Advertising matrices
	Management consulting services
	Merchandising programs
Seasonal discounts	Sales "spiffs"
Mixed carload privilege	Technical assistance
Drop shipping privilege	Payment of sales personnel and demonstrator salaries
Trade deals	Promotional and advertising allowances (with performance requirements)

Financial Assistance

Conventional Lending Arrangements	*Extended Dating*
Term loans	E.O.M. (end of month) dating
Inventory floor plans	Seasonal dating
Notes payable financing	R.O.G. (receipt of goods) dating
Accounts payable financing	"Extra" dating
Installment financing of fixtures and equipment	Post dating
Lease and note guarantee programs	
Accounts receivable financing	

Protective Provisions

Price Protection	*Inventory Protection (cont.)*
Premarked merchandise	Reorder guarantees
"Franchise" pricing	Guaranteed support of sales events
Agency agreements	Maintenance of "spot" stocks and fast delivery
Inventory Protection	*Territorial Protection*
Consignment selling	Selective distribution
Memorandum selling	Exclusive distribution
Liberal returns allowances	
Rebate programs	

SOURCE: Bert C. McCammon, Jr., "Perspectives for Distribution Programming," in Louis P. Bucklin, ed., *Vertical Marketing Systems* (Glenview, Ill.: Scott, Foresman and Company, 1970), 36–37. Reprinted with permission of the author.

grammed merchandise agreements. These agreements have been defined as "a joint venture in which a specific retail account and a supplier develop a comprehensive merchandising plan to market the supplier's product line. These plans normally cover a six-month period but some use a longer duration."[25] Exhibit 5.7 profiles the activities covered in programmed merchandising agreements. Manufacturers that have used programmed merchandising agreements include General Electric (on major and traffic appliances), Sealy (on its Posturepedic line of mattresses), Scott (on its lawn care products), Norwalk (on its upholstered furniture), Keepsake (on diamonds), and Stanley (on hand tools).

Retailers that use this type of an agreement include Sears, Kroger, and Wal-Mart. Sears, for example, administers its relationships with almost all its suppliers. In fact, very few suppliers would have the power to administer to Sears. For example, in hard goods (appliances such as washing machines, dishwashers, and refrigerators), Sears accounts for over 25 percent of all U.S. sales. It is not surprising that Sears dominates its relationship with the manufacturers of these products.

MANAGING RETAILER/SUPPLIER RELATIONS

Retailers that are not part of a contractual system or corporate channel will probably participate in several marketing channels, since they need to acquire merchandise from many suppliers. These marketing channels will be either conventional or administered. If retailers desire to improve their performance in these channels, they must understand the principles of interorganizational management.

Interorganizational management is the management of relationships between organizational entities.[26] In a marketing channel, it involves one member, such as a retailer, managing its relationships with other organizations in the channel, such as wholesalers and manufacturers. The retailer operating in a conventional marketing channel could apply the concepts of interorganizational management to move the channel toward becoming an administered channel. The retailer that participates in an administered channel, on the other hand, needs an understanding of interorganizational management to appreciate the need for one channel member to lead and organize the channel and for all channel members to work in unison.

What are the basic concepts of interorganizational management that a retail executive needs to understand? They are dependency, power, and conflict.

DEPENDENCY

As we mentioned earlier in this chapter, all marketing systems need to perform eight marketing functions through their member institutions; none of the members can isolate itself. Retailer A is dependent on Suppliers X, Y,

EXHIBIT 5.7

Plans and Activities Covered in Programmed Merchandising Agreements

Merchandising Goals

1. Planned sales
2. Planned initial markup percentage
3. Planned reductions, including planned markdowns, shortages, and discounts
4. Planned gross margin
5. Planned expense ratio (optional)
6. Planned profit margin (optional)

Inventory Plan

1. Planned rate of inventory turnover
2. Planned merchandise assortments, including basic or model stock plans
3. Formalized "never out" lists
4. Desired mix of promotional versus regular merchandise

Merchandise Presentation Plan

1. Recommended store fixtures
2. Space allocation plan
3. Visual merchandising plan
4. Needed promotional materials, including point-of-purchase displays, consumer literature, and price signs

Personal Selling Plan

1. Recommended sales presentations
2. Sales training plan
3. Special incentive arrangements, including "spiffs," salesmen's contests, and related activities

Advertising and Sales Promotion Plan

1. Advertising and sales promotion budget
2. Media schedule
3. Copy themes for major campaigns and promotions
4. Special sales events

Responsibilities and Due Dates

1. Supplier's responsibilities in connection with the plan
2. Retailer's responsibilities in connection with the plan

SOURCE: Bert C. McCammon, Jr., "Perspectives for Distribution Programming," in Louis P. Bucklin, ed., *Vertical Marketing Systems* (Glenview, Ill.: Scott, Foresman and Company, 1970), 48–49. Reprinted with permission of the author.

and Z to make sure that goods are delivered on time and in the right quantities. Conversely, Suppliers X, Y, and Z depend on Retailer A to put a strong selling effort behind the goods, displaying the merchandise, and helping to finance consumer purchases. If Retailer A does a poor job, each supplier can be adversely affected; if even one supplier does a poor job, Retailer A can be adversely affected. In all channel alignments, each party depends on the others to do a good job.

When each party is dependent on the others, we say that they are *interdependent*. But interdependence is the root of conflict in marketing channels, and when conflict arises, someone needs to exercise power. However, before we explore the concepts of power and conflict, let us examine the concept of dependence in more detail.

Generally, the retailer's dependence on the supplier is (1) directly proportional to the retailer's motivational investment in goals that the supplier can mediate and (2) inversely proportional to the retailer's alternatives for achieving its goals outside its relationship with the supplier. This relationship can be better understood through a hypothetical example. Assume that the management of Lifestyles, a catalog showroom, is highly committed to achieving a 20 percent return on investment. Lifestyles purchases the majority of its merchandise from a single supplier, which provides a merchandise line that yields a very attractive profit margin. It is clear that this attractive margin will significantly help Lifestyles attain its goal. Further assume that Lifestyles is not able to locate any other suppliers that can supply merchandise lines with such attractive profit margins. Obviously, then, the retailer is very dependent on the supplier. To see whether you understand the concept of dependence, create a situation in which the retailer would *not* be very dependent on the supplier.

POWER

The **power** of the supplier over the retailer is its ability to affect the decision variables of the retailer.[27] The more the retailer depends on the supplier, the more power the supplier has. For example, a powerful beverage distributor could get a dependent convenience store to give its products prime shelf space and special promotional emphasis. It is a fact of life in marketing channels that the more a retailer allows itself to become dependent on a supplier, the more the supplier will be able to influence the retailer's actions.[28]

A second explanation of power is that the more sources of power A has over B, the more power A has over B.[29] In this framework, A could be either the supplier or the retailer. There are five sources of power:

1. **Reward power** is based on the ability of A to reward B.
2. **Expertise power** is based on B's perception that A has some special knowledge.

3. **Referent power** is based on the identification of B with A. B wants to be associated or identified with A.
4. **Coercive power** is based on B's belief that A has the capacity to punish or harm B if B doesn't conform to A's desire.
5. **Legitimate power** is based on A's right to influence B, or B's belief that B should accept A's influence. Legitimate power is most obvious in contractual marketing systems.

The retailer can use the concepts of dependence and power to develop strategies to equalize its power with the supplier, or even to become more powerful than the supplier. Here are some realistic examples of what the retailer might do in this regard:

1. Develop expertise power by obtaining information about consumers' needs and providing this information to suppliers.
2. Maintain multiple sources of supply in order to avoid the coercive power of any single supplier.
3. Use scarce shelf space to reward key suppliers (this is especially true today in supermarkets).
4. Establish referent power by building a market position image so that the consumer becomes more loyal to its store than to a supplier's brand.
5. Develop a strong store brand program to avoid the coercive power of national producers.
6. Band together with other retailers in order to purchase in larger quantities and employ reward power with suppliers.

Over the last decade, large retail organizations such as Kmart, Wal-Mart, and Safeway have gained substantial power over manufacturers by using methods 1 through 5 described previously. The balance of power in the channel has clearly shifted to the retailer over the last decade.

CONFLICT

Conflict between retailers and suppliers is inevitable since retailers and suppliers are interdependent.[30] For example, in Exhibit 5.8 we show the major causes of conflict or disagreement between discount stores and their vendors as identified by each. Interdependence has been identified as the root of all conflict in marketing channels; however, there is more to understanding conflict than its direct tie to interdependence. Exhibit 5.9 provides a model of the conflict process to serve as a frame of reference for the following discussion.

Interdependency and Conflict Potential. As Exhibit 5.9 shows, conflict involves several stages.[31] First, interdependence needs to exist among the retailer and supplier. Dependence on another channel member to achieve your goals results in the other member having power over you. This power can be from

EXHIBIT 5.8

Conflict Between Discount Stores and Their Vendors

Buy only on price	80%	Late deliveries	83%
Unwilling to commit early	67	Lack of communication	52
Ask for too many concessions	53	Lack of promotional support	36
Lack of communication	47	Billing disagreements	33
Special concessions	40	Frequent personnel changes	31
Slow response	20	Rapidly changing terms/allowances	31
Billing disagreements	20	Dealing with manufacturer reps	26
Unable to reach top management	20	Poor quality control	24
Buying committee	20		

Source: Debra Chanil, "Reaching Further Climbing Higher," *Discount Merchandiser* (July 1991): 23.

any of the five different sources. The fact that one channel member is dependent on another member causes the potential for conflict to enter the channel. However, more than just a potential for conflict needs to exist for a retailer and supplier to engage in conflict. Latent sources of conflict are also necessary.

Latent conflict is an underlying situation that, if left unattended, could eventually result in conflicting behavior. In the retailer/supplier dyad, there are three major sources of latent conflict: perceptual incongruity, goal incompatibility, and domain dissensus.

Perceptual incongruity occurs when the retailer and supplier have different perceptions of reality.[32] A retailer may perceive that the economy is entering a recession and therefore may want to cut inventory investments, while the supplier may perceive that the economy will remain strong and therefore may feel that inventory investments should be maintained or possibly increased. Perceptual incongruity is a major source of conflict in the marketing channel. For example, consider the following areas which the retailer and supplier might perceive differently: the quality of the supplier's merchandise, the potential demand for the supplier's merchandise, the consumer appeal of the supplier's advertising, and the best shelf position for the supplier's merchandise.

A second source of latent conflict is **goal incompatibility,** a situation in which achieving the goals of either the supplier or the retailer would hamper the performance of the other.[33] For instance, consider an apparel supplier with a sportswear line that it wants the consumer to perceive as having a status image. A high retail price would be consistent with this goal. However, the retailer might believe that its return on investment goals could be better achieved if the sportswear were heavily discounted and a higher volume could be sold. Clearly, the retailer's profit goals are not compatible with the supplier's image goals.

EXHIBIT 5.9

Conflict Process Role of Channel Interdependency

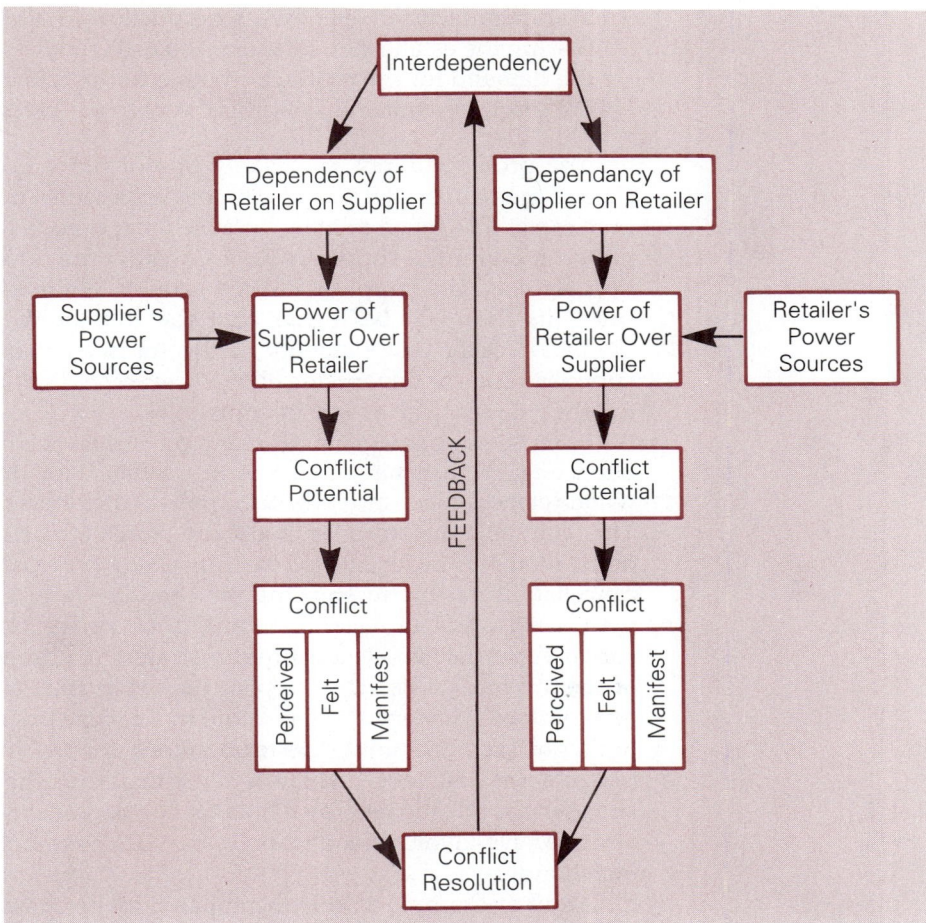

Three other examples of the retailer's goals being incompatible with the supplier's goals are:

1. The manufacturer or wholesaler enters the retail business by opening an outlet store in competition with an established retailer carrying the product line. For example, the nation's largest food wholesaler, Super Value, will occasionally open corporate-owned Cub Super Warehouse Stores. However, to minimize conflict with its existing retail grocers, it offers to franchise its Cub stores. For instance, in 1990, of the 16 Cub stores in Chicago, seven were franchised.[34]
2. The retailer seeks to gain an exclusive territory agreement, when the supplier wants to have as many retailers as possible carrying the line. In Chapter 6 we will discuss the legal issues involved in these agreements.

3. The manufacturer sells excess production to off-price or discount stores, placing the established retailer, who feels that he or she helped to develop the demand for the product, in price competition. Often this will result in the original retailer's replacing the national brand with a private label.

The problem is not necessarily one of profit goals versus image goals. Even if the retailer and supplier both have a return on investment (ROI) goal, they can still be incompatible, because what is good for the retailer's ROI may not be good for the supplier's ROI. Consider the price element in the transaction between the supplier and the retailer. If the supplier obtains a higher price, its ROI will be higher, but the ROI of the retailer will be lower. Similarly, other key elements in the transaction between the retailer and supplier—such as advertising allowances, cash discounts, order quantity, and freight charges—can result in conflict.

Because suppliers have different goals than the retailers they serve, they often engage in behavior that is in conflict with the retailer. For instance, when retailers place orders with suppliers they often give a cancellation date. This date tells the supplier that if the merchandise can't be shipped by that date, then the order should be cancelled. But many suppliers ignore the cancellation dates and ship the merchandise late. What can a gift shop do with a shipment of Valentine cards that arrives on February 15? Another common practice is the substitution of merchandise when the supplier is out of the ordered items. The supplier may substitute colors and styles that the retailer does not want. A fabric store in a college town may place an order for midnight blue and gold, the team colors, for the homecoming celebration. Imagine the retailer's dismay when unpacking the order to find that the supplier has substituted royal blue for the darker shade. Finally, retailers will often receive invoices requesting immediate payment before they receive the merchandise.

Another example of goal incompatibility occurs when an individual franchisee of a fast-food chain is concerned only with selecting the profit-maximizing location for one outlet in a geographic area, while the franchisor is concerned with maximizing its profits from a set of outlets.

A third source of latent conflict is **domain dissensus.** Domain refers to the decision variables that each member of the marketing channel feels it should be able to control. When the members of the marketing channel agree on who should make which decisions, **domain consensus** exists. When there is disagreement about who should make decisions, domain dissensus exists.

Consider the case of an automobile manufacturer and an automobile dealer. The dealer believes it should be able to make decisions regarding employees, local advertising, retail pricing, hours of operation, and remodeling and expansion. However, the manufacturer believes that it should be consulted on hours of operation and remodeling and expansion. As a consequence, there exists some domain dissensus in the auto manufacturer/auto dealer dyad.

Perceived Conflict. **Perceived conflict** is a cognitive stage. It represents the point at which either the supplier or the retailer becomes aware of one or more of the preceding sources of latent conflict. For instance, in our example of the apparel supplier that was pursuing a high-priced, quality image for its sportswear line and the retailer that was heavily discounting the brand to achieve a higher return on investment goal, perceived conflict would not occur until the supplier became aware of the retailer's pricing strategy. Note that none of the three sources of latent conflict are necessarily ever perceived. If they are not perceived, conflict will not progress beyond the latent stage.

Felt Conflict. **Felt conflict** consists of stress, tension, or hostility resulting from perceived conflict. It is the affective dimension of conflict. Not all suppliers and retailers that perceive conflict will experience felt conflict; some may have a high tolerance for perceived conflicts. They may realize that there is a basic source of conflict but feel that it isn't worth becoming upset about.

Manifest Conflict. **Manifest conflict** is the behavioral or action stage of conflict. This stage is often characterized by verbal or written threats or other actions by the supplier or retailer to block the actions of the other. Manifest conflict will not always follow felt conflict, for a variety of reasons. The supplier or retailer may experience felt conflict but determine that there is little to gain by engaging in manifest conflict. Or the retailer may experience felt conflict but also realize that the supplier has considerably more power, rendering any engagement in manifest conflict futile.

Conflict Resolution. Not all conflict in the channel is bad. Sometimes the appearance of conflict may stimulate members to improve channel efficiency. For example, a wholesaler might at first become angry toward a retailer, with whom it has had a long and satisfying relationship, when the retailer seeks to buy certain items directly from the manufacturer. This initial anger might develop into a manifest conflict situation that would destroy the relationship, or it might cause both members to put forth a better effort in the future. In this case, channel efficiency would be improved. In most instances, though, conflict reduces channel efficiency and must go through a resolution process.[35] Manifest conflict threatens the most potential harm to the retailer/supplier dyad and thus needs to be resolved as soon as possible.

There are two major conflict resolution mechanisms—*withdrawal* and *procedural resolution*.[36] In a retailer/supplier conflict, withdrawal should be viewed as a last resort. However, if the retailer and supplier fail, through all reasonable means, to resolve their conflict, then their relationship may be dissolved. In that case, each will need to seek a new channel partner.

Procedural resolution is more common than withdrawal. If the retailer and supplier are each dependent on the other and are interested in a continuing relationship, most conflicts can be resolved. There are three means of procedural resolution: reconciliation, compromise, and award.

Reconciliation is a situation in which "the value systems of . . . the parties so change that they now have common preferences in the joint field: they both want the same state of affairs or position in the joint field and so conflict is eliminated."[37] For example, in the situation discussed earlier, the retailer perceived that a recession was on the horizon and the supplier perceived continued prosperity. As a result, the retailer desired to reduce inventories and the supplier wanted to maintain or even increase inventory. Ultimately, the supplier and retailer got into a heated argument. Finally, the supplier was able to present evidence that caused the retailer to revise its perceptions and come to hold the same view as the supplier. In another situation, retailers that doubt the saleability of a new product might reconcile conflict by securing a "return clause" in order to minimize losses if the item doesn't sell.

A second form of procedural resolution is **compromise.** Compromise is the result of a situation "in which the value systems are not identical and the parties have different optimum positions in the joint field; however, each party is willing to settle for something less than his ideal position rather than continue the conflict."[38] To continue the preceding example, the supplier and retailer, after heated debate, may decide to compromise on their original positions. The retailer may decide not to cut inventory as much as it had initially planned if the supplier will finance more of the retailer's inventory investment by providing 45-day instead of 30-day payment terms. In a conflict resolved by compromise, each party relinquishes part of its initial position. In marketing channels, compromise is the most common form of conflict resolution.

Award is a settlement that is reached "because both parties have agreed to accept the verdict of an outside person or agency rather than continue the conflict."[39] An award is typically the result of a legal trial or arbitration. The courts have settled many conflicts in marketing channels, specifically between retailers and suppliers.

In addition, state and federal legislatures have passed laws to equalize the balance of power between retailers and their suppliers and thus reduce or resolve conflict. For example, when automobile dealers and manufacturers clashed over distribution and marketing policies, state and federal legislation was passed in an attempt to equalize the balance of power between them.[40] Similar legislation resulted in regulating franchisors in the 1970s.[41]

When **arbitration** is used to resolve a conflict, parties voluntarily submit their dispute to a third party whose decision will be considered final and binding.[42] Many franchise channels and administered vertical marketing systems have established formal arbitration boards.[43] These boards consist of industry representatives and are chaired by an independent arbitrator, perhaps a retired judge. This approach "provides for a third party to enter and resolve a dispute before it becomes too difficult to settle in a reasonably friendly fashion."[44] Using arbitration to resolve channel conflicts offers five advantages:

1. *Arbitration is fast.* The parties to a dispute can be quickly informed that a quarrel exists and told the time of a hearing; the evidence can then be heard by a panel and the decision rendered within a few weeks.
2. *Arbitration preserves secrecy.* Outside parties can be banned from the hearings. Decisions that are not matters of public record can be kept secret.
3. *Arbitration is less expensive than litigation,* reducing the cost of a tolerable decision.
4. *Arbitration confronts problems in their incipient stage,* when they are easier to solve. The attitude is, "We have a potential problem here; let's solve it before positions and options get too fixed."
5. *Arbitration often takes place before industry experts.* The arbitrator panel is composed of those who know an industry and its practices. Some argue that this produces a fairer decision than the courts.[45]

Feedback. If you refer to Exhibit 5.9, you will notice that conflict doesn't end with resolution. After the conflict has been resolved, there will be feedback. In other words, the outcome of the conflict will affect the future balance of dependence between the channel members. It will also result in a change in the power each member has over the other. How satisfactory the resolution was to the parties, and what they learned about each other during the entire conflict process, will influence their future behavior toward each other. Also, a retailer's conflict with one supplier may provide useful information about how to handle similar conflicts with other suppliers.[46]

SUMMARY

The system must be viewed as the solution. If the retailer ignores the marketing system in order to maximize short-run profits, then in the long run the system will forget about the retailer. And if the system forgets the retailer, then profits sufficient for survival and growth will vanish.

In learning to work within the marketing system, the retailer needs to recognize the eight marketing functions necessary in all marketing systems: buying, selling, storing, transporting, sorting, financing, information gathering, and risk taking. The retailer can seldom perform all these functions and therefore must rely on other primary and facilitating institutions in the marketing system. Although the marketing functions are pervasive, they can be shifted or divided among the institutions in the marketing system.

The institutions in the marketing system can be arranged into two primary marketing channel patterns—conventional and vertical. A conventional marketing channel is one in which each member of the channel is loosely aligned with the others, each member recognizing those it directly interacts with but ignoring all others. Conventional marketing channels are on the decline in the United States and vertical marketing systems are becoming dominant. In the vertical marketing system, all parties to the channel recognize each other and one party programs the channel to achieve technological, managerial, and promotional economies. Three types of vertical marketing systems are corporate, contractual, and administered.

The retailer, in order to operate efficiently and effectively in any marketing channel, needs to understand the basics of interorganizational behavior. Key concepts that need to be understood are dependence, power, and conflict. By understanding these concepts, the retailer can learn to interact productively with other marketing channel members.

We paid particular attention to conflict in the marketing channel. It was pointed out that the root of all conflict is interdependence between the retailer and its channel partners. Conflict progresses through four stages—latent, perceived, felt, and manifest. Once conflict becomes manifest, it needs to be resolved and can be resolved either by withdrawal from the channel relationship or by one of four procedures—reconciliation, compromise, award, or arbitration.

QUESTIONS FOR DISCUSSION

1. In this chapter we stated that Kmart's marketing channels are in competition with those of Target and Wal-Mart. Would this be the case if both Kmart and Target bought from some of the same suppliers? For example, assume both buy calculators from Texas Instruments.
2. Facilitating marketing institutions are powerless in the marketing channel. Agree or disagree and explain your reasoning.
3. How might a small local chain of five grocery stores increase its power in the marketing channel?
4. Can a retailer lead the marketing channel?
5. During economic recession, conflict in the marketing channel is likely to increase. Agree or disagree and explain why.
6. Using the return on investment model (Exhibit 2.3a) as a frame of reference, show how certain components of the model help explain conflict between retailers and their suppliers.
7. What are the marketing functions performed in a marketing channel?
8. Define and give an example of the three sources of latent conflict.
9. How do wholesaler-sponsored voluntary groups benefit independent retailers?
10. What are the advantages of the franchise form of distribution/marketing to the franchisor and franchisee?
11. What are the advantages of using arbitration to resolve conflict in the marketing channel?
12. What are some of the factors that complicate the study of marketing channels?
13. What is a vertical marketing system?
14. What is the primary difference between a conventional marketing channel and a vertical marketing system?
15. How does sorting overcome the problems inherent in heterogeneous supply and demand?
16. Why would a manufacturer elect to use multiple channels of distribution for the same product?
17. Describe the complex relationship between power and conflict.
18. Define the five sources of power that can be used in a marketing channel.

MANAGEMENT MEMO

You hold the position of treasurer/controller for a manufacturer of swimwear and beachwear with annual sales of $3.8 million. Your firm has regularly sold a large national department store chain $120,000 to $160,000 annually in swimsuits. Merchandise is typically sold on terms of 3/10 EOM net 60 (3 percent cash discount if payment is received 10 days after the end of month or full payment due in 60 days). Payment by the chain was always prompt, but in mid-1990 payments began to be late due to its faltering financial condition and $4.5 billion debt servicing load. Write a memo to the president of your firm, Sandra Hollander, outlining any suggested changes in credit policy or actions to be taken.

BOARDROOM REPORT

Your role is director of distribution for a regional chain of 27 supermarkets operating in five cities in the southwest region of the United States. Annual volume of the chain is $350 million. Procter & Gamble has approached your firm about a program to improve your inventory turnover of their products by 10 to 20 percent. This improved productivity will be accomplished by an electronic data interchange (EDI) system. The firm would electronically send to P & G daily information on sales, and P & G would replenish merchandise based on an agreed retail inventory level. In addition, the firm would be expected to pay its bills to P & G electronically. You are very excited about this proposal because it will improve distribution efficiency and thus profits for the organization. Unfortunately, the director of information systems and the vice-president of finance are opposed to this program with P & G, because they believe sales data should be kept confidential. The president of the firm, Tom Boyt, has asked you to develop a policy statement that would address not only the P & G proposal, but proposals from other suppliers that are likely to occur in the near future. You have five minutes for a presentation at the next board of directors meeting. Prepare a presentation.

SUGGESTED READINGS

Carney, Mick, and Eric Gedajlovic. "Vertical Integration In Franchise Systems: Agency Theory and Resource Explanations." *Strategic Management Journal* (November 1991): 607-29.

Gaski, John. "The Theory of Power and Conflict in Channels of Distribution." *Journal of Marketing* (Summer 1984): 9-29.

Greenland, Steven J., and Peter J. McGoldrick. "From Mail Order to Home Shopping—Revitalising the Non-Store Channel." *Journal of Marketing Channels* no. 1 (1991): 59-85.

Hunt, Shelby D., Nina M. Ray, and Van R. Wood. "Behavioral Dimensions of Channels of Distribution: Review and Synthesis." *Journal of the Academy of Marketing Science* (Summer 1985): 1-24.

Kaufman, Patrick J., and V. Kasturi Rangan. "A Model for Managing System Conflict During Franchise Expansion." *Journal of Retailing* (Summer 1990): 155-73.

"Kmart's Got Flow." *Discount Merchandising* (May 1992): 42-45.

ENDNOTES

1. "Do Drug Makers Give Mail Order Houses a Special Deal?" *New York Times,* (5 November 1989) sec. 3, p. 17.
2. For a more detailed discussion of marketing functions, consult Franklin W. Ryan, "Functional Elements of Market Distribution," *Harvard Business Review* (January 1935): 205-21) and Edmund D. McGary, "Some Functions of Marketing Reconsidered," in Reavis Cox and Wroe Alderson, eds., *Theory in Marketing* (Homewood, Ill.: Richard D. Irwin, 1950), 263-79.
3. "Tuesday Morning Sells 185 Mornings," *Chain Store Age Executive* (April 1991): 26-28. "If There's Anything Left to Buy, It's Tuesday Morning or Christmas Eve." *Wall Street Journal* (23 December 1991): B1, B4.
4. For a further discussion of off-price retailers, see "$1 Store Fills the Bill," *Advertising Age,* 16 December 1991, 26.
5. Alderson was one of the first to discuss the sorting function in detail. See Wroe Alderson, *Marketing Behavior and Executive Action* (Homewood, Ill.: Richard D. Irwin, 1957). Some current authors use the term *standardization and grading* instead of sorting. For example, see E. Jerome McCarthy and William D. Perreault, *Basic Marketing,* 9th ed. (Homewood, Ill.: Richard D. Irwin, 1987), 18 and William F. Schoell and Joseph P. Guiltinan, *Marketing,* 3d ed. (Boston: Allyn and Bacon, 1988), 9.
6. "Sniffing Trouble on Seventh Avenue," *Business Week,* 26 August 1991, 52.
7. U.S. Bureau of the Census, *Statistical Abstract of the United States: 1991,* 111th ed. (Washington, D.C.: Government Printing Office, 1991).
8. "Wal-Mart Set to Eliminate Reps, Brokers," *Wall Street Journal,* 2 December 1991, A3 and "Independent Sales Reps Are Squeezed by the Recession," *Wall Street Journal,* 27 December 1991, B2. "Cutting Out the Middleman," *Forbes* (6 January 1992): 169.
9. Bert C. McCammon, Jr., Alton F. Doody, and William R. Davidson, "Emerging Patterns of

Distribution" (Paper presented at the annual meeting of the National Association of Wholesalers, Las Vegas, January 15, 1969). Reprinted in Bruce J. Walker and Joel B. Haynes, eds., *Marketing Channels and Institutions: Selected Readings,* 2d ed. (Columbus, Ohio: Grid, 1978), 195.

10. "Chrysler to Acquire Dollar Rent A Car, Eyeing Broader Market in Rental Sector," *Wall Street Journal,* 27 June 1990, A4.
11. "Thriving Factory Outlets Anger Retailers as Store Suppliers Turn into Competitors," *Wall Street Journal,* 8 October 1991, B1, B6.
12. "How Managers Can Succeed Through Speed," *Fortune,* 13 February 1989, 54-59.
13. Anthony Baldo, "Food Fight," *Financial World,* 8 January 1991, 40-41.
14. "Wakefern: A Co-op That Works," *Progressive Grocer* (October 1991): 27-31.
15. Louis W. Stern and Adel I. El-Ansary, *Marketing Channels,* 3d ed. (Englewood Cliffs, N.J.: Prentice-Hall, Inc., 1988), 331 and Steve Weinstein, "Climate for Co-ops: Partly Cloudy," *Progressive Grocer* (November 1991): 43-46.
16. This section is based on information obtained from the U.S. Department of Commerce, *Franchise Opportunities Handbook* (Washington, D.C.: Government Printing Office, 1988), xxix.
17. "Medicine Shoppe Has the Rx for Success," *Chain Store Age Executive* (April 1991): 23-24.
18. For additional discussion of the increasing diversity of franchises, see Bruce J. Walker, "Retail Franchising in the 1990s," *Retailing Issues Letter* (January 1991): 2-3.
19. "New Owners of Franchises Belie Mom-and-Pop Image," *Wall Street Journal,* 29 August 1988, 13.
20. Bert Rosenbloom, *Marketing Channels,* 3d ed. (Hinsdale, Ill.: Dryden Press, 1983), 374-76.
21. Ronald Stephenson and Robert G. House, "A Perspective on Franchising," *Business Horizons* (August 1971): 35-42.
22. Better Business Bureau, *Facts on Selecting a Franchise,* 1975 and International Franchise Association, *Answers to the Twenty-One Most Commonly Asked Questions About Franchising,* 5.
23. Stephenson and House, "Perspective on Franchising," 38.
24. Bert C. McCammon, Jr., "Perspectives for Distribution Programming," in Louis P. Bucklin, ed., *Vertical Marketing Systems* (Glenview, Ill.: Scott, Foresman, 1970), 45. Reprinted with permission of the author.
25. McCammon, 48.
26. Several recent examples of literature in this area include: Robert A. Robicheaux, Jule Gassenheimer, and Jay U. Sterling, "Power Source Elasticity: An Assessment of the Differential Effects of Supplier Role Performance on Dealers' Attributed Power, Satisfaction and Future Purchase Intentions," in William Bearden et al., eds., *Enhancing Knowledge Development in Marketing* (Chicago: American Marketing Association 1990), 262; Rajiv P. Dant and Patrick Schul, "Evaluating Relational Exchange Norms in Channels of Distribution," in William Bearden et al., eds., *Enhancing Knowledge Development in Marketing* (Chicago: American Marketing Association 1990), 251; Retha Price, "Channel Leadership Behavior: A Framework for Improving Channel Leadership Effectiveness," *Journal of Marketing Channels* no. 1 (1991): 87-112; and Retha Price, "An Investigation of Path-Goal Leadership Theory in Marketing Channels," *Journal of Retailing* (Fall 1991): 339-61.
27. James R. Brown, Robert F. Lusch, and Darrel D. Muehling, "Conflict and Power-Dependence Relations in Retailer-Supplier Channels," *Journal of Retailing* (Winter 1983): 54.
28. For a more detailed discussion of the power/dependence relationship, see Steven J. Skinner and Joseph P. Guiltinan, "Perceptions of Channel Control," *Journal of Retailing* (Winter 1985): 65-88 and M. Christine Lewis and Douglas M. Lambert, "A Model of Channel Member Performance, Dependence, and Satisfaction," *Journal of Retailing* (Summer 1991): 205-25.
29. J. R. P. French and Bertram Raven, "The Bases of Social Power," in Darwin Cartwright and Alvin Zoner, eds., *Group Dynamics: Research and Theory* (New York: Harper and Row, 1968).
30. For an investigation of conflict across channels rather than within a particular channel, see John Robbins, Thomas Speh, and Morris Mayer, "Retailers' Perceptions of Channel Conflict Issues," *Journal of Retailing* (Winter 1982): 46-67.
31. This process model of conflict relies heavily on Louis R. Pondy, "Organizational Conflict Concepts and Models," *Administrative Science Quarterly* (September 1967): 328-41.
32. Perceptual incongruity is identified as a source of conflict in Morton Deutsch, *The Resolution of Conflict* (New Haven: Yale University Press, 1973), 16; Joseph A. Litterer, "Conflict in Organizations: A Re-Examination," *Academy of Management Journal* (September 1960): 183; and Louis

W. Stern and James L. Heskett, "Conflict Management in Interorganizational Relations: A Conceptual Framework," in Louis W. Stern, ed., *Distribution Channels: Behavioral Dimensions* (Boston: Houghton Mifflin Co., 1969), 294.
33. Goal incompatibility is identified as a source of conflict in Stuart M. Schmidt and Thomas A. Kochon, "Conflict: Toward Conceptual Clarity," *Administrative Science Quarterly,* (September 1972): 359-70; Bertram H. Raven and H. T. Eachus, "Cooperation and Competition in Means-Interdependent Triads," *Journal of Abnormal and Social Psychology* (1963): 307-16; and Stern and Heskett, "Conflict Management in Interorganization Relations," 294.
34. "Retailing: A Wholesale Dilemma," *Progressive Grocer* (November 1990): 35-40.
35. Bert Rosenbloom, "Conflict and Channel Efficiency: Some Conceptual Models for the Decision Maker," *Journal of Marketing* (July 1973).
36. Kenneth E. Boulding, *Conflict and Defense* (New York: Harper and Brothers, 1962).
37. Boulding, 310.
38. Boulding, 310.
39. Boulding, 310.
40. Stuart Macaulay, *Law and the Balance of Power* (New York: Russell Sage Foundation, 1966).
41. Shelby D. Hunt and John R. Nevin, "Tying Agreements in Franchising," *Journal of Marketing* (July 1975): 24-25; Shelby D. Hunt and John R. Nevin, "Full Disclosure Laws in Franchising," *Journal of Marketing* (April 1976): 53-62; and James T. Haverson, "What's in Store at the Federal Trade Commission," *Franchising and Antitrust* (Washington, D.C.: International Franchise Association, 1975), 20-29.
42. Stern and El-Ansary, *Marketing Channels,* 296.
43. Robert F. Weigand and Hilda C. Wasson, "Arbitration in the Marketing Channel," *Business Horizons* (October 1974): 39-47.
44. Weigand and Wasson, 39.
45. Weigand and Wasson, 39.
46. For a discussion of how members' satisfaction is related to the channel's climate, see Patrick L. Schul, Taylor E. Little, Jr., and William M. Pride, "Channel Climate: Its Impact on Channel Satisfaction," *Journal of Retailing* (Summer 1985): 9-38.

CHAPTER 6

UNDERSTANDING THE LEGAL ENVIRONMENT

OVERVIEW

In this chapter we discuss the legal aspects of decisions about pricing, promotion, products or merchandise, marketing channels, and mergers and acquisitions. Our major emphasis is on federal laws since state and local laws vary greatly. You may find it useful to refer to this chapter again when analyzing the various alternatives available to the retail marketing decision maker.

UNDERSTANDING THE LEGAL ENVIRONMENT

I. Pricing Constraints
   A. Horizontal Price Fixing
   B. Vertical Price Fixing
   C. Price Discrimination
      1. Legal Definitions of Price Discrimination
      2. Retailer's Defenses of Price Discrimination
      3. Discrimination in Services
      4. Synthetic Brokerages
   D. Deceptive Pricing
   E. Predatory Pricing
II. Promotion Constraints
   A. Deceitful Diversion of Patronage
   B. Deceptive Advertising
   C. Bait-and-Switch Advertising

        D. Deceptive Sales Practices
        E. Substantiation and Retraction
  III. Product Constraints
        A. Patents
        B. Product Safety
        C. Product Liability
        D. Warranties
  IV. Channel Constraints
        A. Territorial Restrictions
        B. Dual Distribution
        C. Diverting
        D. Exclusive Dealing
        E. Tying Agreements
        F. Franchise Constraints
  V. Mergers and Acquisitions
  VI. Other Federal Laws
  VII. State and Local Laws
  VIII. Summary

We have pointed out in earlier chapters (see Exhibit 1.4, page 15, and Exhibit 3.1, page 72) that the retailer is influenced by several uncontrollable external forces in the retail marketplace. In the past three chapters we have looked at the consumer, competition, and the channel. We will now explore the last of these marketplace forces that have an impact on retail decisions—the legal system. Consider the impact of a city ordinance making it impossible for a certain national pizza chain offering a 30-minute delivery guarantee to operate in the city on the basis of traffic safety,[1] or the impact of state laws that restrict retailers to conduct only one yearly promotional game of chance. What about state "blue laws" that affect the retailer's ability to operate seven days a week? What about those cities that have "sign ordinances" regulating the retailer's use of colors on billboards and even the sign on the retailer's building?[2] What about state regulations restricting the retailer's use of product samples or determining the standards to be used when a retailer advertises a "sale?"[3] Finally, should out-of-state mail-order houses be allowed to omit sales tax, and in effect offer lower prices, when competing with local retailers?[4] All these laws could influence the ability of the retailer to serve the needs of its target market.

    Retailers cannot freely make decisions without regard for the laws society has established to regulate business trade. The legal environment consists of those federal, state, and local laws that limit the retailer's flexibility and freedom in making business-related decisions.

    The dynamic nature of retailing requires that it, like the other sectors, be monitored. Most large retailers maintain legal departments and lobbyists to keep abreast of, interpret, and even influence government regulations. Such activities are usually beyond the resources of small businesses; however, the government and the press do a reasonably good job of keeping businesses informed of pending and new legislation. In addition, retailer associations in most states keep retailers abreast of proposed changes in state laws and attempt to protect the retailers' interests.

Since local and state laws are quite varied, the emphasis of this chapter will be on federal legislation and its impact on retailers' actions. We will comment on some state and local laws, but will, for the most part, leave it up to you to investigate the impact of state and local laws on retail activities in your state and community.

Exhibit 6.1 shows the various constraints that can affect the retailer's decision-making process with regard to pricing, promotion, products, channel relationships, and mergers and acquisitions. Exhibit 6.2 lists the dozen federal laws that have the greatest impact on a retailer's decision-making ability.

PRICING CONSTRAINTS

Retailers continually have to establish prices for the many items they carry. In doing this, they have considerable, but not total, flexibility. The major constraining factors on pricing are summarized in Exhibit 6.3.

EXHIBIT 6.1

Constraints Influencing the Retail Decision Maker

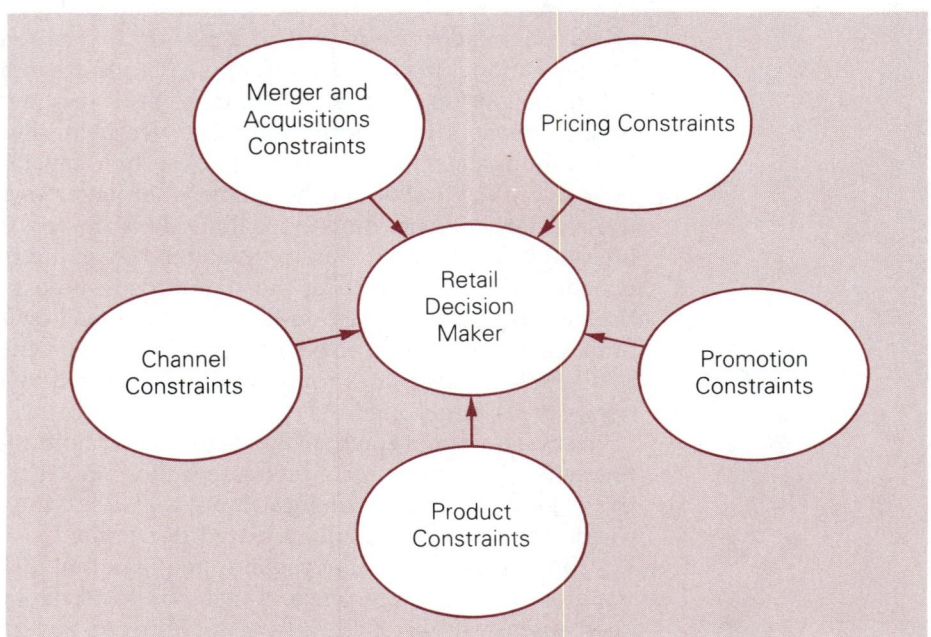

EXHIBIT 6.2

Federal Legislation Affecting Retailing

Sherman Antitrust Act (1890)

Bans (1) "monopolies or attempts to monopolize" and (2) "contracts, combinations, or conspiracies in restraint of trade" in interstate and foreign commerce.

Federal Trade Commission Act (1914)

Establishes the Federal Trade Commission, a body of specialists with broad powers to investigate and to issue cease-and-desist orders to enforce Section 5, which declares that "unfair methods of competition in commerce are unlawful."

Clayton Act (1914)

Adds to the Sherman Act by prohibiting specific practices (e.g., certain types of price discrimination, tying clauses) "where the effect . . . may be to substantially lessen competition or tend to create a monopoly in any line of commerce."

Robinson-Patman Act (1936)

Amends the Clayton Act. Adds the phrase "to injure, destroy, or prevent competition." Defines price discrimination as unlawful (subject to certain defenses) and provides the FTC with the right to establish limits on quantity discounts, to forbid brokerage allowances except to independent brokers, and to ban promotional allowances or the furnishing of services or facilities except where made available to all "on proportionately equal terms."

Wheeler-Lea Act (1938)

Prohibits unfair and deceptive acts and practices regardless of whether competition is injured.

Antimerger Act (1950)

Amends Section 7 of the Clayton Act by broadening the power to prevent intercorporate acquisitions where the acquisition may have a substantially adverse effect on competition.

Automobile Information Disclosure Act (1958)

Prohibits car dealers from inflating the factory price of new cars.

Fair Packaging and Labelling Act (1966)

Makes provision for the regulation of the packaging and labeling of consumer goods. Permits industries' voluntary adoption of uniform packaging standards.

Truth-in-Lending Act (1968)

Requires lenders to state the true costs of a credit transaction. Established a National Commission on Consumer Finance.

EXHIBIT 6.2
(continued)

Magnuson-Moss Warranty/FTC Improvement Act (1975)

Empowers the FTC to determine rules concerning consumer warranties and provides for consumer access to means of redress, such as the "class action" suit. Expands FTC regulatory powers over unfair or deceptive acts or practices.

Equal Credit Opportunity Act (1975)

Prohibits discrimination in credit transactions because of sex, marital status, race, national origin, religion, age, or receipt of public assistance.

Fair Debt Collection Practice Act (1978)

It is illegal to harass or abuse any person and make false statements or use unfair methods when collecting a debt.

HORIZONTAL PRICE FIXING

Horizontal price fixing occurs when a group of competing retailers establishes a fixed price at which to sell their merchandise. For example, all retail grocers in a particular trade area may agree to sell eggs at 94 cents per dozen. Regardless of its actual or potential impact on competition or the consumer, this price fixing violates Section 1 of the Sherman Antitrust Act (1890), which states, "Every contract, combination in the form of trust or otherwise, or conspiracy, in restraint of trade or commerce among the several states, or with foreign nations is declared to be illegal."[5]

It is also illegal for retailers to reach agreements with one another regarding the use of double (or triple) coupons, rebates, or other means of reducing price competition in the marketplace.

Since passage of the Sherman Act, the courts have viewed horizontal price fixing as a restraint of trade. Occasionally, retailers have argued that the Sherman Act does not apply to them, since they operate locally, not "among the several states"—the definition of **interstate commerce.** However, because the merchandise retailer's purchase typically originates in another state, the courts view retailers as involved in interstate commerce even if all their customers are local. Also, most states have laws similar to the Sherman Act, prohibiting such restraints of trade as horizontal price fixing on a strictly local level.

VERTICAL PRICE FIXING

Vertical price fixing occurs when a retailer collaborates with the manufacturer or wholesaler to resell an item at an agreed-on price. This is often referred to as **resale price maintenance** or **fair trade.** Such agreements are illegal.[6] Resale price maintenance does not mean that manufacturers cannot suggest to retailers a price at which they would like to see an item sold. But they cannot establish with the retailers a price for resale, nor can they legally threaten

Chapter 6 Understanding the Legal Environment

EXHIBIT 6.3

Pricing Constraints

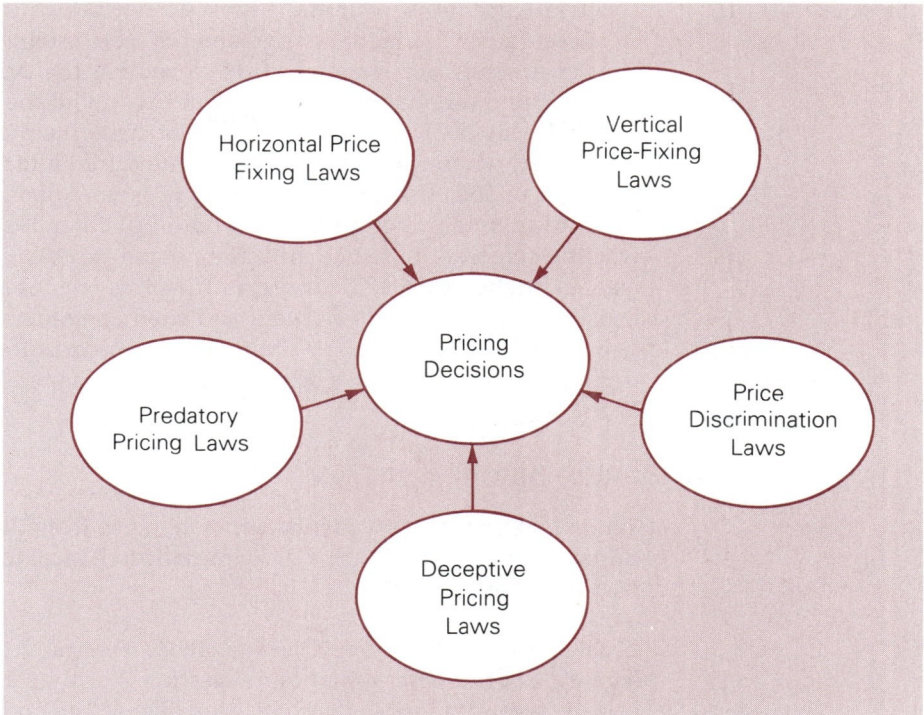

ILLUSTRATION 6.1

Gas stations respond almost instantly to each others' pricing, prompting questions as to whether the market is illegally maintaining prices.

retailers with supply cutoffs if they do not sell at the recommended price.

Resale price maintenance agreements were established during the depression as a means for small retailers to combat the price advantages of chain stores. They were banned by President Ford, with the consent of Congress, in 1976. In May 1988, however, the use of price maintenance was again made quasi-legal when the Supreme Court ruled that a manufacturer's decision to cut off a retailer that is discounting prices isn't illegal, unless it involves an effort to fix retail prices. Since it would be difficult to prove that price fixing was the sole intent of such an action, some experts think that the ruling will lead to higher prices.[7] It appears that this matter will only be settled by legislative action, as discounters and their customers seek congressional aid in preventing a return to fair trade. Now some manufacturers and retailers are urging that fair trade laws be enacted again as a means to combat the inroads of the discounters.[8]

PRICE DISCRIMINATION

When two retailers buy identical merchandise from the same supplier but pay different prices, that is **price discrimination.** Not all forms of price discrimination are illegal.

Legal Definitions of Price Discrimination. Federal legislation addressed the legality of price discrimination in Section 2 of the Clayton Act, which made certain forms of price discrimination illegal.[9] Section 2 was amended and strengthened with passage of the Robinson-Patman Act in 1936.[10] This act had two primary objectives:

1. To prevent suppliers from gaining unfair advantage over their competitors by discriminating among buyers either in setting prices or in providing allowances or services.[11]
2. To prevent buyers from using their economic power to get discriminatory prices from suppliers so as to gain an advantage over their own competitors.

The Robinson-Patman Act, like fair trade laws, grew out of the struggle of small independent retailers to compete with chain store retailers during the 1930s. During this time many small grocers, druggists, and other retailers were quite vocal in complaining to their senators and representatives about how suppliers frequently discriminated in price among different customers. It was quite disheartening to these small retailers that suppliers would often charge chain stores even less than they did the wholesalers that sold to the small, independent retailer. Times have changed, however, and the small, mom-and-pop grocer or druggist is now almost nonexistent. In its place are a large number of well-organized chain store organizations that aggressively compete for market share and large groups of independent retailers that have banded together in cooperatives to be able to have the purchasing economies of the large chain store organizations. Some scholars have thus argued that the Robinson-Patman Act should be repealed,[12] and FTC enforcement of the act is at a minimum.

For the retail manager, Section 2 of the Robinson-Patman Act (actually Section 2 of the amended Clayton Act) is the most important. Section 2(a) of the statute provides:

That it shall be unlawful for any person engaged in commerce . . . to discriminate in price between different purchasers of commodities of like grade and quality . . . where the effect of such discrimination may be substantially to lessen competition or tend to create a monopoly in any line of commerce, or to injure, destroy, or prevent competition with any person who either grants or knowingly receives the benefit of such discrimination, or with customers of either of them. . . .

The retailer should recognize three things regarding this section of the act. First, the transaction must occur in interstate commerce, which the courts see as being almost universal, since customers can come from anywhere. Second, the actual competition does not have to be lessened; only a potential lessening of competition must exist. Third, the retailer that knowingly receives the benefit of discrimination is just as culpable as the supplier granting the discrimination. Thus, retailers should not coerce their suppliers into giving them discriminatory discounts that would put them at an advantage over their competitors. However, this does not mean that retailers can't negotiate the best deal possible; in most instances, retailers don't know what the best deal possible is.

Considerable attention has been given by the courts, as well as retailers and manufacturers, to the phrase "commodities of like grade and quality." What does this phrase mean? Commodities are goods and not services. This implies that discriminatory pricing practices in the sale of services, such as advertising space or the leasing of real estate, are not prohibited by the act. For example, shopping center developers frequently charge varying rates for equal square footage depending on the tenant and the type of merchandise sold. In a case brought by Plum Tree, Inc. (a franchisor of a nationwide chain of retail shops), against the N.K. Winston Corporation (a shopping center developer), Plum Tree charged the developer with price discrimination under the Robinson-Patman Act for charging different rents for equal space. Plum Tree contended that the commodities under the act are equivalent to leaseholds in shopping centers and that a landlord must charge equal rent for equal space. The court held that a lease for real property is not "selling goods, wares, or merchandise."[13]

"Like grade and quality" has been interpreted by the courts to mean of identical physical and chemical properties. This implies that different prices cannot be justified merely because the labels on the product are different. Therefore, private labeling of merchandise does not make it different from identical goods carrying the seller's brand. However, if the seller can establish that an actual physical difference in grade and quality exists, then a price differential can be justified.

Retailer's Defenses of Price Discrimination. The illegality of price discrimination is not clear cut. A variety of defenses are available to buyers and sellers charged with price discrimination. The principal defenses are:

1. A *cost justification* defense, which attempts to show that a differential can be accounted for on the basis of differences in cost to the seller in manufacture, sale, or delivery arising from differences in the method or quantities involved.
2. A *changing market conditions* defense, which attempts to justify the price differential on the basis of danger of imminent deterioration of perishable goods or on the obsolescence of seasonal goods.
3. An argument based on *meeting competition* in good faith. The seller attempts to show that its lower price to a purchaser was made in good faith to meet an equally low price of a competitor provided that this matched price actually existed and was lawful in itself.

Therefore, it is legally possible that one retailer, a large warehouse club purchasing 10,000 cases, for example, might have a lower cost per case than a smaller retailer purchasing only 15 cases. However, the retailer that knowingly receives a discriminatory price from a seller (assuming the goods are of like grade and quality) should be relatively certain that the seller is granting a defensible discrimination based on any of the three preceding criteria.

The cost justification defense is extremely difficult to use because the courts have never defined exactly how costs should be computed. The two most common defenses are changing market conditions and meeting competition in good faith. The courts ruled against a unique interpretation of the good-faith defense by Folger Coffee. The courts found that since Folger allowed retailers partial price reductions for coffee held by retailers in inventory and extended its discounts beyond the time period that its competitors provided discounted prices, it had negated its good-faith argument.[14]

The Supreme Court has recently expanded the protection afforded sellers charging different prices to competing retailers, whether the retailers bought directly from the manufacturer or used a wholesaler, under the meeting competition defense. The case involved a manufacturer, Falls City Brewery, selling beer to wholesalers in Indiana and its neighboring state, Kentucky. Indiana law bans Indiana wholesalers from both buying and/or selling beer to out-of-state businesses and requires brewers to charge the same price throughout the state. Therefore, Falls City was entitled to sell beer at a lower price to Kentucky wholesalers, in order to meet competition, than it was charging wholesalers in Evansville, Indiana (a city on the Ohio River across from Kentucky).[15] This action hurt Indiana wholesalers and retailers as many Indiana consumers were able to cross the river and purchase Falls City beer at a lower price.

Discrimination in Services. Sellers are not only prohibited from discriminating through price, they are also banned from providing different services and payments to different retailers. These services and payments frequently include advertising allowances, displays and banners to promote the goods, in-store demonstrations, and the distribution of samples or premiums. Sections 2(d) and 2(e) of the Robinson-Patman Act deal specifically with these practices and state that such services and payments or consideration must be made available on *proportionately equal terms* to all *competing customers*. Retailers have brought many more enforcement actions under these two sections than under Section 2(a).

Two questions arise in interpreting these sections: (1) Who are competing customers? and (2) What is proportionately equal? Let us illustrate some of the technical difficulties in answering these questions.

A manufacturer of household cleaning detergents is providing a large supermarket chain with an advertising allowance of $2.50 per case purchased. The supermarket chain buys directly from the manufacturer. A small grocer that operates a single store in the ghetto of a large city also sells detergent produced by this manufacturer but is offered no allowance. This small grocer purchases all its merchandise through a local wholesaler and is six miles from the nearest store operated by the large supermarket chain. In reviewing this situation, the courts are most likely to be concerned with whether the small grocer and the chain store supermarket are competing customers.

It could be argued that the small grocer and chain grocer are not both customers of the detergent manufacturer, since the small grocer is, strictly speaking, a customer of a wholesaler. Courts have generally not accepted this argument. Competing customers has been held to *include* those buying for resale from a seller's customer, such as a wholesaler.[16] Another argument that might be presented is that the small grocer and chain grocer do not compete for the same customers. Expert witnesses may testify that consumers typically do not travel more than two to four miles to purchase groceries—especially in an urban environment. Since the two stores are separated by six miles, they could hardly be viewed as competitors. This argument, if carefully constructed and supported by empirical evidence and expert testimony, might be considered plausible by the courts.

Let us now try to illustrate some of the ambiguity of the concept of proportionately equal terms. Assume that a cosmetics manufacturer offers a department store in Chicago a cosmetics demonstrator for one eight-hour day per month. A small drugstore in Chicago also handles this line of cosmetics but sells only one-eighth as much as the department store. The manufacturer believes that it would be impractical to furnish the drugstore a cosmetics demonstrator for one hour per month (a proportionately equal allowance). The drugstore retailer would also probably feel that this would be impractical. However, this does not relieve the manufacturer of its duty to the drugstore retailer to offer *proportionate* promotional service. The service need not be the same. A substitute could be offering a demonstration kit to the drugstore retailer, as long as both agreed this was adequate.

The same problem arises quite frequently in regard to advertising allowances offered retailers. A large appliance manufacturer may offer retailers an advertising allowance to be applied against any television advertising they engage in. This is unfair to the very small appliance retailer, because it cannot afford to advertise on television even if the manufacturer picks up part of the cost. The small retailer has the right to some alternative promotional allowance (perhaps an allowance to be applied to advertising in the newspaper or to be used for window displays or banners). In a similar case, the FTC found that General Motors was unfair to smaller car-rental companies when it supplied millions of advertising dollars to National Car Rental and Avis Rent-A-Car, but little or no money to smaller firms. The judge ruled that GM must advertise the availability of any future ad-support programs in specified publications and offer ad dollars to all interested rental and leasing firms on equal terms.[17]

Synthetic Brokerages. Another aspect of the Robinson-Patman Act with which the retailer needs to be acquainted is Section 2(c). This important section prohibits the development of synthetic brokerages or any type of dummy brokerage payment; that is, any commission or allowance to a person directly or indirectly controlled by the buyer is prohibited. For example, suppose a retailer creates a synthetic brokerage company through which to place its orders. The manufacturer would be instructed by the synthetic broker to ship the goods directly to the retailer and bill the retailer directly. The manufacturer would then remit to the broker a commission that would, in reality, end up in the hands of the retailer. Thus, the effective price that the retailer is paying for the goods is lower than the price competing retailers that transact their business through legitimate brokers are paying. Arrangements involving synthetic brokers are a form of price discrimination and have been treated as violations of the Robinson-Patman Act.

In summary, the Robinson-Patman Act makes it illegal to discriminate in the price of a product in interstate commerce (to sell goods of like grade and quality, but not services, to two nonretail buyers at different prices) if it has the potential to lessen, injure, destroy, or prevent competition or create a monopoly (only the potential of a lessening, not an actual lessening, at any level in the channel is needed). The three defenses for charging different prices are: (1) the seller can show that a cost saving was realized from selling to a particular customer (often difficult to define); (2) the price differential was caused by normal market/price fluctuations (an important defense); and (3) the seller simply matched the equally low price of a competitor (retailers can be found guilty if they provide false information to the vendor).

DECEPTIVE PRICING

Retailers should avoid using a misleading price to lure customers into the store. Advertising goods at a "sale price" or at a discount from "regular price" when the retailer never intended to sell at that regular price, advertising at a price below what the retailer is actually willing to take, or advertising at an artificially low price and then adding hidden charges are deceptive pricing practices that are all unfair methods of competition. The Wheeler-Lea Amendment (1938) of the Federal Trade Commission Act (1914) made illegal all "unfair or deceptive acts in commerce." Not only is the retailer's customer being unfairly treated when the retailer uses deceptive pricing, but the retailer's competitors are potentially being harmed because some of their customers may be deceitfully diverted.

The issue of when a "sale" is really a "sale" has long been a problem for regulators. The FTC's current guidelines, which date from 1964, require that goods be offered for sale at regular prices "for a reasonably substantial period of time . . . honestly and in good faith and not for the purpose of establishing a fictitious higher price." However, some states, such as Colorado, have established stiffer new criteria: Retailers can advertise discounts only from higher prices at which goods *actually were sold*—not just offered for sale.[18] This was the result of a case against May D&F Department Stores. May D&F was accused of misleading consumers by artificially inflating its "original" or "regular" prices, then promoting discounts from those prices to create the illusion of offering bargains on cookware, linens, and other household goods.[19]

Sears was charged by the New York City Department of Consumer Affairs with deceptive pricing when it switched to its "everyday low prices" strategy. The NYCA claimed this strategy created a "false impression" that Sears' prices represented a significant discount from past prices.[20]

No wonder the consumer finds the pricing policies of many retailers deceptive, especially when experts report that as much as 85 percent of some general-merchandise lines are sold "on sale" because the store originally took a higher-than-usual markup in order to take a later markdown or that one jewelry chain has never sold a single item at a regular price. These practices are causing retailers to lose credibility with their customers who no longer know the true price of any product. In addition, such pricing methods

ILLUSTRATION 6.2

In many states, prices advertised in local media must be marked as advertised prices in the store.

actually can hurt retailers by causing the customer to wait for the so-called sale because they know the first price is a phony one. When these people delay their purchases, the retailer runs the risk that a competitor may steal the customer away by offering a better deal sooner, or that the postponed purchase may never be made.

PREDATORY PRICING

If a retail chain charges different prices in different geographical areas in order to eliminate competition, a predatory action, in selected areas, it is in violation of Section 3 of the Robinson-Patman Act. This section forbids the sale of goods at lower prices in one area for the purpose of destroying competition or eliminating a competitor, or sales of goods at unreasonably low prices for such purpose. Deluxe Store, Handy Andy, and a local retail grocer's association won suits alleging that H.E. Butt Grocery Company engaged in predatory pricing in the San Antonio market.[21] A similar charge was filed against Kroger in its hometown of Cincinnati by 16 members of the Independent Grocers Alliance (IGA) Distributing Company. The courts ruled in favor of Kroger, because IGA, while it proved that such action would result in irreparable injury to IGA, failed to prove that Kroger was operating below cost—a test for predatory pricing.[22]

PROMOTION CONSTRAINTS

The ability of the retailer to make any promotion decision is constrained by two major pieces of federal legislation, the FTC Act (1914), especially Section 5, and the Wheeler-Lea Amendment (1938) to the FTC Act. The retailer should be familiar with five promotional practices under the domain of the FTC Act and the Wheeler-Lea Amendment. These areas are deceitful diversion of patronage, deceptive advertising, bait-and-switch tactics, deceptive sales practices, and substantiation and retraction of advertising (see Exhibit 6.4).

DECEITFUL DIVERSION OF PATRONAGE

If a retailer publishes or verbalizes falsehoods about a competitor in an attempt to divert patrons from that competitor, the retailer is engaging in **deceitful diversion of patronage.** The competitor is afforded protection under the FTC Act and could also receive protection by showing that the defamatory statements were libel or slander. In either case, the competitor would have to demonstrate that actual damage to its business had occurred.

Another form of deceitful diversion of patronage is palming off. **Palming off** occurs when a retailer represents merchandise as being made by a firm other than the true manufacturer. For example, an exclusive women's apparel retailer purchases a group of nicely styled dresses at a bargain price and

EXHIBIT 6.4
Promotional Constraints

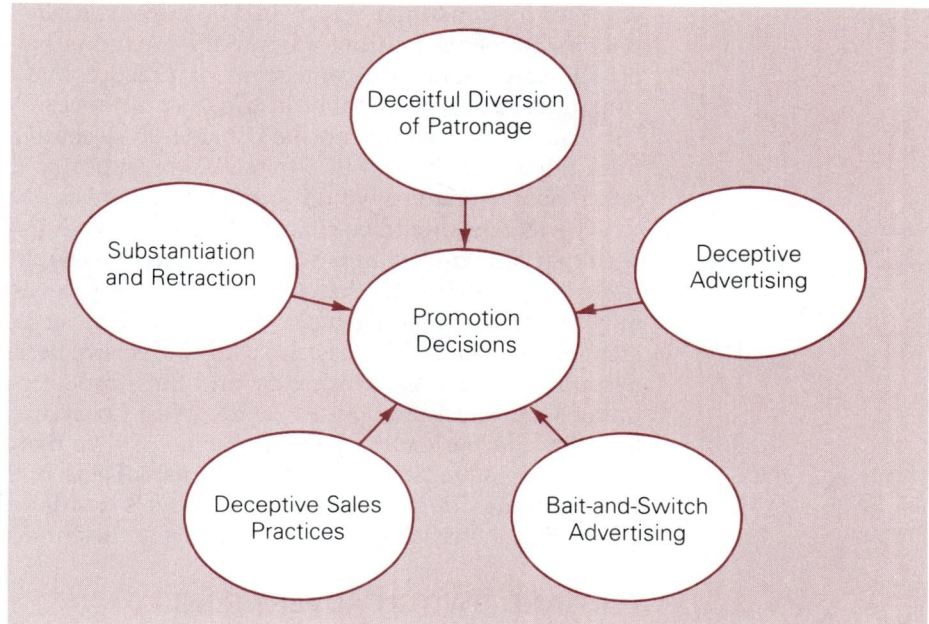

replaces their labels with those of a top designer. This is deception as to source of origin, or palming off, and litigation can be brought under the FTC Act and the Wheeler-Lea Amendment. Also, if the designer's dress label is a registered trademark, protection would also be afforded under the major piece of federal trademark legislation—the Lanham Act (1946). Palming off also has legal and ethical implications when the retailer is offered a "special deal" on name-brand merchandise that the retailer knows is counterfeit.

U.S. firms lose $20 billion a year as a result of the counterfeiting of trademarked U.S. products. Hundreds of different products—all fakes—have been copied overseas and shipped to the United States for retail sale ranging from Batman T-shirts to Nike, L.A. GEAR, Reebok footwear, Rolex watches, Izod shirts, and containers of Vicks Vapo-Rub.

DECEPTIVE ADVERTISING

Deceptive advertising occurs when a retailer makes false or misleading advertising claims about the physical makeup of a product, the benefits to be gained by its use, or the appropriate uses for it. Deceptive advertising is illegal. However, it is often quite difficult to distinguish between what is false or misleading and what is simply puffery, which is not illegal. Saying, "This is an excellent buy, and you can't afford to pass it up" is probably puffery, even though the product may not be an excellent buy by all standards, and you may be able to afford to pass it up! It is important for retailers to recognize that the FTC is concerned not with the intent of the advertiser but with whether the consumer was misled by the advertising. The FTC has adopted a policy statement requiring proof that a consumer has been harmed as a result of a misrepresentation, omission, or practice that is likely to mislead the consumer acting reasonably in the circumstances.[23] For example, an ad for "Danish pastry" would not be considered deceptive simply because "a few misguided souls believe . . . that all 'Danish pastry' is made in Denmark;"[24] a reasonable consumer would know what Danish pastry was.

The retailer should be concerned not only with its own advertising but also with that of manufacturers whose products it sells. If the manufacturer makes misleading statements, then the consumer may develop negative attitudes not only toward the manufacturer, but also toward retailers that carry that manufacturer's products. There is also a legal problem, because retailers are liable for deceptive co-op ads (which they and the supplier paid for jointly). In a Supreme Court decision, Pay 'n' Save, a West Coast drug chain, was found liable for false and misleading advertisements of X-11 diet pills. The ads were prepared by an advertising agency for Porter & Dietsch, the manufacturer of X-11. The Supreme Court ruled that Pay 'n' Save's lack of knowledge of the false and misleading advertising claims was not a sufficient defense.[25]

BAIT-AND-SWITCH ADVERTISING

Bait-and-switch advertising is another type of deceptive advertising involving promoting a product at an unrealistically low price to serve as "bait" and then trying to "switch" the customer to a higher-priced product. Other types of deceptive advertising include failure to have sufficient inventory to cover an advertised "sale," and false competitive-price comparisons. In Retailing in Action 6.1 you can decide whether or not a retailer was involved in bait-and-switch advertising.

DECEPTIVE SALES PRACTICES

Three sales practices are considered to be deceptive and, therefore, illegal: failure to be honest or to omit key facts in sales presentations; advertising the availability of "free merchandise" (buy one, get one free) without disclosing all conditions; and using deceptive credit contracts.

Attorney generals in several states have recently charged health spas with deceptive sales practices. Customers were offered a free week at the health spas but were subjected to intensive sales pitches before getting the temporary memberships. These sales pitches sometimes resulted in high-pressure and fast-moving sales efforts.

With regard to deceptive credit, federal laws attempt to "assure a meaningful disclosure of credit terms so that the consumer will be able to compare more readily the various credit terms available to him and avoid the uninformed use of credit."[26] These laws were a response to unscrupulous practices on the part of retailers attempting to hide the true cost of merchandise by selling at a very low price and then tacking on a high finance charge.

In order to ensure that the consumer can make more informed purchases

RETAILING IN ACTION

6.1 You Be the Judge

After reading all the facts, you decide whether this retailer was guilty of using bait-and-switch advertising.

A Wisconsin television and appliance dealer, whom we will call XYZ, ran the following radio advertisement:

> There are lots of good-quality washers and dryers on the market. But when you ask which ones are the best automatic washers and dryers, well, it's simple. There's Speed Queen, Maytag, and all the rest . . . at XYZ we have both of them and they're on sale for our January white sale. A clearance sale on the finest washers and dryers you can buy. This week a Speed Queen washer and dryer set is reduced to $499 . . . you can buy the finest for less than $500 . . . Why pay more at Sears?

The court determined that the dealer:

1. Lost money on each sale of the advertised set
2. Ordered only 20 of the sale sets, but 133 additional more expensive Speed Queen sets
3. Didn't pay a sales commission on the advertised sets
4. Accepted credit cards for the purchase of the more expensive sets, but not on the advertised sets
5. Only sold four of the advertised sets

Whether the managers of XYZ actually did intend to "bait-and-switch" was never proven. However, they were found guilty.

Source: Based on State of Wisconsin vs. American TV & Appliance of Madison, Inc., 140 Wis. 2d 353, 410 N.W. 2d 596 (Wisc. Ct. App. 1987).

---

when using credit, federal law requires that the customer receive information about:

1. The total amount financed
2. The finance charge as an annual percentage rate (APR)
3. The finance charge in dollars
4. Information about payments (number, amount, due dates, early repayment, etc.)
5. A rundown on any other fees or charges (late payment, insurance, etc.)

If the credit agreement involves merchandise bought on time, creditors are also required to provide:

1. A description of the merchandise
2. The cash price
3. The "deferred payment" price (price plus total interest)
4. The amount of any down payment and/or trade-in

These credit disclosure rules apply not only to in-store selling but also to all promotional activities of the retailer.

SUBSTANTIATION AND RETRACTION

The FTC can request that the retailer substantiate its advertising claims about the safety, quality, or performance of its products. The FTC charged Walgreen with making unsubstantiated claims for Advil, a pain reliever. Walgreen advertised Advil as a "prescription pain reliever . . ." and "anti-inflammatory . . . a source of comfort for people who experience arthritis pain." The FTC argued that Walgreen did not have a reasonable basis for its claims and Advil cannot be substituted for prescription forms of ibuprofen, the product's active ingredient. The commission challenged only Walgreen's claims and not those of Advil's manufacturer, American Home Products.[27]

If the FTC finds that a retailer has made false or deceptive statements in advertising, it may require that a new advertisement be made in which the former statements are contradicted and the truth stated. This is called **retroactive (or retraction) advertising.** The FTC issued a complaint requiring Montgomery Ward to run retroactive advertising. According to the complaint, Ward gave consumers false and confusing information that may have led them to install wood stoves at unsafe distances from combustible walls. The order required that Ward place full-page notices in its October house-clearance catalog and its next spring and summer general catalog, offering to relocate wood-burning heaters to recommended distances from combustible walls.[28]

PRODUCT CONSTRAINTS

A retailer's major activity is selling merchandise. In order to accomplish this goal, it must assure its customers that the products they purchase will not be harmful to their well-being and will meet expected performance criteria. Four areas of the law have a major effect on the products a retailer handles: patents, product safety, product liability, and warranties. They are highlighted in Exhibit 6.5.

PATENTS

In mass retailing, the direct copying of popular product brands or lines is common. Retailers such as Kmart, Ward, and Sears often copy an item that has been a commercial success. Their goal is to produce the item at a lower cost so that they can offer it to the mass market at an attractive price.

Acceptance of competition is so widespread in the United States that this practice is condoned unless a patent right is infringed on. A **patent** gives a 17-year legal monopoly for the marketing of a product or process to the patent holder. A person or company applying for a patent will usually receive it as

EXHIBIT 6.5
Product Constraints

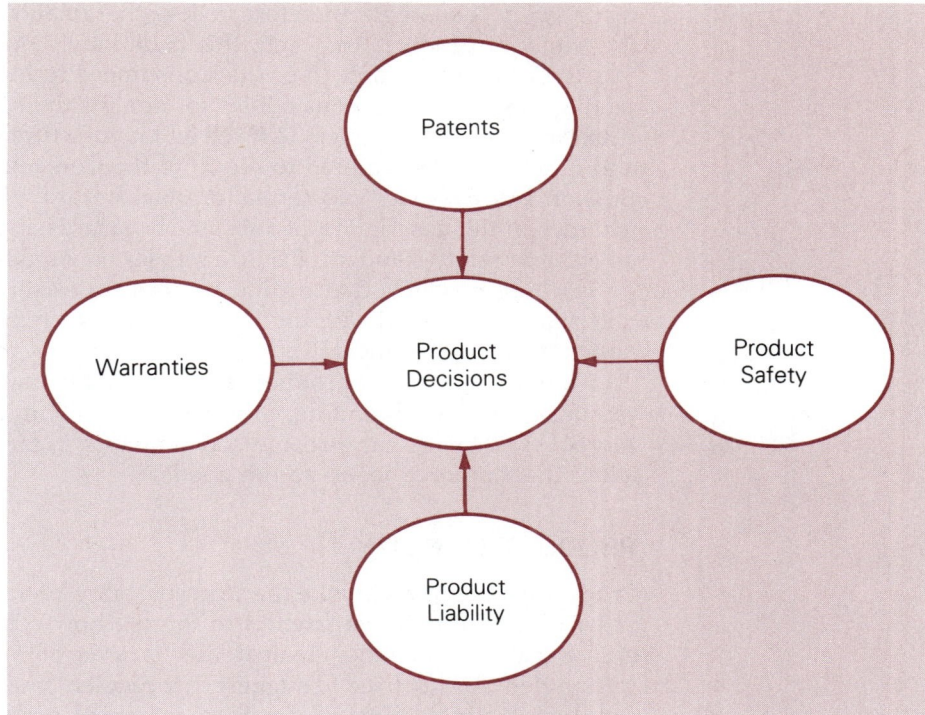

long as application forms are completed properly. However, patent rights can be challenged in court on the basis that the patent was a product or process that didn't serve to advance the general well-being or welfare of society.[29]

An illuminating case in this realm is Sears, Roebuck, and Co. vs. Stiffel Co.[30] Stiffel developed a pole lamp that proved to be a commercial success. Sears then brought out a substantially identical lamp at a much lower price and Stiffel sued for unfair competition, claiming that Sears had caused confusion as to the source of the lamps. The initial judgment was in favor of Stiffel, but Sears appealed and the U.S. Supreme Court reversed the decision. The Supreme Court stressed that a patent could not be given to an article that did not advance the welfare of society. They argued that the pole lamp sold by Stiffel was not entitled to a patent based either on design or mechanical features. Therefore, the pole lamp was in the public domain and Sears had every right to design and sell almost identical lamps. The fact that Stiffel originated the pole lamp and made it popular was irrelevant.

PRODUCT SAFETY

Retailers are in a precarious position when it comes to product safety. Most retailers do not produce the goods they offer for sale but purchase them from wholesalers or manufacturers. Thus, they have little say about product quality or safety. You might therefore believe that retailers are not responsible for the safety of products they sell; this is definitely not the case.

According to Section 15 of the Consumer Product Safety Act (1972), the retailer has specific responsibilities to monitor the safety of consumer products.[31] Specifically, retailers (as well as manufacturers, other intermediaries, and importers) are required to report to the Consumer Product Safety Commission any possible "substantial product hazard." Furthermore, Section 15 includes in the description of substantial hazards any failure to comply with an existing safety standard. Thus, a retailer may unknowingly violate the law by reselling products that do not conform to existing safety standards. Retailers may further violate the law by failing to repurchase from customers nonconforming products.

More than 200 food products are recalled by manufacturers each year for reasons such as misbranding, product deterioration, or criminal adulteration. Moreover, retailers can become codefendants in tampering lawsuits if they allow the tamperer access to the goods.[32]

PRODUCT LIABILITY

Product liability laws invoke the "foreseeability" doctrine, which states that a seller of a product must attempt to foresee how a product may be misused and warn the consumer against the hazards of misuse. The courts have interpreted this doctrine to suggest that retailers must be careful of how they sell their products. This is of particular importance to restaurant, nightclub, and bar owners who fail to consider the consequences of serving a consumer one more drink "for the road." In addition to the federal laws covering product liability, all states have their own regulations.

WARRANTIES

Retailers are also responsible for product safety and performance under conventional warranty doctrines. Under the current warranty law, the fact that the ultimate consumer may bring suit against the manufacturer or processor in no way relieves the retailer from its responsibility for the fitness and merchantability of the goods. The disheartening fact that confronts the retailer is that in many states the buyer has been permitted to sue both the retailer and the manufacturer or processor in the same legal suit.

Retailers can offer expressed or implied warranties. **Expressed warranties** are the result of negotiation between the retailer and the customer. They may be either written into the contract or verbalized. They can cover all characteristics or attributes of the merchandise or only one attribute. An important point for the retailer (and its salespeople) to recognize is that an expressed warranty can be created without the use of the words "warranty" or "guarantee." For example, a car salesperson might tell a buyer, "Everybody to whom we've sold this type of car has gone at least 60,000 miles with no problems whatsoever, and I see no reason why you can't expect the same. I wouldn't be surprised if you go 100,000 miles without any mechanical problems." This statement could create an expressed warranty. The court would, however, be concerned with whether this was just sales talk ("puffery") or a statement of fact or opinion by the salesperson.

Many retailers have resorted to using disclaimers similar to the one in Exhibit 6.6 as a means of reducing their liability.

Implied warranties are not expressly made by the retailer but are based on customs, norms, or reasonable expectations. There are two types of implied warranties (which overlap a bit): an implied warranty of merchantability and an implied warranty of fitness for a particular purpose.

An **implied warranty of merchantability** is made by every retailer selling goods. By offering the goods for sale, the retailer implies that they are fit for the ordinary purpose for which such goods are typically used. The notion of implied warranty applies to both new and used merchandise. For example, imagine that a sporting goods retailer located close to a major lake resort sells used inner tubes for swimming and a customer purchases one. The tube bursts while the person is floating on it, and the person subsequently drowns. This retailer may be held liable. Because of the potential legal liability that accompanies an implied warranty, many retailers will expressly disclaim at the time of sale any or all implied warranties. This is not always legally possible; some retailers will not be able to avoid implied warranties of merchantability.

The **implied warranty of fitness** for a particular purpose arises when the customer relies on the retailer to make or assist in making the selection of goods to serve a particular purpose. Consider a customer who is about to make a cross-country moving trip and plans to tow a two-wheel trailer behind her automobile. She needs a pair of tires for the rear of the automobile and thus asks the local tire retailer for a pair of tires that will allow her to tow the loaded trailer safely. The customer in this regard is ignorant and is relying on the expertise of the retailer. If the retailer sells the customer a pair of tires not suited for the job, then the retailer is liable for breach of an implied warranty of fitness for a particular purpose. This is true even if the retailer did not have

EXHIBIT 6.6
Sample Disclaimer

The following is an example of a disclaimer that attempts to limit a seller's exposure when offering goods and services in the marketplace:

Seller warrants that the goods supplied hereunder will conform to the description stated herein; that it will convey good title thereto, free of all liens of any kind whatever unknown to the buyer; and that such goods will be of merchantable quality. This is seller's sole warranty with respect to the goods. SELLER MAKES NO OTHER WARRANTY OF ANY KIND WHATEVER, EXPRESSED OR IMPLIED: AND ALL IMPLIED WARRANTIES OF MERCHANTABILITY AND FITNESS FOR A PARTICULAR PURPOSE THAT EXCEED THE AFORESTATED OBLIGATION ARE HEREBY DISCLAIMED AND EXCLUDED FROM THIS AGREEMENT.

Source: Steven Mitchell Sack, "Some Words on Warranties . . . ," *Sales and Marketing Management* (December 1986): 52-54.

in stock a pair of tires to perform the job safely but instead sold the customer the best tire in stock.

Consumer product warranties have frequently been confusing, misleading, and frustrating to consumers. As a consequence, the Magnuson-Moss Warranty Act[33] was passed. While nothing in federal law requires a retailer to warrant a product under this act, anyone who sells a product costing the consumer more than $15 and who gives a written warranty (while only written warranties are covered by federal laws, all types of warranties are subject to state laws) is required to provide the consumer with the following information:

1. The identity of the persons to whom the warranty is extended, if the written warranty can be enforced only by the original consumer purchaser or is limited to persons other than every consumer owner of the item during the term of the warranty.
2. A clear description of the products, parts, characteristics, components, and properties covered by the warranty; if necessary for clarity, those items excluded from the warranty must be described.
3. A statement of what the warrantor will do in the event of a defect, malfunction, or failure to conform with the written warranty, including those items or services the warrantor will pay for, and if needed for clarity, those items or services he or she will not pay for.
4. The point in time when the warranty begins (if it begins on a date other than the purchase date) and its duration.
5. A step-by-step explanation of the process the consumer should follow to obtain performance of the warranty obligation and information regarding any informal dispute-settling mechanisms that are available.
6. Any limitations on the duration of implied warranties or any exclusions or limitations on relief, such as incidental or consequential damages, together with a statement that under some state laws the exclusions or limitations may not be allowed.
7. A statement that the warranty gives the consumer certain legal rights, in addition to his or her other rights under state law, which may vary from state to state.

It is the retailer's responsibility to provide the prospective buyer with the written terms of the warranty for review prior to the actual sale. In this regard, the retailer has two options: clearly and conspicuously displaying the text of the written warranty near the product, or making warranties available for examination by consumers upon request and posting signs advising consumers of the presale availability of warranties.

The FTC polices retailers' adherence to the Magnuson-Moss Warranty Act. For example, the FTC took action against a department store chain for not properly making warranties available to consumers prior to the actual sales. The chain agreed to conduct a special training program to instruct its sales personnel about the availability and location of warranty information.[34] A nationwide investigation of warranty practices began in early 1980, shortly after the FTC sent warnings to 17 major chains, such as Sears, Kmart,

Montgomery Ward, Woolworth, and Korvette's, pointing out that failure to disclose warranty terms could subject the firms to fines of up to $10,000 for each violation.[35]

CHANNEL CONSTRAINTS

Retailers are restricted in the relationships and agreements they may develop with channel partners. These restrictions can be conveniently categorized into six areas as shown in Exhibit 6.7.

TERRITORIAL RESTRICTIONS

Territorial restrictions are attempts by a supplier, usually a manufacturer, to limit the geographical area in which a retailer may resell its merchandise. The courts have viewed territorial restrictions as potential contracts in restraint of trade and thus in violation of the Sherman Antitrust Act. Even though the retailer and manufacturer may both favor territorial restrictions because of the lessening of intrabrand competition, the courts frown on such arrangements.[36]

The courts' views on territorial restrictions have changed several times

EXHIBIT 6.7

Channel Constraints

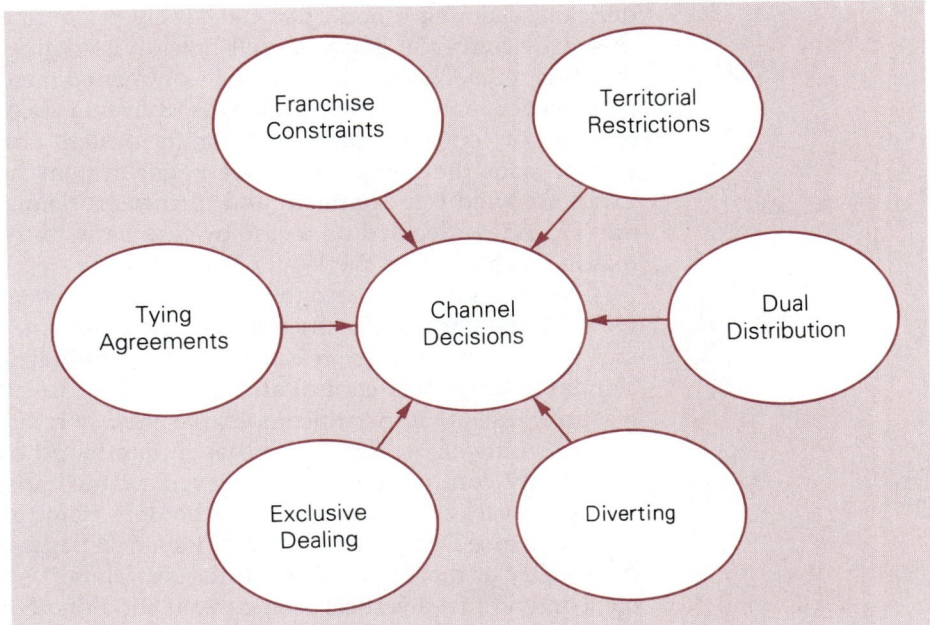

since the early 1960s, making it difficult for retailers and suppliers to know what is legal and what is not. Let us review the changing view of the courts, beginning with the White Motor case.[37] White Motor Company had insisted that its dealers confine their sales to well-defined territories. The legality of this agreement was challenged, and in 1963 the Supreme Court admitted that it did not know "enough of the economic and business stuff out of which the arrangements emerge to be certain" about the appropriate decision.[38] As a result, the Supreme Court decided to send the case to a lower court to assess the competitive consequences of the territorial restrictions. Thus, the Supreme Court was implying by its behavior that territorial restrictions were not a violation of the Sherman Act. Before the lower court could make a decision, White Motor consented to stop the contested practice, and the precedent was set that territorial restrictions would be assessed on their individual merits in regard to their effect or potential effect on competition.

Four years later, in 1967, the Supreme Court decided the Schwinn case, which dealt with territorial restrictions Schwinn, the bicycle manufacturer, had placed on its distributors and franchised retailers.[39] The court stated that suppliers could *not* prevent intermediaries which held clear title to goods from selling to anyone of their choosing. Once title passed, the destination of goods could not be controlled. Not only Schwinn, but most other manufacturers were shocked by this ruling. In essence, the court was stating that territorial restrictions on retailers selling goods to which they have clear title were a per se violation of the Sherman Act.

A decade later, retail executives were again surprised. In 1977, in the GTE Sylvania case, the Supreme Court overruled the precedent of the Schwinn decision, claiming it had acted too hastily.[40] Continental TV, a retailer franchised by Sylvania, began to sell outside its defined territory. As a result, Sylvania refused to continue selling Continental merchandise, and Continental sued Sylvania for treble damages. Sylvania successfully argued that the promise of territorial protection for its dealers strengthened competition, since it made the survival of its marketing system more likely. The Supreme Court accepted this argument and further proclaimed that territorial restriction should be decided on a case-by-case basis, thus reverting to the rule of reason established in the White Motor case.[41]

The courts upheld the right of Adolph Coors to terminate a wholesaler for violating the territorial restrictions of his agreement.[42] The Court, in reinforcing the Sylvania ruling, reasoned that a manufacturer has the right to set standards for quality control and to enforce those standards. In this case, it was concluded that the anticompetitive effect of reducing intrabrand competition was outweighed by an increase in interbrand competition as a result of the quality control standards achieved by territorial restrictions. Congress has, however, exempted soft-drink bottlers from this legislation.[43]

The Justice Department, in 1985, issued 46 pages of guidelines supporting the legality of most vertical territorial restraints.[44] The guidelines, for example, contend that a vertical arrangement shouldn't be challenged if the manufacturer using it controls less than 10 percent of the market for the product it covers. The department also won't try to overturn vertical arrangements covering fewer than 60 percent of dealers or distributors in a specific geographic area.

It is important to note that while vertical territorial restrictions may be valid under the rule of reason, the rule applied to territorial restrictions arrived at by agreement between competitors is different. In such cases, the parties will have contracted, combined, or conspired in restraint of trade, a violation of Section 1 of the Sherman Act. Known as horizontal market allocation, such conduct is an inexcusable violation.[45]

DUAL DISTRIBUTION

A manufacturer that sells to independent retailers and also through its own retail outlets is engaged in **dual distribution.** Thus, the manufacturer manages a corporately owned vertical marketing system that competes with independent retailers, which it also supplies through a conventional, administered, or contractual marketing channel. Retailers tend to become upset about dual distribution when the two channels compete at the retail level in the same trade area. For example, occasionally an oil company will open a dealership close to an independent dealer it sells to as a means to set the retail price.[46] Likewise, Ralph Lauren has wholly owned retail outlets and in addition uses major independent retailers as outlets, and many manufacturers are opening their own retail stores in so-called factory outlet malls. Such actions can have a severe effect on manufacturer/retailer relationships.[47] The current reduction in the number of retailers, a result of the recent merger trend, has caused manufacturers to open these outlets not as a place to unload seconds, but as a means of keeping production up to capacity. In the future, these manufacturers will have to expand beyond outlet malls, which currently are located away from major retail centers, to compete next door to their retail customers.[48] Many manufacturers will be forced to do what OshKosh B'Gosh did in 1991. After building up an image of high quality by selling through pricey department and specialty stores, OshKosh began selling some of its line through volume leaders JCPenney and Sears.[49] Dual distribution also takes place when manufacturers sell similar products under different brand names for distribution through different channels. This kind of dual distribution is common in the retailing of private labels.

Independent retailers argue that dual distribution is an unfair method of competition and thus in violation of the Sherman Act. The courts have not viewed dual-distribution arrangements as violations. In fact, they have reasoned that dual distribution can actually foster competition rather than reduce it. For example, the manufacturer may not be able to find a retailer to represent it in all trade areas; or the manufacturer may find it necessary to operate its own retail outlet to establish market share and remain competitive with other manufacturers. The courts have so far applied a rule-of-reason criteria. An independent retailer suing a manufacturer for dual distribution has to convince the court that it was competed against unfairly and that competition was damaged. The retailer's best strategy would be to show that the manufacturer-controlled outlets were favored or subsidized (for instance, with an excess advertising allowance or lower prices) to an extent that was detrimental to the independent retailer.

DIVERTING

A new channel of distribution was given legal status in 1988, when the Supreme Court legitimized the so-called "diverter market" that discounters exploit to give customers bargain-priced goods. In this channel diverters, which are often authorized U.S. dealers, corporations, universities, and other large purchasers, obtain the goods at large quantity discounts of 30 to 40 percent and then sell the goods to smaller and/or unauthorized retailers at a profit. The diverters can resell these products profitably for less than what a smaller and/or unauthorized retailer would normally pay for these items or sell them to large retailers, such as Kmart, and 47th Street Photo, for slightly less than the largest discounted amount. In many cases, they can make money simply by ordering huge quantities to earn big discounts and then selling the excess at cost. With regard to imported goods, the diverters usually rely on arbitrage. Here, when a strong dollar weakens the German mark against the Japanese yen, importers sometimes can acquire Japanese cameras from Germany at a much lower dollar cost than they could using the "authorized channel" from Japan.[50]

The troublesome thing about these practices is that the unauthorized retailers do not provide service and information. In addition, unauthorized retailers may make unauthorized alterations in the product, or the product may have been produced to another country's specifications. Most importantly, these retailers undermine the efforts of the authorized retailers by getting a free ride on the authorized dealers' efforts to cultivate and educate potential customers. No wonder some retailers were confused when, only a month after ruling that manufacturers don't necessarily violate antitrust laws if they cut off discounters after receiving complaints from full-price retailers, the Supreme Court legitimized "diverting." The ruling allowed diverted imports to be blocked only in about 10 percent of situations.[51]

EXCLUSIVE DEALING

Retailers and their suppliers occasionally enter into exclusive dealing arrangements. In a **one-way exclusive dealing** arrangement, the supplier agrees to give the retailer the exclusive right to merchandise the suppliers' product in a particular trade area. The retailer, however, does not agree to do anything for the supplier; hence, the term *one-way*. A weak manufacturer will often have to offer one-way exclusive dealing arrangements to obtain shelf space at the retail level. Truly one-way arrangements are legal.

A **two-way exclusive dealing** arrangement occurs when the supplier offers the retailer the exclusive distribution of a merchandise line or product if in return the retailer will agree to do something for the manufacturer, such as agree not to handle competing brands. Two-way agreements violate Section 3 of the Clayton Act (1914) if their effect may be to lessen competition substantially or to tend to create a monopoly. Specifically, the courts have been concerned with three potential negative consequences of two-way exclusive dealing agreements. First, strong manufacturers may attract strong retailers, and the strength of the two reinforcing each other could lessen competition from smaller manufacturers and retailers. Second, since there are many more national manufacturers than there are retailers in any given smaller city, there would not be enough retail outlets for all manufacturers to be represented. Third, price competition at the retail level would be reduced, because intrabrand rivalry would be absent or severely restricted. The legality of two-way exclusive dealing agreements is determined case by case on a rule-of-reason basis, usually by considering the three preceding points.

TYING AGREEMENTS

When a seller with a strong product or service forces a retailer to buy a weak product or service as a condition for buying the strong one, a **tying agreement** exists. For example, a large national manufacturer with several very strongly demanded lines of merchandise may force the retailer to handle its entire merchandise assortment as a condition for being able to handle the most popular lines. This is called a **full-line policy.** Alternatively, a strong manufacturer may be introducing a new product, and, as a means of obtaining shelf space or display space at the retail level, it may require retailers to carry the new product in order to purchase better known or established merchandise lines.

Tying arrangements have been found to be in violation of Section 3 of the Clayton Act, Sections 1 and 3 of the Sherman Act, and Section 5 of the FTC Act. The term or concept of tying, however, is not expressly mentioned in any of these acts. Tying is not viewed as a per se violation, but it is generally viewed as illegal if a substantial share of commerce is affected. The courts have noted in recent rulings that it is difficult to prove tying.

> *Even assuming arguments that plaintiff's proof shows that it accepted uneconomic secondary products and that defendant possessed dominant economic power and utilized that power to require plaintiff to buy more of its goods, this is not sufficient a finding of an illegal tying agreement.*[52]

FRANCHISE CONSTRAINTS

Since the early 1960s, the number of franchised retailers has grown rapidly to the point where U.S. franchise outlets now sell $700 billion in goods and services. Associated with this growth have been substantial legal difficulties between franchisors and franchisees.

In principle, a franchise is a relationship between two independent parties, whose rights are determined by the contract existing between them. However, because of the imbalance of power in this relationship (the franchisor has much more), the franchisee should know that certain requirements the franchisor may try to impose will be viewed as illegal in a court of law. Basically, the legal system has attempted to equalize the balance of power between the franchisor and franchisee, and some states are even providing franchisees with more power.[53]

The franchised retailer should keep the following points in mind:

1. Although the franchisor may want the franchisee to set prices at a certain level, generally such agreements will be found in violation of the antitrust laws if tested in court.
2. Requirements that the franchisee purchase materials and supplies from the franchisor when competitive goods of similar quality are available will be viewed as an illegal tying agreement.
3. Geographic limitations may or may not be viewed as unlawful. A rule-of-reason approach will be used.
4. Standards for operating procedures, quality control, and cleanliness are generally legal, since the franchisor has a legitimate interest in maintaining the name or reputation of the franchise.

Thus, the franchisor should not take undue advantage of the franchisee (through tying or price fixing). However, franchising allows for tying arrangements when a product (frozen yogurt or a hamburger) is tied to a trademark (the tying product) since the quality of the final product is at stake. Likewise, the franchisee should also not take advantage of the franchisor (for instance, by not following cleanliness standards).

One way that franchisors could formerly take advantage of franchisees was by unfair *franchise termination*. Traditionally, a franchise contract ran for a short period (typically a year) and the franchisor had great flexibility in cancelling the franchisee. Currently, however, most franchise contracts specify the causes for cancellation (failure to make payments, bankruptcy of franchisee, failure to meet sales quotas). In addition, many franchise contracts now contain an arbitration provision that allows for a neutral third party to make a final and binding decision on whether a breach of contract has occurred and whether it was sufficient to justify cancellation of the franchise. Franchise termination is now quite difficult, because many states have statutes to protect franchisees from arbitrary termination.

Finally, fraud has often occurred in the sale of franchises to unsuspecting potential franchisees. Franchises have been sold to the small investor as get-rich-quick schemes, and the pitches to attract franchisees have been based on misleading statements. Because of these practices, several states have enacted franchise investment laws. Under these laws, a franchisee who is deceived by a misleading statement (typically in a prospectus) may sue for damages.[54]

MERGERS AND ACQUISITIONS

In recent years, a number of retailers were able to achieve explosive rates of growth by acquiring other retail enterprises. Mergers or acquisitions can present legal problems for the retailer. According to Section 7 of the Clayton Act, an acquisition of stock or assets of a company, where the effect may be to substantially lessen competition or tend to create a monopoly in any line of commerce in any section of the country, is illegal. This section of the Clayton Act was strengthened by the Celler-Kefauver Act (1950).

Mergers or acquisitions are not per se violations; rather, the courts use a rule of reason. Debate and arguments[55] tend to revolve around two central issues:

1. What is the line of commerce? For example, is a women's apparel store in the same line of commerce as a men's apparel store or department store?
2. What is the market? Is a shoe retailer in Tucson that acquires a shoe retailer in Phoenix acquiring a firm in the same section of the country?

In each of the preceding issues, the concept of competition is crucial. We could restate the two questions thus: Do different types of merchandise compete? Do retailers in different geographic areas compete?

The retail manager might find Exhibit 6.8 helpful in assessing the likelihood of legal problems surrounding a merger or acquisition. In Exhibit 6.8 we can examine whether the acquisition or merger involves the same or different lines of commerce, and the same or different sections of the country. At least four distinct possibilities exist. The retailer could acquire or merge with a firm in the same line of commerce and in the same section of the country. A dominant furniture retailer in Seattle, Washington, might merge with or acquire another large furniture retailer in Seattle. Such mergers or acquisitions are very likely to be challenged either by existing competitors in that market or by the Justice Department's Antitrust Division. Of course, the challenge is more likely to occur if each firm has a large share of the market. In fact, the larger the market share of the firms involved in an acquisition or merger, the greater the likelihood of antitrust violations irrespective of other

EXHIBIT 6.8

Mergers and Acquisitions

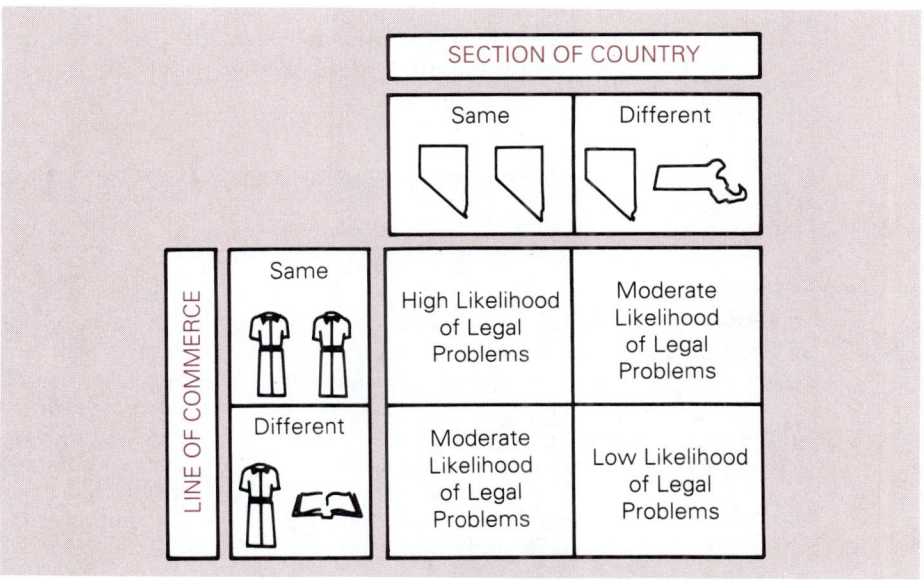

facts surrounding the case. Retailing in Action 6.2 describes how the states are seeking to go beyond the coverage of federal laws dealing with mergers and acquisitions.

Another alternative is the acquisition or merger of two firms that represent different lines of commerce and are currently operating in different sections of the country. For example, a regional department store chain in the Southwest might acquire a petroleum distributor in Oklahoma City and Tulsa. In this situation, the likelihood of violating antimerger provisions of the Clayton or Celler-Kefauver Amendment is relatively small. This example clearly delineates the line of commerce and section of the country. But what if a department store in the Southeast had stores only in cities over 250,000 in population, and it acquired a chain of drugstores that operated in the Southeast but only in towns less than 50,000 in population? Are the lines of commerce and sections of the country different? This is more typical of the questions the courts address.

The third and fourth alternatives in terms of acquisition or merger represent a moderate likelihood of antitrust violations. The third option occurs when a firm acquires or merges with another in the same line of commerce but a different section of the country (a supermarket chain in Colorado acquires a supermarket chain in South Carolina). The fourth option is to acquire a firm in a different line of commerce but in the same section of the country (a supermarket chain in Dallas acquires a retail sporting goods chain in Dallas).

OTHER FEDERAL LAWS

Several other federal laws also affect retailers, but their impact is beyond the scope of this text. One such law deals with the minimum wage law, since labor is a retailer's largest expense; still others pertain to the legal form of

---

RETAILING IN ACTION

6.2 States Expand Their Legal Role in Mergers

A unanimous decision by the Supreme Court in April 1990 gave state governments the same power as the federal government to break up mergers and acquisitions that reduce competition, increase unemployment, and increase prices.

The ruling backed an appeal by the California attorney general, supported by briefs by 30 other states, to block a grocery chain merger between Lucky Stores, the state's largest chain, and American Stores, the fourth-largest chain in California. The appeal was brought after the Federal Trade Commission had approved the transaction.

In addition, two states, Pennsylvania and Massachusetts, passed anti-takeover laws that let directors of firms consider the concerns of communities, consumers, and workers as well as investors.

organization (sole proprietorship, partnership, or corporation) that the retailer operates under; and another set, which will be discussed in Chapter 16, deals with personnel matters. Chapter 12 will consider how the Americans with Disabilities Act, Public Law 101-336, affects the layout and design of the retailer's store.

STATE AND LOCAL LAWS

In addition to federal laws, many state and local municipalities have passed legislation regulating retail activities. Exhibit 6.9 illustrates how state and local laws affect the retailer. Zoning laws, for example, prohibit retailers from operating at certain locations and require building and sign specifications to be met. Many retailers have found these codes to be highly restrictive, especially since some existing firms have been able to influence this type of legislation, thereby protecting their already established local business.

With regard to selling laws, for example, 22 states have sales-below-cost legislation governing the retail distribution of merchandise.[56] The specific content of these laws varies, but usually they prohibit the retailer from selling merchandise below cost plus some fixed percentage markup (6 percent is typical). These state laws are generally unclear as to whether the retailer can give merchandise away or offer prizes or premiums without increasing an item's price as a form of price reduction.

State laws have been generally ineffective in preventing sales below cost. First of all, they usually require that a competitor lodge a complaint or initiate a legal action against the retailer. Most retailers will not do this because they, too, may sometimes sell below cost. A second problem has been that most

ILLUSTRATION 6.3

This handicapped-access ramp is an example of how the Americans with Disabilities Act, Public Law 101-336, affects the layout and design of the retailer's store.

EXHIBIT 6.9

Various State and Local Laws Affecting Retailers

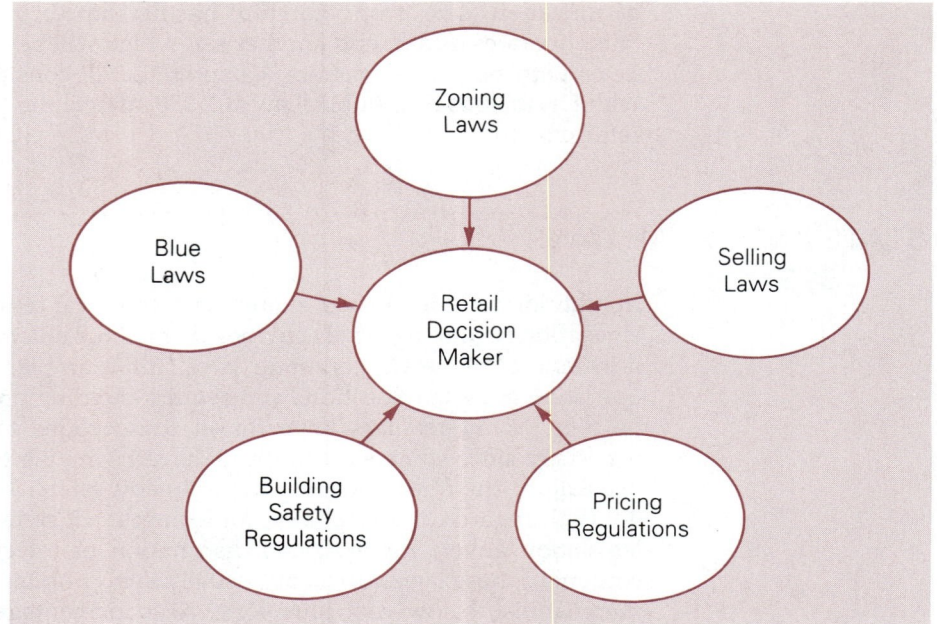

statutes do not clearly define cost. Is a retailer's cost the cash price paid, the invoice price before a cash discount, the delivered price, the average price paid over a year minus any end-of-year rebates, the price less any advertising or promotional allowance, or something else? Because of the technicalities in defining cost, litigation is time consuming and expensive.

In addition, most localities have strong building codes that regulate construction materials, fire safety, architectural style, height and size of building, number of entrances, and even elevator usage. Some states regulate the prices paid to wholesalers by retailers. Other states enforce "blue laws" restricting the sale of certain products on Sundays and have "unfair trade practices" laws regulating the minimum markup a retailer must charge. Various cities have passed Green River ordinances restricting door-to-door selling, excessive use of garage sales, lottery promotions, and sale of obscene materials and dangerous products. In addition, states and cities might require licenses to operate certain retail businesses.

For further information about these various laws, a retailer should consult the local Better Business Bureau, the National Retail Federation, state and local retailing trade associations, or state and local regulatory agencies.

SUMMARY

The purpose of this chapter was to describe the multifaceted legal environment that confronts retailers in the United States. We began by identifying the legal constraints on retailers' activities in seven broad categories: (1) pricing, (2) promotion, (3) products, (4) channel relations, (5) mergers and acquisitions, (6) other federal laws, and (7) state and

Chapter 6 Understanding the Legal Environment

local regulations. Within each of these broad constraints, we summarized some specific activities that are regulated.

With regard to pricing, federal law regulates horizontal and vertical price fixing, price discrimination, deceptive pricing, and predatory pricing. Constraints on a retailer's promotional efforts revolve around deceitful diversion of patronage, deceptive advertising, bait-and-switch advertising, deceptive sales practices, and substantiation and retraction. A retailer's product constraints involve patents, product safety, product liability, and warranties, either expressed or implied, on the products sold. A retailer's relationship with other channel members includes terms of territorial restrictions, dual distribution, diverting, exclusive dealing, and tying agreements. In addition, restrictions concerning franchises and mergers and acquisitions are handled here.

The chapter concluded with a discussion of the impact of the various state and local laws on retail operations.

QUESTIONS FOR DISCUSSION

1. Do you believe retailers will be more or less constrained by the legal environment in the future? Why?
2. A federal grand jury argues that because all major supermarkets in a town are selling milk at the same price there must be a conspiracy to fix prices. Agree or disagree and explain your reasoning.
3. Retail executives should abide by the philosophy "as long as it is legal, it is ethical." Agree or disagree and explain your reasoning.
4. How could two-way exclusive dealing arrangements be harmful to the consumer and competition?
5. Deceptive advertising and pricing harm not only the consumer but also competition. Agree or disagree and explain your reasoning.
6. Why should a retailer be familiar with the Robinson-Patman Act?
7. Why is sales-below-cost legislation usually ineffective?
8. What is deceitful diversion of patronage? Comment on the legality of it.
9. Discuss the concept of exclusive dealing. Are exclusive dealing arrangements in the retailer's best interest? Are they in the consumer's best interest?
10. Explain how a retailer could minimize its legal problems in mergers and acquisitions.
11. What should a retailer do to ensure that it does not violate the customer's rights under the Magnuson-Moss Warranty Act?
12. When are price discounts legal under the Robinson-Patman Act?
13. Is it legal for a manufacturer to tie the sale of one product to the sale of another product? Do the same rules apply to a retailer selling to the final consumer?

MANAGEMENT MEMO

You are the manager of the appliance department of a small department store. Yesterday you overheard a salesperson tell a customer looking at a new washer, "This washer is so good that you could do 20 loads of wash a day for 10 years and the washer would still be running, just like new." Should you be concerned about your sales force making such warranties? If so, prepare a written set of guidelines for your sales force to follow.

BOARDROOM REPORT

As vice-president of sales for a fast-food restaurant chain, you have been approached by your counterpart at a rival chain. The other chain wants to raise the prices of its soft drinks by a nickel for all sizes and wants to know if you would follow suit in this attempt to cover the increase in operating expenses that has affected not only soft drinks but all other food items. The rest of the board wants to follow your rival's lead and has asked for your input at next week's board meeting. Prepare a five-minute report to present to the board outlining your position on this subject.

SUGGESTED READINGS

Huber, Peter W. *Liability: The Legal Revolution and Its Consequences.* New York: Basic Books, Inc., 1988.

Krmenec, Andrew J. "Sales Tax as Property Tax Relief? The Shifting Onus of Local Revenue Generation." *Professional Geographer* 43 (1991): 60-67.

Kumar, V., Roger Kerin, and Arun Pereira. "An Empirical Assessment of Merger and Acquisition Activity in Retailing." *Journal of Retailing* (Fall 1991): 321-38.

Sikora, Martin. "The M & A Bonanza of the 80s—and Its Legacy." *Mergers and Acquisitions* (March-April 1990): 90-95.

Twomey, David P. *Equal Employment Opportunity Law.* Cincinnati: South-Western Publishing Co., 1990.

Also the interested reader is encouraged to consult the "Legal Developments in Marketing" section of recent copies of the *Journal of Marketing* and "Marketing and the Law" in the *Journal of the Academy of Marketing Science.*

ENDNOTES

1. "Domino's Craps out as a Suburb Refuses to Gamble on Safety," *Wall Street Journal,* 4 September 1990, B8.
2. "True Purists, They Rarely Treat It as a Joke if Anything's Off Color," *Wall Street Journal,* 25 June 1991, B1.
3. "Store's Concept of 'Sale' Pricing Gets Court Test," *Wall Street Journal,* 15 May 1990, B1, B13 and "Low Prices or Low Practice? Regulators Cast Wary Eye on Retailers' Many Sales," *Wall Street Journal,* 13 February 1990, B1, B6.
4. "Justices Rebuff States in Taxing Mail-Order Sales," *Wall Street Journal,* (May 27, 1992): A3.
5. Sherman Act, 26 Stat. 209 (1890), as amended, 15 U.S.C. articles 1-7.
6. For a detailed discussion of fair-trade laws, the reader might want to consult L. Louise Luchsinger and Patrick M. Dunne, "Fair Trade Laws—How Fair?" *Journal of Marketing* (January 1978): 50-53.
7. "A Red Flag for Red Tags," *Business Week,* 16 May 1988, 38.
8. "Senate Clears Bill Aimed at Blocking Fixing of Prices," *Wall Street Journal,* 10 May 1991, B2.
9. Clayton Act, 38 Stat. 730 (1914), as amended, 15 U.S.C. articles 12-27.
10. Robinson-Patman Act, 49 Stat. 1526 (1936), as amended, 15 U.S.C. article 13.
11. Under the Robinson-Patman Act, references to sellers or suppliers and buyers, purchasers, or customers exclude the ultimate customer, the consumer. Thus, the buyer, purchaser, or customer is the retailer and the seller or supplier is the manufacturer or wholesaler. There is nothing illegal about a retailer charging different customers different prices for identical goods. For example, two households could go to a local Chevrolet dealer to buy an identical automobile and be charged different prices without any legal fault by the dealer. The Robinson-Patman Act protects competitors and not the final consumer.
12. Edwin A. Elias, "Robinson-Patman: Time for Rechiseling," *Mercer Law Review* 26 (1975): 689-736 and Rom J. Markin, Jr., "The Robinson-Patman Act: Regulatory Pariah," in Robert F. Lusch and Paul H. Zinszer, eds., *Contemporary Issues in Marketing Channels,* (Norman, Okla.: Distribution Research Program, University of Oklahoma, 1979), 121-29.
13. Joseph Barry Mason, "Power and Channel Conflicts in Shopping Center Development," *Journal of Marketing* (April 1975): 33.
14. Indian Coffee Corporation vs. The Folger Coffee Company, D.C.W. PA, Sept. 1982.
15. Falls City Industries, Inc., vs. Vanco Beverages, Inc., CCH 65, 282 (U.S.S.C., March 1983).
16. FTC vs. Fred Meyer Company, Inc., 390 U.S. 341 (1968).
17. "GM Ordered to Open up Car Rental Ad Deals," *Advertising Age,* 17 October 1983, 20.
18. Colorado Consumer Protection Act, C.R.S., 6-1-10, et seq.
19. "Store's Concept of 'Sale' Pricing."
20. "Low Prices or Low Practice?" and "Sears Calls It 'Low Prices,' New York Calls It Misleading," *Wall Street Journal,* 22 December 1989, B1, B3. For a more complete discussion of this subject,

see Sandra L. Schmidt and Jerome B. Kernan, "The Many Meanings (and Implications) of 'Satisfaction Guaranteed,'" *Journal of Retailing* (Winter 1985): 89-108.
21. "Death Among the Pop-Tarts," *Texas Monthly* (August 1982): 90 and "What Does H.E.B. Stand for, Anyway?" *Texas Monthly* (April 1988): 102-105, 144-161.
22. "Court, Council KO Kroger Critics," *Progressive Grocer* (May 1979): 32.
23. FTC (1983) at 690.
24. Dingell Leads Attack of FTC's New Deception Policy," *Broadcasting*, 31 October 1984, 59.
25. "Pay 'n Save Loses Supreme Court Appeal," *Chain Store Age Executive* (July 1980): 10.
26. N.C. Freed Co., Inc. vs. Board of Governors of Federal Reserve System (CA2 NY) 473 F2d 1210.
27. In re Walgreen Co., FTC File No. 852 3066.
28. Ray O. Werner, ed., "Legal Developments in Marketing," *Journal of Marketing* (Spring 1980): 100.
29. When patent laws were developed in the mid-1800s, they were designed to grant patents only to processes or products that advanced the welfare of society. Since the patent office receives so many applications for patents, it has tended to approve applications as long as the applications have been properly prepared. Thus, this generally leaves it up to the court to decide the worthiness of the product or process. In short, most patents are not worth the paper they are written on.
30. Sears, Roebuck & Co. vs. Stiffel Co., 376 U.S. 225 (U.S. Sup. Ct. 1964).
31. United States Public Law 92-573, Consumer Product Safety Act (1972).
32. Fred W. Morgan, "Tampered Goods: Legal Developments and Marketing Guidelines," *Journal of Marketing* (April 1988): 86-96.
33. Magnuson-Moss Warranty Federal Trade Commission Act, Public Law 93-637, 93rd. Congress, 1975.
34. Ray O. Werner, ed., "Legal Developments in Marketing," *Journal of Marketing* (Summer 1980): 112.
35. "FTC Still on Retailing's Case," *Chain Store Age Executive* (September 1980): 50.
36. **Intrabrand competition** is competition between two retailers selling the same brand, whereas **interbrand competition** would be between retailers selling different brands of the same product class. For example, a Chevrolet dealer engages in intrabrand competition with another Chevrolet dealer and interbrand competition with a Ford dealer.
37. White Motor vs. U.S., 372 U.S. 253.
38. White Motor vs. U.S.
39. U.S. vs. Arnold Schwinn and Co., 388 U.S. 365.
40. Continental T.V., Inc. vs. GTE Sylvania, Inc., 433 U.S. 36 (1977).
41. For a suggested approach in vertical restraint cases, see E. F. Zelek, Jr., L. W. Stern, and T. W. Dunfee, "A Rule of Reason Model After Sylvania," *California Law Review* 68 (1980): 801-36.
42. Joe Mendelovitz, d/b/a Eastex Wholesale Beer vs. Adolph Coors Co., and Highland Coors Distributors, Inc., CA-5, Dec. 1982.
43. "Territorial Franchisers Ok'd by House for Soft Drinks," *Supermarket News*, 30 June 1980, 2.
44. U.S. Department of Justice, *Vertical Restraints Guidelines*, (January 23, 1985).
45. "Justice Department Guidelines Support Marketing Restrictions by Makers," *Wall Street Journal*, 24 January 1985, 24.
46. "Pricing Flap: Small Gasoline Dealers Say Big Oil Is Pushing Them out of Business," *Wall Street Journal*, 15 October 1990, A1, A12.
47. "Thriving Factory Outlets Anger Retailers as Store Suppliers Turn into Competitors," *Wall Street Journal*, 8 October 1991, B1, B6.
48. Ibid.
49. OshKosh B'Gosh May Be Risking Its Upscale Image," *Business Week*, 15 July 1991, 140.
50. Dale F. Duhan and Mary Jane Sheffet, "Gray Markets and the Legal Status of Parallel Importation," *Journal of Marketing* (July 1988): 75-83.
51. "A Red-Letter Day for Gray Marketeers," *Business Week*, 13 June 1988, 30.
52. Unijax, Inc., vs. Champion International Inc., D.C., S.N.Y., May 1981.
53. "McDonald's Is Challenging Iowa's New Franchise Law," *Wall Street Journal* (May 14, 1992): B2. "This Franchisee Is at the Edge of the Legal Firestorm in Iowa," *Wall Street Journal* (May 22, 1992): A1.
54. Shelby D. Hunt and John R. Nevin, "Full Disclosure Laws in Franchising: An Empirical Investigation," *Journal of Marketing* (April 1976): 53, 62.
55. "Antitrust Policy After the Steel Veto," *Fortune*, 19 March 1984, 85-98.
56. Willard F. Mueller and Thomas W. Paterson, "Effectiveness of State Sales-Below-Cost Laws: Evidence from the Grocery Trade," *Journal of Retailing* (Summer 1986): 166-85.

Part 3

MERCHANDISING AND PRICING

CHAPTER 7

INTRODUCTION TO MERCHANDISING CONTROL

OVERVIEW

In this chapter we introduce the types of financial records and statements used in retail planning: the merchandise budget, inventory valuation, and accounting statements. We look at how a six-month merchandise budget is prepared and how it is used in making plans for an upcoming merchandise season. Next, we discuss inventory valuation using both the cost and the retail method. Finally, we describe the basic differences among an income statement, balance sheet, and statement of cash flow, as well as how a retailer uses these accounting statements in controlling its merchandising activities.

INTRODUCTION TO MERCHANDISING CONTROL

I. The Merchandise Budget
   A. Determining Planned Sales
   B. Determining Planned BOM and EOM Inventories
   C. Determining Planned Retail Reductions
   D. Determining Planned Purchases at Retail and Cost
   E. Determining The Buyer's Planned Gross Margin

II. Inventory Valuation
   A. The Cost Method
   B. The Retail Method
      1. Calculation of the Cost Complement
      2. Calculation of Reductions from Retail Value

        3. Conversion of Adjusted Retail Book Inventory to Cost
　III. Retail Accounting Statements
　　　A. Income Statement
　　　B. Balance Sheet
　　　C. Statement of Cash Flow
　IV. Summary

The key element in a retailer's planning process is its merchandising and pricing strategy. This is the stake around which all the retailer's other activities revolve. After all, the merchandise in a Wal-Mart or Kmart store in Des Moines looks much the same as in one in Modesto. Only after merchandising decisions are made should retailers concern themselves with store sites and design and selling and promotion activities. However, before we can explain how to make these merchandise decisions, we must discuss the retailer's means of controlling these activities.

Many people believe that the terms "retailing" and "merchandising" are synonymous. They are not. Retailing includes all the business activities that are necessary to sell goods and services to the final consumer. Merchandising, which is the balancing of inventory, sales, margins, and expenses to create a profit, is only one of the retailing activities. High-performance merchandising requires total financial planning and control.

This chapter is divided into three sections: the merchandise budget, retail accounting statements, and inventory valuation.

THE MERCHANDISE BUDGET

Successful retailers must have good financial planning and control of their merchandise. In fact, some have said that a retailer is really a financial control officer. The retailer invests money in merchandise for profitable resale to others. A poor choice of merchandise will result in a low or negative return on investment. Therefore, in order to be successful in retailing, as in any other activity, an individual must have a plan of what is to be accomplished.[1] In retailing this plan of operation is called the merchandise budget. A **merchandise budget** is a plan of projected sales for an upcoming season, when and how much merchandise is to be purchased, and what markups and reductions will likely occur. The merchandise budget forces the retailer to develop a formal outline of merchandising objectives for the upcoming selling season.

In developing the merchandise budget, the retailer must make these five major merchandising decisions:

1. What will be the anticipated sales for the department, division, or store?
2. How much stock-on-hand will be needed to achieve this sales plan, given the level of turnover expected?

ILLUSTRATION 7.1

In developing a merchandise budget, a retailer must decide when and how much to buy, as well as what projected sales will be and what markups and reductions will likely occur.

3. What reductions from the original retail price must be made in order to dispose of all the merchandise brought into the store?
4. What additional purchases must be made during the season?
5. What gross margin (the difference between sales and cost of goods sold) should the department, division, or store contribute to the overall profitability of the retailer?

When preparing the merchandise budget, the high-performance retailer must follow these four rules.

First, a merchandise budget should always be prepared in advance of the selling season. Since the original plan is often prepared by the buyer for a particular department to be approved by the divisional merchandising manager and/or the general merchandising manager, most apparel and hard-goods retail firms begin the process of developing the merchandise budget three to four months in advance of the budget period. This, however, is not always the case with some specialty stores, such as music shops. A new release is only known to the buyer about a month in advance and can be easily reordered if it goes to the top of the charts. These specialty stores also don't have to worry about markdowns since excess quantities can be returned to vendors for full credit. Most retailers operate under a two-season calendar: the spring/summer season, usually February through July, and the fall/winter season, August through January. The buyer will usually begin to prepare merchandise budgets in early April and October for the upcoming seasons.

Second, since the budget is a plan that management expects to follow in the upcoming merchandise season, the language must be easy to understand. The merchandise budget illustration contained in this chapter has only 11 items, although the number of items contained in a budget may vary by company due to their own merchandise and market characteristics. Remember, the budget can serve no useful purpose unless it can be understood by all the decision makers and unless it contains all the information needed for that particular retailer.

Third, the economy today is constantly changing and retailers are not always able to predict these changes. The standing joke among retailers is that "economists have been able to correctly predict eleven of our last three recessions." For example, early in this decade, uncertainties about the future of the economy and what actions the Federal Reserve Bank would take produced a major credit crunch for many small retailers.[2] Nevertheless, despite the uncertainties about the overall economy, the retailer must still budget. Thus, the budget is usually made for a relatively short period of time. Six months is the norm for most retailers, although some use a three-month, or even shorter, plan. Forecasting future sales is difficult enough without complicating the process by projecting for a time period too far into the future. The firm's general management should be concerned with long-term trends and effects on store and personnel needs. The firm's buyers are involved in the more short-term trends and effects that may influence the merchandise budget.

Fourth, the budget should be flexible enough so that changes are not impossible. All merchandise budgets are plans and estimates of predicted future events. However, competition and the consumer are not always predictable, especially in regard to fashion preferences. Thus, any forecast is subject to error.

A blank six-month merchandise budget for the housewares department of a major department store is shown in Exhibit 7.1. Don't be alarmed or confused if Exhibit 7.1 is not clear to you at this time. In the following discussion, as well as in the next two chapters, we will describe why the budget is set up in this form. We will also explain all the analytical tools used by the retailer to calculate the numbers required in developing a six-month merchandise budget or plan.

In Exhibit 7.1 each element of the budget is broken into four parts, last year, plan, revised plan, and actual, to provide the decision maker with complete information. *Last year* refers to last year's sales for the season; *plan* is what the original plan projected; *revised plan* is the result of any revisions caused by changing market conditions after the plan is accepted, and *actual* is the final results.

Exhibit 7.2 presents the same material in a simpler form. Here we show you how and why a retailer develops a six-month merchandise plan. Exhibit 7.2 shows the spring/summer season, February through July, for Two-Seasons Department Store, Department 353, with projected sales of $500,000, planned retail reductions of $50,000 or 10 percent of sales, planned initial markup of 45 percent, and a planned gross margin on purchases made of $208,750.

Chapter 7 Introduction to Merchandising Control

EXHIBIT 7.1

Sample Six-Month Merchandise Budget

		\multicolumn{7}{c}{SIX-MONTH MERCHANDISE BUDGET Housewares Department Fall 199X}	
		FEBRUARY	MARCH	APRIL	MAY	JUNE	JULY	Total
BOM Stock	Last Year							
	Plan							
	Revised							
	Actual							
Sales	Last Year							
	Plan							
	Revised							
	Actual							
Reductions	Last Year							
	Plan							
	Revised							
	Actual							
EOM STOCK	Last Year							
	Plan							
	Revised							
	Actual							
RETAIL PURCHASES	Last Year							
	Plan							
	Revised							
	Actual							
PURCHASES COST	Last Year							
	Plan							
	Revised							
	Actual							
INITIAL MARK-UP	Last Year							
	Plan							
	Revised							
	Actual							
GROSS MARGIN DOLLARS	Last Year							
	Plan							
	Revised							
	Actual							
GROSS MARGIN PERCENTAGE	Last Year							
	Plan							
	Revised							
	Actual							
ON ORDER: END OF MONTH	Last Year							
	Plan							
	Revised							
	Actual							

STOCKTURN: Last Year: _____ Plan _____ Actual _____
ON ORDER - BEGINNING OF SEASON: _____ Plan _____ Actual _____
EOM INVENTORY FOR LAST MONTH: _____ Plan _____ Actual _____
REDUCTION PERCENTAGE: _____ Plan _____ Actual _____
MARKUP PERCENTAGE: _____ Plan _____ Actual _____

EXHIBIT 7.2

A Completed Six-Month Merchandise Budget

Two-Seasons Department Store
Dept. 353
Six-Month Merchandise Budget

	FEBRUARY	MARCH	APRIL	MAY	JUNE	JULY	TOTAL
1. Planned BOM[a] Stock	$225,000	$300,000	$300,000	$250,000	$375,000	$300,000	----
2. Planned Sales	75,000	75,000	100,000	50,000	125,000	75,000	$500,000
3. Planned Retail Reductions	7,500	7,500	5,000	7,500	6,250	16,250	50,000
4. Planned EOM[b] Stock	300,000	300,000	250,000	375,000	300,000	250,000	----
5. Planned Purchases @ Retail	157,500	82,500	55,000	182,500	56,250	41,250	575,000
6. Planned Purchases @ Cost	86,625	45,375	30,250	100,375	30,937.50	22,687.50	316,250
7. Planned Initial Markup	70,875	37,125	24,750	82,125	25,312.50	18,562.50	258,750
8. Planned Gross Margin	63,375	29,625	19,750	74,625	19,062.50	2,312.50	208,750
9. Planned BOM Stock/Sales Ratio	3	4	3	5	3	4	----
10. Planned Sales Percentage	15%	15%	20%	10%	25%	15%	100%
11. Planned Retail Reduction Percentage	10%	10%	5%	15%	5%	21.67%	10%

Planned Total Sales for the Period	$500,000
Planned Total Retail Reduction Percentage for the Period	10%
Planned Initial Markup Percentage	45%
Planned BOM Stock for August	$250,000

[a]BOM refers to Beginning of the Month
[b]EOM refers to the End of the Month

DETERMINING PLANNED SALES

The initial step in developing a six-month merchandise budget is to estimate *planned sales* for the entire season and for each individual month.[3] The buyer begins by examining the previous year's sales records. Adjustments are then made in the planning of sales for the upcoming merchandise budget. A retailer with an excellent record of forecasting sales is San Francisco–based Williams-Sonoma, best known for its *Catalog for Cooks*. Williams-Sonoma's secret for forecasting sales rests on its highly automated mailing lists. Its database of 4.5 million customers tracks up to 150 different pieces of information per customer. With a few simple keystrokes, the retailer can tell you what you've bought from each of its five annual catalogs (an estimated 60 percent of customers have bought from more than one), what time of the year you tend to buy, how often you buy, what category of merchandise you lean toward, and so forth. Through a complex cross-referencing of the data, Williams-Sonoma's two full-time statisticians are able to project, to plus or minus 5 percent accuracy on average, each catalog's sales.[4]

Retailers, when comparing this year's sales to last year's sales, don't always compare to the exact date (i.e., comparing February 2, 1993 sales to February 2, 1992) since the dates fall on different days of the week. For instance, February 2 in 1992 was a Sunday, when the retailer might have been closed, and a Tuesday in 1993. Rather, retailers use a retail reporting calendar, as shown in Exhibit 7.3, which divides the year into two seasons, each with six months as shown. Thus, February 1, 1993, the first Monday of the spring season would be compared to February 4, 1991 and February 3, 1992, which were also the first Mondays of their spring seasons.

By using a retail reporting calendar, fashion goods retailers will eliminate problems in making direct comparison except for one event in each season. These retailers will be affected by the movement of Easter (March 31 in 1991, April 19 in 1992, and April 11 in 1993) when making comparisons in the spring season. Likewise, during the fall season, the period between Thanksgiving and Christmas can vary in length by as much as a week. Since Thanksgiving is the fourth Thursday of November, it can fall between November 22 and November 28. As a result, the number of days in the Christmas shopping season will differ from year to year. For example, in 1991, there were four weekends and 26 days between November 28 and December 25, while, in 1995, there will be five weekends and 31 days between November 23 and Christmas Day.

To return to the example in Exhibit 7.2, after reviewing the data available, the buyer for Department 353 forecasted that $500,000 was a reasonable total sales figure for the future season. June, with a projected 25 percent of total season's sales, and April, with 20 percent, are expected to be the busy months. May, with only 10 percent, is expected to be the slowest month. The remaining months will have equal sales. Since April, May, and June account for 55 percent of total sales, then February, March, and July's total must be 45 percent or 15 percent per month since they are equal. The buyer is able to determine planned monthly sales by multiplying the planned monthly sales percentage by planned total sales. Since we know February's planned monthly sales are 15 percent of the total planned sales of $500,000, February's planned sales must be $75,000 (15% × $500,000 = $75,000).

It is important to use recent trends when forecasting future sales. All too often some retailers in a no-growth market merely use last season's figures for this season's budget. This method overlooks two major influences on projected sales volume: inflation and competition. If inflation was 10 percent and no other changes occurred in the retail environment, then the retailer planning on selling the same physical volume as during the previous year should

EXHIBIT 7.3
Retail Reporting Calendar for 1992 and 1993

WEEK	PERIOD	SPRING 1992							WEEK	PERIOD	FALL 1992						
		SUN	MON	TUE	WED	THU	FRI	SAT			SUN	MON	TUE	WED	THU	FRI	SAT
4	FEB	2	3	4	5	6	7	8	4	AUG	2	3	4	5	6	7	8
		9	10	11	12	13	14	15			9	10	11	12	13	14	15
		16	17	18	19	20	21	22			16	17	18	19	20	21	22
		23	24	25	26	27	28	29			23	24	25	26	27	28	29
4	MAR	1	2	3	4	5	6	7	4	SEP	30	31	1	2	3	4	5
		8	9	10	11	12	13	14			6	7	8	9	10	11	12
		15	16	17	18	19	20	21			13	14	15	16	17	18	19
		22	23	24	25	26	27	28			20	21	22	23	24	25	26
5	APR	29	30	31	1	2	3	4	5	OCT	27	28	29	30	1	2	3
		5	6	7	8	9	10	11			4	5	6	7	8	9	10
		12	13	14	15	16	17	18			11	12	13	14	15	16	17
		19	20	21	22	23	24	25			18	19	20	21	22	23	24
		26	27	28	29	30	1	2			25	26	27	28	29	30	31
5	MAY	3	4	5	6	7	8	9	4	NOV	1	2	3	4	5	6	7
		10	11	12	13	14	15	16			8	9	10	11	12	13	14
		17	18	19	20	21	22	23			15	16	17	18	19	20	21
		24	25	26	27	28	29	30			22	23	24	25	26	27	28
		31	1	2	3	4	5	6	5	DEC	29	30	1	2	3	4	5
4	JUN	7	8	9	10	11	12	13			6	7	8	9	10	11	12
		14	15	16	17	18	19	20			13	14	15	16	17	18	19
		21	22	23	24	25	26	27			20	21	22	23	24	25	26
		28	29	30	1	2	3	4			27	28	29	30	31	1	2
4	JUL	5	6	7	8	9	10	11	4	JAN	3	4	5	6	7	8	9
		12	13	14	15	16	17	18			10	11	12	13	14	15	16
		19	20	21	22	23	24	25			17	18	19	20	21	22	23
		26	27	28	29	30	31	1			24	25	26	27	28	29	30

Chapter 7 Introduction to Merchandising Control

WEEK	PERIOD	SPRING 1993					
		SUN	MON	TUE	WED	THU	FRI	SAT
4	FEB	31	1	2	3	4	5	6
		7	8	9	10	11	12	13
		14	15	16	17	18	19	20
		21	22	23	24	25	26	27
4	MAR	28	1	2	3	4	5	6
		7	8	9	10	11	12	13
		14	15	16	17	18	19	20
		21	22	23	24	25	26	27
5	APR	28	29	30	31	1	2	3
		4	5	6	7	8	9	10
		11	12	13	14	15	16	17
		18	19	20	21	22	23	24
		25	26	27	28	29	30	1
5	MAY	2	3	4	5	6	7	8
		9	10	11	12	13	14	15
		16	17	18	19	20	21	22
		23	24	25	26	27	28	29
		30	31	1	2	3	4	5
4	JUN	6	7	8	9	10	11	12
		13	14	15	16	17	18	19
		20	21	22	23	24	25	26
		27	28	29	30	1	2	3
4	JUL	4	5	6	7	8	9	10
		11	12	13	14	15	16	17
		18	19	20	21	22	23	24
		25	26	27	28	29	30	31

WEEK	PERIOD	FALL 1993					
		SUN	MON	TUE	WED	THU	FRI	SAT
4	AUG	1	2	3	4	5	6	7
		8	9	10	11	12	13	14
		15	16	17	18	19	20	21
		22	23	24	25	26	27	28
4	SEP	29	30	31	1	2	3	4
		5	6	7	8	9	10	11
		12	13	14	15	16	17	18
		19	20	21	22	23	24	25
5	OCT	26	27	28	29	30	1	2
		3	4	5	6	7	8	9
		10	11	12	13	14	15	16
		17	18	19	20	21	22	23
		24	25	26	27	28	29	30
4	NOV	31	1	2	3	4	5	6
		7	8	9	10	11	12	13
		14	15	16	17	18	19	20
		21	22	23	24	25	26	27
5	DEC	28	29	30	1	2	3	4
		5	6	7	8	9	10	11
		12	13	14	15	16	17	18
		19	20	21	22	23	24	25
		26	27	28	29	30	31	1
4	JAN	2	3	4	5	6	7	8
		9	10	11	12	13	14	15
		16	17	18	19	20	21	22
		23	24	25	26	27	28	29

expect a 10 percent increase in this season's dollar sales. Similarly, if the exit of a competitor across town is expected to increase the number of customer transactions by 5 percent, this increase should be reflected in the budget. Suppose that last year's sales were $100,000, inflation is 10 percent, and the retailer expects its market share to increase by 8 percent, while the total market remains stable. What should your projected sales be? A simple equation used in retail planning is

Total sales = Average sale × Total transactions

In the preceding example, average sales would increase by the 10 percent level of inflation to 1.10 times last year's sales and total transactions would increase by the 8 percent gain in market share to 1.08 times last year's total transactions for an increase in total sales of 1.188 times (or 1.10 × 1.08), resulting in a total sales increase of $18,800 to budgeted total sales of $118,800.

DETERMINING PLANNED BOM AND EOM INVENTORIES

Once the buyer has estimated the seasonal and monthly sales for the upcoming season, plans can be made for *inventory requirements.* In order to achieve projected sales figures, the merchant will generally carry stock or inventory in excess of planned sales for the period, be it a week, month, or season. The extra stock or inventory provides a merchandise assortment deep and broad enough to ensure sales. A common method of estimating the amount of stock to be carried is the **stock-to-sales ratio.** This ratio depicts the amount of stock to have on hand at the beginning of each month to support the forecasted sales for that month. For example, a ratio of 5.0 would suggest that the retailer have $5 in inventory (at retail price) for every $1 in forecasted sales. Planned average beginning-of-the-month (BOM) stock-to-sales ratios can also be calculated directly from a retailer's planned turnover goals. For example, a retailer wants a target turnover rate of 4.0. By dividing the number of months in a year (12) by the annual turnover rate, we can compute the average BOM stock-to-sales ratio for the year. In this case,

Number of months/ Turnover rate = BOM stock-to-sales ratio
12 / 4.0 = 3.0

Thus, the average stock-to-sales ratio for the season is 3.0. Generally, these stock-to-sales ratios will fluctuate month to month as sales tend to fluctuate monthly. Nevertheless, it is important to always review these ratios because if they are set too high or too low, too much or too little inventory will be on hand to meet the sales target.

Other methods of determining opening inventory will be discussed in Chapter 8. From experience, a buyer knows how much stock must be maintained in order to generate planned sales. Retail trade associations such as the National Retail Federation conduct surveys and publish industry average

ILLUSTRATION 7.2

Retail trade shows allow retailers to visit the trade show booths of many vendors and compare their merchandise offerings with a minimum expenditure of time and money.

stock-to-sales ratios. Based on data available, the buyer for Department 353 used a planned stock-to-sales ratio of 3.0 for February, April, and June, a ratio of 4.0 for March and July, and a ratio of 5.0 for May. The buyer was able to determine that $300,000 worth of merchandise was needed beginning March 1 due to a planned stock-to-sales ratio of 4.0 and planned sales of $75,000. Two things should be noted. First, stock-to-sales ratios always express inventory levels at retail, not cost. Second, the beginning-of-the-month (BOM) inventory for one month is the end-of-the month (EOM) inventory for the previous month. This relationship can be easily seen by comparing the BOM figures for one month in Exhibit 7.2 with the EOM figures for the previous month.

DETERMINING PLANNED RETAIL REDUCTIONS

All merchandise brought into the store for sale to consumers is not actually sold at the planned initial markup price. Therefore, when preparing the six-month budget, the buyer should make allowances for **reductions** in the dollar values of stock not due to sales. Generally, these planned retail reductions fall into three categories: markdowns, employee discounts, and stock shortages. These items are referred to as reductions because they reduce the department's retail inventory values and the planned gross margin, unless the vendor (a general term used in retailing to refer to the suppliers of merchandise to retailers) makes a corresponding contribution to the retailer. Reductions must be planned because, as the dollar value of the inventory level is reduced, the BOM stock to support next month's forecasted sales will be inadequate unless adjustments are made this month.

A few retailers don't include planned reductions in their merchandise budgets. They simply treat them as part of the normal operation of the store and feel they should be controlled without being part of the total budget. This gives management an understated, conservative planned-purchase figure, thereby having the effect of holding back some purchase reserve until the physical inventory reveals the exact amount of reductions. We have included planned reductions here for two reasons: (1) to reflect the additional purchases needed for sufficient inventory to begin the next month and (2) to point out that taking reductions is not bad. Too often, inexperienced retailers believe that taking a reduction is an admission of error and therefore fail to mark down merchandise until it is too late in the season. Therefore, a buyer must remember that reductions are part of the cost of doing business. Methods available to the retail buyer for minimizing retail reductions caused by retailer mistakes are discussed in Chapter 9.

It should be noted that reductions in our six-month budget are listed as a percentage of sales, not as a percentage of planned sales so as to make calculations easier. The buyer in our example has estimated monthly retail reduction percentages as shown on line 11. To determine planned retail reductions for March (line 3), planned monthly sales are multiplied by the planned monthly retail reduction percentage to yield the planned monthly retail reduction of $7,500 ($75,000 × 10% = $7,500).

Reductions are one of the major items in the merchandise budget subject to constant change. One reason is that the planned reductions may prove inadequate in light of actual conditions encountered by the retailer. If retailers delay too long in taking reductions, they may be forced to take even larger price cuts later on as the merchandise style depreciates even more in value. Alternatively, consider what happens when the department manager does such an effective merchandising job that not all the reduction money is needed for the period. The solution to both these dilemmas is found in the rules for developing a budget; namely, keeping it so flexible it can be intelligently administered.

DETERMINING PLANNED PURCHASES AT RETAIL AND COST

We are now ready to determine what additional purchases must be made during the merchandising season. The retailer will need inventory for (1) planned sales, (2) planned retail reductions, and (3) planned EOM inventory. In the six-month merchandise budget example, the March *planned purchases at retail* for Department 353 are $82,500 (line 5). This figure was derived by (1) adding planned sales, planned retail reductions, and planned EOM inventory and (2) subtracting planned BOM inventory:

$75,000 + $7,500 + $300,000 − $300,000 = $82,500

Once planned purchases at retail are determined, *planned purchases at cost* can be easily calculated. The retail price always represents a combination of cost plus markup. If the markup percentage is given, the portion of retail attributed to cost (or the cost complement) can be derived by subtracting the markup percentage from the retail percentage of 100 percent. Given the markup percentage is 45 percent of retail for Department 353, the cost complement percentage must be 55 percent (100% − 45% = 55%). Planned purchases at cost for March (line 6) must be 55 percent of planned purchases at retail or $45,375 ($82,500 × 55% = $45,375). Planned initial markup for March (line 7) must be 45% of planned purchases or $37,125 ($82,500 × 45% = $37,125).

DETERMINING THE BUYER'S PLANNED GROSS MARGIN

The last step in developing the merchandise budget is determining the buyer's planned gross margin for the period. As we already discussed, the buyer in making plans recognizes that the initial selling price for all the products will probably not be realized and that some reductions will occur. Referring to Exhibit 7.2, the buyer's planned gross margin for February (line 8) is determined by taking planned initial markup (line 7) and subtracting planned reductions (line 3) ($70,875 − $7,500 = $63,375). Notice that the *buyer's* planned gross margin is not the same as the *firm's* gross margin for the month as used in accounting statements, because buyers are only accountable for their own actions. In this case, the buyer is accountable for the purchases made, the expected selling price of these purchases, the cost of these purchases, and the reductions that are involved in selling merchandise the buyer has previously purchased. Thus, in February, the buyer's gross margin is the result not of the $75,000 in sales but of the purchases of $157,500 having an initial markup of $70,875 and reductions of $7,500. The buyer's planned gross margin of $63,375 ($70,875 − $7,500) therefore reflects the amount of gross margin that the buyer's actions will contribute to the firm when the merchandise is sold.

Gross margin is not the same as profit. **Gross margin** is the difference between the total cost of merchandise and net merchandise sales. **Operating profit** is gross margin minus all the operating expenses. **Net profit** is operating profit plus or minus any transactions not directly relating to the firm's retailing activities. Yet, because sales and the cost of goods are essentially controllable by the buying function of the firm, which usually has little or no control over many of the other expenses that affect the profitability of a retail unit, gross margin is still one of the key measures of a retailer's merchandising success.

INVENTORY VALUATION

Due to the many different merchandise lines carried, most retail inventory accounting systems are quite complex. The advent of the scanner and other computer technology, which will be discussed in detail in Chapter 17, has enabled the retailer to both speed up and improve the accuracy of inventory valuation. Nevertheless, these inventory systems must provide the retailer with information such as sales, additional purchases not yet received, reductions for the period, gross margin, open-to-buy, stock shortages, and inventory levels.

Two inventory accounting systems are available for the retailer: (1) the cost method and (2) the retail method. We will describe and analyze both accounting methods on the basis of the frequency with which inventory information is received, difficulties encountered in completing a physical inventory and maintaining records, and the extent to which stock shortages can be calculated.

THE COST METHOD

In the **cost method** of inventory valuation, the cost of each item is recorded in the accounting records by its inventory code number or is coded on the price tag. When a physical inventory is taken, all the items are counted, the cost of each item is taken from the records or the price tags, and the total inventory value at cost is calculated.

One of the easiest methods of coding the cost of merchandise on the price tag is to use the first 10 letters of the alphabet to represent the price. Here A = 1, B = 2, C = 3, D = 4, E = 5, F = 6, G = 7, H = 8, I = 9, J = 0. A product with the code EFIC has a cost of $56.93. This method is useful as an accounting tool as well as for those retailers that allow price negotiations by customers (dollar markup per item is easy to calculate).

The cost method can be used when one is conducting physical or book inventories. A **physical inventory** involves an actual count of merchandise, whereas a **book inventory** depends on bookkeeping entries.

The physical inventory system using the cost method can be illustrated by using the income statement for Fallon Company for the spring season 199X, as shown in Exhibit 7.4. The sales amount is from the store's total receipts during the season. Beginning inventory is calculated by a physical count of all merchandise in stock on February 1 and recorded at cost. Purchases are determined by summing all invoice slips for merchandise received during the season. Ending inventory is the physical count on July 31, at cost.

When using the physical inventory system, gross margin cannot be calculated until after the ending inventory is taken and the cost of goods sold is determined. Because most retailers undertake physical inventories only once or twice a year, the physical method imposes severe limitations on the retailer's merchandise planning. This method also prevents the retailer from calculating (and spotting) inventory shortages resulting from theft, breakage, and so on, because the ending inventory is only determined by the costing of all items in stock.

The book inventory system (sometimes called the perpetual inventory system) avoids the problem of infrequent financial statements by keeping a running total of the cost value of inventory on hand at a given time. In addition, it allows a retailer to calculate shortages at any point in time. A

EXHIBIT 7.4

A Sample Income Statement

The Fallon Company
Income Statement
Feb. 1–July 30, 199X

Sales		$500,000
Less: Cost of Goods Sold:		
Beginning inventory (at cost)	$400,000	
Purchases (at cost)	150,000	
Goods available for sale	$550,000	
Ending inventory (at cost)	325,000	
Cost of goods sold		225,000
Gross Margin		$275,000
Less: operating expenses		
Salaries	$125,000	
Utilities	25,000	
Rent	40,000	
Depreciation (fixtures + equipment)	35,000	
Total Operating Expenses		225,000
Net Profit Before Taxes		$ 50,000

retailer maintains a perpetual system by adding purchases to its current inventory value and subtracting sales to arrive at the new current value of the inventory at cost. Exhibit 7.5 shows how the perpetual inventory system would have worked for our Fallon Company example.

Exhibit 7.5 contains the same financial information—the beginning inventory, total purchases, total cost of goods sold, and ending inventory—for Fallon Company as the income statement in Exhibit 7.4. If sales and operating expenses were given, one could determine the income for the period using the perpetual inventory data.

As shown previously, the book inventory system for retailers using the cost method is superior to the physical inventory system on two counts. First, the book system enables the retailer to know end-of-the-month inventory levels without taking a physical count, and frequent financial statements can be developed. Second, a book inventory value is available for comparison with the physical count to determine shortages.

The cost method of inventory valuation does have several limitations, however. These limitations include:

1. The fact that daily inventories (or even monthly inventories) are impractical

EXHIBIT 7.5

The Fallon Company Perpetual Inventory System

Date	BOM Inventory (at Cost)	+	Purchases (at Cost)	−	Sales (at Cost)	=	EOM Inventory (at Cost)
2/1	$400,000		$ 30,000		$ 45,000		$385,000
3/1	385,000		20,000		40,000		365,000
4/1	365,000		40,000		35,000		370,000
5/1	370,000		10,000		25,000		355,000
6/1	355,000		25,000		40,000		340,000
7/1	340,000		25,000		40,000		325,000
TOTAL			$150,000		$225,000		

2. The difficulties involved in costing out each sale
3. The problems involved in allocating freight charges to the cost of goods sold
4. The difficulty of adjusting inventory values to reflect changes in the demand for the product at the retail level

The cost method is generally used by those retailers with big-ticket items and a limited number of sales per day (i.e., a jewelry store selling expensive items or an antique furniture store), where there are few lines, limited seasonality, infrequent price changes, and low turnover rates.

Two methods of costing inventory are FIFO (first in, first out) and LIFO (last in, first out). The **FIFO** method assumes that the oldest merchandise is sold before the more recently purchased merchandise. Therefore, the merchandise on the shelf will reflect the most current replacement price. During inflationary periods this method allows the retailer to realize "inventory profits" (by selling the less expensive earlier inventory, not the more expensive newer inventory).

The **LIFO** method is designed to cushion the impact of inflationary pressures by matching current costs against current revenues. The cost of goods sold is based on the cost of the most recently purchased inventory, while the older inventory is regarded as the unsold inventory. The LIFO method results in the application of a higher unit cost to the merchandise sold and a lower unit cost to inventory still unsold. In times of inflation most retailers use the LIFO method, resulting in lower profits on the income statement, but also lower income taxes. Most retailers also prefer to use LIFO for planning purposes, since it accurately reflects replacement costs.

The Internal Revenue Service only permits a retailer to change its accounting method once.

THE RETAIL METHOD

Due to the limitations of the cost method, most retailers use the **retail method** of inventory valuation which was created in the early 1900s. The objectives of the retail inventory method are to determine interim inventory amounts and the cost of goods sold and to monitor inventory shortage. This method of inventory overcomes the disadvantages of the cost method by keeping detailed records of inventory based on the retail value of the merchandise. The fact that the inventory is valued in retail dollars, however, makes it a little more difficult for the retailer to determine the cost of goods sold when computing the gross margin for a time period. Some retail consultants, given the sophisticated inventory systems available today, are recommending a switch back to the cost method.[5]

There are three basic steps in computing an ending inventory value using the retail method: (1) calculation of the cost complement, (2) calculation of reductions from retail value, and (3) conversion of the adjusted retail book inventory to cost.

Calculation of the Cost Complement. Inventories, both beginning and ending, and purchases are recorded at both cost and retail levels when using the retail method. Exhibit 7.6 shows an inventory statement for Spengel's Sporting Goods for the fall season.

In Exhibit 7.6 the beginning inventory is shown at both cost and retail. Net purchases, which are the total purchases less merchandise returned to vendors, allowances, and discounts from vendors, are also valued at cost and retail. Additional markups are the total increases in the retail price of merchandise already in stock which were caused by inflation or heavy demand. Freight-in is the cost to the retailer for transportation of merchandise from vendors.

Using the information from Exhibit 7.6, the retailer can calculate the average relationship of cost to retail price for all merchandise available for sale during the fall season. This calculation is called the **cost complement**:

EXHIBIT 7.6

Spengel's Sporting Goods Inventory Available for Sale, Fall Season, 199X

	Cost	Retail
Beginning inventory	$199,000	$401,000
Net Purchases	70,000	154,000
Additional Markups		5,000
Freight-in	1,000	
Total inventory available for sale	$270,000	$560,000

Cost complement = Total cost valuation/Total retail valuation
= $270,000/$560,000 = 0.482

Since the cost complement is 0.482, or 48.2 percent, 48.2 cents of every retail sales dollar is comprised of merchandise cost.

Calculation of Reductions from Retail Value. During the course of retail day-to-day business activities, the retailer must take reductions from inventory. In addition to sales which lower the retail inventory level, retail inventory can be lowered by reductions. These reductions include markdowns (sales and reduced prices on end-of-season, discontinued, or shopworn merchandise), discounts (employee, senior citizen, student, religious, etc.), and stock shortages (employee and customer theft, breakage). Markdowns and discounts can be recorded throughout an accounting period, but a physical inventory is required to calculate stock shortages.

In Exhibit 7.6 we see that Spengel's had a retail inventory available for sale of $560,000 for the 199X fall season. This must be reduced by actual fall season sales of $145,000, markdowns of $12,000, and discounts of $2,000. This results in an ending book value of inventory at retail of $401,000, shown in Exhibit 7.7.

Once the ending book value of inventory at retail is determined, a comparison can be made to the physical inventory to compute the actual stock shortages. If the book value is greater than the physical count, a stock shortage has occurred. If the book value is smaller than the physical count, a stock overage has occurred. Shrinkage, or shortages, are due to thefts, breakages, overshipments not billed to customers, and the most common cause—bookkeeping errors. These errors result from the failure to properly record markdowns, returns, discounts, and breakages. While most consumers believe that shrinkage is caused by theft, it really is employee error, not misdeeds. Many retailers have greatly reduced their original shrinkage estimate by reviewing the season's bookkeeping entries. A stock overage, an excess of

EXHIBIT 7.7

Spengel's Sporting Goods Ending Book Value at Retail, Fall Season, 199X

Inventory available for sale at retail		$560,000
Less reductions:		
Sales	$145,000	
Markdowns	12,000	
Discounts	2,000	
Total reductions		159,000
Ending book value of inventory at retail		$401,000

physical inventory over book inventory, also is usually the result of bookkeeping errors, either miscounting during the physical inventory or improper book entries. Exhibit 7.8 shows the results of Spengel's physical inventory and the ensuing adjustment.

Since a physical inventory must be taken in order to determine shortages (overages) and retailers only take a physical count once or twice a year, shortages (overages) are often estimated in merchandise budgets as shown in Exhibits 7.1 and 7.2. As a rule of thumb, convenience stores use a figure of 1 to 2 percent of sales, while furniture stores use a half percent of sales in estimating monthly shortages.

Conversion of Adjusted Retail Book Inventory to Cost. The final step to be performed in using the retail method is to convert to cost the adjusted retail book inventory figure in order to determine the closing inventory at cost. The procedure involved here is simply multiplying the adjusted retail book inventory ($398,000 in the case of Spengel's) by the cost complement (0.482 in our example):

$$\begin{aligned}\text{Closing inventory (at cost)} &= \text{Adjusted retail book inventory} \\ &\quad \times \text{Cost complement} \\ &= \$398{,}000 \times 0.482 \\ &= \$191{,}836\end{aligned}$$

While this equation does not yield the actual closing inventory at cost, it does provide a close approximation of the cost figure. Now that ending inventory at cost has been determined, the retailer can determine gross margin, as well as net profit before taxes if operating expenses are known. In the Spengel's example, let's use $12,000 for salaries, $1,000 for utilities, $9,000 for rent, and $2,200 for depreciation. These are shown in Exhibit 7.9.

The retail method has several advantages over the cost method of inventory valuation. Among these advantages are:

1. Accounting statements can be drawn up at any time. Inventories need not be taken for preparation of these statements.

EXHIBIT 7.8

Spengel's Sporting Goods, Stock Shortage (Overage) Adjustment Entry, End of Fall Season, 199X

Ending book value of inventory at retail	$401,000
Physical inventory (at retail)	398,000
Stock shortages	$ 3,000
Adjusted ending book value of inventory at retail	$398,000

EXHIBIT 7.9

Spengel's Sporting Goods, Income Statement, Aug. 1–Jan. 31, 199X

Sales		$145,000
Less: Cost of Goods Sold:		
Beginning inventory (at cost)	$200,000	
Purchases (at cost)	70,000	
Goods available for sale	$270,000	
Ending inventory (at cost)	191,836	
Cost of goods sold		78,164
Gross Margin		$ 66,836
Less: operating expenses		
Salaries	$ 12,000	
Utilities	1,000	
Rent	9,000	
Depreciation (fixtures + equipment)	2,200	
Total Operating Expenses		24,200
Net Profit Before Taxes		$ 42,636

2. Physical inventories using retail prices are less subject to error and can be completed in a shorter amount of time.
3. The retail method provides an automatic, conservative valuation of ending inventory as well as inventory levels throughout the season. This is especially useful in cases where the retailer is forced to submit insurance claims for damaged or lost merchandise.

Complaints against the retail method include the fact that it is a "method of averages." That is, closing inventory is valued at the average relationship between cost and retail, and large retailers, such as supermarkets, offer many different classifications and lines with different margins. This disadvantage can be overcome by breaking down the total inventory into smaller homogeneous subsegments with similar margins, or by adjusting the cost complement to account for variations in the mix of purchases versus inventory.

The retail method places a heavy burden on the bookkeeping activities. The true ending book inventory value can be correctly calculated only if there are no errors in recording beginning inventory, purchases, freight-in, markups, markdowns, discounts, returns, transfers between stores, and sales. As noted earlier, many of the retailer's original shortages have later been determined to be bookkeeping errors.

One of the biggest limitations of this method, however, occurs in the dry grocery (dairy, liquor, frozen foods, and cigarettes) and nonfood departments of modern supermarkets. The retail method worked well in earlier times when stores were smaller, had less and more cohesive inventory assortments, and pricing was less promotional or competitive. Modern supermarkets, however, are built around heavy promotional activities and buying programs to ensure that the large retailer gains price advantages. In such an environment, a retailer might pay four different prices, resulting in four different margins, for the same SKU within a month. Here the retail method is inadequate and ineffective without a POS scanner inventory system to track sales and purchases.[6]

RETAIL ACCOUNTING STATEMENTS

Successful retailing also requires sound accounting practices, although the number and types of accounting records needed depend on management's objectives. Large retailers generally require more detailed information based on merchandise lines, departments, branches, or divisions. Small retailers may be able to make first-hand observations of sales and inventory levels and make decisions before financial data are available. Still, the small retailer would be well advised to consult the accounting records to confirm personal observations.

Properly prepared financial records provide measurements of profitability and retail performance. In addition, they show all transactions occurring within a given time period. However, financial records must provide the manager with not only a "look at the past" but also a "look into the future" so the manager can plan. Financial records should indicate whether a retailer has achieved high-performance results and whether growth potential and problem areas lie ahead. They can answer such questions as:

1. Is some merchandise line outperforming or underperforming the rest of the store?
2. Is the inventory level adequate for the current sales level?
3. Is the firm's debt level too high or increasing over time?
4. Are reductions too high a percentage of sales or increasing over time?
5. Is the gross margin adequate for the firm's profit objectives?

In one company where merchandise line X was generating an annual profit of $800,000, and merchandise line Y was losing money at the rate of $600,000, management was totally unaware of the situation, just pleasantly happy to be making $200,000! Management was astounded when a little accounting work revealed the true situation.[7]

INCOME STATEMENT

The most important financial statement a retailer prepares is the income statement (also referred to as the profit and loss statement). The **income**

statement provides a summary of the sales and expenses for a given time period, usually monthly, quarterly, seasonally, or annually. Comparison of current results with prior results allows the retailer to notice trends or changes in sales, expenses, and profits. Many financial institutions base their loan decisions on the retailer's income statement and, as a result, as shown in Retailing in Action 7.1, retailers have found ways to improve their reported financial position without actually improving their situation.

Since income statements can be further subdivided by departments, divisions, branches, and so on, the retailer can evaluate each subunit's operating performance for the period. Exhibit 7.10a shows the basic format for an income statement and Exhibit 7.10b shows the income statement for TMD Furniture.

Gross sales are the retailer's total sales whether or not the sales were for cash or credit. **Returns and allowances** are reductions from gross sales. In Exhibit 7.10b the retailer made adjustments to customers because the customers returned merchandise to the retailer. Since these reductions represent cancellations of previously recorded sales, the gross sales figure must be reduced to reflect them.

Net sales, gross sales less returns and allowances, represent the amount of merchandise the retailer actually sold during the time period.

Cost of goods sold is the cost of merchandise that has been sold during the period. While this concept is easy to understand, the exact calculation of the cost of goods sold is somewhat complex. For example, like their own customers, retailers may obtain some return privileges or receive some allowances from vendors. Also, there is the problem of establishing inventory costs.

Let's study an example of the effect of the LIFO and FIFO methods of inventory valuation on the firm's financial performance. Suppose you began the year with a total inventory of 15 fax machines which you purchased on the

---

EXHIBIT 7.10a

Retailers' Basic Income Statement Format

Gross Sales		$ _____
— Returns and Allowances	$ _____	
Net Sales		$ _____
— Cost of Goods Sold	$ _____	
Gross Margin		$ _____
— Operating Expenses	$ _____	
Operating Profit		$ _____
± Other Income or Expenses	$ _____	
Net Profit Before Taxes		$ _____

EXHIBIT 7.10b

A Sample Income Statement

TMD Furniture, Inc.
Six Month Income Statement
July 31, 199x

				Percentage
Gross Sales			$393,671.79	
Less: Returns and Allowances			16,300.00	
Net Sales			$377,371.79	100%
Less: Cost of Goods Sold				
Beginning Inventory		$ 98,466.29		
Purchases		218,595.69		
Goods Available for Sales		$317,061.98		
Ending Inventory		103,806.23	213,255.75	56.5%
Gross Margin			$164,116.04	43.5%
Less: Operating Expenses				
Salaries & Wages:				
Managers	$18,480.50			
Selling	17,755.65			
Office	7,580.17			
Warehouse & Delivery	6,685.99			
		$ 50,502.31		
Advertising		15,236.67		
Administration and Warehouse Charge		800.00		
Credit, Collections and Bad Debts		1,973.96		
Contributions		312.50		
Delivery		1,434.93		
Depreciation		5,398.56		
Dues		23.50		
Employee Benefits		566.26		
Utilities		3,738.74		
Insurance		3,041.75		
Legal and Auditing		1,000.00		
Mds. Service & Repair		1,439.16		
Miscellaneous		602.00		
Rent		9,080.00		
Repairs & Maintenance		1,576.99		
Sales Allowances		180.50		
Supplies, Postage		1,135.40		
Taxes:				
City, County & State	$ 2,000.00			
Payroll	3,902.90	5,902.90		
Telephone		1,520.09		
Travel		404.92		
Warehouse Handling Charges		12,216.86	118,088.00	31.3%
Operating Profit			$ 46,028.04	12.2%
Other Income:				
Carrying Charges		$ 3,377.48		
Profit on sale of parking lot		740.47	4,117.95	1.1%
Net Profit Before Taxes			$ 50,145.99	13.3%

> ## RETAILING IN ACTION
>
> ### 7.1 Dressing Up the Balance Sheet
>
> Retailers, especially small retailers, learned a long time ago that lenders judge the worth and creditability of a business by the firm's financial statements. Thus, many retailers make their statements look as good as possible. Listed below are a number of things retailers can do to window-dress their books.
>
> First, since ratio analysis, which was explained in Chapter 2, is probably the most common way lenders analyze a balance sheet, retailers may improve their ratios by doing the following. The current ratio (current assets divided by current liabilities) can be improved by paying off current debt before the review. For example, suppose a retailer has $20,000 in cash, $30,000 in other current assets, and $25,000 in current liabilities, for a current ratio of 2:1. If $12,500 of the cash is used to reduce debt, however, the ratio improves significantly to 3:1. The same principle can be used when a retailer exchanges long-term debt for short-term debt.
>
> Another method is to have the retailer borrow against receivables from a bank or a finance company. Retailers normally issue a payment to the lender for any collection on these receivables. As a result, on the day the retailer collects from a customer, the retailer's bank balance is impressive. The next day, however, it is anemic again.
>
> Another common method to improve the balance sheet is to have the lending institution agree to a slower repayment schedule, enabling the retailer to build up its cash balance.
>
> Are the methods legal? Are they ethical? Would you use them?

last day of the preceding year for $300 each. Thus, if the fax machines were the only merchandise you had in stock, your beginning inventory was $4,500 (15 × $300). Suppose also that during the year you sold 12 fax machines for $700 each for total sales of $8,400, that in June you purchased 8 new fax machines (same make and model as your old ones) at $325, and that in November you bought 4 more at $350. Thus, your purchases were $2,600 in June and $1,400 in November for a total of $4,000, and you would still have 15 fax machines in stock at year end. Under the LIFO inventory approach, your ending inventory would be the same as it was at the beginning of the year ($4,500), since we would assume that the 12 fax machines sold were the 12 purchased during the year. However, using the FIFO approach, we would assume that we sold 12 of the original $300 fax machines and had 3 left. These three fax machines, along with June's and November's purchases, result in an ending inventory of $4,900 [(3 × $300) + (4 × $350)]. Now let's see how these approaches can affect our gross margins.

	LIFO	FIFO
Net sales	$8,400	$8,400
Less: Cost of goods sold		
Beginning inventory $4,500		$4,500
Purchases 4,000		4,000
Goods available $8,500		$8,500
Ending inventory 4,500		4,900
Cost of goods sold	4,000	3,600
Gross margin	$4,400	$4,800

Once the retailer makes a determination of the cost of goods sold, the gross margin can be computed. **Gross margin,** as we pointed out earlier, is the difference between net sales and the cost of goods sold, or the amount available to cover operating expenses and produce a profit. We see by this example that using LIFO inventory valuation results in $4,400 in gross margin dollars versus $4,800 when FIFO inventory valuation is used. This supports our earlier statement that during inflationary times LIFO results in lower profits.

Operating expenses are those expenses that a retailer incurs in the operation of the business other than the cost of the merchandise sold (i.e., payroll, rent, utilities, advertising, depreciation, supplies, taxes, interest paid, repairs, and insurance).

Operating profit is the difference between gross margin and operating expenses.

Other income or expenses is income or expense items that the firm incurs, though not in the course of its normal retail operations. For example, a retailer might have purchased some land to use for expansion and after careful deliberation postponed the expansion plans. Now the retailer rents that land. Since renting land is not in the normal course of business for a retailer, the rent received would be considered other income.

Net profit is operating profit plus or minus other income or expenses. Net profit is the figure upon which the retailer pays taxes and thus is usually referred to as net profit before taxes.

Most retailers actually divide the income statement into two sections, the first, or the top half, being those elements above the gross margin total, and the second, the bottom half, being those elements below the gross margin total. Sales and cost of goods sold are essentially controllable by the buying functions of the retail organization, which has less and less control over the operating expenses that are shown below gross margin. In fact, a number of retail organizations have started to include the cost of personnel responsible for the acquisitions of merchandise in the cost of goods sold. This practice does, however, drastically distort the firm's gross margin figures when used in comparison to retailers that don't include those costs.

BALANCE SHEET

The second accounting statement used in financial reporting is the balance sheet. A **balance sheet** shows the financial condition of a retailer's business at a particular point in time, as opposed to the income statement which reports on the activities over a period of time. The balance sheet identifies and quantifies all the firm's **assets** and **liabilities.** The difference between assets and liabilities is **owner's equity** (or **net worth**). Comparison of a current balance sheet with that from a previous time period enables a retail analyst to observe changes in the firm's financial condition.[8]

A typical balance sheet format is illustrated in Exhibit 7.11. As Exhibit 7.11a shows, the basic equation for a balance sheet is

Assets = Liabilities + Net worth

Hence, both sides always must be in balance with each other. Exhibit 7.11b shows the balance sheet for TMD Furniture.

An **asset** is anything of value that is owned by the retail firm. Assets are broken down into two categories: current and noncurrent.

Current assets include cash and all other items that the retailer can easily convert into cash within a relatively short period of time (generally one year). Besides cash, current assets include marketable securities, accounts receivable, notes receivable, inventory, supplies, and prepaid expenses. **Accounts and notes receivable** are amounts that customers owe the retailer for goods and services. Frequently, the retailer will reduce the total receivables by a fixed percentage (based on past experience) to take into account those customers who may be unwilling or unable to pay. **Prepaid expenses** are those items, such as trash collection, for which the retailer has already paid but the service has not been completed. **Retail inventories** comprise merchandise that the retailer has in the store or in storage and is available for sale.

Earlier we discussed the effect that the LIFO and FIFO methods of estimating retail inventory will have on profits. A similar comparison holds true with regard to inventory valuation in the current asset section of the balance sheet. In times of rising prices, the LIFO method reduces the firm's inventory values, while the FIFO method increases the value of inventory. As we mentioned, most retailers favor the conservative LIFO method so as not to overstate assets or profits.

Noncurrent assets are those assets that cannot be converted into cash in a short period of time in the normal course of business. These long-term assets include buildings, parking lots, fixtures (i.e., display racks), and equipment

EXHIBIT 7.11a
Retailers' Basic Balance Sheet Format

Current Assets		Current Liabilities	
Cash	$_____	Accounts Payable	$_____
Accounts Receivable	$_____	Payroll Payable	$_____
Inventory	$_____	Current Notes Payable	$_____
Prepaid Expenses	$_____	Taxes Payable	$_____
Total Current Assets	$_____	Total Current Liabilities	$_____
Noncurrent Assets		Long-term Liabilities	
Building (less depreciation)	$_____	Long-term Notes Payable	$_____
Fixtures and Equipment (less depreciation)	$_____	Mortgage Payable	$_____
Total Noncurrent Assets	$_____		
Goodwill	$_____	Total Long-term Liabilities	$_____
		Net Worth	
		Capital Surplus	$_____
		Retained Earnings	$_____
		Total Net Worth	$_____
TOTAL ASSETS	$_____	TOTAL LIABILITIES and NET WORTH	$_____

EXHIBIT 7.11b
A Sample Balance Sheet

TMD Furniture
Balance Sheet
July 31, 199X

Current Assets			Current Liabilities		
Cash	$ 11,589		Accounts Payable	$57,500	
Accounts Receivable	71,517		Payroll Payable	$ 1,451	
Inventory	103,806		Current Notes Payable	$14,000	
			Taxes Payable	$ 1,918	
Total Current Assets		186,912	Total Current Liabilities		$ 74,869
Noncurrent Assets			Long-term Liabilities		
Building (less depreciation)	$ 61,414		Long-term Notes Payable	$52,750	
Fixtures and Equipment (less depreciation)	$ 11,505		Mortgage Payable	$38,500	
Total Noncurrent Assets		72,919	Total Long-term Liabilities		$ 91,250
Goodwill		100	Net Worth		$ 93,812
TOTAL ASSETS		$259,931	TOTAL LIABILITIES and NET WORTH		$259,931

ILLUSTRATION 7.3
Store "shells" and fixtures represent a retailer's fixed or noncurrent assets, while merchandise represents current assets.

(i.e., air-conditioning system). These items are carried on the books at cost less accumulated depreciation. Depreciation is usually necessary because most noncurrent assets have a limited useful life; the difference between the asset's original cost and depreciated values provides a more realistic picture of the retailer's assets and prevents overstating them.

Some retailers also include goodwill as an asset. **Goodwill** is an intangible asset, usually based on customer loyalty, that a retailer pays for when buying an existing business. The dollar value assigned to goodwill is generally minimal since current accounting regulations require any goodwill to be written off over 40 years, reducing the purchasing retailer's taxable profits.

Total assets equal current assets plus noncurrent assets plus goodwill.

The other part of the balance sheet reflects the retailer's liabilities and net worth. A **liability** is any legitimate claim against the retailer's assets. Liabilities are classified as either current or long term.

Current liabilities are short-term indebtedness payable within one year. Included here are accounts payable, notes payable due within a year, payroll payable, and taxes payable. **Accounts payable** is money owed vendors for goods and services. Payroll payable is money due employees on past labor. Taxes due the government (federal, state, or local) are also considered a current liability. Another current liability that some retailers have is interest due within the year on long-term notes or mortgages.

Long-term liabilities include notes payable and mortgages not due within the year. **Total liabilities** equal current liabilities plus long-term liabilities.

Net worth is the difference between the firm's total assets and total liabilities and represents the owner's equity in the business. Net worth reflects the owner's original investment, plus any profits reinvested in the business, less any losses incurred in the business and any funds that the owners have taken out of the business.

In actuality, the balance sheet doesn't reflect all the retailer's assets and liabilities. Specifically, such items as store personnel can be an asset, or a liability, to the business. These items might not appear on the balance sheet but are extremely important to the success of a high-performance retailer. Other items that could be either assets or liabilities, although not in the strict accounting sense, are goodwill, customer loyalty, and even vendor relationships. Each of these items can contribute to the success or failure of a retailer.

Not all countries use the same accounting rules in preparing accounting statements, as shown in Retailing in Action 7.2. The variations in the use of these rules sometimes put American retailers at a disadvantage.

STATEMENT OF CASH FLOW

A third financial statement that the retailer can use to help understand the business is the statement of cash flow.[9] A **statement of cash flow** explains the changes in cash and cash equivalents (short-term, highly liquid investments that are both readily convertible to known amounts of cash, and so near their maturity that they present insignificant risk of changes in value because of changes in interest rates[11]) from one accounting period to the next by showing all cash inflows and all cash outflows from the operating, investing, and financing activities of the company for the given time period. When cash inflows exceed cash outflows, the retailer is said to have a positive cash flow; when cash outflows exceed cash inflows the retailer is said to be experiencing a negative cash flow. Thus, the purpose of the statement of cash flow is to provide information about the retailer's cash receipts and payments for a given time period and enable the retailer to project the cash needs of the firm. Based on projections, plans may be made either to seek additional financing, if a negative flow is projected, or to make other investments, if a positive flow is anticipated. Likewise, a retailer with a positive cash flow for the period might be able to take advantage of closeouts or other "good deals" from vendors.

A statement of cash flow is not the same as an income statement.[12] In a statement of cash flow, the retailer is only concerned with the movement of cash into or out of the firm, whereas an income statement pertains to the profitability of the retailer after all revenue and expenses are considered. For example, if a retailer were to make a cash sale, this would be reflected on both statements. A credit sale would only affect the income statement since no cash was received. Consider the example of TMD Furniture for the month of August 199X, as shown in Exhibit 7.12b.

RETAILING IN ACTION

7.2 International Retailers Use Different Accounting Rules

As of 1991, 30 International Accounting Standards (IASs) have been adopted by the International Accounting Standards Committee (IASC), with a membership of over 80 professional bodies representing more than 70 countries, addressing such areas as inventory valuation and goodwill.

The IASC recently issued exposure draft E38, which would eliminate LIFO as an alternative costing method in that its primary benefit is only in reducing an applicable company's tax liability. It does not appear to reflect the logical order in which most companies sell their merchandise inventory.

As a result of exposure draft E38, what will be the advantages and disadvantages to U.S. retailers versus U.K. retailers? Since most U.S. retailers utilize the LIFO costing method and U.K. retailers use the FIFO method, the effect would be felt primarily by the U.S. retail establishment. By shifting from LIFO to FIFO, U.S. retailers would show a relatively higher financial statement net income as past inflation becomes reflected in a higher ending inventory value. However, this reporting change would also result in a higher tax liability. Most U.S. retailers will probably be hesitant to comply with this new standard. In addition, any increase in profitability during the transition period would probably be perceived by financial markets only as the result of an accounting method change and not a change in the fundamental profitability of U.S. retailers.

Within the area of intangibles, the maximum period for amortization of goodwill is significantly different between the IASC and current U.S. practices. While the United States allows a maximum period of 40 years, the IASC states that goodwill (the difference between the fair market value of acquired assets and their purchase price) should be amortized over a period not to exceed 5 years *unless* a longer useful life can be justified. This longer useful life should not exceed 20 years. Currently, the United States has not complied with this IAS. An even greater difference exists between the United States and Germany. Along with Spain and Malaysia, Germany does not amortize goodwill at all.[10] What impact does this current difference in accounting have on retailers in the United States? Based on current standards, it is much more attractive for a German retailer to purchase a U.S. retailer because of the preferential goodwill treatment. Because it can amortize goodwill over a 40-year period, the German company's consolidated financial statements should not be significantly affected in the year of purchase. On the other hand, a U.S. retailer interested in buying out a German retailer would have to charge all goodwill to expense in the period of purchase. This additional expense could have a severe negative impact on the relative profitability of the company in the year of purchase. Although the present situation is beneficial to the United States in attracting new foreign investment, it is not beneficial to U.S. retailers that are interested in investing in companies abroad. This competitive disadvantage could have a negative long-run effect on U.S. retailers unless the United States is willing to comply soon with the provisions of the IASC.

Prepared by George Aldhizer of Texas Tech University and used with his permission.

EXHIBIT 7.12a

Classification of Cash Inflows and Cash Outflows

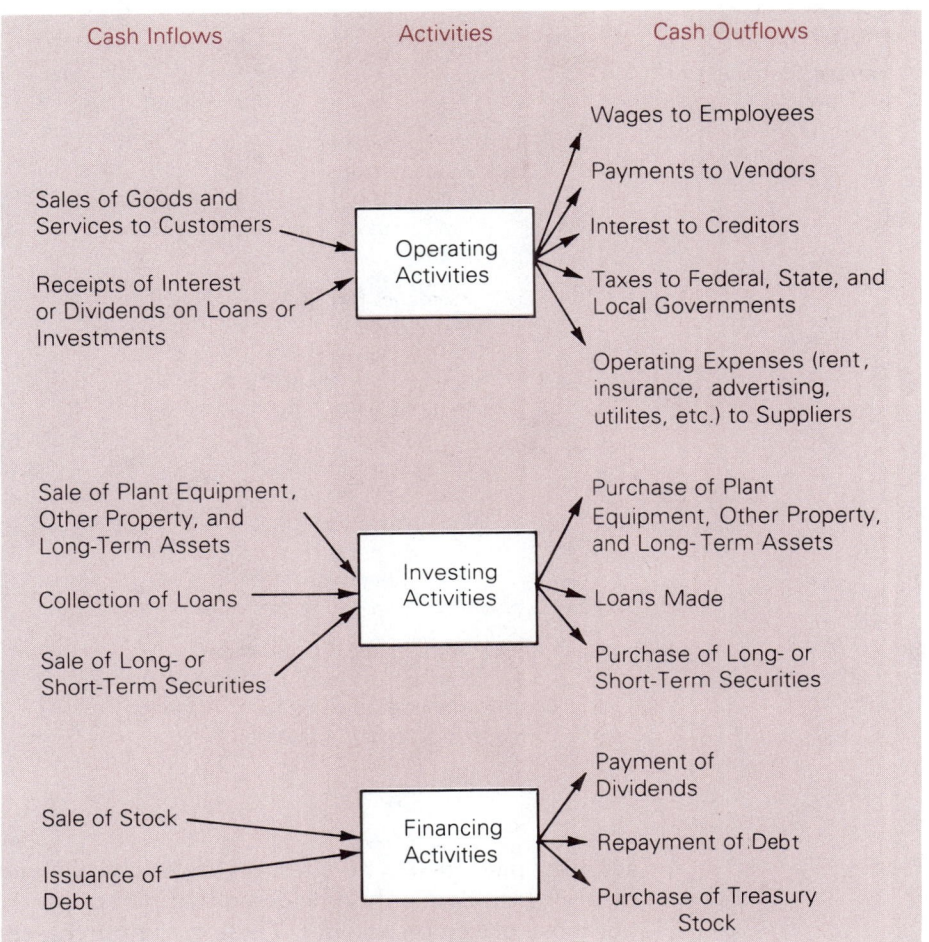

August is a slow month for furniture sales since many customers are taking vacations, and as a result TMD is expecting sales of only $40,000 for the month. However, only $15,450 of that amount will be for cash and TMD expects to collect $24,998 on its accounts receivable. Along with a tax refund check due from the state for $97, TMD has projected a cash inflow of $40,545 for August. However, because August is also the month that several notes and accounts payable are due, TMD Furniture is expecting to have to pay out $48,372 during August. This will result in a negative cash flow for the month of $7,827. TMD has prepared for this by having cash on hand (as reported on the July 31, 199X balance sheet) of $11,589. However, many retailers forget about cash and realize the difference between cash flow and profit only after the coffers are empty. In the case of TMD Furniture, paying off the notes and

EXHIBIT 7.12b

A Sample Statement of Cash Flow

TMD Furniture
Statement of Cash Flow
For August 199X

Cash Flows from Operating Activities			
Cash Receipts from			
Sales		$15,450	
Collection of Accounts Receivable		24,998	
Refund on State Taxes		97	$40,545
Cash Payments for			
Merchandise		$ 5,750	
County Taxes		173	
Payment of Accounts Payable		20,632	
Operating Expenses			
Rent	$1,513		
Salaries	8,483		
Utilities	1,450		
Advertising	2,300		
Supplies	921		
Telephone	150	14,817	41,372
Net Cash Used by Operating Activities			($ 827)
Cash Flows from Financing Activities			
Payment of Note Payable		($7,000)	
Net Cash Flows Used by Financing Activities			($7,000)
Net Increase (Decrease) in Cash			($7,827)

accounts payable had no effect on the income statement. Likewise, the statement of cash flow only considered that part of purchases paid for with cash, not those placed on account. These credit purchasers had no direct effect on the cash flow. Exhibit 7.12b lists the typical retailer's cash inflow and outflow items.

The issue of cash flow is more important than income earned or merchandising issues for some retailers today as a result of poor decisions retailers made in the late 1980s. Then many investors felt retailers had undervalued assets, primarily in real estate. As a result, there were tremendous miscalculations regarding future earnings and cash flow (earnings plus depreciation) of retailers of all sizes. Based on these miscalculated projections, big-name corporations like Toronto's Campeau Corporation, the Hooker Corporation of Sydney, Australia, and Great Britain's B.A.T. Industries acquired major American retailers like Federated Department Stores, Allied Department Stores, Bonwit Teller, B. Altman, Marshall Fields, and Saks Fifth Avenue. The idea was to use the cash flow, from not only the normal retail operations, but also from the sale of some assets, to pay off the heavy interest debts incurred on the purchases. A large percentage of this new debt was "junk bonds" or low-grade investment quality bonds that paid higher rates. The same idea was being used by other retailers at the same time, such as 7-Eleven and Circle K in the convenience store business, Ames in the discount store business, Ethan Allen in the furniture business, Resorts International in the entertainment field, and many small retailers. (Not all retailer takeovers involved such heavy debt load. The Bernard Brennan–led buyout of Montgomery Ward sold off the chain's credit operation, so it could avoid the use of the higher-interest-cost junk bonds.)

At first, all went well for the retailers and their heavy debt burdens. Most did not report huge profits; in fact, most reported losses, but their cash flow more than covered their interest payments. That was all the bankers and investors cared about. Cash flow, not profits, was everybody's concern. Then the economy slowed down in the early 1990s. Cash flow no longer covered debt, and these retailers were limited in their possible responses because of their heavy debt.

The rest is history. The heavy-debt retailers were forced to seek the protection of Chapter 11 of the bankruptcy code, all because they misjudged future cash flows. While Montgomery Ward, even with its large debt, and other retailers, like Home Depot, Wal-Mart, The Limited, and many small local retailers without huge debt burdens, survived these tumultuous times.

SUMMARY

This chapter introduced the different financial statements and their importance in merchandise planning and control. We began our discussion by stating that merchandising is the key to success in today's marketplace and introduced its primary planning and control tool—the six-month merchandise budget. This statement projects sales, when, and how much new merchandise should be ordered, what markup is to be taken, what reductions are to be planned, and the target or planned gross margin for the season. The establishment of such a budget has several advantages for the retailer:

1. The six-month budget controls the amount of inventory and forces management to control markup and reductions.
2. The budget helps to determine how much merchandise should be purchased so that inventory requirements can be met.
3. The budget can be compared with actual or final results to determine the performance of the firm.

We concluded our discussion of the six-month merchandise budget by showing how each of the figures is determined. We illustrated how to estimate sales, inventory levels, reductions, purchases, and gross margin.

The second section of this chapter described two methods of inventory valuation: the cost method and the retail method. The cost method is the simplest to use, but the retail method, despite some new problems, is the most widely used. Either method can use physical or book inventory systems. The physical system involves the actual counting of inventory at stated time intervals, while the book system relies on accurate bookkeeping and a reliable information exchange between the selling floor and the bookkeeping office.

The final part of this chapter explained how the retailer uses three important accounting statements: the income statement, the balance sheet, and the statement of cash flow.

The income statement gives the retailer a summary of the income and expenses incurred over a given time period. A balance sheet shows the financial condition of the retailer at a particular point in time. The statement of cash flow lists in detail the source and type of all revenue and expenditures for a given time period.

QUESTIONS FOR DISCUSSION

1. What are the components of a merchandise budget?
2. Why should a merchandise budget be flexible? When should it be changed?
3. Retailers must carry an amount of inventory in excess of planned sales for an upcoming period. Why?
4. List the advantages and disadvantages the retail method of inventory valuation has over the cost method. What current factors are making the retail method more difficult to use?
5. Define FIFO and LIFO and the reasons for using one or the other. During a period of inflation, how would each affect the income statement and the balance sheet?
6. What is a stock-to-sales ratio?
7. What is the difference between the statement of cash flow and the income statement? Which should a retailer be more concerned with?
8. Why is it difficult to determine the exact value of inventory when preparing financial statements?
9. What is the cost method of inventory valuation and when is it most appropriate to use this method?
10. Mustard's Last Stand, a hot dog stand in South Philadelphia, is trying to determine its net profit before taxes. Use the following data to assist the owners in their endeavor:

Rent	$ 15,000
Salaries	$ 36,000
Purchases	$100,000
Sales	$250,000
Beginning inventory	$ 20,000
Utilities	$ 3,000
Ending inventory	$ 21,000

11. Why is a statement of cash flow needed when most of the information in it is available from comparative income statements and balance sheets?
12. What are the effects of the following on a retailer's statement of cash flow: (a) an increase in accounts receivable, (b) a decrease in inventory, (c) an increase in accounts payable, (d) an increase in wages payable, and (e) an investment in long-term government bonds.
13. Complete the following:
    a. A retailer reports an increase in sales this year of 5.8 percent. If last year's sales were $498,253, what were they this year?
    b. Total sales for a retailer increased this year by 10 percent and the size of the average sale increased by 8 percent. What happened to the number of transactions?
    c. The number of transactions for a retailer decreased by 6 percent when a competitor moved nearby. However, the size of the average sale increased by 8 percent. What happened to total sales?

Chapter 7 Introduction to Merchandising Control

d. If total sales increased by 12 percent and the number of transactions increased by 3 percent, what happened to the size of the average sale?
e. A retailer, which last year had sales of $600,000, experiences an inflation rate of 5.3 percent and an increase in the number of transactions of 7.9 percent. What will planned sales be for this year?

14. Complete the following six-month merchandise plan:

The Smart Shoppe   Date 6/16/9X   Season FALL/WINTER

Six-Month Merchandise Budget							
Spring/Summer	FEB	MAR	APR	MAY	JUN	JUL	SEASONAL TOTAL
Fall/Winter	AUG	SEP	OCT	NOV	DEC	JAN	
1. Planned BOM[a] Stock	225,000						
2. Planned Sales	75,000						
3. Planned Retail Reductions	7,500						
4. Planned EOM[b] Stock	300,000						
5. Planned Purchases @ Retail	157,500						
6. Planned Purchases @ Cost	86,625						
7. Planned Initial Markup	70,875						
8. Planned Gross Margin	63,375						
9. Planned BOM Stock/Sales Ratio	3.0	4.0	3.0	5.0	3.0	4.0	—
10. Planned Sales Percentage	15%	15%	20%	10%	25%	15%	100%
11. Planned Retail Reduction Percentage	10%	10%	5%	15%	5%	10%	8.25%

Planned Total Sales for the Period   500,000

Planned Total Retail Reduction Percentage for the Period   8.25%

Planned Initial Markup Percentage for the Period   45%

Planned BOM Stock for FEB   250,000

NOTE: All dollar signs have been deleted from the merchandise budget grid

[a] BOM refers to Beginning-of-the-Month
[b] EOM refers to End-of-the-Month

MANAGEMENT MEMO

Over the last three years the nation's inflation rate has been around 3 percent. However, the Commerce Department has just issued its projections for next year: an inflation rate of 6.7 percent. Your firm's merchandise costs mirror the nation's inflation rate. You have been asked to prepare a memo for the senior management of your privately held company detailing how this new information will affect the firm's profitability if it continues to use a FIFO method of valuing inventory.

BOARDROOM REPORT

It has been suggested to your board that to improve earnings it must increase the firm's current turnover rate of 4.5 times per year to 5.2 times per year. You have been asked to prepare a report for next week's BOD meeting listing the benefits and costs of such a decision.

ENDNOTES

1. William A. Andres, "Managing Change: A Challenge for Retailers" (Paper presented at Texas A&M Center for Retailing Studies Lecture Series, April 21, 1983).
2. "The Credit Crunch Is Latest Harsh Blow for Small Retailers," *Wall Street Journal,* 9 April 1991, A1, A10.
3. "Time to Ask Hard-Nosed Question," *Sales & Marketing Management,* (October 1989): 88-93.
4. "Preserving the Magic," *Forbes,* 18 February 1991, 60-61.
5. James R. Larson, "Inventory Accounting: The Cost Method Makes Slow but Steady Gains," *Retail Control* (March 1991): 13-18.
6. Robert L. Grottle, "The Store of the Future: Harnessing the Information Opportunities from Automation," *International Trends in Retailing* (Spring 1988): 31-40.
7. Patrick M. Dunne and Harry I. Wolk, "Marketing Cost Analysis: A Modularized Contribution Approach," *Journal of Marketing* (July 1977): 83-84.
8. For more information, see "Early Warnings," *Forbes,* 25 June 1990, 246, 250.
9. For a more detailed description of cash flow, see *Statement of Financial Accounting Standards 95,* "Statements of Cash Flows."
10. Frederick D. S. Choi and Vinod B. Bavishi, "International Accounting Standards: Issues Needing Attention," *Journal of Accountancy* (March 1983): 62-68.
11. Ibid, FAS 95.
12. In actuality, a retailer may choose to present its operating cash flows directly or indirectly. FAS 95 encourages the use of the "direct" method which we used in Exhibit 7.12b and presents major classes of operating cash receipts and cash payments. However, most public companies, retailers included, prefer to use the easier to understand "indirect" method, a format that reconciles net income to net cash flow. Stacy L. Kronquist and Nancy Newman-Limata, "Reporting Corporate Cash Flows," *Management Accounting* (July 1990): 31-36.

CHAPTER 8

THE MERCHANDISE BUYING AND HANDLING PROCESS

OVERVIEW

In this chapter we explain the planning that retailers must do in managing their merchandise selection process. We analyze the way retailers control the amount of merchandise to be inventoried as well as the selection of, and negotiations with, vendors. The security measures used when handling merchandise are covered and merchandising performance evaluation concludes the chapter.

THE MERCHANDISE BUYING AND HANDLING PROCESS

I. Planning and Control
II. Dollar Merchandise Planning
   A. Basic Stock Method
   B. Percentage Variation Method
   C. Weeks' Supply Method
   D. Stock-to-Sales Method
III. Dollar Merchandise Control
IV. Unit Stock Planning
   A. Optimal Merchandise Mix
      1. Variety
      2. Breadth
      3. Depth
   B. Constraining Factors
      1. Dollar Constraints

2. Space Constraints
3. Turnover Constraints
4. Market Constraints
   C. Model Stock Plan
      1. Identify Attributes
      2. Identify Levels
      3. Allocate Dollars or Units
   D. Conflicts in Unit Stock Planning
V. Selection of Merchandise Sources
VI. Vendor Negotiations
   A. Trade Discount
   B. Quantity Discount
   C. Promotional Discount
   D. Seasonal Discount
   E. Cash Discount
   F. Delivery Terms
VII. In-Store Merchandise Handling
   A. Vendor Collusion
   B. Theft
   C. Loss Prevention
VIII. Evaluating Merchandise Performance
   A. Profit Measures
   B. Gross Margin Return on Inventory
   C. GMROI and Space Management
      1. Gross Margin Return on Selling Space
      2. Space Assortments
   D. Direct Product Profit
IX. Summary

One of the major changes in retailing over the past decade has been the added importance placed on merchandise selection. Merchandise and its presentation is what sets retail stores apart from each other. As we noted in the previous chapter, merchandising is the center of the retail operation. If your merchandise doesn't match the needs and wants of your target customer, then the best location, promotion, and management can't save you. Retailing in the 21st century will be about adopting a coherent merchandising mission and objectives aimed at an unsatisfied customer segment, then creating a network of stores, complete with a distribution system, to deliver that merchandise to the targeted customer. Remember, Sam Walton chose his store locations only *after* he developed his Wal-Mart and Sam's merchandising concepts. No wonder there is an old retailing adage that "goods well bought are half sold."

In this chapter we will look at merchandise management, that is, the merchandise buying and handling process and its effect on a store's performance. The next chapter will look at pricing this merchandise.

Merchandise management is the analysis, planning, acquisition, handling, and control of the merchandise investments of a retail operation. "Analysis" is used in our definition because retailers must be able to correctly identify their customers before they can determine their needs and wants to make a good buying decision. "Planning" occurs because, as we pointed out in the previous chapter, merchandise that is to be sold in the future must be bought now. "Acquisition" occurs when the merchandise is purchased from vendors, either wholesalers or manufacturers. "Handling" brings the merchandise where it is needed and in the proper shape to be sold. Finally, "control" of the large dollar investments in inventory is important to ensure for the retailer an adequate financial return.

Whatever your career path in retailing, you cannot avoid some contact with the firm's merchandising activities. Merchandising is the day-to-day business of all retailers. As inventory is sold, new stock needs to be purchased, displayed, and sold once again. Clearly, merchandising, though a subfunction of retailing, is its heart beat. Therefore, retailers that do a superior job at managing their inventory investment will make substantial progress toward achieving their desired high-performance objectives. If a retailer's inventory continues to build up, then the retailer is either missing the sales projected or making poor purchasing decisions and incurring additional carrying costs. Likewise, if the retailer has too little inventory, it might drive customers to other stores with larger selections. Now you know why the business trade press takes such an interest in retail inventory levels as re-

ILLUSTRATION 8.1

The greatest mistake a retailer can make is being out of stock in a merchandising category. Not only are sales lost, but the sight of empty shelves leaves a lasting negative impression with many customers.

tailers approach different seasons, with a special emphasis on Christmas. A Christmas season that normally accounts for 30 to 40 percent of a department store's annual sales can be ruined by having too much or too little inventory to support sales.

It should be obvious that in retailing high-performance results are produced not by investments only in promotion, personnel, buildings, and fixtures (though they help), but by wise investments in inventory. This is not to say that location and display do not contribute to retail success, but the merchant must have merchandise to sell to produce a financial return.

Before we continue our discussion of merchandise management, you may want to review a couple of earlier chapters. Since all retailing activities are aimed at serving the customer's needs and wants at a profit, you may want to review Chapter 3 on the customer. Likewise, because merchandise management is concerned with the acquisition of inventory, you may want to review Chapter 5 on the behavior of the different channel members.

PLANNING AND CONTROL

Merchandise management revolves around planning and control. Since it takes time to buy merchandise, have it delivered, record the delivery in the company records, and properly display the merchandise, it becomes essential to plan. Merchandise managers need to decide today what their stock requirements will be in several weeks, or months, or a merchandising season, or even a year in advance.

If planning occurs, then it is only logical that control be exercised over the merchandise dollars or units that the retailer plans on purchasing. A good control system is vital if the retailer is seeking to obtain high-performance results.

DOLLAR MERCHANDISE PLANNING

Buyers, working with upper management, are responsible for the dollar planning of merchandise requirements. In the previous chapter we described the various factors that must be considered in making the sales forecast, the first step in determining inventory needs. Once planned sales for the period in question have been projected, merchandise managers are then able to use any one of four different methods for planning the dollars to be invested in stock: basic stock, percentage variation, weeks' supply, and the stock-to-sales ratio method. However, before discussing these methods, let's first consider the impact of turnover on inventory performance.

At the outset we emphasized that **inventory turnover,** which may also be called inventory or merchandise stockturn or just turnover, was a key to high performance, which in turn means profits in retailing. The inventory turnover concept tries to capture how long inventory is on hand before it is sold. Items with a high turnover are on hand a short time; those with a low turnover are on hand longer.

Retailers have at their disposal several ways to measure inventory turnover:

1. Net sales/average inventory at retail
2. Cost of merchandise sold/average inventory at cost
3. Units sold/average units in inventory

Methods 1 and 2 are the most frequently used. Method 3 can be misleading unless the units are measured in homogeneous groups. The other methods are better for combining heterogeneous groups of items, because each item can be weighted by its dollar value.

The relationship between turnover and both sales and inventory levels can be shown by taking method 1 and analyzing it in more detail. For example, it can be shown that

Net sales = Turnover × Average inventory at retail

or

Average inventory at retail = Net sales/Turnover

The first equation shows that if a retailer is capable of achieving a given turnover—say six times—and has an average retail inventory of $100,000, then that retailer has the capacity to generate $600,000 in annual sales (6 × $100,000). The second equation could be used to determine inventories needed to support an expected sales volume with a fixed turnover goal. If the retailer has forecast sales of $500,000, and experience has shown that a turnover of four times is reasonable to expect, then the retailer would need to have average inventories at retail of $125,000 ($500,000/4 = $125,000).

It is not true, however, that higher turnover will indefinitely increase profits, and the lowest turnover will not necessarily result in the lowest profits. This point can be brought into sharper focus by examining the advantages and disadvantages of rapid turnover, outlined in Exhibit 8.1.

Rapid turnover enables the retailer to reduce certain expenses; the more rapid the turnover, the lower the average inventory required. Lower inventories will obviously require less capital, and thus the retailer's interest expense will be lower. At the same time, lower inventories will mean lower levels of required insurance coverage, lower inventory taxes on year-end inventories, and lower cost of storage space. However, rapid turnover can also increase expenses and/or reduce revenues. With smaller average inventories on hand, the retailer might suffer a decrease in sales as customers can't find what they want. Likewise, retailers must order more frequently and in smaller quan-

EXHIBIT 8.1

Advantages and Disadvantages of a Rapid Turnover

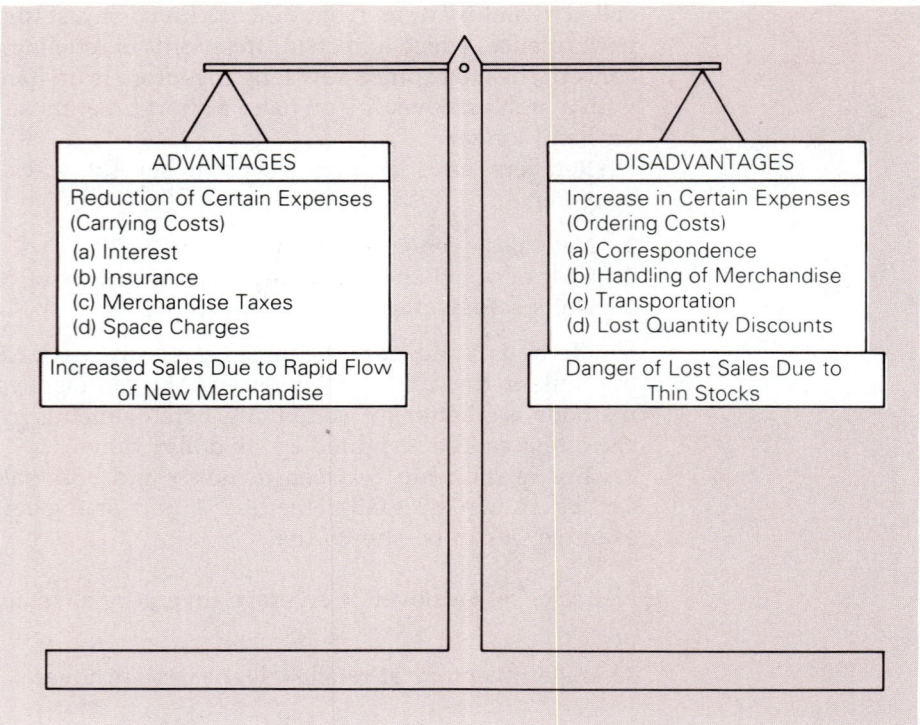

tities, resulting in higher clerical costs, lost quantity discounts, and higher transportation rates. The costs of correspondence, clerical work, and handling will also rise, since more orders will need to be processed over a season or year.

Thus, at one extreme, if the retailer places one large order per year, order placement costs will be low, but since average inventories will be high, the associated inventory carrying costs will be high. At the other extreme, if the retailer orders every week, the ordering costs will be high, but the average inventories and the costs associated with carrying them will be relatively low. In determining the trade-off between these two costs, the retailer must remember that the rate of turnover influences not only the supply side of retailing (cost functions), but also demand (sales or revenue functions).[1]

This discussion demonstrates the importance of the turnover concept to merchandise management. Programming a store to operate on the optimal rate of turnover is a difficult, but necessary, task in propelling the retailer toward the goal of high-performance results. However, turnover is not the only possible measure of performance. Exhibit 8.2 shows the turnover rate by all merchandise lines for large department stores.

EXHIBIT 8.2

Inventory Turnover for All Department Stores with Sales Over $2 Million

Inventory Turnover	
Footwear	1.7
Female Apparel	2.9
Adult Female Accessories	2.2
Mens & Boys Apparel & Accessories	2.3
Infants & Childrens Clothing & Accessories	2.9
Cosmetics & Drugs	2.3
Leisure & Home Electronics	1.7
Home Furnishings	1.5
Other Hard Lines	2.7
All Other Merchandise	4.2

Source: National Retail Federation, Merchandising and Operating Results of Department and Specialty Stores in 1990 (New York: Financial Executives Division, National Retail Federation, 1991): p. 4-5.

BASIC STOCK METHOD

The **basic stock method (BSM)** is used when retailers believe that it is necessary to have a given level of inventory available at all times. It requires that the retailer always have a base level of inventory investment regardless of the predicted sales volume. In addition to the base stock level, there will be a variable amount of inventory that increases or decreases at the beginning of each sales period (one month in the case of the merchandise budget introduced in the previous chapter) by the same dollar amount as the period's sales are expected to increase or decrease. The BSM can be calculated as follows:

Average monthly sales for the season = Total planned sales for the season/Number of months in the season

Average stock for the season = Total planned sales for the season/Estimated inventory turnover rate for the season

Basic stock = Average stock for the season − Average monthly sales for the season

BOM stock = Planned monthly sales + Basic stock

To illustrate the use of the basic stock method, let's look at the planned sales for Department 353 of Two-Seasons Department Store. Assume that the inventory turnover rate for the six months, or the number of times the average inventory is sold, for the season is 2.0.

Average monthly sales for the season = Total sales/Number of months
= $500,000/6 = $83,333

Average stock for the season = Total sales/Inventory turnover = $500,000/2 = $250,000

Basic stock = Average stock − Average monthly sales = $250,000 − $83,333 = $166,667

BOM @ retail (Feb.) = Basic stock + Planned monthly sales
    = $166,667 + $75,000 = $241,667
BOM @ retail (Mar.) = $166,667 + $75,000 = $241,667
BOM @ retail (Apr.) = $166,667 + $100,000 = $266,667
BOM @ retail (May) = $166,667 + $50,000 = $216,667
BOM @ retail (Jun.) = $166,667 + $125,000 = $291,667
BOM @ retail (Jul.) = $166,667 + $75,000 = $241,667

For each month $166,667 of basic stock is added to planned sales to arrive at the BOM stock. In those cases where actual sales either exceed or fall short of planned sales for the month (a rather common occurrence in retailing, unfortunately), the retailer can easily adjust the amount of overage or shortfall to bring the next month's BOM stock back in line by buying more or less stock.

The basic stock method of planning dollar inventory levels works best when a retailer has a low turnover rate or sales are erratic. It fails to perform adequately when the turnover is greater than once every two months, because in this situation the basic stock level for each month would be negative. Therefore, when inventory turnover is greater than three times per six-month season, or six times per year, you should use one of the following methods.

PERCENTAGE VARIATION METHOD

A second commonly used method for determining planned stock levels is the **percentage variation method (PVM).** This method functions when the retailer has a yearly turnover rate of six or more and doesn't desire to have a given level of inventory available at all times but does face fluctuations in sales. It assumes that the monthly percentage fluctuations from average stock should be half as great as the percentage fluctuations in monthly sales from average sales.

BOM stock = Average stock for season × 1/2[1+(Planned sales for the month/Average monthly sales)]

Since the PVM utilizes the same components as the BSM, we can use the data from the previous example.

BOM (Feb.) = $250,000 × 1/2[1+($75,000/$83,333)] = $237,500
BOM (Mar.) = $250,000 × 1/2[1+($75,000/$83,333)] = $237,500
BOM (Apr.) = $250,000 × 1/2[1+($100,000/$83,333)] = $275,000

BOM (May) = $250,000 × 1/2[1+($50,000/$83,333)] = $200,000
BOM (Jun.) = $250,000 × 1/2[1+($125,000/$83,333)] = $312,500
BOM (Jul.) = $250,000 × 1/2[1+($75,000/$83,333)] = $237,500

In the preceding example a turnover rate of 2.0 for a six-month season is equal to an annual turnover rate of 4.0. When the annual turnover rate is 6, the PVM and BSM will produce the same results. When the turnover is less, the PVM will have a greater fluctuation, and when it is higher than 6, the PVM will fluctuate less. Thus, always choose the PVM when your annual turnover rate is greater than 6.0 and choose the BSM when it is less than 6.0.

WEEKS' SUPPLY METHOD

A third method for planning inventory levels is the **weeks' supply method (WSM).** The WSM formula is used by retailers such as supermarkets in which inventories are planned on a weekly, not monthly basis, and where sales do not fluctuate substantially. It states that the inventory level should be set equal to a predetermined number of weeks' supply. The predetermined number of weeks' supply is directly related to the stock turnover rate desired. In the WSM, stock level in dollars vary proportionally with forecasted sales. Thus, if forecasted sales triple, then inventory in dollars will also triple.

To illustrate the WSM, let's return to our earlier problem and use the following formulas:

Number of weeks to be stocked = Number of weeks in the period/Stock turnover rate for the period

Average weekly sales = Estimated total sales for the period/Number of weeks in the period

BOM Stock = Average weekly sales × Number of weeks to be stocked

Thus

Number of weeks to be stocked = 26/2 = 13
Average weekly sales = $500,000/26 = $19,231
BOM stock = $19,231 × 13 = $250,000

With the number of weeks' supply to be stocked at 13 weeks and average weekly sales of $19,231, stock levels can be replenished on a frequent or regular basis to guard against stock-outs. The one major problem with this method is that during weeks in which there is a slow turnover (below average), there will be an excessive buildup of inventory, which will increase costs. Therefore, unless your business is marked by stable sales and a stable turnover, this method is not advisable.

STOCK-TO-SALES METHOD

The final method for planning inventory levels and the one we used in Chapter 7 is the **stock-to-sales method (SSM).** This method is quite easy to use but requires the retailer to have a beginning-of-the-month stock-to-sales ratio. This ratio tells the retailer how much inventory is needed at the beginning of the month to support that month's estimated sales. A ratio of 2.5, for example, would tell retailers that they should have two and one-half times that month's expected sales on hand in inventory at the beginning of the month.

Stock-to-sales ratios can be obtained from internal or external sources. If the retailer has designed a good accounting system and has properly stored historical data so that they can be readily retrieved, the statistics can be obtained internally. The retailer can also often rely on external retail trade associations such as the National Retail Federation and the Menswear Retailers Association. Trade associations collect stock-to-sales ratios from participating merchants and then compile, tabulate, and report them in special management reports or trade publications. Exhibit 8.3 provides an example of beginning-of-the-month stock-to-sales ratios that the National Retail Federation releases to the department store industry.

Inventory turnover is a key factor in a retailer's financial performance. Planned average beginning-of-the-month stock-to-sales goals can be easily

EXHIBIT 8.3

BOM Stock-to-Sales Ratios

Store Volume (millions $)	Feb	Mar	Apr	May	Jun	Jul	Aug	Sept	Oct	Nov	Dec	Jan
Department Stores												
Under $100	6.28	4.78	5.07	5.24	5.07	5.34	5.69	5.48	5.35	5.07	4.26	7.12
$100-$300	6.45	4.10	4.57	5.63	4.91	6.21	5.31	4.55	4.63	4.30	2.41	6.62
$300-$600	5.54	4.48	5.63	5.21	4.43	6.00	4.61	4.86	5.32	5.08	2.89	8.68
Over $600	4.87	3.83	5.03	4.85	4.14	5.11	4.62	3.73	5.18	4.32	2.92	6.43
Specialty Stores												
Under $20	6.43	5.88	6.16	6.58	6.11	6.80	6.05	6.38	7.01	6.22	5.81	8.80
Over $20	5.65	4.63	4.81	4.79	4.06	4.92	5.15	5.04	6.18	5.42	2.72	6.01
Under $5	6.50	5.36	5.85	6.03	5.53	6.24	5.42	5.75	6.55	5.87	3.17	8.08
$5-$20	6.37	6.41	6.48	7.13	6.68	7.36	6.67	7.00	7.47	6.58	8.45	9.52
$20-$100	4.80	4.10	3.24	4.30	4.17	3.23	3.67	4.51	4.14	4.34	3.11	4.32
Over $100	5.82	4.73	5.12	4.89	4.04	5.26	5.44	5.15	6.59	5.63	2.64	6.34

Source: National Retail Federation, Merchandising and Operating Results of Department and Specialty Stores in 1990 (New York: Financial Executives Division, National Retail Federation, 1991): p. 10–11.

calculated using turnover goals. If you divide the number of months in the season by the desired inventory turnover rate, you arrive at an average BOM stock-to-sales ratio for the season. For example, if you desired an inventory turnover rate of 1.8 (3.6 annually) for the upcoming six-month season, your average BOM stock-to-sales ratio would be 3.3 (6/1.8 = 3.3).

DOLLAR MERCHANDISE CONTROL

Once the dollar merchandise to have on hand at the beginning of each month (or season) has been planned, the retailer normally should not make commitments for merchandise that would exceed the dollar plan. In short, the dollars planned for merchandise need to be controlled. This control is accomplished through a technique called open-to-buy. The **open-to-buy (OTB)** represents the dollar amount that a buyer can currently spend on merchandise without exceeding the planned dollar stocks discussed previously. When planning for any given month (or season), the retail buyer will not necessarily be able to purchase a dollar amount equal to the planned dollar stocks for that period. There may be some inventory already on hand or on order but not yet delivered. To illustrate this point, let's compute the open-to-buy for an upcoming month. The basic formula is

1. End-of-month planned retail stock
2. Plus planned sales for month
3. Plus planned reductions for the month
4. Minus stock on hand at retail
5. Equals planned purchases at retail
6. Minus commitments at retail for current delivery
7. Equals open-to-buy at retail

Thus, if the buyer in Department 353 of the Two-Seasons Department Store had merchandise at $15,000 retail on order, but not yet received on February 1, 199X, and planned reductions for February are 10 percent of planned sales, the open-to-buy for the month would be $142,500 at retail.

EOM planned retail stock	$300,000
Plus planned sales for February	+ 75,000
Plus planned reductions for February	+ 7,500
Minus BOM stock	− 225,000
Equals planned purchases at retail	$157,500
Minus commitments at retail for current delivery	− 15,000
Equals open-to-buy	$142,500

The OTB figure should not be a fixed quantity that cannot be exceeded. Consumer needs are the dominant consideration. If sales of a product line, department, or store exceed planned sales, additional quantities should be ordered above those scheduled for purchase according to the merchandise budget. Buyers must have permission of their merchandise manager to purchase additional inventory of fast-moving merchandise; however, this should not be a common occurrence. If it is, the sales planning process is wrong. Either the buyers are too conservative in estimating sales or they are buying the wrong merchandise. In any case, management should always determine the causes of OTB adjustments. Exhibit 8.4 lists some of the common buying errors that retailers, especially new ones, make.

Merchandise planning is a dynamic process subject to many changes. Consider the implications that could arise in planning your stock levels as a result of: (1) sales for the previous month being less or higher than planned, (2) reductions being either higher or lower than planned, and (3) shipments of merchandise being delayed in transit. Understanding the consequences of each of these situations can show you the interrelationship of merchandising activities with the merchandise budget. Such occurrences also serve to make retailing a challenging and exciting career choice.

EXHIBIT 8.4
Some Common Buying Errors

1. Failure to analyze previous year's merchandise results before going to market or making purchases.
2. Failure to have kept records from the previous year.
3. Determining only the quantity and leaving the merchandise selection to the vendor, especially size and color selections.
4. Using too many vendors.
5. Merchandise whose sizes and/or colors were wrongly bought or in too large a quantity or were wrongly delivered and proved to be disproportionate to customer demand at regular price.
6. Not helping out inexperienced buyers.
7. Failure to know the selling season for your market.
8. Buying too many items rather than just a few styles.
9. Buying too many hot, new items.
10. Failure to make small initial purchases, that can be followed up by reorders.
11. Failure to determine if buyer can deliver on time the merchandise ordered or accepting changes by the manufacturer.
12. Buying too broad of a product line.
13. Failure to cancel past due orders.
14. Making the last re-order once too often. The last one may arrive just in time to be marked down.
15. Failure to negotiate all possible discounts from the vendor.
16. Failure to study the market sufficiently so as to know the best quality merchandise and best price.
17. Failure to ask one of the following questions during negotiations: a. "Does your company substitute ship?" b. "Does your company backorder often?" c. "How long has your company been in business?"
18. Failure to shop the competition so as not to buy identical items.
19. Failure to talk with the central office (where applicable) in order to see what other buyer services are offered.
20. Failure to buy enough merchandise, resulting in lost sales volume.
21. Buying your personal preferences, instead of the market's preferences.

UNIT STOCK PLANNING

The dollar merchandise plan is only the starting point in merchandise management. Once the merchandise manager has decided how many dollars can be invested in inventory, the dollar plan needs to be converted into a unit plan. On the sales floor, stock keeping units (SKUs), not dollars, are sold. The assortment of SKUs that will comprise the merchandise mix must then be planned.[2]

Designing the optimal merchandise mix involves a complex decision for which there exists no standard methodological solution. The final mix will be determined by a combination of creative and analytical thought. Consider, for example, a grocery store manager attempting to allocate $250,000 in inventory dollars among 6,000 to 9,000 SKUs. On a strict analytical basis, the manager might try to allocate the $250,000 to the thousands of possible SKUs in order to maximize the combined contribution of all the items to total store overhead and profits. It does not take a genius to quickly conclude that without knowledge of the demand functions for each of the SKUs, the task could not be accomplished using only analytical techniques. Thus, creative thought processes must accompany analytical thinking in designing the optimal merchandise mix.

OPTIMAL MERCHANDISE MIX

As we begin our discussion of the optimal merchandise mix, it is important to remember something that Stanley Marcus, one of this country's greatest merchandisers, noted about the state of merchandising affairs today.

Some customers insist on an attractive store ambiance; most want polite and knowledgeable service; all expect satisfaction from the merchandise they purchase. In today's economy of abundance, many customers are buying for wants and not needs. They are looking for excitement, and for merchandise that is unusual and different. Instead they are finding standardized stocks of the same merchandise everywhere they shop.

No wonder customer loyalty has dropped. There is little reason for a shopper to go across town to a store when it's a foregone conclusion that she'll find the same merchandise in store C that she has already seen in stores A and B. I fully expect to come upon a headline in the newspaper that proclaims, "Customer Found Bored to Death in the Sportswear Department of the XYZ Department Store."

The sameness of merchandise emanates from the educational limitations of the buyers who have been taught to play it safe by avoiding risky fashions, to play it cautiously by buying from a limited number of standard vendors who sell the same "packages" to all of their major accounts, to play it for a profit by advertising only those goods supported by manufacturers' advertising allowances.

Many retailers erroneously believe that their objective is to make a profit and fail to realize that a profit is the result of having produced goods or services that are so satisfactory that the customer is willing to pay a bonus, or a profit, over and above the distributors' cost.

This may sound like an exercise in semantics, but the recognition and practice of this concept has a tremendous effect on those engaged in trade at all levels. Once accepted, it forces the seller to an ever-present consciousness that it's up to him to make the transaction so satisfying that a profit is earned . . .

There is little doubt in my mind that "customer-driven" stores will consistently have better stocks of merchandise, more satisfaction and broader and deeper styles and sizes.[3]

Exhibit 8.5 shows the three dimensions of the optimal mix that Mr. Marcus felt offered today's retailer a chance to differentiate its wares: variety,

EXHIBIT 8.5

Dimensions of and Constraints on Optimal Merchandise Mix

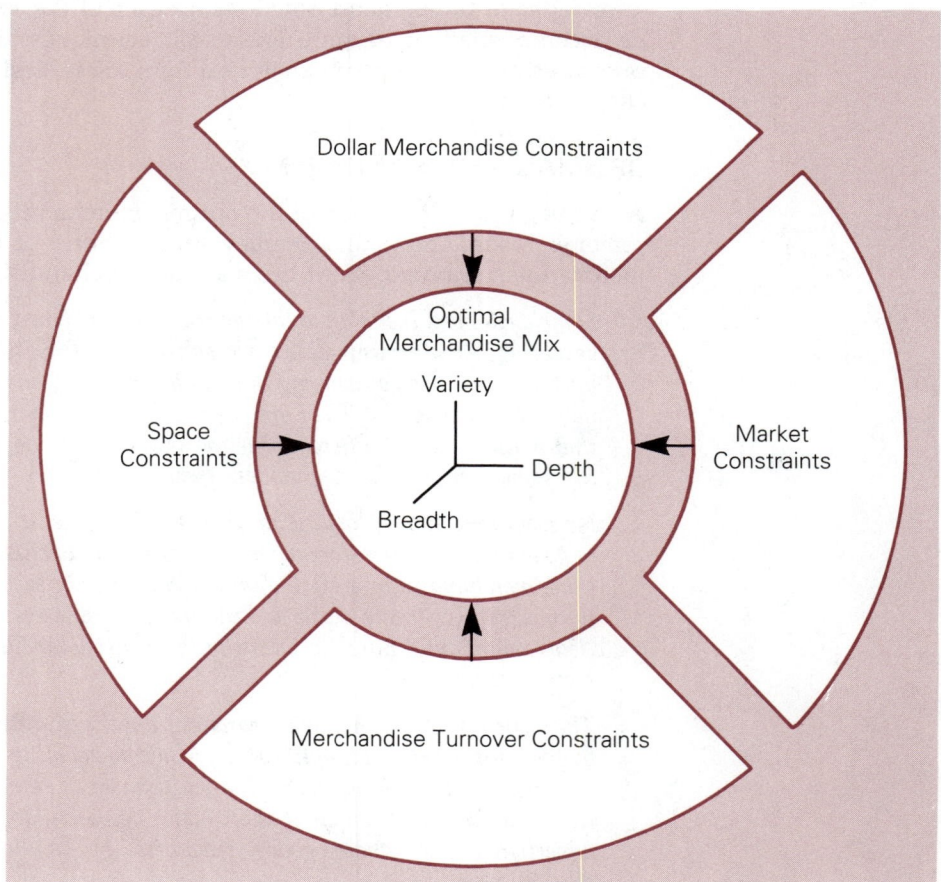

breadth, and depth. Each of these dimensions needs to be defined; however, we need first to define merchandise line. A **merchandise line** consists of a group of products that are closely related because they are intended for the same end use (all televisions), are sold to the same customer group (junior miss clothing), or fall within a given price range (budget women's wear).

Variety. The **variety** of the merchandise mix refers to the number of different lines the retailer stocks in the store. For example, department stores have a large variety of merchandise lines. Some have over 100 departments, carrying such lines as menswear, women's wear, children's clothing, infants, toys, sporting goods, appliances, cosmetics, and household goods.

On the other hand, Foot Locker, a specialty chain, carries only one basic merchandise line: athletic shoes. In the middle of these two would be a retailer like Sportsmart selling a complete range of sporting goods.

Breadth. **Breadth,** also called **assortment,** refers to the number of merchandise brands that are found in the merchandise line. For example, a supermarket will have a large amount of breadth, or assortment, in the number of different brands of mustard that it carries: six or seven national or regional brands, a private brand, and a generic brand. A 7-Eleven or Circle K convenience store, however, will offer very little breadth, generally carrying only the most popular brand and size in any merchandise line. One of the many reasons that led to Circle K's bankruptcy in early 1990 was its inability to control breadth. At the time of bankruptcy, Circle K was found to be carrying six brands of dog food, seven brands of aspirin, and a large selection of hair nets (this last despite the fact that females made up only a small percentage of

ILLUSTRATION 8.2

The smaller bread display at a convenience store (*left*) does not make as strong a merchandising and price statement as the much larger display a supermarket (*right*) can afford to make.

its customers). This type of breadth was entirely inappropriate for a retailer selling convenience goods and already heavily in debt.[4]

Depth. Merchandise **depth** refers to the average number of SKUs within each brand of the merchandise line. The supermarket manager must decide which sizes and types of French's mustard to carry. The convenience store will probably carry only the regular nine-ounce jar of French's.

Research has shown that the depth of a retailer's product assortment has a strong association with consumers' purchasing behavior—the larger the assortments, the lower the loyalty toward individual brands and the higher the sensitivity to promotion.[5] Thus, retailers need to select their merchandise line strategy carefully and only after noting the behavior of their target market.

CONSTRAINING FACTORS

With these definitions of variety, breadth, and depth in mind, we can refer back to Exhibit 8.5 to observe the four constraining factors that influence the design of the optimal merchandise mix.

Dollar Constraints. There seldom will be enough dollars to emphasize all three dimensions of variety, breadth, and depth. If the decision is made to emphasize variety, it would be unrealistic also to expect great breadth and depth.

For instance, assume for the moment that you are the owner/manager of a local gift store. You have $30,000 to invest in merchandise. If you decide that you want a lot of variety in gifts (jewelry, crystal, candles, games, cards, figurines, ashtrays, clocks, and radios), then you obviously could not have much depth in any single item, such as crystal glassware.

Some retailers try to overcome dollar constraints by shifting the expense of carrying inventory back on the vendor. When a retailer buys a product on **consignment,** the vendor retains ownership of the goods, usually establishes the selling price, and is paid only when the goods are sold. Or the retailer might try to obtain **extra dating,** whereby the vendor allows the retailer some extra time before paying for the goods. For example, most textbook publishers either sell their books on consignment or give the bookstores an extra 60 days in which to pay. In this way your campus bookstore orders its books in early July for an early August delivery and sells them in late August and early September. However, because the books were sold on consignment or with extra dating, the bookstore doesn't have to pay the publisher until October.

Space Constraints. The retailer must also deal with space constraints. If depth or breadth is wanted, space is needed. If variety is to be stressed, it is also important to have enough empty space to separate the distinct merchandise lines. For example, consider a long counter containing cosmetics, candy, fishing tackle, women's stockings, and toys. This would obviously be an unsightly and unwise arrangement. As more variety is added, empty space becomes necessary to allow the consumer to distinguish clearly among distinct product lines.

Some retailers, especially in the grocery business, realizing their importance in the distribution channel, have begun to turn this space constraint into an advantage by charging the manufacturers a "slotting fee," or a fixed charge per each new SKU per store that the retailer agrees to handle. Supermarkets, faced with more than 15,000 new food products each year, were the first to charge such fees. After all, supermarkets have the shelf space manufacturers need. Compounding the issue is the fact that so many new products fail to live up to the manufacturers' promises. When a product does fail, the retailer has not only lost money on the investment in the new product; it has also lost the opportunity to use its valuable shelf space on a profitable product.

The slotting fee, often ranging up to $3,000 per SKU, is the retailers' way of guaranteeing at least some profit for taking on the new brand, size, or variety. Retailers claim that the manufacturers, while not happy about this new cost, are paying it. One big retail chain said its $15-per-store fee to shelve a new item brings in $50 million a year. In an industry with a net profit margin under 2 percent, slotting fees can have a major impact on the bottom line.

Other retailers insist that the manufacturer buy any unsold products, at full retail price, if the new item does not meet sales objectives.

Either way, supermarket managers realize that they are the gatekeepers to the consumers and that "manufacturers had better not mess with them."[6]

Turnover Constraints. As the depth of the merchandise increases, the retailer will stock more and more variations of the product to serve smaller and smaller segments. Consequently, inventory turnover will deteriorate and the chances of being out of stock will increase. One does not have to minimize variety, breadth, and depth to maximize turnover, but one must know how various merchandise mixes will affect inventory turnover.

Market Constraints. Market constraints should also affect decisions on variety, breadth, and depth of the merchandise mix. The three dimensions have a profound effect on how the consumer perceives the store, and consequently on the customers the store will attract. Someone searching for depth in a limited set of merchandise lines such as formal menswear will thus be attracted to a menswear retailer specializing in formal wear. On the other hand, the consumer perceives the general-merchandise retailer such as Montgomery Ward or Sears as a store with lots of variety and breadth in terms of merchandise lines, but with more constrained depth. Therefore, someone who needs to make purchases across several merchandise lines and is willing to sacrifice depth of assortment would be more attracted to the general-merchandise retailer.

These constraining factors make it almost impossible for a retailer to emphasize all three dimensions. However, if you are going to lose customers, lose the less profitable ones by properly mixing your merchandise in terms of variety, breadth, and depth within the dollar, space, turnover, and market constraints. The retailer should remember that the top 20 percent of customers produce 80 percent of the retailer's profits. Likewise, the bottom tier of customers isn't likely to be too profitable for a retailer. However, even this simple rule is difficult for some retailers. Sears, despite all its recent efforts, is probably never going to be noted for its trendy fashion image, so why use valuable dollars and inventory space courting this market? With nearly 70 percent of its sales coming from appliances, why should it have its stores located in malls where customers are usually shopping for fashion? These are the reasons JCPenney, which was almost identical to Sears in merchandise, switched its emphasis during the 1980s. JCPenney dropped its appliance line in favor of fashion to blend in with its locations.[7]

This problem is even more evident in the supermarket industry. In an industry where the average retailer can stock 24,000 to 29,000 SKUs, the supply of new products can still outrun the store's ability to handle them. In 1991, over 15,000 items were introduced to the supermarket trade.[8] Existing products had to be dropped to make way for the new items. The reasons most often cited as influencing supermarket buyers to try a new product are: introductory terms (including slotting fees), including ad/display allowances and discounts; consumer ad plans; consumer promotions; and perceived consumer demand.[9]

MODEL STOCK PLAN

After deciding the relative emphasis to be placed on the three dimensions of the merchandise mix, the retailer needs to decide what merchandise lines and items to stock. This can be an overwhelming task for the novice, but even for the experienced retailer it is time consuming and often frustrating. Units are planned using a **model stock plan,** which gives the precise items and quantities that should be on hand for each merchandise line. A separate model stock plan needs to be compiled for each line of merchandise.

Exhibit 8.6 shows a hypothetical menswear retailer attempting to develop a unit plan for men's shirts. It has already prepared a dollar plan and has allocated $30,000 at retail for men's shirts. Since the average retail price of a shirt for the store is $30, 1,000 shirts will need to be stocked. The model unit plan will reveal how many shirts of each kind the retailer should keep in stock. While Exhibit 8.6 only shows the breakdown within one attribute (casual shirts), the same procedure would be followed for all types of shirts.

Identify Attributes. The first thing the menswear retailer should do is to identify what attributes the customer considers in purchasing shirts. Exhibit 8.6 shows that the retailer has identified six: (1) type of shirt (dress, casual, sport, or work), (2) size, (3) sleeve length, (4) collar type, (5) color, and (6)

EXHIBIT 8.6

A Partial Model Unit Plan for Men's Shirts

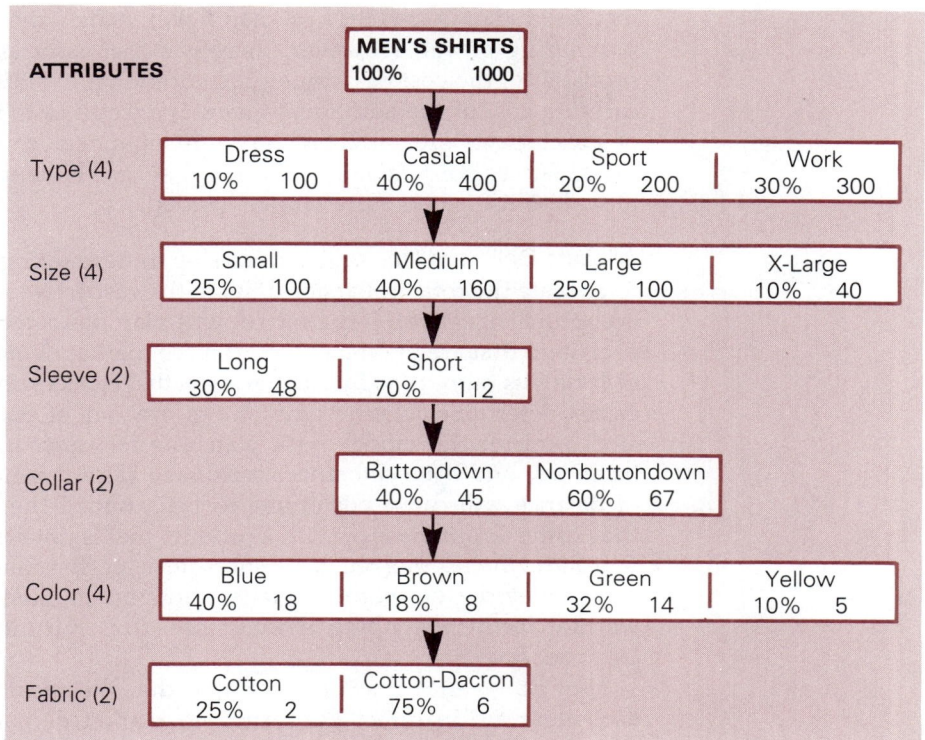

fabric. Are any key attributes left out? What about price? If customers shop for shirts by price point, then price should also be a product attribute.

Identify Levels. The second step is to identify the number of levels under each attribute. The retailer in Exhibit 8.6 has selected four types of shirts to stock, four sizes, two sleeve lengths, two collar types, four colors, and two fabrics.

In relation to the first two steps in the construction of a model stock plan, a basic principle of merchandise management can be identified: Stocking requirements will grow explosively as product attributes are added and expanded levels are offered on each. If the retailer offers four shirt types, four sizes in each type, two sleeve lengths, two collar styles, four colors, and two fabrics, then it will have to stock 512 shirts (4 × 4 × 2 × 2 × 4 × 2), just to stock one unit of each. More importantly, if the retailer now decides to offer two price points instead of one, the stocking requirements double to 1,024 items. But this example assumes that only 1,000 shirts can be stocked. Obviously, the retailer has a problem if it wants to feature six or seven attributes and several price points in each attribute.

The preceding discussion illustrates the need for a basic trade-off in merchandise management. As more attributes are featured, the probability is increased that a product on hand will match the customer's needs and purchasing power. However, there is a cost associated with increasing this probability, the cost of carrying the additional inventory. At some point, the carrying cost of the additional inventory required to increase the probability of purchase is greater than the profit obtained from those additional unit sales. Successful retailers know that they will have to allow some customers to walk out of their store empty handed.

Allocate Dollars or Units. The third step in developing the model stock plan is to allocate the total dollars or units to the respective item categories. There is an optimal allocation if the model unit plan has recommended quantities for each item that are in direct proportion to market demand patterns. If the plan reflects this ratio, then by comparing actual stocks with model stocks, one can easily determine whether the stocks are out of balance. The more actual stocks mirror the model stock plan, the more accurately the stocks will be balanced, and balanced stocks maximize sales potential. Stocks that are out of balance will cause customers to walk out of the store without the item they came to purchase or with a product that is not well suited to their needs. The latter helps the retailer's short-term performance. However, the consumer may decide that the retailer's interest in "just getting a sale" doesn't warrant further shopping at that store, thus hurting the retailer's long-run performance.

But how can a retailer determine that the recommended quantities for each item are in direct proportion to market demand patterns? The most useful thing to do is to analyze past sales records. Exhibit 8.7 shows the sales experience of our hypothetical menswear retailer in reference to the last 500 shirts sold. This exhibit, derived from past sales records, shows the demand density for different types and sizes of shirts. This simple analysis forms the basis of planning unit stocks in the model plan. Changing the data in Exhibit 8.7 to percentage form, we can see that 10 percent of our shirt sales were dress, 40 percent casual, 20 percent sport, and 30 percent work. Furthermore, of the casual shirts, 25 percent were small, 40 percent medium, 25 percent large, and 10 percent extra large. The percentage derived from such a sales analysis can then be used in the model stock plan (Exhibit 8.6). Thus, of the 1,000 shirts we plan to stock, 100 will be dress, 400 casual, 200 sport, and 300 work. A similar procedure determines how many to stock in each size, sleeve length, collar type, color, and fabric.

One should not always allow past sales results to solely determine future stocking patterns. In the past, quantities not in proportion to demand patterns may have been stocked and in fact sold—but probably at a loss. The pure sales statistics will not reveal this. In addition, new products that come into the market may feature attributes previously not stocked, and the demand for these may be so hot that the item must be stocked in order to compete. Strict analysis of past statistics alone cannot dictate the model stock plan; insight and creative power must be used where appropriate. In one study, senior buyers, in their analysis, were found to place greater emphasis on selling history and markup, than advertising allowance.[10]

EXHIBIT 8.7

A Sales Analysis of Men's Shirts

TYPE	SIZE			
	Small	Medium	Large	X-Large
Dress	XX	XXXX	XXX	X
Casual	XXXX XXXX XX	XXXX XXXX XXXX	XXXX XXXX XX	XXXX
Sport	XXXX X	XXXX XXXX X	XXXX X	X
Work	XXXX XXXX	XXXX XXXX XXX	XXXX XXX	XXXX

KEY: Each X=5 shirts

So far, we have ignored the problems of individuals opening their first store with no past sales records to rely on. In this situation, does one use only intuition and creativity in developing a model stock plan? Certainly not! Of the three steps, the first two pertain as much to the entrepreneur as to any existing retailer. For the third step, the new retailer can obtain trade or other external sources on consumer purchasing patterns. For example, in the food industry, one could consult the Towne-Oller Index, which measures actual sales and the sales rank of each product and shows the number of different products needed to meet the demand of a certain percentage of the buying public for that particular product line. For instance, one might see that if meeting 80 percent of the demand preferences for mouthwash is the retailer's desired goal, the four leading brands would need to be stocked.

CONFLICTS IN UNIT STOCK PLANNING

Unit stock planning is an exercise in compromise and conflict. The conflict is multidimensional because everything cannot be stocked. The dimensions of conflict are presented in Exhibit 8.8 and summarized as follows:

1. Maintain a strong in-stock position on genuinely new items while trying to avoid the 90 percent of new products that fail in the introductory stage. One of the greatest myths in retailing is that the successful retail innovator is a wild risk taker.[11] The wise retailer will want to have on hand the types of new products that will satisfy customers. This can only be done if the retailer knows who its customers are. The successful retailer is a prudent

EXHIBIT 8.8

Conflicts in Building a Model Stock Plan

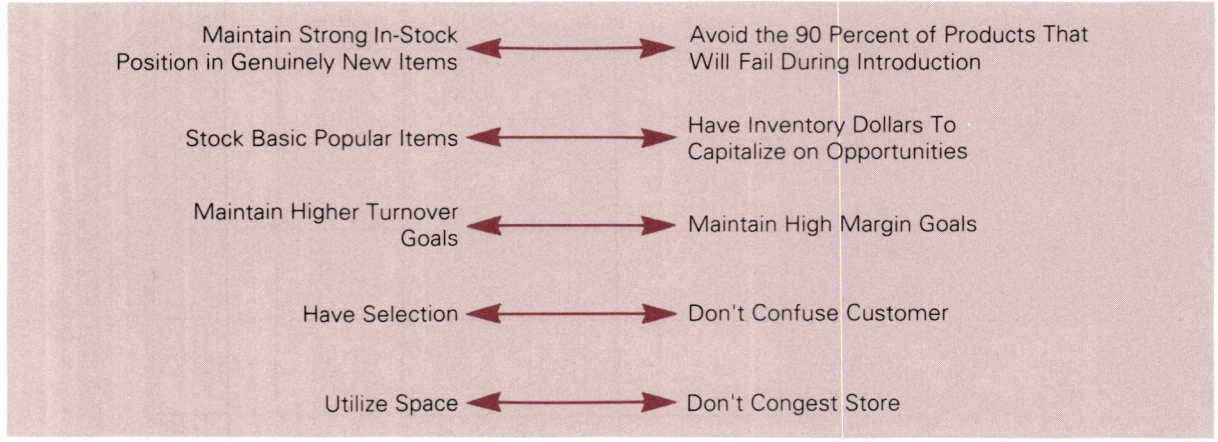

risk taker that knows that if the consumer is sold a poor product, it hurts the retailer. The challenge is to screen out poor products before they reach the customer. Any screening device, however, has error; the retailer might end up stocking some losers and turning down some winners. Thus, a basic conflict arises, but even the best of buyers will make a mistake only to be forced to use markdowns or watch a competitor have the missed-out hot, new item.

2. Maintain an adequate stock of the basic popular items while having sufficient inventory dollars to capitalize on unforeseen opportunities. Many times, if we fill out the model stock plan with recommended quantities, there is little if any money left over for the super buy that is just around the corner. But if we hold out that money and cut back on basic stock, we may lose customers, and that super buy may never surface.

3. Maintain high merchandise turnover goals while maintaining high margin goals. This is perhaps the most glaring conflict. Items that have a rapid turnover generally have thinner profit margins. Therefore, trying to build a unit plan that will accomplish both objectives will surely be challenging.

4. Maintain adequate selection for customers while not confusing them. If customers are confronted with too many similar items, they will not be able to make up their minds and they may leave the store empty handed and frustrated. On the other hand, if the selection is inadequate, the customer will again leave empty handed. Thus, a delicate balance needs to be struck between too little and too much selection.

5. Maintain space productivity and utilization while not congesting the store. Take advantage of buys that will utilize the available space, but avoid buys that cause the merchandise to spill over into the aisles. Unfor-

tunately, some of the best buys come along when space is already occupied.

As should be readily evident at this point, unit stock planning is no easy task. Equally challenging is the selection of vendors from whom to purchase the merchandise.

SELECTION OF MERCHANDISING SOURCES

After deciding on the type and amount of inventory to be purchased, the next step is to determine the source. All too often people have misconceptions about how retailers choose and negotiate with vendors. Many times we have heard people say, "I would love to be a buyer. After all, I have been told I have good fashion tastes, and besides I love to travel." Buying isn't that simple. However, with proper planning and control it can be a very rewarding experience, especially when your customers react positively to your merchandise selection. However, no matter how rewarding your buying experience is, it will also be grueling. Not only must you determine what merchandise lines to carry, you must also select the best possible vendor to supply you with these items and then you must be able to negotiate the best deal possible with that vendor.

When selecting a merchandise source, the retailer must consider many criteria depending on the type of store and merchandise sold. Generally, the following seven criteria, which may vary across merchandise lines, should always be considered: selling history, product quality, reliability of delivery, steady source of supply, markup, quality, and fashionability. Service, reputation, and country of origin have been found not to have a major impact on vendor selection[12] (although, as discussed in Retailing in Action 8.1, this may soon change). In cases where a co-op is offered, the amount of price reduction, advertising, and display support have been shown to have a significant effect on the purchase decision.[13] The smart apparel retailer might check to see whether the same merchandise will be made available to a nearby competitor; in such cases, it may be advantageous for the retailer to consider using a private label. Also, the buyer should check to see whether the merchandise could be purchased at a better price from a diverter.

One of a retailer's greatest assets when dealing with a vendor is the retailer's past experiences with that vendor. A small retailer doing all its own buying or a new buyer for a large chain should always approach vendors with two important pieces of information: the vendor profitability analysis statement and the confidential vendor analysis. The **vendor profitability analysis statement** (see Exhibit 8.9) lists the record of all purchases made last year, the discount granted by the vendor, the transportation charges paid, the original markup, markdowns, and finally the season-ending gross margin on that vendor's merchandise. The **confidential vendor analysis** (see Exhibit 8.10)

> **RETAILING IN ACTION**
>
> ### 8.1 More Than License Plates Are Made in Some Prisons
>
> While research has shown that country of origin does have some influence on product evaluation by the consumer, it is not very important in the purchasing decisions of the retail buyer. However, this could change in the near future. A recent State Department document revealed that the Chinese may be exporting up to $100 million of merchandise made by prisoners, including many political prisoners. The importation of such merchandise violates American laws, yet, most U.S. importers are unaware of the problem. While Chinese officials have denied using prisoners to make goods for export, the only way U.S. retailers can be sure that they aren't buying prison-made merchandise is to inspect all suppliers, down to the smallest subcontractors. Such careful vigilance would be expensive and it is doubtful whether American consumers would be willing to bear the cost.
>
> Sources: "China's Ugly Export Secret: Prison Labor," *Business Week,* 22 April 1991, 42–46; Richard Ettenson, Janet Wagner, and Gary Gaeth, "Evaluating the Effect of Country of Origin and the 'Made in the USA' Campaign: A Conjoint Approach," *Journal of Retailing* (Spring 1988): 85–100; Sung-Tai Hong and Robert S. Wyer, Jr., "Effects of Country-of-Origin and Product-Attribute Information on Product Evaluation: An Information Processing Perspective," *Journal of Consumer Research* (September 1989): 175–87; Janet Wagner, Richard Ettenson, and Jean Parrish, "Vendor Selection Among Retail Buyers: An Analysis by Merchandise Division," *Journal of Retailing* (Spring 1989): 58–79.

lists the same companies as in the profitability analysis statement but also provides a three-year financial summary as well as the names, titles, and negotiating points of all the vendor's sales staff. This last piece of information is based on notes taken by the buyer after the previous season's buying trip.

Based on the information obtained in these two reports, some retailers classify vendors into five categories.

Class A vendors. These are the vendors from which the retailer purchases large and profitable amounts of merchandise. The retailer may distinguish them from others by purchasing a certain minimum quantity from them. These vendors and the retailer work together as partners.

Class B vendors. These are the vendors that generate satisfactory sales and profits for the retailer. They occasionally develop a strong product offering for the retailer.

Class C vendors. These are the vendors who carry outstanding lines but do not currently sell to the retailer. This is the type of vendor that the store buyer desires as a supplier.

Class D vendors. These are the vendors from whom the retailer purchases small quantities of goods on an irregular basis. Because of the expense of small orders, it is doubtful whether purchases from these vendors produce any profits for either the retailer or the vendor.

Class E vendors. These are the vendors with which the retailer has had an unfavorable experience. Only after the approval of top store officials can orders be placed with these vendors.

EXHIBIT 8.9

Two-Seasons Vendor Profitability Analysis Period Ending 01/03/9X Dept. 135

Vendor Name	Purchases		Discount and Anticipation %	Freight %	Markup % Landed Loaded	Markdown		Gross Margin Percentage	Vendor No.
	Cost	Retail				$	%		
Anderson Sports	62,481	129,861	7.1	1.4	50.7	20,211	15.6	46.2	273359
Jack Frost, Inc.	26,921	53,962	8.0	1.3	49.4	3,233	6.0	50.5	818922
Sue's Fashions	25,572	51,930	8.1	1.8	49.9	6,667	12.8	47.1	206284
Jana Kantor Asso.	14,022	29,434	8.0	.8	52.0	481	1.6	55.1	050187
Pierce Mills	12,761	25,438	9.5	1.7	49.8	7,858	30.9	33.1	132886
Ray, Inc.	2,196	4,416	8.0	1.8	49.4	754	17.1	43.8	148296
Dusty's Place	2,071	4,332	8.0	1.3	51.6			55.4	662411
Lady Carole	1,050	2,100	8.0	2.1	48.9			52.9	676841
Jill Petites	740	1,584	10.4	.5	54.2	640	40.5	29.2	472977
Andrea's	198	410	8.0	.8	51.1			55.0	527218

Cost: your cost
Retail: your original selling price
Discount and anticipation %: discount received for early payments
Freight %: your shipping expenses
Markup % Landed Loaded: [Retail selling price − (Cost + Freight)]/Retail Selling
Markdown: Amount original selling price is reduced
Gross Margin %: [Actual selling price − (Cost + Freight)]/Actual Selling

EXHIBIT 8.10

Confidential Vendor Analysis, Retail

Trip Dates: Fall Market City: Dallas Buyer's Name: Cooper Dept. Name: Women's Wear Dept. No.: 491

Vendor/Address Phone No./Floor No.		Volume History 199X 199X 199X			Markup History 199X 199X 199X			Markdown History 199X 199X 199X			Vendor Executives & Titles	Remarks
West Texas Blouse	Spring	590.5	719.4	330.8	47.5	47.7	46.7	2.4	5.3	4.4	Name: Larry Wilcox (VP)	
	Fall	1002.8	706.7		47.3	47.5		3.4	7.8		Julie Davin	Prone to co-op
	Year	1593.3	1426.1		47.4			3.1			Ted Rombach	
	Objectives:											
	Results: As of 5/22											
Flatland Fashions	Spring	224.5	230.2	210.8	47.7	50.0	47.2	6.5	8.5	3.8	Name: Joe Hall (P)	
	Fall	175.8	230.5		47.3	47.6		17.0	9.0		Richard Reel	Will deal on
	Year	400.3	460.7		47.5	48.8		11.1	8.7			transportation
	Objectives:											
	Results As of 5/22:											
Southern	Spring	-0-	42.3	50.7		48.4	45.4	-0-	9.1	4.2	Name: Jackie Poteet (SM)	
	Fall	37.0	69.2		47.1	42.3		7.7	7.8		Boonie Hanley	"Quantity"
	Year	37.0	112.5		47.1	44.7		7.7	8.2		Carol Little	
	Objectives											
	Results: As of 5/22											
Gallo	Spring	21.7	195	55.6	46.9	50.0	48.3	1.3	0.2	1.2	Name: Ruth Wilson (P)	
	Fall	-0-	13.9		-0-	46.7		-0-	2.0		John Murphy	Easier of
	Year	21.7	33.4		46.9	48.6		1.3	0.9			the two
	Objectives											
	Results: As of 5/22											

Even buyers who do not go to market but have the vendors come to them must evaluate their vendors. For years, many grocers felt that firms like Procter & Gamble treated retailers poorly. These grocers needed the many products that P & G manufactured, but they didn't like P & G's "We win, you lose" attitude. P & G was a Class B vendor, at best. Recently, however, P & G has developed a program in which it helps all its customers in developing their merchandise plans for the next months. It has even moved some offices to the retailer's hometown (for example, P & G has a Wal-Mart team in Bentonville, Arkansas) so that it can work in a true partnership with the retailer. This new attitude of "Let's both win" has encouraged many supermarkets to reevaluate P & G as a Class A vendor. P & G knows that it can only be as successful as its retailers let it be.[14]

Some buyers may elect to use the services of a resident buying office. **Resident buying offices (RBOs)**, whether retailer-owned and operated or independent, are usually located in important merchandise centers (New York City for women's clothing, High Point, North Carolina, for furniture) and enable the participating retailers to have better contacts with vendors. In addition, RBOs supply valuable and timely information to the participating retailers.

Specifically:

1. The RBO keeps the retailer informed of new merchandise. Bulletins are sent out in a timely fashion making the participating retailer aware of new products and where they can be obtained. These mailings usually contain all specifications and information concerning the availability of the merchandise. The women's specialty store in Kalamazoo or Modesto is as aware of new merchandise as the retailer in New York City. If given the authority, the RBO can place a trial order for the goods.
2. The RBO provides the out-of-town retailer with an office when making a market buying trip. In addition, because the RBO is able to determine which vendors will best suit the participating retailer's needs, personnel at the RBO can save time by arranging appointments for the out-of-town retailer.
3. The RBO makes the participating retailer aware of macro developments in retailing through its marketing research department. The RBO keeps the retailer constantly abreast of critical subject areas, like changes in styles or legal developments.
4. The RBO provides support services to help the retailer in its promotional activities and other areas such as store design and layout and information systems.
5. Because of the rapid growth of imported merchandise from the Far East, the RBO sends its personnel to these markets, and the participating retailer is able to stock imported goods at higher than normal markups. Based on its client needs, the RBO can determine the type of goods to be manufactured, maintain a desired level of quality, and ensure timely delivery of merchandise. Merchandise of this type usually has to be

ordered at least six months prior to delivery. Also, participating retailers can develop their own brand names, thereby developing a degree of product differentiation.

After selecting vendors, the retailer still must make a decision on the specific merchandise to be bought. Some products, such as the basic items for the particular department in question, are easy to purchase. Other products, especially new items, require more careful planning and consideration. Retailers should concern themselves with several key questions, among them:

1. Where does this product fit into the strategic position that I have staked out for my department within my firm?
2. Will I have an exclusive with this product or will I be in competition with nearby retailers?
3. What is the estimated demand for this product in my target market?
4. What is my anticipated gross margin for this product?
5. Will I be able to obtain reliable, speedy replacement stock?
6. Can this product stand on its own, or is it merely a "me-too" item?
7. What is my expected turnover rate with this product?
8. Does this product complement the rest of my inventory?

VENDOR NEGOTIATIONS

The climax of a successful buying plan is active negotiation with suppliers. The effectiveness of the buyer/vendor relationship depends on the negotiation skills of the buyer and the economic power of the firms involved.

The retail buyer must negotiate price, delivery dates, discounts, shipping terms, and return privileges. All these factors are significant because they affect both the firm's profitability and cash flow.

Manufacturers as well as retailers have in recent years become increasingly aware of the cost of carrying excess inventory. Likewise, both parties have also become more concerned with the time value of money and its resulting effect on the firm's cash flow. Since each party is trying to shift costs to the other, most negotiations do produce some conflict. However, successful negotiation is usually accomplished when buyers realize that vendors are really their partners in the upcoming merchandising season. Since both are seeking to satisfy the retailer's customers better than anybody else, buyers and vendors must resolve their conflicts and differences of opinion, remembering that negotiation is a two-way street and a long-term profitable relationship is the goal. After all, the vendor wants to develop a long-term relationship as much as the retailer does with its customers.

What can be negotiated? There are many factors (prices, freight, delivery dates, method of shipment and shipping costs, exclusivity, guaranteed sales, markdown money, promotional allowances, return privileges, and discounts) and life is simplest when there are no surprises. Therefore, the smart buyer leaves nothing to chance and discusses everything with the vendor before hand. The buyer and seller together work out the upcoming merchandising plans using the buyer's merchandise budget and planned turnover. The buyer and seller should seek to make negotiations a "win–win" situation in which both sides win and neither feels like a loser. The essence of negotiation is to trade what is cheap to you but valuable to the other party, for what is valuable to you but cheap to the other party.[15]

The smart buyer puts all the upcoming areas of negotiations and previous agreements in letter form and sends it out before market. This helps to eliminate any misunderstandings afterward.

Price, of course, is probably the first factor to be negotiated. Buyers should attempt to purchase the desired merchandise at the lowest possible net cost but should not expect unreasonable discounts or price concessions.

The buyer must be familiar with the prices and discounts allowed by each vendor. This is why past records are so important. However, the buyer must remember that bargaining power is a factor in his or her *planned* purchases from the vendor. As a result, a large retailer may be able to purchase goods from a vendor at a lower price than a small, mom-and-pop retailer. There are five different types of discounts to be negotiated.

TRADE DISCOUNT

A **trade discount,** sometimes referred to as a **functional discount,** is a form of compensation the buyer may receive for performing certain services for the manufacturer. The size of the discount will vary with the service. Thus, variations in trade discounts are legally justifiable on the basis of the different costs associated with doing business with various buyers.

Trade discounts can either be a single discount (for instance, 20 percent off list) or a chain of discounts applied to the list price in successive order. For example, a discount of 40/10/5 means the retailer receives 40 percent off the list price, the merchant wholesaler receives 10 percent off the balance, and the manufacturer's agent earns 5 percent off the second balance. Assume that the list price of an item is $1,000 and that the chain of trade discounts is 40/20/10. The manufacturer's agent actually pays $432 for this item, while the merchant wholesaler pays $480, and the retailer pays $600 for the item which will retail for $1,000. The computations would look like this:

List price	$1,000
Less 40%	− 400
	$ 600
Less 20%	− 120
	$ 480
Less 10%	− 48
Manufacturer's selling price	$ 432

Let's look at how the various chains of discount permit a vendor to compensate the members of the distribution channel for their marketing activities. Assume that the manufacturer sells through a channel system that includes manufacturers' agents, service wholesalers, and small retailers. The purchase price of $432 is accorded to the manufacturer's agent who negotiates a sale between the manufacturer and the service wholesaler. The manufacturer's agent then charges the service wholesaler $480 for the item, realizing $48 for rendering a number of marketing functions. The service wholesaler, in turn, charges a retailer $600 for the item, thus making $120. The retailer then sells the item at the suggested list price of $1,000, making $400 in gross margin to cover expenses and profit.

Trade discounts are legal where they correctly reflect the costs of the intermediaries' services. Sometimes large retailers want to buy directly from the manufacturer and, in our example, pay only $432, instead of $600. This action would enable the large retailer to undercut the competition and would be illegal, unless one of the three defenses of the Robinson-Patman Act explained in Chapter 6 could be applied.

QUANTITY DISCOUNT

A **quantity discount**[16] is price reduction offered as an inducement to purchase large quantities of merchandise. There are three types of quantity discounts available:

1. **Noncumulative quantity discount.** A discount based on a single purchase.
2. **Cumulative quantity discount.** A discount based on the total amount purchased over a period of time.
3. **Free merchandise.** A discount whereby merchandise is offered in lieu of price concessions.

Quantity discounts can be legally justified by the manufacturer if its costs are reduced because of the quantity involved or if the manufacturer is meeting a competitor's price in good faith. Most vendors would have a difficult time justifying cumulative quantity discounts, since many small orders could be involved, thereby reducing the vendor's savings.

In addition, cumulative quantity discounts can be shown to be anticompetitive. For example, consider the following cumulative quantity discount schedule for widgets costing $10:

Order Quantity	Discount from List Price
1–999	
1,000–9,999	5%
10,000–24,999	8%
25,000–49,999	10%

If a retailer that had already purchased 500 units for $5,000 earlier this year wanted another 800 units, it would have to pay $8,000 (800 × $10) to purchase the units from a different vendor. However, the retailer would receive a 5 percent discount on all 1,300 units, and pay only $7,350 (1,300 × $9.50 minus the $5,000 already paid), if the additional 800 units were purchased from the original vendor using a cumulative pricing policy.

Recent research has shown that quantity discounts might not always be in the seller's best interest and should always be viewed as an invitation for further negotiations. Consider this price schedule published by IBM for a computer.

Quantity	Unit Price
1–19	$5,795
20–49	$5,099
50–149	$4,636
150–249	$4,486

Let's say that as a buyer for a retail chain you want 18 of these computers and your cost is $104,310 (18 × $5,795). But 20 would only cost $101,980 (20 × $5,099). What do you do? You actually have four choices: (a) order 20 computers at $5,099 and keep the extra two, (b) order 20 computers at $5,099 but have IBM ship 18 and keep the other two, (c) order 20 but tell IBM to ship you only 18 and to credit you for two computers at $5,099 each, or (d) negotiate a purchase price.[17] In summary, whenever quantity discounts are offered, the buyer should always check to see whether ordering more might lower the total purchase price.

PROMOTIONAL DISCOUNT

A third type of discount is a **promotional discount** given when the retailer performs an advertising or promotional service for the manufacturer. For example, a vendor might offer a retailer 50 extra jeans free if the retailer purchases 1,250 jeans during the season and runs two newspaper advertisements featuring them. These discounts are legal as long as they are available to all competing retailers on an equal basis.

The use of promotional discounts has caused some manufacturers to sell as much as 40 percent of their annual production of certain products to wholesalers and retailers during the six weeks when those products were given promotional allowances. Results such as this are the reason that manufacturers are beginning to view the retailer as their merchandising partner.[18] Special promotions can also allow the retailer to use a strategy known as "forward buying," that is, buying several months' supply ahead of time to take advantage of the price. Many times retailers can make a quick profit on special promotional deals, buying excess products by utilizing quantity discounts and selling the extra merchandise to a diverter. The diverter, who is not an authorized member of the marketing channel, will be able to purchase these goods more cheaply from the retailer than from the manufacturer and can sell this excess merchandise to other retailers. Consider the retailer discussed previously that needs only 18 computers and purchases 20 computers. The retailer that sold the two computers to a diverter for $3,500 apiece would be better off by $9,330 than if it bought only 18 computers at $5,795 each (18 × $5,795 = $104,310; 20 × $5,099 = $101,980 − $7,000 = $94,980). The diverter can now profit by selling these two computers to another retailer for $4,000 each. No wonder diverters, who are not doing anything illegal, are becoming respectable members of the retailer's channel.[19] However, as shown in Retailing in Action 8.2, not all manufacturers feel the same way about them and are seeking means to stop them.

SEASONAL DISCOUNT

Retailers can earn a **seasonal discount** if they purchase and take delivery of the merchandise in the off season (e.g., buying swimwear in October). However, this does not mean that all seasonal discounts result in the purchase of merchandise out of season. Retailers in resort areas often take advantage of these discounts since swimwear is never out of season for them. As long as

---

RETAILING IN ACTION

8.2 Can Manufacturers Stop Diverters?

There doesn't appear to be any way that manufacturers can stop the spread of diverters if they continue to use quantity discounts. What was once confined to the supermarket industry has now spread through the electronics industry, into department stores via the cosmetic goods channels, and even to automobile dealers.

Let's consider some of the strategies computer manufacturers have used in the past to prevent their current channel members from acting as diverters, and ways diverters have gone around them.

Maintenance/Field Service

Manufacturers feel that "only we can sell and maintain the product." They believe that by not giving out the shop repair manual they can force customers to return to authorized dealers for repair and warranty. Obtaining the manual is usually no problem, however, since many suppliers provide one directly to customers. Diverters will often throw in a manual to close a deal. Remember, if the manufacturer can't control inventory and prices, how can it expect to control a manual, especially with all the photocopiers around.

Distributor Training

The manufacturer may only train repair people at its headquarters. Here the diverter simply hires a trained person away from an authorized dealer or subcontracts the dealer to moonlight.

Warranty/Guaranty Agreements

Often the warranty is voided if the product is purchased at an "unauthorized dealer." This is easy to overcome. Does the buyer know or care who authorized dealers are? If the product breaks down, the buyer will hold the manufacturer responsible. Besides, most products experience problems only after the warranty expires.

Cash Rebates Directly to the Customer

This is a potentially effective countermeasure. If the manufacturer makes a point of advertising the rebate widely, those diverters that don't have the rebate card or whose place of purchase will prevent the manufacturer from honoring the card will be forced to explain this to the customer, jeopardizing the sale.

Some diverters will either honor the rebate directly from their profits or simply not carry the line during the rebate time period. After all, no manufacturer will continue such a program indefinitely. Some diverters send in the card for the customer and list the authorized dealer they themselves purchased the product from.

Cumulative Discounts and "Year End" Bonuses
Deleting the Channel Members Who Don't Cooperate

While these two ideas might make sense for manufacturers at first, unfortunately the FTC would consider such actions a means of price control or fixing, restraint of trade, and collusion.

Thus, about the only thing a manufacturer can do to prevent diverters from becoming unauthorized members of its channel is to stop using quantity discounts.

Source: Based on "Auto Club Finds Agency's Ruling Less Than AAA," *Wall Street Journal*, 12 April 1991, B1 and Roy Howell, Robert Britney, Paul Kuzdrall, and James Wilcox, "Unauthorized Channels of Distribution: Gray Markets," *Industrial Marketing Management* (1986): 257-63. Used with the permission of the authors.

the same terms are available to all competing retailers, seasonal discounts are legal.

CASH DISCOUNT

The final discount available to the buyer is a **cash discount** for prompt payment of bills. Cash discounts are usually stated as 8/10, net 30, which means that an 8 percent discount is given if payment is received within 10 days of the invoice date and the net is due within 30 days.

Although the cash discount is a common method for encouraging early payment, it can also be used as a negotiating tool by delaying the payment due date. This future-dating negotiation may take many forms. Several of the most common are:

1. End-of-month (EOM) dating allows for the cash discount and full payment period to begin on the first day of the following month instead of on

the invoice date. (End-of-month invoices dated *after the 25th* of the month are considered to be dated *on the first* of the following month.)
2. Middle-of-month (MOM) dating is similar to EOM except the middle of the month is used as the starting date.
3. Receipt-of-goods (ROG) dating allows the starting date to be the date goods are received by the retailer.
4. Extra dating merely allows the retailer some extra or free days before the period of payment begins.
5. A final discount form is anticipation. Anticipation allows a retailer to pay the invoice in advance of the expiration of the cash discount period and earn an extra discount. Anticipation is usually figured at an annual rate of 7.0 percent.

One of the major advantages that high-turnover/low-margin retailers such as warehouse clubs have is that their rapid turnover rate enables them to sell merchandise twice before the cash discount period expires on the first purchase. For example, Procter & Gamble offers all customers, regardless of size, the same cash discount terms: 2/30 net 31. Sam's Club has a turnover rate of 15, which means it must replace its entire inventory every 24 days. Thus, Sam's could purchase several truck loads of P & G products, sell them in 24 days, sell some of the replacements during the next six days, and still earn the discount on the original purchase. This is even more valuable in the apparel industry where the standard cash discount is 8/10, net 30, EOM. In this case, the retailer could purchase something on the first of the month, reorder and sell it two more times, and still earn the discount by paying for it before the 10th day of the next month.

Many vendors have eliminated the cash discount, since some large-volume retailers, realizing that vendors don't want to endanger such sales, have been taking 60 to 120 days to pay and still deduct the cash discount. Also, most vendors are requiring new accounts to pay up front until credit is established.

DELIVERY TERMS

Delivery terms are important because they specify when title to the merchandise passes to the retailer, whether the vendor or buyer will pay the freight charges, and who is obligated to file any damage claims. The three most common shipping terms are:

1. *Free on board (FOB) factory.* The buyer assumes title at the factory and pays all transportation costs from the vendor's factory.
2. *Free on board (FOB) shipping point.* The vendor pays the transportation to a local shipping point, but the buyer assumes title there and pays all further transportation costs.
3. *Free on board (FOB) destination.* The vendor pays the freight and the buyer takes title on delivery.

IN-STORE MERCHANDISE HANDLING

The retailer will need to have some means of handling incoming merchandise. For some types of retailers (like grocery stores), this need will be significant and frequent; for others (like jewelers), it will be relatively minor and infrequent. A retailer with a frequent and significant amount of incoming merchandise needs to do considerable planning of merchandise receiving and handling space. To illustrate, consider that a full-line grocery store will need to build receiving docks to which 40-to-60-foot semitrailers can be backed up. Space may also be needed for a small forklift to drive between the truck and the merchandise receiving area to unload the merchandise. Subsequently, the merchandise will need to be moved from the receiving area, where it is counted and marked, to a storage area, either on the selling floor or in a separate location.

The point at which incoming merchandise is received can be a high theft point. Although various figures have been reported on the losses incurred by employee and customer theft, a recent study by the U.S. Chamber of Commerce estimates that employee theft alone amounts to some $40 billion a year.[20] The retail manager needs to design the receiving and handling areas in order to minimize this problem. Several types of theft occur and most can be controlled.

VENDOR COLLUSION

Vendor collusion includes losses that occur when the merchandise is delivered. Such losses typically involve the delivery of less merchandise than is charged for, the removal of good merchandise disguised as old or stale merchandise, and the theft of other merchandise from the stockroom or the selling floor while making delivery. Vendor collusion often involves both the delivery people and the retail employee who signs for the delivery, with the two splitting the profit. Most fencing operations pay 25 percent of the ticketed price for stolen merchandise.[21]

THEFT

Employee theft occurs when employees believe that free merchandise is part of their pay. Although some of the stolen goods come from the selling floor, a larger percentage is taken from the stockroom to the employee lounge and lockers, where it is kept until the employees leave with it at quitting time. Statistics show that while shoplifters caught outnumber employees caught by 92,212 to 8,197, shoplifters had only $57.31 worth of merchandise compared to the employee's $890.[22] Employee theft is most prevalent in food stores, department stores, and discount stores. Considering that these types of stores are usually larger in size, sales volume, and number of employees, the lack of close supervision might contribute to this problem.

LOSS PREVENTION

Stealing merchandise from the stockroom and receiving area may be easier than taking it from the selling floor for several reasons. First, much of the stockroom merchandise is not ticketed, so it is easier to get it through electronic antishoplifting devices. Second, once the thief enters the stock area, there is very little antitheft security. Most security guards watch the exits and fitting rooms. Third, there is usually an exit in the immediate area of the stockroom through which the thief can carry out the stolen goods. Many such exits have now been wired to set off an alarm when opened without a key, helping to reduce theft somewhat.

The retailer must be aware that there is an excellent opportunity for receiving, handling, and storage thefts to happen. Therefore, steps should be taken to help cut down on these crimes.[23] The retailer cannot watch everybody every minute to see whether or not he or she is honest, but some surveillance is helpful. One study reported that subliminal messages in the background music, such as "I am an honest person. I do not steal" can reduce theft by 20 percent.[24] Others have found that having the shoplifter pay a civil penalty of $100 to $200 to cover the cost of antishoplifting devices, in addition to returning the merchandise, works in lieu of having criminal charges filed to produce a "sudden and dramatic drop in juvenile theft." At present, 39 states have passed such statutes.[25]

EVALUATING MERCHANDISE PERFORMANCE

Up to this point, we have discussed the importance of merchandise planning, the amount of merchandise to stock, issues that can be negotiated with vendors, and ways to protect the merchandise once received. However, we have ignored the most important aspect of merchandise—how it performs in terms of generating sales and profits for the retailer. In this section we shall examine various measures of merchandise performance.

PROFIT MEASURES

Some retailers still insist on measuring performance in terms of a productivity measure such as sales or inventory turnover rate. But the ultimate test of merchandising performance should be a profit criterion. A retailer could produce excellent sales or turnover by giving the merchandise away—but that is not the name of the game. Sales without sufficient profit margins don't let retailers cover their overhead or operating expenses. Thus, the role of the retail executive is to manage demand and supply factors in order to achieve a return on investment sufficient for survival and future growth. We need profit margins to cover overhead and to purchase additional merchandise for resale.

How profitable are a retailer's merchandising decisions? To answer this, we need to define profit. Merchandise managers may use three measures of profitability when assessing merchandising performance.

1. **Gross margin** is net sales less cost of goods sold. This measure is useful if there are no expenses besides the cost of merchandise that can be directly related or traced to the merchandise. For example, it may not be possible to directly tie any advertising or sales expenses to particular lines of merchandise.
2. **Contribution margin** is defined as net sales less cost of goods sold and any expenses that are directly traceable to that product.[26] In this case, items such as advertising expense can be related to specific product lines.
3. **Operating profit** is net sales less cost of goods sold, direct expenses, and a share of all indirect expenses the retailer incurs. This method is not useful unless the indirect expenses can be equitably allocated. Typically, however, they cannot, since it is difficult to allocate such expenses as the president's salary or clerical and office expenses to merchandise lines without doing it on an arbitrary basis.

All three profit figures can be related to a sales base, to obtain profit margin statistics such as:

Gross margin percentage = Gross margin/Net sales
Contribution margin percentage = Contribution margin/Net sales
Operating profit percentage = Operating profit/Net sales

Of the available profit measures, gross margin is the most widely used in retailing to assess merchandising performance. There are two reasons for this. First, it is the most accurate number to work with, since both sales and cost of merchandise sold can be measured by merchandise line, or even merchandise item, with minimal error. This is a significant advantage over the contribution margin and operating profit methods, since both of them require decisions as to which expenses, besides cost of merchandise, should be subtracted from net sales. Second, many industry trade associations regularly report data on gross margins by merchandise line, making it possible for the retailer to compare its performance to the experience of others. Exhibit 8.11 is the gross margin data by merchandise line for a major department store chain.

GROSS MARGIN RETURN ON INVENTORY

Gross margin return on inventory (GMROI) incorporates into a single measure both inventory turnover and profit.[27] It can be computed as follows:

(Gross margin/Net sales) (Net sales/Average inventory at cost)
= (Gross margin/Average inventory at cost)

EXHIBIT 8.11

Maintained Markup or Gross Margin for a Large Department Store Chain

Department Description	Gross Margin Percentage	Department Description	Gross Margin Percentage
Better Coats	43.0	Inexpensive Coats	46.2
Women's Dresses	42.9	Special Occasion	36.2
Ms. Budget Separates	48.1	Petite Dresses	42.4
Better Sportswear	37.5	Ms. Sweaters	44.1
Jewelry	49.8	Bridge Jewelry	46.1
Footwear & Bodywear	47.7	Fragrance	39.2
Junior Tops	45.6	Junior Bottoms	45.6
Young Juniors	43.4	Lamps	40.6
Foundations	53.4	Loungewear	46.3
Girls Wear (4 to 6X)	45.6	Girl's Lingerie	46.6
Newborn	45.5	Boys Furnishings	44.1
Mens Suits	37.5	Mens Active Wear	43.3
Young Mens	41.6	Mens Better Sportswear	35.5
Mens Furnishings	51.2	Mens Neckwear	55.1
Toys	36.4	Electric Floor Care	24.6
Cookware	39.6	Towels and Rugs	44.4
Sheets and Pillowcases	37.8	Pillows and Accessories	44.3
Notions	43.5	Casual Furniture	37.1
Upholstered Furniture	42.4	Furniture Accessories	34.5
Rugs	44.3	Silverware	41.2
Boys Clothing	40.2	Gift Shop	43.8

In this simple model the gross margin percentage (gross margin/net sales) is multiplied by the sales-to-stock ratio* to obtain a gross margin return on inventory. Thus, if a particular merchandise line has a gross margin of 35 percent and an inventory turnover rate of 3.9, its sales-to-stock ratio would be 6.0 [3.9 ÷ (100% − 35%)] and a GMROI of $2.10 ($0.35 × 6). That is, for each dollar invested in inventory, on average, the retailer obtains $2.10 in gross margin annually. These gross margin dollars can be used to pay store operating expenses and help yield a profit for the retailer. Exhibit 8.12 lists the median GMROI for the large department stores by merchandise lines.

The GMROI model is not complex but it does tell the retailer three things:

1. The principal goal in managing merchandise investments (inventory) should be a *return on investment* goal—specifically, gross margin return on inventory investment. Gross margin and inventory turnover are not

---

*The sales-to-stock ratio is similar to inventory turnover except the average inventory is expressed at cost rather than at retail. The sales-to-stock ratio is used in GMROI instead of inventory turnover, since the denominator of a return on investment measure should reflect the cost of the investment. Inventory turnover is obtained by multiplying net sales/average inventory at cost times (100 − gross margin percentage).

EXHIBIT 8.12

GMROI for All Department Stores with Sales Over $2 Million

Footwear	$1.1
Female Apparel	$2.5
Adult Female Accessories	$2.3
Mens & Boys Apparel & Accessories	$1.8
Infants & Childrens Clothing & Accessories	$2.4
Cosmetics & Drugs	$1.3
Leisure & Home Electronics	$0.5
Home Furnishings	$1.0
Other Hard Lines	$1.0
All Other Merchandise	$2.3

Source: National Retail Federation, Merchandising and Operating Results of Department and Specialty Stores in 1990 (New York: Financial Executives Division, National Retail Federation, 1991): 4-5.

goals; they are worth pursuing only to the extent that they enhance GMROI.
2. There are two principal decision making areas in merchandise management. The first is *gross margin management* and the second is *inventory turnover management.*
3. Merchandise managers who effectively interrelate gross margin management and inventory turnover management will be able to achieve *high-performance results.*

GMROI AND SPACE MANAGEMENT[28]

Merchandise assortments must be effective if the retail store is to prosper. An effective assortment is one that creates good financial returns. Assortments should be planned at the stockkeeping unit level, with special consideration given to the inventory or merchandise intensity, sales, and space attributable to each SKU or group of similar SKUs.

Gross Margin Return on Selling Space. Many retailers do assortment planning using only GMROI. Thus, an SKU or group of SKUs with a high GMROI receives more merchandising emphasis. However, this can be a questionable emphasis at times. The key resource with which a retailer should be concerned in planning assortments is space, not dollars of inventory investment. The influence of merchandise assortments on gross margin return on selling space (GMROS) is thus often more important than their influence on GMROI.

In merchandise assortment planning, all SKUs should be examined in terms of their need for space. The SKUs that contribute most to the effectiveness of the assortment plan are those that have a high inventory investment per unit of space they occupy (inventory intensity—often also referred to as merchandise intensity) and also have a high GMROI. Inventory intensity and GMROI are key correlates of retail productivity and profitability.

Three factors (gross margin, sales-to-stock ratio, inventory intensity) when multiplied together yield **space productivity** (defined as gross margin per square foot of selling space), as shown in Exhibit 8.13. For example, at a storewide level, a retailer with a gross margin of 30 percent, a sales-to-stock ratio of 5.0, and a $20 inventory investment per square foot of selling space will achieve $30 in gross margin per square foot of selling space (30% × 5 × $20 = $30 gross margin per square foot of selling space).

Let's examine how GMROI, when seen in isolation, can be misleading. Consider two merchandise lines—A and B. Line A has a GMROI of 180 percent and line B has a GMROI of 150 percent. Line A is best by GMROI standards. However, assume A has an inventory intensity (inventory investment per square foot) of $20 and B has a $40 inventory intensity. Line A has a $36 gross margin return on space (180% × $20), and line B has a $60 gross margin return on space (150% × $40), assuming a gross margin of 30% and a sales-to-stock ratio of 5. The real winner is line B, not line A.

Space Assortments. Not all SKUs can be expected to have high space productivity. Collectively, however, the total assortment of SKUs must yield respectable storewide space productivity. A useful frame of reference for space

EXHIBIT 8.13
Space Productivity Model

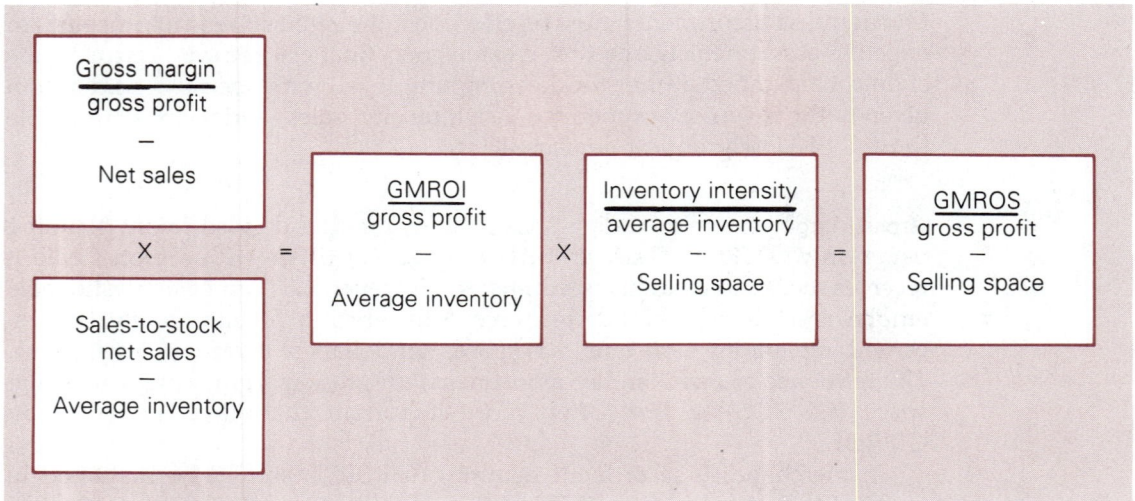

Source: Robert F. Lusch, "Two Critical Determinants of Retail Profitability," *Zale Retailing Issues Newsletter* 2, no. 1 (April 1986): 1 and The Center for Retailing Studies, Texas A&M University.

allocation is the assortment planning matrix presented in Exhibit 8.14. This is a 2-by-2 matrix. One dimension is GMROI and the other is inventory intensity. Each dimension is divided into low and high categories, resulting in four types of assortments in terms of their use of space: golden assortments, space-effective assortments, inventory-effective assortments, and competitive assortments.

A **golden assortment** consists of items that are blessed with both high GMROI and high inventory intensity. The golden assortments are the cash cows of the store. They can often generate enough profit to pay most of the store's operating expenses. Retail managers should do everything possible to protect the favorable performance characteristics of their golden assortments.

An example of a discount department store's golden assortment is costume jewelry, because both GMROI and inventory intensity are high. It is not unusual for the inventory investment to be over $60 per square foot for costume jewelry.

A second type of assortment is **space-effective assortment.** These assortments have a low GMROI, but they are not space hogs and thus have high inventory intensity. This results in reasonable (but not spectacular) space productivity. Cameras and photographic equipment and supplies are examples of space-effective assortments in discount department stores. The GMROI on this assortment is generally low because of the price leader position many discount stores take in these items. But the inventory investment is often over $70 per square foot, which results in respectable space productivity.

The third type of assortment is **inventory-effective assortment.** These assortments have a high GMROI but are heavy users of space; that is,

EXHIBIT 8.14
Assortment Planning Matrix

		GMROI	
		Low	High
Inventory intensity	Low	Competitive assortments	Inventory effective assortments
	High	Space effective assortments	Golden assortments

Source: Robert F. Lusch, "Two Critical Determinants of Retail Profitability," *Zale Retailing Issues Newsletter* 2, no. 1 (April 1986): 2 and The Center for Retailing Studies, Texas A&M University.

ILLUSTRATION 8.3

The costume jewelry department in many discount stores represents a profit center that produces high sales and high margin.

inventory intensity is low. Nonetheless, their high GMROI allows them to generate a reasonable level of space productivity. An excellent example of inventory-effective assortments in discount department stores is stationery and school supplies. These items have a high GMROI (except during back-to-school sales) but are rather bulky in relation to their value and thus are not effective space users. Inventory investment per square foot is often in the $20 to $25 range, which is less than half that for the costume jewelry and photography examples.

The fourth type of assortment is the **competitive assortment.** This merchandise consists of SKUs that are offered only for competitive reasons. They are poor profit performers because they have a low GMROI and are heavy users of space. The result is low space productivity. A naive analyst would drop all items with these characteristics. This would be a mistake if the competitive realities of the marketplace dictated that they be offered.

In a discount department store, the linens and domestics are competitive-merchandise assortments. Linens and domestics have a low GMROI because of a low sales-to-stock ratio. These items also occupy a lot of space in relation to their value and thus the net result is poor performance. To discontinue carrying linens and domestics, however, would be disastrous.

The key message is that the competitive realities of the marketplace dictate that a retailer must plan the store's total space assortment to have a mix of these four categories with the goal being to maximize the number of SKUs in golden assortments. Each SKU or group of similar SKUs should be monitored regularly to determine whether one of the three "hot" buttons of space productivity (gross margin, sales-to-stock ratio, inventory intensity) can be pushed to improve its performance. Looking at each SKU independently will likely lead to suboptimization and a failure to meet customer needs. This is the real weakness of GMROI and GMROS if they are not applied in a total system context.

DIRECT PRODUCT PROFIT

Direct product profit (DPP) was introduced in 1986[29] to be used in the retail food industry as a means of reducing costs and controlling product proliferation. Some retailers worried that, since GMROI measures product performance based on gross margin, it could hide important differences in the costs of selling merchandise. DPP, therefore, focuses on the contribution margin of individual retail items in individual stores. DPP equals an item's gross margin dollars, plus discounts and allowances earned, less direct handling, selling, and inventory holding costs. DPP can be aggregated to enable the retailer to develop results for brands, categories, departments, stores, and so on, thus forming the basis for merchandising decisions.

Because DPP is felt to be a much more accurate measure of an SKU's true contribution toward fixed-cost and pretax profit by incorporating interim differences in sales, margins, and costs associated with storing, transporting, shelving, and labor-intensive merchandising activities such as pricing, it is replacing gross margin in making merchandising decisions, not only in the retail food industry, but also for mass and general merchandisers. Exhibit 8.15 shows how DPP allows a retailer to go past historical measures (dollar sales, sales per square foot, gross margin percentage, and GMROI) by including all the variable costs of handling a product. By including these costs, the retailer can arrive at the product contribution, or DPP, of each individual product, in our example $9.19 or $35.51 per square foot per week.

By expressing DPP against a common unit of measure (floor space), retailers can compare the performance of products of different physical proportions. Since retail space is usually limited, DPP can be used for:

1. Item selection (high-DPP items should generally be added, and low ones reviewed for possible pruning)
2. Store/shelf location (high-DPP items should be given prime location)
3. Promotion (total DPP can be improved by increasing the sales of high-DPP products)

High-performance retailers such as Kmart, Wal-Mart, and almost all supermarket chains now make extensive use of DPP to better manage their operating costs, identify the most efficient channel, and identify SKUs that are poor profit contributors. Kmart, for example, uses DPP to evaluate different pricing strategies, new store layouts, and new advertising programs.

EXHIBIT 8.15

Computing Direct Product Profit for an Individual Product

Retail price	$ 25.00
Less: Cost	12.50
Equals: Gross margin dollars	12.50
Plus: Discounts and allowances earned	
Payment discount	.45
Merchandise allowances	1.10
Equals: Adjusted gross margin	$ 14.05
Less: Direct handling costs	
Freight in	.11
Promotion expenses	.38
Retail direct labor	2.13
Retail inventory expense	.16
Retail operating expense	.97
Distribution center direct labor	.78
Distribution center inventory expense	.14
Distribution center operating expense	.19
Equals: DPP per unit	$ 9.19
Times: Number of units/week	51
Equals: DPP per week	$468.69
Divide: Square feet used	13.2
Equals: DPP per square feet per week	$ 35.51

However, DPP is time intensive and expensive to calculate, and it can be difficult to interpret. Thus, along with growing support, DPP has started to come under criticism. Some question the additional value DPP provides over indexes such as turnover or GMROI. Others cite the difficulties encountered in obtaining the 40 product inputs and over 70 cost components required to run the DPP model. Recent research shows that other product indexes are still more commonly used to make merchandising decisions such as dropping/adding, pricing, and promotion. One study examined whether decisions made without DPP would be any different if DPP were used, and whether a quickly calculated combination of commonly available indexes could approximate an item's DPP.[30] The research indicated that in some cases gross margin or movement indicators had a strong relationship with DPP, but the results were not consistent enough across categories to justify replacing DPP with any one measurement. The study did find that the relationship between an item's DPP and a weighted combination of gross-margin dollars, dollar sales, unit sales, and square feet of space allocation was extremely close. In fact, in most categories, a simple combination of gross-margin dollars and unit movement was all that was required to come close to an SKU's DPP.

Chapter 8 The Merchandise Buying and Handling Process

SUMMARY

Merchandise management is the analysis, planning, acquisition handling, and control of merchandise in a retail enterprise. An understanding of the principles of merchandise management is essential to good retail management.

A major part of merchandise management is planning. The retailer needs to plan, first, the dollars to invest in inventory and, second, the units of merchandise to purchase with these dollars. These two forms of planning are called dollar merchandise planning, for which we discussed the basic stock, percentage variation, weeks' supply, and stock-to-sales inventory methods, and unit stock planning, for which we discussed the conflicts between the optimal level of inventory and the various constraints on it. Obviously, planning should be followed by control.

In addition to deciding what and how much to purchase, successful merchandise management must also consider vendor selection and negotiations. In this chapter we reviewed what factors are important in the selection of a vendor, how a merchandise manager prepares for a buying trip, and what factors can be negotiated. In addition, we looked at various means of handling the merchandise once it is received in the stores. We concluded the chapter by pointing out that good retail management of the merchandising function cannot occur unless the retailer's merchandising performance can be evaluated. Evaluative techniques include GMROI (gross margin return on inventory) and DPP (direct product profit).

QUESTIONS FOR DISCUSSION

1. Why is merchandise planning so important to a retailer's success?
2. What is the difference between inventory turnover rate and sales-to-stock ratio?
3. A retailer has a target GMROI for a particular merchandise line of $2.40 and believes that it can be achieved with a sales-to-stock ratio of 6.0. What must its target gross margin be?
4. If a retailer's annual turnover rate is 15 times, which inventory stock level method should it use and why? If the annual inventory turnover rate were 4, would your answer remain the same? Why?
5. What is the chief reason for diverters to operate in a retailer's channel of distribution?
6. What is the difference between the sales-to-stock ratio and the stock-to-sales method when discussing inventory?
7. What does the term open-to-buy mean? How can it be used to control merchandise investments?
8. Do you think it would be more difficult to make a merchandise plan for a supermarket or a dress shop? Why?
9. How can merchandise lines have too much breadth, yet not enough depth?
10. Would it require more inventory investment to support a supermarket doing $10 million in annual sales or a furniture store with the same amount of annual sales? Why?
11. Why is both dollar merchandise planning and unit stock planning necessary?
12. What type of measures can a buyer use to evaluate her job performance?
13. What are the major constraints in designing the optimal merchandise mix?
14. Compute the ratios in the GMROI model for the following three product lines:

Merchandise Line	Sales	Average Inventory at Cost	Gross Profit
A	$120,000	$35,000	$31,000
B	$130,000	$34,000	$42,000
C	$115,000	$50,000	$38,000

15. Herb's Hardware is attempting to develop a merchandise budget for the next 12 months. The target inventory turnover is 4.8 and forecasted sales are as follows:

Month	Forecasted Sales
1	$27,000
2	26,000
3	20,000
4	34,000
5	41,000
6	40,000
7	28,000
8	27,000
9	38,000
10	39,000
11	26,000
12	28,000

Develop a monthly merchandise budget using the basic stock method (BSM) and the percentage variation method (PVM).

16. A buyer is going to market and needs to compute her open-to-buy. Here is the relevant data: Planned stock at end of March is $319,999 (at retail prices); planned March sales are $149,999; current stock-on-hand (March 1) is $274,000; merchandise on order for delivery is $17,000; planned reductions are $11,000. What is the buyer's open-to-buy?

17. A retailer has a target GMROI for a particular merchandise line of $1.44 and believes that it can competitively price the line to obtain a gross margin of 32 percent. What must its target sales-to-stock ratio on this line be?

18. If the inventory turnover rate is 4.0 for a line of merchandise and the gross margin for this merchandise is 50 percent, what is the sales-to-stock ratio?

19. If one of your buyers has a negative OTB, should you do anything about increasing it or merely tell the buyer not to go to next week's market?

20. Explain how cumulative quantity discounts can be considered to be anticompetitive.

MANAGEMENT MEMO

It is early September and the local economy is starting to slow, which will affect sales in your department. As the store's newest buyer, you moved into your current position in early March, you don't want to make any merchandising mistakes in your first Christmas season. Today, you receive a memo from the president stating, "I would rather lose sales, than get stuck with a tremendous overhang of merchandise and end up giving it away come December. So cut back your OTB by 25 percent." After reading this memo several times, you decide to respond to the president. What would your response say?

BOARDROOM REPORT

Your firm, Worldwide Computer Sales, has long been acting as a diverter since manufacturer pricing policies encourage it. Now some members of the board are becoming concerned that the manufacturers may take some sort of action to prevent retailers from making a profit by diverting. You have been asked to prepare a report for next week's board meeting on this subject. This report is to discuss what possible actions the manufacturers could take to stop the diverting of their products and to develop a strategy for Worldwide to use if the manufacturers actually take such actions.

SUGGESTED READINGS

Farris, Paul, James Oliver, and Cornelius DeKluyer. "The Relationship Between Distribution and Market Share." *Marketing Science* (Spring 1989): 107-28.

Matthews, Ryan. "DPP: Dead or Alive." *Grocery Marketing* (July 1989): 14-15.

Monroe, Kent B., and Albert J. Della Bitta. "Models for Pricing Decisions." *Journal of Marketing Research* (August 1990): 413-28.

Wilcox, James B., Roy D. Howell, Paul Kuzdrall, and Robert Britney. "Price Quantity Discounts: Some Implications for Buyers and Sellers." *Journal of Marketing* (July 1987): 60-71.

ENDNOTES

1. John T. Mentzer and R. Kirshnan, "The Effect of the Assumption of Normality on Inventory Control/Customer Service," *Journal of Business Logistics* 6 (1985): 101-20.
2. Frank Burnside, "Merchandise Assortment Planning," in R. Patrick Cash, ed., *The Buyer's Manual* (New York: National Retail Merchants Association, 1979), 245-71.
3. Stanley Marcus, "Merchandise for the 1990s," *Retailing Issues Letter* (July 1990).
4. "Karl Eller of Circle K Always Pushing Luck, Now Lives to Regret It," *Wall Street Journal,* 3 April 1990, 1, 5.
5. Kapil Bawa, Jane T. Landwehr, and Aradhna Krishna, "Consumer Response to Retailers' Marketing Environments: An Analysis of Coffee Purchase Data," *Journal of Retailing* (Winter 1989): 471-95.
6. "Supermarkets Demand Food Firms' Payment Just to Get on the Shelf," *Wall Street Journal,* 1 November 1988, A1, A22. "Not Everyone Loves a Supermarket Special," *Business Week,* 17 February 1992, 64-67.
7. "Penney Moves Upscale in Merchandise but still Has to Convince Public," *Wall Street Journal,* 7 June 1990, A1, A10.
8. "Another 15,000 New Products Expected for U.S. Supermarkets," *Marketing News,* 10 June 1991, 8.
9. "Life in the Food Chain Becomes Predatory," *Advertising Age,* 9 May 1988, S-2.
10. Richard Ettenson and Janet Wagner, "Retail Buyers' Saleability Judgements: A Comparison of Information Use Across Three Levels of Experience," *Journal of Retailing* (Spring 1986): 41-63.
11. George A. Rieder, "Mythbusters: Keys to Creating a Climate for Innovation and Risk-Taking," *Retailing Issues Letter* (May 1989).
12. Janet Wagner, Richard Ettenson, and Jean Parrish, "Vendor Selection Among Retail Buyers: An Analysis by Merchandise Division," *Journal of Retailing* (Spring 1989): 58-79; Richard Ettenson, Janet Wagner, and Gary Gaeth, "Evaluating the Effect of Country of Origin and 'Made in the USA' Campaign: A Conjoint Approach," *Journal of Retailing* (Spring 1988): 85-100; Sally K. Francis and Daniel J. Brown, "Retail Buyers of Apparel and Appliances: A Comparison," *Clothing and Textiles Research Journal* 4 (1985-1986): 1-8; and Elizabeth C. Hirchman, "An Exploratory Comparison of Decision Criteria Used by Retail Buyers," in *Retail Patronage Theory,* R. F. Lusch and W. R. Darden, eds., (Norman, Okla: University of Oklahoma Printing Services), 1-5.
13. Rockney G. Walters, "An Empirical Investigation into Retailer Response to Manufacturer Trade Promotion," *Journal of Retailing* (Summer 1989): 253-72.
14. "America's Best Sales Forces: Six at the Summit," *Sales & Marketing Management* (June 1990): 62, 72.
15. Roger Dickinson, "Supplier-Retailer Negotiations: The Negotiation Ratio," *Proceedings of a Joint Conference of the American Collegiate Retailing Association and the Academy of Marketing Science* (Charleston, 1988) 29.
16. For a look at the sophisticated use of these discounts, see Ashok Rao, "Quantity Discounts in Today's Markets," *Journal of Marketing* (Fall 1980): 44-51.
17. Roy Howell, Robert Britney, Paul Kuzdrall, and James Wilcox, "Unauthorized Channels of Distribution: Gray Markets," *Industrial Marketing Management* (November 1986): 257-63.
18. "Retailers Buy Far in Advance to Exploit Trade Promotions," *Wall Street Journal,* 9 October 1986, 31.
19. "Diverting Gets Respectable," *Supermarket Business* (April 1988): 23.
20. "Your Credit Record Could Cost You Your Job," *Sales & Marketing Management* (March 1991): 28.
21. "Chicago Retailers' 'Sting' Aims to Put Shoplifting Professionals out of Business," *Wall Street Journal,* 5 June 1990, B1, B2.
22. "Some Customers Are Always Wrong," *The New York Times Magazine,* 10 June 1990, 19, 56-57.

23. Warren A. French, Melvin R. Crask, and Fred H. Mader, "Retailer's Assessment of Shoplifting Problem," *Journal of Retailing* (Winter 1984): 108-15.
24. "Some Customers."
25. "Antishoplifting Statutes Grow More Popular in the States," *Wall Street Journal,* 15 October 1990, B2.
26. Patrick Dunne and Harry Wolk, "Marketing Cost Analysis: A Modularized Contribution Approach," *Journal of Marketing* (July 1977).
27. Daniel J. Sweeney, "Improving the Profitability of Retail Merchandising Decisions, *Journal of Marketing* (January 1973): 60-68.
28. This section is based on Robert F. Lusch, "Two Critical Determinants of Retail Profitability," *Zale Retailing Issues Newsletter* (April 1986).
29. *Direct Product Profit Manual* (Washington, D.C.: Food Market Institute, 1986).
30. Norm Borin and Paul Farris, "An Empirical Comparison of Direct Product Profit and Existing Measures of SKU Productivity," *Journal of Retailing* (Fall 1990): 297-314.

CHAPTER 9

PRICING IN THE RETAIL OPERATION

OVERVIEW

This chapter begins by examining how pricing interacts with all other retail decisions. We discuss both demand- and supply-oriented pricing, then look at why initial markups and maintained markups are different. We next examine how an initial markup is established and why and how a retailer should take markdowns during the normal course of business. We then discuss the various pricing objectives a retailer may choose. The chapter concludes with a complete discussion of the pricing policies and strategies available to achieve those objectives.

PRICING IN THE RETAIL OPERATION

I. Interactive Price Decisions
   A. Merchandise
   B. Location
   C. Promotion
   D. Credit
   E. Customer Services
   F. Store Image
   G. Complementary Products
   H. Legal Constraints
II. Demand-Oriented Pricing
   A. Population Density
   B. Consumer Travel Costs

1. Actual Travel Costs
2. Opportunity Travel Costs
3. Psychic Travel Costs
4. Pricing Implications
5. A Note on Nonstore Retailing
    C. Maximum Demand Price
        1. Environmental Demand Variables
        2. Household Demand Variables
        3. Managerial Demand Variables
III. Supply-Oriented Pricing
    A. Cost Curves
    B. Profit
IV. Using Markups and Markdowns
    A. Calculating Markup
    B. Markup Methods
    C. Using Markup Formulas when Purchasing Merchandise
V. Planning Initial Markups
    A. Initial Markup Equation
    B. Markup Determinants
VI. Maintained Markup Percentage
VII. Markdown Management
    A. Buying Errors
    B. Pricing Errors
    C. Merchandising Errors
    D. Promotion Errors
VIII. Markdown Policy
    A. Early Markdown Policy
    B. Late Markdown Policy
    C. Markdown and GMROI
    D. Amount of Markdown
IX. Pricing Objectives
    A. Profit-Oriented Objectives
        1. Target Return
        2. Profit Maximization
    B. Sales-Oriented Objectives
    C. Status Quo Objectives
X. Pricing Policies and Strategies
    A. Pricing at Market Levels
    B. Pricing Above the Market
        1. Services Provided
        2. Merchandise Offerings
        3. Convenient Locations
        4. Extended Hours of Operation
    C. Pricing Below the Market
XI. Specific Pricing Strategies
    A. Customary Pricing

B. Variable Pricing
C. Flexible Pricing
D. One-Price Policy
E. Price Lining
F. Odd Pricing
G. Multiple-Unit Pricing
H. Leader Pricing
I. Bait Pricing
J. Private-Brand Pricing
XII. Summary

Perhaps the most common question facing retailers today is "What price should I charge for this product?" It should *not* be a difficult decision if the retailer has analyzed its market position correctly. Pricing, which is the final step in the retailer's merchandising strategy, is really an interactive decision made in conjunction with the firm's mission statement, its goals and objectives, its strategy, and the other elements of the retail mix.

Other strategy and policy decisions are affected by a retailer's pricing actions. If a retailer is to be a sales leader, and its strategy is aimed at the entire middle-class market with the goal of achieving a 30 percent market share, a sales-to-stock ratio of 9.0, and a GMROI of $3.00, it certainly would be easy to see that this retailer should not use high prices to capture a large market share and have a high turnover rate. Rather, the retailer should probably use prices that are below those of the competition. Below-market pricing actions work best when customers are highly sensitive to price. Retailers can also use low prices to discourage competition. Compare this to the retailer that wants a highly specialized, high-fashion, prestige image and uses an above-market pricing policy. This is appropriate when the target market is insensitive to price and little or no competition is at hand. Here the retailer attracts those customers who prefer status over price.

While many examples can be cited of retailers failing to consider the importance of price in the overall strategy of the firm, one of the more interesting is the case of fair trade laws (resale price maintenance laws) which were discussed in Chapter 6. These laws were originally proposed as a means for small independent retailers to combat the pricing policies of larger chain stores. Small retailers felt secure in charging the manufacturer's suggested list price, knowing that they did not have to make price decisions and that everyone was charging the same price and thus making pricing a nondecision.

At a time when consumers were unaware of or insecure in their knowledge of pricing and quality comparisons,[1] fair trade laws allowed consumers to compare the discounters' prices with the full "fair trade" prices of the traditional retailers. What was in fact happening was that this law, which enabled some ineffective retailers to weather the economic depression of the 1930s, was giving impetus to discount stores.[2]

Recent data indicate that marketing decision makers—retailers included—still rate pricing decisions as one of their two most important functions. Yet they spend less time working with pricing decisions, and have lower levels of confidence in these decisions, than in those involving other business functions.[3]

INTERACTIVE PRICE DECISIONS

As shown previously, pricing decisions are related to other retail decisions. Specifically, the decision to price an item at a certain level should interact with the retailer's decisions on lines of merchandise carried, location, promotion, credit, customer services, the store image the retailer wishes to convey, and the legal constraints we discussed in Chapter 6.

MERCHANDISE

Retailers should not set prices without carefully analyzing the attributes of the merchandise being priced. Does the merchandise have attributes that differentiate it from similar merchandise carried by competitors? What is the value of these attributes to the consumer? Consider, for example, the menswear retailer that has purchased 100 men's suits for the fall selling season. What are the attributes of these suits (size, color, type of fabric, cut or style, brand label, quality of workmanship, quality of fabric)? How does the consumer value these attributes? Is a Hickie Freeman label more valuable than a Stanley Blacker label, a Hart-Shafner Marx label, or the retailer's private label? Is good workmanship worth more? Are better-quality fabrics worth more? The an-

ILLUSTRATION 9.1

A consumer usually places a high value on the Pendleton brand name. Thus, Pendleton merchandise can be priced higher. This is known as an interactive price decision.

swers to all these questions are not obvious; they depend on the market the retailer is targeting.

Merchandise selection presents the retailer with one other attribute to consider: the range of price points to be made available to the consumer. Remember, the retailer's controllable element of price can be either the cost of goods sold or the gross margin added to the cost. The retailer, in deciding to buy to a price point, may either purchase lower-cost merchandise and have a high gross margin, or purchase more expensive goods and reduce the gross margin to come in at the same price point. It is for this reason that retailers try to educate their customers to move up to a higher price point. This enables the retailers to maintain their gross margin percentage, buy a better grade of merchandise to be sold at a higher price, and increase both total sales and profits.

LOCATION

The location of the retail store, as pointed out in Chapter 4 and as will again be emphasized in Chapters 10 and 11, will have a significant effect on the prices that can be charged. The closer the store is to competitors with identical or similar merchandise, the less pricing flexibility it will have. The distance between the store and the customer is also important.

PROMOTION

In Chapter 14 we will illustrate how promotion can be a significant demand generator. Here we will show how pricing can generate demand. Pricing and promotion decisions are not independent.[4]

If the retailer promotes heavily and is also very price competitive, it may generate a cumulative increase in demand greater than the high promotion and lower price strategies would produce independently. Imagine, for example, the retailer establishing low prices but not promoting them in the marketplace. Or, imagine heavy promotion but no cut in prices. Obviously, each will generate demand, but the interactive and cumulative effect of both would be much greater. One exception to this general rule is the nation's number-one retailer Wal-Mart. According to Paul Higham, Wal-Mart's vice-president for marketing and sales promotion, "It's true our advertising spending is limited. Our objective is to keep advertising expenses as low as possible. The lower our expenses are, the better we serve our customers with low prices. We hope that our service level and prices are so attractive to the people who shop in our stores that they enjoy the experience and come back."[5]

CREDIT

For a given price level on merchandise, the retailer selling on credit will often be able to generate greater demand than the retailer not selling on credit. Likewise, the retailer selling merchandise on credit may be able to charge a slightly higher price than the retailer not selling on credit and still generate the same, if not a higher, demand as the noncredit retailer. Credit-granting retailers often do charge higher prices, as shown by the recent move by some retailers to offer special discounts for cash-paying customers.[6] This move is an attempt by the retailer to eliminate the 1.5 to 4.5 percent that banks charge retailers on credit card purchases and to shift the credit costs back onto the customers actually using the credit. It is not that the retailers do not want to accept credit cards; they know they increase sales. They just don't want to pay the high fees. In 1991, American Express, the king of charge cards, faced a revolt by Boston restauranteurs protesting the high fees they paid to honor AmEx cards. The restauranteurs wanted the 3.25 percent charge American Express levied on restaurants lowered to the same 2.5 percent fee that larger-volume customers were levied.[7] It took several months for AmEx and the restauranteurs to finally reach a compromise.

CUSTOMER SERVICES

Retailers that offer many customer services (product demonstrations, product use recommendations, delivery, gift wrapping, alterations, more pleasant surroundings, sales assistance) tend to have higher prices. A decision to offer many customer services will automatically increase operating expenses and thus prompt management to establish higher retail prices. However, this policy could result in higher profits. Consider the case of women's dresses. Customer service used to be common in department stores that initially marked up all incoming merchandise by 60 to 65 percent, but pricing pressure by discounters caused department stores to respond by cutting markups and service. The smaller specialty stores have picked up on this change and as a result many offer the consumer greater assistance in selecting and trying on a dress, something unheard of in most department stores. Many women are willing to pay more for this extra service. It is important to remember that customer service decisions interact significantly with pricing decisions.

STORE IMAGE

One of the most obvious cues the customer receives from a store is its prices. Prices aid the customer (either consciously or subconsciously) in developing an image of the store. If an exclusive, high-fashion women's apparel store started to discount its merchandise heavily, it simply would not be the same store in the eyes of the customers. Merchandise, store decor, and personnel may remain unchanged, but a change in pricing strategy will significantly alter the overall store image.

Consumers often choose to patronize a store based on their perceptions of the store's overall price level, that is, its position relative to the competition. A recent study by Cox and Cox[8] suggests that a retailer can do several things with pricing to shape its image or position. A store can enhance its reputation for low overall prices by using reference prices. A retailer can feature mostly name-brand items in its ads, risking the image of being high priced but enhancing its high-quality position. Finally, despite a common trend toward the use of "everyday low prices," consumers are still impressed by "specials" or reduced prices. Thus, pricing policies and strategies interact with store image policies and strategies.[9]

COMPLEMENTARY PRODUCTS

Prices charged for one product can adversely affect retailers of complementary products when there is a high cross-elasticity of demand. For example, a price war on air fares in the summer of 1992 helped two industries that rely heavily on air travelers—car-rental companies and hotels.

Car-rental companies and many resorts experienced large increases in their business due to lower air fares. For hotels the timing couldn't have been better: Many properties were just recovering from a long dry spell, caused by a huge surplus of hotel rooms. Things were even better for the car-rental industry, where seven of ten rentals are made to air travelers. During the summer of 1992, many hotel and motel chains offered rooms as low as $39 a night to customers who made advance registrations. Car-rental companies offered free mileage and special weekend rates to attract leisure customers. And many hotels and car-rental firms tried to drum up business by offering special corporate discounts. Yet until the airline price war of 1992, nothing seemed to work. However, once air travel picked up, so did the auto rental and hotel businesses.[10]

LEGAL CONSTRAINTS

Pricing decisions must only be made with an understanding of the legal environment, especially if state laws are involved and the retailer wants to operate in more than one state. As pointed out in Chapter 6, a retailer may not set a price in conjunction with a competitor, can sell below the manufacturers' suggested retail price, may offer different prices to different retail customers, may not sell below cost, and may not claim or imply in any ads that a price had been reduced unless it really has.

The other environmental factors we discussed in Part 2 (consumer behavior, competitor behavior, the socioeconomic environment, and conflict in the channel) should also be considered when the retailer is developing its overall pricing and market strategy.

DEMAND-ORIENTED PRICING

When establishing prices, retail decision makers should be demand oriented. They should conscientiously take into account customers and their wants, needs, preferences, and ability to purchase the merchandise.

A frame of reference for the demand-oriented retailer is the three-dimensional demand model in Exhibit 4.2. That model suggested that the retailer pay particular attention to population density, consumer travel costs, and the maximum demand price.

POPULATION DENSITY

Since retailers attract customers from a given geographic area, they should be concerned with the number of potential customers in that area. In high-population-density areas, the retailer will not have to draw customers from as great a distance in order to generate a given level of total revenue; thus, there will be less need to lower prices to attract customers from greater distances. Of course, a low price strategy may still be profitable.

Assume that you are a retailer operating in a city with a population density of 3,000 households per square mile, and you are currently attracting patrons within a two-mile radius of your store. The geometric area of your trade area would be equal to πr^2 (the formula for the area of a circle) or (22/7)4, which equals 12.57 square miles. Therefore, the potential number of households in your trade area is 12.57 × 3,000, or 37,710. Assume now that you could lower prices sufficiently to attract households from a 2.5-mile radius; then your trade area would be 19.64 [(22/7)6.25] square miles, and the number of potential households in the trade area would be 58,920. Notice that by increasing the radius half a mile, you increase the number of potential households in your trade area by over 50 percent.

CONSUMER TRAVEL COSTS

The three-dimensional demand model tells us that consumer travel costs are important determinants of shopping behavior at retail stores. Consumer travel costs consist of the actual dollar costs of transporting oneself to the store and back, the time involved, which is related to opportunity costs (what else could you be doing with your time, and what value do you attach to those alternative activities?), and the psychic costs of traveling to the store and back. The retailer needs to know that lower prices can offset the negative effect on quantity demanded of all three of these travel costs. For example, in the 1950s, the low prices offered by Schwegmann's Supermarkets in New Orleans in its battle against "fair trade" prices[11] led to volume declines in Mobile, 150 miles away. Today, the same thing happens when a Sam's or Price Club enters a new market.[12]

Actual Travel Costs.
Consumers demand goods that offer form, possession, and place utility. To obtain the possession utility, the customer needs to travel to the store. To obtain the place utility, the customer usually needs to transport the goods home. Assume that the customer would be willing to pay $25 for the item in order to obtain the total package of form, place, and possession utility. If the customer is 5 miles from the store (10 miles round trip) and the

cost per mile of travel is $0.20, then the actual travel cost would be $2.00. Thus, if the retailer had a price on the item above $23, in theory this consumer would not purchase the item.

Opportunity Travel Costs. Travel takes time, and time is money. As the number of two-income households increases in the United States, time will become even more scarce for many households. Consumers dislike waiting in lines to purchase merchandise and thus attach to their time an opportunity cost (loss of benefits to be gained by engaging in other activities).[13] In addition, if consumers perceive that their time is limited, they make fewer unplanned, as well as fewer planned, purchases when they do shop.[14] Consider once again the consumer who is willing to pay $25 for an item. The round-trip distance to the store is 10 miles, and it takes an hour to visit the store and purchase the item. The actual travel cost is $0.20 per mile, and let us say the opportunity cost per hour is $4.75. In this case, the highest price the customer would pay is $18.25.

Psychic Travel Costs. Traveling may also involve psychic costs or benefits. On the cost side of the equation, travel may be punishing. Consider, for example, travel to a store in a metropolitan area where the traffic arteries or public transportation is very congested and indeed at some points quite dangerous. On the other hand, the travel may represent net psychic benefits. Consider, for example, the first warm day after a dreadfully cold winter, on which the consumer decides that an afternoon drive to a regional shopping mall, on a quiet back country road, would actually be enjoyable. These psychic travel costs (or benefits) are difficult to measure, but they will influence how much the consumer is willing to pay to acquire an item.

Pricing Implications. All these components of consumer travel costs have implications for retail pricing policies. Consider the following suggestions, derived from the preceding discussion:

1. "Park and shop" or "free transit" coupons effectively lower the price to consumers and can be a strong force attracting them to the store.
2. Paying the cost of gasoline to the store and back can induce distant customers to travel to the store.
3. Special discounts for multiple-item purchases allow the customer to economize on time—already a scarce resource.
4. The store design can offer a net psychic benefit. This is the logic behind the theatrical atmosphere of some department stores, specialty shops, and large banks that in an attempt to attract large-volume customers have opened special clubs or lounges for them where they are pampered with special privileges not available to others. For example, Neiman Marcus has a gold card for customers who spend $3,000 per year. It's called the "InCircle Club" and is a sophisticated frequent-shopper program whose members receive a quarterly newsletter, travel discounts, perfume, maga-

zine subscriptions, toll-free member services, invitations to special events, and awards that have included a trip to Barcelona for the Olympics.[15]

A Note on Nonstore Retailing.[16] From the customer's perspective, one of the most significant advantages of nonstore retailing (catalogs, cable television shopping channels, direct sellers, etc.) is the absence of travel costs. Nonstore retailers should thus be able to demand a higher price for merchandise similar to that offered by traditional retailers. This assumes that, on all other dimensions, the customer would view the nonstore and traditional retailer the same way. Some consumers might want immediate possession, something not all nonstore retailers are able to provide. These consumers would incur a higher cost in using nonstore settings. Since nonstore retailers tend to have lower operating costs than traditional retailers and are not yet required to charge a sales tax to out-of-state customers (which does increase demand for their products over that of traditional local retailers),[17] and since the customer would be willing to pay at least the same as in a traditional retail store, nonstore retailers have the potential of increasing their market share during the remainder of this century. Offsetting this advantage, however, is the fact that direct sellers such as Tupperware, Avon, and Mary Kay have found that economic conditions can drastically affect the supply of part-time salespeople available. Likewise, the "party sales" concept is on the verge of change. Many consumers don't want, or have the time, to attend a party in order to make a purchase. Soon more and more of these sales will result from phone orders or orders received from parties held in offices over lunch hours.

MAXIMUM DEMAND PRICE

The **maximum demand price** is the highest price (inclusive of all transportation costs) that a consumer would be willing to pay for one unit of the product. What factors tend to make the consumer willing to pay a higher maximum demand price for an item? There are three basic determinants. The first is the utility or satisfaction the customer expects to receive from the product. This boils down to the attributes of the product and the value the consumer attaches to each attribute. The second is the consumer's income or budget. How much money does the consumer have at this time to allocate to the purchase of goods and services? The third effect upon the maximum demand quantity is the price at rival stores. Is a competitor offering the same merchandise for a lower price?

These basic determinants of maximum demand price can be influenced by three variables: environmental, household, and managerial.

Environmental Demand Variables. Demand variables beyond the control of the individual household and external to the individual retailer are called environmental. Some examples are traffic congestion, weather patterns, and population density. Environmental demand variables can have either a positive or a negative effect on demand, depending on the product type and the direction of change in the variable. Consider, for example, weather patterns and the demand for snow tires, swimsuits, overcoats, and even grocery products.[18] In fact, weather can have a major effect on the demand for almost all goods, because bad weather keeps people indoors and makes shopping trips less likely. Many retailers subscribe to weather service forecasts to help them plan for downturns or upturns in demand.

Household Demand Variables. Variables that characterize the household can affect demand. Typical household characteristics are age, income, education, and sex of the head of household. For example, two-income households have higher income levels but often have little time to make the purchase; thus they place heavy reliance on brand names. The education level of the household, while often similar to the income level, will have a significant influence on the way consumers spend their leisure time. Finally, as more and more men and women are becoming single heads of households, retailers and manufacturers alike are developing special marketing programs for them. Consider the department store that runs special cooking classes "for men only" and the home-improvement centers that run how-to classes for women. Consider what the change in demand might be for a store selling prerecorded music if more households with teenage children moved into its trade area.

Managerial Demand Variables. Any variable under the control of the retailer that can influence demand is a managerial demand variable. Some of the more common are promotion, credit, customer services, and price. By treating price as a demand determinant, we can introduce the concept of **demand elasticity of price.** This is the percentage change in quantity demanded divided by the percentage change in price. It can be formally defined as follows*:

$$E_p = -(\Delta Q/Q) / (\Delta P/P) = -(P/Q)(\Delta Q/\Delta P)$$

where: E_p = demand elasticity of price
$\Delta Q/Q$ = percentage change in quantity demanded
$\Delta P/P$ = percentage change in price

Let us develop an example of demand elasticity of price. Assume that a retailer has an item priced at $10 and sells 100 units a month; this would result in sales of $1,000 ($10 × 100). If demand elasticity of price is 1.5 and price is cut by 10 percent, what will happen to total sales? Using the preceding equation, we could derive the percentage of change in quantity demanded: 15 percent (10% × 1.5). As a result, the quantity demanded would rise from 100 to 115 as the price fell from $10 to $9. The new sales volume would be $1,035

---

*Note: Since quantity demanded and price vary inversely, a positive change in price will be accompanied by a negative change in quantity demanded. Thus, in order to make the coefficient of price elasticity positive, a "minus" sign is added to the equation.

($9 × 115), which is an increase from the previous month's sales volume of $1,000. However, just because the retailer experienced a $35 increase in sales doesn't mean that profits also increased by $35. Assume that the retailer's cost was $5 per item. In prior months this resulted in a dollar gross margin of $500 (sales minus cost or $1,000 − $500); now the retailer's dollar gross margin is only $460 ($1,035 − $575). Thus, while discussion of price elasticity is important as a tool for analyzing the relationship between sales and price changes, the retailer must not overlook the effect of a price change on gross margin either. A retailer should not become very excited about a huge increase in total sales if the new selling price is not sufficient to cover costs.

If the demand elasticity of price coefficient takes on a value less than 1.0, then demand is price inelastic. A 1 percent change in price results in a less than 1 percent change in the opposite direction for quantity demanded. Thus, if demand is price inelastic, a cut in price will yield a drop in total revenues, and a rise in price will yield an increase in total revenue. On the other hand, if the coefficient is greater than 1.0, demand is price elastic. A 1 percent change in price results in a more than proportionate change in quantity demanded. Thus, a drop in price will raise total revenues and a rise in price will lower total revenues. Notice that this is merely a review of basic microeconomic price theory.

SUPPLY-ORIENTED PRICING

Up to this point, we have considered how demand influences price. Now, let's consider the influence of supply on price.

Retail decision makers should study and analyze their supply or cost curves when establishing and changing prices. Typical cost curves for a retail store were presented in Exhibits 4.3 and 4.4; take a moment to review them. For our purposes, however, we can view costs in retailing as fixed and variable.

COST CURVES

Fixed costs are those that do not change in the short run as a result of an increase in volume. Most retailers have relatively high fixed costs, which include telephone, heating, lighting, air conditioning, insurance, taxes, rent, and wages for most types of employees. The presence of high fixed costs in retailing suggests that retailers have high break-even points. The logic of this can be made clearer if you consider that to open a store each morning one needs to have a staff or employees on hand, the lights and heating or air conditioning operating, and so on. All these costs must be incurred regardless of whether any customers enter the front door.

Variable costs are those that change with volume. The major variable cost in retailing is that of the merchandise sold. Another might be some portion of wages, since retail salesclerks are often paid on commission. Still another example could be promotional expenses.

PROFIT

In a sense, desired profit represents a cost. The profit the retailer desires can be viewed as a cost on the use of its capital and payment for taking risks. In other words, profit can be thought of as an opportunity cost. If a retailer took its capital and invested it in a relatively safe fashion (say, U.S. Treasury securities), how high a return could it obtain? Desired profit should equal this return plus a premium for taking risks.

Regardless of the specifics, the basic fact remains that the retailer cannot use its capital or that provided by stockholders or creditors without programming into its supply function a fair return on that capital. In short, profit is a necessary cost of doing business.

USING MARKUPS AND MARKDOWNS

A retail buyer, using both a demand and a supply orientation, should be able to calculate rapidly whether a proposed purchase will provide an adequate markup or gross margin to produce a profit at the level of demand faced. The markup can be expressed in dollars or as a percentage of either the selling price or the cost of the good. There are times, too, when a lack of demand forces a retail buyer to compute a markdown for the product, which is a reduction in the selling price of the goods. Markdowns are made in order to move certain merchandise.

CALCULATING MARKUP

To calculate the selling price (or retail price), the retailer should begin with the following basic markup equation:

$SP = C + M$

where: C = dollar cost of merchandise per unit
M = dollar markup per unit
SP = selling price per unit

Thus, if the retailer has a cost per unit of $16 on a calculator and a dollar markup of $14, then the selling price per unit is $30. In other words, **markup** is simply the difference between the cost of the merchandise and the selling price, which is the same as gross margin.

This markup is intended to cover all the operating expenses incurred in the sale of the product (wages, rent, utilities, promotion, credit, etc.) and still provide the retailer with a profit. Occasionally, a retailer will sell a product without a markup high enough to cover the cost of the merchandise in order to generate traffic or build sales volume. This chapter will only be concerned with using markup to produce a profit on the sale of each item.

MARKUP METHODS

Markup can be expressed as either a dollar amount or a percentage of the selling price or cost. It is most useful when expressed as a percentage of the selling price, because it can then be used in comparison with other financial data such as last year's sales results, reductions in selling price, and even the firm's competition. The equation for expressing markup as a percentage of selling price is

Percentage markup on selling price = (SP − C)/SP = M/SP

While some businesses, usually manufacturers or small retailers, express markup as a percentage of cost, this method is not widely used in retailing because most of the financial data the retailer uses are expressed as a percentage of selling price. Nevertheless, when expressing markup as a percentage of cost the equation is

Percentage markup on cost = (SP − C)/C = M/C

Several problems occur when we attempt to equate markup as a percentage of selling price with markup as a percentage of cost. Since the two methods use different bases, we really are not comparing similar data. However, there is an equation to find markup on selling price when we know markup on cost:

Percentage markup on selling price = Percentage markup on cost/(100% + Percentage markup on cost)

Likewise, when we know markup on selling price, we can easily find markup on cost:

Percentage markup on cost = Percentage markup on selling price/(100% − Percentage markup on selling price)

The preceding equations are conversions, converting percentage markup on cost to percentage markup on selling price or vice versa. Exhibit 9.1 shows a conversion table for markup on cost and markup on selling price. Let's go back to our original example of the calculator and see how easy it is to determine markup on selling price when we know the markup on cost and vice versa.

The retailer purchased the calculator for $16.00 and later sold it for $30.00. The difference between the selling price and the cost is $14.00. This $14.00 as a percentage of selling price (markup on selling price) is 46.7 percent

EXHIBIT 9.1

Markup Conversion Table

Markup Percent of Selling Price	Markup Percent of Cost	Markup Percent of Selling Price	Markup Percent of Cost	Markup Percent of Selling Price	Markup Percent of Cost
4.8	5.0	18.0	22.0	32.0	47.1
5.0	5.3	18.5	22.7	33.3	50.0
6.0	6.4	19.0	23.5	34.0	51.5
7.0	7.5	20.0	25.0	35.0	53.9
8.0	8.7	21.0	26.6	35.5	55.0
9.0	10.0	22.0	28.2	36.0	56.3
10.0	11.1	22.5	29.0	37.0	58.8
10.7	12.0	23.0	29.9	37.5	60.0
11.0	12.4	23.1	30.0	38.0	61.3
11.1	12.5	24.0	31.6	39.0	64.0
12.0	13.6	25.0	33.3	39.5	65.5
12.5	14.3	26.0	35.0	40.0	66.7
13.0	15.0	27.0	37.0	41.0	70.0
14.0	16.3	27.3	37.5	42.0	72.4
15.0	17.7	28.0	39.0	42.8	75.0
16.0	19.1	28.5	40.0	44.4	80.0
16.7	20.0	29.0	40.9	46.1	85.0
17.0	20.5	30.0	42.9	47.5	90.0
17.5	21.2	31.0	45.0	48.7	95.0
				50.0	100.0

($14/$30). This same $14.00, however, represents 87.5 percent ($14/$16) of the cost (markup). In this example, if all we knew was that the calculator had an 87.5 percent markup on cost, we could determine that this was the same as a 46.7 percent markup on selling price:

Percentage markup on selling price = Percentage markup on cost/(100% + Percentage markup on cost)
= 87.5%/(100% + 87.5%) = 46.7%

Likewise, if we knew we had a 46.7 percent markup on retail, we could easily determine markup on cost:

Percentage markup on cost = Percentage markup on selling price/(100% − Percentage markup on selling price)
= 46.7%/(100% − 46.7%) = 87.5%

In Exhibit 9.2 you can see that dollar markup does not change as the percentage changes when markup is expressed based on cost or selling price. Dollar markup is presented as a percentage of a different base—cost or selling price.

USING MARKUP FORMULAS WHEN PURCHASING MERCHANDISE

Although quite simple in concept, the basic markup formulas will enable you to determine more than the percentage of markup on a particular item. Let us work with the markup on selling price formula to illustrate how an interesting and frequent question might be answered. If you know that a particular type of item could be sold for $8 per unit and you need a 40 percent markup on selling price to meet your profit objective, how much would you be willing to pay for the item? Using our equation for markup on selling price, we have:

$$\text{Percentage markup on selling price} = (SP-C)/SP$$
$$40\% = (\$8-C)/\$8$$
$$C = \$4.80$$

Therefore, you would be willing to pay $4.80 for the item. If the item cannot be found at $4.80 or less, it is probably not worth stocking.

Likewise, if a retailer purchases an item for $12.00 and wants a 40 percent markup on selling price, how would the retailer determine the selling price?

EXHIBIT 9.2
The Relationship of Markups—Expressed on Selling Price and Cost

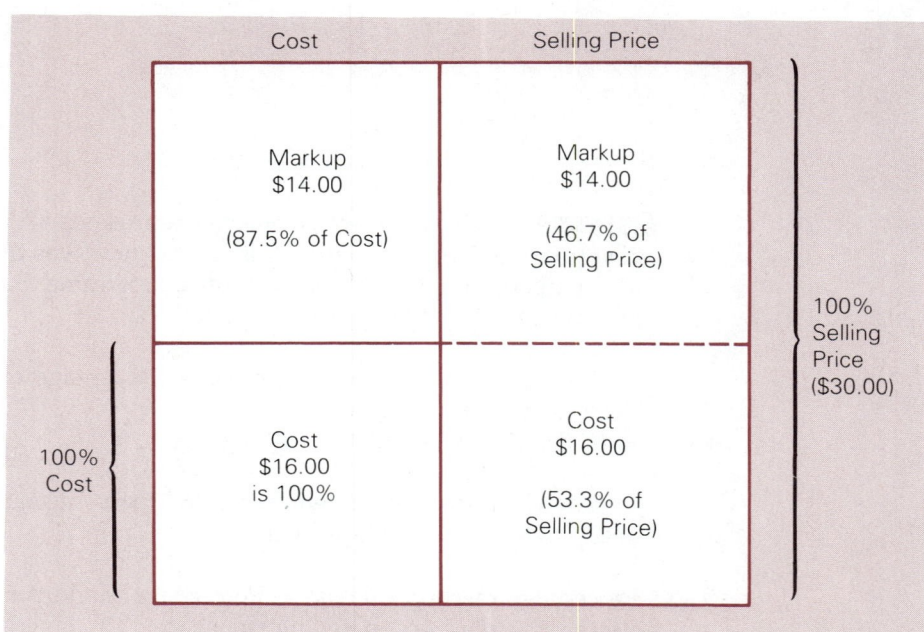

Returning to our original equation (SP = C + M), we know that SP = C + 0.40SP since markup is 40 percent of SP. If markup is 40 percent of selling price, cost must be 60 percent since cost and markup are the complements of each other and must total 100 percent. Thus, if

60% SP = $12.00

(divide both sides by 60%), then

SP = $20.00

PLANNING INITIAL MARKUPS

As the previous discussion illustrates, retailers do not casually arrive at an initial markup percentage; it must be carefully planned. Markups must be great enough to cover all the operating expenses and still provide a reasonable profit to the firm. In addition, markups must provide for markdowns, shortages, employee discounts, and alteration expenses (together referred to as total reductions), which reduce net revenue. Likewise, cash discounts taken decrease cost and must be included.

INITIAL MARKUP EQUATION

To determine the initial markup, use the following formula:

Initial markup percentage = (Operating expenses + Net profit + Markdowns + Stock shortages + Employee and customer discounts + Alteration costs − Cash discounts)/(Net sales + Markdowns + Stock shortages + Employee and customer discounts)

This equation can be simplified if we remember that markdowns, stock shortages, and employee and customer discounts are all total retail reductions from stock levels. Likewise, gross margin is the sum of operating expenses and net profit. This produces a simpler formula:

Initial markup percentage = (Gross margin + Alteration costs − Cash discounts + Reductions)/(Net sales + Reductions)

Since many retailers record cash discounts as other income and not as a cost reduction in determining initial markup, the formula can be simplified one more time:

Initial markup percentage = (Gross margin + Alteration costs + Reductions)/(Net sales + Reductions)

Regardless of which of the three formulas is used, when planning initial markup the retailer must always remember the effect of each of the following items: operating expenses, net profit, markdowns, stock shortages, employee and customer discounts, alterations costs, cash discounts taken, and net sales.

Assume a retailer plans to achieve net sales of $1 million and expects operating expenses to be $270,000. The net profit goal is $60,000. Planned reductions include $80,000 for markdowns, $20,000 for merchandise shortages, and $10,000 for employee and customer discounts. Alteration costs are expected to be $20,000, and cash discounts $10,000. What is the initial markup percentage that should be planned? What is the cost of merchandise to be sold?

The initial markup percentage can be obtained by using the original equation:

Initial markup percentage on retail = ($270,000 + $60,000 + $20,000 − $10,000 + $80,000 + $20,000 + $10,000)/($1,000,000 + $80,000 + $20,000 + $10,000) = 40.54%

The cost of merchandise sold can also be determined. We know that gross margin is operating expenses plus net profit ($330,000). This gross profit is equivalent to net sales less cost of merchandise sold; cost of merchandise sold includes alteration costs less any cash discounts. Thus, in the problem at hand, we know that $1 million less cost of merchandise sold (including alteration costs and subtracting cash discounts) is equal to $670,000. Since the alteration costs are planned at $20,000 and cash discounts at $10,000, the cost of merchandise is equal to $660,000 ($670,000 − $20,000 + $10,000).

We can verify our answer by returning to the basic initial markup formula: asking price minus cost divided by asking price. The asking price is the planned net sales of $1 million plus planned reductions of $110,000 ($80,000 for markdowns, $20,000 for shorts, and $10,000 for employee and customer discounts). The cost is the cost of merchandise before the alteration costs and prior to cash discounts, or $660,000. Using the basic initial markup formula, we obtain ($1,110,000 − $660,000)/$1,110,000, or 40.54 percent. This is the same result we achieved earlier.

The preceding computations resulted in a markup percentage on retail selling price for merchandise lines storewide. Obviously, not all lines or items within lines should be priced by mechanically applying this markup percentage. Ideally, you would like to be able to increase the demand for all your merchandise by shifting the three-dimensional demand curve we discussed in Exhibit 4.2 outward, attracting more customers from a wider area who are willing to pay more. However, this does not always happen since the actions of competitors will affect what prices you are able to charge for each merchandise line. Thus, you will want to price the mix of merchandise lines in such a fashion that a storewide markup percentage is obtained. To achieve this, some lines may be priced with considerably higher markups and others with substantially lower markups than the storewide average.

MARKUP DETERMINANTS

In planning initial markups, it is useful to know some of the general rules of markup determination. These are summarized as follows:

1. As goods are sold through more retail outlets, the markup percentage decreases. On the other hand, selling through few retail outlets means a greater markup percentage.
2. The higher the handling and storage costs of the goods, the higher the markup should be.
3. The greater the risk of a price reduction due to the seasonality of the goods, the greater the magnitude of the markup percentage early in the season.
4. The higher the demand inelasticity of price for the goods, the greater the markup percentage.

Although these rules are common to all retail lines, there are others unique to each line of trade that are only learned through experience in the respective lines, such as how much to mark up produce in a supermarket during different seasons.

MAINTAINED MARKUP PERCENTAGE

While retailers would prefer to have their **initial markup** (the markup placed on the merchandise when the store receives it) equal the **maintained markup** or **achieved markup** (the actual selling price less the cost), this seldom occurs. Usually, the actual selling price for some of the firm's merchandise is lower than the original retail price, making the firm's maintained markup lower than the initial markup. Maintained markup, thus, differs from initial markup by the amount of reductions:

Initial markup = (Original retail price − Cost)/Original retail price
Maintained markup = (Actual retail price − Cost)/Actual retail price

Five reasons can account for the difference between initial and maintained markups. First is the need to balance demand with supply. Since most markup formulas are cost oriented rather than demand oriented, adjustments in selling prices will occur. This is especially true when consumer demand changes and the only way for retailers to reduce their inventory and make their merchandise saleable is by taking a markdown or reduction in selling price. A second reason is stock shortages. Shortages can occur from theft by employees or customers, or by mismarking the price when merchandise is received or sold. In either case, the selling price received for the goods will be less than the price carried in the inventory records. In fact, clerical error probably accounts for more stock shortages than theft. Third, there are employee and customer discounts. Employees are usually given some discount privileges after they have worked for the firm for a specified period of time. Also, certain customer groups (i.e., religious and senior citizen groups) may be given special discount privileges.

Fourth is the cost of alterations. Some fashion apparel items require alterations before the product is acceptable to the customer. While men's clothing is often altered free of charge, there is usually a small charge for altering women's wear. Nevertheless, this charge usually doesn't cover all alteration costs, and therefore alterations are actually a part of the cost of the merchandise.

A fifth and final reason that initial markup may be different from maintained markup is cash discounts. Cash discounts are offered to retailers by manufacturers or suppliers to encourage prompt payment of bills. Cash discounts reduce the cost of merchandise and therefore make the maintained markup higher than the initial markup, just the opposite result of the first four factors.

Some large retailers ignore cash discounts in calculating initial markup, because the buyer may have little control over whether or not the discount is taken. Achieving discounts through prompt payment is the result of financial operations and not merchandising decisions, and therefore the buyer should not be penalized if the discounts are not taken or rewarded if they are.

Next, let's look at how the maintained markup percentage is determined. A discounter purchases the calculator used in an earlier example for $16 with the intent of selling it for $25 (an initial markup of 36%). However, the calculator did not sell at that price and the retailer reduced it to $20 in order to sell it. This would result in a maintained markup of 20 percent:

Maintained markup = (Actual selling price − Cost)/(Actual selling price)
= $4/$20 = 20%

The following formula can also be used to determine maintained markup percentage:

Maintained markup percentage = Initial markup percentage
− [(Reduction percentage) (100% − Initial markup percentage)]

where:
Reduction percentage = Amount of reductions/Net sales

In the above example
Maintained markup percentage = 36% − [($5/$20) × (100% − 36%)] = 36% − 16% = 20%

MARKDOWN MANAGEMENT

Thus, maintained markup (sometimes referred to as gross margin or just plain gross) is the real key to profitability because it is the difference between the actual selling price and the total cost of that merchandise. This means that for effective retail price management, markdowns should be planned. Pricing is not a science with high degrees of precision but an art form with considerable room for error. If retailers knew everything they needed to know about demand and supply factors, they could use the science of economics to establish a price that would maximize profits and ensure the sale of all the merchandise. Unfortunately, retailers do not possess perfect information about supply and demand factors. As a result, the entire merchandising process is subject to error which then makes pricing difficult. Four basic errors can occur: (1) buying errors, (2) pricing errors, (3) merchandising errors, and (4) promotion errors.

BUYING ERRORS

Errors in buying occur on the supply side of the pricing question. They result when the retailer buys the wrong merchandise (wrong styles, sizes, colors, patterns, or price range) or buys the right merchandise in too large a quantity (demand was overestimated or an economic slowdown was not foreseen). Whatever the cause of the buying error, the net result is a need to cut the price to move the merchandise. Sometimes the resulting prices are below the actual cost of the merchandise to the retailer. Thus, buying errors can be quite costly. As a consequence, you might expect that the retail manager would wish to eliminate buying errors. However, this is not strictly the case. The retailer could eliminate errors only by being extremely conservative, buying just what it knew the customer wanted and what it could be certain of selling, but at the expense of lost profit opportunities on some riskier types of purchase decisions. Recall that when we reviewed the determinants of markups, we mentioned that the greater the risk of potential price reductions, the higher the markup percentage. This is simply another way of recognizing that taking a gamble on some purchases that represent buying errors can be profitable if initial markups are appropriately high.

PRICING ERRORS

Errors in pricing merchandise can be another cause of markdowns. Pricing errors occur when the initial price of the item is too high to move the product at the speed and in the quantity desired, creating purchase resistance on the part of the typical customer. An overly high price is often relative to the pricing behavior of competitors. Perhaps in principle the price would have been acceptable, but if competitors price the same item substantially lower, then the original retailer's price becomes too high.

MERCHANDISING ERRORS

While many new retailers believe that carrying over seasonal or fashion merchandise into the next merchandising season is the most common merchandise error, it really isn't. Failure by the buyer to inform the sales staff about how the new merchandise relates to the current stock, ties in with the store's image, and satisfies the needs of the store's target market is the most common merchandising error. A key point in this error category is failure to keep the department manager and sales force informed about the new merchandise lines, so that these goods will be available to the customer. Too many times the new merchandise is left in the storeroom, or the salespeople are not informed about the key features of the new item, and thus the customer never becomes excited about it.

Another merchandising error is improper handling or ineffective visual presentation of the merchandise by the sales staff, such as failure to stock the new merchandise behind old merchandise whenever possible. Simply misplacing the merchandise all too often creates an unintended slow seller.

PROMOTION ERRORS

Finally, it is often the case that even when the right goods were purchased in the right quantities and were priced correctly, the merchandise fails to move as planned. In this situation, there is most often a promotion error and the consumer has not been properly informed about or prompted to purchase the merchandise. The advertising, personal selling, sales promotion activities, or in-store displays were too weak or sporadic to elicit a strong response from potential customers.

ILLUSTRATION 9.2

When merchandise is not moving as planned, it is important to mark the price down and move it out quickly. Sales are often held to move odds and ends and slow-moving merchandise quickly.

MARKDOWN POLICY

Retailers will find it advantageous to develop a markdown timing policy to guide the two crucial decisions: when and how much of a markdown to take.[19] In principle, there are two extremes to a markdown timing policy: early and late.

EARLY MARKDOWN POLICY

Most retailers that concentrate on high inventory turnover pursue an early markdown policy to speed the movement of merchandise and enable the retailer to take less of a markdown per unit to dispose of the goods. The dollars obtained from selling the merchandise can then be used to help finance more saleable goods. At the same time, the customer seems to benefit, since markdowns are offered quickly on goods that some consumers still think of as fashionable. Another advantage of the early markdown policy is that it allows the retailer to replenish the stock of lower-priced lines from the higher ones that have been marked down. For instance, many women's wear retailers will regularly take slow-moving dresses from higher-priced lines and move them down to the moderate- or lower-priced lines. Other retailers mark goods down at regular intervals until the merchandise is sold.

LATE MARKDOWN POLICY

Allowing goods to have a long trial period before a markdown is taken is called a late markdown policy. This policy avoids disrupting the sale of regular merchandise by too frequently marking goods down. As a consequence, customers will learn to look forward to a semiannual or annual clearance, in which all or most merchandise is marked down. Thus, the bargain hunters or low-end customers will be attracted only at infrequent intervals. As we pointed out in Chapter 2, regardless of which timing policy is followed, the retailer must plan for these reductions.

MARKDOWN AND GMROI

The profit effect of varying markdown policies on merchandise can be analyzed in relation to the gross margin return on inventory (GMROI), which was introduced in the previous chapter. GMROI suggests that inventory investments be gauged in terms of the multiplicative effect of gross margin percentage and the turnover rate. The important thing to recognize is that the more quickly merchandise is marked down, the more rapidly inventory will sell, but at the expense of gross margin. On the other hand, if markdowns are postponed, gross margins will remain high but inventory will sell slowly.

Let us assume that the retailer purchases $40,000 in merchandise and expects to be able to sell the merchandise in 12 weeks without using any markdowns, at a retail value of $50,000. The average investment in inventory annually is

Average inventory investment = [(Beginning inventory + Ending inventory)/2](Inventory turnover in weeks/52 weeks)
= [($40,000 + 0)/2] (12/52) = $4,615

The annual sales-to-stock ratio would be sales divided by average inventory investment ($50,000/$4,615), or 10.83 times. Since the gross margin is 20 percent ($10,000/$50,000), one would obtain a GMROI of $2.17, or (20% × 10.83).

Now let us assume that the merchandise is marked down by $3,000 after three weeks and liquidated in another three weeks. Consequently, average inventory investment annually would be

[($40,000 + 0)/2] (6/52) = $2,308

The sales-to-stock ratio would be ($47,000/$2,308), or 20.36 times, the gross margin would be ($7,000/$47,000), or 14.89 percent, and GMROI would be (14.89% × 20.36), or $3.03. Thus, the markdown of $3,000 was profitable, since it bolstered GMROI from $2.17 to $3.03.

AMOUNT OF MARKDOWN

An issue related to the timing of markdowns is their magnitude. If the retailer waits to use a markdown at the last moment, then the markdown should probably be large enough to move the remaining merchandise. With an early markdown, however, the reduction only needs to be large enough to give sales a stimulant. Once sales have been stimulated, the retailer can watch merchandise movement; when it slows, the retailer can give the merchandise another stimulant by again marking it down. Which is the more profitable strategy depends on the GMROI effect. One rule of thumb for markdowns is that "prices should be marked down at least 20% in order for the consumer to notice."[20] However, the markdown percentage should vary with the type of good, time of season, and competition.

Many times retailers are able to have their suppliers supplement their markdown losses with "markdown money," or some other type of price reductions. Here's how it works: Let's say Acme Clothing Company delivers 100 sweaters to Judy's Dress Shop at the wholesale price of $40 each. Judy in turn plans to take her customary markup of 50 percent on selling price in order to sell each sweater for $80, thus producing a gross margin of $4,000.

However, after three months Judy still has 50 sweaters in stock, which she puts on sale for $50 each in order to move the merchandise. After selling the remaining sweaters, Judy's gross margin is only $2,500 [(50 × $80) + (50 × $50) − (100 × $40)].

The following month Judy goes to market and visits the Acme showroom. Judy wants Acme to pay her the $1,500 she lost in taking the markdowns on its sweaters. She threatens Acme with a loss of future orders if they don't cover her losses. Does this sound fair to you?

Actually, this scenario happens quite frequently when buyers go to market. The buyers maintain that manufacturers should share in the responsibility when the merchandise doesn't sell as promised. They claim that if the supplier cannot deliver the gross margin they want, there is no reason to reorder from them. From the retailers' standpoint, when the manufacturer contributes markdown money, the manufacturers are really asking for a second chance to prove the saleability of their lines.

Markdown money can be of a cash payment or a discount on future purchases.

PRICING OBJECTIVES

The pricing objectives of retailers should be in agreement with their mission statement and other merchandising policies. Some objectives may be profit oriented, some may be sales oriented, and some may be to leave things just the way they are. However, by beginning with the proper pricing objectives, the retail manager can establish pricing policies that will complement the store's image and assist in attracting the desired target customers.

PROFIT-ORIENTED OBJECTIVES

Many retailers establish the objective of either achieving a certain rate of return or maximizing profits.

Target Return. A **target return objective** sets a specific level of profit as an objective. This amount is often stated as a percentage of sales or a percentage of the retailer's capital investment. A target return for a supermarket might be 2 percent of sales. In 1990, Wal-Mart decided against further expansion in the hypermarket field when its returns on its current hypermarkets failed to meet its objectives.[21]

Profit Maximization. A **profit maximization objective** seeks to obtain as much profit as possible. Some people claim that this pricing policy "charges all the traffic will bear." This objective doesn't always lead to the retailer's charging high prices; a retailer might find that its profit maximization price is low because of the high volume that such a price generates.

Retailers know that if they follow a high price policy, they are inviting competitors to enter the market. However, in some cases, a retailer may have a temporary monopoly and want to take advantage of it. The first video-rental stores, knowing that others would follow shortly, often charged high rental fees, only to lower them when competition did enter the market. This is **skimming,** or trying to sell at the highest price possible and recovering your investment faster before settling on a more competitive level. Other retailers may take the opposite approach and use a **penetration price,** which seeks to establish a loyal customer base by entering the market with a low price.

SALES-ORIENTED OBJECTIVES

Sales-oriented objectives seek some level of unit sales, dollar sales, or market share but do not mention profit. Two of the types most commonly used in retailing are growth in market share and growth in dollar sales.

While both these objectives are common with retailers today, especially smaller ones, the achievement of either doesn't necessarily mean that profits will also increase. After all, if a retailer lowers prices, gross margin will go down, sales may improve, but the retailer may not make more money. Many retailers that used junk bonds to finance their buyouts, such as Macy's, Federated, and Allied Stores, adopted sales-oriented policies in the early 1990s in an effort to increase cash flow so they could make interest payments. They were more worried about getting the sales to finance cash flow than about profit.

STATUS QUO OBJECTIVES

Retailers that are happy with their market share and level of profits sometimes adopt **status quo objectives,** or "don't rock the boat" pricing policies. Many supermarkets gave up on the extra profits and increases in market share that "double coupons" might have brought because they were afraid of what competitive actions would have resulted.

Also, some retailers prefer to compete on grounds other than price. Fast-food chains, like McDonald's and Burger King, want the consumer to focus on nonprice issues such as quality of food, service, and convenient locations.[22]

PRICING POLICIES AND STRATEGIES

Pricing policies are rules of action, or guidelines, that ensure uniformity of pricing decisions within a retail operation. A large retailer has many buyers who are involved in pricing decisions. By establishing the store's overall pricing policies, the top merchandising executives provide these buyers with a framework for adopting specific pricing strategies for the entire organization.

A retail store's pricing policies should reflect the expectations of its target market. Very few retailers can appeal to all segments of the market. Low-income consumers are usually attracted to low-priced discount stores. The middle-class market often shops at moderate-priced general-merchandise chains. Affluent consumers are frequently drawn to high-priced specialty stores that provide extra services. Only supermarkets are able to cross the various income lines, and even then there is some basis for segmentation. Successful retailers carefully position themselves in a market and then direct their specific pricing strategies toward satisfying the needs and wants of their target markets. Many times the proper pricing policies influence consumers to patronize one store over another.

In establishing a pricing policy, retailers must decide whether they should price at market levels, above market levels, or below market levels.

PRICING AT MARKET LEVELS

Most merchants want to be competitive with one another. The use of comparison shoppers—that is, employees who visit competitive retail outlets in order to compare prices—stems from this basic premise. Competitive pricing involves a **price zone,** a range of price points for a particular merchandise line that appeals to customers in a certain demographic group, such as Kmart selling women's tops for $9.99 to $19.99. Marshall Fields does not need to match the prices of Kmart but should establish prices on a level with its competitor, Saks Fifth Avenue. And Kmart should be competitively priced with Wal-Mart and Target.

The size of a retail store affects its ability to compete on a price basis. Small retailers usually pay more for their merchandise and have higher expenses as a proportion of sales than larger retailers. Although some small retailers have joined voluntary cooperative chains to reduce their expenses through quantity discounts, they continue to experience a cost disadvantage. For these reasons small retailers, such as mom-and-pop grocery stores and convenience stores, often stress convenience and service strategies rather than price in their retailing mix. Even in this case, the price cannot be too far out of line.[23]

PRICING ABOVE THE MARKET

Some retailers, either by design or by circumstance, follow a policy of pricing above the market. Retailers that charge higher prices benefit from maintaining stable prices over time because consumers tend to be less price sensitive when prices are less variable.[24] Certain market sectors are receptive to this policy because nonprice factors are more important to customers than price. For example, Nordstrom offers such outstanding service that it has minimal price competition. Other retailers, such as small neighborhood drug and hardware stores, are forced to price above the market because of their high cost structure. Some conditions that permit retailers to price above market levels are services provided, merchandise offerings, convenient locations, and extended hours of operation.

Services Provided. In many communities there are service-oriented merchants with a loyal group of customers willing to pay higher prices for an array of services ranging from wardrobe counseling to delivery. Nordstrom's clerks have a habit of doing special things like dropping off purchases at a customer's home, sending "thank you" notes to loyal customers, or even ironing a newly purchased shirt so the customer can wear it that day. These services put Nordstrom in a nonprice competitive sector of retailing. Even when the firm's employees complained that they were forced to be so "overtly nice," it only reemphasized the company's distinctive service image.[25]

Merchandise Offerings. Some consumers will pay higher-than-average prices for specialty items, for an exclusive line, or for unusual merchandise. Prestige retailers such as Gucci or Neiman Marcus carry high-priced specialty items. An exclusive line, such as Christian Dior, permits higher-than-average prices. Unusual merchandise, such as in Neiman Marcus' annual Christmas catalog of one-of-a-kind gifts, is normally not price compared.

Convenient Locations. The convenient location of gift shops in hotels and airline terminals allows them to charge high prices. Knowing that consumers value time, fast-food retailers select sites adjacent to residential areas. Retailers in metropolitan office buildings often charge premium prices because of their accessible locations. In addition, consumers may have no other place to shop. For example, a consumer at Chicago's O'Hare Airport has to eat lunch there or not eat. There are no alternatives.

Extended Hours of Operation. By remaining open while other stores are closed, some merchants are able to charge higher-than-average prices. All-night pharmacies justify their higher prices by never closing.

PRICING BELOW THE MARKET

Because a large market sector buys mainly on a price basis, a below-market pricing policy is attractive to many retailers such as TJX, which is discussed in Retailing in Action 9.1, Wal-Mart, Dollar General, and many of the warehouse clubs. When retailers consistently price below the market, they must rely on the high volume generated by low prices to produce satisfactory profits. However, as academic research studies[26] and Sears, Roebuck's lack of success with just "everyday low prices"[27] have shown, retailers must support this policy with sales and reference points.

In order to offer low prices, these retailers are compelled to reduce their markups and to buy wisely, which may include closeouts and seconds. In addition, these stores stock fast-selling merchandise, curtail customer services, and operate from modest facilities. Also, some of them stock private brands extensively and enhance their low-price image by promoting the price differences between their private brands and similar national brands.

RETAILING IN ACTION

9.1 Off-Price Retailers: Are Their Days Numbered?

Off-price retailers, an innovation of the 1970s, are value-oriented merchants relying on rapid inventory turnover and using a sophisticated distribution network, selling quality brand merchandise at least 25 percent off retail, and able to entice customers to become everyday shoppers. While some experts believe that the off-price retailer's days are numbered as traditional retailers become more competitive, the management at TJX Companies, Inc. believes just the opposite.

TJX operates four distinct off-price retail divisions: T.J. Maxx, which features excellent values in family apparel, domestics, gifts, women's shoes, and fine jewelry; Hit or Miss, which caters to the working woman's needs for career and weekend fashions at affordable prices; Chadwick's of Boston, aimed at working women with the convenience of catalog shopping and off-price values; and Winners Apparel Ltd., a Toronto-based operation offering off-price apparel for the entire family. Each division has its own unique statement of mission, management, target market, operations, distribution network, and merchandising program.

How has TJX kept pace with the competition? Let's consider what the firm's divisions did in fiscal year 1991. T.J. Maxx, with 393 units operating mostly in western states, developed a coordinated sportswear area in its stores to reaffirm it as a place to find great values, not only for the home, but for the shopper. In addition, the division tested an expanded giftware/houseware department called "Home Collections." The chain undertook an extensive marketing research program to reposition its Hit or Miss division. TJX also sought to improve the execution of Hit or Miss's merchandising, marketing, and operational efforts. Chadwick's increased the productivity of its catalogs with focus books such as "Career Advantages." Finally, the chain acquired Winners in mid-year as a means to tap the Canadian market.

Source: Based on information contained in TJX's annual reports.

SPECIFIC PRICING STRATEGIES

Various pricing strategies are adopted by retailers in their effort to achieve certain pricing objectives. The pricing strategies should be in accord with the other components of the store's retail mix: location, promotion, display, service level, and merchandise assortment.

CUSTOMARY PRICING

Customary pricing occurs when a retailer sets prices for goods and services and seeks to maintain those prices over an extended period of time. Candy bars, newspapers, movies, and vending machine products are all items that use customary pricing. For such products, the retailer seeks to establish prices that customers can take for granted for long periods of time.

VARIABLE PRICING

Variable pricing is used when differences in demand and cost force the retailer to change prices in a fairly predictable manner. Flowers tend to be higher priced when demand is greater around Mother's Day and Valentine's Day. Tuesday and Wednesday nights tend to have lower demand for movies, so many theaters offer $2 specials on those nights. Fresh fruits tend to sell for less during their growing seasons when the retailer's costs are down.

Some retailers vary their prices by giving discounts to special consumer groups such as senior citizens, students, and the clergy. Even some employee groups—for example, credit unions—have negotiated price discounts with selected retailers.

FLEXIBLE PRICING

Flexible pricing means offering the same products and quantities to different customers at different prices. Retailers generally use flexible pricing in situations calling for personal selling. The advantage of using flexible pricing is that the salesperson can make price adjustments based on the customer's interest, a competitor's price, a past relationship with the customer, or the customer's bargaining ability. Most jewelry stores and automobile dealerships use this pricing policy, although not all customers like it. This policy can increase costs as customers begin to bargain for everything, or find that they paid more than a friend did for the same product.

ONE-PRICE POLICY

Under the **one-price policy** a retailer charges the same price for an item to all customers. A one-price policy may be used in conjunction with customary or variable pricing. All people buying a dozen roses on Valentine's Day will pay the same price. John Wanamaker, founder of Wanamaker's Department Store in Philadelphia, allegedly adopted the one-price policy because it meant efficiency and fairness in handling customer transactions in a large store. In a large organization, the selling activity is delegated to salespersons who have varying degrees of loyalty to the retailer. If salespersons were permitted to bargain over price, customers who were shrewd and assertive could conceivably negotiate terms that are unprofitable to the retailer.

A one-price policy does speed up transactions and reduce the need for highly skilled salespeople. Most catalog operators adopt a one-price policy, since they are forced to retain their prices until the expiration date of the catalog, which can be six months from its issuance.

PRICE LINING

To simplify their pricing procedures and to aid consumers in making merchandise comparisons, some retailers establish a specified number of price lines or price points for each merchandise classification. Once the price lines have been determined, these retailers purchase goods that fit into each line. This is called **price lining.** For example, in men's slacks the price lines could be limited to $29.95, $39.95, and $49.95. The monetary difference between the price lines should be large enough to reflect a value difference to consumers. This makes it easier for a salesperson to either trade up or trade down a customer. (Trading up occurs when a salesperson moves a customer from a lower-priced line to a higher one. Trading down occurs when a customer is initially exposed to higher-priced lines but expresses the desire to purchase a lower-priced line.)

Retailers select price lines that have the strongest consumer demand. By limiting the number of price lines, a retailer achieves broader assortments, which leads to increased sales and fewer markdowns. For example, a retailer that stocks 150 units of an item and has 6 price lines would have an assortment of only 25 units in each line. On the other hand, if the 150 units were divided among only 3 price lines, there would be 50 units in each line.

When retailers are limited to certain price lines, they become specialists in those lines. This permits them to concentrate all their merchandising and promotional efforts on those lines, thus defining their store image more clearly. In addition, they direct their purchases to vendors who handle those lines. The vendors in turn provide favored treatment to their large-volume retailing customers. Other advantages of price lining include the ability to buy more efficiently, simplify inventory control, and accelerate inventory turnover. From the shopper's perspective, it is easy to shop when price lining is used, because differences are perceived among the various price points.

An analysis of a store's best-selling price lines is essential before any decision is made to alter them. Generally the middle-priced lines should account for the majority of sales. When the bulk of sales occurs at the extremes of the price lines, the retailer should take certain corrective actions. These include altering the assortments in the present price lines, changing the price lines, redirecting the salespersons' efforts, developing more effective promotions, and adjusting the total marketing mix to a new target market.

ODD PRICING

It has been suggested that the rightmost, or ending, digits of a price can carry connotations about various attributes of a product or a retailer. For example, the ending 00 may connote high quality, 63 may mean a carefully determined price, and 99 a discount or special value.[28] The practice of setting retail prices that end in the digits 5, 7, and 9, such as $29.95, $49.97, or $9.99, is called **odd pricing.**

A quick look at retail advertisements in newspapers will reveal that many retailers use an odd pricing policy. Retailers feel that odd prices produce significantly higher sales because the consumer supposedly perceives these

ILLUSTRATION 9.3

While it is controversial, many retailers believe that odd pricing, which ends in digits 5, 7, and 9, makes customers believe the merchandise offers a better value.

odd prices as substantially lower. That is, $489 seems more like $400 than like $500, and $4.99 seems more like $4.00 than $5.00. Whether this is indeed true is debatable. In fact, the empirical research is inconclusive.[29] However, if the consumer perceives that 79 cents is a better price than 78 cents, the retailer should never forego the penny by pricing at 78 cents. Retailing in Action 9.2 reviews the historical reasons for the development of odd pricing.

Because odd prices are associated with low prices, they are typically used by retailers that sell either at prices below the market or at the market. Retailers selling above the market, such as Neiman Marcus and Nordstrom, usually end their prices with even numbers that have come to denote quality. These retailers would likely sell an item for $90.00 rather than $89.99. Prestige-conscious retailers are not seeking bargain hunters as customers.

MULTIPLE-UNIT PRICING

In **multiple-unit pricing**, the price of each unit in a multiple-unit package is less than the price it would carry if it were sold singly. Grocery retailers use multiple-unit pricing extensively in their sales of cigarettes, light bulbs, candy bars, and beverages. Apparel retailers often sell multiple units of underwear, hosiery, and shirts.

Retailers use multiple-unit pricing to encourage additional sales, because consumers will buy the quantity suggested by the multiple-unit pricing,[30] and to increase profits. The gross margin that is sacrificed in a multiple-unit sale is more than offset by the savings that occur from reduced selling and handling

> **RETAILING IN ACTION**
>
> ### 9.2 The Origin of Odd Pricing
>
> The predisposition to favor the use of certain "odd prices," based on the belief that $9.99 sounds much less formidable to the customer than $10 and 49 cents sounds better than 52 cents, has never been proven with any conclusive research. Another theory suggests that the use of an odd price means the price is at the lowest level possible, thus encouraging the customer to purchase more units. Still a more plausible explanation for the adoption of odd pricing goes back to the early part of this century before there was a sales tax. In those days, when merchandise was priced at even dollars, it was very easy for salesclerks to pocket an occasional one-, five- or ten-dollar bill or gold piece since they didn't have to make change for the customer.
>
> When Marshall Field caught on to this, he devised the first odd pricing system to stop the practice. Field ruled, "We'll charge 99 cents instead of even dollars. This will force the clerks to ring up the sales, open the cash register, put the money in and give the customer a receipt and change."
>
> Perhaps, this explains why, despite the lack of supportive research, odd pricing is such a standard in retailing today.

expenses. Generally, multiple-unit pricing can be effectively employed for items that are either consumed rapidly or used together.

LEADER PRICING

In **leader pricing** a high-demand item is priced low and advertised heavily in an effort to attract consumers into a store. The items selected for leader pricing should be widely known and bought frequently. In addition, information should be available that will permit consumers to make price comparisons. National brands of convenience goods, such as Crest toothpaste, Mitchum antiperspirant, Maxwell House coffee, and Coca-Cola, are often designated as leader items.

Leader pricing is usually part of a promotional program intended to increase store traffic. A successful program will produce additional sales for all areas of a store. In many instances the price of the leader item is reduced only for a special promotion. However, there are retailers such as supermarkets that regularly feature leader items.

A retailer using leader pricing should carefully evaluate its usefulness. If consumers are limiting their purchases to only the leader items, then the policy is ineffective. Because the leader items may be sold at or near a retailer's cost, higher-markup items must also be sold to generate a profit for the retailer. An item that is sold below a retailer's cost is known as a **loss leader.** For example, every Thanksgiving many supermarkets sell turkeys at a loss in hopes of attracting consumers to their stores and making a profit on the rest of their purchases.

BAIT PRICING

The practice of advertising a low-priced model of a shopping good, such as a washing machine or a refrigerator, to lure shoppers into a store is called **bait pricing.** Once the shoppers are in the store, a salesperson tries to persuade them to purchase a higher-priced model.

Bait pricing is considered by the Federal Trade Commission to be an illegal practice when the low-priced model used as bait is unavailable to shoppers. In one ruling, which was discussed in Chapter 6, the courts found a retailer guilty of bait pricing when these facts were considered as a whole: The retailer ordered only 20 of the low-priced products and 133 of the higher-priced ones; the retailer lost money on each low-priced unit sold; the retailer did not pay a commission on the low-priced units; and the retailer did not accept credit cards on the lower-priced units but did accept them on the higher-priced units.[31]

PRIVATE-BRAND PRICING

A private-brand item often can be purchased at a cheaper price, be marked up higher, and still be priced lower than a comparable national brand—a practice known as **private-brand pricing.** Private brands permit the retailer a large degree of pricing freedom because consumers find it difficult to make exact comparisons between private brands and national brands of similar goods. In the early 1990s, supermarkets experienced their greatest growth in several categories with private labels.[32] Mervyn's and Kmart price their private brands below the market, while Saks Fifth Avenue and Marshall Field price theirs above the market. Sometimes having too many private labels only confuses the customer. In 1991, Limited stores dropped three in-house brands in favor of a new "Limited" label.[33]

SUMMARY

Pricing decisions are among the most frequent a retailer must make. It is therefore prudent to understand pricing concepts and techniques. Price decisions cannot be made independently; they interact with the merchandise, location, promotion, credit, customer service, and store image decisions.

Retail decision makers should be demand oriented when establishing prices. A useful frame of reference is the three-dimensional demand model introduced in Chapter 4. This model suggests that the retailer pay particular attention to several important demand variables: population density, consumer travel costs, and the maximum demand price. Demand elasticity is product specific and refers to the change in quantity demanded that is due to a change in a demand determinant. Demand variables may be environmental, household, or managerial.

Retailers should also be supply oriented when setting prices. They should know both their fixed and variable cost curves and recognize their need for profit. The profit needed can be viewed as a cost of the use of the retailer's capital and payment for taking risks.

A useful frame of reference for supply-oriented pricing is the markup equation, which simply states that, per unit, the retail selling price is equal to the dollar cost plus the dollar markup. Since the initial price may not be attractive enough to sell all of the merchandise, the initial markup may need to be reduced. When we talk of actual selling prices versus initial prices, we are discussing the difference between an initial and a maintained markup.

Markups should be planned. The initial markup percentage can be determined by using operating expenses, net profit, alteration costs, cash discounts, markdowns, stock shortages, employee and customer discounts, and sales. The retailer must recognize that not all items can be priced by mechanically applying this markup percentage. Some items will need to be priced to yield a considerably higher markup, and others a substantially lower markup depending on the retailer's objectives. The initial markup is seldom equal to the maintained markup because of three kinds of reductions: markdowns, shortages, and employee and customer discounts.

Because the retailer does not possess perfect information about supply and demand, markdowns are inevitable. They are usually due to errors in buying, pricing, merchandising, or promotion. The retailer needs to establish a markdown policy. Early markdown speeds the movement of merchandise and also allows the retailer to take less of a markdown per unit to dispose of merchandise. Late markdown avoids disrupting the sale of regular merchandise by too frequent markdowns. The best policy from a profit perspective depends on how the markdown influences GMROI.

Retailers' pricing objectives should be in agreement with their mission statements and other merchandising policies. There are broad categories of objectives: profit oriented, including target return and profit maximization; sales oriented; and status quo objectives.

We concluded the chapter with a discussion of the various pricing policies (pricing at, below, or above the market) and strategies retailers can use to achieve their objectives. These strategies include customary pricing, variable pricing, flexible pricing, one-price pricing, price lining, odd pricing, multiple-unit pricing, leader pricing, bait pricing (which may be illegal in some circumstances), and private-brand pricing.

QUESTIONS FOR DISCUSSION

1. What is the relationship between a household's travel cost and a retailer's pricing decisions?
2. Explain how markdowns can be profitable.
3. What effect should fixed costs have on retail price decisions?
4. A buyer buys 228 raincoats at $442/dozen. If the department markup on selling price is 54 percent, what should be each raincoat's retail price?
5. When may an initial markup be equal to the maintained markup?
6. Would it be easier for a mail-order retailer or a department store retailer to conduct a price experiment? Explain by developing an example.
7. In a practical sense, how should retailers establish price levels?
8. Compute the markup on selling price for an item that retails for $29.95 and costs $15.20.
9. An item has a markup on cost of 83 percent; what is its markup on retail?
10. Assume that a retailer plans to achieve a net sales of $1.5 million and expects operating expenses to be $375,000. The net profit goal is $100,000. Planned reduc-

tions include $88,000 for markdowns, $38,000 for merchandise shortages, and $14,000 for employee and customer discounts. Cash discounts from suppliers are expected to be $30,000. At what percentage should initial markups be planned?

11. A buyer plans to achieve net sales of $500,000 with operating expenses of $95,000, total retail sales reductions of $40,000, and a profit goal of $55,000. What should the average initial markup be?
12. How can location and promotion decisions influence the demand for a retailer's product line?
13. A retailer hopes to make $50,000 on sales of $600,000 next year. If operating expenses are estimated to be $115,000 and planned total retail sales reductions are $25,000, what should the average initial markup be?
14. Why should a retailer plan on taking markdown during a merchandising season?
15. Complete the following:

	Dress Shirt	Sport Shirt	Belt
Selling price	$60.00	$29.95	$22.50
Cost	$36.00	$14.35	$10.50
Markup in dollars	_____	_____	_____
Markup percentage on cost	_____	_____	_____
Markup percentage on selling price	_____	_____	_____

16. You have just purchased some blouses for $23.44 each and you want to sell them at a 56 percent markup on selling price. What should your selling price be?
17. Your selling price is $14.95 and your markup is 40 percent on selling price. What is your cost and markup in dollars?
18. Your markup is 45 percent on selling price and your cost is $437.50. What is your selling price?
19. Complete the following:

Selling price	_____	_____	$75.00	$80.00	$44.00
Cost	$15.00	$25.00	_____	_____	$33.00
Markup in dollars	$10.00	_____	_____	$20.00	_____
Markup on selling Price percentage	_____	40%	50%	33⅓%	_____	_____

20. Intimate Apparel wants to produce a 12 percent operating profit this year on sales of $460,000. Based on past experience, the owner made the following estimates:

Net alteration expenses	$ 800	Employee discount	$ 3,400
Markdowns	27,000	Operating expense	215,000
Stock shortages	4,200	Cash discounts earned	2,100

Given these estimates, what average initial markup should be asked for the upcoming year?

21. A retailer wants to produce a 10 percent operating profit on sales of $380,000. Based on past experience, the owner made the following estimates:

Alteration revenues	$ 325	Customer discounts	$ 450
Alteration expenses	1,425	Operating expenses	128,000
Stock shortages	2,150	Markdowns	40,000
Employee discounts	1,100	Cash discount earned	150

Chapter 9 Pricing in the Retail Operation

Given these estimates, what average initial markup should be used for the upcoming season?

22. While at market, the vendor offers you a choice of discounts. You may have either a 2 percent cash discount or an extra 2 percent in merchandise. Which one would you choose and why?

MANAGEMENT MEMO

You have just been hired to be the merchandise manager of a small chain (four stores) of women's apparel stores. The chain caters to working women, and five of its six buyers have less than a year's experience. In looking over the records, you notice that these buyers have been late in taking markdowns. As a result, the chain's GMROI has suffered. In talking with the buyers, you detect a sense of fear in taking markdowns. They believe that a markdown is an admission of an error in their buying and that if they make too many errors, their jobs will be in jeopardy. You decide to write the buyers a memo regarding markdowns.

BOARDROOM REPORT

Congress has recently been considering the idea of returning to resale price maintenance or fair trade laws. Your firm operates 15 traditional full-line department stores in four states. The BOD has asked you to prepare a report on what position it should take on this issue. The board's chairperson is expecting to meet with one of the state's U.S. senators this weekend at a fund raiser.

SUGGESTED READINGS

Dickson, Peter R., and Alan Sawyer. "The Price Knowledge and Search of Supermarket Shoppers." *Journal of Marketing* (July 1990): 42-53.

Fabricant, Ross A. "Special Retail Services and Resale Price Maintenance: The California Wine Industry." *Journal of Retailing* (Spring 1990): 101-18.

Mazumdar, Tridib, and Kent B. Monroe. "The Effects of Buyers' Intentions to Learn Price Information on Price Encoding." *Journal of Retailing* (Spring 1990): 15-32.

Oxenfeldt, Alfred R. *Pricing for Marketing Executives.* San Francisco: Wadsworth Publishing Co., 1961.

Ozment, John, Dave L. Kuntz, and Kenneth E. Clow. "How Consumers Form Expectations of Service Quality Prior to a First Time Purchase." *Proceedings of the 1991 Retail Patronage Behavior Symposium,* Baton Rouge, Louisiana State University, 1991.

Rao, Akshay R., and Kent B. Monroe. "The Effect of Price, Brand Name, and Store Name on Buyers' Perceptions of Product Quality: An Integrative Review." *Journal of Marketing Research* (August 1989): 351-57.

ENDNOTES

1. Tibor Scitovsky, "Some Consequences of the Habit of Judging Quality by Price," *Review of Economic Studies* (1945): 100-105.
2. L. Louise Luchsinger and Patrick M. Dunne, "Fair Trade Laws—How Fair?" *Journal of Marketing* (January 1978): 50-53.
3. Patrick Dunne and Rajaram Baliga, "Pricing Decision: Who Makes Them and How," Working Paper, 1989.

4. Joseph N. Fry and Gordon H. McDougall, "Consumer Appraisal of Retail Price Advertisements," *Journal of Marketing* (July 1974): 64-67.
5. "Wal-Mart's Way," *Advertising Age,* 18 February 1991, 3, 48.
6. "Gas Cash Discounts Fades," *Advertising Age,* 25 March 1991, 6.
7. "The War of Plastic," *Business Week,* 15 April 1991, 28-29.
8. Anthony Cox and Dena Cox, "Competing on Price: The Role of Retail Price Advertisements in Shaping Store Price Image," *Journal of Retailing* (Winter 1990): 428-45.
9. Robert F. Lusch, Syed H. Akhter, and Warren L. Dickson, "Social Class and Income, Not Social Class vs. Income: A Study of Retail Store Patronage Behavior," in William R. Darden, Robert F. Lusch, and J. Barry Mason, eds., *The Cutting Edge II* (Baton Rouge: Louisiana State University, 1992), 271-82.
10. "Hotels, Resorts Reap a Windfall From Air Fares," *Wall Street Journal,* 5 June 1992, B1. "Oh, What a Lovely Fare War," *Business Week,* 29 June 1992, 37.
11. Schwegmann Brothers vs. Calvert Distillers Corp., 314 U.S. 384 (1951).
12. Albert Bates, "Pricing for Profit," *Retailing Issues Letter* (September 1990).
13. See Zarrel V. Lambert, "An Investigation of Older Consumers' Unmet Needs and Wants at the Retail Level," *Journal of Retailing* (Winter 1979): 35-57; Leonard L. Berry, "The Time-Buying Consumer," *Journal of Retailing* (Winter 1979): 58-69; and Rebecca H. Holman and R. Dale Wilson, "Temporal Equilibrium as a Basis for Retail Shopping Behavior," *Journal of Retailing* (Spring 1982): 58-81.
14. C. Whan Park, Easwar S. Iyer, and Daniel C. Smith, "The Effects of Situational Factors on In-Store Grocery Shopping Behavior: The Role of Store Environment and Time Available for Shopping," *Journal of Consumer Research* (March 1989): 422-34.
15. "Department Stores Score BIG Linking FM to Credit Cards," *Colloquy* (April 1991): 1, 12-13.
16. For a more complete discussion of nonstore retailing, see Robert Peterson, Gerald Albaum, and Nancy M. Ridgway, "Consumers Who Buy from Direct Sales Companies," *Journal of Retailing* (Summer 1989): 273-86.
17. John C. Mowen, Joshua Weiner, and Clifford Young, "Consumer Store Choice and Sales Taxes: Retailing, Public Policy, and Theoretical Implications," *Journal of Retailing* (Summer 1990): 222-42.
18. Robert Mittelstaedt and Robert Stassen, "Market Richness, Seasonality, and the Diversity Within Retail Markets" (Paper presented at the Symposium on Patronage Behavior and Retail Strategic Planning, Baton Rouge, May 1991).
19. Phillip G. Carlson, "Fashion Retailing: The Sensitivity of Rate of Sale to Markdown," *Journal of Retailing* (Spring 1983): 67-76.
20. Stewart Henderson Britt, "How Weber's Law Can Be Applied to Retailing," *Business Horizons* (February 1975): 24.
21. "Wal-Mart Gets Lost in the Vegetable Aisle," *Business Week,* 28 May 1990, 48.
22. "Casualties in the Fast-Food Price Wars," *Wall Street Journal,* 23 October 1989, B1; "McDonald's, Faced with Competition on Prices, Plans Program of Discounts," *Wall Street Journal,* 4 October 1989, B6; "Fast-Food Joints Are Getting Fried," *Business Week,* 8 January 1990, 90; and "Restaurants: Doing Well by Being Big," *Business Week,* 14 January 1991, 92.
23. "Convenience Chains Pump for New Life," *Advertising Age,* 23 April 1990, 80; "Stop N Go's Van Horn Wants to Reinvent the Convenience Store," *Wall Street Journal,* 6 February 1991, A1, A10; and "Troubled Circle K is Turning This Way and That," *Business Week,* 20 November 1989, 78-80.
24. Kapil Bawa, Jane Landwehr, and Aradhna Krishna, "Consumer Response to Retailers' Marketing Environments: An Analysis of Coffee Purchase Data," *Journal of Retailing* (Winter 1989): 471-95.
25. Douglas Tigert, Stephen Arnold, Lonnie Powell, and Kathleen Seiders, "Service, Service, and Service: Why Nordstrom Is so Successful" (Presentation given to the Symposium on Patronage Behavior and Retail Strategic Planning, Baton Rouge, May 1991).
26. Cox and Cox, ibid; Donald R. Lichtenstein and William O. Bearden, "Contextual Influences on Perceptions of Merchant-Supplied Reference Prices," *Journal of Consumer Research* (June 1989): 55-66; and P. Rajan Varadarajan and James H. Leigh, "Consumers' Behavioral Response to Alternative Coupon Price Promotions" (Paper presented at the Patronage Behavior and Retail Strategic Planning Symposium, Baton Rouge, May 1991).
27. "Can Sears Recover?" *U.S. News & World Report,* 13 May 1991, 55-56.
28. Robert Schindler, "Symbolic Meanings of a Price Ending," *Advances in Consumer Research* (1991): 794-801.

29. Robert Blattberg and Scott Neslin, *Sales Promotion: Concepts, Methods, and Strategies* (Englewood Cliffs, N.J.: Prentice-Hall, Inc., 1990), chap. 12; Zarrel V. Lambert, "Perceived Prices as Related to Odd and Even Price Endings," *Journal of Retailing* (Fall 1975): 13-21, 78; and "Strategic Mix of Odd, Even Prices Can Lead to Increased Retail Profits," *Marketing News,* 7 March 1980, 24.
30. Ibid.
31. State of Wisconsin vs. American TV & Appliance of Madison, Inc., 140 Wis. 2d 353, 410 N.W. 2d 596 (Wisc. Ct. App. 1987).
32. "Making a Name for Selves: Store Brands Proving Stiff Competition for Marketers," *Advertising Age,* 6 May 1991, 36 and "What's in a Name? Increasingly, Little, Research Suggests," *Wall Street Journal,* 10 December 1990, B5.
33. "Limited Inc. Stores to End 'Confusion' Over 3 Brands," *Wall Street Journal,* 12 April 1991, B4.

Part 4

THE SELLING ENVIRONMENT

CHAPTER 10

IDENTIFYING ATTRACTIVE MARKETS FOR RETAIL STORES

OVERVIEW

In this chapter we examine how to identify attractive markets in which to locate retail stores. We introduce three theoretical frameworks: retail gravity theory, central place theory, and saturation theory, which each help to identify the most attractive geographic markets. We next discuss how to identify demand factors that might help determine the attractiveness of a market and also do the same for supply factors. We conclude with a detailed example of how to use secondary data to evaluate the attractiveness of a market area.

IDENTIFYING ATTRACTIVE MARKETS FOR RETAIL STORES

I. Steps in the Retail Location Decision
II. Theories of Market Identification
    A. Retail Gravity Theory
        1. Reilly's Law
        2. Converse's Revision
    B. Central Place Theory
    C. Contributions from Reilly and Christaller
    D. Saturation Theory
III. Demand Factors
    A. Market Potential
        1. Population Characteristics
        2. Buyer Behavior Characteristics

B. Household Characteristics
   1. Household Income
   2. Household Age Profile
   3. Size of Household
C. Community Characteristics
   1. Community Life Cycle
   2. Population Density
   3. Mobility
D. A Recap on How to Use Demand Factors
IV. Supply Factors
    A. Square Feet per Store
    B. Square Feet per Employee
    C. Growth in Stores
    D. Quality of Competition
    E. A Recap on How to Use Supply Factors
V. Secondary Sources of Information
VI. A Simple Example
VII. Summary

Traditionally, retailers have viewed location as the single most important decision affecting success. In fact, a retail executive once said that the three major success factors in retailing are location, location, and location. We believe that this perspective is outdated and is in fact one of the primary reasons for the failure of many of today's retail establishments. Retailers have traditionally tended to view the location decision, once made, as an "external uncontrollable" factor with which they are stuck, and to which they must therefore adapt a merchandising strategy. However, as we learned in Chapters 7 through 9, the most critical and pivotal element of the retailer's market positioning strategy is its merchandise and the pricing of that merchandise.

The merchandising and pricing decisions do have a major influence on the location decision. First, a retailer should tailor the merchandise and its price to a well-defined customer segment. Second, most individuals have a primary place of residence and work (except the homeless). So for the merchandise to be accessible to the target customer segment, the location decision is critical. Furthermore, depending on the type of merchandise, the customer will be willing to travel varying distances. This was illustrated in Chapter 3 when we discussed convenience, shopping, specialty and unsought goods and again in Chapter 4 when we presented a model of retailer's three-dimensional demand function (Exhibit 4.2, page 123). Again location does influence success.

Certainly, it is also clear that the retail location is not easily changed. A retailer can easily adjust prices, promotions, customer services, or even merchandise assortment but is constrained by lease commitments, space requirements of the business, or the unavailability of a better and more affordable location. Nonetheless, retailers sometimes watch their market shrink due to the entry of competitors, changes in population makeup, or the addition of a major traffic artery blocking access to their location when in fact they should probably relocate instead. In these situations the retailer will often fail because it does not quickly decide to close the store and find a more appropriate location.

Some retail analysts believe location is a problem for Sears. Sears has historically been known for its hard-goods merchandise (appliances, furniture, tools, automotive parts, etc.), and customers today do not go to shopping malls for these items; however, that is where Sears is primarily located. Sears continues to try to make these locations work by adjusting merchandise, prices, and promotion rather than by making the difficult decision to close these locations and find locations more appropriate for a primarily hard-goods retailer.

STEPS IN THE RETAIL LOCATION DECISION

The retail location decision involves three sequential steps. First, the retailer must identify the most attractive markets in which to operate. Some retailers, such as Woolworth, Toys "R" Us, Sears, Benetton, and McDonald's, are international, and thus when they think of new locations they consider the

ILLUSTRATION 10.1

The size and prosperity of the United States consumer market attracts many international retailers such as Benetton.

attractiveness of geographic expansion into foreign countries. Many retailers such as Wal-Mart and Sharper Image are taking a new look at Mexico, since it has its inflation under control and is discussing a free-trade agreement with the United States.[1] Other retailers such as County Seat Jeans or Kroger concentrate on a single country, the United States, and thus when considering new locations they evaluate the attractiveness of the 50 states of the United States. Finally, some retailers concentrate on a small region of the United States or possibly a single state or city. You can probably easily identify some local retailers unique to the city or state where you reside.

The second step in the retail location decision is to evaluate the density of demand and supply within each market and identify the most attractive sites that are available within each market. Essentially, this means the identification of the sites most consistent with the retailer's market positioning statement for which the market is not already overstored or in which competition is not overly intense.

The third step is the selection of the best site (or sites) available. This stage involves estimating the revenue and expenses of a new store at various locations and then identifying the most profitable new locations.

These three steps are illustrated in Exhibit 10.1. This chapter will discuss the first step, and Chapter 11 will detail steps 2 and 3.

EXHIBIT 10.1

Selecting a Retail Location

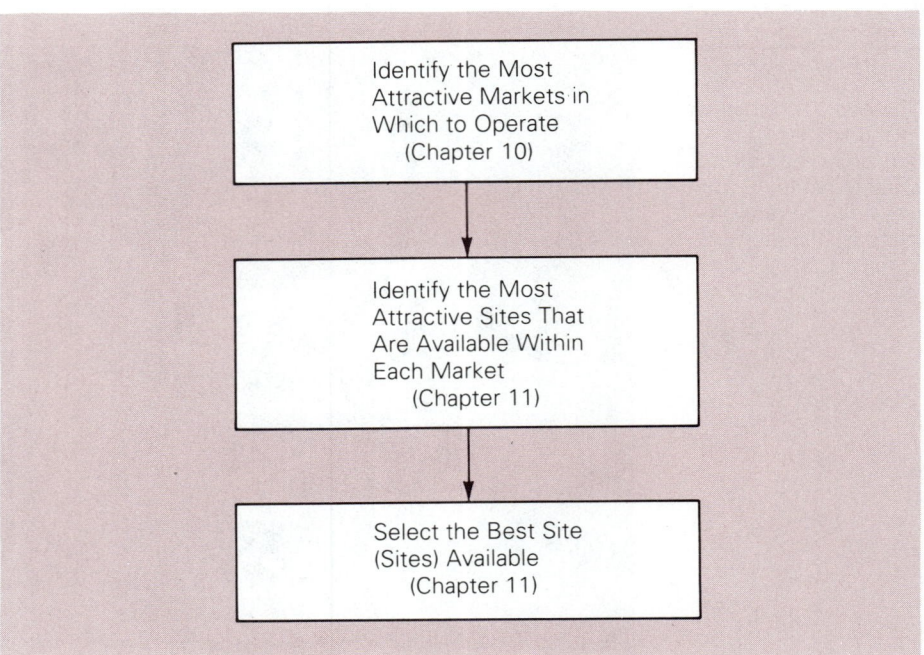

THEORIES OF MARKET IDENTIFICATION

The first step toward making a good retail location decision is to identify the most attractive markets in which the retailer could locate. We will describe three theories for identifying the best markets. The first two are useful in delineating the size, shape, and total trade area of a potential location, while the third enables the retailer to evaluate how the demand of this potential trading area is being served by current retail establishments.

RETAIL GRAVITY THEORY

Research on store location started just after World War I. Two groups of social scientists—one theoretical, the other pragmatic—believed that there were underlying consistencies in shopping behavior that would yield to mathematical analysis and prediction, based on the concept of gravity.

Reilly's Law. William J. Reilly, who described himself as a "sometime marketing specialist" as well as a "professor," published the first trading area model in 1929.[2] **Reilly's law of retail gravitation** dealt with how large urban areas attracted customers from smaller communities serving the rural hinterland. As its name implies, Reilly's law had Newtonian gravitational principles as its core: Two cities attract trade from an intermediate place approximately in direct proportion to the population of the two cities and in inverse proportion to the square of the distance from these two cities to the intermediate place, or

$$\left(\frac{B_a}{B_b}\right) = \left(\frac{P_a}{P_b}\right) \times \left(\frac{D_b}{D_a}\right)^2$$

B_a = business City A draws from the intermediate place
B_b = business City B draws from the intermediate place
P_a = population of City A
P_b = population of City B
D_a = distance from City A to intermediate place
D_b = distance from City B to intermediate place[3]

Mansfield, a small town of 800 people, has only a gas station and a convenience store and thus virtually all retail shopping is out of town. Mansfield is 25 miles from Levelland and 40 miles in the opposite direction from Norwood. Levelland's population is 100,000 and Norwood's is 200,000.

Using Reilly's equations, we can see that the retailers in Levelland attract 1.28 times as much business from the citizens of Mansfield as do the retailers in Norwood.

$$\left(\frac{B_a}{B_b}\right) = \left(\frac{100{,}000}{200{,}000}\right) \times \left(\frac{40}{25}\right)^2 = 1.28$$

Since we know that Mansfield's citizens spend 1.28 dollars in Levelland for every dollar spent in Norwood, we can say that Levelland has a 56 percent share of the Mansfield market and Norwood has a 44 percent share:

$$\frac{1.28}{1.28 + 1.00} = 56\% \qquad \frac{1.00}{1.28 + 1.00} = 44\%$$

Converse's Revision. Two decades later Paul Converse revised Reilly's original law in order to determine the boundaries of a city's trading area or to establish a "point of indifference" between two cities.[4] The **point of indifference** is the point at which shoppers would be equally willing to shop at either city. Converse's formulation of Reilly's law can be expressed algebraically as

$$D_{ab} = \frac{d}{1 + \sqrt{\frac{P_b}{P_a}}}$$

where:
D_{ab} = breaking point from City A, measured in miles along the road to City B
d = distance between City A and City B along the major highway
P_a = population of City A
P_b = population of City B

Referring to our earlier example, the breakpoint of indifference between Levelland and Norwood would be 26.9 miles from Levelland and 38.1 miles from Norwood. This means that if you lived 20 miles from Levelland and 45 miles from Norwood, you most probably would choose to shop in Levelland since it is within your zone of indifference and Norwood is beyond your zone of indifference. You might want to figure this out yourself, using Norwood as City A and Levelland as City B:

$$D_{ab} = \frac{65}{1 + \sqrt{\frac{200{,}000}{100{,}000}}}$$

This formula can also be used with more than two cities. Consider the population and distances separating Cities A, B, C, and D in Exhibit 10.2a. City A is the largest, with a population of 240,000, and it is surrounded by three smaller cities. City B is 18 miles away and has a population of 14,000; City D is 5 miles away and has a population of 30,000; and City C is 14 miles away and has a population of 21,000. We will assume that the roads on Exhibit 10.2a are the only ones connecting the smaller cities with the larger City A.

EXHIBIT 10.2
A Community's General Trading Areas

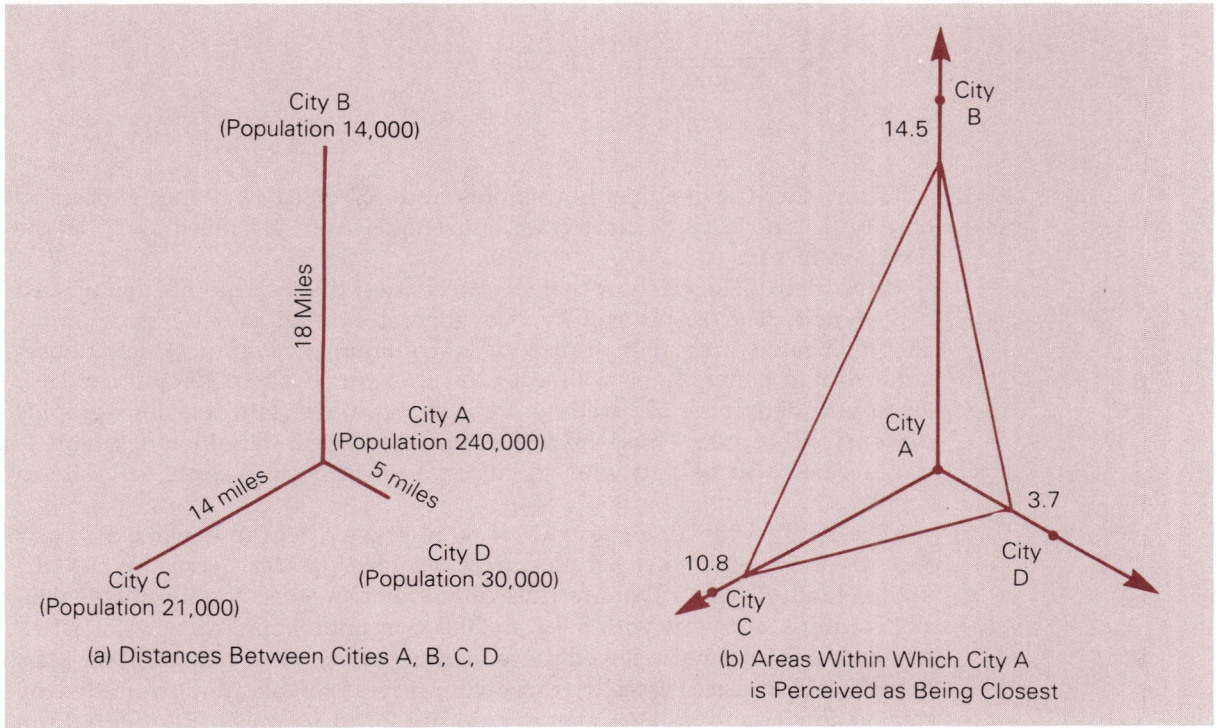

(a) Distances Between Cities A, B, C, D

(b) Areas Within Which City A is Perceived as Being Closest

Converse's revision of Reilly's law will allow us to determine the distances from which each of the smaller cities will be able to attract households. The complement of this finding is the distances from which City A will be able to attract households in the direction of Cities B, C, and D.

For example, if we consider Cities A and B we would have

$$D_b = \frac{18}{1 + \sqrt{\frac{240{,}000}{14{,}000}}} = 3.5 \text{ miles}$$

City B is able to attract households from 3.5 miles away in the direction of City A. Since A and B are 18 miles apart, we could also conclude that A could attract customers from 14.5 miles (18 − 3.5) away in the direction of B.

Applying the same equation but using relevant data on Cities C and D yields

$$D_c = \frac{14}{1 + \sqrt{\dfrac{240{,}000}{21{,}000}}} = 3.2 \text{ miles}$$

$$D_d = \frac{5}{1 + \sqrt{\dfrac{240{,}000}{30{,}000}}} = 1.3 \text{ miles}$$

Thus, City C can attract households from 3.2 miles away in the direction of City A, and City D can attract households from 1.3 miles away in the direction of City A.

In Exhibit 10.2b we show that we can connect the three points that we just determined. The result is City A's general **trading area,** a geographically delineated area that surrounds a community, within which households would generally be willing to travel to purchase goods and services. Once you determine the trading area, you can ascertain the demographic makeup of that area. Thus, the retailer now has a clear definition of where its trading area will be and who its customers will be if it elects to locate in City A.

The Reilly and Converse laws of retail gravity help to explain the early success of Sam Walton's location decision for Wal-Mart stores. Wal-Mart, until recently, located Wal-Mart discount stores in small communities—usually county seat towns with 5,000 to 20,000 in population. More established retailers such as Kmart viewed these markets as too small to enter. Wal-Mart thought otherwise. Typically, these county seat towns are surrounded by smaller towns and villages that extend out 20 to 35 miles. Residents from these smaller towns and villages would travel to the county seat town to shop, and with the addition of a 50,000-to-75,000-square-foot discount department store such as Wal-Mart the county seat towns became even more of a magnet. What Wal-Mart realized is what Reilly and Converse showed mathematically: The trade area can and often does include residents from outside the town or city. Interestingly, firms such as Kmart, Target, McDonald's, and Red Lobster are now viewing smaller towns as attractive markets.[5]

Reilly's law and Converse's revision rest on two assumptions: that the two competing cities are equally accessible from the major road; and that population is a good indicator of the differences in goods and services available in different cities. Consumers are attracted to larger population centers not because of the city's size, but because of the greater number of store facilities and larger product assortment available. The increased selection makes the increased travel time worthwhile.

The law of retail gravitation was an important contribution to trading area analysis because it is easy to use when other data are not available or when the costs of obtaining these data are too high. However, Reilly's law does have several limitations. First, population doesn't always reflect available shopping facilities. For example, two neighboring cities, each with a population of 10,000 and similar demographics, would be reflected equally in Reilly's law even though one of the cities had a Wal-Mart-based shopping center and the other didn't. This would result in a serious prediction error using Reilly's law since the presence of the Wal-Mart would add substantially to the merchandise assortment present in a community and thus its drawing power. Second, distance is measured in miles, not in the time required for the consumer to travel or the consumer's perception of the distance or time. Given our present highway system, this limitation is significant. Traveling 30 miles on an interstate to a mall located at an exit is easier than the stop-start travel involved in going six miles through downtown traffic. Some retailers using Reilly's law substitute travel time for mileage. Another important limitation is that the size of the trading area is totally dependent on the corner cities selected. If City E, with a population of 50,000, is 20 miles past City B on the same highway from City A as shown in Exhibit 10.3, then City A's trading area will be different. Finally, while the law works reasonably well in rural areas, where distance is a major decision factor, it isn't flawless. Recent

EXHIBIT 10.3

New Trading Area for City A After Substituting City E for City B

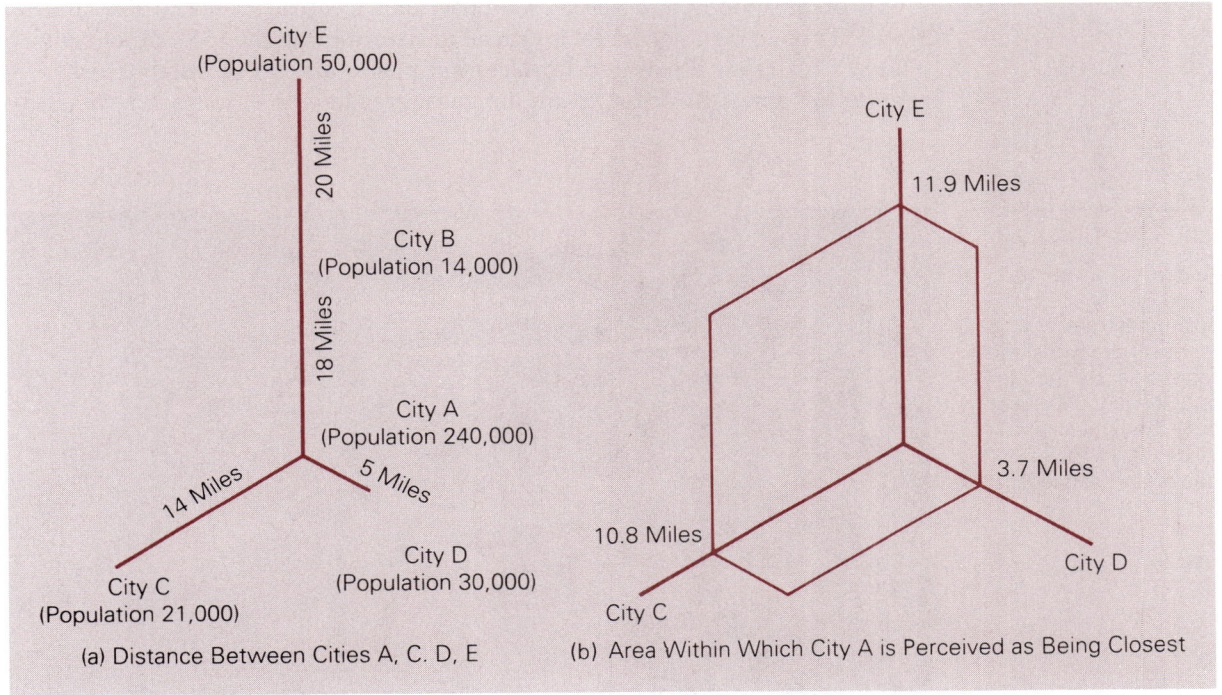

(a) Distance Between Cities A, C, D, E
(b) Area Within Which City A is Perceived as Being Closest

research on **outshopping,** that is, leaving your community to shop from rural areas suggests that factors other than those considered by retail gravity theory are important. Some of these factors include perceived differences between local and other trading centers, variety seeking behavior, and other services provided including medical services and/or entertainment facilities.[6] Also, gravity theory is less useful in metropolitan areas where consumers typically have a number of shopping choices available within the maximum distance they are willing to travel.

CENTRAL PLACE THEORY

At the same time that Reilly was publishing his work in the United States, Walter Christaller in southern Germany was developing a theoretical model to evaluate the spatial arrangement of stores required for the distribution of a single good to a dispersed population. Christaller's work was titled *Central Places in Southern Germany.*[7] According to Christaller, a central place is a center of commerce—a village, town, or city—consisting of a cluster of retail institutions. **Central place theory** ranks communities according to the assortment of goods available in each. At the bottom of the hierarchy are communities that represent the smallest central places. They provide the most basic assortment of goods and services, the necessities of life. Farther up the hierarchy are larger central places, which carry all the goods and services found in lower-order central places plus more specialized ones that are not as necessary.

To obtain goods and services, households need to travel to the central places. Thus, consumer travel is crucial in determining the location of central places. Christaller illustrated how central places should be established in a geographic space in order to minimize aggregate travel costs for the con-

ILLUSTRATION 10.2

According to central place theory, consumers are willing to travel great distances for specialized goods and services because only the larger central places have those goods and services.

sumer. The more basic the good or service, the shorter the distance the consumer should need to travel to purchase it. On the other hand, the typical household could expect to travel a great distance for specialized goods and services, since only the larger central places have them.

It is important to recognize that Christaller's theory is not directly used by retail location analysts; however, it has contributed some useful concepts that are often used. Two important ones are the range and the threshold of a good. The **range** is the maximum distance a consumer is willing to travel for a good or service, and as such it determines the outer limit of a store's trade area. The real estate and site location departments of large retail chain organizations frequently do consumer research to determine the range. For example, a fast-food restaurant (in the United States) may find that its range is 2 to 3 miles or 5 to 8 minutes travel time. However, even the range is dependent on such things as the economic geography of the area and consumer demographics. In a rural community the range for a fast-food restaurant would be much higher (perhaps as high as 15 miles or 30 minutes), while in a large and congested city such as New York it would be much less (perhaps as little as 2,000 feet or 5 minutes walking time). **Threshold** is the minimum amount of consumer demand that must exist in an area for a store to be economically viable. In spatial terms, this threshold is equal to the radius of the area containing the population that can just support the store.

Let's develop an example where these two concepts might be used. If a fast-food restaurant needs a population base of 15,000 to be successful, and if the population per square mile in a particular market area is 800, then the number of square miles of geographic space needed to account for 15,000 people is 15,000/800 or 18.75 square miles. Now if we assume that a trade area is a circle, and given we know the area of a circle is πr^2 (where r is the radius), we then know that

$$\pi r^2 = 18.75$$
$$(22/7)r^2 = 18.75$$
$$r^2 = 5.966$$
$$r = 2.44$$

Thus, the threshold, in spatial terms, for this fast-food restaurant is 2.44 miles.

According to Christaller, the range must be greater than the threshold if the store is to be economically feasible. In the preceding example the range is 2 to 3 miles and the threshold 2.44 miles. Thus, it is very unlikely that the fast-food restaurant would be economically feasible. However, what if the population per square mile were 2,000? Then we see that the square miles of trade area needed is 15,000/2,000 or 7.5 miles. Again if we assume a circular trade area we have

$$\pi r^2 = 7.5$$
$$r^2 = 7.5(22/7)$$
$$r = 1.54$$

We now see that the threshold is 1.54 miles, and this is well within the range of 2 to 3 miles. What have we learned from this exercise? This hypothetical fast-food chain should look for market areas where the population density is greater than 2,000 people per square mile.

The preceding discussion of Christaller's theory and the concepts of range and threshold explain why firms, shopping centers, or communities offering only convenience goods will be more numerous and closer together than those offering more specialized but less frequently purchased goods or services that must attract consumers from a much wider geographic area Consumers also prefer to visit a single location for a variety of needs, rather than traveling to different places for each item. This forces firms to group together as a community of businesses in order to serve as many different needs as possible from a single location. Thus, the communities most centrally located in a region attract the more specialized and largest number of firms.

Although Christaller developed his theory to describe the location of retail activity in southern Germany in the 1930s, modern retailing experts agree that central place models offer a "powerful explanation of the spatial distribution of retail facilities and market centers and the pattern and extent of market areas."[8] In fact, Christaller's theory helps to explain the success of hypermarkets in Europe. The European hypermarkets are often over 150,000 square feet and stock a wide variety of food as well as soft and hard goods.

What are the implications of central place theory for the identification of the best markets? There are three:

1. Not all communities will be able to support all types of retailing activity. The more basic or necessary the goods are, the more communities the seller can consider potential markets. If the retailer is selling very specialized goods such as furs and jewelry, then it need only consider the larger communities. This explains why very specialized medical doctors (such as brain surgeons) and lawyers (such as securities lawyers) are located only in large cities.
2. Central place theory tells the retailer which types of retail activity a growing community will most likely need in the future. For example, a small community with only a gasoline service station and a grocery store will probably need a restaurant next.
3. The theory tells us that a single trip to a higher-order central place will replace the need to make separate trips to several lower-order centers. This suggests that the larger central places will do a disproportionately larger amount of business. When consumers from small communities travel to a larger central place, they will be able to purchase not only specialized goods and services but also basic ones. The implication is simply that large central places tend to be more attractive in terms of potential demand. This has been demonstrated often in small-town America, where the arrival of a Wal-Mart draws other retailers toward Wal-Mart's location and away from the old downtown business district.

Christaller's work had one major limitation. A number of studies have found that, contrary to the central place assumptions, consumers will sometimes bypass closer shopping opportunities to visit agglomerated centers that are farther away in order to shop for different types of goods on the same trip. Multipurpose shopping trips account for between 30 to 50 percent of all shopping today; however, central place theory ignores the relationship that exists among different types of retail firms.

Ghosh, the recent editor of the *Journal of Retailing*, recognizing that multipurpose shopping patterns presented a strong economic incentive for low-order retailers to agglomerate with higher-order ones wherever possible, developed a model of consumer shopping that determines the optimal shopping itinerary of individual consumers. While the actual model developed is beyond the scope of this chapter, it is important to point out that a number of Ghosh's predictions regarding the spatial organization of retailing are consistent with reality. For example, Ghosh predicts that consumers living close to the low-order stores will make more frequent trips to those stores. Ghosh's model provides the underlying rationale for the agglomeration of dissimilar retailing firms in shopping centers and malls and determines the benefits of such actions for both retailers and consumers.[9]

CONTRIBUTIONS FROM REILLY AND CHRISTALLER

Reilly and Christaller looked at the issue of retail location from different perspectives, and each made a significant contribution to its early development. (Reilly was probably unaware of Christaller's early work since it was not published in an English translation until 1966.) Reilly's contribution was a statistical model based on empirical observation, and Christaller's was a theoretical model showing the relationship of the different ingredients in a location process. It was not until the translation of the work of Losch[10] that a mathematical model of Christaller's theory was produced. Losch argued that since the real price of a good increases with distance traveled, the quantity demanded will decrease correspondingly as we pointed out in Exhibit 4.2.

Another important contribution of these pioneers in location studies was that for the first time, retailers were able to predict the shape of their market areas. Based on the work of Christaller, the locations of the various market centers were assumed to be in a hexagonal pattern. Hexagons are the nearest geometrical equivalents to circles that will allow all geographic areas and consumers to be served by a center. (A network of circles around a central place would result in some areas being overlapped by two central place cities and/or other areas not being covered.) Christaller's argument, however, was only theoretical in nature and could be distorted by natural or artificial barriers to travel, political uncertainties, or nonuniform population patterns.

Given the location of the largest cities, the locations of the next level of communities will occur exactly at the apex of three of the largest cities. Exhibit 10.4 shows that every plan contains two B-level communities for every A-level city. Since the method by which successive orders of communities are

EXHIBIT 10.4

The Arrangement of Trade Centers and Trade Areas According to Christaller's Model of Central Place

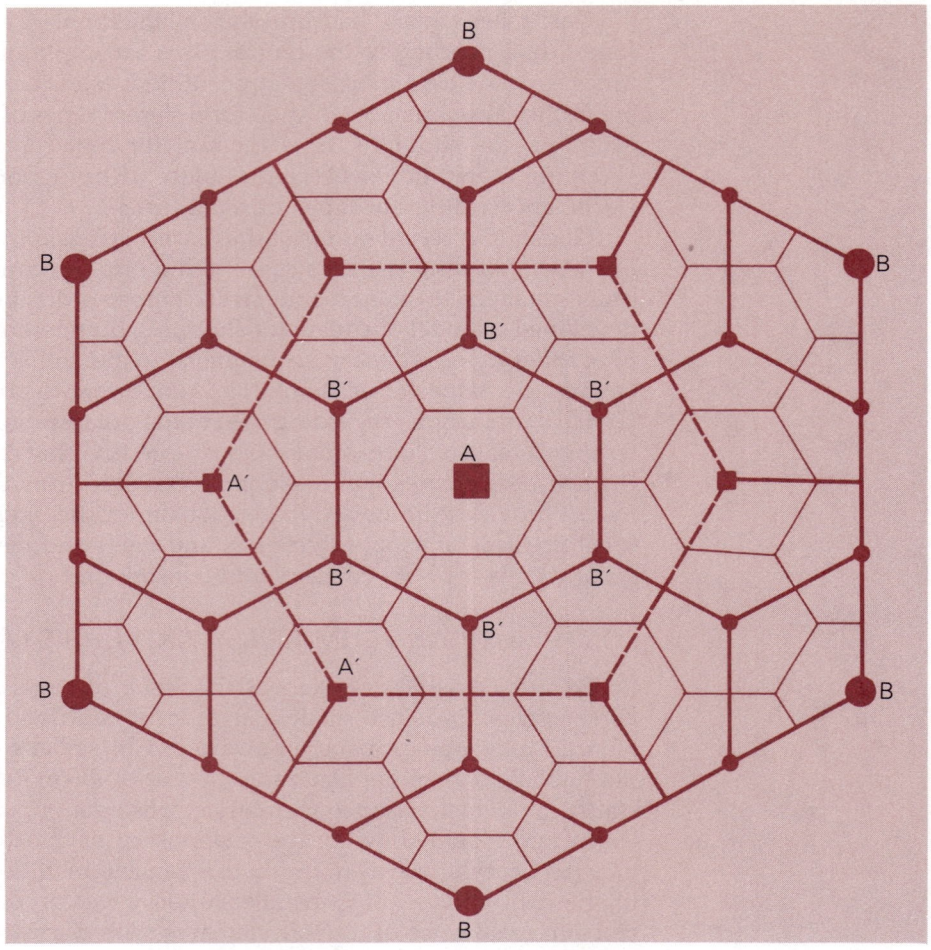

added does not change, it will always be true that the number of communities in a given order will equal twice the number of communities in all higher levels combined. In other words, 1:2:6:18:54:162, and so on.

These numbers can be proved by looking closely at Exhibit 10.4 and assuming that A (the central city) is the largest city. At the corners of A's market area are six B-level cities. Each B, however, is located at the junction of the market areas of three A cities, so that each B city may be counted only as 1:1 in calculating the ratio of A to B cities (or 2:1).[11]

SATURATION THEORY

A third theoretical concept that can help to determine the attractiveness of different market areas is retail saturation. William Applebaum and Saul Cohen define **store saturation** as follows[12]:

Store saturation of a market is a condition under which existing store facilities are utilized efficiently and meet customer needs. Saturation exists for a given type of store when a market has just enough store facilities of a given type to serve the population of the market satisfactorily and yield a fair return to the owners on their investments without raising prices to the customer to achieve this return. When a market has too few stores to provide satisfactorily the needs of the customer, it is under-stored. When a market has too many stores to yield a fair return on investment, it is over-stored. Saturation, as defined here, implies a balance between the amount of existing retail store facilities and their use (which in turn is a reflection of need).

A possible indicator of under- versus overstored markets is the **index of retail saturation (IRS).**[13] The IRS can be calculated as follows:

$$IRS = \frac{H \times RE}{RF}$$

where:
IRS = index of retail saturation for area 1
H = number of households in area 1
RE = annual retail expenditures for a particular line of trade per household in area 1
RF = square feet of retail facilities of a particular line of trade in area 1 (including square footage of proposed store)

When the IRS has a high value in comparison with the line of trade in other cities, it indicates that the market is not saturated and that a potentially attractive opportunity exists. A low value indicates a saturated market, without significant opportunity.

As an example of how the index of retail saturation is used, consider an individual planning on opening a dry cleaner in either City A or City B. This individual has the following information: Residents of both cities spend $75.36 annually on dry cleaning. Total households are 17,000 in City A and 22,000 in City B. City A has 2,000 square feet of dry-cleaning facilities, City B has 2,500, and the size of the proposed dry cleaner is 500 square feet. Given this information and using our formula for IRS, we can find the IRS for each city:

$$\text{IRS (City A)} = \frac{17{,}000 \times 75.36}{2{,}000 + 500} = 512.45$$

$$\text{IRS (City B)} = \frac{22{,}000 \times 75.36}{2{,}500 + 500} = 552.64$$

Thus, based solely on these two factors of demand (number of households and average expenditure for products by each household) and one factor of supply (the number of square feet of retail space serving this demand), the individual would choose to locate in City B.

You should notice two things about the IRS formula. First, the IRS informs the retail analyst that market-entry decisions should be based on supply and demand factors. In fact, the IRS is simply the ratio of aggregate household demand ($H \times RE$) to aggregate retail space supply (RF). The higher the ratio of aggregate demand to aggregate supply, the more attractive the market opportunity. Second, the IRS is essentially a measure of average sales per square foot of the existing retail establishments in the market. With this statistic, the analyst can derive an estimate of profits by working with known gross margin and operating expense ratios for the industry.

The computed IRS value can be compared to the sales dollars per square foot needed by the retailer to break even in a new location. Even if one city under consideration has a much higher value than the other cities, if that value isn't greater than the break-even costs of operation, the retailer should reject the city. Some retail scholars have questioned the usefulness of this index, because even markets with a low IRS value may be attractive places to enter if existing retailers are not satisfying consumer desires. Nevertheless, the IRS is still widely used in retailing today.[14]

The concept of retail saturation forces the retailer to assess demand and supply in analyzing various markets. Let us now identify the major demand and supply factors that were not explicitly recognized in the IRS.

DEMAND FACTORS

The major demand factors that should be carefully analyzed, in addition to retail sales per household (as defined in the IRS), are market potential and household and community characteristics. Household characteristics include income, age profile, and size. Community characteristics include life cycle, population density, and mobility.

MARKET POTENTIAL

The major components of market potential to be considered are population and buying behavior. These same characteristics define the market position the retailer hopes to attract (see Chapter 2).

As we study the following characteristics, keep in mind that the analysis of market potential is not always an easy process since data may not be available. For example, McDonald's had little hard data to suggest that it would be successful in Russia. The company was more interested in building an image than in sending profits home. Consequently, McDonald's was patient over the 14 years it spent structuring the joint venture and in accepting to do business only in rubles.[15] Because rubles could not be converted into dollars on the open market, McDonald's had to agree to reinvest its rubles in further expansion or other activities in Russia.

Population Characteristics. Population characteristics are the criteria most often used to segment markets. The decennial census of population is the most important source of these data for both large and small communities, providing a uniform set of data for intercommunity comparisons. Exhibit 10.5 shows data from the 1990 Census. The basic data, called "complete count" or "100 percent," come from the questions asked of every person. Other items are based on sample estimates. In general, the larger the city, the greater the amount of detail available in the census reports.

Although total population figures and their growth rates are of primary importance to a retailer in examining potential markets, the executive can obtain a more detailed profile of a market by examining school enrollment, education, age, sex, occupation, race, and nationality. Retailers should try to match a market's population characteristics to the population characteristics of the people it desires to attract. For example, a child day care center such as Kinder Care or LaPetite would want to identify markets where there were a high proportion of dual-income families with moderately high incomes and children under 8 years of age. Consequently, it would find unattractive communities that were primarily for retirement, where a low proportion of

EXHIBIT 10.5

Population Data Available from 1990 Census of Population and Housing

Sample Population Items	100 Percent Population Items
School enrollment	Household relationship
Education attainment	Sex
State or country of birth	Race
Citizenship and year of immigration	Age
Current language and English proficiency	Marital status
Ancestry	Spanish/Hispanic origin or descent
Place of residence 5 years ago	
Activity 5 years ago	
Veteran status and period of service	
Presence of disability or handicap	
Children ever born	
Marital history	
Employment status last week	
Hours worked last week	
Place of work	
Travel time to work	
Means of transportation to work	
Persons in carpool	
Year last worked	
Industry, occupation, and class of worker	
Work in 1989 and weeks looking for work in 1989	
Amount of Income by source in 1989	

households had two income earners, or where total household income was relatively low. National Planning Data Corporation provides a service to retailers called "Consumer Clout," which is a method for estimating the expenditures on over 400 specific product categories by geographic area. Consumer Clout could be used to estimate the market potential for a particular trade area around a proposed site, or for an entire city, county, or state in the United States.

Retailing in Action 10.1 examines how CACI Marketing Systems has taken the 1990 Census and put it in easy-to-use packages to help the retailer make location decisions.

Buyer Behavior Characteristics. Another useful criterion for analyzing potential markets is the buying behavior characteristics of the market. Such characteristics include store loyalty, consumer lifestyles and psychographics, store patronage motives, geographic and climatic conditions, and product benefits

---

RETAILING IN ACTION

10.1 CACI Marketing Systems Paves the Way for Easy Use of 1990 U.S. Census Data

The U.S. Census Bureau collects an amazing amount of data during its decennial census. However, the government leaves it to the private sector to add value to these data and help industry solve marketing problems with the data.

The 1990 Census will be especially useful to retailers because it will feature the government's Topologically Integrated Geographic Encoding and Referencing system, referred to as TIGER. TIGER is a detailed coding of natural, political, and statistical boundaries—every street, road, subdivision, stream, bridge, and tunnel in the United States. In addition, the Census Bureau will make the complete U.S. Census available on 37 CD-ROM at a cost of less than $10,000. Since the TIGER files are essentially a series of codes and numbers meaningless to most, specialized software is required to allow the retailer to zoom in on meaningful geographic areas. CACI Marketing Systems is one such provider of software.

CACI's InSite.USA is a desktop-computer-based system that allows retailers to analyze and interpret data on relevant geographic areas quickly and easily. For example, McDonald's has used such a system to help determine new restaurant locations, and Dairy Queen uses it to pinpoint neighborhoods with the greatest demand potential for soft ice cream.

Retailers that want to start with a noncomputer-based system can order printed reports on certain geographic areas that list information such as age, income, race, occupation, education, and other demographic data. In addition, one could order CACI's annual Sourcebook of Zip Code Demographics, containing demographic data on every ZIP code in the United States.

Source: Various CACI advertisements.

sought. If one were expanding a chain of barbecue restaurants, one would need to identify those individuals whose lifestyles were consistent with patronage of barbecue restaurants. One research firm clusters all neighborhoods in the United States into 40 types that describe the lifestyle and psychographics of the neighborhood. Two of these 40 neighborhood types are "Norma Rae-Ville," which represents lower-middle-class mill towns and industrial suburbs mainly in the South, and "Shotguns and Pickups" which represents crossroads villages serving the nation's lumber and breadbasket needs. The expansion-minded chain of barbecue restaurants would probably want to evaluate sites in the Norma Rae-Ville and Shotguns and Pickups neighborhoods, since these neighborhoods represent the highest market potential for barbecue restaurants.

HOUSEHOLD CHARACTERISTICS

Household Income. The average household income and the distribution of household income can significantly influence demand for retail facilities. Further insights into the demand for retail facilities are provided by **Engel's laws.** These are generalizations about a household's response to an increase in income. They imply that spending increases for all categories of products as a result of an income increase, but that the percentage of spending for some categories increases more than for others. According to Engel's laws, as average household income rises, the community will exhibit a greater demand for luxury goods and a more sophisticated demand for necessity goods. Consider the demand for food. Regardless of household income, as long as it is above the poverty level, individuals will consume the same approximate quantity of food. At low incomes they may consume pinto beans, hot dogs, and bread; at higher-income levels they may eat asparagus, sirloin steak, and fancy dinner rolls.

The distribution of household incomes in a community can influence the demand for retail facilities. If all households in a community had an identical income (an unlikely phenomenon), then the same type of retail facility within any given line of trade would probably appeal to all households. There would be no opportunity to segment the market based on income. For example, if all households had relatively low incomes, then an upscale women's apparel store would face little opportunity, even though there might be a need for an additional women's apparel store. On the other hand, if the average household had a low income, but there were also a fair number of households with high incomes, then some potential might exist for such a store.

Household Age Profile. The age composition of households can be an important determinant of demand for retail facilities. In communities where households tend to be young, the preferences for stores may be different than in communities where the average household is relatively old. For example, in communities with a disproportionate number of young households, the demand for restaurants will be heavily oriented toward fast food. In communities with a disproportionate number of older households, the demand will be more oriented toward leisurely dining. Age will help determine the demand for a wide range of retail facilities such as furniture stores, jewelry stores, and apparel stores.

Size of Household. If we hold income and age constant and change the average size of households, we will be able to identify another determinant of the demand for retail facilities. Consider two young households with moderate incomes: One household contains a husband and wife and the other a husband, wife, and three children. For the second household, the moderate income level loses much of its buying power because of the larger household size. This will influence the distribution of retail expenditures between food stores, apparel stores, furniture stores, restaurants, auto dealers, and so on. It will also influence the demand for specific types of retailers (e.g., discount department store versus full-service, conventional department stores). To illustrate this point further, imagine yourself as the head of a household with an income of $34,000 and consider how you would spend that money if you had no children and then if you had three children. As Exhibit 10.6 points out, important household data are readily available from census data.

COMMUNITY CHARACTERISTICS

Community Life Cycle. Communities tend to exhibit growth patterns over time. It has been suggested that:

> *Over a span of time, growth patterns of communities may be of four major types. These include the pattern of rapid growth, the pattern of continuous growth, the pattern of relatively stable growth and the pattern of decline. The rapid growth pattern can be found largely in communities located along the Gulf Coast, in the Southwest and in the West. The continuous growth pattern is appearing in communities that are developing new industries and expanding established industries. The slow or constant-level growth pattern can be found when a city has developed an established economy that remains in a relatively stable position. The diminished or declining growth pattern is often associated with the exhaustion of resources or a shift in technology.*[16]

The retailer should identify communities that are in a rapid or continuous growth pattern, since they will represent the best long-run opportunities.

Population Density. The population density of a community can be defined either as the number of persons per square mile or the number of households per square mile. In either case, empirical research suggests that the higher the population density, the larger the average store in terms of square feet and thus the fewer the number of stores that will be needed to serve a population of a given size.[17] However, it is also clear that when population density

EXHIBIT 10.6
Housing Data Available from 1990 Census of Population and Housing

Sample Items	100 Percent Items
Condominium status	Number of housing units at address
Plumbing	Number of rooms in unit
Year unit built	Tenure (whether the unit is owned or rented)
Year moved into this house	Condominium identification
Source of water	Value of home (for owner-occupied units and condominiums)
Sewage disposal	
Heating equipment	Monthly rent (for renter-occupied units)
Fuels used for home heating, water heating, and cooking	
Costs of utilities and fuels	Vacant for rent, for sale, etc., and period of vacancy
Kitchen facilities	
Number of bedrooms and bathrooms	
Telephone	
Air conditioning	
Number of automobiles	
Number of light trucks and vans	
Home owner shelter costs for mortgage, real estate taxes, and hazard insurance	

becomes too high then consumer mobility declines due to increased congestion and under these circumstances the stores may be in fact smaller in size. Therefore, it is important that retailers consider the population density of markets they are evaluating.

Mobility. The easier it is for people to travel, the more mobile they will be.[18] When people are mobile they are willing to travel greater distances to shop, and therefore there will be fewer but larger stores in the community. Thus, a community whose households are highly mobile will need fewer retailers than a community whose mobility is low. Mobility cannot be directly determined, but there are surrogate indicators. One popular indicator is the number of automobiles per household. As this number rises, households become more mobile. Other indicators are the availability of public transportation and the amount of traffic congestion. Households may have cars, but if the roadways are inadequate to handle the quantity of traffic, congestion will hamper mobility. Thus, more stores are needed, and they should be closer together.

A RECAP ON HOW TO USE DEMAND FACTORS

How does a retail location analyst use all the preceding information about demand factors to help evaluate market areas? The answer is quite simple. The analyst needs to sit down with senior management and identify the top four to seven demand factors that are important to determining the success of new stores. These factors will be in part a function of the retailer's market positioning and in part a function of factors that may positively influence demand for the type of merchandise it will sell. For example, of the preceding items reviewed, a chain of home appliance stores might identify the following five items as important:

1. Population growth of 20 percent over the last 10 years—because rapidly growing areas have more new home construction.
2. Average age of household head between 25 and 35—because this is the prime time when heads of households acquire appliances.
3. Greater than 70 percent home ownership—because renters purchase fewer appliances.
4. Population density over 1,500 persons per square mile and 30,000 total population in trade area—because this is needed to make a new outlet financially viable.
5. Average household income over $35,000—because this gives the household the purchasing power to acquire more appliances.

The retail analyst could then either gather data that are publicly available in U.S. Census publications or use the data services of firms such as National Planning Data Corporation, Urban Decision Systems, or CACI. These firms allow the analyst to connect to its computers via modem and print out relevant data.

SUPPLY FACTORS

The IRS formula used an aggregate measure of supply: total square feet of retail facilities by line of trade in a community. Although this is a useful indicator, there are many others—square feet per store, square feet per employee, growth in number of stores, and quality of competition.

SQUARE FEET PER STORE

It is helpful if the retail analyst has data on the square feet per store for the average store in the communities that are being analyzed. Whether a community tends to have large- or small-scale retailing is important in terms of assessing the extent to which the retailer's store would blend with the existing structure of retail trade in the community. This does not mean that a retailer should only consider locating small stores in communities that presently tend to have small stores. But if there currently are only small stores in a community, then before entering with a large store the retailer should make certain that the demand factors would support a large establishment.

SQUARE FEET PER EMPLOYEE

A measure that combines two major supply factors in retailing—store space and labor—is square feet of space per employee. A high number for this statistic in a community is evidence that each employee is able to handle more space. This could be due to either a high level of retail technology in the community or more self-service retailing. Since retail technology is fairly constant across communities, any difference in square feet per employee is most often due to the level of service being provided. In communities currently characterized by retailers offering a high level of service, there may be a significant opportunity for new retailers oriented toward self-service because such retail enterprises can offer lower prices to compensate for the self-service by the customer.

GROWTH IN STORES

The analyst should look at the rate of growth in the number of stores over the last one to five years. When growth is rapid, then on average the community will have better-located stores with more contemporary atmospheres. Recently located stores will better match the existing demographics of the community. Also their atmosphere will better suit the current tastes of the marketplace and they will tend to incorporate the latest in retail technology. The strength of retail competition will be greater when the community has recently experienced rapid growth in the number of stores.

QUALITY OF COMPETITION

The three supply factors discussed previously reflect the quantity of competition. Analysts also need to look at the strength or quality of competition. They should attempt to identify the major retail chains or local retailers in each market and evaluate the strength of each. Answers to questions such as the following would provide valuable insights: What is their market share or profitability? How promotion and price oriented are they? Are they customer oriented? Do they tend to react to new market entrants by cutting prices, increasing advertising, or improving customer service? A retailer would think twice before competing with Wal-Mart on price, Bloomingdale's on fashion, or Nordstrom on service. Retailing in Action 10.2 illustrates how supply and demand factors in a community influence the retailer's strategy developments.

A RECAP ON HOW TO USE SUPPLY FACTORS

How does the analyst use these supply factors to assess market attractiveness? The analyst must determine what configuration of supply factors yields an attractive market from a supply point of view. Consider the hypothetical

RETAILING IN ACTION

10.2 How the Great Atlantic & Pacific Tea Company, Inc. Tailors Its Strategy to Community Characteristics

The most attractive food market in the United States is the New York metropolitan area. However, this area, with more than 10 million people, is comprised of communities with quite different characteristics. Consequently, A&P has designed its stores and their merchandising strategy to target the characteristics of local communities. In brief, the firm has recognized the critical role location plays in the development of strategy. Let's review how this segmented marketing approach has been used in the New York metropolitan area.

With its Food Emporium stores, A&P has a strategy of providing convenience and service in an upscale urban market. The approach is to be a combination supermarket and gourmet store. Food Emporium is a favorite among discriminating Manhattan shoppers, and has also developed a loyal following in affluent Westchester County, Long Island, and Connecticut suburbs. These stores have become known as supermarkets with a distinctive gourmet flair and a cosmopolitan product assortment attuned to the city's many cultural influences.

Waldbaum's, another A&P division, "continues to appeal to New York's real melting pot—the hard-working, no-nonsense shoppers who demand value yet respect their longstanding heritage . . ." Several Waldbaum's prototypes exist; however, each is designed for promotional, high-volume merchandising, as communicated by the chain's advertising slogan, "Come Share Our Values." The Waldbaum's chain serves Long Island, Westchester County, and all the boroughs of New York, outside Manhattan.

A&P is also developing its own superstores under its A&P logo. "In the more affluent, executive communities of New York's Westchester County and New Jersey, A&P continues to develop superstores incorporating the Food Emporium-style emphasis on upscale product selection, service and shopping atmosphere, but spread across a much greater variety of product lines and sizes."

A&P has also developed the Sav-A-Center superstore format with a strong price emphasis to appeal to more price-sensitive population groups. The more "densely populated suburbs of New York generally pose different demographics—more 'traditional' households, greater ethnic concentrations, young couples starting out in condominium or garden apartment developments, more senior citizens, and generally more moderate incomes. The A&P Sav-A-Centers have massive product displays, metal grocery racking and bold price signage."

Finally, A&P maintains its traditional neighborhood stores. The "smaller, neighborhood markets continue to compete effectively-and-profitably—by bridging the price/variety/service gap between larger and smaller competitors. Easy access and a tailored product assortment enable these stores to fill a variety of shopping needs . . . But, the popularity of the neighborhood supermarket is based on more than location and convenience. By sponsoring recreational and civic activities, heading local food donation programs and supporting other charitable endeavors, A&P stores become focal points in their communities . . . a degree of involvement that develops friendships as well as customers."

Source: The Great Atlantic & Pacific Tea Company, Inc. Annual Report to Stockholders, 1989.

ILLUSTRATION 10.3
Many large retailers create different store formats, such as A&P's Sav-A-Center, for different types of retail locations.

appliance retailer we have been discussing. It might be decided that the following supply factors would characterize an attractive market:

1. Average store size of less than 7,500 square feet. This retailer plans to open 15,000-square-foot stores and wants to be twice as large as the average appliance retailer.
2. Average square feet of floor space per employee of more than 1,200. The retailer plans to have one employee for each 600 square feet of floor space in order to offer roughly twice the customer service level as the average competitor.
3. Growth in appliance stores of less than 15 percent over the last 10 years. Recall that the potential markets were screened to rule out any markets that had growth in population of less than 20 percent over the last 10 years. This retailer wants to enter a market where the growth in stores has *not* kept pace with the growth in population.
4. The quality of competition is not as important; however, it would be ideal if it were low to average. This retailer believes that if markets exist where the preceding demand and supply criteria are met, the quality of competition should not be a deterring factor.

SECONDARY SOURCES OF INFORMATION

Our discussion of retail gravity theory, central place theory, saturation theory, and demand and supply factors has provided us with a frame of reference for identifying the most attractive markets to consider for a store site. More complete, statistically based frameworks are available, but they are beyond the scope of this text. The most important point to keep in mind is that before retailers select a location, they should identify the communities that represent attractive opportunities. The data necessary to do this type of analysis are available in publications such as *Census of Retail Trades, County and City Data Book, Census of Housing and Population, Sales Management's Survey of Buying Power,* and *Editor & Publisher Market Guide.* Let's look at an example of a retailer using the data from these publications and the tools presented earlier in this chapter.

A SIMPLE EXAMPLE

XYZ Corporation, a retail chain specializing in general-merchandise goods, is considering expansion. The firm is looking at two different trading areas for possible location of its new store. These trading areas were found by using Reilly's law and are Peoria and Joliet, Illinois. For each area, the firm will develop a **buying power index (BPI)**, a single-weighted measure combining effective buying income (personal income less all tax and nontax payments such as Social Security), retail sales, and population size into an overall indicator of a market's potential. Generally, business firms use the following formula, which was developed by *Sales and Marketing Management* magazine, for BPI:

$$\text{Buying power index} = 0.5(\text{the area's percentage of U.S. effective buying income}) \\ + 0.3(\text{the area's percentage of U.S. retail sales}) \\ + 0.2(\text{the area's percentage of U.S. population})$$

Using data that can be easily obtained from the previously named publications, we can develop the BPI for each city:

$$\begin{aligned} \text{BPI (Joliet)} &= 0.5(0.1652) + 0.3(0.1213) + 0.2(0.1567) \\ &= 0.1503 \\ \text{BPI (Peoria)} &= 0.5(0.1537) + 0.3(0.1396) + 0.2(0.1347) \\ &= 0.1456 \end{aligned}$$

As you can see, the BPI for Joliet is more attractive. However, the three components that make up the BPI should be carefully studied. Joliet has more of the U.S. population than Peoria although it has a lower percentage of the retail sales. At the same time it has a larger percentage of the effective buying income in the United States than does Peoria. All this suggests that Joliet may be a better opportunity for XYZ Corporation to locate within. However, it should be noted that we have not looked at supply factors and to make this analysis complete we would need to determine the amount of retail selling space (in square footage) available in each of these communities and relate this to the number of households or population so we could assess if one market is more or less saturated than the other.

SUMMARY

Store location decisions are important because of their short-run and long-run natures, their investment requirements, and their effects on the other elements of the retail mix. The location decision is often considered to be uncontrollable, that is, impossible or very difficult to change. However, merchandising and pricing decisions are paramount, and location decisions should be adapted to these key retail strategy variables.

The choice of retail location involves three decisions: (1) identifying the most attractive markets, (2) evaluating the demand and supply within each market, and (3) selecting the best site (or sites) available. This chapter has concentrated on the first decision.

We began our analysis of market selection by looking at three location theories and how these theories can aid in the location decision. Reilly's law of retail gravitation assumed that the population size of a community served as a magnet for the surrounding areas and drew customers into its business district. Christaller assumed communities could be ranked by looking at goods and services available within them. The third theory, the index of retail saturation, compares the total demand for the product under question with the availability of retailers to service or supply that product. We concluded our discussion on market selection by looking into other factors that could influence a community's supply (square feet per store, square feet per employee, growth in stores, and quality of competition) or demand (market potential and household and community characteristics).

QUESTIONS FOR DISCUSSION

1. Explain the importance of the concepts of range and threshold as they relate to retail location decisions.
2. A chain of dry cleaners has done some research that suggests that people will not travel more than 5 miles from their place of residence to patronize a dry cleaner. Furthermore, it believes that it needs a population of 22,000 to be successful. It is considering establishing a policy of only opening outlets in communities that have a population density of at least 600 people per square mile. Evaluate the reasonableness of this policy.
3. Christaller assumed that the market area surrounding a market center was hexagonal. Based on your own experience do you believe that this is true today?
4. What is the index of retail saturation? How can it be used in making location decisions?
5. What is the buying power index (BPI)? How is it used?
6. Calculate the buying power indexes for the following three cities:

City	Percentage of U.S. Effective Buying Income	Percentage of U.S. Retail Sales	Percentage of U.S. Population
Arkon City	0.005	0.006	0.004
Binghamtown	0.006	0.004	0.005
Cochran	0.004	0.005	0.007

7. Compute the index for retail saturation for the following three markets:

	A	B	C
Retail expenditures per household	$510	$575	$610
Square feet of retail space	600,000	488,000	808,000
Number of households	112,000	91,000	147,000

Which market is most attractive? What additional data would you find helpful in determining the attractiveness of the three markets?

8. Temple is 64 miles from Beckville (population 220,000) and 32 miles in the opposite direction from Waco (population 110,000). Using Reilly's law, how much money will the citizens of Temple spend in Beckville for every dollar they spend in Waco?

9. If we say that location is an uncontrollable factor for a retailer, does this mean that a retailer with 15 years remaining on his or her lease should make an immediate study of the trends expected 15 years from now, or that he or she should do nothing since location is beyond his or her control?

10. Using Reilly's law, construct a general trading area for your community.

11. For a pair of cities of your choosing, attempt to gather as much secondary data on food stores as possible. Consider both supply and demand factors. Collect the following data: (a) average square feet per store, (b) square feet per employee, (c) growth in stores, (d) average household income, (e) average household size, (f) population density, and (g) age profile of population growth over the last five to ten years. Compare these cities on the basis of the data you gather. Identify the opportunities for grocery retailers in each city.

MANAGEMENT MEMO

Your grandparents started a grocery store in Springerville in 1928 when the town had 4,000 people. In 1962, when your father graduated from college, he went to work in the business and in 1969 purchased the store from his parents. Springerville continued to be a small community, and in 1980 it had only 4,400 people. At this time, the sales per square foot at the store were $210. The 1980s, however, were a period of spectacular growth, and by 1990 the town had a population of 9,400 people in 3,800 households, and sales per square foot had reached $685 at the store. The growth was due both to increased employment from a paper goods factory that raised its employment from 120 to 300 people during the 1980s, and an increasing number of families from a large metropolitan area of 700,000 people, 48 miles to the north building homes in Springerville due to the low cost of real estate. Six hundred people in Springerville work in this distant community. During the summer you were in Springerville working at the grocery store. You mentioned that Springerville was understored in terms of grocery stores and that you wouldn't be surprised if someone else built a store in the community. Your Dad looked surprised and asked you to put down your thoughts in a one- or two-page memo.

BOARDROOM REPORT

Home Depot is a warehouse-style chain of home-improvement centers that appeals to active do-it-yourself home repair/remodeling enthusiasts and local contractors/builders. As a recent recruit into its management training program, you have been singled out to present a brief report to the board of directors on reasons why the firm should not ignore foreign market expansion. Prepare a three-to-five-minute report on the rationale for considering foreign market expansion and suggestions on how Home Depot might begin to consider this type of location decision.

SUGGESTED READINGS

Carn, Neil, Joseph Rabianski, Ronald Rocater, and Maury Seldin. *Real Estate Market Analysis: Techniques and Applications.* Englewood Cliffs, N.J.: Prentice-Hall, Inc., 1988.

Clapp, John M., and Stephen D. Messner, eds. *Real Estate Market Analysis: Methods and Applications.* New York: Praeger, 1988.

Ghosh, Avijit, and Charles A. Ingene, eds. *Spatial Analysis in Marketing: Theory, Methods, and Applications.* Greenwich, Conn.: JAI Press, Inc., 1991.

Ghosh, Avijit, and Gerald Rushton, eds. *Spatial Analysis and Location Allocation Modeling.* New York: Van Nostrand Reinhold, Inc., 1987.

ENDNOTES

1. "A 1980s Style Book Is Just Now Reaching an Awakening Mexico," *Wall Street Journal,* 18 December 1991, A1, A12. "Wal-Mart Plans to Enlarge Mexico Venture," *Wall Street Journal,* 1 June 1992, B3.
2. William J. Reilly, "Methods for the Study of Retail Relationships," Research Monograph no. 4 (Austin, Tex.: Bureau of Business Research, The University of Texas, 1929).
3. Reilly, 48-49.
4. P. D. Converse, "New Laws of Retail Gravitation," *Journal of Marketing* (January 1949): 379-84.
5. "Podunk Is Beckoning," *Business Week,* 23 December 1991, 76.
6. Michael Jay Polonsky, Denise G. Jarratt, and Charles Sturt, "An Expenditure Based Estimate of Outshopping and Its Implications for Rural Areas: The Australian Case," in Terry Childers et al., eds., *1991 AMA Winter Educators' Conference: Marketing Theory and Applications* (Chicago: American Marketing Association 1991), 90-98.
7. Walter Christaller, *Central Places in Southern Germany,* Carlisle W. Baskin, trans. (Englewood Cliffs, N.J.: Prentice-Hall, Inc., 1966). This is a translation of Christaller's 1935 book.
8. C. Samuel Craig, Avijit Ghosh, and Sara McLafferty, "Models of Retail Location Process: A Review," *Journal of Retailing* (Spring 1984): 6.
9. Avijit Ghosh, "The Value of a Mall and Other Insights from a Revised Central Place Model," *Journal of Retailing* (Spring 1986): 79-97.
10. A. Losch, *The Economics of Location,* W. Woglam and W. Stopler, trans. (New Haven: Yale University Press, 1943).
11. John Urquhart Marshall, *The Location of Service Towns: An Approach to the Analysis of Central Place Systems* (Toronto: University of Toronto Press, 1969), 18-21.
12. William Applebaum and Saul B. Cohen, "Trading Area Networks and Problems of Store Saturation," *Journal of Retailing* (Winter 1961-1962): 35-36. Reprinted with permission of the *Journal of Retailing.*
13. Bernard LaLonde, "The Logistics of Retail Location," in William D. Stevens, ed., *Fall American Marketing Proceedings* (Chicago: American Marketing Association, 1961), 572.
14. Charles A. Ingene, "Structural Determinants of Market Potential," *Journal of Retailing* (Spring 1984): 37-64 and Charles A. Ingene and Robert F. Lusch, "Market Selection Decisions for Department Stores," *Journal of Retailing* (Fall 1980): 21-40.
15. "A Great Place to Invest—If You Don't Mind the Wait," *Business Week,* 1 October 1990, 145.
16. Rom J. Markin, Jr., *Retailing Management* 2nd ed. (New York: Macmillan, 1977), 150.
17. Charles A. Ingene and Robert F. Lusch, "A Model of Retail Structure," in Jagdish Sheth, *Research in Marketing* 5 (1981): 101-64.
18. Mobility can be viewed as either a household characteristic or a community characteristic. We chose to treat it as a community characteristic because the design of the community, the availability of public transportation, and the cost of operating an auto in any given area are determinants of mobility and are themselves characteristic of the community.

CHAPTER 11

STORE SITE ANALYSIS

OVERVIEW

This chapter completes the discussion of our retail location decision process by describing how to identify the most attractive sites in each market and then how to select the best one or ones available. We begin by considering the three basic types of location: central business district, shopping center, and freestanding units. Next, the chapter looks at how a retailer analyzes the demand and supply alternatives within a given market for the merchandise offerings under consideration. We follow with a discussion of the various attributes retailers consider as they select a specific site in a target market and finally look at how to compute a pro forma return on investment model for a store at a proposed site.

STORE SITE ANALYSIS

I. Types of Location
    A. Central Business District
    B. Shopping Center
    C. Freestanding Locations
    D. A Note on PUDs
    E. A Note on Service Retailing
II. Evaluation of Demand and Supply Within the Market
    A. Size of Trading Area
    B. Description of Trading Area
    C. Demand Density

D. Supply Density
E. Site Availability
III. Site Selection Decision Process
A. The 100 Percent Location
B. Nature of Site
C. Traffic Characteristics
D. Type of Neighbor
E. Lease versus Buy
F. Terms of Lease
G. Pro Forma Return on Investment Model
1. Total Sales
2. Total Assets
3. Net Profit
4. Return on Assets
IV. Measuring Performance
V. Summary

In Chapter 10 we discussed several methods for evaluating and identifying the most attractive markets for a retail store. Once retailers have identified several good markets, the next task is to perform a more detailed analysis of each. This analysis should consist of an evaluation of the demand and supply within each market, by census tract or other meaningful geographic area, and should be augmented by an identification of the most attractive sites currently available within each market. The third and final step will be the selection of the best possible site. We refer to these second and third steps in the retail location decision process as the **within-market opportunity analysis.**

TYPES OF LOCATION

Before retailers can begin to evaluate the different sites available, they must first decide what type of location is best suited for their product offerings. For example, Claires (a retailer of costume jewelry) has decided that it will locate in shopping centers and not in freestanding stores, because it sells intercept merchandise and relies on the high traffic in a shopping mall for its patronage. Given that this fundamental decision has been made, Claires need only look at the available or planned shopping centers within markets for potential sites. Note that this type of location decision doesn't have to be made each time the retailer decides to enter a new market. Rather, the decision can be made once, and if market conditions remain unchanged, it can guide all future expansion.

A retailer can select from three basic types of location: the central business district, the shopping center, and freestanding units. No single type of location is always better than the others. Many retailers have been successful in all three location types (e.g., McDonald's and Radio Shack). Each type of location has its own characteristics relating to the composition of competing stores, parking facilities, affinities with nonretail businesses (such as office buildings, hospitals, universities), and other factors.

CENTRAL BUSINESS DISTRICT

Historically, many retailers were located in the **central business district (CBD),** usually an unplanned shopping area around the geographic point at which all public transportation systems converge. Many traditional department stores are located in the CBD along with a good selection of specialty shops. The makeup or mix of retailers in a CBD is generally not the result of any planning but depends on history, retail trends, and luck.

In 1991, Sony opened an innovative store in downtown Chicago on North Michigan Avenue and plans similar stores in New York City and Los Angeles. The stores are called "Sony Gallery of Consumer Electronics" and are intended not to sell merchandise but to offer in-depth product information and demonstrations in elaborate "lifestyle" settings. In addition, these Sony stores will showcase new Sony technologies that most retail stores don't yet carry. To avoid competing with other retailers that sell its products, the Sony Gallery will sell only at full price and cheerfully refer visitors to discount retailers that handle Sony products. By locating on North Michigan Avenue in downtown Chicago, Sony has been able to generate very high quality traffic and thus use the store to bolster its image.[1]

ILLUSTRATION 11.1

Many retailers still operate in central business districts and other urban locations.

The CBD has several strengths and weaknesses to consider. Among its strengths are easy access to public transportation; wide range of product assortment; variety in images, prices, and services; and proximity to commercial activities. Some weaknesses are inadequate (and usually expensive) parking, older stores, high rents and taxes, traffic and delivery congestion, potentially high crime rate, and the generally decaying conditions of many inner cities. Higher rents are an especially unattractive feature. For example, in some CBDs such as in Chicago, Los Angeles, or New York, rents of $75 per square foot are not unusual.

Often, the weakness of CBDs has resulted in a retail situation known as "inner-city" or "ghetto" retailing, which occurs when only the poorest citizens are left in an urban area. Traditionally, product and service offerings in these areas have decreased, while prices have held steady or even increased. However, good merchandise selection, careful security, and heavy public relations are evident some retailers, such as First National Supermarkets and Woolworth's, which operates 450 of its 1,000 variety stores in inner-city areas.[2] Such retailers have found success in these markets by tailoring their inventories to the special needs and tastes of inner-city residents. In Retailing in Action 11.1 we explore some of the opportunities in ghetto retailing.

A newer type of central business district is being created in larger cities by the expansion of secondary business districts and neighborhood business

RETAILING IN ACTION

11.1 Ghetto Retailing: Ethics and Profits

Many of America's inner cities have become ghettos that large national and regional retail chains have avoided. At the same time, free enterprise and U.S. capitalists view Poland, Bolivia, and China as market opportunities. Is this ethical? Why ignore opportunities in the United States that are probably no more risky than ventures in politically unstable developing economies?

The fact is that America's inner cities are often the province of government and represent as much socialism and government intervention as are found just about anywhere. The ghettos are starved for private investment and entrepreneurial spirit. And the opportunity exists! For example, East Harlem has a median household income of $14,500, which—although it is only one-half the national median—results in an aggregate neighborhood income of $1.35 billion annually. And that doesn't include income from the underground economy and purchasing power from food stamps.

Not all retailers ignore this opportunity. For example, Woolworth operates close to one-half its 1,000 variety stores in predominately minority areas (including Harlem). In these areas, the firm does extremely well because the competition is weak—Woolworth can offer lower prices, better merchandise, and better service than many mom-and-pop stores.

Source: Based in part on "The Ghetto's Hidden Wealth," *Fortune*, 24 July 1991, 167-74.

districts. A **secondary business district (SBD)** is a shopping area that is smaller than the CBD and that evolves around at least one department or variety store at a major street intersection. A **neighborhood business district (NBD)** is a shopping area that evolves to satisfy the convenience-oriented shopping needs of a neighborhood. The NBD generally contains several small stores, with the major retailer being either a supermarket or a variety store, and is located on a major artery of a residential area.

The factor that distinguishes these business districts from a shopping center is that they are largely unplanned. Like CBDs, SBDs and NBDs usually evolve partially by planning, partially by luck, and partially by accident. No one planned that there would be two department stores, four jewelry stores, two camera shops, three leather shops, twelve apparel shops, and one theater in an SBD. That happened by chance, and there is nothing to stop the camera shop from selling out to a popcorn store. Long-range planning comes about only when the business district is under someone's control.

SHOPPING CENTER

A **shopping center** is a centrally owned or managed shopping district that is planned, has balanced tenancy (the stores complement each other in merchandise offerings), and is surrounded by parking facilities. A shopping center has one or more **anchor stores** (major department stores that are expected to draw customers to the center) and a variety of smaller stores. To ensure that these smaller stores complement each other, the shopping center often specifies the proportion of total space that can be occupied by each type of retailer. Similarly, the center's management places limits on the merchandise lines that each retailer may carry. A unified, cooperative advertising and promotional strategy is followed by all the retailers in the center.

A shopping center location can offer a retailer several major advantages over a CBD location. Among them are:

1. Heavy traffic resulting from the wide range of product offerings
2. Proximity to population
3. Cooperative planning and sharing of common costs
4. Access to highways and availability of parking
5. Lower crime rate
6. Clean, neat environment

Despite these favorable reasons for locating in a shopping center, retailers in shopping centers face several disadvantages. Among the limitations are:

1. Inflexible store hours; the retailer must stay open the hours of the center and can't be open at other times (e.g., after 10 p.m.)
2. Higher rents
3. Restrictions as to the merchandise the retailer may sell
4. Inflexible operations and required membership in the center's merchant organization

5. Possibility of too much competition and the fact that much of the traffic is not interested in a particular retailer's product offering
6. Dominance of the smaller stores by the anchor tenant
7. Inattention to amenities that make shopping more enjoyable and easy, such as convenient and easy to find restrooms, drinking fountains, and sitting areas

Despite the fact that these restrictions are common, exceptions are sometimes negotiated. For instance, Chick-fil-A operates fast-food restaurants in shopping centers but does not open on Sunday since it is against corporate policy.

Central place theory assumes that consumers patronize the nearest outlet; however, it has been shown that 30 to 50 percent of consumers tend to make a disproportionate number of trips to large shopping centers. Shopping center image and shopping center personality all attract various subsets of consumers, giving retailers located at these centers a competitive advantage over other retailers. Therefore, it is extremely important that a retailer considering a shopping center location be aware of the makeup, image, preferences, and personality of the center under consideration. One study of a specialty apparel chain found that the chain would have lower sales and profits in shopping centers with Sears, JCPenney, or Montgomery Ward stores. This was attributed to the fact that the chain sold moderately priced fashion apparel for the youthful figure, which was easily compared to the three general merchandisers with their larger stores and assortments of similar merchandise.[3]

There are six different types of shopping centers, each with a distinct function.

1. A **neighborhood center** provides for the sale of convenience goods (foods, drugs, and sundries) and personal services (laundry and dry cleaning, barbering, shoe repairing, etc.) for the day-to-day living needs of the immediate neighborhood. In the past such a center had a supermarket as the principal tenant; now the supermarkets are often being replaced by home-improvement centers or discount department stores. The neighborhood center is the smallest type of shopping center and, as a rule of thumb, has approximately 50,000 square feet in gross leasable space.
2. The **community center** is next in size. In addition to the convenience goods and personal services of the neighborhood center, community centers provide a wider range of facilities for the sale of soft lines (apparel for men, women, and children) and hard lines (hardware and appliances). In addition to a supermarket, community centers are built around a junior department store (not a full-line one), a variety store, or a discount department store as the major tenant. The typical size is 150,000 square feet of gross leasable area, but this can vary. About two-thirds of all shopping centers in the United States are neighborhood or community types, and they account for about one-third of total retail sales.
3. **Regional centers** provide for the sale of general merchandise, apparel, furniture, and home furnishings, as well as a range of services and

recreational facilities. They are built around one or two full-line department stores of generally not less than 100,000 square feet each. Their typical size is considered to be 400,000 square feet of gross leasable area. The regional center is the second-largest type of shopping center. It provides services typical of a central business district but is not as extensive as a super-regional.

4. **Super-regional centers** provide extensive variety in general merchandise, apparel, furniture, and home furnishings, as well as a variety of services and recreational facilities. They are built around at least three major department stores of generally not less than 100,000 square feet each. The typical size of a super-regional is between 600,000 and 1,400,000 square feet of gross leasable area. Super-regionals, while making up only 1 percent of the total number of centers, account for over 10 percent of sales. The *Guinness Book of World Records* ranks the 110-acre West Edmonton Mall (Alberta, Canada) as the world's largest, with over 800 shops, several dozen restaurants, 34 theaters, an 18-hole miniature golf course, a 10-acre water park for swimming and sunning under tanning lamps, two dozen amusement rides, and a 360-room hotel for extended stays. It's all indoors, under one roof.[4] Next on the list is the 4.2-million-square-foot "Mall of America" in Bloomington, Minnesota (the twin cities area of Minneapolis/St. Paul). This center, which opened in 1992, has an amusement park, over 400 stores, and 12,000 parking spaces.

5. **Theme centers** are shopping centers located in places of historical interest and where a lot of tourist traffic is generated. An example of a theme center is Faneuil Hall in Boston. Theme centers vary in size but are usually

ILLUSTRATION 11.2

The creation of theme centers, such as Faneuil Hall in Boston, has become a popular method of converting old, existing real estate in urban areas.

at least 100,000 square feet and less than 500,000 square feet. They often consist of specialty stores and have no anchor tenant such as a department store. Merchandise is heavily concentrated on intercept merchandise and especially the type of items that people will purchase on vacation, such as T-shirts, low-to-moderate-priced jewelry and giftware, sports clothing, and specialty foods.

6. **Factory outlet centers** specialize in manufacturer's outlets that dispose of excess merchandise and factory seconds. Traditionally, factory outlet stores were freestanding locations near their respective manufacturer's factory. However, in the mid-1980s, they began to gather together in specially designed malls located away from the factories. In 1982, there were fewer than 20 factory outlet malls in the United States; 10 years later there were over 100.[5] A typical center will have 20 to 80 stores and will be located away from major retail centers to avoid competing with other retailers. For example, San Marcos, Texas (a college town) has a factory outlet mall with about 75 manufacturer-owned stores that sell big-name goods at 25 to 75 percent off regular retail prices.

The preceding categorization of shopping centers is not exhaustive, since exceptions and innovations always develop. For example, recently many larger airports have developed shopping concourses. And enterprising retailers have seen these locations as excellent for store expansion. Bloom-

ILLUSTRATION 11.3

Factory outlet centers and stores, such as Outlets Ltd., have become a popular and successful distribution channel for manufacturers.

ingdales of New York opened its first Bloomie's Express in New York's Kennedy Airport in 1986 and now has stores in airports in Phoenix, Baltimore/Washington, and Cleveland. Benjamin Books is located in over 25 airports and Pizza Hut, Burger King, and Dunkin' Donuts are realizing the value of locating in airport shopping concourses. Other shopping centers are developing that only offer automobile repair services. Here a group of independent firms such as a muffler shop, a tire store, a transmission repair shop, a paint and body shop, a tune-up shop, and so forth will locate in a shopping center especially designed to offer auto repair services. It is interesting to note that although auto dealers historically sought freestanding locations, there is a trend toward auto-malls in which 5 to 15 dealers all locate their dealerships on a common ground with uniform landscaping, amenities, and operating hours. And other innovations will no doubt develop as shopping centers evolve into new formats.

Shopping centers are popular locations for retailers. They first appeared in 1950 and now account for nearly 55 percent of all retail sales, excluding automobile dealers and gasoline service stations, in the United States.

The central role of shopping centers in America is further illustrated by the following facts[6]:

- In a typical month, over 172 million adults shop at shopping centers—94 percent of the population over 18 years of age.
- 70 percent of the adult population shops at regional malls and does so an average of 3.9 times per month.
- 89 percent of the adult population shops at community and neighborhood centers and does so an average of 7.1 times per month.
- 9.9 million people are employed in shopping centers, equal to about 1 of every 10 nonfarm workers in the United States.

Despite the popularity of shopping malls as retail locations, they are often difficult for a new retailer to get into. Shopping mall owners, especially for regional and super-regional malls, are very risk averse and do not like to gamble on an unproven retail format unless it was developed by a large, well-known retail organization. For example, Rebecca Matthias, owner of a chain of maternity wear stores called Mothers Work, had a very difficult time getting into a mall. "The malls are like an expensive club," she says. "If you're not a member, you can't join."[7] Rebecca finally got her first mall store in 1988 in an upscale mall in King of Prussia (a suburb of Philadelphia). Since business boomed, she has developed a track record and now regularly receives offers from malls looking to lease space. There is, however, one method by which a fledging retail entrepreneur can enter a shopping center without too much difficulty. This method involves using a kiosk or push cart in a shopping center. Shopping centers will allow a certain number of such merchants as temporary tenants in their mall. They may sell giftware, T-shirts, or food or provide services such as monogramming. Kiosks or push carts are excellent for selling intercept merchandise.

Anchor stores are extremely important to the success of a center. They attract customers and project images. Anchors tend to be either mass merchandisers with national reputations and distribution (JCPenney, Sears, Montgomery Ward) or branches of national, regional, or local department stores (Bloomingdale's, Dillard's, Robinson's, and Famous-Barr). Neighborhood centers typically use a major supermarket chain for anchors. The center's other tenants rely on anchors to draw customers for their target markets to the centers.

However, department stores in shopping centers today are the same as the old retail giants of the downtown era and are facing another crisis: How do you change a high-volume organization that offers "more of everything" into a much smaller branch anchor? Even the largest branch store is seldom more than 250,000 square feet—less than half the size of its downtown predecessor. In many areas today, we have now seen a decrease in the importance of the center's department stores because, as a group, the center's specialty stores have more space and are far more effective in penetrating specific target markets.[8] Thus, the center or mall of the future will be identified not so much by the anchor but as a single location with a combination of stores.

Two other factors will affect the typical mall's appearance over the next decade. Many malls were built in the early 1970s, most with original leases lasting for 20–25 years. That fact, combined with the advancing age of the population, means changes are sure to occur in shopping centers. Shopping centers and malls in the year 2000 must be ready to respond to these changes. The tenant mix will be changing over the next decade. The number of service-oriented tenants, such as health-care clinics, banks, insurance offices, travel agencies, athletic clubs, and so on, will probably increase so that shopping, health-care, financial, and recreation needs can be met in one place. Also, the architecture and physical layout of the centers will have to consider the needs of the older population.

FREESTANDING LOCATIONS

The last location alternative available to the retailer is to locate as a freestanding store. A **freestanding retailer** generally locates along major traffic arteries, without any adjacent retailers selling competing products to share traffic. Freestanding retailing offers several advantages, which include:

1. Lack of direct competition
2. Generally lower rents
3. Freedom in operations and hours
4. Facilities that can be adapted to individual needs
5. Inexpensive parking

Freestanding retailing does have some limitations:

1. Lack of drawing power of complementary stores

2. Difficulties in attracting customers for the initial visit
3. Higher advertising and promotional costs
4. Operating costs that cannot be shared with others
5. Need to build in some cases rather than rent
6. Restrictive zoning laws may limit some activities

The difficulties of drawing customers to an isolated or freestanding store and then holding onto them is the reason only large, well-known retailers should attempt it. Small retailers may be unable to develop a loyal customer base, since customers may be unwilling to travel to a freestanding store that does not have a wide assortment of products and a local or national reputation. Furthermore, only retailers that primarily sell destination merchandise should consider freestanding locations. Kmart and Wal-Mart, as well as many convenience stores and gasoline stations, have used freestanding locations successfully in the past, and discount appliance centers and wholesale clubs are using them today.

A NOTE ON PUDS

A location alternative that could involve either a freestanding location, a shopping center, or a neighborhood business district is a **planned urban development (PUD).** A PUD is a totally conceived and supervised community including housing, retail, and business activity. One of the pioneers in developing PUDs is Mission Viejo Company, which developed Mission Viejo, California, in the mid-1960s. Recently, it completed its last retail phase in Mission Viejo—Trabaco Hills Center, a 154,000-square-foot mixed-use center to contain retail stores, restaurants, a cinema, auto service and gas station, and medical/professional offices. The advantages of a PUD include controlled retail competition and planned population demographics. PUDs are more common in California, Arizona, and Texas, but they are occurring even in the East. For example, North Shore Properties is a 2,150-acre PUD in eastern Long Island that will be developed during the 1990s.[9]

A NOTE ON SERVICE RETAILING

The location decision is just as important to service retailers as it is to the retailers of physical products. Some service retailers are an exception, however, since their products are delivered directly to the consumer. Some examples of services for which location is not important are plumbers, house painters, repair services, and lawn care firms. In these cases, the retailer's location is the consumer's home or office, and travel time to the consumer might be the only location consideration involved.

Most service retailers are visited by the consumer, however, and location is important. Car washes, dry cleaners, shoe repair stands, and rental retailers are all examples of service retailers that must be concerned about the convenience of their locations. For this reason, many shoe repair stores are beginning to pay a premium to locate in busy shopping malls, just as car-rental agencies pay airport managements. Most consumers do not want to go out of their way to have their shoes repaired but will do it only if it is convenient. Essentially shoe repair is an intercept service and thus traffic is critical to the success of a shoe repair stand.

After deciding which type of location is most desirable based on an analysis of existing locations (if available), competitor's actions, and the firm's overall strategy, retailers—of both services and products—can begin to evaluate the various sites available in each market.

EVALUATION OF DEMAND AND SUPPLY WITHIN THE MARKET

Once retailers have identified the top-ranking markets in terms of opportunity and made the decision as to the type of location desired, they next need to perform a more detailed analysis of the desired markets to determine site location.[10] This analysis consists of evaluating the density of demand and supply of various areas within the chosen market by census tract, ZIP code, or some other meaningful geographic area, and then identifying the most attractive sites available for new stores within each market.[11]

One of the advantages of using census tract data is that such data are published regularly by the Census Bureau. Census tracts are relatively small statistical subdivisions that vary in population from about 2,500 to 8,000 and are designed to include fairly homogeneous populations. They are most often found in cities and in counties of metropolitan areas, that is, the more densely settled portions of the nation. In addition, about 3,000 census tracts were established in 221 nonmetropolitan counties, along with five states that were entirely tracted: Connecticut, Delaware, Hawaii, New Jersey, and Rhode Island. In all, there are over 43,300 census tracts. However, with the development of the TIGER system (discussed in Retailing in Action 10.1), it is possible for firms such as CACI to provide the retailer with detailed demographics on geographic areas much smaller than a census tract. Data can also be provided on different configurations of trade areas. For instance, if the retailer wants to know the demographics within a 1-, 3- or 5-mile radius of a proposed site, these data can be easily generated by CACI or other demographic supply houses; if the retailer decides the trade area is not a circle but is a polygon or some other shape, the data can be just as easily generated. The TIGER files have made retail site analysis considerably easier.

SIZE OF TRADING AREA

In Chapter 10 we discussed the general trading area of a community. Now we will examine how to determine and evaluate the trading area of specific sites within markets. In short, we will show how to estimate the geographic area from which a store located at a particular site will be able to attract customers.

At the same time that Reilly and Christaller were developing theories to determine the trading area for communities, William Applebaum designed a technique built around **customer spottings** to determine and evaluate trade areas. For each $100 in weekly store sales, one customer was randomly selected or "spotted" for an interview. These spottings usually didn't require much time since the interviewer only asked about demographic information, shopping habits, and some pertinent consumer attitudes toward the store and its competitors. After the home addresses of the shoppers were plotted on a map, the analyst could make some inferences about trading area size and the competition.[12]

Other techniques used to define a trading area include analysis of checks customers write, credit records, and license plates to see who purchases and where they reside. Today, it is possible for some retailers that have fully computerized their point-of-sale systems to assign each regular customer an identification number that can be captured at point-of-sale and thus regularly update their trading area maps.

It is relatively easy using one of the preceding techniques to define the trading area of an existing store. For a new store, the task is not so easy. The conventional wisdom about the correlates of trading area size can be summarized as follows:

1. Stores that sell convenience goods have smaller trading areas than those that sell shopping or specialty goods.
2. As consumer mobility increases, the size of the store's trading area increases.
3. As the size of a store increases, its trading area increases because it can stock a broader and deeper assortment of merchandise, which will attract households from greater distances.
4. As the distance between competing stores increases, their trading areas will increase.

In Exhibit 11.1 we illustrate how the size of the trading area is influenced by these four factors.

Natural and artificial obstacles such as railroads, rivers, mountains, and freeways can abruptly alter the boundaries of a trading area. This is illustrated in Exhibit 11.2.

One of the most widely accepted approaches to defining and estimating a store's trading area was developed by David Huff,[13] a marketing professor at the University of Texas-Austin. Huff defines a **trading area** as "a geographically delineated region containing potential customers for whom there exists a probability greater than zero of their purchasing a given class of products or services offered for sale by a particular firm or by a particular agglomeration of firms."[14] Thus, a trading area can be thought of as a series of *demand gradients* or zones in which, as the distance from the retailer increases, the probability of a household's purchasing or shopping declines. In Exhibit 11.3 this way of viewing a trading area is graphically presented.

EXHIBIT 11.1

Determinants of Trading Area Size

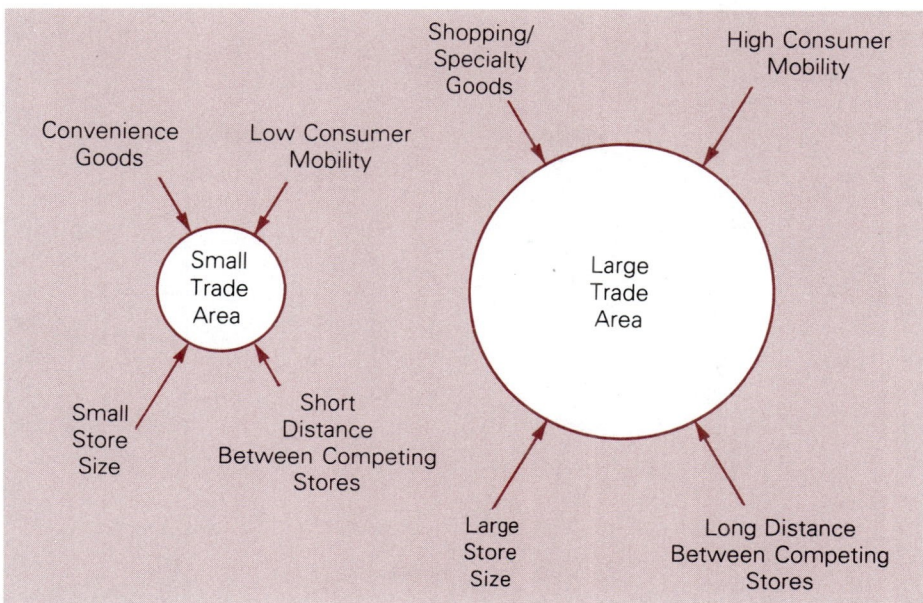

EXHIBIT 11.2

The Impact of a Natural/Artificial Barrier on Trade Area Size

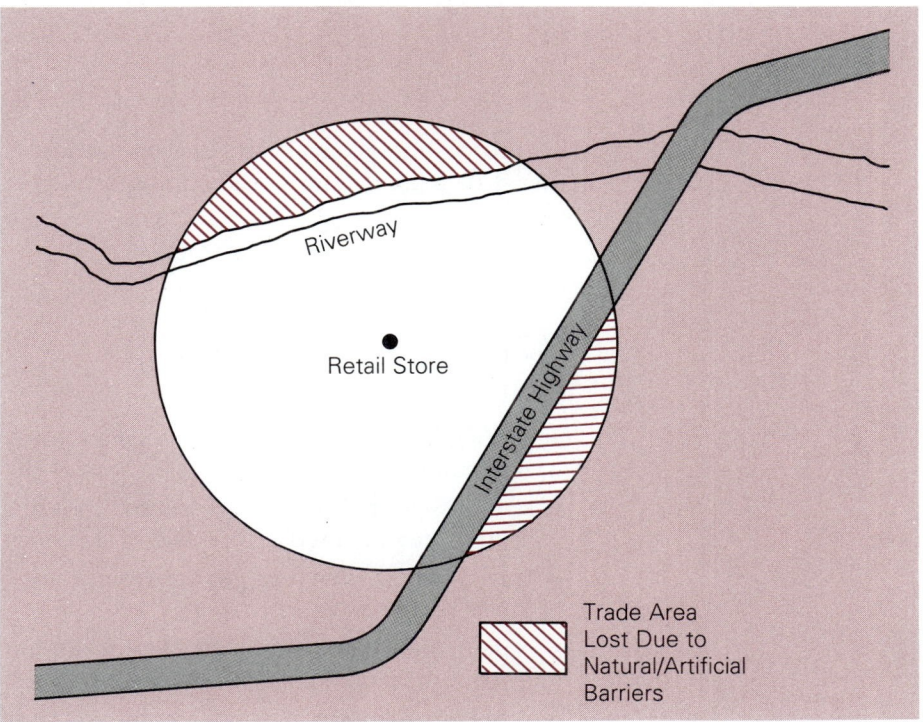

EXHIBIT 11.3

Retail Trade Area Shown by Probability Contours

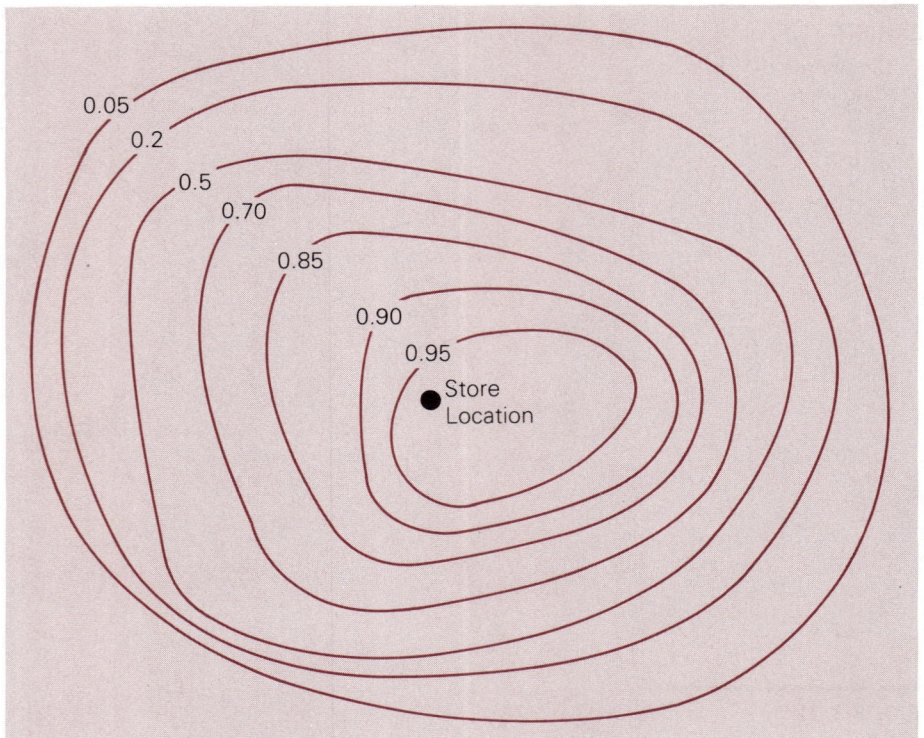

The probability of any particular household shopping at a retail site (whether it be a single store or shopping center) can be calculated with the following formula[15]:

$$P_{ij} = \frac{S_j/T_{ij}^\lambda}{\sum_{j=1}^{n} (S_j/T_{ij}^\lambda)}$$

where:
- P_{ij} = probability of a household at a given point of origin i traveling to a particular retail center j
- S_j = size of the retail center j (measured in terms of the square footage of selling area devoted to the sale of a particular class of goods)
- T_{ij} = travel time involved in getting from a household's travel base i to a given retail center j
- λ = a parameter to be estimated empirically to reflect the effect of travel time on various kinds of shopping trips
- n = number of competing retail centers or stores

With this formula, the retailer can calculate the size of its trading area in terms of the expected number of households that will be attracted to the retail site.[16] This can be done by summing the number of households in each demand gradient and multiplying this by the probability of their shopping at the retail center. More specifically, the equation is[17]:

$$TA_j = \sum_{i=1}^{n} (P_{ij} \times H_i)$$

TA_j = trading area of the particular firm or agglomeration of firms; that is the total expected number of households within a given region that is likely to patronize j for a specific class of products or services

P_{ij} = probability of an individual household residing within a given gradient i shopping at j

H_i = number of households residing within a given gradient i

Naturally, there are other approaches to determining trading areas, including the buyer behavior of various retail locations. However, the Huff approach is quite useful, so let us look at the example developed in Exhibit 11.4.

DESCRIPTION OF TRADING AREA

Local newspapers, as part of their service to advertisers, can often provide retailers with information concerning the trading area for various retail locations, as well as the buyer behavior of the trading area. The following information is based on a 1989 PRIZM study provided retailers in the Los Angeles area by the Marketing Research Department of the *Los Angeles Times*.[18] PRIZM is a registered trademark of Claritas Corp.; PRIZM data for trading areas can also be provided by National Planning Data Corporation.

The PRIZM system is based on the belief that birds of a feather flock together. In other words, even though the total makeup of the U.S. marketplace is very complex and diverse, neighborhoods tend to be just the opposite. People tend to feel most comfortable living in areas with others who are like them. Think for a moment of the place where you are living now as a student and of your parent's home, and you will most likely see the truth of this.

There are many possible reasons consumers usually live in neighborhoods with their own kind. One may be income, because people must be able to afford to live in a particular neighborhood. Factors such as age, occupation, family status, race, culture, religion, population density, urbanization, and housing types also distinguish neighborhoods and thus are important for the retailer to consider.

EXHIBIT 11.4

A Numerical Example of Huff's Model

Ted Stafford is considering opening a new 40,000-square-foot grocery store in Centerville, a midwestern town of 15,000 households. Currently, there are two grocery stores, one in the northeast part of Centerville and the other in the southwest part of Centerville. Ted is considering locating his new store approximately halfway between these stores. The location of the proposed new store and the two existing stores is shown in Exhibit A. The households in Centerville tend to cluster in three areas. In area a, where the new store would be located, there are 3,000 households within 1 mile of the new store, on average 3 miles from Store B in the southwest and 4 miles from Store C in the northeast. In area b, where a 60,000-square-foot store exists, there are 8,000 households on average 1 mile from Store B, 3 miles from the proposed new Store A, and 7 miles from Store C in the northeast part of Centerville. In area c, where a 30,000-square-foot store exists, there are 4,000 households on average 1 mile from Store C, 4 miles from the proposed new store, and 7 miles from Store B.

Exhibit A

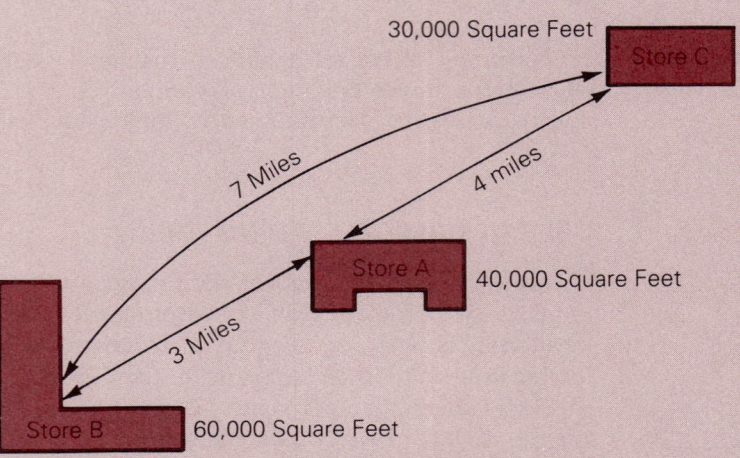

Ted wants to forecast the sales for the new store. How should he proceed? Follow him through the next three steps. (Note that in the following computations we assume that λ is 2.0 in the Huff model.)

1. Determine the probability that a household in each of the three areas of Centerville will shop at the new store.
    a. For area a of Centerville,
    $$P = \frac{40{,}000/1^2}{40{,}000/1^2 + 60{,}000/3^2 + 30{,}000/4^2}$$
    $$= 0.824$$
    b. For area b of Centerville,
    $$P = \frac{40{,}000/3^2}{40{,}000/3^2 + 60{,}000/1^2 + 30{,}000/7^2}$$
    $$= 0.068$$

> c. For area c of Centerville,
>
> $$P = \frac{40{,}000/4^2}{40{,}000/4^2 + 30{,}000/1^2 + 60{,}000/7^2}$$
>
> $$= 0.074$$
>
> 2. Estimate the number of households from each area of Centerville that will shop at the new store.
>   a. Cluster A = 3,000 (0.824) = 2,472
>   b. Cluster B = 8,000 (0.068) = 544
>   c. Cluster C = 4,000 (0.074) = 296
>
>   Total households = 3,312
>
> 3. Determine the total expected annual sales.
>
>   3,312 households × $1,540 annual expenditures = $5,100,480
>
> Thus, Ted can expect annual sales of $5.1 million and the key question then becomes can he make a sufficient profit at this sales volume to make the new store an attractive investment opportunity. We will address this issue later in the chapter.

In distinguishing between neighborhood types, Claritas uses two basic criteria. First, each type of neighborhood must be different enough from all the others to make it a distinct market segment. Second, there must be enough people living in each type of neighborhood to make it a segment worthwhile to retailers. Utilizing Census Bureau data, the study found 40 neighborhood types in the United States. These types are distinguished from each other in many ways. Some distinctions are based primarily on income, some are family oriented, some are race oriented, some are urban, some suburban, and some rural. Most combine two or more distinguishing demographic characteristics. Exhibit 11.5 identifies the 40 neighborhood types PRIZM uses, ranked in socioeconomic order from highest to lowest. Each is identified by a group identifier, an identification number, and a nickname.

The nicknames try to capture the essence of the neighborhood and provide an easy way of remembering distinctions. The identification number is assigned randomly and is used as a reference tool. The group identifier consists of a letter that stands for the degree of urbanization and a number that reflects the level of affluence. An S stands for suburban; U, urban; T, town; and R, rural. Affluence is scaled from 1 (highest) to 4 (lowest). There is more than one neighborhood type for each group identifier.

Exhibit 11.6 provides brief descriptions of several neighborhood types starting with the highest socioeconomic rank, Blue Blood Estates, and ending with the lowest, Public Assistance. Neiman Marcus would probably locate near Blue Blood Estates and Dollar General would probably choose Norma Rae-Ville.

Retailing in Action 11.2 provides an example of the factors a service retailer considers in its location process.

EXHIBIT 11.5

Percentage Distribution of U.S. Households by PRIZM Neighborhood Types

Neighborhood Types			Households Percent Distribution	Neighborhood Types			Households Percent Distribution
Group	Number	Nickname		Group	Number	Nickname	
S1	28	Blue Blood Estates	0.64%	T2	16	Middle America	4.76%
S1	8	Money & Brains	1.14	U2	36	Old Yankee Rows	1.80
S1	5	Furs & Station Wagons	2.44	T2	29	Coalburg & Corntown	2.55
U1	21	Urban Gold Coast	0.45	R1	19	Shotguns & Pickups	2.53
S2	7	Pools & Patios	3.28	T3	33	Golden Ponds	3.06
S2	25	Two More Rungs	1.03	R1	34	Agri-Business	4.28
S2	20	Young Influentials	3.02	U2	14	Emergent Minorities	2.07
S3	24	Young Suburbia	5.63	U2	26	Single City Blues	2.08
T1	1	God's Country	2.97	T3	22	Mines & Mills	1.85
S3	30	Blue-Chip Blues	5.19	R2	10	Back-Country Folks	4.29
U1	37	Bohemian Mix	0.81	T3	13	Norma Rae-Ville	2.95
S4	27	Levittown, U.S.A.	4.51	T3	18	Smalltown Downtown	1.95
S4	39	Gray Power	2.26	R1	35	Grain Belt	1.43
U1	31	Black Enterprise	1.21	U3	4	Heavy Industry	1.95
U1	23	New Beginnings	4.77	R2	38	Share Croppers	3.65
T2	40	Blue-Collar Nursery	1.70	U3	11	Downtown Dixie-Style	2.30
T1	17	New Homesteaders	5.08	U3	9	Hispanic Mix	1.52
U2	3	New Melting Pot	1.33	R2	15	Tobacco Roads	0.96
T1	12	Towns & Gowns	2.18	R2	6	Hard Scrabble	1.02
S4	2	Rank & File	1.07	U3	32	Public Assistance	2.30
						TOTAL	100.00%

Source: Reprinted with permission of the Los Angeles Times Marketing Research Department.

DEMAND DENSITY

The extent to which potential demand for the retailer's goods and services is concentrated in certain census tracts, ZIP codes, or parts of the community is called **demand density.** To determine the extent of demand density, retailers need to identify the major variables influencing their potential demand. One method of identifying these variables is by use of a regression model, a series of mathematical equations that show the relationship between sales and a variety of independent variables for each existing store. The variables identified should be standard demographic variables, such as age, income, and education, since data will be readily available. Let us construct an example.

RETAILING IN ACTION

11.2 Using Demand Factors in Location

Retailers have long realized that not all locations are equal when it comes to choosing store sites. As a result, some retailers have developed elaborate computer programs to aid in location planning, while other, smaller retailers make their decision by locating near a McDonald's or 7-Eleven. They know that these large franchise operations do an extensive study of traffic patterns and growth projections before deciding on a location. But what about retailers that do not necessarily need to make a location decision based solely on traffic flow: Is one site better than another for them? Consider the case of Kinder Care Learning Centers, a firm with more than 1,200 day-care centers for children aged 6 weeks to 12 years.

Kinder Care bases its location decisions on demographic factors. It looks for growth areas, new construction, new homes, and two wage-earning adults. The ideal location is near a new housing development where both husband and wife must work to meet the mortgage payments. The couple is usually in their late 20s or early 30s, earn approximately $30,000 per year, have children, and are planning on having more.

Apartment area locations are out because of the high percentage of singles, as are neighborhoods with a high concentration of older people whose child-rearing years are over.

A retailer is evaluating the possibility of locating in a community whose geographical boundaries are shown in Exhibit 11.7. It consists of 23 census tracts. The community is bordered on the west by a mountain range, on the north and south by major highways, and on the east by railroad tracks. The retailer has determined through a series of statistical models it has constructed from data on existing stores that three variables are especially important in determining the potential demand: median household income over $22,000, households per square mile in excess of 1,200, and average growth in population of at least 3 percent per year over the last three years. Exhibit 11.7 maps the extent to which these three conditions are met for each of the 23 census tracts in the community undergoing evaluation, so the potential demand is readily apparent in each tract. Only three tracts (6, 10, 17) meet all three conditions; four tracts (1, 5, 11, 16) meet two; five tracts (8, 9, 14, 15, 18) meet only one; and eleven tracts (2, 3, 4, 7, 12, 13, 19, 20, 21, 22, 23) meet none of the conditions.

Demand density maps similar to the one shown in Exhibit 11.7 are available at modest cost from firms such as CACI Marketing Systems, R. L. Polk and Co., National Planning Data Corporation, and Urban Decision Systems, Inc. The retail analyst could also construct such maps using data from the Census Bureau, yellow pages, or city and county data sources.

Another method of looking at potential demand for a retailer's product is to use the *Los Angeles Times* data mentioned earlier when discussing neighborhood types. Suppose a high-fashion women's apparel chain wanted to enter

EXHIBIT 11.6

Brief Description of Several Neighborhood Types

TOBACCO ROADS
Cluster 15 is found throughout the South from Virginia to Texas. However, its greatest concentrations are seen in the river basins and coastal, scrub-pine flatlands of the Carolinas, Georgia and Gulf states. It is half Black and a fifth English stock. There is some light industry, but poor, unskilled labor predominates. Still dependent upon agriculture, Cluster 15 ranks last in white-collar employment.

Number 15 —

NORMA RAE-VILLE
Cluster 13s are concentrated in the South, with their geocenter in the Appalachian and Piedmont regions. They include hundreds of industrial suburbs and mill towns with a great many in textiles and other light industries. The residents are county folk with minimal educations. They are unique among the T3s in having a high index for Blacks and lead the nation in nondurable manufacturing.

Number 13 —

GRAY POWER
This is a new cluster, representing over a million upscale senior citizens who have chosen to pull up their roots and retire among their peers. Primarily concentrated in sunbelt communities of the South Atlantic and Pacific regions, they are the nation's most affluent, elderly, retired and widowed neighborhoods. They have the highest concentration of childless married couples living in mixed multi-units, condos and mobile homes with non-salaried incomes.

Number 39 —

PUBLIC ASSISTANCE
With 70% of its households Black, Cluster 32 represents the "Harlems" of America. These are the nation's poorest neighborhoods with twice its unemployment level and five times its share of public assistance incomes. Cluster 32s have been urban-renewal targets for three decades, and show large, solo-parent families in rented, public high-rise buildings interspersed with aging tenement rows.

Number 32 —

BLACK ENTERPRISE
Another new cluster, Black Enterprise is 60% Black with median Black household incomes well above average and consumption behavior to match. A few downscale pockets can be found, exhibiting five-plus person households, divorces and separations, single parents and female breadwinners. However the majority of these Blacks are educated, employed and solidly set in the upper-middle class.

Number 31 —

FURS & STATION WAGONS
Third in socioeconomic rank, Cluster 5 is typified by "new money." living in expensive new neighborhoods in the green-belt suburbs of the nation's major metros coast to coast. These are well educated, mobile professionals and managers with the nation's highest incidence of teenage children. They are winners — big producers and big spenders.

Number 5 —

Reprinted with permission of the Los Angeles Times Marketing Research Department.

Chapter 11 Store Site Analysis

EXHIBIT 11.6
(Continued)

BACK-COUNTRY FOLKS
You can't get much farther out than Guntersville, Alabama; Elkins, Arkansas; Saltville, Virginia; or Caribou, Maine. Cluster 10 abounds in such remote, rural towns geocentered in the Ozark and Appalachian uplands. It is predominantly White and leads the nation in concentration of persons of English ancestry, some of whom are descendents of original colonists and still speak in Elizabethan dialect.

Number 10 —

HARD SCRABBLE
The term "hard scrabble" is an old phrase meaning to scratch a hard living from hard soil. Cluster 6 represents our poorest rural areas from Appalachia to the Ozarks, Mexican border country and Dakota Badlands. With very few Blacks, Cluster 6 leads the nation in American Indians, including many Indian reservations. It also shows a high index for both Mexican and English ancestries.

Number 6 —

MINES AND MILLS
Industry is king in Cluster 22, including both light and heavy industry. Cluster 22 gathers hundreds of mining and mill towns scattered throughout Appalachia from New England to the Pennsylvania/ Ohio industrial complex and points south. It ranks first in total manufacturing and in total blue-collar occupations. It has very few Black or Hispanic minorities.

Number 22 —

BLUE BLOOD ESTATES
America's wealthiest socio-economic neighborhoods, populated by super-upper established managers, professionals and heirs to "old money" accustomed to privilege and living in luxurious surroundings. One in ten millionaires can be found in Cluster 28, and there is a considerable drop from these heights to the next level of affluence.

Number 28 —

MONEY AND BRAINS
Cluster 8 enjoys the nation's second-highest socioeconomic rank. These neighborhoods are typified by swank townhouses, apartments and condos with relatively few children. Many of these neighborhoods contain private universities and a mix of upscale singles. They are sophisticated consumers of adult luxuries including apparel, restaurants, travel and others.

Number 8 —

LEVITTOWN, USA
The post-World War II baby boom caused an explosion of tract housing in the late 40's and 50's in brand new suburbs for young white-collar and well-paid blue-collar families. As with "Pools & Patios," the children are now largely grown and gone. Aging couples remain in comfortable middle-class suburban homes. Employment levels are still high, including double incomes allowing for "easy living" in these neighborhoods.

Number 27 —

EXHIBIT 11.7

Demand Density Map

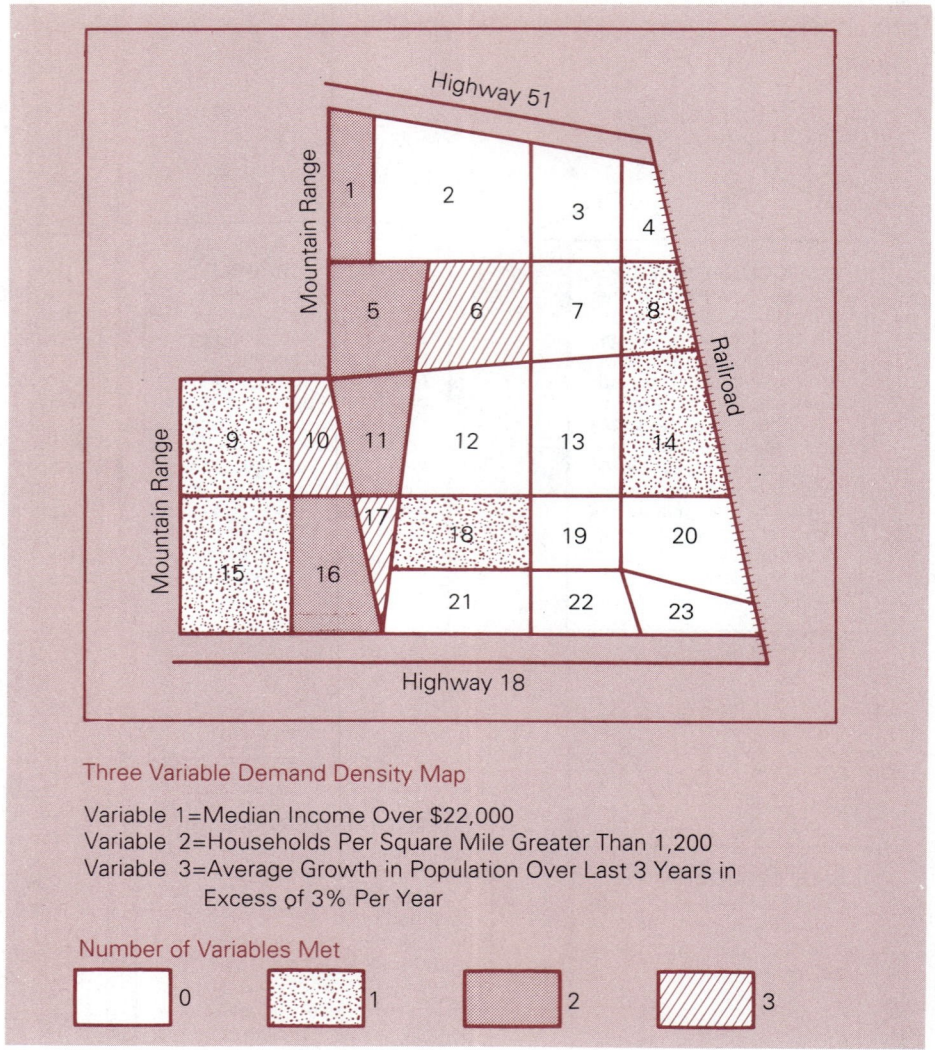

the Los Angeles market. The chain would first determine, from its own records, which neighborhood types accounted for the largest percentage of its sales in comparison to the national average for its product categories. In this case, neighborhood types 5, 8, and 28 all spend at least three times the average per capita amount for the chain's product line. Neighborhood types 25, 20, and 7 spend at least twice the average, and neighborhood types 1, 3, 12, 23, 24, 26, 37, and 39 would spend up to twice the average. In the remaining 26 neighborhoods, sales for the chain's products would be less than the national average.

SUPPLY DENSITY

The demand density map allows us to identify the areas within a community that represent the highest potential demand, but the location of existing retail establishments should also be mapped. This allows us to examine the **density of supply,** or the extent to which retailers are already concentrated in different areas of the market under question.

Exhibit 11.8 shows the density of stores in the community we saw in Exhibit 11.7. Examination of Exhibit 11.8 reveals that two of the three most attractive census tracts (10 and 17) lack stores. Also, in the census tracts with fairly attractive demand density (two of the three conditions met), there are currently no retail outlets (see tracts 1 and 5).

SITE AVAILABILITY

Just because demand outstrips supply in certain geographic locations does not mean that stores should be located in there. Sites must be available.

A map should be constructed of available sites in each community being analyzed. We have done this in conjunction with the supply density map in Exhibit 11.8. The only available site in the top six census tracts (in terms of demand density) is in census tract 10. In tracts 1, 5, and 17, which currently

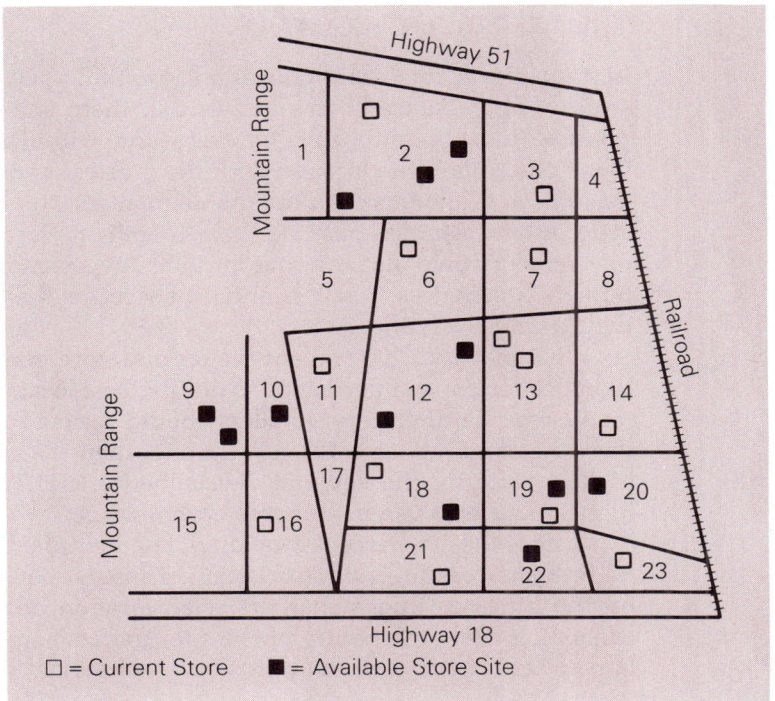

EXHIBIT 11.8

Store Density and Site Availability Map

have no retail outlets, no sites are available, which may explain the present lack of stores in these areas; perhaps these tracts are zoned for residential use.

Although Exhibit 11.8 seems to show only one good potential site, several more may exist. Census tract 9 borders high-density tract 10, in which there are no stores at present and in which one site is available for a new store. Tract 9 has two available sites. Furthermore, tract 12 has an available site close to the borders of tracts 11 and 17, which are both attractive but lack available sites.

SITE SELECTION DECISION PROCESS

After completing the analysis of each segment of the desired market and identifying the best available sites within each, retailers are ready to make the final decision regarding location: selecting the best site (or sites) available.[19] Retailers are well advised to use the assistance of a real estate professional in this step, even if they have done all the analysis to this point. In fact, more and more large retail firms are setting up separate corporations just to handle their real estate transactions.[20]

THE 100 PERCENT LOCATION

In principle, all retailers should attempt to find a **100 percent location** for their stores: "The essence of this idea is that there is a location that is the best possible (most optimum) site for every store within a given shopping district. Generally, this is the location with the greatest amount of the kind of traffic desired."[21] While this condition for all retailers would be considered the ideal state, it has been demonstrated that there is no location from which at least one retailer could not improve profitability by moving to a different location.[22] Nonetheless, retailers should strive for the 100 percent location for their product offering.

What may be a 100 percent site for one store may not be for another. The best location for a supermarket is not the best location for a discount department store. Furthermore, retailers should realize that if two or more stores view the same site as a 100 percent site, then the retailer willing to pay the highest price for the site will determine its use. This is what is called the highest and best use in resource economics.

How is the 100 percent location or site identified? Unfortunately, there is no best answer to this basic question. There is, however, general agreement on the types of things that the retail location analyst should consider in evaluating sites: the nature of the site, traffic characteristics, type of neighbors, size of trade area, and pro forma return on investment model.

NATURE OF SITE

Is the site currently a vacant store, a vacant parcel of land, or the site of a planned shopping center? Many available retail sites are vacant stores, because 10 to 15 percent of all stores go out of business each year. Often the reasons for a retailer's failure at a given location make that site a bad choice for another store, especially if the prior occupant of the store was in the same line of retail trade. If Supermarket A fails at a particular store site, then the probability is significantly increased that Supermarket B will also fail at that site. When a store location is vacant for an extended period of time, the rent or price may be lowered, but a cut in price will not make an unattractive site attractive.

When the retail site is a vacant parcel of land, the retailer needs to investigate why it is vacant. Why have others passed up the site? Was it previously not for sale? Was it priced too high? Or is there some other reason? For instance, many supermarkets abandon 20,000-square-foot locations to move to newer 65,000-square-foot sites. These abandoned sites usually are available at lower costs and are not necessarily bad locations.

Finally, the site may be part of a planned shopping center. In this case, the retailer can usually be assured that it will have the proper mix of neighbors, adequate parking facilities, and good traffic. Sometimes, of course, the center has not been properly planned, and the retailer needs to be on the lookout for these special cases.

TRAFFIC CHARACTERISTICS

The traffic that passes a site, whether it be vehicular or pedestrian, is an important determinant of the potential sales at that site. But more than just traffic flow is important. The retailer must also determine whether the population and traffic are of the type desired. For example, a retailer of fine furs and leather coats may be considering two alternative sites—one in the central business district and the other in a group of specialty stores in a small shopping center in a very exclusive residential area. The CBD site may generate more aggregate traffic, but the small shopping center may generate more of the right type of traffic.

The retailer should evaluate two other traffic-related aspects of the site. The first is the availability of sufficient parking, either at the site or nearby. One of the advantages of shopping centers is the availability of adequate parking. If the site is not a shopping center, then the retailer will need to determine whether parking will be adequate. It is difficult to give a precise guideline for the space that will be needed. Generally, it is a function of four factors: size of the store, frequency of customer visits, length of customer visits, and availability of public transportation. As a rule of thumb, shopping centers estimate that there should be four and a half parking spaces for every

1,000 square feet of selling space in medium-sized centers and five spaces per 1,000 square feet in large centers.

A second traffic-related factor the retailer should consider is the ease with which consumers can reach the store site. Are the roadways in good shape? Are there traffic barriers (rivers with limited number of bridges, interstates with limited crossings, one-way streets, or congestion limiting access to the site)? Remember, customers will generally avoid congested shopping areas and shop elsewhere in order to minimize driving time and difficulties.

Sufficient parking and ease of travel are critical factors in selecting locations for home-improvement centers such as Home Depot, Builders Square, and Scotty's. Since the do-it-yourself household will be taking home a lot of merchandise, a freestanding location with immediate adjacent parking becomes critical. And since the car or truck is likely to be heavily loaded, being able to get to the parking lot and home easily and safely on well-built roads is critical.

TYPE OF NEIGHBOR

What are the neighboring establishments that surround the site? There can be good and bad neighbors. The type of store that one is considering operating at the site determines what a good or bad neighbor is. Suppose you plan to open a children's apparel store and are considering a pair of alternative sites. One site has a toy store and a gift shop as neighbors. The other site has a bowling alley and an adult book store as neighbors. It is obvious who the good and bad neighbors are.

A good neighboring business is compatible with the retailer's line of trade. When two or more businesses are compatible, they can actually help generate business for each other. For example, a paint store, hardware store, and an auto parts store located next to one another may increase total traffic that benefits them all.

The **principle of compatibility** has been formalized as follows:

Two compatible businesses located in close proximity will show an increase in business volume directly proportionate to the incidence of total customer interchange between them, inversely proportionate to the ratio of the business volume of the larger store to that of the smaller store, and directly proportionate to the sum of the ratios of purposeful purchasing to total purchasing in each of the two stores.[23]

This relationship can be more explicitly summarized as follows:

$$V = I\,[V_s\,(P_L\,V_s + P_s\,V_L)\,/\,V_L]$$

V_L = volume of larger store

P_L = purposeful purchasing in larger store

V_s = volume of smaller store

P_s = purposeful purchasing in smaller store
V = increase in total volume of two stores
I = degree of interchange

Consider this example.

If there are two retail stores side by side and one customer in a hundred makes purchases in both, the rule indicates that together they will do 1 percent more business than if separated by such a distance as to make this interchange impossible or unlikely. If one customer in ten makes purchases in both stores, their total increase in business will be about 10 percent. Theoretically, if every customer bought in both stores, their total business volume would double, if both businesses did about the same dollar volume.

However, a very large store and a very small store would not show the same total increase as two stores of equivalent size. For example, if a department store doing $5,000,000 worth of retail volume a year were next door to a variety store doing $500,000 a year, their total would not double even with a 100 percent interchange of customers. If their customer interchange were on the order of 25 out of 100, the total increase in business for the two establishments would be directly proportionate to the interchange, or 25 percent, but inversely proportionate to the ratio of their volumes, which is 10:1. Thus the total increase would equal one tenth of 25 percent or 2.5 percent. If, however, interviews showed purposeful purchasing at the department store and the variety store to be respectively, on the order of 90 percent and 15 percent of total purchasing, the 2.5 percent increase would have to be multiplied by 105 percent. Thus, these two stores together would show a business increase of 2.5 × 1.05 = 2.625 percent of the total of $5,000,000, or an additional $144,375. This is not a measure of market potential. All compatibility determinations assume that an adequate market exists.[24]

When Nordstrom entered the Washington, D.C., market in 1988 with a store projected to do a dizzying $100 million in first-year sales, the neighboring Hecht's branch had a 35 percent sales increase. Likewise, Marshall Field's enjoyed a double-digit sales increase when Bloomingdale's joined it in downtown Chicago.[25]

LEASE VERSUS BUY

Sometimes the retailer has the option of purchasing a site and building or leasing. (However, if the retailer locates in a shopping center, it will usually need to lease.) The lease versus buy decision is one of economics and flexibility. Leases are generally more flexible and do not lock a retailer into a location for as long a period of time. At the same time purchasing a site and building on it requires more initial capital investment, which may be difficult for a rapidly growing retail organization to obtain. Another factor to consider is that lease payments are fully deductible as a business expense, whereas only depreciation on a building is deductible for tax purposes. One advantage of buying is that if real estate goes up in value the retailer will have a more valuable asset; however, if real estate values decline just the opposite will occur. Since retailers are primarily in the business of selling merchandise and services and not in the brick and mortar business, most retailers have decided that leasing is the preferred option.

TERMS OF LEASE

A final consideration for the retailer is lease terms. The retailer should review the length of the lease (it could be too long or too short), the exclusivity clause (whether or not the retailer will be the only one allowed to sell a certain line of merchandise), the guaranteed traffic rate (there could be a reduction in rent if the shopping center fails to achieve a targeted traffic level), and an anchor clause (which allows for a rent reduction if the anchor store in a developing center doesn't open on time).

PRO FORMA RETURN ON INVESTMENT MODEL

The final step in site selection analysis is construction of a pro forma return on investment model for each possible site. The return on investment model comprises three crucial variables: profit margin, asset turnover, and return on assets.

For the purpose of evaluating sites, the potential return on owner's equity is not important. This is true because the financial leverage ratio (total assets divided by owner's equity) is a top-management decision, which represents how much debt the retail enterprise is willing to assume. Most likely, the question of how to finance new store growth has already been answered or at least contemplated. The retailer should already have determined that it has or can obtain the capital to finance a new store. It is therefore reasonable and appropriate to evaluate sites on their potential return on assets and not return on equity.

If the retailer is to evaluate sites on their potential return on assets, it will need at least three estimates: total sales, total assets, and net profit.

Total Sales. The sales that can be generated from a proposed store at a particular site are not easy to estimate with precision. One method is to use the Huff model as we illustrated in Exhibit 11.4. Quantitative techniques, such as regression, can also be employed,[26] but in practice the estimation is often done less rigorously. Whatever the procedure, the retail analyst should consider all the factors discussed earlier as part of the within-market opportunity analysis and site selection analysis. Of the array of considerations under these headings, the most important in estimating sales is the potential trading area of the site.

Given a well-defined trading area, the retailer will know how many potential households are in the area. Next, the retailer will seek to determine what percentage of these potential households it will actually serve. One method, used by many small retailers, is to assume that the new store will achieve a percentage of sales equal to its retail selling space as a percentage of total selling space in the trading area. The retailer divides the proposed store's selling space by the trading area's selling space with the new store's space included. This figure will give the retailer a reasonable estimate of what market share it will achieve. Next, the retailer should multiply total households by market share, and then multiply that figure by the average expenditure per household. This gives the estimated total annual sales for the store. The estimate of average expenditures per household can be developed from past experience in similar settings, from industry averages, or from formal quantitative techniques.[27]

While forecasting can take many forms, it must be attempted in order to determine cash, inventory, and employee needs for the future. Consider an example. A supermarket retailer is evaluating a site expected to have a trading area of 36,000 households. The proposed store will have 100,000 square feet of selling space, and the other stores in the trading area have a combined selling space of 900,000 square feet. The retailer estimates that annual sales per household will be $1,600. Its expected total annual sales are therefore $5.76 million [36,000 × (100,000 square feet/100,000 square feet + 900,000 square feet) × $1,600].

Total Assets. The retail analyst must next estimate total dollar investment needed to conduct business at the site. If the site is to be purchased and a store constructed on it, these costs must be considered. The cost of sites can vary considerably, as can the cost of constructing similar buildings on alternative sites. The costs of inventory, fixtures, lighting, and parking facilities must also be estimated. In addition, if the store is not expected to break even for several months or longer, then anticipated losses should be considered as asset dollars or capital needed to commence operations. In short, the retailer must estimate the total capital needed to begin operations. Generally, the estimate of capital (asset dollars) is much more accurate than the sales estimate, because the retailer can obtain fairly accurate data on what it will cost to acquire various assets.

In the supermarket example, let us assume that the total capital needed to start operations is $1.9 million. This includes the cost of the land, building, fixtures, parking lot, inventory, and other working capital. If the retailer estimated annual sales at $5.76 million, it follows that its expected rate of asset turnover is 3.03 ($5,760,000/$1,900,000).

Net Profit. If the retailer has done a good job of estimating total sales and assets, the estimate of net profit should not be too difficult. Net profit equals total sales less fixed and variable costs. (Recall that fixed costs are those that remain constant regardless of the level of sales; variable costs change in proportion to sales.)

Most fixed costs in retailing are related to the size of the store, which is in turn tied to total assets. As the store becomes larger, it requires more employees, it takes more energy to heat and cool, it requires higher interest costs to finance capital, it incurs higher insurance premiums, and it incurs more dollars of depreciation.

The major variable expense will be the cost of merchandise sold. Obviously, as more is sold, the total cost of merchandise becomes higher. There is often a fairly linear relationship between cost of merchandise and sales. If the retailer can estimate how much the goods cost as a percentage of sales, it can easily estimate the total cost of goods sold by multiplying the cost of goods sold percentage by the estimated total sales.

Several other expenses may be expected to vary with total sales (e.g., some labor and advertising expenses). Past experience or industry standards can give the retailer a reasonable estimate of operating expenses that vary with sales. These expenses can also be stated as a percentage of sales.

In our supermarket example, we established that the supermarket had expected sales of $5.76 million and would need $1.9 million in assets. Assume that the annual fixed costs of operating the supermarket are estimated to be $471,000 and the cost of goods sold is expected to be 78.7 percent of sales. In addition, other variable operating expenses are estimated at 9.4 percent of sales. Through analysis of these numbers we can determine the expected net profit:

$$\begin{aligned}\text{Net Profit} &= \text{Sales} - \text{Fixed costs} - \text{Variable costs} \\ &= \$5{,}760{,}000 - \$471{,}000 - (0.787 + 0.094)(\$5{,}760{,}000) \\ &= \$214{,}440\end{aligned}$$

Thus, the overall profit margin (net profit divided by sales) would be ($214,440/$5,760,000) or 3.72 percent.

Return on Assets. For each site being evaluated, the expected return on assets should be computed. The computation of return on assets is simple if sales, assets, and net profit have been estimated. The appropriate data can be inserted into the return on assets equation:

$$\frac{\text{Net profit}}{\text{Total sales}} \times \frac{\text{Total sales}}{\text{Total assets}} = \frac{\text{Net profit}}{\text{Total assets}}$$

Using our supermarket example, we can compute the expected return on assets as

$$\frac{\$214{,}000}{\$5{,}760{,}000} \times \frac{\$5{,}760{,}000}{\$1{,}900{,}000} = \frac{\$214{,}440}{\$1{,}900{,}000}$$

$(0.0372) \times (3.032) = (0.11286)$

If the supermarket is located at the site under consideration, it can be expected to have a profit margin of 3.72 percent and a rate of asset turnover of 3.03, which will yield an 11.29 percent return on assets. All these figures are before taxes. Thus, assuming a 40 percent tax rate, the return on assets would drop to less than 7 percent. This is hardly an attractive return on assets given the cost of capital facing most supermarket retailers. The retailer should probably search for a better site.

MEASURING PERFORMANCE

At last the site has been chosen and the store is open. In the early weeks of operation, careful attention needs to be given to sales performance. Are sales materializing at the level anticipated? If not, why not? Is it a management or merchandising failure, or is it due to having selected a poor site? If the performance is attributable to poor management or merchandising, then corrective action needs to be taken as soon as possible. If a poor site was selected, then the retailer can only hope to learn from its error. If retailers carefully plan new locations, then errors in site location should be minimal. Chains can usually learn from their errors, while individual store owners go out of business. This is one reason for the high number of retail failures each year.

After the first month or two of operations, retailers will want to analyze not only their sales performance but also their expense performance. If any expenses are not in line with expectations, then an investigation of the deviation will be worthwhile. The cause of the deviation is typically either poor expense control or poor initial planning. Quite frequently, since the expense estimates are approximate (because there is no prior experience in operating at the site), the cause will be poor expense planning. But if the cause is poor management control of the expense item, then corrective action should be taken as quickly as possible.

SUMMARY

This chapter continues the location decision discussion in Chapter 10. We began by reviewing three location alternatives available: the central business district, the shopping center, or a freestanding unit.

The central business district is generally an unplanned shopping area around the geographic point where a city originated and grew up. As cities have grown, we have witnessed an expansion of two new types of central business districts—the secondary business district and the neighborhood business district.

A shopping center is a centrally owned or managed shopping district which is planned, has balanced tenancy, and is surrounded by parking facilities. It has one or more anchor stores and a variety of smaller stores. Because of the many advantages shopping centers offer the retailer, they now account for nearly 55 percent of all retail sales in this country.

A freestanding retailer generally locates along major traffic arteries without any adjacent retailers selling competing products to share traffic.

After reviewing these three location alternatives, we discussed the second of our three steps in the location process: evaluating the density of demand and supply within each market and identifying the sites that are available in the markets under study.

Next, the retail location analyst should conduct a site selection analysis of the top-ranking sites in each market. The goal is to select the best site or sites. The following factors should be considered: nature of the site, traffic characteristics, type of neighbors, lease versus buy, terms of lease, and pro forma return on investment model.

After all relevant sites have been analyzed and the best one selected, then the process becomes an ongoing one—measuring sales, expense, and profit performance of the store once it begins operations. Any significant deviations from expectations should be investigated and corrective action taken.

QUESTIONS FOR DISCUSSION

1. Identify the factors you would consider most important in locating a fast-food restaurant. Compare them with the factors you would use in selecting a site for a furniture store.
2. Why are discount department stores such as Wal-Mart usually not located in large shopping centers?
3. How can the return on investment model be used to assist in location decisions?
4. Explain the concepts of demand density and supply density. Why are they important to retail decision making?
5. Compute the expected return on assets for a proposed supermarket with the following characteristics:
   - 4,400 households in trading area
   - 18,000 total square feet of store space
   - Expected annual sales per household of $1,400
   - Land costs of $280,000
   - Construction costs of $40 per square foot
   - Costs to develop land of $38,000
   - Inventory investment per square foot of $10
   - Equipment and fixture costs of $400,000
   - Gross margin of 23.4 percent
   - Operating expenses (variable) of 12.4 percent of sales
   - Fixed operating costs per year (including depreciation) of $340,000

   What other factors, besides expected return on assets, should be considered in deciding whether to build the proposed supermarket?
6. What are the differences among the major location types discussed in this chapter?
7. Nearly 55 percent of all retail sales, excluding automobile dealers and gasoline service stations, occur in shopping centers. Does this mean that the shopping center's future is bright, or does it face problems in the coming decade?
8. What criteria should a small retailer use in selecting a type of location?
9. What does the principle of compatibility reveal about retail stores locating next to each other?
10. What are four major determinants of the size of a retailer's trading area?
11. A new hardware store is being considered for Maryville, a town of 22,000 people. Currently, there is only one hardware store and it is 8,000 square feet. The new store that is being planned will be 18,000 square feet and is 4 miles to the east of the existing hardware store. A thriving new subdivision of 150 houses is being built 2 miles from the existing hardware store and 4 miles from the new proposed store. What is the probability that residents of the new subdivision will shop at the existing hardware store? The new hardware store?

MANAGEMENT MEMO

As marketing director of a large regional shopping mall of 1,000,000 square feet, you have become increasingly concerned about the rowdiness of heavy teenage traffic on weekends and during summer months. Last Saturday afternoon was an especially disturbing day because within two hours there were two fist fights in the food court. In one of the episodes, a police officer was injured when attempting to break up the brawl. Your fear is that this type of behavior is starting to negatively influence store traffic from the community and thus sales. Write a one- or two-page memo to the managers of the 83 stores in the mall suggesting a policy to curb teen traffic.

BOARDROOM REPORT

The 38 tenants of a 425,000-square-foot regional mall will be meeting in three days with the management board of the center. A topic they wish to discuss is "rent relief." Since sales at the mall are down 9 percent for the first six months of the year compared to last year, they are proposing a cut in rent. Your boss, Eve Clements, has asked you as the marketing manager of the mall to propose instead a program of free management consulting. The mall has worked with a local retail consultant, whom Eve wants to put on retainer, to advise the tenants on tactics and strategy for improving sales. Prepare a five-minute report to be presented to the tenants at the board meeting.

SUGGESTED READINGS

Curry, Bruce, and Luiz Moutinho. "Expert Systems and Marketing Strategy: An Application to Site Location Decisions." *Journal of Marketing Channels* 1 (1991): 23-38.

Eroglu, Sevgin, and Gilbert D. Harrell. "Retail Crowding: Theoretical and Strategic Implications." *Journal of Retailing* (Winter 1986): 346-63.

Finn, Adam, "Characterizing the Attractiveness of Retail Markets." *Journal of Retailing* (Summer 1987): 129-62.

Fram, Eugene Ho, and Joel Axelrod. "The Distressed Shopper." *American Demographics* (October 1990): 44-45.

Green, Howard L. "Retail Sales Forecasting Systems." *Journal of Retailing* (Fall 1986): 227-30.

Turchiano, Francesca. "The Unmalling of America." *American Demographics* (April 1990): 36-39.

ENDNOTES

1. "Sony's 'Gallery' Has Retailers Hearing Footsteps," *Business Week,* 23 December 1991, 29.
2. "Finast Finds Challenges and Surprising Profits in Urban Supermarkets," *Wall Street Journal,* 8 June 1992, A1, A4. "The Ghetto's Hidden Wealth," *Fortune* (29 July 1991): 167-174.
3. Patricia M. Anderson, "Association of Shopping Center Anchors with Performance of a Nonanchor Specialty Chain's Store," *Journal of Retailing* (Summer 1985): 61-74.
4. "Edmonton's Eighth Wonder of the World," *American Demographics* (February, 1986): 20.
5. "Thriving Factory Outlets Anger Retailers as Store Suppliers Turn into Competitors," *Wall Street Journal,* 8 October 1991, B1, B6.
6. *The Scope of the Shopping Center Industry In the United States 1990* (New York: International Council of Shopping Centers, 1990).
7. "New Retailers Face Struggle Getting in Malls," *Wall Street Journal,* 24 July 1990, B1, B2.
8. George Sternlieb and James W. Hughes, "The Demise of the Department Store," *American Demographics* (August 1987): 31-33, 59.
9. "The PUD Market Guarantee," *Chain Store Age Executive* (April 1991), 31-38.
10. For a more detailed discussion of site selection, consult Avijit Ghosh and C. Samuel Craig, "Formulating Retail Location Strategy in a Changing Environment," *Journal of Marketing* (Summer 1983): 56-68.
11. Martha Farnsworth Riche, "Computer Mapping Takes Center Stage," *American Demographics* (June 1986): 26-31, 64-65 and Matthew A. Rose, "What's New?" *Direct Marketing* (March 1988): 26. The reader might also want to consult Roland T. Rust and Julia A. N. Brown, "Estimation and Comparison of Market Area Densities," *Journal of Retailing* (Winter 1986): 410-30 for a new method for estimating density of customers around a single retail center.
12. The essence of Applebaum's work, plus contributions from several of his students, can be found

in "William Applebaum and Others," Curt Korhblau, ed., *Guide to Store Location Research with Emphasis on Supermarkets* (sponsored by Super Market Institute, Addison-Wesley, 1968).
13. David L. Huff, "Defining and Estimating a Trading Area," *Journal of Marketing* (July 1964): 34-38.
14. Huff, 38.
15. Huff, 26.
16. The Huff model has been extended to include image and other competitive variables. For example, see John R. Nevin and Michael J. Houston, "Image as a Component of Attraction to Intraurban Shopping Areas," *Journal of Retailing* (Spring 1980): 77-93 and Thomas J. Stanley and Murphy A. Sewell, "Predicting Supermarket Trade: Implications for Marketing Management," *Journal of Retailing* (Summer 1978): 13-22, 91, 92.
17. Huff, "Defining and Estimating," 38.
18. Reprinted with permission of the *Los Angeles Times*.
19. Computer-based expert systems are being developed to aid in this process; see Bruce Cuny and Luiz Moutinho, "Expert Systems and Marketing Strategy: An Application to Site Location Decisions," in Terry L. Childers et al., eds., *1991 AMA Winter Educator's Conference: Marketing Theory and Applications* (Chicago: American Marketing Association, 1991), 256-62.
20. "Bonanza Firm to Separate Its Operation," *Lubbock Avalanche Journal*, 5 July 1983, 10A.
21. Rom J. Markin, *Retailing Management* (New York: Macmillan, 1977), 177.
22. Tjalin C. Koopmans and Martin Beckman, "Assignment Problems and the Location of Economic Activities," *Econometrica* (January 1957): 69.
23. Richard L. Nelson, *The Selection of Retail Locations* (New York: F. W. Dodge, 1958): 66. A *purposeful purchase* is one made by a shopper who, when interviewed, states that a visit to the store was a major purpose of the shopping trip. Total purchases, of course, include incidental and impulse purchases as well.
24. Nelson, 67.
25. "Store Wars Break out All Around the Beltway," *Business Week*, 10 October 1988, 140 and Francine Schwadel, "Bloomingdale's Foray into Chicago Has Competitors Polishing Their Acts," *Wall Street Journal*, 4 October 1988, B6.
26. G. I. Heald, "The Application of the Automatic Interaction Detector (A.I.D.) Program and Multiple Regression Techniques to the Assessment of Store Performance and Site Selection," *Operations Research Quarterly* (December 1972): 445-57.
27. Charles A. Ingene and Robert F. Lusch, "A New Frame of Reference for Managing Retail Profitability," in *Proceedings of the Sixth International Research Seminar in Marketing* (Gordes, France, June 4-8, 1979).

CHAPTER 12

STORE PLANNING, DESIGN, AND MERCHANDISING

OVERVIEW

In this chapter we discuss the place where all retailing activities come together—the retail store. The store not only represents a retail organization's largest fixed asset, it can be the most meaningful form of communication between the retailer and its customers. Most importantly, the store is where sales happen—or fail to happen. We will see that with all its hundreds of elements, the store has two primary roles: creating the proper market position image and increasing the productivity of the sales space. We identify the most critical elements in creating a successful retail store and describe the art and science of store planning, merchandising, and design.

STORE PLANNING, DESIGN, AND MERCHANDISING

I. Introduction
   A. Elements of the Store Environment
   B. Objectives of the Store Environment
      1. Engineering the Market Position Image
      2. Increasing Sales Productivity
   C. Creating the Store Environment
      1. Who Creates the Store Environment
      2. Steps in Creating a Store
II. Store Planning
   A. Allocating Space

1. Types of Space in the Store
   a. Back Room
   b. Offices and Other Functional Spaces
   c. Aisles, Service Areas, and Other Nonselling Areas
   d. Floor Merchandise Space
   e. Wall Merchandise Space
2. Space Allocation Planning
   a. Space Allocations for a New Store
   b. Enhancing Space Productivity in Existing Stores
   B. Store Layout
      1. Adjacencies
      2. Bubble Planning
      3. Block Planning
   C. Circulation
      1. Free Flow
      2. Grid
      3. Loop
      4. Spine
   D. Shrinkage Prevention
III. Fixture Selection and Merchandise Presentation Planning
   A. Fixture Types
      1. Hardlines Fixtures
      2. Softlines Fixtures
      3. Wall Fixtures
   B. Merchandise Presentation Planning
      1. Methods of Merchandise Presentation
      2. Psychology of Merchandise Presentation
         a. Value/Fashion Image
         b. Angles and Sightlines
         c. Vertical Color Blocking
   C. Selecting the Proper Fixtures and Merchandising Methods
   D. Merchandise Capacity Calculations
   E. Visual Merchandising
IV. Store Design
   A. Storefront Design
   B. Interior Design
   C. Lighting Design
   D. Total Sensory Marketing: Sounds and Smells
V. Visual Communications
   A. Name, Logo, and Retail Identity
   B. Institutional Signage
   C. Directional, Departmental, and Category Signage
   D. Point-of-Sale (POS) Signage
   E. Lifestyle Graphics
IV. Summary

INTRODUCTION

So far, we have discussed the nature of retailing, the retailer's competitive environment, merchandising and pricing, and where to locate stores. Now we discuss the retail store itself. Virtually all management activity is directed at making sure the right things happen in the store, and that the right customers enter the store, shop, and spend money. Simply put, for retailers the store is where the "rubber meets the road."

Though a store is composed of literally thousands of details, we will introduce two primary objectives around which all activities, functions, and goals in the store revolve: **market position image** and **sales productivity**. We will first define these objectives, then discuss how effective planning, merchandising, and design can help achieve them.

ELEMENTS OF THE STORE ENVIRONMENT

It is important to identify elements that compose the store environment, each of which will be discussed in detail in this chapter. Exhibit 12.1 shows how these many elements interact.

The first decision the retailer must make in planning a store is how to allocate the scarce resource, space. Next, the retailer must create a store layout, which shows the location of all merchandise departments and the placement of circulation aisles to allow customers to move through the store. The merchandise must catch and hold customers' attention, be easy to understand, and encourage shoppers to browse, evaluate, and buy. Therefore, the

EXHIBIT 12.1

Elements of Selling Environment

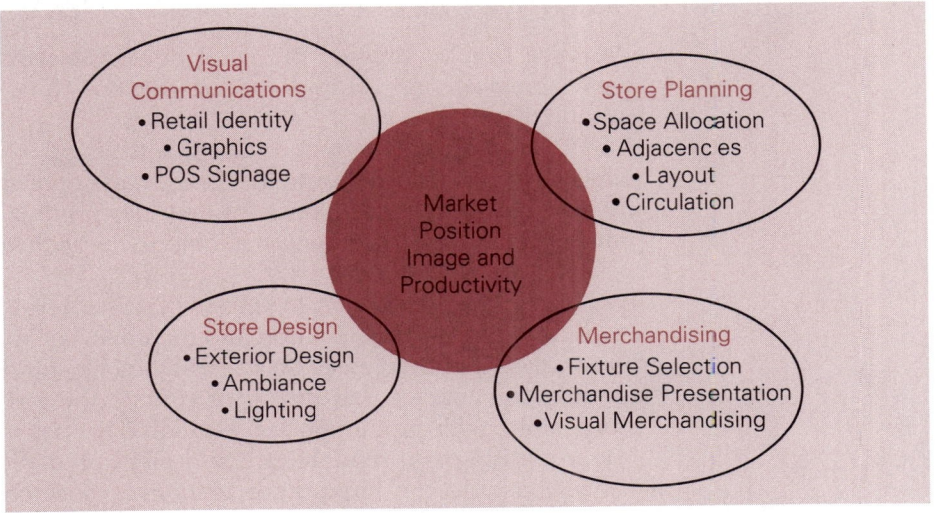

presentation of the merchandise—or **merchandising,** as it is often called—is one of the most critical factors in the sales power of a store. Book retailers have found, for instance, that by displaying books with the covers facing out, rather than the spines, they can sell more. However, "face-outs" take up more horizontal shelf space than "spine-outs," so the retailer must carefully balance the increased selling power of this technique against the reduced amount of inventory that can be carried.

At the same time, merchandise presentation has a significant impact on the market position image the store conveys. A bookstore with a high percentage of face-outs, for example, can create the image of being a specialty book boutique that carries a limited selection of exclusive titles and is therefore a rather pricey place to shop. A bookstore with virtually all spine-outs is often perceived as cramming in a huge selection of titles sold at low prices. So merchandise presentation is a critical factor in both the market position image and productivity of a store and will be discussed in detail later in the chapter.

Most shoppers are accustomed to noticing the design of the store, which comprises all elements affecting the human senses of sight, sound, smell, and touch. An effective store design, including storefront and interior, creates a comfortable environment that enhances the merchandise and entices shoppers to browse and buy. One aspect of design is lighting, which not only helps create the proper image but draws customers' eyes around the store and onto merchandise. Lighting design will be discussed in some detail.

Finally, in-store graphics such as art, photography, and signs form an important visual communication link between the store and its customers by providing much needed information on how to shop in the store.

OBJECTIVES OF THE STORE ENVIRONMENT

We have already stressed the two primary objectives of the store environment, creating the desired market position image and increasing sales productivity.

These objectives amount to a simple description of the retailer's mission, which is to get customers into the store (market position image) and influence them to buy merchandise once inside (sales productivity). The store planner must constantly balance these two objectives, as they are sometimes at odds.

Engineering the Market Position Image.
In Chapters 3 and 4 we discussed the retail customer and competition and the importance of creating the appropriate market position image in the customer's mind. The starting point in creating this market position is, of course, the merchandise carried in the store, along with promotion and selling. The store itself also serves a critical role in creating and reinforcing the desired market position image.[1]

To illustrate the importance of market position image, consider for a moment the words 7-Eleven. For most people, these words represent more

ILLUSTRATION 12.1

All visual and sensory communications made by a store send a message about its market position. The black mansard roof and dark colors of 7-Eleven's older stores (*left*) communicate a different message than the cleaner, more colorful new stores (*right*).

than just two numbers. Together, they form the name of one of the most ubiquitous retailers in the United States, the chain of more than 6,000 convenience stores.

The thoughts and emotions this logo evoke in customers constitute 7-Eleven's market position image. Regardless of what its managers would like its market image to be, regardless of what image they have tried to create, the store's actual market image exists only in the heads and hearts of consumers. Many factors influence that image.

First, the name itself has a great influence. If the stores were called "8-Twelve," we all might have a different image in our heads. (The name was created in 1946 to stress the stores' operating hours, 7 a.m. to 11 p.m. every day, then unheard of in retailing.[2]) The rhythm and rhyme of seven and eleven allow the name to roll easily off our tongues and be more memorable. The orange and green colors of the logo suggest to us certain things about the chain's quality. The storefront, historically a large black mansard roof, conveys a heavy, masculine appearance, and the windows plastered with price savings signs suggest a promotional environment. When you walk in the store, a buzzer warns clerks of entering shoppers, suggesting a concern about safety and theft. The smell of cheese nachos and the sight of sausages and hot dogs rolling up and down on the hot dogger create a certain atmosphere. Even the uniforms worn by the store clerks leave an impression, which joins all other impressions on the five senses to create 7-Eleven's store image in our minds. The market position image is an amalgam of dozens of in-store variables perceived by the consumer.[3]

Recently, in fact, 7-Eleven has conducted experiments to change its market position image to that of a higher-quality provider of service foods. Managers have altered not only the merchandise mix but such store variables as colors, layout, light levels, and aisle widths to affect the consumer's perception of 7-Eleven's market position.[4]

This is why planning the store environment is so important to a retailer. While advertising and other communications are all important in establishing a desired market position image, the store itself makes the most significant and lasting impression on our collective consciousness and it is here that the retailer must focus great energy on creating the right image.

This effort is complicated by the knowledge that consumers are extremely fickle, able to change their feelings about retailers at any time for little substantive reason, and the fact that today there are more stores than ever vying for limited consumer dollars. It is not surprising that **image engineering**—the ability to create and change market position image—becomes more important every day for a retailer's survival. Retailing in Action 12.1 shows how Sears has been very successful using store design to create a new market position image for its stores in Mexico City but has not been able to do so in the United States.

RETAILING IN ACTION

12.1 Image Repositioning in Mexico City

How important is a retailer's market position image to sales and profit? Sears, Roebuck, which had been the world's largest retailer for most of this century until losing that title to Wal-Mart in 1991, discovered the power of image repositioning in one of its international divisions.

Sears' Mexico division, Sears de Mexico, operates some 33 stores throughout the country, including 10 stores in Mexico City, now the world's largest city with more than 21 million residents. In 1988, Sears de Mexico began investigating ways to increase the productivity of its Mexico City stores, most of which were located in large shopping centers housing several other department stores. In the United States we know Sears as a lower-priced provider of good value, but Sears in Mexico carries higher-priced, brand-name fashion merchandise. Still, despite carrying much the same merchandise at lower prices than its competition, Sears de Mexico was not viewed by consumers as occupying the same market position. In other words, Sears' market positioning *image* did not match its intended market position. As shown in Exhibit 1, consumer research indicated that Sears' image differed from its competition in the important dimensions of quality and price. Sears had two choices: upscale its image to match its merchandise assortment or downscale its merchandise mix to match its current market position image.

Sears de Mexico decided to upscale the image of its Mexico City stores, based predominantly on store planning, merchandising, and design. Sears dramatically changed the store design from neutral beige tones to a contemporary, bold design featuring neon, video screens, and sophisticated lighting. The front entrance was converted into a grand atrium by cutting through the first and second floors. This atrium, anchored by a 32-screen video wall playing seductive perfume and fashion apparel videos, drew customers off the mall concourse and encouraged vertical movement through the store. The main floor, which housed men's and women's fashions, was organized into small boutique shops adorned heavily with marble floors, rich design materials, and expensive cove lighting. The lower level was converted into a dynamic youth store with young fashions shops circulating around a central core housing consumer electronics. Bright colors, unexpected architectural angles and elements, video terminals, and unique merchandising all contribute to an atmosphere of fun and excitement which attracts youthful buyers.

By dramatically modifying its store planning, merchandising, and design, Sears de Mexico was able to reposition its image to be more in line with the merchandise offering made by both its own stores and those of competitors. The result was a significant increase in sales, ranging from 100 to 175 percent in some stores. While the cost of remodeling the stores was great, doubling sales produced significant profit increases which quickly paid for the investment.

EXHIBIT 1

Image Repositioning of Sears de Mexico

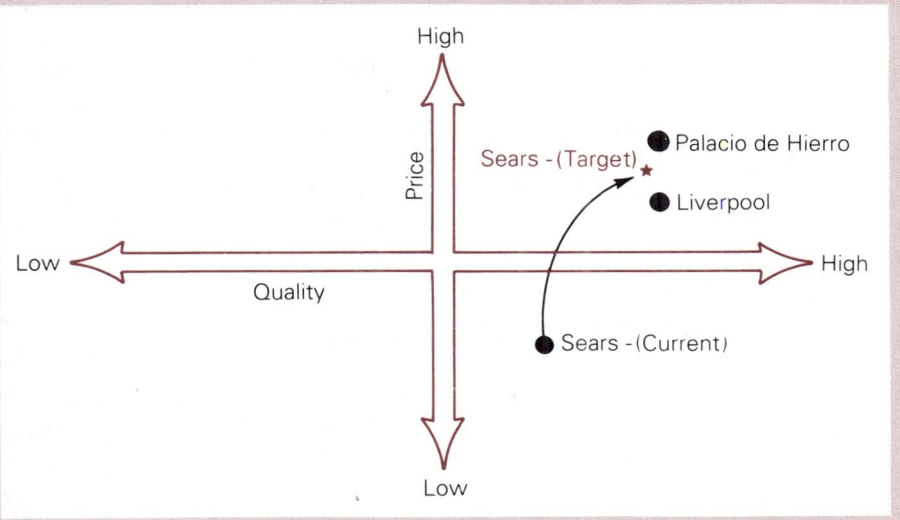

Increasing Sales Productivity. The image of a store attracts customers and keeps them coming back, but while they are there, the store must also convince shoppers to purchase. Therefore, the second major objective of the store environment is to increase the sales productivity of the store, a goal which is summarized in a simple but powerful truism in retailing: *The more merchandise customers are exposed to, the more they tend to buy.* Through careful planning of the store environment, the retailer can encourage customers to flow through the entire store and see a wide variety of merchandise.[5]

Many retailers are focusing more attention on **in-store marketing,** based on the theory that marketing dollars spent inside the store—in the form of store design, merchandising, visual displays, or in-store promotions—should lead to significantly more sales and profit increases than marketing dollars spent in advertising and other out-of-store vehicles such as public relations and promotions. It is easier to get a consumer who is already in your store to buy more merchandise than planned, than to get a new consumer to get in the car and make a trip to your store.[6]

One factor which detracts from sales productivity is **shrinkage,** or the loss of merchandise through theft, loss, and damage. (It is called shrinkage, because you usually don't know what happened to the missing items, only that the inventory level in the store has somehow shrunk.) Even stores which move customers through the entire space and effectively use in-store marketing techniques to maximize sales can fall victim to high shrinkage. Remember, when a store sells an item for $1.29, it earns only a small percentage of that sale, perhaps ranging from 15 to 60 cents. When that item is stolen, lost, or damaged, however, the store loses the entire $1.29, and this loss is deducted from the store's overall sales. Shrinkage ranges from 1 to 4 percent of retail sales. While this may seem like a small number, consider that many retailers' after-tax profit is little more than 2 percent, so high shrinkage alone can make the difference between a profit and a loss. National statistics indicate that shrinkage amounts to more than $27 billion in losses annually.[7]

Therefore, to enhance sales productivity, retailers must incorporate planning, merchandising, and design strategies which minimize shrinkage by avoiding hidden areas of the store which shoplifters can take advantage of, and reduce the number of times merchandise must be moved, during which damage and loss can occur.

CREATING THE STORE ENVIRONMENT

Who Creates the Store Environment. Creating the store environment requires a seemingly endless list of tasks, some very strategic in nature and some simply the nuts and bolts that hold a store together. But who actually designs and creates the store environment?

In most retail organizations, the store environment is seen as a strategic issue, the responsibility for which ultimately rests with the chief executive officer or president. Many CEOs, who often spend great amounts of time visiting competitive stores, initiate projects to enhance or revise the store format to be used throughout the store chain. In most organizations with more than 11 or so stores, the retailer develops a **prototype** store format that is then repeated in all stores, with minor adaptations to local merchandising or market conditions.

But the CEO's involvement typically ends with setting broad strategic directions and reviewing concepts once they are developed, for the store planning process is extremely detailed and could easily consume too much of the CEO's time. The CEO must also attend to merchandise buying, distribution, promotion, and financial management issues to keep the whole operation running. From there, most retail organizations have a dedicated store planning and design staff responsible for development of the store concepts. Within the store planning and design department are store planners (usually architects or architectural draftspersons who have specialized in space utilization and developing floorplans) and interior or industrial designers. There are also often specialists in fixture selection and merchandise presentation.

As an adjunct to these internal staffs, an entire industry of retail design firms has emerged to work with retailers on special projects, usually the development every several years of a new prototype to guide stores over a four- to seven-year period. These design firms range from architectural firms with expertise in retail design to so-called "space productivity firms" that specialize in store planning and merchandise presentation and their impact on increasing sales.

Steps in Creating a Store. We now turn to the actual tasks and functions in developing an effective store. As you review these functions, it might be helpful to consider that designing an effective retail store is like creating an effective piece of writing, and that moving through a store as a customer is much like reading through an article or a chapter in a book. The words are like the merchandise, which are there for you to review, understand, and consume. Just as a book needs more than words to make sense, a store needs more than merchandise to be shoppable.

The layout and organization of the store is like the organization of chapters, sections, and subsections in this book. Grouping the words and thoughts into "mental chunks" makes the book easier to digest and understand. A store that is not broken into departments and categories would be impossible to shop. The pants would be mixed in with the shovels, the socks would be mixed in with the garden plants, and you wouldn't know where to begin.

Signs and graphics are like the headlines and punctuation, which give you cues to understanding the organization of both a book and the merchandise in a store. Without headlines and subheadlines, this chapter would be a stream of words, very difficult—and worse, boring—to read and understand. Similarly, without signs, a store would seem like an endless sea of racks and merchandise difficult to understand and shop.

Finally, the illustrations, exhibits, and charts in this book have a retail equivalent in the visual displays and focal points—or areas where the merchandise is pulled off the shelf or racks and displayed in theatrical vignettes— that successful retailers use to break up the store space, illustrate merchandise opportunities in the store, and visually demonstrate how certain merchandise goes together or can work in your life. Like illustrations and exhibits in a book, these visual displays elaborate on the text, or the bulk of merchandise on the racks, to make editorial statements.

Most importantly, a retail store and a piece of writing are very similar in the way they affect the consumer. Many writing coaches teach aspiring writers that each time an uncommon word is used, or a punctuation mark is missing, the reader hits a "speed bump" in the writing and must mentally pause to consider what is meant. After hitting three speed bumps, readers may conclude that the writing is too difficult to understand and quit reading.

It is the same in a retail store. All cues must work subliminally to organize the merchandise and guide the shopper effortlessly through the store. Each time shoppers become a bit confused as to where they are, where they need to go, how much an item costs, or where certain merchandise is, they become frustrated. The first or second instance may not be noticed, but the shopper quickly becomes frustrated and may conclude the store is too hard to shop.

Most shoppers cannot consciously identify the elements of a good store, but certainly they recognize when they are missing.[8] We have all experienced the feeling that a store seems to "really have it together." It's easy to shop, fun, and exciting; the merchandise is easy to understand; the associates seem friendly. You conclude that this store is a "good shop" and, with any luck, are completely oblivious to the thousands of little details that have guided you through the shopping experience.

STORE PLANNING

The term "store planning" has a special meaning in retailing, referring to floorplanning, or developing the layout of the store. The floorplan, like an architectural blueprint, indicates where merchandise and customer service departments are located, how customers circulate through the store, and how much space is dedicated to each department. The floorplan serves as the backbone of the store and is the fundamental structure around which every other element of the store environment takes shape. Therefore, the store layout must be carefully planned to meet the strategic merchandising goals of the organization, make the store easy to understand and shop, and allow merchandise to be effectively presented.

ALLOCATING SPACE

As with most elements of the store environment, there is both an art and a science to creating the store layout. This is true because the starting point of store planning is determining how the available store space—usually measured in square footage—will be allocated to various departments, and this allocation can be based on mathematical calculation of the returns generated by different types of merchandise. So for most retailers, the store planning process begins with determining how to allocate space. Before describing this process, however, we must understand the various types of space in the store.

Types of Space in the Store. Shoppers are most familiar with the sales floor, but this is not the only element in a retail store with which the planner must contend. There are five basic types of space in a store: back room; office and other functional spaces; aisles, service areas, and other nonselling areas of the main sales floor; wall merchandise space; and floor merchandise space. The store planner must balance the quest for greater density of merchandise presentation with the shoppability and functionality of the store. Since space is the retailer's ultimate scarce resource, rarely can the store planner achieve all of his or her desired goals. Rather, most store planners find themselves compromising one or more dimensions, carefully weighing the priorities, strategic goals, and special constraints of their company. In reviewing each of these categories of space, the goal should be to make the largest possible amount of space available to hold merchandise and be shoppable.

Back Room. To operate virtually any type of retail store, some space is required as back room, which includes the receiving area to process arriving inventories and the stockroom to store surplus merchandise. The percentage of space dedicated to the back room varies greatly depending on the type of retailer, but the amount of space is shrinking for all types. Historical back-room percentages have ranged from nearly 50 percent in some department stores, to as little as 10 percent in some small specialty and convenience stores. General-merchandise stores have historically dedicated about 15 to 20 percent of their store space to the back room. The need to squeeze more sales out of expensive retail space, coupled with new distribution methods allowing smaller, more frequent merchandise deliveries from suppliers (called **quick response** inventory control), have allowed retailers to shrink their back rooms, with department stores cutting back to about 25 percent, and others cutting back to 5 percent or even less.

Some recent retail formats, such as warehouse clubs, have only receiving areas but virtually no back-room stock capacity. In these stores, the store fixtures are usually large "warehouse racks" that carry shoppable inventory at reachable heights (up to 84 inches), and carry large palettes or cartons of excess inventory at higher levels. These racks can go as high as 15 feet.

There is an important store planning lesson here. Warehouse clubs are taking advantage not only of the width and depth of the store, but also the height. In other words, while retailers pay expensive rents for their store space, as measured in square footage, the store and the merchandise can be stacked as high as possible at little additional cost, using the *cubic* footage of the store. The ability of shoppers to reach does limit the height at which shoppable merchandise can be stacked, but it does not limit the use of this high space to carry excess inventory. The same inventory carried in the back room would consume additional square footage, either causing higher rent or reducing the amount of shoppable space. Essentially, the sales floor doubles as the back room. Most importantly, this stocking method visually creates a dramatic low-cost image in the store, which can be advantageous to value-oriented retailers, but detrimental to fashion or high-end retailers.

Offices and Other Functional Spaces. Every store must contain a certain amount of office and other functional space. This often includes a break room for associates, a training room, offices for the store manager and assistant managers, a cash office, bathroom facilities for both customers and employees, and perhaps other areas. While necessary, the location of such functional spaces receives a lower priority than the location of the sales floor and stockroom. Often they are located on mezzanines over the front of the store or over the back stockroom, or in side spaces too small to be stockrooms.

Aisles, Service Areas, and Other Nonselling Areas. Even on the main sales floor, some space must be given up to nonselling functions, the most obvious of which is moving large numbers of shoppers through the store. The store planner's first step, particularly in larger stores, is to create main aisles through which shoppers will flow on their way through the store, and secondary aisles that draw customers back into the merchandise. These aisles must be wide enough to accommodate peak crowds, and in large stores may be as wide as 15 feet. The amount of space dedicated to aisles can be significant. For instance, a 15-foot aisle running around the perimeter of an 80,000-square-foot store (the size of a typical discount store) may consume 12,000 square feet, or 15 percent of the entire space!

In addition to aisles, space must be given to dressing rooms, layaway areas, service desks, and other customer service facilities that cannot be merchandised. While the store planner always attempts to minimize the amount of nonselling space, customer service is an equally important part of a store and should not be short-changed.

Floor Merchandise Space. Finally, we come to the store space with which we as shoppers are most familiar, the floor merchandise space. Here, many different types of fixtures are used to display a wide variety of merchandise. Generally speaking, retailers use so-called "bulk" fixtures on the floor to carry large quantities of merchandise. But increasingly, retailers are realizing that the best goal isn't just to cram the largest possible amount of merchandise on the floor, but to attractively and effectively display the largest amount customers can understand and shop.

Wall Merchandise Space. The walls are one of the most important elements of a retail store. They serve as fixtures holding tremendous amounts of merchandise, as well as serving as a visual backdrop for the merchandise on the floor.

Space Allocation Planning. To determine the most productive allocation of space, the store planner must first analyze the productivity and profitability of various categories of merchandise. In Chapter 2 we introduced various methods for measuring merchandise performance, such as gross margin return on inventory (GMROI) and gross margin return on space (GMROS). No matter what type of productivity analysis is done, the results must somehow be related to the space in the store, in order to determine the best allocation of the square footage. There are two situations with which a retailer may have to deal: planning a new store and revising the space allocation of an existing store.

Space Allocations for a New Store. When a retailer is creating a new store format, no productivity and profitability data are available on which to base the allocation of space. In most cases, the retailer bases space allocation on industry standards, previous experience with similar formats, or more frequently, the space required to carry the number of items specified by the buyers. Once a detailed assortment plan has been created, typical stock levels are estimated based on minimum and maximum quantities. The store planner can then determine the amount of shelf space required to carry this merchandise. By determining the space for each item, then for each category, then for each department, the store planner can create a space allocation plan for the entire store, as well as the total square footage required for the store. As you can imagine, this is a grueling process.

Enhancing Space Productivity in Existing Stores. When a retailer has been in business for some time, it can develop a sales history on which to evaluate merchandise performance, refine space allocations, and enhance space productivity. Exhibit 12.2 shows a **merchandise productivity analysis,** which relates GMROI, GMROS, and square footage for various merchandise categories. The final column shows the **space productivity index,** which compares the ranking of the gross margin of a particular category to its percentage of space utilized. An index rating of 1.0 would be an ideal department size. If the index is greater than 1.0, the category is performing somewhat better than should be expected, and consideration should be given to allocating additional space to it. If the index falls below 1.0, the category is underperforming relative to other categories, and it should perhaps be reduced in size. The merchandise productivity analysis shown in Exhibit 12.2 indicates that in this store, softlines categories are performing very well and should be given more space (index of 1.29), and hardlines are underperforming and should be downsized (index of 0.86). Overall, the store is performing fairly well, with a space productivity index of 1.05.

Of course, as with all financial analysis, the space productivity index is simply a tool to help management make decisions, not a decision-making formula. Even though a certain category may have a low index, senior management may retain its full space because a new buyer has just been hired, or because the category is an important image builder. A high-index category might not be given more space if management expects a hot fashion trend to cool off soon and believes the space productivity index for that category will drop accordingly.

STORE LAYOUT

The next step in planning the store is developing the store layout, a two-dimensional floorplan that visually describes where each of the store elements listed previously will be located. The steps in this process are deciding

EXHIBIT 12.2
Merchandise Productivity Analysis

Category	Total Sales	Sale as % Total	Total Sq. Ft.	Sq. Ft. % Total	Sales per Sq. Ft.	Total G.M. $	G.M. $ % Total	GM$/s.f. (GMROS)	Average Inventory Cost	Turnover (sales/Avg. Invent.)	Inventory Intensity ($/sq.ft.)	G.M. $/ Avg.Inv. (GMROI)	Space Productivity Index
Juniors	259,645	3.9	1,602	2.9	162.05	211,497	4.57	132	49,531	5.24	31	4.27	1.58
Dresses	47,829	0.7	608	1.1	78.70	33,426	0.72	55	15,057	3.18	25	2.22	0.66
Misses	512,458	7.7	3,702	6.7	138.44	429,403	9.29	116	79,372	6.46	21	5.41	1.39
Womens	170,819	2.6	1,934	3.5	88.34	148,899	3.22	77	44,714	3.82	23	3.33	0.92
Boys	184,485	2.8	2,542	4.6	72.59	144,866	3.13	57	66,452	2.78	26	2.18	0.68
Mens	751,604	11.3	3,591	6.5	209.29	603,330	13.05	168	236,600	3.18	66	2.55	2.01
Infants	204,983	3.1	1,658	3.0	123.67	142,545	3.08	86	78,754	2.60	48	1.81	1.03
Toddlers	47,829	0.7	497	0.9	96.19	43,261	0.94	87	14,566	3.28	29	2.97	1.04
Girls	191,318	2.9	2,542	4.6	75.28	157,573	3.41	62	63,282	3.02	25	2.49	0.74
Lingerie	273,311	4.1	2,431	4.4	112.43	262,548	5.68	108	110,314	2.48	45	2.38	1.29
Accessories	245,980	3.7	1,602	2.9	153.52	238,735	5.16	149	78,274	3.14	49	3.05	1.78
Jewelry	129,823	1.9	829	1.5	156.65	123,484	2.67	149	82,323	1.58	99	1.50	1.78
Total Softlines	3,020,084	45.2	23,537	42.6	128.31	2,539,566	54.92	1,246	919,239	3.29	39	2.76	1.29
Domestics	498,792	7.3	4,531	8.2	110.10	407,745	8.82	90	326,196	1.53	72	1.25	1.08
HBA	464,628	6.8	1,989	3.6	233.60	153,153	3.31	77	228,587	2.03	115	0.67	0.92
Housewares	457,795	6.7	3,591	6.5	127.48	254,979	5.51	71	190,283	2.41	53	1.34	0.85
Cosmetics	75,160	1.1	608	1.1	123.67	55,913	1.21	92	67,365	1.12	111	0.83	1.10
Tobacco	140,187	2.1	221	0.4	649.27	37,349	0.81	169	4,857	28.86	22	7.69	2.02
Candy	144,944	2.2	387	0.7	371.01	88,179	1.91	228	37,364	3.88	97	2.36	2.72
Sporting Goods	184,485	2.8	2,652	4.8	69.56	129,948	2.81	49	175,605	1.05	66	0.74	0.59
Stationery	307,475	4.6	2,763	5.0	111.30	254,150	5.50	92	171,723	1.79	62	1.48	1.10
Furniture	75,160	1.1	1,547	2.8	48.58	60,333	1.30	39	50,700	1.48	33	1.19	0.47
Home Entertainment	601,284	9.0	2,265	4.1	265.44	255,973	5.54	113	324,017	1.86	143	0.79	1.35
Toys	300,642	4.5	2,431	4.4	123.67	143,429	3.10	59	174,913	1.72	72	0.82	0.70
Seasonal	145,333	2.2	2,652	4.8	54.11	90,168	1.95	34	39,203	3.71	15	2.30	0.41
Hardware/Paint	163,986	2.5	2,100	3.8	78.11	111,274	2.41	53	163,638	1.00	78	0.68	0.63
Pet Supplies	13,666	0.2	55	0.1	247.34	13,094	0.28	237	4,424	3.09	80	2.96	2.83
Auto Accessories	81,993	1.2	1,271	2.3	64.52	29,227	0.63	23	85,963	0.95	68	0.34	0.27
Total Hardlines	3,655,480	54.8	29,061	52.6	125.79	2,084,914	45.08	1,426	2,044,837	1.79	70	1.02	0.86
Total Stores	6,675,564	100.0	55,250	95.2		4,624,480	100.00	2,672	2,964,076	2.25	54	1.56	1.05

on adjacencies, developing a **bubble plan,** and refining the bubble plan into a **block plan.**

Adjacencies.
The space allocations determined through merchandise productivity analysis deal with quantities, but not qualities; they are simply numbers that represent the "science" of store planning. The "art" comes in when it is time to create the **adjacencies plan,** which determines which categories will be placed adjacent to each other. The adjacencies plan forms the foundation for a successful selling environment, because placement of certain categories adjacent to one another can enhance the sales of one or both, while certain adjacencies can actually decrease sales. Fashion retailer Ann Taylor, for instance, formerly carried an expensive line of Joan & David shoes, a category which produced mediocre margins but increased overall store sales by attracting traffic.[9] The store planner must learn the art of adjacencies planning through years of study and experience.

A good example of the power of adjacencies is seen in most discount stores, which often group together costume jewelry, cosmetics, and fashion accessories such as handbags. Though this grouping might seem natural to us now, it was not always so. Though the three categories are purchased by different buyers and seem unrelated, over time store managers realized they were quite similar in the role they play in customers' lives—helping women enhance their appearance—and grouped them together. Now the store created a market position image of catering to shoppers' fashion needs, and customers shopping for one fashion accessory were exposed to others, creating add-on sales.

Bubble Planning.
The extensive thought process devoted to planning adjacencies is reduced to paper in the form of the **bubble plan,** which shows the rough placement and adjacency of key elements of the proposed store. Exhibit 12.3 shows a sample bubble plan. As you can see, the bubble plan does not contain a great deal of detail, but it shows the approximate size and shape of the store building (also called the "footprint") and the size and placement of back room and functional spaces, main areas or "worlds" of merchandise, and customer service areas.

Usually, several alternative bubble plans are prepared and then presented to management. Bubble plans should demonstrate a general interpretation of the retailer's strategic goals. For instance, if the retailer wants to improve its image in fashion apparel, fashion departments might be located in more visually prominent parts of the store. If consumer research has revealed a poor service image, the customer service desk might be located in a more visible location. If traffic flow has been a problem, main aisles may be widened and a more defined customer circulation pattern indicated. These variables are discussed with management, and one or two bubble plans are identified as going in the right strategic direction. These plans then become the subject of block planning.

EXHIBIT 12.3

Sample Bubble Plan

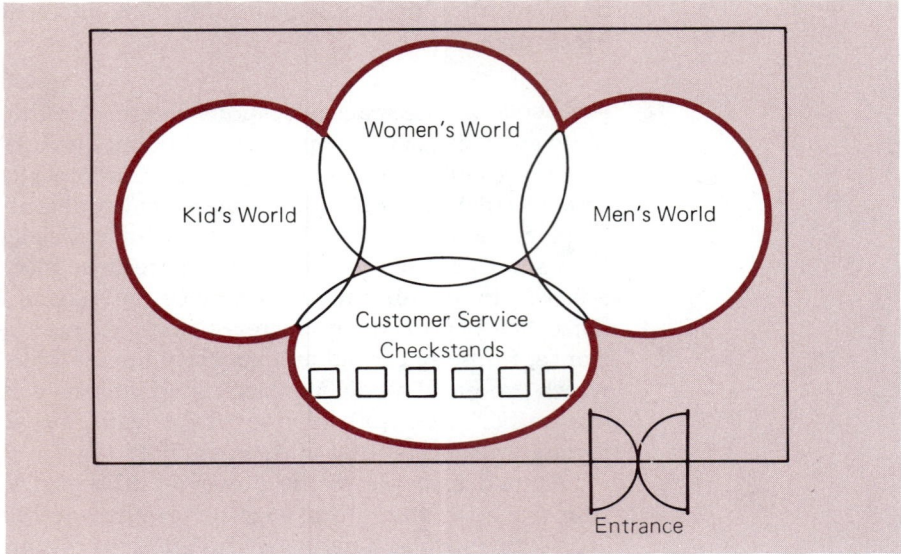

Block Planning. The **block plan** delineates the actual sizes and shapes of all store components. Here, as shown in Exhibit 12.4, the relatively large "bubbles" in the bubble plan are broken down into their component departments and categories, and the previously determined square footage allocations are applied. Each department is laid in and measured for accurate square footage. Each customer service area, back-room space, and functional element is configured according to its recommended size and functional requirements. While determining the placement of fixtures is not a primary goal of block planning, a limited number of fixtures may be indicated to demonstrate how fixtures can fit into the departments.

Again, management reviews several alternative block plans to determine how they satisfy strategic objectives and functionality. Often, in this more detailed stage of planning, some promising bubble plan ideas are determined to be unachievable due to space constraints or physical impediments such as the locations of supporting columns, and are eliminated.

CIRCULATION

The **circulation pattern** not only ensures efficient movement of large numbers of shoppers through the store, exposing them to more merchandise, but also determines the character of the store. There are four basic types of layout in use today—the free flow, grid, loop, and spine—each of which is described in the following discussion. Shoppers have been trained to associate certain circulation patterns with different types of stores, so in reading these descriptions, try to think of how they are used in different stores you shop and the store image they evoke in your mind.

EXHIBIT 12.4

Sample Block Plan

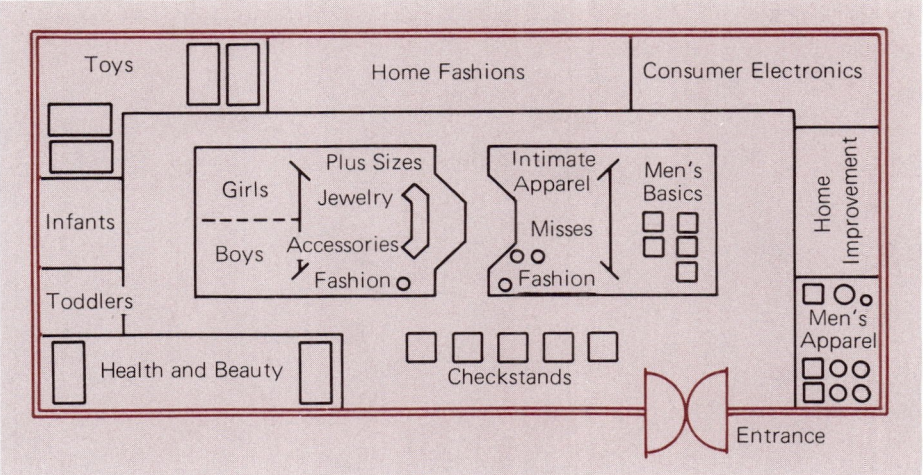

Free Flow. The simplest type of store layout is a **free-flow layout** (Exhibit 12.5), in which fixtures and merchandise are grouped into free-flowing patterns on the sales floor. Customers are encouraged to flow freely through all the fixtures, since there are usually no defined traffic patterns in the store. This type of layout works well in small fashion stores, usually smaller than 5,000 square feet, in which customers wish to browse through all of the merchandise. Generally, all the merchandise is of the same type, such as all fashion apparel, perhaps categorized only into tops and bottoms. If there is a greater variety of merchandise (for instance, men's and women's apparel, bedding, and health and beauty aids), a free-flow layout fails to provide cues as to where one department stops and another starts, confusing the shopper.

Grid. Another traditional form of store layout is the **grid layout,** in which the counters and fixtures are placed in long rows or "runs," usually at right angles, throughout the store. In a grid layout (Exhibit 12.6) customers circulate up and down through the fixtures, and, in fact, the grid layout is often referred to as a "maze." The most familiar examples of the grid layout are supermarkets and drugstores.

The grid is a true "shopping" layout, best used in retail environments in which the majority of customers wish to shop the entire store. In supermarkets, for instance, many shoppers flow methodically up and down all the fixture runs, looking for everything they might need along the way. However, if the shopper wishes to find only several specific categories, the grid can be confusing and frustrating, because it is difficult to see over the fixtures to where other merchandise is located (especially today, as fixtures have become higher). Of course, retailers like the idea of moving customers through the entire store, but forcing customers to do this when they don't want to may frustrate customers and lead to less rather than more sales.

EXHIBIT 12.5
Free-Flow Layout

EXHIBIT 12.6
Grid Layout

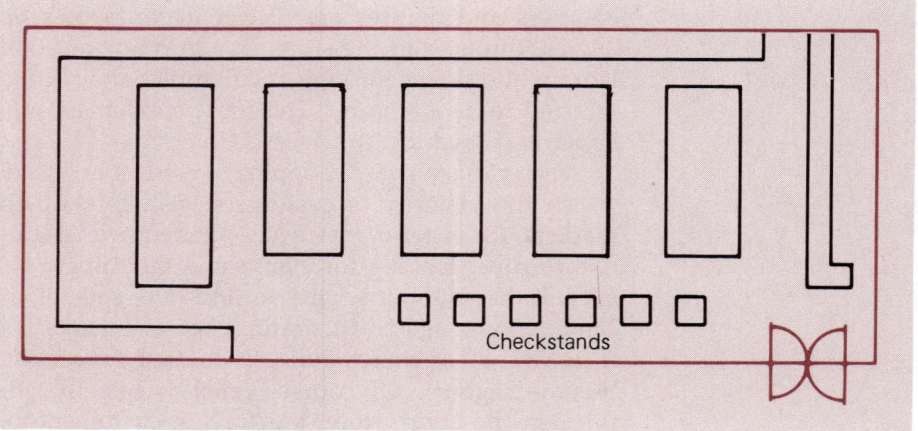

Loop. Over the past 15 years, the **loop layout** (sometimes called a "racetrack") has become popular as a tool for enhancing the productivity of retail stores. Defined simply, a "loop" (Exhibit 12.7) provides a major customer aisle which begins at the entrance, "loops" through the store, usually in the shape of a circle, square, or rectangle, and then returns the customer to the front of the store. While this seems like a simple concept, the loop can be a powerful sales productivity tool.

The strategic foundations of the loop are found in the key objective of a store: exposing shoppers to the greatest possible amount of merchandise. An effective circulation pattern must first guide customers throughout the store to encourage browsing and cross-shopping. Along the way, shoppers must be able to easily see and understand merchandise to the left and right, so ideally the main aisle should never stray more than 60 feet from any merchandise. The way to simultaneously accomplish these two goals is to create a main circulation loop that mirrors the configuration of the outside walls of the store, and is never more than 60 feet from the outside wall. In larger stores, the interior island of the loop can itself be too large to easily see across, and internal walls may be created to shorten sightlines to merchandise.

Spine. The **spine layout** (Exhibit 12.8) is essentially a variation of the free-flow, grid, and loop layouts and combines the advantages of all three in certain circumstances. A spine layout is based on a single main aisle running from the front to the back of the store, transporting customers in both directions. On either side of this spine, merchandise departments branch off toward the back or side walls. Within these departments, either a free-flow or

EXHIBIT 12.7

Loop Layout

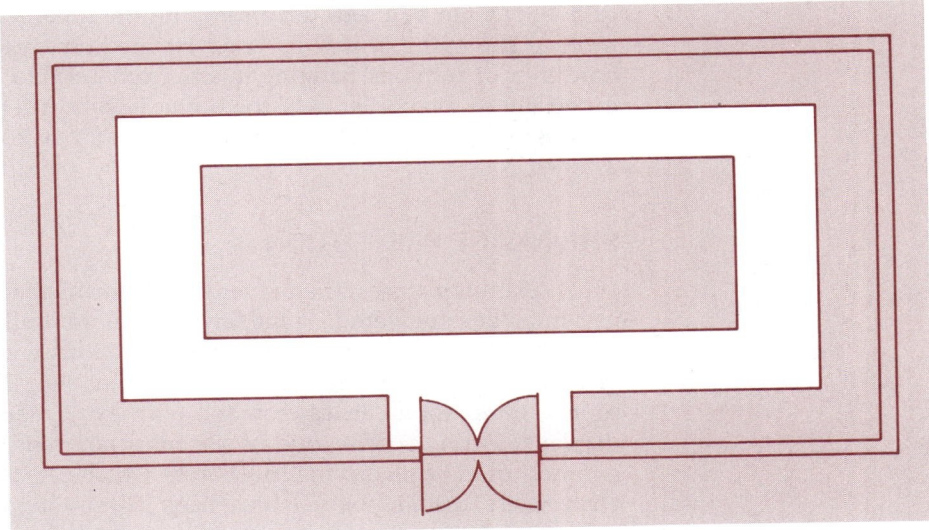

EXHIBIT 12.8

Spine Layout

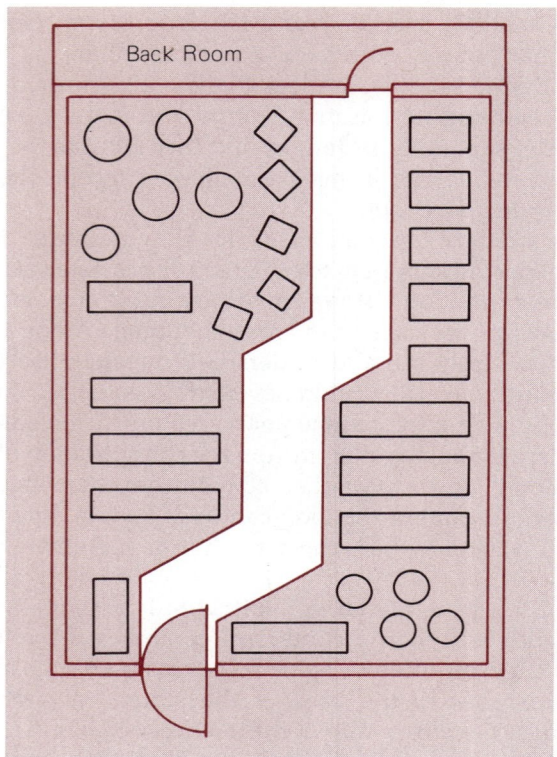

grid layout can be used, depending on the type of merchandise and fixtures in use. The spine is heavily used by medium-sized specialty stores, either hardlines or softlines, ranging in size from 2,000 to 10,000 square feet. Often, especially in fashion stores, the spine is subtly set off by a change in floor coloring or surface and is not perceived as an aisle, even though it functions as such.

SHRINKAGE PREVENTION

When planning stores, the prevention of shrinkage due to theft, damage, and loss must be considered. Some layouts will minimize vulnerability to shoplifters. One of the most important considerations when planning the layout is visibility of the merchandise. Most customer shoplifting takes place in fitting rooms, blind spots, aisles crowded with extra merchandise, or behind high displays. Fitting rooms, one of the most common scenes of the shoplifting crime, should be placed in visible areas which can be monitored by associates. Historically, display fixtures have been kept no higher than eye level, to allow store associates to monitor customers in other aisles. Recently, mass merchandisers have found that increased sales from the greater merchandise intensity of higher fixtures outweighs the increase in shoplifting due to reduced visibility. This depends greatly on merchandise type, however. Expensive items which are easily placed into pockets and handbags, such as compact discs, are high-theft items, and are usually kept on low fixtures to discourage shoplifting. The manager's office and other security windows can be an excellent deterrent to shoplifting if they are placed in an obvious area above the sales floor level, where managers can easily see the entire store. Electronic security systems, including sensor tags and video cameras, have become very popular, and are usually located in a highly visible location to serve as a deterrent.

FIXTURE SELECTION AND MERCHANDISE PRESENTATION PLANNING

It has often been said that retailing is theater, and in no area is that more true than in merchandise presentation, or merchandising, as it is often called. Retailers have emphasized merchandising over the past 15 years, as competition has grown and stores must squeeze more sales out of existing square footage. There are two basic types of merchandising, visual merchandising and on-shelf merchandising. In the "theater" of retailing, visual merchandising displays are analogous to the props which set scenes and serve as backdrops, while on-shelf merchandising represents the stars.

As you might expect, merchandising is a complex activity best learned on the retail floor. While this text will not attempt to teach the art and science of merchandising, you should be familiar with a number of basic components of merchandising and their potential impact on store image and sales, including fixture type and selection and certain techniques and methods of on-shelf merchandising.

As its name implies, on-shelf merchandising describes the merchandise which is displayed on and in counters, racks, shelves, and fixtures throughout the store. This is the merchandise that the shopper actually touches, tries on, examines, reads, understands, and hopefully buys. Therefore, on-shelf merchandising must not only present the merchandise attractively, it must display the merchandise in a manner that is easy to understand and accessible to the shopper. Further, it must be reasonably easy to maintain, with customers themselves able to replace merchandise so it is equally appealing to the next shopper.

FIXTURE TYPES

There are many different types of store fixtures, and more are being developed every day, but they fall into a few basic categories with which you should be familiar—hardlines, softlines, and wall fixtures.

Hardlines Fixtures. The workhorse fixture in most hardlines departments is known as the gondola, so named because it is a long structure consisting of a large base, a vertical spine or wall sticking up as high as eight feet, fitted with sockets or notches into which a variety of shelves, peghooks, bins, baskets, and other hardware can be inserted. The basic gondola, shown in Exhibit 12.9, can hold a wide variety of merchandise—in fact, virtually all hardlines—by means of hardware hung from the vertical spine. If you think of your last trip to a discount store or supermarket, the long, heavy duty fixtures fitted predominantly with shelves are gondolas. In fact, you can probably recall gondolas in virtually every store you have visited recently, as they are the most pervasive fixture in retailing. For sturdiness, flexibility, and functionality, the gondola simply can't be beat.

For hardlines, there are only a few other types of fixtures in common use today. Tables, large bins, and simple flat-base decks are used to display bulk quantities of merchandise when the retailer wants to make a high-value statement. These fixtures are commonly used in promotional aisles to display advertised or other special value merchandise.

Softlines Fixtures. Of course, the bulky gondola is inappropriate for fashion-oriented softlines merchandise. A large array of fixtures have been developed to accommodate the special needs of softlines, which often are hung on hangers. As shown in Exhibit 12.10, the four-way feature rack and the round rack are the two fixtures most heavily used today. These smaller, more specialized fixtures have replaced the straight rack, a long pipe with legs on

EXHIBIT 12.9
Gondola

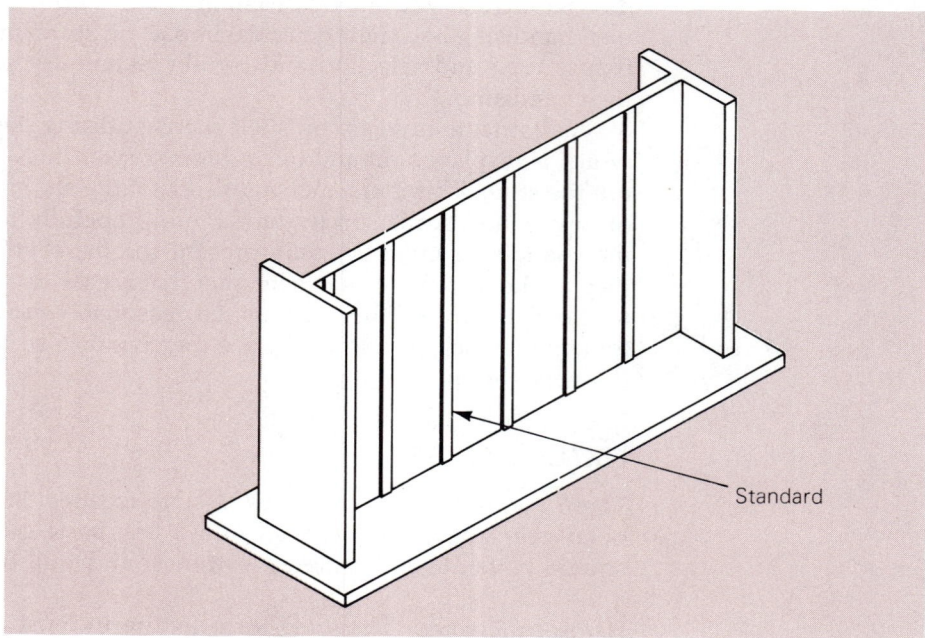

each end from which rows of apparel were hung, which for generations was the most prevalent softlines fixture. While it held a great quantity of garments and was easy to maintain, the straight rack provided few opportunities to differentiate one style or color of garment from another, which merchants have found is the key to selling more. A straight rack is like the hanger rod in your closet, and if you think of what you see when you open your closet, it is nothing more than sleeves. You know your own clothes, so sleeves are enough to tip you off to what the rest of the garment looks like. When you are shopping, however, the more of the garment you are exposed to—and the more varieties of size, silhouette (shape), and color—the more you are going to buy. So merchants prefer "face out" presentations over "sleeve out" presentations. Of course, face-outs take up more space than sleeve-outs, so it is impractical to face out all or even a high percentage of the total merchandise on the floor.

The round rack is known as a **bulk or capacity fixture** and is intended to hold the bulk of merchandise without looking as heavy as a long straight rack of merchandise. While it is smaller than the straight rack, it too allows only sleeve-outs unless fitted with special hardware. The four-way rack, on the other hand, is considered a **feature fixture,** because it presents merchandise in a manner which features certain characteristics of the merchandise (such as

EXHIBIT 12.10

4 Way Feature Rack (*left*) and Round Rack (*right*).

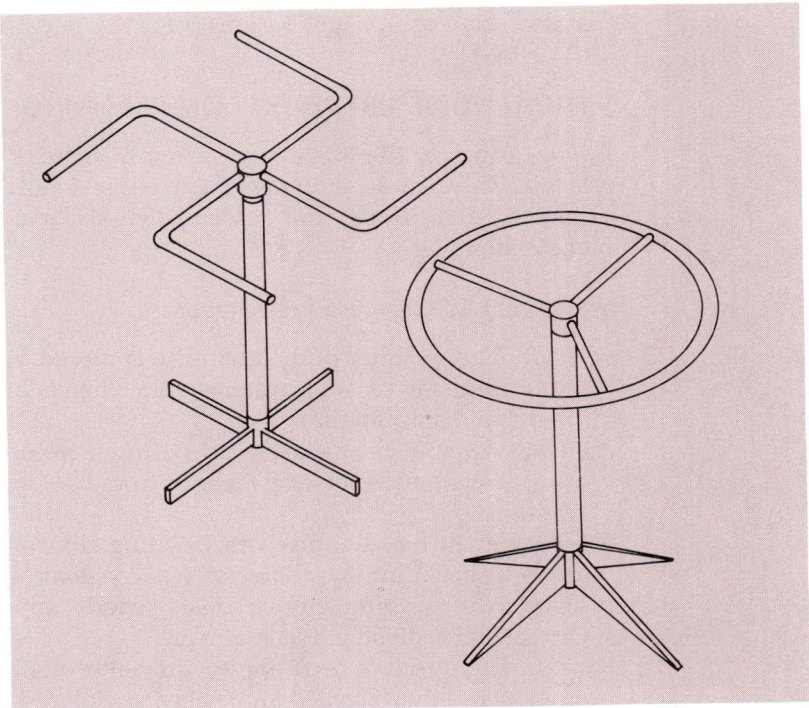

color, shape, or style). The ingenious design allows it also to hold a large quantity of merchandise on the hanger arms behind the four face-outs. However, to be easily shopped, all the merchandise on one arm must be the same type of garment with variations only in color and size. When poorly merchandised so that the front garment doesn't match those behind it, the four-way leaves the customer in the same quandary as the straight rack.

Wall Fixtures. The last type of fixture are those designed to be hung on the wall. To make a plain wall merchandiseable, it is usually covered with a vertical skin that is fitted with vertical columns of notches similar to those on the gondola, into which a variety of hardware can be inserted. Shelves, peghooks, bins, baskets, and even hanger bars can be fitted into wall systems. Hanger bars can be hung parallel to the wall, much like your closet bar, so that large quantities of garments can be "sleeved out," or they can protrude perpendicularly from the wall, either straight out (straight-outs) or angled down (waterfalls), to allow merchandise to be faced out. The primary quality to remember about wall systems is that walls can generally be merchandised much higher than floor fixtures. Whereas on the floor, round racks are kept to a maximum of 42 inches so that customers can easily see over them to other merchandise, garments can be hung on the wall as high as customers can reach, which is generally about 72 inches. This allows walls to be "double hung" with two rows of garments, or even "triple hung" with smaller children's apparel. Therefore, walls not only hold large amounts of merchandise, but also serve as a visual backdrop for the department.

MERCHANDISE PRESENTATION PLANNING

As you can see, there is a large array of fixtures and hardware for use by retailers. This may seem to present an endless variety of ways to merchandise products, but there are essentially six methods of merchandising presentation.

Methods of Merchandise Presentation.

Shelving. The majority of merchandise is placed on shelves that are inserted into gondolas or wall systems. Shelving is a flexible, easy-to-maintain merchandising method.
Hanging. Apparel on hangers can be hung from softlines fixtures, such as round racks and four-way racks or from bars installed on gondolas or wall systems.
Pegging. Small merchandise can be hung from peghooks, which are small rods inserted into gondolas or wall systems. Used in both softlines and hardlines, pegging gives a neat, orderly appearance, but can be labor intensive to display and maintain.
Folding. Higher-margin or large, unwieldy softlines merchandise can be folded and then stacked onto shelves or placed on tables. This can create a

Chapter 12 Store Planning, Design, and Merchandising 427

ILLUSTRATION 12.2

Shelving is one of the six predominant methods of merchandising products. The way in which merchandise is displayed affects how the customer perceives the merchandise — whether trendy, exclusive, pricey, or value-oriented.

high-fashion image, such as when bath towels are taken off peghooks and neatly folded and stacked high up the wall.

Stacking. Large hardlines merchandise can be stacked on shelves, the base decks of gondolas, or "flats," which are platforms placed directly on the floor. Stacking is easily maintained and gives an image of high volume and low price.

Dumping. Large quantities of small merchandise can be dumped in bins or baskets inserted into gondolas or wall systems. This method can be used in softlines (socks, wash cloths) or hardlines (batteries, candy), and creates a high-volume, low-cost image.

Psychology of Merchandise Presentation. The method of merchandise presentation can have a dramatic impact on image and sales effectiveness. While none of us likes to admit it, different merchandising methods can strongly influence our buying habits and cause us to purchase more. In other words, there is a certain **psychology of merchandise presentation,** which must be carefully considered in developing merchandise presentation schemes. The following are a number of key psychological factors to consider when merchandising stores.

Value/Fashion Image. One of merchandising's most important psychological effects is to foster an image in the customer's mind of how trendy, exclusive, pricey, or value oriented the merchandise is. For each of the merchandising methods mentioned previously, we discussed its effect on price image. By changing the merchandise presentation method, we can change the perception of our towel display from common, high-volume, high-value, to an exclusive selection of high-fashion merchandise, which presumably will be at higher prices.

This is very much a psychological effect, though perhaps it is social rather than individual psychology. There is nothing innate in large, bulk merchandise displays that says they must be low cost, but American consumers have been trained over many years to associate large quantities with mass production and consumption, and therefore low cost.

Angles and Sightlines. Research has shown that as customers move through a retail store, they view the store at approximately 45 degree angles from the path of travel, as shown in Exhibit 12.11, rather than perpendicular to their path. While this seems logical, most stores are set up at right angles because it is easier and consumes less space. Therefore, merchandise and signage often wind up being at a 90 degree angle to the main aisle. Exhibit 12.11 also shows how four-way feature racks can be more effectively merchandised by being turned to meet the shoppers' sightlines head-on.

Vertical Color Blocking. To be most effective, merchandise should be dis-

EXHIBIT 12.11

45-Degree Customer Sightline

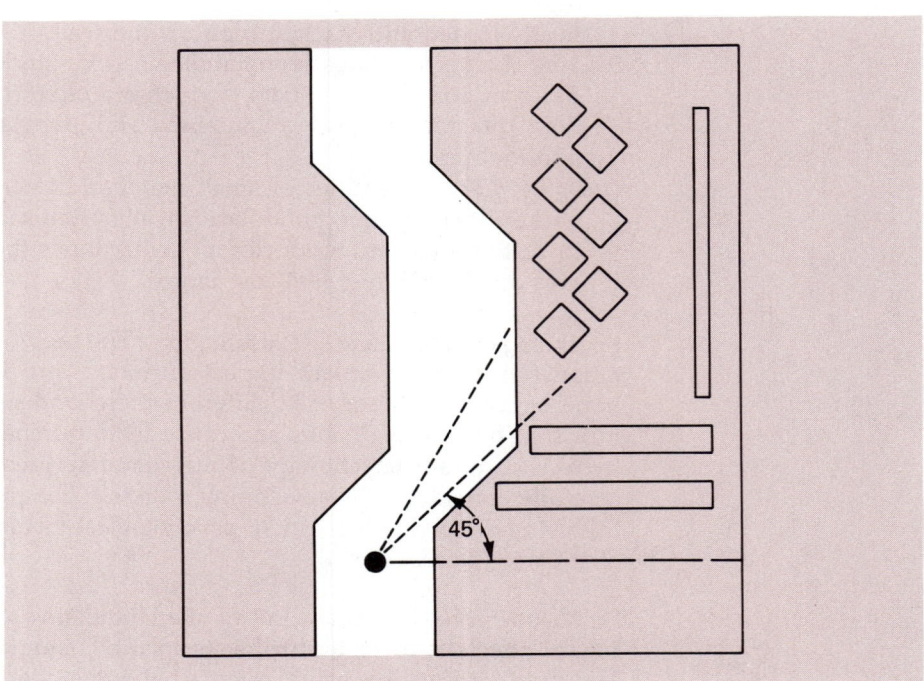

played in vertical bands of color wherever possible. As customers move through the store, their eyes naturally view a "swath" approximately two feet in height, parallel to the floor, at about eye level. This is shown in Exhibit 12.12. To cover a broader vertical visual pattern, shoppers would constantly have to bob their heads up and down. If merchandise is displayed in vertical bands, as shown at the right of Exhibit 12.12, customers are exposed to a greater number of SKUs, whereas in horizontal merchandising, as shown at the left of Exhibit 12.12, they are naturally exposed to only one SKU. Within the same merchandise item, color should be used to create vertical ribbons, which are more attractive and eye-catching. Once again, the more merchandise items we expose shoppers to, the more they will buy.

SELECTING THE PROPER FIXTURES AND MERCHANDISING METHODS

Now that you understand some of the basic types of fixtures, we will discuss some of the variables considered when deciding which fixture to use in a specific situation. Proper fixtures emphasize the key selling attributes of merchandise while not overpowering it. While it is not always possible to follow, a good guideline for selecting fixtures is to *match the fixture to the merchandise, not the merchandise to the fixture*. This means you should only use fixtures which are sensitive to the nature of the merchandise, but all too often, retailers are forced to put merchandise on the wrong fixture.

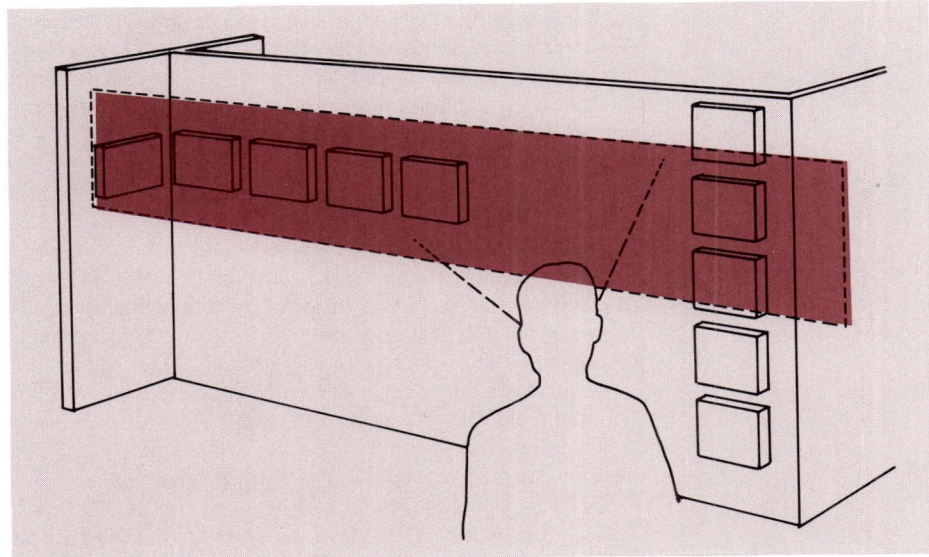

EXHIBIT 12.12
Vertical Color Blocking

RETAILING IN ACTION

12.2 Will the Real Retailer Please Stand Up[15]

Will retailers be retailers in 10 years, or simply landlords? Will manufacturers take their place as the true retailers?

These two questions are begging for an answer as recent trends in retailing suggest that manufacturers are taking increasing amounts of responsibility—and gaining greater control—in retail distribution channels.

As an example, "retailer/vendor partnerships," in which retailers and manufacturers ostensibly work together to increase sales and profitability, have become the rage of the industry. While the partners may have mutual goals—better front-end planning of merchandise lines, cooperative buying and financing terms, sharing of sales information, and more efficient distribution systems—their motivations are quite different. Retailers are looking for marketing and financial participation from their suppliers, while manufacturers are looking to gain shelf space, market share, and ultimately greater control over the merchandising of their goods.

In fact, based on this rush to create partnerships with retailers, many leading manufacturers have begun development of fixturing and merchandising systems. The result: a new generation of manufacturer-supplied merchandising systems, based on innovative fixturing, presentation, lighting, and communications techniques.

While in some cases major retailers have asked key vendors to create merchandising systems, many manufacturers have unilaterally invested time and money to develop superior merchandising systems, then offered them to retailers. The response of retailers has been mixed, with at least one major retailer rejecting such displays because they "junk up the store." But several manufacturer-designed merchandising systems have created significant sales increases and, coupled with full vendor distribution support, have increased margins by enhancing in-stock position. Retailers will not be able to ignore the sales power of these strategies for long.

More importantly, neither will manufacturers ignore the power of these programs. Bolstered by better balance sheets, marketing budgets, higher margins—and more to lose!—manufacturers will become increasingly aggressive in developing and selling their own merchandising programs. They will put their money where their mouth is, paying for fixtures, signage, and ultimately huge shelf placement fees in order to gain and protect market share.

There are some early indicators that this shift in responsibility may extend further. A toy manufacturer was recently asked by several major retailers to begin maintaining its own product on store shelves, effectively absorbing another channel function. Soon, the manufacturer may take full control of all elements of distribution, to ensure the right product is in the right store, presented effectively. The result is a subtle shift in responsibility, cost, and control of key channel activities from retailers to manufacturers.

The crucial question is how long retailers, many of them in weak financial condition, can hold off this key industry trend. And when retailers give in, will they become simply landlords, selling their square footage and shelf space to manufacturers, who become the true retailers of their own products?

Source: This retailing in action first appeared as an article by Randall E. Gebhardt in National Retail Federation's Annual Conference Exhibitor's Guide, January 1992.

Consider intimate apparel, for instance. This is a fast-selling, high-margin merchandise category that can enhance a retailer's image in fashion merchandising. Though retailers entering into this business might be tempted to dump intimate apparel onto existing shelves on a gondola. However, the large, metal, bulky appearance of the gondola will overpower the small, delicate intimate apparel, and therefore reduce sales potential. They would be well served to consider special fixtures to enhance the delicate qualities of intimate apparel. More delicate fixtures made of softer materials will enhance sales. Similarly, it would not make sense to bulk stack fragile merchandise, since the weight of items might damage those lower in the stack. It would not make sense to peghook large, bulky items, because they take up too much room and might be too heavy for the peghook.

Another key factor in choosing fixture type and merchandising method is the gross margin generated by the merchandise, since certain merchandising methods require more labor, and therefore more cost, to stock and maintain. For instance, a small novelty key chain is a low-ticket item generating pennies in margin, while an electronic component for cleaning videotape recorders may cost $10 and generate four dollars in margin. Both items seem ideal for peghooks inserted on a gondola wall, since that display will present the merchandise most effectively to the customer. However, pegging merchandise is a labor-intensive display method, since each item must be lifted individually and hung on the peg. Further, as merchandise is moved around by customers, peghook displays must be constantly reblocked to maintain a good appearance. This labor is justified for the high-margin VCR component, but not for the key chain. Instead, the key chains should be simply dumped into bins hung on the gondola, which takes just seconds. The customer can then pick through the key chains, and as merchandise is sold, no further attention is needed until the bin is nearly empty.

MERCHANDISE CAPACITY CALCULATIONS

While the store planner looks at allocation of square footage, the retailer is more interested in merchandise capacity, because different fixtures and merchandising methods can hold different capacities of merchandise in the same square footage. The average gondola, for instance, may be 4 feet wide and 32 feet long, for a total floor space of 128 square feet. But the gondola also goes up and, depending on its height, it may contain various numbers of shelves. Since shelves are what actually hold the merchandise, retailers are most interested in how many linear feet of shelf space a fixture will have. If the gondola holds five shelves (including the base deck), for instance, it can hold five times 32 feet, or 160 linear feet of shelf space on each side. Since it has a front and a back, the gondola holds 320 linear feet of shelf space in its 128 square feet of floor space. Round racks and other softlines fixtures can be rated in linear footage, garments held, or some other measure of merchandise carrying capacity.

VISUAL MERCHANDISING

We have spent considerable time discussing on-shelf merchandising, which is the display of merchandise customers shop. Now we will briefly discuss the second type of merchandising, **visual merchandising,** which is the artistic display of merchandise and theatrical props used as scene-setting decoration in the store. While on-shelf merchandising must be tastefully displayed to encourage shopping, a store with just on-shelf merchandising would be boring. In fact, many lower-end stores contain little visual merchandising, and indeed they do appear more boring than their upscale cousins in fashion retailing, which concentrate heavily on visual merchandising displays, or "visuals," as they are often called.

A visual merchandising display has several key characteristics. Visual displays are not typically associated with a shoppable fixture, but are located in a focal point, feature area, or other area remote from the on-shelf merchandising and perhaps even out of reach of the customer. Visual merchandising is meant to be visual, not shoppable. Its goal is to create a feeling in the store conducive to buying merchandise.

Another key characteristic of visual merchandising is its use of props and elements in addition to merchandise. In fact, visuals don't always include merchandise—they may just be interesting displays of items somehow related to the merchandise offering or to a mood the retailer wishes to create. It may be a wooden barrel, a miniature airplane, or a mock tree with autumn leaves. As we said earlier, visuals are like the illustrations and design elements in a book that make it interesting and tell you whether this is an upscale, serious shopping experience, a frivolous, fun shopping experience, or a down and dirty, low-price shopping experience.

To be most effective, however, visuals should incorporate relevant merchandise. In apparel retailing, mannequins or **figure forms** are used to display merchandise as it might appear on a person, rather than hanging limply on a hanger. This helps the shopper visualize how these garments will enhance her or his appearance. Good fashion visuals include more than just one garment, to show how tops and bottoms go together and how belts, scarves, and other accessories can be combined to create an overall fashion look. This is called **accessorization.** When successful, visuals help the shopper translate the merchandising from "garments on a rack" to "fashionable clothes that will look good on me."

One of the most successful visual merchandisers is The Limited. In all its divisions, The Limited stresses visual merchandising as the heart and soul of the fashion offerings in its stores. Long ago, The Limited decided that its stores needed to convey a strong sense of fashion and excitement and, realizing that fashion trends change frequently, decided the fashion story is better told through visual merchandising than store design. While all Limited stores are designed tastefully, they are carefully planned to be a stage against which theatrical stories can be told with the merchandise and visual props.

Retail MARKETING

▲ One of the most important roles of the selling environment is to create the proper marketing positioning image. Several years ago, this large music store chain realized it needed to reposition from a traditional music store (left) to an entertainment center. The bold colors, flowing neon, exciting fixtures, and central video wall work together to create a memorable image of a store which caters to total entertainment needs.

Source: Retail Planning Associates, 645 South Grant Avenue, Columbus, OH 43206

▶ A second major goal of the selling environment is to maximize exposure of merchandise to customers, which generally leads to increased sales. The store planner's first step in meeting this goal is developing an effective floor plan, such as the loop layout for this hardware store. The loops encourage customers to circulate through the entire store. Since no department extends more than 30 feet from the main isle, the merchandise is more visible to the shoppers. In this store, the core categories of electrical, hand and power tools, plumbing, and hardware are placed in the center core of the store to increase their visibility and enhance the store's image as a full-service hardware store.

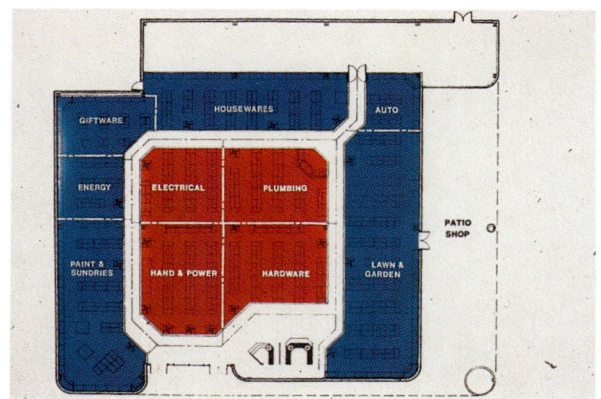

◀ While maximizing exposure of the merchandise, store planners must guard against excessive theft. In high-theft departments such as consumer electronics- which includes many small, expensive items that are easily shoplifted - store planners often deter theft by placing counters together to form a "bullpen." The bullpen forms an enclosed security area which is easier for associates to monitor.

▶ In order to maximize exposure of merchandise, a variety of fixtures is used for different purposes. The white multi-shelved table and four-way fixtures along the aisle in this store serve as feature racks which highlight the special selling characteristics of apparel. The large round racks in the middle of the department serve to carry the bulk of the stock; the special fixtures on the wall both carry large quantities of merchandise and serve as high visual displays that attract passing shoppers.

▲ Merchandisers must be aware that customers view selling environments at angles that naturally meet their sightlines. When merchandise is displayed perpendicular to aisles (left), customers often see sleeves and parts of hangars which do not encourage sales. The same merchandise angled at 45 degrees better meets shoppers' sightlines and displays the critical selling features of color and silhouette (shape).

◀ Another technique often used by merchandisers is to create vertical ribbons of colors, which attract attention and help shoppers differentiate various styles of merchandise. It is often best to let the merchandise tell its own story through creative and carefully planned presentation techniques.

▶ Visual displays, such as this children and giraffe vignette, set a mood which is conducive to selling the type of merchandise located in the adjacent department. Visual displays, which often include theatrical props, can be an effective way to demonstrate how merchandise can function in a shopper's life and encourage additional sales by accessorizing basic merchandise with related items.

◀ Lighting is critical to creating the proper buying mood and directing shoppers' eyes to merchandise. In this store, the neon serves as accent lighting, while spotlights create bright areas which attract shoppers' attention to floor and wall merchandise.

▶ Interior design, including the architectural shapes and design finishes, creates the proper mood and market positioning image that attracts customers and complements merchandise. This bookstore uses rich wood tones and fabric chairs to create the image of a home den; this encourages browsing and invites customers to stay longer - and buy more.

◀ Signs play an important role in the selling environment by providing a road map which customers can follow. Different types of signs, such as the departmental "Toys" sign in this store, serve different purposes in an overall signage program designed to assist customers and increase sales.

◀ The exterior design of a store must attract attention and create an image which is consistent with the merchandise and service offering inside. This is particularly important for retailers of services, such as this restaurant, because in lieu of a tangible product to purchase, customers evaluate service quality based on their pre-use expectations, which are often formed by the appearance of the store. The traditional architecture of this restaurant (Chippendale roof, white picket fence) suggest "home-style cooking at a good value."

▶ The store image can be used to create expectations regarding pricing that are easily met and exceeded. The store creates a very rich image which suggests high prices, so customers are pleased to find the merchandise is very moderately priced. A low-image store which creates low price expectations could find great resistance to charging high prices.

▲ This store, which sells everything for one dollar, creates a simple, though not downscale, image by using basic colors, metal fixtures, and design elements. Customers expect good prices but accept the merchandise as being good quality.

▲ Retailers of services must use special techniques to create tangible messages about their intangible services. These banks have increased sales by creating signage and photopanels which describe their many services and encourage customers to ask about these services.

▲ The United States Postal Service is another example of a service retailer which has many intangible, and some tangible, products. The USPS has developed a new postal-store-of-the-future which places self-service machines near the front for convenience oriented shoppers, teller lines at the back for traditional customers, and "The Postal Store" - a wall of mail-related merchandise customers are willing to buy in a post office - between the two. By making merchandise and services more visible, this postal store can increase sales.

▶ Retailers often find that their differential advantage over competition is an intangible service, and they must find a way to make it tangible. This paint store, whose special skill is mixing paint colors, merchandises this differential advantage by creating "The Pro Shop," a custom paint mixing center which leaves a lasting visual impression on customers.

▲ Similarly, many photo processing shops have added high-speed processing and printing equipment to allow them to provide one-hour service. These shops often merchandise this differential advantage by putting the processing equipment in a display window.

▶ Making an intangible service tangible often requires the use of graphics. These graphics must be organized into a hierarchy of merchandising information which guides the customer through the buying process. This store uses large departmental signs placed very high in the store, smaller category signage placed lower, and even smaller policy and merchandise-specific signage to educate customers, draw them through the store, and focus their attention on merchandise.

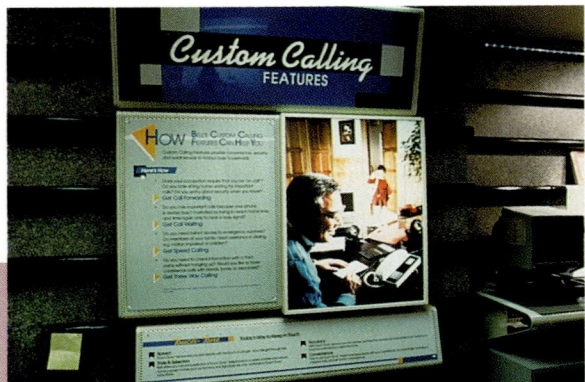

◀ This service store uses the hierarchy of merchandising information to attract attention to its custom calling features; educate shoppers to various options and benefits; and provide specific instructions on how to order the services.

▶ Since services must be produced and consumed simultaneously, service retailing often involves customer waiting lines. Service retailers can utilize this time by placing messages about their services and differential advantages in areas where customers wait. This bank places tangible service messages in its 24-hour automated teller vestibule, where customers wait in line.

◀ Similarly, some banks have transformed the traditional velvet rope queuing line into a service information center. While they wait, customers can occupy their time by reading about services offered by the bank.

Chapter 12 Store Planning, Design, and Merchandising   433

ILLUSTRATION 12.3
Visual displays use theatrical props to set a scene conducive to selling the nearby merchandise.

Many times, visual merchandising managers for The Limited see an interesting art object somewhere in the world, photograph it, and produce an inexpensive (not cheap) replica, which is sent to all the stores. The next time you are in a successful fashion store, take special notice of the artfulness and creativity of the many visual displays.

STORE DESIGN

Store design is important to a successful store because it is the element most responsible for the first of our two goals in planning the store environment—creating a distinctive and memorable market positioning image. Store design encompasses both the exterior and the interior of the store. On the exterior, we have the storefront, signage, and entrance, all of which are critical to attracting passing shoppers and enticing them to enter. On the inside, store design includes the architectural elements and finishes on all surfaces, such as wall coverings, floorcoverings, and ceiling. There are literally hundreds of details in a store's design, and all must work together to create the desired store **ambiance,** which is the overall feeling or mood projected by a store through its aesthetic appeal to human senses.

STOREFRONT DESIGN

If the retail store can be compared to a book, then the storefront or store exterior is like the book cover. It must be noticeable, easily identified by passing motorists or mall shoppers, and memorable. The storefront must clearly identify the name and general market positioning of the store and give some hint as to the merchandise inside. Generally, the storefront design includes all exterior signage and the architecture of the storefront itself.

In many cases, the storefront includes display windows, which serve as an advertising medium for the store. Store windows must arrest the attention of passing shoppers, enticing them inside the store. Therefore, windows should be maintained in exciting visual displays that are changed frequently, are fun and exciting, and reflect the merchandise offering inside.

INTERIOR DESIGN

Unless you have ever been responsible for redecorating a house or room, you may be unaware of the dozens of design elements that go into a physical space. We can break interior design into two types of elements: architectural shapes and the finishes applied to surfaces. Think of all the elements from the floor to the ceiling. First, we have some type of floorcovering placed over either a concrete or wood floor—at the least paint, but more frequently vinyl floorcovering, carpet, ceramic tile, or marble. Each of these different surfaces leaves a different impression on the shopper. An unpainted concrete floor conveys a low-cost, no-frills environment. Vinyl floorcovering makes another statement, which, depending on its quality, sheen, color, and design pattern, can vary from very downscale to very upscale. Carpet suggests a homelike atmosphere conducive to selling softgoods. Ceramic tile and especially marble suggest an upscale, exclusive, and probably expensive shopping experience.

From there we have even more options for covering the walls, from paint and wallpaper to hundreds of types of paneling. The ceiling must also receive a design treatment, whether it is finished drywall (a very upscale image because it is expensive to do), or a suspended ceiling (very common and economical, though not distinctive), or perhaps even an open ceiling with all the pipes and wires above painted black (which suggests a low-price warehouse approach). Then, there are thousands of types of moldings that can be applied to the transitions from floor to wall to ceiling, and hundreds of architectural design elements that can be incorporated.

LIGHTING DESIGN

We have reserved a special discussion for lighting, one of the most important—though often overlooked—elements in a successful store design. Retailers have come to understand lighting as an independent science that can greatly enhance store sales. A young Sam Walton, for instance, learned early on that increasing the light levels in his Walton's 5 & 10 store in Bentonville, Arkansas, resulted in increased sales.[10] Department stores, on the other hand, have found that raising lighting levels in fashion departments can actually discourage sales, because bright lighting suggests a discount store image.

Lighting design, however, is not limited to simple light levels. Contemporary lighting design requires an in-depth knowledge of electrical engineering and the effect of light on color and texture. Not only have retailers learned that different types and levels of lighting can have significant impact on sales, but the types of light sources available have multiplied quickly. Today, there are literally hundreds of light fixtures and lamps (bulbs) from which to choose.

The two most important characteristics of lighting systems are the quantity of light they produce, which is measured in footcandles, and the quality of light, measured in terms of a temperature scale (degrees Kelvin). The temperature of light affects the ways certain colors and textures will appear. For comparison, the general illumination of a typical home is around 50 footcandles of light, and the temperature of an incandescent house lamp is around 2,700 degrees Kelvin. Stores are typically lit to about 60 to 100 footcandles of general illumination, often using inexpensive, long-lasting, and energy-efficient fluorescent lights, which emit temperatures of around 4,200 degrees Kelvin. Higher-temperature lighting makes colors appear dull, lifeless, and flat, while lower-temperature lighting enhances colors and textures and makes a store more comfortable to shop. Generally, customers associate higher-temperature light sources and fluorescent lighting with discount stores and lower prices, and lower-temperature incandescent light sources with more upscale and fashion environments. Recently, lighting manufacturers have begun producing lower-temperature fluorescent lamps that emit light in the 3,200 to 3,500 degrees Kelvin range. Many discount stores have quickly converted to these lamps, which combine the enhanced energy efficiency and longer life of fluorescent lamps with more comfortable shopping environments and better color rendition.

TOTAL SENSORY MARKETING: SOUNDS AND SMELLS

We said at the outset that effective store design appeals to all human senses of sight, sound, smell, and touch. Obviously, the majority of design activity in a retail store is focused on affecting sight. Research has shown that the other senses can be very important, too, and many retailers are beginning to engineer the sounds and smells in their stores.

Retailers have piped music into their stores for generations, believing that a musical backdrop will create a more relaxing environment and encourage customers to stay longer. Increasingly, music is being seen as a valuable marketing tool, since the right music can create an environment which is both soothing and reflective of the merchandise being offered. Researchers believe that while the tempo of music affects how long shoppers stay in a store, the type of music may be just as influential on how much they purchase.[11] For instance, while classical music is soothing and has been shown to encourage customers to shop longer,[12] it may be inconsistent with the desired ambiance of a trendy fashion store catering to high school girls.

Many retailers have also begun to use smell as a key in-store marketing tool. Victoria's Secret, a division of The Limited, has deployed potpourri cachés throughout its store—and in fact now sells them—to create the ambiance of a lingerie closet. The Knot Shop, a men's tie store catering to female shoppers buying ties as gifts, employ scent tiles impregnated with leather and tobacco scents to create the ambiance of a men's store, with the goal of making female customers feel the store is the type of store in which their male friend or spouse would buy his own tie.[13]

VISUAL COMMUNICATIONS

The store is, above all else, a selling environment, and a key to selling is communication. In Chapter 15 we dedicate an entire chapter to personal selling, the role of sales associates in helping customers evaluate and purchase merchandise. But sales associates can't always be available to assist customers, particularly in this era of increased competitive pressure and reduced gross margins, when many retailers have found it necessary to cut costs by reducing their sales staffs. Even department stores, which staked their reputations on high levels of personal customer service, have had to reduce their service levels and learn to rely on alternative service strategies. How then, can retailers provide good selling communications and high customer service while controlling labor costs?

The answer is **visual communications,** in the form of in-store signage and graphics. Retailers can plan the store environment to incorporate signs, large photopanels, and other visual devices that serve as silent salespersons, providing shoppers with much needed information and directions on how to shop the store, evaluate merchandise, and make purchases. Since these visual communications are inanimate objects that stay permanently in place, they require only a one-time installation cost, low maintenance, and can always be relied on to perform their function, the same way, for every shopper. Unlike sales associates, visual communications are never late for work, are never in a bad mood, and never mistreat customers. Of course, neither are they as effective as a good sales associate, who provides the personal touch that makes customers feel welcome and comfortable. But when carefully balanced with personal service, visual communications—with their reliability and low cost—can create an effective selling environment and are therefore becoming an important tool in the store designer's toolbox.

Earlier we likened a retail store to a well-written book. Visual communications are akin to the headlines, subheads, illustrations, and captions that give the reader direction and illustrate the written descriptions. Without visual communications, a store would be like a newspaper full of words but no headlines, a jumbled, incomprehensible mess of merchandise. An effective visual communications program includes a range of messages, from those large and bold in nature, used sparingly to provide cues to the gross organization of the space, to the smaller, more specific and plentiful messages that describe actual merchandise. A visual communications program includes the following important elements.

NAME, LOGO, AND RETAIL IDENTITY

The first and most visible element in a comprehensive visual communications program is the retailer's identity, composed of the store name, logomark, and supporting visual elements. The name and logo are seen not only on the storefront and throughout the store, but also in advertising and all communications with the consumers, and therefore they must be catchy, memorable, and most of all, reflective of the retailer's merchandising mission. Historically, many retail companies have taken the name of their founders, as is the case with most department stores. That practice has fallen out of vogue, however, as retailing has become a game of crafty market positioning and catchy retail identities. A founder's name rarely captures the merchandising spirit of a company as well as names such as Home Depot and Toys "R" Us. With advertising messages bombarding customers more than ever and the effectiveness of each message waning,[14] retailers have found it necessary for their names to be highly descriptive of their unique offerings.

ILLUSTRATION 12.4

This Toys "R" Us store front is an example of the highly descriptive nature of successful retail outlets' names and supporting visual elements.

Once a name has been chosen, a logo is developed to visually portray the name in a creative and memorable manner. Again, the key is to keep the logo simple and easy to understand at a glance, while making it exciting enough to leave a lasting image in the customers' minds. The logo is often accompanied by taglines that provide more description of the store concept, such as "Fashions for the Home."

The logo's most prominent placement is on the outside of the store or on tall pylon signs by the roadside. These are critical to attracting customers and creating high store traffic. This is another reason why the store name and logo should be succinct and descriptive—their most important role is often played to motorists passing at 45 miles per hour.

INSTITUTIONAL SIGNAGE

Once inside the store, the first level of visual communications is known as **institutional signage,** or signage that describes the merchandising mission, customer service policies, and other messages on behalf of the retail institution. This signage, is usually located at the store entrance, to properly greet entering customers, and at service points such as the service desk, layaway window, and cash registers. In addition, some retailers place customer ser-

ILLUSTRATION 12.5

Institutional signage is usually located at the store entrance and at service points such as the service desk, layaway window, and cash register, as well as throughout the store in some cases.

vice signage throughout the store, to reinforce special policies several times during the shopping trip. This signage might include messages such as "Lowest Price Guaranteed" or "All Major Credit Cards Accepted."

DIRECTIONAL, DEPARTMENTAL, AND CATEGORY SIGNAGE

Directional and departmental signage serve as the highest level of organization in an overall signage program. These signs are usually large and placed fairly high, so they can be seen throughout the store. They help guide the shopper through the shopping trip and locate specific departments of interest. Not all stores use directional signage, particularly in smaller store environments where it is not necessary, but virtually all stores larger than 10,000 square feet in size use some type of departmental signage. Once a shopper locates and moves close to a particular department, **category signage** is used to call out and locate specific merchandise categories. Category signage is usually smaller in size, since it is intended to be seen from a shorter distance and is located on or close to the fixture itself. For instance, the departmental sign might say "Sporting Goods," and be two feet high and six feet wide, and hang from the ceiling. On the other hand, the category signage might be only six inches high and two feet wide, affixed to the top of the gondola, and read "Hunting," "Tennis," or "Fitness."

POINT-OF-SALE (POS) SIGNAGE

The next level of signage is even smaller, placed closer to the merchandise, and known as **point-of-sale signage,** or POS signage. Since POS signage is intended to give details about specific merchandise items, it usually contains more words and is affixed directly to fixtures. POS signage may range in size from 11-by-17 inches to a 3-by-5-inch card with very small words describing an item. Always, however, the most important function of POS signage is to clearly state the price of the merchandise being signed, as shown in Exhibit 12.13.

POS signage includes a set of sign holders used throughout the store, along with a variety of printed signs that can be inserted into the hardware. Store associates mix and match the signage and hardware as directed by management, so that POS signage changes frequently. Special POS signs for sales, clearance, and "as advertised" are often a different color than the normal price signage to highlight these special values. In some states, consumer protection laws require that all merchandise advertised as being on sale must be so marked in the store, and this is accomplished through the highly flexible POS sign package.

LIFESTYLE GRAPHICS

Visual communications encompass more than just words. Many stores incorporate large graphics panels showing so-called lifestyle images in important departments. These photo images portray either the merchandise, often as it

EXHIBIT 12.13
Point-of-Sale Signage Program

is being used, or simply images of related items or models that convey an image conducive to buying the product. In a high-fashion department, lifestyle photography might show a scene of movie stars arriving at a nightclub in very trendy fashions, suggesting that similar fashions are available in that department. In sporting goods, a lifestyle image might show an isolated lake surrounded by autumn colored trees, with mist rising off the water and the sun rising in the background.

Retailers must be careful when choosing lifestyle photography, for as the saying goes, "beauty is in the eye of the beholder." One person's lifestyle is not necessarily another's, so lifestyle photography must be kept very general in nature so as to be attractive to the majority and offensive to none. Increasingly, photopanels and lifestyle imagery, which can be expensive to create, are being provided free of charge to retailers by merchandise vendors, who are looking to gain an advantage for their products on the retail floor.

SUMMARY

In this chapter we have focused on the retail store—the most tangible and memorable form of communication between a retailer and its target customers. The store must effectively convey the market position image desired by the retailer, and provide a shopping environment which is conducive to high sales. The guiding principle in effective store planning, merchandising, and design is that the more merchandise customers are exposed to, the more they tend to buy.

Step one is to entice customers to enter. This depends largely on image engineering, or planning the name, logo, and visual appearance of the store to convey a desired market position image. While retail organizations work diligently to influence their images, true market position image is an amalgam of all messages consumers receive, from advertising, to stories they hear from friends, to the store itself.

Store planning refers to developing a plan for the organization of the retail store, indicating the location of all selling and nonselling areas. First, the retailer must decide how to allocate the precious square footage available, which is usually accomplished by conducting a mathematical analysis of the productivity of various merchandise categories. By comparing the sales and gross margin produced by various categories with the space they take and the cost of carrying the inventory, the retailer can develop a plan for the optimal allocation of available space. The floorplan is then created, showing the placement and adjacencies of all merchandise departments. Experience has shown that certain departments sell more when they are adjacent to one another, because they are related to each other in the shopper's mind, and so store planning is a complex problem of aligning spaces to optimize both qualitative and quantitative performance.

Fixture selection and merchandising are critical to exposing customers to the maximum amount of merchandise. There are many types of store fixtures, as well as specific methods of merchandise presentation, which have been shown to maximize merchandise exposure and lead to increased sales. Particularly, there is a "psychology of merchandise presentation" which utilizes customer's natural shopping behaviors and adopts merchandise presentation to match them. In addition to maximizing sales, fixture selection and merchandise presentation must conform to operational constraints and be easy to maintain.

The most visible element of the store is the storefront and interior decor. The storefront or exterior must be eye-catching, inviting, and reflective of the merchandise offering inside. The interior design must be comfortable, put the shopper in the proper buying mood, and provide a backdrop that enhances but does not overpower the merchandise. The store designer must always remember that shoppers are there to look at the merchandise, not the store design.

Finally, a successful selling environment is based on effective communications with the customers. Since shoppers require information even when sales associates are not available, visual communications must be used throughout the store to provide direction, specific information, and prices. A visual communications program begins with the store name and logo and includes a range of interior signage that walks the customer through the buying experience.

There are literally hundreds of details in a successful retail store, and all must be carefully coordinated to create a cohesive, targeted store image that reflects the retailer's mission.

QUESTIONS FOR DISCUSSION

1. Discuss the two primary objectives of the store environment and how these are achieved.
2. Distinguish between market position and market position image. How does the store environment relate to these two concepts?
3. Discuss some of the constraints retailers face when trying to change their market position.
4. Define the term merchandising and discuss how it is used in the store, as well as the impact it has on customers.
5. What is the simple but powerful truism in retailing that store planners can use as a guide to increasing the sales productivity of a store environment?

6. Why are retailers focusing increasingly on in-store marketing? Discuss some in-store marketing strategies and their effect on customers.
7. Why do chief executive officers become involved in the seemingly unimportant task of store planning, merchandising, and design?
8. What lessons can store planners draw from an effectively written book?
9. Discuss the various types of space in a retail store, describing the role of each.
10. Describe the steps in the space allocation and store planning process.
11. What is adjacencies planning and why is it important to retailers?
12. Identify the four main types of store layouts, discussing their differences and impact on customers.
13. In the theater of retailing, discuss the differences between the "props and visual backdrops" and the "stars."
14. Discuss the different uses of bulk or capacity fixtures and feature fixtures.
15. What is the psychology of merchandise presentation and how is it used?
16. What are the goals of interior and exterior design?
17. Why is lighting design important to store planners?
18. What are the goals of visual communications? Discuss different types of visual communications, how they are used, and their effect on customers.

MANAGEMENT MEMO

You have just been made the new manager of Cardinal Sports Shops. One of your first duties as manager of this "all-sports" equipment retailer is to develop a floorplan for the new mega-sized store. The main categories in the store are: women's athletic apparel, men's athletic apparel, children's athletic apparel, team-related apparel (football jerseys, etc.), athletic equipment for female-oriented sports, athletic equipment for male-oriented sports, children's games, and heavy exercise equipment. You know that exercise equipment and children's games are the two big destination items that draw traffic, and the apparel categories tend to be intercept purchases. (The concept of destination and intercept merchandise was first introduced in Chapter 3.) The grand opening for the square, 35,000-square-foot store is scheduled for September 1. Your job is to prepare a memo for senior management stating the type of layout you suggest, and the adjacencies and category locations you feel are appropriate. Be sure to include in your memo why various layout types (or combinations) might work or not work, how you plan to maximize merchandise exposure, specific adjacencies which will lead to add-on sales, and how the destination and intercept merchandise can be strategically located to increase sales.

BOARDROOM REPORT

You are the director of facilities planning for a small chain of women's apparel stores. Your flagship store, a 15,000-square-foot store located in a rapidly growing section of town, has seen consistent sales increases in recent years, and the company president believes the store is missing even more sales. He has budgeted about $400,000 for capital improvements to capture these additional sales. The vice-president of operations has recommended that the $400,000 be used to buy new fixtures to increase the merchandise capacity of the existing store. His idea is to shrink the width of all aisles, fit more bulk fixtures on the floor, and double stack all merchandise. You believe merchandise is already crammed in too tightly, and there are too few feature presentations of your fashion apparel. You suggest the key to increasing sales is not cramming more merchandise in, but increasing the store size. You know the 5,000-square-foot store next door in the strip center is empty, and for the same $400,000, you could acquire its lease, open the wall between the stores, and improve and merchandise the new space. The board of directors is meeting later this week, and has asked both of you to make five-minute presentations supporting your recommendations. Be sure to include in your report specific reasons why increasing store space, which will take longer and be more difficult, will lead to greater sales and customer satisfaction than adding more fixtures.

SUGGESTED READINGS

Eroglee, Sevgin, and Gilbert D. Harrell. "Retail Crowding: Theoretical and Strategic Implications." *Journal of Retailing* (Winter 1986): 346-63.

Owens, Jan P. "Store Atmosphere: An Environmental Psychology Approach Revisited." In *The Cutting Edge II*, (edited by William R. Darden, Robert F. Lusch, and J. Barry Mason, 37-49. Baton Rouge: Louisiana State University, 1992).

ENDNOTES

1. David Maursky and Jacob Jacoby, "Exploring the Development of Store Images," *Journal of Retailing* (Summer 1986): 145-65.
2. Alan Liles, *Oh Thank Heaven! The Story of The Southland Corporation*, (Dallas: The Southland Corporation, 1977).
3. Edward M. Tauber, "Why Do People Shop?" *Journal of Marketing* 36 (October 1972): 46-59.
4. "Some 7-Elevens Try Selling a New Image," *Wall Street Journal,* 25 October 1991.
5. Iyer, Easwar S. "Unplanned Purchasing, Knowledge of the Shopping Environment," *Journal of Retailing 88:1* (Spring 1989): 40-57.
6. "Influencing Shoppers During the Moment of Decision," *Wall Street Journal,* 18 August 1991.
7. "Some Customers Are Always Wrong," *New York Times Magazine,* 10 June 1990, 19, 56-57.
8. Jan P. Owens, "Store Atmosphere: An Environmental Psychology Approach Revisited" in *The Cutting Edge II* (edited by William R. Darden, Robert F. Lusch, and J. Barry Mason). Baton Rouge, La.; Louisiana State University, 1992, pp. 37-49.
9. "Trouble Stalks the Aisles at Ann Taylor," *Business Week,* (9 December 1991), 38.
10. Vance H. Trimble, *Sam Walton: Founder of Wal-Mart* (New York: Dutton Books, 1990), 63.
11. Gordon C. Bruner II, "Music, Mood, and Marketing," *Journal of Marketing* (October 1990): 94-104.
12. Ronald E. Milliman, "Using Background Music to Affect Behavior of Supermarket Shoppers," *Journal of Marketing* 46 (Summer 1982): 86-91.
13. "No One's Sniffing at Aroma Research Now," *Business Week,* 23 December 1991, 82-83.
14. "The Party's Over," *The Economist,* 1 February 1992, 69-76.

CHAPTER 13

RETAILING OF SERVICES

OVERVIEW

When most of us think about retailing, we think about the selling of physical products—or merchandise—to consumers. By our definition, however, retailing occurs each time the end consumer spends money, whether it's on a tangible good, an intangible service, or even an idea. Today, in fact, more than half of all consumer dollars are spent on intangible services and ideas, such as dry cleaning, weight loss programs, or chances to win a million-dollar lottery. In this chapter we will review the importance of services in our national economy, discuss the unique challenges involved in the retailing of services, and present specific marketing strategies for increasing sales and customer satisfaction for retailers of services. We will see that since customers do not distinguish between retailers of services and the services they provide, as they often do between merchandise and retailers, retailers of services must pay special attention to the selling environment to ensure that it creates the appropriate consumer expectations and encourages them to purchase and use services.

RETAILING OF SERVICES

I. The Retailing of Services
   A. Why Retailing of Services Is Important
      1. Services Play an Important Role in Our Lives
      2. Services Represent a Large Portion of the Economy
   B. The Selling Environment's Role in Retailing of Services
   C. All Retailing Is a Service

II. The Nature of Services and the Retailing of Services
    A. How Services and Goods Differ
        1. Intangibility
        2. Perishability
        3. Inseparability
        4. Heterogeneity
    B. Unique Challenges in the Retailing of Services
        1. Services, Retailers of Services, and the Selling Environment Are Intertwined
        2. Corporate Image Influences Customer Expectations of Services
        3. Intangible Services Are Undetectable
        4. Services Are Indistinguishable from One Another
        5. Customers Have Difficulty Shopping for Services
        6. Service Delivery Often Forces Customers to Wait
III. Service Quality in the Retail Environment
    A. High-Quality Service Leads to Increased Sales and Profits
    B. Definition of Service Quality
    C. Attracting and Retaining Customers Through High-Quality Service
    D. How Consumers Form Expectations
    E. How Consumers Evaluate Services in the Retail Environment
        1. Time
        2. Convenience
        3. Merchandise or Service Offering
        4. Personal Service
        5. Pricing
        6. After-Sales Service
IV. Strategies for Enhancing Retailing of Services
    A. Using the Selling Environment to Help Form Customer Expectations
    B. Creating Tangible Evidence of Services
    C. Merchandising a Differential Advantage
    D. Creating a Hierarchy of Merchandising Information
    E. Utilizing Dwell Time
V. Summary

THE RETAILING OF SERVICES

Throughout most of this text we have been discussing the retailing of physical products, which are tangible in nature and can be seen, touched, and held by consumers. But not all retailing involves tangible goods. In fact, you may remember from your introductory marketing class that products can be physical products—which we call goods—or intangible services and ideas. Consumers purchase services and ideas just as they do goods, so the selling of services must be considered retailing just like the selling of tangible goods.

Though both are retailed, tangible goods and intangible services differ in many ways, and the manner in which they are retailed must also differ. One of the key differences is that due to the intangibility of services, the selling environment becomes even more important in the retailing process. In this chapter we focus on the *retailing of services,* and explore specific retail marketing strategies based on the differences between tangible goods and intangible services.

WHY RETAILING OF SERVICES IS IMPORTANT

Retailing of services is rarely set out as a separate subject in retail textbooks. However, we feel that recent changes in the nation's economy, lifestyle trends, and a focus on service quality in the marketing fields, all call for a special focus on the retailing of services. Many industries which have traditionally not considered themselves retailing (such as funeral homes, discussed in Retailing in Action 13.1) have found it necessary and highly beneficial to begin using merchandising and retailing strategies—in short, to become retailers. Furthermore, as the chain retailing industry has matured and reached a state of parity in which most merchandise is available at many retail outlets at similar prices, retailers themselves have realized that the key to differentiation is providing superior service. In this section we will review in more detail some of the forces that have made the 1990s the decade for the retailing of services.

Services Play an Important Role in Our Lives. Think about your life during the past 24 hours. Perhaps you began your day by stopping at a restaurant for breakfast. Then you stopped by a laundromat on your way to class and since you were short of time, left your clothes for cleaning, pressing, and folding by the cleaning company. You dropped off a roll of film at the one-hour photo processing center, then stopped by the campus travel agent to begin planning your spring break. After class, you dropped off some mail at the post office, went to the copy center to have a copy of your term paper made, then visited

---

RETAILING IN ACTION

13.1 Funeral Homes Learn to Merchandise Their Services

Virtually all consumer-oriented industries face increased competition in the 1990s, and this often results in traditional merchandising and retailing strategies being introduced in new ways. In one of the more dramatic and curious examples, the funeral service industry has seen bold new strategies take hold that even five years ago would have seemed inappropriate.

Increased competition, changing consumer demands, and deregulation have created a new market environment for funeral service providers. Historically, funeral services were provided by local, family-owned businesses in which the local undertaker's children were trained to take over the business. A traditional funeral service and burial could cost as much as $5,000 to $10,000, with a relatively small percentage of less expensive cremations being performed. In 1984, however, the Federal Trade Commission prohibited the sale of packaged funeral services, which listed only one lump sum for an entire funeral. Instead, elements of the funeral service—such as embalming, casket, funeral service, rental of the funeral parlor, and burial—had to be priced separately. Consumers became aware of the high cost of certain specific elements, and began balking at paying often exorbitant markups—as much as 900% for caskets, for instance. A new price consciousness evolved in a market in which the grief-stricken had historically taken high prices for granted. At the same time, social and demographic trends—such as higher education and an older, more mobile population less tied to their birthplace—generated more interest in cremations, which have nearly doubled as a percentage of all death-related services since 1980 and are expected to reach nearly 30% by 2010.

This more competitive market has fostered a new breed of aggressive, innovative funeral service providers who use creative merchandising and retailing strategies to gain a competitive advantage. One company sells off-price caskets through a discount casket retail store at prices sometimes less than half what funeral homes charge. Another offers production of a video memorial of the deceased for presentation at funeral services, which are increasingly held without the body present. At the price-conscious level, one company in Houston offers an $895 no-frills cremation service through its toll-free telephone number. At the other end of the price spectrum, some companies are developing special—and more costly—rituals for cremations.

To underscore the increased price sensitivity of consumers regarding funeral services, one company offers grave site funeral services which cut out the funeral parlor—and its related costs. This service runs newspapers advertisements on obituary pages proclaiming, "Why pay $1,000 to $2,000 more for a funeral home . . . ?" Instead of owning or leasing a large, expensive funeral home or other facility, this company sells it funeral services through a small store in a strip center. As with all consumer goods and services, the retail facility can change to reflect the offering.

Many firms have realized they are not selling products—such as embalming, caskets, and burials—as much as a service, namely the coordination and facilitation of the beginning of the grieving process following the death of a loved one. Accordingly, they are offering grief counseling services along with the services related to disposal of the deceased's body.

As discussed in this chapter, services are most effectively retailed when they respond directly to the expectations of customers. Traditional funeral homes offer one type of funeral service, whether customers want it that way or not. By providing nontraditional variations and lower prices, the new breed of funeral service providers are adapting to changing consumer expectations. As one industry professional summarized poignantly, " . . . the public is giving us a message: 'We don't want what we're being told we have to have.' Now we have to figure out what it is they do want."

Source: Based on authors' insights into industry and Joshua Levine and Seth Lubove, "Cash and Bury," *Forbes* (11 May 1992): 162-166.

your favorite hair salon to have your hair cut or styled. On your way home you picked up your developed film, as well as your neatly folded clothes.

What do these activities have in common? First, they all make use of services. Second, since you as a consumer undoubtedly paid for each of the services, you were involved in retailing.

Services Represent a Large Portion of the Economy. Retailing of services is fast becoming one of the most important types of retailing, largely because services are becoming more important in our economy. In just the past five years, in fact, services have become the largest portion of the U.S. economy, representing as much as 75 percent of the nation's gross domestic product.[1] More dramatically, studies have shown that services account for as much as 83 percent of jobs in the economy,[2] including nine out of every ten jobs created.[3]

Services not only play an important role in our overall economy, but represent a large portion of retail activity as well. Estimates have suggested that more than half of all consumer dollars are spent on services, which seems very possible when you consider telephone bills, household utilities, insurance, and other services.

There are numerous reasons for the growth of services, many of them the key demographic, social, and economic changes introduced in Chapter 3. Some researchers have focused attention on three key trends: additional wealth, changes in leisure time, and an increase in the number of two-career families.[4] Certainly, there is a dramatic increase in the number of two-career families, in which both spouses are working. In fact, the Labor Department reports that among households headed by married couples, the number with two or more people at work has risen 10 percentage points in the past generation to 65 percent.[5] Theoretically, this provides more disposable income while decreasing the amount of time each family member has to do household chores such as housecleaning or lawn care, which can be done by service providers.

The most controversial of the factors leading to increased service spending is the amount of leisure time Americans have now compared to past generations. Researchers can't seem to agree on whether Americans have more or less leisure time.[6] One researcher reports that diary studies show Americans are working less now than they did a generation ago, and yet more of them report "feeling hurried."[7] Various explanations have been offered for this apparent discrepancy between reality and consumer perception. The most plausible seems to be that while each individual worker may be working fewer hours, the family unit, comprising both working parents, may be working more hours. A study comparing the work habits of Japanese and American men, for instance, found that while both work about 56 to 58 hours each week, American men work 44 hours at a job and 14 doing household chores, and Japanese men spend 52 hours on the job and only four doing household chores.[8] With each spouse working in America, less time is available in the total family unit to complete household maintenance tasks, which have not diminished.[9]

Regardless of the underlying reasons, and whether the time poverty is real or imagined, consumers' perceptions of time poverty have created many opportunities for retailers of all kinds, especially retailers of services. Some sociologists credit decreased time for parents to spend with children as one reason why toy sales have skyrocketed in recent years, tripling from 1960 to 1990 to an average of $421 per child.[10] Day care centers, personal shopping services, and car detailing services are all examples of service retailers that have taken advantage of changing consumer lifestyle patterns and perceptions. This is another important example of a concept first introduced in Chapter 3: Reality is not always as important as consumer perceptions, because it is perceptions that drive consumer spending activities.

THE SELLING ENVIRONMENT'S ROLE IN RETAILING OF SERVICES

The retailing of services presents many challenges due to the unique qualities of services, which are intangible and difficult for customers to observe and understand. Therefore, the selling environment becomes even more important, because it serves as a proxy or substitute in the consumer's mind for the services being offered. Research indicates, for instance, that consumers have more difficulty forming expectations about a service than they do a physical product, primarily because the service is intangible. Expectations about a service often wind up being made based on the consumer's perception of the physical environment through which it is offered.

Research also shows that when deciding whether to try a new service, consumers rely heavily on information they have received personally, through their own senses and from family and friends (as opposed to nonpersonal information such as advertising). One of the primary sources of such personal information is the consumer's own observations of the physical facility through which the service is offered, especially the exterior which is frequently seen by passing consumers.

Consumers also base their expectations of and evaluate services by comparing them to other service providers of which they have knowledge. Consumers observe various competitors and place them mentally on a continuum of low-quality expectations to high-quality expectations. Since the selling environment is often the only tangible perception a consumer has of various service retailers, it plays a critical role in helping consumers evaluate alternatives.

Finally, there is evidence that consumers evaluate services differently than goods. For goods, functionality seems to be of prime importance, but for services the process of receiving the service is just as important as the functionality of the service. When an accounting service prepares your tax return, for instance, your satisfaction with the service is based not just on how much tax you save, but also how you were treated during the process. Did a private office make you feel like you were being cared for personally, or did an open room with many metal desks make you feel like "just another set of numbers" to the tax preparer? Did the tax preparer's work environment, which is simultaneously his or her selling environment, inspire confidence in you or leave you wondering if this is a fly-by-night operation? Because the process is just as important as the result in evaluating a service, and because the service environment plays a critical role in the process, the selling environment is even more critical for retailers of services than it is for retailers of goods.

ALL RETAILING IS A SERVICE

You may recall from your introductory marketing course that it is difficult to classify most marketing transactions as strictly involving goods or services, because most products involve both physical characteristics and some intangible service. This is especially true in retailing, because all retailers—whether they are selling goods, services, or ideas—are providing services to customers, and therefore all retailers can benefit from the service strategies suggested in this chapter. Retailers generally do not manufacture goods, but rather provide a forum for consumers and products to come together, thereby facilitating transactions and allowing exchanges to take place. Rather than providing products, retailers really are providing time and place value to consumers. They are collecting products from around the world, arranging for their shipment, providing a store or other forum for the transaction, and providing information consumers need to make purchase decisions. By performing these tasks for thousands of consumers, retailers spread the expense and reduce the cost to each consumer.

In fact, in today's saturated retail market, many stores carry essentially the same merchandise mix and brand names. What differentiates them is the level of service they provide. All retailers can therefore be considered service providers, and can benefit from the service strategies discussed in this chapter.

THE NATURE OF SERVICES AND THE RETAILING OF SERVICES

Services are different than goods, and accordingly, the retailing of services requires some specialized strategies. In this section we will review the fundamental differences between goods and services and then discuss some retail implications of the special characteristics of services.

HOW SERVICES AND GOODS DIFFER

To fully appreciate the unique requirements in the retailing of services, we must first review the important ways in which goods and services differ. A host of researchers have articulated these differences and organized them into four key areas.

Intangibility. The first and most obvious difference between goods and services is that goods are tangible and services are *intangible*. Goods can be boxed, stored, placed on shelves, carried around, examined, and once purchased, often returned if defective. None of these qualities applies to services. But perhaps the most dramatic implication of the intangibility of services is the consumer's inability to perceive them through the human senses. We can perceive a tangible good through sight, smell, hearing, touch, and taste and can generally agree on what the good is. On the other hand, services cannot be directly perceived through the senses and can therefore go undetected by consumers, or may be perceived differently by different consumers.

Perishability. We mentioned previously that goods can be produced or manufactured, boxed, stored, and shelved. A key implication is that goods can endure through time. They can be manufactured today, stored tomorrow, and sold to the end consumer next week. While all goods are ultimately *perishable*—lettuce much sooner than, say, a shovel—services are much more perishable than goods, primarily because they generally have no material qualities. In fact, services theoretically perish the moment they are produced. Once a dry cleaner has provided the cleaning service, the service itself is essentially gone. The result of the service—clean, pressed garments—remains for some time, but even that perishes once the clothes are worn.

Inseparability. Closely related to perishability is *inseparability*, or the concept that there can be no separation between production and consumption of a service. They occur simultaneously. This is in contrast to a good, which can be manufactured days, weeks, even years before it is actually used. Due to inseparability, service retailers do not have the luxury of hiding the messy or unpleasant process of production from the consuming public. For instance, consider hot dogs, a manufactured food product. While the process of making hot dogs may be perfectly clean and natural, many consumers would just as soon not know the many ingredients that go into them. Service providers must often perform the service, with all its potential unpleasantries, in the presence of the purchaser. Some service providers have turned this fact into a differential advantage. To speed service, McDonald's prepares many of its food products in full view of its customers. Realizing that cleanliness is a major concern of customers, McDonald's early on designed its stores with stainless steel and porcelain surfaces that are easily cleaned, do not discolor with age, and shine and sparkle when clean. This design technique emphasizes to viewing customers that McDonald's is very clean, so clean that it is not afraid to expose its kitchen and food preparation areas. McDonald's turned a potential disadvantage into a differential advantage, and then proudly displayed this advantage to customers, much as goods retailers merchandise their products.

An implication of both perishability and inseparability is that service providers cannot stockpile their products as manufacturers can. While the vast majority of consumer goods are purchased during normal retail hours

ILLUSTRATION 13.1

Inseparability is the concept that there can be no separation between production and consumption of a service. That is, services are produced at the same time they are being consumed.

(roughly 12 hours a day), a manufacturer may find that it needs more than 12 hours a day to produce all the demanded product. Manufacturers can simply put on a second shift, producing and stockpiling goods during the night. Service providers must simultaneously produce and sell their products at the precise moment consumers demand them. If the service provider cannot keep up, sales opportunities are lost and cannot be recovered.

Another important implication of inseparability is that service providers don't get a second chance. All manufacturers expect a certain amount of incorrectly manufactured product—often called scrap—due to human error or deviations in raw materials. They simply discard this scrap or if possible recycle it into future product, building the cost into the price of saleable goods. Service providers can't do this. If a service is provided incorrectly, it has by virtue of inseparability already been delivered to the consumer, who is likely already dissatisfied. Have you ever tried a new hair stylist and been disappointed with the results? There is little you can do except wait for your hair to grow back.

Heterogeneity. Generally speaking, services are provided by human beings, who are by nature subject to inconsistent performance. This results in *heterogeneity*, or a variation in the service from day to day and from server to server. Even the most accomplished service providers are occasionally subject to subpar performance. This is known as single-server heterogeneity. In addition, services are performed not by one but by many different servers, resulting in variations in the way the service is delivered. This is known as multiple-server heterogeneity.

Since services are naturally subject to heterogeneity, and yet service providers cannot catch and remove substandard services before they are delivered as manufacturers handle scrap, retailers of services must be even more attentive to creating and maintaining high-performance standards. Each step in the service process must be carefully programmed and controlled so that every individual server can perform the process in a similar manner, time after time. In some businesses, such as fast food, this requires simple and clearly defined job duties and an emphasis on discipline rather than creative thinking. To see this concept in action, try ordering a hamburger at Wendy's with onions, catsup, mustard, and pickle. Invariably, the order take will call out your order as "catsup, onion, pickle, mustard"—precisely in that order—because employees are trained to always call the condiments in a specific order to reduce confusion.

Many service providers have developed elaborate training programs to instill this consistency, direction, and discipline, such as the employee "universities" operated by McDonald's and Walt Disney Company. In fact, Disney University has been so successful in empowering employees to provide good customer service that it now offers paid training seminars to other companies.

In other businesses, service retailers have found they cannot anticipate and program every service requirement, so they instead instill their employees with simple epithets such as "Always do whatever it takes to satisfy the customer." One national department store chain known for its high customer service reportedly has a simple, three-part code of conduct for its employees:

1. Always satisfy the customer.
2. Don't steal from the company.
3. Never chew gum.

By not burdening its employees with rules and regulations, this retailer empowers them to use their best judgment in satisfying customers. Of course, at times an employee may use poor judgment and give away more than required to a customer, but retailers that are highly focused on customer service will not discourage them. As one Disney executive said:

> *It's okay if the customer gets away with something, because the alternative is that we [Disney] might be wrong. And if we're wrong, it might cost us a fortune, because that guest will go away and tell everyone he knows that Disney is cheap.*

UNIQUE CHALLENGES IN THE RETAILING OF SERVICES

The basic characteristics of services make them somewhat more difficult to retail. It is important for retailers of services—and indeed all retailers who hope to provide superior service to their customers—to understand the following unique challenges. Strategies for overcoming these challenges will be presented later in this chapter.

Services, Retailers of Services, and the Selling Environment Are Intertwined. A key characteristic of retailing of services is that consumers often don't make a distinction between the service, which is intangible, and the retailer of services. When a tangible good is purchased but is unsatisfactory, the consumer often blames the manufacturer and forgives the store where the item was purchased—assuming the store treated the customer well. This is rarely true for services, which are seen as integral to the stores that provide them. For example, tax preparers such as H&R Block offer services through a retail facility. If a particular preparer makes a mistake on a tax return, most affected customers would not view H&R Block as a generally good tax preparer which just had one bad employee that year. Instead, most customers would be soured on H&R Block in general. Therefore, as we shall see in this chapter, all messages which retailers of services communicate to consumers are critical to attracting, satisfying, and retaining customers. To a greater extent than is seen in consumer goods, the image and tangible communications of a retailer of services are one and the same as the service itself.

As an outgrowth of the fact that consumers identify retailers of services with their services, the selling environment is also integral to the service itself. Consumers will sometimes purchase a name-brand packaged good from a dark, dingy store with a substandard environment, feeling that once they get the product home it will be the same as one purchased at a fancy department store. The same cannot be said of services, the use and evaluation of which goes hand in hand with the selling environment. Most people, for instance, prefer not to eat in restaurants which have a dated, unkept appearance, for fear the food will be unclean or low quality. As we will see throughout this chapter, service providers must pay careful attention to their selling environment, which helps customers form expectations about the service, encourages them to use more services, and is an integral part of their evaluation of the quality of the service.

Corporate Image Influences Customer Expectations of Services. Remember that service quality ratings depend first and foremost on customer expectations. Quality-minded retailers maintain a vigilant watch on customers' expectations and make sure all external communications are coordinated to foster the appropriate expectations. This process begins, of course, with the retailer's mission, which delineates what the retailer wants to be. The retailer must carefully consider what it can do well, relative to the competition, and just as importantly what it cannot do well. All external communications must then foster high customer expectations regarding areas where the retailer performs well and downplay expectations where it cannot do well. Conversely, the retailer must also identify areas where consumers already expect it to perform well—perhaps because of expectations created by competitors—and ensure that it does perform well in these areas. If a retailer is spending large amounts of time and money to improve its performance in areas where customers don't have high expectations—either because it isn't an important attribute to customers or because they don't expect the retailer to perform well on it—the retailer must carefully consider whether its effort will yield an advantage over competition. Perhaps these resources could be applied to other areas where a greater increase in customer service ratings can be achieved.

One important area of building expectations we have discussed is corporate image, composed of all external communications received by consumers. Of course, retailers have long viewed corporate image and awareness as critical to attracting customer traffic. The concept of service quality suggests that it is just as important in retaining customers and ensuring repeat visits, by helping to establish the expectations customers use to evaluate the quality of their retail shopping trip.

While corporate image is important for all retailers, it is especially important for retailers of services, because the consumer's image of a firm and its services are one and the same. Research has suggested that when forming expectations about the image of a service, consumers base their perceptions mostly on word-of-mouth information received from family and friends, and the physical facility they have seen in the past. Surprisingly, promotional materials and advertising by the retailer of services have considerably less effect on consumers' image perceptions.[11] Image perceptions in turn create expectations regarding the retail facility, its product and service offering, personal service, and price, all of which dramatically affect a customer's evaluation of the eventual shopping trip.[12] This suggests two strategies retailers should employ:

1. Retailers must try to gain favorable expectations through the retail facility and word-of-mouth communications. Since word of mouth is strongly influenced by past customers' evaluation of service quality, retailers should be very aware of customer expectations and consistently meet and exceed them.
2. Retailers must ensure that their physical facility, especially the exterior, not only attracts attention, but also communicates messages consistent with the store's performance. The decor should not suggest an upscale shopping environment if the merchandise, service, and pricing are not consistent. Whatever image and expectations are created by the facility, the retailer must be able to meet or exceed them to achieve high customer service evaluations, which in turn leads to more return visits and better word-of-mouth communications.

Intangible Services Are Undetectable. The most basic difference between services and goods is that services are intangible. In the retailing environment, the implication of this difference is that services are, by themselves, undetectable by the customer. They have no qualities which can be perceived by the human senses. Therefore, retailers of services must create tangible messages which serve as proxies or substitutes for the services in the customer's mind. These tangible cues alert customers to the availability of various services;

describe them, their characteristics, and their potential benefits; and provide details on how customers can order and/or use them. Without these tangible cues, a store that sells only services would be little more than an empty room with a human salesclerk, through whom all information about the services would come. In fact, this is exactly what many service retailing environments have historically been. Banks, post offices, car showrooms, airline counters, and other service centers were simply rooms with counters and service people. If customers didn't ask for a service—often because they didn't know it existed—it didn't get sold. If a salesperson suggested an additional service, customers often felt like they were being railroaded into spending more money by high-pressure sales tactics. Today, progressive service centers have become service *stores* by creating tangible messages which communicate the full range of services, and information about them, to customers, who feel they are educating themselves about services and then asking for rather than being sold the service. This leads to not only greater sales, but greater customer satisfaction.

Services Are Indistinguishable from One Another. Because services are intangible, they have no physical qualities which customers can use to independently distinguish one from another. Without further explanation, a shoe shine is a shoe shine. Of course, every shoe shiner has a different technique, and some are better than others. Some have created different names for different kinds of shines. A sign in one airport shoe shine shop listed a wax shine for $2, buff and polish for $2.50, and a spit shine for $3. The sign is a good start at creating tangible cues which differentiate various levels of service, for it encourages customers to ask for the higher-priced shine. The prices help you determine that a spit shine must be, if you'll pardon the phrase, the mother of all shoe shines (though the name might make you think just the opposite). But without further description about the features and benefits, it is impossible to determine why the spit shine is worth the extra 50 cents, and most importantly, why this shoe shine's spit shine is better than that of the shoe shine down the hall. It is very difficult for consumers to differentiate one service from another, and to be successful, service retailers must communicate specific reasons why their service is unique or somehow offers an advantage over that of a competitor.

Customers Have Difficulty Shopping for Services. Whether customers like it or not, shopping is a necessary prerequisite to buying. Shoppers must identify and learn about options which are available, make decisions regarding the benefits and cost of alternatives, make a purchase decision, and complete a transaction. This is easy in a store offering purely tangible goods, because the goods themselves often provide the information necessary to shop. Produce can be squeezed to determine ripeness. Boxes can be read to determine specifications or ingredients. In a store selling services, however, customers often have difficulty shopping. If you have ever entered a service store and felt awkward because you weren't even sure where to stand to wait for help, you have experienced the difficulty shopping for intangible services. Therefore, the service retailer must provide not only tangible cues which substitute for services, but they must organize these cues in a manner which provides a rational shopping process for the customer to follow. If a hardware store carried four types of hammers but placed each of them in a different part of the store, customers would find it very difficult to shop. Similarly, if a retailer of services hangs four signs about similar services at disparate points in the store, the customer will become confused.

Service Delivery Often Forces Customers to Wait. The inseparability and perishability of services means that they must be produced simultaneously as they are sold, and cannot be stockpiled for later sale. Accordingly, for many service purchases customers must wait for the service to be performed, and when several customers request a service at the same time, they wind up waiting in line. Further, many services are subject to inconsistent demand. Restaurants obviously have peak demand points during breakfast, lunch, and dinner. Dry-cleaning shops have peak pickup times right after work hours, when customers stop on their way home. Supermarkets have demand peaks on Saturdays, and even certain days of the month coinciding with pay days.

To retailers, these peak periods and the lines of waiting customers present both difficulties and opportunities. Certainly, it is difficult to economically operate a facility designed for peak crowds, but which operates well below peak much of the time. Supermarkets cannot call in extra employees for the two-hour rush and send them home with only two hours' pay, or workers would quit. On the other hand, lines of waiting customers present an opportunity to communicate many positive messages about the retailers and the goods and services it offers. Many retailers put so-called impulse merchandise in waiting areas where customers have **dwell time.** Similarly, service retailers can use dwell time to communicate messages about various services, leading to increased sales.

SERVICE QUALITY IN THE RETAIL ENVIRONMENT

We now understand some of key characteristics of services, as well as some of the unique challenges confronting retailers of services. Due to their intangibility, perishability, inseparability, and heterogeneity, services cannot stand alone—they go hand in hand with the retailer that sells and provides them, and the selling environment through which they are sold and consumed. For this reason, it is impossible to discuss specific strategies for the retailing of services without first introducing the concept of **service quality,** which is an area of study that has developed to define and describe how services can be delivered in such a manner as to satisfy the recipient.

Service quality, which in the retail world equates to customer service and satisfaction, is central to the success of the retailer. It is closely associated with personal selling, discussed in Chapter 15, the merchandising concepts discussed in Chapters 7 through 9, and the selling environment concepts discussed in the other chapters in this part. In fact, customer satisfaction has implications for virtually all chapters because it is so central to retailing. We choose to discuss it in this chapter, because of our view that all retailers are really selling service, rather than physical products. The manufacturers are selling the products; the retailer is selling the time and place value of bringing the right products to the right people at the right time and cost.

In this section we will discuss why providing high-quality service is so important to retailers, how it is defined, and how customers evaluate service in the retail environment.

HIGH-QUALITY SERVICE LEADS TO INCREASED SALES AND PROFITS

Throughout this text we have stressed the concept that over the next generation, population growth will be slower, growth in consumer spending will be slower, and many retailing sectors will reach maturity. In the struggle to grow and remain profitable in the future, retailers will find it difficult to increase sales through the historical growth strategy of adding new stores. Instead, they will be forced to generate greater productivity and profit out of their existing stores. By understanding and applying the concepts of service retailing, retailers can increase the quality of their service, and therefore their sales and profits.

In their extensive work on service quality, Zeithaml, Berry, and Parasuraman have shown that firms that offer superior quality often achieve greater sales and profitability.[13] High quality is particularly important in the retailing of services because consumers are often more loyal in service purchasing than they are in the purchase of tangible goods.[14]

There is little doubt that quality is very important in the retailing of services. But retailers of services face a quandary: Maintaining high quality is simultaneously more important and more difficult for services than for goods. Because of the intangibility, heterogeneity, perishability, and inseparability of services, it is more challenging for service providers than goods manufacturers to develop and adhere to quality standards. While manufacturers can develop tangible standards for their tangible products, such as weight, size, or strength, service providers can establish only nontangible standards, which are difficult to define, observe, and measure.

For the same reasons, ironically, it is even more important for service providers to establish and meet quality standards. Since each delivery of a service is subject to human error and varying consumer perceptions, service providers must try even harder to delineate and follow standards for the quality of their service. Due to the dramatic growth of services in our economy, and the increased importance and difficulty of quality standards, the concept of service quality has received great attention in the past five years. Retailers of services must understand service quality concepts and apply them in managing their corporate image, store exterior, selling environment, service assortment, and pricing, in order to attract and retain customers. This section discusses some of the latest thinking on maintaining service quality in service retailing.

DEFINITION OF SERVICE QUALITY

Just what is service quality? Intuitively, it seems as simple as providing good service that satisfies customers. But how do providers of services achieve this simple goal? How do you know what customers want? How do you ensure that possibly hundreds of different human beings providing the service do it the right way, time after time? And how do you know when customers are really satisfied, especially since some dissatisfied customers may be more likely to just not come back than to express their displeasure?

High-quality service is defined as delivering service which meets or exceeds customers' expectations. In this definition there is no absolute quality service, but only service that is perceived as high quality because it meets and exceeds the expectations that customers have. For example, suppose a consumer has dinner one night at a restaurant he or she expects to have slow service and is served in 10 minutes. The next night, the same consumer eats dinner at a restaurant he or she expects to have fast service and again is served in 10 minutes. Even assuming that other factors such as cleanliness, friendliness, and food quality are the same, this consumer might report the service quality to be better in the first restaurant, because the 10-minute service was faster than expected, and report lower service quality in the second restaurant because the 10-minute service was slower than expected. On an absolute basis, the service was the same in each case—good food in 10 minutes—but the customer's evaluation was different due to different expectations.

Much of the current research on service quality focuses on the gaps between what customers want and what they get. According to the gap theory, high-quality service entails first knowing what customers expect of your service or organization and then meeting or exceeding these expectations. This has prompted research on how customers form their expectations, how service providers can measure such expectations, how organizations can set and enforce standards that ensure services are provided in a manner responsive to customer expectations, and how customers form evaluations or perceptions of the service after it has been provided and consumed. Initial research has shown that all these tasks vary greatly from their counterparts in the manufacturing and retailing of tangible goods.[15]

ATTRACTING AND RETAINING CUSTOMERS THROUGH HIGH-QUALITY SERVICE

Understanding how consumers form expectations of and evaluate services is important to retailers of services for two reasons. First, expectations can either lead to initial store visits or dissuade consumers from visiting a store. If customers expect they will receive poor service, they obviously will not visit the store except in an emergency. Second, as seen previously in our example of the two restaurants, prior expectations of service have a dramatic effect on the consumer's evaluation of the service once it is provided, which naturally influences whether he or she will return in the future or recommend the store to others.

One is reminded of stand-up comedian Stephen Wright, who often complained in the 1980s of arriving at a 24-hour convenience store just as the store clerk was locking the door to go home. "But your sign says you're open 24 hours," Wright said to the clerk. The clerk, he reported in his comic routine, gave him a blank stare and said dryly, "Not in a row." Customer expectations are greatly influenced by the physical selling environment, signage, and corporate image, and these expectations in turn influence customer satisfaction.

Remember that this concept applies not just to retailers of services, but to all retailers, which by our definition are providing a service and are subject to the gap theory of service quality. All retailers can obtain new customers and retain existing ones by meeting and exceeding customer expectations—our definition of service quality.

HOW CONSUMERS FORM EXPECTATIONS

Customers can form expectations in one of two situations: before they have ever tried the service, and then before and after every subsequent use. Not surprisingly, customers have some difficulty forming expectations prior to their first use of a service, since they have no direct experience to go by.[16] Research has shown that consumers have more trouble forming first-time expectations with services than they do with goods,[17] and that they form prior expectations about services using slightly different inputs than for tangible goods.[18]

Consumers often base their decision whether to try a new retailer of services on images they have formed from many messages. While advertising and word-of-mouth information can be important, the selling environment, which is the most tangible form of communication between a service retailer and consumers, also plays a major role. In New York and other large cities, retailers have for generations used window displays to help consumers form expectations, realizing that to passing pedestrians these tell more about the service experience inside than would dramatic architecture. In other parts of the country, particularly suburban locations, retailers have focused their communication more on architecture than window displays.

As you undoubtedly have experienced, purchasing a service can seem somewhat more risky than purchasing a packaged good. While a good can usually be returned or exchanged, a service is consumed as it is produced, and it is generally too late to return it. Therefore, consumers rely more heavily on personal information sources, such as recommendations from friends and family, than on nonpersonal sources such as promotional material and advertising, which they are not sure whether to trust. They also are influenced by their personal observations of external, tangible cues of the service organization, such as corporate identity and physical facilities.[19]

In one study conducted by the authors, more than half of car buyers were observed to conduct extensive information gathering before deciding on a car to purchase and a dealership at which to purchase it. Included in this information search were discussions with family and friends not only about the car being considered, but also about the repair and service capabilities of dealerships being considered.

The decision to visit a particular retailer of services is partially driven by customer expectations. But customers have trouble forming expectations prior to their first visit and, therefore, many retailers of services attract first-time users by offering free trials. Movie theaters often hand out free passes, amusement parks offer discounts, and professionals such as chiropractors and lawyers offer free consultations to determine how they can help. These trial offers allow customers to form positive expectations through personal experience at little risk, and encourage both initial visits and continued patronage. Since consumers tend to be more loyal in their use of services than in the purchase of goods, the minimal cost of the initial giveaway is quickly offset by ongoing patronage.

Research also shows that consumers form expectations of retailers of services based not just on characteristics of that retailer, but also on where that retailer fits on a continuum of other firms that consumers consider to be competitors.[20] So, consumers' expectations regarding a retailer of services can be influenced not just by its own image, but how it stacks up against other competitive firms. Retailers are therefore wise to be fully cognizant of competitors' market images and position themselves to play off these images positively.

In one famous example, the Kroger Company adapted to the introduction of highly competitive Cub Stores, a division of Super Valu. Cub Stores are large food warehouses that offer very low prices. When Cub entered the Indianapolis market, Kroger, which had operated many stores in the area for years, tried to compete directly with Cub based on price, advertising its own low prices. However, Kroger was not able to match the volume and low prices offered by the huge Cub Stores, and it lost many customers. Several years later when Cub entered Columbus, another Kroger stronghold, Kroger preceded Cub's store openings with six months of extensive advertising touting Kroger's extra services, such as carrying groceries to the customer's car. When Cub opened, many customers were programmed to perceive Cub's low price advertising as an admission that service wouldn't be as high as Kroger's, and they stayed with Kroger. Kroger had learned and applied an important lesson in how to place itself on the continuum of customer service against a powerful competitor.

As the perceived risk of a service purchase decision goes up, so does the consumer's reliance on personal knowledge and observations. For this reason, corporate image can be more important for a service firm than for a goods manufacturer,[21] since it serves as a key factor in consumers' formation of expectations regarding not just the company, but also the services it provides. Corporate image, of course, can be influenced by the external visual cues a company communicates—such as its name, logo, corporate colors, slogans, and advertising—as well as by uncontrollable communications such as news articles and word of mouth.

Zayre Corporation, which had been a leading regional discount chain for 25 years in the Northeast, went out of business early this decade. By not changing its merchandise mix, selling environment, and customer service policies for many years, Zayre gained a reputation for being a stale, low-service retailer. One of the main cues which customers used to form this low-quality image of Zayre was the generally old and outdated stores. Since Zayre was one of the earliest discount store chains, its stores were older and smaller than the newer competition, and Zayre did not invest the money to upgrade them quickly enough. Haphazard merchandise presentation with little organization failed to communicate that Zayre was a dominant source for any particular merchandise category, instead suggesting Zayre was a generalist with odds and ends of merchandise. However, Zayre continued to run two advertising circulars per week promoting large discounts on specific items. Customers continued to visit Zayre despite its reputation, but research showed customers had virtually no interest in browsing or shopping because they thought the store had little to offer. Instead, they bought only items on

ILLUSTRATION 13.2
Providing extra services may enable a retailer to hold onto its customers when a new retailer advertising lower prices enters the market.

sale and left the store. While sales continued to rise at Zayre till the very end, its margins shrank until it was no longer profitable. In its final months, Zayre prepared two alternative advertising campaigns touting special values and a promise of fast movement through checkout registers. When they conducted focus groups to see which commercials would have the most positive effect on customers, Zayre's management found that customers didn't believe anything Zayre said, because it had made and broken too many promises over the years.

HOW CONSUMERS EVALUATE SERVICE IN THE RETAIL ENVIRONMENT

Service quality was defined as meeting and exceeding customer expectations, and since we have already discussed how consumers form expectations, we will now look at how services are evaluated by consumers once they have been used. This process is somewhat different for services than for tangible goods, and research has shown that it is more difficult for consumers to form evaluations of services than goods.[22]

In one study, customers who were satisfied by a service were shown to be more likely to describe the service in emotional rather than functional terms.[23] In other words, customers reported positive feelings in terms of how they felt about the service process, rather than just the technical quality or functionality of the service. It appears that the process of receiving the service is just as important as, or perhaps more important than, the outcome of the service itself. It is almost as though customers view satisfaction of their functional needs as a prerequisite of the service, rather than an advantage. The difference between different service providers, then, is often the satisfaction with the *service process* that they provide.

An easy way to think of the factors consumers consider when evaluating the quality of retailers of services is to think of all the types of expectations consumers form about retailers. Customers come to expect a shopping visit to take a certain amount of time and to be convenient. They expect the right selection of goods and services to be available, the right amount of personal service, appropriate prices, and the right amount of after-sale service such as money-back guarantees. We will look at these key factors in more detail.

Time. An important factor in the evaluation of services is the amount of time it takes to wait for, order, receive, and use the service. Whether it is the number of minutes waiting to see a doctor or the number of days waiting for a car to be repaired, customers have specific expectations of how long a service should take. For years, catalog retailers have operated under the assumption that home shoppers are willing to wait longer to receive their goods through the mail and do not demand the instant delivery they receive in a store. More recently, as catalog retailers have introduced rushed and overnight delivery as a differential advantage, fast delivery has become more an expectation than an advantage. Many catalogs now offer next day delivery by Federal Express, U.P.S., or other parcel post service.

For many retailers, one of the most critical aspects of service quality is the time customers must wait in the checkout lane. Most retailers use this as a critical gauge of their customer service, and in fact the supermarket industry spends millions of dollars on research and technology to streamline what it calls front-end operations.

Interestingly, one study showed that customers' perceptions of the waiting time can be influenced by how quickly they are moving through the line or by activities they can perform while in the line.[24] Amusement parks often employ clowns or other simple entertainment to occupy the minds of customers waiting in long lines. The implication is that consumers don't mind the actual wait, but rather the notion that service is being provided slowly. As long as they have a sense that service is being provided quickly—as evidenced by a fast-moving checkout line—customers in many types of stores are willing to wait a little longer before becoming frustrated. In fact, customers may relate long checkout lines to high volume and low prices in some stores and are content to shop there as long as the lines move quickly.

Many retailers of services use this concept to create an image of fast service. Banks, fast-food restaurants, theme parks, and airlines use centralized checkout lines that feed to many different service points. While any number of stations may be open, the entire line moves each time a new window comes open, as opposed to the slower movement of separate lines. This gives the impression of rapidly provided service, even though the total waiting time may be the same. Of course, while the single serving line emphasizes fast-moving service, it can just as easily emphasize slow service. Recall how infuriating it is to wait in an airline counter line during a holiday weekend, when the line never seems to move.

Convenience. Closely related to time is convenience, or how easy it is for the customer to order, receive, and use the service. Factors in the consumers' perception of convenience may include location of the store, ease of parking, length of walk, ease in locating and selecting merchandise or services, ease of payment, ease of delivery, and ease of use. Customers form expectations regarding each of these factors, and much of their satisfaction with a particular shopping trip depends on how the trip stacks up against these expectations.

To encourage sales during times which are less convenient, retailers of services often offer special values which offset the inconvenience. Matinees at movie theaters at lower ticket prices, special dinner values prior to 6 p.m. at restaurants, and price reductions by a chimney sweep in the spring and summer season when most consumers don't want to bother with their fireplaces, are all examples of service providers trading off price for convenience.

Of course, an entire retail industry was formed in the United States to provide convenience. Southland Corporation's 7-Eleven, Circle K, and many

ILLUSTRATION 13.3

One way in which retailers provide convenience to customers is by offering merchandise or services at locations where the customer has already stopped—like this convenience store that also sells gas.

other convenience stores—commonly called "c-stores"—were created to fill a void left when small corner markets were forced out of business by large supermarkets. Convenience stores offered a wide variety of merchandise with extended hours and easy in-and-out service, though the prices were significantly higher. Supermarkets eventually responded, however, by introducing longer hours, express lanes, and in some cases even mini-convenience stores near the front entrance, to encourage convenience shopping. At the same time, corner gas stations realized that convenience can be provided by offering merchandise where the customer already must stop—to get gas—and created so-called "g-stores," which offer gas customers a smaller selection of convenience products. This combined competitive response cut significantly into the convenience store industry, forcing the two industry leaders and several others into Chapter 11 bankruptcy. By the early 1990s, both 7-Eleven and Circle K had streamlined their companies, merchandise mix, and operations and emerged from Chapter 11 with refreshing new formats.

The consumer's demand for convenience sometimes conflicts with the reality of providing services, which by virtue of inseparability can be less predictable and therefore less subject to planning than manufacturing goods. Home repair services, for instance, often do not know the exact nature of a repair problem before arriving at the home, and therefore can only estimate the time required to make the repair. After several of these unpredictable repair calls, a service person's schedule can vary by minutes or hours, causing delays in arriving at later appointments. As a result, many repair services will not schedule an exact time for a repair or home delivery, often specifying only a morning or afternoon appointment. Consumers are obviously frustrated by having to wait for several hours, particularly when both spouses have jobs outside the home, but repair services have found this system frustrates customers less than showing up two hours late for a set appointment. By creating only expectations they can be sure to meet, such as showing up within a four-hour period, repair services are attempting to maximize their service quality.

Merchandise or Service Offering. Not surprisingly, consumers' evaluations of whether they receive good service in a store depend on whether they found the merchandise or services they were seeking. Again, the critical factor in this evaluation is not just what merchandise or services were available, but what the customer was expecting. Think about your own experience. You have undoubtedly been disappointed by not finding, say, an electronics component in an all-purpose electronics store, where you expected the item to be. Conversely, you have probably been pleasantly surprised to find an item in a store where you didn't expect it, and concluded the store provided good service by saving you a trip to another store. Likewise, service customers can be disappointed when they find their favorite service provider is unexpectedly off duty or busy, or a necessary piece of equipment, such as a shoe resoler, is broken.

This is one reason why retailers and service providers must constantly change their merchandise offering, creating new reasons for customers to shop there. Retailers should establish a core merchandise mix on which customers can depend and then experiment with new and exciting offerings—both goods and services—that keep their stores exciting and fresh. If we know nothing else about retail customers, we know that their needs, desires, and expectations constantly change, and a stale merchandise mix is a sure way to lose your customer franchise, as did Zayre. Many supermarkets, for instance, now offer U.S. postage stamps and automated teller machines, simple services that save the shoppers another trip while earning the supermarket customer loyalty, if not incremental profit. Many convenience stores attempted to add services such as check cashing, money orders, lottery sales, and other customer services to entice more shoppers. However, some found these services simply slowed down the checkout lane—thereby compromising their primary offering of time convenience—while adding little profit. Service offerings must be carefully matched to the type of retail environment, target customer, and shopping occasion.

Personal Service. It may seem obvious that high levels of personal service always result in high service evaluations of a retailer. This is not necessarily so because such evaluations are made not on an absolute basis but relative to the customer's expectations. In certain stores, customers expect high levels of personal service and may be fairly unimpressed when it is provided. In other stores, particularly self-service discount stores and supermarkets, customers want to be left alone to shop. They don't want to be pressured into buying things they don't need, so too much personal service can actually be viewed as a negative. Of course, service associates must always be available should a customer develop a question or the customer will feel unserved, so staffing and operating such stores can be tricky.

Wal-Mart has addressed this problem by placing a friendly people-greeter at the entrance to every store. The greeter's job is simply to welcome all entering shoppers, answer any immediate questions they have, and most of all, offer them a shopping cart to fill. This creates an immediate image of customer service. While shopping the store, customers may not see another associate before checking out, but that image of customer service remains. Recently, Wal-Mart instituted a store policy that requires associates to personally walk confused customers to their desired item rather than just pointing to it or giving an aisle number. In Nordstrom's stores, the many associates on the floor are trained to introduce themselves, tell the customer they are standing by if help is needed, and then back away rather than pressure the customer.

Pricing. Although pricing is one of the most obvious expectations customers form about stores, it is not always appreciated for its role in service quality. Consumers probably have strong expectations regarding price levels in most stores they enter, and how actual prices compare to these expectations can play a critical role in the consumer's evaluation of service quality. Therefore, retailers must always be aware of customer's expectations regarding their pricing, as well as their actual pricing and that of their competitors.

The physical facility and selling environment can make a dramatic contribution to achieving high customer service by creating the appropriate price image. If the corporate image, store exterior, layout, design, merchandising, and graphics create the appropriate image, customers will develop price expectations in line with the retailer's actual pricing levels. Discount stores, for instance, shy away from the sophisticated lighting and expensive decor used in many department stores, because they create an inappropriate price image that intimidates their target customer base. Department stores must be careful to match the level of their architecture and decor to the quality and price levels of their merchandise. Merchandise sold in Gucci stores would not sell well in a lower-level specialty store environment, and vice versa. The Gap and The Limited, meanwhile, create a classy though not pretentious selling environment reflective of their "affordable fashions" merchandise offering.

In some special cases, the selling environment can be used to create a deceptively high-price image. It is then easy for the retailer to meet and exceed the customer's price expectations. For instance, the Metropolitan Museum of Art stores use expensive ceiling soffits, sophisticated lighting, and rich design finishes including dark wood to create a high-price image. The merchandise is displayed in recessed shelving, much as it would be in a museum. This creates the illusion that the merchandise includes rare highly priced art pieces, when in fact most items are moderately priced reproductions. Customers are pleasantly surprised to find the prices well below the expectations fostered by the selling environment, and they often purchase out of a sense of relief. This is sometimes referred to as "reverse sticker shock." Of course, creating the illusion of higher prices can be a risky venture, as it will scare away rather than entice customers in many merchandise lines.

In a telling example of how important it is to match the price image conveyed by the selling environment with actual price levels, Sears encountered severe difficulties when it attempted to switch pricing strategies from highly promotional (regular high margins with frequent low-margin sales) to "every single day pricing" with sustained lower margins. Sears closed all its U.S. stores one weekend in March 1989 and launched a massive television advertising campaign stating that when they reopened, Sears stores would offer a different shopping experience with lower everyday prices. When the stores reopened, the prices had indeed been changed, but most of the merchandise and the merchandising methods remained the same. Shoppers who had been trained by discount stores to believe low prices only come in massive quantities refused to believe that Sears' prices were really low because the merchandise was not presented in mass displays. In fact, the Sears organization was not experienced in creating and maintaining mass displays and encountered difficulty creating a selling environment that conveyed the promised price image.[25]

After-Sales Service. Whether consumers are purchasing goods or services, they generally expect certain after-sale assurances from the retailer. These may include warranties or guarantees to ensure the product or service will be replaced if defective, a method for repairing a good if it should fail later, delivery or installation, follow-up service, and more often these days, a price-matching guarantee should the customer find the good or service for less money elsewhere. Consumers don't always demand each of these items, but they certainly form expectations about a store relative to each of them. If a retailer meets or exceeds a customer's expectations on one or more of these after-sale service items, the store's service image can be enhanced.

STRATEGIES FOR ENHANCING RETAILING OF SERVICES

In the preceding discussions of how customers form expectations about and evaluate retailers, there are many hints about how retailers of services can enhance their quality by helping shoppers form appropriate expectations. We will look at a number of key strategies that all retailers, as service providers, should employ.

USING THE SELLING ENVIRONMENT TO HELP FORM CUSTOMER EXPECTATIONS

A common theme in this section is the consumer's use of outward, tangible cues to form expectations about intangible services. One of the most important of these tangible cues is the physical facility through which it is simultaneously retailed and produced. The retailer can therefore plan the physical appearance of a store, especially its exterior (which customers frequently see prior to their first use), to be a key tangible cue which helps form appropriate customer expectations. The store provides information that helps consumers form a perception of the service provider's image and the types of services the retailer provides.[26] In addition to the exterior and interior design or appearance, the store location and layout can provide important tangible cues that customers use to form expectations about a service provider.

One service industry that has prospered in recent years is weight loss guidance centers. Many such centers, including Physician's Weight Loss Centers based in Akron, Ohio, offer medically supervised diets in which routine checkups by doctors and registered nurses and an implied sanctioning by the medical community serve as the differential advantage. Though a doctor may be present as little as two hours a week, Physician's Weight Loss Centers designs and locates its facilities to mimic a physician's office. Centers are often located in medical or professional buildings alongside doctors and dentists, and even when located in strip centers, they are designed with a patient waiting room in front and private examination rooms in the back. Service associates often wear white smocks like those found in doctor's offices.

Bob Evans Restaurants has successfully built a chain that offers "down-home cooking" and traditional dishes. The restaurants themselves are an architectural representation of this service offering. The dramatic red and white wood siding with Chippendale facade creates an eyecatching exterior that suggests traditional, high-quality service. Recently, Bob Evans introduced a new Mexican restaurant format called Cantina Del Rio, and the architecture of this facility is equally committed to creating an image reflective of the service offering inside. Varied roof lines, colored lights, bricks exposed through stucco, and other design features suggest an authentic Mexican environment. While some Mexican Americans have suggested the restaurant does not truly reflect Mexican architecture, it at least reflects many perceptions of Mexico. Once again, market position image is often more critical than reality.

CREATING TANGIBLE EVIDENCE OF SERVICES

Customers cannot see and touch services, since they are intangible. However, to form expectations of and evaluate services—a process central to customer satisfaction—customers must be able to sense their availability and performance through the five human senses. Therefore, retailers should strive to create tangible cues that describe their services. By *tangibilizing their services*, retailers can make more customers aware of their existence, create and influence customers' expectations regarding them, and to some extent influence customers' perceptions about their performance.

For example, deregulation in the 1980s made the financial services industry dramatically more competitive, and many banks turned to traditional retailing principles to gain a competitive advantage. While most banks offer many services, most customers use only two or three, and these are often the bank's less profitable transaction-related products such as check cashing. Banks needed to find ways to entice their regular transaction-based customers to use more profitable services, such as loans, financial planning, and investment assistance. By creating elaborate signage systems which advertised these services in appealing ways, banks exposed their intangible products to more customers, thereby increasing sales. By tangibilizing their services, banks became more successful retailers, as further detailed in Retailing in Action 13.2.

Another retailer of services that draws heavy, though not very profitable, transaction traffic is the U.S. Post Office. Like banks, the post office offers many services and products, though customers often view it only as a place to buy stamps and mail letters, neither of which are very profitable for the U.S.P.S. Research showed that many postal customers would be interested in purchasing shipping materials, collectors' stamps, Americana such as posters, and other merchandise while visiting a post office. The post office already carried many of these items but kept them behind the teller counter, out of sight, for security reasons. Recently, the U.S.P.S. developed a "Postal Store of the Future," which places the teller line at the back of the selling environment and draws transaction customers past self-service displays of the many product and service offerings. Not surprisingly, sales of these more profitable items have risen sharply in these postal stores, and customers report being more satisfied by the post office. In the 1990s, the U.S.P.S. continues to experiment with this store concept as a means to better satisfy customers and raise revenues and profits in the face of increased competition from commercial delivery services.

MERCHANDISING A DIFFERENTIAL ADVANTAGE

All service retailers enjoy some advantage over competitors in one or more specific attributes. Perhaps their checkout lanes are quicker, their location or parking more convenient, their pants pressing more crisp, or their paint-mixing ability more complete. In many cases, this differential advantage is an intangible service that cannot be directly sensed by shoppers. Retailers should create tangible cues of this service and merchandise their differential advantage.

In a simple yet powerful example, Fuller O'Brien Paints faced the challenge of creating a store that attracted not only the professional painters who were a strong customer franchise for Fuller O'Brien, but also retail customers. Fuller O'Brien, a premier paint manufacturer, knew that one of its key selling attributes was the store's ability to mix thousands of shades of paint almost instantly. Rather than placing the paint-mixing equipment in the backroom, as is done in many paint stores to hide the mess, Fuller O'Brien created a new store prototype that featured a glass-enclosed "Pro Shop" behind the checkout counter. In this Pro Shop, associates mix many different paint colors on

RETAILING IN ACTION

13.2 Deregulation Prompts Banks to Become Retailers

For generations, banks had been seen as service institutions rather than retailers. Prior to 1980, government regulated which types of financial institutions could offer certain financial services, thereby limiting the availability of services and regulating the way in which they were retailed. With deregulation, however, more institutions were allowed to offer a wider variety of financial services, and the market became highly competitive. Today, the average bank branch offers some 135 different financial services, though the average bank customer uses between two and three. Most bank visits are for so-called transaction services, such as withdrawals and deposits, which produce low margins for the financial institution. Historically, there was no way for customers to know about the other 130 or so financial services offered by the bank unless they asked, and the industry referred to "platform officers" as those people who sat behind mahogany desks on the raised service platform, just waiting for customers to ask for help.

In the more competitive environment of the 1990s, banks are realizing they must do more than just wait to be asked. They must actively market their services to their customers, and to do this, they have begun to tangibilize their services through visual communications in the bank, which is now referred to as a store.

In one of the early examples of a retail-oriented bank branch, Bank One, one of the nation's 10 largest banks with branches in Ohio, Indiana, Wisconsin, and Texas, introduced a "financial marketplace" concept that utilized many merchandising principles. As customers entered, they first encountered a greeter station where a receptionist welcomed them and directed them through the branch according to their needs. The teller line was strategically located at the rear of the selling environment, and a circular aisle forced customers to circulate through the store on their way to and from the tellers. Along the way, shoppers were exposed to modular offices dedicated to specific services such as mortgage, financial planning, realty, and travel services. Each of these "departments" was boldly identified with stylized neon signs and large photographs, alerting transaction-oriented customers to other services they could purchase and use at the branch. The Bank One financial marketplace was highly successful because it created tangible evidence of Bank One's many services, and it was mimicked by bank branches all over the country.

---

demand, putting on a show at the same time. While not all customers have paint mixed each visit, the Pro Shop creates a lasting visual image, and the next time customers need paint, this image reminds them of Fuller O'Brien. By merchandising its differential advantage—an advantage that was an intangible service rather than a tangible good—Fuller O'Brien created a competitive advantage.

Similarly, many one-hour photofinishing stores now place the photofinishing equipment in plain view of customers, often in a store front window for passersby to see as well. While the photofinishing process is not all that exciting, the brightly colored machine creates a lasting visual impression that merchandises the store's key differential advantage over competitors that don't have one-hour service.

CREATING A HIERARCHY OF MERCHANDISING INFORMATION

Customers must not only be aware of available goods and services; they also must be able to understand what they are, why they should use them, and how to buy them. Successful retailers create a **hierarchy of merchandising information** that leads the customer through the shopping and buying process. This is important in all retail stores, but especially in those that offer predominantly services, since it is the primary way by which customers become aware of the services available.

To create the hierarchy of merchandising information, retailers must understand the way human beings sense and evaluate their environment. People entering a facility usually look at high levels and great distances to obtain an overall orientation to the space. Once they understand how it is organized, they look for specific messages as to the merchandise opportunities available. They then make a choice and begin heading in a particular direction, at which time their sightlines often drop to lower levels, and they begin looking for closer messages. As they move through the space and choose a specific area to shop, their eyes drop further, and they look for very close messages regarding goods or services available in the immediate area. The rest of the store is now unimportant to them, but as soon as they are done with the immediate good or service, they will look high and far once again to find messages about where to go next.

To communicate effectively, messages must be not only in the right place, but in the right form. Generally, the farther the message is from the customer, the larger the message—whether words, pictures, or merchandise—must be. Messages placed high in the store need to be visible from long distances and must be very large. As messages drop down in the hierarchy, they tend to become smaller, since customers will be reading them from shorter distances. Signage on a fixture explaining merchandise right next to it is often very small.

Another merchandising concept is to understand that words are often not the most effective way to communicate with human beings, who see so many words they begin to ignore them. Often the merchandise itself, or a picture of the merchandise, is a more effective way to communicate. Imagine, for instance, a hardware store that identified its paint department either with a two-foot-by-six-foot sign that said, "Paint," or a 20-foot-high-by-10-foot-wide stack of paint cans. Most customers would more quickly notice the stack of paint cans, which just as effectively communicates the location of the paint department.

Finally, effective merchandisers understand that customers do not really want to buy the good or service itself, but rather the benefits it brings them. If they are buying paint, customers are really seeking a different color house or room. If they are buying dry-cleaning services, they really want clean clothes.

Messages in the merchandising hierarchy are often pictures depicting the benefit of the service or good. This helps customers visualize how the good or service can enhance their lives.

To utilize these merchandising strategies, retailers should create a systematic hierarchy of merchandising information, which is translated into physical messages such as signage, pictures, and merchandise displays. These messages are placed strategically throughout the facility to draw customers through the store, help them stay oriented to the space and find the goods and services they seek, provide information required to make purchase decisions, and actually enter them into the transaction process.

Bell Canada, the primary provider of phone equipment and services in Canada, operates stores that rely heavily on a hierarchy of merchandising information. In the past, all phone customers had to visit a Bell Canada "service center" to purchase or rent equipment, or add services such as a phone line, call waiting, or speed dialing. Customers often waited in long lines to talk with a service associate, who either completed a transaction or informed the customer—after a lengthy wait—that the service was not available. Many customers were dissatisfied with the long waits and what they perceived as poor service. To improve customer service, Bell Canada developed a service store which tangibilized many services through signage and created a hierarchy of merchandising information. This allowed customers to learn about available services and products, make purchase decisions, and then report to sales associates only to complete transactions. Different areas in the store were dedicated to various "departments," such as the rental center, purchase center, custom calling features area, and application center. Customers were drawn initially by large photopanels and signage which identified and distinguished the departments. As a shopper approached a department of interest, smaller signage provided specific information regarding the services available, features and benefits, and costs. For services, clipboards were provided with order forms which the customer could fill out and take to the checkout area. Merchandise, such as phones and answering machines for rent and purchase, was located in convenient displays showing color and style options, with boxes of the product available directly below samples on display. Sales increased because customers were exposed to more products and services, and customer satisfaction was enhanced because shoppers felt more in control and the shopping process was quicker and easier.

UTILIZING DWELL TIME

As we discussed earlier, even customer waiting time can influence expectations and evaluations of service quality. While customers understand that certain waiting periods are required in service retailing, they must be kept busy so as not to perceive that slow service is being provided. Retailers can *utilize dwell times* as prime opportunities to communicate messages regarding services available in the store, and at the same time entertain waiting customers. Dwell time messages can be used to tangibilize services, merchandise differential advantages, and show elements of the hierarchy of merchandising information.

CitiBank has developed very effective merchandising systems that utilize dwell time in the lines at many of its branches. Instead of simple velvet ropes or other queuing guides, Citibank installed structured mini-merchandising walls to guide customers through the line. These mini-walls were lined with photographs and brochures describing many available services and showing how they could enhance a shopper's life. By tangibilizing these services and placing them in the line, Citibank utilizes dwell time to merchandise its services and increase sales. Similarly, CoreStates Bank in Philadelphia placed large graphic panels in its 24-hour automatic teller areas that alert waiting ATM customers to service offerings available inside.

SUMMARY

While much of this text has focused on the retailing of tangible goods, the retailing of intangible services is also an important part of the retail industry. Retailing of services has become more important in recent years, as the nation's economy has transitioned from a manufacturing to a service economy in which nearly three-fourths of all expenditures are made on organizational and consumer services. In fact, service retailers touch most of our lives everyday, among them restaurants, health clubs, shoe shine stands, and dry cleaners. It is also important to remember that all retailers are really providing services (time and place value) to their customers, and are therefore retailers of services which can benefit from the strategies outlined in this chapter.

Services differ from goods in four significant ways—intangibility, perishability, inseparability, and heterogeneity—which present unique challenges for retailers of services to overcome. Because services are intangible and cannot be produced in advance of consumption, service providers and retailers of services are really one in the same. Consumers therefore do not distinguish between a service and the retailer providing it, as they sometimes do between goods and a store. The retail environment plays a critical role in the retailing of services by helping consumers form expectations about services and evaluate the process in which they are received. This process in which consumers form expectations about services and then evaluate their performance is the essence of high service quality, which is defined as meeting and exceeding customers' expectations. Providing high-quality service leads to increased patronage, sales, and profit for retailers of services, partly because consumers tend to be more loyal in their use of services than in their purchase of goods. Consumers form expectations about services based primarily on personal information they have received from personal observation or through friends and family, and evaluate retailers of services based on factors such as time, convenience, merchandise or service offering, personal service, pricing, and after-sales service.

Based on the unique characteristics of services and the manner in which consumers form expectations and make evaluations, retailers of services can utilize their retail environment to employ specific marketing strategies that increase sales and customer satisfaction. The retail environment must first be carefully planned to create an image and expectations which are consistent with a merchandise and service offering the retailer can deliver. Graphics and visual displays can be used to tangibly represent intangible services, which helps customers become aware of and shop for additional services. Visual displays and store design can also be used to merchandise the retailer's differential advantage,

Chapter 13 Retailing of Services

which is often an intangible service rather than a tangible, and therefore self-evident, good. The signage and other visual communications must create a hierarchy of merchandising information that leads the customer through the shopping process. Finally, service environments often require waiting times by customers, and the retail environment should be planned to take advantage of such dwell time to both occupy customers' minds and make them aware of additional services.

Retailing of services presents some unique challenges for retailers, challenges which can be viewed as opportunities to plan a retail environment which leads customers to appropriate expectations, exposes them to more merchandise and services, and helps them satisfy their needs. The result is increased sales and more satisfied customers.

QUESTIONS FOR DISCUSSION

1. Why is the selling of services considered retailing?
2. Why is the retailing of services an important consideration in the study of retailing? What role do services play in our nation's economy, and how has this changed in recent years?
3. Try to name at least 20 retailers of services that you have seen or patronized in the past few days.
4. What is the retail environment's role in the retailing of services. Is this role different from the retailing of physical products? Explain.
5. Why and how can all retailers benefit from the strategies discussed in this chapter for use by retailers of services?
6. Why are industries not traditionally considered retailing, such as funeral homes and banks, beginning to become retailers by adopting merchandising and retailing strategies?
7. Describe the four ways in which services differ from goods.
8. Describe some of the unique challenges faced by service retailers.
9. Define high service quality. Why are corporate image and a store's exterior so important to service quality?
10. Why does high service quality depend on a retailer's market positioning relative to its competition?
11. List and describe some of the factors consumers use to evaluate the service performance of retailers?
12. Describe the concept of tangibilizing a service and give an example you have noticed recently in a retail store offering goods, services, or both.
13. Describe the concept of merchandising a differential advantage and give an example you have noticed recently in a retail store offering goods, services, or both.
14. What is a hierarchy of merchandising information and how does it function to increase a store's sales and customer satisfaction?
15. Discuss examples of how retailers can utilize dwell time. Discuss the potential effect of this practice on both sales and customer satisfaction.

MANAGEMENT MEMO

You are the director of strategic planning for a regional bank company with 150 bank branches throughout Illinois. Recently, the chief executive officer has challenged senior management to come up with strategies for increasing sales of key profit-making services such as car loans, home mortgages, home equity loans, financial planning, and investment assistance. Consumer studies show that transaction traffic at your bank branches is strong relative to the competition, and that customers feel you provide good customer service. The vice-president of operations has suggested that more service staff be hired, so that they can dedicate more time to servicing customers and selling these additional services. The vice-president of facilities, on the other hand, feels money should be invested in signage systems communicating the availability and benefits of the additional services. The CEO has asked you to prepare a memo discussing the advantages and disadvantages of these alternative strategies, considering their short-term and long-term cost, potential impact on sales of the additional products, and their likely effect on customer satisfaction.

BOARDROOM REPORT

You have recently been hired as president of a 100-store chain of budget apparel stores called Bradley's which, like many other retailers, was forced to file for Chapter 11 bankruptcy protection in 1992 and is scheduled to emerge from Chapter 11 in the next six months. You joined the company despite its current financial status because of existing plans to cut the total merchandise assortment from 13,000 SKUs to less than 7,000, bring in more brand names, lower margins dramatically, rename the stores to Bradley's Bargain Basement, and begin an aggressive advertising program. You believe the new merchandising program will be well received by customers as offering strong value, and believe your new company has unique buying advantages over its competition. New financing has been put in place providing $20 million in capital funding to improve the stores in the next year, in order to tell consumers that a new store has emerged. Only one part of the plan bothers you. Most of the new merchandise changes and pricing strategy will not be in place for nine months, due to the lag in buying merchandise, but the store remodeling program is scheduled to begin immediately with all stores renamed by the time Bradley's emerges from Chapter 11 in six months. You're not sure whether the stores should be remodeled and renamed before the merchandise and pricing changes are in place, and have been asked to make a presentation to the board of directors next week detailing your concerns. Be sure to discuss the potential positive or negative impact of these changes, and their timing, on customer expectations and satisfaction, as well as on sales. What alternative strategies can you offer for the timing of changes? What kind of store changes should be made before or after the merchandise and pricing changes?

SUGGESTED READINGS

Albrecht, Karl, and Ron Zemke. *Service America*. (Homewood, Ill.: Dow-Jones-Irwin, 1985).

Bitner, Mary Jo. "Servicescapes: The Impact of Physical Surroundings on Customers and Employees." *Journal of Marketing* (April 1992): 57-71.

Brown, Stephen W., Evert Gummersson, B. Edwardson, and Bengtove Gustavsson, eds. *Service Quality: Multidisciplinary and Multinational Perspectives*. (Lexington, Mass.: D.C. Heath and Company, 1991).

Zeithaml, Valerie A., A. Parasuraman, and Leonard L. Berry. *Delivering Quality Service: Balancing Customer Perceptions and Expectations*. (New York: The Free Press, 1990).

ENDNOTES

1. Valerie A. Zeithaml, A. Parasuraman, and Leonard L. Berry, *Delivering Quality Service: Balancing Customer Perceptions and Expectations* (New York: The Free Press, 1990), 1.
2. James L. Heskett, *Managing in the Service Economy* (Boston: Harvard Business School Press, 1986).
3. Zeithaml, Parasuraman, and Berry, *Delivering Quality Service*, 1.
4. Douglas J. Dalrymple and Leonard J. Parsons, "Services in Marketing," *Marketing Management, Strategy and Cases*, 5th ed. (Toronto: John Wiley & Sons, 1990), 444-61.

5. "If the U.S. Work Ethic Is Fading, Alientation May Be Main Reason," *Wall Street Journal,* 7 February 1992, 1.
6. "Overworked Americans?" *Newsweek,* 16 March 1991, 50.
7. John P. Robinson, "The Time Squeeze," *American Demographics,* 12 February 1990, 30-33.
8. "If the U.S. Work Ethic Is Fading," 1.
9. Juliet Schor, *The Overworked American: The Unexpected Decline of Leisure Time* (New York: Basic Books, 1991).
10. "The Growing Gets Tough," *Forbes,* 13 April 1992, 68-70.
11. Kenneth E. Clow, Dave L. Kurtz, and John Ozment, "How Customers Form Expectations of Service Quality Prior to a First Time Purchase," in *The Cutting Edge II,* William R. Darden, Robert F. Lusch, and J. Barry Mason, eds. (Baton Rouge, La.: Louisiana State University, 1992), 99-110.
12. Ibid.
13. Valerie A. Zeithaml, Leonard L. Berry, and A. Parasuraman, "Communication and Control Processes in the Delivery of Service Quality," *Journal of Marketing* 52 (1988): 35-48.
14. Angela Rushton and David J. Carson, "The Marketing of Services: Managing the Intangibles," *European Journal of Marketing,* 19 (May 1985): 19-45.
15. Valerie A. Zeithaml, "How Consumer Evaluation Processes Differ Between Goods and Services," in *Marketing of Services,* James H. Donnelly and William R. George, eds. (Chicago: American Marketing Association, 1981), 186-90. Also Keith B. Murray, "A Test of Services Marketing Theory: Consumer Information Acquisition Activities," *Journal of Marketing* 55 (January 1991): 10-25.
16. Clow, Kurtz, and Ozment, "How Consumers Form Expectations," 99-110.
17. Zeithaml, "How Consumer Evaluation Processes Differ," 186-90.
18. Clow, Kurtz, and Ozment, "How Consumers Form Expectations," 99-110.
19. Ibid.
20. Ibid.
21. R. M. Bessom and D. W. Jackson, "Service Retailing: A Strategic Marketing Approach," *Journal of Retailing* (Summer 1975).
22. Robert F. Young, "The Advertising of Consumer Services and the Hierarchy of Effects," in *Marketing of Services,* James H. Donnelly and William R. George, eds. (Chicago: American Marketing Association, 1981), 196-99. Also Keith B. Murray, "A Test of Services Marketing Theory," 10-25.
23. John E. Swan and Linda J. Combs, "Product Performance and Consumer Satisfaction: A New Concept," *Journal of Marketing* 40 (April 1976): 25-33.
24. "Retailing Excellence: The Customer's Perspective," Study commissioned by the International Mass Retail Association and conducted by Ambassador Cards division of Hallmark, Kansas City, May 1989.
25. "Sears' Plan on the Ropes," *Advertising Age,* 8 January 1990, 1 and "Sears Weathering Bumpy EDLP Transition," *Discount Store News,* 2 July 1990, 89.
26. Mary Jo Bitner, "Evaluating Service Encounters: The Effects of Physical Surroundings and Employee Responses," *Journal of Marketing* 54 (April 1990): 69-82.

Part 5

PROMOTION AND SELLING

CHAPTER 14

RETAILING ADVERTISING AND PROMOTION

OVERVIEW

Promotion is the major generator of demand in retailing. This chapter focuses on the role of advertising, sales promotion, and publicity in the operation of a retail business. Retail selling, another important element of the retailer's promotional mix, will be discussed in Chapter 15. Our discussion is directed not at how to design and create successful promotional campaigns, but at how to manage a firm's promotional resources.

RETAIL ADVERTISING AND PROMOTION

I. The Retail Promotion Mix
II. Integrated Effort
III. Promotion and the Marketing Channel
IV. Law, Ethics, and Promotion
V. Promotion and Creativity
VI. Promotion Strategy
VII. Promotion Objectives
    A. Long-Run Objectives
        1. Store Image and Positioning
        2. Public Service Promotion
    B. Short-Run Objectives
        1. Increased Patronage from Existing Customers
        2. Attraction of New Customers

        C. Interdependence
- VIII. Retail Advertising Management
  - A. Types of Retail Advertising
  - B. Sponsorship
    1. Vertical Cooperative Advertising
    2. Horizontal Cooperative Advertising
  - C. Advertising Objectives
    1. Not a Panacea
    2. What Advertising Can Accomplish
  - D. Setting a Budget
    1. Affordable Method
    2. Percentage-of-Sales Method
    3. Task-and-Objective Method
  - E. Allocation of Advertising Dollars
    1. Gross Margin Percentage
    2. Advertising Elasticity of Demand
    3. Market Share Dominance
    4. Sales Displacement and Substitution
    5. Backup Resources
    6. Critical Mass
  - F. Media Alternatives
    1. Newspaper Advertising
    2. Radio Advertising
    3. Television Advertising
    4. Magazine Advertising
    5. Direct Mail
    6. Miscellaneous Media
  - G. Media Selection
  - H. Scheduling of Advertising
  - I. Advertising Results
- IX. Sales Promotion Management
  - A. Role of Sales Promotions
  - B. Evaluating Sales Promotions
- X. Publicity Management
- XI. Summary

Up to this point, we have discussed how retailers develop a merchandising plan targeted to the needs of a previously unsatisfied consumer group and then create a store, or a network of stores, to serve this targeted group. Retailers use promotion to generate sales from this targeted group by making it aware of their offerings.

Some sales can occur without the retailer spending any money on promotion. For instance, households close to the retailer might like its convenience; passersby might occasionally visit the store for an impulse purchase. Some retailers, such as the traditional department stores, believe that they must use heavy advertising in order to generate their desired sales levels. Others, such as Wal-Mart, spend only a small percentage of their sales on promotion. They believe that lower prices are more important than location and heavy promotional expenditures in generating traffic levels.

Most retailers, however, use a combination of location, price levels, and promotion as a means to generate store traffic and sales. Specifically, stores such as The Limited and The Gap that operate out of prime mall locations will trade off unspent advertising dollars against rent dollars and use the mall to generate traffic, with the mall's own promotional campaigns and in combination with other merchants. Direct promotional expenditures are, therefore, not a prerequisite to generating sales. Rather, they are a means of achieving sales above those that could be obtained merely from offering a certain price range or location or having a certain traffic flow.

THE RETAIL PROMOTION MIX

Retailers need to manage at least four basic promotion components: advertising, sales promotion, publicity, and personal selling. Collectively, these components comprise the retailer's promotion mix. Each component is defined as follows and will be discussed from a managerial perspective.

1. **Advertising** is "paid, nonpersonal communication through various media by business firms, nonprofit organizations, and individuals who are in some way identified in the advertising message and who hope to inform and/or persuade members of a particular audience; includes communication of products, services, institutions, and ideas."[1] Retail advertising's function is primarily to inform potential buyers of the problem-solving utility of a retailer's offering, with the objective of developing consumer preferences for a particular retailer.[2] Retailers most commonly use the following advertising media: newspapers, radio, television, and printed circulars.
2. **Sales promotions** "involve the use of media and non-media marketing pressure applied for a pre-determined, limited period of time at the level of consumer, retailer or wholesaler in order to stimulate trial, increase consumer demand, or improve product availability."[3] The most popular sales promotion tools in retailing are point-of-purchase displays and consumer premiums such as free gifts, trading stamps, and games.
3. **Publicity** is "non-paid-for communications of information about the company or product, generally in some media form."[4] Popular examples are Macy's Thanksgiving Day Parade and 7-Eleven's sponsorship of the Jerry Lewis Telethon on Labor Day.
4. **Personal selling** is "selling that involves a face-to-face interaction with the consumer."[5] Most retail employees are involved in personal selling discussed in detail in the next chapter.

ILLUSTRATION 14.1

Displays are one of the most popular sales promotion tools in retailing. Sales promotions, advertising, publicity, and personal selling are the components of retail promotion.

All four components of the retailer's promotion mix need to be managed in a systems perspective. That is, they need to be mixed together and managed together to achieve the retailer's promotion objectives. Each must reinforce the others. If the advertising conveys quality and status, so must the personal selling, publicity, and sales promotion. Otherwise, the consumer will receive conflicting or inconsistent messages about the retailer, which will result in confusion and loss of patronage.

INTEGRATED EFFORT

The management of promotional efforts in retailing must fit into the retailer's overall plan. Promotion decisions relate to and must be integrated with other decision areas such as location, merchandise, price, credit policy, building and fixtures, and customer service. For example:

1. There is a maximum distance consumers will travel to visit a retail store. Thus, a retailer's location will help determine to whom to promote. Basically, the most effective promotion dollars are those directed toward households in the retailer's primary trading area.
2. Retailers need high levels of store traffic to keep their merchandise rapidly turning over. Promotion helps build traffic.
3. A typical retailer's credit customers are more store loyal and purchase in larger quantities. Thus, they are an excellent target for specialized promotional efforts based on their past purchase history.

4. A retailer confronted with a temporary cash flow problem can use promotion to increase short-run cash flow by having a special event lasting anywhere from a couple of hours ("Midnight Madness") to a week or more ("Summer Bargain Days").
5. A retailer's promotional strategy must be reinforced by its building and fixture decisions. Promotional creativity should complement the style of the building, fixtures, and store layout.
6. Unless the retailers have an "exclusive" arrangement with the manufacturer, their ads should push not product features, but price and availability. A retailer with an exclusive product will, however, talk features, service, and image rather than price. Most retailers lack exclusive arrangements and therefore do feature price in their advertising.
7. Promotion provides customers with more information, which will help them make better purchase decisions because risk is reduced. Promotion, therefore, can actually be viewed as a major component of customer service.

The retailer that systematically integrates its promotional programs with other retail decision areas will be better able to achieve high-performance results. Exhibit 14.1 is a set of decision rules that retailers should consider when developing their promotional programs.

EXHIBIT 14.1

Rules for Retail Promotion

Try to utilize only promotions that are consistent with and will enhance your store image.
Review the success or failure of each promotion to help in developing better future promotions.
Wherever possible, test new promotions before making the major investment of using them on a broader scale.
Use appeals that are of interest to your target market and that are possible to attain. For example, double couponing offers everybody a reward; a sweepstakes has only one winner.
Make sure your objectives are measurable.
Make sure your objectives are obtainable.
Develop total promotional campaigns, not just ads.
The lower the rent, the higher the promotional expenses generally needed.
New stores need higher promotional budgets than established stores.
Stores in out-of-the-way locations require higher promotional budgets than stores with heavy traffic, such as in malls.

Source: Based on a handout prepared by Louis Bing.

PROMOTION AND THE MARKETING CHANNEL

The retailer is not the only marketing channel member that uses promotion. Suppliers (wholesalers and manufacturers) also invest in promotion for many of the same reasons retailers do—to move merchandise more quickly, to speed up cash flow, and to better serve customers. However, the promotional activities of the retailer's channel partners may not be in harmony with the retailer's promotional objectives.

As discussed in Chapter 5, suppliers and retailers sometimes look at the channel from two different viewpoints. Let us consider the case of an automobile channel. Assume that the general rate of real economic growth has slowed considerably and that industry auto sales are off 21 percent from last year. The manufacturer believes that the recession will be short-lived and, therefore, does not want to offer any price rebates or special promotions from the factory. However, the automobile dealers believe that the recession will be fairly prolonged. They feel that advertising by the manufacturer should be increased and that special allowances should be given for increased local advertising. They would also like to see the manufacturer tie in this increased advertising program with an $800 rebate from the factory. Because the manufacturer and dealer have different beliefs about the future, there can be serious conflicts between them.

Conflict between channel members can also occur when the manufacturer, through the use of promotion, seeks to attract a high-quality, high-price, status-symbol image to its brand, while the retailer wants to be known as the price leader and advertises "I will not be undersold!" In such a case, the manufacturer's and the retailer's promotional efforts are not interwoven and again a serious conflict can develop between them.

LAW, ETHICS, AND PROMOTION

In Chapter 6 we discussed the regulation of promotion; a review of this material might be helpful to you. Retail managers should become familiar with the legal constraints on promotion in retailing. At the same time, a strong ethical philosophy (an understanding of what is right and wrong practice in retail promotion) should be developed by retail managers early in their careers. Promotion decisions in retailing are probably the most ethically oriented decisions that a retailer will encounter, as pointed out in Retailing in Action 14.1.

PROMOTION AND CREATIVITY

Promotional programs and decisions by the retailer cannot be determined solely by analytical and scientific methods. On the contrary, promotion offers the opportunity for highly creative thought. In fact, creativity can enable the promotion mix to differentiate a store from its competitors. (Remember, how IKEA was able to avoid a price war with its Christmas tree promotion, as

> **RETAILING IN ACTION**
>
> ### 14.1 Some Vendors Don't Want Their "Specials" Promoted
>
> Most airline, hotel/motel, and even car-rental companies offer special discounts to large groups traveling together or going to the same location for a conference, meeting, or convention. These special discounts are made available by assigning a special code for the group members to use when making reservations. For example, in August 1991, if an individual were going to the American Marketing Association meeting in San Diego, American Airline's special 45 percent discount code was Star #S09Z1K1 and the Delta code was File #U0232. An individual attending the Alpha Kappa Psi Convention in Denver during the same time period and desiring to rent a car could use code 79242, Group G3 at Alamo Car Rental for an extra discount. These travel companies, however, don't want members of the general public to be able to use their codes to reduce travel costs.
>
> One retailer, a New York travel agency, has nevertheless used these codes to generate a substantial sales increase by publishing a newsletter featuring an extensive list of meetings and the fare codes needed to gain the discount. Several airlines objected to this action, but the travel agency obtained an injunction preventing them from stopping the newsletter.
>
> Is this an ethical promotional strategy for the travel agent?

discussed in Retailing in Action 4.1.) Usually, however, despite the fact that promotion offers the greatest opportunity for being creative, most retail promotional programs miss that opportunity.

One need only read the daily newspapers from several large metropolitan areas to quickly notice that retailers have a terrible habit of copying one another. Most retailer advertising looks the same. In addition, retailers freely copy each other in selecting the items to promote. When one department store has a sale on men's suits, the competing department stores follow. One appliance retailer has a sale on color televisions; so do its competitors. Imitation also applies to other facets of the promotional mix. If one shopping mall has an arts-and-crafts show, other shopping malls will have competing shows.

Retailers, unfortunately, do not always take the time to think of ways to differentiate themselves. Creativity does not come from hurried executives trying to meet deadlines. If we decide on Tuesday afternoon that we want to move more merchandise this weekend and thus need to deliver an advertisement to the newspaper by noon on Wednesday, we cannot expect that ad to be creative. Creativity requires time to think without worrying about other problems. This may sound idealistic, and retailers may argue that the pressures and fast pace of retailing do not allow for the luxury of time to think and be creative. But if retailers want a good return on their promotional expenditures, then each promotional event must be different and creative; it must attract traffic to the store and must be talked about by the consuming public.

Another reason for lack of creativity is the difference between large retailers and their smaller counterparts. Large retailers with their own advertising staff can at least strive for some level of creativity. They can attempt to design ads with a consistent graphic approach that is readily recognizable even if the store logo is missing from the ad. However, even large retailers suffer in that many of the best creative people in advertising prefer working for a multiclient agency instead of for a retailer. They feel that the work is more diversified, the pay is better, and the advancement potential is greater. Small retailers generally have no advertising personnel and tend to rely on the advice and assistance of the media salesperson in the preparation of their ads. Also, when using co-op advertising, small retailers often make more use of the materials and copy supplied by the manufacturer which is not always very creative.

A final reason for the lack of creativity in retail ads is that it is difficult to be creative when using only a price appeal, which all too many retailers are doing today. To survive into the 21st century, retailers must learn to use something other than price to differentiate themselves. After all, price is the easiest element of the retail mix to copy.

If price is going to be used as the competitive weapon, the retailer is advised to follow the suggestions of a recent academic study.[6] This study found that the most profitable price promotions include: (1) Items with high markups make the most attractive candidates for periodic promotions; (2) for some items, an "everyday-low-price" approach is more profitable than promotions; (3) the longer the time between promotions, the larger the markdown should be; and (4) promotions should be held during positive seasonal periods; for example, ties and shirts right before Father's Day.

PROMOTION STRATEGY

What is involved in developing a promotion strategy? The elements of the retailer's promotion strategy are just a part of the total company's strategy. As we already noted, a retailer's promotion program cannot be determined by analytical and scientific methods alone. It is an eight-step process:

1. Determining the promotional objectives
2. Determining whether there is a means of differentiating the offering in order to provide a promotional opportunity or advantage
3. Selecting the target
4. Selecting the message
5. Setting a budget
6. Allocating promotional dollars
7. Measuring the performance
8. Organizing the firm to perform the promotional functions

We have already discussed some of these functions in previous chapters; others of great importance to retailers will be discussed in the remainder of this chapter.

PROMOTION OBJECTIVES

To efficiently manage the promotion mix, the retail manager must first establish promotion objectives. These should be the natural outgrowth of the retailer's operations management plans. All promotion objectives should ultimately improve the retailer's financial performance, since this is what strategic and administrative plans are intended to accomplish.

As Exhibit 14.2 shows, promotion objectives should relate to financial performance objectives and can be established to help improve both long- and short-run financial performance.

LONG-RUN OBJECTIVES

The retailer can establish two long-term promotion objectives: store image and positioning objectives, and public service objectives.

Store Image and Positioning. This first objective is intended to reinforce in the consumer's mind the store image and position the retailer wants to project.

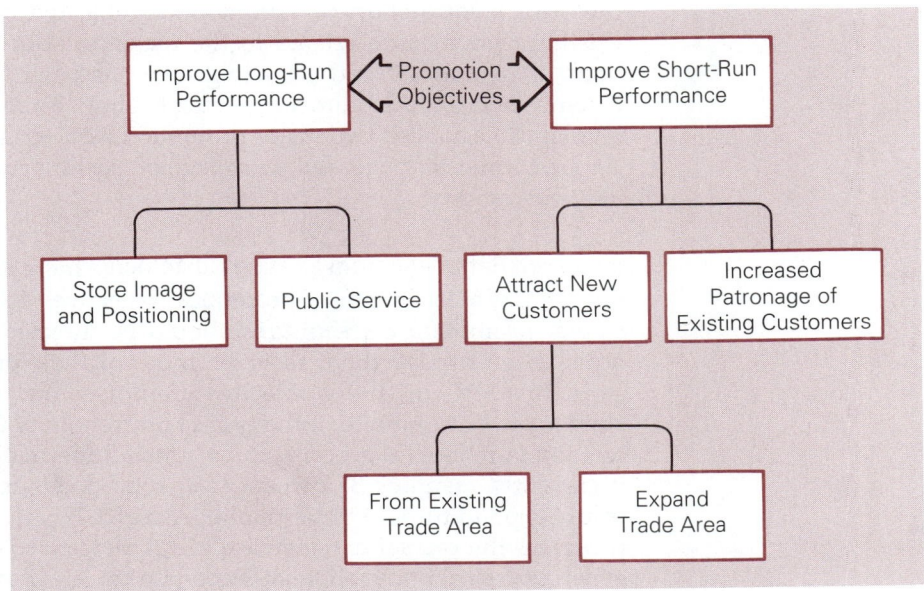

EXHIBIT 14.2
Possible Promotion Objectives in Retailing

For example, the consumer who thinks of Neiman Marcus or Nordstrom perceives an elegantly designed store featuring the top names in fashion backed by excellent service and a helpful sales staff. Promotion directed at fulfilling this objective will have its major impact on improving the retailer's long-run financial performance. However, as you might expect, it will also assist the retailer in the short run, as when a consumer is seeking to purchase a gift for a special friend. The promotional efforts of a store, especially in creating an image, have been found to be a key predictor of store choice when gift shopping.[7]

Public Service Promotion. The second long-run objective is directed at convincing the consumer to perceive the retailer as a good citizen in the community. Retailers may sponsor public service advertisements to honor local athletes and scholars. For example, some retailers offer meeting rooms for use by local civic organizations; some supermarkets have begun publishing consumer newsletters with health, cooking, safety, and beauty tips; many malls now let senior citizens in early each morning, before the stores open, so that they may exercise by "walking-the-mall" and not having to brave the elements outside; while other retailers provide public service announcements and sponsor programs on public television stations.

SHORT-RUN OBJECTIVES

Exhibit 4.2 showed the three ways demand for a product could be increased. We discussed one of those ways in Chapter 9 on pricing. Now we can relate the other two to short-run promotional objectives: Increasing patronage of existing customers is related to the maximum-quantity-demanded propositions of Exhibit 4.2 and attracting new customers relates to the maximum distance or effort a customer is willing to shop. Therefore, in the short run the retailer can establish two major promotional objectives to help improve financial performance: increased patronage of existing customers and attraction of new customers.

Increased Patronage from Existing Customers. Increased patronage is probably one of the most common promotion objectives found in retailing. Simply stated, promotion expenditures should be directed at current customers in order to encourage them to make more of their purchases at the retailer's store. In other words, this objective attempts to make present customers more store loyal. For example, if the typical household of four spends $4,800 a year on food purchases at grocery stores, and if Supermarket A's average customer is currently spending 37 percent of its food dollar at Supermarket A, then its yearly expenditures at Supermarket A are $1,776. If, with a good promotional program, the retailer can increase the 37 percent to 43 percent, then average expenditures per household at Supermarket A will rise from $1,776 to $2,064, for an increase of $288 per year. If the supermarket is serving an equivalent of

4,100 four-person households, then the net increase in the retailer's annual sales would be 4,100 × $288, or $1,180,800. There is, however, some question about the advantages of catering only to the loyal shopper. Research has shown that those consumers who regularly shop more than one supermarket spend up to 50 percent more for groceries overall than the loyal shopper.[8]

Attraction of New Customers. A second major short-run promotion objective is to increase the number of customers that can be attracted to the store. One approach is to try to attract new customers from the retailer's existing trading area. There are always some households within the existing trading area that, for a variety of reasons, do not patronize the retailer. Perhaps they do their shopping at a retailer close to their place of employment, or perhaps they simply do not think the retailer's store is attractive. Perhaps they once had a bad experience while shopping there and vowed never to return. A second approach is to expand the trading area by attracting customers from outside it. In this case, the retailer might want to consider the selection of different advertising media so as to expand the geographic coverage of its promotional efforts. A third type of new customer is the customer just moving into the retailer's market area. Mobile consumers are generally more prone to use national retailers, since they are familiar with their stores, unless local retailers use promotions to inform them of their offerings.

INTERDEPENDENCE

The arrow in Exhibit 14.2 suggests that although promotion objectives can be established to improve long- or short-run financial performance, programs designed to achieve either objective will actually benefit the other as well. Promotional efforts to build long-run financial performance will begin to have an effect almost immediately but will also have a cumulative effect over time. Similarly, efforts to promote short-run financial performance will carry over to affect the long-run future of the retailer.

RETAIL ADVERTISING MANAGEMENT

The following discussion develops in some detail a perspective for managing the advertising component of the retailer's promotional mix. Throughout the discussion you should remember that the best advertising decisions are integrated with other promotional decisions.

TYPES OF RETAIL ADVERTISING

Retail advertising can be classified in several ways, but the most popular system categorizes it as institutional or promotional. Institutional advertising is most beneficial in increasing long-run retailer performance; it attempts to sell the store rather than the merchandise in it, building the store image and creating a unique position for the retailer in the consumer's mind. On the other hand, promotional advertising attempts to bolster short-run performance by advertising product features or price as a selling point.

Although dividing retail advertising into institutional and promotional ads is useful and intuitively appealing, it can be somewhat artificial. Good retail advertisers have come to learn that all advertising should have institutional overtones. Most would agree with the statement, "Any ad for merchandise that does not place the store in a favorable image is a mistake."

SPONSORSHIP

Advertising is a paid form of nonpersonal presentation. The actual sponsor who pays for the advertising can be the retailer, the supplier, or any combination thereof. Most retail advertising is paid for solely by the retailer. In some cases manufacturers or vendors pick up part or all of the cost of advertising. This is called **vertical cooperative advertising.** If several retailers share the cost of advertising, it is called **horizontal cooperative advertising.**

Vertical Cooperative Advertising.

Vertical cooperative advertising allows the retailer and other channel members to share the advertising burden. For example, the manufacturer might pay up to 40 percent of the retailer's cost for advertising the manufacturer's products, up to a ceiling of say 4 percent of annual purchases by the retailer. If the retailer spent $10,000 on advertising the manufacturer's products, then it could be reimbursed 40 percent of this amount or $4,000, as long as the retailer purchased at least $100,000 during the last year from the manufacturer.

The responsibilities of each party in a vertical cooperative advertising arrangement are typically specified by means of a contract. In general, the manufacturer has a good degree of control over the general content of the advertising, considerably constraining the distinctiveness of the retailer's advertising. To illustrate, consider the relatively high possibility that in a large city (over 250,000 in population), two or more retailers in the same area of the city would cooperate with the same manufacturer on a particular merchandise line. In this situation their advertisements will appear very similar to the consumer.

There is a strong temptation among retailers to view vertical co-op advertising money as free (although most will acknowledge that getting their money back from the manufacturer is a hassle).[9] Retailers must remember that even if the supplier is putting up 50 percent of the money, they must put up the other 50 percent. Another way to look at it is that since the supplier exercises considerable control over the content of the advertising, retailers are actually paying 50 percent of the supplier's cost of advertising rather than vice versa. In addition, most media offer lower rates to local retailers than are offered to national manufacturers.

Because the amount of co-op money can be so large, retailers sometimes fall into the trap of advertising the products with the largest co-op deal, even though those products might not be the best products to attract consumers to their store.

Retailers must decide whether they can achieve a better return on their money with vertical co-op dollars or by assuming total sponsorship of the advertising. Many times it can be more profitable for the retailer to pass up the co-op deal on one product line and spend the money on another line, where the increased ad dollars will have a higher sales impact. Assume, for example, that the retailer is considering the possibility of advertising two alternative merchandise lines. The retailer has $5,000 to spend on advertising either line A or line B. With line A, the vendor has offered a co-op deal, which roughly translates into the supplier's paying 50 percent of the cost of the advertising. This would allow the retailer to purchase $10,000 of advertising for a $5,000 investment. No co-op deal is being offered by the supplier of line B, but line B is an increasingly popular line among consumers, and the retailer believes it could benefit substantially from $5,000 in advertising. What should the retailer do?

The answer to the preceding question will depend on two major factors. First, how much will the sales of line A increase with $10,000 in advertising as against the amount the sales of line B might increase with the $5,000 in advertising that can be spent on it? Second, what is the gross margin percentage for each line? Generally, any given merchandise line will be a more attractive candidate for increased advertising if its sales are more responsive to increased advertising expenditures and its gross margin percentage is higher. For the situation at hand, let us examine some specific (if hypothetical) figures. Line A has 50 percent gross margin and line B has 60 percent gross margin. Currently, line A has sales of $80,000, and it is expected that a $10,000 advertising program will push sales up to $110,000. At the present time, line B has sales of $18,000 and it is expected that a $5,000 advertising program will increase the sales volume to $60,000. Exhibit 14.3 shows the preceding sales response functions for lines A and B.

Notice that line B, although its current sales are relatively low, is very responsive to advertising expenditures in relation to the responsiveness of merchandise line A. The numerical analysis that will help you determine which line to advertise is as follows:

	Line A		Line B	
	Before	After	Before	After
Sales	$80,000	$110,000	$18,000	$60,000
Cost of merchandise	40,000	55,000	7,200	24,000
Gross margin	40,000	55,000	10,800	36,000
Advertising	0	5,000[a]	0	5,000
Contribution profit	$40,000	$50,000	$10,000	$31,000

---

[a] Actually, $10,000 was spent, but the net cost to the retailer was $5,000 since the supplier paid the other $5,000.

EXHIBIT 14.3

Sales Response Curves for Two Lines

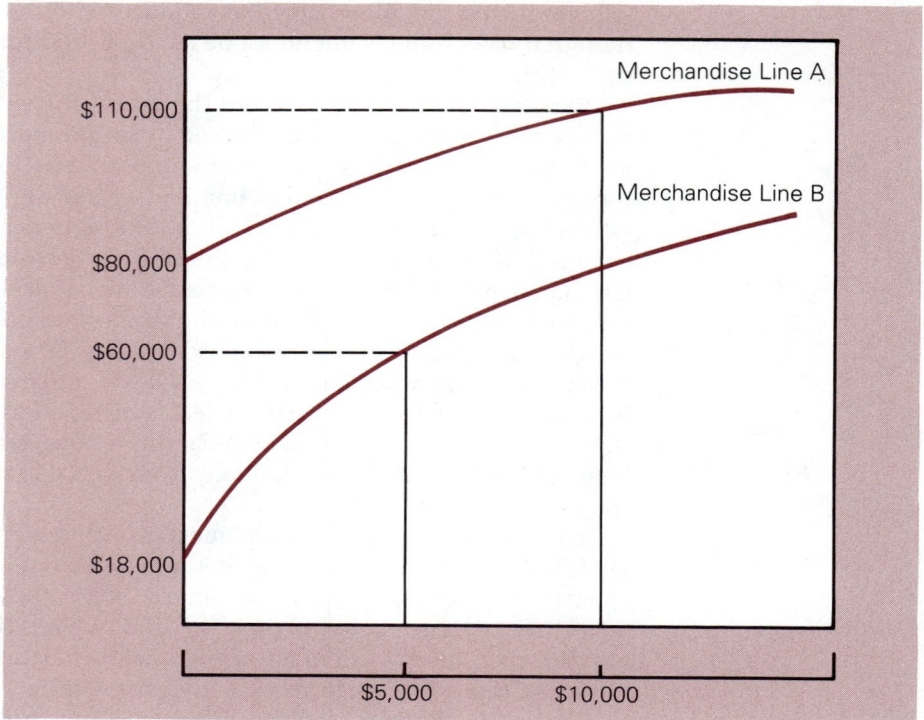

The numerical analysis suggests that it would be more profitable for the retailer to pass up the co-op deal on line A and spend the $5,000 on advertising line B.

Horizontal Cooperative Advertising. With **horizontal cooperative advertising,** two or more retailers band together to share the cost of advertising. Significantly, this tends to give small retailers more bargaining power in purchasing advertising. Also, if properly conducted, it can create substantially more store traffic. For example, retailers in shopping centers will often jointly sponsor multiple-page spreads in newspapers promoting special sales events such as a "Presidents' Day" or "Moonlight Madness" sale, while downtown merchants usually gather and jointly sponsor "Sidewalk Days" or "Downtown Days" sales. These events are good traffic generators. They pull significantly more people to the shopping area than any individual merchant's advertising could expect to, and thus all retailers benefit from the increased traffic in the shopping area. Exhibit 14.4 shows the various horizontal cooperative campaigns planned for one shopping mall for an upcoming year.

Chapter 14 Retail Advertising and Promotion

EXHIBIT 14.4

Next Year's Promotional Campaign for Large Shopping Mall

19XX		
January	**February**	**March**
Thou$and Dollar $ale (Coupon) Misspelled Word Contest Christmas Card Return Mad Hatter Sale	Presidents' Day Sale (One Day) Open Market Health Fair	Do It Yourself Sale (Demos/Paint/Clean/Fix) Art Show - Easter is March 30
April	**May**	**June**
Fashions in the Mall Midnight Madness The Great Trade-In Sale Funny Bunny Munny	Mother's Day Free Gift Wrapping Sports Show (Exhibition) Safety Town (Tots) (Bikes)	Pop's Our Pet Senior Citizen Salute Craft Show
July	**August**	**September**
Dog Days (Sale/Dog Show/Trade-In Sale)	Back to School Coupon Days Girl Scout Camp-In/Show	Fall Music Festival (4 Weeks) Harvest Sale (Farm Group Exhibition) Open Market Safety City (Law Enforcement Show) High School Football Night
October	**November**	**December**
Birthday Sale (Sidewalk Clowns/Music) Oktoberfest (Costumes/Travel Exhibits) Spook Parade Midnight Madness	Detroit City (New Car Show) Gobbler Give-Away (Silver $$) Gift Guide (Tabloid) Santa Arrival (Day After Thanksgiving)	Last Minute Gift Guide (Tabloid) Santaland Caroling for Charity

ADVERTISING OBJECTIVES

Advertising objectives should flow from the retailer's promotion objectives, but they should be more specific because advertising itself is a specific element of the promotion mix. Advertising objectives will suggest how advertising will help retailers achieve their overall promotional objectives.

ILLUSTRATION 14.2

Groups of independent retailers, such as these six members of Independent Grocers of America (IGA), often band together to place horizontal cooperative advertising, reducing the cost to each independent and permitting more dominant advertisements than each grocer could afford alone.

Not a Panacea. Before we explore the specific advertising objectives the retailer might develop, we need to stress that advertising is not a panacea. Many retailers incorrectly believe that heavy doses of advertising can cure their minor as well as major problems. Advertising, regardless of its quality, can simply not do the following:

1. Advertising cannot sell merchandise that people do not want to buy.
2. Advertising cannot sell merchandise in profitable quantities without the backing of every other division of the store (credit department, janitorial services, and so on).
3. Advertising cannot succeed to the fullest extent unless it is used continuously.[10]

What Advertising Can Accomplish. Although advertising is not a panacea, it can be powerful if properly used. All retail advertising will be either institutional or promotional, but this refers to its purpose and not to its more specific objectives. The objectives advertising can accomplish are many and varied. Examples include the following:

Increase traffic during slow periods
Move old merchandise at the end of a selling season
Explain store policies
Attract newcomers in the community to the store
Strengthen the store's image or reputation
Identify the store with nationally advertised brands
Reposition the image of the store in the minds of consumers
Cultivate new customers

Consider how creative advertising was used by Mazzio's Pizza, a midwestern pizza chain, to successfully reposition itself in the minds of consumers. The pizza chain carried products similar to those carried by Pizza Hut and Domino's. Rather than compete head-on with Pizza Hut and Domino's by using discounts and 2 for 1 promotions, Mazzio's sought to position itself as the "premium" alternative to the other chains. Television ads were created to reposition Mazzio's as the pizza retailer that offered real value for the price, with the theme "Mazzio's means more." The chain not only increased traffic and sales but gained over a 50 percent market share in key markets.[11]

SETTING A BUDGET

A well-designed retail advertising program requires money that could also be spent on other areas (such as more merchandise or higher wages for employees). The retailer hopes that the dollars spent on advertising will bring back many more dollars, which can then be used to finance other areas of the retail enterprise. The amount to spend on advertising in any given budget period should be determined only after the retailer considers several factors that are unique to retailing and that will influence not only the advertising budget, but the promotion budget as well. These factors are:

1. *Age of store.* New stores or stores seeking to rebuild a lost image need more advertising.
2. *Store location.* Stores in poor locations need more advertising.
3. *Types of goods sold.* Retailers selling high-image fashion goods generally require more advertising than discounters normally use. Discounters will need greater personal selling support in order to increase turnover.
4. *Level of competition.* The greater the level of competition, the more advertising and other promotional activities are needed.
5. *Market area size.* The size of the market will often dictate the type and extent of the media that can be used. Also, the larger the market the greater the need for promotional activities.
6. *Supplier support.* Suppliers may provide advertising and other promotional

support that enable the retailer to reduce its expenditures for those activities.[12]

After considering all these factors, the retailer can use the three following methods to determine the amount to be spent on advertising: the affordable method, the percentage-of-sales method, or the task-and-objective method.

Affordable Method. Many small retailers use the **affordable method** by allocating all the money that they can afford for advertising in any given budget period. This may lead to an inadequate appropriation or to a budget that is not related to actual needs. The logic of this approach suggests that advertising does not stimulate sales or profits but rather is supported by sales and profits. However, some retailers have little choice but to use this approach. A small retailer cannot go to the bank and borrow $100,000 to spend on advertising. This is unfortunate, because the small retailer might benefit more from advertising than from more inventory or equipment. Thus, we can see that although the affordable method may not be ideal in terms of advertising theory, it is certainly defensible given the financial constraints that confront the small retailer.

Percentage-of-Sales Method. In the **percentage-of-sales method** of budgeting for advertising, the retailer targets a specific percentage of forecasted sales to be used for advertising.

The percentage of sales that should be used is frequently determined by industry data or the retailer's past experience. Industry data, such as shown in Exhibit 14.5, are often published by trade associations. These figures are averages, however, and they do not reflect the unique circumstances and objectives of a particular retailer. A more suitable guide to the level of advertising appropriations is the retailer's past sales experience. The average ratio of advertising expenditures to sales for the past several years can be applied to the current year.

An obvious weakness of the percentage-of-sales method is that the amount of sales becomes the factor that influences the advertising outlay. In a correct cause-and-effect relationship, the level of advertising should influence the amount of sales. In addition, this technique does not reflect the retailer's advertising goals. One furniture retailer was quoted as saying that he never saw business so bad that he "couldn't buy all of it he wanted." By that he meant that when business slowed and all his competitors reduced their ad budgets, he would increase his ad expenditures. Without the clutter of competitor ads, consumers became more aware of his ads and his furniture sales increased, despite the general sales slowdown.

Percentage of sales does, however, provide a controlled, generally affordable amount to spend, and if the money is spent wisely, it may work out well in practice.

EXHIBIT 14.5

Advertising Expenditures as a Percentage of Sales

Line of Trade	Ad Dollars as Percentage of Sales
Apparel and accessory stores	2.4%
Auto and home supply stores	2.3
Buildling materials, hardware, garden	4.0
Catalog, mail-order houses	5.7
Computer and software stores	0.9
Department stores	2.9
Drug and proprietary stores	1.5
Eating places	3.3
Electronic parts, equipment	1.6
Family clothing stores	1.9
Furniture stores	7.1
Grocery stores	1.3
Hardware, plumbing, heat equipment	1.4
Hobby, toy and game shops	1.6
Home furniture and equipment stores	5.0
Lumber and other building materials	1.8
Miscellaneous general merchandise stores	3.1
Miscellaneous shopping goods stores	3.7
Radio, TV consumer electronics stores	5.3
Record and tape stores	1.4
Retail stores	5.8
Shoe stores	2.8
Variety stores	1.9
Women's clothing stores	2.7

Source: Schonfeld & Associates, 1 Sherwood Drive, Lincolnshire, IL 60069, 1990. Reprinted with permission.

Task-and-Objective Method. With the preceding budgeting methods, advertising seemed to follow sales results. With the **task-and-objective method,** the logic is properly reversed; advertising leads to sales or some other measure of financial performance. Basically, the retailer establishes its advertising objectives and then determines the advertising tasks that need to be performed to achieve those objectives. Associated with each task is an estimate of the cost of performing the task. When all these costs are totaled, the retailer has its advertising budget. In short, this method begins with the retailer's advertising objectives and then determines what it will cost to achieve them.

Exhibit 14.6 gives an example of the task-and-objective method. Notice that the retailer has five major advertising objectives and a total of 11 tasks to perform to accomplish these objectives. The total cost of performing the tasks is $99,020. While the task-and-objective method of developing the advertising budget is the best of the three methods from a theoretical and managerial

EXHIBIT 14.6

The Task-and-Objective Method of Advertising Budget Development

Objective and Task		Estimated Cost
Objective 1:	Increase traffic during dull periods.	
Task A:	15 full-page newspaper advertisements to be spread over these dates: February 2-16; June 8-23; October 4-18	$22,500
Task B:	240, 30-second radio spots split on two stations and spread over these dates: February 2-16; June 8-23; October 4-18	4,320
Objective 2:	Attract new customers from newcomers to the community.	
Task A:	2,000 direct-mail letters greeting new residents to the community	1,000
Task B:	2,000 direct-mail letters inviting new arrivals in the community to stop in to visit the store and fill out a credit application	1,000
Task C:	yellow-page advertising	1,900
Objective 3:	Build store's reputation.	
Task A:	weekly 15-second institutional ads on the 10 P.M. television news every Saturday and Sunday	20,800
Task B:	one half-page newspaper ad per month in the home living section of the local newspaper	9,500
Objective 4:	Increase shopper traffic in shopping center.	
Task A:	cooperate with other retailers in the shopping center in sponsoring transit advertising on buses and cabs	3,000
Task B:	participate in "Midnight Madness Sale" with other retailers in the shopping center by taking out 2 full-page newspaper ads—one in mid-March and the other in mid-July	3,000
Objective 5:	Clear out end-of-month, slow-moving merchandise.	
Task A:	run a full-page newspaper ad on the last Thursday of every month	18,000
Task B:	run 3, 30-second television spots on the last Thursday of every month	14,000
Total advertising budget		**$99,020**

control perspective, not all retailers use it that could. Most retailers, especially the smaller ones, do not use ad agencies and lack the sophistication required to adequately implement the task-and-objective approach.

ALLOCATION OF ADVERTISING DOLLARS

Regardless of the method by which the retailer determines its budget, the firm will subsequently need to decide how to allocate its advertising dollars. It will probably not be profitable to heavily advertise all merchandise lines or departments. Even if it were, most retail advertising budgets would not be large enough to do so. Thus, in either case, some conscious decision on where to spend advertising dollars is necessary.

Deciding which lines or departments to spend advertising dollars on is not easy. Advertising theory would suggest that the retailer's limited advertising funds be allocated to products or departments that maximize the retailer's overall profitability. In practice, due to uncertainty and inadequate information, such a theoretical rule is difficult to implement. Rather, the retailer must settle for an allocation that is approximately correct.

It is important for the retailer to become familiar with the factors that indicate a merchandise line or department is a candidate for a high advertising allocation. These are summarized in Exhibit 14.7.

Gross Margin Percentage. Merchandise lines or departments that have a high gross margin percentage are potentially better able than others to benefit or produce a profit from high levels of advertising. If a merchandise line has a gross margin of 20 percent, then to pay for each dollar of advertising at least five dollars in merchandise needs to be sold. If the merchandise line has a gross margin of 50 percent, then only two dollars in sales have to be created for each dollar of advertising.

Advertising Elasticity of Demand. The product's advertising elasticity of demand is the percentage of change in sales as a result of a 1 percent change in advertising. For example, an advertising elasticity of demand of 3.8 suggests that as advertising is increased by 1 percent, sales will rise by 3.8 percent. When demand is more elastic, demand is more expandable, and therefore the product is a better candidate for a high advertising expenditure.

Market Share Dominance. Retailers have found through experience and limited empirical research that a close correlation exists between market share by

EXHIBIT 14.7

Factors in Allocating Advertising Dollars

HIGH ADVERTISING ALLOCATION

- High Gross Margin Percentage
- High Advertising Elasticity of Demand
- Dominant or Potentially Dominant Market Share in Department or Merchandise Line
- Good Backup Resources (Space, Inventory, Accounts Receivable, People)
- Willingness to Allocate Enough to Achieve "Critical Mass"

LOW ADVERTISING ALLOCATION

- Low Gross Margin Percentage
- Low Advertising Elasticity of Demand
- Low Market Share and Limited Potential for Being Dominant Market Share Department or Line
- Poor Backup Resource (Space, Inventory, Accounts Receivable, People)
- Unwillingness to Allocate Enough to Achieve "Critical Mass"

merchandise classification and profit.[13] Also, retailers with large market shares enjoy an unusually large consumer franchise that can be protected only with high levels of advertising. Thus, retailers with dominant market share merchandise lines or departments should allocate a disproportionate share of advertising to them. The same also applies to lines or departments that are growing rapidly and have the potential of being dominant in terms of market share.

Sales Displacement and Substitution. Retail promotions, including price reductions, have been shown to increase current period sales substantially. However, in addition to increasing current sales of the advertised brand, retail promotions may also reduce sales of the brand during subsequent nonpromotional periods, referred to as **sales displacement** and reduce current and future demand for competitive brands, referred to as **substitution effect.** If a promoted brand causes extensive substitution effects, for example, the retailer may be worse off when consumers switch purchases from high-margin unpromoted brands to low-margin promoted ones. Likewise, sales displacement may have deleterious effects on the retailer's sales if consumers switch from a potentially high-margin time period to low-margin promotional periods.[14]

Backup Resources. A merchandise line or department should not receive a heavy dose of advertising unless it is supported sufficiently by other resources. Adequate inventory needs to be in stock to handle sales generated from the advertising, and there needs to be sufficient space to display the goods and employees to serve the customers when they visit the store. If the type of merchandise advertised is often sold on credit, then the retailer should have adequate funds to finance the consumer credit or some method by which to get it quickly.

Critical Mass. The retailer needs sufficient funds to allocate to a department or merchandise line so that the advertising can really make a difference in the line's or department's performance. The question is not whether a line should receive a high proportion of a retailer's advertising budget, but whether that high proportion is sufficiently high in absolute dollars to make things happen. Otherwise, the dollars are better spent on another line or department.

MEDIA ALTERNATIVES

The retailer has many media alternatives from which to select. Each has strengths and weaknesses, shown in Exhibit 14.8. Let us briefly review them here.

Newspaper Advertising. The most frequently used advertising medium in retailing is the newspaper, for the following reasons: First, most newspapers are local. This is advantageous since most retailers appeal to a local market or

EXHIBIT 14.8

Advantages and Disadvantages of Media Alternatives

Advantages	Media Alternative	Disadvantages
Local, well-defined distribution Low technical skill required for design and creation of ads Short time required between copy and deadline and appearance of ad	Newspaper 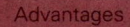	Low attention value Short life Poor reproduction quality Wasted coverage when market is small Short exposure
Ability to segment audiences Can effectively employ sound and volume to create distinction and appeal	Radio 	Low attention due to passive nature of media Clutter Short life Limited to sound (no visual appeal)
Offers both sight and sound Broad coverage Local cable offers competitive prices for local retailers	Television 	High cost Greater coverage than required by local advertisers Clutter
High reproduction quality Longer life than newspaper Longer exposure than newspaper Specialized vehicles can create appropriate mood for purchase	Magazine 	Long lead time prevents use of price advertising
Good audience selection Offers means of personal contact Does not directly compete with competitors' messages Results are easily measured	Direct Mail 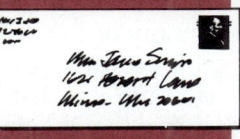	High cost per contact Dependence on quality of mailing list Junk mail perception

a trading area within a local market. Second, a low technical skill level is required to create advertisements for newspapers. This is helpful because the majority of retailers are small and relatively unsophisticated in the design and creation of ads. Third, newspaper ads require only a short time between copy deadline and publication. Since most retailers do a poor job at planning their advertising program over a prolonged period, and since they tend to use advertising to respond to crises (poor cash flow, slackening of sales, need to move old merchandise), the short lead time for placing newspaper ads is a significant advantage.[15]

Retail newspaper advertising also has its disadvantages: (1) The fact that a consumer was exposed to an issue of a newspaper does not mean the consumer read or even saw the retailer's ad[16]; (2) the life of any single issue of a newspaper is short—it's read and discarded; (3) the typical person spends relatively little time with each issue, and that time spent is spread over many items in the newspaper; (4) newspapers have poor reproduction quality, which leads to ads with little visual appeal; and (5) if the retailer has a small target market, much of its advertising money will be wasted, since newspapers tend to have a broad appeal. In fact, seldom does the retailer's trading area match the circulation of any newspaper. It is either larger in the case of small communities or smaller in the case of large metropolitan newspapers. The exception to this is chain stores which do much of their advertising using preplanned newspaper copy. Retailers such as Mervyn's, Wal-Mart, and Kmart rely almost exclusively on newspaper inserts.

Radio Advertising. Many retailers prefer to use radio because it can target messages to select groups. In most communities there are five to ten or more radio stations, each of which tends to appeal to a different demographic group. Radio is also good for developing distinctive and appealing messages through the use of proper variations in volume, music, and types of sounds. In short, there is a lot of flexibility. Also, many radio audiences develop strong affection and trust for their favorite radio announcers. When these announcers endorse the retailer, the audience is impressed.

Radio advertising also has its drawbacks. It is frequently listened to during work hours or while driving to and from work (a period called **drive time**) and tends, over time, to become part of the background environment. Active listeners eventually become passive listeners as the blare of the radio blends into whatever they are doing. Radio also is increasingly suffering from carrying too many ads. Because people listen to radio for the music or programming and not for the ads, they become annoyed when ads are too frequent and learn to selectively block them. When people do perceive the ad, their memory of it is rather short, and unfortunately once they forget the ad, they can't go back in time and hear it again. Another disadvantage is that radio is nonvisual. It is impossible to demonstrate effectively or show the merchandise that is being advertised. And, finally, radio signals tend to cover an area much larger than a retailer's trading area. Therefore, a good portion of the retailer's advertising dollars may be wasted.

Television Advertising. Retailers in the 1990s are turning to television advertising as a means of creating an image or position in the marketplace and not just as a medium to induce direct action or immediate response.[17] Research suggests that, over time, pictures retain their effects on consumer memory and evaluations to a greater extent than the verbal messages from media such as radio.[18] However, television advertising is expensive, and dollar for dollar print advertising still is best for retailers.[19] A half-dozen well-designed television ads may use up the retailer's total ad budget. In addition, for the small- or even intermediate-sized retailer, a television ad would reach well beyond its trading area. A final disadvantage of television advertising is that competition for the viewer's attention is high. During advertising periods, the viewer may take a break and leave the room, change to another channel, or be exposed to several ads, one right after another—often advertising different brands of the same product or different retailers in the same line of trade.

In spite of its drawbacks, television advertising can be a powerful tool for generating higher sales. The American public spends more time relaxing in front of the television than in any other recreational activity. Television has broad coverage; over 98 percent of homes in the United States have at least one television set. Most of these sets are color and offer the retailer a vehicle in which both sight and sound can be used to create a significant perceptual and cognitive effect on the consumer.

Recently, the widespread development of cable television has made television more attractive to local retailers. Local cable operators have been selling retailers advertising on cable channels. The cost of advertising on such programs is quite competitive with that of newspaper advertising. However, retailers just starting to use television advertising may be hard-pressed to find a niche since so many others have already been seeking to fill niches, too. This is probably the reason that most of the current advertising by local retailers on cable channels is so poor.

Magazine Advertising. Relatively few local retailers advertise in magazines, unless the magazine has only a local circulation. Nationally based retailers such as Sears or JCPenney will allocate some of their advertising budget to magazines. Typically, the retail ads that these retailers place in magazines are institutional.

Magazine advertising can be quite effective. In relation to newspapers, the other major print medium, magazines perform well on several criteria. They have better reproduction quality than newspapers; they have a longer life than newspapers per issue; and consumers spend more time with each issue of their magazine than with their newspaper. An added benefit is that featured articles in a magazine can put people in the mood for a particular product class being advertised. For example, a feature article on home remodeling in *Better Homes and Gardens* can put people in a frame of mind to consider purchasing wallpaper, carpeting, tiling, draperies, paint, and other home-improvement items. The major disadvantage of using magazines is that the long lead time requirements prevent price appeal advertising.

Direct Mail. With direct mail, the retailer can precisely target its message at a particular group as long as a good mailing list of the target population is available. Also, direct marketing can be a powerful addition to the retailer's promotional strategy. One study found nine specific reasons for retailers to use direct mail[20]:

1. To cultivate new customers
2. To minimize or reduce inventory investment
3. To take advantage of unique, but limited, merchandise offerings
4. To intensify cross-selling
5. To convert infrequent purchasers to frequent purchasers
6. To help develop, maintain, or alter store image
7. To derive an additional source of revenue
8. To bring customers into the store
9. To secure sales leads

While these can be achieved using other media as well, direct mail provides retailers with personal contacts with individual consumers who share certain valued characteristics. Also, these messages can reach the consumer without being noticed by the competition. Finally, direct-mail results can generally be easily measured, thus providing the retailer with important feedback information.

On the negative side, direct-mail advertising is relatively expensive per contact or message delivered. Also, the retailer's ability to reach the target market depends entirely on the quality of the mailing list. If the list is not kept current, advertising dollars will be wasted. A related problem is the high incidence of unopened or unexamined mail, especially when it is addressed to "occupant" or arrives via third-class mail.

Miscellaneous Media. The retailer can advertise using media other than those previously identified: yellow pages, outdoor advertising, transit advertising (on buses, cabs, subways), electronic information terminals, specialty firms such as Welcome Wagon, and shopping guides (newspaper-like printed material, but with no news). Each of these is usually best used to reinforce the other media and should not be relied on exclusively unless the retailer's advertising budget is minimal. Most retailers look upon these media vehicles as geared more toward particular product advertising by manufacturers. However, that doesn't mean a retailer can't make good use of them.

MEDIA SELECTION

To select the best media, the retailer needs to remember the strengths and weaknesses of each medium (which we have summarized in Exhibit 14.8) and determine the coverage, reach, and frequency of each.

Coverage refers to the *theoretical* maximum percentage of a retailer's target market that can be reached by a medium—not to the percentage actually reached. For example, if a newspaper is circulated to 70 percent of the 20,000 households in a retailer's trading area, the coverage is 14,000 households.

Reach, on the other hand, refers to the actual total number of target customers who come into contact with the ad message. Another useful term is **cumulative reach,** which is the actual number accumulated over a given time period.

Frequency is the average number of times each person who is reached is exposed to an advertisement during a given time period.

Different media can be evaluated by combining knowledge about the cost of ads in a medium with the medium's reach and cumulative reach. The most commonly used measure for doing this is the **cost per thousand (CPM) method.** We compute the CPM by dividing the cost for an ad or series of ads in a medium by the reach or cumulative reach. If a newspaper ad costs $500 and the cumulative reach was 13,860, then the cost per thousand is $36.08 [($500/13,860) × 1,000)]. The newspaper may have actually reached 38,200 households in the community, but if only 13,860 were reached in the retailer's trading area, then that is the relevant statistic.

The CPM is useful for comparing similar-sized advertisements in the same media type, for example, two local newspapers. But when comparing different media (television versus newspapers), the CPM can be misleading. A medium such as television may cost more based on CPM, but if it has a significantly greater impact, it may be the better buy. **Impact** refers to how strong an impression an advertisement makes and how effectively it ultimately leads to a purchase.

SCHEDULING OF ADVERTISING

When should a retailer schedule its advertisements? What time of day, day of week, week of month, and month of year should the ads appear? No uniform answer to these questions is available for all lines of retail trade. Rather, the following conventional wisdom should be considered:

1. Ads should appear on, or slightly precede, the days when customers are most likely to purchase. If most people shop for groceries Thursday through Saturday, then grocery store ads might appear on Wednesday and Thursday.
2. Advertising should be concentrated around the times when people receive their payroll checks. If they get paid at the end of each month, advertising should be concentrated at that point.
3. If the retailer has limited advertising funds, it should concentrate its advertising during periods of highest seasonal demand. For example, a lawn and garden retailer would concentrate its advertising in the spring and early summer months and perhaps the early fall. Along similar lines, a muffler repair shop would be well advised to advertise during drive time on Thursday and Friday, when the consumer is aware of his or her muffler problem and has Saturday available for the repair work.
4. The retailer should try to minimize advertising during periods of bad weather, since poor weather keeps people indoors and few sales will bring

them outdoors. For this reason, some retailers subscribe to weather forecasting services.
5. The retailer should time its ads to appear during the time of day or day of week when the best CPM will be obtained. Many small retailers have found the advantages of late-night television.[21]
6. The higher the degree of habitual purchasing of a product class, the more the advertising should precede the purchase time.[22]
7. The greater the carryover effect—the more the ad is remembered and influences sales in the future—the more the timing of the advertising should precede the purchase time.[23]
8. Retailers must be especially careful about how they integrate their pricing and promotional strategies. On one hand, consumers appear to be attracted to retailers whose prices are presented as discounts from "regular" prices. On the other hand, as more retailers use discounting, consumers are apt to expect discounts, and the amount of discount needed to generate a positive impression will have to increase.[24]

Many retailers use advertising to react to crises. Of course, if this is the situation, the timing of ads cannot be planned in advance. This is unfortunate and a source of much inefficiency in retail advertising.

ADVERTISING RESULTS

Will the advertising produce results? It depends on how well designed the ads are and how well the previously mentioned advertising decisions were made. A consistent record of good retail advertising decision making comes about only if the retailer effectively plans its advertising program.

Some retailers will try systematically to assess the effectiveness and efficiency of their advertising. **Advertising effectiveness** refers to the extent to which advertising has produced the desired result (i.e., helped to achieve the advertising objective). **Advertising efficiency** is concerned with whether the advertising result was achieved with minimal effort.

If effectiveness and efficiency are assessed in some systematic fashion, then typically certain quantitative or statistical tools are used. Some tools are multiple regression, experimental design, and computer simulation. It should be mentioned, however, that developments in electronic point-of-sale terminals and universal product codes have significantly increased the retailer's ability to obtain valid and timely data to put into mathematical models. Recently, a supermarket discovered a brand new "breed" of customers after analyzing its scanning data. Increases in multiple wage-earning families, and single-person households and increasing career opportunities for women have swelled the ranks of the "after-five shopper." This shopper wants "one-stop" shopping advantages and prepared foods, seldom uses coupons or reads newspaper ads, and hates a crowded checkout line. The media solution to reaching this customer group—drive time radio—was not the most effective for other target groups.

Too many retailers, especially the smaller ones, make little or no effort to evaluate the effectiveness of their advertising. Often this results from the retailer's believing that at least some amount of advertising is necessary and that there are no good ways to measure advertising's effectiveness. However, several methods are available to retailers of all sizes.

One simple check tracks unit sales of the featured items for a limited time after the ad runs. However, this method fails to measure the future loss of sales for the featured item if consumers only view the sale as an opportunity to "stockpile" the featured item (sales displacement) or to substitute it for another brand not on sale (substitution effect).

Another, more advanced, method is to make use of the new scanning technology available. For example, A.C. Nielsen has developed analysis procedures that relate purchase decisions to stimuli, measure the competitive impact, and evaluate advertising and promotion effectiveness. In evaluating the relative results of each promotional event, Nielsen seeks to define the

- Net extra cases sold as a result of each ad or promotion
- Net extra gross margin and cost per each event
- Consumption/inventory impact of the promotion schedule

Nielsen's method for doing this is logical and straightforward. The actual results of the promotional event are compared to an estimated volume for the event period and post-event period assuming that the promotion did not occur.[25]

The effectiveness or efficiency of a retailer's advertising can also be assessed on a subjective basis. Simply ask yourself: Are you satisfied with the results produced? Do you believe you achieved those results at the least cost? Most, but not all, ineffective advertising is due to 10 common errors:

1. The retailer may be bombarding the consumer with so many messages and sales that any single message or sale tends to be discounted. A retailer that has a major sale every week will tend to wear out its appeal.
2. The advertising may not be creative or appealing. It may be just "me too" advertising in which the retailer does not effectively differentiate itself from the competition.
3. The advertising may not give the customers all the information they need. The store hours or address may be absent because the retailer assumes that everyone already knows this information. Or information may be lacking on sizes, styles, colors, and other product attributes.
4. The advertising dollars may have been spread too thinly over too many departments or merchandise lines.
5. There may have been poor internal communications between salesclerks, cashiers, stock clerks, and management. For example, customers may come to see the advertised item, but salesclerks may not know the item is on sale or where to find it, and cashiers may not know the sale price.
6. The advertisement may not have been directed at the proper target market.

7. The retailer didn't consider all media options. A better buy was available, but the retailer didn't take the time to find out about it.
8. The retailer made too many last-minute corrections in the advertising copy, increasing the cost of the ad. Or—worse yet—as shown in Retailing in Action 14.2, retailers frequently fail to find their own errors.
9. The retailer took co-op dollars just because they were "free" and therefore thought they represented a good deal.
10. The retailer used a medium that reached too many people not in the target market. Thus, too much money was spent on advertising to people who were not potential customers.

RETAILING IN ACTION

14.2 International Promotion Isn't Just Translating an Ad

There are usually significant differences between domestic and foreign retail markets. Nowhere have international retailers had more problems recognizing these differences than with regard to promotional activities. For example, consider the following:

In Quebec, television commercials, by law, cannot be aimed at children.
Comparative advertising is banned in Germany.
Brazil doesn't regulate the number of advertisements that can be shown consecutively on television.

However, the real errors in international promotion usually result from retailers trying to write signs and instructions in a foreign language. Sometimes, poor knowledge of the customer's language results in unintentionally interesting promotions. Consider the following errors by foreign retailers trying to translate promotions into English:

Mexico City discount store: AMERICAN WELL SPEAKING HERE.
Paris dress shop: DRESSES FOR STREET WALKING.
Hong Kong dentist: TEETH EXTRACTED BY LATEST METHODISTS.
Rome laundry: LADIES, PLEASE LEAVE YOUR CLOTHES HERE AND SPEND THE AFTERNOON HAVING A GOOD TIME.
Tokyo hotel: THE FLATTENING OF UNDERWEAR IS THE JOB OF THE CHAMBERMAID—TO GET IT DONE, TURN HER ON.
Bangkok dry cleaner: DROP YOUR TROUSERS HERE FOR BEST RESULTS.
Amsterdam hotel: YOU ARE ENCOURAGED TO TAKE ADVANTAGE OF OUR CHAMBERMAIDS.
Hong Kong tailor shop: ORDER YOUR SUMMER SUIT NOW. BECAUSE OF BIG RUSH WE EXECUTE CUSTOMERS IN STRICT ROTATION.
Stockholm furrier: FUR COATS MADE FOR LADIES FROM THEIR OWN SKIN.

However, even Americans have trouble using their own native language. Robert Kahn in his *Retailing Today* (October 1991) newsletter reported seeing an ad for a California shop advertising a "PRE-GRAND OPENING CLEARANCE SALE." Or what about the New York car wash offering a "fully automated hand wash."

SALES PROMOTION MANAGEMENT

The most popular sales promotions used by retailers are consumer premiums such as gifts or trading stamps, games of chance, product demonstrations, and samples. In-store displays, another type of sales promotion, were discussed in detail in Chapter 12.

ROLE OF SALES PROMOTIONS

Sales promotion tools are excellent demand generators. Many can be used on relatively short notice and can help the retailer achieve its overall promotion goals. Furthermore, sales promotions can be significant in helping the retailer differentiate itself from competitors. Retailers have long known that consumers will change their shopping habits and brand preferences to take advantage of sales promotions, especially those that cut prices or offer rebates.[26] Exhibit 14.9 lists the various types of sales promotions used by retailers today. A noted authority has suggested,

> It takes more than merchandise to make a store take wing and rise above others, and some of that buoyancy is the excitement of in-store happenings. Chop them out, chop the stuff that makes them happen, and you've chopped visibility. You've chopped some of the very things that lift one store above and beyond all others.[27]

In the retailer's overall promotion mix, the role of sales promotion is quite large and often represents a larger expenditure than advertising. Many retailers do not recognize this because of their poor record-keeping systems. They know the cost of advertising because most of that is paid to parties outside the firm. Therefore, promotions warrant more attention by retail decision makers than is typically given.

EXHIBIT 14.9

Examples of Retail Sales Promotion Tools

Free Gifts. Receipt of a gift with the purchase of a particular item or a certain dollar amount.
Rebates. The refund of a fixed amount from the purchase price.
Coupons. An advertising vehicle that enables the consumer to purchase a product at a reduced price based on specific terms and conditions.
Games of Chance. Games in which no skill is required to win.
Trading Stamps. Premiums or stamps issued with purchases that can be redeemed for merchandise or cash.
Samples. Customers are given the opportunity to use the product on a limited basis before purchasing.
Product Demonstrations. Customers are given the opportunity to observe the product's benefits and performance before purchasing.
Contests. Games in which skill influences the outcome.
Premiums. A good that is either given free or sold at a reduced price to customers to encourage the purchase of other, more expensive goods.

The role of sales promotions in the retail organization should be consistent and reinforce the retailer's overall promotion objectives. Most sales promotions are not institutional although they should have institutional overtones; they are promotional—as their name implies. They also tend to be directed at improving the retailer's short-run performance.

EVALUATING SALES PROMOTIONS

Since sales promotions are intended to help generate short-run increases in performance, they should be evaluated in terms of their sales and profit-generating capability. Like advertising, sales promotions can also be evaluated with sophisticated mathematical models. However, the development and use of such models are usually not cost effective.

A simpler approach is to monitor weekly unit volume before the sales promotion and compare it to weekly unit volume during and after the promotion. The before measure provides the retailer with a benchmark that can be compared to results during the sales promotion. But this comparison should be adjusted by the information provided in the after measure, since the sales promotion may have borrowed sales from future time periods. Consider a grocery store retailer that featured Tide detergent in an end-of-aisle display for two weeks. Before the display, typical weekly movement of Tide was 8 cases. During the display, movement accelerated to 13.2 cases per week. But for the four weeks after the sales promotion, movement was 4.8, 5.3, 6.7, and 7.1 cases per week. In the fifth and subsequent weeks, movement returned to 8 cases per week. Thus, the net impact of the sales promotion was to move an additional 2.3 cases over the two-week display period.* Most of the increase in sales was due to customers' buying for future needs. This helps to illustrate a general point about sales promotions: For staple and necessity items, sales promotions will generally encourage people to stock up, but seldom will it encourage them to consume more. Thus, the value of sales promotions for these goods rests on their ability to expand the retailer's trading area and capture customers who would have purchased these items elsewhere. Selling more to existing customers at the expense of their buying less in the future will not economically justify the promotion. It is more difficult to evaluate service promotions since the retailer cannot stockpile the service.

PUBLICITY MANAGEMENT

Publicity was defined at the outset of this chapter as non-paid-for communications of information about the company or products, generally in some media form.[28] In part, this definition is misleading. Although the retailer does

---

*The 2.3 cases are obtained by the following computation: Movement during promotion period minus normal movement during promotion period if there had been no promotion minus sales borrowed from future periods; numerically, $(13.2 \times 2) - (8 \times 2) - (8 - 4.8) - (8 - 5.3) - (8 - 6.7) - (8 - 7.1) = 2.3$.

not directly pay for publicity, it can be very expensive to have a good publicity department that plants the commercially significant news in the appropriate places. It may be even more expensive to create the news that is worth reporting. For example, Hudson's Thanksgiving Day Parade in Detroit, 7-Eleven's sponsoring a car in the Indianapolis 500 race, and McDonald's Ronald McDonald Houses represent significant dollar expenditures. They create favorable publicity, but they are expensive. Whether the money could be better spent in other ways is debatable.

We will not pursue a detailed discussion of publicity management, since most retail enterprises do not formally have a publicity department or even a person in charge of publicity. Rather, let us mention that publicity (like other forms of promotion) has its strengths and weaknesses. Perhaps the major advantages are that it is objective and credible and appeals to a mass audience. The major disadvantages are that publicity is difficult to control and time. Publicity-related events are hard to plan, and if they are to be planned, the cost can become exorbitant. In addition, sometimes retailers can experience bad publicity in the form of rumors. Only in very rare circumstances does one ever find out who started these false stories about successful retailers. In the past, there have been rumors about snakes being found in one discounter's overcoats and about a well-known fast-food chain using worms in its hamburgers. It seems that the events never happen to the individual telling the story, but always to a friend of a friend. Recently, there was a false story involving IKEA, the furniture and houseware chain.[29] It went like this: An unsuspecting shopper, usually a woman, brings an IKEA cactus home.

ILLUSTRATION 14.3

This giant inflatable panda is an example of publicity—Furniture Liquidator's attempt to appeal to a mass audience.

After a few days, she notices that the plant is moving and—could it be?—breathing. She calls IKEA, and someone from the store commands: "Get out of the house—now." Later, two men arrive and confiscate the cactus. The reason: It's filled with tarantula eggs and about to explode, spewing deadly insects.

"Every time we open a new store, [the rumor] hits," Pam Diaconis, IKEA's head of PR, notes. "We have yet to have anyone call who actually has one. It's always a friend of a friend."

The truth is, tarantulas just don't camp out in cacti. But it was a great story until the facts got in the way. Still, such examples do point out the need for retailers to plan for the unexpected, in case something goes wrong. For example, supermarkets should be prepared to handle stories (true or false) of someone's having tampered with packaged items. Similarly, a restaurant might need to be prepared to handle a hepatitis outbreak.

If publicity is formally managed in the retail enterprise, it should be integrated with other elements of the promotion mix. In addition, all publicity should reinforce the store's image.

SUMMARY

Retail promotion is made up of advertising, sales promotions, publicity, and personal selling. All four components must be integrated. In addition, the promotion mix itself must be integrated with other retail decisions such as location, merchandise, credit, cash, building and fixtures, price, and customer service. Using its retail management model as a backdrop, the retailer should establish promotion objectives that are either directly or indirectly related to improving financial performance.

Retail advertisements can be institutional—attempting to sell the store—or promotional—attempting to bolster short-run performance by advertising product features or price. However, all good retail advertising should have institutional overtones. Any ad that does not give the store a favorable image is a mistake.

In budgeting advertising funds, retailers tend to use the affordable method, the percentage-of-sales method, or the task-and-objective method. Once the budget has been established, it should be allocated in such a way that it maximizes the retailer's overall profitability. In determining allocations, retailers can choose from a variety of media alternatives, primarily newspapers, radio, television, magazines, and direct mail. Each medium has its own advantages and disadvantages. To choose among the media, the retailer should know their strengths and weaknesses, coverage and reach, and the cost of an ad. After the retailer selects a medium, it must decide when its ad should appear.

The ability of advertisements to produce results depends on how well the retailer plans its advertising program. Advertising results can be assessed in terms of efficiency and effectiveness. Effectiveness is the extent to which advertising has produced the result desired. Efficiency measures whether the result was achieved with minimal cost.

Sales promotion is a second component of the retail promotion mix. The most popular forms are consumer premiums, games of chance, and product demonstrations and samples. They can be used to help the retailer bolster its short-run performance. As with advertising, the retailer should evaluate the effectiveness and efficiency of sales promotions.

Publicity is the final component of the retail promotion mix discussed in this chapter. (Retail selling will be discussed in Chapter 15.) Although the retailer may not directly pay for publicity, the indirect cost can be quite significant. Most retail enterprises do not have formal publicity departments or directors, but some of the larger retailers do. The major advantages of publicity are that it is objective and credible and appeals to a mass audience. The major disadvantage is that publicity is difficult to control and schedule.

QUESTIONS FOR DISCUSSION

1. What is the relationship between retail promotion decisions and the marketing channel?
2. How should advertising and sales promotions be evaluated?
3. What methods should a retailer use in making the media selection decision?
4. What is sales promotion? How is it different from advertising?
5. Do you agree or disagree with the following statement? "A retailer should always make use of every dollar of co-op advertising available." Explain your answer.
6. Define the term publicity. How does publicity fit into a retailer's promotional efforts?
7. What is the first thing a retailer should do when developing its promotional strategy? Why?
8. Explain how a long-run promotional objective can affect the firm over the short run.
9. What are the two different types of retail advertising?
10. What is cooperative advertising? When should it be used?
11. Describe the three methods available to the retailer for determining the amount to spend on advertising.

MANAGEMENT MEMO

Your chain is offered a co-op advertising deal from a major supplier. The supplier will pay 60 percent of your advertising expense as long as the advertising uniquely features the supplier's product line. The general merchandise manager is considering spending $8,000 on advertising the supplier's line, since the supplier will pick up $4,800. The product line has a gross margin of 64 percent, and the GMM expects the advertising to increase sales by 30 percent. Current sales are $100,000 and no other supplier is offering a co-op program. Today the GMM asks you to prepare a memo on whether the chain should participate in this program or not.

BOARDROOM REPORT[30]

The chair of the board of directors for a regional supermarket chain has just received the following memo from a new store manager and wants you to prepare a report on the subject for next week's board meeting.

> *After only three months on the job, I have observed a rather strange phenomenon and was wondering whether the company had a policy regarding it.*
>
> *Occasionally, I have my employees attach signs marked "Everyday Low Price" in front of two or three randomly selected brands in several different product categories throughout the store, leaving the prices unchanged. Sales for these randomly selected items usually double during the period the signs are used. I was so taken by this finding that I had some store associates poll customers immediately after they selected these EDLP items. Most were unaware that the items selected weren't on sale and assumed that the sign meant there was a "special sale."*

Do we want to continue this practice of having our customers making suboptimal decisions and run the risk of some bad publicity in the future? Or should we discontinue the use of all signage unless a real "Price Cut" is involved?

SUGGESTED READINGS

Blattberg, Robert C., and Scott A. Neslin. *Sales Promotion: Concepts, Methods, and Strategies.* Englewood Cliffs, N.J.: Prentice-Hall, Inc., 1990.

Kelley, J. Patrick, "Retailers' Uses of Cooperative Advertising, Slotting Allowances, and Promotional Allowances: Impact on Retail Pricing." *Proceedings of 1989 Patronage Behavior and Retail Symposium.* Baton Rouge: Louisiana State University, 1990.

McCann, John, Ali Tadlaqui, and John Gallagher. "Knowledge Systems in Merchandising: Advertising Design." *Journal of Retailing* (Fall 1990): 257-77.

Taraba, Tibor. "How to Select an AD Agency—In 10 Easy Steps." *Sales & Marketing Management* (October 1990): 166-67.

ENDNOTES

1. *Dictionary of Marketing Terms* (Chicago: American Marketing Association, 1988), 4. Reprinted with permission of the American Marketing Association.
2. Robert E. Wilkes and James B. Wilcox, "Recent FTC Actions: Implications for the Advertising Strategist," *Journal of Marketing* (January 1974): 55.
3. *Dictionary of Marketing Terms,* 179. Reprinted with permission of the American Marketing Association.
4. *Dictionary of Marketing Terms,* 164. Reprinted with permission of the American Marketing Association.
5. *Dictionary of Marketing Terms,* 144. Reprinted with permission of the American Marketing Association.
6. Dale Achabal, Shelby McIntyre, and Stephen Smith, "Maximizing Profits from Periodic Department Store Promotions," *Journal of Retailing* (Winter 1990): 383-407.
7. Bruce E. Mattson, "Situational Influences on Store Choice," *Journal of Retailing* (Fall 1982): 46-58.
8. "It's Worth Wooing 'Disloyal' Shopper; She's a Big Spender," *Supermarket News* (August 1980): 1.
9. "Getting Your Money's Worth," *Sales & Marketing Management* (May 1991): 64-68.
10. Charles M. Edwards, Jr., and Russell A. Brown, *Retail Advertising and Sales Promotion,* 3rd ed. (Englewood Cliffs, N.J.: Prentice-Hall, Inc., 1959), 14.
11. Susan Garland, "Mazzio's Positions Itself in New Market," *Advertising Age,* 3 August 1987, 24.
12. David L. Hurwood and James K. Brown, *Some Guidelines for Advertising Budgeting* (New York: Conference Board, 1972).
13. Bert C. McCammon, Jr., et. al., "The New Parameters of Retail Competition: The Intensified Struggle for Market Share," in Ronald W. Stampfl and Elizabeth Hirschman, eds., *Competitive Structure in Retail Markets: The Department Store Perspective* (Chicago: American Marketing Association, 1980), 108-18.
14. Mark M. Moriarty, "Retail Promotional Effects on Intra- and Interbrand Sales Performance," *Journal of Retailing* (Fall 1985): 27-48.
15. William O. Bearden, Donald R. Lightenstein, and Jessee E. Teel, "Comparison Price, Coupon, and Brand Effects on Consumer Reactions to Retail Newspaper Advertisements," *Journal of Retailing* (Summer 1984): 11-34.
16. Lawrence C. Soley and William L. James, "Estimating the Readership of Retail Newspaper Advertising," *Journal of Retailing* (Fall 1982): 59-76.
17. Charles R. Taylor, Gordon Miracle, and Kyu Yeol Chang, "Retail Television Advertising: Is It Really Unsophisticated?" *Proceedings of the 1991 Retail Patronage Behavior Symposium* (Baton Rouge: May 1991).
18. Meryl P. Gardner and Michael J. Houston, "The Effects of Verbal and Visual Components of Retail Communications," *Journal of Retailing* (Spring 1986): 64-78.
19. "Ads on TV: Out of Sight, out of Mind," *Wall Street Journal,* 14 May 1991, B1, B8.
20. Martin Topol and Myron Gable, "A Teaching Module: Introducing Direct Marketing into the

Retailing Course," in *Retailing: Its Present and Future* (1988 Combined Academy of Marketing Science and American Collegiate Retailing Association Proceedings), 155-60.
21. "Big Advertisers Are Working to Benefits of Late-Night TV," *Wall Street Journal*, 9 February 1984, 27.
22. This principle is discussed in more detail in Lawrence Jacobs, *Advertising and Promotion for Retailing: Text and Cases* (Glenview, Ill.: Scott, Foresman, 1972), 92.
23. Jacobs, *Advertising and Promotion*, 92.
24. Anthony Cox and Dena Cox, "Competing on Price: The Role of Retail Price Advertisements in Shaping Store Price Image," *Journal of Retailing* (Winter 1990): 428-45.
25. "Customer Needs," *The Role of Media in Nielsen Scantrack* (A.C. Nielsen Co., 1987), 16, 17; "Supplementing the Value of Nielsen Data Through Computer Technology," *The Nielsen Researcher*, no. 4 (1982): 8-11; and "Scan Data Quality: The Nielsen Approach," *The Nielsen Researcher*, no. 2 (1987): 2-9.
26. "A Penny Saved Is a Penny Earned," *Advertising Age*, 2 April 1990, 33.
27. M. Seklemaian, *Sek Says* (New York: Retail Reporting Bureau, 1979), 71.
28. *Dictionary of Marketing Terms*, 164. Reprinted with permission of the American Marketing Association.
29. "So, Let's Go Hunt Alligators in the Sewers," *Business Week*, 11 February 1991, 32.
30. This boardroom report is based on J. Jeffrey Inman, Leigh McAlister, and Wayne D. Hoyer, "Promotion Signal: Proxy for a Price Cut?" *Journal of Marketing Research* (June 1990): 74-81.

CHAPTER 15

PERSONAL SELLING

OVERVIEW This chapter discusses how retail selling can be used in conjunction with other operational functions of the firm to increase demand. The most effective personal selling occurs when salespeople are carefully selected, well trained, and properly managed.

PERSONAL SELLING

I. Determining the Level and Types of Sales Personnel
   A. Store Characteristics
   B. Competition
   C. Type of Merchandise
   D. Price Image
   E. Target Market Income
   F. Cost of Services
II. Retail Selling
   A. Types of Retail Selling
   B. Labor Force Management
   C. Salesperson Selection
      1. Criteria
      2. Predictors
         a. Demographics

b. Personality
c. Knowledge and Intelligence
d. Experience
D. Salesperson Training
1. Customer Types
2. Merchandise
3. Store Policies
4. Customer Choice Criteria
a. No Active Product Choice Criteria
b. Inadequate or Vague Choice Criteria
c. Choice Criteria in Conflict
d. Explicit Choice Criteria
E. The Selling Process
1. Prospecting
2. Approach
3. Sales Presentation
4. Closing the Sale
5. Suggestion Selling
F. One Retailer's Selling Program
G. Selling in the Service Sector
H. Salesperson Evaluation
1. Performance Standards
2. Conversion Rate
3. Sales per Hour
4. Use of Time
5. Data Requirements
III. The Customer Service and Sales Enhancement Audit
IV. Summary

DETERMINING THE LEVEL AND TYPES OF SALES PERSONNEL

Having the right number of properly trained retail salespersons on the sales floor at any one point in time is a difficult accomplishment. Theoretically, however, one could argue that a retailer should add sales personnel until the incremental revenue generated equals the incremental cost of providing this staff. In short, this argues for establishing the level of staffing that maximizes profitability. Of course, the effect on long-run profits should be the overriding concern since, in the short run, profits can usually be increased by cutting back on costly selling services which could hurt long-run profits.

However, even when the retailer has the correct number of sales personnel on hand and the shoppers can easily find a salesperson, it is possible that the salesperson hasn't had even rudimentary training in the basics of salesmanship to prevent shoppers from walking out without making a purchase. In the fall of 1991, shoppers, despite a downturn in the economy, continued to appear in the stores. But many retailers, not having properly trained sales personnel, continued to make purchasing an obstacle.

Nowhere are the effects of too few salespeople or with too little training shown better than in a study by Marvin Rothenberg.[1] Rothenberg, a well-known retailing consultant, studied what happened in four companies operating a total of 68 stores and found that 131,328,000 sales opportunities a year (2.4 million shoppers who averaged 1.9 shopping visits per month going into 2.4 departments per trip), produced only 38 million transactions. Thus, 93 million departmental shopping visits resulted in "no sale."

In fact, 49 million of the departmental shoppers who made no purchase didn't even have contact with a salesperson or a cashier. Another 44 million had contact but didn't buy anything. And among these two segments of 93 million shoppers already in the departments, 28 million came into the department with the intent to make a specific purchase! In total, 71 percent of all the departmental shopping visits resulted in shoppers either having no contact with sales personnel or if they had contact, it was probably the wrong kind, and no purchase was made. No wonder Rothenberg, in another study, found that one-third of customers who entered a store with the expressed intent of making a specific purchase walked out without making any purchase.[2] It is obvious that a small increase in converting these nonpurchasing shoppers into buyers will increase sales dramatically, even if the shopper is only in the store as a means to combat loneliness.[3]

For example, if these retailers did nothing more than just contact half the 49 million customers who had no sales contact, and if the conversion rate among this group was only half what it was among those who had contact, the number of sales transactions, currently 38 million, would increase by 15 percent (half of 49 million who had no contact multiplied by half of the conversion rate for those who had contact equals 5.7 million more sales transactions). That's an opportunity to add 15 percent to sales . . . by doing nothing more than what is already being achieved when customers contact a salesperson.

As illustrated in Exhibit 15.1, six factors help retailers determine the type and level of their sales staff: the store characteristics, the selling services offered by the competition, the type of merchandise handled, the price image of the store, the income of the target market, and the cost of providing the service. It is the retailer's job to study these six areas to arrive at the selling mix that will increase long-run profits by keeping present customers, enticing new customers, and projecting the right type of store image. Above all else, retailers must remember to be realistic and not expect to satisfy the wants and needs of all customers. No strategy could be less profitable than trying to satisfy everybody. What the retailer is really trying to do is to use its sales staff as the conduit between the vendor's and customer's expectations, as shown in Exhibit 15.2.

EXHIBIT 15.1

Factors That Determine the Type and Level of Sales Staff

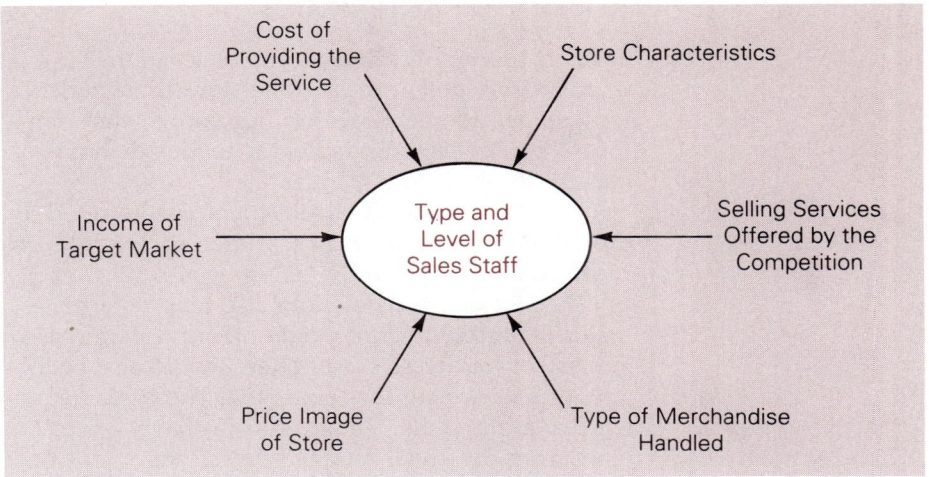

EXHIBIT 15.2

How the Retailer's Salesforce Meets the Expectations of Both Vendors & Customers

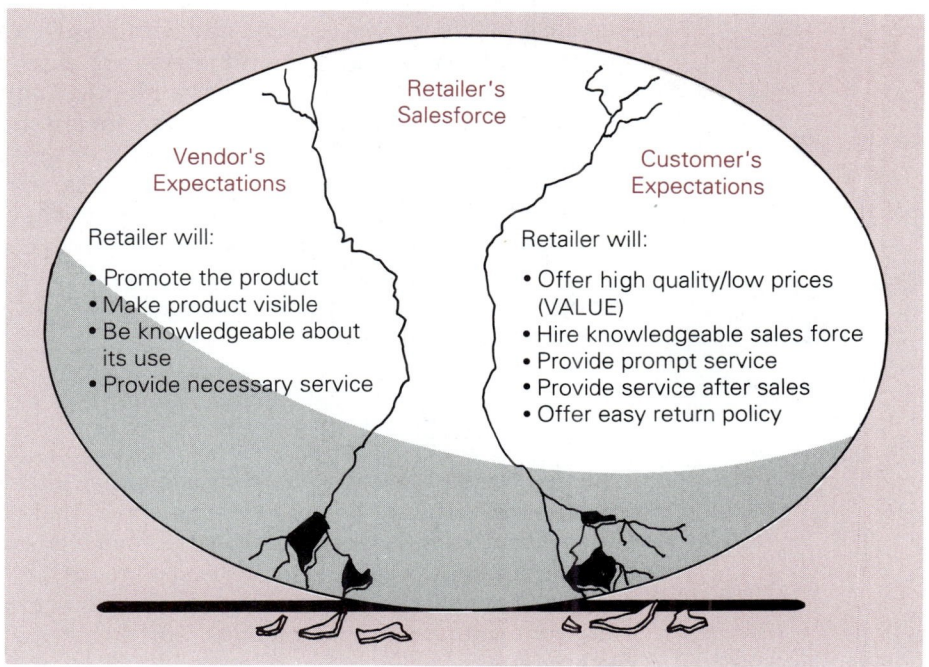

STORE CHARACTERISTICS

Store characteristics include store location, size, and type. It is especially important to look at these three store characteristics when considering salesforce expectations. Research has shown that employee perceptions of customer service are fundamental to the delivery of quality service and are consistent predictors of sales.[4]

The type and level of sales personnel offered by a clothing retailer in the downtown financial area of a large city would probably be different from those offered by a clothing store in a rural center.

The size and type of store also help determine which services to offer. A major department store would offer a different assortment of services than a grocery or hardware store. There would also be a difference between a large and a small store of the same type. The customer would expect more services from a large retailer's staff, and probably fewer but more personalized services from the small retailer's salesforce.

COMPETITION

The services offered by competitors will have a significant effect on the type and level of selling services offered. The effective retailer must offer similar services, suitable substitutes, or lower prices.

Suppose, for example, that there are three clothing stores of the same general type, price range, and quality within a given area. Store A and Store B offer free gift wrapping, standard alterations, bank card credit, and a liberal return policy. Store C, on the other hand, offers only store credit and has an exchange-only return policy. Customers who are shopping for gifts generally frequent Stores A and B over C because they feel confident that whatever they purchase will ultimately be just right. It can even be gift wrapped there at the store. If the gift isn't suitable, the recipient can have it altered to fit, exchange it, or even receive a cash refund. In this situation, Store C can do two things to compete: It can either add services or lower prices. Retailing in Action 15.1 gives an example of a retailer whose reputation for service is second to none.

TYPE OF MERCHANDISE

The merchandise lines carried can be another indication of the types of selling services to offer. The principle reason is that certain merchandise lines benefit from knowledgeable sales personnel; for example, would you want a less-than-knowledgeable salesperson to assist you in purchasing an engagement ring for the woman of your dreams? Or worse yet, would you want your boyfriend buying your engagement ring at a self-service discounter?

RETAILING IN ACTION

15.1 This Store's Return Policy Is Unbeatable

In the highly competitive world of department stores, Seattle-based Nordstrom has turned exacting standards of customer service into something legends are made of. Nordstrom, an apparel, shoe, and soft-good retailer on the West Coast since 1901, recently expanded to the East Coast.

A major ingredient in Nordstrom's success (earnings of $116 million on 1991 sales of $3 billion) is the quality of its salesforce. Nordstrom's employees are better paid and better trained than the competition's and are encouraged to do almost anything within reason to satisfy customers. One salesclerk personally ironed a customer's newly purchased shirt so it would look fresher for an upcoming meeting.

However, the big part of the legend is the firm's return policy laid down by the president, James Nordstrom: "Replace anything on demand, no matter how expensive, no questions asked." Although the policy is sometimes abused by shoppers (who may, for example, order an expensive dress, wear it to a party, and then return it), it has made Nordstrom a symbol of customer satisfaction. There is even a story—which the company doesn't deny—about a customer who got his money back on a tire. Since Nordstrom doesn't sell tires, this was a testament to Nordstrom's simple one-page training manual for new associates:

Welcome to Nordstrom

We're glad to have you with our Company. Our number one goal is to provide outstanding customer service. *Set both your personal and professional goals high. We have great confidence in your ability to achieve them. Nordstrom Rules: Rule #1:* Use your good judgment in all situations. *There will be no additional rules. Please feel free to ask your department manager, store manager or division general manager any question at any time.*

PRICE IMAGE

Generally, customers will expect more attention from personnel in a store with a high-price image than from a discount retailer. When a customer perceives a store as having high prices, it also sees the store as possessing an air of pampering. Therefore, the sales staff should convey that pampering style of luxury or status.

On the other end of the scale, discount stores needn't offer a lot of sales assistance, because customers who shop there are seeking low prices, not customer service.

TARGET MARKET INCOME

The higher the income of the target market, the higher the maximum demand prices that consumers will pay. The higher the prices consumers will pay, the more sales help the retailer, such as Nordstrom, can profitably provide. Some customers may expect more services than they are able to afford, but the retailers, such as 50%-Off or Dollar General, must avoid the strong temptation of providing costly assistance to such consumers. In the long run, the retailer will have to raise prices to pay for the services and then it will quickly lose its share of low-income customers.

COST OF SERVICES

It is imperative to know the cost of a service in order to know how much in additional sales need to be generated to pay for it. For example, if a customer service were expected to increase costs by $20,000 per year and the store operated on a gross margin of 25 percent, then you would have to expect that the service would stimulate sales by at least $80,000 ($20,000/0.25). In this sense, customer services are evaluated like promotional expenditures. The key criterion becomes the financial effect of adding or deleting a service.

Another way of expressing the cost of having poor service from your salesforce is to examine what the costs would be if you didn't have a good one. If the salesforce of a 100-store supermarket chain alienated only one customer per day per store, the chain would lose $94.9 million in annual revenue. This is based on the assumption that grocery business is repeat business and that the real cost is the $50 a customer spends weekly.[5]

RETAIL SELLING

Retail salespersons and the services they provide are a major factor in consumer purchase decisions and a reflection of the store's image. For example, when the retail salesperson is busy helping someone else, is rude, or is not helpful, customers will often walk out of the store empty handed. When the salesperson is available, friendly, and helpful, customers will often be influenced to enter into a transaction with the retailer. The management of the retail salesforce plays a crucial role in the success or failure of a retail operation.

The importance of personal selling is even greater in the retailing of services, since consumers of services, as opposed to consumers of tangible products, seldom know exactly what they want or need due to their inability to see the final product before purchasing. These consumers generally don't know what they are really purchasing until they don't get it. If the home owner's rugs were cleaned properly, that is fine. This is passive satisfaction—from getting something that's expected. However, let the rugs still have the stain from last weekend's party and the customer is no longer passive. Therefore, it is extremely important for the sales personnel of a service retailer to (1) understand exactly what the customer expects, (2) explain what the retailer is able to provide, and (3) balance these two expectations together at the completion of the service to ensure that the promises made to obtain the sale were fulfilled. The sales staffs of tangible-product retailers generally don't become this involved in a retail transaction.

TYPES OF RETAIL SELLING

In many retail settings, the employees who are called salespeople are **order takers** and sell only regular in-stock merchandise. For example, consider the role of salespeople in a typical discount department store such as a Wal-Mart, Kmart, or Target. The employees might show the customer where the merchandise is located in the store or may go to the storeroom to get an item that is not on the shelf, but seldom, if ever, do they attempt to sell the merchandise or demonstrate its use. In fact, according to one discounter's president, it is his firm's policy to provide "next-to-no-sales help." Discounters "don't want to get into the business of person-to-person selling." These stores are appealing to those customers who want value instead of service.[6] Whether these employees should be called salespeople is debatable. Perhaps they should be referred to as retail clerks. Nonetheless, one must recognize that these order takers can influence demand, especially in a negative manner. If you are in a store such as Target and cannot find a retail clerk to assist you when you need help, you may become frustrated and leave the store without making a purchase.

Retail employees who are most appropriately labeled salespeople should be order getters as well as order takers. **Order getters** are involved in conversation with prospective purchasers for the purpose of making a sale. They

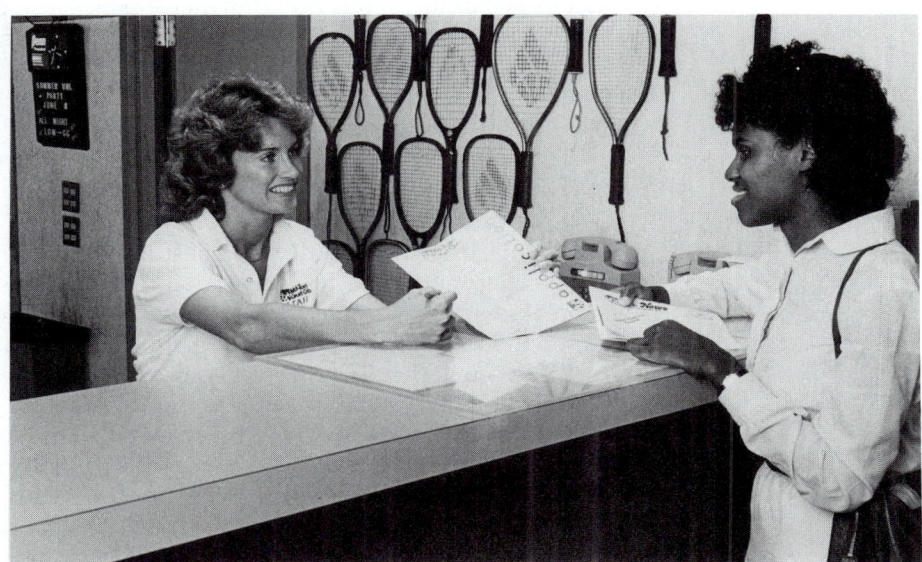

ILLUSTRATION 15.1
Order-getters inform, guide, and persuade the customer in order to sell a product or service.

will inform, guide, and persuade the customer in order to culminate a transaction either immediately or in the future.

The degree of emphasis the retailer places on its employees' being order getters depends on the line of retail trade and the retailer's strategy. Retailers that concentrate on the sale of shopping goods (e.g., automobile dealers, furniture retailers, computer retailers, and appliance retailers) will want their salespeople to be both order getters and order takers. In lines of retail trade where convenience goods are predominantly sold (gasoline service stations and grocery retailers), the role of the salesperson (or what many may call the retail clerk) will be that of an order taker. In terms of strategic orientation, it is generally true that retailers with high margins and high levels of customer service will place more emphasis on order getting. Those with low margins and a low customer service policy will tend to emphasize order taking.

Clearly, however, regardless of the line of retail trade or the retailer's strategic thrust, all retail enterprises must carefully evaluate the role of the salesperson in helping to generate demand.

LABOR FORCE MANAGEMENT

While there has been debate recently on how to measure the productivity of retail labor,[7] no one will argue with the fact that no matter how it is measured, retail labor productivity has been declining over the past decades. Retailers appear to be caught in a vicious circle in which the relatively low wages they offer have attracted low-quality employees, which tends to perpetuate the low-wage/low-quality cycle. In fact, it might even be argued that "Americans have developed utter contempt for the retail clerk."[8]

Let us elaborate on this point further. Retail salespeople are not motivated by low wages and thus quickly lose morale. Consequently, many of them become disgruntled, and employee turnover rises and productivity falls. The decline in productivity and the prospect of continued high turnover prompts retailers to keep wages low. In short, retailers have created a self-fulfilling prophecy. It is not surprising, therefore, that in some retail stores the salesforce you see today is totally different from the one you would have seen last year or the one you will see next year.

The profit impact of increased salesforce productivity in retailing is dramatic. As we mentioned in earlier chapters, retailers operate very close to their break-even point due to the relatively high costs of opening the store doors each morning. Therefore, a 10 to 15 percent increase in salesforce productivity—whether measured in sales per employee hour, gross margin per employee hour, value added per employee hour, or gross margin minus sales commission per employee hour—would, for the most part, directly translate into a proportional improvement in store profits. Consequently, retail managers should accept a major performance imperative to increase salesforce productivity in the future.

To program operations to increase salesforce performance over forthcoming budget periods, a retailer needs to develop frames of reference for the following personnel decision areas: selection, training, compensation, size, scheduling, and evaluation. In this chapter we will discuss the selection, training, and evaluation of the retail salesforce. In the next chapter we will discuss the other topics in detail.

SALESPERSON SELECTION

Selecting retail salespeople should involve more than casually accepting anyone who answers an ad or walks into the store seeking gainful employment. In fact, the casualness with which many retailers have selected people to fill sales positions is one cause of poor productivity.

Criteria. To select salespeople properly, retailers must decide what their criteria will be. What is expected of retail salespeople? Are the retailers looking for a work force that has low absenteeism, the ability to generate a high volume of sales, or some other qualities? Unless you know what you are looking for in salespeople, you will be certain not to acquire a salesforce that possesses the proper qualities.

However, high-performance results depend not only on the salesperson's characteristics but on how the sales job was designed and how satisfied the salesperson is with the job.[9] One study has shown that retail selling jobs should be designed so that they have high levels of variety (the ability to perform a wide range of activities), autonomy (the degree to which an employee determines the work procedures), task identity (the degree to which an employee is involved in the total sales process), and feedback from supervisors and customers.[10] An earlier study indicated that retail salespersons perceived greater job satisfaction when they were closely supervised and in highly structured positions.[11]

Predictors. Once retailers have determined the criteria, they must then identify potential predictors to meet the chosen criteria.[12] The most common predictors used in selecting retail salespeople are demographics, personality, knowledge, intelligence, and prior work experience. The criteria for selecting management trainees will be discussed in more detail in Chapter 16.

Demographics. Depending on the specific line of retail trade, demographic variables can be important in identifying good retail salespeople. For example, a record and stereo store appealing to teens will probably benefit from having retail salespeople under 30 years of age. A high-fashion women's apparel store appealing to 30-to-50-year old, career-oriented, upwardly mobile females would probably not desire 18-year-old salespeople from lower social class backgrounds. And a motorcycle shop would probably not want 60-year-old salespeople. Obviously, there are exceptions to each of the preceding rules, especially when avoiding discrimination in hiring practices (which are discussed in the next chapter), but the essential point is that retailers can use demographic variables to help screen applicants for sales

ILLUSTRATION 15.2

Salespeople should reflect the social, demographic, and merchandise characteristics of a store in order to relate to the clientele and be able to provide valuable information related to the merchandise.

positions. One study found that convenience store employee turnover was related to experience and age. The study concluded that convenience store executives could reduce turnover by developing a strategy of hiring older and more experienced individuals.[13]

Personality. An individual's personality can reflect on his or her potential as a retail salesperson. The retailer would most likely prefer salespeople who are friendly, confident, stable, and empathetic. These personality traits can be identified either through a personal interview with the applicant or by computerized personality inventory tests. In most lines of retail trade the personal interview will be sufficient.

Knowledge and Intelligence. Many products that retailers sell are technically complex. Consider, for example microcomputers, solid-state televisions, microwave ovens, 35-mm cameras, and 10-speed bicycles. Salespeople with knowledge of these products will be better able to sell them. Similarly, to be able to respond to customer inquiries in a logical fashion, retail employees will need to possess some level of intelligence as well as an educational level compatible with the job description.

Experience. One of the most reliable predictors of success is prior work experience, especially selling experience and prior ethical behavior in selling situations. It is better for a firm not to hire applicants who may be prone to using unethical sales techniques in the first place, than to have to handle the resulting disciplinary actions when such behavior occurs.[14] If applicants have performed well in prior jobs, there is a good chance they will perform well in the future. The correlation is not perfect, however. Also, many applicants for retail selling jobs will be young and have no prior work experience of any magnitude. These applicants are better assessed on their personal character and apparent ambition, drive, and work ethic.

SALESPERSON TRAINING

Some retailers consider themselves fortunate if they retain 50 percent of new salespeople for two to three years, since employee training and turnover costs can range from $1,000 to $2,000 per salesperson. To reduce turnover and improve performance, after salespeople have been selected, they should be exposed to some form of training. This is true even if they have selling experience. In their training programs retailers should explain their store policies and help inexperienced salespeople become familiar with and knowledgeable about the retailers' merchandise, the different customer types they may have to deal with, and the selling strategies available for different customer choice criteria. Even order takers need training in greeting and thanking customers and using a point-of-sale terminal.

Customer Types. The greatest myth about selling is that product knowledge is the key to successful selling. In reality, market and customer knowledge and selling skills are higher priorities than product knowledge.[15] Retail salespeople can be taught how to identify and respond to certain customer types, described in Exhibit 15.3. By knowing how to handle each of these customers, the salesperson can generate added sales. Too many times retailers tend to dwell on handling the machinery of a job rather than the feelings of a customer. One car-rental clerk was quoted as saying: "The computer training was real good. I know how to do all this technical stuff, but nobody prepared me for dealing with all these different types of people."[16]

Merchandise. If the merchandise includes shopping goods, which we defined in Chapter 3, the retailer will want to train its salespeople to be familiar with the strengths and weaknesses of the merchandise. This will allow salespeople to assist customers in shopping for the best goods to meet their needs. It also suggests that the salesperson should become knowledgeable about the competitor's merchandise offerings and their strengths and weaknesses.

Increasingly, retail salespeople need to be familiar with the warranty terms on merchandise the retailer handles and also the serviceability of the merchandise. This implies that the salesperson should know something about the reputation of each manufacturer the retailer represents. Exhibit 15.4 lists in greater detail the specific information that a retailer generally expects its salespeople to know about its products.

EXHIBIT 15.3

Various Customer Types

Characteristics	Basic Types	Recommendations
Doesn't trust any salesperson. Resists communication due to a dislike of others. Generally uncooperative and will explode at slightest provocation.	Defensive 	Avoid mistaking silence for openness to your ideas. Avoid any arguments. Stick to basic facts. Tactfully inject product's advantages and disadvantages.
Intense, impatient personality. Often interrupts salespersons and has a perpetually "strained" expression. Often, driven and successful person who wants results fast.	Interrupter 	Don't waste time. Move quickly and firmly from one sales point to another. Avoid overkill since customer knows what he or she wants.
Confident in ability to make decisions and stay with them. Open to new ideas but wants brevity. Highly motivated by self-pride.	Decisive	Avoid canned presentations. The key is to assist. Don't argue or point out errors in judgment.
Worries about making the wrong decision; therefore tends to postpone all decisions. Wants salesperson to make decision.	Indecisive	Avoid becoming frustrated yourself. Determine as early as possible the need and concentrate on that. Avoid presenting too many alternatives. Start with making decisions on minor points.
Friendly, talkative type who is enjoyable to visit with. Has time on his or her hands (e.g., retirees). Usually resists the close.	Sociable 	You may have to wait out these customers. Listen for points in conversation where you can interject product's merits. Pressure close is out. Subtle friendly close needed.
Quick to make decisions. Impatient; just as likely to walk out as to walk in.	Impulsive 	Close as rapidly as possible. Avoid any useless interaction. Avoid any oversell. Highlight product merits.

EXHIBIT 15.4

Summary of Merchandise Information Needed by Salespersons

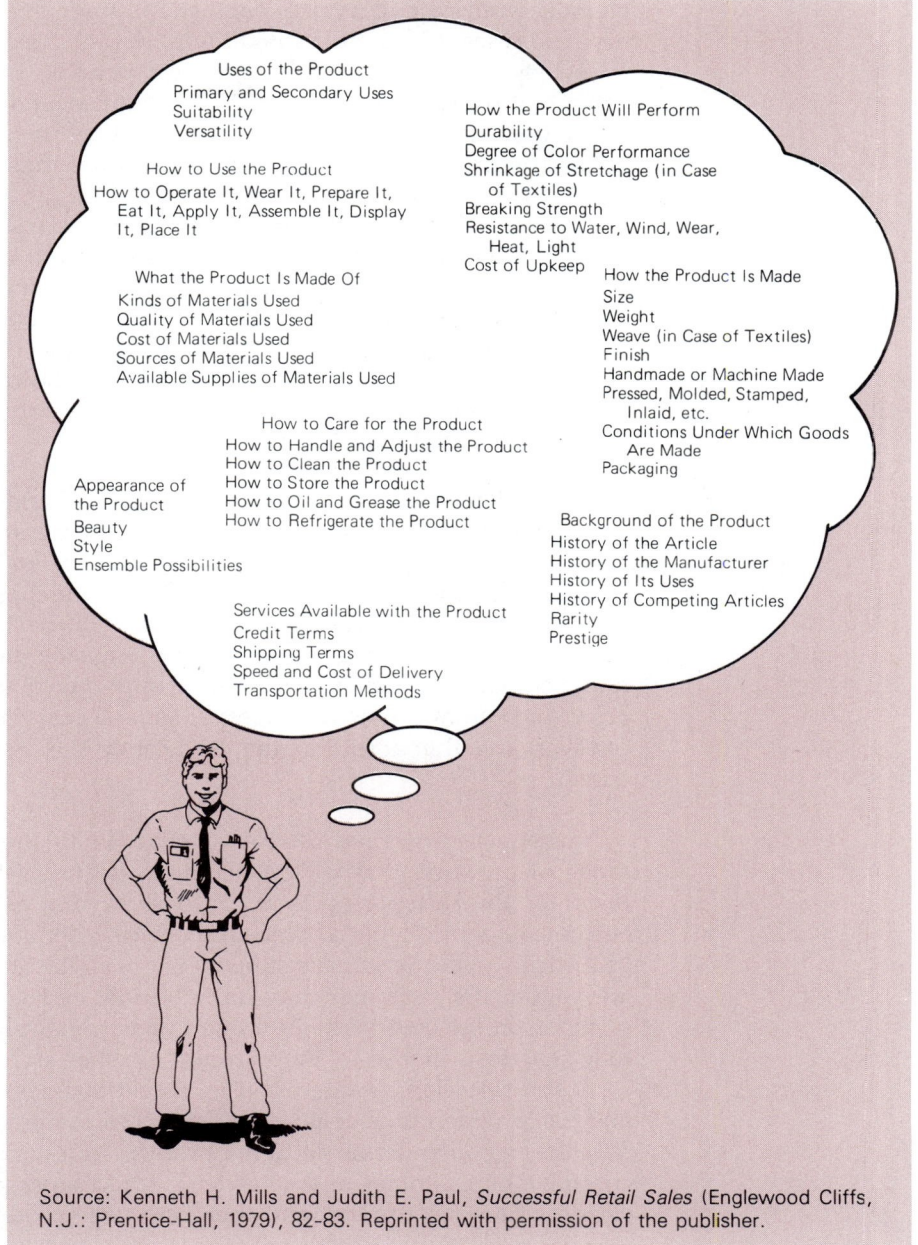

Source: Kenneth H. Mills and Judith E. Paul, *Successful Retail Sales* (Englewood Cliffs, N.J.: Prentice-Hall, 1979), 82-83. Reprinted with permission of the publisher.

Store Policies. In most situations, the connection between the customer and the retailer takes place through the salesperson. It is thus important for the salesperson to become familiar with the store policies, especially those that involve the customer directly. Some of these policies would relate to merchandise returns and adjustments, shoplifting, credit terms, layaway, delivery, and price negotiating. In addition, the retail salesperson should become knowledgeable about work hours, rest periods, lunch and dinner breaks, commission and quota plans, nonselling duties, and standards of periodic job evaluation. It might also be useful and motivating to inform sales employees about criteria used for promotion and advancement within the firm.

Customer Choice Criteria. The retail salesperson should also learn how to identify the customer's choice criteria and how to respond to them.[17] There are four choice criteria situations: (1) The customer has no active product choice criteria; (2) the customer has product choice criteria but they are inadequate or vague; (3) the customer has product choice criteria but they are in conflict; and (4) the customer has product choice criteria that are explicit and well defined. For each situation there is an appropriate selling strategy the salesperson should learn.

No Active Product Choice Criteria. The best sales strategy when the customer does not have a prior criteria set is to educate the customer about the best choice criteria and how to weigh them. For example, a prospective customer enters an automobile dealership to purchase a used automobile but does not know what criteria to use to select the best car. The car salesperson may present convincing arguments for why the customer should consider four criteria in the following order of importance: warranty, fuel economy, price, and comfort. Once the salesperson and customer agree on this list, they can work together at finding the used car on the dealer's lot that best fits the criteria.

Inadequate or Vague Choice Criteria. When the criteria are vague, the range of products that will satisfy them is often wide. Perhaps the easiest thing for the salesperson to do is to show that a particular product fits a customer's choice criteria. Since the choice criteria are vague this would not be difficult and little actual selling would be involved. But because the criteria are vague, the customer may have trouble believing that the product the salesperson selected is the best one to meet his or her needs. The customer may therefore choose to shop around at other stores.

If the salesclerk is interested in repeat business and customer goodwill and has a wide range of products to sell, a preferable strategy would be to help the customer define his or her problem in order to arrive at a set of choice criteria. The customer and salesclerk would work together in defining the criteria of a good product and then select the product that best fits them.

Choice Criteria in Conflict. Prospective customers with choice criteria that are in conflict frequently have trouble making purchase decisions. There are two basic ways in which choice criteria can be in conflict. First, the customer may want a product to possess two or more attributes that are mutually exclusive. For example, someone purchasing a 10-speed bicycle may wish it to be of high quality and low price. This person will quickly find that these two attributes do not exist in common. The best strategy in this situation is for the salesperson to play down one of the attributes and play up the other.

A second kind of conflict between choice criteria occurs when a single attribute possesses both positive and negative aspects. Consider a person thinking of purchasing a high-performance automobile. High-performance automobiles have both positive aspects (status, speed, and pleasure fulfillment) and negative aspects (high insurance and low mileage per gallon). For this type of conflict, the best selling strategy is to enhance the positive aspects and deemphasize the negative ones.

Explicit Choice Criteria. When the customer has well-defined, explicit choice criteria, the best selling strategy is for the salesperson to illustrate how a specific product fits those criteria. "The salesclerk guides the customer into agreeing that each attribute of his product matches the attributes on the customer's specification. If, at the end of the sales talk, the customer does not agree to the salesclerk's proposition, he appears to be denying what he has previously admitted."[18]

THE SELLING PROCESS

Several basic steps occur during the retail selling process. The length of time that a salesperson spends in each of these steps depends upon the product type, the customer, and the selling situation. Exhibit 15.5 details the process model we will now discuss.

Prospecting. Prospecting is the search for those who have the ability and willingness to purchase your product. It is particularly important when the store is full of customers because a salesperson doesn't want to waste time on a looker while a purchaser is left alone. A salesperson should be aware that good prospects generally display more interest in the products than poor prospects who are "just looking." Salespeople should take advantage of the behavioral cues shown in Exhibit 15.3.

Approach. The salesperson may meet hundreds of customers a day, but the customer is only going to meet the salesperson one time. Therefore, it is extremely important that the first 15 to 30 seconds set the mood for the sale. Never begin the sales presentation with "May I help you?" or any other question to which the customer can respond in the negative. A simple good morning (afternoon, evening) or any other greeting acknowledging the customer's presence should do.

This is a period for the salesperson to begin to develop a mood of trust and rapport through what one expert calls hypnotic pacing. This involves statements and gestures that adjust to a customer's pace. By playing back a customer's experience, observation, or behavior, the pacing becomes a relax-

EXHIBIT 15.5

The Selling Process in the Retail Environment

Step 1—Prospecting

Who can benefit from your product

a. Finding prospects

b. Qualifying prospects. (Determining whether a prospect has the ability, buying power, and willingness to make a purchase.)

▼

Step 2 — Approach

The first 15 seconds are the key because they set the mood for the sale.

a. Never say "May I help you?"
A simple "hello," "good morning" or "what may I show you" makes customers realize that you are glad they are in your store.
b. Determine as early as possible the customer's needs.
Listen - *What you hear* is more important than anything you could possibly tell your customer. Ask a few well-chosen questions.
  1. New customer has need or problem to be solved.
  2. User of the product

▼

Step 3 — The Sales Presentation

Getting the customer to want to buy your product/service

a. Pick the right price level.
If uncertain - ask "Is there a price range you have in mind?" Remember, you can't pick out the right product for the uncertain customer if the price is wrong.
b. Pick the right product
Match user and need with product. Show the customer at least two items.
c. Show the merchandise in an appealing manner.
Make the merchandise stand out.
Show the item so that its good points will be seen.
Let the customer handle the merchandise.
Stress the features of the products.
Explain the benefits of these features.
Appeal to the customer's emotions.
d. Help the customer decide.
Handle objections
Replace unneeded items
Watch for unconscious clues
Stress features and benefits of "key" product

▼

Step 4 — Closing the Sale

Reaching an agreement

a. Find out what is going on in the customer's mind.
b. Four effective ways to close:
  1. Make the decision for the customer.
  2. Assume the decision has already been made.
  3. Ask the customer to choose.
  4. Turn an objection around.

▼

Step 5 — Suggestion Selling

Follow up leads to other sales

ing mirror, suggesting that the customer and salesperson are similar and in sync.[19]

Discover as early as possible what the customer's needs are. Discovering begins with listening. What the salesperson hears about the customer's problem or need is more important than anything the salesperson can possibly contribute at this point. Ask a few well-chosen questions to find out more about the need or problem to be solved. The salesperson, in seeking to determine the customer's needs, should find out whether the user is a different individual from the customer. If it is, find out about the user. Remember, the salesperson should ask only as many questions as needed, let the customer do the talking.

Sales Presentation. Once the initial contact has been established, the salesperson is in a position to present the merchandise and sales message correctly. The way the salesperson presents the product or service depends on the customer and the situation. The key, however, is to convince the customer to want to buy your product or service. People will respond better if the salesperson is able to appeal to their pride, their emotions, and their feelings. A little warmth goes a long way toward making that sale.[20] Begin by determining the right price range of products to show the customer. A price too high or too low will generally result in a lost sale. If uncertain, ask the customer about the price range desired.

Next, because the salesperson knows the merchandise and where it is located in the store, he or she should pick out what he or she believes will be the right product or service to satisfy the customer's needs. The salesperson should be careful not to show the customer so many products as to confuse.

The salesperson should tell the customer about the merchandise in an appealing way, stressing the features that are outstanding qualities or characteristics of the product and allowing the customer to handle the merchandise.

This is the best place to deal with any objections the customer might have. For example, if the customer states that a competitor offers better service after the sale, the salesperson should assure the customer that there haven't been any complaints about the retailer's own service program and talk of previous satisfied customers.[21]

Replace any inappropriate or unneeded items, and continue to stress the features and benefits of the product the customer seems most interested in. Remember also that with a well-planned, focused, and effective sales presentation you can speed the customer's acceptance. Even if speed does not induce all the customers to say "yes" every time, it can improve the sales success rate by exposing the sales personnel to more customers in a day.[22]

Closing the Sale. Closing the sale is a natural conclusion to the selling process. However, for many salespersons it is the most difficult part. Remember the salesperson is there to help the customer solve a problem, so he or she should not be afraid to ask for the sale. The key to closing is to determine what is going on in the customer's mind. Exhibit 15.6 lists some of the things a

EXHIBIT 15.6

Some Closing Signals the Salesperson Should Be on the Lookout For

> The customer reexamines the product carefully.
> The customer tries on the product (i.e., trying on a sports coat or strapping on a wristwatch).
> The customer begins to read the warranty or brochure.
>
> The customer makes the following statements:
> I always wanted a compact disc player.
> I never realized that these were so inexpensive.
> I bet my wife would love this.
>
> The customer asks the following questions:
> Does this come in any other colors?
> Do you accept Discover cards?
> Can you deliver this tomorrow?
> Do you have a size 7 in this style?
> Do you accept trade-ins?
> Do you have any training sessions available?
> Do you have it in stock?
> What accessories are available?
> Where would I take it to get it serviced?
> Is it really that easy to operate?

salesperson should be on the lookout for at this stage of the selling process. If he or she waits too long or is too impatient, the customer will be gone before the salesperson realizes it. There are four effective ways to close a sale: (1) make the decision for the customer, (2) assume that the decision has been made and ask whether it will be cash or charge, (3) ask the customer to choose which product or service to purchase, and (4) turn an objection around (for instance, by stressing that while the initial cost might be high the product's longer life span will reduce total cost).

One recent study of the lack of selling skills among retail salespeople found that the top two errors were failure to use closing techniques and not encouraging the customer to make the purchase.[23] Retailing in Action 15.2 lists a few unusual but successful closing techniques.

Suggestion Selling. A good salesperson uses suggestions to continue selling even after the sale has been completed. There is always the possibility of an additional sale. The salesperson should find out whether the customer has any other needs or knows of anybody with needs that can be solved with the salesperson's product line. A good example of this occurs when, following the sale to a young college student of a Valentine gift for his girlfriend, the salesperson asks whether he needs help with a gift for his mother.

Suggestion selling after a sale has proven to be an effective way for a retailer to increase sales and profits. Good order getters have always practiced

RETAILING IN ACTION

15.2 Close That Sale: Tips that Work!

One salesperson claims that a single gesture is the best signal for when to close the sale. When the customer touches his or her chin, he or she is ready to close. It doesn't have to be a big gesture, maybe it's just a quick flick. The sales expert can't explain why the "chin watch" works but claims it has a 100 percent accuracy rate.

A New England furniture store increased its closing rate by 40 percent simply by giving customers instant Polaroid photographs of the furniture and accessories they were considering. Customers who leave with the photos are also more likely to leave a deposit on the merchandise.

General Motors' Cadillac division has authorized its dealers to give weekend rentals to shoppers who test drove its models at dealerships, but weren't quite ready to close. "It's another way of getting people into our cars," a Cadillac spokesman said of this closing technique.

Source: Based on "Best Advice," *Sales & Marketing Management* (January 1990): 34 and "Living with a Car Before Committing to It," *Wall Street Journal,* 17 July 1990, B1.

ILLUSTRATION 15.3

Free samples are often offered in stores as a form of suggestion selling.

suggestion selling, but with many retailers becoming self-service operations, suggestion selling has become neglected in recent years. Cashiers, who do not perceive themselves as salesclerks, have become the customer's only contact. Therefore, retailers need to develop planned programs in which suggestion selling becomes a formal aspect of the cashier's tasks.

Development of this type of program for stores requires attention to several important considerations. These are:

1. The items chosen should not be costly, nor should they require an active selling effort. They should lend themselves to impulse buying.
2. The presentation should be canned and no longer than 30 seconds. Cashiers should learn the presentations and give them each time a sale is made.
3. During very busy sales periods, when there may be considerable queuing at the checkout counters, suggestion selling presentations should be halted. (The decision should be made by the store manager, not by the cashier.) These situations should not arise too frequently, and even during the Christmas season, there would be no reason to stop the program except for busy times during the day.
4. Management needs to make certain that this program is being carried out in all stores. When programs are developed at the home office, there is a tendency for slippage at the store level. The program can be monitored by territorial or regional managers or through the use of an independent shopping service.
5. An incentive system should be used in implementing the program so that cashiers receive some form of reward for making sales presentations. While there is no ideal incentive system, rewards are desirable in securing behavior modification.
6. Each item should be used for promotion for two weeks. If an item is promoted for a longer period of time, a customer might have to hear the same canned presentation more than once. There is no reason why an item could not be used a second time; however, there should be a six-month hiatus.
7. Measuring the success or failure of this program by determining sales increases or decreases over a previous sales period can be misleading because fluctuations in sales will have a direct relationship to the number and quality of "hits" that are around at a given time.

ONE RETAILER'S SELLING PROGRAM

Consumer attitudes about a retailer are frequently determined by contact with salespeople at the store level. For this reason, Kmart has developed its "GLAD TO" selling system to make sure that customers' first impressions are positive ones. "GLAD TO" is an acronym that stands for Greet, Listen, Ask, Determine needs, Tell and show benefits, and Offer to sell. Following are specific instructions for Kmart salespeople[24]:

GREET the person. "Be friendly and sincere. Introduce yourself. Let the customer know you on a first-name basis. Using an open-ended question encourages a customer to tell you what he is looking for. Body language and eye contact are also very important. Look alert and interested. Always acknowledge the waiting customer."

LISTEN to the customer. "Listening is one of the most critical steps in the process. Most of us don't listen effectively. It has been estimated that we only listen at about 25 percent of our potential. We ignore, forget, distort, or misunderstand 75 percent of what we hear. We can break the listening process down to four steps: hearing, interpreting, evaluating, and responding. It's important that you concentrate on the customer and what is being said. Make sure you have all the important information before you decide how to respond. Let the customer know you are listening."

ASK questions. "If you listen closely to what the customer said, but you still don't have enough information to recommend a product, asking good questions will provide the answer. It's better to start with broad general questions rather than ask for price ranges or brand preferences right away. Start with general questions and then become specific. For example, a customer is looking for a rod and reel. Ask if it's for him rather than assuming so. Ask which type he's interested in, open or closed face, and if he's right- or left-handed. If he's not an experienced fisherman, don't offer to show a bait cast rod and reel. Make suggestions. When finally asking what he wants to spend, refer to price ranges."

DETERMINE the customer's needs or wants. "This is where you evaluate what you have learned during the previous steps in order to define the customer's needs. You also identify which product you will present to the customer to meet those needs. To prepare your presentation, you must understand the customer's wants and needs.

"For instance, a woman comes in to buy a sweater. Is she buying it because she needs clothing to keep warm or because she wants to be fashionable? Probably both, but before you present it, you want to know which feature you should emphasize. If she asks questions about the fabric, how warm it is and so on, it's more of a need. On the other hand, if she asks about colors and styles, she probably wants to look fashionable."

TELL and show benefits. "There are some simple rules to remember. Know how to operate the product yourself before you demonstrate it. Otherwise, you could make the customer think it's too complex to use. Next, think about your presentation and structure it in a logical way. That way you won't jump around and confuse the customer.

"A customer is looking for a basic video recorder that must be easy to operate because it will be for the entire family's use. Don't just say it's VHS with three speeds and HQ. Always relate a product feature to a customer benefit. So rather than saying it's VHS with three speeds, tell him he can record for two, four, or six hours on one tape and get a better picture. Use the manufacturer's name for a feature. Involve the customer whenever possible. Let him push buttons and operate whatever you're demonstrating. Never overwhelm a customer with too much information. Never oversell a customer. Conclude by providing two or three options."

OFFER to sell. "This is also known as closing the sale. Often new salespeople find closing to be the most difficult step in the process. Remember, the customer actually expects you to close the sale. Some signs that the customer is ready for the close are: He slows down the pace. He asks more questions. He responds enthusiastically to your questions. He requests further demonstration.

"You can be direct when you close. You can allow him to make a small choice. You can make it easier to buy. You can point out a deadline or let him close himself. If he doesn't want it, don't pester him to buy the product. Just thank him for his time and for coming to Kmart. If you treat the customer right, he'll come back in the future."

SELLING IN THE SERVICE SECTOR

As we mentioned earlier, the teaching of proper selling techniques is even more important in the retailing of services. First of all, it is difficult to attract new customers since they cannot try the product, inspect it, or test it. Second, once they have purchased the service, they only know if it *didn't* satisfy them or solve their problem. They are generally not happy with a purchase, only dissatisfied if the service was not what they were led to believe it would be.[25] One study concluded that the retailer of services needs to understand what benefit the customer is really buying. For example, it is important for the salesforce to remember that hospitals market health care, not operations, and colleges market educational attainment, not classes.

Third, not only is it important to know what benefit is sought, but the provider must consider how to help the customer achieve that benefit—a different task from simply providing the service. For example, a plumber is not merely selling the ability to unclog sink pipes but also informing consumers about what they can do to keep the sink pipes running freely. This enables the consumer to become involved and to feel a sense of accomplishment.

Fourth, the retailer should determine how to change the service so as to produce positive customer satisfaction. A consumer might not feel anything if the security firm guarding the household property is merely checking the property daily with routine inspections and nothing bad happens. However, consider the positive customer satisfaction that could be gained if the security firm also involved the customer in the process with a self-defense class.

Finally, remember that with services the goal is to preclude dissatisfaction, since that is the best remembered aspect of a service purchase. Here again it is important for the sales staff to be aware that the end result should match the customer's expectations. Remember, consumers will never forget a poor service job.[26] Research on service selling suggests that future sales opportunities depend mostly on the trust and satisfaction established. The ability to convert these opportunities into sales hinges more strongly on conventional salesperson characteristics, such as expertise and similarity.[27]

SALESPERSON EVALUATION

Salesperson evaluation seeks to determine each salesperson's value to the firm. It is important as a basis for salary adjustments, promotions, transfers, terminations, and sales reinforcement. The retailer should develop a systematic method for evaluating both individual salespeople and the total sales staff. Rather than subjectively evaluating performance, the manager should develop standards.[28]

Performance Standards. Several standards can be developed to measure sales performance. Some of them apply only to individual effort, whereas others assess both individual and total salesforce effort.

Conversion Rate. The conversion rate is computed by dividing the total number of customers who walk out of the store with a purchase, by the total number of customers who entered the store. The measure reflects the percentage of shoppers who were converted into customers and the overall salesforce performance. This is a measure of the salesforce's performance, not an individual's.

A poor conversion rate can be caused by a variety of factors. Perhaps there were not enough clerks on hand when customers needed them. This could have resulted in a high degree of unassisted search and long customer waiting times, with many customers exiting the store without making a purchase. Or the number of salespeople could have been adequate to handle the flow of customers but the salespeople may not have done a good selling job. A poor selling job can be caused by a variety of factors, such as salespeople being poorly qualified, giving inadequate product information to the customer, disagreeing or arguing too strongly with the customer, demonstrating the product poorly, having an unfriendly attitude, or giving up too early. However, all these factors are really related to *poor training*, which is often an underlying reason for poor sales. A low conversion rate may also be due to factors beyond the salesperson's control, such as inadequate stock of merchandise. The important point is that when a substandard conversion rate exists, the retailer should try to identify the causes and remedy the situation.

Sales per Hour. Perhaps the most common measure of a salesperson's or salesforce's performance is sales per hour, which is computed by taking total dollar sales over a particular time frame and dividing by total salesperson or salesforce hours. With a well-designed record-keeping system, a retailer can compute this simple measure for each salesperson, any group of salespeople, or the entire salesforce.

When employing this measure, remember that standards should be specific to the group or person being evaluated for a particular time period. For example, in a department store the sales per hour of selling effort cannot be expected to be the same for the toy department as for the jewelry department. Nor could one expect the same sales per hour during July as during December, because of the heavy Christmas demand for toys and jewelry.

Use of Time. Standards can be developed for how salespeople should spend their time. A salesperson's time can be spent in four ways:

1. *Selling time* is any time spent in assisting customers with their needs, whether talking, demonstrating, writing sales receipts, or working with the customer in other potentially profitable ways.
2. *Nonselling time* is any time spent on the nonselling tasks, such as stocking inventory.
3. *Idle time* is time the salesperson is on the sales floor but is not involved in any productive work.
4. *Absent time* occurs when the salespeople are not on the sales floor. They may be at lunch, in the employee lounge, in another part of the store, or in some inappropriate place.

A retailer's standard time allocations may suggest that salespeople spend 60 percent of their time selling, 28 percent on nonselling activities, 5 percent idle, and 7 percent absent. Any deviation from these standards should be investigated and corrective measures taken if necessary.

One of the nation's most successful, yet least known, retailers is Tres Mariposas, an El Paso fashion specialty store. Its owner expects his sales personnel to be accountable for their time. To that end, he has regular contests to test their knowledge of every item in the store, as well as of the art of selling to upscale consumers. Also, rather than leaning on counters while waiting for customers to enter the store, the sales staff is expected to call at least three customers a day to tell them about newly arrived merchandise. No wonder the store's sales have increased from $200,000 in 1980 to $2.25 million in 1991.[29]

Data Requirements. To establish proper standards of performance, the retailer needs data. What are good standards for the conversion rate? sales per hour? time allocation? Only data will help answer these questions. The data can come from retail trade associations, consulting firms, or the retailer's own experience.

Once the retailer has obtained the data on which to base standards, it must continually (or at least periodically) collect additional data on actual performance. The actual conversion rate, sales per hour, and time allocation must be contrasted to their respective standards. If the actual data differ significantly from the standard, an investigation of the cause is warranted. Both favorable and unfavorable variances should be investigated, because you may learn just as much from unusually good performance as from unusually poor performance.

THE CUSTOMER SERVICE AND SALES ENHANCEMENT AUDIT

Up to this point, we have discussed the level and type of sales personnel needed in a retail operation; the types of retail selling; the selection, training, and management of the salesforce; and the factors to consider when evaluating individual salespeople. These are microapproaches to improving the productivity of retail selling. How do we get macro answers for the performance of a whole department or a whole store? Remember our example at the beginning of this chapter about those retailers who had 49 million possible buyers walk out of their stores without any salesperson contact. One solution is the Customer Service and Sales Enhancement Audit.[30]

The Customer Service and Sales Enhancement Audit provides the direction that enables retailers to capture the unrealized potential of customers who walk out without salesperson contact. It analyzes current levels of performance by selling area within each company store, revealing how customers shop the store and the extent of the service they receive. It is *not* an attempt to learn what the customers want (i.e., "friendly and competent salespeople," "low prices," etc.); instead, it concentrates on the facts of their shopping experience. The objectives of the audit are to:

Identify the service, salesmanship and sales enhancement methods that will produce more sales from the existing shopping traffic.
Target the methods, by store and selling area, that will produce the most significant improvements.
Determine the added sales that can be generated by improving the accepted service level, salesmanship, and sales enhancement programs.

The **Customer Service and Sales Enhancement Audit** provides management with a detailed analysis of current sales activity by location and by selling area. It identifies how and where additional sales volume is available. These are the specific factors that are measured, analyzed, and reported:

Basic Service

1. *Customer contact.* In stores that purport to offer service, there can be no sale if the shopper has no contact with a salesperson or a cashier. The more shoppers that are approached, the more that are likely to buy.
2. *Salesperson-initiated contact.* Motivated salespeople, those who do not wait for customers to approach them, can prevent walkouts and generate more sales from those shoppers who otherwise might have to spend shopping time looking for a salesperson.
3. *Customer acknowledgment.* Greeting customers within a short time frame also prevents walkouts and provides more shopping time. It keeps the shopper in a favorable buying mood.

Salesmanship

4. *Merchandise knowledge.* A salesperson with product knowledge can answer shopper's questions, enhance the transaction, help to consummate the sale, prevent lost sales, and even add to the purchase.
5. *"Needs" clarification.* Asking the proper questions enables the salesperson to present and show the proper merchandise.
6. *Active selling.* Actively selling the merchandise and volunteering advice about the use and care of the goods, as well as stating the advantages of ownership, helps to consummate the sale.
7. *Suggestion selling.* Suggesting additional and/or complementary merchandise increases the value of the sale when successful. (Measurement is also made of the number of times that it is successful.)

Sales Enhancement

8. *Impulse purchasing.* Proper selection of merchandise, packaging, location within a department, presentation, then servicing the transaction will increase the productivity of shopping traffic.
9. *Walkouts.* Retaining sales that would be otherwise lost is one of the most direct and immediate routes to sales improvement. Offering the desired goods is the most obvious method for reducing walkouts. However, customer contact and salesmanship can be a major deterrent of walkouts among those who come to buy.

These elements of service, salesmanship, and sales enhancement are measured and reported by selling area within each company store, enabling management to apply targeted training programs. It is usually not necessary to spend the money to train or retrain all personnel in each store for each of the techniques.

However, when applied, the method can add significantly to the value of each transaction. For example, in the four companies mentioned at the beginning of the chapter, the incremental sales transactions for the average salesperson after the audit were:

10% . . . when the salesperson initiated the contact with the shopper.
 3% . . . when the salesperson acknowledged the customer's presence in a timely manner.
12% . . . when the salesperson was able to answer the customer's questions.
14% . . . when the salesperson asked questions to clarify the shopper's needs.
18% . . . when the salesperson actively "sold" the merchandise.
48% . . . when the salesperson suggested additional or complementary merchandise and the suggestion was taken.

No incremental addition to the average salesperson can be calculated for increasing contacts with shoppers, for improving the rate of impulse buying, or for reducing walkouts. The reason is obvious: When these techniques are applied and are successful, an entirely new transaction is created!

To provide management with an action program, the Customer Service and Sales Enhancement Audit includes a series of exception reports showing specifically what improvement is necessary within each selling area at each company store. The dollar value is listed, too, so that management can know the added volume that is available by applying targeted retraining programs. For walkouts, the report lists the causes for each selling area at each location. Management therefore receives an analysis of current performance by selling area at each company location and the specific action necessary to capture unrealized potential. The dollar opportunity is also calculated to highlight the value of each improvement. Exception reports make it easy to implement the program.

Every day within all types of stores there are "acres of diamonds in their own backyards." Shoppers are continuing to come in to stores in large numbers . . . many of them willing, able, and anxious to be converted into buyers. Management's task is to identify where and how that can be accomplished. That is the function of the Customer Service and Sales Enhancement Audit!

SUMMARY

The best level and type of sales personnel for any retailer should be determined on a long-run profit perspective, because in the short run, retailers can always increase bottom-line performance by reducing services. In the long run, however, this strategy could be unprofitable if a significant number of customers switch their shopping patronage to another retailer that offers a more satisfactory selling effort. Conventional wisdom suggests that in establishing the combination of sales personnel the retailer should consider six factors: store characteristics, competition, type of merchandise, price image, target market income, and cost.

Retail salespeople play a role in demand generation whether they are primarily order getters or order takers. However, the role played by the order getter is obviously more critical and crucial in stimulating demand.

The productivity of retail salespeople has been stagnant over the past two decades. This problem can be traced to low wages, poor morale, high turnover, and a general inability of retailers to properly manage their salespeople. Finally, the criteria to be used in the selection of a selling staff and its training program was discussed as well as how the staff should be evaluated both on a micro and macro level.

QUESTIONS FOR DISCUSSION

1. What should retail salespeople know about consumer behavior?
2. A major retail discount department store chain has analyzed the annual sales per salesperson in 20 of its stores located in different cities across the United States. On a storewide basis, the sales per salesperson range from a low of $91,000 to a high of $134,000. Develop the list of factors that might help to explain this wide variation.
3. Is it possible to increase expenditures on salespeople as a percentage of sales and increase the overall profitability of the firm?
4. What should retail salespeople know about customer choice criteria?
5. Develop a list of predictor variables you would use to screen applicants for a sales

position in (a) a jewelry department in a high-prestige department store, (b) a used-car dealership, (c) a health club, (d) an antique shop.
6. Someone once said that "selling is selling regardless of the product being sold." Do you agree with this statement? How would your answer change if we were to compare the selling of services to the selling of physical products?
7. How can it be said that while other retailers are beginning or extending their self-service operations, it may be profitable for a retailer to offer more sales support?
8. Provide examples of suggestion selling in a discount store, such as Kmart.
9. How can a small retailer evaluate the performance of its two salespeople?
10. Why is the approach important in retail selling? Does it really matter how a salesperson greets a customer?

MANAGEMENT MEMO

Rodger Strom has been in appliance retailing for over 20 years. He started out with a single-store "Ma-and-Pa" operation that his father founded in 1966. In the past several years, under his management, the operation has grown to five stores. Because the business simply "evolved" into its present status, Rodger had never actually provided formal training for his salespeople. Yesterday while walking through his newest store, Rodger overheard two salespeople commenting to each other about the way they sold merchandise. According to the one doing all the talking, the only thing a store like theirs should do is to accept bankcards, have a good selection of merchandise available, and treat the customers well, but never use a hard close or force a customer to buy a product. These remarks lead Rodger to believe that now is the time for that training. As the manager of his largest and most profitable store, he has asked you to "prepare a memo that outlines what closing a sale is all about."

BOARDROOM REPORT

At a recent board meeting for a department store, a fellow vice-president recommended that since profits have been declining recently, the firm could improve its bottom line by reducing services for the next merchandise season. The president has asked you to make a report on this subject at next week's meeting.

SUGGESTED READINGS

Bitner, Mary Jo. "Evaluating Service Encounters: The Effects of Physical Surroundings and Employee Responses." *Journal of Marketing* (April 1990): 69-82.
Bitner, Mary Jo, Bernard H. Booms, and Mary Stanfield Tetreault. "The Service Encounter: Diagnosing Favorable and Unfavorable Incidents." *Journal of Marketing* (January 1990): 71-84.
Brown, Gene, Robert E. Widing, II, and Ronald Coulter. "Customer Evaluation of Retail Salespeople Utilizing the SOCO Scale: A Replication, Extension, and Application." *Journal of the Academy of Marketing Science* (Fall 1991): 347-52.
Krapfel, Robert E., Jr. "Customer Complaint and Salesperson Response: The Effect of the Communication Source." *Journal of Retailing* (Summer 1988): 181-98.
Swan, John E., and Richard L. Oliver. "Postpurchase Communications by Consumers." *Journal of Retailing* (Winter 1989): 516-33.

ENDNOTES

1. Information provided the authors by Marvin J. Rothenberg, Marvin J. Rothenberg Retail Marketing Consultants, Inc., Fair Lawn, NJ 07410 and used with permission.
2. *Ibid.*
3. Andrew M. Forman and Ven Sriram, "The Depersonalization of Retailing: Its Impact on the 'Lonely' Consumer," *Journal of Retailing* (Summer 1991): 226-43.

4. William Weitzel, Albert B. Schwartzkopf, and E. Brian Peach, "The Influence of Employee Perceptions of Customer Service on Retail Store Sales," *Journal of Retailing* (Spring 1989): 27-39.
5. "The Real Cost of Losing Customers," *Incentive* (May 1988): 8.
6. "Many Stores Abandon 'Service with a Smile,' Rely on Signs, Displays," *Wall Street Journal*, 16 March 1981, 1, 20.
7. A special issue of the *Journal of Retailing* (Fall 1984) under the guest editorship of Dale Achabal was devoted to the issue of productivity in retailing. The reader should review: Charles Ingene, "Productivity and Functional Shifting in Spatial Retailing: Private and Social Perspectives"; Robert Lusch and Soo Young Moon, "An Exploratory Analysis of the Correlates of Labor Productivity in Retailing"; Roy Thurik and Nico van der Wijst, "Part-Time Labor in Retailing"; and Dale Achabal, John Heineke, and Shelby McIntyre, "Issues and Perspectives on Retail Productivity."
8. "Many Stores Abandon . . . ," 1.
9. Charles M. Futrell and A. Parasuraman, "The Relationship of Satisfaction and Performance to Salesforce Turnover," *Journal of Marketing* (Fall 1984): 33-40.
10. Alan J. Dubinsky and Steven J. Skinner, "Impact of Job Characteristic on Retail Salespeople's Reactions to Their Jobs," *Journal of Retailing* (Summer 1984): 35-62.
11. R. Kenneth Teas, "A Test of Model of Department Store Salespeople's Job Satisfaction," *Journal of Retailing* (Spring 1981): 1-22.
12. For a good discussion of how data can be systematically used to select retail salespeople, see J. N. Mosel and R. R. Wade, "A Weighted Application Blank for Reduction of Turnover in Department Store Salesclerks," *Personnel Psychology* (1951): 177-84 and Robert F. Hartley, "The Weighted Application Blank Can Improve Retail Employee Selection," *Journal of Retailing* (Spring 1970): 32-40.
13. William R. Darden, Ronald D. Hampton, and Earl W. Boatwright, "Investigating Retail Employee Turnover: An Application of Survival Analysis," *Journal of Retailing* (Spring 1987): 69-88.
14. Joseph A. Bellizzi and Robert E. Hite, "Supervising Unethical Salesforce Behavior," *Journal of Marketing* (April 1989): 36-47.
15. Jack Falvey, "The Top Ten Sales Training Myths," *Small Business Reports* (March 1990): 68-77.
16. "Pul-eeze! Will Somebody Help Me?" *Time,* 2 February 1987, 52.
17. Much of the following is based on John O'Shaughnessy, "Selling as an Interpersonal Influence Process," *Journal of Retailing* (Winter 1971-72): 32-46.
18. O'Shaughnessy, "Interpersonal Influence Process," 41.
19. "Hypnotic Selling," *Sales & Marketing Management* (September 1989): 32.
20. "How to Handle People," *American Salesman* (June 1991): 24-25.
21. "I Hunt for Dissatisfied Customers," *American Salesman* (June 1991): 3-5, 25.
22. "Bridging the Communication Gap," *Sales & Marketing Management* (August 1991): 62-65.
23. Lawrence B. Chonko, Marjorie J. Calallero, and James R. Lumpkin, "Do Retail Salespeople Use Selling Skills?" *Review of Business & Economic Research* (Spring 1990): 36-46.
24. This information has been provided by Kmart and is used with its permission.
25. Theodore Levitt, "Marketing Intangible Products and Product Intangibles," *Harvard Business Review* (May-June 1981): 100.
26. Betsy Gelb, "How Marketers of Intangibles Can Raise the Odds for Consumer Satisfaction," *The Journal of Consumer Marketing* (Spring 1985): 60.
27. Lawrence A. Crosby, Kenneth R. Evans, and Deborah Cowles, "Relationship Quality in Services Selling: An Interpersonal Influence Perspective," *Journal of Marketing* (July 1990): 68-81.
28. For a more complete coverage of this topic, see Robert P. Bush, Alan J. Bush, David J. Ortinau, and Joseph F. Hair, Jr., "Developing a Behavior-Based Scale to Assess Retail Salesperson Performance," *Journal of Retailing* (Spring 1990): 119-36.
29. "One Store Where Selling Is Still in Style," *Sales & Marketing Management* (September 1989): 31-32.
30. The material in this section was developed by Marvin Rothenberg and is used with his permission.

Part 6

RETAIL OPERATIONS AND ADMINISTRATION

CHAPTER 16

MANAGEMENT OF HUMAN RESOURCES

OVERVIEW

In this chapter we examine the role human resources play in a retail firm's success. To carry out retail marketing strategies successfully, retailers must have the proper number and mix of human resources. Thus, managers must plan for human resources; evaluate employee performance; hire, train, and develop; compensate human resources; improve the job environment; and finally, organize their human resources for maximum efficiency.

MANAGEMENT OF HUMAN RESOURCES

I. Human Resource Management
II. Planning for Human Resources
   A. Task Analysis
      1. Marketing Functions
      2. Identifying Tasks
      3. Mapping Tasks into Jobs
      4. Development of Job Descriptions and Job Specifications
   B. Long-Range and Short-Range Analysis
III. Hiring the Right Person for the Job
   A. Sources
   B. Screening and Selection
      1. Application Blanks
      2. Personal Interview
      3. Testing

4. References
IV. Training and Development
V. Performance Appraisal
VI. Employee Motivation
   A. Content Theories
      1. Maslow's Hierarchy of Needs
      2. Herzberg's Two-Factor Theory
      3. Theory X and Theory Y
   B. Process Theories
      1. Expectancy Theory
      2. Goal Setting
VII. Human Resource Compensation
   A. Common Types of Compensation Programs for the Sales Force
      1. Straight Salary
      2. Salary Plus Commission
      3. Straight Commission
   B. Supplemental Benefits
      1. Employee Discounts
      2. Insurance and Retirement Benefits
      3. Child Care
      4. Push Money
   C. Compensation Plan Requirements
VIII. Job Enrichment
IX. Organizing Human Resources
   A. Organizing Modes
   B. Which Mode?
      1. Target Market
      2. Decision Making
      3. Employees
   C. Organizing Around Functions
      1. One-Function Organization
      2. Two-Function Organization
      3. Three-Function Organization
      4. Four-Function Organization
      5. Complex Structures
   D. Organizing Around Merchandise
   E. Organizing Around Location
   F. Multi-Mode Organizations
   G. Branch-Store Organizations
      1. Brood Hen and Chick
      2. Separate Store
      3. Equal Store
   H. Chain Store Organizations
      1. Coordination and Control
      2. Buying and Selling
   I. Ownership Groups
X. Summary

HUMAN RESOURCE MANAGEMENT

A wise retailer once observed that there are only three simple principles to follow to be successful in retailing:

First, success depends on your location, location, and location.
Second, the customer is ALWAYS right.
Third, when the customer is WRONG, refer to the second principle.

The first principle was fully discussed at the beginning of Chapter 10. The second and third principles are not as easy to follow as it might at first seem. After all, how can the customer be made to feel like a king or queen, if the salesperson waiting on him or her isn't happy with the job. The successful retailer of the 21st century will be the one that does the best job of increasing the productivity of its employees. Employees, especially the salesforce which we discussed in the last chapter, represent the retailer and its merchandise, which was covered in Chapters 7 through 9, to its customers and thus have the ability to propel the firm to high-performance results or failure. Since good human resources are in short supply, the proper planning and management of these resources is a key correlate of a retailer's ultimate performance level.

After all, the impact of increased salesforce productivity on profit in retailing is dramatic. For example, the use of suggestion selling, a lost art discussed in Chapter 15, can often be the difference between success and failure for many retailers. Retailers operate very close to their break-even

ILLUSTRATION 16.1

Stores must be careful to have proper staffing at peak times in order to provide rapid checkout service.

points due to the relatively high costs of opening the store doors each morning. Therefore, a 10 to 15 percent increase in salesforce productivity—be it measured in sales per employee hour, or gross margin less sales commission per employee hour—would directly translate into a proportional improvement in store profits. Consequently, retail managers should accept a major performance imperative to increase human resource productivity, especially in the salesforce.

In addition, the declining birthrates of the late 1970s and early 1980s mean that the pool of young adults available to enter the retail labor force will be smaller in the latter part of the 1990s. Paradoxically, the recent increase in the birthrate since 1989 could keep more women at home with their young children.[1] The resulting labor shortage will further complicate the retailer's hiring plans. Retailers, like other employers, will be forced to replace the relatively cheap labor previously offered by young adults and women without children and seek to improve labor productivity to match the higher pay scale on which they will operate. High-performance results will thus be achieved not with low-cost labor, but with improved management of human resources. Retailers must also be aware that demographic changes could result in an increase in unionization activities by retail workers in the latter part of this decade.[2] Not surprisingly, as pointed out in Retailing in Action 16.1, labor is the number one issue facing retailers around the world.

Retailers use different methods for planning and managing human resources. Nevertheless, there is a common core of knowledge regarding planning and managing human resources in retailing, and this common core will be the focus of this chapter.

PLANNING FOR HUMAN RESOURCES

Planning for human resources means deciding now what human resources will be needed later in order to achieve the firm's goals and objectives.

TASK ANALYSIS

The starting point for a retailer's human resource planning is task analysis. **Task analysis** simply involves identifying all the tasks the retailer needs to perform and breaking those tasks into jobs. Four steps should be followed: *identifying the functions* within the marketing system that retailers need or wish to perform; *identifying the tasks* that need to be performed within each function; *mapping the tasks into jobs*; and *developing the job descriptions and job specifications.*

Marketing Functions. In Chapter 5 we stressed that retailers need to view themselves as a part of a larger marketing system. Retailers are but one institution in a marketing channel that, as a system, must perform eight

RETAILING IN ACTION

16.1 Labor: The Number 1 Issue Facing Retailers Around the World

A 1991 study of supermarket chief executives around the world by the Food Marketing Institute and Coca-Cola, Inc. found labor to be the most critical issue they expect to face over the coming decade. The ratings reported below were based on an eight-point scale; the lower the number, the more important the issue.

	Global	Europe	Latin America	North America	Pacific Rim	Australia/ New Zealand
Labor	2.55	2.66	3.14	2.03	2.27	2.41
Competition	3.77	4.02	3.38	4.24	2.93	4.59
Economy	4.07	4.78	1.86	5.36	3.29	3.22
Technology	4.41	4.32	4.75	4.28	5.15	4.36
Government	4.64	4.53	3.69	4.61	4.00	4.87
Nutrition/ Safety	5.08	4.88	6.25	4.74	5.07	5.13
Financial	5.19	4.88	5.08	6.31	5.54	4.39
Environment	5.28	4.52	6.75	4.03	6.92	4.50

marketing functions: buying, selling, storing, transporting, sorting, financing, information gathering, and risk taking. Since the eight functions can be shifted and divided, no single institution in the marketing channel will typically perform all of them.

The starting point for good human resource planning is for the retailer to decide which and how much of the eight marketing functions it will perform. Today, many retailers are attempting to push the performance of some of these functions back to the vendors, solely as an expense-saving device. Such actions may produce short-run savings, but they can also result in turning over to vendors the vital control of the functions that should be retailer-directed. Therefore, only those functions should be shifted in which loss of control will not seriously affect the business and which the vendor can perform more efficiently than the retailer. In fact, we may even conclude that in the interest of channel performance, the retailer should take over some of the the vendor's functions. As retailers assume responsibility for more of these marketing functions, which the vendor had been performing, they will require more human resources.

Identifying Tasks. Once retailers have established the amount of each marketing function to perform, they must identify all the tasks that will need to be performed. Functions are broad classifications of activities; tasks are specific activities. For example, selling is a function that may involve the tasks of customer contact, customer follow-up, advertising in newspapers, and pricing merchandise.

Exhibit 16.1 provides a list of typical tasks that most retailers perform—ranging from transporting goods to cleaning the floors and windows of the store.

Mapping Tasks into Jobs. The next step is the mapping of tasks into jobs. Retailers want a job to be comprised of a relatively similar set of tasks. Since most retail tasks are not similar, retailers will need to find those tasks that are most similar and group them together. The smaller the retail firm, the less this will be possible. In a mom-and-pop store the owner does everything from purchasing supplies and merchandise, preparing financial statements, contacting customers, to even washing windows.

As stores grow in size and add more employees, specialization can occur. As a retailer grows, the tasks of granting credit, billing customers, paying bills, and preparing financial statements will be placed in the hands of an accounting or financial clerk. Similarly, the tasks of handling customer complaints, repairing and altering merchandise, and gift wrapping may be placed in the hands of a director of customer services. When the retailer was smaller, these tasks may have been handled by the same person, even though they weren't similar in nature. At the other extreme, if the retailer becomes large enough, each task may be performed by a separate individual and ultimately there may be many employees handling a single task. For instance, Sears needs hundreds of employees just to bill customers, and thousands more just to purchase merchandise.

Development of Job Descriptions and Job Specifications. Once the tasks have

EXHIBIT 16.1
Typical Tasks Retailers Perform

Searching for merchandise	Following up on customers	Contacting customers	Doing customer research
Packaging	Handling customer complaints	Transporting inbound merchandise	Preparing press releases
Gift wrapping	Cleaning store	Transporting outbound merchandise	Preparing financial statements
Advertising	Controlling inventory	Paying bills	Storing merchandise
Purchasing supplies	Hiring and firing employees	Handling cash	Preparing merchandise statistics
Purchasing merchandise	Training employees	Altering merchandise	Maintaining the store
Granting credit	Selling	Repairing merchandise	Providing store security
Billing customers	Supervising employees	Forecasting sales	
Building merchandise assortments	Displaying merchandise		
Pricing merchandise			

been mapped into jobs, job descriptions and job specifications should be developed so that human resource managers know what the job applicant should be able to do, the skills required to do the job, and the kind of training that should be provided the employee. Job descriptions and specifications also can help determine the sources that should be used to recruit applicants, the selection procedures that should be used in evaluating applicants, and the training and development that should be given new employees in order to maximize performance.

LONG-RANGE AND SHORT-RANGE ANALYSIS

Retailers generally use two different time frames in planning their human resource needs. On a long-range time horizon (two to five years), the major factor will be the retailer's projected growth in sales volume and number of stores. Frequently, the growth in sales and number of stores depends on the availability of good human resources. In analyzing long-range growth trends, retailers should pay particular attention to the speed and predictability of sales growth, the geographical dispersion of growth, and the amount of growth related to line-of-trade diversification.

Most retailers are more concerned with the short-range time frame which is usually less than one year and in many cases may be weekly, monthly, or seasonal. Retailers should forecast any short-run swings in sales and then adjust human resource inputs appropriately. For instance, if retailers forecast a recession in the next quarter, they might postpone new hiring for the near term, so that if the recession does materialize, no employees will need to be fired or laid off.

It is wise to analyze any recurring seasonal trends. If retailers always do a strong business during the Christmas season, they should plan to have adequate human resources during this period each year. Similarly, if they always experience more traffic on Friday and Saturday, they should plan to have the necessary human resources to serve this increased traffic.

Periodic and predictable increases in short-run demand for human resources can be handled either by utilizing part-time employees or by having existing employees participate in job sharing. Part-time employees for peak periods such as Christmas or weekends can help retailers serve more customers. One way of attracting good part-timers is to send out stuffers to your charge account holders, those customers who already use and probably like the store, offering part-time employment for the Christmas season with the standard employee's discount privileges. However, the peak business can often be handled by having existing employees share jobs, such as having managers waiting on customers, or by having some employees work overtime. However, using overtime is not a long-term solution. Research has shown that at 60 hours a week, a worker's performance declines by 25 percent.[3]

HIRING THE RIGHT PERSON FOR THE JOB

Retailers must remember that human resources are acquired in a competitive marketplace. Good employees are not waiting around to be hired, and seldom will they come pounding at your door. In fact, when good workers or managers are looking for employment, they will seldom think of contacting retail firms, simply because of the reputation many retailers have for low starting wages. Therefore, retailers must aggressively seek out and recruit good employees; in so doing, they must compete with other industries for labor resources.

SOURCES

What are the sources from which retailers can obtain human resources? The seven sources shown in Exhibit 16.2 are the most common: competitors, walk-ins, employment agencies, schools and colleges, former employees, advertisements, and recommendations.

Retailers sometimes have to resort to using a different type of labor pool in order to match personnel with business demand. For example, several years ago, when Best Western International was faced with a shortage of reservation takers, it turned to a most unconventional source of employees—the Arizona Department of Corrections.[4]

SCREENING AND SELECTION

Regardless of the specific source, all job applicants should be subject to a formal screening process to sort the potentially good from the potentially bad employees. As with any judgment process, some mistakes will happen. But fewer errors occur when screening is used.

Retailers tend to vary in the amount of screening they use. In principle, as shown in Exhibit 16.3, there are four screens: application blanks, personal interview, testing, and references. The total applicant pool for a particular job is progressively reduced as the applicants are subjected to each screen.

Application Blanks. As a matter of procedure, all applicants should be asked to fill out an application blank. The application blank should capture conveniently and compactly the individual's identity, training, and work history that will relate to his or her performance of the job tasks. Title VII of the Civil Rights Act of 1964 prohibits employers from discrimination in employment on the basis of race, color, religion, sex, or national origin; the Age Discrimination in Employment Act of 1967 (ADEA) prohibits employers from discrimination in employment on the basis of age; and the Americans with Disabilities Act of 1990 prohibits employers from discrimination in employment on the basis of handicap/disability. Moreover, laws and regulations in many states also prohibit discrimination on other bases, such as marital status, ancestry, arrest record, credit record, prior accidents on the job, disabilities

EXHIBIT 16.2
Sources of Retail Employees

Competitors. Competitors are the most common source for middle to upper management personnel, particularly when the retailer does not have someone to promote from within the firm due to geographic or line-of-trade conditions.

Walk-ins. Often a source for clerical, sales, and custodial positions, but seldom for managerial or supervisory employees. Walk-ins are most frequent during periods of high unemployment, when retailers need additional human resources least.

Employment Agencies. All states provide public employment services, which are typically available free of charge to both job seekers and employers. They are a reasonable, if not good, source for unskilled employees. At the same time, they are an excellent source for minority, handicapped, and veteran employees. This can help retailers meet their commitment to help achieve a specific policy of equal employment opportunities for all persons.

Private employment agencies, which may charge either the hiring company or the applicant a fee, are generally a much better source for managerial and white-collar employees, especially top executives. Two examples are Retail Executive Search, Inc., based in Chicago and Retail Recruiters based in New York City. Both are good sources for suitable candidates for top management retail positions.

Schools and Colleges. High schools that have Distributive Education Clubs of America (DECA) chapters provide an excellent source for operating-level employees. Many such employees have the basic talent, skills, and ambition to become shift managers or assistant department managers within a one- or two-year period.

Junior-college graduates, because of their college training, can begin in some low-level supervisory roles, such as assistant night manager of a store.

Four-year college graduates, and in some cases MBAs, expect and receive higher starting salaries due to educational experiences that enable them to move quickly into management positions.

Former Employees. Since retail organizations are always changing, there may come a time when a position is open for which a former employee would be excellent. It is not uncommon for a person to leave one retail organization as an assistant buyer to take a job as a sales rep for a supplier or as a buyer at another retail organization and then return to the initial retailer several years later as divisional merchandise manager.

Advertisements. Advertisements are a good source for salesclerks, cashiers, and janitors and occasionally buyers and managers. This is especially true when a retailer is entering a new geographic area and wants to make sure that employees at other retail firms in the area are aware that the new retailer is really interested in obtaining personnel with knowledge of the local market and not merely transferring existing personnel.

Recommendations. Current employees and vendors may have acquaintances or friends with an interest in applying for the jobs that are open. This source is good for filling jobs at all levels in the organization. Salesclerks as well as store managers, vice-presidents, and sales reps may know of others seeking employment at a variety of ranks or positions.

unrelated to ability, weight, height, and so forth. Thus, the employer is effectively prohibited from asking any questions whose answer could be used to discriminate between two different groups of applicants. For example, if it

EXHIBIT 16.3

Employee Screening Process

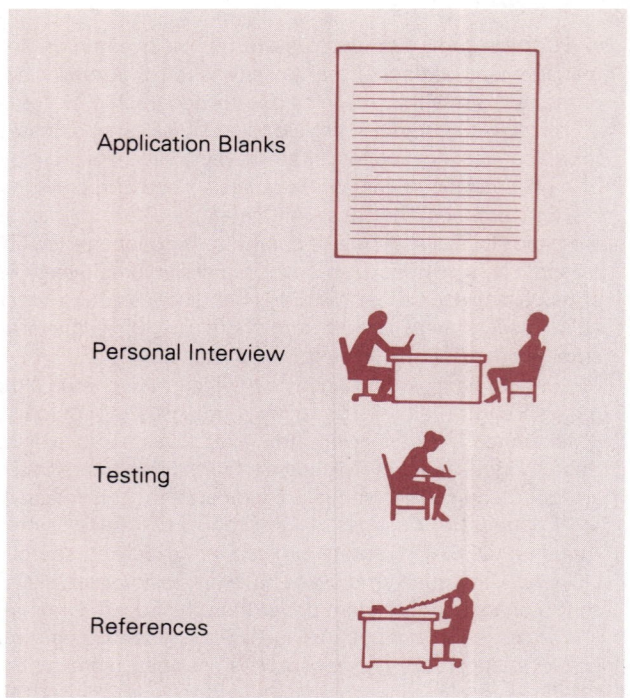

could be shown that certain minorities have a higher arrest record or that they change residences more often than nonminorities, then questions concerning such information would be illegal; they could be used to discriminate and normally do not elicit data indicative of likely job performance. Occasionally, exceptions may be made where religion, sex, or national origin (but not race or color) is a **bona fide occupational qualification (BFOQ)** that is reasonably necessary to the narrow operation of a particular enterprise.[5] Examples using a BFOQ are a restaurant on the Mexican border hiring bilingual personnel or a women's apparel store hiring only females as dressing room attendants.[6]

Based on a recent study[7] of the existing laws, the court interpretations thereof, and current practices of a national sample of department store retailers with regard to development and use of employment application blanks, 98 percent of retailers responding were using "suspect" questions on their application blanks. Exhibit 16.4 shows some specific questions by area of discrimination that retailers were using in 1991. Retailers should make every effort to avoid using such questions.

From the list of qualified applicants who filled out applications, the retailer must select the best possible subset of candidates for each job.

Personal Interview. Those applicants who possess the basic characteristics needed to perform the job should be personally interviewed. This important

EXHIBIT 16.4

Specific Problem Questions to Be Avoided by Area of Discrimination

Race
  Length of time at current residence
  Do you own or rent?
  What languages, other than English, can you speak, write, or read?
  What is your race?
  Number of children and/or dependents?
  Have you ever been arrested?
  Have you ever been convicted of a crime?
  Name of schools attended
  Number of years you attended school
  Name of school and location
  Name and address of relative to contact in case of emergency
  Name of individual to contact in case of emergency
  Were you in the military service?
  What type of discharge did you earn?
  What did you do in the service?

Age
  How old are you?
  Date of birth
  Dates attended school
  Years in military service
  List all jobs and years worked

Sex
  Height
  Weight
  Is spouse working for retailer?
  Marital status
  Number of children and/or dependents
  Is your spouse employed?
  Do you prefer being called Mr., Mrs., Miss, or Ms.?
  What is your sex?

Handicaps
  How is your health in general?
  Prior worker's compensation claims?
  Do you have physical or mental handicaps?
  Do you have any handicaps that could limit your performance?

Religion
  If you are hired, do you have a request for regular days or certain times off?
  Membership in professional organizations
  Membership in social clubs
  Name of a pastor, minister, or rabbi
  Name of school attended

step allows the retailer to assess how well qualified the applicants are for the job. By its very nature an interview is subjective, but in a well-structured interview one can obtain information or at least gain insight into the attitudes, personality, motives, and job aspirations of the interviewee.

Many interviewers overlook the fact that the interview should be a two-way communication process. Not only does the retailer want to gather information about the applicant, but the applicant may desire information about the retailer. Allowing time for the applicant to ask questions is essential if the retailer is competing for the talents of highly desired applicants. In fact, part of the interview time may actually be used by the interviewer to try to sell the applicant on the retailer as well as honestly explaining what the job entails so as not to lead to job dissatisfaction or possible legal complications based on misunderstandings.

A new trend is to use the computer for gathering information about the applicant during the interview phase. Research has shown that more correct information is obtained this way. Since the responses were to the computer directly rather than on paper or given to the interviewer, respondents felt that the information was more readily subject to instant checking and verification with other databases. Thus, to avoid potential embarrassment, applicants were more truthful.[8] In recent years, Bloomingdale's has asked entry-level sales, stock, and clerical candidates to sit down with a computer and answer multiple-choice questions about their background. They found that people feel at ease "talking" to a computer and that their answers are also more accurate. Marriott Hotels found that workers screened by computers tend to remain with Marriott for a longer period of time.[9]

Testing. Sometimes formal tests will be administered to those applicants who received favorable ratings in their personal interviews. These tests may look for certain characteristics, such as intelligence, interests, leadership potential, personality traits, or honesty. Since 1989 retailers have not been permitted by federal law to use lie detector tests. While most retailers never used polygraph tests, some, especially in the jewelry business, relied heavily on their results. Many retailers have switched to other types of tests.[10] These include credit checks with local credit bureaus, checks of prior worker's compensation claims, and drug tests. However, because each state has different laws on the use of these types of tests, especially drug tests, the retailer should consult with an attorney before using them. In addition, some tests could violate the applicant's rights if he or she isn't advised of such inquiries ahead of time and given the opportunity to consent, or if the tests run afoul of the anti-discrimination laws' protections for minorities and the handicapped. Besides, in many cases these tests have been found not only to violate the applicant's rights but also to give error-ridden information about the applicant.[11]

References As a general rule, retailers should not ask for or check the references the applicant has provided until the applicant has been screened or filtered through the preceding stages. If references were obtained and verified on all initial applicants, the cost would be excessive.

Negligent hiring is one of the hottest issues in current employment law. The premise is that an employer can be held responsible for an employee's unlawful actions if it did not reasonably investigate an employee's background and then placed the employee in a position where he or she caused harm to a customer.[12] When references are obtained and checked, the retailer should try to assess the honesty and reliability of the applicant. The reason for leaving the prior place or places of employment should also be investigated. The retailer should be interested in finding out what type of person will vouch for the prospective employee. Although most references provided by the applicant can be expected to give a neutral or favorable recommendation (if they give one at all), the reference check does give the retailer a means to verify the accuracy and completeness of the application. Also, as a point of information, many retailers have found greater success using telephone interviews instead of asking for written replies. This method enables retailers to gather more complete and honest evaluations than do letters, even if it is only in what the reference doesn't say about the applicant.

One final comment on checking references: The retailer must tread carefully here to avoid breaking federal and state laws. The personnel manager will be well advised to visit the firm's legal staff yearly to determine the firm's and the applicant's legal rights. New laws are regularly being made in the courts, Congress, and state legislatures.

TRAINING AND DEVELOPMENT

Human resources, both new and existing, should receive training and development if retailers wish a good return on their investment. Recall that human resource planning is deciding in the present what will be the human resource requirements in the future. Training and development fit nicely into this scheme, because they provide a vehicle for enhancing the quality of both existing and new human resources so that they will better be able to meet the future needs of the organization. The importance of proper training and development was shown in a report by a B. Dalton executive. B. Dalton reported a 20 percent reduction in store manager turnover as a result of more realistic job previews in the training process, as well as increased salaries and opportunities for managers to gain recognition.[13]

Training and development is an area where retailing has traditionally lagged behind other forms of business. Previously, retailers used the "sink or swim" method, whereby the new employee was thrust into the job and had to learn in any way possible or else quit or get fired, or the "sponsorship" method, in which training consisted of assigning the new employee to a senior employee for instruction on the job to be performed. Today, however, retail personnel directors are developing more sophisticated approaches to meeting their human resource needs. These approaches are geared to transforming college graduates into assistant buyers and area managers rather than into buyers and store managers. New programs teach such hands-on skills as operations and merchandising and make extensive use of training manuals, classroom sessions, computer-based simulation games, video tapes, role-playing, and case studies. Many entering the retailing profession after college graduation will spend the first month(s) on the job going through such a training program.

This program is not a one-time event, however. Retailers today view training as a process of continuing education. Thus, as an individual's responsibilities increase, so does the training and development. Employees are taught not just technical skills but administrative and "people" skills as well. Each phase of development is built on the training that preceded it and includes training in merchandising, operations management, motivation, decision making, problem analysis, and time management.

In addition to developing a pool of future managers and assisting employees with present duties, training and development programs enable the employees to know where they are and how they are doing. After all, because of its long hours, not being able to take vacation time around Christmas and Thanksgiving, and job pressures a career in retailing is not for everybody. Also, a career in retailing is different from careers in other business fields. In the beginning it is like a pyramid, with the employee becoming increasingly specialized so as to achieve the status of buyer, the ultimate specialist. Afterwards, the goal is to increase breadth, not specialty, so as to become a manager (store or division).

Retailers should view their salespeople and managers as a strategic resource and invest resources in their training and development. This means, among other things, providing new salespeople with information about the company and its goals, plans, and policies. The more they understand the firm's objectives and policies, the more salespeople are prepared to communicate to both present and potential customers the message that the retailer wants its customers to hear. Training and development for salespeople is an ongoing process and should include such topics as: product knowledge, different selling approaches, code of ethics, communication theory, planning and problem-solving skills, and self-assessment and understanding. If you think of employees as "clerks," that's probably just what you will have. It is not an accident that the nation's largest retailer, Wal-Mart, does not have "employees" or "clerks" but hires "associates" working for (and with) senior management, as pointed out in Retailing In Action 16.2.

Finally, the results of all training programs should be evaluated. The reasons for conducting this evaluation are:

1. To determine whether the program is accomplishing its objectives
2. To identify the program's strengths and weaknesses
3. To calculate the cost/benefit ratio of the program
4. To establish a reference point for future decisions about the program

Training programs can be evaluated with a variety of methods. The most popular is to analyze questionnaires completed by the trainees after the program. In the case of salespeople, professional shoppers sometimes pose as

RETAILING IN ACTION

16.2 Wal-Mart's People Approach

Wal-Mart might be the nation's largest retailer, but it considers itself to be not in the retailing business but in the people business. The late Sam Walton wanted his employees treated with dignity, respect, and responsiveness up and down the line.

In making sure that employees are the chain's "number one asset," Wal-Mart seeks to provide an environment in which employees grow, not just from training classes, but from on-the-job challenges. The chain also involves its associates in several unique operations:

Each spring, managers hold extensive "grass roots" meetings with all associates to listen to the associates' problems and ideas. They make immediate responses to these suggestions.

Associates are involved in assisting in key decisions as quickly as possible. Hourly associates are included in the screening process on all job applications.

Managers are encouraged to take breaks with associates, keep an open door, engage in two-way communication, and gain respect for each other.

However, probably the one factor that sets Wal-Mart employees apart from other retailing employees is that they are all owners as part of their compensation program. Thus, every store has a sign that reads: "Today's Wal-Mart Stock Quote: $XX.XX. Tomorrow's Depends on You."

Based on Von Johnston and Herff Moore, "Pride Drives Wal-Mart to Service Excellence," *HRMagazine* (October 1991): 79–82 and information supplied by the people division during the authors' visit to Wal-Mart's headquarters in Bentonville, Arkansas.

---

customers and report on their experiences with a sales trainee. Remember, the best training and development program devised is useless unless management adopts a philosophy of complete support. In the past, many retail executives became so involved in merchandising concerns, they forgot about human resources.

PERFORMANCE APPRAISAL

Performance appraisal and review is the formal, systematic assessment of how well employees are performing their jobs in relation to established standards, and the communication of that assessment to employees. Employees place a great deal of importance on appraisals, and the way the appraisal system operates affects morale and organizational climate in significant ways. Moreover, the appraisal system also has an impact on other human resource processes, such as training and development, compensation, and promotion.

ILLUSTRATION 16.2

Wal-Mart places a greeter at the entrance of every one of its stores, a practice first initiated by a floor-level associate that was picked up and made company-wide policy.

Informal appraisals tend to take place on an ongoing basis within the retail firm as supervisors evaluate their subordinates' work on a daily basis and as subordinates appraise each other as well as their supervisors. However, the formal, systematic appraisal of an individual is likely to occur at certain intervals throughout the year or when the employee is being considered for a wage increase, a promotion, a transfer, or an opportunity to improve job skills.

Retailers of all sizes should try to use objective criteria for the appraisal and review process wherever possible. A form for the objective review and appraisal of salespeople is shown in Exhibit 16.5. However, not every item that the retailer might want to evaluate can be quantified. Larger retail operations use a committee, frequently consisting of the vice-president of human resources and one or two other executives, to evaluate each employee. Some retailers, especially smaller ones, sometimes forego the formal evaluation process and judge a salesperson on the basis of dollar sales, number of transactions, errors, on-time performance, ratio of returned merchandise, and customer complaints.[14]

It is important to recognize several key factors in conducting performance appraisals. First, the process should be an ongoing affair, not just a periodic review. Regularly scheduled review times should not keep supervisors from

EXHIBIT 16.5

Criteria to Be Used in Appraisal and Review Process

Merchandise Procedures:	Employee's accuracy in counting and inventorying merchandise.
	Prevents merchandise shrinkage due to mishandling of merchandise.
	Keeps merchandise in a neat and orderly manner on sales floor.
	Knows the design and specifications of warranties and guarantees of the merchandise groups.
	Gets merchandise on sales floor quickly after merchandise arrival.
Customer Service Ability:	Provides courteous service to customers.
	Handles customer complaints and/or service problems as indicated by store procedure.
	Follows proper procedures concerning merchandise returns and lay-aways when conducted through credit transactions.
	Suggests add-on or complementary merchandise to customers.
Sales Ability:	Has strong ability to close the sale.
	Promotes sale of merchandise items having profit margins.
	Acts as a resource to other departments or other salespeople needing assistance.
	Works well with fellow workers in primary merchandise department.
Product-Merchandise Knowledge:	Knowledgeable of design, style, and construction of merchandise group.
	Knowledgeable of special promotions and/or advertised sale items.
	Knowledgeable of material (fabrics), color coordination, and complementary accessories related to returned merchandise.
	Provides accurate and complete paperwork related to returned merchandise.
Store Policy:	Provides accurate and complete paperwork related to work schedules.
	Provides accurate and complete paperwork for cash and credit transactions.
	Shows up on time for work, sales meetings, and training sessions.
	Accurately follows day-to-day instructions of immediate supervisor.
	Employee's overall job-related attitude.

Source: Robert P. Bush, Alan J. Bush, David J. Ortinau, and Joseph F. Hair, Jr., "Developing a Behavior-Based Scale to Assess Retail Salesperson Performance," *Journal of Retailing* (Spring 1990): 119-36.

appraising or coaching their subordinates whenever necessary. Second, employees seek feedback, or information about how well they are doing their jobs, and this feedback should be provided on a timely and relevant basis. Third, the person doing the review should know what the job being reviewed entails and the performance standards. Many times employees can become upset with the review process when the reviewer is not aware of problems and limitations of the job under review. Fourth, different supervisors are likely to rate personnel with different degrees of leniency or severity. Therefore, not only should the person making the review understand the performance standards, but at least two people should make the review. Finally, research has shown that the particular method of reviewing the employee doesn't matter. Retailers have found success in various types of measures including the rating scale, checklist, free-form essay, and rankings.

EMPLOYEE MOTIVATION

Human resource management goes beyond selecting, training, and compensating the employees. It also means motivating them to improve current performance. A high-performance retailer today must constantly encourage the salesforce, as well as all other employees, to strive for higher sales figures, to decrease expenses, to communicate company policies to the public, and to solve problems as they arise. This is achieved through the proper use of motivation.

Motivation is the drive within a person to excel, either individually or as a member of a firm. Several theories on motivation have been developed. These can be divided into **content theories,** which ask "What motivates an individual to behave," and **process theories,** which ask "How can I motivate an individual." Among the content theories we will discuss are Maslow's hierarchy of needs, Herzberg's two-factor theory of motivation, and McGregor's Theory A and Theory Y. In our discussion of the process theories, we will look at two of the most widely used: expectancy theory and goal-setting.

CONTENT THEORIES

Maslow's Hierarchy of Needs. Abraham Maslow, a noted psychologist, developed a model, which is shown in Exhibit 16.6, that suggests people have different types of needs and that they satisfy lower-level needs before moving to higher levels. The first level is the basic physiological need, which can be satisfied by the employee's cash wages. Once a sales force becomes content at this level, it becomes concerned with safety and security needs. Retailers have satisfied these needs with such benefits as security patrolled parking locations. The third level of needs, that of belongingness and social needs, can be satisfied with "employee or salesperson of the month" awards. A similar

EXHIBIT 16.6

How Retailers Can Use Maslow's Hierarchy of Needs

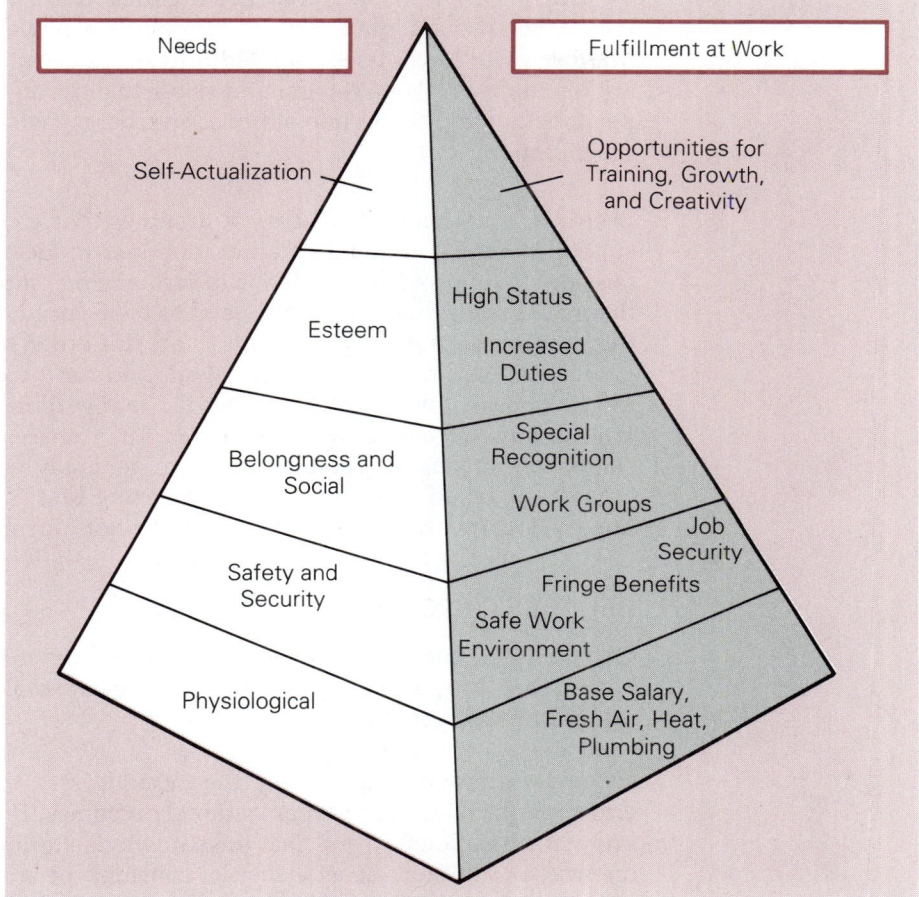

approach can be used at the fourth level of needs, esteem, with fancier offices and job titles. The highest need level is self-actualization or "becoming all you can be" in this life. Here retailers can provide seminars to help broaden the horizons of salespeople. Maslow's hierarchy thus provides retailers with ideas that can appeal to the basic needs of their employees.

Herzberg's Two-Factor Theory. Herzberg offered another perspective on motivations. Herzberg suggested that two factors operate as motivators: hygiene factors and motivators. Hygiene factors are extrinsic to the individual and can be organizationally determined. Examples of hygiene factors in a retail setting are pay, verbal praise, and special name badges. Motivators, on the other hand, are intrinsic to the individual and include the feeling of self-accomplishment or the desire to excel.

Thus, Maslow's and Herzberg's theories as to what motivates an individual to behave are quite similar. Herzberg's hygiene factors are basically Maslow's two lower levels of need (physiological and safety) and motivators are his top two levels (esteem and self-actualization). Maslow's third level of need, belonging, can fit into either of Herzberg's two categories depending on the situation.

Theory X and Theory Y. Theory X assumes that employees must be closely supervised and controlled and that economic inducements (salaries and commissions) will provide the means of influencing employees to perform. This theory assumes that employees need to be induced or coerced to work since they are inherently lazy. Theory Y, on the other hand, assumes that employees are self-reliant and enjoy work and can be delegated authority and responsibility. Over the past decade, many different retailing employee groups have foregone wage increases for a share of management. These "employee managed" retail stores have generally experienced an increased organizational effectiveness, thus supporting Maslow's, Herzberg's, and the Theory Y contention that money alone is not a primary motivator.

PROCESS THEORIES

On the other side of content theories are process theories which, as we said earlier, are concerned with how to motivate employees to behave in the retailer's best interest.

Expectancy Theory. Expectancy theory addresses the relationship between effort, performance, and organizational outcomes. It assumes that employees know this relationship and that this knowledge influences them to behave in one way or another. As an example, consider the situation of retail salespeople. More specifically, expectancy theory states that a salesperson's motivation to expend effort on some task depends on whether (1) the salesperson expects that the effort will lead to a sale (performance), (2) the sale will likely lead to a reward or bonus (outcome), and (3) the reward or bonus is desirable (valued). Obviously, the critical consideration is how much value the salesperson attaches to the reward or bonus, be it cash, prizes, promotions, fancier offices, increased job status, better conditions, or a greater sense of achievement.

Expectancy theory appears to provide a logical answer to the question "how to motivate a sales staff." If a salesperson likes to travel and thinks he or she can reach quota, he or she will work hard to win a trip.

Goal Setting. Goal setting is a way to obtain the firm's objectives that depend on inducing a person to behave in the desired manner. The goals must be attainable; too difficult a goal, such as an increase in sales of 50 percent, will not motivate a salesperson because the chances of achieving the target are slim. Likewise, too easy a goal, such as a 1 percent increase, is often demotivating and unchallenging. The time frame is also important. Too long a time frame is generally demotivating. Just as you would put off a term paper due in four months, the salesperson might do the same with a year-long sales goal. A 10 percent increase in yearly sales might be broken down into either the two seasons or 12 months, with changes made at stated intervals based on market conditions.

Remember, it is the retail manager's job to motivate employees in a manner that yields job satisfaction, low turnover, low absenteeism, and high-performance results.

HUMAN RESOURCE COMPENSATION

As all businesspeople know, human resources are not free goods. They are expensive, and in retailing their cost typically represents 50 percent of operating expenses. We will not discuss here how to control labor expenses but merely highlight some important aspects about compensating human resources.

Compensation is one of the major variables in attracting, retaining, and motivating human resources. The quality of employees that can be attracted, whether as salesclerks or executives, is directly proportional to the compensation package offered. The better the human resource, the higher the price. Naturally, other things besides compensation are important to employees, but compensation still stands out as the most important aspect in most employees' feelings of job satisfaction. A study by the Hay Group reported that knowledge about the employee benefit program and about the pay policies and procedures was more important than any other types of information the employer could give the employee. Knowledge about the firm's plans for the future was third.[15]

Competitive compensation is just as important to retaining good employees as it is to attracting them. In this regard, the retailer needs to realize that if it invests more money in training and developing employees, these employees will actually increase in value, not only to the retailer, but also to competitors who may try to hire them. Thus, as the retailer invests money to train and develop employees, it must also make a commitment to provide them with more compensation, or the retailer will be training and developing employees for its competitors.

Here the term **compensation** includes direct dollar payments (wages, commissions, and bonuses) and indirect payments (insurance, vacation time, and retirement plans). For most retail executives, the subject of compensation packages means collective bargaining with union negotiators, as most lower-level retail employees are already, or are becoming, members of unions. For example, almost 70 percent of all supermarket chains employ unionized personnel.

Compensation plans in retailing can have up to three basic components: a fixed component, a variable component, and a fringe benefit component. The **fixed component** typically is composed of some base wage per hour, week, month, or year. The **variable component** is often composed of some bonus that is received if performance warrants it. Salesclerks may be paid a bonus of 10 percent of sales above some established minimum; department managers may receive a bonus based on the profit performance of their department. Workers in restaurants often receive tips, a variable component that the retailer does not control. Finally, a **fringe benefit package** may include such things as health insurance, disability benefits, life insurance, retirement plans, the use of automobiles, and financial counseling.

Each of the three components helps the retailer to achieve a different human resource goal. The fixed component helps it to ensure that its employees have a source of income to meet their most basic financial obligations. This helps to fulfill the employees' *physiological needs*. The variable component allows the retailer to offer its employees an incentive for higher levels of effort and commitment, which helps to fulfill a *belongingness and social need* among employees for special recognition in return for high performance. The fringe benefit component allows the retailer to offer employees *safety and security*. Retail employees have a need to be protected and cared for when they are faced with difficult times or when they become too old to provide for themselves. Also, certain employees (especially executives) have a need for prestige and status.

The best combination of fixed, variable, and fringe compensation components depends on the person, the job, and the retail organization. There is no set formula. Some top retail executives prefer mostly salary, others thrive on bonuses, still others would rather have more pension benefits. The same holds for salesclerks. Therefore, the compensation package needs to be tailored to the individual. We now focus our attention on compensation of the salesforce, but the same principles will apply to managers.

COMMON TYPES OF COMPENSATION PROGRAMS FOR THE SALESFORCE

Retail salesforce compensation programs can be conveniently broken into three major types: (1) straight salary, (2) salary plus commission, and (3) straight commission, each with advantages and disadvantages.

Straight Salary. In the straight-salary program, the salesperson receives a fixed salary per time period (usually per week) regardless of the level of sales generated or orders taken. However, over time, if the salesperson does not help generate sales or take enough orders, he or she will likely be fired for not performing adequately. Similarly, over time, if the salesperson helps to generate more than a proportionate share of sales or fills more than a proportionate number of orders, the retailer will be unable to retain the employee without a raise.

Many small retailers use this compensation method, because they typically assign stock rearranging, merchandise display, and other nonselling duties to their salespeople. If these employees were paid on a commission basis, they would spend little if any time on their nonselling duties, and the retail organization would suffer. Many promotional and price-oriented chain stores whose salespeople are merely order takers will use the straight-salary method because the salesperson is not much of a causal factor in generating sales. Also, most clerks and cashiers, as well as other lower-level retail personnel, are almost always paid straight salaries.

The salesperson may view this plan as attractive because it offers income security, or as unappealing because it gives little incentive for extraordinary effort and performance. Thus, for this method, which is also the easiest plan for the employee to understand, to be effective it must be combined with a periodic evaluation so that superior salespeople can be identified and singled out for higher salaries.

Salary Plus Commission. Sometimes the salesperson is paid a fixed salary per time period plus a percentage commission on all sales or on all sales over an established quota. The fixed salary here is lower than that of the salesperson working on a straight-salary plan, but the salary plus commission structure offers the potential to earn more than the straight-salary plan. In fact, most salespeople on the salary plus commission program earn more than their counterparts on straight-salary programs.

This plan gives the employees a stable base income—and thus incentive to perform nonselling tasks—but it also encourages and rewards superior effort. Therefore, it represents a good compromise between the straight-salary and the straight-commission programs. In many cases, top management receives a salary and a bonus based on overall store or department performance.

Quotas in this plan must be properly established. Developing the quota-based commission plan requires four steps:

1. *Determining the quota for the time period.* This is usually based on past sales, with adjustment for changed conditions and for seasonal fluctuations. If $5,000 has been the average weekly sales in the past, this figure may be used as the quota. To be a sales stimulus, the quota should remain within the reach of practically all the salespeople. Yet it cannot be too low or everyone will reach it without much effort.
2. *Establishing a base salary.* Base salary is usually determined on the basis of the past wage/cost ratio, that is, if the ratio in the past had been about 9 percent, the base salary might be established at 9 percent of the quota, or $450 on a $5,000 quota.
3. *Setting the commission rate for sales in excess of the quota.* In practice, this commission is usually set considerably below the store's average wage cost, frequently, about 3 percent.
4. *Deciding between a cumulative and a noncumulative plan.* Noncumulative plans, which are used by most retailers today, offer a "fresh start" in

reaching quota in each new time period. When sales people who fail to make their quota in one period have to fill the deficiency before becoming eligible for a bonus in the next period, the plan is cumulative. This type of plan tends to discourage employees who for reasons beyond their control fail to reach quota during two time periods in a row.

Straight Commission. Income of some salespeople is limited to a percentage commission on each sale they generate. The commission can be the same percentage on all merchandise, or it can vary depending on the profitability of the item. Retail salespeople working on a straight commission typically receive commissions of 2 to 9 percent of the selling price of the product.

The straight-commission plan provides substantial incentive for retail salespeople to generate sales. However, when the general business climate is poor, retail salespeople may not be able to generate enough volume to meet their fixed-payment obligations (mortgage payment, auto payment, food expenses). For this reason, most retailers slightly modify the straight-commission plan to allow the salesperson to draw wages against future commissions up to some specified amount per week. For instance, the employee may be able to draw $200 per week, to be paid back from future commissions.

A major problem with the straight-commission plan is that it may provide the retail salesperson with too much incentive to sell. As a result of the income insecurity of this plan, the employee may begin to use pressure tactics to close sales, hurting the retailer's image and long-run sales performance. Similarly, the employee may not be willing to perform other duties such as

ILLUSTRATION 16.3

Retail jewelry salespeople are typically paid a salary plus commission on sales.

helping customers with returned merchandise or helping to set up displays, because after all, compensation is paid to sell and not to handle customer complaints or displays. Generally, sales personnel for high-priced merchandise such as automobiles, real estate, jewelry, and furniture, as well as for goods and services requiring the sales personnel to prospect or seek out potential customers, (insurance and door-to-door selling) are paid this way.

The 1990 Ernst & Young survey reported that 51 percent of the retailers polled used a salary plus commission plan and 38 percent used straight commission.[16] Exhibit 16.7 summarizes the attributes of each of these plans. However, during the economic slowdown of the early 1990s, many retailers began to reduce the commission portion of employee compensation plans and increase the salary portion. This was an attempt to reduce consumer distaste for what was perceived to be "high pressure."[17]

SUPPLEMENTAL BENEFITS

In addition to regular wages (salary, commission, or both), retail salespeople can also receive four types of supplementary benefits: employee discounts, insurance and retirement benefits, child care, and push money (or spiffs).

Employee Discounts. Almost all retailers offer their employees discounts on merchandise they purchase for themselves or their immediate family. About

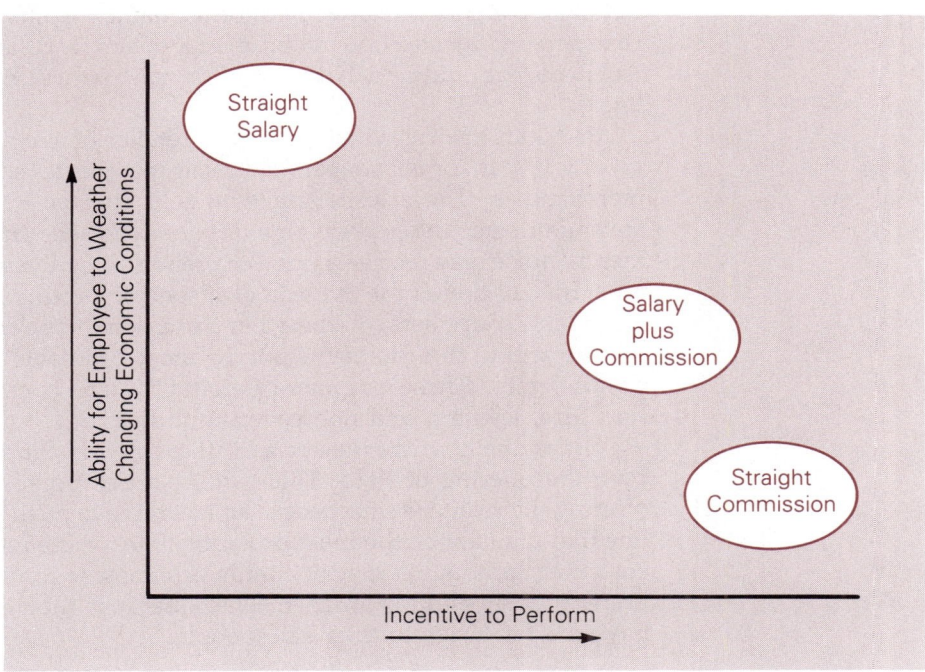

EXHIBIT 16.7
Attributes of Compensation Plans

the only line of trade where these discounts are not offered is grocery retailing, because grocery retailers operate on relatively thin gross margins. In other lines of retail trade, the discounts can range from 10 to 40 percent.

Insurance and Retirement Benefits. Historically, retail personnel were not provided any insurance or retirement benefits. In some situations, this is still the case. However, many retailers are providing their employees with either free or low-cost group health and life insurance. Still others are making profit sharing, stock ownership, and retirement programs available to long-tenure salespeople. These benefits are valued between $50 and $190 a month per individual.

Child Care. In an effort to attract employees from two-wage-earner families, some U.S. businesses have begun to provide child care for employees' offspring during working hours. Retailers have just started providing child care, a program that experts agree will be a necessity in the late 1990s. However, with health-care costs rapidly increasing in the early 1990s, some retailers have delayed plans to add child care due to the added expenses. Hardee's Food Systems in early 1991 eliminated its successful pilot child-care subsidy at six Raleigh, North Carolina, restaurants.[18]

Push Money. A final type of supplementary benefit is "push money," which some may call "prize money," "premium merchandise," or just plan "PM." Retailers commonly call it by another name, "spiffs." The PM, paid to the salesperson, in addition to base salary and regular commissions, is said to encourage additional selling effort on particular items or merchandise lines.

PMs can be offered either by the retailer or the supplier. A retailer may give a PM in order to persuade salespeople to sell old or slow-moving merchandise. The salesperson who sells the most may win a free trip to Hawaii or some other prize, or everyone who sells an established quantity of merchandise may receive a prize or premium. Or the retailer may simply offer an extra $10 bonus for the sale of a specific product, for example, a dining room table. Suppliers, on the other hand, tend to offer PMs to retail salespeople for selling the top-of-the-line or most profitable items in the suppliers' product mix. These supplier-offered PMs are common in the appliance, furniture, jewelry, and floorcovering industries.

Occasionally, there may be a conflict between the supplier and the retailer over the offering of PMs. This conflict arises because the supplier may be offering the retailer's salespeople an incentive to push an item or merchandise line that may not be the most profitable line for the retailer or the best for the customer, although it may be highly profitable to the supplier. Some retailers prefer to keep all PMs for themselves, because they believe they are already paying a fair wage to their salespeople.

COMPENSATION PLAN REQUIREMENTS

Regardless of what method a retailer ultimately determines to use in compensating its employees, the method should meet the following general requirements:

1. *Fairness:* The plan should not favor one group or division over any other or enable any group to gather rewards disproportionate to its contribution. It must also keep wage costs under control so that they do not put the store at a competitive disadvantage.
2. *Adequacy:* The level of compensation should enable the employee to maintain a standard of living commensurate with job position, and to maintain job satisfaction.
3. *Prompt and regular payments:* Payments should be made on time and in accordance with the agreement between employer and employee. In incentive plans, greater stimulation is provided when the reward closely follows the accomplishment.
4. *Customer's best interest:* The plan should not reward any actions by an employee that could result in customer ill will.
5. *Simplicity:* The plan must be easy to grasp so as to prevent any misunderstanding between employee and employer that could generate ill will. It should also enable management to minimize the labor-hours needed to determine compensation levels.
6. *Balance:* Pay, supplemental benefits, and other rewards must provide a reasonable total reward package.
7. *Security:* The plan must fulfill what Maslow called the individual's two basic needs: physiological and safety and security.
8. *Cost effective:* The plan must not result in excessive payments, given the retailer's financial condition.

While none of the three plans we discussed previously fully satisfies all these requirements to the maximum level, keeping the requirements in mind will help the retailer select the best plan given the individual circumstances. In fact, it is not uncommon for the same retailer to use more than one plan in the same store as different divisions or departments have different needs.

JOB ENRICHMENT

Job enrichment is the process of enhancing the core job characteristics for the purpose of increasing worker motivation, productivity, and satisfaction. Five core job characteristics should be enhanced:

1. *Skill variety:* The degree to which an employee can use different skills and talents.

2. *Task identity:* The degree to which a job requires the completion of a whole assignment that has a visible outcome.
3. *Task significance:* The degree to which the job affects other employees.
4. *Autonomy:* The degree to which the employee has freedom, independence, and discretion in achieving the outcome.
5. *Job feedback:* The degree to which the employee receives information about the effectiveness of his or her performance.[19]

Job enrichment programs have their base in Maslow's need hierarchy theory and Herzberg's motivation/hygiene theory. These theories suggested that job factors themselves, such as challenge, independence, and responsibility, are powerful motivators.

Retail management has long recognized that paying attention to job descriptions, work scheduling, job sharing, and employee input programs will have a positive effect on employee productivity and satisfaction. Some of the many things retailers are doing today to provide enrichment for their employees include: flex time, job sharing, child care, and employee assistance programs for drug and alcohol abuse.

ORGANIZING HUMAN RESOURCES

If you were the owner/manager of a retail organization, you could not merely plan for and hire human resources and then let them run loose to do their own thing. Havoc would result! Rather, you would need to organize your staff to work efficiently toward your organization's objectives and goals. For this, you would need an organization structure.

An organization structure is an arrangement of human resources in terms of lines of authority and responsibility. There are, of course, formal and informal organization structures. The **formal organization structure** represents the way employees *should* behave in terms of lines of authority and responsibility. The **informal organization structure** depicts how the employees within the retail organization *actually* behave. All retail enterprises have both formal and informal organization structures—and both are useful.

ORGANIZING MODES

Retailers tend to organize their human resources around one of three modes: function, merchandise line, and geography. Organizing around *function* means delineating the functions the retailer performs (buying, selling, transporting, storing) and structuring the human resources so that there are specific tasks, responsibilities, and lines of authority covering the performance of each function. Organizing around *merchandise lines* is a similar process. What are the major merchandise lines to be handled (produce, meats, etc.)? How should the human resources be structured to perform tasks related to each of the lines while receiving the appropriate levels of responsibility and authority? To organize around *geography* one might ask: What are the major geographic areas in which tasks need to be performed? Which human resources should perform these tasks in each geographic area?

WHICH MODE?

How does one decide which mode is best suited for a specific retail enterprise? The answers to three other questions help resolve this fundamental one.

1. What is the retailer's target market?
2. Where do decisions need to be made?
3. What is best for employees?

Target Market. After the merchandising decisions are made, all retail organizations must seek out customers or markets to serve. These customers or markets provide the transactions that help make the retailer profitable or unprofitable. Whether human resources are organized around functions, merchandise, or geography, the human resources will ultimately be concerned with retaining and attracting new customers to the retail enterprise. Therefore, the retailer must carefully define its target market if it is going to design a good retail organization structure that is customer oriented.

Decision Making. Where will most of the decisions be concentrated? If we are referring to a 200-unit women's apparel chain with stores spread over 30 states, then it is likely that many decisions will have to be made at each location or region. Such a retailer might organize around geographic regions. On the other hand, decision making in a local department store may center on its departments and their respective merchandise lines. That store might therefore organize around merchandise lines. Other retailers, whose decisions most often concern functions, might organize around function.

Employees. Which organizing mode would be best for employee morale, productivity, and protecting the retailer's investment in human resources? Let us assume that a local sporting goods retailer is growing rapidly and expects to open five stores in nearby cities over the next three years. If this retailer is organized around merchandise lines, then it may not be developing its human resources so that middle managers (merchandise managers) can become store managers in the near future. This retailer needs to develop a group of managers who understand all the functions within the retail enterprise, and a merchandise line organization may not be its best organization structure.

As another example, consider a retailer organizing its human resources so that each person performs a specialized function and nothing else, such as greeting customers, assisting customers, persuading customers, and collecting payment from customers. This specialization may, in theory, increase productivity, but if it is too extreme employees may become bored, and morale and productivity may be harmed. If a separate clerk were employed for each subfunction, then regardless of how much productivity could increase in theory, the practical problems of employee boredom and morale would block the theoretical productivity gains.

ORGANIZING AROUND FUNCTIONS

Regardless of how retailers organize around functions and the number of functions that are formally incorporated into the organization structure, the basic tasks that need to be performed in retailing still remain. For example, assume you are the owner/manager of a local hardware store. In your organization you may formally recognize only one function—to manage the store. In practice, however, you will have as many tasks and related functions to perform as there are formally delineated in the organization charts of some of the largest retail organizations in the world.

Let's look at one-, two-, three-, four-, and five-function retail organization structures. Keep in mind that there is a direct correlation between the size of the retailer and the number of functions formally recognized in the organization structure.

One-Function Organization. Exhibit 16.8 shows a typical organizational structure of small, single-unit retailers. The small, local, two-to-four-employee hardware store, record store, drugstore, gasoline station, and floral shop are good examples. As illustrated in Exhibit 16.8, these organizations are headed by a store owner or a manager; these are most often the same person. Reporting directly to the manager/owner is a head salesperson; this suggests that the major function of the retail organization is to sell merchandise. Almost all small retail enterprises, when initially established, will find themselves organizing around the selling function. Reporting to the head salesperson are two employees, labeled the second and third salespeople (obviously, there could be more).

Two-Function Organization. As retail organizations grow, they may find that the basic one-function organization structure has become obsolete. With an increase in size, a modest degree of specialization can be obtained by establishing a two-function organization structure. Typically when this occurs, the two functions that are formally delineated are merchandising and operations.

Each function is handled by a unit headed up by a manager; reporting to both the merchandise and the operations manager is a set of subordinates, each of whom is assigned certain duties. In general, the merchandise manager handles all activities related to the buying and selling of merchandise, whereas the operations manager assumes responsibility for activities related to maintaining the store in good working order and tasks that assist in serving

EXHIBIT 16.8

One-Function Retail Organization

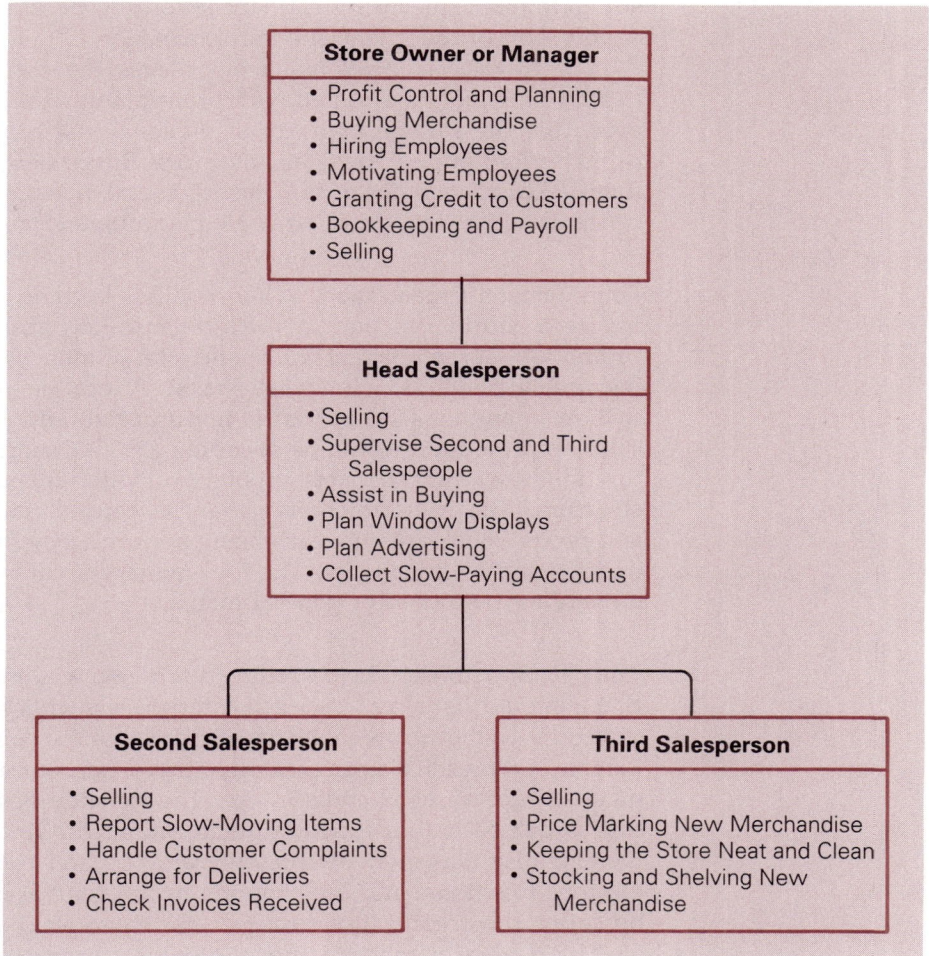

customers (delivery and stocking merchandise). With the two-function organization, the owner/manager still retains primary responsibility for profit control and planning but may have some assistants to help in record keeping.

Three-Function Organization. Once again, the driving force for adding more functional specialization is growth. As the retailer grows, the amount of paperwork and record keeping actually grows more than proportionately. Tighter financial controls are needed as the number of employees grows, because the opportunity for embezzlement and theft of merchandise grows rapidly. It is not surprising, therefore, that the next function to be formally added to retail enterprises is financial control, performed by a unit under the supervision of the financial control manager.

The financial control manager relieves the owner/general manager of much of the work associated with profit planning and control. Notice, however, that the general manager or owner is still responsible for the overall profit performance of the retail enterprise. But by delegating some control to a financial control manager, the owner/general manager will have more time to concentrate on long-range strategic planning and growth goals.

Four-Function Organization. When retailers become sufficiently large to formalize a fourth function in their organization structure, it most often is promotion. Large retailers will spend a lot of money on promotion (advertising, public relations, window displays). A local department store doing $10 million in annual sales (which is not unusual) and allocating 3½ percent of sales on promotion would be spending $350,000 annually. Such an expenditure might warrant the addition of a promotion manager to the organization structure. The four functions—financial control, merchandise, operations, and promotions—are now each being performed by separate units, with each unit headed by a manager. The four managers, all with equal status, report directly to the owner or general manager.

Complex Structures. The preceding discussion was intentionally simplified so that we could visualize how retail enterprises might change their organization structures as they grow. Now we are ready for the complexity of Exhibit 16.9. Exhibit 16.9 presents a complex organization structure for a large, corporately owned, general-merchandise store. The skeleton of this organization structure is our basic four-function organization: the financial control manager, merchandise manager, promotion manager, and operations manager head the four functions, and each reports to the general manager. At this point, however, the organization becomes more complex.

The general manager is not the owner, because we are dealing with a corporately owned organization; the stockholders are the owners. Between the stockholders and the general manager are a board of directors, president, and vice-president. Both the president and vice-president tend to concentrate on strategic and administrative planning matters, with a staff to assist and advise. The president's staff includes an executive secretary, a legal counselor, and a treasurer. The vice-president has an executive secretary, research director, and director of planning on his or her staff.

We also see complexity in the number of subordinates reporting to each of the four functional managers. Still, however, we have not shown all of the complexity of a retail organization. For example, the accounts payable manager who reports to the assistant controller would have a staff of several people, or even, in a retailer as large as Sears, over a hundred accounts-payable clerks. And notice we only show the subordinates for one division merchandise manager, whereas each would actually have a number of buyers and department managers reporting to him or her.

EXHIBIT 16.9

Complex Organization for a Large, Corporate-Owned, General-Merchandise Store

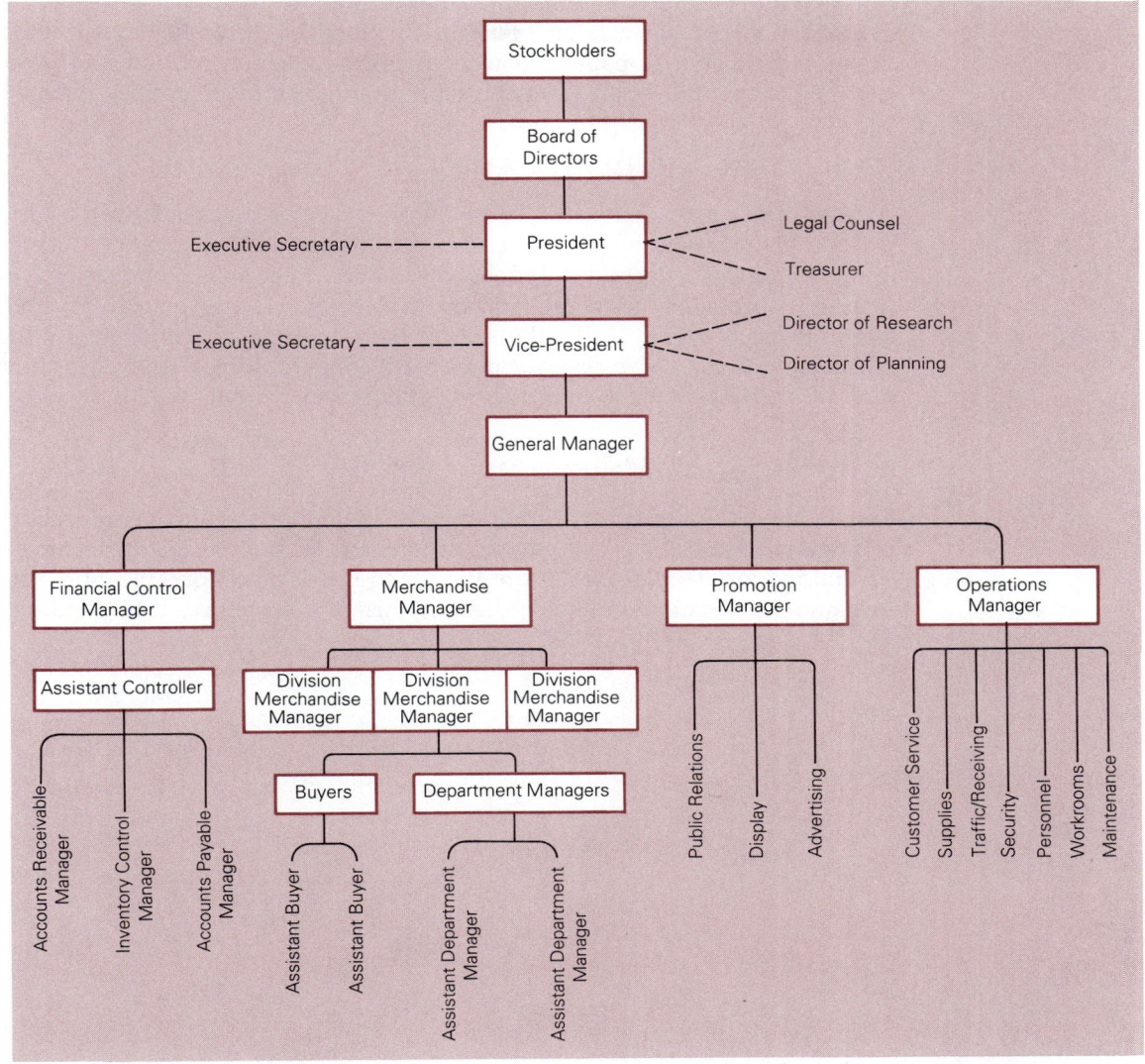

Source: Parts of this exhibit are adapted from Paul M. Mazur, *Principles of Organization Applied to Modern Retailing* (New York: Harper, 1927), frontispiece.

ORGANIZING AROUND MERCHANDISE

Retailers that offer a wide variety and assortment of goods will sometimes organize their enterprise around the main merchandise categories they handle. By organizing around distinct merchandise categories, the retailer is implying that separate merchandise categories require unique managerial skills, and that these skills are more crucial than skills in managing specific functions. Exhibit 16.10 shows a basic, merchandise-oriented retail organization for a home-improvement center. Reporting directly to the store owner or general manager are a lawn and garden manager, a lumber and building materials manager, a paint and wall covering manager, a hand and power tool manager, and a hardware, plumbing, and electrical supplies manager.

ORGANIZING AROUND LOCATION

A retail enterprise that has a large number of stores spread over a broad geographic area will often find it advantageous to structure its organization around geographic locations. It does this in order to be able to quickly address operating problems on a regional or local level. Having good managerial talent in each region, with the appropriate amount of responsibility and authority, means that decisions can be made more rapidly. The basic location-oriented retail organization structure is shown in Exhibit 16.11

MULTI-MODE ORGANIZATIONS

Retailers need not only organize around a single mode—functions, locations, or merchandise categories—but can organize their human resources around several modes. Two examples are the functional-location organization structure and the locational-merchandise organization structure. While a discus-

EXHIBIT 16.10

Merchandise-Oriented Retail Organization

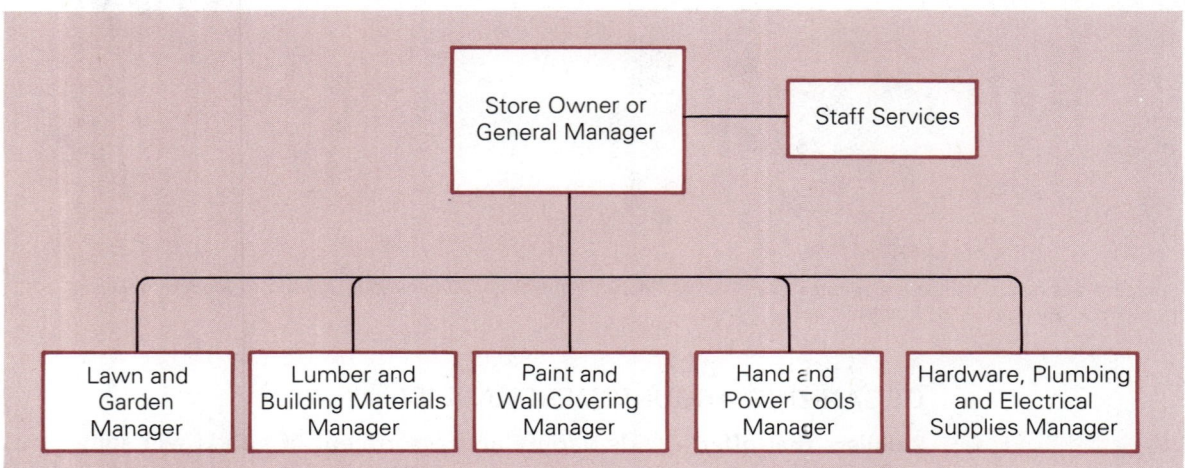

EXHIBIT 16.11

Location-Oriented Retail Organization

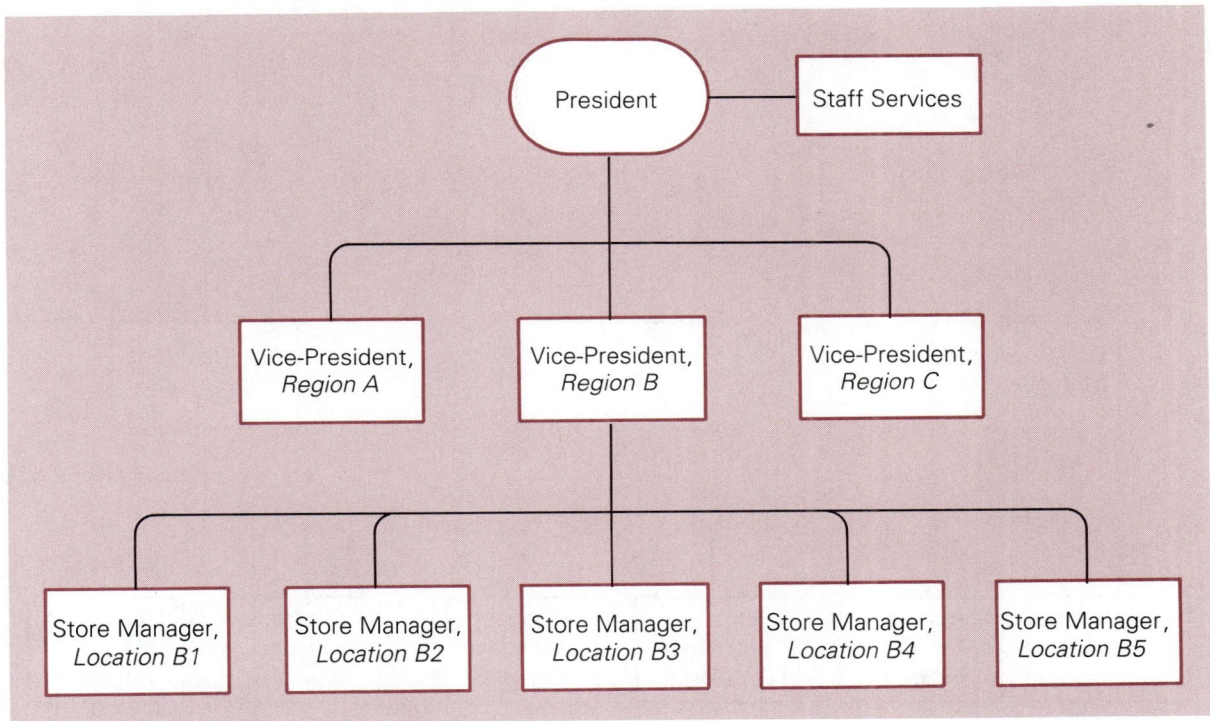

sion is beyond the scope of this text, two examples are depicted in Exhibits 16.12 and 16.13.

BRANCH STORE ORGANIZATIONS

When a single-unit retailer decides to add a second store in the same city, it typically refers to this as a branch store. In fact, the first several branch stores represent coordination and control problems. There is no best way to handle these problems in terms of organization structure, but several alternatives are available. Duncan, Hollander, and Savitt call these the "brood hen and chick" organization, the "separate store" plan, and the "equal store" structure.[20]

Brood Hen and Chick: When a retailer first begins to expand by opening new stores, and when these new stores are substantially smaller than the parent store, the brood hen and chick plan is often followed. In principle, the parent store operates the branch. Each key executive at the parent store performs or supervises the functions of related personnel in the branch. For example, the

EXHIBIT 16.12

Functional-Locational Retail Organization

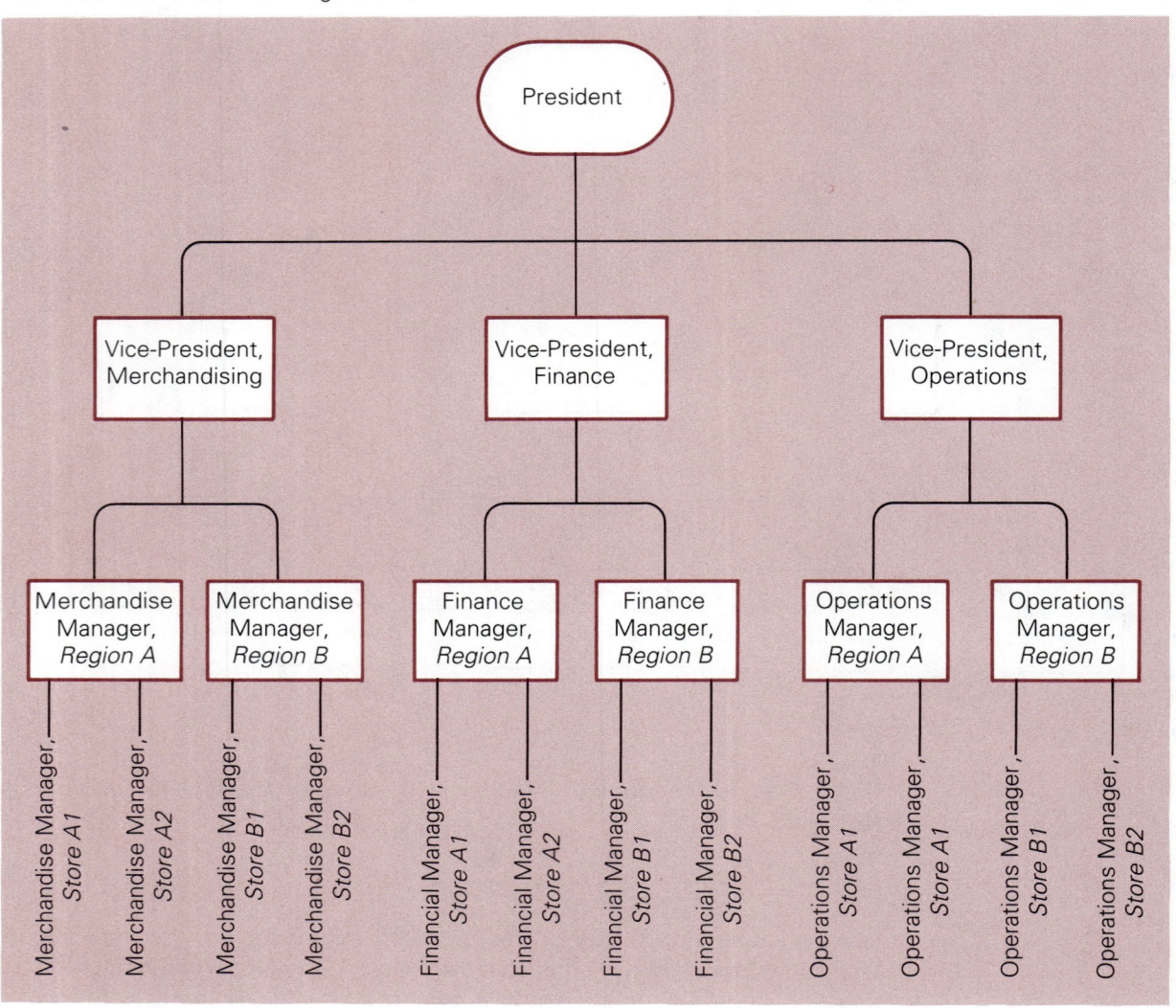

financial control manager of the parent store is also the controller of branch operations.

Separate Store. If too many branches are added or if the branch becomes too large, the workload on the executives at the parent store will become too heavy. At this point, the retailer may create a separate management group and staff for the branch. However, if each branch has its own management

EXHIBIT 16.13

Locational-Merchandise Retail Organization

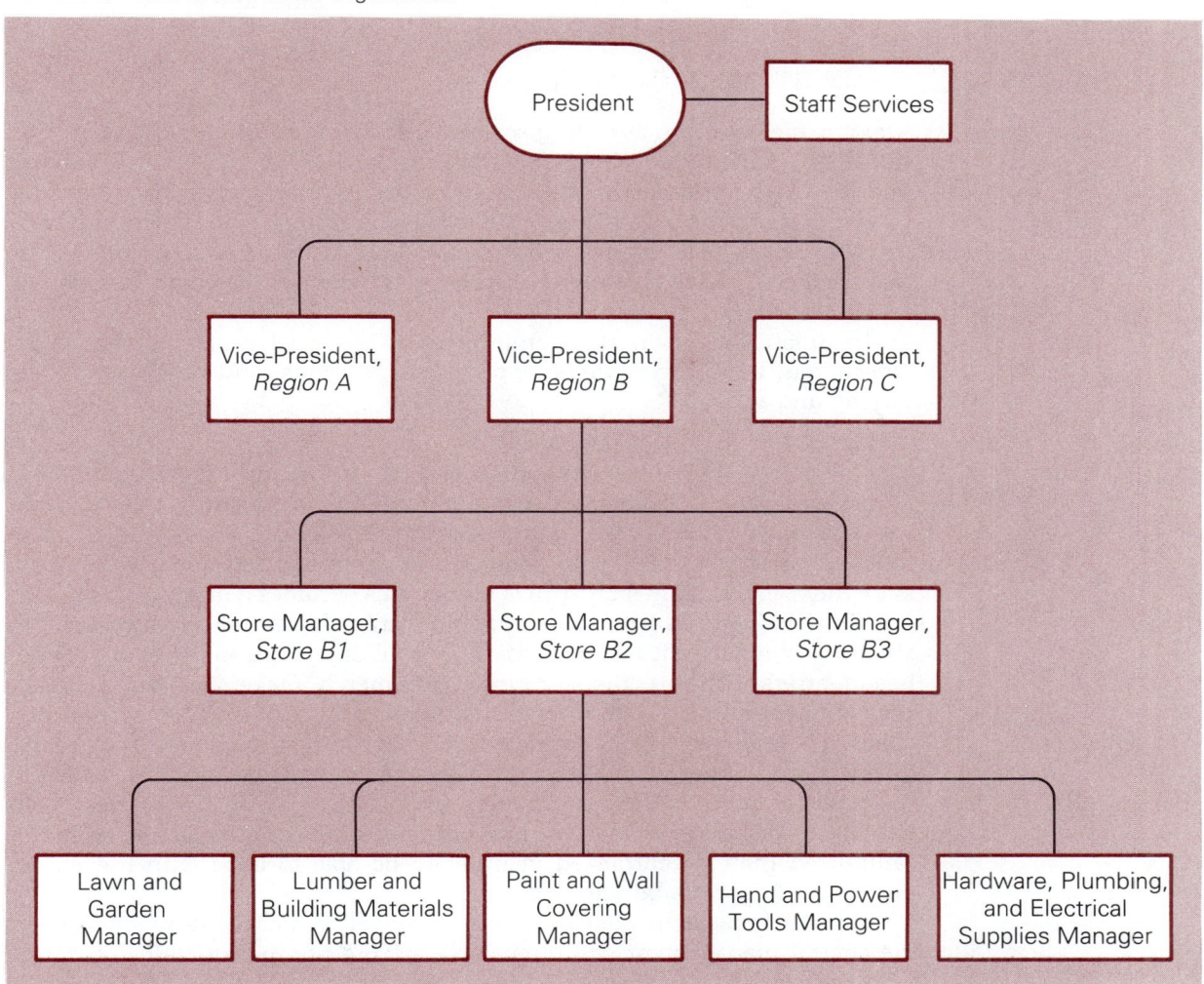

group and staff, there may easily result a duplication of efforts and therefore an inefficient use of human resources.

Equal Store. It is possible to move in the opposite direction from that which we outlined previously; that is, all major management functions may be centralized at a single headquarters. The management group and staff at headquarters will treat all stores as equal in terms of organizational status. The first store is given no special treatment or attention merely because it was the parent. The major problem under this plan is that many of the unique problems of the individual stores—parent or branch—cannot be given special attention, because most decisions are centralized and made at headquarters.

CHAIN STORE ORGANIZATIONS

Most of the concepts already discussed also apply to chain store organizations. The major point to keep in mind is that chains have 11 or more outlets, and therefore coordination and control become crucial. However, there is no precise pattern for organizing chain store enterprises. The structure developed by a particular chain depends on the organizational philosophies of top management, merchandise lines carried, and whether the chain is national, regional, or local.

In organizing chain store enterprises two special problems should be considered: how to coordinate and control decisions, and how to separate buying and selling.

Coordination and Control. The central problem in organizing chain store enterprises is one of coordination and control of individual stores. In fact, what we want to do with the organization structure is to create a system in which a network of stores, each with human and economic resources, will work smoothly. As the chain store grows in size, this becomes a more difficult feat.

Most chain stores have developed an extremely centralized organization structure in which all major decisions for all stores are made at the chain headquarters. In short, the store managers merely make sure that policies, procedures, and directives from headquarters are followed. The system becomes a bureaucracy, with store managers responding to memos from headquarters and filling out numerous reports (daily, weekly, monthly) to keep headquarters aware of the store's performance. Obviously, chain stores will vary in the degree to which they are centralized. But all are going to be more centralized than decentralized in order to be able to cope with the major problems of coordination and control.

In order to facilitate coordination and control in a chain store enterprise, the central management will often have a large number of staff personnel who are specialists in a number of key functional decisions. Staff personnel could include:

- Consumer research specialists
- Merchandise statistics specialists
- Real estate specialists
- Legal counselors
- Public relations specialists
- Tax planning specialists
- Pension plan specialists
- Consumer advocate advisors

Obviously, only the size and complexity of chain store enterprises can justify this type of management specialization and investment in human resources. In fact, there is often even a specialist in human resource management.

Buying and Selling. The second major problem in designing chain store organization structures is deciding whether to separate buying and selling. In other words, should buying be totally centralized—with headquarters buying all merchandise for all the stores—while the stores are responsible for selling the merchandise? By centralizing all buying, the chain store can obtain significant buying economies because it can purchase in large quantities. The problem with this approach is that all stores receive a standard merchandise mix that, by definition, will not be tailored to the trade area of each store. This is obviously less of a problem for supermarkets than for fashion apparel chains. But in either situation, it is a problem.

Some chain store organizations have responded to this problem by allowing local stores to purchase a certain percentage (perhaps up to 20 percent) of their merchandise. This still gives each store, regardless of location, a core of standard merchandise, but it allows some tailoring of the merchandise mix to local demands and preferences. The major problem is that as each local store is allowed to buy a higher percentage of its own merchandise, the presentation of a consistent image for the chain's stores becomes increasingly difficult. For example, a person who generally shops at a store of Chain X in Georgia may not recognize the chain's store in Michigan.

It is still the dominant industry practice in chain store retailing to centralize decisions, and to perform 100 percent of the buying at headquarters and most of the selling on a local level. Any selling at the headquarters relates to designing or placing national or regional advertisements and occasionally managing local advertising.

OWNERSHIP GROUPS

Ownership groups are retail enterprises that have purchased previously independent retailers and in some cases other retail chains. The ownership group allows individual stores to maintain their prior image and management and merchandising procedures. Any changes that are made typically relate to centralizing certain staff services, such as legal services or long-range planning. Examples of ownership groups are Federated Corporation, May Company, Woolworth Company, Dayton-Hudson Corporation, and Mercantile Stores Company.

Ownership groups, as opposed to chain store organizations, allow their stores to be relatively autonomous. One important area in which they are not autonomous is opening new outlets, adding additional space, or remodeling. This is the case because all positive cash flow goes to headquarters, and the top management of the ownership group allocates capital back to the respective divisions according to need and the long-range plans that each division has developed in consultation with the ownership group. Obviously, some divisions will receive more financial capital than they generated, and others less. Some divisions, based on their location, image, or strategic advantage, will be better positioned for profitable growth opportunities. This is why it was such a major news item in the mid-1980s when Federated's top management decided to let Bloomingdale's expand into Foley's Texas market. Federated based its decision on the fact that with 11 major department store chains operating in Texas, and with Bloomingdale's and Foley's projecting different images, there was room for both operations. Since then, Campeau Corporation has acquired Federated and sold Foley's to the May Company.

SUMMARY

Our discussion of human resource planning and management focused on five major dimensions: planning for human resources, human resource acquisition, training and development, human resource compensation, and organizing human resources.

To properly plan for human resources, the retailer should first identify the myriad of tasks that need to be performed. A useful frame of reference is the marketing functions. Which functions and how much of each does the retailer desire to perform? Each function can then be broken into tasks, and the tasks into jobs.

In long-range planning, the retailer should carefully examine its projected speed of growth and the predictability of this growth. It should also carefully examine its plans to diversify geographically or by line of trade. Finally, it should conduct a human resource audit. In short-run human resource planning, the retail executive should attempt to forecast any weekly, monthly, or seasonal swings in sales activity and then adjust human resource inputs appropriately.

Hiring occurs in a competitive labor market. There are many available sources of applicants; the more common include competitors, walk-ins, employment agencies, schools and colleges, former employees, advertising, and recommendations from existing employees. Once the applicants are obtained, they must be properly screened. We suggested a four-step screening process: application blanks, personal interview, testing, and reference check.

Expenditures on training and development are intended to increase the productivity of human resources. These programs should be ongoing as the employees' responsibilities first become specific (the buyer function), then increase in breadth (the store manager).

The employee's performance should be subjected to an ongoing, formal and systematic review process. This process will enable the employer to make better decisions concerning wage increases, promotions, transfers, and improvement in job skills.

Employee motivation is also a topic of great importance. Two schools of thought are represented by the content models and the process models. While the content models are older, retailers have made more use of the process models in that they have tried to link together the task, the outcome, and the reward.

Compensation is crucial to attracting, retaining, and motivating retail employees. A good compensation program includes a fixed component to provide income, a variable component to motivate employees, and a fringe benefit component to provide security and prestige. Special attention was paid to the advantages and disadvantages of the three types of compensation plans: straight salary, straight commission, and a combination of the two.

Chapter 16 Management of Human Resources

Job enrichment is the process of increasing the skill variety, task identity, task significance, autonomy, and feedback from the job in an effort to improve worker motivation, productivity, and satisfaction.

Retailers can organize their enterprises around functions, merchandise lines, or geographic location. Some of the larger retail enterprises will organize around more than one of these. In deciding which way to organize, the retailer should ask, What is my target market? Where do decisions need to be made? and What is best for my employees?

We concluded by discussing several alternatives for organizing branch stores, including the brood hen and chick organization, the separate store plan, and the equal store structure. In addition, we commented on organizing chain stores and ownership groups.

QUESTIONS FOR DISCUSSION

1. What are the various methods of compensating retail employees?
2. Why do retailers need an organization chart?
3. Discuss the alternative methods for organizing branch stores.
4. Can retailers increase the productivity of their employees only if they pay them higher wages? Explain your answer.
5. What is the best way to compensate (a) a retail salesperson, (b) a store manager, (c) a buyer? Explain your answer.
6. What are the major problems in centralizing the buying function in a chain organization?
7. What are the advantages and disadvantages of paying salespeople in a furniture store strictly on a commission basis?
8. Why is it so important for a retailer to screen an applicant before hiring?
9. If you were the regional personnel director for Wal-Mart, what traits or characteristics would you look for in a college senior under consideration for your management training program?
10. Why must training be an ongoing operation?
11. Develop a list of predictor variables you would use to screen applicants for a sales position in (a) a jewelry department in a high-prestige department store, (b) a used-car dealership, (c) a health club, (d) an antique shop.

MANAGEMENT MEMO

As the manager of a women's apparel store near the campus, you are seeking to find ways to increase both sales productivity and morale. However, the first solution that comes to mind—increasing wages—is out of the question due to economic circumstances. Nevertheless, you believe that if you give the store owner a memo outlining other possibilities, she will go along with your plans. Prepare such a memo suggesting ways, other than a pay increase, to improve the productivity and morale of the employees in your store.

BOARDROOM REPORT

A bedding vendor has approached your firm, a 14-unit furniture/appliance chain, wanting to know if it can pay push money to your salespeople. At the present time, your chain has a policy of not accepting any push money or spiff offers. However, competitors in most of your markets do accept them. The owner has asked that you prepare a policy statement on the subject for next week's board meeting. Be sure to include the pros and cons of spiffing in your statement.

SUGGESTED READINGS

Coleman, Lyon G. "Salesforce Turnover Has Managers Wondering Why." *Marketing News*, 4 December 1989, 6.

Darden, William R., Ronald Hampton, and Roy D. Howell. "Career Versus Organizational Commitment: Antecedents and Consequences of Retail Salespeoples' Commitment." *Journal of Retailing* (Spring 1989): 80-106.

Fern, Edward F., Ramon A. Avila, and Dhruv Grewal. "Salesforce Turnover: Those Who Left and Those Who Stayed." *Industrial Marketing Management* no. 18 (1989): 1-9.

Sager, Jeffrey K., P. Rajan Varadarajan, and Charles M. Futrell. "Understanding Salesperson Turnover: A Partial Evaluation of Mobley's Turnover Process Model." *Journal of Personal Selling & Sales Management* (May 1988): 20-35.

Twomey, David P. *Equal Employment Opportunity Law*. Cincinnati: South-Western Publishing Co., 1990.

Wotruba, Thomas R. "The Effect of Goal-Setting on the Performance of Independent Sales Agents in Direct Selling." *Journal of Personal Selling & Sales Management* (Spring 1989): 22-29.

Weitzel, William, Albert Schwartzkopf, and E. Brian Peach. "The Influence of Employee Perceptions of Customer Service on Retail Store Sales." *Journal of Retailing* (Spring 1989): 27-39.

ENDNOTES

1. "Do More Babies Mean Fewer Working Women?" *Business Week*, 5 August 1991, 49-50.
2. Patrick Dunne and Alan Levin, "Unionization: How Retailers Should Prepare for the Coming Challenge" (Paper presented at the National Retail Federation/American Collegiate Retailing Association Conference, New York, 1992).
3. "Letter from a Productive Lover of Leisure," *U.S. News & World Report*, 5 August 1991, 6.
4. "Dial 800-Prison," *Sales & Marketing Management* (February 1991): 34.
5. Section 703(e) of Title VII.
6. *Dothard v. Rawlinson*, 433 U.S. 321, 15 FEP 10 (1977).
7. Patrick Dunne, Alan Levin, James Wilcox, and Roy Howell, "Avoid Discrimination Hassles when Recruiting New Personnel," *NARDA News* (October 1991): 16, 58-60 and "Employment Application Blanks: Are Retailers Using Them Correctly?" (Working paper, 1991).
8. Christopher Martin and Dennis Nagao, "Some Effects of Computerized Interviewing on Job Applicant Responses," *Journal of Applied Psychology*, 74, no. 1 (1989): 72-80.
9. "Computer Takeover," *Wall Street Journal*, 15 July 1986, 1.
10. "More Employers Check Credit Histories of Job Seekers to Judge Their Character," *Wall Street Journal*, 30 May 1990, B1, B5; "Polygraph Restraints," *Wall Street Journal*, 11 January 1989, A1; and "Employer's Use of Accident Records Raises Spector of Blacklisted Workers," *Wall Street Journal*, 16 July 1990, B1, B6.
11. "Credit Bureaus: Consumers Are Stewing—and Suing," *Business Week*, 29 July 1991, 69, 70.
12. Joseph Ambash, "Knowing Your Limits: How Far Can You Go when Checking an Applicant's Background?" *Management World* (March/April 1990): 8-10.
13. Fredrick Ford, "An Analysis of Store Manager Turnover" (Paper presented at the 1983 National Retail Merchants Association Meeting, New York).
14. "Chain Finds Incentives a Hard Sell,: *Wall Street Journal*, 5 July 1990, B1, B4.
15. "Tell Me More," *Wall Street Journal*, 9 August 1985, 17.
16. *An Ernst & Young Survey: People in Retail* (September 1990): 11.
17. "Distressed Shoppers, Disaffected Workers Prompt Stores to Alter Sales Commissions," *Wall Street Journal*, 1 July 1992, B1.
18. "Employers Report Gains from Babysitting Aid," *Wall Street Journal*, 22 July 1991, B1.
19. J. Richard Hackman and Greg R. Oldham, *Work Redesign* (Reading, Mass., Addison-Wesley, 1980), 77-80.
20. Delbert J. Duncan, Stanley C. Hollander, and Ronald Savitt, *Modern Retailing Management*, 10th ed. (Homewood, Ill.: Richard D. Irwin, 1983), 159-61.

CHAPTER 17

RETAIL INFORMATION SYSTEMS

OVERVIEW

This chapter describes the role of information in retail planning and management. Strategic plans can only be implemented and kept in tune with the retail marketplace through resources, both human and information. We focus on two types of problems the retail information system can address: first to identify problems and second to solve them. Information, and its availability in usable form, has become a major resource and competitive tool in retailing.

RETAIL INFORMATION SYSTEMS

I. Introducing the Retail Information System
   A. The Need for Information
   B. The Amount and Timeliness of Information
II. Sources of Retail Information
   A. Internal Information
   B. External Information
   C. Integrating Internal and External Sources
III. The Scope of a Retail Information System
IV. The Problem Identification Subsystem
   A. Behavioral Trends: Monitoring Consumers
      1. Purchase Probabilities
      2. Consumer Attitudes
      3. Customer Satisfaction

    B. Behavioral Trends: Monitoring the Marketing Channel
        1. Merchandise Sources
        2. Facilitating Agencies
        3. Financial Performance of Channel Partners
        4. Channel Conflict
    C. Behavioral Trends: Monitoring Competitors
        1. Market Saturation
        2. Pricing
        3. Merchandise Mixes
        4. Promotion
        5. Market Share
        6. Trading Area
    D. Environmental Trends: Monitoring the Socioeconomic Environment
    E. Environmental Trends: Monitoring the Legal Environment
    F. Environmental Trends: Monitoring the Technological Environment
    G. Operating Performance Trends: Monitoring Assets
        1. Performance Standards
        2. Auditing Assets
    H. Operating Performance Trends: Monitoring Revenues and Expenses
        1. Income Statement
        2. Segmental Reporting
        3. Fine-Line Merchandise Report
V. The Problem Solution Subsystem
    A. Strategic Planning Problems
        1. Mission and Objectives
        2. Faltering Strategy
        3. Inadequate Contingency Plans
    B. Administrative Management Problems
        1. Financial Resources
        2. Human Resources
        3. Location Resources
    C. Operations Management Problems
        1. Assets
        2. Revenues and Expenses
VI. Organizing the RIS
VII. Future Developments in RIS
    A. Integrated Information Management Systems
    B. Expert Systems
VIII. Summary

The ideas and strategies of successful retailers are quickly imitated by competitors. Thus, enduring success in retailing can come only from having a better understanding of the whys and hows of the marketplace. A strategy based on detailed understanding of the retail marketplace can produce high-performance results before competition is able to react. But unless retail decision makers have all possible relevant information, their decisions might not be successful in today's highly competitive retail marketplace. Decisions made in the absence of information can cause disaster. In addition, information exchange between suppliers and retailers is increasingly important to serving the customer and maintaining and increasing financial performance. In this chapter we will focus on how a retailer can use a retail information system (RIS) to gather the knowledge necessary to make, execute, and monitor strategic plans.

INTRODUCING THE RETAIL INFORMATION SYSTEM

A RIS can consist of a store owner regularly reading retail trade association magazines, talking to customers to determine how satisfied they are with merchandise and service, and studying quarterly income statements and balance sheets. Or it can be much more extensive, encompassing vendor reports, exchanging information with vendors using electronic data interchange (EDI), market research, and charge account records. However, we wish to define a RIS not in terms of what it might be in a typical retail enterprise, but in terms of what it should be in a model retail enterprise. A **retail information system (RIS)** is a blueprint for the continual and periodic systematic collection, analysis, and reporting of relevant data about any past, present, or future developments that could influence or have influenced the retailer's performance. Several prominent features of a RIS are:

1. Both *continual* and *periodic collection* of relevant data should occur. Data should be continually collected on those activities that are always in a state of flux, such as the retailer's financial performance or competitor behavior. Data should be periodically collected when a nonrecurring problem arises, such as a capital budgeting or an excessive employee turnover problem.
2. The data collection activities should be *systematic* and *relevant*. The world is drowning in data. Retailers must decide what information they need and collect only that information in an orderly fashion.
3. *Analysis* and *reporting* of data are important parts of the RIS. The data cannot merely be dumped on the executive's desk: They must be analyzed and put in a reportable format. A computer file with 3,000,000 bits of data is not usable information until it has been analyzed and placed in a reportable format that the executive can understand.
4. The data can be about the *past, present,* and/or *future,* all of which can be relevant for retail decision making. Most accounting information is historical: It tells where the retailer has been. However, point-of-sale (POS) terminals provide data on what is happening now (present), and six-month monetary projections by the Federal Reserve System tell what will likely happen to interest rates in the future.

This is an ideal definition of a RIS, and it describes what the retailer should strive for.

One of the most sophisticated retail information systems in use today is the one developed by Dillard Department Stores. Dillard's goal was to design a system with on-line ability to enter and update data, as well as to inquire at the needed level of detail about all the firm's operations. Here is how Dillard uses this system for planning, tracking, and controlling.

1. *Planning.* Management is able to develop operating and merchandise plans on line to determine projected net profit. This planning includes historical data from several years prior to the planning period: actual expenses, sales, merchandise levels, turnover rates, markup percentage, shrinkage, and ROI. Management planning also includes simulating various environmental change data to test alternative plans.
2. *Tracking.* Actual performance tracking is reported for expenses, sales, and merchandise levels and compared with planned expenses, sales to inventory levels, markup dollars and percentage, markdowns, freight expenses, shrinkage, and gross margin dollar and percentage. Actual reporting is daily and weekly. Operating expense tracking includes monitoring of payroll, receivables, collections, credit scoring, and even the phone system. As part of its merchandise tracking system, Dillard uses magnetic tickets to capture the department, description, quantity, and price of all sales. Current daily sales are reported by division, department, and store on "flash sales" reports. Orders are placed on line, instantly updating open-to-buy, or are automatically generated by the inventory system. Receiving discrepancies between orders and receipts are resolved by the receiving system. Invoices are entered online and matched to the receipts in batch processing.
3. *Controls.* The register audit system validates the previous day's sales, including Dillard's charge card and bankcards. This system processes only the exceptions, so that by 3 p.m. the next day management knows the audited sales for the entire chain and payments on Dillard accounts. Audited sales data are then passed to billing clerk production, sales and stock, inventory systems, general ledger, employee planning, merchandise planning, and bankcard receivables. Inventory sales data are analyzed to identify early trends in order to reorder merchandise before unnecessary stockouts occur, either by repeating the merchandise on-line order and receiving cycles, or by marking down the merchandise through the retail price change system. Merchandise assortment plans are monitored at the department level so that Dillard can better assess vendor, department, and item profitability. This results in the ability to reduce inventory levels while improving the level of service and sales.

This chapter will elaborate on what an ideal RIS should look like. It will not, however, discuss the many procedures for the systematic collection and analysis of data. These topics are best covered in many of the fine books on marketing research, accounting, and management information systems.

THE NEED FOR INFORMATION

Previous chapters have repeatedly demonstrated the need managers of businesses in retailing have for information. Refer back to the model of strategic planning introduced as Exhibit 2.1. As this model clearly shows, information resources are necessary for both the development of a retail strategy and the implementation and control of that strategy.

Because of the critical role that information plays in retail decision making, retailers are spending a fair portion of their funds on retail or management information systems. For example, a recent study showed that retailers on average spend 0.80 percent of sales on information systems; for department stores, this figure was 0.87 percent.[1] Thus, a department store with annual sales of $100 million spends $870,000 on information systems. We believe that high-performance retailers in the 1990s will need to spend at least 1 percent of sales on information systems.

Assume that you are the general manager of a local chain of three apparel stores called Leslie's. You need to develop a new strategy. Could you develop it without information? Perhaps, but you could develop a better strategy by obtaining information about your competitors, consumers in your trading area, the local economic climate, and recent technological developments in retailing. Now place yourself in other decision-making roles—needing to adjust prices, reevaluate your current promotional policy, or borrow additional capital. Making any of these decisions without information would be unwise. In short, whatever retail decisions need to be made can be made better with information.

THE AMOUNT AND TIMELINESS OF INFORMATION

All decision making in retailing can be improved with more information. Unfortunately, however, retail executives cannot usually obtain complete information. Complete or perfect information is extremely expensive and sometimes impossible to obtain—for example, the sales of a competitor. The cost of information is counted not only in terms of direct dollar outlay but also in terms of the time needed to gather and analyze it. This extended period can represent another cost, that of postponing a decision. For example, if you own and operate a Mexican restaurant and you want to open a second restaurant in the same city, you may decide to gather data on the best location. The longer you take to gather the information on the best possible site, the longer you will postpone opening a potentially profitable restaurant. If you wait too long, your competition may open another restaurant or restaurants, which could saturate the proposed market and lower the likelihood that your new restaurant will be profitable. In Exhibit 17.1 we show the

EXHIBIT 17.1

Time Value of Information

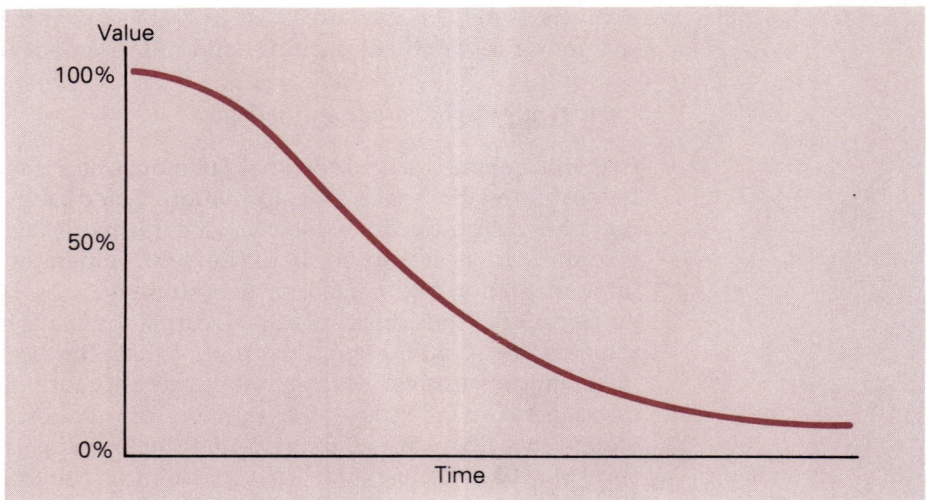

time value of information. Generally, the value of information declines rapidly as its timeliness declines.

SOURCES OF RETAIL INFORMATION

The two major sources of retailing information are internal and external. Both need to be utilized and properly integrated into one retail information system.

INTERNAL INFORMATION

Internal information is found within the retailer's own records. Retailers generate a wide range of useful information in the normal course of their business (operating or income statements, sales records, credit reports, shipping records, purchasing invoices, inventory records, customer charge account records, personnel records, accounts payable and receivable, and past merchandise budgets). By applying certain statistical and analytical procedures, retailers can generate information about a number of different topics.

An example of a source of useful internal information for retailers is shown in Exhibit 17.2. This exhibit shows the actual payroll summary for a 13-week period. A closer look at this exhibit will show that 12 outlets are under budget. This could mean that the budget was wrong, or that service at these stores is poor due to a lack of employees. In either case, this is as serious as being over budget.

EXHIBIT 17.2

Payroll Summary 13 Weeks Ended September 25, 1991

LI/Metro NY

Store	Spvsr	Actual Hours	Budget Hours	Actual Dollars	Budget Dollars	Dollars (Over)/Under Budget	Actual Sales	Act % To Sales	Avg Hrly Rate
Americana	DB	6,120	6,760	31,698	37,047	5,349	547,000	5.79%	5.18
Bayside	DB	2,605	2,600	13,601	13,601	0	119,400	11.39%	5.22
Brooklyn	DB	4,650	4,810	27,103	28,048	945	191,700	14.14%	5.83
Cedarhurst	DB	2,661	2,340	14,780	13,000	(1,780)	130,700	11.31%	5.55
Centereach	SC	3,496	4,030	18,235	20,501	2,266	237,500	7.68%	5.22
Commack	SC	3,776	4,160	20,750	23,829	3,079	277,800	7.47%	5.50
Forest Hills	DB	4,411	4,160	23,974	22,256	(1,718)	264,600	9.06%	5.44
Green Acres	DB	5,569	5,200	28,498	28,402	(96)	350,200	8.14%	5.12
Hicksville	SC	4,039	5,070	23,205	26,390	3,185	294,600	7.88%	5.75
Holbrook	SC	3,822	3,900	23,041	24,248	1,207	261,900	8.80%	6.03
Madison	DB	4,588	4,680	27,364	28,002	638	266,300	10.28%	5.96
Riverhead	SC	2,669	2,860	14,763	16,192	1,429	173,400	8.51%	5.53
Roosevelt	DB	11,472	14,300	67,280	81,868	14,588	1,168,700	5.76%	5.86
Sands	SC	3,628	3,900	19,761	20,722	961	248,300	7.96%	5.45
S. S. M.	SC	5,455	6,760	27,960	34,710	6,750	516,900	5.41%	5.13
Walt Whitman	SC	6,485	8,190	34,711	43,521	8,810	633,900	5.48%	5.35
Wheatley	DB	4,116	3,965	26,771	26,332	(439)	280,200	9.55%	6.50
Total		79,562	87,685	443,495	488,669	45,174	5,963,100	7.44%	5.57

EXTERNAL INFORMATION

External information is obtained from sources outside the firm. This information includes:

1. *Published statistics.* A vast amount of statistical data is published by a variety of public and private sources. The major public source is the federal government; however, private publishers, such as *Sales and Marketing Management's Survey of Buying Power,* are also useful. Exhibit 17.3 provides a more complete listing of these sources.
2. *Standardized retailing information services.* Many research agencies compile data on market trends and consumer behavior and sell the data in standardized form to interested retailers. The *Nielsen Retail Index,* for example, tracks data on individual brands and their price, market share, and promotion. *The Nielsen Retail Index* is based on a sample of 1,600 supermarkets, 750 drugstores, and 150 mass merchandisers.
3. *Publicly circulated research reports.* These usually appear in business journals or are published by trade associations. Many retail trade associations, such as the National Retail Federation, conduct annual studies of operating results that show the average operating performance of the retailers belonging to the trade association. These studies can help the retailer develop standards. Exhibit 17.4 is an example of one of these reports from the American Floorcovering Association.

EXHIBIT 17.3

Sources of Retail Information from Publications

Advertising Age	Home Furnishing Daily
Ad Week	Juvenile Merchandising
American Fabrics and Fashion	Luggage and Leather Goods
Auto Merchandising News	Marketing & Media Decisions
Beverage World	Mart Magazine
Business Week	Merchandising Week
Chain Store Age	Modern Jeweler
Clothing and Textiles Research Journal	Office Products Dealer
Clothes	Office Products News
Discount Merchandiser	Progressive Grocer
Distribution	Retail Advertising Week
Drug Topics	Retail Control
Dun's Business Month	Retail Technology
DYI Retailing	Sales and Marketing Management
Floor Covering Weekly	Sports Merchandiser
Florist	Stores
Fortune	Supermarket Business
Furniture News	Supermarket News
Hardware Age	Visual Merchandising
Hardware Merchandiser	Volume Retail Merchandising
Hardware Retailing	Wall Street Journal
Harvard Business Review	Women's Wear Daily

EXHIBIT 17.4

Composite Income for Floorcovering Retailers and Various Segments

	All Firms	High Profit Firms	Retail Oriented Firms	Contract Oriented Firms	Sales Volume			
					Under $500,000	$500,000 to $1 Mil	$1 Mil to $2 Mil	Over $2 Mil
Number of Firms Reporting	202	47	137	65	17	53	64	68
Typical Sales Volume ($1,000's)	$1,371.9	$1,129.3	$1,167.7	$2,000.9	$394.2	$741.3	$1,378.3	$3,136.7
Income Statement								
Net Sales	100.0%	100.0%	100.0%	100.0%	100.0%	100.0%	100.0%	100.0%
Cost of Goods Sold	69.8	69.9	68.7	72.0	64.3	68.2	70.3	71.9
Gross Margin	30.2	30.1	31.3	28.0	35.7	31.8	29.7	28.1
Operating Expenses:								
Salaries, Wages & Bonuses	14.0	12.5	13.7	13.1	9.1	12.5	13.4	14.1
Payroll Taxes	1.1	0.9	1.2	1.3	0.7	1.1	1.3	1.0
Employee Benefits	0.7	0.8	0.7	0.7	0.8	0.7	0.8	0.8
Advertising & Sales Promotion	2.1	1.7	2.7	1.2	3.1	2.2	1.8	1.9
Samples	0.5	0.7	0.7	0.4	1.1	0.7	0.6	0.3
Utilities & Telephone	1.0	0.9	1.1	0.8	1.8	1.2	1.1	0.8
Rent or Occupancy Expense	2.7	2.1	3.0	2.2	4.9	3.0	2.4	2.3
Depreciation & Amortization	0.9	0.6	0.9	0.8	1.7	1.3	0.9	0.6
Bad Debt Expense	0.1	0.2	0.1	0.3	0.1	0.2	0.2	0.1
All Other Operating Expenses	4.5	4.1	4.8	4.3	6.5	5.8	4.6	4.0
Total Operating Expenses	27.6	24.5	28.9	25.1	29.8	28.7	27.1	25.9
Operating Profit	2.6	5.6	2.4	2.9	5.9	3.1	2.6	2.2
Other Income	0.4	0.3	0.3	0.4	0.0	0.3	0.5	0.3
Interest Expense	0.5	0.2	0.4	0.6	1.3	0.5	0.3	0.6
Other Expenses	0.0	0.0	0.0	0.0	0.0	0.0	0.0	0.0
Profit Before Taxes	2.5	5.7	2.3	2.7	4.6	2.9	2.8	1.9
Income Taxes	0.5	1.1	0.4	0.5	0.3	0.2	0.6	0.3
Profit After Taxes	2.0%	4.6%	1.9%	2.2%	4.3%	2.7%	2.2%	1.6%
Forecasted Sales Increase ('88 versus '87)	11.6%	11.9%	11.7%	11.1%	26.1%	11.4%	13.2%	10.2%

Source: Reprinted with permission of the American Floorcovering Association.

4. *Market research studies.* The retailer can contract for a specialized research study of its markets or customers. A variety of national market research firms such as Walker Research and Burke Research and local market research firms can conduct such studies.

INTEGRATING INTERNAL AND EXTERNAL SOURCES

Retailers have generally done a poor job of integrating internal and external information sources. This is unfortunate because most retail decisions require consideration of both internal and external factors. For example, to make merchandising decisions merely on the basis of past financial performance of different merchandise lines or items is naive. These decisions need to be made by also considering competitive information and consumer information. Coopers & Lybrand is developing a system called WISDOM, which will integrate both internal and external information. "One technology that makes this possible is multi-media databases that can store and integrate sound, color, video, images, text, and data. Thus, in a multi-media environment, information processing will change from data entry to scanning data, from collecting magazine clippings to scanning images, from word-of-mouth to video clips, and from guesses to external databases."[2] The goal of these integrated information systems is for the retailer not only to understand the external environment, but also to influence it, for instance by using information to influence consumer behavior.

THE SCOPE OF A RETAIL INFORMATION SYSTEM

A retail information system should have a broad scope. Exhibit 17.5 shows a model RIS from which you can see that a RIS should have two major subsystems. One subsystem should be reserved for the identification of problem or potential problems confronting the retail enterprise. This subsystem should be designed to continuously compile information on events affecting the retail enterprise. The other subsystem should be dedicated to the solution of recurring or nonrecurring problems that the retailer faces.

An inspection of the RIS in Exhibit 17.5 will show that the problem identification subsystem monitors and scans trends in behavioral, environmental, and operating performance areas. In the behavioral area, three patterns are monitored: consumers, channels, and competitors. In the environmental domain, three environments are scanned: legal, socioeconomic, and technological. Finally, in the area of operating performance, asset, revenue, and expense trends are monitored.

The problem solution subsystem can be utilized to obtain information on recurring or nonrecurring problems in strategic planning, administrative management, and operations management. Strategic planning problems relate to mission, goals, and objectives; opportunity analysis; or contingency

EXHIBIT 17.5

The Retail Information System

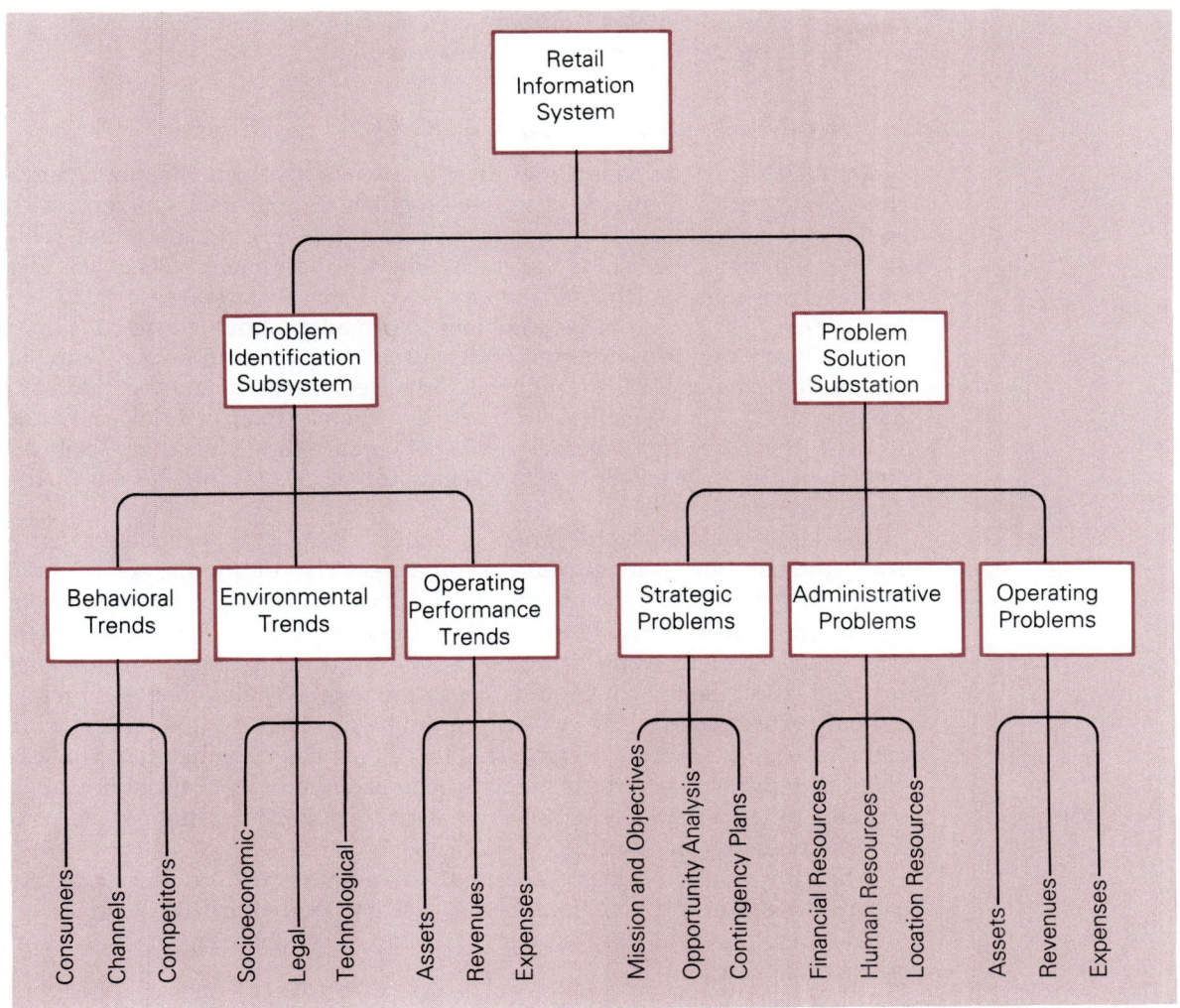

planning. Administrative management problems involve capital structure and generation, organization structure, human resources, or location analysis. Operations management problems are related to either assets or revenue and expense management.

Let us discuss each component of the model RIS, for a general understanding of the information requirements of retail decision makers.

THE PROBLEM IDENTIFICATION SUBSYSTEM

The central goal of the problem identification subsystem is to highlight for the retail executive, on a continuing basis, major problems that the retailer is about to encounter or is presently encountering.

BEHAVIORAL TRENDS: MONITORING CONSUMERS

Most retailers scan the behavior of their customers in a casual manner. Small retailers may simply listen to customer complaints or casually converse with regular customers about their needs, wants, and levels of satisfaction. This can be quite cost effective for the small, single-outlet retailer. Other retailers may read magazines such as *Chain Store Age, Home Furnishings Daily, Stores,* and *Progressive Grocer* in order to obtain information about future consumer trends. Others might use more formal means to foresee the future. Some of these include the analysis of purchases, charge account customers, and consumer panels. Many small service retailers merely look at local economic forecasts. It is important for small retailers to realize that while more sophisticated methods may provide a better monitor, they may not be worth the expense involved.

The larger the retail enterprise, the more likely it is to benefit from a formal and continuous monitoring of consumer behavior trends. As the retail enterprise grows, its decision makers become increasingly removed from regular face-to-face contact with the consumer. Most large-scale retail enterprises would benefit from continual monitoring of consumer behavior patterns. One top executive of a leading department store stated that by monitoring charge card records, the store noticed a heavy influx of mail orders from customers in Texas and Chicago. This led management to research the feasibility of expansion into these markets. The decision maker cannot obtain an accurate understanding of changes in consumer behavior unless the consumer is regularly monitored.

When the retailer decides that a continual monitoring of consumer behavior patterns is warranted, regular market research studies are needed on three crucial consumer behavior variables: purchase probabilities, attitudes, and consumer satisfaction.

Purchase Probabilities Information about purchase probabilities indicates how likely a consumer is to purchase a particular product within the next six months, which allows the retailer to keep apprised of the products it should stock and promote. The Survey Research Center at the University of Michigan reports quarterly on the future plans of American consumers to purchase major durables like automobiles. On the local level, many city newspapers provide continuing consumer surveys of their market areas as a service to advertisers. For example, the *Des Moines Register and Tribune* covers the shopping behavior and purchase intentions not just of Des Moines area consumers but of the entire state. Thus, a Des Moines car dealer, armed with knowledge about the target market's purchase probabilities, can develop special promotions and merchandising programs to attract car-purchasing consumers. The same kind of information is used by home builders and real estate firms to determine home purchase probabilities. One retail consultant has even developed a probabilities model to show that if consumers pay X dollars for an item, they will then purchase a companion product costing Y dollars. For example, if a consumer pays between $75 to $120 for a blazer, she will want to purchase a skirt costing $60 to $80 and shoes costing $41 to $61. This model enables the retailer to identify price ranges and inventory levels given previous purchases.[3]

Consumer Attitudes. Consumer attitudes toward the retailer's store and operation can be a significant determinant of patronage behavior. Changing attitudes can forewarn the retailer of problems on the horizon.

Some retailers find it useful to break consumer attitudes down in terms of the attributes of the store. Using marketing research techniques, they measure the importance of each attribute and how well the store performs. The result might resemble the four quadrants in Exhibit 17.6. The upper-right quadrant characterizes attributes of above-average importance on which the retailer is doing an above-average job. The message here is keep up the good work. The lower-right quadrant addresses attributes that are above average in importance, but for which performance is below average. The message here is get to work to improve performance. In our example the retailer needs to develop action plans to improve the informativeness of advertising and the convenience of store hours and parking. The third quadrant, in the lower left, represents attributes of below-average importance and performance. This area can be left alone. Finally, in the upper-left quadrant, the retailer has above-average performance on attributes that are of below-average importance. Here management should consider deemphasis or reallocating some effort to more important attributes.

Customer Satisfaction. Information about customer satisfaction with both the merchandise and service will indicate whether the customer's visit to the store was a good experience or a bad experience. If there is dissatisfaction with both the merchandise and service, the customer is less likely to choose that store in the future, thus decreasing sales. Retailers have found that customer dissatisfaction is usually the result of discrepancies between:

1. What the consumer actually expected and what the retailer thought the consumer wanted in terms of service and merchandise
2. What the retailer thought the consumer wanted and what the store actually delivered in terms of service and merchandise
3. What the retailer promised in its promotional messages and what it delivered

EXHIBIT 17.6

Importance/Performance Attitudinal Analysis

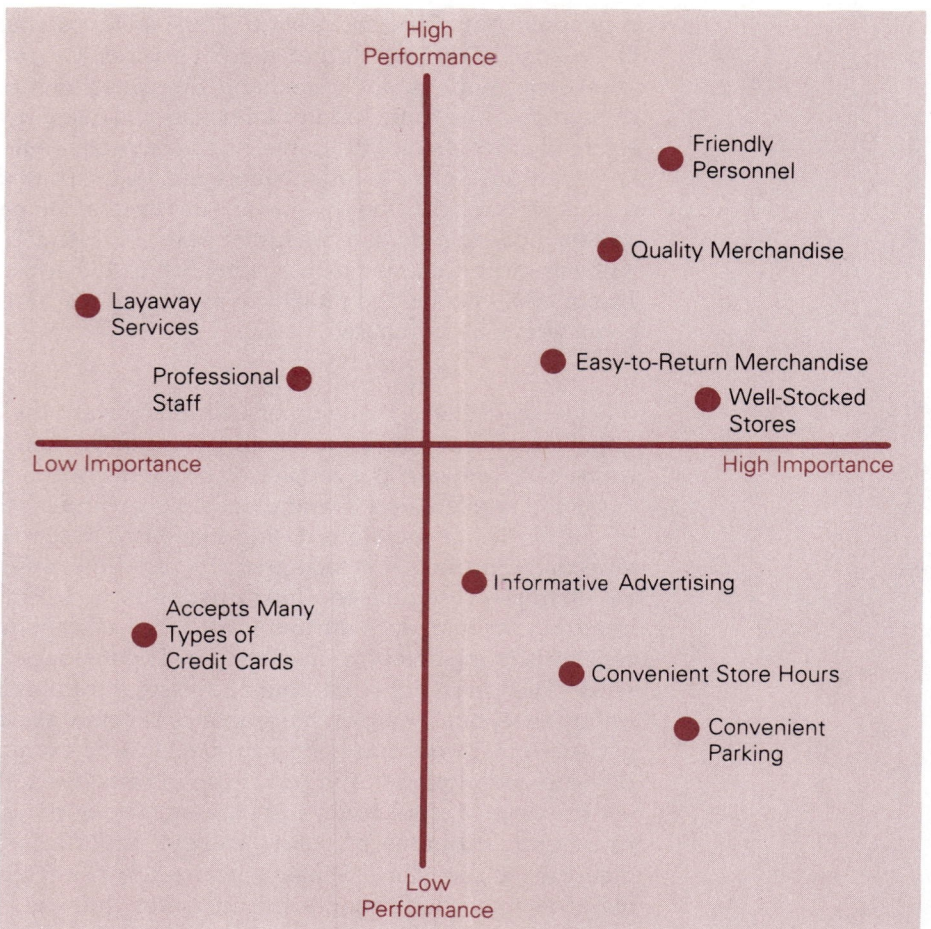

In an effort to eliminate, or at least reduce, the first type of discrepancy, retail managers must spend time on the sales floor, interacting with customers and checking to see whether their expectations of what customers want is correct. When this is not possible, management should at least talk regularly to customer contact personnel. It is important for the retailer's expectations of customers' wants to be shaped by the personnel with hands-on experience.

The second type of discrepancy reflects a lack of commitment to the customer. By making the customer secondary to profits, gross margin, market share, price points, or cost reduction, management tells employees that the expected service or merchandise shouldn't be delivered unless the other objectives are achieved first. Many motels and restaurants ask their patrons to fill out a brief questionnaire on how satisfied they were with their visit or meal. Many auto dealers and furniture retailers send recent customers a letter encouraging them to call a toll-free number if they are dissatisfied with their purchase. These retailers obtain information about customer satisfaction at a relatively low cost and take corrective action if dissatisfaction seems to be rising.

The final type of discrepancy occurs when retailers exaggerate the quality of their merchandise or services, resulting in customers expecting more than the retailers provide. This exaggerated promise could come from the retailers' ads, in-store displays, or salesforce. Again, retail managers can become aware of this type of discrepancy by spending time on the sales floor or conferring with customer contact personnel.

BEHAVIORAL TRENDS: MONITORING THE MARKETING CHANNEL

The retailer is part of a channel system that few retailers can control. Most retailers must adapt to the behavior of other organizations in the channel and, therefore, need to monitor that behavior.

In Chapter 5 we discussed some of the intricacies of adapting to the marketing channel. Here, let us focus on obtaining information about alternative merchandise sources, alternative facilitating agencies, the financial performance of channel partners, and channel conflicts.

Merchandise Sources. If retailers become too dependent on a few sources of merchandise, their ability to bargain and negotiate with the suppliers will be hampered, and the suppliers may even try to dictate how the retailers should conduct their business. The best way to avoid this limitation is to be continually aware of alternative supply sources. Even if retailers have found that Supplier X always has the best merchandise for the lowest price, they should not become complacent and stop looking for a better deal, especially if they rely heavily on foreign manufacturers. Delivery times and currency fluctuations make it extremely important to keep updating information about these sources of merchandise.

Every retailer should have an ongoing system of information collection to alert the retailer to the best deals. For instance, many supermarkets constantly evaluate their wholesale sources of supply against alternatives. This helps them assess the terms of their present suppliers, who will usually be more cooperative if they know the retailer is keeping abreast of the terms being offered by their competitors.

Finally, retailers need to be aware of consumer-led boycotts against certain products. In the recent past, boycotts have been carried out against Coors beer, California grapes, Campbell soups, and *Playboy* magazine.[4] Retailers selling these products need to be aware of these situations, not only to prevent picketing outside the store but also to prepare alternative sources of supply.

Facilitating Agencies. Most retailers rely on a number of facilitating agencies (banks, ad agencies, brokers, and insurance firms). Just as retailers should monitor alternative merchandise supply sources, they should also monitor the availability, strengths, and weaknesses of alternative facilitating agencies. Are there public warehouses or advertising agencies that can do a better job at a more competitive price? Retailers should have access to any information that can help answer such basic questions.

Financial Performance of Channel Partners. As much information as possible should be obtained about the financial performance of channel partners. What is happening to their profit margins, inventory turnover, credit policy, cash flow, labor, and productivity sales growth? Often when a member of a marketing channel begins to have financial problems, it will start to squeeze its channel partners (for instance, cutting credit terms, increasing minimum order size, or raising prices) to increase its performance at the expense of the retailer. By monitoring channel member performance, retailers can have countermoves already developed to minimize any unfair pressure from poorly performing suppliers. Certainly, retailers can help a supplier in need, but they should not allow a supplier to take advantage of them.

One possible approach is to convince suppliers that they should be the retailer's partner. The retailer should seek ways that the supplier and retailer can work together to improve each other's performance. One example is the development of quick-response distribution systems that can be profitable for both the retailer and its channel partners. A quick-response system applies concepts from logistics theory, industrial engineering, and computer science to create an industry pipeline allowing retailers to forecast today what they will sell tomorrow. The early 1990s witnessed an explosion in retailer interest in quick-response distribution systems. We predict by the late 1990s virtually every retailer in the United States will be utilizing a quick-response distribution channel.

To implement quick response, three technologies are required:

1. Point-of-sale scanning and the universal product code (UPC) enable retailers to track merchandise at the item level.
2. Electronic data interchange (EDI) allows partners in the distribution channel to electronically transmit business documents.
3. Shipper container marking (SCM), when used in conjunction with EDI, supports the flow of merchandise through the retailer's distribution center.

However, technology will mean little unless retailers and vendors develop an attitude of cooperation and trust. Their partnership must be based on understanding each other's objectives, opportunities, and constraints.[5] If such a partnership develops, then both partners (retailer and supplier) can improve their financial performance.

Retailers may be able to obtain more information about suppliers than they may realize. Most large suppliers are publicly held corporations, and any stockholder of record can receive annual and quarterly financial statements. Also, any publicly held corporation must file a 10K report with the Securities

ILLUSTRATION 17.1

Point-of-sale scanners that read UPC codes have combined with electronic cash register systems to revolutionize retailing, greatly enhancing the efficiency of retailers by providing more immediate information on merchandise movement.

and Exchange Commission (SEC). The 10K report, which is a matter of public record, is available through the SEC or directly from the reporting company. The 10K report contains a wealth of financial information that is typically not provided in the standard annual report to stockholders, and retailers do not have to hold stock in a supplier to obtain this information. Disclosure, Inc., will provide a copy of any corporation's 10K or annual report at a modest cost. Investors Management Service, based in Denver, can provide similar data on computer laser disc for more than 10,000 publicly held companies in the United States.

Channel Conflict. The final area of channel behavior that should be monitored is the level of conflict. For every significant channel interface, retailers should identify potential sources of conflict. Specifically, they must regularly ask themselves the following questions: To what extent do the channel partners have goals that are not compatible with ours? To what extent does each channel partner try to unduly control aspects of our business? To what extent do channel partners perceive significant events in the economic, social, legal, and technological environments differently than we do? It is better to anticipate potential conflict than to learn about it after the conflict has become manifest and is more difficult to resolve. Some manufacturers, such as Ford Motor Company, invite a group of retail dealers to sit on a Dealer Council, which serves as a source of information to inform the manufacturer of the concerns of its retailers. In addition, sitting on such a council can provide the retailer with useful information about the manufacturer's perspective and view.

BEHAVIORAL TRENDS: MONITORING COMPETITORS

Almost all retail executives will tell you that they are more interested in what their competitors are doing than in how channel partners or consumers are behaving, but all three behaviors are equally important.

All executives have some means of monitoring competitors' activities. At the simplest level, this may consist of reading or listening to competitors' ads and shopping their stores personally to inspect merchandise, prices, displays, and store decor. Many decades ago James Cash Penney, the founder of JC Penney, was well known for visiting competitors' stores, Sam Walton visited Wal-Mart's competitors, and today Wal-Mart senior executives visit these stores. More sophisticated monitoring can include systematic collection and analysis of data on all relevant aspects of competitor market shares and trading areas.

Market Saturation. The extent to which a particular trading area is populated with retailers in a particular line of trade is called **market saturation.** One measure of market saturation is the **index of retail saturation.**[6] The index is found by multiplying the number of households in the market area by the average household retail expenditures per line of trade, then dividing that figure by the square feet of retail selling space for the line of trade. This index was discussed in Chapter 10.

The IRS is a good indicator of potential profits in a particular market area. The higher the IRS, the greater the profit potential. When the IRS is low in comparison with the product line in other market areas, the market is saturated with retail space and competitors compete more aggressively for consumer expenditures.

Pricing. The retailer should determine a bundle of goods on which it desires to be most competitive. For example, a grocery store may identify 150 items out of the 6,000 it stocks on which it wants to be visibly price competitive. Once the bundle has been established, the retailer should compute price indexes that show its price for each item compared to the price each of its major competitors is charging. These indexes should be constructed regularly, probably weekly or monthly. Trends in these price indexes will vividly demonstrate the extent to which the retailer is price competitive.

Merchandise Mixes. How strong is the retailer's assortment of merchandise in relation to key competitors? Is it deeper, wider, and of a higher quality? How has it changed over time? In short, are the retailer's assortments of merchandise competitive? Only ongoing data collection can provide a meaningful answer to this important question. Retailers should regularly shop competing retailers for the answers.

Promotion. There are two fundamental questions retailers will want their information system to answer regarding competitors' promotional efforts.

First, how much are competitors spending on promotion? Second, what is the quality of competitors' promotional activities?

Neither question is easily or inexpensively answered. A detailed analysis of competitors' advertising, sales promotion activities, publicity efforts, and personal selling would be necessary to answer these questions completely. Because such a task would be a burden, most retailers collect data on a regular basis only on competitors' advertising, and in some cases on their sales promotion activities. For example, many apparel retailers have a file of competitors' newspaper advertising. Competitors' ads are clipped daily and placed in this file and then once a month the intensity and quality of competitors' advertising is analyzed. It is now possible to scan these advertisements into a microcomputer, store them on a laser disc, and retrieve them instantly for careful study. This simple process, whether done with a computer or in a more conventional fashion, allows the retailer to spot any significant deterioration in its advertising in relation to competitors.

Market Share. What are the respective market shares of the retailer and its competitors, and how are these changing? One indicator of future profit performance is market share. If retailers observe their market share slipping, that is a warning of future profitability problems.

Retailers that sell a wide range of merchandise should ideally obtain market share data by merchandise line. Rather than only comparing competitors' market shares as a whole, a department store manager may find it most useful to have market share data on particular departments: household furnishings, menswear, women's apparel, children's clothes, sporting goods, jewelry, toys, and lawn and garden equipment. However, the collection of such information is extremely expensive, and the cost must be carefully compared to the value.

Trading Area. Is the retailer's trading area stable, shrinking, or expanding? A shrinking trading area is a bad omen; an expanding one is good. Market saturation, competitive pricing, competitive merchandise assortments, and competitive promotional strength all affect trading area size. The less competitive the retailer's pricing, merchandise assortment, and promotion, the more its trading area will shrink. The more saturated the market, the more the trading area will shrink.

It is relatively easy to obtain information about the trading area. With the addresses of store patrons, the retailer can easily construct a trading area map. One owner/manager of a record store continually held contests in which patrons of the store filled out entry blanks with their names and addresses to qualify for a weekly drawing of a free album. At the end of each month, the owner could plot on a map where patrons came from, enabling him to notice quickly any change in the size or nature of his trading area.

One type of information system component that is increasing in popularity is the geographic information system (GIS). GIS allows one to construct computerized maps of geographic areas that reveal a wealth of information. Some of the more sophisticated systems are linked to satellite data, U.S. Census data, and the firms' own internal databases. For example, a GIS when used for a chain store could take satellite pictures of a city and identify all the stores in the chain and their competitors. In addition, census data or other commercially available data could show the population characteristics surrounding each store. Finally, the financial and merchandising performance of each store could be integrated into the map. The possibilities are endless since satellite photos cold be taken several times a day—making it possible to count the number of cars in the parking lots of competitor stores over time and thus estimate sales. Some of the firms providing GIS products are: Intergraph Corporation of Huntsville, Alabama; Geo Vision with offices in North America, Europe, Asia, and Australia; ESRI of Redlands, California; TYDAC Technologies Corp. of Arlington, Virginia; and UGC Consulting of Englewood, Colorado.

ENVIRONMENTAL TRENDS: MONITORING THE SOCIOECONOMIC ENVIRONMENT

Events in the socioeconomic environment that should be monitored can be categorized into demographic, psychographic, and economic trends.

Major demographic trends that can be particularly useful to monitor are changing household size, educational levels, age distribution of household members, population growth, and geographic migration. Psychographic trends that yield insights are changes in leisure time activities, work habits, and religious, family, and cultural values. Economic trends that should be followed are changes in disposable personal income, household expenditure patterns, discretionary income, and the use of credit.

Highly personalized, continuous data on demographic, psychographic, and economic trends is not cheap. National data are readily available, but they tell retailers little about the socioeconomic dynamics of their trading area. Data on a particular area may be available from a local newspaper; see Retailing in Action 17.1 for an example. Such surveys collect data on a large number of demographic, economic, and in some cases psychographic variables. If the retailer advertises in the newspaper conducting the survey, much of the data can be obtained free or at modest cost.

The United States Census Bureau can provide a wealth of demographic data on census tracts. However, these data are collected only once every 10 years and are quickly dated. Trade associations and publications like *Sales and Marketing Management* publish some of these data on an annual basis. Occasionally, local governments or universities will conduct special surveys to obtain current demographic data. Finally, demographic supply houses such as National Planning Data Corporation and Urban Decision Systems provide annual updated estimates of demographics for areas as small as a neighborhood and as large as a county or state.

RETAILING IN ACTION

17.1 Retailers Should Make Use of Newspaper Research Staffs

Most large-city newspapers provide their advertisers with various types of market research to assist with their advertising strategies. Two such types of research are shown below. The first study shows demographic data for a retail chain's downtown Los Angeles store, as well as the circulation data for the newspaper in reaching this market.

The second study shows the percentage of Los Angeles households that visited various regional shopping centers within the last 30 days and a comparison with an earlier study. The study also shows a comparison of one shopping center's customer profile with the total Los Angeles market.

First Study
Demographic data for: STORE #1—DOWNTOWN

Housing Tenure			*Condominiums*	
Own	23.4%		Percent of total dwelling units	1.2%
Rent (including no cash rent)	76.6			
Total Occupied Units	100.0%		*Household Type*	
			1 person household	27.9%
Rent			2 or more persons: family	66.6
No cash rent	1.3%		2 or more persons: non-family	5.5
Less than $200	69.1		Total Occupied Dwelling Units	100.0%
$200–$299	23.2			
$300–$399	4.9		*Presence of Children*	
$400–$499	1.0		Have children under 18	45.1%
$500 or more	.5		No children under 18	54.9
Total Specified Renter Occupied Dwelling Units	100.0%		Total Occupied Dwelling Units	100.0%
			Marital Status of Persons Age 15 and Over	
Median Rent	$143		Married	42.3%
			Single	37.4
Number of Units at Address			Widowed, divorced, separated	20.3
1	54.5%		Total	100.0%
2–9	21.6			
10 or more	23.7		*Sex of Population*	
Mobile home	.2		Male	50.3%
Total Dwelling Units	100.0%		Female	49.7
			Total	100.0%

First Study
Data for: **STORE #1—DOWNTOWN**   Los Angeles Times

Current Population	Current Occupied Dwelling Units	Circulation Distribution		Percent Coverage	
		Weekday	Sunday	Weekday	Sunday
777,661	233,136	47,774	37,722	21.15%	16.9%

Age of Population		*Education—Persons Age 25 and Over*		*Household Income*	
Under 6	12.3%			Under $15,000	68.9%
6-13	13.6	Less than 4 years		$15,000-$19,999	12.4
14-17	6.9	high school	61.3%	$20,000-$24,999	7.6
18-24	16.0	4 years high school	20.2	$25,000-$34,999	6.9
25-34	17.7	1-3 years college	11.0	$35,000-$49,999	3.0
35-44	10.1	4+ years college	7.5	$50,000-$74,999	.8
45-54	7.9	Total	100.0%	$75,000 and over	.4
55-64	6.7				
65 and over	8.8	Median School		Total	100.0%
Total	100.0%	Years Completed	9.8	Median Household Income	$10,889
Median Age	25.7	*Employment—Employed Persons Age 16 and Over*			
Race of Population		Professional specialty	5.1%	*Home Value*	
White	40.5%	Exec, Administrator, Mgr	4.7	Under $50,000	51.1%
Black	19.4	Tech, Sales; Adm support	22.9	$50,000-$79,999	33.9
Asian-Pacific Islander	7.4	Precision prod, Craft/Repair	12.3	$80,000-$99,999	8.2
All Other	32.7	Operators, Laborers	36.2	$100,000-$149,999	5.1
Total	100.0%	All Other	18.8	$150,000-$199,999	1.1
(Spanish/Hispanic origin)	61.5%	Total	100.0%	$200,000 and over	.6
				Total Specified Owner Occupied Dwelling Units	100.0%
				Median Home Value	$48,951

ENVIRONMENTAL TRENDS: MONITORING THE LEGAL ENVIRONMENT

Although it is disquieting to most retailers, the legal environment is always in a state of flux. To avoid costly legal errors, the RIS should be designed to keep the retailer apprised of changes in the legal environment. The larger the retail enterprise, the higher priority this area should receive.

No retail manager or store owner can be expected to monitor all the relevant changes in the legal environment. Fortunately, all the major retail trade associations devote a fair amount of space in their publications to the

Second Study
Percent of Los Angeles Households Shopping Specified Regional Shopping Centers in the Last 30 Days

	Current			Two Years Ago		
	Rank	Percent of Households	Number of Households	Rank	Percent of Households	Number of Households
South Coast Plaza	1	8.8%	311,572	1	7.9%	273,146
Glendale Galleria	2	8.7	308,032	7	5.5	190,165
Del Amo Fashion Center	3	8.2	290,329	2	7.0	242,028
Los Cerritos Center	4	5.9	208,895	4	6.0	207,452
Fox Hills Mall	5	5.5	194,733	8	4.6	159,047
Westminster Mall	5	5.5	194,733	4	6.0	207,452
Beverly Center	7	5.4	191,192	32	2.0	69,151
Lakewood Center Mall	8	5.1	180,570	3	6.3	217,825
Northridge Fashion Center	9	4.8	169,949	6	5.7	197,080
Santa Monica Place	10	4.7	166,408	10	4.4	155,132
Brea Mall	11	4.4	155,786	14	3.6	124,471
Santa Anita Fashion Park	12	4.1	145,164	9	4.5	155,589
Puente Hills Mall	13	3.7	131,002	12	3.9	134,844
Topanga Plaza	14	3.2	113,299	13	3.8	131,386
West Covina Fashion Plaza	15	3.0	106,218	11	4.0	138,302
Buena Park Mall	16	2.8	99,137	17	3.2	110,641
Sherman Oaks Galleria	17	2.7	95,596	15	3.3	114,099
Century City Shopping Center	17	2.7	95,596	23	2.6	89,896
Fashion Island	19	2.5	88,515	21	2.7	93,354
Huntington Center	19	2.5	88,515	17	3.2	110,641
Hawthorne Plaza	19	2.5	88,515	23	2.6	89,896
Eagle Rock Plaza	22	2.2	77,893	*	*	*
Stonewood Shopping Center	23	2.1	74,353	25	2.5	86,438
Laguna Hills Mall	24	2.0	70,812	27	2.4	82,981
Mission Viejo Mall	24	2.0	70,812	29	2.3	79,523

*Less than 2.0%.

retail implications of pending legislation at both federal and state levels. Many large retail enterprises even have a legal staff to keep top management aware of changes in the legal environment. Sears, JCPenney, Dayton Hudson, and McDonald's all have sizeable legal staffs.

The legal area of most immediate practical concern to the retailer is tax

Second Study
Del Amo Fashion Center
Percent Distribution of All Los Angeles Households and Los Angeles Households Shopping Del Amo Fashion Center in the Last 30 Days by Selected Demographics

	All Los Angeles Households	Households Shopping Del Amo Fashion Center
Annual Household Income		
$50,000 or more	17.5%*	22.5%**
$35,000–$49,999	18.8	23.2
$25,000–$34,999	18.9	24.5
$20,000–$24,999	12.4	10.4
$15,000–$19,999	10.6	6.9
Under $15,000	21.8	12.5
Total	100.0%	100.0%
(Base)***	(4,956)	(432)
Median income	$27,721	$33,208
Age, Household Head		
Under 30	20.3%	22.1%
30–39	25.5	28.5
40–49	18.6	20.5
50–64	21.8	18.8
65 or over	13.8	10.1
Total	100.0%	100.0%
(Base)***	(5,776)	(474)
Median age	42.3	39.8
Education, Household Head		
College graduate or more	32.7%	39.8%
Some college	28.0	29.7
High school graduate	27.4	25.9
Some high school or less	11.9	4.6
Total	100.0%	100.0%
(Base)***	(5,790)	(475)

law. Changes in tax laws generally have a significant effect on retail decisions. For example, a favorable change in the investment tax credit can make store remodeling or expansion attractive. Tax laws can influence decisions about inventory valuation methods, executive compensation plans, or recording of credit sales. The large public accounting firms such as Price Waterhouse and Ernst and Young keep retailers constantly updated on changing tax laws and the impact on retailing.

> **Second Study—Continued**
> **Del Amo Fashion Center**
> **Percent Distribution of All Los Angeles Households and Los Angeles Households Shopping Del Amo Fashion Center in the Last 30 Days by Selected Demographics**
>
> | | All Los Angeles Households | Households Shopping Del Amo Fashion Center |
> |---|---|---|
> | *Occupation, Household Head* | | |
> | Professional/technical | 19.8% | 24.9% |
> | Manager/official/proprietor | 20.1 | 21.1 |
> | Clerical/sales | 13.6 | 15.1 |
> | Craftsman/foreman/operative | 13.7 | 12.5 |
> | Retired | 16.7 | 12.9 |
> | All others | 16.1 | 13.5 |
> | Total | 100.0% | 100.0% |
> | (Base)*** | (5,674) | (465) |
>
> *Example: 17.5% of all Los Angeles households have an annual household income of $50,000 or more.
> **Example: 22.5% of the Los Angeles households shopping Del Amo Fashion Center in the last 30 days have an annual income of $50,000 or more.
> ***Excludes refused/don't know responses.
>
> Source: Los Angeles Times Marketing Research Department, estimates based on data supplied by various governmental agencies, Southern California Association of Governments. Reprinted with permission of the Los Angeles Times.

Retail corporations that are publicly held should also stay informed of the regulations of the Securities and Exchange Commission (SEC) and the accounting standards established by the Financial Accounting Standards Board (FASB). All publicly held retailers must abide by the SEC guidelines in reporting to stockholders. The FASB develops the generally accepted accounting principles (GAAP). These are not legal requirements, but retailers that want their financial statements to receive an unqualified opinion by a certified external auditor will follow GAAP.

ENVIRONMENTAL TRENDS: MONITORING THE TECHNOLOGICAL ENVIRONMENT

Technology is the application of science to develop new methods of doing things. It is always at work, slowly but continually changing the nature and scope of retailing.

The retailer can monitor the technological environment at the basic science stage or the applied science stage. In either case, the retailer will want to monitor technology as related to four areas of innovation: management techniques, merchandising techniques, equipment and fixtures, and construction and building.

A retailer desiring to monitor any of the four areas at the basic science stage could read academic journals in the fields of management, marketing, engineering, computer science, or architecture. For example, to monitor management and merchandising at the basic science level, the retailer might read such journals as the *Journal of Finance, Journal of Retailing, Journal of Marketing,* or *Administrative Science Quarterly.* Unfortunately, most topics and concepts discussed in academic business journals are a long way from being applied, and many practical problems of implementation need to be worked out. For example, the use of experimental designs to test the effectiveness of promotional displays was proposed in the *Journal of Marketing Research* in the 1960s and is just now receiving widespread acceptance by retailers.

Generally, it is more beneficial for the retail executive to monitor technology at the applied level. To do this most effectively, executives should regularly attend trade shows and read trade-related publications.

Rosenbloom and Tripuraneni found that technology was fourth behind competition, consumer behavior, and the economy (and ahead of government regulation) in environmental factors monitored by retailers' strategic planning committees. The authors concluded that "perhaps the very rapid developments in recent years in POS systems, computerized billing, and inventory control, as well as the dramatic changes in consumer electronics products, have made a strong impression on retailers."[7] Keeping up with technology can make the difference between achieving and not achieving high-performance results.

OPERATING PERFORMANCE TRENDS: MONITORING ASSETS

The accounting system should be part of the RIS, since it can be an important source of information about operating performance trends.[8]

A RIS should have the capability to monitor the retailer's assets continually. At the most basic level, a retailer may design the RIS to construct a balance sheet at the end of each operating period (typically a month or a quarter) for assessing the magnitude and composition of its assets. By comparing the current balance sheet to prior ones, retailers can assess the growth of their asset base and changes in the composition of their assets. More detailed analysis of period-to-period balance sheets and the general ledgers used to construct them will provide information about the sources and uses of capital. The balance sheet is one of the most useful pieces of information available to retailers.

A RIS can also provide a merchandise management report as shown in Exhibit 17.7. This report shows the total inventory available at retail, at cost, and in units.

EXHIBIT 17.7

A Merchandise Management Report

King Stores	** Merchandise Management Report **
Merchandise Group 81–87 All Stores	Week From 02/06/91
Beginning Inventory at Retail	$973,683,744.23
Purchases at Retail	$192,845,605.70
Vendor Returns at Retail	$.00
Net Sales at Retail	$32,700.00
Customer Returns at Retail	$.00
Authorized Point of Sale Markdowns at Retail	$.00
Unauthorized Point of Sale Markdowns at Retail	$1,500.00
General Markdowns at Retail	$560,210.60
Price Adjustments at Retail	$.00
Distributions and Transfers at Retail	$.00
Unit Adjustments at Retail	$329,400.00
Planned Shrinkage at Retail (Memo)	$98.10
Ending Inventory at Retail	$1,166,264,339.33
Beginning Inventory at Cost	$439,874,795.48
Purchases at Cost	$92,584,883.70
Vendor Returns at Cost	$.00
Freight and Duty at Cost	$303,000.00
Net Sales at Cost	$14,534.00
Customer Returns at Cost	$.00
Authorized Point of Sale Markdowns at Cost	$.00
Unauthorized Point of Sale Markdowns at Cost	$666.00
General Markdowns at Cost	$351,243.73
Vendor Discounts and Allowances at Cost	$.00
Price Adjustments at Cost	$58,907.93
Distributions and Transfers at Cost	$.00
Unit Adjustments at Cost	$146,400.00
Planned Shrinkage at Cost (Memo)	$43.60
Ending Inventory at Cost	$532,298,543.38
Beginning Inventory in Units	2,952,012
Purchases in Units	7,557,434
Vendor Returns in Units	0
Net Sales in Units	760
Customer Returns in Units	0
Authorized Pos Markdowns in Units (Memo)	0
Unauthorized Pos Markdowns in Units (Memo)	300
Distributions and Transfers in Units	0
Unit Adjustments in Units	7,320
Planned Shrinkage in Units (Memo)	0
Ending Inventory in Units	516,006

One service retailer that does an excellent job of using a RIS to monitor its assets is Avis. Avis employs what it calls a rate-shoppers' guide. The specifics are secret, but, in general, the Wizard system (Avis' reservation system) allows agents to quote up-to-the-minute prices that change with the availability of the fleet at a particular location. If the cars aren't moving, a lower price will kick in. If the fleet is tight, the price stays up. Avis, the first rental car company to unveil a computerized reservation system in 1972, is now using the power of its RIS much more creatively.[9]

Performance Standards. Using basic balance sheet data, the retail analyst can compute financial ratios to evaluate its **liquidity,** the firm's ability to meet its current payment obligations. Liquidity is important to the retailer because it protects the company from economic downturns and potential insolvency and provides the needed flexibility to capitalize on unexpected merchandising opportunities.

Financial analysts generally use three financial ratios to evaluate liquidity: the current ratio, the quick ratio, and the acid-test ratio. The most popular is the **current ratio** which measures current assets to current liabilities. This ratio is the basic measurement of a retailer's solvency. Conventional wisdom suggests that retailers should maintain a current ratio of approximately 2.0. A second ratio is called the **quick ratio** and is computed as current assets, less inventory, divided by current liabilities. The quick ratio is a more stringent measure of a firm's ability to repay its current debt. Conventional wisdom suggests that retailers should maintain a quick ratio of 1.0. The third and final ratio, the **acid-test ratio,** is cash and its equivalent divided by current liabilities. Analysts contend that a retailer's cash should equal 15 to 20 percent of current liabilities.

In any RIS, retailers must first have some target level for each of these three ratios. That is, they must have a desired level of liquidity, probably based on industry norms. Generally, the goal reflects a desired range for the financial ratio; for instance, the target current ratio may be 1.9 to 2.1. Second, retailers must compare actual performance to targeted performance and note any significant deviation from the target. Third, significant deviations from targeted performance should be investigated. This third step takes us into the problem solution subsystem of the RIS.

Exhibit 17.8 gives a control chart for the current ratio of King Bing's Furniture Sales. The dashed lines show that management wants the current ratio to fall between 1.9 and 2.1. Between 1987 and 1991, it fell within this range, but, in 1992, it fell below 1.9. Management needs to investigate the cause of this significant drop in liquidity. A careful investigation of the possible causes might reveal that credit customers have significantly slowed their rate of payment on installment sales.

Retailers can also use data from the balance sheet, in conjunction with other data, to measure how well they are utilizing their assets. Some popular measures are:

EXHIBIT 17.8

Control Chart for Current Ratio for King Bing Furniture Sales

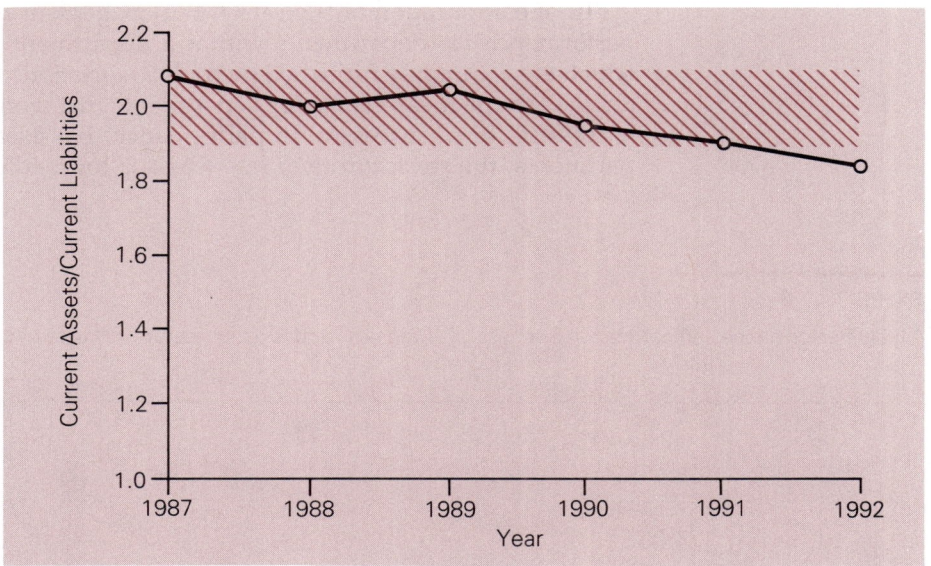

1. *Sales per dollar invested in inventory* (total dollar sales divided by average inventory investment). This is a measure of inventory turnover that shows how productive the retailer's investment in inventory has been. A high rate of turnover is better than a low one if everything else is held constant.
2. *Sales per square feet of selling space* (total dollar sales divided by square feet of selling space). This is a measure of space productivity. The higher its value, the more productively the retailer is using its selling space.
3. *Sales per dollar invested in assets* (total dollar sales divided by total dollars invested in assets). This is a basic measure of asset productivity. It shows how much the retailer has generated in sales for each dollar invested.
4. *Credit sales per dollar invested in accounts receivable* (total dollar credit sales divided by average accounts receivable). This measure shows how quickly retailers are collecting from customers who purchase on credit. The larger the measure, the better.

For each of these measures, the retailers should develop standards of performance. After these performance measures have been established, one method of control is the **Steering Marketing Control Model (STEMCOM)**.[10] STEMCOM predicts a final outcome and then monitors progress toward that outcome. The model is open looped, which means that the identification of factors that cause the process to go out of control and the necessary corrective action are external to the model. STEMCOM alerts managers to deviations from some specified level of performance. Management must then determine the cause of the deviation and whether or not corrective action is necessary.

In one application of STEMCOM, management specified 12 indicators of performance for departments within a department store. These indicators, which are commonly furnished by trade associations, are listed in Exhibit 17.9 along with the mean scores for departments that were successful, moderately successful, or unsuccessful in performance. For example, for successful departments, the stock turnover rate was 4.2; for medium performance depart-

EXHIBIT 17.9

Mean Performance Indicators for Successful, Medium, and Unsuccessful Indicators in a Retail Department Store

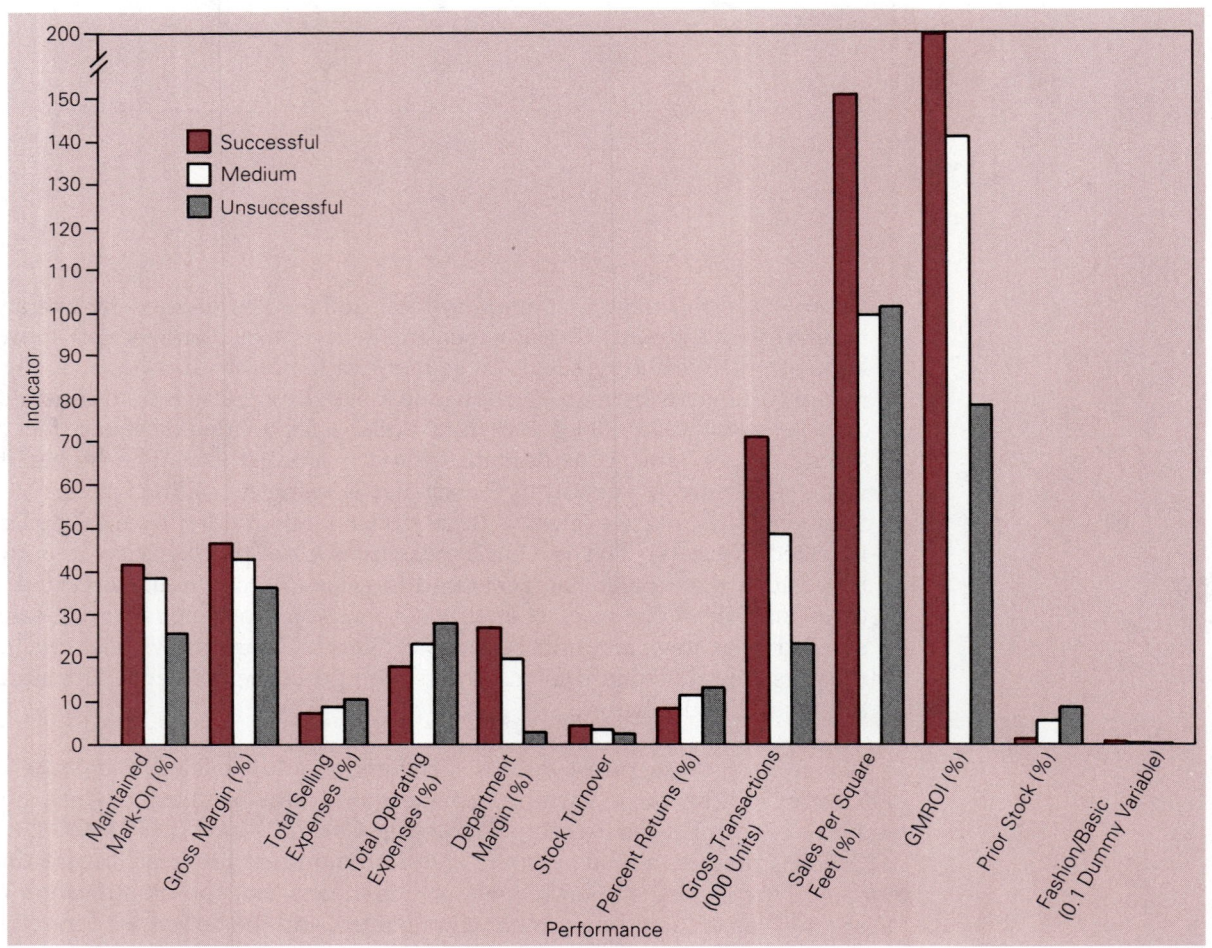

SOURCE: Subhash Sharma and Dale D. Achabal, "STEMCO: An Analytical Model for Marketing Control," *Journal of Marketing,* (Spring 1982), pp. 104–113. (Reprinted with AMA permission.)

ments, the rate was 3.2; and for unsuccessful departments, the rate was 2.7. These indicators were combined into a composite performance index. For successful departments, the composite index value ranged from 1 to 2. Management could monitor the performance of a given department and if the performance index dropped below 1, examine why the deviation occurred and what, if any, corrective action was necessary.

The major objective of STEMCOM is to indicate to management whether actual performance has deviated from target performance. A control chart similar to those used in quality control can be developed (see Exhibit 17.10). The standard control chart consists of a central line indicating the average or target performance and other lines indicating upper and lower control limits. An actual performance index is plotted onto the control chart. If the performance lies within the control limits established, performance is said to be in control. Where the performance index falls outside the control limits, management is alerted that corrective action may be needed. The control chart can also be used to observe trends in the actual performance index. A downward trend would indicate a deterioration in performance over time, and management may decide to take corrective action before performance falls below an acceptable level.

Auditing Assets. Imagine yourself as a retail executive making decisions based on accounting information. You would want to be sure that you have valid information, especially if you were a top executive for a large chain, since you would not be able to visit each store regularly. You would have to rely totally on accounting data to keep you informed of what was happening

EXHIBIT 17.10

Control Chart for STEMCOM (1976-1979)

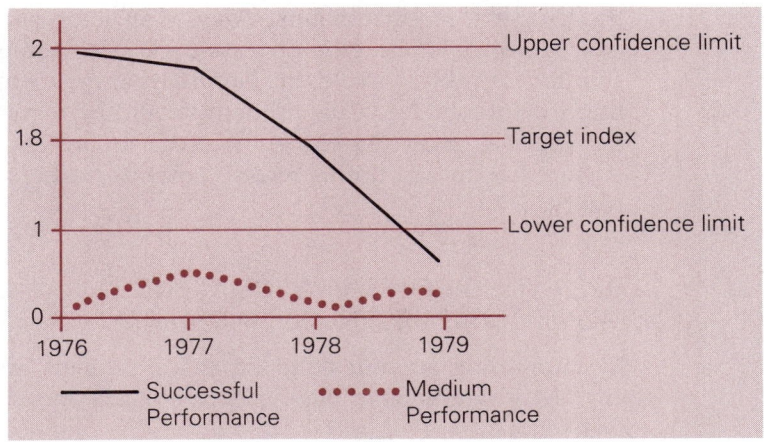

Source: Subhash Sharma and Dale D. Achabal, "STEMCOM: An Analytical Model for Marketing Control," *Journal of Marketing* (Spring 1982): 104-13. (Reprinted with AMA permission.)

at each store. If the balance sheet tells you that there is $4 million in inventory on hand, how do you know this is true? Unless you count the inventory yourself, you probably don't.

For these reasons, the retailer should regularly obtain an independent audit of its accounting records and system to ensure their validity. In fact, the SEC requires an independent audit of the annual financial statements to stockholders of publicly held corporations.

Retailers would also be well advised to implement an ongoing internal audit, to ensure continual protection of its assets. The internal audit department could regularly answer such questions as:

- Are merchandise shipments made only on the basis of approved instructions?
- Are stringent physical controls and paperwork procedures exercised over in-store transfers?
- Are departmental inventory records maintained in total and on an individual store basis?
- Are merchandise units that show erratic or unusually high shrinkage policed on an interim basis?
- Are customer refunds properly approved and controlled?
- Are sales drawers locked while a cashier is on break?
- Does electronic surveillance equipment receive a daily check?
- Are physical inventories of store fixtures and equipment taken periodically, with discrepancies reported to management?[11]

Retail managers should also be concerned with some nonmerchandising questions. For example, what is the market value of the property purchased in 1948 for our downtown store? Is it the $140,500 carried on the books, or is the property worth millions today? Can it be used to finance other retail operations via some type of lease-back sales agreement? What can the accounts receivables be sold for? Naturally, these are only a few of the questions that the internal audit department should be regularly answering. In short, the internal audit department's job is to protect the retailer's assets and ensure that the accounting records and information derived from them reflect reality.

OPERATING PERFORMANCE TRENDS: MONITORING REVENUES AND EXPENSES

By monitoring revenues and expenses, retailers are able to readily identify any significant gaps in planned profit levels and develop appropriate remedial actions.

Income Statement. All the revenue and expense data about which the retailer needs to be kept informed can be presented in a detailed income statement, which was discussed in Chapter 7. Thus, at the most fundamental level of analysis, retailers will want to design their RIS to regularly generate a detailed income statement.

Since the dollars on a retailer's income statement can change from period to period, it is best to have the income statement constructed in both dollars and percentiles (in which sales are equal to 100 percent). The percentile income statement facilitates the comparison of operating periods over time. Thus, a retail executive can quickly tell whether advertising, utilities, wages, or any expense is behaving differently in relation to sales than it has historically.

The percentile income statement allows a retailer to apply standards of performance. If the retailer develops a standard income statement in which each expense is defined as a percentage of sales, actual expenses can then be compared to the standard in order to gauge performance and identify problem areas. Many retail trade associations conduct annual studies of operating results, which show the average operating performance of member retailers. These studies can help the retailer develop standards.

It is important that retailers give careful consideration to the frequency with which their RIS generates income statement data. The income statement should be prepared often enough to allow management to take corrective action if an expense is out of control or if revenues are below standard. An annual income statement will not suffice; monthly or bimonthly statements are better. If you were a retail manager, you would not want to find out about a problem months after it occurred; at that point it may be too late.

Segmental Reporting. In most cases, it is advantageous for retailers to develop individual income statements for separate segments of the enterprise. For example, if a retailer's enterprise consists of a chain of 48 drugstores, it would be beneficial to prepare a separate income statement for each drugstore and a composite income statement for all 48. This allows performance problems to be pinpointed more easily. Another method of segmental reporting is to look at which divisions of a large retail corporation accounted for what percentage of sales, operating profits, assets utilized, and capital expenditures. Exhibit 17.11 shows the performance of various segments of the Dayton Hudson Corporation for a recent year.

Segmental reporting can also be implemented by merchandise line. A chain of home-improvement centers may wish to analyze separately the profit performance of its lumber products, lawn and garden products, small tools and appliances, and home decorating and fixtures. It may construct an income statement for each category, assigning expenses to each.

Sears has a system that allows it to accurately measure the performance of each merchandise group. In the late 1980s, the Sears system was refined and updated so the costs such as warehousing, distribution, and employee health costs could be traced to each merchandise group. This new system revealed that many items Sears was selling were not as profitable as the firm had believed.[12] Many other large chain retailers are also beginning to employ segmental reporting and planning as part of their RIS.

EXHIBIT 17.11

Performance Profiles by Segments of Dayton Hudson (1990)

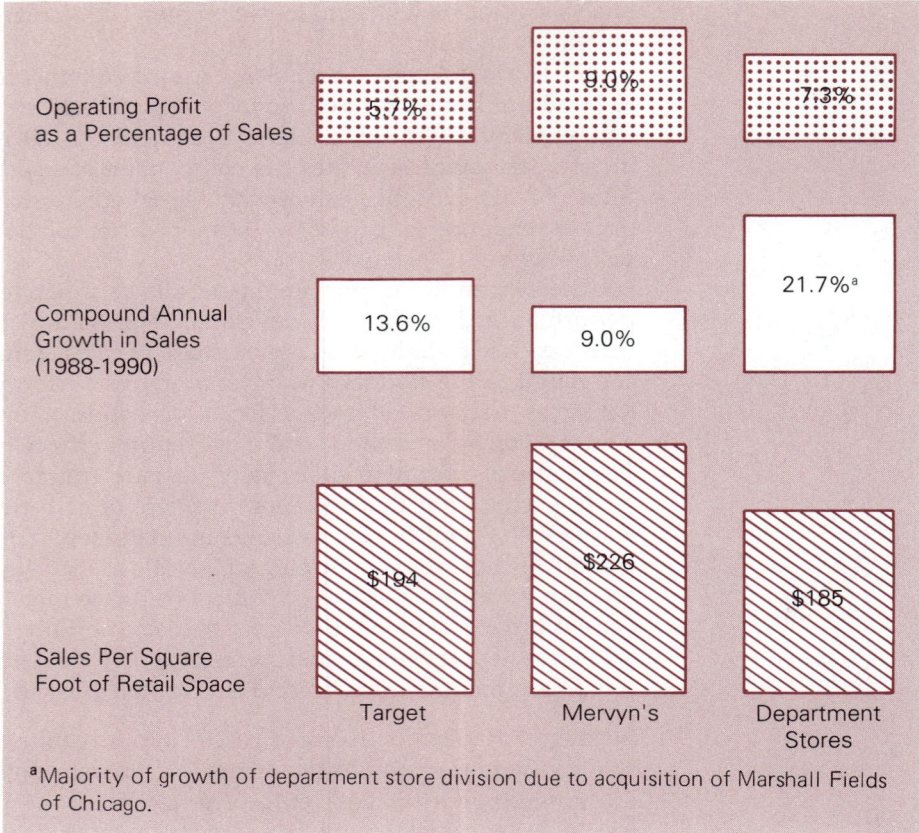

Fine-Line Merchandise Report. Merchandising performance data can only be useful if they can be acted upon. The more detailed and the finer the merchandising data, the more effectively someone can be assigned responsibility to act on them. In Exhibit 17.12 we show the six levels of data aggregation on which merchandising performance can be analyzed; these are: total chain, region, store, department, merchandise line, and SKU. The higher the level of aggregation, the more the truth is hidden. Let's see how this can be the case. If we were to examine chainwide sales last week, we would see they were $13,784,000. This is useful information, especially if it were compared to chainwide sales for the previous year. However, if we look at a finer breakdown, we might study sales by geographic area, and in this example we see that sales in the southeastern region were the highest at $5,917,000. Of course, we might wish to know at which store in the southeast were sales the best. The highest sales were at the Lenox Square store, which had sales of

EXHIBIT 17.12
Fine-Line Merchandising Reporting Week of April 1–5, 1991

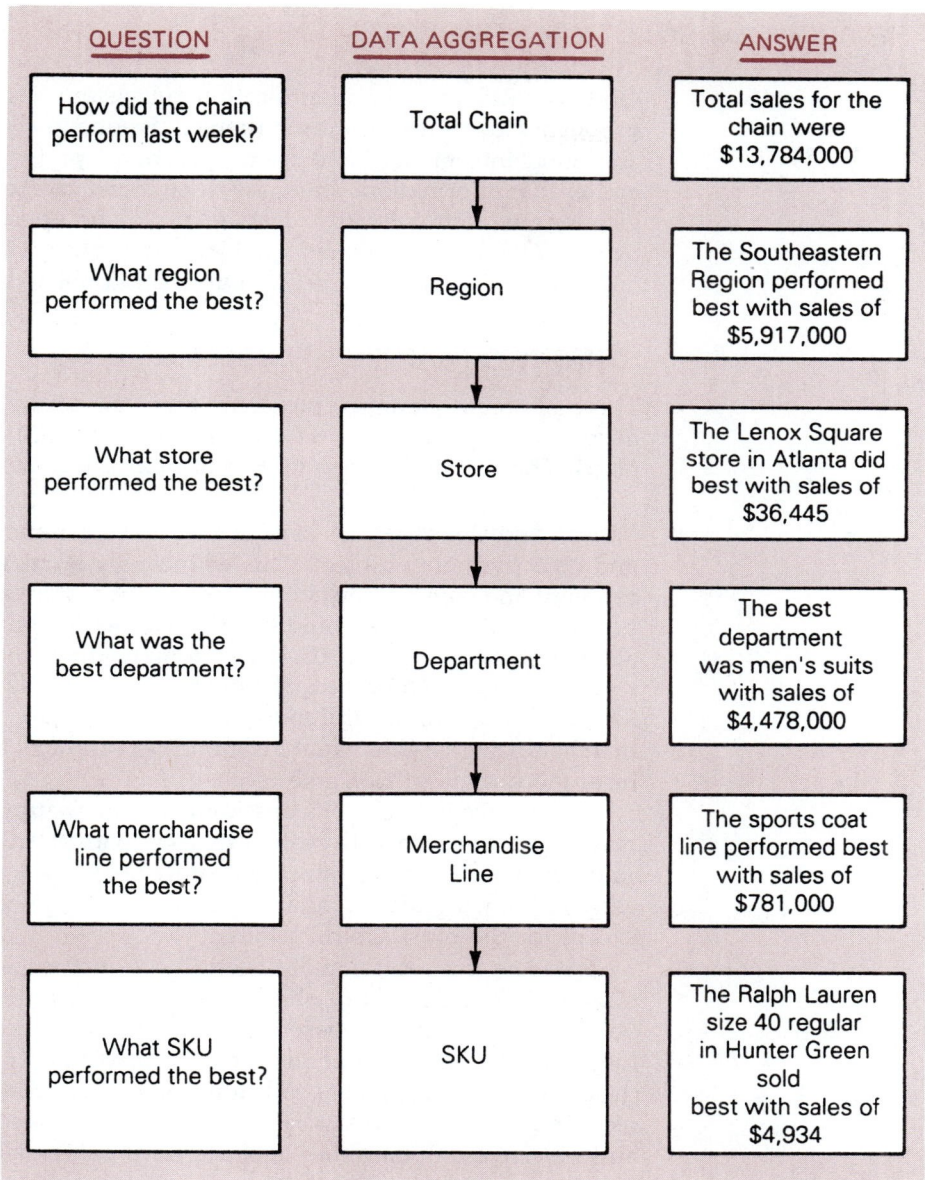

$36,445. The analysis can still become more refined. We see that the best performing department was men's suits with weekly sales of $4,478,000, and that the sports coat merchandise line with weekly sales of $781,000 performed best. Finally, the finest analysis is the SKU. The highest-performing SKU was the Ralph Lauren size-40 regular in hunter green with weekly sales of $4,934.

THE PROBLEM SOLUTION SUBSYSTEM

Once the RIS problem identification subsystem has been used to spotlight problems, the problems must be solved. Frequently, problem solving requires additional information, and it is the role of the problem solution subsystem to gather that information. There are three broad categories of problems: strategic planning, administrative management, and operations management. Let us look at some of the major problems that can occur in each of these areas and briefly discuss the types of information needed to solve them.

STRATEGIC PLANNING PROBLEMS

Three strategic planning problems that can occur are (1) obsolescence of mission or objectives, (2) faltering strategy, and (3) inadequate contingency plans. The retailer can use its RIS to help solve each type of problem.

Mission and Objectives. A retailer may have serious problems if its mission and objectives are obsolete. This will usually occur when the retailer's environment and competition change significantly. For example, most drugstores between 1910 and 1950 could have had a mission of providing their immediate neighborhood (a 10-to-12-block radius) with its medicinal needs. But such a mission today would be questionable given the advent of the combination food and drug stores with more than 60,000 square feet of space, capable of merchandising a wide variety of nondrug products and drawing consumers from more than a three-mile radius.

Alternatively, a retailer's mission may still be appropriate but its objectives may be out of touch with reality. In 1980, with an inflation rate of more than 15 percent, a 20 percent return on equity objective was reasonable. But in the early 1990s, with rates of inflation below 4 percent, this goal was unobtainable except for the most skillful retailer.

Retailers may occasionally need to conduct research on the appropriateness of their mission and objectives. A change in the retailer's mission and objectives should not be based only on intuition. The entire planning process hinges on the statement of mission and objectives; if they are not appropriate, the entire planning process will suffer. It is in a retailer's best interest to spend money and time to collect relevant information before restating its mission and objectives. Some retail analysts have contended that the fundamental problem with Sears is that it needs to seriously reassess its mission and objectives before it develops yet another new strategy.

Faltering Strategy. Retailers may be comfortable with their missions and objectives but uncomfortable with the ability of their present strategy to fulfill them. Therefore, a detailed search for new strategic opportunities may be warranted. It is even possible that the retailer needs to develop a new market positioning image. For example, in the early 1980s, JCPenney was viewed as a general merchandiser of both soft goods and hard goods appealing to upper lower and lower middle classes. However, this market positioning image was not generating sufficient profits. The company decided to reposition itself as a more fashion-oriented specialty department store with a focus on the lower middle and upper middle classes. Consequently, it sold off its automotive service centers and reduced its hard goods emphasis to focus on soft goods and especially apparel.

Using data on significant behavioral and environmental trends obtained from the RIS, retailers may be able to readily identify several significant opportunities. Once opportunities have been identified, retailers will need to collect additional information on each and thoroughly analyze and evaluate the information. Finally, the best opportunities will be selected for strategic development and implementation. Consider the case of Dayton Hudson Corporation, which is serving the full-service department store market (stores are Hudson's and Dayton's), the limited-service department store market (Mervyn's), and the discount department store market (Target). Each of these operations is the result of a strategy that was developed after thoroughly reviewing market opportunities.

Inadequate Contingency Plans. Perhaps a retailer is satisfied with its mission and objectives and its current strategy. However, upon analysis of data from the problem identification subsystem of its RIS, the retailer notices considerable turbulence in the social, economic, and legal environments. It begins to question how well it is positioned against negative developments in these environments. In short, a retailer may see that although it is currently very successful, it does not have any contingency plans. The retailer must conduct special research to help formulate contingency plans before it is too late. A good example is the case of a retailer in the Southwest which, realizing that 30 percent of its business came from Mexican citizens, had contingency plans for almost any government interference in currency valuation or trade agreements. When the peso dropped by 30 percent overnight and a limit was imposed on currency exchanges, the retailer was ready with plans A and B. Plan A was to use a Mexican supplier as an alternative source for some merchandise. The retailer could accept the Mexican peso from its customers, instead of the restricted dollar, and then use the peso to pay the Mexican supplier for merchandise. Plan B involved the use of another American business firm operating in Mexico. This other business used Mexican laborers for certain operations in Mexican communities. The retailer had made arrangements to sell its business pesos at a slight reduction from the official exchange rate, in return for dollars. As a result of this planning, the retailer survived what would have been an economic nightmare.

ADMINISTRATIVE MANAGEMENT PROBLEMS

Administrative management problems are related to the acquisition and management of the resources the retailer needs to carry out its strategy. Three types of resources are especially prone to problems: financial, human, and locational.

Financial Resources. The problem identification subsystem of the RIS can identify financial resource problems that the problem solution subsystem of the RIS can help solve. For example, monitoring of economic trends using the problem identification subsystem may alert a retailer to the fact that interest rates are rising rapidly and are expected to remain high for at least a year. Or monitoring of the balance sheet may alert the retailer that a $10 million bond issue is maturing in six months. This pair of events should trigger problem recognition. The problem, which must be solved with the help of the problem solution subsystem, is how to generate $10 million in capital to retire the bond issue and subsequently restructure the balance sheet. Obviously, additional information will need to be collected to solve this complicated problem.

Other examples of capital-related problems that require a special research effort are evaluation of how to finance the construction of a new warehouse, analysis of the economics of factoring accounts receivable, exploration of new technology for increasing the productivity of capital invested in inventory, and evaluation of a new cash management system.

Human Resources. The problem solution subsystem can also be used to help solve the retailer's human resource problems. Once again, the problem identification subsystem may have been instrumental in calling to the retail executive's attention the presence of a human resource problem—such as deteriorating sales per employee. But it is the problem solution subsystem that must obtain the necessary information to solve the problem.

Human resource problems can include morale problems, motivation problems, productivity problems, turnover problems, conflict problems, and organizational design problems. Often, these problems can best be solved by using the talents of external consulting organizations, which provide an independent analysis and opinion of the cause. People in the retail organization are often too close to the human element of the problem to be objective researchers. Using outside consultants to conduct the research falls within the domain of the RIS. The retail manager needs to recognize that information is needed, but that it can obtain the most valid information by contracting with an independent consulting agency to conduct the research and analyze the results.

Location Resources. A retailer's location is one of the most valuable resources in its arsenal. But this resource can change in value as the retailer's trading area changes. A retailer may discover that its once-valuable location is no longer optimal.

To solve a location problem, retailers need information to help them evaluate alternatives. Reasonable alternatives may be to close the store, modify the merchandise mix and store image, or keep the store operating as is but seek a new location. We strongly recommend that when a retailer finds a location to be inappropriate it not try to solve the problem by making a drastic change in the merchandise mix and thus store image. Merchandise is the critical element that determines the market position image and supports the retailer's mission. If the demographics of the trade area are not consistent with the merchandising strategy, then it may be best to seek a new location.

OPERATIONS MANAGEMENT PROBLEMS

Operations management problems relate to day-to-day management activities. Most can be quickly and effectively solved by an experienced and talented retail manager. However, for the occasional unique problem, special information is needed. Most operations problems are related to assets, revenues, or expenses. Let us briefly examine these problem areas.

Assets. Operations problems can be related to any of the individual assets the retailer must manage on a day-to-day basis. Consider the following problems:

- Inventory is disappearing from the stockroom daily.
- There has been a significant slowdown in customers paying their bills.
- The roof of the store has developed a leak.
- The air-conditioning system repeatedly breaks down.

To solve these problems properly, the manager may require information that is not readily available; he or she will thus turn to the RIS.

Let us illustrate a typical problem in more detail. Assume you are a store manager and the air conditioner regularly breaks down. Would you conclude that the old air conditioner needs to be repaired or replaced with a new unit? Let us say that careful analysis of the technological environment reveals a wealth of new air-conditioning technology, which can have a significant effect on operating costs. At the same time, these lower operating costs must be compared to the higher initial cost of a technologically superior air-conditioning system. Also, there may be less tangible costs and benefits. What will be the effect of a new air-conditioning system on employee morale and customer loyalty? Even an apparently simple problem like this cannot be properly solved in the absence of substantial information.

Revenues and Expenses. Other operating problems that arise can be related to various revenue and expense items. The ability to solve these problems may require more information than the manager has at his or her disposal. What might be some of these problems? Consider the following:

- Sales of a previously popular merchandise line drop 8 percent.
- Employee overtime hours increase by 14 percent in a single month.
- Gross margin declines by 3 percent.

Retail managers would probably only have hunches about the causes of these problems unless the situations had been closely studied. Additional information is required to determine which hunch is correct. In one fast-food restaurant chain, sales of new products accounted for a decline in the previously popular items. In addition, overtime was caused by employees inexperienced with handling the new lines. Management, when presented with all the information, developed new operations procedures so that the new products, although reducing the sales of the previously popular items, drew additional customers, resulting in a profit increase of more than 10 percent the following year

When we discussed the problem identification subsystem, we explained it as a framework for comparing standard with actual performance. This framework can be a good source for identifying significant revenue and expense problems. The problem solution subsystem can then be used, if needed, to gather additional information to solve these problems.

ORGANIZING THE RIS

How should the RIS be organized in a retail enterprise? The answer depends on the scope of the RIS. If the RIS is nothing more than a beefed-up accounting system, then the company controller is probably the best person to manage the system. However, if the RIS is a comprehensive system consisting of both problem identification and problem solution subsystems, a RIS manager may be needed.

A RIS manager directs both RIS subsystems with input from the controller, the legal counsel, the store or department managers, the buyers, and anyone else in the enterprise who is either a potential user or a potential provider of information to the RIS. The RIS manager has to be a very talented individual. In order to interact on a broad array of topics with a wide range over which he or she has little authority, the manager has to be persuasive and diplomatic as well as knowledgeable about aspects of the retail enterprise. The RIS manager must be equally comfortable conversing with a store manager, a warehouse manager, a buyer, and a corporate lawyer.

A RIS manager is not a necessity. The RIS manager's contribution to the organization must justify the cost. If the RIS manager—or even the RIS itself—won't help make decision makers make more profitable decisions, then the position is an unnecessary luxury.

Obviously, the retailer with only a few employees cannot justify a comprehensive RIS, much less a RIS manager. But small retailers should be cognizant of changes in consumer, competitor, and channel behavior; of changes in the socioeconomic, legal, and technological environments; and of changes in asset, revenue, and expense performance. Further, when significant problems occur, even small retailers should try to obtain the best data available within their established cost constraints to solve the problem.

FUTURE DEVELOPMENTS IN RIS

INTEGRATED INFORMATION MANAGEMENT SYSTEMS

Many developments are occurring in computer software, especially in the development of artificial intelligence and expert systems. These new technologies are paving the way for an information system that integrates all aspects of the retailer's operations and as a result will lessen the need for middle managers. Let us examine the building blocks.

Point-of-sale (POS) scanning systems and computerized registers are already very common in retailing.[13] These systems allow the retailer to continuously collect sales data by item. To use scanning technology, items must be marked with a product code symbol. The most dominant coding technology is the universal product code (UPC).[14] In the future, not only products but customers will have codes. This will be voluntary, so not all customers will participate; however, those that do will be given some sort of incentive such as discount coupons, free prizes, and so forth. By being able to capture both product data and customer data at the point of sale, the retailer can construct a data base of awesome potential. For instance, a supermarket will be able to determine which customers prefer a particular brand and when they are most likely to purchase it based on past purchase patterns. This information would allow the retailer to more effectively and profitably manage inventory investments.

A second component of an **integrated information management system (IIMS)** is **electronic data interchange (EDI)**.[15] EDI allows the retailer's computer to "talk" directly to the supplier's computer to transmit intercompany transactions. The primary advantage of EDI is the increased speed of doing business with suppliers—replenishment orders can be transmitted instantaneously. If replenishment is based on monitoring sales via POS systems, speed is increased even more. Currently, only 10 percent of retailers are using EDI, but by 2005, 90 percent of all retailers will be participating.[16] The most important factor in determining the growth of EDI will be cooperation between retailers and suppliers. If retailers and suppliers are going to have access to each other's computers, trust and cooperation will be important.

The customer will become a part of an IIMS through either in-home shopping or traditional shopping at a store. In a store, customers will have the opportunity to check themselves out of the store via **automatic checkout machines (ACMs)**. This phenomenon has already occurred in banking with automatic teller machines (ATMs). With ACMs the customers will scan their own purchases with the POS system, enter their customer identification card (similar to an ATM card), and receive clearance to exit the store. This information could then be transmitted to suppliers with EDI technology.

The entire IIMS technology will rely heavily on **electronic funds transfer (EFT)**. EFT, which has been in use since the late 1970s, allows banks to be electronically linked with their customers in order to make and receive pay-

ILLUSTRATION 17.2
Integrated information management systems such as Electronic Data Interchanges (EDI) link retailers, shippers, and manufacturers to make the entire retail distribution channel more efficient.

ments. EFT will allow customers to check themselves out of the store and pay for their merchandise by having their purchases automatically debited from their bank accounts.

In Retailing in Action 17.2, we see how information systems are on the leading edge of developments in retail technology.

EXPERT SYSTEMS

One important software development that will enable the IIMS to become dominant by 2005 is **expert systems.** These systems will be able to make important recurring retail decisions without human interference by modeling the decision rules of retail experts. We believe that this software development will occur within the next decade.[17] Specifically, we predict that:

1. *Space manager (SM)*. The space manager will be an expert system that automatically analyzes customer demand and matches this with product availability to constantly realign space in the store to maximize financial returns. The space manager software will have the ability to conduct its own experiments and statistically analyze the results. For instance, it could decide to reduce the space assigned to 7-Up, increase the space assigned to Kellogg's Rice Krispies, and then assess the results to determine the effectiveness. Based on the results of this experiment, store personnel would be directed by the computer to alter space configurations on a more permanent basis.

RETAILING IN ACTION

17.2 Developments in Information Technology Lead Retail Technology

The majority of advances in retail technology in the 1990s are occurring in information technology. In 1990, the winners of the Retail Innovation Technology Award (RITA) were as follows:

- JCPenney was named top winner for its catalog division's sales forecasting system.
- Caldor was named first runner-up for its Purchase Order Worksheet (POW) application, which is installed on laptop computers that soft-lines buyers take when they travel overseas. The application has greatly reduced the amount of time spent on paperwork.
- U.S. Shoe received second runner-up honors for its use of the REACT target marketing system, a database that captures and maintains complete purchase histories of millions of customers.

The following entries were cited for honorable mention:

- Price Chopper Supermarkets was cited for pioneering the use of uniform communication standards (UCS) for the electronic invoicing of direct store delivery (DSD) items.
- Hook-Super Rx was acknowledged for its Rx Watch network, which checks for drug interactions when prescriptions are filled and alerts customers to possible problems.
- Big 5 Sporting Goods was recognized for using a sophisticated multimedia system from Learning Systems Sciences to assist in employee training.

Source: "RITA: A Spotlight on Excellence," *Chain Store Age Executive* (September 1991): 57.

---

2. *Replenishment manager (RM).* This piece of software will automatically reorder merchandise and handle all billing, payment, receipt, and stocking. The replenishment manager software will manage delivery dates and assign personnel to receive, mark, and stock the merchandise. Primitive forms of this system have appeared already. More sophisticated software will enable the replenishment manager to communicate with new suppliers to assess purchasing opportunities for frequently stocked items.
3. *Demand manager (DM).* The demand manager software will analyze sales patterns and decide when to mark down merchandise and how long to maintain the markdown. In addition, the demand manager will select the items to advertise, prepare the advertisements, and schedule the advertisements. The demand manager will also have a customer database to keep track of customer purchases by item, price, and time of purchase to make better pricing and promotion decisions. The demand manager will interact with the replenishment manager and space manager.

4. *Human resource manager (HRM)*. All retail personnel will be assigned tasks by the human resource manager software. The time taken to complete these tasks will be monitored. The HRM will report to senior management and recommend corrective actions when value judgments are required. For routine personnel matters, the HRM will act on its own, for example, hiring more part-time help for a holiday season or compiling weekly schedules.
5. *Working capital manager (WCM)*. The working capital manager software will manage the current section of the balance sheet for individual stores or an entire chain of stores. It will interact with the replenishment manager in determining when to pay suppliers and with the customer manager in determining when to offer credit to customers. The investment of cash in short-term income-earning financial instruments will also be managed by the WCM.

Of these developing software types the most advanced to date deals with space management. For decades, retailers planned their allocation of merchandise to space with a planogram, showing where and how merchandise items should be displayed in a store and in what quantities. Traditionally, planograms were constructed by hand using many judgment rules, and the same planogram was used for all stores in a chain. In the mid-1980s, computer technology began to change this approach. There now exist computer hardware and software systems that allow the retailer to scientifically construct a planogram for a specific store to maximize profits. These systems essentially view space as the scarce resource and then allocate merchandise to the space in order to generate the highest level of profits per unit of space.

Although considerable progress has been made with computer-generated planogram systems over the last five to seven years, technology will continue to improve and refine these systems. One major improvement will be in a reduction in cost so that even the small locally owned retailer will be able to afford them. In the early 1990s, the better of these systems cost $60,000 to $100,000 and thus were beyond the reach of small independents. By the mid- to late 1990s, these systems will drop in price to the $10,000 to $25,000 range. At the same time, the more sophisticated of these systems will include voice recognition computer chips. Furthermore, as is already occurring, these systems will have video imaging so retailers will be able to see precisely what the store will look like when merchandise is rearranged on the shelf or floor. In addition, we can expect that consumer research will be brought into the more sophisticated systems. For example, when a customer is standing in front of a display, how will he or she perceive the display. Currently, computer-generated planograms ignore this critical element.[18]

SUMMARY

In this chapter we delineated the nature and scope of a retail information system (RIS). A RIS was defined as a blueprint for the continual and periodic systematic collection, analysis, and reporting of relevant data about past, present, or future developments that influence the retailer's performance.

ILLUSTRATION 17.3

The instantaneous flow of information is now so important in retailing that many large retail chains have invested in elaborate satellite communication systems to transfer sales data and internal communications among stores, distribution systems, and headquarters.

A RIS should have two major operating subsystems. The problem identification subsystem should provide constant feedback on behavioral, environmental, and operating performance trends in order to identify current or potential problems. Behavioral monitoring means scanning the behavior of consumers, competitors, and channel members. Environmental monitoring covers the socioeconomic, legal, and technological environments. Monitoring operating performance includes regular analysis of the retailer's assets, revenues, and expenses.

The problem solution subsystem should be designed to generate information to help solve special management problems in strategic planning, administrative management, and operations management. For each, special research may be necessary for effective problem solving.

The types of strategic planning problems for which the problem solution subsystem may need to generate information are related to reformulation of the retailer's mission and objectives, identification and analysis of strategic opportunities, and development of contingency plans. Administrative management problems that might involve special data collection can be categorized as capital, human resource, and location problems. Finally, operations management problems can be asset, revenue, or expense related.

Finally, we suggested that the key development in the 1990s will be the integration of retail information systems. This will be facilitated by the development of sophisticated software that will include expert systems which will eliminate many middle-management positions. These software systems will manage space, inventory, and human resources and in addition help to manage working capital and demand generation activities.

QUESTIONS FOR DISCUSSION

1. The well-known French philosopher Paul Valery has stated, "Once, destiny was an honest game of cards which followed certain conventions with a limited number of cards and values. Now the player realized in amazement that the hand of his future contains cards never seen before and the rules of the game are modified by each play." Comment on the relevance of this statement in regard to the need for and design of retail information systems.
2. How is the problem identification subsystem different from the problem solution subsystem?

3. How much information should retail decision makers have at hand when making decisions? Does your answer vary depending on the type of decision being made?
4. Who should manage the retail information system?
5. Is it more crucial to monitor the consumer, the marketing channel, or the competition?
6. If you were the owner/manager of a local furniture store, how would you obtain information about your competitors?
7. Explain how operating performance standards can be used to help identify key management problems in retailing.
8. What are the various external information sources available to all retailers?
9. Assume you are the owner/manager of a local hardware store in a city of 140,000 people. You wish to design a basic, low-cost retail information system. What should be the major subcomponents of this system? Prioritize your information needs (i.e., what is the most important information you desire, the second most important, and so on).
10. Obtain copies of the local newspaper for the last two weeks. Clip all the supermarket ads. Analyze the ads for content and write a 500-word statement on the competitive behavior of several of the supermarkets in your city.
11. Obtain copies of the last 12 issues of *Chain Store Age Executive* and *Stores*. What information can you obtain on technology, legal developments, and the socio-economic environment as related to retailing?
12. Visit a small independent merchandise retailer, a small independent service retailer, and a large chain retailer, and discuss their use of RIS. What suggestions could you offer any of these retailers?
13. What is importance/performance analysis and how does it relate to retail information systems?

MANAGEMENT MEMO

You have just received your store's monthly printout of sales and expenses from the home office. Your store is one of 37 furniture stores of a national chain, and while your sales are down 5 percent from budget, labor costs are down 11 percent. You begin to wonder whether there is some relationship between sales and labor costs, so you decide to write a memo to the retail information system manager. In your memo, be sure to include all the reasons why (and why not) such a relationship might occur and a request for the internal data that might help you answer your question.

BOARDROOM REPORT

A major manufacturer of grocery products, with whom your firm does over $2.5 million a year in business, has proposed that it be allowed to link to your computer. In return, the manufacturer would eliminate the need for your firm to carry warehouse inventory for its best-selling products. The manufacturer will use your scanner data to develop a just-in-time delivery system for these products. However, some board members are concerned that by allowing the manufacturer to hook up, your firm will be giving away important information. As the vice-president of operations, you have been asked by the board for your advice. Compose an outline for your presentation stating the pros and the cons of such a venture, and conclude with your recommendation.

SUGGESTED READINGS

Bolfing, Claire P., and Sandra L. Schmidt. "Utilizing Expert Database Services." *Industrial Marketing Management* (1988): 141-51.

"Ernst & Young's Survey of Retail Information Technology Expenses and Trends." *Chain Store Age Executive* (September 1991): sec. 2.

Lodish, Leonard. "A Marketing Decision Support System for Retailers." *Marketing Science* (Winter 1982): 31-56.

McCann, John M., Ali Tadlavůi, and John Gallagher. "Knowledge Systems in Merchandising: Advertising Design." *Journal of Retailing* (Fall 1990): 257-77.

Zimmerman, Robert. "Technology in the Year 2000." *Discount Merchandiser* (May 1991): 76-80.

ENDNOTES

1. "Ernst & Young's Survey of Retail Information Technology Expenses and Trends," *Chain Store Age Executive* (September 1991), sec. 2.
2. "Technology in the Year 2000," *Discount Merchandiser* (May 1991): 76-80.
3. "Information System Helps Retailers to Mine Overlooked 'Acres of Diamonds,' " *Marketing News,* 11 May 1984, 4.
4. Dennis E. Garrett, "The Effectiveness of Marketing Policy Boycotts: Environmental Opposition to Marketing," *Journal of Marketing* (April 1987): 46-57.
5. This section is based on Paul Larson and Robert F. Lusch, "Quick Response Retail Technology: Integration and Performance Measurement," *The International Review of Retail, Distribution, and Consumer Research* (October 1990): 17-32, and Section 3 of the March 1991 issue of *Chain Store Age Executive* which is devoted to quick-response technology.
6. Bernard LaLonde, "The Logistics of Retail Locations," *Proceedings of the AMA Educators Conference* (1961): 572.
7. Bert Rosenbloom and Ravi V. Tripuraneni, "Strategic Planning in the One Hundred Million Club," *Proceedings of Retail Workshop on Research and Teaching in Retailing* (1984): 20.
8. Robert Stevens, "Using Accounting Data to Make Decisions," *Journal of Retailing* (Fall 1975): 23-28.
9. "Vittoria in the Driver's Seat," *American Way* (August 1988): 44-52.
10. Subhash Sharma and Dale D. Achabal, "STEMCOM: An Analytical Model for Marketing Control," *Journal of Marketing* (Spring 1982): 104-13.
11. These questions are only a few of hundreds of questions suggested in *A Retailer's Guide to Accounting Controls* (New York: Price Waterhouse).
12. "Sears' Need: More Speed," *Fortune,* 15 July 1991, 88-90.
13. "NRMA's New POS Study," *Stores* (April 1987): 67-73.
14. "Update on the UPC," *Stores* (March 1987): 48-57.
15. "EDI: Another Competitive Edge for Retailers," *Discount Merchandiser* (October 1987): 78-79 and "A One-Store Development Takes on Electronic Marketing," *Progressive Grocer* (June 1991): 39-44.
16. "Retail MIS Field Reflects Technology Trends," *Chain Store Age Executive* (March 1988): 100.
17. Harris Gordon, "Trends in Retailing—A Look at the Future," *Retail Control* (June-July 1986): 16-26.
18. For additional discussion on this topic, see "Making Space Management Work," *Progressive Grocer* (May 1991): 107-14 and "Computerized Space Management: A Strategic Weapon," *Discount Merchandiser* (March 1991): 64-65.

CASES

CASE 1

Jack Gifford
Miami University
Pat Gifford
Elder-Beerman Stores

TOM BORCH TRADITIONAL CLOTHIER*

The Carltons were at a turning point in the late fall of 1986. Sales volume at their store, Tom Borch Traditional Clothier, was erratic. Cash flow was poor and profits for the second quarter were not looking good. However, plans had been made for better merchandise and financial controls for 1987, and new promotions were envisioned. Would this be enough to warrant continued efforts to maintain the business, possibly with additional bank loans and/or injections from Mr. and Mrs. Carlton's personal resources? Mr. Carlton was particularly concerned that they were falling behind planned sales. If sales were not strong through the fall, Mrs. Carlton was afraid they would have to consider closing the store.

History of the Business

Tom Borch Traditional Clothier was located in Bowling Green, Ohio, a small college community in the north-central part of the state. Steve Carlton, the owner, opened his business August 15, 1984. His parents had just died leaving him two farms in south-central Ohio. He was not interested in farming, having spent several years in retailing following his graduation from Kent State University in 1975. He was able to lease the farms and wanted to use the proceeds to finance the opening of his own business. After two years investigating various areas, Mr. Carlton settled on Bowling Green as a location.

Owing to his expertise in the field, Carlton wanted to open a traditional menswear store. He had spent six years buying menswear for L.L. Bean and two years managing a menswear store in Maine. Bowling Green had only three men's specialty clothing stores at the time. A fourth successful men's traditional store had recently closed because the building in which it was located had to be razed.

Mr. Carlton leased a freestanding building on Dover Street, one block off Main Street, the main thoroughfare of Bowling Green. At the time this was

---

*This case was prepared as a basis for class discussion rather than to illustrate either effective or ineffective handling of a retail situation. All names—persons, location, university, stores—have been changed to ensure the confidentiality of the retailer.

the best location and building he could find, although he had heard that businesses off Main Street often suffered from lack of visibility and low student pedestrian traffic. Tom Borch's custom fixturing and furnishings were in the country gentry style. Clothing and accessories were traditional and of very good quality. As an afterthought, Mr. Carlton added some women's clothing to his stock which he was able to obtain through his menswear suppliers. When the store opened, about 85 percent of the merchandise was for men and 15 percent for women.

Business was slow and most of the traffic was female. Within a short time Mr. Carlton knew that he needed to find a place on Main Street and change his merchandise split to favor women. By August 1985, Mr. Carlton was able to negotiate an agreement to get out of his lease and secure a spot on Main Street. He moved into the lower level of a newly constructed brick building between a new restaurant and a camera/art/card store. The building had three levels; all were open to the street with outside stairways connecting them. The interiors were long and narrow, about 18 feet by 55 feet. There was a gift store on the second level and a quick print shop on the third level. A three-year lease at $750 a month was negotiated for this space. Fifty percent of Mr. Carlton's new stock was women's apparel. Sales began to improve dramatically.

Mr. Carlton was married in the spring of 1986. His wife, Dawn, was a former buyer at Symphony, an exclusive Toledo women's specialty store, and also had experience in computer hardware and software sales. Her expertise proved to be a great asset for the business. She became full-time manager of Tom Borch in August 1986.

During the spring of 1986, Mr. and Mrs. Carlton made the decision to go entirely into women's wear, beginning with the fall 1986 season because they would be able to offer a better selection to women, who continued to make up the vast majority of their business. The fall season got off to a slow start in August and continued to be soft in September and October, producing a sales volume decline from the same months in the previous year.

Merchandising Strategy

Bowling Green is located 35 miles south of Toledo, Ohio. Its permanent residents number 9,226, while the student population of Bowling Green State University's residential campus is 15,100. Bowling Green merchants traditionally have targeted their merchandise offerings primarily to the student population, with permanent Bowling Green residents as a secondary market. There has been some success in drawing summer visitor traffic from the nearby Maumee State Park, but June, July, and early August are usually slow selling periods.

A September 1986 survey of Bowling Green residents' buying habits conducted by Bowling Green University marketing students revealed that of the 570 students surveyed, 11.7 percent made their last purchase of women's clothing in Bowling Green, and 6.2 percent made their last purchase of men's clothing in Bowling Green. Of the 559 permanent residents surveyed, 17.8 percent made their last purchase of women's clothing in Bowling Green, while 12.3 percent made their last purchase of men's clothing in Bowling Green. A large proportion of the students bought their clothing at home before they came to school, and a majority of the Bowling Green permanent residents shopped in Toledo or Maumee shopping malls.

The Carltons had identified their target market over time through conversations with other local merchants and observations of customers in their store.

Market Centers

There were two major shopping areas in Bowling Green, the uptown area and Southgate Mall. The uptown area was adjacent to the main entrance of Bowling Green University. It was six blocks long, with the vast majority of businesses facing Main Street, the main east/west thoroughfare, or the side streets, extending one block north or south of Main Street. The primary north/south thoroughfare, Phillip Street, was three blocks from campus and tended to be an invisible barrier for student pedestrian traffic. Bowling Green merchants who expected to cater primarily to student pedestrian traffic felt that it was necessary to locate within the three blocks of Main Street closest to campus. Businesses in the uptown area included fast-food restaurants; restaurant/bars; bookstores; stationery and art supply stores; drugstores; florists; movie theaters; gift shops; copying services; ice cream shops; services such as banks and insurance and travel agencies; and two gas stations. In terms of apparel, Lee's Bookstore carried some junior women's and men's clothing. Hudson's College Shop (a division of Minneapolis-based Dayton Hudson's Department stores) retailed junior and women's fashions and accessories; The Nutmeg was a chain that carried traditional women's apparel; David Brood's Shoes sold men's and women's shoes; and finally there was Tom Borch Traditional Clothier.

Southgate Mall had a mix of service retailers and merchandise retailers. A new Kroger's superstore had replaced a smaller Kroger's at that location in the summer of 1986. There were also a Super-X drugstore, a Kmart, Penney's catalog store, a card store, beauty shops, a fabric store, two dentists' offices, a Radio Shack, and miscellaneous small convenience stores. The mall was a mile and a quarter from the main business district and two miles from the center of campus.

Sales Volume

The fiscal year for Tom Borch accounting records ran from August 15, 1984 to June 30, 1985, and July 1, 1985 to June 30, 1986. Although these periods are not exactly the same in length, they were used for purposes of comparison. The beginning of the second fiscal year coincided roughly with the opening of the second location; thus, the two sets of fiscal data are valuable in comparing the success of the two locations, especially in terms of sales volume. Sales for Tom Borch rose dramatically from 1985 to 1986 (Exhibit 1). Higher traffic and a year's experience in the Bowling Green market enabled the Carltons to better assess the needs of their customers and make the necessary adjustments to inventory. Mr. and Mrs. Carlton also started to cultivate customers from Toledo and other surrounding areas, which may have contributed a small amount to the increased volume. Sales volume was closely tied to the academic year and holidays.

EXHIBIT 1

Tom Borch Traditional Clothier Monthly Credit and Cash Sales

	1984	1985	% Change 1984–1985	1986	% Change 1985–1986
January					
Credit		$ 593.00	N/A	$ 120.00	−79.76
Cash		10,295.00	N/A	21,790.00	111.66
Total		$ 10,888.00	N/A	$21,910.00	101.23
February					
Credit		$ 1,449.00	N/A	$ 440.00	−69.63
Cash		15,878.00	N/A	15,113.00	−4.82
Total		$ 17,327.00	N/A	$15,553.00	−10.24
March					
Credit		$ 134.00	N/A	$ 476.00	225.22
Cash		5,836.00	N/A	8,506.00	45.75
Total		$ 5,870.00	N/A	$ 8,982.00	50.45
April					
Credit		$ 1,168.00	N/A	$ 455.00	−61.04
Cash		12,374.00	N/A	16,033.00	29.57
Total		$ 13,542.00	N/A	$16,488.00	21.75
May					
Credit		$ 1,684.00	N/A	$ 457.00	−72.86
Cash		8,816.00	N/A	10,633.00	20.61
Total		$ 10,500.00	N/A	$11,090.00	5.62
June					
Credit		$ 486.00	N/A	$ 278.00	−42.80
Cash		2,991.00	N/A	6,636.00	121.87
Total		$ 3,477.00	N/A	$ 6,914.00	98.85
July					
Credit		$ 586.00	N/A	$ 364.00	−37.88
Cash		6,882.00	N/A	10,127.00	47.15
Total		$ 7,468.00	N/A	$10,491.00	40.48
August					
Credit	$ 455.00	$ 881.00	93.63	$ 734.00	−16.69
Cash	1,972.00	17,424.00	783.57	14,968.00	−14.10
Total	$ 2,427.00	$ 18,305.00	654.22	$15,702.00	−14.22

Continued

EXHIBIT 1
Continued

	1984	1985	% Change 1984-1985	1986	% Change 1985-1986
September					
Credit	$ 299.00	$ 581.00	94.31	$ 1,226.00	111.02
Cash	6,538.00	18,840.00	118.16	9,490.00	−49.63
Total	$ 6,837.00	$ 19,421.00	184.06	$10,716.00	−44.82
October					
Credit	$ 315.00	$ 1,469.00	366.35		N/A
Cash	12,018.00	21,653.00	80.17		N/A
Total	$12,333.00	$ 23,122.00	87.48		N/A
November					
Credit	$ 834.00	$ 900.00	7.91		N/A
Cash	8,460.00	20,304.00	140.00		N/A
Total	$ 9,294.00	$ 21,204.00	128.15		N/A
December					
Credit	$ 1,418.00	$ 2,121.00	49.58		N/A
Cash	16,004.00	21,333.00	33.30		N/A
Total	$17,422.00	$ 23,454.00	34.62		N/A
Overall Total	$48,313.00	$174,678.00	261.55		N/A

Cost Structures

Mr. Carlton conceded that he was the type of person who worked on hunches and gut feelings concerning the store, and he believed that he had been lucky with the business to this point. He was, however, beginning to see the need for closer control over the financial and merchandising aspects of the business. The financial accounting procedures were performed by an accountant on retainer by the corporation. Mr. Carlton relied on him for advice and assistance, but communication was difficult as both were very busy. No specific goals were set in terms of the cost structures. The accountant was simply to suggest cost-saving measures and keep taxes at a minimum. Exhibit 2 provides income statements for fiscal 1985 and 1986.

The Carltons hoped to increase their profits for 1987. They also wanted to draw $20,000 in salaries from the business ($10,000 more than last year), which would add to current expenses. The projected income statement is included in Exhibit 2.

Financing

Tom Borch was owned by Mr. Carlton as a corporation under Subchapter S. The corporation had limited liability, limited stockholders, and shareholders were taxed as individuals. Mr. Carlton sustained a loss during his first year of business and has not had to pay taxes on the corporation since its inception, due to the loss carry-forward provisions of the IRS (see Exhibit 2).

Case 1 Tom Borch Traditional Clothier

EXHIBIT 2

Tom Borch Traditional Clothier Income Statement for June 30, 1985 and 1986

	Fiscal 1985	Fiscal 1986	Projected 1987
Income			
Sales	$ 87,641.22	$195,780.70	$240,000.00
Alterations	542.57	3.00	0.00
Miscellaneous	260.09	4,391.69	9,000.00
Returns & Allowances	(1,965.15)	(2,414.74)	(3,000.00)
Total Income	$ 86,478.73	$197,760.65	$246,000.00
Less Cost of Goods Sold	$ 64,726.58	$132,652.88	$155,000.00
Gross Profit	$ 21,752.15	$ 65,107.77	$ 91,000.00
Selling & Admin. Expenses			
Officer's Salaries	$ 1,473.49	$ 10,000.00	$ 20,000.00
Office Salaries	7,436.13	11,055.40	12,000.00
Cleaning and Sanitation	53.40	125.00	125.00
Telephone	1,174.40	1,701.30	1,800.00
Utilities	1,568.77	1,450.07	1,500.00
Insurance	1,527.75	1,838.61	2,000.00
Travel & Entertainment	0.00	0.00	0.00
Office Supplies & Postage	368.72	521.55	650.00
Selling and Admin. Expenses			
Legal & Accounting	607.50	1,371.55	900.00
Advertising	3,263.12	1,118.06	1,500.00
Dues & Subscriptions	910.31	733.00	750.00
Bad Debts	0.00	0.00	0.00
Auto & Travel Expenses	163.50	63.38	100.00
Depreciation	777.42	2,888.02	3,500.00
License Fees	10.00	0.00	0.00
Employee Welfare	0.00	0.00	0.00
Interest	0.00	0.00	330.00
Miscellaneous	875.00	1,557.84	1,975.00
Employment Insurance	183.77	539.87	540.00
Workman's Compensation	0.00	0.00	0.00
Payroll Taxes	2,473.95	2,259.29	2,300.00
Personal Property Taxes	0.00	410.86	450.00
City Income Taxes	0.00	0.00	0.00
Real Estate Taxes	0.00	0.00	0.00
Supplies	895.65	670.08	700.00
Freight	382.20	195.99	200.00
Rent	7,675.00	11,952.74	9,000.00
Bank Charges	9.35	0.00	0.00
Repairs	89.50	0.00	0.00
Refunds	224.18	499.38	650.00
Discounts Allowed	22.05	120.23	150.00
Contract Labor	2,137.13	6,082.72	800.00
Total S & A Expenses	$ 34,302.29	$57,154.94	$ 61,920.00
Net Profit or Loss	$(12,550.14)	$ 7,952.83	$ 29,080.00

Investment requirements for Tom Borch include cash, accounts receivable-trade, inventory, prepaid expenses (the first year only), furniture, leasehold improvements, and a car (see Exhibit 3). Tom Borch had no formal store charge accounts under most circumstances. A few preferred customers deferred half of the purchase price for two weeks and then paid the remainder biweekly. These instances were few and did not show up on accounts receivable on the balance sheets from either year. Stockholders equity, which included common stock, retained earnings, and profit (loss), was not sufficient to cover the investment requirements. Mr. Carlton had to contribute to the business from his personal funds in the form of an officer's loan.

The Carltons had made it a practice to pay for all merchandise purchases within the discount period (usually 10 days from the receipt of invoice) in order to receive a reduction in the cost of merchandise. This reduction was usually 8 percent. The ability to gain these discounts had required adequate cash flow. When current sales did not adequately cover the business needs, Mr. Carlton dipped into his personal assets to pay the bills. In mid-September of 1986, Mr. Carlton was in a temporary cash bind for the business and decided to borrow money personally from the bank in order to pay his business bills within the discount period and take care of a personal financial need. His track record was such that he had no difficulty obtaining the two-year loan which totaled $11,200, $8,000 of which was for the business. Interest on the loan was "prime" (which was 13 percent) plus 2 percent variable at the first of each month.

Merchandise

Mr. Carlton conceived Tom Borch as a fine, traditional apparel store, targeted at college students and townspeople who had discriminating taste in quality clothing at a reasonable price. The interior of the store was designed to create a casual but tasteful atmosphere, an appropriate backdrop for the merchandise. The original women's line included slacks, shirts, sweaters, a few suits, and outerwear jackets. Resources were Thomson, David Brooks, Robert Scott, Aston, and Sero. Belts and canvas bags rounded out the store. Later some dresses and nightgowns by Lanz were added to the women's line.

As the first months of operation passed and Mr. Carlton found that he had more female customers than he had anticipated, he began to increase the proportion of women's clothing and tried a few dresses and more sweaters and pants. He found that the market for traditional men's clothing was not as great as he had earlier thought. He guessed that male students were only interested in jeans and T-shirts and that the taste level and price of his merchandise wasn't matched to the needs of the majority of professors on moderate budgets with a need for practical clothing.

Most of the brands carried by Tom Borch during the first year and a half were available at better department stores—often at lower prices than Mr. Carlton could afford to sell his merchandise. After the 1985 fall season, Mr.

Case 1 Tom Borch Traditional Clothier

EXHIBIT 3

Tom Borch Traditional Clothier Balance Sheets, Year End FPR 1985 and 1986

	Balance Sheet as of 1985	Balance Sheet as of 1986
Assets		
Current Assets		
Cash in bank	$ 3,616.19	$ 2,136.59
Accounts Receivable—Trade	1,501.13	1,688.21
Inventory	47,089.62	48,077.75
Prepaid Expenses	2,110.00	0.00
Total Current Assets	**$54,316.94**	**$51,902.55**
Noncurrent Assets		
Furniture & Fixtures	$ 851.00	$ 9,656.96
Less: Accum. Depn.	(85.10)	(1,005.80)
Leasehold Improvements	3,173.25	3,173.25
Less: Accum. Depn.	(317.32)	(634.64)
Auto	8,531.36	8,531.36
Less: Accum. Depn.	(375.00)	(2,025.00)
Total Noncurrent Assets	**$11,778.19**	**$17,696.13**
Total Assets	**$66,095.13**	**$69,598.68**
Liabilities		
Current Liabilities		
Accounts Payable—Trade	$ 1,026.17	$ 0.00
Accrued Payroll Taxes	313.86	505.12
Accrued Sales Tax	817.44	294.12
Notes Payable—Bank	8,887.80	3,132.26
Estimated Federal Income Taxes	0.00	0.00
Total Current Liabilities	**$11,045.27**	**$ 3,931.50**
Noncurrent Liabilities		
Notes Payable—Officers	$62,600.00	$65,264.49
Total Noncurrent Liabilities	62,600.00	65,264.49
Total Liabilities	**$73,645.27**	**$69,195.99**
Stockholders Equity		
Common Stock	$ 5,000.00	$ 5,000.00
Retained Earnings	0.00	(12,550.14)
Current Profit or Loss	(12,550.14)	7,952.83
Total Stockholders Equity	**$ (7,550.14)**	**$ 402.69**
Total Liabilities & Stockholders Equity	**$66,095.13**	**$69,598.68**

Carlton took a hard look at the store and its directions for the future. By this time he had moved to the new location, sales had picked up, and business seemed to be better, but there were still things that needed to change.

He was by now doing quite well selling women's wear, with 60 to 65 percent of his stock in female apparel. But the men's business was doing poorly. Mr. Carlton had direct competition on much of his women's wear from The Nutmeg Shop, located down the street. That store carried many of the same brands of sweaters, pants, and skirts as Tom Borch, had a broader selection, and sometimes had lower prices. The Bowling Green Nutmeg was part of a 15-store chain and had buying power that Tom Borch did not have as a single unit. Mr. Carlton joined a resident buying office in New York in March 1986 and was hoping to reap the benefit of experts in the market.

During the first few months of 1986, the Carltons made their decision to go entirely into women's wear, to drop many of the suppliers they shared with nearby stores, and to try to forge a new, more unique merchandise line for Tom Borch. The new strategy was initiated with the fall 1986 line. Mrs. Carlton, the store manager since late summer of 1986, and then buyer for the store, planned to develop this more unique, sophisticated merchandise look for the spring and beyond. She found that the college students bought their everyday sweaters and corduroys at other stores but were coming to Tom Borch for "special" clothes, and that Bowling Green women were beginning to look at Tom Borch for "something different." Many parents who visited their children at college were delighted to find Tom Borch and frequently bought for themselves as well as their daughters. New merchandise lines added in the fall included raincoats, a few more one- and two-piece dresses, several two- or three-of-a-kind sweaters and sweater dresses, and more accessories—ties, belts, purses, briefcases, umbrellas, and a limited line of jewelry. Generally, there was a broader range of all merchandise. New resources were Boston Trader, Jason Younger, Needleworks, Scotland Yard, Numa, and British Khaki. For spring 1987, Mrs. Carlton again sought the unusual and ordered many interesting fabrications in styles with a new twist.

Merchandise Control

During the first two years of operation, Mr. Carlton did all the buying for the store. He visited the New York apparel market twice a year, once for his fall line and once for his spring line. He also ordered some merchandise from sales representatives who visited the store and by phone through the buying office. Mr. Carlton did not use a formal buying plan when he went to market. He normally had some idea of what he wanted, worked the market to see what was offered, and ordered what he concluded to be the appropriate merchandise. He did not attempt to control for the cost or the specific units of merchandise purchased.

Mrs. Carlton, from her previous experience in retail buying, was aware of the need for greater controls and was in the process of setting up procedures for inventory control in the store. She also attempted a more organized method of planning her spring purchases during her market trip for spring 1987. The Carltons have never taken a physical inventory. Mr. Carlton did not know why his accountant never asked for one for tax purposes and assumed that he had used the book inventory to derive data for income statements and balance sheets.

Pricing

Mr. and Mrs. Carlton generally priced merchandise with a 50 percent markup, assuming that this would cover expenses and provide some profit. Virtually all the merchandise in the store was priced at what is considered the upper end of "moderate" or the low end of "better." Mr. Carlton estimated that his annual reductions were 27 percent of net sales.

Promotion

The Carltons changed their promotional emphasis over the two years of operations and drastically reduced their advertising costs from 1985 to 1986. They reduced expensive (and ineffective) newspaper advertising in local university and community newspapers. They decided to focus on such things as gift certificates for new sorority pledges; sponsorship of various Greek activities, including style shows; ads in selected playbills and game programs; and only occasional newspaper advertising. Tom Borch did not advertise on the radio. Mrs. Carlton did some direct mailing for special store events. In addition, she tried to reach customers outside the immediate Bowling Green area, by hosting Sunday brunches in the store. She was considering fashion shows, direct mailing, and perhaps special events directed at women in Bowling Green and nearby towns.

The Carltons took great pride in their store and the Bowling Green community. They were members of the Chamber of Commerce and the Bowling Green Retail Merchants Association. They made special efforts to generate goodwill in their store, with other businesses, and the community in general.

QUESTIONS

1. How well have the Carltons integrated the merchandise assortment, pricing, promotion, financial, and control elements of their business? Are there specific problems or inconsistencies?
2. What methods of data collection and control are needed and feasible for this small retailer in order to improve performance?
3. What methods for determining merchandise preferences of target customers are available to the small retailer?
4. Given the 1987 financial projections, what is the break-even point for the store? Have any expenses been omitted? Are the projections realistic? What are the odds of the Carltons successfully competing in Bowling Green in 1987? What specific recommendations would you make to Mr. and Mrs. Carlton?

CASE 2

Michael W. Little
Virginia Commonwealth University
Heiko de B. Wijnholds
Virginia Commonwealth University

CITY DRUGSTORES, INC.

Background

Michael James is vice-president of City Drugstores, a privately owned pharmacy chain headquartered in Fairfax, Virginia. Recently, Michael commissioned a feasibility study for a new site location. He has mixed feelings about the location, however, believing there are better opportunities elsewhere. There is some difference of opinion between Michael and his father, Morton James, who is president.

Until now, little market research has been used for store locations. In the past, Michael's father would locate a store near a major supermarket chain or in a university town. Michael strongly believes market analysis must replace this outdated type of location analysis. Michael and his father have agreed that before a decision is made on the proposed site, research will be done.

Over the years, City Drugstores has grown from a single store in Fairfax to a profitable corporation with 62 stores located in central cities throughout Virginia. This expansion was due to a combination of acquisitions, mergers, and new store construction.

City Drugstores enjoys a good reputation because of its convenient locations, competitive prices, and branded product lines. Like many drugstore chains, City Drugstores has four core departments. The most profitable is prescription drugs, followed by over-the-counter drugs (OTC), cosmetics, and toiletries. Requests for prescription drugs must be presented to a registered pharmacist with a doctor's written order, whereas OTC drugs, such as pain relievers and vitamins, can be sold without such restrictions. Cosmetics and toiletries are referred to as health and beauty aids and add to a drugstore's product mix. A medium-sized store must register approximately $750,000 in sales annually to break even. A profitable store will produce $150 in annual sales per square foot of selling space, with prescription drugs as the product line most instrumental in generating volume.

The Proposed Location

Michael's father has asked him to consider a site near the local university, a state-supported institution with 15,000 students located in Fairfax. Morton James graduated from the Pharmacy School there in 1949. Recently, a fellow graduate, who is owner of Paramount Pharmacy and who wishes to retire, offered to sell James his drugstore.

Paramount Pharmacy is within one block of the university's three student residence halls and is located on the corner of a busy one-way street heading to the downtown business district. If this site were purchased, Paramount Pharmacy would be razed and a modern City Drug unit built in its place. Estimated construction costs are $950,000 and other capital needs (assets) would amount to $475,000. Annual fixed costs for operating a new drugstore are $160,000, with cost of goods expected to be 67 percent of sales and other variable costs estimated at 5 percent of sales.

Paramount Drugstore attracts a small but loyal group of low- to middle-income customers and some university students and faculty. It has not been very profitable or competitive in recent years, however, despite being the only drugstore within the immediate area. For example, Paramount has not taken advantage of university health service contracts for prescription drugs, which are based on bidding. Often these contracts include prescriptions for several hundred students during the academic year.

Upon Michael James' urging, marketing faculty at the university were contracted for the study he and his father agreed to undertake. It was decided that a telephone survey of a representative sample of 200 residents living within census tracts surrounding the present Paramount Drugstore and university fringe would be questioned. In addition, a survey was mailed to 250 college students living in the nearby dorms. An estimate was to be made of the traffic flow past the planned store and the proportion of customers it could attract from this traffic. A guesstimate was also to be provided on walk-in traffic from other students, faculty, and staff. With this information, annual sales potential for the proposed site could be estimated.

The Jameses must decide within 30 days whether or not to buy Paramount Drugs and build one of their own drugstores. Michael has reviewed the data that the researchers collected and needs to make a recommendation to his father.

Research Findings

A summary of responses to some key questions in the resident survey are presented in Exhibit 1.

The data in Exhibit 1 are responses from households represented by randomly selected adults (18 years and older). The expenditure data represent individual purchases and have to be converted to household expenditures by multiplying by the average number of adult spenders, that is, 1.18. The average overall household size amounts to 2.27. (Hint for estimating expenditures: try to substitute average dollar amounts for the tabulated ranges.)

According to the latest U.S. Census data, the number of people living in the target area is 2,949. Unfortunately, these data are four years old. The City's Planning Department has estimated that this mostly low-income population has been declining at an approximate rate of 1 percent per annum. According to the survey, the average household makes approximately 65 percent of all its drugstore purchases at one store (average purchase ratio).

In the student survey, on-campus dormitory students, as a whole, appear to have little store preference when buying prescription drugs. Approximately 28 percent of the respondents didn't purchase prescription drugs. When buying health and beauty aids, however, a significant number of respondents shop near campus. More than half the students surveyed buy something at a drugstore at least twice a week. More than one-third buy at least once a month. This indicates a sizable number of students who are

EXHIBIT 1
Summary of Responses to Resident Survey

1. Do you buy Prescription Drugs? (N = 201)

	N	%
Yes	134	67
No	67	33

2. Where Do You Buy Prescription Drugs? (N = 174)

	N	%
People's Drugs	46	34
City Drug	37	28
Paramount	19	14
Revco	19	14
Other	53	40

(Scores do not add up to 100% due to multiple responses.)

3. Buying Frequency and Expenditures on Drugstore Items (N = 179)

Frequency	Expenditures				
	Under 3	$3-$5	$5-$15	> $15	Total
Daily	2	1	1	2	6
Twice per week	3	3	2	3	11
Once per week	9	8	19	2	38
Twice per month	7	10	14	9	40
Once per month	12	9	17	19	57
Other**	5	11	6	5	27
Total	38	42	59	40	179

*Assume none over $25
**Assume once per six months on the average

4. Would You Shop at Modern Drugstores?

	N	%
Yes	107	55
No	52	27
Don't know	37	18

5. Would You Shop at City Drugstores?

	N	%
Yes	166	84
No	15	8
Don't know	15	8

6. Why Would You Shop at City Drugstores?

	N	%
Close and Convenient	142	71
Cheaper Prices	52	26
Products	21	11
Already Loyal to City Drug	28	14
Loyal to Paramount	8	4
Other	29	10

(Scores do not add up to 100% due to multiple responses.)

frequent purchasers of drugstore products. In fact, on their last visit to a drugstore, these students spent approximately $5 on the average.

When asked if they would shop at a modern drugstore at the Paramount site, half the dormitory student respondents were not sure, implying price, product offerings, and distance as factors in their decision to shop. If the drugstore were City Drug, almost two-thirds would shop there, with about one-third undecided.

Based on the survey data, the dormitory students' total monthly per capita expenditure in drugstores is estimated at $21.80 during the regular academic year. (Academic year is 7.5 months due to Christmas and other holidays.) The average purchase ratio was found to be 60 percent while 62 percent of the students indicated they would shop at the new drugstore.

According to university records, the fall and spring dormitory population is 2,232 (all singles). During the three summer months, approximately 20 percent of this number attends school and stays in the dorms. Summer students spend approximately the same (per capita) monthly amount in drugstores as regular students. Some decline in student population, including dormitories, is expected during the next 10 years.

Traffic flow past the new store is estimated at 5,000 per day for approximately 300 days per year (allowing for Sundays, holidays, and bad weather). This figure includes an estimated 20 percent duplication of the student population discussed previously. It is estimated that 5 percent of this traffic results in actual store visits and purchases averaging $5 per trip.

Based on a very limited survey and some rough estimates, walk-ins, representing faculty, staff, and other students, are expected to spend roughly $30,000 per annum at drugstores in the vicinity of the intended new store.

QUESTIONS

1. Estimate the market potential for all drugstore sales in the area and, using this figure as a base, estimate the sales potential for the new City Drugstore.
2. Determine the expected profitability of the proposed store.
3. What are the main arguments for and against locating a City Drug unit on the intended site?
4. Based on your answers to the previous questions, what should Michael James do? Why?

CASE 3

William A. Staples
University of Houston
John I. Coppett
University of Houston

COMPETITECH LEARNS TO USE TELEMARKETING

Brenda Johnson, vice-president of marketing, was confronted with a major problem. Her company, Competitech, a retailer of computer supplies, had recently started to feature a toll-free 800 number in all of its advertisements, direct-mail pieces, and catalogs. The public was responding very well to this easy-to-use, economical method of ordering products. Response rate reports indicated that sales should have been up by 12 to 15 percent. Actual sales, however, were just about the same as before Competitech started using telemarketing. As Ms. Johnson studied the report, she saw that her three telemarketing service representatives had received approximately 4,000 calls during the last 20 working days. While Ms. Johnson was pleased to note that about 50 percent of the callers had never previously purchased anything from Competitech, the fact that the telephone was ringing but the cash register wasn't was cause for deep concern.

Later that day Ms. Johnson called a meeting of the managers of the telemarketing operation, the shipping and inventory management group, the mail-order department, and customer service department. The meeting focused on determining where and how business was being lost. The managers spent most of the time discussing the steps of order processing as depicted in Exhibit 1.

The telemarketing personnel, when they received a call for a computer part or a software package, recorded the customer's name, address, product identification information, and credit card information, and then they asked the caller where he or she had seen a Competitech advertisement or other promotional information. This last bit of information was considered vital by Ms. Johnson to learn which media were stimulating the most responses. At the end of the workday, the telemarketers forwarded all orders to the mail-order department where that day's orders were totaled. The orders were then passed on to the shipping and inventory management department. Shipping and inventory verified credit worthiness if necessary and then order pickers filled each request and prepared the products for shipment.

If the requested merchandise was out of stock, a written notice of the shortage and the customer's name and address were forwarded to customer service. Customer service sent a letter apologizing for the temporary delay in completing the order and indicated when Competitech anticipated the back-ordered product could be shipped.

The telemarketing group was beginning to receive calls from customers stating that they did not want to wait for back-orders and wished to cancel their orders. Some customers angrily said that if they had known about this delay they would have never done business with Competitech.

Ms. Johnson realized that Competitech was not only losing an opportunity to capitalize on the new business, but, even worse, was alienating some customers. She wondered whether telemarketing might hold the solution to some of the problems.

QUESTIONS

1. What could the telemarketers do if they had on-line computer access to inventory status information?
2. How could telemarketing be used to more efficiently support the customer service function?
3. What information does Ms. Johnson need to determine where the problem(s) are in Competitech?
4. Assuming the telemarketing representatives knew what the inventory status was of every product Competitech sold, how could Ms. Johnson motivate the telemarketing personnel to sell more?

EXHIBIT 1
Order Processing Operations

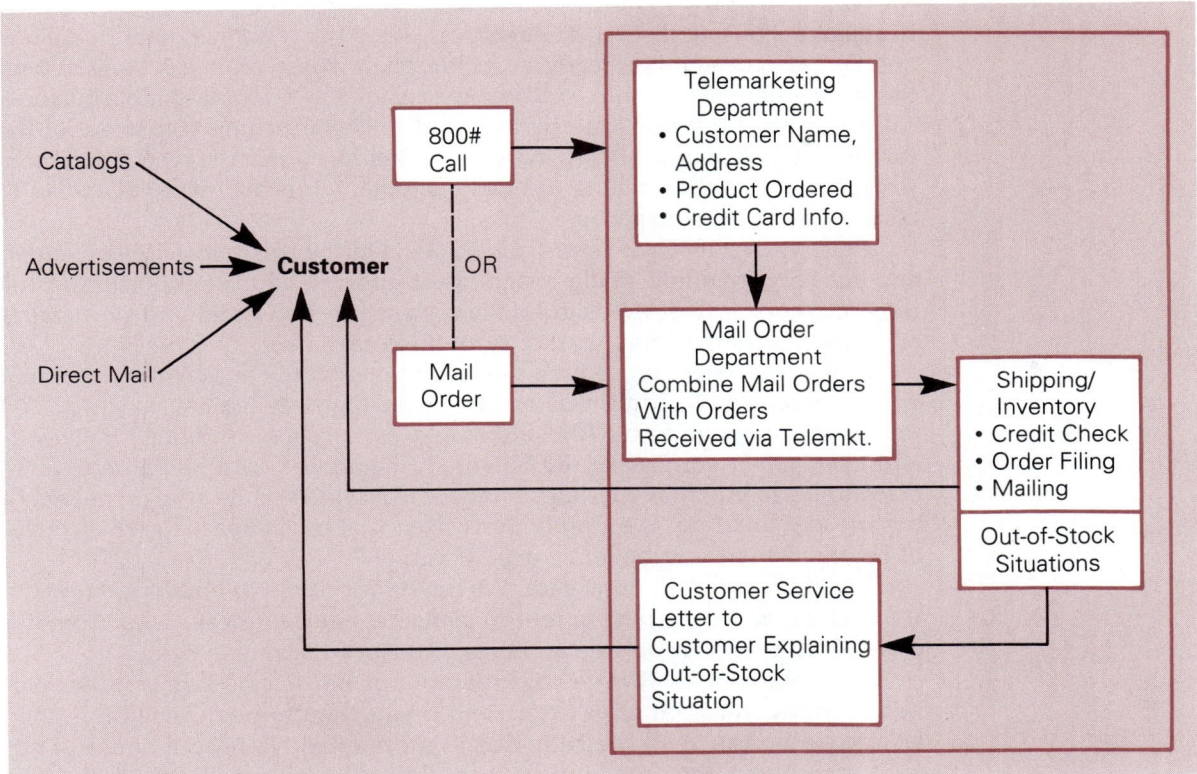

CASE 4

Robert F. Lusch
University of Oklahoma

FREY'S FLOORCOVERING

Over the last 11 years, Stephen Frey has catapulted Frey's Floorcovering from a small one-person operation to a business with more than $1 million in annual sales and a staff of 10 employees (including Stephen). Stephen, now approaching his 35th birthday, is having visions of transforming Frey's into a chain of floorcovering stores.

Background

Stephen is the sole owner of Frey's and proud of it. He single-handedly started the firm in a mid-western town of 81,000 people, in February 1979, immediately after completing a two-year program at a local junior college. Before college, Stephen had spent four years in the Air Force and managed to save $4,000. After completing college, Stephen had close to $5,000 and with that and a $2,500 loan from a local bank he started Frey's Floorcovering. One month later he married Sally Tiedeman.

Originally, Frey's was located in a 50-year-old 1,500-square-foot building near a warehousing district. The rent was cheap but retail customers were few and far between. In those early years, Stephen would often ask Sally to tend the store while he went out to search for customers. He built quite a business calling on local builders, and by year end 1979 was selling 40 percent of the carpet installed in new houses in the area. Selling to builders resulted in more slender margins than selling to retail customers, but they were adequate to cover out-of-pocket expenses.

Frey's ended 1980 with sales of $130,000. During this year, Stephen added another employee and made a significant effort to capture a portion of the retail market. Several thousand dollars were put into radio and newspaper advertising and the retail market responded favorably.

In late 1981, Stephen spotted an old building on the outskirts of town that was for sale. The building was on the major highway leading to town. The price was reasonable, but the building was in poor condition. Sally was strongly against purchasing the building. She argued with Stephen: "You're crazy to try to buy that building. The roof leaks and it is five times the size of our present building. We simply don't need that much space to sell a couple of hundred thousand dollars worth of carpet."

Stephen replied, "I don't care. We must own our own building. How can we ever get ahead by paying rent to someone else? Anyway, who cares if it costs $85,000 as long as we can borrow most of the money?"

Sally interrupted, "We've paid rent on our house since we've been married. If you don't want to pay rent, and if you want to own something, then let's buy a house. With the baby due in six months we need a house of our own more than that old run-down building!" Stephen didn't reply. The conversation was over. Sally hoped that she had made her point.

Two days later when Stephen came home from work, he informed Sally that he had put a $6,000 down payment on the building. For a few years it was rough. At first, the building *was* too large. It was not until 1986, when sales surpassed the $500,000 mark, that space was beginning to be efficiently utilized. In 1989, when sales exceeded $1 million, the building decision finally seemed right. Exhibit 1 profiles the annual sales history of Frey's Floorcovering.

Current Situation

By 1989, Stephen and Sally had their own home and two children. Things looked splendid. Frey's Floorcovering made more than $12,000 in profit for 1989, after Stephen drew a $30,000 salary for himself. Sales were in excess of $1 million, with 42 percent coming from the building contract market and 58 percent from residential sales.

EXHIBIT 1

Sales Growth Profile (1979-1989)

Year	Sales
1979	$ 82,000
1980	130,000
1981	197,000
1982	231,000
1983	260,000
1984	257,000
1985	408,000
1986	548,000
1987	711,000
1988	903,000
1989	1,114,000

Stephen had worked hard to get his business to the $1 million sales level. His next goal was to start a chain of floorcovering stores. He had determined that there were 20 towns with populations between 30,000 and 60,000 within a 100-mile radius of his base operation, none of which had their own floorcovering store.

This plan was simple, Stephen would convert his existing outlet into a warehouse that would supply all the stores. With one truck and driver, he felt that supplying up to 20 stores within a 100-mile radius would be not problem. Since his existing outlet would be converted to a warehouse, Stephen planned to build a new retail outlet for his existing business or possibly try to rent a vacant building temporarily.

The first additional outlet—besides the warehouse and Stephen's own new outlet—would be opened in a town 30 miles to the southeast with a population of 41,000. Stephen's brother-in-law, Scott Stern, would be the manager. Scott, who recently married Stephen's younger sister, is a high school graduate and has been managing the produce department in a local supermarket for the last two years.

Stephen felt he could open at least one new outlet per year over the next 10 years. By the time he reaches age 45, he would like to have 10 or more outlets, with total sales surpassing $5 million. Stephen doesn't want any partners. He wants to be the owner and ultimate decision maker. Scott recently suggested, "Why don't we form a partnership on the store you want me to manage? I've been able to save $10,000, which I was planning to use as a down payment on a house, but that can wait."

Stephen immediately rejected this suggestion: "I need people, not capital. I can get all the money I need from the bank. I've never been late on a payment, even though sometimes it's been extremely close." Stephen has a good credit standing with the largest bank in the county. He has a revolving line of credit of $75,000 at two points over the prime rate—presently about 12 percent. In addition, he has a long-term note with an outstanding balance of approximately $86,000. This note has an interest rate of 10 percent.

In January 1990, Stephen set up an appointment with his banker. At the meeting he presented Jack Black, vice-president of commercial loans, with his idea of transforming Frey's Floorcovering into a full-fledged chain store enterprise. Stephen talked of 10 stores in 10 years as a reasonable goal. Jack Black appeared to be taken by surprise. He seemed to hesitate; no reassurance was forthcoming. Stephen spoke again, "Don't you see how we can both make money on this deal?"

Jack firmly responded, "Stephen, you're a valuable customer, but your balance sheet and income statement will simply not justify expansion at this time. To open even one additional outlet you would need at least $30,000, and that is if you can find a store to rent rather than purchase."

Stephen stood up. "Mr. Black, I've built Frey's to more than $1 million in sales without defaulting on any loans and you say my balance sheet and income statement are too weak!"

Jack responded in a soft and reassuring voice, "Don't get irrational, Stephen. We can work something out, but first sit down and let me tell you something." Stephen reluctantly sat down, although still uneasy. "With sales

EXHIBIT 2

Operating Statements for Frey's and a High-Performance Floorcovering Retailer

Item	Frey's	High Performance Floorcovering Retailer
Net sales	100.00%	100.00%
Cost of sales	70.58	70.28
Gross margin	29.42%	29.72%
Operating expenses		
Payroll	12.82%	15.90%
Advertising	2.99	2.81
Samples	.33	—
Utilities and telephone	1.71	.65
Rent or occupancy	3.98	1.44
Depreciation (trucks, fixtures, and equipment)	.44	.41
Bad debt losses	—	.30
Interest paid	1.64	.66
All other	3.53	2.62
Total operating expenses	27.44%	24.79%
Operating profits	1.98%	4.93%
Net other income	(.33)	(.52)
Net profits (before taxes)	1.65%	4.41%
Net profits (after taxes)	1.10%	2.95%

of $1 million you should be walking home with a lot more than $42,000 per year. You may have built sales, but your profit performance is dismal. Take my advice, Stephen, try to squeeze more profit out of your current operation; then let's sit down together in another year or two and discuss your expansion plans more seriously."

Stephen went home disgusted and had trouble sleeping that night. He was going to show Jack Black that now was the time to expand, not in another year or two. The next day at the office he ran across a copy of the *Operating Results Study of Floorcovering Retailers* prepared by a major trade association. While reading the report, Stephen saw a section of the report entitled "High Performance Retailing." In this portion of the report a typical high-profit floorcovering retailer in the $2 million range was profiled in terms of operating performance. Relevant data from this profile are presented in Exhibits 2 through 4 with comparable data on Frey's Floorcovering.

When Stephen was driving home that evening, he was pondering how he could use these data to show Jack Black how his performance was respectable or, alternatively, how he could use the data in this report to better program

EXHIBIT 3

Balance Sheets for Frey's and a High-Performance Floorcovering Retailer

Item	Frey's	High Performance Floorcovering Retailer
Assets		
Current assets		
Cash (including marketable securities)	10.39%	10.30%
Accounts receivable	30.00	39.38
Inventory	45.42	40.47
All other	1.29	—
Total	87.10%	90.15%
Fixed assets	12.90	9.85
Total assets	100.00%	100.00%
Liabilities and net worth		
Current liabilities		
Accounts payable	23.80%	23.33%
Notes payable	13.43	7.78
Customer deposits	4.87	—
All other	5.93	4.34
Total	48.03%	35.45%
Long-term liabilities	21.05	—
Net worth	30.92	64.55
Total liabilities and net worth	100.00%	100.00%

EXHIBIT 4
Productivity Ratios for Frey's and a High-Performance Floorcovering Retailer

Item	Frey's	High Performance Floorcovering Retailer
Net sales per dollar invested in inventory	$ 5.94	$ 10.55
Net sales per square foot	128.99	168.32
Net sales per full-time salesperson*	222,806.00	364,695.00
Net sales per full-time employee*	111,403.00	136,761.00
Net sales per dollar invested in assets	2.70	4.30

*Two part time employees equal one full-time employee.

Frey's for high-performance results. When he got home, Scott Stern was there. Sally had told Scott about the turndown by the bank. Scott blurted out, "Stephen, I want you to know that I still have the $10,000 if you want to form a partnership on that new outlet."

QUESTIONS

1. Is Frey's financially able to grow and become a multiple-outlet operation?
2. Using the data from the Operating Results Study, identify Frey's major operating problems.
3. Should a partnership with Scott Stern be formed?
4. Can you develop a strategy that would allow Frey's to generate enough capital internally to finance new outlets?
5. Would you say that Frey's problems are in most part strategic or operating?

CASE 5

HEALTH-MORE PHARMACIES, INC.

Robert F. Lusch
University of Oklahoma

Jane Hoover is the president and principal stockholder of Health-More Pharmacies, Inc. She is in a quandary over how to reorganize the corporation so that it will be able to continue its rapid growth. In six years the firm has grown from a single pharmacy to a group of five pharmacies. Ms. Hoover is finding it increasingly difficult to manage and control the five stores.

Background

In 1983, Jane Hoover graduated from college with a degree in pharmacy and immediately took a job as a pharmacist for Walgreen Drugs. It didn't take her long to recognize that the day-to-day activities of a pharmacist were not very exciting and challenging. She frequently found herself daydreaming about operating her own drugstore.

In April of 1985, while visiting a friend in a nearby city, Mrs. Hoover accidentally ran across a small drugstore for sale. The present owner had operated the store for 22 years and was nearing retirement. The store was located in a neighborhood shopping center and was easily accessible to many households within eight blocks of the store. Luckily for Mrs. Hoover, the owner was having difficulty finding a buyer, and she was able to purchase the store (which had a five-year lease remaining) for the book value of the inventory (which was $70,000) and $12,000 for fixtures and equipment. The owner was willing to finance most of the $82,000 purchase price, and Hoover purchased the drugstore with only $9,000 of her own funds. By June 1985, she was in business for herself.

Mrs. Hoover operated the drugstore with the help of two part-time clerks while she served as the full-time pharmacist. Although the new venture did not free her from her role as a pharmacist, she was enjoying herself since there were many other duties to perform besides filling prescriptions. The accounting records had to be kept, employees supervised, merchandise bought and priced, and sales promotions planned. Not surprisingly, she quickly found herself taking night courses at a local university in accounting and marketing.

By October 1986, Mrs. Hoover had spotted another small drugstore for sale. It, too, was located in a neighborhood shopping center. The price was $120,000 and the owner would not finance any of the purchase price. She acquired outside capital by incorporating and selling stock to friends and acquaintances who had been impressed with how well she had managed the first store. She was able to convince the existing owner of the store to take $20,000 of the purchase price in stock of Health-More Pharmacies, Inc.

The first store was turned over to a manager and the new store was managed by Mrs. Hoover. Also at this point she added a part-time bookkeeper to handle the records for both stores.

In 1988, 1989, and 1990, three more drugstores were acquired—all from individual proprietors desiring to get out of the drugstore business. The two most recently acquired stores were located in a city of 47,000 people 21 miles from the first three stores. Stores acquired in 1988, 1989, and 1990 were financed through retained earnings and Health-More Pharmacies, Inc., stock issued to the prior owner. Every time a store was acquired, Mrs. Hoover would become the manager and turn the store she was presently managing over to a new manager.

Current Situation

As 1991 ended, Mrs. Hoover began to recognize that she did not have the time to keep a close watch over all the stores. At the beginning of 1989, she had hired a full-time assistant to help her with the buying and in late 1989 added a full-time accountant. But still there were too many problems that required her special attention and that were taking her away from managing a store. She also wished she had more time to follow up on other possible drugstore acquisitions. Recently she heard of a small group of four drugstores for sale in a city 54 miles away.

The income statements and balance sheet for Health-More Pharmacies, Inc., are provided in Exhibits 1 and 2. These financial statements reflect the composite performance for all five stores as of the end of 1991. All five stores are located in neighborhood centers and are 4,000 to 5,000 square feet in size. Approximately 40 percent of sales were prescription drugs and the remainder was divided among the following product categories: health and beauty aids, magazines, books, newspapers, tobacco, candy, greeting cards, and small gifts ($5 to $25). Each store carries 9,500 SKUs. An item is defined as one size of one product. For example, a bottle of vitamin pills containing 200 tablets is considered one item, even though there may be a dozen bottles of that size and description in stock.

Drugstores are complicated in terms of legal regulations. There are state and federal laws with which druggists must comply since they handle products with dangerous ingredients. Also licenses need to be obtained from the State Board of Pharmacy. In addition, some dangerous drugs need to be ordered by serial number and regularly inventoried and reported to government agencies.

QUESTIONS

1. What are the advantages and disadvantages of a multiple-store organization?
2. How should Health-More Pharmacies, Inc., be reorganized to improve control and give Mrs. Hoover the time she needs to direct the corporation?
3. Analyze the financial performance of Health-More Pharmacies, Inc.
4. Does Mrs. Hoover have a strategy for Health-More Pharmacies, Inc.?

EXHIBIT 1
Health-More Pharmacies, Inc., Income Statement (1991)

Item	Dollars
Net Sales	$2,711,142
Cost of Goods Sold	1,764,954
Gross Margin	946,188
Operating Expenses	
Wages	509,695
Rent	67,779
Advertising	32,534
Utilities and Phone	32,245
Insurance	27,111
Legal and Professional Fees	13,555
Delivery	10,845
Repairs	29,822
Interest	24,400
Bad Debt	8,133
Miscellaneous	78,623
Total Expenses	$ 837,742
Profit (before taxes)	108,446
Taxes	41,209
Profit (after taxes)	$ 67,237

EXHIBIT 2
Health-More Pharmacies, Inc., Balance Sheet (12/31/91)

Assets		Liabilities and Net Worth	
Current Assets		Current Liabilities	
Cash	$ 33,113	Accounts Payable	$123,246
Accounts Receivable	106,510	Notes Payable	49,451
Inventory	426,037	Other	39,560
Other	74,979	Total	$212,257
Total	$640,639	Long-Term Liabilities	$130,101
Fixed Assets		Net Worth	418,422
Equipment	$ 87,130	Total Liabilities	
Leasehold Improvements	33,011	and Net Worth	$760,780
Total	$120,141		
Total Assets	$760,780		

CASE 6

Robert F. Lusch
University of Oklahoma

A.B. KING'S

In mid-1992, Vance Womack, menswear buyer at A.B. King's, requested permission from the general-merchandise manager to change the present pricing policy on men's suits. Womack felt that a change in pricing was necessary due to increased local competition in this merchandise category.

Background

A.B. King's is a locally owned and operated full-line department store in a midwestern city of approximately 250,000 inhabitants. The store was founded by Alfred Bailey King in 1902. The store remains in its original downtown location and is still primarily owned and operated by the King family. Tom King, the grandson of A.B. King, is the current president and chief executive officer. In 1991, annual sales approached $12 million. The company has consistently shown a profit every year since 1902 except 1932, 1933, 1957, and 1990.

Since 1978, competition intensified in King's trading area, which happens to be the entire MSA. Sears remodeled its downtown store and opened another store in a regional shopping mall on the outskirts of the city. In addition Kmart has built three new stores since 1980. Specialty store competition has also intensified, especially in women's apparel and menswear. A.B. King's has always been one of the most fashionable places for upper-middle and upper-class residents to purchase their clothing. Several generations of families have purchased their clothes at King's.

In the area of menswear, one competitor that has grown to be a dominant market leader is Franklin's. Franklin's is a locally owned company founded in 1969. The store sells only menswear and women's apparel in about a 65/35 mix. Franklin's first store was located downtown, directly across the street from A.B. King's. In 1980, its sales were $1.8 million. Today, Franklin's has a total of five stores, and in 1991 its sales were $8.3 million. Franklin's sells moderate- to good-quality clothing at a relatively low markup. It is very promotion- and price-oriented and concentrates on high inventory turnover. Recently, Franklin's introduced a line of high-grade men's suits priced at $249, which most local retailers (including A.B. King's) sell in the $300 to $350 price range. This line has been heavily promoted in the local newspaper.

Current Situation

Vance Womack is concerned about the sales performance of the men's suit lines at A.B. King's. In 1987, King's sold 1,445 suits, but in 1989 that number had dropped to 1,208, and in 1991 suit sales were only 940. The results for 1992 look even less promising.

On July 24, 1992, Vance wrote a memo to John Starr, the general-merchandise manager, about this slackening of demand.

> *Memorandum*
> *TO: John Starr, General-Merchandise Manager*
> *FROM: Vance Womack, Buyer, Menswear*
>
> *It is time we came up with a strategy to combat our declining sales of men's suits. The inroads that Franklin's and other specialty stores are making into our market share is increasingly becoming a problem. We continue to hold on to our loyal patrons, but the transient, bargain-seeking shopper is being intercepted by competition. The problem is not one of poor buying. We have as good a selection and assortment of suits as anyone in town. And our sales assistance and alteration departments are superior. In short, I believe we are simply not price-competitive. Given the level of competition, our present prices are simply too high.*

Starr immediately phoned Womack and told him that he concurred with his observation. He instructed Womack to put together relevant merchandising statistics for men's suits for the first six months of 1992 and also to develop hypothetical merchandising statistics based on his proposed price changes. These statistics are provided in Exhibits 1 and 2.

After Womack had started to compile these statistics, he realized that A.B. King's did not have the selection he had initially thought it had, especially in the moderate- to lower-price range. In fact, it currently had no suits priced under $189. As a result, two lower-priced lines were added—one at $129 and another at $98, and the $189 line was reduced to $169. Neither of these lines was expected to be a best-seller, but Womack thought they might help to generate more traffic in the menswear department.

Womack also suggested an increased level of advertising. Currently, advertising of men's suits had been averaging 1.9 percent of net sales. Womack proposed this be increased to 3.8 percent of net sales. Most of the

EXHIBIT 1

Merchandising Statistics for Men's Suits (1/1/92–6/30/92)

Price Line	Cost Range (billed cost)	Average Markup[a]	Average Unit Stock	Unit Sales	Workroom Cost Per Unit	Cash Discounts (as percentage of billed cost)	Retail Reductions (as percentage of original retail)[b]
$419	$200–240	$213	60	50	$21	2%	8.1%
329	160–199	155	90	108	18	2	9.8
259	125–159	118	120	154	13	2	18.1
189	90–124	80	70	47	12	2	19.4

[a] Average markup represents original markup over original billed cost.
[b] Retail reductions include markdowns, employee discounts, and shortages as a percent of original retail.

EXHIBIT 2

Projected Annual Performance on Men's Suits

Price Line	Cost Range (billed cost)	Average Markup[a]	Planned Unit Stock	Planned Unit Sales	Planned Workroom Cost Per Unit	Cash Discounts (as percentage of billed cost)	Planned Reductions (as percentage of original retail)[b]
$398	$200–240	$192	78	140	$20	2%	3.1%
298	160–199	124	96	312	16	2	6.2
219	125–159	78	128	420	12	2	10.4
169	90–124	60	96	164	11	2	9.8
129	74–89	48	96	140	9	2	6.1
98	54–73	37	78	116	9	2	5.1

[a] Average markup represents original markup over original billed cost.
[b] Retail reductions include markdowns, employee discounts, and shortages as a percent of original retail.

advertising would be directed at the $298 and $398 lines and the $98 and $129 lines. Some consideration was given to putting the $98 line in a new "bargain basement" department of the store, but Womack felt this would defeat the purpose of generating more traffic in the upstairs menswear department.

QUESTIONS

1. Why did A.B. King's wait so long to respond to its declining sales volume in men's suits?
2. Will the price cuts be profitable?
3. How will competition react to the price cuts?
4. What are the pros and cons of adveritising both high- and low-priced men's suits?
5. What are the pros and cons of starting a "bargain basement" department?

CASE 7

OAKLAND DEPARTMENT STORE

Robert F. Lusch
University of Oklahoma

Rodney Hayes is merchandise manager of the shoe department for Oakland Department Store, located in a large metropolitan city of more than 750,000 people in the southwestern United States. Oakland has 250,000 total square feet of floor space, and 80 percent is selling space. In 1990, the store had $42 million in sales, and 3.8 percent of this total was attributed to the shoe department. The shoe department occupies 6,500 square feet of selling floor space. The 1990 income statement for Oakland Department Store is presented in Exhibit 1.

Currently, Hayes is in the process of preparing a merchandise budget for the fall/winter 1991 selling season. The fall/winter season consists of the months August through January; the spring/summer season consists of February through July. The distribution of sales for the fall/winter season for the last three years is presented in Exhibit 2.

Toni McClain, the store controller, has informed all department managers that overall store sales in 1991 should be 5 to 6 percent above 1990. This forecast is based on an assumption of continued moderate inflation and increased competition. Oakland Department Store has been especially hard hit by a growing number of price- and promotion-oriented retailers such as

EXHIBIT 1
Oakland Department Store 1990 Income Statement

Gross Sales	$43,210,000
Less: Return and Allowances	1,210,000
Net Sales	42,000,000
Less: Cost of Goods Sold	27,510,000
Gross Profit	14,490,000
Less: Operating Expenses	11,760,000
Net Profit (before taxes)	2,730,000

EXHIBIT 2

Oakland Department Store Shoe Department Distribution of Annual Sales by Month

Year	August	September	October	November	December	January
1988	10.1%	9.2%	6.3%	8.4%	8.0%	5.9%
1989	10.1	9.1	6.5	8.2	8.1	6.0
1990	9.9	9.4	6.4	8.3	8.2	5.8

Mervyn's and factory outlet malls. Also, a growing number of specialty shoe stores, such as Thom McAn, Athlete's Foot, and Open Country have had a detrimental impact on the performance of the shoe department at Oakland. Over the last 10 years, the shoe department has generally experienced a rate of annual growth in sales lower than the overall growth in store sales (see Exhibit 3).

Since 1986 the shoe department has used a 55 percent planned initial markup for preparing its seasonal merchandise budget. However, Hayes is considering raising this to 60 percent because of the increased level of markdowns over the last several years, the result of increasing competition. When Hayes mentioned to McClain his desire to raise the initial markup to 60 percent, she suggested that a better solution may be to cut the initial markup to 50 percent. She argued that lower everyday prices should reduce the need for markdowns and might also result in higher sales. Actual reductions from the initial markup for the 1990 fall/winter season are presented in Exhibit 4.

In prior years, the seasonal merchandise budget for the shoe department was prepared using the beginning-of-the-month stock-to-sales ratios as shown in Exhibit 5. This year Hayes is contemplating using the basic stock method to develop the seasonal merchandise plan because this method al-

EXHIBIT 3

Oakland Department Store Sales Growth (1981–1990)

Year	Total Store	Shoe Department
1981	6.4%	5.2%
1982	11.8	10.3
1983	12.1	11.4
1984	10.3	10.1
1985	4.9	5.0
1986	6.2	5.7
1987	7.9	6.3
1988	11.2	9.8
1989	10.1	6.9
1990	7.3	5.4

EXHIBIT 4
Oakland Department Store Shoe Department Reductions from Initial Markup (1990)

Reductions	Aug.	Sept.	Oct.	Nov.	Dec.	Jan.
Markdowns	12.1%	12.4%	18.2%	11.5%	11.0%	17.5%
Discounts	5.0	4.0	4.5	5.0	5.0	3.0
Shortages	1.0	.9	1.0	1.0	1.0	.9

lows him to plan for a target stockturn. Hayes is especially concerned about achieving a planned stockturn of 2.5 times per year because this is one of the standards by which senior management will evaluate his performance. Management has also established a 40 percent target gross margin for the shoe department. Hayes was told to plan to have beginning-of-the-month retail stock of $400,000 for February 1991.

Hayes is somewhat concerned about his ability to achieve a 40 percent gross margin and retail stockturn of 2.5, since he has no control over advertising expenditures. In 1990, his department was allocated $25,000 for advertising for the fall/winter season. Hayes believes that if he could double his advertising, sales would grow by at least 20 percent.

It was five days before his merchandise budget was due to McClain when Hayes realized that his long-run future at Oakland was to be largely determined by his ability to reverse the declining performance of the shoe department. He wanted to develop a no-nonsense merchandise budget to convince McClain that his department required special resources and attention.

EXHIBIT 5
Oakland Department Store Shoe Department BOM Stock-to-Sales Ratios

Month	BOM Ratio
Aug.	5.34
Sept.	5.01
Oct.	4.45
Nov.	5.95
Dec.	5.84
Jan.	4.10

QUESTIONS

1. Prepare two seasonal merchandise budgets for the Oakland shoe department, using the BOM stock method and the basic stock method. Which budget should Hayes submit to McClain?
2. How can Hayes convince McClain of the need to double the advertising budget for the shoe department?
3. What should the planned initial markup be?

CASE 8

Robert F. Lusch
University of Oklahoma

TAYLOR'S FURNITURE

Taylor's Furniture is located in a city of roughly 200,000 in the southwestern United States. The company is owned and operated by Tom Prescott, who acquired the company in 1983 from Benny Taylor. Over the last five years, Prescott has experienced success in owning and operating Taylor's. In 1987, sales were $997,000, which produced a profit (after taxes) of $26,500 in addition to a salary of $36,000 Prescott paid himself for managing the store. Prescott, with the help of seven full-time and three part-time employees, operates all aspects of the firm. Sales volume since 1987 has grown at an annual rate of 12.1 percent. Unfortunately, however, first-quarter results for 1988 were not as encouraging. Sales were off 2.1 percent from the corresponding 1987 quarter, and profits were a mere 0.6 percent of sales.

Background

Since Prescott acquired Taylor's in 1983, he has worked at positioning the firm as a promotion-oriented home furnishings retailer with a liberal credit policy and a broad assortment of merchandise. Approximately 7 percent of sales are spent on advertising, which is considerably above the industry average for home furnishing retailers. In addition, 70 percent of all sales are made on credit. The installment credit plan that Prescott designed requires that the customer put at least 10 percent down on an item and that the balance be paid off in six, nine, or twelve equal monthly installments. The interest charge is 1.5 percent per month on the unpaid balance. In every year since 1983, Taylor's has made money on its credit operation. That is, interest income has more than offset the cost of capital, bad debts, and expenses of administering the credit program.

Prescott believes that Taylor's risks in selling on credit are relatively low because of the financial stability of Taylor's target market. Taylor's typical customers are 25 to 44; have at least some college; have a household size of three or four members; own rather than rent; are self-employed, professional, or managerial; and have an annual income of more than $25,000. The quality of this target market has resulted in bad debt expense typically being only 1.4 percent of sales.

Current Situation

In early 1988, the local economy began to slow down. Most households had overspent for Christmas. Interest rates began to climb. Taylor's itself was facing a 12 percent cost of capital from its local bank just to finance inventory during the slowdown. Prescott believed that if Taylor's could move inventory more rapidly, even if it did so by selling the merchandise on credit, it would be better off.

Prescott felt the time was never better for households to purchase major appliances and home furnishings. Manufacturers and retailers were cutting prices to move inventory, and retail credit, in terms of its cost to the consumer could not go beyond its present level of 18 percent annually thanks to state usury laws. Also consumers could be almost certain that prices of furniture and appliances would be significantly higher in the future.

Prescott believed that consumer resistance could be overcome with a strong 30-day promotional program. He felt that up to $10,000 could be committed to this promotional campaign with the goal of moving $150,000 (at retail) of excess and old inventory. Part of the promotional campaign would consist of direct-mail advertising to all past charge customers over the last 24 months, or about 1,600 households. The second part of the promotional campaign would consist of heavy radio advertising for 30 consecutive days. Radio was selected because it offered the best potential for communicating with a specific target market. To assist the firm in selecting the best station on which to advertise, Prescott ordered the most recent copy of the Radio Audience Profile (RAP) from the Marketing and Economic Research Corporation in Oklahoma City. Selected data from this RAP report are presented in Exhibits 1 and 2. All the radio stations had special-package buys, typically consisting of 180 to 360 spots over a 30-day period at a substantial discount over the single-spot price. Relevant data on these special buys are provided in Exhibit 3.

Prescott is not sure which items he should try to promote most heavily. He has even considered not promoting any specific merchandise lines but rather merely advertising storewide savings. Prescott requested that his controller prepare merchandise statistics for 1988 so that he could better decide which merchandise lines might warrant special attention. These statistics are displayed in Exhibit 4.

EXHIBIT 1

Listening Profile of Seven Radio Stations in Metropolitan Area (First Quarter 1988)[a]

Station	Age		Education		Family Size			Residence	Occupation	Income
	25-34	35-44	Some College	College Graduate	2	3	4	Single Family	Professional, Managerial, or Self-Employed	Over $25,000
KEGN-AM	32.2%	17.9%	35.7%	14.3%	14.3%	32.1%	17.9%	78.6%	28.6%	43.1%
KEGN-FM	35.8	14.8	37.5	22.5	34.6	19.8	21.0	71.6	35.8	52.0
KFDE-AM	7.8	22.1	11.8	11.8	35.1	15.6	11.7	76.6	32.9	44.1
KFDE-FM	19.6	21.5	25.5	15.7	27.5	23.5	9.8	78.4	33.4	44.8
KBDI-FM	15.6	18.8	27.0	33.3	34.9	17.5	17.5	88.9	36.5	53.3
KOKE-AM	30.7	21.8	30.7	28.7	31.0	25.0	19.0	87.1	44.5	51.6
KBCT-AM	25.0	3.6	38.1	8.3	31.0	23.8	15.5	68.7	33.5	43.2

[a] All station names are disguised.

EXHIBIT 2

Anticipated Purchasers in Seven Radio Station Audiences in Metropolitan Area[a]

Item	KEGN-AM	KEGN-FM	KFDE-AM	KFDE-FM	KBDI-FM	KOKE-AM	KBCT-AM
Mattress or box springs	700	700	3,300	500	1,700	1,900	2,100
Major household appliances	1,400	4,000	2,400	2,900	1,400	3,100	5,700
Antiques	1,200	1,400	1,700	1,900	2,100	3,800	3,600
Furniture	1,400	5,700	2,400	2,100	3,100	7,400	6,900
Carpeting	1,700	3,300	2,100	1,900	1,900	3,800	4,800
Draperies or other interior decorating items	1,900	5,500	3,600	3,600	4,000	6,900	6,700
Major home remodeling	500	1,900	1,700	1,900	2,400	3,300	1,700
Television	700	2,600	1,700	1,900	1,900	1,900	3,800
Radio or stereo	3,100	6,700	1,000	2,600	700	5,500	8,600
Buying a house	1,700	4,000	2,100	2,100	1,200	3,800	6,400

[a]Responses in the categories above indicate that one or more persons in the respondent's household is considering purchasing or spending money on an item in the indicated category within the next three months. The numbers reported are projected households in the survey area (rounded to the nearest hundred) anticipating a purchase. All station names are disguised.

QUESTIONS

1. Does it make sense for Taylor's to try to shift some of its inventory investment into accounts receivable?
2. Should Taylor's use radio as the major media vehicle for its special 30-day promotional campaign?
3. What would be Taylor's best radio buy?
4. What should Taylor's try to communicate through its 30-day promotional program?

EXHIBIT 3

Radio Station Rates for 30-Second Spots

Station	Program Format	30-Second Spot	180/30/30 Buy[a]	240/30/30 Buy	360/30/30 Buy	720/30/30 Buy
KEGN-AM	Contemporary	$ 6	$ 972	$1,152	$1,512	$2,592
KEGN-FM	Contemporary	9	1,539	1,836	2,592	4,860
KFDE-AM	Modern country	9	n/a	1,944	2,592	4,536
KFDE-FM	Progressive country	8	n/a	1,824	2,448	4,320
KBDI-FM	Beautiful music	7	1,197	1,512	2,142	3,780
KOKE-AM	Middle-of-the-road	9	n/a	1,836	2,430	3,888
KBCT-AM	Album-oriented rock	10	n/a	1,920	2,340	3,600

A 180/30/30 buy consists of 180, 30-second spots broadcast over 30 days; other combinations are similarly coded. All station names are disguised.

EXHIBIT 4
Taylor's Merchandise Statistics (1987)

Merchandise Line	Net Sales to Total Sales	Inventory Turnover[a]	Gross Margin	Percentage of Purchases on Installment Credit
Living room furniture	32.4%	3.4x	42.8%	83.1%
Dining room furniture	8.7	1.6	40.7	78.0
Bedroom furniture	11.3	2.0	41.3	76.4
Bedding	9.1	3.7	43.4	10.8
Kitchen furniture	3.1	2.5	47.1	70.4
Floor coverings	6.1	2.9	34.6	65.8
Draperies and Curtains	2.5	3.1	39.1	48.1
Radio and stereo	3.0	2.2	37.0	87.2
Television	5.6	2.6	24.2	83.4
Washers, dryers, irons	4.8	2.5	32.0	67.1
Lamps and shades	2.1	1.1	48.1	21.4
Refrigerators	2.9	3.1	29.1	79.4
Stoves and ranges	4.9	3.0	33.7	80.7
All other	3.5	1.8	36.7	58.1

[a]Sales divided by inventory at cost.

CASE 9

EAST TOWNE MALL

Myron Gable
Shippensburg University

During the early spring of 1991, Kathy Mathis, the executive director of East Towne Mall, was concerned about how the mall was perceived by shoppers. The mall is located in the mideastern United States, adjacent to a city of approximately 75,000 people. The mall has 125 stores, including two nationally known department stores, three major chain operations, and a substantial number of chains in specific merchandise lines. In addition, there are approximately 75 independent retailers. With the exception of a supermarket, all types of retail stores are represented at the mall.

In the late spring of 1991, under the direction of Dr. Ron Ratliff, a professor of marketing at a nearby state college, a survey was conducted at East Towne Mall. The major findings of this study are found in Exhibits 1 through 4. Frequent shoppers were defined as those shopping at the mall four or more times monthly. Of the total of 756 female shoppers, 337 were classified as frequent; the balance being infrequent shoppers.

Approximately 80 percent of all shoppers traveled less than 30 minutes driving time to the shopping center; 93 percent of frequent shoppers traveled 30 minutes or less. Exhibit 1 indicates that infrequent shoppers spend a greater time traveling. In fact, 31 percent travel 30 minutes or longer. The

EXHIBIT 1

Driving Time to East Towne Mall (in minutes)

Driving Time	All Shoppers #	All Shoppers %	Frequent Shoppers #	Frequent Shoppers %	Infrequent Shoppers #	Infrequent Shoppers %
Less than 10	111	14.7	85	25.2	26	6.2
10–14	179	23.7	97	28.8	82	19.6
15–19	176	23.2	84	24.9	92	22.0
20–29	137	18.2	48	14.3	89	21.2
30–59	88	11.6	19	5.6	69	16.4
60 or more	65	8.6	4	1.2	61	14.6
Total	756	100.0	337	100.0	419	100.0

trading area of the mall was, therefore, quite large. With regard to Statement 1 in Exhibit 2, frequent and infrequent shoppers agree that East Towne Mall is a nice place to shop, with the frequent shoppers ranking it a little higher. The results indicate the stores at the mall keep shoppers reasonably well informed; frequent shoppers feeling they are better informed. Shoppers are reasonably pleased with product assortment, but the results indicate improvement is needed. Shoppers like to read ads or receive flyers before going to shop. Statement 5 in Exhibit 2 indicates that, overall, shoppers do look for sale items with infrequent shoppers seeking them out to a greater degree than frequent shoppers. According to Exhibit 3, approximately 46 percent of all

EXHIBIT 2

Shoppers' Opinions Toward Attitudinal Statements

Statement	Mean Score All Shoppers	Mean Score Frequent Shoppers	Mean Score Infrequent Shoppers
1. Compared to other malls, East Towne Mall is one of the nicer places to shop.	4.201	4.27	4.14
2. The stores at the Mall keep me informed by their advertisements and shopping flyers.	3.53	3.73	3.37
3. I can always find whatever product I am seeking at the Mall.	3.37	3.46	3.30
4. I like to read ads or receive shopping flyers before going to shop.	3.81	3.88	3.77
5. When going shopping, I basically look for sale items.	3.59	3.51	3.65

*A mean score close to 5 indicates strong agreement, while a score close to 1 indicates strong disagreement.

EXHIBIT 3

Age of Shoppers

Age	All Shoppers		Frequent Shoppers		Infrequent Shoppers	
	#	%	#	%	#	%
20 and under	120	15.9	59	17.5	61	14.6
21 to 30	230	30.4	98	29.1	132	31.5
31 to 40	120	15.9	44	13.1	76	18.1
41 to 50	112	14.8	45	13.3	67	16.0
over 50	131	17.3	67	19.9	64	15.3
No Response	43	5.7	24	7.1	19	4.5
Total	756	100.0	337	100.0	419	100.0

shoppers are under the age of 30, with 62 percent under 40. According to Exhibit 4, the average family income of infrequent shoppers was slightly higher than that of frequent shoppers. A survey at a similar-sized mall in another part of the state indicated 33 percent in the $30,000 and over category.

In early 1992, Ms. Mathis again contacted Dr. Ratliff. She wanted him to conduct another study focusing on shoppers' attitudes toward the stores at the mall and to ascertain whether a different type of shopper was now coming to the mall. She was interested in the following types of information:

1. How long did it take the shopper to drive to the mall?
2. Does the shopper have a price or quality orientation toward merchandise?
3. How many shopping trips does the shopper make each week?
4. Does the shopper rely on advertising media? If so, which media?
5. What is the age and income of shoppers coming to the mall?
6. What type of image do shoppers have of the West Mall?

Dr. Ratliff, in deciding on the type of questionnaire to use, thought of semantic differential rating scales. See Exhibit 5 for a partial listing of these scales and their dimensions.

EXHIBIT 4

Annual Family Income of Shoppers (in dollars)

Income Level	All Shoppers		Frequent Shoppers		Infrequent Shoppers	
	#	%	#	%	#	%
Under $20,000	132	17.5	63	18.7	69	16.5
From $20,000–$30,000	372	49.3	170	50.4	202	48.3
Over $30,000	159	21.0	70	20.8	89	21.2
No Response	93	12.2	34	10.1	59	14.0
Total	756	100.0	337	100.0	419	100.0

EXHIBIT 5

A Partial Listing of the Scales and Their Dimensions

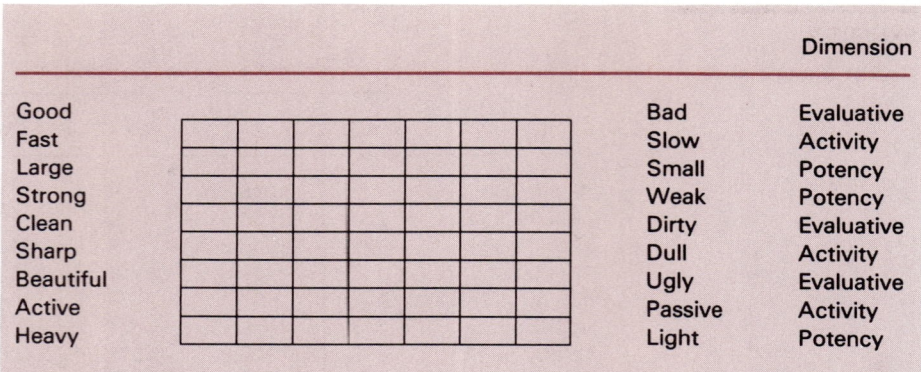

	Dimension
Good — Bad	Evaluative
Fast — Slow	Activity
Large — Small	Potency
Strong — Weak	Potency
Clean — Dirty	Evaluative
Sharp — Dull	Activity
Beautiful — Ugly	Evaluative
Active — Passive	Activity
Heavy — Light	Potency

[1]C. Osgood, G. Suci, and P. Tannenbaum, *The Measurement of Meaning* (Urbana, Illinois: University of Illinois Press, 1957) 37.

QUESTIONS

1. Do you think that the semantic differential would provide a good way to ascertain shoppers' opinions? Defend your answer.
2. What are the elements of the image of a shopping mall? Explain why you selected these elements.
3. What is the consumer profile of the frequent shoppers and infrequent shoppers at East Towne Mall? Describe.
4. Formulate a research recommendation to Kathy Mathis.

CASE 10

ZIG ZAG

Virginia Newell Lusch

In May 1987, two friends who had met in college, Tina Rhodes and Art Ramirez, decided to become partners in a retail venture. The retail enterprise they jointly envisioned would be a specialty store of modest size but, they hoped, sufficient magnitude to provide them with a reasonable income while allowing them both to pursue careers they felt would be fulfilling. Tina had just completed her undergraduate degree in art with an emphasis in fashion design. She believed that the retail venture would be a good vehicle for using her creative talents. Art had just finished a two-year junior college program in business administration. He was eager to try the skills he had acquired in college in the real world and envisioned the retail enterprise in which he and Tina planned to be partners as a way to apply his analytical training.

The store would be located in a coastal city in Texas of approximately 300,000 people. It would cater to the young adult (18 to 26) of moderate income. The merchandise mix would feature unisex clothing (custom T-shirts and Mexican and other imported clothing) and also custom-made beach wear. In addition to the clothing, the store would carry unique accessories for men and women, handmade jewelry, candles, and gift items. The store would be called Zig Zag.

Several months later, on a sultry Friday morning, Zig Zag was opened. But before opening day, Tina and Art had done considerable planning and preparation. After conceptualizing the store, they had to go through all the legal paperwork involved in establishing a partnership: find a location, obtain financing, buy merchandise, develop advertising messages, and much more. They quickly found out that the planning and preparation was more time consuming and complex than they had anticipated. Nonetheless, the big day finally arrived and they held their Grand Opening on August 1 and 2, 1987.

The building they had chosen was located, according to Art's calculations, in an excellent spot to attract its target customers. The store was in a neighborhood shopping center composed of specialty shops, a nationally affiliated supermarket, and a movie theater. The center was on one of the main highways leading out of the city in the direction of one of the busiest beaches in the metropolitan area. The building was only five years old, in excellent condition, and the right size for Zig Zag (2,400 square feet). It had previously been used by a real estate firm, which had recently moved its office to a more central location. The store was located near the end of the strip of shops, between a shoe store and an exclusive dress shop.

During the planning and preparation stages, Art had handled most of the financial and marketing problems while Tina concentrated on the store decor and layout. Her artwork decorated the walls and storefront. Exhibit 1 shows the storefront Tina designed and Exhibit 2 illustrates the layout she developed for Zig Zag.

EXHIBIT 1
Storefront of Zig Zag

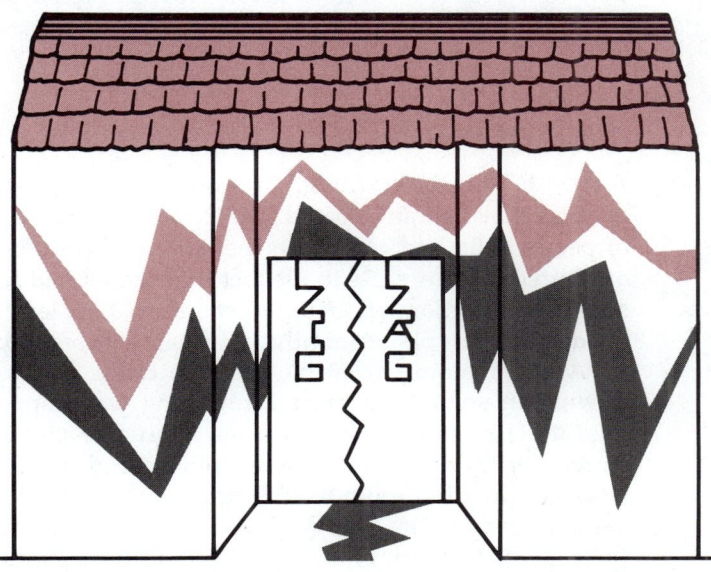

EXHIBIT 2

Interior Layout of Zig Zag

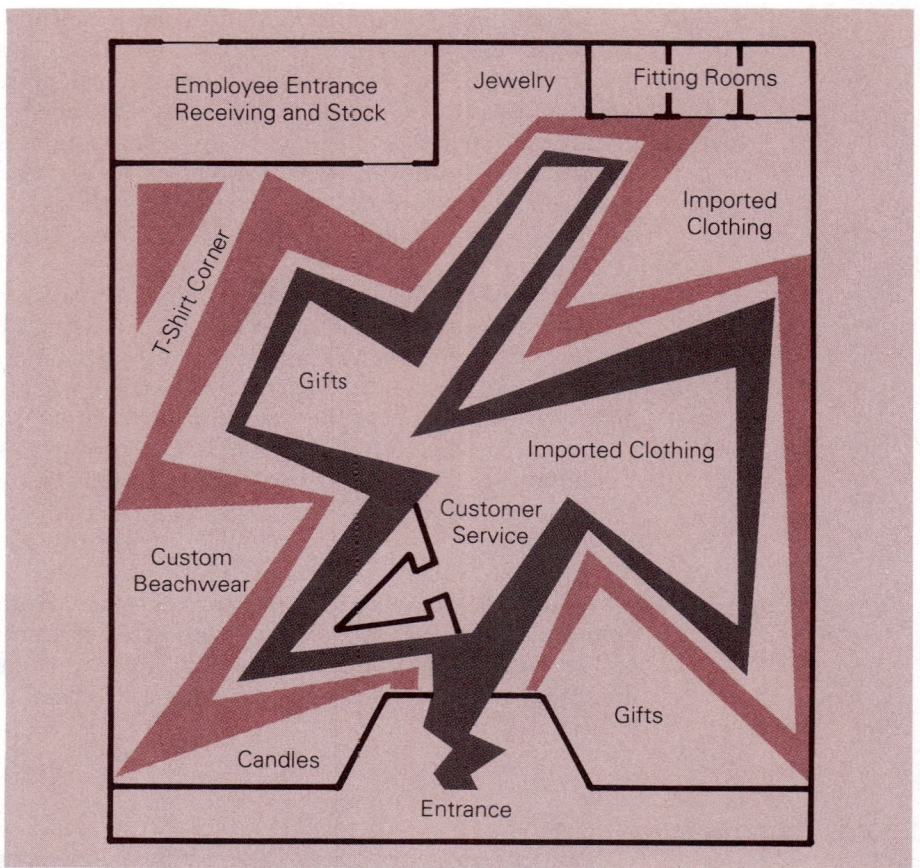

Current Situation

A month after the opening, Art announced that sales had not been quite as good as they had anticipated (see Exhibit 3). Ironically, however, the number of people who had come into the store had been greater than expected. Art attributed the low sales to the fact that school had recently started and that a significant portion of their target group had less discretionary income to spend for a couple of months. "Things will pick up," he assured Tina.

Another month went by, and the traffic began to drop off. Sales were down, but something more astounding was happening. Merchandise was missing. Tina first noticed this one afternoon after four teenage girls left the store after trying on some new embroidered tops. When Tina went back to clear the dressing room for the day, she discovered several empty hangers. Discouraged by this, she went into the storage room to unpack some more of the tops. On entering, she spied an old purse stuffed under some shelves. When she bent to pull it out she knocked several boxes of T-shirts off the

EXHIBIT 3

Zig Zag Daily Sales Volume (First Two Months of Operation)

8/1	$248.16	8/17	Closed (Sunday)	9/1	$ 29.21	9/16	$ 58.41
8/2	311.37	8/18	$ 61.38	9/2	41.73	9/17	71.29
8/3	Closed (Sunday)	8/19	60.41	9/3	48.48	9/18	98.81
8/4	54.18	8/20	88.39	9/4	99.77	9/19	134.47
8/5	84.13	8/21	96.38	9/5	151.47	9/20	149.35
8/6	98.46	8/22	136.31	9/6	147.28	9/21	Closed (Sunday)
8/7	164.72	8/23	178.74	9/7	Closed (Sunday)	9/22	40.55
8/8	168.98	8/24	Closed (Sunday)	9/8	49.43	9/23	51.79
8/9	189.47	8/25	73.18	9/9	57.30	9/24	98.71
8/10	Closed (Sunday)	8/26	84.71	9/10	62.28	9/25	224.49
8/11	59.79	8/27	109.41	9/11	89.99	9/26	288.37
8/12	87.41	8/28	279.34	9/12	119.30	9/27	290.41
8/13	94.70	8/29	271.87	9/13	149.47	9/28	Closed (Sunday)
8/14	161.37	8/30	346.38	9/14	Closed (Sunday)	9/29	58.71
8/15	198.32	8/31	Closed (Sunday)	9/15	41.32	9/30	92.91
8/16	182.44						

shelves. "This really isn't my day!" she muttered. Picking up the boxes she noticed how light in weight they were. Opening them, she found them empty. At this moment the bells on the entrance jangled, indicating a customer. She left the storeroom and reentered the sales area.

Two middle-aged women had just entered and were looking at the gifts. Tina wished that Art would return from the bank so that she could show him what she had discovered in the storeroom but, putting on a happy face, she approached the two women. "May I help you?" she asked, smiling.

One of the women turned to her and answered, "No, I don't think you have anything here that we want. We were at Marcelle's next door and thought your store looked interesting. We have appointments at the beauty salon across the street every week, and we usually come over here to do a little shopping while waiting for the bus. This is a cute place, but we have to go now. Goodbye."

Several days later, Art was beginning to close for the night when a couple in their late teens entered.

"Hi," said Art, "Can I do something for you?"

"Yes," said the girl. "My boyfriend wants to buy me a custom bikini for my birthday. I heard that you have them here."

"Right over here," Art indicated. "Pick out the style and size from the samples hanging on the rack, then choose the fabric. The prices are on the tags. Let me know if I can help you. The fitting rooms are in the back. Just follow the Zig Zag Rainbow carpet. Closing time is in 15 minutes, but if you need a little extra time it's OK."

Art went back to straightening the imported tops and jeans and overheard the two young people as they made their way to the fitting rooms.

"Wow!" exclaimed the boy "I see what Sheila meant when she said that this place was weird. This "follow the Zig Zag Rainbow" routine sounds like something out of the *Wizard of Oz*. Who does this turkey think he is anyway? I think I would like you in style D made out of the blue flowered Hawaiian stuff. What do you think?"

The girl replied, "That would be super. It would be the prettiest suit at the beach, but did you see the price?"

"Don't worry about that. Mr. Zig Zag Rainbow must be loaded. All the people in this shopping center are rich. He doesn't need our money." "Excuse me, sir," the boy called, "My girlfriend likes one of the suits. Can you help her decide on the fabric?"

Putting the overheard conversation out of his mind, Art replied, "Sure. Let's go back to the beachwear area and I'll show you some samples."

Together they went back to the beachwear area where Art unfolded the five fabric samples the girl indicated and laid them on the counter. Among them was the blue flowered Hawaiian material they had discussed earlier.

"We like this one," stated the boy, indicating a multicolored striped cotton, "but don't you have it in any other color combinations?"

"I don't think so," Art replied, "but here's a print that's nice for that suit."

"No, we like the stripes. Is this all your sample stock?"

"Well, no. Actually, I just received a shipment this afternoon that isn't unpacked yet. If you can come back tomorrow I'll show it to you. I'm certain there are several striped pieces in the order."

"We can't do that! This place is 10 miles from her house and I have to work tomorrow. Anyway, today's her birthday, and I'd really like to do it now. Couldn't you check and see if the stripes are there? We can wait."

"OK," said Art, "I'll be right back."

"We'll just look around while you look."

Art went back to the storeroom and opened the box from the fabric mill. He was right. There were several different striped samples. When he returned to the sales area, the couple was looking at the T-shirts.

"Here are the samples," Art called as he went back to the beachwear area.

"We're coming," laughed the girl, "along the Zig Zag Rainbow."

The couple ordered a suit made out of a multishade green fabric and left 15 minutes past closing time.

Art was tired, but at least, he thought to himself, he had closed a sale for his extra effort. As he refolded the fabrics he had shown them, he noticed that the blue Hawaiian print was missing, and as he found out later, so was the style D, size 9 sample unit, several T-shirts, a hand-hammered copper chain, and a belt. He felt sick. Looking at the order form for the custom suit, he realized that the address given was for the public library.

After only two months of operation, Art and Tina realized that Zig Zag had a real problem. The location was good, but the store just wasn't drawing the right customers. The middle-aged women who shopped in the other

EXHIBIT 4

Zig Zag Profit and Loss Statement (8/1/87–9/30/87)

Sales		$ 6635
Less: Cost of goods sold		3666
Gross profits		$ 2969
Less: Operating expenses		
Rent	$2400	
Advertising	600	
Wages	2000	
Theft and pilferage	749	
Utilities	343	
Insurance	200	
Phone	96	
Interest	884	
Miscellaneous	371	
Total operating expenses		7643
Profits or (loss)		$(4674)

stores or frequented the beauty salon were coming in but rarely purchasing anything. There were also numerous young teens who came in packs from the school nearby. Some of them made purchases, and most seemed really turned on to the store atmosphere, but there was a problem with theft that Art and Tina couldn't seem to control.

Art decided something had to be done. He spent the entire weekend taking physical inventory to identify all thefts and preparing a profit and loss statement for the first two months of operation (Exhibit 4) and a balance sheet as of September 30, 1987 (Exhibit 5). In addition, he spent considerable time developing some merchandise operating statistics for the seven major merchandise lines Zig Zag handled (Exhibit 6).

EXHIBIT 5

Zig Zag Balance Sheet (9/30/87)

Assets			Liabilities and Net Worth	
Current assets			Current liabilities	
Cash	$ 483		Accounts payable	$ 3,443
Inventory	22,292		Note payable	30,000
Total	$22,775		Total	$33,443
Fixed assets			Long-term liabilities	0
Equipment and fixtures	$ 9,400		Net worth	$ 1,107
Leasehold improvements	2,375			
Total	$11,775		Total liabilities and net worth	$34,550
Total assets	$34,550			

EXHIBIT 6

Zig Zag Operating Statistics (First Two Months of Operation)

Merchandise Line	Square Feet[a]	Dollar Sales	Average Inventory (at Cost)	Gross Margin Percent[b]
Candles	150	876	$1,732	45.3
Custom beach wear	170	375	692	47.1
T-shirts	222	1,291	1,608	31.3
Gifts	388	429	9,240	39.2
Jewelry	137	1,647	4,659	43.7
Accessories	93	1,408	3,043	29.4
Imported clothing	400	609	3,038	34.0

[a]Total square feet was 2,400; that not devoted to merchandise lines was for aisles, checkout, fitting rooms, and the stockroom.
[b]Gross margin percent equals sales minus cost of goods divided by sales.

After his long weekend with the books and paperwork, Art informed Tina that they were losing almost as much money as they were taking in. Somewhat depressed, he bluntly told her they could probably get out of their six-month lease, close the doors, and take their losses. Alternatively, he mentioned, they could try to hold things together for a couple more months while rapidly making some changes to try to improve sales and profits.

QUESTIONS

1. What do you see as the major problems that have afflicted Zig Zag?
2. What steps should Art and Tina take to correct their problems? Should they close the doors and quit?
3. Draw a new store layout that would improve efficiency and security while promoting the proper atmosphere.

CASE 11

HOMEWORLD-AMERICA*

Virginia Newell Lusch

This scene takes place during a board meeting of HomeWorld-America. HomeWorld-America was started by two brothers in 1956 and has steadily grown over the years from one small general store in Ohio to a highly profitable national chain of 518 stores in medium to small towns, selling mostly American-made products for the home and family. A profit and loss statement for last year is shown in Exhibit 1.

Although there is no standard store format or type, the stores have some common characteristics. They range in size from 40,000 to 85,000 square feet,

*This case was prepared as a basis for class discussion rather than to illustrate appropriate or inappropriate handling of a retail situation. The name and other pertinent facts of the actual retail organization have been disguised.

EXHIBIT 1

Homeworld-America Profit and Loss Statement (December 31, 1991)

Sales	$6,104,321,000
Cost of merchandise	4,803,491,000
Gross profit	1,300,830,000
Operating expenses	
Salaries/wages/fringe benefits	622,641,000
Occupancy/utilities	214,973,000
Advertising	108,190,000
Depreciation	57,418,000
Other	56,810,000
Net profit (before tax)	240,798,000
Taxes	94,634,000
Profit	$ 146,164,000

a typical store is 55,000. Each store employs between 75 and 125 full- and part-time people. The average number of full-time-equivalent employees per store is 83, with 41 of them full time and 84 part time. Of the nonmanagement nonsupervisory staff, 70 percent are female. The average work week for this level of employee is 26 hours for part time and 40 hours for full time. The managerial and supervisory level is composed of one manager, three assistant managers, and eight supervisors per store. The male/female ratio at this level varies by location but averages 65 percent male and 35 percent female. All workers at this level are full time, and their average work week is close to 60 hours. In the last few years, managers have been reporting problems with low employee morale, absenteeism, and high turnover of workers. A committee was assigned to look into this problem and its head, Ms. Jacoby, human resources director, presented the following report.

Ms. Jacoby: As you all know, our committee has been studying the problem of low morale, absenteeism, and turnover among company employees. In doing so, we discovered the following:
1. Ninety-six percent of employees who quit during the last six months stated personal or family problems as their reason for leaving Home-World-America. On further investigation, the problems were found to fall into five major categories.
   a. not enough time for career and family
   b. child-care expenses
   c. inflexibility of employer when dealing with personal issues
   d. money (needing more money to fulfill needs)
   e. personality conflicts.
2. HomeWorld's employee turnover rate of 61 percent is very high compared to national averages for our line of business. What is most interesting is the fact that for women between the ages of 25 and 44 with one or more children under 13, our turnover rate is 87 percent.

Stated alternatively, this employee group is likely to stay with the company only a little over one year.

3. Absenteeism was reported in all age groups with the highest three groups being college-age part-time employees, full-time women employees with children under age 5, and full-time male employees over age 60.

Mr. Burnhardt: May I interrupt a minute, Ms. Jacoby? I don't see what you are getting at. Your committee was told to find out why people are quitting and why they are unhappy here at HomeWorld-America not to figure out *who* is unhappy. We already know who is unhappy . . . the people who quit.

Ms. Jacoby: If you please, Mr. Burnhardt, I am getting to that . . .

Mr. Watson: We don't need to hear about baby sitters and class schedules. Get down to the meat. What are the employees upset about? Not enough coffee breaks? Are the shelves too high for women to stock easily? Should we quit hiring so many working mothers? Is the lunch hour too short? Don't they like the color of the smocks? You know . . . the basics.

Mr. Simpson: I think you are thinking too small, Mr. Watson. There are big issues here that we need to address. We promote our company as being family oriented and socially and environmentally conscious. We go out of our way to sell recyclable products, buy American, support the local economy and schools, and reward excellence among our employees. Isn't it time to address family problems as they conflict with career choices? Please gentlemen and ladies, let's allow Ms. Jacoby to finish.

Ms. Jacoby: Thank you, Chairman Simpson. As I was saying, the problems among our workers at all levels of employment seem to be centered around family versus career struggles. We therefore suggest that a new department be created to handle these problems. This is something that needs more than just a committee or task force. The employees need to know that management understands and wants to help them solve their problems. Exhibit 2 contains some suggestions and costs for beginning to deal with the problems of low morale, absenteeism, and high turnover. We must realize that this is an ongoing and ever-evolving situation and that it is only going to become more serious as fewer people enter the

EXHIBIT 2

Possible Actions to Overcome Low Morale, Absenteeism, and High Turnover

- *On-site child care facilities*—set up and maintained by the company at each store location for the children of employees. The estimated setup cost of such a facility would be $500,000 per store and the annual operating costs would be between $130,000 and $180,000 per facility depending on its location (the average being $155,000). Each facility would have the capacity to handle 40 to 60 children age 3 months to 12 years.

- *Newsletter* — containing employee suggestions and concerns and company suggestions. We already have a company newsletter so we would only need to add a new section to it at minimal cost.
- *Flexible time* — employee works up his or her own weekly schedule as long as the total number of hours stays constant. There is no added cost for doing this and it allows employees flexibility within their week so they are more productive when they are working.
- *Job sharing* — two employees work part time to share one full-time position. Benefits are shared as well, and some companies have actually saved money because they don't have as much turnover and training costs when employees are happier with their jobs.
- *Creation of a permanent department for career/family concerns* — this would be a top-management-level department for coordinating all the career/family concerns of all employees in all the stores with an assistant manager in each store to carry company policy to employees and employee concerns back to top management. Costs of the creation of this department would include hiring or promotion of new staff, office expenses, etc., but it should pay for itself in a short time.
- *Seminars for employees on family matters, career counseling, fitness and health matters* — these can be conducted at a minimal cost by having volunteer agencies present the programs. Yet, the contribution to employee morale is high, because employees feel the company cares about them as people.
- *Weekly personal time* — up to two hours per week of time to take care of personal matters that can only be handled during the employees' regularly scheduled work week; time not used can be accumulated and applied toward an extended annual vacation.
- *Family resource center* — books, tapes, and videos on family issues; annual costs of $300 to $1,000 per location.
- *Before- and after-school programs for children of employees* — a safe place for school age children of employees to stay before and after school so employees need not worry about their getting to and from school safely and on time. Average cost of the program ($50 per month per employee) could be paid by employees.
- *Summer "camperships"* — the company could provide vouchers to children of employees for summer camps in the area. Costs would vary depending on location, but the company could offer $300 camper vouchers for employees who have worked over one year and $500 camperships for employees who have worked over five years.
- *Extended maternity/paternity/family leave* — mother or father could receive up to one year of leave to care for babies or other family members needing full-time care, and return to pre-leave-level position.
- *Biweekly working parent exchange groups* — employees can interact and discuss problems and solutions of trying to juggle careers and families; minimal cost to stores which simply provide a meeting place.

QUESTIONS

service industries. A higher proportion of those available will be working mothers, older adults, and working adult children who are caring for aging parents.

1. As the general population and work force becomes older what long-term problems do you foresee for retailers? What solutions might HomeWorld-America be ready to offer?
2. Construct an employee survey to measure the problems of and concerns about the quality of work life of HomeWorld-America employees.
3. Is the creation of a special department for family/career concerns a good idea? Why or why not?
4. What possible short-term solutions might HomeWorld-America offer its employees?
5. One member of the board of directors, Mrs. Jane Juarez, has come out strongly in favor of HomeWorld-America's building on-site child-care facilities. As chairman of the board, write her a letter explaining why you support or cannot support this suggestion.

CASE 12   COMPETITECH B*

William A. Staples
University of Houston

This discussion is occurring one year after the difficulties described in the original Competitech case were resolved. Brenda Johnson, vice-president of marketing, is meeting with Frank Thomas, the telemarketing center manager.

Johnson: Frank, after we solved the problem of how to coordinate our telemarketing order processing activity with the work of inventory control people, our sales and profits have really increased. Our sales are up almost 30 percent over last year and customer problems are greatly reduced. Top management is very pleased with your department.

Thomas: Thanks, Brenda, I'll pass that on to the people on the phones. You know I've been in the telemarketing business for almost 10 years and this is the best group of people I have ever worked with. They're really customer oriented.

Johnson: I know. Last week I was at an AT&T seminar, and one of the things they mentioned got me thinking about our center and how we could do an even better job with telemarketing.

Thomas: What do you have in mind?

Johnson: Well, right now all our business is generated by incoming calls. Customers call us after they see one of our ads or receive one of our catalogs. The customer is taking the initiative in these situations. What the AT&T people were recommending was an "out-call" sales program.

---

*Background material for this case is provided in Case 3. Students should read the first Competitech case before analyzing Competitech B.

Rather than just waiting for incoming calls to be placed, they recommended we also make calls from our center to prospective customers. In that way, we can use our center more efficiently and increase sales even more. We would still be selling the same products. What do you think?

Thomas: There's a big difference between being an order taker and being an order getter. Let me get back with you next week with a plan that will test the feasibility of this.

Johnson: Good!

QUESTIONS

1. What are the major factors that Frank Thomas needs to consider as he designs a plan?
2. Describe some of the major "people problems" that will need to be anticipated by Thomas if this expansion occurs.
3. Assuming that it is technically feasible for Competitech to proceed with this expanded use of telemarketing, with what target market would you suggest it start?
4. How would you suggest that the telemarketing operators secure new leads from which additional business might be secured?

CASE 13

PORSCHE AG*

Roger A. Kerin
Southern Methodist University

Peter Schultz seemed to have everything going his way. In the three years since he became president of Porsche AG, the Porsche model 944 had become a resounding success since it was introduced in mid-1982, and Porsche sales in the United States had more than doubled. Nevertheless, Mr. Schultz had expressed concerns about Porsche's distribution effort in the United States and was contemplating a change.

Since 1969, Volkswagen of America (VWoA), a subsidiary of Volkswagenwerk AG, had handled all aspects of Porsche's automotive business in the United States, including importing, advertising, sales, and service when it established a Porsche/Audi Division. VWoA sold the Porsche line through 323 independent franchised dealers. These dealers also sold Audis, produced by a Volkswagenwerk AG subsidiary. According to industry sources, VWoA made $40 million importing Porsches into the United States in 1983.

Porsche's contract with VWoA was due to expire in August 1984, and Mr. Schultz felt the time was right to make the "single most important decision in the company's entire history": whether to change the way Porsche sold, warehoused, and repaired its cars in the United States. Several factors combined to lead Mr. Schultz to consider a change. First, he had heard that successful dealers in need of cars often had to buy Porsches from other

---

*This case was prepared as a basis for class discussion rather than to illustrate either effective or ineffective handling of a retail situation.

dealers at premium prices, which inflated the price paid by consumers. Second, he felt a mass-market retailer such as a Porsche/Audi dealer was the wrong outlet for low-volume, high-priced ($21,400 to $44,000 list price) Porsche cars. Third, he believed the Japanese would soon enter the high-performance sports car market in the United States, and Porsche needed a distribution system that would compete against them. These factors led him to conclude that a new distribution arrangement was necessary to bring the Porsche factory closer to its customers. Furthermore, he believed sales in the United States would increase if customers could be assured of obtaining cars more readily with the special features they desired.

The new distribution plan envisioned by Mr. Schultz contained four major points:

1. Porsche AG would withdraw from its contract with VWoA in August 1984 and would stop selling its cars through the VWoA dealer network.
2. Porsche would recruit and use agents to sell its cars rather than Porsche/Audi dealers. These agents would not have to buy cars and inventory them at a fixed location as dealers do. Therefore, they would not have to tie up cash in a car inventory, incur interest costs on that inventory, and operate a dealership.
3. Porsche would operate two warehouses in the United States, one in Reno, Nevada, and the other in Charleston, South Carolina.
4. Forty distribution and repair centers would be operated in the United States, where the Porsche population was highest. These 40 distribution centers would also sell Porsches. The distribution company would be called Porsche Cars North America.

The Company

Porsche AG was founded by Ferdinand Porsche in 1931. Based in Stuttgart, Germany, Porsche AG is primarily engaged in the development, manufacturing, and marketing of sports cars, in four-, six-, and eight-cylinder models, both for domestic consumption and for export. Porsche AG is also well known for its development of racing car models. For example, in 1983, Porsche cars swept nine of the first ten places at LeMans.

Porsche AG recorded net sales of $841 million with record earnings in fiscal 1983. One of the factors in this recent success was the Porsche 944—a high-performance model with an enticing $18,450 price, well below the $33,000 average sticker price for Porsche cars. Another factor in Porsche's record year was a more prosperous U.S. economy, since 53 percent of company sales came from the United States. The introduction of the Porsche 944 and the rebound in the U.S. economy resulted in sales of 21,831 cars in the United States in 1983, compared with 14,407 cars in 1982 and only 11,200 cars in 1981. Summary financial statements for fiscal 1983 are shown in Exhibit 1.

EXHIBIT 1

Porsche AG Financial Statement Summary (in DM 1,000)*

Income Statement Summary
(for the Year Ended July 31, 1983)

Net sales	DM*	2,133,679
Gross margin		758,674
Other income		43,066
Depreciation and amortization		73,148
Operating expenses		449,919
Taxes		124,945
Net income	DM	69,600

*Deutsch Mark (i.e., the German currency)

Balance Sheet Summary
(as of July 30, 1983)

Assets		
Current assets	DM	511,098
Fixed assets (including participatives and deferred charges)		355,452
Total assets	DM	866,550
Liabilities and equity		
Current liabilities	DM	630,105
Long-term debt		15,700
Equity		220,745
Total liabilities and equity	DM	866,550

Distribution Plan

The plan envisioned for the distribution of Porsche cars in the United States was based in part on consumer research indicating that the Porsche buyer was different from the so-called typical car buyer. For example, Porsche owners were not impulse buyers but, rather, approached the decision to buy a Porsche in a deliberate manner. They compared products and considered the purchase of a Porsche as an investment. Furthermore, Porsche owners were viewed as working 60 to 80 hours per week, having high standards of excellence and high expectations, and earning at least $75,000 per year. These data buttressed Mr. Schultz's opinion that Porsche customers could be better served by a different distribution arrangement. He was quoted in *Automotive News* (February 20, 1984, p. 1) as saying:

> *It is our firm belief that Porsche cannot hope to be viable as a manufacturer of high-technology, high-performance sports cars that are distributed by a traditional automotive marketing organization that is basically structured to serve a volume market with traditional service and sales activities.*

He added: "It must be as much fun to acquire a Porsche as it is to drive one." Details of the plan follow.

Agents versus Dealers

A central element of the new distribution plan was the change from conventional car dealers to agents that would represent Porsche Cars North America. Under the arrangement with VWoA, Porsches were inventoried and sold through Porsche/Audi dealers, which typically received a 16 to 18 percent margin on new Porsche cars. In addition, these dealers operated (1) a service department for routine and other car maintenance and repair needs and (2) a preowned, or used, car lot.

Under the new plan, Porsche Cars North America would sell its cars through agents that would be formed as limited partnerships. Every current Porsche dealer would receive an 8 percent commission on new cars sold. Each agent would receive four Porsches for demonstration purposes as part of the limited-partnership fee, but would not inventory new Porsches or operate used-car lots. An agent could offer car servicing or rely on Porsche Cars North America distribution centers to perform Porsche service. Agents would be allowed to set prices for new cars; but the 40 distribution centers located in areas of high Porsche ownership would list a suggested retail price and sell its cars only at the list price. According to a Porsche executive, the establishment of a fixed list price would mean that "A customer that is aware [of the list price] doesn't have to pay over list price; he has an alternative."

Distribution Centers

A second element of the new distribution plan included distribution centers. Forty distribution centers were planned, to be located in areas of high Porsche ownership. The distribution centers would assume many of the functions performed by conventional car dealers, including preparation, delivery, and service of new cars. In addition, distribution centers would operate a used-car program for buyers wishing to purchase a preowned Porsche. However, used-car sales would not be handled in the usual way. The major difference would be that Porsche Cars North America would refurbish cars for the purpose of increasing their value.

Warehouse Locations

West Coast and East Coast warehouses would be operated for new cars and parts. The West Coast warehouse would be located in Reno, Nevada, and the East Coast warehouse in Charleston, South Carolina. Reno, Nevada, would also house the corporate offices of Porsche Cars North America.

Each warehouse would be situated on the premises of an airport, since parts are shipped by air and plans were underway to ship cars by air as well. The plan involved transporting 250 cars per week via Boeing 747 cargo planes. Five flights per week were planned. These cars would serve as a buffer stock for distribution centers and agents. A schematic representative of the proposed distribution system is shown in Exhibit 2.

EXHIBIT 2

Porsche Cars North America Three-Tiered Distribution System

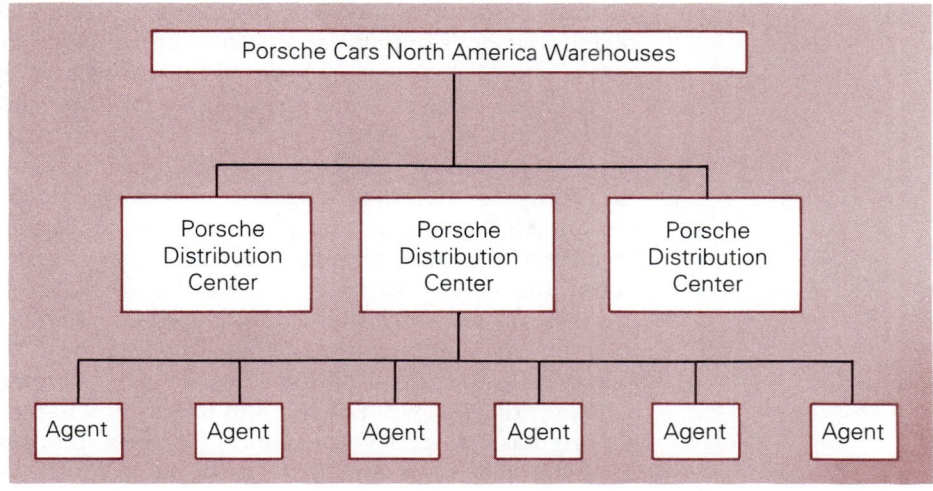

Buyer and Agent Ordering

The ordering of new or used cars would proceed as follows. A customer would go to an agent or distribution center and arrange to buy a car. Once a car was sold, a request for the model would be made through a computer link to Reno or Charleston. The customer would then go to either location to pick up the car and drive it home. Alternatively, an agent or distribution center employee could pick up the car for the buyer.

Cost

The total cost associated with the new system would include the costs of operating the two warehouses and distribution centers as well as importing, advertising, and servicing Porsche cars in the United States. It is estimated that Porsche AG would have to invest $350 million to start the operation and hire at least 275 people. Approximately $22 million would be spent to set up the Reno, Nevada, warehouse alone.

Distribution Plan Issues

The plan outlined by Peter Schultz represented a significant departure from past practices and could affect long-standing relationships with Volkswagenwerk AG. For example, the management of Porsche AG and Volkswagenwerk AG shared numerous family ties. Ferdinand Porsche, the company's founder, designed the Volkswagen "Beetle" that established Volkswagenwerk AG. Ferdinand Porsche's son, Ferry, is chairman of the board of Porsche AG; his son-in-law, Anton Piech, was Volkswagenwerk's first chairman of the board. Anton Piech's widow and children are still active in Volkswagenwerk affairs and own a Volkswagen distributorship and retail outlets in

Austria. Ferdinand Porsche's grandson, Ferdinand Piech, is director of research and development at Volkswagenwerk's Audi subsidiary. In short, a break with Volkswagenwerk could mean severing family ties.

Another issue was the response by Porsche/Audi dealers in the United States and VWoA. When Peter Schultz presented his idea to 300 Porsche/Audi dealers on February 15, 1984, in Reno, Nevada, the response was cool. According to a *Fortune* magazine report (April 16, 1984, p. 64) ". . . the dealers felt betrayed by the abolition of franchises and insulted by Schultz's invitation for them to invest in limited partnerships that would finance Porsche centers." Within a month of Mr. Schultz's announcement, Porsche AG was put on notice that it could face legal action by Porsche/Audi dealers totaling over $1 billion in penalties. In addition, VWoA filed protests against Porsche AG with the California and Nevada Departments of Motor Vehicles.

By April 1984, Mr. Schultz had to decide whether or not to proceed with his original plan or some variation. He was fully aware of the fact that the August 31 date for renewing the distribution contract with VWoA was quickly approaching.

QUESTIONS

1. Will channel conflict develop as a result of the proposed new distribution plan for Porsche automobiles in the United States?
2. Do you believe the proposed distribution plan will help Porsche be a stronger retail competitor in the United States?
3. How do you believe the customer will react to the new distribution system?

Source: This case is based solely on published information which includes: "Porsche Is Doing Great—So Changes Course," *Fortune,* 5 March 1984, 59; "Porsche to Cancel VW of America's Import Contract," *Wall Street Journal,* 30 January 1984, 13; "Porsche Gets Set to Go It Alone in the US," *Business Week,* 27 February 1984, 46–47; "Porsche to End Pact with VWoA," *Automotive News,* 6 February 1984, 3, 7; "Porsche Casts a Pall on Franchise System," *Automotive News,* 20 February 1984, 1, 57; "Porsche Moves Ahead on New Set-Up," *Automotive News,* 7 May 1984, 1, 8; "Porsche Forms Its Own US Distribution Unit to Sell and Service Cars," *Wall Street Journal,* 16 February 1984, 44; *Moody's International Manual* (New York: Moody's Investors Service, 1984); "Suits Against Porsche Could Top $1 Billion," *Automotive News,* 12 March 1984, 1, 57; "Ad Agency to Drop Porsche After Porsche Drops VWoA," *Automotive News,* 6 February 1984, 3, 7.

CASE 14

Robert F. Lusch
University of Oklahoma

SMITH'S IGA: PART A

Fred Smith, the owner and manager of Smith's IGA, was quite proud of his new 48,000-square-foot supermarket, which was doing $345,000 in weekly volume. Fred started the store 10 years ago in a 20,000-square-foot store that Safeway had vacated. After several remodels and expansions, the store was now large enough to compete in a wide variety of merchandise lines that traditional supermarkets ignored. For example, the store had a large section of automotive goods, small appliances, flowers, and kitchenware.

In the past, Fred did all the merchandising, but with the recent expansion to a 48,000-square-foot store, he hired a general merchandise manager, Helen

Demarais. Helen has been on the job for 13 months and has made a lot of changes, and generally Fred is quite impressed with her skills and initiative. After six months on the job, Helen asked for additional help and was given two assistant store managers to help her with merchandising decisions. Henry Barnes was assigned the frozen-food merchandising and Chung Liew the meat and produce departments. Helen handled all other areas of merchandising.

One of the first things Helen did was to insist that the firm purchase a merchandising software program that could help the firm keep track of the 9,500 stockkeeping units (SKUs) merchandised. She had intentionally delayed relying too heavily on the reports this software generates until she had 12 months of data. Now that the software has been in place for 12 months, Helen was anxious to use it to generate reports that could help her begin to remerchandise the store. She first wanted to become proficient with it before she instructed Henry and Chung in its use. In addition, Fred Smith had just mentioned to Helen that he thought the coffee line needed some attention. Fred was concerned that eight linear feet of aisle space (each aisle has five shelves of space or 40 linear feet) was being devoted to coffee and that the space and inventory investment was not justified given the level of coffee sales. In fact, coffee sales had recently declined—3 percent last year and 4 percent the prior year. This occurred despite an increase in shelf space of two linear feet of aisle space over the last three years. Fred knew from industry sources that this was a common trend. Young people were drinking less coffee and generally consuming fewer products with caffeine.

Helen felt it was important to establish some criteria for deciding more systematically which SKUs to drop and which to add. She knew Fred had some ideas on this, so together they sat down and brainstormed last Wednesday afternoon. The meeting resulted in the following criteria:

1. Each SKU should be profitable and this they decided should be stated in terms of gross margin return on inventory. The storewide goal was 120 percent ($1.20) and therefore each SKU should have at least a 75 percent GMROI.
2. An SKU that sells fewer than 1.5 units per week should be strongly considered for deletion or not added to begin with. These products might generate a sufficient GMROI but nonetheless tie up shelf space needlessly. An SKU that sells fewer than 1.5 units per week usually translates into four or fewer cases per year.
3. SKUs that are always associated with a supermarket should be stocked regardless of their profitability. For example, if sugar were not meeting the preceding two criteria, it should still be handled.

With these three criteria in mind, Helen sat down at her computer terminal and requested a report on the 53 coffee SKUs currently stocked. The report is presented in Exhibit 1. In the report were data on: product name, package size, units per case, unit cost, unit price, average weekly unit movement, number of facings on the shelf, and units per facing. For some reason the computer did not report the average inventory investment, but Helen was not too concerned because she knew she could compute that in 10 minutes with the data in Exhibit 1.

As she began to work on resetting the coffee line, Helen encountered another unanticipated issue. She felt that she needed to know not only the average weekly movement but also how this varied from week to week. After running a computer analysis of each of the 53 SKUs, she concluded that the weekly movement could be twice or occasionally three times the average weekly movement, and thus she decided that the store should always stock a shelf with at least six times the average weekly movement. She set the level at six times average weekly movement instead of three because the coffee line is restocked every two weeks.

EXHIBIT 1
Performance of Coffee SKUs

Product Name	Size (oz)	Case Pack	Unit Cost	Unit Price	Weekly Unit Movement	Number Facings	Units/ Facing
A1 DECAF	2	12	2.08	2.29	1.5	1	28
B1 DECAF	2	18	1.62	1.89	1.7	1	16
C1 INSTANT	2	24	1.62	1.87	2.0	1	16
A2 REG 2	2	12	1.94	2.18	4.1	1	42
D1 INST	2	24	1.45	1.72	15.4	4	16
C2 FREEZE DRIED INST	4	12	3.52	3.89	0.4	2	12
E1 FREEZE DRIED	4	12	3.38	3.85	1.0	1	12
F1 INSTANT	4	12	2.83	3.19	1.3	2	10
G1 INSTANT COFFEE	4	12	2.67	3.42	1.4	4	7
A3 INSTANT	4	12	3.59	3.89	1.7	3	14
H1 COLOMBIAN INSTANT	4	12	2.43	2.97	2.4	5	6
B2 INSTANT	4	24	2.54	2.90	2.9	2	12
D2 DECAF INSTANT	4	15	1.76	3.16	3.1	2	14
A4 DECAF FR DR	4	24	3.62	3.90	3.2	2	14
H2 INST COFFEE	4	12	2.13	2.45	3.5	4	6
A5 FREEZ DRY C	4	24	3.40	3.72	8.2	3	14
D3 INST COFE CRYST	4	24	2.54	2.86	14.5	8	10
I1 SGRFRE CAFE AME	4.5	12	2.69	3.04	1.3	1	21
I2 SGRFRE CAFE IRS	4.5	12	2.68	3.05	2.0	1	21
I3 SGRFRE IRSH MOC	4.5	12	2.68	3.05	2.7	1	21
I4 SGRFRE CAFE	4.5	12	2.69	3.06	3.0	1	21
I5 SGRFRE CAPPUCCI	4.5	12	2.69	3.05	3.3	1	21
I6 SGRFRE SWISS MO	4.5	12	2.69	3.05	3.5	1	21
H3 S-F VANILLA MOCHA	6	12	1.72	2.05	2.1	1	21
H4 S-F FUDGE MOCHA	6	12	1.72	2.00	2.5	1	21

Product Name	Size (oz)	Case Pack	Unit Cost	Unit Price	Weekly Unit Movement	Number Facings	Units/ Facing
H6 COLOMB	7	12	5.47	5.99	0.6	2	6
A7 INSTANT	7	12	3.59	3.82	1.3	1	14
J1 INST CEREAL BEV	7	6	3.19	3.57	4.7	3	5
K1 DEC	8	12	4.28	5.14	0.5	2	6
L1 FREEZE DRIED	8	12	4.35	5.10	0.7	2	10
F2 INS	8	12	3.35	4.05	1.3	3	6
M1 INST COFF	8	12	3.37	3.84	1.5	3	6
I7 DOUBLE DUTCH	8	12	2.52	2.78	1.6	1	21
B3 DECAF	8	12	4.61	5.09	1.7	2	10
N1 COFFEE FLVR	8	12	2.96	3.23	2.3	3	6
D4 DECAF INST	8	18	4.58	5.23	2.7	2	10
C3 INSTANT	8	18	4.37	5.15	3.1	2	10
I8 CHOC MINT	8	12	2.51	2.77	3.4	1	21
B4 INST COFFEE	8	18	3.57	3.81	4.3	4	10
N2 INSTANT	8	12	2.96	3.24	5.3	3	6
I9 CAFE	8	12	2.50	2.78	5.7	1	21
H5 INST COFFEE	8	12	2.69	3.17	6.4	4	6
I10 MOCHA INST CO	8	12	2.50	2.77	7.4	3	21
D5 INST COFFEE	8	18	3.75	3.95	18.7	9	10
A8 DECAF	9	20	4.40	6.25	1.7	2	12
A9 FRZ DRY	9	20	5.11	5.77	4.7	3	12
I11 VIENNA	10	12	2.50	2.76	6.5	1	21
I12 CAPPUCCINO	10	12	2.50	2.76	8.4	1	21
B5 INST COFFEE	12	12	5.25	5.95	1.0	3	4
A10 REG	12	12	7.17	7.87	2.0	4	5
D6 INST COFFEE	12	12	5.12	5.83	7.3	9	4
M2 SWISS MO	12.5	12	2.20	2.73	1.8	1	14
M3 VIENNA INST CO	12.5	12	2.06	2.99	3.3	1	14

QUESTIONS

1. How would you reconfigure the coffee line? What SKUs should be expanded, curtailed, or deleted?
2. How would you go about cutting the aisle space devoted to coffee from eight linear feet to six linear feet?
3. Is there any additional data that could be included in the merchandising report that would help assess the performance of an SKU?

CASE 15

Robert F. Lusch
University of Oklahoma

SMITH'S IGA: PART B

Helen was excited to share her results with Fred Smith. She scheduled a meeting on Monday afternoon and spent two hours going over her recommendations with Fred. At the end of the meeting, she was quite frustrated because Fred did not want to talk much about coffee but insisted on looking at the bigger picture. Part of a conversation that took place is summarized as follows.

Fred: "Helen, I know you are very excited about implementing some of your ideas for the coffee line, but let's not worry about that now. There is something bigger that we need to consider and that is how we will be using these merchandising reports in the future. I don't want us to go off and make some decisions on coffee using a particular approach and then find that we made the wrong decision because our merchandising report didn't include all the data we need."

Helen: "Fred, I thought we agreed on the criteria to use to evaluate SKUs. When we met last Wednesday we brainstormed and sorted out these issues. I think the real problem is that you are uncomfortable with trying to look more systematically at merchandising performance."

Fred: "Helen, that couldn't be further from the truth. You're doing a great job and I hired you because I wanted to upgrade our capabilities . . . I wouldn't have authorized the purchase of the merchandising software and would not have assigned Chung and Henry to work with you if I didn't want progress. Let's simply try to consider, one more time, what we may have forgotten to include in our merchandising report."

Helen: "The best way to do that is for us to go ahead and make some decision on coffee; after all, I spent 15 hours over the weekend coming up with some recommendations, then we can gradually modify our merchandising reports in the future as we learn, until we get them the way you would like them."

Fred: "You didn't hear me, Helen. We are going to get those reports refined before we begin to use them."

Helen: "OK, you're the boss. What do you think we left out?"

Fred: "Well, I'm not sure but I am a bit uncomfortable that we are only dealing with gross margin percentage. Space is very expensive, the recent expansion cost $288,000, and all that money was borrowed. It occurs to me that we need to charge each SKU with a space charge, and this should be relatively easy to do."

Helen: "If that is the issue, it can be easily handled. There is an option on our merchandising software that will allow us to compute the direct product profitability for each SKU. Frankly, I didn't bring that up earlier because I thought it was becoming a little too sophisticated too quickly."

Fred: "Well, let's try it, but first tell me a little more about how it works."

Helen: "Essentially, each SKU is charged any costs that can be reasonably traced to it. For example, we can charge each SKU for space depending on its usage of the shelf, and we can also allocate extra energy costs to the frozen-food department. Let me get to work and see what I can develop for the coffee line."

After considerable work Helen developed the direct product profitability for each SKU in the coffee department, presented in Exhibit 1. With these data in hand she sat down to develop some new merchandising recommendations for the coffee line.

EXHIBIT 1

Unit Direct Product Profitability Coffee SKUs

Product Name	Unit DPP	Product Name	Unit DPP
A1 DECAF	0.123	J1 INST CEREAL BEV	0.304
B1 DECAF	0.179	K1 DEC	0.556
C1 INSTANT	0.154	L1 FREEZE DRIED	0.513
A2 REG 2	0.189	F2 INS	0.564
D1 INST	0.237	M1 INST COFF	0.346
C2 FREEZE DRIED INST	0.059	I7 DOUBLE DUTCH	0.166
E1 FREEZE DRIED	0.314	B3 DECAF	0.354
F1 INSTANT	0.238	N1 COFFEE FLVR	0.188
G1 INSTANT COFFEE	0.644	D4 DECAF INST	0.534
A3 INSTANT	0.194	C3 INSTANT	0.674
H1 COLOMBIAN INST	0.462	I8 CHOC MINT	0.199
B2 INSTANT	0.265	B4 INST COFFEE	0.164
D2 DECAF INSTANT	0.322	N2 INSTANT	0.225
A4 DECAF FR DR	0.178	I9 CAFE	0.231
H2 INST COFFEE	0.261	H5 INST COFFEE	0.429
A5 FREEZ DRY C	0.263	I10 MOCHA INST CO	0.225
D3 INST COFE CRYST	0.281	D5 INST COFE	0.154
I1 SGRFRE CAFE AME	0.242	A8 DECAF	1.672
I2 SGRFRE CAFE IRS	0.290	A9 FRZ DRY	0.572
I3 SGRFRE IRSH MOC	0.304	I11 VIENNA	0.213
I4 SGRFRE CAFE	0.308	I12 CAPPUCCINO	0.217
I5 SGRFRE CAPPUCCI	0.301	B5 INST COFFEE	0.477
I6 SGRFRE SWISS MO	0.303	A10 REG	0.538
H3 S-F VANILLA MOCH	0.255	D6 INST COFFEE	0.643
H4 S-F FUDGE MOCHA	0.221	M2 SWISS MO	0.449
H6 COLOMB	0.214	M3 VIENNA INST CO	0.870
A7 INSTANT	0.100		

QUESTIONS

1. Use the direct product profitability data to establish merchandising recommendations for the coffee line. How do your recommendations differ from what you recommended using only gross margin data?
2. Develop a recommendation for how a merchandising report should look for each product line Smith's IGA handles. Also develop a set of guidelines for adding or deleting SKUs.

CASE 16

CENTRAL CITY SAVINGS BANK

Virginia Newell Lusch

Central City Savings Bank was created in 1988 through the consolidation of City Bank and Central Savings Bank. Both were small independent banks operating in a college town in Oklahoma, a state which until recently did not allow branch banking. Most Oklahoma consumers were therefore used to having numerous small, independent banks and were reluctant to accept the big national banks with many branches throughout the country. They knew and trusted their small-town bankers and didn't like the idea of being controlled by "somebody in New York or Chicago or Tokyo." However, the savings and loan crisis and the oil economy depression of the 1980s forced many Oklahoma banks into bankruptcy and consolidation, and gradually larger banks and branch banks began creeping into the lifestyles of Oklahoma townspeople.

Central City Savings Bank, through its conservative investing policy and friendly atmosphere, has captured 13.9 percent of the banking business in College City, Oklahoma, but wants to do an even better job serving its customers and attracting new customers. To this end, Dr. Suzanne King, a marketing professor at the college, proposed to Larry Ellis, the president of the bank, that the bank commission a marketing research study to determine the following:

1. Who are the bank's current customers?
2. Who should the bank target as future customers?
3. What product mix should the bank offer?
4. Where should the bank put its advertising dollars?

The data upon which the study is based were compiled from a stratified, randomly selected sample of residents of College City, using a computer-

EXHIBIT 1

Satisfaction of College City, Oklahoma's Financial Institution Customers

Institution	Percentage Responding Customers	Very Satisfied	Satisfied	Somewhat Satisfied	Not Satisfied
Central City Savings Bank	13.4	59.2	38.9	0.0	1.9
First National Bank	12.9	73.1	23.1	1.9	1.9
Employee Credit Union	10.7	69.8	14.0	14.0	2.2
Bank of Oklahoma	9.9	34.1	36.6	19.5	9.8
First Interstate	9.2	50.0	33.3	11.1	5.9
Liberty Bell Bank	6.9	70.3	25.9	3.8	0.0
U.S. Bank & Trust	4.2	50.0	41.7	8.3	0.0
Sooner Savings & Loan	3.2	61.5	30.8	7.7	0.0
Federal Savings & Loan	2.5	60.0	40.0	0.0	0.0
"Other" Credit Unions	3.9	71.4	14.3	14.3	0.0
Republic Bank	2.2	88.9	11.1	0.0	0.0
Riverside Savings & Loan	1.2	40.0	20.0	20.0	20.0
First Federal Savings	0.7	100.0	0.0	0.0	0.0
All Other	12.7	No response	No response	No response	No response
Do not use financial institution	5.7				
Refused to answer	0.7				
	100%				

generated list of 405 working residential telephone numbers. This sample provides a reliability coefficient of 95 percent with a sampling error of ±5 percent. The results of the survey are given in Exhibits 1 through 11. After reviewing the data, Dr. King made the following recommendations to Larry Ellis.

1. Central City Savings Bank should set a goal of obtaining a 20 percent market share within the next three years. To help achieve this, it should:
    a. Continue professional but friendly service
    b. Maintain convenience of drive-in and ATM facilities
    c. Entice the 20 to 50 age group with special promotions
    d. Stay involved in community activities, especially those benefiting current customers, target customers, and neighborhoods around the bank
    e. Offer special incentives and educational programs to students.
2. Since most people choose a financial institution through word-of-mouth advertising, the best growth strategy is to keep current customers happy so they will spread the word. The publicity received through participation

EXHIBIT 2

Customers' Rating of Selected Services

	Rating							
	Good		Fair		Poor		Don't Know/ Not Applicable	
Service	All	CCSB	All	CCSB	All	CCSB	All	CCSB
Convenient parking	68.0	59.3	16.8	16.7	5.7	11.1	9.5	12.9
Friendly employees	86.9	94.4	8.5	3.7	1.5	1.9	3.1	0.0
Available credit/loans	45.5	46.3	12.7	11.1	2.8	1.9	39.0	40.0
Attractive lobby	68.7	70.4	20.9	22.2	1.1	0.0	9.3	7.4
Convenient drive-in hours	72.4	79.6	12.1	7.4	2.6	5.6	12.9	7.4
Progressive policies	51.5	48.2	24.5	24.1	3.1	1.9	20.9	25.9
Professional employees	80.2	88.9	13.9	7.4	2.1	0.0	3.8	3.7
Informative advertising	41.8	46.3	22.9	14.8	5.7	1.9	29.6	37.0
Drive-in service	74.2	87.0	9.8	1.9	3.4	1.9	12.7	9.2
Lobby service	75.1	66.7	11.7	11.1	1.6	0.0	11.7	22.2
Community activity	35.6	68.5	14.4	5.6	3.9	0.0	46.1	25.9
Levels of service charges	50.1	42.6	32.8	40.7	8.5	5.6	8.5	11.1
Lobby hours	58.5	50.9	22.0	13.2	3.6	3.8	15.8	32.1
Accessible drive-in	76.9	81.5	6.7	3.7	3.6	1.9	12.7	13.0
Level of interest on savings	41.5	31.5	31.4	25.9	3.9	1.9	23.2	40.7
Level of interest on loans	26.5	29.6	25.8	27.8	2.6	0.0	45.1	42.6
Average	59.6	62.0	17.9	14.8	3.5	2.5	19.0	20.7

and support of community activities and causes increases visibility and name recognition. However, in order to attract new customer groups, informative newspaper advertisements would be helpful.
3. The bank should work harder to attract auto and home mortgage loans. After all, while 57.4 percent of CCSB customers think the level of interest charged on loans is good or fair, CCSB has only a small percentage of customers in the 20 to 50 age range, the prime group for auto and home mortgage loans. If the bank finances a home or car for a person, the customer will likely be willing to bank at CCSB as well.

EXHIBIT 3
Length of Time of Patronage of Major Financial Institution

Time	Percentage All Respondents	Percentage CCSB Respondents
5 years or less	54.5	31.5
6–10 years	21.0	18.5
11–15 years	8.6	9.3
16 or more years	15.9	40.7
	100%	100%

EXHIBIT 4
Financial Services Used by Customers During Past 12 Months

Service[a]	Percentage
Purchased certificate of deposit	19.4
Opened trust account	3.7
Obtained auto loan	16.4
Obtained safe deposit box	10.2
Purchased stocks and/or bonds	13.9
Obtained home mortgage	5.4
Obtained credit card	13.9
Purchased travelers checks	23.1
Purchased life insurance policy	6.4
Obtained money market account	12.2
Obtained NOW account	5.0
Obtained passbook savings account	12.2
Obtained debt consolidation loan	1.0
Obtained education loan	5.7
Obtained small business loan	1.7
Obtained home improvement loan	0.5
None	32.8

[a] Making deposits and withdrawals not included.

EXHIBIT 5
Frequency of Use of ATM Card in Past Month[a]

Frequency	Percentage
None	23.5
1-3 times	18.8
4-6 times	22.5
More than 6 times	34.7
Don't know	0.5

[a]Fifty-nine percent of respondents have an ATM card.

EXHIBIT 6
Types of Advertising Used to Select a Financial Institution

Type	Percentage All Respondents	Percentage CCSB Customers
None	32.5	35.2
Direct mail	2.5	3.7
Newspaper	13.2	13.0
Radio	1.7	1.9
Billboard	0	0
Television	3.2	1.9
Yellow pages	4.5	0
Word-of-mouth	37.2	38.9
Other[a]	5.2	5.5

[a]Other includes brokers, friends, personal contacts, and magazines.

EXHIBIT 7
Newspaper Section Most Often Read

Section	Percentage
News	37.3
Sports	15.7
Advertising	4.2
Editorials	3.7
Women's section	2.6
Comics	2.6
Births and deaths	0.8
Other[a]	33.1

[a]Other includes "all sections," marriages and divorces, business, entertainment, travel, TV and radio, front page, local area news.

EXHIBIT 8
Sex of Customers

Sex	Percentage All Respondents	Percentage CCSB Customers
Male	47.9	48.9
Female	52.1	51.1

EXHIBIT 9
Age Distribution of Heads of Households (percent)

Age	All Respondents[a]	CCSB Customers[b]	First National Customers	Employee Credit Union Customers	Bank of Oklahoma Customers
Under 20	1.1	1.8	2.1	0.0	2.5
20–29	27.6	20.4	27.7	16.7	17.5
30–39	28.6	14.8	23.4	40.5	22.5
40–49	20.7	14.8	10.6	16.7	17.5
50–59	13.8	20.4	12.8	23.8	20.0
60+ over	8.2	27.8	23.4	2.4	20.0

[a]Median age head of household for all respondents = 37.8 years.
[b]Median age head of household for CCSB customers = 47.9 years.

EXHIBIT 10
Occupation of Heads of Households (percent)

Occupation	All Respondents Male	All Respondents Female	CCSB Customers Male	CCSB Customers Female
Professional/technical	27.2	20.8	31.7	16.3
Managerial	10.1	6.3	14.6	8.2
Trades	24.0	23.7	31.7	4.1
Services	11.1	6.9	2.4	18.4
Homemaker	0.0	18.4	0.0	22.4
Military	1.9	0.0	0.0	0.0
Retired	10.7	10.8	12.2	24.5
Student	9.8	9.9	7.3	6.1
Unemployed	4.6	2.6	0.0	0.0
Refused to answer	0.6	0.6	0.0	0.0

EXHIBIT 11

Annual Household Income Before Taxes

Income Range	Percentage All Respondents[a]	Percentage CCSB Customers[b]
Less than 12,000	17.1	14.8
12,000–14,999	4.0	5.6
15,000–19,999	10.2	14.8
20,000–29,999	14.4	11.1
30,000–49,999	25.6	24.1
50,000–59,999	8.2	9.2
60,000 and above	10.4	7.4
Refused to answer	10.2	13.0

[a]Median household income all respondents = $33,850.
[b]Median household income CCSB customers = $33,700.

QUESTIONS

1. Based on the data, identify the strengths and weaknesses of CCSB.
2. Compose a profile of the bank's current customer.
3. Identify three groups the bank should target as future customers.
4. Make a list of 10 services (in descending order of importance) you look for when choosing a financial institution. Make a second list for the CCSB customer you profiled in question 2. How do the lists differ and why?
5. Design a newspaper advertisement for Central City Savings Bank to attract each of the three target groups you identified in question 3.
6. Write a memo to the board of directors promoting a community activity in which you think the bank should become involved. Explain the activity and show why the bank's participation would be beneficial to both the community and the bank.
7. Larry Ellis has asked you to react in memo form to the recommendations of Dr. King. As the bank's director of marketing, write Mr. Ellis a 1-to-2-page memo outlining your reaction.

CASE 17

TOYS "R" US INTERNATIONAL

Virginia Newell Lusch

Toys "R" Us International is a growing division of Toys "R" Us, the world's largest and fastest-growing children's specialty retail chain. The international toy market is about twice as large as that of the United States, and about 80 percent of the merchandise sold internationally is the same as that sold in the United States. Like Toys "R" Us United States, most stores in other countries are freestanding buildings in areas people drive to, with parking at the store. Studies have shown that people tend to buy more if they can put their purchases directly into their cars. This is especially true of toys which often tend to be big, heavy, or bulky to carry.

As of January 1991, Toys "R" Us International operated in eight countries: Canada (32 stores), France (10), Germany (18), United Kingdom (28), Hong Kong (3), Malaysia (2), Singapore (2), and Taiwan (2), for a total of 97 locations. Puerto Rico is considered a U.S. location and is included as two of Toys "R" Us United States' 451 locations.

Toys "R" Us United States has been profitable even in times of recession partly due to its ability to "clone" existing stores into similar markets and use centralized warehouses to cut down on distribution costs. The toy market has also been stronger than some other markets because of the number of women in the work force, for although women are generally having fewer children and are waiting longer to have them, these women are spending more on their own children and on gifts for friends and relatives than when the families were larger and there was only one income for support. The international division expects similar trends.

As a recent college graduate, you accepted a position in the merchandis-

EXHIBIT 1

Population Trends

Country	Population in 1988 (millions)	Estimated Population in 2021 (millions)	Urban Population as Percentage of Total	Percentage Population Under 15 Years Old (1990)
Argentina	31.96	40.19	84.6	29.9
Australia	16.53	20.34	85.5	22.2
Belgium	9.92	10.04	96.3	18.1
Brazil	144.43	207.45	72.7	35.2
Canada	**25.95**	**30.20**	**75.9**	**20.9**
France	**55.87**	**59.43**	**73.4**	**20.2**
Germany	**77.87**	**79.53**	**85.5**	**17.4**
Hong Kong	**5.68**	**6.74**	**92.4**	**22.0**
Italy	57.44	57.29	67.4	17.1
Ivory Coast	11.61	26.49	N/A	49.4
Japan	122.61	131.68	76.7	18.5
Kenya	23.88	53.47	19.7	52.1
Malaysia	**16.92**	**23.69**	**38.2**	**36.2**
Netherlands	14.76	15.32	88.4	17.8
Singapore	**2.65**	**3.12**	**100.0**	**26.5**
Spain	39.05	41.83	75.8	20.4
Taiwan	**19.90**	**26.72**	**N/A**	**N/A**
Thailand	54.54	71.59	19.8	32.7
Turkey	52.42	76.64	45.9	34.3
United Kingdom	**57.08**	**57.56**	**91.7**	**18.9**
United States	**246.33**	**281.22**	**73.9**	**21.5**
Venezuela	18.75	30.1	87.6	38.3

Source: *The Economist Book of Vital World Statistics* (1990), 16–17, 18–19.

ing area of Toys "R" Us International. Although you enjoyed the work, you were delighted to be transferred to the marketing research/planning area of the firm. You have been presented with the data in Exhibits 1 through 4 and asked for your analysis and recommendations concerning possible expansion into additional countries.

Note that on all exhibits, the countries where Toys "R" Us is currently doing business are highlighted in **bold** type, and information not available is indicated by N/A.

EXHIBIT 2

Income and Education Ratios (1987-1990)

Country	Income Ratio[a]	Percentage Population Working	Percentage Income Spent on Leisure	High School Enrollment as a Percentage of Relevant Age Group
Argentina	11.3	37.4	7.8	74
Australia	8.7	47.4	23.1	98
Belgium	4.6	42.7	18.0	99
Brazil	33.7	42.0	11.5	38
Canada	**7.5**	**51.1**	**26.2**	**104[b]**
France	**7.7**	**44.3**	**20.4**	**92**
Germany	**5.0[c]**	**47.9**	**23.9**	**99**
Hong Kong	**8.7**	**50.0**	**15.0**	**74**
Italy	7.1	41.7	24.1	75
Ivory Coast	25.6	N/A	23.0	19
Japan	4.3	49.8	29.5	95
Kenya	25.0	N/A	10.4	23
Malaysia	**14.4**	**N/A**	**9.1**	**59**
Netherlands	4.4	55.0	25.2	104[b]
Singapore	**N/A**	**47.9**	**21.5**	**71**
Spain	5.8	36.8	21.6	102[b]
Taiwan	**N/A**	**N/A**	**14.6**	**N/A**
Thailand	8.8	53.0	15.9	28
Turkey	16.3	36.2	N/A	46
United Kingdom	**5.7**	**48.3**	**30.8**	**83**
United States	**7.5**	**50.0**	**25.5**	**98**
Venezuela	18.2	34.4		54

[a] Income ratio measures the ratio of the richest 20 percent of the population to the poorest 20 percent (generally the larger the ratio, the poorer the country). For example, the richest 20 percent of the people in Argentina have incomes that are 11.3 times the income level of the poorest 20 percent of the people.
[b] Percentages may be over 100 percent if children of other age groups attend.
[c] Includes West Germany (pre-1990) only.
Source: *The Economist Book of Vital World Statistics* (1990), 194-95, 204-205, 229-32.

EXHIBIT 3
Private Vehicle Use (1985-1988)

Country	Number of Vehicles Owned (000s)	Total Vehicle Kilometers per Year per Kilometer of Road (000s)
Argentina	5,232.7	236.6
Australia	9,221.1	N/A
Belgium	3,936.6	373.3
Brazil	16,605.6	N/A
Canada	**15,400.0**	**168.8**
France	**27,090.0**	**459.6**
Germany	**35,302.9**	**843.8**
Hong Kong	**324.1**	**4,705.7**
Italy	25,490.0	923.4
Ivory Coast	238.0	N/A
Japan	52,450.2	497.0
Kenya	265.0	N/A
Malaysia	**2,681.2**	**N/A**
Netherlands	5,788.8	761.4
Singapore	**395.0**	**N/A**
Spain	12,475.0	291.9
Taiwan	**1,450.0**	**N/A**
Thailand	2,667.8	408.7
Turkey	1,725.0	69.6
United Kingdom	**24,499.6**	**929.6**
United States	**183,468.0**	**494.2**
Venezuela	3,548.0	N/A

Source: *The Economist Book of Vital World Statistics* (1990), 108-10.

EXHIBIT 4
Media Exposure and Advertising Expenditures (1985-1988)

Country	Television Advertising (millions)	Number of Televisions per 1,000 Population	Print Advertising (millions)	Newspapers per 1,000 Population
Argentina	325.2	217	318.1	N/A
Australia	932.9	483	1,300.2	264
Belgium	106.2	320	341.8	221
Brazil	1,057.7	191	837.9	48
Canada	**890.4**	**577**	**2,360.4**	**225**
France	**1,708.3**	**333**	**3,383.3**	**193**

Germany	902.1	570	6,560.8	344
Hong Kong	286.4	241	181.6	N/A
Italy	2,189.4	257	1,825.9	99
Ivory Coast	N/A	5	N/A	8
Japan	8,257.4	587	8,350.9	566
Kenya	N/A	6	N/A	13
Malaysia	69.2	140	83.6	N/A
Netherlands	240.8	469	1,878.2	N/A
Singapore	50.9	N/A	92.7	357
Spain	1,050.3	368	1,705.9	75
Taiwan	246.5	N/A	416.9	N/A
Thailand	115.9	103	75.4	15
Turkey	N/A	172	N/A	N/A
United Kingdom	3,069.6	434	5,835.9	421
United States	23,946.2	811	37,327.9	259
Venezuela	265.2	142	148.1	N/A

Source: *The Economist Book of Vital World Statistics* (1990), 126, 130.

QUESTIONS

1. What three countries would you recommend to the board as possible areas for Toys "R" Us International to enter? Why did you choose these three over the others?
2. Are there any countries on the list that you think Toys "R" Us should stay out of for the near future? Why or why not?
3. Is there additional data you would like to obtain? If so what other information do you want and why?

CASE 18

HIGBY'S HARDWARE

Virginia Newell Lusch

Higby's Hardware is a small, mom-and-pop-type hardware store in a rural eastern town of 5,000. It was established in the mid-1800s and has always been family owned and operated. Higby's has never made much of a profit, but being the only hardware store in town, it has managed to stay in business. Harold Higby, the current owner, is a portly, timid widower in his late 50s with no children. He feels overworked, underpaid, and frightened that the store is slowly losing ground and, since he has no heirs, the future of Higby's rests on his shoulders. He currently employs Rachel Goldsby as his "office staff." She is 23 years old and joined Higby's upon completion of an office management course at a nearby junior college. Rachel shares an apartment with Tiffany Butler, a beautician who is remodeling an old farmhouse with her fiance, Kenneth Simms. Tiffany and Kenneth plan to marry in three more months and move into their newly renovated house. Kenneth had been working for his uncle at the lawn and garden supply store in a neighboring town, but on Rachel's recommendation, he landed the assistant manager's position at Higby's Hardware. Mr. Higby was impressed with Kenneth's experience as well as with the shining character reference provided by Rachel, which mentioned Kenneth's helpfulness, generosity, intellect, and ability to make or fix just about anything. Harold hired him immediately with dreams of letting Kenneth run things and ultimately taking over while he, himself, took things easier. A good manager, he mused, could make all the difference.

After one week of training, Harold handed Kenneth the keys and announced that he was taking a short vacation and would return in five or six days. He felt confident that Kenneth and Rachel could handle things until he returned. After all, they had experience. Forty-five minutes after Harold left, Kenneth announced that he needed to check on a couple of things at the house but would be back before closing to lock up. Rachel spent the rest of the day as the only employee, handling sales, office, and loading area duties. Kenneth returned just before closing and apologized for taking so long.

"You're a real gem, Rachel," he said. "I ran into a couple of problems at the house and just couldn't leave until I figured out how to solve them. You understand. I'll come in early tomorrow to make up my time."

When Rachel arrived at work the following morning, she found the doors still locked at 8:50. Higby's always opened promptly at 8 and several angry customers were grumbling at Rachel as she unlocked the door to open up. She couldn't imagine what had happened to Kenneth and started to envision all sorts of accidents. By 9:30 she had things running smoothly again, the customers had been served, and she finally had the time to start hunting for Kenneth. She called his home phone.

"Hello," a groggy voice answered.

"Kenneth! This is Rachel. Are you OK? Why aren't you here? Are you sick? Kenneth, what's going on?"

"Oh wow, what time is it?" replied Kenneth, still sounding half asleep.

"Kenneth!" shouted Rachel. "Get to work. It's after 9:30 and you were supposed to be here early this morning. I had to open the store when I came to work. It's a good thing I was a few minutes early, but you're really going to catch it for this when Mr. Higby gets back. There were customers here waiting . . . and they weren't happy. Now, get in here and help me."

"OK, OK. Stop screeching at me. I had a late night last night. I'll be there shortly."

At 12:15 Kenneth appeared wearing a grin and handed Rachel a bouquet of two dozen yellow roses.

"Thanks for hanging in and covering for me," he said. "You've done a great job and I really appreciate it. Why don't you knock off early this afternoon? You deserve it."

"That's OK," replied Rachel. "Thanks for the flowers. You know they're my favorite. I think I will take a couple hours off, if you're sure you can handle everything here by yourself."

"What's to handle?" he smiled back and went to help a customer.

Things ran smoothly for a couple of days until Rachel arrived at work one morning to see two police cars parked in front of the store.

"What's going on?" she cried, running through the door to see Kenneth talking to the officers.

"Oh, we had a little break-in last night. Not too bad, the best I can figure, but we need you to go over the records with the officers to see how much was actually taken. Most of the stuff seems to be from the order we got in yesterday afternoon. I didn't have it all tagged and put away yet, so I guess it was real easy to take. Did we have an itemized invoice for that?"

"It should be on my desk. Wait a minute and I'll get it. Has anyone told Mr. Higby about this?" Rachel asked.

"No, he wasn't at home. I think he's fishing somewhere for the next couple of days. He'll find out about it soon enough. There's no reason to bother him. We can handle everything. He'll be pleased we didn't ruin his little vacation," replied Kenneth.

Rachel went to look for the invoice only to find that the office had been vandalized. Papers were everywhere, her desk overturned, the file cabinet destroyed, and the money box empty.

She returned to the officers and explained that since everything was in such a mess, she was unable to locate the invoice. She told them it would take a day or two to clean up and get the office back in order and that she would have a list assembled before Mr. Higby returned on Monday. She forgot to mention the empty money box.

Friday and Saturday Rachel spent most of her time cleaning up and assembling a list of stolen merchandise for the police, the insurance company, and Mr. Higby. Kenneth was in and out of the store "taking care of a few things," he said. Much of the paperwork had been destroyed beyond repair, but as nearly as she could figure the thief had gotten away with about $1,200 worth of wood paneling, 60 gallons of paint and varnish, 2 large-capacity hot-water heaters, a roll of copper tubing, a roll of electrical wire, a container of electrical boxes, a crate of nails, a box of hand-hammered copper drawer pulls and brackets, and $756 in cash. There also seemed to be other miscellaneous items missing from the store, but without precise records, Rachel wasn't sure about the accuracy of her memory and did not tie them to the burglary.

"Poor Mr. Higby," thought Rachel. "Just when he thought things were going to fall into place for him. Well, at least insurance will cover the merchandise and repairing the back door and office."

Insurance did cover the loss, but Harold's dreams of Kenneth's turning things around and taking over for him were shattered. After three months, profits hadn't improved at all. In fact, Kenneth seemed to be buying at higher prices and selling fewer big-ticket items. Customers were complaining of short orders, overcharging, inferior merchandise, and unfriendly service. Rachel had noticed cash register receipts with incorrect prices, missing price tags, boxes of bulk goods that seemed lighter than usual, invoices for items she didn't remember ordering, and Kenneth leaving the store whenever

Harold wasn't around. She began to suspect that perhaps Kenneth was responsible for many of the problems, but she hated to say anything since he was her roommate's fiance and he had been so nice to her in the past. She kept her suspicions to herself.

Kenneth and Tiffany were married in the early summer and moved into their "dream house." It was just the way they wanted it. Rachel was their first guest. She marveled at all Kenneth had been able to accomplish in the last four or five months. It was beautiful, but Rachel couldn't help wondering how they could afford some of the fixtures. She knew what they cost because Higby's handled them.

"Beautiful garden," remarked Rachel, trying to draw her mind back from her suspicions.

"Oh yes, isn't it!" gushed Tiffany. "Kenneth's uncle told him to take whatever he wanted from the lawn and garden store. Isn't that nice? Employee privileges, he called it."

"Yeah, nice."

Tiffany was so excited about the house that she wanted to show Rachel everything including the extra-large water heaters (one on each end of the house so they would have lots of hot water), and the special-effect lighting that took Kenneth "hours and hours to figure out" (not to mention all the extra wiring it took). But the most special room of all was Kenneth's study.

"Just wait until you see this, Rachel," she said. "Kenneth designed it himself." She took Rachel into the small paneled study.

"Nice," said Rachel.

"No, wait," bubbled Tiffany. "It's a study but you don't see a desk or files or computer or anything, do you?"

"No."

"Watch this," Tiffany laughed as she touched the edge of one of the wooden panels. The panel popped open, revealing a built-in desk, computer center, bar, and filing cabinet, all with hand-hammered copper brackets and drawer pulls.

"Kenneth always wants this closed so nobody knows it's here," Tiffany whispered, "but it's so beautiful and so ingenious I just had to show it to you."

"Yes," replied Rachel. "Very ingenious, all right."

QUESTIONS

1. Put yourself in Rachel's place. Do you have sufficient reasons to believe Kenneth is being dishonest? If so, how would you handle the situation? If not, what additional evidence would you need before you felt you needed to act?
2. What controls should Harold Higby have had in place at his store to minimize the types of thefts that occurred?
3. Rachel is Mr. Higby's employee and Kenneth's wife's friend. What sort of conflicts do you think she feels? What are her responsibilities to her employer? What are her responsibilities to her friend?

CASE 19 QUALITY MARKETS

Richard M. Petreycik

As a customer was leaving the new Quality Market in Lakewood, New York, Randy Sweeney noticed the shopper had left a package of cold cuts in her shopping cart. Sweeney grabbed the cold cuts and ran outside after the woman.

"Ma'am, I think you forgot this," Sweeney called after the customer.

"Why thank you very much," said the woman.

When Sweeney came back inside he said to a visitor, laughing, "See how friendly we are? I don't even know whether she paid for them."

Such displays of customer service are not unusual at Quality Market. "We're interested in our customers more than we're interested in the supermarket," says Sweeney, who is vice-president of sales for 24-store Quality Markets, based in Jamestown, New York. "We want to show our customers that we're interested in the things that are important to them."

Since opening less than six months ago, the store has done just that by becoming involved in three community events: a radio marathon fund raiser for the American Heart Association, free transportation and food for a local Winter Special Olympics group, and a hefty donation to the American Red Cross.

The store has also made an impression with aggressive promotional activities. For example, a two-day Italian sausage campaign pushed out 6,500 pounds of sausage at 99 cents a pound. During a "Lobster Maine-ia" promotion, 800 lobsters sold for $3.99 a pound.

Other promotions included a giveaway featuring a refrigerator filled with dairy products, a trip to Disney World, a baby derby, a pizza party complete with party favors, a "Taste of Jamestown" food sampling promotion, appearances by members of the Buffalo Bills, and a home and garden show.

In addition, two company employees participate in a popular cooking show featured on a nearby Jamestown cable television station. "These girls can't even go into a store without people constantly huddling around them," says Sweeney. "It's good to get the exposure. When customers come to a new location, they expect more."

And, that's just what they've gotten. The 42,000-square-foot Quality Market features a floral shop, fresh seafood, bakery, deli, cheese island, salad and soup bar, and a takeout pizza and sub shop.

Although this particular store is new to Lakewood, Quality Markets is not. The new unit is located across the street from the company's 20-year-old store, which was closed when the new Quality Market opened.

Sweeney says the old 22,000-square-foot store just wasn't large enough. The Lakewood area was growing quickly as a result of the heavy tourist trade from the nearby Chautauqua Lake community. "A developer came to us and said, 'We're building a strip center across the street. Are you interested?' We said yes," says Sweeney.

The store's extra space has allowed the company to expand departments as well as add new sections such as seafood and pizza. Linear footage in most departments was doubled in the new store, says Sweeney.

"Everything in the older store was on a much smaller scale," he says. "For example, our dairy and frozen food departments were easily doubled. They were both a problem in the older store, especially the dairy department. We couldn't fit everything into the departments."

Space is not the only thing there's more of in the new store. Sales have nearly doubled since the move across the street. *Progressive Grocer* estimates the new store's weekly volume is averaging about $350,000. This figure is particularly strong, considering that two Bells stores and a Super Duper are located within a three-mile radius.

Sweeney attributes the new store's success to more than just its increased size and emphasis on customer service and community relations. Quality, variety, and freshness are also important, he says. The strong decor package is another factor.

A boutique-like atmosphere greets shoppers as they enter the low-ceilinged "Market Square" area. This section extends along the right side of the store and includes florals, produce, deli, seafood, and bakery.

Each Market Square department features a different layout and decor. For example, seafood sports a blue and white tiled prep area. A blue fishnet is hung loosely from the ceiling above the refrigerated cases.

The produce department features a very different decor. The walls are made of oak, which is milled locally. Red brick-colored chalkboards containing product and pricing information are mounted above the low-profile product cases.

Although the perishables departments were changed considerably, compared with the old store, the section that experienced the greatest growth in the new store is General Merchandise, Health and Beauty Aids (GM/HBA). The department consists of 444 linear feet, or approximately 26 percent of the store's grocery shelving.

"We added photo albums, picture frames, cosmetics, automotive accessories, telephone jacks, speaker wire, home repair supplies, and other items," says Smith. "We did it to try and capture the drugstore and mass-merchandise categories. We have three drugstore chains in the area, but we really didn't expand our GM/HBA section to take anything away from anyone. We just wanted a better position. We wanted a better share."

Despite the increased size of the new store, management was determined not to lose sight of its No. 1 priority: to service all its customers in the best way possible.

Maintaining the store's level of service meant some adjustments in its operations following the move. One change involved the parcel pickup service. The old Quality Market provided this service, which was especially popular with senior citizens, who comprise almost 28 percent of the area's population. However, because many departments were expanded in the new store, there was no room for parcel pickup. To make up for that, employees now carry out customers' groceries.

Senior citizens are only one of the many groups that make up the area's diverse population. Quality Market's customers represent many backgrounds and income levels. To appeal to this diverse base, the company has kept its advertising and promotional strategies general, rather than targeting just one or two groups.

Products advertised on special are carefully selected to appeal to everyone. "For example, during the summer months we'll merchandise basics like soft drinks, hot dogs, snack items, ground beef, and rolls," says Sweeney.

Smith adds that "We target our advertising toward the season, not toward types of people like blue-collar groups or upscale groups. We want all our customers' business, not just one group."

The area's population includes an upscale tourist trade. The store is located near the Chautauqua Institution, a 750-acre national historic landmark. The institution is a well-known cultural and educational center offering activities for all ages.

"It's a town in itself," says store manager Steve Lombardo. "We get 5,000 summer residents in two weeks. The institution brings a lot of talented people into the area, making it more upscale during the summer."

Quality Markets is a division of Penn Traffic, based in Johnstown, Pennsylvania, which owns and operates more than 500 supermarkets, including P&C, Big Bear, Riverside, and Grand Union.

However, Randy Sweeney, Quality Market's vice-president of sales, says the company maintains a high degree of autonomy. "We're able to do what we see best," he says. "Whatever decisions Penn Traffic makes center around financial matters involving the entire corporation. But as far as day-to-day business decisions are concerned, they're done by Quality Markets."

What this means, says Steve Smith, Quality Market's vice-president of store operations, is that Quality still has to set certain goals, which Penn Traffic must approve. If approved, Quality is free to pursue those goals in whatever fashion it sees fit, as long as the goals are met. "The goals revolve around sales projections, payroll, and other capital expenditures," says Smith. "Penn Traffic acts as overseer of the entire operation."

Exhibits 1a and 1b show the layout of the Lakewood Village Quality Market and explanations of the 11 areas. Exhibit 2 is a detailed breakdown of the Lakewood Village Center Quality Market.

Source: Richard M. Petreycik, "Nice Guys *Can* Finish First," Store of the Month, *Progressive Grocer* (February 1991): 95-99. Reprinted with permission of Progressive Grocer.

QUESTIONS

1. Randy Sweeney needs to design the upcoming in-store promotions for the October–December period and it is now July 1. Design promotions for Columbus Day, Veterans Day, Halloween, Thanksgiving, and Christmas.
2. How do you propose that the promotions you designed be evaluated for their effectiveness?

EXHIBIT 1A

Layout of Lakewood Quality Market

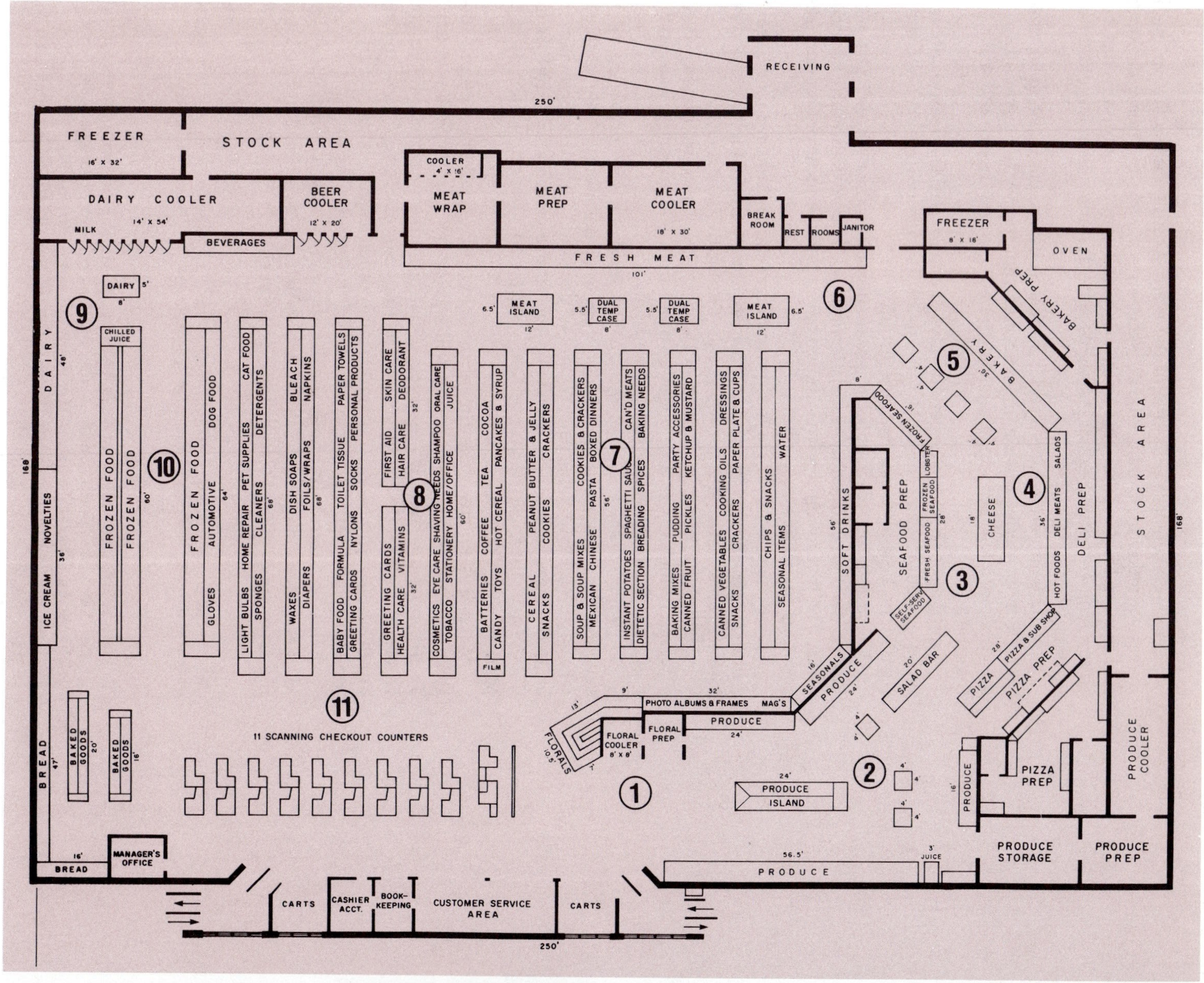

EXHIBIT 1B

Eleven Areas Explained

1. *Florals*. Florals, which is part of the produce department, is the first section customers see when they enter Quality Market's "Market Square." The focal point is an oak-paneled display section that houses a variety of plants. Popular items include azaleas and mums. Produce specialist Dave Holmberg says 60 percent of floral sales are in fresh bouquets and arrangements. "Green plants and potting plants make up 35 percent of the business, and potting soil makes up the additional 5 percent," he says. Low oak-paneled display cases are used for seasonal displays.

2. *Produce*. The produce department features about 180 items and comprises 7.1 percent of sales. The department is highlighted by oak-paneled walls and low-profile cases. Holmberg says customers' interest in health and nutrition has benefited the store's salad bar. The salad bar features more than 60 items, including taco meat with salsa, marinated vegetable salad, German cole slaw, and bacon-brocoli-cauliflower salad. One of the more popular salad bar items is a "Fruit Pizza," which consists of a pie crust covered with peaches, strawberries, kiwi, grapes, vanilla pudding, and whipped cream. "We brought the idea back from a share group meeting with our parent company, Penn Traffic," says Steve Smith, vice-president of store operations. "The idea originated with one of our sister companies, Big Bear in Columbus, Ohio." The produce department also features many locally grown vegetables, especially during the summer months. Some of these items include tomatoes, corn, and yellow squash.

3. *Seafood*. Seafood accounts for 1.5 percent of sales. The biggest seller is shrimp, which contributes 20 percent of department sales. Seafood specialist Joe Jessey says orange roughy and North Atlantic whitefish are next in popularity, followed by salmon fillets. Product and pricing information is written in bright colors on blackboards, which are hung on the department's tiled wall. In addition to fresh seafood, the department includes an 8-foot service case that houses frozen items such as breaded scallops at $7.99 a pound and stuffed flounder at $4.29 a pound. The department also contains a 16-foot case for frozen packaged fish. "This case helps support the overall department," says Smith. "It shows our customers that they can buy all the seafood items they want in one place."

4. *Deli*. The deli department contains a pizza and sub section (called "The Hot Spot"), hot foods, cold cuts, and salads. According to Joanne Nalbone, manager of the pizza and sub section, pizza can be made to order and so far, customers have been responding well. "Lunch and dinner are the busiest periods, and customers like the fact that they can buy pizza whole or by the slice," she says. A hot-food menu featuring daily lunch and supper specials is published each week. Selections include stuffed peppers, vegetable lasagna, and breaded pork chops. Deli manager Sharon Foti says health-conscious shoppers like "the healthy deli," which features low-sodium and low-cholesterol products, such as ham, Lorraine cheese, and Jarlsberg cheese. These items are identified with pink signs. A cheese case features prepackaged domestic and international cheeses. Popular international cheeses include Brie and blue nego, which is a Brie combined with blue cheese. The deli department accounts for 4.8 percent of total store sales.

EXHIBIT 1b
Continued

5. *Bakery.* The bakery, also known as the "Pastry Shop," features cookies, pastries, and doughnuts that are piled on yellow trays in European-style cases. Popular items include cream puffs priced at two for $1.29, cream cannoli at 69 cents apiece, and brownies featured at three for $1. Wooden racks display rolls, bagels, and crusty breads, which Foti says are growing in popularity. The bakery department accounts for 2.2 percent of sales.

6. *Meat.* Meat cutter Ron Johnson says the trend in meat these days is toward poultry or lean beef. "People are on this diet kick," he says. "Turkey is selling better than ever, especially products like turkey sausage." Johnson also notes that a lot of his customers want smaller-sized packages and convenience-oriented meat items, such as strip steaks, tenderloins, cube steaks, and top and bottom rounds. "Ninety percent of our customers know exactly what they want," he says. "If a recipe book calls for 12 ounces of beef, that's what they want. They want to just put it in the oven and eat it." The new store features more than 100 feet of multi-deck cases, compared with single-deck cases in the old store. The department also features four dual-temperature coffin cases for frozen or refrigerated meat products. Meat comprises 14.7 percent of sales.

7. *Grocery.* "A lot of effort goes into facings and appearance in the grocery department," says Smith. Shelves are constantly replenished and squared down to give a full appearance. "It's an image that says we're ready for business," says Smith. Shelved endcaps reinforce the store's full appearance by giving more depth to product arrangements. Grocery accounts for 48.3 percent of sales.

8. *GM/HBA.* The nonfoods department underwent a large expansion in the new store. In addition to adding items, Smith says the magazine section was expanded to include hardcover books. "We brought in clay-colored formica book displays and put in 20 feet of magazine racks," says Smith. "We also expanded our greeting card offerings." The low-profile greeting card fixture features a lighted canopy. The GM/HBA section accounts for 5.6 percent of sales.

9. *Dairy.* The dairy department accounts for 8.1 percent of sales, 70 percent of which comes from low-fat milk. "Milk is promoted very heavily in New York state," says Randy Sweeney, vice-president of sales. "And 1 percent milk is becoming a very strong item because people are more health conscious." The department's milk section is loaded from the rear and is housed beneath a yellow canopy that says "The Milk House." Other strong movers include low-salt cheeses, juices, gelatin and pudding products, and yogurt.

10. *Frozens.* Suspended signs identifying frozen poultry, meat, dinners, and vegetables make it easy for customers to find items behind the department's 54 doors. Sweeney says shoppers continue to look for quick entrees that are low in sodium and cholesterol. In addition, frozen yogurt is doing well. "It takes time for people to try it, but once they do, they find out they like it," says Sweeney. The frozens department accounts for 7.7 percent of sales.

11. *Front end.* The front end features 11 checkout counters equipped with side-scanning registers. Craig Howard, director of store systems, says the registers are designed so that if the main office controller goes down, each scanner has the capability of operating on its own. The front end also features an EFT system that honors Visa, MasterCard, and Discover cards.

EXHIBIT 2

Detailed Breakdown of Lakewood Village Quality Market

Date opened	September 30, 1990
Type of location	Strip plaza
Overall area	42,000 square feet
Selling area	29,000 square feet
Hours of operation	24 hours, 7 days a week
Parking capacity	418 spaces
Architect	Reinhart & Schwartz
Design	In-house
Cost of store (incl. equipment and fixtures)	$3.4 million
Grocery/nonfood shelving	1,683 linear feet
Display cases (linear feet)	
Produce	168
Florals	48
Salad bar	20
Deli	100
Bakery	36
Meat	182
Frozens	220
Dairy	110
Estimated weekly volume	$350,000
Number of employees	183
Wholesaler	Penn Traffic
Store manager	Steve Lombardo

Trade Area Statistics

Median age	33.2 years
Average household size	2.6 people
Average household income	$28,221
Median education	12.4 years
Percentage owner-occupied housing	60.2%
Percentage working women	42.0%
Percentage blue collar	51.4%
Percentage single-family dwelling units	63.3%

Percentage Sales by Department

	Quality Market	Industry Average
Grocery	48.3%	40.1%
Meat	14.7	17.0
Dairy	8.1	7.8
Frozens	7.7	6.0
Produce	7.1[a]	9.8[b]
GM/HBA	5.6	8.2
Deli	4.8	2.7
Bakery	2.2	1.6
Seafood	1.5	N/A

[a] Including florals and salad bar.
[b] Including florals only.

CASE 20

James W. Camerius
Northern Michigan University

WAL-MART: STRATEGIES FOR MARKET DOMINANCE*

It's dusk in the foothills of the Ozark Mountains in northwest Arkansas. A battered red 1980 Ford pickup minus two hubcaps with a hunting dog named Buck seated inside the cab, is headed down the rural road for some coffee and conversation with friends at Fred's Hickory Inn in Bentonville. Inside the truck, driving, is one of the most successful retailing entrepreneurs in modern history, who continues to be down-to-earth and old fashioned in his views of the past, the present, and the future. "I didn't sit down one day and decide that I was going to put a bunch of discount stores in small towns and set a goal to have a billion-dollar company some day," Sam Walton says. "I started out with one store and it did well, so it was a challenge to see if I could do well with a few more. We're still going and we'll keep going as long as we're successful." From these humble beginnings, Wal-Mart has emerged as a modern retail success story.

An Emerging Organization

Wal-Mart Stores, Inc., in 1991, with corporate offices at Bentonville, Arkansas, had completed its 28th consecutive year of growth in both sales and earnings records. The firm operated stores under a variety of names and retail formats including: Wal-Mart stores which existed as discount department stores; Sam's Clubs which were wholesale/retail membership warehouses; and Hypermarket*USA which were combination grocery and general-merchandise stores in excess of 200,000 square feet. It operated Wal-Mart Super Centers, scaled-down versions of hypermarkets; Dot Discount Drugstores, a super discount drug chain; and Bud's, off-price outlet stores. In sales volume, it was not only the nation's largest discount department store chain, but had recently surpassed Sears, Roebuck and Company as the largest retail organization in the United States.

The Sam Walton Spirit

Much of the initial and continuing success of Wal-Mart was attributed to the entrepreneurial spirit of its founder and recent chairman of the board, Samuel Moore Walton. Sam Walton or "Mr. Sam" as some referred to him, traced his down-to-earth, old-fashioned, homespun, evangelical ways to growing up in rural Oklahoma, Missouri, and Arkansas. Although he was remarkably blasé about his roots, some suggested that it was a simple belief in hard work and ambition that had "unlocked countless doors and showered upon him, his customers, and his associates . . . , the fruits of . . . years of labor in building [this] highly successful company." "Our goal has always been to be the very

---

*This case was prepared as a basis for class discussion rather than to illustrate either effective or ineffective handling of a retail situation. All rights reserved to the authors. Copyright © 1992 by James W. Camerius.

best," he said in an interview, "and, along with that, we believe you've got to make a good situation and put the interests of your associates first. If we really do that consistently, they in turn will cause . . . our business to be successful, which is what we've talked about and espoused and practiced." "The reason for our success," Sam Walton said, "is our people and the way that they're treated and the way they feel about their company." Many have suggested it is this "people first" philosophy, which guided the company through the challenges and setbacks of its early years, and allowed the company to maintain its consistent record of growth and expansion in later years.

There was little about Walton's background that reflected his amazing success. He was born in Kingfisher, Oklahoma, on March 29, 1918, to Thomas and Nancy Walton. Thomas Walton was a banker at the time and later entered the farm mortgage business and moved to Missouri. Sam Walton, growing up in rural Missouri in the depths of the Great Depression, discovered early that he "had a fair amount of ambition and enjoyed working," he suggested in a company interview. He completed high school at Columbia, Missouri, and received a Bachelor of Arts Degree in Economics from the University of Missouri in 1940. "I really had no idea what I would be," he said, adding as an afterthought, "at one point in time, I thought I wanted to become president of the United States."

A unique, enthusiastic, and positive individual, Sam Walton was called "just your basic home-spun billionaire" by *Business Week* magazine. One source suggested that: ". . . Mr. Sam is a life-long small-town resident who didn't change much as he got richer than his neighbors." Walton drove an old Ford pickup truck, would grab a bite to eat at Fred's Hickory Inn in Bentonville, and as a matter of practice would get his hair cut at the local barbershop. He had tremendous energy, enjoyed bird hunting with his dogs, and flew a corporate plane. When the company was much smaller, he could boast that he personally visited every Wal-Mart store at least once a year. A store visit usually included Walton leading Wal-Mart cheers that began "Give me a W, give me an A . . . ." To many employees, he had the air of a fiery Baptist preacher. Paul R. Carter, a Wal-Mart executive vice-president, said, "Mr. Walton has a calling." He became the richest man in America, and by 1991 had created a personal fortune for his family in excess of $21 billion.

For all that Walton's success has been widely chronicled, its magnitude is hard to comprehend. Sam Walton was selected by the investment publication, *Financial World* in 1989 as the "CEO of the Decade." He had honorary degrees from the University of the Ozarks, the University of Arkansas, and the University of Missouri. He also received many of the most distinguished professional awards of the industry like "Man of the Year," "Discounter of the Year," "Chief Executive Officer of the Year," and was the second retailer to be inducted into the Discounting Hall of Fame. He was recipient of the Horatio Alger Award in 1984 and acknowledged by *Discount Store News* as "Retailer of the Decade" in December of 1989. "Walton does a remarkable job of instilling near-religious fervor in his people," says analyst Robert Buchanan of A.G.

Edwards. "I think that speaks to the heart of his success." In late 1989, Sam Walton was diagnosed as having multiple myeloma, or cancer of the bone marrow. He remained active in the firm as chairman of the board of directors until his death in 1992.

The Marketing Concept

Genesis of an Idea

Sam Walton started his retail career in 1940 as a management trainee with JCPenney in Des Moines, Iowa. He was impressed with the Penney method of doing business and later modeled the Wal-Mart chain on "The Penney Idea" as reviewed in Exhibit 1. The Penney Company had found strength in calling employees "associates" rather than clerks. Founded in Kemerer, Wyoming, in 1902, Penney's for decades located on the main streets of small towns and cities.

Following service in the U.S. Army during World War II, Sam Walton acquired a Ben Franklin variety store franchise in Newport, Arkansas, which he operated successfully until losing the lease in 1950. He opened another store under the name of Walton's 5 & 10 in Bentonville, Arkansas, the following year. By 1962, he was operating a chain of 15 stores.

The early retail stores owned by Sam Walton in Newport and Bentonville, Arkansas, and later in other small towns in adjoining southern states, were variety store operations. They were relatively small operations of 6,000 square feet, were located on "main street," and displayed merchandise on plain wooden tables and counters. Operated under the Ben Franklin name and supplied by Butler Brothers of Chicago and St. Louis, they were characterized by a limited price line, low gross margins, high merchandise turnover, and concentration on return on investment. The firm, operating under the Walton 5 & 10 name, was the largest Ben Franklin franchise in the country in 1962.

EXHIBIT 1

The Penney Idea (1913)

1. To serve the public, as nearly as we can, to its complete satisfaction.
2. To expect for the service we render a fair remuneration and not all the profit the traffic will bear.
3. To do all in our power to pack the customer's dollar full of value, quality, and satisfaction.
4. To continue to train ourselves and our associates so that the service we give will be more and more intelligently performed.
5. To improve constantly the human factor in our business.
6. To reward men and women in our organization through participation in what the business produces.
7. To test our every policy, method, and act in this way: "Does it square with what is right and just?"

Source: Vance H. Trimble, *Sam Walton: The Inside Story of America's Richest Man* (New York: Dutton, 1990).

The variety stores were phased out by 1976 to allow the company to concentrate on the growth of Wal-Mart stores.

Foundations of Growth

The original Wal-Mart discount concept was not a unique idea. Sam Walton became convinced in the late 1950s that discounting would transform retailing. He traveled extensively in New England, the cradle of "off-pricing." "He visited just about every discounter in the United States," suggested William F. Kenney, the retired president of the now-defunct Kings Department Stores. He tried to interest Butler Brothers executives in Chicago, in the discount store concept. The first Kmart, as a "conveniently located one-stop shopping unit where customers could buy a wide variety of quality merchandise at discount prices" had opened in 1962 in Garden City, Michigan. His theory was to operate a discount store in a small community and in that setting, he would offer name-brand merchandise at low prices and would add friendly service. Butler Brothers executives rejected the idea. The first "Wal-Mart Discount City" opened in late 1962 in Rogers, Arkansas.

Wal-Mart stores would sell nationally advertised, name-brand merchandise at low prices in austere surroundings. As corporate policy, they would cheerfully give refunds, credits, and rain checks. Management conceived the firm as a "discount department store chain offering a wide variety of general merchandise to the customer." Early emphasis was placed upon opportunistic purchases of merchandise from whatever sources were available. Heavy emphasis was placed upon health and beauty aids (HBA) in the product line and "stacking it high" in a manner of merchandise presentation. By the end of 1979, there were 276 Wal-Mart stores located in 11 states.

The firm developed an aggressive expansion strategy as it grew from its first, 16,000-square-foot discount store in Rogers. New stores were located primarily in towns with populations of 5,000 to 25,000. The stores' sizes ranged from 30,000 to 60,000 square feet with 45,000 being the average. The firm also expanded by locating stores in contiguous areas, town by town, state by state. When its discount operations came to dominate a market area, it moved to an adjoining area. While other retailers built warehouses to serve existing outlets, Wal-Mart built the distribution center first and then spotted stores all around it, pooling advertising and distribution overhead. Most stores were less than a six-hour drive from one of the company's warehouses. The first major distribution center, a 390,000-square-foot facility opened in Searcy, Arkansas, outside Bentonville in 1978.

National Perspectives

At the beginning of 1991, the firm had 1,573 Wal-Mart stores in 35 states with expansion planned for adjacent states. Wal-Mart became the largest retailer and the largest discount department store by continuing to follow the unique place strategy of first locating discount stores in small-town America and later in suburban markets.

As a national discount department store chain, Wal-Mart Stores, Inc., offered a wide variety of general merchandise to the customer. The stores were designed to offer one-stop shopping in 36 departments which included family apparel, health and beauty aids, household products, electronics, toys, fabrics and crafts, automotive supplies, lawn and patio, jewelry, and shoes. In addition at certain store locations, a pharmacy, automotive supply and service center, garden center, or snack bar were also operated. The firm operated its stores with an "everyday low price" as opposed to putting heavy emphasis on special promotions, which called for multiple newspaper advertising circulars. Stores were expected to "provide the customer with a clean, pleasant, and friendly shopping experience."

Although Wal-Mart carried much the same merchandise, offered similar prices, and operated stores which looked much like the competition, there were many differences. In the typical Wal-Mart store, employees wore blue vests to identify themselves, aisles were wide, apparel departments were carpeted in warm colors, a store employee followed customers to their cars to pick up their shopping carts, and the customer was welcomed at the door by a "people greeter" who gave directions and struck up conversations. In some cases, merchandise was bagged in brown paper sacks rather than plastic bags because customers seemed to prefer them. A simple Wal-Mart logo in white letters on a brown background on the front of the store served to identify the firm. In consumer studies it was determined that the chain was particularly adept at striking the delicate balance needed to convince customers its prices were low without making people feel that its stores were too cheap. In many ways, competitors like Kmart, sought to emulate Wal-Mart by introducing people greeters, by upgrading interiors, by developing new logos and signage, and by introducing new inventory response systems. In 1989, sales per square foot of retail space at Wal-Mart were $227. Kmart, in contrast, sold only $139 per square foot worth of goods annually.

A "Satisfaction Guaranteed" refund and exchange policy was introduced to allow customers to be confident of Wal-Mart's merchandise and quality. Technological advancements like scanner cash registers, hand-held computers for ordering of merchandise, and computer linkages of stores with the general office and distribution centers improved communications and merchandise replenishment. Each store was encouraged to initiate programs which would make it an integral part of the community in which it operated. Associates were encouraged to "maintain the highest standards of honesty, morality, and business ethics in dealing with the public."

The External Environment

Industry analysts had labeled the 1980s as an era of economic uncertainty for retailers. Some firms faced difficulty upon merger or acquisition. After acquiring U.S.-based Allied Department Stores in 1986 and Federated Department Stores in 1988, Canadian developer Robert Campeau was declared bankrupt with over $6 billion in debt. Several divisions and units of the organization upon reevaluation were either sold or closed. The flagship downtown Atlanta store of Rich's, a division of Federated, was closed after completing a multimillion dollar remodeling program. Specific merchandise programs, in divisions like Bloomingdale's, were reevaluated to lower inventory and to raise cash. The notion of servicing existing debt became a significant factor in the success or failure of a retailing organization in the later half of the decade. Selected acquisition of U.S. retailers by foreign firms over the past decade are reviewed in Exhibit 2.

Other retailers experienced changes in ownership. The British B.A.T. Industries PLC sold the Chicago-based Marshall Field department store division to the Dayton Hudson Corporation. L.J. Hooker Corporation, the U.S. arm of Australia's Hooker Corporation, sold its Bonwit Teller and Sakowitz stores; it liquidated its B. Altman chain after fruitless sale efforts. The R.H. Macy Company declared bankruptcy after saddling itself with $4.5 billion in debt as a result of acquiring Bullock's and I. Magnin specialty department stores. Chicago-based Carson, Pirie, Scott & Company was sold to the P.A. Bergner & Company, operator of the Milwaukee Boston Store and Bergner Department Stores. Bergner declared a Chapter 11 bankruptcy in 1991.

Many retail enterprises confronted heavy competitive pressure by lowering prices or changing merchandise strategies. Sears, Roebuck, and Company, in an effort to reverse sagging sales and less than defensible earnings, unsuccessfully introduced a new policy of "everyday low pricing" (EDLP) in 1989. It later introduced name-brand items such as Whirlpool alongside its traditional private-label merchandise like Kenmore and introduced the "store within a store" concept to feature the name-brand goods. Montgomery Ward and to a lesser extent Kmart and Ames Department Stores followed similar strategies. The JCPenney Company, despite repositioning itself as a more upscale retailer, felt an impending recession and concerns about the Persian

EXHIBIT 2

Selected Acquisitions of U.S. Retailers by Foreign Firms (1980–1990)

U.S. Retailer	Foreign Acquirer	Country of Acquirer
Allied Stores (general merchandise)	Campeau	Canada
Alterman Foods (supermarkets)	Delhaie-Le Leon	Belgium
Bonwit Teller (general merchandise)	Hooker Corp.	Australia
Brooks Brothers (apparel)	Marks & Spencer	Great Britain
Federated Department Stores (diversified)	Campeau	Canada
Great Atlantic & Pacific (supermarkets)	Tengelmann	West Germany
Herman's (sporting goods)	Dee Corp.	Great Britain
International House of Pancakes (restaurants)	Wienerwald	Switzerland
Talbots (apparel)	Jusco Ltd.	Japan
Zale (jewelry)	PS Associates	Netherlands

Source: Barry Berman and Joel R. Evans, *Retail Management: A Strategic Approach*, 4th ed. (New York: Macmillan Publishing Company, 1989).

Gulf War had combined to erode consumer confidence. "As a result," the company noted in its 1990 Annual Report, "sales and profits within the industry were more negatively impacted than at any time since the last major recession of 1980–82."

The discount department store industry by the early 1990s had changed in a number of ways and was thought to have reached maturity by many analysts. Several formerly successful firms like E.J. Korvette, W.T. Grant, Atlantic Mills, Arlans, Federals, Zayre, Heck's, and Ames had declared bankruptcy and as a result either liquidated or reorganized. Regional firms like Target Stores and Shopko Stores began carrying more fashionable merchandise in more attractive facilities and shifted their emphasis to more national markets. Specialty retailers such as Toys "R" Us, Pier 1 Imports, and Oshmans were making big inroads in toys, home furnishings, and sporting goods. The "superstores" of drug and food chains were rapidly discounting increasing amounts of general merchandise. Some firms like May Department Stores Company with Caldor and Venture and F.W. Woolworth Co. with Woolco had withdrawn from the field by either selling their discount divisions or closing them down entirely.

Several new retail formats had emerged in the marketplace to challenge the traditional discount department store format. The superstore, a 125,000-square-foot operation, combined a large supermarket with a discount general-merchandise store. Originally a European retailing concept, these outlets were known as "malls without walls." Kmart's Super Kmart, American Fare, and Wal-Mart's Super Center Store and Hypermarket were examples of this trend toward large operations. Warehouse retailing, which involved some combination of warehouse and showroom facilities, used warehouse principles to reduce operating expenses and thereby offer discount prices as a primary customer appeal. Home Depot combined the traditional hardware store and lumber yard with a self-service home-improvement center to become the largest home center operator in the nation.

Some retailers responded to changes in the marketplace by selling goods at price levels (20 to 60 percent) below regular retail prices. These off-price operations appeared as two general types: (1) factory outlet stores like Burlington Coat Factory Warehouse, Bass Shoes, and Manhattan's Brand Name Fashion Outlet, and (2) independents like Loehmann's, T.J. Maxx, Marshall's, and Clothestime which bought seconds, overages, closeouts, or leftover goods from manufacturers and other retailers. Other retailers chose to dominate a product classification. Some super specialists like Sock Appeal, Little Piggie, Ltd., and Sock Market offered a single narrowly defined classification of merchandise with an extensive assortment of brands, colors, and sizes. Others, as niche specialists, like Kids Mart, a division of F.W. Woolworth, and McKids, a division of Sears, targeted an identified market with carefully selected merchandise and appropriately designed stores. Some retailers like Silk Greenhouse (silk plants and flowers), Office Club (office supplies and equipment), and Toys "R" Us (toys) were called "category killers" because they had achieved merchandise dominance in their respective product categories. Firms like The Limited, Victoria's Secret, and The Banana Republic became mini-department specialists by showcasing new lines and accessories alongside traditional merchandise lines.

Wal-Mart became the nation's largest retailer and discount department store chain in sales volume in 1991. Kmart Corporation, now the industry's second largest retailer and discount department store chain, with over 2,300 stores and $32,070,000,000 in sales in 1990, was perceived by many industry analysts and consumers in several independent studies as a laggard, even though it had been the industry sales leader for a number of years. In the same studies, Wal-Mart was perceived as the industry leader even though according to the *Wall Street Journal:* "they carry much the same merchandise, offer prices that are pennies apart and operate stores that look almost exactly alike." "Even their names are similar," noted the newspaper. The original Kmart concept of a "conveniently located, one stop shopping unit where customers could buy a wide variety of quality merchandise at discount prices," had lost its competitive edge in a changing market. As one analyst noted in an industry newsletter, "They had done so well for the past 20 years without paying attention to market changes. Now they have to." Wal-Mart and Kmart sales growth over the past 10 years is reviewed in Exhibit 3. A competitive analysis is shown of four major retail firms in Exhibit 4.

Some retailers like Kmart had initially focused on appealing to professional, middle-class consumers who lived in suburban areas and who were likely to be price sensitive. Other firms like Target, which had adopted the discount concept early, attempted to go generally after an upscale consumer who had an annual household income of $25,000 to $44,000, Fleet Farm and Menard's served the rural consumer, while firms like Chicago's Goldblatt's Department Stores returned to their immigrant heritage to serve blacks and Hispanics in the inner city.

EXHIBIT 3
Competitive Sales and Store Comparison

	Kmart		Wal-Mart[a]	
Year	Sales (000)	Stores	Sales (000)	Stores
1990	$32,070,000	2,350	$32,601,594	1,573
1989	29,533,000	2,361	25,810,656	1,402
1988	27,301,000	2,307	20,649,001	1,259
1987	25,627,000	2,273	15,959,255	1,114
1986	23,035,000	2,342	11,909,076	980
1985	22,035,000	2,332	8,451,489	859
1984	20,762,000	2,173	6,400,861	745
1983	18,597,000	2,160	4,666,909	642
1982	16,772,166	2,117	3,376,252	551
1981	16,527,012	2,055	2,444,997	491
1980	14,204,381	1,772	1,643,199	330

[a]Wal-Mart fiscal year ends January 31. Figures are assigned to previous year.

EXHIBIT 4

An Industry Competitive Analysis (1991)

	Wal-Mart	Sears, Roebuck	Kmart	JCPenney
Sales (thousands)	$32,601,584	$55,972,000	$32,070,000	$17,410,000
Net income (thousands)	$1,291,024	$902,000	$756,000	$577,000
Net income per share	$1.14	$2.63	$3.78	$4.33
Dividends per share	$0.14	$2.00	$1.72	$2.64
Number of stores (see note)	1,724	1,765	4,180	3,889
Percentage sales change	26.0%	1.2%	0.6%	2.1%

Note: Wal-Mart and subsidiaries (number of outlets)
    Wal-Mart Stores—1,573
    Sam's Club—148
    Hypermart USA—3
Sears, Roebuck and Company
    Sears Merchandise Group (number of outlets)
        Department stores—863
        Paint and hardware stores—98
        Catalog outlet stores—101
        Western Auto—504
        Eye Care Centers of America—94
        Business Systems Centers—65
        Pinstripes Petites—40
    Allstate Insurance Group
    Dean Witter Financial Services Group
    Coldwell Banker Real Estate Group
Kmart Corporation (number of outlets)
    General Merchandise—2,350
    Specialty retail stores—1,830
        PACE Membership Warehouse
        Builders Square
        Payless Drug Stores
        Waldenbooks
        The Sports Authority
JCPenney Company, Inc. (number of outlets)
    Stores—1,312
        Metropolitan market stores—697
        Geographic market stores—615
    Catalog Units—2,090
        JCPenney stores—1,312
        Freestanding sales centers—626
        Drug stores—136
        Other, principally outlet stores—16
    Drugstores (Thrift Drug or Treasury Drug)—487

In rural communities Wal-Mart's success often came at the expense of established local merchants and units of regional discount store chains. Hardware stores, family department stores, building supply outlets, and stores featuring fabrics, sporting goods, and shoes were among the first to either close or relocate elsewhere. Regional discount retailers in the Sunbelt states like Roses, Howard's, T.G. & Y, and Duckwall-ALCO, which once enjoyed solid sales and earnings, were forced to reposition themselves by renovating stores, opening bigger and more modern units, remerchandising assortments, and offering lower prices. In many cases, stores like Coast-to-Coast, Pamida, and Ben Franklin closed upon a Wal-Mart announcement to build in a specific community. "Just the word that Wal-Mart was coming made some stores close up," indicated a local newspaper editor.

Corporate Strategies

The corporate and marketing strategies that emerged at Wal-Mart to challenge a turbulent and volatile external environment were based upon a set of two main objectives which had guided the firm through its growth years in the decade of the 1980s. In the first objective the customer was featured, "customers would be provided what they want, when they want it, all at a value." In the second objective the team spirit was emphasized, "treating each other as we would hope to be treated, acknowledging our total dependency on our Associate-partners to sustain our success." The approach included: aggressive plans for new store openings; expansion to additional states; upgrading, relocation, refurbishing, and remodeling of existing stores; and opening new distribution centers. The plan was to not have a single operating unit that had not been updated in the past seven years. In the 1991 Annual Report to stockholders, the 1990s were considered: "A new era for Wal-Mart; an era in which we plan to grow to a truly nationwide retailer, and should we continue to perform, our sales and earnings will also grow beyond where most could have envisioned at the dawn of the 80s."

In the decade of the 1980s, Wal-Mart developed a number of new retail formats. The first Sam's Club opened in Oklahoma City, Oklahoma, in 1983. The wholesale club was an idea which had been developed by other firms earlier but which found its greatest success and growth in acceptability at Wal-Mart. Sam's Club featured a vast array of product categories with limited selection of brand and model, cash-and-carry business with limited hours, large (100,000 square foot), bare-bone facilities, rock-bottom wholesale prices, and minimal promotion. The limited membership plan permitted wholesale members who bought membership and others who usually paid a percentage above the ticket price of the merchandise. At the beginning of 1991, there were 148 Sam's Clubs open in 28 states. Effective February 2, 1991, Sam's Clubs merged the 28 units of The Wholesale Club, Inc., of Indianapolis, Indiana, into the organization.

The first Hypermarket*USA, a 222,000-square-foot superstore which combined a discount store with a large grocery store, a food court of restaurants, and other service businesses such as banks or video tape rental stores, opened in 1988 in the Dallas suburb of Garland. A scaled-down version of Hypermarket*USA was called the Wal-Mart Super Center, similar in merchandise offerings, but with about half the square footage of the hypermarts. These expanded store concepts also included convenience stores and gasoline distribution outlets to "enhance shopping convenience." The company proceeded slowly with these plans and later suspended its plans for building any more hypermarkets in favor of the super-center concept.

The McLane Company, Inc., a provider of retail and grocery distribution services for retail stores, was acquired in 1991. In October 1991, management announced that it was starting a chain of stores called Bud's, which would sell damaged, outdated, and overstocked goods at discounts even deeper than regular Wal-Mart stores.

Several programs were launched to "highlight" popular social causes. The "Buy American" program was a Wal-Mart retail program initiated in 1985. The theme was "Bring It Home to the USA" and its purpose was to communicate Wal-Mart's support for American manufacturing. In the program, the firm directed substantial influence to encourage manufacturers to produce goods in the United States rather than import them from other countries. Vendors were attracted into the program by encouraging manufacturers to initiate the process by contacting the company directly with proposals to sell goods which were made in the United States. Buyers also targeted specific import items in their assortments on a state-by-state basis to encourage domestic manufacturing. According to Haim Dabah, president of Gitano Group, Inc., a manufacturer of fashion discount clothing which imported 95 percent of its clothing and now makes about 20 percent of its products here, "Wal-Mart let it be known loud and clear that if you're going to grow with them, you sure better have some products made in the U.S.A." Farris Fashion, Inc. (flannel shirts), Roadmaster Corporation (exercise bicycles), Flanders Industries, Inc. (lawn chairs), and Magic Chef (microwave ovens) were examples of vendors that chose to participate in the program.

From the Wal-Mart standpoint the "Buy American" program centered around value—producing and selling quality merchandise at a competitive price. The promotion included television advertisements featuring factory workers, a soaring American eagle, and the slogan: "We buy American whenever we can, so you can too." Prominent in-store signage, and store circulars were also included. One store poster read: "Success Stories—These items formerly imported, are now being purchased by Wal-Mart in the U.S.A."

Wal-Mart was one of the first retailers to embrace the concept of "green" marketing. The program offered shoppers the option of purchasing products that were better for the environment in three respects: manufacturing, use, and disposal. It was introduced through full-page advertisements in the *Wall Street Journal* and *USA Today*. In-store signage identified those products which were environmentally safe. As Wal-Mart executives saw it, "customers are concerned about the quality of land, air, and water, and would like the opportunity to do something positive." To initiate the program, 7,000 vendors were notified that Wal-Mart had a corporate concern for the environment and to ask for their support in a variety of ways. Wal-Mart television advertising showed children on swings, fields of grain blowing in the wind, and roses. Green and white store signs, printed on recycled paper, marked products or packaging that had been developed or redesigned to be more environmentally sound.

Wal-Mart had become the channel commander in the distribution of many brand-name items. As the nation's largest retailer and in many geographic areas the dominant distributor, it exerted considerable influence in negotiation for the best price, delivery terms, promotion allowances, and continuity of supply. Many of these benefits could be passed on to consumers in the form of quality name-brand items available at lower than competitive prices. As a matter of corporate policy, management often insisted on doing business only with a producer's top sales executives rather than going through a manufacturer's representative. Wal-Mart had been accused of threatening to buy from other producers if firms refuse to sell directly to it. In the ensuing power struggle, Wal-Mart executives refused to talk about the controversial policy or admit that it existed. As a representative of an industry association representing a group of sales agencies representatives suggested, "In the Southwest, Wal-Mart's the only show in town." An industry analyst added, "They're extremely aggressive. Their approach has always been to give the customer the benefit of a corporate saving. That builds up customer loyalty and market share."

Another key factor in the mix was an inventory control system that was recognized as the most sophisticated in retailing. A high-speed computer system linked virtually all the stores to headquarters and the company's distribution centers. It electronically logged every item sold at the checkout counter, automatically kept the warehouses informed of merchandise to be ordered, and directed the flow of goods to the stores and even to the proper shelves. Most important for management, it helped detect sales trends quickly and speeded up market reaction time substantially.

Decision Making In a Market-Orientated Firm

One principle that distinguished Wal-Mart was the unusual depth of employee involvement in company affairs. Corporate strategies put emphasis on human resource management. Employees of Wal-Mart became "associates," a name borrowed from Sam Walton's early association with JCPenney. Input was encouraged at meetings at the store and corporate level. The firm hired employees locally, provided training programs, and through a "Letter to the President" program, management encouraged employees to ask questions, and made words like "we," "us," and "our" a part of the corporate language. A number of special award programs recognized individual, department, and division achievement. Stock ownership and profit-sharing programs were introduced as part of a "partnership concept."

The corporate culture was recognized by the editors of the trade publication, *Mass Market Retailers*, when it recognized all 275,000 associates collectively as the 1989 "Mass Market Retailers of the Year." "The Wal-Mart associate," the editors noted, "in this decade that term has come to symbolize all that is right with the American worker, particularly in the retailing environment and most particularly at Wal-Mart . . . ." The "store within a store" concept, as a Wal-Mart corporate policy, trained individuals to be merchants by being responsible for the performance of their own departments as if they were running their own businesses. Seminars and training programs afforded them opportunities to grow within the company. "People development, not just a good 'program' for any growing company but a must to secure our future," is how Suzanne Allford, vice-president of the Wal-Mart people division, explained the firm's decentralized approach to retail management development.

"The Wal-Mart Way" was a phrase that was used by management to summarize the firm's unconventional approach to business and the development of the corporate culture. As noted in the 1991 Annual Report referring to a recent development program, "We stepped outside our retailing world to examine the best managed companies in the United States in an effort to determine the fundamentals of their success and to 'benchmark' our own performances." The name "Total Quality Management" (TQM) was used to identify this "vehicle for proliferating the very best things we do while incorporating the new ideas our people have that will assure our future."

The Growth Challenge

David Glass, 53 years old, had assumed the role of president and chief executive officer at Wal-Mart, the position previously held by Sam Walton, founder of the company. Known for his hard-driving managerial style, Glass gained his experience in retailing at a small supermarket chain in Springfield, Missouri. He joined Wal-Mart as executive vice-president for finance in 1976. He was named president and chief operating officer in 1984.

And what of Wal-Mart without Mr. Sam? "There's no transition to make," said Glass, "because the principles and the basic values he used in founding this company were so sound and so universally accepted." "As for the future," he suggested, spinning around in his chair at his desk in his relatively spartan office at corporate headquarters in Bentonville, "there's more opportunity ahead of us than behind us. We're good students of retailing and we've studied the mistakes that others have made. We'll make our own mistakes, but we won't repeat theirs. The only thing constant at Wal-Mart is change. We'll be fine as long as we never lose our responsiveness to the customer."

Wal-Mart Stores, Inc., had for over 30 years experienced tremendous growth and as one analyst suggested, "been consistently on the cutting edge of low-markup mass merchandising." Much of the forward momentum had come from the entrepreneurial spirit of Samuel Moore Walton. Mr. Sam remained chairman of the board of directors and corporate representative until his death in 1992. A new management team was in place. As the largest retailer in the country, the firm had positioned itself to meet the challenges of the next decade as an industry leader. The question now was: Could the firm maintain its blistering growth pace—outmaneuvering the competition with the innovative retailing concepts that it has continued to develop better than anyone else?

Case 20 Wal-Mart: Strategies for Market Dominance

QUESTIONS

1. Identify and evaluate the marketing strategies that Wal-Mart pursued to maintain its growth and marketing leadership position. What factors should a firm consider in the development of its marketing strategy?
2. Discuss the importance of changes in the external environment to an organization like Wal-Mart.
3. What conclusions can be drawn from a review of Wal-Mart's financial performance

---

APPENDIX A
Wal-Mart Stores, Inc.
Financial Performance 1991–1982
1991 Annual Report[a]

Ten-Year Financial Summary[b]
(Dollar amounts in thousands except per share data)

	1991	1990	1989	1988	1987
Earnings					
Net sales	$32,601,594	$25,810,656	$20,649,001	$15,959,255	$11,909,076
Licensed department rentals and other income-net	261,814	174,644	136,867	104,783	84,623
Cost of sales	25,499,834	20,070,034	16,056,856	12,281,744	9,053,219
Operating, selling, and general and administrative expenses	5,152,178	4,069,695	3,267,864	2,599,367	2,007,645
Interest costs					
Debt	42,716	20,346	36,286	25,262	10,442
Capital leases	125,920	117,725	99,395	88,995	76,367
Taxes on income	751,736	631,600	488,246	441,027	395,940
Net income	1,291,024	1,075,900	837,221	627,643	450,086
Per share of common stock					
Net income	1.14	.95	.74	.55	.40
Dividends	.14	.11	.08	.06	.0425
Stores in operation at the end of the period					
Wal-Mart Stores	1,573	1,402	1,259	1,114	980
Sam's Clubs	148	123	105	84	49
Financial Position					
Current assets	6,414,775	4,712,616	3,630,987	2,905,145	2,353,271
Net property, plant, equipment, and capital leases	4,712,039	3.430,059	2,661,954	2,144,852	1,676,282
Total assets	11,388,915	8,198,484	6,359,668	5,131,809	4,049,092
Current liabilities	3,990,414	2,845,315	2,065,909	1,743,763	1,340,291
Long-term debt	740,254	185,152	184,439	185,672	179,234
Long-term obligations under capital leases	1,158,621	1,087,403	1,009,046	866,972	764,128
Preferred stock with mandatory redemption provisions					
Shareholder's equity	5,365,524	3,965,561	3,007,909	2,257,267	1,690,493

APPENDIX A
Continued

Ten-Year Financial Summary[b] (Dollar amounts in thousands except per share data)	1986	1985	1984	1983	1982
Earnings					
Net sales	$8,451,489	$6,400,861	$4,666,909	$3,376,252	$2,444,997
Licensed department rentals and other income-net	55,127	52,167	36,031	22,435	17,650
Cost of sales	6,361,271	4,722,440	3,418,025	2,458,235	1,787,496
Operating, selling, and general and administrative expenses	1,485,210	1,181,455	892,887	677,029	495,010
Interest costs					
Debt	1,903	5,207	4,935	20,297	16,053
Capital leases	54,640	42,506	29,946	18,570	15,351
Taxes on income	276,119	230,653	160,903	100,416	65,943
Net income	327,473	270,767	196,244	124,140	82,794
Per share of common stock					
Net income	0.29	0.24	0.17	0.11	0.08
Dividends	0.035	0.0263	0.0175	0.0113	0.0082
Stores in operation at the end of the period					
Wal-Mart Stores	859	745	642	551	491
Sam's Clubs	23	11	3		
Financial Position					
Current assets	1,784,275	1,303,254	1,005,567	720,537	589,161
Net property, plant, equipment, and capital leases	1,303,450	870,309	628,151	457,509	333,026
Total assets	3,103,645	2,205,229	1,652,254	1,187,448	937,513
Current liabilities	992,683	688,968	502,763	347,318	339,961
Long-term debt	180,682	41,237	40,866	106,465	104,581
Long-term obligations under capital leases	595,205	449,886	339,930	222,610	154,196
Preferred stock with mandatory redemption provisions	4,902	5,874	6,411	6,861	7,438
Shareholder's equity	1,277,659	984,672	737,503	488,109	323,942

[a]Wal-Mart Annual Report, January 31, 1991.
[b]On beginning year balance.

over the decade of the 1980s? From this review, what can you conclude about the financial future of the firm?

4. Speculate on how much impact the death of Samuel Moore Walton will have on the forward momentum of the organization. What steps should be taken by management to continue Mr. Sam's formula for success?

5. What evidence is there to suggest that the marketing concept was understood and applied at Wal-Mart?

REFERENCES

"A Supercenter Comes to Town," *Chain Store Age Executive* (December 1989): 23-30+.
Abend, Jules, "Wal-Mart's Hypermart: Impetus for U.S. Chains?" *Stores* (March 1988): 59-61.
"Another Record Year at Wal-Mart," *Chain Store Age, General Merchandise Edition* (June 1984): 70.
Bard, Ray, and Susan K. Elliott, *The National Directory of Corporate Training Programs* (New York: Doubleday Publishing, 1988), 351-52.
Barrier, Michael, "Walton's Mountain," *Nation's Business* (April 1988): 18-20+.
Beamer, Wayne, "Discount King Invades Marketer Territory," *National Petroleum* (April 1988): 15-16.
Bergman, Joan, "Saga of Sam Walton," *Stores* (January 1988): 129-30.
Blumenthal, Karen, "Marketing with Emotion: Wal-Mart Shows the Way," *Wall Street Journal,* 20 November 1989, B3.
Bradford, Michael, "Receiver Sues to Recoup Comp Payments," *Business Insurance,* 11 September 1989, 68.
Bragg, Arthur, "Wal-Mart's War on Reps," *Sales & Marketing Management* (March 1987): 41-43.
Brauer, Molly, "Sam's: Setting a Fast Pace," *Chain Store Age Executive* (August 1983): 20-21.
Brookman, Faye, "Will Patriotic Purchasing Pay Off?" *Chain Store Age, General Merchandise Trends* (June 1985): 95.
Caminiti, Susan, "What Ails Retailing," *Fortune,* 30 January 1989, 63-64.
Cochran, Thomas N., "Chain Reaction," *Barron's,* 16 October 1989, 46.
Corwin, Pat, Jay L. Johnson, and Renee M. Rouland, "Made in U.S.A.," *Discount Merchandiser* (November 1989): 48-52.
"David Glass's Biggest Job is Filling Sam's Shoes," *Business Month* (December 1988): 42.
"Discounters Commit to Bar-Code Scanning," *Chain Store Age Executive* (September 1985): 49-50.
Edgerton, Jerry, and Jordon E. Goodman, "Wal-Mart for Hypergrowth," *Money* (March 1988): 12.
Endicott, R. Craig, " '86 Ad Spending Soars," *Advertising Age,* 23 November 1987, S-2+.
Endicott, R. Craig, "Leading National Advertisers (Companies Ranked 101-200)," *Advertising Age,* 21 November 1988, S-1+.
"Explosive Decade," *Financial World,* 4-17 April 1984, 92.
"Facts About Wal-Mart Stores, Inc.," Press Release, Corporate and Public Affairs, Wal-Mart Stores, Inc.
Fisher, Christy, and Patricia Strand, "Wal-Mart Pulls Back on Hypermart Plans," *Advertising Age,* 19 February 1990, 49.
Fisher, Christy, and Judith Graham, "Wal-Mart Throws 'Green' Gauntlet," *Advertising Age,* 21 August 1989, 1+.
Gilliam, Margaret A., "Wal-Mart and the Investment Community," *Discount Merchandiser,* (November 1989): 64+.
"Glass is CEO at Wal-Mart," *Discount Merchandiser* (March 1988): 6+.
"Great News: A Recession," *Forbes,* 8 January 1990, 194.
Gruber, Christina, "Will Competition Wilt Rose's," *Chain Store Age, General Merchandise Edition* (May 1984): 40.
Hartnett, Michael, "Resurgence in the Sunbelt," *Chain Store Age, General Merchandise Trends* (October 1985): 13-15.
Helliker, Kevin, "Wal-Mart's Store of the Future Blends Discount Prices, Department-Store Feel," *The Wall Street Journal,* 17 May 1991, B1, B8.
Higgins, Kevin T., "Wal-Mart: A Pillar in a Thousand Communities," *Building Supply Home Centers* (February 1988): 100-102.
Huey, John, "America's Most Successful Merchant," *Fortune,* 23 September 1991, 46-48+.
Huey, John, "Wal-Mart, Will It Take Over the World?" *Fortune,* 30 January 1989, 52-56+.
Huey, John, "Hypermart USA Makes a Few Adjustments," *Chain Store Age Executive* (May 1988): 278.
"In Retail, Bigger Can Be Better," *Business Week,* 27 March 1989, 90.
"Jack Shewmaker, Vice Chairman, Wal-Mart Stores, Inc.," *Discount Merchandiser,* (November 1987): 26+.
Jacober, Steve, "Wal-Mart: A Boon to U.S. Vendors," *Discount Merchandiser* (November 1989): 41-46.
Jacober, Steve, "Wal-Mart: A Retailing Catalyst," *Discount Merchandiser* (November 1989): 54-58.
Johnson, Jay L., "Are We Ready for Big Changes?" *Discount Merchandiser* (August 1989): 48, 53-54.
Johnson, Jay L., "Hypermarts and Supercenters—Where Are They Heading?" *Discount Merchandiser* (November 1989): 60+.
Johnson, Jay L., "Hypermart USA Does a Repeat Performance," *Discount Merchandiser* (March 1988): 52+.

Johnson, Jay L., "Internal Communication: A Key to Wal-Mart's Success," *Discount Merchandiser* (November 1989): 68+.
Johnson, Jay, L., "Supercenters: Wal-Mart's Future?" *Discount Merchandiser* (May 1988): 26+.
Johnson, Jay L., "The Future of Retailing," *Discount Merchandiser,* (January 1990): 70+.
Johnson, Jay L., "The Supercenter Challenge," *Discount Merchandiser* (August 1989): 70+.
Johnson, Jay L., "Walton Honored by Harvard Business School Club," *Discount Merchandiser* (June 1990): 30, 34.
Keith, Bill, "Wal-Mart Places Special Emphasis on Pharmacy," *Drug Topics,* 17 July 1989, 16-17.
Kelly, Kevin, "Sam Walton Chooses a Chip off the Old CEO," *Business Week,* 15 February 1988, 29.
Kelly, Kevin, "Wal-Mart Gets Lost in the Vegetable Isle," *Business Week* 28 May 1990, 48.
Kerr, Dick, "Wal-Mart Steps Up 'Buy American,'" *Housewares,* 7-13 March 1986, 1+.
Klapper, Marvin, "Wal-Mart Chairman Says His Buy American Program Working," *Women's Wear Daily,* 3 December 1985, 8.
"Leader in New Construction," *Chain Store Age Executive* (November 1985): 46.
Levering, Robert, *The 100 Best Companies to Work for in America* (Reading, Mass.: Addison-Wesley, 1984), 351-354.
Lloyd, Bruce A., "Wal-Mart to Build Major Distribution Center in Loveland, Colo.," *Site Selection,* (June 1989) 634-635.
"Management Style: Sam Moore Walton," *Business Month,* (May 1989): 38.
Marsch, Barbara, "The Challenge: Merchants Mobilize to Battle Wal-Mart in a Small Community," *Wall Street Journal,* 5 June 1991, A1, A4.
Mason, Todd, "Sam Walton of Wal-Mart: Just Your Basic Homespun Billionaire," *Business Week,* 14 October 1985, 142-143+.
McLeod, Douglas, "Miro Exceeded Authority on Wal-Mart Cover: Judge," *Business Insurance,* 20 July 1987, 28.
McLeod, Douglas, "Transit Liquidator Can't Collect from Wal-Mart, Court Rules," *Business Insurance,* 3 October 1988.
"$90 Million Expansion Bill at Wal-Mart," *Chain Store Age Executive* (November 1982): 73.
"Number of Units Set to Climb by 62%," *Chain Store Age Executive,* (November 1983): 34.
"Our People Make the Difference: The History of Wal-Mart," Video Cassette, (Bentonville, Arkansas: Wal-Mart Video Productions, 1991).
Padgett, Tim, "Just Saying No to Wal-Mart," *Newsweek,* 13 November 1989, 65.
"Perspectives on Discount Retailing," *Discount Merchandiser,* (April 1987): 44+.
Peters, Tom J., and Nancy Austin, *A Passion for Excellence* (New York: Random House), 266-67.
Rawn, Cynthia Dunn, "Wal-Mart vs. Main Street," *American Demographics* (June 1990): 58-59.
Reed, Susan, "Talk About a Local Boy Making Good! Sam Walton, The King of Wal-Mart, Is America's Second-Richest Man," *People,* 19 December 1983, 133+.
Reier, Sharon, "CEO of the Decade: Sam M. Walton," *Financial World,* 4 April 1989, 56-57+.
"Rex Chase—Pure Wal-Mart Lore," *Chain Store Age, General Merchandise Edition* (March 1983): 35.
Rudnitsky, Howard, "How Sam Walton Does It," *Forbes,* 16 August 1982, 42-44.
Rudnitsky, Howard, "Play It Again, Sam," *Forbes,* 10 August 1987, 48.
"Sam's Wholesale Club Racks Up $1.6 Billion Sales in 1986," *Discount Merchandiser* (February 1987): 26.
"Sam Moore Walton," *Business Month* (May 1989): 38.
"Sam Walton, The Retail Giant: Where Does He Go from Here?" *Drug Topics,* 17 July 1989, 6.
Saporito, Bill, "The Mad Rush to Join the Warehouse Club," *Fortune,* 6 January 1986, 59+.
Schachner, Michael, "Wal-Mart Chief Fined $11.5 Million for Court Absence," *Business Insurance,* 9 January 1989, 1+.
Schwadel, Francine, "Little Touches Spur Wal-Mart's Rise," *Wall Street Journal,* 22 September 1989, B1.
Sheets, Kenneth R., "How Wal-Mart Hits Main St.," *U.S. News & World Report,* 13 March 1989, 53-55.
"Small Stores Showcase Big Ideas," *Chain Store Age, General Merchandise Trends* (September 1985): 19-20.
"Small Town Hit," *Time,* 23 May 1983, 43.
Smith, Sarah, "America's Most Admired Corporations," *Fortune,* 29 January 1990, 56+.
Sprout, Alison L., "America's Most Admired Corporations," *Fortune,* 11 February 1991, 52+.
Taub, Stephen, "Gold Winner: Sam M. Walton of Wal-Mart Stores Takes the Top Prize," *Financial World,* 15 April 1986, 28+.
Taylor, Marianne, "Wal-Mart Prices Itself in the Market, *Chicago Tribune,* 28 April 1991, sec. 7, p. 1+.

Taylor, Marianne, "Tending Wal-Mart's Green Policy," *Advertising Age,* 29 January 1991, 20+.
The Almanac of American Employers (Chicago: Contemporary Books, Inc., 1985), 280.
"The Early Days: Walton Kept Adding 'a Few More' Stores," *Discount Store News,* 9 December 1985, 61.
"The Five Best-Managed Companies," *Dun's Business Month* (December 1982): 47.
Thurmond, Shannon, "Sam Speaks Volumes About New Formats," *Advertising Age,* 9 May 1988, S-26.
Trimble, Vance H., *Sam Walton: The Inside Story of America's Richest Man* (New York: Dutton, 1990).
"Wal-Mart's 1990 Look," *Discount Merchandiser* (July 1989): 12.
"Wal-Mart Associates Generate Over $5.5 Million for United Way," Press Release (January 2, 1990), Corporate and Public Affairs, Wal-Mart Stores, Inc.
"Wal-Mart Beats the Devil," *Chain Store Age* (August 1986): 9.
"Wal-Mart Expands; Tests New 'Wholesale' Concept," *Chain Store Age, General Merchandise Trends* (June 1983): 98.
"Wal-Mart's Glass to Reps: 'That's a Bunch of Baloney!,'" *Discount Merchandiser* (September 1987): 12.
"Wal-Mart's Goals," *Discount Merchandiser* (January 1988): 48-50.
"Wal-Mart Goes on Its Own," *Progressive Grocer* (June 1987): 9.
"Wal-Mart's 'Green' Campaign to Emphasize Recycling Next," *Adweek's Marketing Week,* 12 February 1990, 60-61.
"Wal-Mart Has No Quarrel with 1984," *Chain Store Age, General Merchandise Trends* (June 1985): 36.
"Wal-Mart on the Move," *Progressive Grocer* (August 1987): 9.
"Wal-Mart Policy Asks for Supplier Commitment," *Textile World* (May 1985): 27-28.
"Wal-Mart Raises Over $3 Million for Children's Hospital," Press Release (June, 1989), Corporate and Public Affairs, Wal-Mart Stores, Inc.
"Wal-Mart Rolls Out Its Supercenters," *Chain Store Age Executive,* (December 1988): 18-19.
"Wal-Mart Stores Penny Wise," *Business Month* (December 1988): 42.
"Wal-Mart: The Model Discounter," *Dun's Business Month* (December 1982): 60-61.
"Wal-Mart to Acquire McLane, Distributor to Retail Industry," *Wall Street Journal,* 2 October 1990, A8.
Weiner, Steve, "Golf Balls, Motor Oil and Tomatoes," *Forbes,* 30 October 1989, 130-131+.
Weiner, Steve, "Pssst! Wanna Buy a Watch? A Suit? How About a Whole Department Store?" *Forbes,* 8 January 1990, 192+.
"Wholesale Clubs," *Discount Merchandiser,* (November 1987): 26+.
"Why Wal-Mart Is Recession Proof," *Business Week,* 22 February 1988, 146.
"Work, Ambition—Sam Walton," Press Release, Corporate and Public Affairs, Wal-Mart Stores, Inc.
Zweig, Jason, "Expand It Again, Sam," *Forbes,* 9 July 1990, 106.

CASE 21

A NEW MALL FOR MANKATO*

Carolyn J. Hanka
Mankato State University

Mankato, Minnesota

Mankato appears to be the latest target chosen for a new shopping mall to be built by General Growth Company. General Growth Company is the fourth-largest mall manager in the United States.[1]

Mankato, Minnesota, a small community in south central Minnesota, is made up of Mankato on one side of the Minnesota River and North Mankato

---

*This case was prepared as a basis for class discussion rather than to illustrate either effective or ineffective handling of a retail situation. All rights reserved to the author. Copyright © 1991 by Carolyn J. Hanka.

on the other side. The combined population is 41,607, with 75 percent of the population in Mankato. The population in 1988 was 78,820 within 15 miles of Mankato and 132,859 within 25 miles.[2] This regional center attracts people from a radius of 40 to 60 miles to work, conduct business, shop, enjoy recreational activities, attend college, or visit medical facilities. Mankato was described as one of the best small cities in the United States by Cheryl Russell in an article published in *American Demographics*.[3] Mankato ranked number nine among cities of at least 15,000 people in counties of at least 40,000 that are not part of a metropolitan area according to Russell. A major metropolitan area, Minneapolis–St. Paul and suburbs, is located about 75 miles northeast of Mankato.

Mankato and North Mankato currently have approximately one million square feet of retail space encompassed in two enclosed malls, five strip malls, and many free standing retailers and older, traditional shopping areas. The locations of these shopping areas are shown on the map of Mankato–North Mankato (Exhibit 1) and the three enclosed malls are described in Exhibit 2 and in the following discussion.

Madison East Mall

In 1970, an enclosed mall, Madison East, was built on the east side of town at the junction of Highways 14 and 22, about four miles from downtown. This 350,000-square-foot mall is anchored by Sears at one end, Woolworth at the opposite end, and includes about 58 other retailers.[4] When the mall was built, some local stores moved from downtown to this new mall, and national chains located retail outlets there. Madison East continues to attract shoppers, although it has not had a major facelift in 20 years.

Mankato Mall

A short time after Madison East Mall opened its doors, the downtown merchants decided to turn the old downtown area into an enclosed mall. Some of Mankato's retailers owned multistory buildings located on both sides of Front Street, the main shopping street and also the original north-south artery through Mankato, State Highway 169. Traffic was rerouted via a new location for the highway and a new street around the mall. Three-story buildings were enclosed in a structure one and one-half blocks in length and extending from alley to alley in width. A three-level parking ramp was built adjacent to the mall. The street and building construction took more than two years. During this time, shoppers and downtown workers had to contend with street and utility relocation and construction, new one-way streets, temporary street closings, dirt, and confusion. Out-of-towners avoided downtown and concentrated their shopping trips to or near Madison East Mall.

The downtown Mankato Mall was completed in 1978 and included two anchors, JCPenney and Bretts Department Store. Bretts is the headquarters

EXHIBIT 1

Mankato–North Mankato Major Shopping Areas

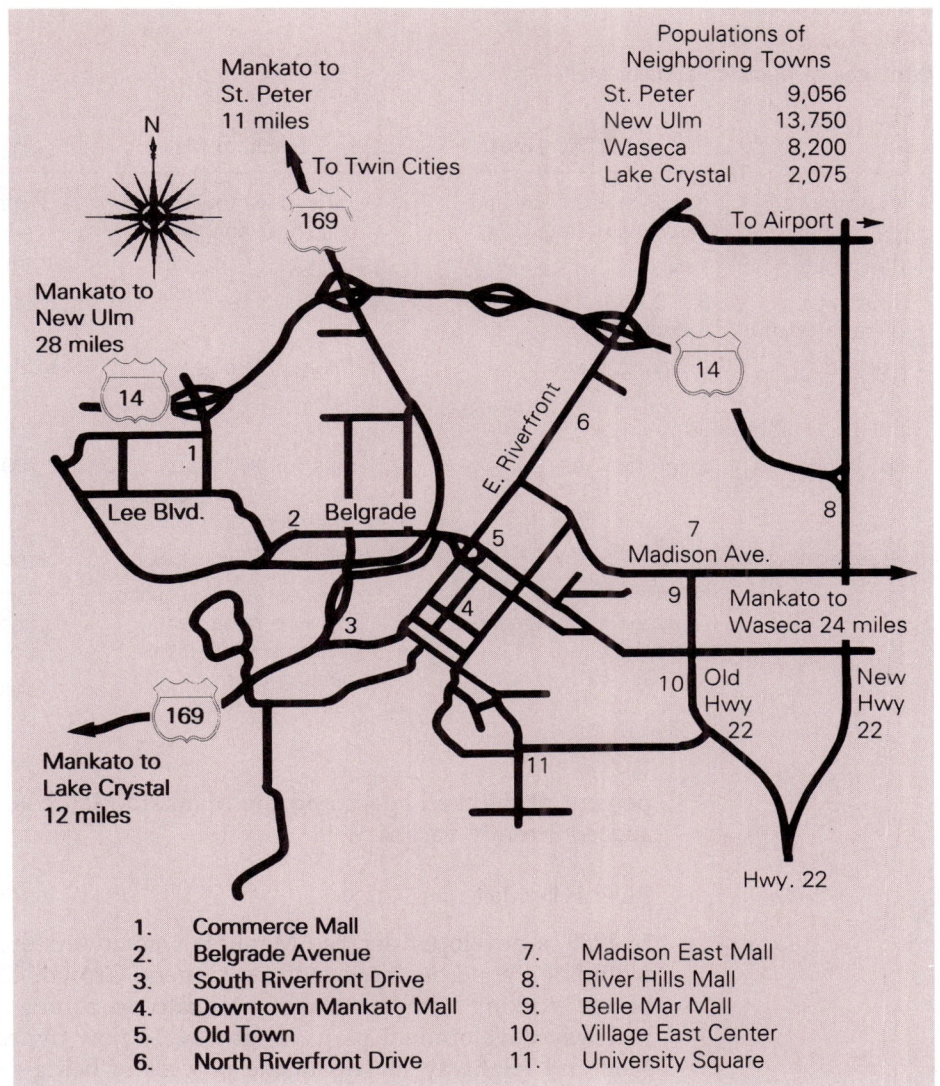

and original location of a small, regional chain and is family owned. Both Bretts and JCPenney own their multilevel buildings. Other tenants of the Mankato Mall include local and national specialty shops, a four-screen theater, two restaurants, one snack bar, and services including a beauty shop, travel agency, brokerage firm, Social Security office, and accounting and insurance firms.[5] The total mall area is 400,000 square feet. Four banks, other shops, a Hy-Vee Supermarket, and business services are located in close proximity to the Mankato Mall. Madison East vacancies include about 5

EXHIBIT 2

Attributes of Mankato's Major Malls

	Madison East	Mankato Mall	River Hills
Appearance	Single-story, brick and steel structure	Original downtown buildings, enclosed	Contemporary, with window wall
Constructed	1968	1978	1991 (planned)
Total area (square feet)	350,000	400,000	600,000
Anchors	Sears, Woolworth	JCPenney, Bretts	JCPenney, Herberger's, Target
Specialty shops	58	65	110
Parking	Large lot, free	Ramps for 1610 cars, @ 30 cents per hour, meters on street	2,700 cars, free
Pedestrians	None	Downtown employees	None
Extras	Night club, snack bar, two restaurants, meeting rooms	Four-screen theater, snack bar, two restaurants, performance court, meeting room	11-screen theater, 12 snack shops, 2 performance courts, meeting room

percent of the mall space and the Mankato Mall has about 10 percent of its space currently vacant.

River Hills Mall

In 1988, a developer decided Mankato was understored and that a new mall would be a good business venture. General Growth Company of Des Moines began working with the city of Mankato on zoning, building permits, and highway development plans. Highway 14 now bypassed the Madison East Mall and Highway 22 was in the process of being moved one mile east to intersect at the new junction of Highway 14. This is the corner General Growth Company chose as a site for the new River Hills Mall. The city planned to annex the area to control the development. The existing Mankato malls opposed the plan and brought suit against General Growth Company based on environmental concerns that the carbon dioxide created by the traffic would harm a nearby small lake and wildlife refuge area.[6]

General Growth Company's proposal is to build a 600,000-square-foot mall with three anchors, 110 retail shops, 12 specialty food shops, and a multiscreen movie theater. The parking lot would hold 2,700 cars.[7] Rent in the new mall is estimated to be about $27.00 per square foot for specialty shops, nearly three times as much as in the existing malls. JCP Realty, a subsidiary of JCPenney, is a 30 percent owner of the mall developer, General

EXHIBIT 3

Mankato Area and Eau Claire Comparative Statistics: Population, Effective Buying Income, Retail Sales, and Buying Power Index (in thousands)

County	Population	Households	1989 EBI[a]	1989 Retail Sales	BPI[b]
Blue Earth	52.1	18.8	561,338	487,032	0.0212
Nicollet	29.3	9.8	358,333	101,279	0.0095
Eau Claire	85.5	32.1	906,727	598,521	0.0311

[a] Effective buying income (EBI) is a dollar amount combining personal income from all sources minus taxes and nontax payments (i.e., personal contributions for social security insurance).

[b] The buying power index (BPI) is a weighted measure of an area's potential based on 0.5 (EBI), 0.3 (percentage of U.S. retail sales), and 0.2 (percentage of U.S. population). BPI is expressed as a percentage of the total U.S. buying power.

Source: The Survey of Buying Power Data Service (Sales and Marketing Management Magazine, 1990).

Growth Company, and JCPenney will move from the downtown Mankato Mall into a 62,690-square-foot space in the River Hills Mall.[8] Another anchor will be Herberger's, a regional department store based in St. Cloud Minnesota.[9] Dayton Hudson's Target will be the third anchor.

General Growth Company opened a similar-sized mall in Eau Claire, Wisconsin, in 1986. The demographics and makeup of Eau Claire and Mankato are similar, and that mall is described as a success by Tom Reiter, Eau Claire's city planner.[10] Comparative retail statistics are available from the Survey of Buying Power Service (see Exhibit 3). Since the Mankato retail area includes parts of Blue Earth and Nicollet Counties, statistics from those counties should be combined to reflect Mankato's trading area.

General Growth Company has several hurdles to jump before it can build its proposed mall including zoning ordinances, highway access, the lawsuit, and securing tenant leases.

QUESTIONS

1. Should the Mankato city council approve the zoning request to annex the area where General Growth Company wants to build its River Hills Mall?
2. Is Mankato understored based on the data in the case and exhibits?
3. Are the size and location of the River Hills Mall appropriate for Mankato? See Exhibit 1.
4. Should current Mankato Mall and Madison East Mall tenants consider relocating in the new mall? Consider Bretts Department Store, locally owned specialty shops, and national specialty chain outlets.
5. Using Reilly's law of retail gravitation, calculate the distance along each of the major highways on the map from which people from St. Peter, Lake Crystal, Waseca, and New Ulm will gravitate to the smaller community to shop.
6. Using Huff's law, calculate North Mankato residents' propensity to shop at Mankato Mall, Madison East Mall, and the proposed new River Hills Mall. Use an estimated parameter of 2 to denote the importance of the shopping trip. A purchase requiring less time uses a higher parameter value. The distance from

central North Mankato to the Mankato Mall is 1 1/2 miles, to Madison East Mall the distance is 3 1/2 miles, and to the River Hills Mall location the distance is 4 1/2 miles.

REFERENCES

Anderson, Jim, "An Object Lesson for Mankato; How a General Growth Mall Changed a Wisconsin City," *The Free Press*, 10 July 1989, 1A.

Anderson, Jim, "New Mankato Mall Will Be Getting Big Metro Siblings," *The Free Press*, 3 October 1989, 1A.

Editor & Publisher Market Guide (New York: The Editor & Publisher Co., 1990).

Huff, David L., and Rowland T. Rust, "Measuring the Congruence of Marketing Areas," *Journal of Marketing*, 48 (Winter 1984): 68-74.

Mankato Area Chamber of Commerce, *Welcome to the Mankato-North Mankato Area: Community Profile* (1990).

Mason, J. Barry, and Morris L. Mayer, *Modern Retailing* 5th ed. (Homewood, Ill.: Irwin, 1990) 679-81.

Russell, Cheryl, "The Best Small Cities in America," *American Demographics* (May 1990): 32-34, 53.

Spear, Joe, "JCPenney's to Move," *The Free Press*, 18 September 1990, 1A.

The Survey of Buying Power Data Service (Sales and Marketing Management Magazine, 1990).

ENDNOTES

1. Jim Anderson, "An Object Lesson for Mankato; How a General Growth Mall Changed a Wisconsin City," *The Free Press*, 10 July 1989, 1A.
2. Mankato Area Chamber of Commerce, *Welcome to the Mankato-North Mankato Area: Community Profile* (1990).
3. Cheryl Russell, "The Best Small Cities in America," *American Demographics* (May 1990): 32-34, 53.
4. *Editor & Publisher Market Guide* (New York: The Editor & Publisher Co., 1990).
5. *Editor & Publisher Market Guide*.
6. Joe Spear, "JCPenney's to Move," *The Free Press*, 18 September 1990, 1A.
7. Spear, 1A.
8. Spear, 1A.
9. Spear, 1A.
10. Jim Anderson, "An Object Lesson for Mankato."

CASE 22

SONIC CORP.*

Robert F. Lusch
University of Oklahoma

Introduction

Sonic Corp. operates and franchises drive-in restaurants under the name "Sonic" that feature fast service and a limited menu of moderately priced, cooked-to-order items. In 1984, the Company hired a new management team that began a program to improve its operations by selling underperforming and geographically remote Company-owned restaurants, implementing advertising and food purchasing cooperatives, and refurbishing the appearance

---

*This case was prepared as a basis for class discussion rather than to illustrate either effective or ineffective handling of a retail situation. This case was based on a Prospectus to offer 3,700,000 shares of common stock during early 1991. Some parts of the Prospectus have been deleted in this case study for brevity. The underwriters were The First Boston Corporation and Stephens, Inc.

of Sonic Restaurants. As a result, average annual sales of Company-owned restaurants increased from $264,000 in 1984 to $459,000 in 1990 and average annual sales of all Sonic restaurants increased from $292,000 in 1984 to $445,000 in 1990.

The Company's strategy is to continue enhancing the profitability of Sonic restaurants, to develop new franchised restaurants, and to increase the number of Company-owned restaurants through the acquisition of existing restaurants from franchisees and the opening of new Company-owned restaurants.

To accomplish its goals and to pay off a debt, the Company plans to offer 3,700,000 shares of common stock between $10 and $12 per share.

The Company

Sonic Corp. operates and franchises drive-in restaurants under the name "Sonic" that feature fast service and a limited menu of moderately priced, cooked-to-order items. The original operations of the Company were conducted as a sole proprietorship from 1959 until 1974 when the Company was incorporated.

In 1984, C. Stephen Lynn joined the Company as President and Chief Executive Officer, and recruited an experienced management team. Management implemented programs to support and service its franchisees more effectively and to improve the profitability of Company-owned restaurants. In 1986, an investor group that included management (the "1986 Investor Group") acquired the Company in a leveraged-buyout transaction.

In 1988, members of management and investors affiliated with MAST Resources, Inc., a New York–based investment firm ("MAST"), recapitalized the Company (the "1988 Transaction") through a predecessor of the Company that exchanged cash, stock, and subordinated notes for the stock owned by the 1986 Investor Group. In addition, the Company assumed indebtedness of certain members of the 1986 Investor Group. The funds obtained to complete the 1988 Transaction consisted of $2 million invested by the MAST investor group and $18.8 million obtained under a $24 million revolving credit facility from First National Bank of Boston ("Bank of Boston"). Following the 1988 Transaction, management of the Company and Troy Smith, Sr., a founder and stockholder of the Company, owned together 47.5 percent of the Common Stock of the Company on a fully diluted basis, and the investors affiliated with MAST owned together 47.5 percent of the Common Stock of the Company on a fully diluted basis. The present officers, directors, 5 percent stockholders of the Company, and the investors affiliated with MAST now hold subordinated notes of the Company in the aggregate amount of $5.3 million. These notes and all of the debt owed to Bank of Boston will be repaid with proceeds of the Offering.

Investment Considerations

In addition to the other information in this Prospectus, prospective investors should carefully consider the following investment considerations relating to the Company and its Common Stock before making an investment.

The Quick-Service Restaurant Industry

The quick-service restaurant industry is highly competitive and can be significantly affected by many factors, including changes in local, regional, and national economic conditions, changes in consumer tastes, consumer concerns about the nutritional quality of quick-service food, and increases in the number of, and particular locations of, competing quick-service restaurants. Factors such as inflation, increases in food and energy costs, and the availability of an adequate number of hourly paid employees can also affect the quick-service restaurant industry. The Sonic chain competes primarily on the basis of food quality, price, and speed of service. Major chains, many of which have substantially greater financial resources than the Company, dominate the quick-service restaurant industry. A significant change in pricing or other marketing strategies by one or more of these competitors could have an adverse impact on the Company's sales, earnings, and growth. In addition, with respect to the sale of franchises, the Company competes with many franchisors of restaurants and other business concepts.

Reliance on Key Personnel

The Company believes that its continued success will depend to a significant extent upon the efforts and abilities of certain senior management, in particular those of C. Stephen Lynn, President and Chief Executive Officer, Robert P. Flack, Executive Vice-President and Chief Operating Officer, and Dennis H. Clark, Vice-President of Restaurant Operations. The loss of the services of any of these people could have a material adverse effect upon the Company, including the Company's ability to maintain good relations with its franchisees. See "Management."

Control by Management and Principal Stockholders

Following completion of the Offering, the directors and officers of the Company and their affiliates and the investors affiliated with MAST will beneficially own in the aggregate approximately 52 percent of the outstanding Common Stock. Accordingly, such persons will likely be able to elect the entire Board of Directors of the Company and to continue to direct the affairs of the Company. These persons could propose a recapitalization of the Company similar to the 1988 Transaction, although they have no current plans to do so. The Company will submit any proposal for a recapitalization that is similar to the 1988 Transaction to a special committee consisting of independent members of the Company's Board of Directors for review. Certain provisions of the Company's Certificate of Incorporation and Bylaws could delay or frustrate the removal of incumbent directors and could make more difficult a merger, tender offer, or proxy contest involving the Company, even if such events would be beneficial to the interests of the stockholders.

Proceeds

The Company will not receive any of the proceeds from the sale of the 1,100,000 shares (1,360,150 shares if the over-allotment option is exercised in full) to be sold by the Selling Stockholders. The proceeds from the sale of the

2,600,000 shares (2,709,850 shares if the over-allotment option is exercised in full) to be sold by the Company will be used by the Company to repay indebtedness to Bank of Boston of $16.9 million and indebtedness to shareholders and affiliates of the Company totaling $7.3 million, all of which was incurred in the 1988 Transaction.

Seasonality

The Company's business is seasonal, with revenues historically lower during the winter.

Dilution

The purchasers of the shares of Common Stock offered hereby will experience immediate and significant dilution. The purchase price of the Common Stock offered hereby will exceed the pro forma net tangible book value of the Common Stock immediately following the Offering. See "Dilution."

Lack of Public Market; Shares Eligible for Future Sale

Prior to the Offering, there has been no public market for shares of the Company's Common Stock and there can be no assurance that an active trading market will develop or be sustained. No predictions can be made as to the effect, if any, that market sales of shares or the availability of shares for sale will have on the market price prevailing from time to time. Sales of substantial amounts of shares in the public market following the Offering could adversely affect the market price of the Common Stock and could impair the Company's future ability to raise capital through an offering of equity securities. Excluding shares of Common Stock offered by this Prospectus, pursuant to Rule 144 promulgated under the Securities Act of 1933, as amended, approximately 250,000 shares may be sold immediately following the Offering and approximately 3,363,150 shares may be sold 90 days after the completion of the Offering. The holders of these shares have agreed that, without the consent of the Representatives of the Underwriters, they will not sell any shares of Common Stock held by them during the 180-day period immediately following the completion of the Offering.

Use of Proceeds

The net proceeds to the Company from the Offering will be used (i) to repay all loans outstanding from Bank of Boston, of which approximately $16.9 million was outstanding at November 30, 1990, at an interest rate equal to the prime rate of interest of Bank of Boston plus 1 1/2 percent (11.5 percent at November 30, 1990) and subject to an amortization schedule requiring principal payments through 1995, and (ii) to repay the $7.3 million subordinated debt held by certain stockholders of the Company and others, which bears interest at 12 percent per annum and matures on January 10, 1996, January 10, 1997, and December 12, 1998. Any remaining net proceeds will be used as a part of the Company's working capital.

The Company intends to establish a new line of credit of $10 million with a financial institution after the Offering is completed. Funds under this line of credit will be available and may be used to (i) repay any remaining outstanding balance of the subordinated debt, (ii) finance an increase in the number of Company-owned restaurants, primarily through the acquisition from franchisees of majority interests in existing franchised restaurants and to a lesser extent the opening of new restaurants, and (iii) provide funding for general corporate purposes. The Company has received from Bank of Boston a written indication of interest to provide this new line of credit on a secured basis with interest at the prime rate of interest of Bank of Boston plus 1/2 percent. For the first two years, loans would be on a revolving credit basis. After two years, the outstanding balance would convert to a term loan that would be due and payable on December 1, 1997.

The Company will not receive any proceeds from the sale of the shares of Common Stock offered by the Selling Stockholders.

Dilution

At November 30, 1990, the net tangible book value of the Company was $(16,061,700) or $(3.16) per share of Common Stock outstanding. The negative net tangible book value of the Company resulted from the accounting treatment of the 1988 Transaction and not as a result of continuing business operations. Net tangible book value per share is determined by dividing the Company's tangible net worth (tangible assets less liabilities) by the number of shares of Common Stock outstanding. After giving effect to the sale by the Company of 2,600,000 shares of Common Stock offered hereby, based upon an initial public offering price of $11.00 per share and after deducting the underwriting discount and estimated offering expenses of $2,634,400, the pro forma net tangible book value of the Company at November 30, 1990 was $9,903,900, or $1.29 per share of Common Stock. This represents an immediate increase in net tangible book value of $4.45 per share to existing stockholders and an immediate dilution of net tangible book value of $9.71 per share to new investors. The following illustrates this per share dilution:

Assumed public offering price		$11.00
Net tangible book value per share at November 30, 1990	$(3.16)	
Increase in net tangible book value per share attributable to new investors	4.45	
Pro forma net tangible book value per share after the Offering		1.29
Dilution per share to new investors		$ 9.71

The following data set forth as of November 30, 1990 the number of shares purchased from the Company, the total consideration paid, and the average price per share paid by the existing holders of Common Stock and the price to be paid by the new investors, based upon an initial public offering price of

$11.00 per share. The following computations do not reflect the sale of shares of Common Stock by the Selling Stockholders:

	Shares Purchased		Total Consideration		Average Price per Share
	Number	Percentage	Amount	Percentage	
Existing stockholders	5,075,150	66.1%	$ 2,558,360	8.2%	$ .50
New investors	2,600,000	33.9%	$28,600,000	91.8%	$11.00
Total	7,675,150	100%	$31,158,360	100%	

Dividend Policy

During the historical reporting periods covered by this Prospectus, the Company has not paid a dividend on Common Stock. The declaration and payment of future dividends will be at the sole discretion of the Board of Directors and will depend upon the Company's profitability, financial condition, cash requirements, future prospects, and other factors deemed relevant by the Board of Directors. The Company presently intends to retain earnings for working capital and general corporate purposes and does not expect to pay any cash dividends in the foreseeable future. The Company's loan agreement with Bank of Boston contains restrictions on the Company's ability to pay dividends. These restrictions will terminate when the Bank of Boston loans are repaid with the proceeds of the Offering, although a new loan agreement currently being discussed by the Company with Bank of Boston may contain similar restrictions.

Selected Financial Data

The financial data presented in Exhibit 1 for the five years ended August 31, 1990 are derived from Consolidated Financial Statements of Sonic Corp. (and its predecessor) which have been audited by Ernst & Young, independent auditors. The selected financial data for the three-month periods ended November 30, 1989 and 1990 are derived from unaudited consolidated financial statements. The unaudited financial statements include all adjustments, consisting of normal, recurring accruals, which Sonic Corp. considers necessary for a fair presentation of the financial position and the results of operations for these periods. Operating results for the three months ended November 30, 1990 are not necessarily indicative of the results that may be expected for the entire year ending August 31, 1991. The selected financial data should be read in conjunction with the Consolidated Financial Statements of the Company included elsewhere in this Prospectus.

Financial Condition and Results of Operations

The Company's revenues are derived primarily from sales by Company-owned restaurants, royalty fees from franchisees, and restaurant equipment sales. The Company also receives revenues from initial franchise fees, area

EXHIBIT 1

Selected Financial Data (in thousands, except per share data)

	Predecessor									Three Months Ended November 30,	
	Year Ended August 31,			Three Months Ended November 30, 1988	Nine Months Ended August 31, 1989	Pro Forma Year Ended August 31, 1989[a]	Year Ended August 31, 1990			1989	1990
	1986	1987	1988								
Income Statement Data											
Sales by Company-owned restaurants	$18,446	$16,581	$17,842	$4,869	$17,185	$22,054	$30,574			$7,004	$8,333
Franchised restaurants											
Franchise fees and royalties	3,252	3,871	4,926	1,451	4,573	6,024	7,765			1,892	2,279
Equipment sales	1,065	4,452	3,643	1,078	3,673	4,751	6,419			1,807	1,399
Other	901	905	804	267	789	1,056	1,102			249	289
Total revenues	23,664	25,809	27,215	7,665	26,220	33,885	45,860			10,952	12,300
Cost of restaurant sales	15,161	13,584	14,487	3,861	13,495	17,356	23,726			5,523	6,516
Cost of equipment sales	783	3,808	3,080	924	3,111	4,035	5,398			1,520	1,164
Selling, general, and administrative	4,872	4,413	5,212	1,433	4,787	6,245	7,540			1,638	1,682
Depreciation and amortization	1,263	1,229	1,051	262	1,175	1,584	1,793			442	460
Minority interest in earnings of restaurant partnerships	579	674	885	249	964	1,213	1,888			401	497
Other expenses	284	415	670	250	126	376	333			73	49
Income from operations	722	1,686	1,830	686	2,562	3,076	5,182			1,355	1,932
Interest expense	1,663	1,318	1,072	387	3,106	4,124	3,684			923	890

Interest income	(677)	(691)	(647)	(189)	(476)	(665)	(178)	(48)	(76)
Aquisition-related expenses	—	—	—	2,197	—	2,197	—	—	—
Income (loss) before income taxes	$(264)	$1,059	$1,405	$(1,709)	$(68)	$(2,580)	$1,676	$480	$1,118
Net loss income	$(231)	$453	$878	$(1,201)	$(311)	$(2,051)	$941	$270	$637
Income (loss) per common share[b]					$(0.06)	$(0.41)	$0.19	$0.05	$0.13
Weighted average shares outstanding[b]					5,000	5,000	5,018	5,263	5,018
Balance Sheet Data									
Working capital	$1,675	$1,788	$1,335		$1,421	$1,421	$1,371	$1,243	$1,577
Property, equipment, and capital leases	8,865	6,475	6,513		8,511	8,511	9,382	8,554	9,261
Total assets	18,576	16,628	16,742		31,579	31,579	31,631	31,713	32,460
Obligations under capital leases, net of current portion	4,159	3,920	3,597		4,449	4,449	4,347	4,336	4,317
Long-term debt	8,338	5,907	4,629		26,523	26,523	25,582	25,353	24,829
Stockholders' equity (deficit)	2,349	2,802	3,680		(5,837)	(5,837)	(5,186)	(5,457)	(4,549)

[a]The pro forma income statement data for the year ended August 31, 1989 is presented as though the 1988 Transaction had been completed as of September 1, 1988. The pro forma adjustments for 1989 include additional management fees, incremental interest expense on the increase in outstanding debt, and additional depreciation and amortization.

[b]Earnings (loss) per share is calculated based on the weighted average number of shares outstanding during the period and gives effect to the exchange of predecessor common stock for 25 shares of Sonic Corp. common stock subsequent to August 31, 1990.

development fees, and the leasing of signs and real estate. Cost of Company-owned restaurant sales and minority interest in earnings of restaurant partnerships relate directly to Company-owned restaurant sales, while the cost of restaurant equipment sales relates to sales of restaurant equipment. Other expenses, such as depreciation and amortization and general and administrative expenses, relate to both Company-owned restaurant operations and restaurant equipment sales as well as the Company's franchising operations. The Company's revenues and expenses are directly affected by the number and sales volumes of Company-owned restaurants. The Company's revenues and, to a lesser extent, expenses are also affected by the number and sales volumes of franchised restaurants. Restaurant equipment sales and initial franchise fees are directly affected by the number of restaurant openings.

Exhibit 2 sets forth the percentage relationship to total revenues, unless otherwise indicated, of certain items included in the Company's statement of operations. Exhibit 2 also sets forth certain restaurant data for the period indicated.

Business

Sonic Corp. operates and franchises drive-in restaurants under the name "Sonic," that feature fast service and a limited menu of moderately priced, cooked-to-order items. Sonic restaurants, located principally in the south central United States, comprise the largest chain of quick-service, drive-in restaurants in the country. At a typical Sonic restaurant, the customer drives into one of 24 covered parking spaces, orders through an intercom from a menu featuring hamburgers, hot dogs, french fries, onion rings, and specialty beverages, and has the food delivered by a carhop within an average of five minutes.

The Company's strategy is to continue enhancing the profitability of Sonic restaurants, to develop new franchised restaurants, and to increase the number of Company-owned restaurants through the acquisition of existing restaurants from franchisees and the opening of new Company-owned restaurants. From time to time, the Company has considered the acquisition of other restaurant chains.

SONIC RESTAURANTS

General. The Sonic restaurant philosophy stresses a partnership relationship between restaurant owners and managers in which managers at all Company-owned and most franchised restaurants own an equity interest in the restaurant. The Company believes that this structure is unique in the restaurant industry and provides a substantial incentive for restaurant managers to operate their restaurants profitably and efficiently.

Off-premises consumption of food prepared at quick-service restaurants has more than doubled since 1982. "Off-premises" consumption includes food that is not consumed by the customer inside the restaurant building. The

EXHIBIT 2

Percentage Results of Operations and Restaurant Data

	Year Ended August 31,			Three Months Ended November 30,	
	1988	Pro Forma 1989[a]	1990	1989	1990
Income Statement Data					
Revenues					
Sales by Company-owned restaurants	65.6%	65.1%	66.7%	63.9%	67.7%
Franchised restaurants					
Franchise fees and royalties	18.1	17.8	16.9	17.3	18.5
Equipment sales	13.4	14.0	14.0	16.5	11.4
Other	2.9	3.1	2.4	2.3	2.4
	100.0%	100.0%	100.0%	100.0%	100.0%
Costs and expenses					
Company-owned restaurants[b]	81.2%	78.7%	77.6%	78.9%	78.2%
Equipment sales[c]	84.6	84.9	84.1	84.1	83.2
Selling, general, and administrative	19.2	18.4	16.4	15.0	13.7
Depreciation and amortization	3.9	4.7	3.9	4.0	3.7
Minority interest in earnings of restaurant partnerships[b]	5.0	5.5	6.2	5.7	6.0
Interest expenses	3.9	12.2	8.0	8.4	7.2
Other expenses	2.5	1.1	0.7	0.7	0.4
Income from operations	6.7	9.1	11.3	12.4	15.7
Net income (loss)	3.2	(6.1)	2.1	2.5	5.2
Restaurant Operating Data (sales in thousands)					
Company-owned restaurants[d]	50	65	69	65	70
Franchised restaurants[d]	930	931	974	947	987
Total	980	996	1,043	1,012	1,057
Systemwide sales	$341,135	$390,195	$454,790	$106,958	$121,840
Systemwide average sales per restaurant	356	395	445	106	116
Systemwide comparable average sales per restaurant[e]	348	387	441	103	114
Company-owned average sales per restaurant	370	416	459	108	119
Company-owned comparable average sales per restaurant[e]	373	423	470	108	121

[a]The pro forma information for the year ended August 31, 1989 is presented as though the 1988 Transaction had been completed as of September 1, 1988. The pro forma adjustments for 1989 include additional management fees, interest expense on the incremental increase in debt outstanding, and additional depreciation and amortization.
[b]As a percentage of sales by Company-owned restaurants.
[c]As a percentage of equipment sales.
[d]Number of restaurants open at end of period.
[e]Represents sales for restaurants open in both the reported and prior periods.

Company believes that the drive-in format of Sonic restaurants positions the Sonic chain to take advantage of current consumer trends toward off-premises consumption.

Sonic restaurants enjoy a dedicated customer base with visit frequency rates greater than those of other major quick-service hamburger restaurants. In addition, while other major quick-service chains have seen little or no growth in customer traffic in recent periods, Sonic restaurants have experienced significant growth in customer traffic.

Menu. At Sonic restaurants, all food is freshly prepared and cooked to order to customer specifications. The Company's business strategy is to have a limited menu of popular items in order to streamline restaurant operations, lower food costs, and promote uniform food quality. Standard menu items include hamburgers, hot dogs, corn dogs, steak, chicken and fish sandwiches, onion rings, french fries, soft drinks, specialty beverages, and ice cream. Each restaurant also has the option of offering one or two regional specialties. During the three-month period ended May 31, 1990, the average ticket price per customer was $2.25, which does not materially differ from other major quick-service restaurant chains located in the south central United States.

Restaurant Design and Construction. The standard Sonic restaurant consists of a kitchen housed in a one-story building flanked by two canopy-covered rows of parking spaces, each space with its own intercom and menu board. Sonic restaurants typically do not provide an indoor eating area.

Based on information provided to the Company by franchisees, the current average cost to start up a new Sonic restaurant is approximately $370,000, considerably less than the start-up costs of most other major quick-service restaurants. Of this amount, $100,000 is typically spent on land, $145,000 on building and site work, $85,000 on equipment, $25,000 for working capital, and $15,000 for the initial franchise fee. The average first-year sales of a new Sonic restaurant were $613,000 for the 12-month period ending July 31, 1990, resulting in an average ratio of first-year sales to capital costs of 1.7:1, which management believes compares favorably to other major restaurant chains. However, the costs associated with land acquisition in the south central United States (where the Sonic chain is predominantly located) may be lower than comparable costs of restaurant chains based in other parts of the United States.

In 1985, the Company developed a program to renovate and refurbish Sonic's older restaurants, some of which were nearly 30 years old. This "retrofit" program was designed to add a more appealing, contemporary design to Sonic restaurants at a modest cost. The retrofit typically adds a new exterior facade, vestibule, accent lighting and neon signs, and increased energy efficiency. In many cases, franchisees implementing the retrofit programs have made additional capital expenditures on their own initiative that have increased the operating efficiency of their restaurants. A basic retrofit package takes about two weeks to complete, with no material interruption of business, and costs between $25,000 and $30,000. As of August 31, 1990, 71 percent of all Sonic restaurants featured the more contemporary design of the retrofit package. The Company believes that this design has contributed to increased revenues at the restaurants that have adopted it.

Equipment Sales. The Company sells restaurant equipment manufactured by third parties to existing Sonic restaurants and a significant majority of new Sonic restaurants. The Company assembles a complete package of equipment needed to start up a restaurant and arranges for shipment to the restaurant location.

In 1987, the Company sold its equipment sales division to a third party in exchange for notes and common stock of the buyer. In 1988, when the buyer defaulted on the notes, the Company repossessed the division. During the period 1987 to 1990, this transaction and the litigation that followed resulted in approximately $1.2 million of losses and expenses to the Company, of which $500,000 was attributable to loss on equity investment and $700,000 arose from litigation expenses.

The Company intends to continue to sell restaurant equipment to franchisees. The equipment operation, which was profitable in 1990, does not account for a significant percentage of the Company's profits.

Royalties and Signs. Each Sonic restaurant, including Company-owned restaurants, operates under a franchise agreement that provides for payments to the Company of a graduated percentage of the gross revenues of the restaurant. Approximately 94 percent of Sonic restaurants are subject to a form of franchise agreement adopted in 1984 (the "1984 Form") which provides for a royalty that begins at 1 percent of gross revenue and increases to 3 percent as the level of gross revenues increases. The current average royalty rate for all Sonic restaurants covered by the 1984 Form is 1.75 percent. The 79 Sonic restaurants placed in operation since September 1, 1989 have been paying average royalties under this agreement equal to approximately 2.1 percent of gross revenues. A new form of franchise agreement adopted in 1988 (the "1988 Form") provides for graduated royalty rates that begin at 1 percent of gross revenues and increases to 4 percent. This new agreement is in effect for seven Sonic restaurants. The Company estimates that 20 percent of all new restaurants opened in fiscal year 1991 will be subject to the 1988 Form. Not all new restaurants will be governed by this new agreement because many developers of new restaurants have options that entitle them to open restaurants governed by the 1984 Form. The Company believes that in coming years a progressively greater percentage of new restaurants will be governed by the 1988 Form.

All restaurants are required to display a Sonic drive-in sign manufactured in accordance with Company specifications. In virtually all cases, the Company owns this sign and leases it to the restaurant at a monthly rental rate of between $76 and $150, depending on the age of the lease. Among other remedies, the Company is entitled to remove this sign if the franchisee is in breach of its franchise agreement.

Advertising. Starting in 1984, the Company sponsored the formation of advertising cooperatives among restaurant owners to pool and direct advertising expenditures in local markets. Under the 1984 Form, franchisees are required to contribute 0.375 percent of their gross revenues to a central media production fund and expend an additional 1.125 percent of gross revenues on advertising, either directly or through Company-sponsored cooperatives. For the fiscal year ended 1989, franchisees participating in cooperatives contributed an average of 2.15 percent of revenues to Sonic advertising cooperatives, exceeding the required 1.125 percent. The following table reflects the extent of participation in advertising cooperatives by all Sonic restaurants and the total amounts spent on media production and purchases (principally television):

Fiscal Year	Number of Participating Restaurants	Percentage of All Restaurants	Funds Spent on Media Production and Purchase
1986	330	35%	$ 880,000
1987	498	52	2,266,000
1988	682	70	4,018,000
1989	788	79	5,810,000
1990	870	84	7,937,000

The table does not reflect amounts that were spent by individual restaurants on forms of advertising other than electronic media, such as newspaper advertisements. From 1986 to 1990, based on information supplied to the Company by franchisees, systemwide expenditures in this latter category have ranged between $4.5 million and $5 million per year.

Marketing Programs. On an annual basis, the Company and its advertising agency develop a marketing plan that, for the most part, promotes Sonic's signature items, such as onion rings, its cooked-to-order format, and the personal manner of service by carhops. The marketing plan includes monthly promotions to be offered throughout the Sonic chain. These promotions are generally supported by television commercials that correspond with the nature of the promotion.

One of the Company's more successful marketing campaigns is the "Brown Bag Special." This meal is delivered in a brown paper bag displaying the Sonic logo and includes two hamburgers, two orders of french fries, and two soft drinks, priced significantly less than the cost of these items purchased individually. The Brown Bag Special has met with success each time it has been promoted.

Sonic television commercials often feature characters and scenes that capitalize on an interest in 1950s nostalgia. Since 1987, the Company has retained Frankie Avalon to appear in Sonic commercials and at the Company's annual franchisee convention and other special Sonic events.

Food Purchasing Cooperatives. In 1984, the Company began sponsoring the formation of purchasing cooperatives among restaurant owners to negotiate bulk orders of food and supplies and enter into long-term supply contracts for beef and cooking oil. These purchasing cooperatives have achieved cost savings, improved food quality and consistency, and helped decrease the volatility of supply costs for Sonic restaurants. The average cost of food and paper supplies for a Sonic restaurant has decreased as a percentage of sales from 36.4 percent in 1986 to 35.3 percent in 1990. The Company believes that the food purchasing cooperatives contributed to these results and have allowed restaurants to avoid menu price increases that might otherwise have occurred.

In recent years, a planned reduction in the number of food and paper product distributors has improved the Sonic chain's ability to negotiate more advantageous purchasing terms and to maintain more uniform products. The following table illustrates the extent of such consolidation and the extent of participation in purchasing cooperatives by all Sonic restaurants:

End of Fiscal Year	Number of Food Services Distributors	Percentage of All Restaurants
1986	70	22%
1987	56	34
1988	30	73
1989	22	89
1990	18	92

Geographic Territory. Sonic drive-in restaurants are located principally in the south central United States. The eight contiguous states of Oklahoma, Texas, Louisiana, Mississippi, Arkansas, Tennessee, Missouri, and Kansas contain 86 percent of all Sonic restaurants. The following table sets forth by state the number of franchised restaurants and Company-owned restaurants, respectively, as of November 30, 1990:

State	Franchised	Company-Owned	Total
Texas	287	35	322
Oklahoma	136	13	149
Arkansas	80	—	80
Tennessee	78	—	78
Missouri	64	11	75
Louisiana	66	6	72
Mississippi	71	—	71
Kansas	60	5	65
New Mexico	49	—	49
Kentucky	15	—	15
Alabama	14	—	14

State	Franchised	Company-Owned	Total
Arizona	14	—	14
Colorado	13	—	13
North Carolina	10	—	10
California	9	—	9
Georgia	7	—	7
South Carolina	4	—	4
Nevada	3	—	3
Florida	3	—	3
Nebraska	3	—	3
Illinois	1	—	1
	987	70	1,057

Company-Owned Restaurants

Company-owned restaurants are those Sonic restaurants owned by partnerships in which the Company is the majority partner. A minority interest in the partnership is owned by managers ("management partners") who are involved in the day-to-day management and operation of the restaurant. Under the standard partnership agreement, the Company has the right to purchase the interests of any management partner on short notice. The partnerships operate on a cash basis and distribute net income to partners on a monthly basis. Each management partner contributes his or her pro rata portion of all operating expenses, including franchise fees, royalties, sign expenses, as well as the initial equity (typically an aggregate of $40,000 in the case of new restaurants), which is used to cover start-up costs. Equipment is usually purchased with borrowed funds, the repayment of which the Company and all management partners guarantee. The Company alone guarantees any real estate lease entered into for the site.

In addition to the advertising and food purchasing cooperatives discussed previously, the Company has taken the following steps since 1984 to revitalize the operations of Company-owned restaurants:

- Through 1987, selling 36 underperforming restaurants to third parties, generally existing franchisees.
- Since 1987, opening seven restaurants and acquiring 17 existing restaurants.
- Clustering Company-owned restaurants to facilitate better Company supervision and control.
- As a management incentive, increasing from 19 percent in 1986 to 41 percent in 1990, the average aggregate ownership by management partners in Company-owned restaurants.

As a result of these changes, operating margins of Company-owned restaurants have improved significantly thereby improving the Company's profitability. The following table illustrates this trend and provides information on the number of Company-owned restaurants opened and closed during the past five years:

	1986	1987	1988	1989	1990
Company-owned restaurant data					
Average revenues per Company-owned restaurant	$266,000	$302,000	$370,000	$416,000	$459,000
Average operating profit per Company-owned restaurant	$13,600	$24,300	$39,600	$56,000	$67,200
Average operating profit as a percentage of average revenues	5.1%	8.1%	10.7%	13.5%	14.6%
Newly opened and reopened restaurants	3	2	2	4	1
(Sold to) purchased from franchisees	(21)	(15)	3	11	3
Closed	(2)	(2)	(1)	–	–
Total open at year end	61	46	50	65	69

During the 1991 fiscal year, the Company expects to open five new Company-owned restaurants and to acquire seven restaurants from franchisees.

Franchised Restaurants

General. Franchised restaurants are Sonic restaurants owned by third parties. Of the 987 franchised restaurants, the Company owns a minority interest in 25. In most franchised restaurants, the managers own an equity interest in the restaurants.

The following table summarizes the number of franchised restaurants opened, purchased from or sold to the Company, and closed over the last five years:

	1986	1987	1988	1989	1990
Franchised restaurant data					
New restaurants	18	27	41	30	53
Purchased from (sold to) the Company	21	15	(3)	(11)	(3)
Closed and terminated, net of reopenings	(41)	(20)	(17)	(18)	(7)
Total open at year end	887	909	930	931	974

In addition to the advertising and food purchasing cooperatives and marketing programs discussed previously, the Company provides various services to its franchisees in addition to those required by franchise agreements, including the following:

- Assisting with quality control through field representatives, to assure that each franchise is consistently delivering high-quality food and service.

- Assisting in selecting sites for new restaurants using demographic data and studies of traffic patterns.
- Providing five-week training seminars for new restaurant managers which emphasize quality food preparation, quick service, cleanliness of restaurants, and consistency of service.
- Providing one-stop shopping for all equipment needed to open a new restaurant. This equipment, a package of which has been designed by the Company for restaurant use, is manufactured by third parties. The Company assists in selecting the equipment and arranging for delivery.
- Making financing available through a third-party source to qualified franchisees for purchasing restaurant equipment.

In 1989, certain franchisees, who together own approximately 400 Sonic restaurants, organized a Sonic franchisee association. The Company believes it has good relations with its franchisees and the Sonic franchisee association.

Future Expansion. Traditionally, growth in the number of franchised restaurants has occurred when existing franchisees have increased the number of their restaurants on a single restaurant basis. The Company expects that most new Sonic restaurants will be developed in this fashion for the next two to three years. The Company has initiated a strategy to develop multiple franchised restaurants through area development agreements with third parties. Each area development agreement gives a developer the exclusive right to construct, own, and operate Sonic restaurants within a defined area. In exchange, each developer agrees to open a minimum number of Sonic restaurants in the area within a prescribed time period. Since 1984, the Company has entered into 37 area development agreements, and 80 Sonic restaurants have been opened under these agreements. The Company believes that its experience with franchisees who commit to develop Sonic restaurants under area development agreements has been favorable, although there can be no assurance that future performance by developers under these agreements will be successful.

One area development agreement in effect covers the southern half of Florida and requires that 150 new Sonic restaurants be opened by 1996. To date, one restaurant has been opened under this agreement, and one restaurant is under construction.

Competition

The Company competes in the quick-service restaurant industry, which is highly competitive in price, service, restaurant location, and food quality, and is often affected by changes in consumer trends, economic conditions, demographics, traffic patterns, and concerns about the nutritional content of quick-service foods. The Company competes primarily on the basis of price, food quality, and speed of service. In selling franchises, the Company also competes with many franchisors of restaurants.

Employees

As of November 30, 1990, the Company had 97 employees. None of these employees is covered by a collective bargaining agreement. Company-owned restaurants employ approximately 1,400 persons, none of whom are employees of the Company. The Company believes that its labor relations are good.

Trademarks and Service Marks

The Company owns numerous trademarks and service marks. Many of these, including the "Sonic" logo and trademark, are registered with the United States Patent and Trademark Office. The Company believes that its trademarks and service marks have significant value and are important to its marketing efforts.

Government Regulation

The Company is subject to Federal Trade Commission ("FTC") regulation and several state laws that regulate the offer and sale of franchises. The Company is also subject to a number of state laws that regulate substantive aspects of the franchisor/franchisee relationship. The FTC's Trade Regulation Rule on Franchising (the "FTC Rule") requires that the Company furnish prospective franchisees with a franchise offering circular containing information prescribed by the FTC Rule.

State laws that regulate the franchisor/franchisee relationship presently exist in a substantial number of states. Such laws regulate the franchise relationship by, for example, requiring the franchisor to deal with its franchisees in good faith, prohibiting interference with the right of free association among franchisees, and regulating discrimination among franchisees in charges, royalties, or fees. These laws have not precluded the Company from seeking franchisees in any given area. Although such laws may restrict a franchisor in the termination of a franchise agreement by, for example, requiring "good cause" to exist as a basis for the termination, advance notice to the franchisee of the termination, an opportunity to cure a default and repurchase of inventory, or other compensation, these provisions have not had a significant effect on the Company's operations.

Each Sonic restaurant is subject to regulation by federal agencies and to licensing and regulation by state and local health, sanitation, safety, fire, and other departments. Difficulties or failures in obtaining the required licenses or approvals could delay or prevent the opening of a new restaurant.

Sonic restaurants are subject to federal and state environmental regulations, but these have not had a material effect on their operations. More stringent and varied requirements of local governmental bodies with respect to zoning, land use, and environmental factors could delay or prevent development of new restaurants in particular locations.

The owners of Sonic restaurants are subject to the Fair Labor Standards Act and various state laws governing such matters as minimum wages, overtime, and other working conditions. Significant numbers of food service personnel in Sonic restaurants are paid at rates related to the federal minimum wage, and accordingly, increases in the minimum wage would increase labor costs at these locations.

Properties

Of the 70 Company-owned restaurants, 61 are located on property leased from third parties and 9 are located on property owned by the Company. These restaurant leases expire on dates ranging from 1991 to 2007, with the majority of the leases providing for renewal options. All leases provide for specified periodic rental payments, and some call for additional rentals based on sales volume. Most leases require the Company to maintain the property and pay the cost of insurance and taxes.

The Company's executive offices are located in 33,918 square feet of leased office space in Oklahoma City, Oklahoma. The lease for this property expires in July 1995 and the Company has an option to extend the lease for two additional five-year terms. The Company also leases, for its equipment sales operations, approximately 12,500 square feet of office and warehouse space in Oklahoma City under a lease that expires in July 1994.

Litigation

From time to time, the Company is involved in litigation relating to claims arising out of its normal business operations. The Company is not now engaged in any legal proceedings that are expected, individually or in the aggregate, to have a material adverse effect on the Company.

Management

Executive Officers and Directors

The following table sets forth certain information regarding the executive officers and directors of the Company:

Name	Age	Position
C. Stephen Lynn	43	President, Chief Executive Officer and Director
Robert P. Flack	52	Executive Vice-President and Chief Operation Officer
Dennis H. Clark	44	Vice-President, Restaurant Operations
J. Clifford Hudson	36	Vice-President, Corporate Development, General Counsel and Secretary
Jerry W. Grizzle	37	Vice-President and Treasurer
Raymond N. Fain	44	Vice-President and Controller
K. Keith Sutterfield	54	Vice-President, Marketing
Warner L. Van Sciver	51	Vice-President, Franchise Services
Marc C. Bergschneider	39	Director
Leonard Lieberman	62	Director

The Board of Directors of the Company is divided into Class A, Class B, and Class C directors. Each director is elected to serve for a period of three years, except that the initial term of Class A directors expires in 1991 and the initial term of Class B directors expires in 1992. There is no fixed term of office for the Company's officers.

Mr. C. Stephen Lynn has been President and Chief Executive Officer of the Company since November 1983. Mr. Lynn is a member of the boards of directors of The International Franchise Association and CityBank & Trust of Oklahoma City.

Mr. Robert P. Flack has been Executive Vice-President and Chief Operating Officer of the Company since September 1, 1990. From June 1989 until that time, Mr. Flack was Vice-President in charge of franchise development for the Company. From 1982 to 1989, Mr. Flack was Executive Vice-President of El Chico Corporation, a full-service restaurant chain. Mr. Flack's primary responsibilities with the Company are the management of its franchise network.

Mr. Dennis H. Clark has been Vice-President, Restaurant Operations since 1987. Mr. Clark became a franchisee of the company in 1986. From 1982 to 1986, Mr. Clark was a joint venture partner and President of Farmer Brown's Inc., a regional restaurant chain. He also served as Divisional Director of Operations of Taco Bell from 1979 to 1982 and as Regional Vice-President for Jericho, Inc., the franchisor of Long John Silver's, from 1976 to 1979. Mr. Clark's primary responsibilities with the Company are the management of Company-owned restaurants.

Mr. J. Clifford Hudson has been Vice-President, Corporate Development, General Counsel, and Secretary of the Company since September 1, 1990. From June 1985 to that time, Mr. Hudson was Vice-President, General Counsel, and Secretary of the Company.

Mr. Jerry W. Grizzle has been Vice-President and Treasurer of the Company since 1986. From 1984 to 1986, Mr. Grizzle was Controller of the Company.

Mr. Raymond N. Fain has been the Company's Vice-President and Controller since 1986. Prior to that time, Mr. Fain served at various times as Vice-President of Finance, Treasurer, and Controller of the Company. He has been employed by the Company since 1978. Mr. Fain is a certified public accountant. He directs the Company's corporate accounting, restaurant accounting, franchise compliance auditing, and business planning process.

Mr. K. Keith Sutterfield has been Vice-President, Marketing of the Company since September 1987. From 1985 to 1987, he was Director of Advertising and Senior Director of Marketing of the Company.

Mr. Warner L. Van Sciver has been Vice-President, Franchise Services since April 1988. From 1980 to 1988, Mr. Van Sciver was Vice-President of Southeastern Operations for Jericho, Inc., the franchisor of Long John Silver's, where he was responsible for the operation of 125 company-owned and 90 franchise restaurants located in eight southeastern states.

Mr. Marc C. Bergschneider has been a Director of the Company since 1988. Mr. Bergschneider is the President of MAST, a position he has held since 1988. Mr. Bergschneider is also the President of New Charleston Capital, Inc., a New York-based merchant banking firm. From 1985 to 1988, Mr. Bergschneider was a Managing Director with Drexel Burnham Lambert, Inc. Mr. Bergschneider is a director of American Vision Centers, Inc.

Mr. Leonard Lieberman has been a Director of the Company since 1988. Mr. Liberman was the Chief Executive Officer and a director of Supermarkets General Corporation from 1983 to 1987. From 1987 to the present, Mr. Lieberman has been a private investor. In January 1991, Mr. Lieberman was elected Chairman, President, and Chief Executive Officer of Outlet Communications, Inc. Mr. Lieberman is also a director of Outlet Communications, Inc. and of Republic New York Corporation.

The Company intends to designate additional directors prior to the effective date of this Prospectus. Board members (other than members of management) will be entitled to receive $5,000 per annum and $1,000 per meeting and will be granted options to purchase shares of Common Stock.

Committees

The Company expects that the Board of Directors will establish an audit committee and a compensation committee prior to the effective date of this Offering. No additional fees will be paid to directors for serving on committees.

QUESTIONS

1. Evaluate Sonic's strategy since 1984. What are the firm's prospects for the 1990s?
2. Does Sonic have any other options for financing growth other than by issuing common stock? How reasonable are these other options?
3. Evaluate Sonic's financial performance from 1986 through 1990.

CASE 23

Deborah Zizzo
University of Oklahoma

CIRCLE K CORPORATION*

Introduction

The rise and fall of Circle K is a story of a quiet regional company which grew to be the largest publicly owned convenience store chain in the United States—before collapsing into bankruptcy. In 1983, Circle K operated 1,221 stores in 12 states with sales just over $750 million. A crucial change in leadership that year sparked the company's voracious appetite, and it began devouring other convenience stores, from profitable operations to what one seller termed "a bunch of crap." By 1989, the company boasted 4,685 convenience stores in 32 states and sales were over $3 billion. To finance this growth, Circle K gorged on the money readily available through the junk bond market, until it became bloated with debt. In its consuming quest for

---

*Reprinted with permission of Deborah Zizzo.

growth, the company apparently ignored the competitive environment and, worse, neglected operations of its own stores. Yet almost until the very end, the investment community applauded and rewarded Circle K's flashy growth. Apparently, no one suspected that this series of management lapses would lead Circle K to the brink of demise.

The Convenience Store Industry

The convenience store concept originated in 1927 in Dallas, Texas, when "Uncle Johnny" Jefferson Green began stocking bread, milk, and eggs at the Southland Ice Dock he operated. This dock was open 16 hours a day, 7 days a week, and Green had realized that customers often needed these and other staples after local grocery stores had closed. This type of store and others of similar format increased modestly in number for many years. They were more successful in warmer climates, partly because of their open storefronts.

The number of convenience stores began to grow more rapidly after World War II. As the increased ownership of automobiles helped spur the growth of the suburbs, downtown supermarkets became less accessible to consumers. New supermarkets were much larger than before and often could no longer provide the customer with quick service. Convenience stores stepped in to fill this gap. Stores were small, usually containing between 1,600 and 2,400 square feet, were built in residential areas, and offered fast service and extended hours of operation. Products sold usually included dairy products, bakery items, snack foods, beverages, tobacco, health and beauty aids, and candy. As the larger supermarkets also began to drive "mom and pop" corner groceries out of business, convenience stores again filled in. By 1960, there were 2,500 convenience stores in operation which accounted for less than 1 percent of total U.S. grocery sales.

The 1960s were growth years for the convenience store industry (see Exhibit 1). The increasing mobility of the population as well as the growing number of working women led to time-pressured, dual-income families. Convenience stores rushed to build stores in suburban neighborhoods, where they saw consumers, especially commuters, with more discretionary income and less time to spend it. During the mid-1960s, convenience stores introduced coffee, slush drinks, 24-hour operations, and, most important, self-service gasoline. At first, the retail industry attributed little significance to the installation of self-service gasoline at convenience stores, especially since it seemed to invite so many problems. Several states banned self-service as a fire hazard and often town ordinances were restrictive. Pumping facilities were not especially inviting or attractive, and equipment was unreliable. Convenience stores did not offer gasoline at discount prices, and few customers elected to pump their own when it was only 30 cents per gallon. Still, since equipment was relatively inexpensive, many companies installed it. By 1970, there were 13,250 convenience stores which accounted for nearly 3 percent of grocery sales. The number of these stores selling gasoline was not even noted at the time.

EXHIBIT 1

Growth of the Convenience Store Industry

Year	Number of Convenience Stores	Number of Convenience Stores Selling Gasoline	Convenience Store Sales (millions)	Convenience Store Gasoline Sales (millions)	Number of Service Stations
1960	2,500	n/a	$400	n/a	220,200
1965	6,000	n/a	$990	n/a	221,000
1970	13,250	n/a	$2,600	n/a	222,000
1975	28,500	5,871	$7,100	$500	189,480
1980	44,100	17,861	$24,500	$6,800	158,240
1981	47,900	20,693	$31,200	$9,600	151,250
1982	51,200	23,706	$35,900	$12,200	144,690
1983	54,400	28,288	$41,600	$15,800	136,570
1984	57,300	28,650	$45,600	$16,300	132,080
1985	61,000	33,550	$51,400	$18,200	124,600
1986	64,000	38,400	$53,900	$17,900	120,510
1987	67,500	39,825	$59,600	$20,500	115,870
1988	69,200	40,828	$61,200	$22,000	112,000
1989	70,200	45,630	$67,700	$27,100	n/a

Source: National Association of Convenience Stores and Dollars per Day Survey.

The 1970s were the big boom years for the convenience store industry, due in large part to this almost reluctant addition of gasoline to the product mix. When the Arab oil embargo of 1973 tripled the price of gasoline, consumers suddenly became willing to pump their own in order to save money. Convenience stores could and did under-price their competitors on gasoline in order to lure customers into the store to purchase another, more profitable, item. Oil companies, especially, keenly felt this loss of gasoline sales at a time when their traditional gas service stations were most vulnerable. Service stations had historically obtained most of their profits from car repairs and sales of tires, batteries, and other accessories. Yet during this time, specialty stores and the national chains, including Midas Muffler and Sears, had taken much of that business. As a result, the major oil companies were forced to close many of their neighborhood service stations, most of which were located on corner sites. The glut of these sites on the market forced prices to drop, in many cases by as much as one-half between 1972 and 1975, and convenience stores quickly bought these locations.

For convenience stores, gasoline had become an important element of the product mix and an even more important customer draw. From 1975 to 1980, gasoline as a percentage of total sales rose from 7 to 28 percent. Industry estimates indicated that between 30 and 40 percent of customers purchasing gasoline also bought at least one more item inside the store. By the end of the decade, traffic counts had replaced household density counts as the primary determinant of site selection for convenience stores. Many said that convenience stores located on streets in suburban, residential areas were "doomed" and that primary locations, that is, corner sites on high-traffic intersections, would become prerequisites for survival.

History of Circle K

In 1951, Fred Hervey purchased three neighborhood stores in El Paso, Texas, operating under the name "Kays Drive-In Grocery." In keeping with the regional flavor, he created a brand-type logo for his stores by encircling the "K." The company adopted the name Circle K Food Stores in 1957 and, in 1963, made an initial public offering of common stock. Hervey built the company steadily, from 43 stores in 1961 to 423 stores by 1970. During the convenience store boom years of the 1970s, Circle K nearly tripled in size, and by 1980, operated 1,200 stores in 12 states, as well as 3 in Japan. Recognizing the increasing importance of gasoline sales and hoping to ensure a stable supply of it, in September 1980, Circle K purchased a 13.2 percent stake in Nucorp Energy, Inc., an oil and gas exploration company. The following year Circle K was reorganized into a holding company to permit greater flexibility in acquiring other oil and gas companies, although none were ever purchased. In 1982, Nucorp filed for Chapter 11 bankruptcy, and Circle K took a $30 million write-down on their investment, resulting in a loss for the fiscal year ending April 30, 1982. By the end of the next fiscal year, the company operated 1,221 stores in Arizona, California, Texas, New Mexico, Idaho, Oregon, Montana, Oklahoma, Washington, Utah, Colorado, and Nevada. In July 1983, founder Fred Hervey, at age 73, turned over the company to Karl Eller, a long-time friend and business associate, stating

> *I have put 32 years into the development of Circle K, and it is time for me to turn things over to someone who can carry the company into its next generation of growth. I don't know anyone who has demonstrated better ability to manage growth and expansion than Karl Eller.*[1]

Karl Eller

Karl Eller was an Arizona native and born entrepreneur. As a student at the University of Arizona in the early 1950s, he sold other students class notes for $4.00. He began his career selling billboard space and as an account supervisor before becoming president of Eller Outdoor Advertising. In 1968, he began acquiring small outdoor advertising, broadcasting, and publishing companies, which he formed into Combined Communications Corporation. During this venture, he met and teamed up with Carl Lindner, a Cincinnati, Ohio, financier, who was to play an important role in Eller's tenure at Circle K. By the time Eller sold Combined Communications to the Gannett Company in 1979, it had become one of the country's largest outdoor advertising companies. After a short stay with Gannett, Eller went to Charter Company, an oil corporation wanting to build up its media division. In February 1981, he became president of the communications division of Columbia Pictures Industries and initiated the talks which eventually led to Coca Cola Co.'s acquiring Columbia. From 1982 until he became president of Circle K, he ran Karl Eller Company Financial Consultants in Phoenix.

The Competitive Environment in the Early 1980s

By 1980, there were 35,800 convenience stores throughout the United States, nearly half of which sold gasoline. These stores accounted for 5.6 percent of grocery sales overall, and up to 12 percent in some markets. However, some markets were becoming saturated with convenience stores, especially southern states with warm weather and heavy tourist traffic. Consequently, convenience stores began to compete with each other, as well as with companies in the grocery, gasoline, fast food, and other retail sectors of the economy. Clearly the boom years for convenience stores were ending.

Supermarkets had begun to strike back at convenience stores by increasing hours of operation and installing "express" lanes. Some supermarket companies, using their food merchandising expertise, began to open and operate their own convenience stores, although they usually did not offer gasoline. In addition, discount department stores and drugstores were attempting to grab some grocery dollars by carrying selected food items.

By 1982, convenience stores accounted for 8 percent of the total amount of gasoline pumped in the Untied States.[2] Despite this significant inroad convenience stores were making in marketing gasoline, oil companies had made only feeble attempts to add convenience store operations to their facilities. By 1982, six oil companies operated convenience stores at only 2,000 locations. Oil companies lacked the necessary marketing expertise to merchandise the thousands of products carried in a convenience store. Yet they retained many prime corner locations, usually with garages which could be converted into stores, and they certainly had deep pockets.

In theory, the demographics for convenience stores looked strong. The increasing number of time-constrained, dual-income households appeared to be building a solid base of convenience store customers. Yet the typical customer was an 18-to-34-year-old male in a blue-collar occupation. Convenience stores recognized the need to attract more women and upscale customers, but they faced an image problem. Shoppers considered them to be dirty, high-priced (except for gasoline), crime-infested stores. Indeed, many stores had never been refurbished and looked run-down and cluttered. So companies began extensive, expensive remodeling programs to improve lighting, brighten colors, and increase street visibility in hopes of attracting more women and upscale customers. To combat their high-priced image, many convenience stores began offering staples at competitive prices and advertising these and other special promotions aggressively. The combination of more expensive sites, increased capital expenditures for remodeling, reduced prices on staples, and aggressive advertising began to impact profits for convenience stores.

Convenience stores were also facing potential trouble with their product mix (see Exhibit 2). Pinball machines, delicatessen and sandwich counters, fountain drinks, microwave ovens, and self-service fast foods had been introduced in the 1970s. During the 1980s, convenience stores began offering car washes, videocassette rentals, automatic teller machines, upscale merchandise, and extensive fast-food service. Still, in 1983, four products accounted for 66 percent of sales: gasoline, tobacco, alcoholic beverages, and soft drinks. Of these categories, only soft drinks appeared immune to increasing regulatory or legislative pressure. The Environmental Protection Agency had begun to study the effects of underground gasoline storage tanks and lines. Sales of alcoholic beverages, especially through outlets that also sold gasoline, were coming under attack from groups such as Mothers Against Drunk Driving. The tobacco industry was facing intensified pressures, especially regarding advertising, and the number of smokers continued to decline. Even fast-food operations, predicted to be the growth vehicle for the 1980s much like gasoline was in the 1970s, were becoming more labor intensive and often included on-site preparations, subject to local health regulations (see Exhibit 3).

EXHIBIT 2

Convenience Store Sales by Product Category

Product Category	1975	1980	1981	1982	1983	1984	1985	1986	1987	1988	1989
Tobacco products	14.2%	10.5%	10.2%	11.0%	10.9%	11.6%	11.5%	13.2%	13.6%	13.8%	14.0%
Alcoholic beverages	14.8	9.4	9.3	10.4	9.7	9.6	9.8	10.1	9.8	8.5	8.9
Fast foods	4.6	5.2	4.9	4.9	4.2	4.7	6.8	7.2	7.0	7.8	5.3
Soft drinks	9.4	7.9	7.8	7.7	7.3	7.3	6.6	6.9	6.4	5.7	5.9
Dairy products	8.9	7.1	6.7	4.9	4.3	4.4	4.3	3.9	3.8	3.5	3.1
Candy and gum	3.8	3.8	3.7	3.3	3.0	3.1	3.2	3.3	3.5	3.2	3.2
Groceries	10.5	6.7	6.4	6.5	5.7	5.8	3.8	3.7	3.7	3.2	2.3
Fountain drinks	0.4	0.5	0.6	1.1	1.3	1.5	1.7	2.4	1.6	1.8	2.2
Health and beauty aids	4.0	3.7	3.3	2.2	2.1	2.1	2.2	2.0	2.0	1.7	1.4
All other	17.5	11.6	10.9	8.2	7.9	7.8	6.3	4.4	5.8	5.1	6.2
Total merchandise sales	93.0%	72.2%	69.2%	66.0%	62.0%	64.3%	64.6%	66.8%	65.6%	64.0%	60.0
Gasoline sales	7.0	27.8	30.8	34.0	38.0	35.7	35.4	33.2	34.4	36.0	40.0
Total sales	100.0	100.0	100.0	100.0	100.0	100.0	100.0	100.0	100.0	100.0	100.0

Source: National Association of Convenience Stores and Distribution Research Program, The University of Oklahoma.

EXHIBIT 3

Convenience Store Gross Margins on Selected Products (1985)

Hot beverages	61%	General merchandise	39%	Wine and liquor	30%
Fountain drinks	58%	Ice cream	39%	Beer	27%
Ice	53%	Health and beauty aids	37%	Eggs	23%
Frozen beverages	44%	Groceries	35%	Dairy products	22%
Delicatessen	43%	Cookies and snacks	35%	Magazines	21%
Candy and gum	41%	Soft drinks	32%	Gas (company-owned)	8%
Sandwiches	39%	Tobacco products	30%	Gas (on consignment)	5%

Source: National Association of Convenience Stores.

Karl Eller Takes Over At Circle K

By the time Karl Eller arrived at Circle K, the easy growth years had ended. The company's rate of sales growth had slowed due to the 1980 and 1981–1982 recessions and increased competition. To boost sales, in early 1983, Circle K launched "an aggressive marketing and advertising program . . . designed around a more competitive pricing posture on selected items such as milk, cigarettes, and beer plus an increase in seasonal promotions and advertising."[3] Circle K had just opened its own commissary to produce sandwiches and other fast foods for its stores, and, with its own distribution system, was better positioned than many to ride the fast-food wave. Eller announced ambitious expansion plans. He predicted the company would grow 15 to 20 percent per year and would become a national chain operating 5,000 stores by 1990 (see Exhibit 4).

His first acquisitions came within five months when he purchased two outdoor advertising companies in Texas and Idaho. He explained that these acquisitions would benefit a convenience store chain because of "logical synergism—for every corner where a Circle K is located, there is the potential for an outdoor billboard."[4] In fact, the company's 1984 10K report announced Circle K's intentions to "seek acquisitions of additional outdoor advertising or other media or communications businesses." In October 1983, Circle K issued $50 million in debentures to finance its growth.

Rumors of Circle K's becoming another media conglomerate quieted when, in December 1983, Eller acquired the UtoteM Corp. from American Financial Corporation, the company run by his friend, Carl Lindner. UtoteM, headquartered in Houston, Texas, operated 959 convenience stores in 12 states and was a major competitor of Circle K in some states. The acquisition almost doubled the number of Circle K stores and expanded operations into seven new states: Alabama, Arkansas, Florida, Kansas, Kentucky, Missouri, and Ohio. UtoteM stores were located primarily in single- or multi-family

EXHIBIT 4

Increase in Number of Circle K Stores

Fiscal Year (4/30)	Number of Stores at End of Fiscal Year	Number of Stores Acquired During Year	Number of Stores Opened During Year	Number of Stores Closed During Year	Number of Stores Selling Gasoline
1970	423	a	81	2	—
1975	1,024	a	89	12	516
1980	1,200	3	61	22	726
1981	1,194	2	19	28	741
1982	1,211	16	9	8	768
1983	1,221	12	8	10	798
1984	2,185	985	10	31	1,436
1985	2,669	456	61	33	1,719
1986	3,372	632	166	95	2,293
1987	3,507	123	161	149	2,433
1988	4,077	573	252	255	3,011
1989	4,685	557	263	212	3,600

aIncluded in number of stores opened during year.

residential areas or along heavily traveled local streets. Although 64 percent of these store sold gasoline, they did so primarily on a consignment basis. UtoteM's dairy and snack foods businesses had been sold earlier by AFC, but UtoteM continued to operate three ice plants (see Exhibit 5).

The total cost of $226.8 million consisted of $100 million in cash, $75 million in 12½ percent installment notes, $50 million in newly issued Circle K preferred stock, and $1.8 million in common stock purchase warrants. The consignment gasoline operations at 395 stores were purchased for approximately $12 million. Four months later, 370 UtoteM stores were sold to and subsequently leased back from AFC for $98.6 million, part of which paid off the $75 million note. Circle K retained, among others, three top-level executives from that chain, including the president, James Williamson, Jr., who was named president of Circle K Convenience Stores.

In October, 1984, Eller purchased the chain of Little General Stores from General Host Corporation. Little General operated 435 convenience stores in six southern and southeastern states, primarily in Florida. The acquisition pushed the company into four new states: Georgia, Louisiana, Mississippi, and North Carolina. Little General's stores were located in dense residential areas, primarily along homeward bound routes, and 52 percent sold gasoline. Little General operated one ice plant, but did little warehousing. The purchase price of $132.2 million consisted of $112.3 million in cash and $19.9

EXHIBIT 5
UtoteM, Inc.

	12/31/80	12/31/81	12/31/82
Sales	$321,817	$387,709	$438,968
Net profits	$4,324	$6,533	$14,093
Total assets	$168,391	$163,999	$177,386
Net worth	$78,102	$80,835	$89,510
Number of states	12	12	12
Number of stores	931	949	959
Number of stores selling gasoline	558	600	618

million in assumed liabilities. None of the senior management of Little General was retained (see Exhibit 6).

By January 1985, the three top executives from UtoteM had left Circle K. To fill the critical gaps in his executive offices, Eller appointed three outsiders, including Robert Reade, from the outdoor advertising division of the Gannett Company, who was named senior vice-president of real estate.

The 1985 Annual Report noted that the company's "growth has been a quality growth of manageable proportions." Economies of scale were being realized for distribution, buying, and administrative functions as acquired businesses were integrated into the Circle K system. The company launched an extensive remodeling program and announced plans to become a leader in new product and service introductions. The commissary was beginning to supply all stores acquired in the acquisitions, thus reducing dependence on local distributors for fast-food products.

In September 1985, Circle K acquired Shop & Go, Inc., for $166.6 million in cash. Shop & Go operated 406 convenience stores in central Florida and 40 stores in southern Georgia. Stores were located on the outskirts of rapidly growing cities, with some in strip shopping centers. Approximately 74 percent of Shop & Go stores sold gasoline, and one-third were located on corner sites. The company operated ice and sandwich manufacturing facilities and distributed some items under its own label. Shop & Go's founders and majority stockholders, Robert and Lorena Jaeb, were 74 and 65 years old, respectively, when they sold their shares to Circle K (see Exhibit 7).

EXHIBIT 6
Little General Stores

	12/26/81	12/25/82	12/31/83
Revenues	$177,745	$181,791	$205,769
Operating profits	$8,331	$11,552	$14,298
Identifiable assets	$49,287	$56,245	$71,012
Number of states	7	6	6
Number of stores	462	431	435
Number of stores selling gasoline	208	208	226

EXHIBIT 7
Shop & Go, Inc.

	3/31/83	3/29/84	3/28/85
Sales	$201,956	$254,183	$294,868
Net profits	$6,421	$8,944	$10,205
Total assets	$52,400	$71,006	$81,910
Net worth	$32,258	$39,653	$48,036
Number of states	2	2	2
Number of stores	415	430	446
Number of stores selling gasoline	286	307	328

Although internally generated funds still covered portions of the acquisition costs, Circle K increasingly began to rely on outside sources of capital. The bond market in the early and mid-1980s was eager to lend money. High-yield, speculative bonds (later known as "junk" bonds) were fashionable and a readily available means of raising capital. In May 1985, the company issued $100 million in 8¼ percent convertible subordinated debentures and, in October 1985, issued $125 million in 12¾ percent senior subordinated debentures. Both offerings were rated by Moody's in the *Ba* category, as containing speculative elements.

In March 1986, Circle K acquired 224 convenience stores, including 38 closed stores, from National Convenience Stores, Inc., of Houston, Texas. National Convenience was facing difficult times due to the oil bust in its largest market, Houston, and had decided to concentrate its resources on fewer markets where it had a strong presence. Circle K purchased stores in Arkansas (23), Texas (53), Louisiana (24), Oklahoma (8), Colorado (23), Mississippi (31), and another new state for the company, Tennessee (25). The purchase price was $51.8 million in cash plus $5.6 million in assumed obligations. The president of National Convenience Stores announced later that he had sold Eller "a bunch of crap."[5]

Circle K's 1986 Annual Report admitted it "was not an easy year." The company blamed poor economic conditions in Texas and the Gulf Coast states, acquisition-related expenses, and increased liability insurance premiums. Circle K stated that it would "maintain a competitive edge by providing our customers with as many different products and services as possible—even those items infrequently purchased." In November 1986, Robert Reade, senior vice-president of real estate, became president (see Exhibit 8).

In terms of acquisitions, 1987 was a comparatively quiet year, although Eller did pick up 123 stores in California, Texas, and Oklahoma. The company raised the capital by issuing bonds and selling and leasing back stores (see Exhibit 9).

In April 1988, Eller was presented with an irresistible opportunity. Circle K's chief competitor had always been the Southland Corporation, operators of 7-Eleven stores, the largest convenience store chain in the nation. In

EXHIBIT 8

Summary of Circle K Bonds Issued

Date	Type of Bond	Amount (millions)	Yield	Moody's Initial Rating
Oct 83	Convertible subordinated debentures	$50	9%	Ba-3
May 85	Convertible subordinated debentures	$100	8¼%	Ba-3
Sep 85	Convertible subordinated debentures	$75	8¾%	—
Oct 85	Senior subordinated debentures	$125	12¾%	Ba-2
Nov 86	Convertible subordinated debentures	$150	7¼%	Ba-3
Dec 87	Junior subordinated debentures	$72	13%	B-1
Oct 88	Senior secured notes	$200	10.7%	—

December 1987, Southland had been acquired by the founding family through a leveraged buyout. Struggling under a huge debt burden, the company was forced to sell assets to raise cash. Southland agreed to sell Circle K all of its stores in Alabama, Arkansas, Georgia, Louisiana, and South Carolina, as well as stores in Arizona, Florida, North Carolina, Tennessee, and Texas. The total transaction involved 473 stores and 90 closed facilities and cost Circle K $151.4 million. This acquisition had a dilutive effect on Circle K's earnings. Still, Eller insisted these stores would be profitable, once personnel duplications were eliminated, once they were supplied with Circle K manufactured products, and once the company's increased volume purchasing power was realized.

In September 1988, Eller made his final acquisition: Charter Marketing Group from Charter Co., where he had previously worked. Charter had recently emerged from three years of bankruptcy proceedings, which had left Carl Lindner as chairman of the board and AFC holding the majority of stock. Charter operated 538 convenience stores, primarily in the Southeast, but also in six states new for Circle K: Michigan, Indiana, Maine, New Hampshire, Connecticut, and Massachusetts. Although in 1986 Eller had said he didn't envision the company "going into the Upper Midwest or Northeast because our path has always been here in the Sunbelt,"[6] the 1988 Annual Report

EXHIBIT 9

Summary of Stores Sold and Leased Back

Date	Number of Stores	Price (millions)
Apr 84	370	$98.6
Mar 85	122	$38.4
Apr 85	132	$39.1
Oct 85	97	$38.0
Apr 86	238	$80.0
Apr 87	250	$100.0
Fiscal 88	147	$106.0

EXHIBIT 10

Charter Marketing

	12/31/85	12/31/86	12/31/87
Revenues	$552,179	$482,964	$506,396
Operating profits	$9,329	$21,043	$8,957
Identifiable assets	$103,084	$92,920	$114,860
Number of states	9	9	13
Number of stores	411	407	538

claimed this acquisition took Circle K into the "economically attractive New England area." The purchase price of $125.6 million consisted of $75.6 million cash and $50.0 million in newly issued preferred stock and left AFC owning 38.4 percent of Circle K (see Exhibit 10).

At the end of fiscal 1988, Circle K appeared to be riding the crest of the wave, with earnings at a record $60.4 million. With Southland now privately held, the company could proclaim itself to be the largest publicly owned convenience store operator in the United States and an industry leader and pacesetter as well. A joint venture in branded fast foods with Dunkin' Donuts appeared successful and was slated for expansion. Circle K continued testing new products and services including a microwavable ice cream sundae and Federal Express drop boxes. The company's videocassette rental program was available in 65 percent of stores, and Circle K attributed its mixed results to temporary supplier problems (see Exhibit 11).

In short, from 1983 to 1988, Circle K had grown from 1,221 stores in 12 states to 4,685 stores in 32 states, and sales had increased from $750 million to nearly $3.5 billion. In February 1989, Eller proposed hiring an investment banker firm to assess the company's value for possible sale. On that news, the company's stock price jumped, eventually trading at $16.25. In May 1989, Circle K officially announced that it was for sale, and Eller indicated that he was considering purchasing the company himself in a leveraged buyout. Financial analysts estimated the company's value at between $16.00 and $18.00 per share, despite Circle K's disclosure that it expected to post a loss for the fourth quarter ending April 30, 1989 (see Exhibit 12).

EXHIBIT 11

Summary of Circle K Major Acquisitions

Date	Company	Number of Stores	Price (millions)
Dec 83	UtoteM	959	$226.8
Oct 84	Little General	435	$132.2
Sep 85	Shop & Go	446	$166.6
Mar 86	(from) National Convenience	224	$57.6
Apr 88	(from) Southland Corporation	563	$151.4
Sep 88	Charter Marketing	538	$125.6

EXHIBIT 12

Circle K Corporation Selected Financial Data (1983-1989)

	4/30/83	4/30/84	4/30/85	4/30/86	4/30/87	4/30/88	4/30/89
Operating Statement							
Merchandise sales	$460.5	$646.7	$1,090.0	$1,368.4	$1,558.2	$1,649.2	$1,962.4
Gasoline sales	$287.3	$382.2	$592.1	$742.9	$731.2	$964.6	$1,479.0
Other revenues	$5.9	$6.3	$14.2	$20.2	$27.3	$42.9	$53.5
Total revenues	$753.7	$1,035.2	$1,696.3	$2,131.5	$2,316.7	$2,656.7	$3,494.9
Cost of sales	$573.1	$783.1	$1,252.7	$1,551.5	$1,649.5	$1,893.1	$2,580.4
Operating and administrative expense	$149.7	$205.9	$362.3	$467.1	$537.4	$627.6	$822.3
Interest and debt	$5.6	$7.9	$21.8	$36.6	$41.6	$56.6	$95.9
Operating profit (loss)	$25.3	$38.1	$59.6	$76.3	$88.3	$79.5	($5.5)
Gain on sale of assets	—	—	—	—	$5.9	$8.2	$32.3
Other expenses[a]	($3.7)	—	—	($6.7)	—	—	—
Earnings before income taxes	$21.6	$38.1	$59.6	$69.6	$94.3	$87.7	$26.8
Income taxes	$5.8	$17.7	$25.9	$30.4	$44.9	$32.8	$11.4
Gain from change in accounting method	—	—	—	—	—	$5.5	—
Net earnings	$15.8	$20.4	$33.7	$39.2	$49.4	$60.4	$15.4

Balance Sheet

Assets							
Cash	$12.3	$16.5	$22.3	$19.9	$24.8	$44.2	$38.5
Accounts receivable	$3.5	$7.2	$11.1	$12.5	$25.7	$34.4	$36.3
Inventory	$42.3	$79.0	$107.1	$135.8	$160.2	$191.0	$239.9
Other current assets	$22.1	$20.6	$39.5	$108.9	$148.2	$109.9	$94.3
Total current assets	$80.2	$123.3	$180.0	$277.1	$358.9	$379.5	$409.0
Fixed assets	$91.6	$189.4	$252.5	$345.7	$451.8	$708.3	$1,068.5
Intangibles[b]	$0.0	$67.2	$109.0	$173.1	$235.2	$247.1	$405.8
Other assets	$2.9	$32.3	$38.3	$59.9	$90.6	$200.9	$161.6
Total assets	$174.7	$412.2	$579.8	$855.8	$1,136.5	$1,535.8	$2,044.9
Liabilities							
Notes payable[c]	$15.9	$14.7	$6.1	$56.6	$18.0	$65.4	$98.9
Accounts payable	$23.8	$42.3	$61.1	$77.1	$84.6	$112.1	$134.9
Other current liabilities	$14.6	$42.6	$48.0	$54.2	$66.8	$103.1	$116.6
Total current liabilities	$54.3	$99.6	$115.2	$187.9	$169.4	$280.6	$350.4
Long-term debt	$40.5	$157.0	$269.4	$382.9	$536.6	$844.1	$1,103.8
Other long-term liabilities	$8.2	$12.1	$20.4	$34.9	$73.0	$80.1	$212.8
Preferred stock	$0.0	$50.0	$50.0	$50.0	$47.5	$47.5	$47.5
Stockholder's equity	$71.7	$93.5	$124.8	$200.1	$310.0	$283.5	$330.4
Total liabilities	$174.7	$412.2	$579.8	$855.8	$1,136.5	$1,535.8	$2,044.9
Dividends on common stock	$8.2	$8.4	$8.9	$9.9	$13.0	$13.0	$12.2
Dividends on preferred stock	$0.0	$1.0	$4.0	$4.0	$4.0	$3.8	$5.1
Capital expenditures	$18.9	$56.9	$95.4	$150.8	$264.1	$268.9	$193.3

[a]Expenses related to Nucorp sale and litigation.
[b]Intangibles include excess costs over acquired net assets and favorable leases acquired.
[c]Notes payable include due to bank and current portion of long-term debt and capital lease obligations.
Source: Circle K Corporation Annual Reports.

Problems Begin To Surface

As the investment bankers scrutinized Circle K, they discovered more problems with the company than had been previously suspected. In August, when Circle K released its Annual Report for the year ending April 30, 1989, the outside community became aware of some of these problems.

Circle K was strapped for cash. The acquisition binge and store construction and remodeling program had skyrocketed the company's debt from $40.5 million in 1983 to more than $1.1 billion by 1989. Nearly one-third of this debt was subject to fluctuations in interest rates, and rates had risen. The company had been forced to renegotiate credit lines and loan terms with its banks and faced suspension of its dividend should profitability requirements not be met. In addition, late in 1988, the Environmental Protection Agency had tightened regulations on underground storage tanks, and Circle K estimated it would need $150 million to comply.

The company was attempting to generate funds, but options were becoming limited. The junk bond market, particularly in the depressed convenience store industry, collapsed. In October 1988, the company was able to raise $200 million in a private placement of notes, but only by putting up 425 stores and an office complex as collateral. Circle K was running out of assets to divest. The two outdoor advertising companies had been sold for $16.2 million. (Eller was one of the buyers.) The ice manufacturing and distribution operations brought in $32 million. The commissary was sold for $28 million, although Circle K immediately entered into an agreement to purchase its products at market prices. The company even sold the future rights to its name in Japan for $55 million. In addition, the majority of Circle K stores already had been sold and leased back.

Increased competition made funds from operations scarce. Oil companies finally had launched their own strategic assault on convenience stores, and accounted for virtually all of the growth in the industry since 1986.[7] By 1989, oil companies owned 7 of the 20 largest convenience store chains. Their stores were newer and more attractive, and often they would discount food items to sell more gasoline. Even their small kiosk and mini-mart operations stole profitable sales from convenience stores. In addition, other retailers such as Blockbuster Video (which had 17 stores in 1985 and 1,079 in 1989) had devastated many convenience stores' videocassette rental programs. Despite heavy investments in these programs, convenience stores were unable to compete with the specialty retailers' wide selections.

Most important, Circle K suffered serious operating problems. The company's decision to carry all items, even infrequently purchased ones, left many slow-moving products on the shelves. Many stores even carried multiple brands of these unwanted items, ranging from hair nets to dog food. In addition, the company did not even know what was in many of its stores. During the 1970s and 1980s, many retailers had invested heavily in electronic technology to help their merchandising operations. Scanning equipment, for example, reduced checkout time and allowed merchants to monitor product sales by store, enabling them to tailor product mixes to individual markets. However, most convenience stores, including Circle K, had not invested in technology, believing it was unnecessary since their stores offered quick enough service and sold so many "unscannable" items, such as fast foods and fountain drinks. Due to obsolete inventory management systems, Circle K did not know what was selling in its stores and had no cost-effective way to find out.

Because Circle K had retained none of the senior executives from any of the chains it had acquired and the company's top officers had no experience in convenience store management, operations had been essentially neglected. Needing someone to handle day-to-day operations, Eller turned to another business associate, Richard Smith, chairman of Steve's Homemade Ice Cream, Inc. Eller designated Smith an "unpaid consultant" to Circle K and gave him far-reaching authority. Smith was allowed to set company policy on purchasing, marketing, advertising, pricing, training personnel, and negotiating with vendors. This highly unusual arrangement raised conflict-of-interest questions, since Smith's company sold ice cream to Circle K and Eller owned 16.6 percent of Steve's.

Smith convinced Eller that Circle K could improve its operating performance by getting tough with suppliers, raising prices, reducing promotions and eliminating regional deviations by centralizing marketing efforts. In its 1989 Annual Report, the company announced plans to do those things. Circle K felt it wielded enough volume purchasing power to justify putting additional pressure on vendors to lower their prices. Although Smith's negotiations brought discounts from some suppliers, others were antagonized. The company believed that raising prices and reducing promotions would generate more cash, which was needed desperately to cover debt payments. Once prices were uniformly raised, the reasoning went, then promotions could be offered more selectively and would be more successful. Prices were raised approximately six percent at all stores, and gross margins did improve. However, sales began to drop, slowly at first, but as customers flocked to competitors, sales plunged.

By September 1989, no one, including Eller, had stepped forward with an offer to buy Circle K. The investment advisers indicated that no one probably would, due to the depressed junk bond market and Circle K's weak financial performance and severe operating problems. When it became clear that no one was interested, Circle K announced it was no longer for sale and suspended its common stock dividend. As the jilted company revealed plans to devote its full energies to strengthening operations, the stock price fell to $7.75.

Postscript

Circle K's troubles did not end with its failure to locate a buyer. The bills for the acquisition binge were coming due, despite frantic negotiations with creditors for time to sell off assets and develop a strategic plan. The board of directors began to assert themselves, particularly the major stockholder, Carl Lindner. Smith was "fired" and Lindner brought in another AFC executive, Robert Dearth, to manage operations. Dearth immediately moved to slash prices, revamp the product mix, and return authority to local managers, but it was too late. By March 1990, Circle K stock traded at $1.75. Eller admitted "when you look back, we probably grew too fast at the time . . . I did the best I knew how. Somebody has to be the hero when you're doing good, and the fall guy when things are going bad. I deserve all the credit, and all the woes."[8] A final plan to swap junk bond debt for common stock fell through at the last minute when lenders decided to cut their losses in Circle K, apparently not confident that the company could continue as a viable firm in the intense retail competitive environment.

In April 1990, the company reported a loss of $772.9 million for the year. In May, Eller resigned. One week later, Circle K filed for protection under Chapter 11 of the U.S. bankruptcy code.

QUESTIONS

1. What were the major changes in consumer, channel, and competitor trends that influenced the growth of convenience food stores?
2. When did it become evident that Circle K was headed for financial trouble? What were the danger signs? What measures of financial performance would have provided management with additional useful information?
3. What were the primary causes of the bankruptcy of the Circle K Corporation?

ENDNOTES

1. Circle K Corporation, *1983 Annual Report*, 3.
2. "Look Who's a Champ of Gasoline Marketing," *Fortune*, 1 November 1982, 150.
3. *1983 Annual Report*, 2.
4. "Seems Like Old Times," *Forbes*, 5 December 1983, 58.
5. "Stop N Go's Van Horn Wants to Reinvent the Convenience Store," *Wall Street Journal*, 6 February 1991, A10.
6. "Circle K Breaking New Ground with Acquisitions, Fast Foods," *National Petroleum News* (February 1986): 48.
7. "Why C-Store Chains Are Getting Squeezed," *National Petroleum News* (September 1988): 41.
8. "Karl Eller of Circle K, Always Pushing Deals, May Have Overdone It," *Wall Street Journal*, 28 March 1990, A1.

CASE 24

IKEA NORTH AMERICA: THE VIKINGS REDISCOVER AMERICA

G. Peter Dapiran

Introduction

It was early 1990 and Bjorn Boyle, president of IKEA North America, was remembering that exciting day in July 1985—the opening, which had gone off with extraordinary success, of the first American IKEA store at Plymouth Meeting, 20 miles from Philadelphia. The roads had been jammed with traffic for miles around. The event had been covered on television and had drawn 100,000 people in the first four days. Customers had lined up around the building, waiting their turn to shop. IKEA, a lifestyle furniture retailer from

Sweden, specialized in ready-to-assemble furniture. Now, three more stores later with plans to have 10 stores in the United States by 1992, was a time to reflect on the entry strategy for the United States and to assess the planned expansion strategy.

From Fish to Furniture

In 1947, at the age of 22, an entrepreneurial Ingvar Kamprad quit his home deliveries of fish and milk to start selling flower seeds and ballpoint pens by mail order to customers in his native Sweden. Fired by the success of this venture, he turned his attention to the local furniture industry. He saw opportunities to improve the distribution methods and to sell the products at lower prices. He began to sell the furniture output of the local carpenters through his catalog at prices 30 to 50 percent lower than his competitors. He achieved the low prices by having the furniture manufactured in a knock-down form for his customers to assemble at home.

His strong competition earned him the boycott of the local industry and he was forced to seek suppliers beyond his native Sweden. This was the start of a supply strategy that eventually led to a broad base of 1,500 suppliers in 50 countries. To maintain low manufacturing costs, a piece of furniture could be assembled from components sourced from a number of different suppliers. For example, the cover, frame, and metal fittings of a chair could come from three different suppliers. Kamprad emphasized low cost, not only in product design, but also in all facets of operations, as the basis for success.

Six years later, he opened the first IKEA showroom in the small southern Swedish town of Almhult.

IKEA, a name coined by the founder from the initial letters of his name, together with the names of the farm, Elmtaryd, and the parish, Agunnaryd, in which he grew up, prospered.

He opened his second store outside Stockholm, Sweden. This site was to become the flagship and the largest IKEA store in the world at 463,000 square feet.

Stores in Norway and Denmark followed. It was not until 1973 that IKEA ventured beyond Scandinavia, with a store near Zurich in Switzerland.

European expansion, restrained to ensure it was always within the financial capability of the organization, continued into Germany, Austria, France, and Belgium. By the mid-1980s, IKEA had 85 stores in 19 countries in Europe and as far afield as Australia, Kuwait, and Hong Kong. By 1984, 14 percent of sales were derived outside Europe and Scandinavia. With growth opportunities declining in the European and home markets, and with the experience gained in a variety of foreign locations, it was time to tackle the larger American market.

The U.S. Furniture Market

The total American retail furniture market was considered to be about $35 billion, as depicted in Exhibit 1.

EXHIBIT 1
The Furniture Market

Value of Product Shipments for House Furniture (in millions of dollars)				
SIC[a]	1987	1988	1989	1990[b]
2511 Wood furniture	$7,421	$7,421	$7,310	$7,164
2512 Upholstered	4,895	4,944	4,894	4,796
2514 Metal furniture	1,893	1,912	1,874	1,846
2515 Mattresses	2,706	2,773	2,801	2,801

Total New Supply of House Furniture (in millions of dollars)			
	1987	1988	1989
Domestic	$17,765	$18,610	$19,063
Imports	2,889	2,910	2,765

[a]SIC = Standard industrial classification. [b]Forecast.
Source: Adapted from *U.S. Industrial Outlook 1990*, U.S. Department of Commerce, January 1990.

Expenditure on furniture was closely tied to the well-being of the housing sector and the real growth in disposable income. Cost of credit also had an impact, as furniture was more likely to be financed than nondurable consumer goods. The forecast into the middle 1990s was for a slight growth in domestic furniture shipments.

Another set of factors of significance in the American economy into the 1990s was the aging of the baby boomers, those born between 1945 and 1965. As the decade progressed, these people would move into the 30 to 49 age bracket. This shift would bring with it peak earnings, higher disposable incomes, a propensity to buy more expensive furniture, and a lifestyle that emphasized quality of life, family values, and a focus on the home, as shown in Exhibit 2.

One of the challenges facing the furniture industry was how to convert these demographic changes into actual higher spending on furniture.

The North American Assault

The mode of entry into a market is a crucial decision that faces any potential exporter. The possibilities are numerous, and nearly all had been used by European companies entering the U.S. market. (See Exhibit 3.)

IKEA was aware of the factors deemed by former successful entrants from Europe to be important for success in the United States. (See Exhibit 4.)

In the mid-1970s, IKEA established itself in the Canadian market through a franchising arrangement as it had done in some of the other more remote locations such as Australia. Canada was considered important not only for its own sake but also because it was seen as a test market for the much larger U.S. market.

EXHIBIT 2
The Furniture Buyers

Annual Expenditures on Furniture by Age of Householder (in millions of dollars)

	1985	1990	1995	2000
Under 25	$1,017	$ 872	$ 807	$ 831
25 to 34	7,286	7,711	7,253	6,553
35 to 44	6,503	7,903	8,897	9,426
45 to 54	4,761	5,440	6,799	8,144
55 to 64	2,954	2,782	2,765	3,142
65 to 74	1,997	2,148	2,209	2,119
75 and older	431	515	583	656

Percentage of College-Educated Adults by Age by Type of Store where They Would Expect to Find Furnishings That Would Appeal to Them

Store Type	Age			
	Total	Less than 30	30 to 49	50 +
Furniture store	47%	46%	46%	52%
Specialty store	29	37	31	18
Department store	16	14	15	20
All about equal	3	1	3	3
Other	3	1	3	3
Not sure	2	1	2	3

Source: Adapted from "Sitting Pretty," J. Schlossberg, *American Demographics* (May 1988): 24-28. Reprinted with permission © *American Demographics*, May 1988.

The franchises were not successful, partly because, it was thought, the franchises chose to sell a limited number of lines. This prevented the store from conveying the IKEA concept effectively. IKEA bought out the Canadian franchisees.

IKEA's strategy for success was to make shopping an easy and pleasurable experience, and to offer well-designed, functional, quality furniture at low prices.

The target segment was considered to be the active urban adults of 25 to 35 years with an annual household income of more than $50,000.

The American plan was to open two to three stores a year grouped in five to six stores per region, each region serviced by a separate distribution center, management team, and maybe even a marketing staff. IKEA planned to have 10 stores in the United States by 1992.

The first American store was opened with great fanfare in June 1985. The opening was promoted heavily through a mailing based on household income. Local promotion through television, radio, newspapers, and even the backs of buses, was extensive. One million catalogs were distributed for the event.

EXHIBIT 3

Selected European Companies with U.S. Involvement

> Company (Origin): Core retail business—Main U.S. interest.
> *Ahold* (Netherlands): Food—Owns three supermarket chains (Bi-Lo, Giant Food Stores, First National Supermarkets).
> *Asko* (West Germany): Food—Minority stake in Furr's Supermarkets.
> *Austin Reed* (U.K.): Men's apparel—Licensing agreement with Hartmax Corporation of Chicago to make and sell Austin Reed.
> *Benetton* (Italy): Fashion knitwear—Approximately 700 franchised stores.
> *BAT* (U.K.): Department stores, catalog showrooms—Owns Saks Fifth Avenue and Marshall Field's.
> *Dixons* (U.K.): Home electrical—Owns Silo.
> *Dunhill* (U.K.): Menswear—Chain of company-owned stores.
> *Fastframe* (U.K.): Picture framing—Twenty-eight franchised stores.
> *GIB Group* (Belgium): Department stores, food, DIY—Owns Scotty's DIY 164-store chain.
> *Printemps* (France): Department stores—One store trading as a joint venture in Denver.
> *Tie Rack* (U.K.): Neckties—Thirty-one company-owned stores; further expansion through franchising.
> *Vendex International* (Netherlands): Department stores, home furnishings, apparel, food—50% stake in Barnes & Noble bookstores, minority stake in Dillard Department Stores.
>
> Source: Adapted from "Global Links in U.S. Retailing," *Discount Merchandiser* (September 1989): 26-31. Reprinted with permission.

The 165,000-square-foot store was located at Plymouth Meeting just outside Philadelphia, away from the crowded city center. The location was consistent with IKEA's idea of the ideal site—a low-cost real estate suburban site away from city traffic congestion, allowing large parking lots and easy access to and from the motorways.

A second store of 156,000 square feet was opened in Washington in the fall of 1986, followed by the 200,000-square-foot Baltimore store at the end of summer 1988.

Pittsburgh was the site of the fourth store, which opened in the summer of 1989.

IKEA established two large distribution centers in Montreal, Canada, and Philadelphia to service the East Coast of America and was looking for suitable sites to establish its West Coast attack.

The IKEA Shopping Experience

A key IKEA philosophy was that shopping had to be made a relaxed and pleasant event. Its large accessible parking lots at sites away from crowded city centers initiated this experience for the potential IKEA customer.

EXHIBIT 4

Some Opinions of Success Factors for European Retailers in the United States

Americans have already shown that they like a total-concept store. You can't always transplant a store as it existed in Europe. Any European retailer is in danger the first three years. There is the product risk, the location risk, and the management risk if the company franchises.

J.M. Loubier, Director, International Division, Descamps (Home textiles).

"Americans like big shopping areas."

S. Fischer, Director, Public Relations, Benetton (Fashion casual wear).

"Here [in the United States], advertising is a very big deal. Names are important in America but not in Europe. You have to sell a look and an image. Any European company that does not hire an American to run its U.S. operation deserves to fail. You can't understand a country unless you're of that country. Business today is in the mass market. . . . Lower price points attract a bigger market. A lot of Europeans who come here make big mistakes and have trouble adapting. . . . With proper adjustments, you can build a success."

P. Dora, President, Conran's (Home furnishings).

"The diversity of consumers and the extensive amount of advertising required to achieve market penetration were hurdles that (British based BAT, French Agache-Willot, German Hugo Mann—all retailers) failed to overcome."

Source: Adapted from N.M. Miller, "The New Immigrants," *Chain Store Age Exectutive* (February 1986): 16-18.

Supervised child minding and indoor play areas, together with a restaurant offering Swedish food, were all elements of IKEA's philosophy of pleasurable shopping undisturbed by the demands of otherwise bored children.

Pencils, paper, tape measures, and a product catalog inside the front entrance were designed to make shopping easy. Unobtrusive staff, located in a central service area, could be called upon for assistance if necessary, but otherwise customers were left to consider the merchandise in their own time.

The spacious stores decorated with colorful banners had a carnival atmosphere. Furniture was laid out in room settings where customers could see and try the products in a simulated home environment. Swing tags on each piece of furniture clearly indicated the style and model names, product dimensions, and price.

The furniture, 90 percent of which was designed in-house, was upscale modern Scandinavian—functional with simple lines and forms. It was available exclusively in knockdown form in flat packs and was ready to be assembled at home by the customer with only a simple tool, which came with each pack. IKEA had a commitment to product quality. To this end, furniture was tested and appropriately labeled with the Swedish testing authority tag.

Although furniture was the main product category, it was complemented with merchandise that included housewares, home textiles (bed and bath, fabric, rugs), lighting, bedding, floor tiles, china, cutlery, glassware, and wallpaper. A total of 14,000 product lines helped the customer create the IKEA home.

All products were described in a catalog that IKEA considered to be a key marketing tool. Half of the marketing budget of an estimated $10 million was devoted to the lavishly produced catalog. It clearly displayed the products, indicated module sizes, provided instructions for calculating needs, and listed price information. The catalog was designed not simply to communicate IKEA's products and prices but also to serve as the principal communication device in conveying the difference between IKEA and its competitors. It conveyed the IKEA concept.

Prices were fixed for 12 months. This allowed customers to plan their interior design at home by using the catalog and then space their purchases over the year. Price credibility was maintained by having a single sale of selected lines just before introduction of the new catalog each September. IKEA offered unconditional return of goods within 14 days if the customer was dissatisfied.

After the customers made their selection in the showroom, information on the swing ticket directed them to a location in the well-signed warehouse where they picked up their own orders and placed them on trollies. This transfer of warehouse labor to the customer contributed to IKEA's low-cost operation and eliminated a typical warehouse problem and its associated costs—that of errors in picking out merchandise. The customers then wheeled their purchases out through checkout points to their car. Home delivery could be arranged with an independent carrier at the store exits. IKEA made no money from this arrangement; it simply provided space for an external carrier organization as an added service to its customers. Alternatively, car roof-racks were available for purchase at the checkout. Point-of-sale cash registers captured sales movement to aid in the electronic reordering of stock.

The Competition

IKEA saw as its competition not simply the furniture store down the road, but, more broadly, as all those big expenditures that made a claim on a household's disposable income, such as vacations, a videocassette recorder, even a night out on the town.

More prosaically, a range of furniture sellers competed for the same customers as IKEA. The leading American furniture specialist, Levitz, had annual sales of over $879 million (Exhibit 5). Furniture sales of each of the top three department stores, leading with Sears, with annual furniture sales of more than $780 million (Exhibit 6), dwarfed even the second-largest furniture specialist, Seaman's.

EXHIBIT 5

Sales of Selected Furniture Stores

Company and Rank	1986 Sales (millions of dollars)	1987 Sales (millions of dollars)	Stores[a]	Per Square Foot[b]
1. Levitz	$840	$879	105	$413
2. Seaman's	230	254	30	406
3. W.S. Badcock	210	247	251	96
4. Rhodes	235	240	89	109
5. Haverty's	189	218	79	N/A
6. Breuners	215	198	19	107
7. Wickes	135	177	16	221
8. Value City	101	150	32	213
9. Helig-Meyers	141	142	259	90
10. Nebraska Furniture Mart	132	142	1	676
12. Pier I	182	117	350	12
13. Art Van	110	113	15	N/A
16. Scandinavian Design	108	101	68	345
21. IKEA	50	77	2	N/A
27. Conran's	47	65	15	14
33. Jordan's	30	55	3	570

[a]Number of stores in 1987.
[b]Sales per square foot in dollars.
Source: Adapted from "Balancing the Retail Equation," *HFD—The Weekly Home Furnishings Newspaper,* 20 June 1988.

EXHIBIT 6

Furniture Sales of Selected Department Stores (in millions of dollars)

Rank	Company	1986 Sales	1987 Sales	Branches
1	Sears	$750	$788	480
2	Montgomery Ward	530	543	302
3	JCPenney	400	401	300
4	Macy's New York/New Jersey	154	162	24
5	Bloomingdale's	70	81	13
6	Dayton Hudson	68	71	16
7	Macy's California	65	67	15
8	The Broadway	56	57	10
9	Abraham & Straus	54	56	13
10	Burdines	50	55	17
11	Marshall Field's	40	44	16
46	Dillard's	8	10	67

Source: Adapted from "Balancing the Retail Equation," *HFD—The Weekly Home Furnishings Newspaper,* 20, June 1988.

The department stores found that they could achieve better sales per square foot from other products in the same high-cost space taken up by the furniture sections of their stores. This created a trend toward freestanding furniture outlets, which also served to enhance the department store presence in the furniture market. At the same time, these freestanding specialist stores could be seen to be more readily in direct competition with IKEA.

Ready-to-assemble (RTA) furniture, distributed through a variety of channels, was starting to come into its own with annual sales of over $3 billion in 1988, as depicted in Exhibit 7.

Besides the traditional department stores and furniture stores, discounters, specialty stores, home centers (which saw themselves as natural outlets for RTA furniture), and wholesale clubs also sold RTA furniture, often in combination with a self-service warehouse environment.

Heilig-Meyers, which offered a range of home furnishings, including electronics, appliances, and lawn and garden implements, saw RTA furniture as an avenue to their expansion and upscaling strategy.

EXHIBIT 7

Sales of Selected Ready-to-Assembly (RTA) Furniture Retailers (in millions of dollars)

Rank	Company	1988	Category
1	Kmart	$110	Discounter
2	Wal-Mart	95	Discounter
3	IKEA	90	Lifestyle
4	Target	85	Discounter
5	Ames/Zayre	80	Department store
6	Sears	80	National retailer
7	Bombay Company	60	Lifestyle
8	Service Merchandise	45	Catalog showroom
9	Best	40	Catalog showroom
10	Venture	35	Discounter
12	Conran's	32	Lifestyle
14	STOR	30	Lifestyle
16	JCPenney	27	National retailer
19	Levitz	23	Furniture retailer
20	Pier I	21	Lifestyle
21	Meijer	20	Discounter
22	Price Club	19	Wholesale club
25	Montgomery Ward	17	Department store
26	Pergament	16	Home center
36	Radio Shack	11	Electronics
42	Helig-Meyers	10	Furniture retailer
43	Office Depot	10	Office furniture
67	Macy's New York	4	National retailer
Top 80 RTA retailers		$1,500	
Total RTA market		$3,000	

Source: Adapted from "Top 80 RTA Retailers," *HFD—The Weekly Home Furnishings Newspaper*, 10 July 1989.

The nature of RTA furniture also made it a natural for sale through mail-order catalogs. The products were ideal for shipment by United Parcel Service and hence, rapidly available for home assembly and use. The whole range of JCPenney RTA furniture was sold through its catalog.

One of the biggest challenges facing the industry was overcoming the negative attitude of the American consumer toward RTA furniture. This was being tackled to some extent by application of manufacturing techniques that did not make the furniture look knockdown. An additional problem was that of missing parts. IKEA was not immune from this with a return rate of 1.6 percent of sales in the latest 1987 survey—a decline from 3 percent in the early 1980s.

IKEA, however, saw itself as being unique in the RTA field in two respects: It presented a complete range of furniture and not just the limited number of pieces offered by most of the other retailers, and it was marketing a concept, not simply selling a collection of knockdown furniture.

Specialty stores, such as Pier 1, and more especially Conran's, and the large department stores were seen as IKEA's key competitors. Conran's, however, felt that it catered to the more upscale customer.

The Future

IKEA was considered to be the world's multinational furniture chain. This status was attributed to the logistics savings made possible by its flatpack furniture and the innovative channel possibilities that this had opened up, and the low costs achieved through its sourcing policies and the transfer to the customer of assembly and warehouse costs. Only Conran's, of the UK, could also be considered a multinational furniture store operation.

The flatpack design concept also provided a number of customer benefits: the ability to carry home and enjoy the purchase immediately, considered a particular advantage by the target market that was thought to be in constant search of instant gratification; and the low prices that flowed from the low costs. A continuing commitment to product quality also helped to alleviate the concerns about RTA furniture as a concept.

A Newark, New Jersey, store opened in the spring of 1990; one opened in Los Angeles, California, in October 1990; and one in Long Island, New York, in 1991.

At this stage, IKEA did not offer a mail-order service like its competitors.

Also, other furniture makers had adapted their merchandise to fit different regional needs. IKEA resisted this line of approach, preferring to push its so-far-successful formula.

Recently, IKEA decided to establish a U.S. buying office to boost the volume of product sourced from the United States. Its current level is 20 percent of the line.

A new and rapidly growing segment that appeared in the marketplace was that of home office furniture. IKEA was not strong in this area.

There were a number of issues to be resolved about the future. Bjorn Boyle sat there and thought.

QUESTIONS

1. What are the success factors that help in making IKEA the largest multinational furniture specialist?
2. Discuss the international distribution channel for furniture.
3. Discuss the options available to IKEA for its expansion in the U.S.

REFERENCES

Arbose, J., "The Folksy Theories That Inspire Lifestyle Merchant IKEA," *International Management*, (November 1985): 51–59.

Moore, S. D., "IKEA Bucks Home-Furnishings Trends," *Wall Street Journal*, 23 February 1990, A7D.

Reynolds, J., "IKEA: A Competitive Company with Style," *Retail & Distribution Management*, (May–June 1988).

"Why Competitors Shop for Ideas at IKEA," *Business Week*, 9 October 1989.

CASE 25

SEARS: A GIANT IN TRANSITION

David J. Frayer

Introduction

In September 1989, Edward A. Brennan, Chairman of Sears, Roebuck and Company, was confronted with a difficult situation. Faced with mediocre profits over a period of years in the merchandising segment and the threat of a hostile corporate takeover, Brennan had championed numerous changes in the late 1980s. Sears introduced brandname products to compete with existing private-label brands, streamlined its sales and distribution system to reduce expenses, slashed overhead by reorganizing its headquarters and store staff into six autonomous business units, and examined alternative specialty retailing formats to recover lost customers. Perhaps the most heralded of all Brennan's moves culminated on March 1, 1989, when Sears reopened its 827 stores after having permanently reduced prices on 75 percent of the merchandise. This new "everyday low pricing" strategy was designed to make Sears more competitive in its traditional retail segments. However, analysts were skeptical. Lauren Lambert of Drexel Burnham Lambert stated that Sears has "changed more since the beginning of this year than they have in a long time. It's not going to turn on a dime. I think the company's agility could be improved."[1]

Company Background

In 1886, Richard W. Sears began his career in the retailing business while working as a railroad agent in Minnesota. Through a consignment agreement, he managed to sell an entire shipment of watches that had been refused by a local merchant. After experimenting with other products, he eventually quit his job and founded the R.W. Sears Watch Company. The business grew quickly and in 1887 he moved his company to Chicago.

In an effort to expand profits, Sears decided to buy component parts and assemble the watches himself. He advertised for a watchmaker in the *Chicago Daily News*, and Alvah C. Roebuck joined the firm. Sears sold the business to

Roebuck in March of 1889 for $72,000 and later formed another watch and jewelry company that he eventually sold to Roebuck in 1891. Within a few weeks, Sears sought to rejoin the company and became an equal partner with Roebuck. Soon thereafter, the company published its first catalog, which included 32 pages of watches and an 8-page insert of jewelry and sewing machines. By the following year, the catalog included 140 pages and a wider selection of products, most of which were less expensive than other stores could offer.

Sears' early success relied almost entirely on ever-increasing sales that were often the result of exaggerated claims. Roebuck, unsure of the business's future potential, sold his portion of the company to Sears in 1895 for $25,000. Julius Rosenwald joined the firm that same year and provided stringent financial controls as the business expanded. In 1906, the company issued its first preferred stock to help finance growth. By 1908, the business climate had changed and Sears was forced to adjust its marketing tactics by providing more accurate, highly detailed descriptions of products. Sears became chairman of the board in 1908, but rarely took an active part in business operations. He resigned in 1913.

While not the first catalog company, Sears, by 1917, was publishing two large general-merchandise editions and several hundred specialty catalogs. General Robert E. Wood joined Sears in 1924 after leaving rival Montgomery Ward and immediately decided to expand the business into retail outlets. While the catalogs had successfully penetrated the rural markets, the retail stores sought to capitalize on the growing metropolitan areas. The first retail merchandise store opened in 1925 in the Chicago Catalog Merchandise Distribution Center. By 1929, Sears had opened 324 stores, and in 1931, retail sales surpassed catalog sales for the first time.

By 1931, Sears realized the growing importance of the automobile in shaping American lifestyles and began to offer low-cost auto insurance through the mail. The Allstate Insurance Company, named after a popular line of Sears' tires, was founded to handle these transactions which were solicited through the general catalog. In 1933, Sears introduced over-the-counter insurance sales by expanding Allstate operations into Sears' retail outlets. This move broke with prevailing customs and provided another avenue for Sears' continued growth. In 1945, Sears' yearly sales exceeded $1 billion for the first time.

Following World War II, Sears embarked on a second period of retail expansion. While other retailers hesitated in fear of a postwar recession, Sears anticipated growth in the suburbs and moved quickly to capitalize on delayed consumer spending. In 1953, Sears introduced the revolving charge account, which expanded the purchasing power of consumers. Beyond merchandise sales, Allstate added life insurance to its growing portfolio of products in 1957, and the company was soon setting growth records.

As Sears continued to support its corporate growth strategy through additional retail outlets and an expanded product and service offering, profits continued to soar. Management began to search for attractive uses for the firm's financial resources. In 1961, Allstate purchased a California Savings and Loan Institution to further diversify its insurance operations. Sears continued to develop retail shopping centers and embarked on a plan to consolidate its operations in a single location. During the 1960s, Sears passed A & P to become the world's largest general-merchandise retailer. Sears' corporate stature reached a pinnacle with completion of the Sears Tower in 1973. The leading retail and insurance firm had constructed a corporate headquarters that dwarfed other buildings in the Chicago skyline, much like Sears towered over its nearest competitors.

By 1980, Sears recognized that the traditional financial services system was not providing adequate service to its customers. Already an established presence in insurance and personal banking, Sears in 1981 acquired Coldwell Banker for real estate and Dean Witter for investments to create a new kind of broad-based consumer-oriented financial services institution. Allstate, Coldwell Banker, Dean Witter, and Sears Savings Bank (formed in 1984) were assembled as members of the Sears Financial Network, a partnership of leading firms working in collaboration to develop and distribute unique financial services. Sears Financial Network Centers were established in retail outlets and many services were introduced, including the Discover Card in 1985.

While Sears developed into a major participant in the financial services arena, retail operations relied on outdated merchandising strategies to extend corporate growth. Following a series of merchandising mistakes in the late 1970s, Sears reported a $7 million retailing loss in the first quarter of 1980. Sears had lost much of its market to Kmart and other retailers, as merchandising operations slipped further behind the highly profitable insurance segment. By 1982, it became apparent that major changes were necessary. The "Store of the Future" debuted in 1983 as an attempt to minimize the adverse effects of competition from national discounters and specialty retailers. To stimulate sales, Sears renovated its stores and introduced new product lines. However, as Sears entered its second century in 1986, it remained under attack from all sides. The strategic advantages that had transformed this small mail-order watch operation into the world's largest retailer appeared to have become liabilities.

Industry Developments as of January 1988

Despite the initial success of Sears' "Store of the Future" campaign, sales remained relatively flat. Selling expenses as a percentage of sales continued to lead the industry. In 1988, Sears' selling and administrative costs were 32 percent of sales, compared with 24 percent at Kmart, 23 percent at Wal-Mart, and 17 percent at The Limited. "You don't get an expense structure until you're 100 years old," joked Joseph Batogowski, an executive vice-president of merchandising for Sears, Roebuck and Company.[2] In reality, the company had trailed far behind industry competitors in most measures of retail productivity for quite some time. Despite belt-tightening efforts, Sears' costs had continued to grow faster than sales every year since 1985 and Sears' market share had declined almost 33 percent since 1980. Only about 55 percent of Sears' floor space in its largest stores was devoted to sales, while Kmart and many other department stores approached 80 percent.

Retail merchandising, though, was not the only area that suffered. Sears' catalog sales had declined as a percentage of total company sales and had shown only marginal gains during a period when the consumer mail-order industry grew over 44 percent. Exhibit 1 contains selected financial data for the years 1979 through 1988.

Sears traditionally used its size to derive scale economies through mass purchasing and combined staff organizations. For several years, a centralized approach to marketing resulted in advertising and product decisions originating exclusively in Chicago. Power struggles between headquarters staff groups and store managers often slowed and distorted implementation of even the simplest ideas. Sears' giant bureaucracy had even failed to recognize regional weather patterns, attempting to sell space heaters in Hawaii and distributing catalogs in Miami with heavy winter parkas on the cover. Despite a strong brand franchise, Sears continued to lose customers to discounters and specialty stores (see Exhibit 2). However, in 1987, Sears established a network of 25 consolidated retail regions which brought merchandising strategy to the local level.

In a 1985 interview with *Chain Store Age*, Joseph Batogowski confirmed the retailer's historic commitment to private-label merchandise. In reference to Kenmore, Sears' highly successful line of home appliances, Batogowski commented, "I doubt you'll ever see another [brand of] washing machine on our floor."[3] Such confidence in Sears' traditional approach to consumer marketing was prevalent among corporate executives even as Sears faced critical challenges from a number of new sources. Specialty retailers like The Limited and Toys "R" Us made Sears' private-label merchandise appear shabby and neglected, while low-overhead discounters such as Kmart and Wal-Mart utilized efficient networks to attack Sears' prices. Sears' position as the nation's leading retailer was clearly in jeopardy, but other external threats provided a more dangerous and complex challenge for the firm's management.

Continued poor performance by Sears' merchandising group had focused the attention of Wall Street investors on the value of Sears' diversified portfolio. Despite its size, $48.4 billion in 1987 corporate sales, Sears was not invulnerable to a hostile takeover. The recent buyout of RJR Nabisco had proven that even corporate giants could become suitable targets. By summer of 1988, investors were preparing breakup analyses, indicating that Sears' stock was undervalued by as much as 50 percent. Sears' chairman, Edward A. Brennan, insisted that the value of Sears was greater than the sum of its parts (Sears' Merchandise Group, Dean Witter, Coldwell Banker, and Allstate Insurance). However, to reestablish a 15 percent corporate return on equity, Brennan needed to improve the merchandising group's 12.2 percent return on equity.

EXHIBIT 1

Selected Financial Data for Sears, Roebuck and Company

Reported in Millions of Dollars, Except for Common-Share Data

Operating results	1988	1987	1986	1985	1984	1983	1982	1981	1980	1979
Revenues	$50,251	$45,904	$42,303	$39,349	$37,898	$35,257	$29,559	$27,243	$25,082	$24,301
Costs and expenses	$45,617	$41,222	$38,139	$35,384	$33,766	$31,751	$26,866	$25,182	$23,170	$22,323
Nonrecurring expenses	$ 751	$ 105	—	—	—	—	—	—	—	—
Interest	$ 2,937	$ 2,721	$2,653	$ 2,629	$ 2,528	$ 1,703	$ 1,628	$ 1,520	$ 1,133	$ 918
Operating income	$ 946	$ 1,856	$ 1,511	$ 1,336	$ 1,604	$ 1,803	$ 1,065	$ 541	$ 693	$ 1,060
Other income	$ 157	$ 239	$ 282	$ 277	$ 246	$ 66	$ 28	$ 101	($11)	$ 43
Income from continuing operations before income taxes, minority interest, and equity in net income of unconsolidated companies	$ 1,103	$ 2,095	$ 1,793	$ 1,613	$ 1,850	$ 1,869	$ 1,093	$ 642	$ 682	$ 1,103
Income taxes										
Current operations	$ 54	$ 521	$ 444	$ 306	$ 498	$ 565	$ 238	$ 10	$ 98	$ 317
Fresh start and deferred tax benefits		($172)			($60)					
Income from continuing operations	$ 1,032	$ 1,726	$ 1,336	$ 1,280	$ 1,422	$ 1,326	$ 866	$ 646	$ 604	$ 820
Income (loss) from discontinued operations	($122)	($93)	$ 3	$ 14	$ 30	$ 11	($5)	$ 4	$ 6	$ 10
Cumulative effect of change in accounting for income taxes	$ 544									
Net income	$ 1,454	$ 1,633	$ 1,339	$ 1,294	$ 1,452	$ 1,337	$ 861	$ 650	$ 610	$ 830
Percentage return on average equity	10.5	12.3	10.8	11.4	14.0	14.4	10.1	8.2	8.1	11.4

Financial Position

Investments	$29,136	$25,120	$22,183	$19,249	$17,203	$15,434	$13,497	$12,229	$11,336	$ 9,985
Receivables	$28,685	$26,026	$21,417	$18,942	$17,565	$15,511	$11,532	$10,827	$ 8,956	$ 8,967
Property and equipment, net	$ 5,179	$ 4,790	$ 4,593	$ 4,541	$ 4,361	$ 3,938	$ 3,396	$ 3,312	$ 3,153	$ 3,061
Merchandise inventories	$ 3,716	$ 4,115	$ 4,013	$ 4,115	$ 4,530	$ 3,621	$ 3,146	$ 3,103	$ 2,715	$ 2,680
Total assets	$77,952	$75,014	$66,009	$66,426	$57,073	$46,177	$36,541	$34,406	$28,218	$26,904
Insurance reserves	$17,329	$13,169	$10,014	$ 8,090	$ 6,919	$ 6,262	$ 5,667	$ 5,161	$ 4,407	$ 4,075
Short-term borrowings	$ 8,978	$ 7,055	$ 4,306	$ 3,996	$ 3,887	$ 4,596	$ 2,820	$ 3,233	$ 4,436	$ 4,293
Long-term debt	$ 9,736	$ 9,562	$10,067	$ 9,907	$ 9,531	$ 7,405	$ 5,816	$ 5,324	$ 2,965	$ 2,966
Total debt	$18,714	$16,617	$14,373	$13,903	$13,418	$12,001	$ 8,636	$ 8,557	$ 7,401	$ 7,259
Percentage of debt to equity	133	123	110	118	123	123	98	103	97	97
Shareholder's equity	$14,055	$13,541	$13,017	$11,776	$10,903	$ 9,782	$ 8,812	$ 8,269	$ 7,665	$ 7,446

Shareholder's Common-Stock Investment

Book value per share (year end)	$37.75	$35.77	$33.90	$31.66	$29.46	$27.59	$25.08	$23.77	$24.32	$23.44
Shareholders	351,999	328,446	319,686	326,201	340,831	339,644	350,292	354,050	349,725	339,459
Average shares outstanding (millions)	379	378	369	363	358	353	350	316	316	320
Net income per share										
Income from continuing operations	$2.72	$4.55	$3.57	$3.47	$3.92	$3.76	$2.47	$2.05	$1.91	$2.57
Income (loss) from discontinued operations	($0.32)	($0.25)	$0.01	$0.04	$0.08	$0.03	($0.01)	$0.01	$0.02	$0.03
Cumulative effect of change in accounting for income taxes	$1.44									
Net income	$3.84	$4.30	$3.58	$3.51	$4.00	$3.79	$2.46	$2.06	$1.93	$2.60
Dividends per share	$2.00	$2.00	$1.76	$1.76	$1.76	$1.52	$1.36	$1.36	$1.36	$1.28
Dividend payout percentage	52.1%	46.5%	49.2%	50.1%	44.0%	40.1%	55.3%	66.0%	70.5%	49.2%
Market price (high-low)	46-	59.5-	50.4-	41.1-	40.4-	45.1-	32-	20.8-	19.5-	21.6-
	32.3	29.8	35.9	30.9	29.5	27	15.8	14.9	14.5	17.9
Closing market price at year end	40.9	33.5	39.8	39	31.8	37.1	30.1	16.1	15.4	18
Price earnings ratio (high-low)	12-8	14-7	14-10	12-9	10-7	12-7	13-6	10-7	10-8	8-7

Source: 1988 Sears, Roebuck and Company Annual Report.

EXHIBIT 2
Comparison of Top Retailers

	Revenue (in billions of dollars)	Share of Top Five Retailers (%)
	1971	
Sears, Roebuck	$10.1	44
JCPenney	4.8	21
Kresge (now Kmart)	3.1	13
Woolworth	2.8	12
Montgomery Ward	2.3	10
	Revenue (in billions of dollars)	Share of Top Five Retailers (%)
	1988	
Sears, Roebuck	$30.2	29
Kmart	27.3	26
Wal-Mart	20.6	20
JCPenney	15.2	14
Dayton-Hudson	12.2	11

Source: *Business Week,* 10 July 1989.

The extent of Sears' logistic requirements also became an operational issue. In 1984, Sears purchased products from over 6,000 domestic sources whose accounts were handled through a computerized billing system. Sears, a leading advocate of transportation deregulation, was able to reduce the number of carriers from 4,200 to about 180 by 1984. More efficient transportation also permitted Sears to reduce the number of distribution centers from a high of 110. Joseph Batogowski conceded that the company still needed to improve distribution and inventory controls by approaching a just-in-time delivery system. On average during 1986, merchandise required 18 weeks to reach the stores once a buyer had ordered it. By cutting the average delivery time by a single day, Sears could save an estimated $43 million per year. Overall, Sears' distribution costs remained a shocking 8 percent of sales in 1987, compared with approximately 2 percent for both Kmart and Wal-Mart. To help reduce some of these costs, Sears planned to close five more of its twelve remaining distribution centers by 1989, idling 5,700 of the company's 18,500 distribution center employees.

In the fall of 1987, Sears finally organized perhaps its best marketing tool, the Sears Household File. This computerized database contains information on the buying habits of every household in America that does business with Sears. Approximately three-quarters of all U.S. households are involved, a healthy 68.3 million total. According to Allan Stewart, senior vice-president for planning, "The key . . . is to increase multiple relationships."[4] This means persuading Die-Hard battery buyers, Craftsman tool customers, and Kenmore washing-machine families to trust Sears with their investment money as well. Sears must recapture a generation of children who began to shop elsewhere for more modern merchandise. As these children establish their own families, Sears must provide them with goods and services that meet their criteria of value and style.

When Sears celebrated its diamond jubilee year in 1961, management felt: "The ultimate test of value is not Sears' judgment, but the customer's response. It is the customer who renders the final verdict."[5]

By January 1988, Sears' customers were responding by shopping elsewhere. If Sears was to remain competitive in the retail segment, comprehensive changes were needed to revitalize the company's merchandising operations. Sears' entire cost structure required dramatic reductions, while logistics operations needed to be more carefully integrated. Poor management of Sears' sales and distribution channels had resulted in an inefficient corporate structure. A strong performance by the companies of Sears' Financial Network made strategic decisions even more critical in light of the firm's breakup value. Now, more than ever, Sears needed to capitalize on the firm's internal synergies.

Establishing Synergies Through Networks

In January 1988, Sears reorganized its principle businesses into two distinct operating units, the Sears Financial Network and the Sears Retail Network (see Exhibit 3). The restructured company was the culmination of an intensive, organizationwide evaluation of the various business units and was designed to implement the firm's refocused strategy. The overriding objective was to ensure that Sears would achieve increased shareholder value through distinct competitive advantages lasting well into the 1990s. As outlined in the 1988 annual report:

> *Among the key elements of the consumer focused direction are the revitalization of the Merchandise Group, broadening it into the Sears Retail Network, and the focusing of our financial services on the consumer.*
>
> *The "network" concept that has existed among our financial services companies for several years includes a wide range of distribution channels—from traditional branch offices to locations in Sears stores. Research developed during our strategic evaluation shows that while Coldwell Banker, Dean Witter and Allstate each have strong identities as individual companies, consumers say their strength is enhanced through their collective membership in the Sears Financial Network.*
>
> *Employing the same network concept, the Merchandise Group has established several distinct businesses, creating the Sears Retail Network which capitalizes on the trust, integrity and financial strength of Sears.*

EXHIBIT 3

Sears' Organization Chart

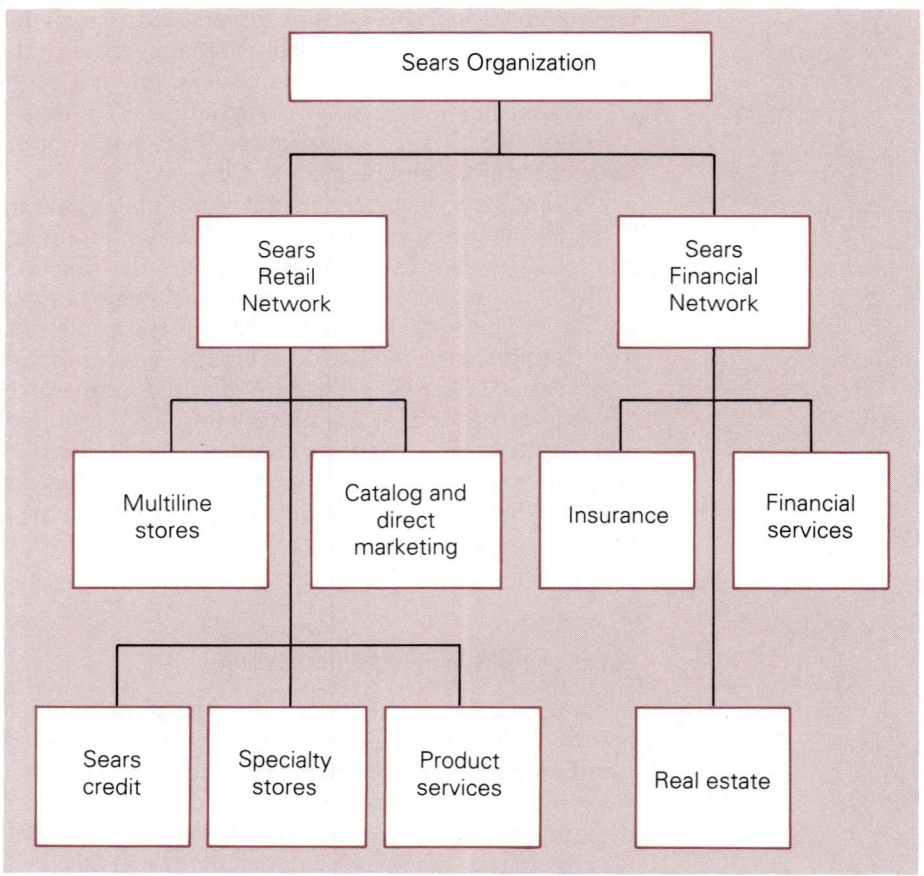

Source: *1988 Annual Report*, Sears, Roebuck and Company.

The end result is two powerful, interrelated organizations—the Sears Retail Network and the Sears Financial Network. They are the vehicles through which the company will implement the revitalization of the Merchandise Group and the refocusing of financial services on the consumer.[6]

Sears Financial Network

The Sears Financial Network includes several businesses that operate in three primary areas: insurance, financial services, and real estate. Through the Allstate Insurance Group, Sears offers policies covering life, auto, home, and business. Financial services are the primary focus of the Dean Witter Group whose operations include retail brokerage, investment banking, consumer lending, and the Discover Card. The Coldwell Banker Group provides real estate services, products, and financing through its three primary business units: Coldwell Banker Residential Group, Sears Mortgage Group, and Homart Development Co.

The corporate reorganization that took place in January 1988 focused the attention and resources of the Sears Financial Network companies on the consumer. Commercial businesses were divested or restructured to better support consumer businesses. A number of key changes are outlined in the 1988 annual report:

- Allstate's group life and health business has been sold. The Allstate Life Insurance Company will concentrate on individual life products, annuities, pensions, and direct response marketing products.
- Allstate's business insurance division has been refocused to direct its attention to the small to midsize market, and its national accounts business is being de-emphasized.
- Coldwell Banker's commercial division is being divested. Homart will continue to create value for shareholders by developing and managing quality real estate projects.
- Sears Mortgage Company's business has been transferred from Dean Witter to Coldwell Banker, which will permit more efficient offering of mortgages to residential clients.
- Dean Witter has restructured its securities-related organization. Dean Witter Financial will concentrate on sales and marketing and Dean Witter Capital will focus on investment banking and product development.
- Discover Card has been aligned as a stand-alone unit reporting directly to the chairman of Dean Witter.[7]

The companies of the Sears Financial Network have strong market positions individually and through powerful affiliations with one another. The linking of programs, such as selling Allstate investment products through Dean Witter account executives, helped provide critical business synergies to strengthen the entire Financial Network.

Sears Retail Network

While the Sears Financial Network was created as an alliance of separate but interrelated companies, the Sears Retail Network attempted to distinguish among several distinct businesses that were formerly integrated within the Sears Merchandise Group. These businesses include multiline stores, specialty stores, product services, catalog and direct-marketing operations, and Sears credit.

Conventional Sears retail outlets that carry a broad assortment of product lines in numerous departments were identified as multiline stores. The selected merchandise categories build upon Sears' established market strengths: home appliances, home improvement, automotive goods, home fashions, men's and children's apparel, and women's apparel. When coupled with updated merchandising strategies, this structure increased accountability by product line, streamlined decision making, and improved competitiveness in each merchandise category.

Specialty stores were the newest enterprises in the Sears Retail Network. These outlets were developed both internally and externally and included McKids stores, sleep shops, paint and hardware stores, eye-care centers, and freestanding auto centers. This segment was designed to increase Sears' total market share in selected merchandise categories through acquisition and management of growing companies.

The provision of selected product services permitted Sears to capitalize on a nationwide organization of 850 service facilities, 19,000 technicians, and 14,000 service vehicles. Sears' reputation in product repair coupled with expansion of service capabilities to include brand-name merchandise provided significant marketing opportunities within this segment.

The final two business segments included in the Sears Retail Network can be easily distinguished as independent operations. The catalog and direct-marketing organization was established as a business independent of the retail structure. Such a format allowed Sears to leverage its historic strength in catalog sales to provide improved performance across the segment. Sears' credit operation was the first Merchandise Group business to be separately organized. This distinction permitted clear performance measures to be established and monitored more effectively.

The network structure, which had been so effective in the financial services organization, was intended to improve performance among the merchandise businesses. By providing customers with the right goods at the right price and at convenient locations, management expected to raise corporate returns through increased profitability in each market segment. However, structural change alone was not sufficient to achieve these objectives.

Strategic Response

In order to support the extensive structural changes that created the Sears Retail Network, the Merchandise Group simultaneously developed its retail, catalog, and service strategies for the 1990s. Four primary strategic responses emerged—power formats, everyday low pricing, vertical business accountability, and corresponding logistics support—which operated within the framework of intense cost containment necessary for success in a highly competitive environment. Michael Bozic, chairman and chief executive office of Sears Merchandise Group, insisted that each of these new strategies was "aimed at delivering quality, value, trust and integrity to the consumer."[8] However, the success of these strategic responses depended on two key assumptions:

1. Sears can properly implement and control these programs.
2. These responses address the fundamental problems that have resulted in the Merchandising Group's declining market share and reduced return on investment.

A careful examination of each strategic response highlights key areas of concern.

Power formats were designed to convert Sears' retail outlets into "stores of superstores." They were developed in key areas, including: automotive, lawn and garden, home improvement, home fashions, men's clothing, and women's apparel. The concept debuted in 1988 with the introduction of Brand Central. This area featured home appliances and home entertainment equipment in a dramatic new setting surrounded by improved signs and an expanded product assortment. To enhance Sears' appeal and strengthen the store's competitive position, over 50 national brands including Whirlpool, General Electric, Sony, RCA, and Zenith were added, while the Kenmore franchise remained in place. Since Kenmore commanded gross margins in excess of 30 percent, Sears' primary source of profit appeared threatened. To protect this revenue, Sears planned to heavily advertise Kenmore appliances and provide sales staff incentives to push high-margin products.

Results from initial market tests in 18 Indiana and Kentucky stores reinforced the decision to expand Brand Central into 400 additional stores during 1989. Carpet departments were also converted to a power format during early 1989. After several months of testing in three markets, well-known national brands replaced the house label in 726 Sears stores. Exclusive marketing agreements with McDonald's and Walt Disney Studios turned Sears into a formidable competitor for Kids "R" Us. By providing a greater selection and improved service, Sears hoped to attract consumers from both national and local discount chains.

In conjunction with these power formats, Sears adopted an everyday low pricing strategy. After being tested in three Wichita stores during the fall of 1988, the plan was implemented nationwide on March 1, 1989. It was hoped that lower prices everyday would encourage customers to shop more often and more widely rather than wait for promotions. This resulted in more consistent shopping patterns, which permitted better control of inventories, reduced operating costs, and lighter work loads at all levels in the organization. A new advertising campaign was developed to support the pricing program. "Your Money's Worth and a Whole Lot More" expressed Sears' desire to create power formats that delivered quality, value, trust, and integrity. The campaign emphasized the price/quality relationship between Sears' merchandise and various value-enhancing programs such as dedicated customer service, credit options, delivery, merchandise installation, and product repair. The combination of reduced prices and after-sale service created a value-based mix that Sears believed few discounters could match completely.

With the third strategic element introduced by the Merchandise Group Sears recognized the need to carefully manage each business segment according to the merchandise, services, and other characteristics of that business. Through vertical business accountability, headquarters and field organizations were aligned to become more responsive to market changes and were evaluated based on specific performance measures. This concept is critically linked with the structural organization of the Merchandise Group into the

Sears Retail Network. The future success of power formats and catalog operations was closely tied to vertical accountability, which has been tested within the credit organization.

Effective integration of merchandise planning, inventory management, and physical distribution was a primary concern of Sears' Merchandise Group, which sought improved logistics efficiency and support for merchandising operations. One major consideration for this fourth strategic response was development of systems to serve the newly separated retail and catalog businesses. Inventories, which had previously been consolidated, were handled separately after mid-1989. This focused on reduced overhead through elimination of seven catalog distribution centers by mid-1990. Simultaneously, Sears' distribution facilities were divided based on the desired product flow. Major appliances purchased in a retail outlet were sent directly to the consumer's home from a distribution facility, while smaller "take-with" items were distributed to stores. This improved product flow reduced inventories while providing better customer service. Central to improved logistics was Sears' commitment to convert to a standardized electronic language for communication with suppliers and a state-of-the-art system for processing customer orders, managing inventory, and operating distribution facilities. Through creation of a distribution system that grew with the business, Sears hoped to avoid frequent stockouts on popular items. Such channel management systems were critical in providing adequate support for Sears' merchandising activities.

Two additional strategies designed to enhance Sears' logistics system included expanded distribution and further development of specialty merchandising formats. In 1988, Sears opened 13 new multiline stores and relocated 18 others. By 1994, the Merchandise Group plans to increase the number of multiline stores to 1,050 from the 1988 year-end total of 824, including 226 new locations and 87 relocations. A portion of this expansion is designed to improve market penetration in underserved suburban and urban areas through creation of Sears Ltd., with complete power formats selected for local market demographics. Expansion of speciality merchandising formats occurred primarily through acquisition of Western Auto Supply, Eye Care Centers of America, and Pinstripes Petites. In addition, the focus of Sears Business Systems Centers was adjusted to emphasize small and medium-sized businesses, while improving service to the consumer market.

Preliminary Results Through August 1989

When Sears, Roebuck and Company slashed prices permanently on 75 percent of the items sold in its 827 stores March 1, 1989, management had hoped to reverse five years of dismal sales. As expected, the preliminary results did not indicate the plan was an immediate success. Same-store sales in March were up 9.6 percent over March 1988, and April gained 6.8 percent over April

1988. Revenues, however, dropped a shocking 2.4 percent in July and 1.1 percent in August across stores that had been open at least one year (see Exhibit 4). Industry observers expected Sears' aggressive new pricing policies to primarily impact sales in discount stores. While Kmart registered a 1 percent drop in same-store sales in April, Wal-Mart, Hills, and Target posted solid gains. According to analyst Wayne Hood of Prudential Bache Securities, "They still have a long way to go to convince the consumer that day in and out you can find lower prices at Sears."[9]

Despite advertising claims, Sears' prices were not always the lowest in town. In one market, a Magnavox 13-inch color television cost $269 at Sears, while the same television sold for $249 at Kmart across town.

In May 1989, a series of surveys conducted by Impact Resources of Columbus, Ohio, indicated that in many markets Sears had failed to convince consumers that it was indeed a price leader. In Cleveland, Chicago, and Buffalo more shoppers cited price as a reason for picking Sears, while the percentage of shoppers who rated price as their primary motivator in selecting Sears declined in Milwaukee, Kansas City, and Denver.

Still, optimism remained high at Sears Tower in Chicago. When an angry shareholder scolded management for squandering its hold over the American consumer, Edward Brennan, chairman and chief executive officer, replied; "Give us a try. We want you back."[10]

EXHIBIT 4

Percentage Change in Same-Store Revenue (from the Previous Year)

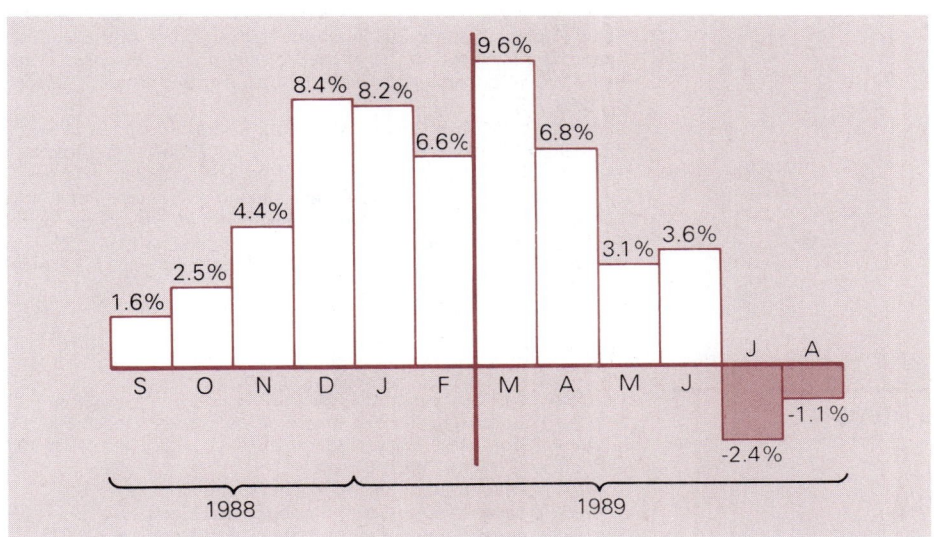

Source: "Slow Start for Pricing Strategy," USA TODAY, 7 September 1989. Copyright 1989, USA TODAY. Reprinted with permission.

QUESTIONS

1. Describe the primary strategic advantages Sears used to support corporate growth from 1886 through 1979. Will these strategic advantages remain viable tools for Sears to support merchandising activities in the 1990s? Why or why not?
2. Explain the network concept as applied at Sears, Roebuck and Company. Why are networks important? Can Sears develop the operating synergies alone, or will it require participation by other channel members? Why or why not?
3. How do channel management issues relate to the crisis facing Sears in 1988? How have these changed by August 1989? What additional problems do you foresee? Provide solutions where possible.
4. How have the changes instituted at Sears between 1985 and 1989 changed the strategic positioning of the firm? What are the implications of these changes for Sears' channel strategy, logistics channels, supplier evaluation and selection, and relationships with suppliers? In particular, consider the impact on channel relations of closing five distribution facilities.

SUGGESTED READINGS

1961 Annual Report, Sears, Roebuck and Co., 9-13.
1984 Annual Report, Sears, Roebuck and Co., 5-14.
1988 Annual Report, Sears, Roebuck and Co., 1-41.
"The Big Store's Big Trauma," *Business Week,* 10 July 1989, 50-55.
"Brands to Join Kenmore in Test," *Chain Store Age,* (December 1987): 11.
"Master Plan to Revitalize Sears Still Under Scrutiny," *Chain Store Age Executive* (January 1989): 38-40.
"Minding the Store," *Forbes,* 7 April 1986, 31-32.
"On the Rebound," *Forbes,* 20 June 1983, 12.
"Sears' Big Book: Dinosaur of Phoenix?" *Direct Marketing* (July 1986): 71-74.
"Sears Faces a Tall Task." *Business Week,* 14 November 1988, 54-55.
"Sears' Family Stores Leap into New Century," *Chain Store Age,* (December 1985) 11-91.
"Sears Pricing Strategy Still in Doubt," *Chain Store Age Executive* (October 1989): 124.
"Sears: Trimming the Worst of the Corporate Fat," *Business Week,* 16 March 1987, 39.
"Sears Works on Appeal to Make Up for Five Bad Years," *Lansing State Journal,* 11 September 1989, B5.
"Shaking Sears Right Down to Its Work Boots," *Business Week,* 17 October 1988, 84-87.
"Slow Start for Sears' Price Strategy," *USA Today,* 7 September 1989, B1-B2.
"They Buy Their Stocks Where They Buy Their Socks," *Forbes,* 7 March 1988, 60-67.
"Today, Each of the Big Three Travels along a Different Path," *Stores* (July 1987): 23-24.
"Too Early to Gauge 'New' Sears Impact," *Chain Store Age Executive,* (June 1989): 85.
"Transportation: Making It Work," *Stores* (February 1984): 38.
"Will the Big Markdown Get the Big Store Moving Again?" *Business Week,* 13 March 1989, 110-14.

ENDNOTES

1. *USA Today,* 7 September 1989, B2.
2. *Chain Store Age,* General Merchandise Trends (December 1985): 12.
3. *Chain Store Age,* General Merchandise Trends (December 1987): 11.
4. *Forbes,* 7 March 1988, 61.
5. *1961 Annual Report,* Sears, Roebuck and Company, 12.
6. *1988 Annual Report,* Sears, Roebuck and Company, 5.
7. *1988 Annual Report,* Sears, Roebuck and Company, 7-8.
8. *1988 Annual Report,* Sears, Roebuck and Company, 10.
9. *Lansing State Journal,* 11 September 1989, B5.
10. *Business Week,* 10 July 1989, 55.

CASE 26

Ray R. Serpkenci

FOOD4LESS STORES, INC.*

In September 1985, Bob Allison, senior vice-president of store operations and corporate planning, and his newly hired staff specialist, Richard Wold, assistant marketing controller, were listening to the final details of a major market research study being presented by a group of outside consultants. The two-day session, with all the other senior executives of Food4Less present, had been a draining exercise. The Market and Performance Assessment Project was easily the most ambitious study ever undertaken by the Food4Less organization. The year-long research, commissioned in late 1984, had two key objectives: In the short run, the research findings would be used to establish guidelines for the rehabilitation of ailing stores; and for the longer run, the results of the study would provide new strategic insights for both new store development and market positioning.

This last meeting with the consultants was especially important for Allison and Wold, since they had been assigned the task of organizing the upcoming "store owners meeting" that was scheduled for November 14, 1985. At that time, the Food4Less senior management was expected to report on the results of the Market and Performance Assessment Project, and to present the general outlines of a new strategic plan for the Food4Less operation for the 1990s.

After the consultants' presentation, Mr. Allison turned to Rick Wold and commented:

> We have to get the findings of the consultants organized quite tightly for the November meeting. I think we should get together later this evening for a planning meeting. I am very disturbed at some of the findings, and we will have to put together a consistent program for the owners. As these guys [consultants] presented their stuff, things are all over the map. This surely won't go well with the owners.

Food4Less Organization

Though the individual Food4Less stores and their owners had been in business for a fairly long time, Food4Less Stores, Inc. in its present form was a relatively young operation. The supermarket chain had acquired a "cooperative" status early in 1980, following the initiative of several independent operators who decided to band together for buying, merchandising, and marketing efficiencies.

---

*This case was prepared as a basis for class discussion rather than to illustrate either effective or ineffective handling of a retail situation. No part of this publication may be reproduced, stored in a retrieval system, or transmitted in any form or by any means—electronic, mechanical, photocopying, recording, or otherwise—without the permission of the author. Copyright © 1987 Ray R. Serpkenci and Faculty of Management, University of Toronto.

The *co-ops*, as they were commonly known in the trade, have become a major force in retail distribution, especially in the supermarket industry. The original concept had emerged as a response to the appearance and rapid growth of corporate chains in the early 1940s. At that time, (corporate) chain stores, with their massive scale in buying and distribution efficiencies, had been a major dislocative force in food retailing, forcing independents to realign themselves considerably. Later in its life cycle, however, the scope of co-op operations had been significantly expanded to include a vast number of integrated programs, such as centralized consumer advertising and promotion, store design, location and layout expertise, employee and member training programs, financing and accounting systems, and, in some cases, a complete package of support services.

Food4Less Stores, Inc. was a cooperative exhibiting many of the more advanced elements of this form of channel organization. The individual operators of Food4Less stores not only owned their wholesale company (and several distribution centers), but also used a uniform and standardized storefront and logo, and generally adhered to common advertising, promotional, and operating practices. They had, for example, a vigorous private label and generics program in place, a centralized equipment and store fixture procurement system, as well as a real estate and store engineering staff which all members could turn to for assistance from time to time.

The executive group in the corporate office coordinated all of these activities and were appointed by the co-op general assembly. The executives in the corporate office reported directly to the board of directors which included a number of Food4Less store owners as well as members appointed from the outside. Through the years, the corporate office had grown to become a source of both innovative ideas and a driving force in the formulation of major strategic decisions for the co-op.

As of the end of fiscal year 1985, there were nearly 200 affiliated Food4Less stores located in several eastern states, with combined revenues close to $2.0 billion, and a work force of nearly 14,000 full- and part-time employees. (Some of the key elements from their financial and operating profile are provided in Exhibits 1 through 3.)

The individual Food4Less stores were a mixed breed in terms of their size and physical configuration. Some of the affiliated stores were as small as 10,000 square feet, while others were much larger at 40,000 square feet of gross space. Furthermore, not all member stores had all the major departments in their stores. Newer units, for example, had added fresh-fish and bakery departments which most of the smaller units could not support. Also, depending on local ordinances, some stores could not carry wine or beer while others chose not to do so. Predictably, the smaller Food4Less stores carried a narrower assortment of grocery items of nearly 10,000 to 12,000 SKUs, while larger stores were very much like superstores, with close to 20,000 to 25,000 SKUs. Exhibits 2 and 3 provide some of the key operating statistics, and outline the sales contribution and gross margins by individual departments for all the Food4Less stores.

EXHIBIT 1

Market and Performance Assessment Project: An Operational and Financial Profile of Food4Less Stores

Operational Statistics	All Stores	Net Sales per Square Foot of Selling Area				
		$450 or Less	$451-$600	$601-$699	$700 and Over	
Full-time employees per store	22.3[a]	15.3	18.3	23.8	29.9	
Part-time employees per store	57.4	40.3	51.8	59.1	73.6	
Weekly hours per part-time employee	22.7	22.2	23.8	23.2	21.9	
Weekly hours per full-time employee	47.7	49.8	47.2	47.3	47.0	
Annual rate of labor turnover	38.23%	43.69%	31.79%	40.41%	37.89%	
Average hourly wage rate	$8.48	$8.27	$8.74	$8.51	$8.37	
Selling area per store (square feet)	16,343	17,159	16,411	16,160	15,835	
Gross leasable area per store (square feet)	21,991	23,750	22,328	21,468	20,814	
Customer checkout counters per store	9.0	7.7	8.1	11.4	9.2	
Customer parking spaces per store	171.9	230.0	183.9	144.8	139.5	
Age of store	11.6	10.9	13.1	10.7	11.7	
Years since last store remodeling	3.2	2.9	4.4	1.7	3.4	
Store hours per day	16.1[b]	13.6	16.2	17.0	17.0	
Store hours per week	109.3	92.7	110.3	115.8	115.7	

Store Sales and Investment

Net store sales per week	$189,347.97	$125,307.53	$165,213.14	$202,211.27	$247,854.57	
Average inventory investment per store	$348,731.47	$317,339.07	$341,272.06	$354,628.26	$373,658.61	
Fixtures, equipment and leasehold improvements						
Net book value	$501,597.04	$236,028.40	$511,831.62	$642,797.67	$575,884.93	
Gross book value	$928,176.09	$533,119.00	$939,492.35	$1,120,770.52	$1,089,313.11	
Estimated size of transaction per customer	$16.34	$14.73	$15.92	$16.87	$17.46	

[a]Read: An "average" Food4Less store has 22 full-time employees.
[b]Read: An "average" Food4Less store is open for 16 hours per day.

EXHIBIT 2

Market and Performance Assessment Project: Summary of Operating Results

Store Revenue and Gross Margin	Net Sales per Square Foot of Selling Area				
	All Stores	$450 or Less	$451–$600	$601–$699	$700 and Over
Net sales	100.00%	100.00%	100.00%	100.00%	100.00%
Cost of sales	77.63%	78.56%	77.51%	77.31%	77.33%
Gross margin	22.37%[a]	21.44%	22.49%	22.69%	22.67%
Store Operating Expenses					
Salaries and wages	9.29%	9.52%	9.97%	8.94%	8.75%
Payroll taxes and benefits	2.59%	2.54%	2.71%	2.59%	2.50%
Rent	1.08%	1.39%	1.06%	1.01%	0.94%
Utilities	1.53%	2.03%	1.67%	1.38%	1.17%
Advertising and promotion	1.76%	1.87%	1.71%	1.82%	1.68%
Other store expenses	3.87%	4.08%	4.09%	3.65%	3.68%
Total operating expenses	20.12%	21.43%	21.21%	19.39%	18.72%
Corporate overhead	2.11%	1.97%	1.94%	2.25%	2.26%
Total operating expenses and overhead	22.23%	23.40%	23.15%	21.64%	20.98%
Store Profitability					
Operating income	0.14%	(1.96)%	(0.66)%	1.05%	1.69%
Other income (expense)	0.60%	0.84%	0.54%	0.49%	0.57%
Profit before taxes	0.74%	(1.12)%	(0.12)%	1.54%	2.26%
Estimated breakeven volume as a percentage of current sales	100.64%	114.61%	105.73%	94.21%	90.78%

[a] Read: An "average" Food4Less store operates on a 22 percent gross margin.

Except for the largest stores, most Food4Less members were located in strip centers, typically in high-density, urban locations. Most of the larger stores, on the other hand, were stand-alone units with ample customer parking spaces. Also, a few of the operators had recently switched to a seven days a week, 24-hour format. Most Food4Less stores, however, were open about 16 hours per day, 8 a.m. until midnight.

Despite the common themes in advertising, promotion, sales support, and training, Food4Less stores at the local level were fairly independently run. In part due to their entrepreneurial spirit, and in part due to the considerations unique to their immediate market environment, Food4Less stores had historically operated, at times, according to the whims of their owners. A few of the operators did own more than one store. However, by and large, the independent owner/operator was the norm rather than the exception in the Food4Less operation.

EXHIBIT 3

Market and Performance Assessment Project: Departmental Sales Contribution and Margins

		Net Sales per Square Foot of Selling Area			
Contribution to Store Sales	All Stores	$450 or Less	$451–$600	$601–$699	$700 and Over
Prepared meats department	15.33%a	15.27%	15.28%	15.31%	15.45%
Butcher shop	0.92%	n/a	0.40%	0.86%	1.23%
Produce department	7.75%	7.61%	7.38%	7.88%	8.09%
Frozen foods department	6.91%	6.97%	6.87%	6.87%	6.94%
Deli and appetizers shop	4.61%	4.88%	4.61%	4.74%	4.31%
Dairy products department	13.25%	13.65%	13.60%	12.55%	13.16%
In-store bakery	1.42%	1.24%	1.43%	1.63%	1.41%
Fresh fish department	1.35%	0.90%	1.25%	1.80%	1.26%
Wine and beer store	7.28%	n/a	9.08%	4.89%	n/a
All other grocery	41.18%	49.48%	40.10%	43.47%	48.15%
Gross Margin Performance					
Prepared meats department	21.45%b	20.86%	21.69%	21.23%	21.81%
Butcher shop	22.63%	n/a	22.74%	21.56%	23.65%
Produce department	31.38%	30.74%	30.10%	32.17%	32.44%
Frozen foods department	26.53%	27.81%	25.98%	25.65%	26.57%
Deli and appetizers shop	39.46%	37.37%	39.70%	39.48%	40.68%
Dairy products department	21.54%	20.36%	21.77%	21.14%	22.42%
In-store bakery	44.57%	45.64%	45.39%	42.75%	44.15%
Fresh fish department	22.63%	24.52%	22.50%	21.62%	22.97%
Wine and beer store	23.33%	n/a	26.40%	19.25%	n/a
All other grocery	19.42%	18.72%	19.57%	19.80%	19.48%

aRead: On average, prepared meats department contributes 15 percent of store sales.
bRead: On average prepared meats department generates a 21 percent gross margin.

Food Store Competition On The Eastern Seaboard

As in most other parts of the country, the food store competition on the East Coast was intense. Following the "oil bust" and the heavy reverse migration from the Sunbelt in the early to mid-1980s, several national chains had either expanded their existing stores and/or opened new stores in the region. Though there was certainly a new vigor in the marketplace, the level and nature of competition in this region was not particularly different from that found in other regions of the country. Notwithstanding this general observation, it was also true that some of the Food4Less stores operated in relatively mature markets of the Eastern seaboard, while others were in sprawling new suburbs. Shoprite and Pathmark, the two key competitors of the Food4Less organization, had both larger, and in some cases, newer stores in or near Food4Less stores' trading areas. These and other competitors also had aggressive pricing policies in the market, which Food4Less had tried to counter with double couponing since early 1982.

Given the high density of population on the Eastern seaboard, it was inevitable that most competitors had overlapping trading areas. Hence, it was not unusual for competing stores to be located within a 1-to-3-mile radius of each other. Also in this region, the food stores typically had higher sales per store compared to conventional stores in other parts of the country. This was, in major part, a reflection of the higher cost of living in this region in general. [Exhibits 4 through 6 summarize some of the key measures of market and competitive structure in the primary trading areas (PTAs) of Food4Less stores.]

There was also some "leakage" of food dollars away from the traditional supermarkets toward the local green grocers and fresh meat/butcher shops.

EXHIBIT 4

Market and Performance Assessment Project: Population and Housing Profile in the Primary Trading Areas

Population and Household Statistics	Net Sales per Square Foot of Selling Area				
	All Stores	$450 or Less	$451–$600	$601–$699	$700 and Over
Population of the primary trading area	36,243[a]	44.467	28,975	37,771	35,712
Number of households in the PTA	12,599	15,688	10,000	13,163	12,291
Average household size	2.89	2.85	2.92	2.86	2.91
Proportion of 1–2 person households	49.41%	50.82%	48.26%	50.80%	48.39%
Proportion of 3+ person households	50.59%	49.18%	51.74%	49.20%	51.61%
Total Number of families in PTA	9,435	11,400	7,590	9,871	9,352
Average family size	3.35	3.36	3.36	3.31	3.37
Proportion of married couples	80.65%	77.39%	82.62%	81.58%	80.52%
Proportion of nonfamily households	22.92%	24.54%	22.13%	23.00%	22.42%
Proportion of African Americans	12.34%	14.21%	10.50%	11.61%	13.17%
Proportion of Irish Americans	15.19%	13.76%	16.41%	15.48%	14.91%
Proportion of Italian Americans	15.32%	14.91%	13.82%	14.81%	17.39%
Proportion white collar	58.57%	53.84%	60.32%	58.61%	60.36%
Median household income	$21,100.29	$18,648.85	$22,276.64	$20,586.90	$22,186.04
Average household income	$24,304.43	$21,754.05	$25,655.76	$23,344.19	$25,639.75
Automotive vehicles per household	1.72	1.62	1.76	1.70	1.76
Median school years completed	12.52	12.31	12.64	12.49	12.60
Proportion completed college	32.60%	28.75%	35.76%	30.91%	33.79%
Rate of unemployment	6.79%	7.87%	6.22%	7.14%	6.26%

Housing Statistics

Proportion of housing units					
Owner occupied	60.62%	52.83%	64.89%	62.40%	61.05%
Renter occupied	33.43%	39.93%	30.01%	29.47%	34.82%
Vacant	4.05%	5.27%	4.09%	4.05%	3.13%
Average housing value	$66,428.99	$60,223.30	$70,422.76	$63,629.38	$69,395.46
Average rent	$259.94	$242.25	$265.36	$249.48	$275.57
Proportion of households who moved to the trading area					
Prior to 1960	19.04%	16.76%	18.06%	19.60%	21.12%
During 1960-1969	20.73%	17.96%	20.38%	21.41%	22.50%
During 1970-1980	60.23%	65.28%	61.56%	58.99%	56.38%
Proportion of housing units built	19.04%	16.76%	18.06%	19.60%	21.12%
Prior to 1960	63.99%	63.64%	59.16%	63.10%	69.20%
During 1960-1969	21.00%	18.41%	22.69%	20.30%	21.86%
During 1970-1980	15.01%	17.95%	18.15%	16.60%	8.94%

[a]Read: The primary trading area for an "average" Food4Less has a population of 36,243 individuals.

Especially in the more heavily ethnic neighborhoods, where there is traditionally stronger store loyalties, these small independents posed a threat to all supermarket operations.

Motivation For The Market and Performance Assessment Project

Each year, the affiliated members get together for a general business meeting to discuss the plans for the coming year, exchange data, and swap stories. According to Bob Allison:

> *In our last year's meeting, a general consensus emerged that we should reassess the status quo, with an eye on the future. Some of the owners were getting nervous upon hearing stories on warehouse or PriceClub-type concepts making inroads onto the East Coast. At the time, there did not appear to be a significant penetration [from these new-wave competitors]. But given the small size of some of our member operators, they were naturally quite concerned. For many, the investment in a Food4Less is their entire life savings. In any case, none of us wanted to be caught with our pants down.*

With these thoughts and other considerations in mind, in late 1984, the corporate office hired a group of consultants, and for the next few months an intense research planning activity ensued. One of the key questions that Food4Less corporate, as well as the individual operators were asking was whether there were certain key conditions, either internal or external, that resulted in superior operating performance; and conversely what, if any,

EXHIBIT 5

Market and Performance Assessment Project: Competitive Market Structure in the Primary Trading Areas

PTA Competitive Market Structure	Net Sales per Square Foot of Selling Area				
	All Stores	$450 or Less	$451–$600	$601–$699	$700 and Over
Annual supermarket volume [$000]	$54,823.1[a]	$54,928.0	$49,597.1	$57,251.8	$57,779.3
Supermarket sales as a percentage of incomes in PTA	21.88%	23.76%	20.44%	23.37%	20.71%
Population per retailer	8,396	9,412	8,039	8,029	8,258
Households per retailer	2,923	3,311	2,774	2,842	2,839
Total competitive retail space (square feet)	86,805	100,130	90,107	80,620	78,993
Population per [000] square foot of retail space	442	430	406	510	430
Households per [000] square foot of retail space	154	152	140	179	149
Aggregate PTA income per retailer	$65,984.7	$63,528.8	$67,001.0	$64,793.0	$67,725.1
Retail square footage per person	3.71	4.70	3.77	3.34	3.23
Retail square footage per household	11.14	14.25	11.43	9.94	9.57
Profile of Competitive Supermarkets					
Number of direct competitors in PTA	3.93	4.45	3.35	3.90	4.11
Average distance from Food4Less (miles)	2.24	2.11	2.27	2.40	2.20
Average number of years in PTA	11.33	10.07	12.68	10.81	11.62
Average size of store (square feet)	22,387	24,450	25,515	20,630	19,599
Average share of space	22.95%	24.90%	22.61%	22.33%	22.55%
Annual sales volume [$000]	$12,322.8	$14,199.8	$12,871.9	$11,604.8	$11,223.1
Weekly sales volume	$236,979.60	$273,072.55	$247,537.34	$223,170.07	$215,829.24
Average share of sales	23.72%	26.01%	22.61%	24.05%	22.86%
Annual sales per selling square foot	$540.69	$480.34	$497.33	$573.62	$595.89
Weekly sales per selling square foot	$10.40	$9.24	$9.56	$11.03	$11.46
Retail square footage per person	2.92	3.80	2.86	2.59	2.58
Retail square footage per household	8.78	11.57	8.67	7.80	7.63

[a] Read: Estimated yearly supermarket sales in the primary trading area for an "average" Food4Less is $54.8 million.

were the conditions that impacted a store's performance adversely. Coming to grips with such factors was significant for several reasons:

- First, to the extent such determinants could be isolated, store location or relocation decisions could be augmented considerably. If, for example, certain demographic and competitive conditions, in themselves or in combination, generally resulted in poor sales or profit performance, such market areas could be avoided in future store location decisions. Conversely, those areas with superior performance potential could be more actively sought.
- Second, if such parameters could be found, the corporate office would have a much easier time providing guidelines for improvement to those members who had negative contribution to the group. Or, if there were significant barriers for improvement, a case could be made for closing or relocating a store.

To the extent that an affiliated member was not performing well, it impacted the more profitable operators since they would be contributing more than their fair share of the group overhead. For a typical Food4Less, the

EXHIBIT 6

Market and Performance Assessment Project: Food4Less Stores Market Position in the Primary Trading Areas

Food4Less Competitive Position in PTA	Net Sales per Square Foot of Selling Area				
	All Stores	$450 or Less	$451–$600	$601–$699	$700 and Over
Share of sales in PTA	27.09%[a]	23.06%	33.73%	23.32%	26.65%
Share of space in PTA	27.68%	22.69%	32.39%	29.10%	25.82%
Share of PTA incomes	4.08%	2.91%	4.10%	4.38%	4.67%
Weekly sales as a percentage of PTA average	97.09%	65.73%	89.12%	97.31%	126.70%
Selling space as a percentage of PTA average	109.29%	105.53%	102.93%	108.85%	118.22%
Age of store as a percentage of PTA average	147.39%	160.22%	202.29%	109.59%	123.96%
Aggregate PTA income per GLA square foot	$14,642.34	$16,321.26	$11,935.06	$15,548.93	$15,180.39
Aggregate PTA income per selling square foot	$19,045.61	$21,432.20	$15,842.19	$19,734.66	$19,684.32
Population per [1000] square foot of GLA	1,182	2,455	1,400	1,953	1,849
Households per [1000] square foot of GLA	657	881	474	685	640

EXHIBIT 6

Continued

Food4Less Versus the Top Competitor[b]	Net Sales per Square Foot of Selling Area				
	All Stores	$450 or Less	$451–$600	$601–$699	$700 and Over
Location	3.3	2.6	2.8	3.9	4.0
Accessibility	3.5	2.8	3.4	3.7	3.8
Perceived prestige	3.6	3.2	3.4	3.9	3.9
Cleanliness	4.9	4.7	4.8	4.8	5.3
Availability of parking	2.9	2.7	2.6	3.1	3.0
Speed of customer checkout	4.2	3.7	4.1	4.2	4.7
Interior design	3.7	3.6	3.8	3.8	3.8
Displays	4.6	4.0	4.4	5.0	5.0
Store atmosphere	4.2	4.0	4.0	4.0	4.6
Store size	2.6	2.2	2.6	2.6	2.9
Assortments	3.2	3.0	2.9	3.4	3.4
Number of checkouts	3.0	2.4	2.9	3.1	3.3
Amount of advertising	3.5	3.3	3.4	3.5	3.6
Overall prices	3.3	3.0	3.4	3.5	3.2
Value for money	3.6	3.3	3.4	4.2	3.6
Weekly specials	3.5	3.1	3.6	3.7	3.4
Deli department	4.5	3.6	4.1	5.2	4.9
Bakery department	3.4	3.2	3.4	3.7	3.4
Produce quality	4.7	4.2	4.6	4.8	5.0
Meat quality	5.0	4.7	5.1	5.0	5.0
Quality of employees	4.3	4.6	4.1	4.3	4.3
Courtesy of employees	4.9	4.8	4.8	4.5	5.3

[a] Read: An "average" Food4Less has 27 percent of supermarket sales in the primary trading area.
[b] Average of ratings given to Food4Less stores (compared to their key competitor in their PTA) by each store manager: A score of 1–2 indicates a "very unfavorable" rating. A score of 6–7 indicates a "very favorable" rating for the Food4Less store in question.

current contribution rate for corporate overhead averaged about 2 to 3 percent of gross store sales.

Presently, there were a number of Food4Less members who had been consistently losing money over the past several years, while others were generating sales per square foot in excess of $1,000—equaling or exceeding the highest quartile performers in the industry. This disparity in operating performance was one of the key reasons for the group members to push for a major research effort. Given the favorable economics of the region in recent years, there was also the fear that, if some of these stores could not be turned around, they probably would be unable to survive in an increasingly more competitive environment. This situation, of course, could potentially have an adverse effect on all Food4Less stores, because some of the efficiencies and scales realized by the corporate organization would be eroded significantly.

The Research Plan

In order to provide some answers to these and other questions, a significant amount of information on the financial and operating characteristics of each store, as well as data on a number of market-based factors, were needed. Working with the consultants, the following research plan and associated instruments were devised:

1. *A survey of store operations* was to be implemented at the store level for every member. This survey would include a complete income statement for each store for its most recent fiscal year and a balance sheet for the corresponding year end. Also, this instrument would have a sales breakdown by individual departments, as well as margin information for each of the departments in the store. Furthermore, an operating profile of the stores, including such items as the number of customer checkout counters, part- and full-time employees; annual staff turnover; parking spaces available to the customers, and a host of other variables, would also be obtained for each store in the group.

2. *A competitive audit* was also to be implemented for each store, with the purpose of collecting information on all the competitors in the primary and secondary trading areas. Thus, for each Food4Less location, there would be information on the size of each of the competitors, their weekly and yearly volumes; and their location and distance to the focal Food4Less. Furthermore, a qualitative evaluation of the top three competitors on some 20-odd dimensions would be obtained, comparing each competitor with the Food4Less store of interest. These measures could then be used in better understanding the competitive position of each vis-à-vis their major competitors, in their respective market areas.

3. *A demographic survey* of each store's trading area was also to be undertaken. The data for this purpose would include the standard socio-economic scales (e.g., income, occupation, ethnic composition, etc.), as well as population and household count and size distribution, level of employment, and mobility (migration) into or out of the trading area. Also to be included as part of this survey was a housing profile, including such information as the number of housing units, average values of homes or rents, and vacancy rates.

4. *A consumer research study* was to be implemented to gather information on primary and secondary customers' store choice criteria in the general market area where Food4Less stores were clustered. Given the number of stores, and the required sample sizes to make reasonable inferences, it was decided that it was best to gather these data for a limited number of stores in key states and in those market areas where Food4Less had significant membership.

Execution of Research

Following the establishment of basic research objectives and parameters, all effort was directed, for the first six months in 1985, toward the collection of the data and the verification of the collected data.

For the research effort to have a uniform basis for comparison at the store level, the consultants, along with the corporate staff, carefully reviewed each store's trading area. An exit study of shoppers in each Food4Less, sampled randomly, was used to determine the primary trading areas (PTAs) of each of the stores. Operationally, the PTA was defined as the geographical boundary within which the focal store drew 80 percent or more of its revenues. Predictably, many stores had quite distinct trading area shapes and boundaries, which in some cases, closely approximated a circle with a 1- or 2-mile radius, while for others quite diverse shapes and sizes emerged. Ultimately, these boundaries were used to complete both the competitive audit and the population and housing surveys. In this fashion, both the competitive audit data and the demographic data could be merged and mixed to produce new measures of interest, such as retail space per household or aggregate household income or population per square mile (see Exhibits 4 and 5).

By early August 1985, the consultants had finished their work on data collection and analyses. Throughout the months of August and September, a number of executive briefing conferences were set up to discuss the findings of the research with the senior executives (and a few key owners sitting on the board). Today's meeting attended by Bob Allison and Rick Wold was the last briefing conference in the series. The next meeting, which was to take place in mid-November, was the annual owners conference, at which time the key conclusions from the research undertaken had to be communicated to the affiliated members, and a new strategic plan had to be unveiled for the next five years.

Monday Night Meeting

After a long and exhaustive day, Bob Allison and Rick Wold got together in Bob's hotel suite to discuss the game plan for the upcoming annual meeting. Throughout the year, Rick Wold had been gathering a variety of reports from the Market and Performance Assessment Project, but he was especially keen on a series of exhibits that the consultants had prepared for the meeting earlier in the day. (Some of key elements from these exhibits are reproduced here as Exhibits 1 through 6.)

In these exhibits, each Food4Less store was assigned into one of four space productivity groups (calculated on sales area of each store) ranging from very low to low, and from high to very high. In effect, each of these columns contained a "profile" of the *poorly performing* ($450/square foot or less); *low performing* ($451–$600/square foot); *good performing* ($601–$699/square foot); and *excellent performing* ($700/square foot or more) Food4Less operations. Also included in each exhibit was a column representing all

Food4Less Stores that could be used as a "base-line case" for all figures to be compared.

Though such breakdowns were available based on many other performance criteria, Rick Wold wanted to limit the discussion to sales per square foot as the critical dependent variable. According to Wold's "reading," nearly all of the other measures, such as net or gross profit as a percentage of sales, profits per square foot, or return on (controllable) assets [ROCA], appeared to support similar conclusions.

Though Allison was in general agreement, he thought one of the "limitations" of these exhibits was that they had no information from the consumer research study (of Food4Less customers). Wold was quick to point out, however, that the consumer research in six Food4Less regions had indicated that the store choice behavior among the Eastern seaboard consumers was quite consistent with research results already widely reported in various trade and academic journals. There was, according to Wold, no "new" news there for the owners. Allison agreed, but he still believed that some of the implications of this research should be tied to the information presented in the exhibits Wold had put together. (Some of the highlights from the Consumer Research Study are summarized in Exhibit 7).

Looking at these exhibits and other results from the consultants' work, Allison was decidedly more enthusiastic: "There may be a simple story-line to all this mass of data after all," he mused to himself. Looking at the reams and reams of data and listening to the consultants early in the day, he had become increasingly disturbed, and at times, utterly confused as to what to make of this "stuff." The exhibits Rick Wold had gathered certainly made it easier to put together a comprehensive and consistent action plan which hopefully would be well received by the corporate and the owners. As it passed midnight, Bob Allison turned to Rick Wold:

> *Rick, I think we have here the beginnings of a dynamite report for the owners. I also think we can make a strong case as to why some stores are doing well while others are doing so miserably. Since you seem to have made more headway in putting these things together, you should generate a first draft of an* Executive Briefing Document *that we can circulate to the senior people at Corporate, before we go "public" with it to the owners. I think there is more than enough meat here for you to work with. I will let you decide on the format as to how this report should be organized. However, I think the first section of your report should include a review of the determinants of performance for Food4Less, and based on your conclusions in this section, you should also outline a plan of action for the next planning horizon.*

That evening, Rick Wold returned to his hotel suite well past midnight. Having agreed to generate a first draft by early November, he knew he had not much time to waste. He called room service for a double Chivas and laid out all the exhibits on his bed. "If we can't win this thing on style," he thought, "we sure will get them [owners] on content."

EXHIBIT 7

Food4Less Consumer Research Study: Selected Findings

Supermarkets Shopped

- One-third (33 percent) of Food4Less' regular customers shopped at a Shoprite store during the past four weeks, while one-quarter (25 percent) shopped at a Pathmark store.
- Thirty-five percent of Shoprite's regular customers shopped at a Food4Less store while almost a third (32 percent) visited a Pathmark store within the past month.
- Thirty-two percent of Pathmark's regular customers shopped at a Food4Less store, while 41 percent shopped at a Shoprite store.
- Over the past six months to a year there has been a slight drop in the percentage of Shoprite and Pathmark customers "occasionally" shopping at Food4Less stores.

Reasons for Store Patronage

- The major reason for customers to *shop at Food4Less regularly* continues to be *"convenient location."* The primary reasons for shopping regularly at Shoprite and Pathmark remains *"convenient location"* and *"price."*
- As in previous years, *high prices* continue to be the primary reason for *shopping at Food4Less only occasionally and not regularly;* however, "price" complaints appear to have declined since early 1985.
- "Inconvenient location," "more familiar with another store," "pick up odds and ends", "and poor selection and variety" are also mentioned frequently as the major reasons for *shopping at Food4Less only occasionally.* "Inconvenient location" and "high prices" continue to be the major reasons for *not shopping Food4Less at all.*

Store Ratings

- A comparison of the regular customers of Food4Less rating Food4Less "excellent" to the same ratings by the regular customers of Shoprite and Pathmark show that:
  - Food4Less continues to rate superior to both Pathmark and Shoprite in the area of *"convenient location."* Food4Less also rates superior to Shoprite and Pathmark in *"courteous/helpful employees," clean store,"* and *"always having ad items in stock."*
  - Food4Less's ratings are lower than Pathmark's and Shoprite's on the following 7 [of the 23] supermarket characteristics considered:
    - All needs under one roof
    - Large variety/selection
    - Advertised sales/specials
    - Money's worth in fresh produce
    - Good prices private label
    - Low everyday prices
    - Low grocery prices

> - Food4Less rates lower than Pathmark on the following eight supermarket characteristics:
>   - Convenient store hours
>   - Clean stores
>   - Fresh produce
>   - Good coupons (excluding doubles and triples)
>   - Good quality private label
>   - Always carrying items wanted
>   - Money's worth in meats
> - There is no statistically significant difference between the percentage excellent ratings of Food4Less versus Pathmark and Shoprite on the following characteristics
>   - Pleasant shopping environment
>   - Delicatessen selection/quality
>   - Top quality meats
>   - Quick checkout
>   - Never running out of items wanted
>
> Source: Consumer Tracking Study, Food4Less Stores, Inc., internal report, Spring 1985.

QUESTIONS

1. Based on the research findings, identify the key determinants of space productivity (sales per square foot).
2. To be able to compete more effectively in the future, do you believe Food4Less should change its market positioning?
3. What additional services might the co-op provide to store owners to help them compete more effectively?

CASE 27

Kenneth L. Bernhardt
Georgia State University

RICH'S DEPARTMENT STORE*

The executive committee meeting had been a lengthy session, lasting through most of the morning, but Mr. Dick Mills, vice-president and sales promotion director of Rich's Department Store, had returned to his office knowing that a major advertising decision was still not ready to be made. In addition, Mr. Mills realized that it would be his responsibility to submit a final recommendation on media strategy at the next meeting.

Mr. Mills stared at the two neatly bound research reports that he had placed side by side on his desk. The pair of documents represented summaries of the two presentations that had been made to the Rich's executive committee that morning. These studies had been based on exactly the same

---

*© 1988. Used with permission.

data, drawn from the same in-store survey of Rich's customers. Each report had been prepared by an experienced and professional marketing researcher. Mr. Mills had expected the strong self-interests of the researchers to be reflected in their presentations and interpretations of the survey results, but he was confident that neither man would misrepresent the actual facts.

Mr. Mills had to admit to himself that he had been very surprised at the apparent major contradictions between the two presentations that he had heard earlier that morning. Mr. Mills and the research director of Rich's, who had also attended the morning presentations by the two outside researchers, had discussed the situation briefly after the meeting. The two men had decided to separately review the written reports and, then, to meet later in the afternoon to decide what additional steps to take.

Before rereading the reports, Mr. Mills thought back over the events of the past three months that had eventually led to this situation.

Rich's Department Store was both the largest merchant and the largest single advertiser in Atlanta, Georgia. The store had been founded in 1867 and had grown to an annual sales volume of approximately $200 million through its downtown store and six branch stores located in major suburban shopping centers. The Rich's market share was 40 percent of department store sales in Atlanta and 25 percent of all general-merchandise sales.

The Rich's advertising strategy in the past had been to emphasize newspaper advertising for specific sales items and to utilize broadcast media primarily for image purposes. Newspaper was also used for some image-oriented advertising, with occasional direct mailings used to promote specific sales items of merchandise. Rich's is the largest local advertiser in both print and broadcast media.

The two principal daily newspapers in Atlanta are the *Atlanta Journal* (evenings) and the *Atlanta Constitution* (mornings). These are two of the largest circulation newspapers in the South, and both have distinguished journalism traditions, including Pulitzer Prizes. Although both newspapers are owned by the same company, Atlanta Newspapers, Inc., there is little overlap of readership except for the combined Sunday morning edition.

There are 6 television stations and 40 radio stations in the Atlanta market. However, broadcast media are dominated by WSB-TV and WSB Radio, both of which are owned by Cox Broadcasting Corporation.

Mr. Mills recalled that several months earlier, executives of Cox Broadcasting and of their two local stations had met with key executives of Rich's. One topic discussed at the meeting had been possible use of broadcast media to promote individual sales items. WSB had offered to participate with Rich's in a market test to determine the abilities of different media to sell specific items of merchandise.

As a result of these discussions, Mr. Mills had held a series of meetings with Mr. Jim Landon, research director of WSB-TV and Radio, and Mr. Ferguson Rood, research director of the Atlanta Newspapers, Inc., to design the market test. It was eventually decided to conduct the test during Rich's annual Harvest Sale, which has been the merchandising highlight of the year since 1925. This sale runs for two weeks each fall. The test was to center on 10 specific items of merchandise which would be advertised in both print and broadcast media during the first three days of the sale. During the same period, in-store interviews would be conducted by professional interviewers, with all purchasers of these 10 items in three representative stores (see the appendixes for detailed survey design, sample questionnaire, and media plan).

At the conclusion of the survey period, the research departments of both Atlanta Newspapers, Inc., and WSB were furnished duplicate computer disks by Rich's containing survey data. It was these data that served as the basis for the presentations that Jim Landon and Ferguson Rood had made to the Rich's executive committee. Excerpts from *the Atlanta Journal* and *Constitution* are presented in Appendix A, and excerpts from the WSB report are presented in Appendix B.

These were the two presentations that Mr. Mills would have to reconcile to arrive at a decision about future media strategy for Rich's. Mr. Mills knew that a decision would have to be made quickly, in view of television production lead times, if any change in media mix were to be considered for the upcoming Christmas sales season.

QUESTIONS

1. What are the major conclusions that can be drawn from the Atlanta Journal and Constitution research report? What conclusions can be drawn from the WSB research report? Are there any conflicts or discrepancies in these two research reports and their findings?
2. Should Rich's Department Store change its media mix?

APPENDIX A An Analysis of Rich's In-Store Study of Advertising Effectiveness on Specific Purchase Decisions*

Foreword

This report is the result of an innovative research study conducted by Rich's Department Store in partnership with Atlanta Newspapers, Inc., and Cox Broadcasting Corporation.

The study was designed to measure:

1. The relative performance of newspapers, television, and radio as a source of influence on shoppers' decisions to purchase specific items.
2. Shoppers' exposure to specific item advertising messages.

---

*Presented by the Atlanta Journal and Constitution Research and Marketing Department.

The advertising period covered in this study consisted of the first three days (beginning Sunday, September 20) of Rich's annual Harvest Sale.

A total of 2,176 interviews were made on Monday and Tuesday, September 21 and 22. The interviews were made in three of Rich's seven stores—Downtown, Lenox Square, and Greenbriar, and focused on the 10 departments in each store where the advertised items were sold.

An Atlanta interviewing firm was employed by Rich's to interview shoppers in each department immediately after they made their purchase. To qualify for the survey, shoppers had to purchase the specific advertised item or a directly related item.

Summary and Interpretation

- More than 9 out of 10 shoppers covered in this survey had the specific purchase in mind before going to Rich's, or knew it was on *special*.
- Three-fourths of all shoppers recalled being recently exposed to advertising messages for specific items.
- More than half of all shoppers' decisions to purchase specific items were attributed to advertising.
- Attributions to newspapers were more than twice those of television and radio combined in influencing specific item purchase decisions (71 percent versus 33 percent).
- Dollar for dollar . . . newspapers delivered more than three times the influence on specific item purchase decisions than television and radio combined.
- The advertising schedule placed in newspapers . . . was conspicuously more effective and more efficient . . . in influencing specific purchase decisions . . . than the saturation schedule placed on television and radio.

The results of this report are based on an analysis of the data presented in Exhibits A.1 through A.16.

EXHIBIT A.1
Newspaper Advertising Schedule[a]

	Sunday Journal and Constitution (inches)	A.M. Constitution (inches)	P.M. Journal (inches)
Sunday	1,064		
Monday		172	247
Tuesday		0	505
Total	1,064	172	752

[a] 1,989 column inches, the equivalent of 11.6 pages, made up the newspaper schedule covered in this survey.

Case 27 Rich's Department Store

EXHIBIT A.2
Broadcast Schedule[a]

	Television			Radio		
	Sunday	Monday	Tuesday	Sunday	Monday	Tuesday
6 a.m.		x			x	x
7		x			x	x
8		x	x		x	x
9		x	x	x	x	x
10		x		x	x	x
11		x			x	x
12		x	x	x	x	x
1 p.m.	x	x	x	x	x	x
2	x	x	x	x	x	x
3	x	x	x	x	x	x
4	x	x	x	x	x	x
5	x	x	x	x	x	x
6	x	x		x	x	
7	x	x		x	x	
8	x	x				
9	x	x				
10	x	x				
11	x	x				
Total spots	42	86	49	53	121	87
Average number per schedule hour	3.8	4.8	6.1	5.3	8.6	7.2

[a]438 thirty-second spots were scheduled to run on five television and five radio stations, for an average of eight spots per hour, between 6 a.m. and 11 p.m. over the three-day period.

EXHIBIT A.3
Comparison of Advertising Schedule and Budget

	Broadcast Spots			Newspaper Space (inches)
	Television	Radio	Total	
Hard goods				
Mattresses	12	19	31	35
Carpeting	12	23	35	150
Draperies	16	26	42	407
Vacuum cleaners	15	22	37	172
Color televisions*	0	0	0	150
Soft goods				
Handbags	15	27	42	189
Girdles†	15	27	42	0
Shoes	15	27	42	398
Shirts*	56	64	120	86
Pant sets	21	26	47	400

EXHIBIT A.3 Continued

	Broadcast Spots			Newspaper Space (inches)
	Television	Radio	Total	
Total 10 departments				
Sunday	42	53	95	1,064
Monday	86	121	207	420
Tuesday	49	87	136	505
Total	177	261	438	1,989
Budget			$27,158	$16,910

*The original broadcast schedule included 20 TV and 24 radio spots for the color television sets to run Tuesday. Since all the sets were sold on Monday, this commercial time was switched to shirts.
†While no Playtex girdle ads were scheduled to run in newspapers, other foundation advertising during the test period supported the influence.

EXHIBIT A.4 Interviews

	Number	Percentage
Total	2,175	100%
Women	1,764	81
Men	380	18
Couples	31	1
Under 35	963	44
35–49	817	39
50 and over	394	18
White	1,966	90
Nonwhite	209	10
Hard goods	527	24
Mattresses	71	3
Carpeting	45	2
Draperies	123	6
Vacuum cleaners	134	6
Color televisions	154	7
Soft goods	1,649	75
Handbags	284	13
Girdles	249	11
Shoes	393	18
Shirts	483	22
Pant suits	240	11
Distribution of interviews by store		
Downtown	683	31
Lenox Square	848	39
Greenbriar	645	30

EXHIBIT A.5
Question 1

"Before coming to Rich's today, did you have in mind buying this specific brand/item, or did you decide after you came into the store?"

- Sixty-three percent of all shoppers had the specific purchase in mind before going to Rich's.

These shoppers described the following as sources of influence on their buying decision when asked: "What was it that gave you the idea to buy this brand/item?"

Advertising	52%
Needed or wanted it	23
Past experience with it	16
Outside source suggestion	6
Other	7

EXHIBIT A.6
Question 2

"Was the store having a special on this specific brand/item today, or were they selling at the regular price?"

Eighty-four percent of all shoppers said the brand/item was on special.

These shoppers gave the following sources when asked: "Where did you learn about that?"

Advertising	63%
Store display/crowds	27
Outside source	6
Other	4

EXHIBIT A.7
Advertising Influence

Fifty-five percent of all shoppers attributed their specific purchase decision to advertising. Of these, 71 percent attributed their purchase to newspapers, 33 percent to broadcasts (28 percent to television and 9 percent to radio), and 9 percent to mail circulars.

Newspapers and broadcast accounted for 94 percent of all advertising influence. Sixty-one percent of these influences were attributed to newspapers exclusive of broadcast. Twenty-three percent were attributed to broadcast exclusive of newspapers, and 10 percent were attributed to both.

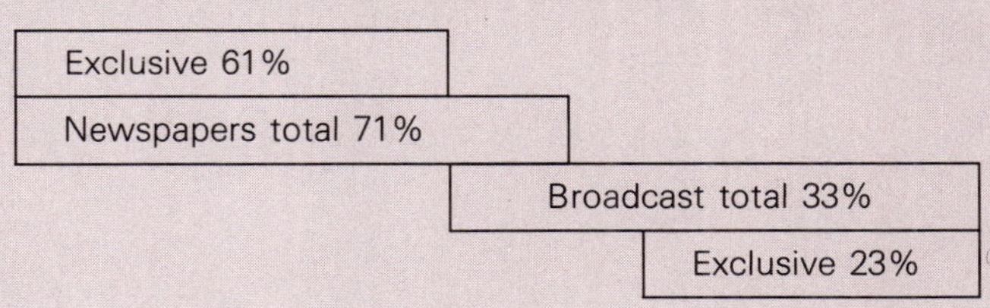

```
| Exclusive 61%        |
| Newspapers total 71%    |
            | Broadcast total 33%  |
                | Exclusive 23% |
```

EXHIBIT A.8
Advertising Influence

Newspapers and television accounted for 90 percent of all advertising influence. Sixty-two percent of these influences were attributed to newspapers exclusive of television. Nineteen percent were attributed to television exclusive of newspapers, and 9 percent were attributed to both.

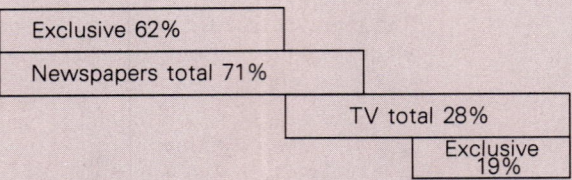

Newspapers and radio accounted for 77 percent of all advertising influence. Sixty-eight percent of these influences were attributed to newspapers exclusive of radio. Six percent were attributed to radio exclusive of newspapers, and 3 percent were attributed to both.

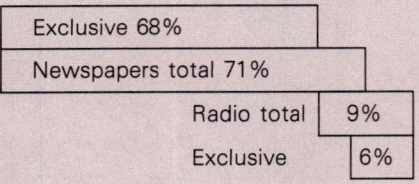

EXHIBIT A.9

Advertising Influence—By Shopper Demographics (among the 55 percent of all shoppers who were influenced by advertising)

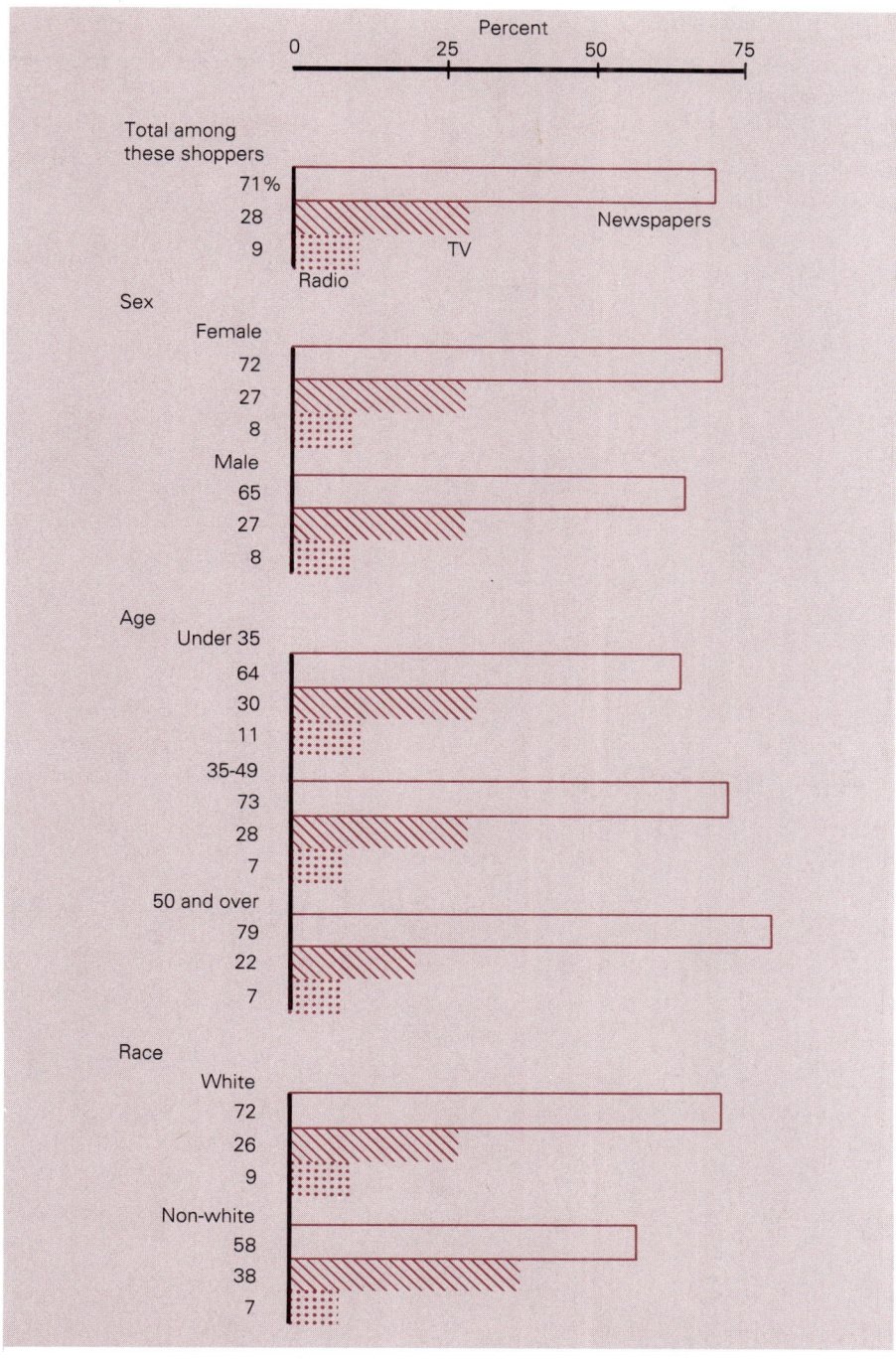

EXHIBIT A.10

Advertising Influence—By Shopper Patterns (among the 55 percent of all shoppers who were influenced by advertising)

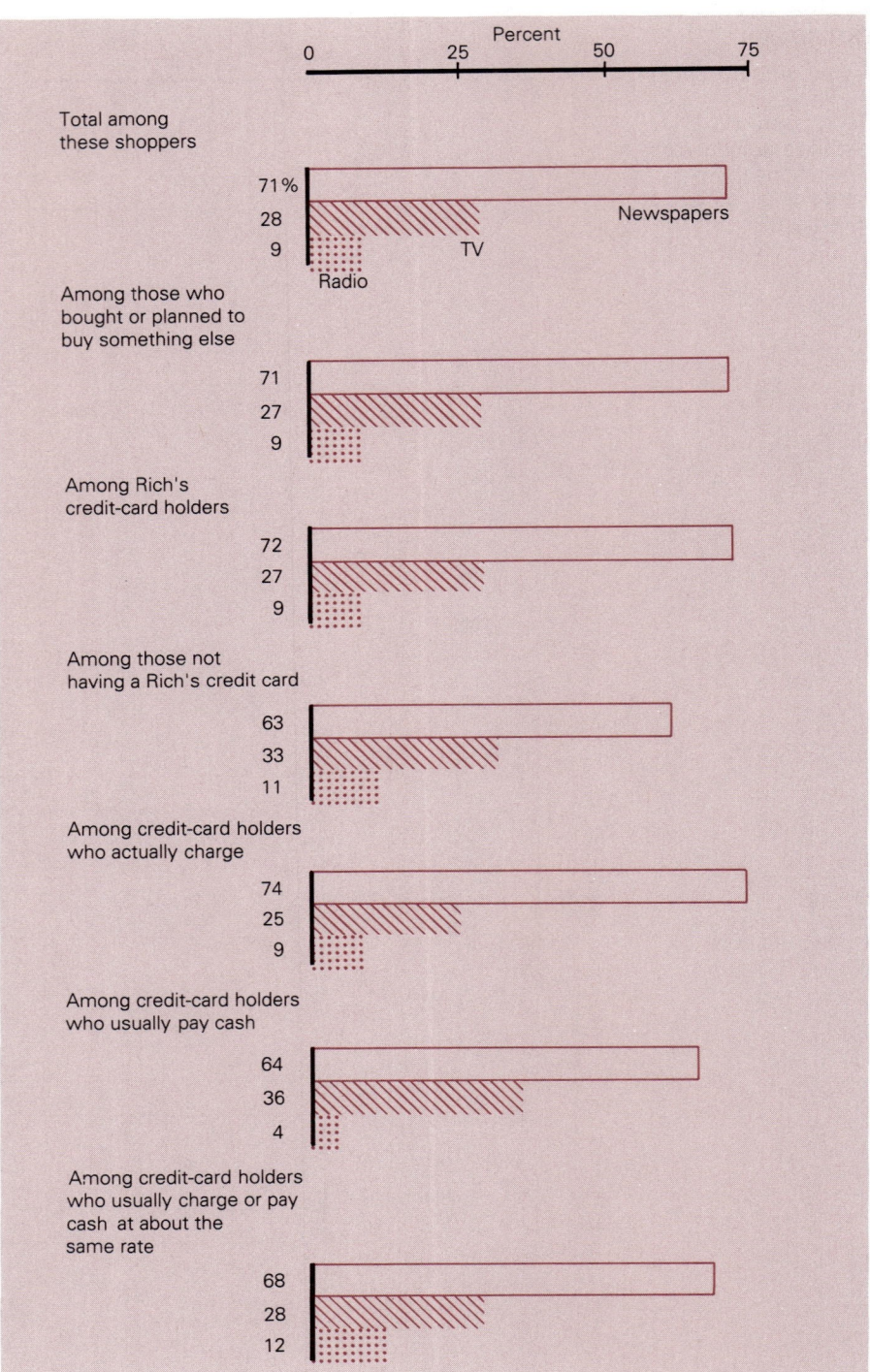

EXHIBIT A.11

Share of Budget Versus Share of Influence

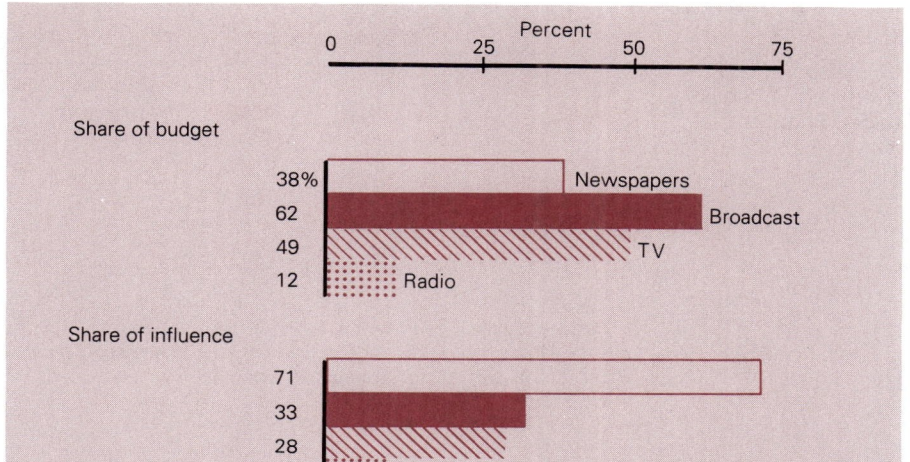

EXHIBIT A.12

Newspapers/Broadcast Share of Influence Versus Share of Budget by Departments

	Newspapers		Broadcast	
	Share of Influence	Share of Budget	Share of Influence	Share of Budget
Total	71%	38%	33%	62%
Hard goods	77	45	30	55
Mattresses	43	11	69	89
Carpeting	83	39	23	61
Draperies	83	56	22	44
Vacuum cleaners	70	25	45	75
Color televisions	99	100	1	—
Soft goods	68	34	34	66
Handbags	68	41	27	59
Girdles	28	—	74	100
Shoes	87	54	25	46
Shirts	63	12	36	88
Pant suits	82	53	16	47

EXHIBIT A.13

Comparison of Advertising Schedule/Budget/Shopper Influence[a]

	Broadcast Spots		Newspaper Space		
	Television	Radio	Journal-Constitution	Constitution	Journal
Schedule					
Sunday	42	53	1,064		
Monday	86	121		172	248
Tuesday	49	87		0	505
	177	261	1,064	172	753

[a]438 broadcast spots versus 1,989 inches; budget—$27,158 for broadcast spots versus $16,910 for newspaper space; and shopper influence—33 percent for broadcast spots versus 71 percent for newspaper space.

EXHIBIT A.14

Advertising Exposure

- 74 percent of all shoppers recalled being exposed to specific advertising messages within the past day or two. Of these, 79 percent recalled newspapers, 53 percent recalled broadcasts (46 percent television, 18 percent radio), and 24 percent recalled mail circulars.
- Newspapers and broadcast accounted for 96 percent of all advertising messages. Forty-three percent recalled newspapers exclusive of broadcast. Seventeen percent recalled broadcast exclusive of newspapers, and 36 percent recalled both.

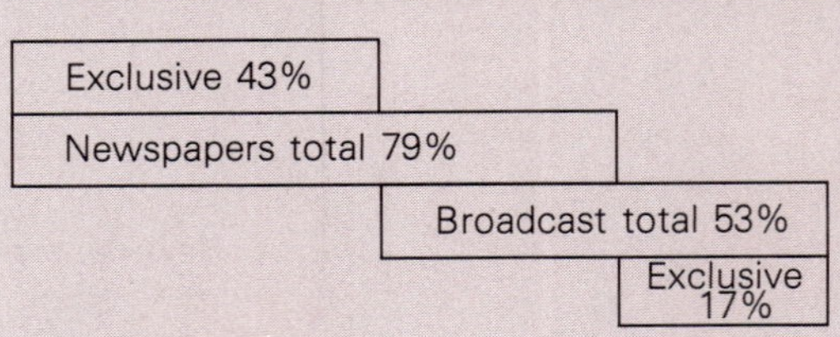

```
┌─────────────────────────┐
│ Exclusive 43%           │
├─────────────────────────┴──────┐
│ Newspapers total 79%           │
└────────────┬───────────────────┴────────┐
             │ Broadcast total 53%         │
             └──────────────────┬──────────┤
                                │ Exclusive│
                                │   17%    │
                                └──────────┘
```

EXHIBIT A.15

Advertising Exposure

- Newspapers and television accounted for 93 percent of all advertising messages. Forty-seven percent recalled newspapers exclusive of television. Fourteen percent recalled television exclusive of newspapers, and 32 percent recalled both.

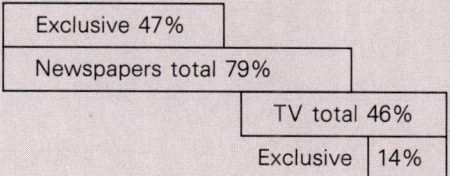

- Newspapers and radio accounted for 85 percent of all advertising messages: Sixty-seven percent recalled newspapers exclusive of radio. Six percent recalled radio exclusive of newspapers, and 12 percent recalled both.

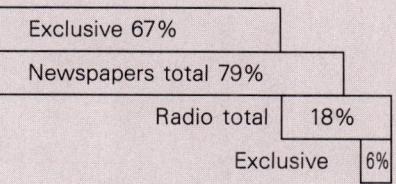

EXHIBIT A.16

Harvest Sale In-Store Customer Survey

Questionnaire   HARVEST SALE IN-STORE CUSTOMER SURVEY

Interviewer Name: _____ (1-2)   STORE: ....Downtown.........Lenox..........Greenbriar (3)
                                                                                                                1   2   3

DATE: M   T   W   TIME OF INTERVIEW _____ DEPARTMENT _____ (6)
            1   2   3   (4)   (5)

Hello. We're conducting a short survey among RICH'S customers:

1. What did you buy in this department today? _____ (7-8)
                                                                                 (PROBE, BRAND, STYLE)

2. Before coming to RICH'S today, did you have in mind buying this specific brand/item, or did you decide after you came into the store?

    HAD IN MIND.......☐1   DECIDED IN STORE.......☐2   SKIP TO Q. NO. 3   (9)

    What was it that gave you the idea to buy this brand/item? _____

    (IF APPROPRIATE, ASK: Where did you learn about that?) _____ (10-11)

3. Was the store having a special on this specific brand/item today, or were they selling at the regular price?

    SPECIAL.......☐1   REGULAR PRICE.......☐2   SKIP TO Q. NO. 4   (12)

    Where did you learn about that? _____ (13-14)

4. Do you recall seeing or hearing any advertising within the past day or two on radio or in the newspapers or in a mail circular that may have reminded you or helped you decide to buy this _____ today?

    YES.......☐1   NO.......☐2   SKIP TO Q. NO. 5   (15)

    a. Where did you see or hear it?   (16)

	4a. UNAIDED RECALL	5. AIDED RECALL	
		YES	NO, DK
RADIO	1	1	2	(17)
NEWSPAPERS	2	1	2	(18)
TELEVISION	3	1	2	(19)
MAIL CIRCULAR	4	1	2	(20)
OTHER, DON'T KNOW	5		

ASK FOR EACH MEDIUM NOT CHECKED IN Q. NO. 4a.

5. Did you happen to see or hear any of the following within the past day or two: A radio commercial for this specific _____ ? A newspaper ad for this specific _____ ? A television commercial for this specific _____ ? A mail circular for this specific _____ ?

6. Have you bought anything else at RICH'S today, or do you plan to buy anything else at RICH'S today?
    YES.......☐1   NO.......☐2

7. Do you (or your wife/husband) have a RICH'S credit card?   YES.......☐1   NO.......☐2   (21-22)

    a. Do you usually charge or pay cash for most of your purchases at RICH'S?
    CHARGE.......☐1   CASH.......☐2   SAME.......☐3   (23)

8. What is the name of the county where you live? _____ OUT-OF-STATE.......☐ (24-25-26)

    ESTIMATE AGE   UNDER 35 YEARS.......☐1   SEX: FEMALE...☐1   RACE: WHITE............☐1   (27)
                              35 – 49...................☐2   MALE ....☐2   NONWHITE...☐2   (28)
                              50+...........................☐3   (29)

APPENDIX B An Analysis of Rich's In-Store Survey*

Introduction

First, we would like to state that WSB television and radio were pleased to have the opportunity to participate in this research effort with Rich's. We have one basic characteristic in common with Rich's—both WSB-TV and WSB Radio, like Rich's, are dominant in the Atlanta market. Like Rich's, we are an Atlanta institution and have enjoyed dominance since our origination.

In this presentation, we will not attempt to interpret the results of your research from a marketing standpoint. You have your own market research department, and we are sure that it has done a capable job of analyzing and interpreting the results of the study from that aspect. Instead, we will concentrate on interpreting the results from a media standpoint, which is our particular area of experience.

The following pages contain our detailed analysis of this research for Rich's management.

Pre-Harvest Sale Advertising Weight

Rich's pre–Harvest Sale was heavily promoted with a "mix" of three media: radio, television, and newspaper.

On the broadcast side, Rich's ran 261 radio spots on five stations and 177 television spots on five stations promoting 10 different items during a three-day period. It can be estimated that the total radio campaign reached about 90 percent of the Atlanta adult metro population, with the average listener exposed to seven commercial announcements (all products combined). The total television campaign also reached an estimated 90 percent of the Atlanta adult population, with the average viewer exposed to 10 commercial announcements.

The newspaper campaign consisted of 13 ads for the specific items and 11 ads for related (same item but different price than in the radio and television commercial) items, or a total of 24 ads representing 1,987 inches of space in the *Journal* and *Constitution*. Rich's also ran 6,140 inches of other newspaper advertising during the three-day period. We have no way of estimating the reach and frequency of the newspaper ads.

Pre-Harvest Sale A Success

Rich's total advertising effort helped make the store's pre–Harvest Sale a tremendous success.

---

*Presented by WSB-TV, WSB Radio, and Cox Broadcasting Research.

Monday, September 21, and Tuesday, September 22, were two of Rich's biggest days of the year according to traffic and sales volume. As far as we know, the departments participating in the test were all up considerably in sales volume compared to a year ago.

Unfortunately, sales results for the *specific items* tested were not available. However, it is our understanding that the departmentwide sales results reflected the success of the individual items in those departments that were tested.

The advertising effort for the pre-Harvest Sale represented one of the few times that Rich's has used a media mix for *item selling*. Radio and television have been used extensively by Rich's for institutional advertising and to announce sale events, but item selling has been limited in the past primarily to newspaper and direct mail. *The media mix for item selling worked from a sales results standpoint.*

Summary of Media Recall Findings

After analyzing the results of the survey, we found the following to be the most significant findings:

1. Because of the confusion and particularly the conditioning factor regarding newspaper, the three media cannot be completely compared in recall.
2. Recall for both radio and television was significantly higher on Tuesday versus Monday, indicating that the broadcast media were building in impact on customers. Sales results were also generally better on Tuesday versus Monday.
3. Both radio and television did *best* in recall (compared to newspaper) for items having the *least* amount of newspaper advertising. Radio and TV did *poorest* for items having the *greatest* amount of newspaper advertising.
4. In general, items where radio and television did *best* in recall (compared to newspaper) had better sales results than items where radio and television did poorest.
5. All three media performed better among high-priced items and for items where customers decided to buy before coming into the store.
6. Radio and television balanced newspaper quite well by reaching younger adults than the print medium.

See Exhibits B.1 through B.3.

Three Types of Media Recall in the Study

The questionnaire used in Rich's in-store survey obtained information about customers' recall of advertising media in three areas:

1. *Idea to buy.* For customers purchasing the item being tested, those that indicated having in mind buying that specific merchandise before coming to the store were asked *what gave them the idea to buy the item.* In this question, answers involving media came from top-of-mind recall (not

EXHIBIT B.1
Summary of Newspaper Recall

Item	Budget	Day/Ads			Got Idea	Learned of Special	Direct Recall
Draperies	$4,412	Sun/2	Tues/2		48%	68%	81%
Pant suits	3,359	Sun/2	Mon/1	Tues/3	50	56	63
Shoes	2,834	Sun/1	Mon/2	Tues/1	48	55	72
Handbags	1,670	Sun/1	Tues/1		30	30	60
Carpeting	1,503	Sun/1			61	63	80
Color televisions	1,503	Sun/1			62	68	66
Dress shirts	859	Sun/1			40	40	54
Vacuum cleaners	780	Mon/4			36	62	64
Mattresses	260	Tues/1			30	37	54
Career shirts					19	27	45
Girdles					12	15	16
Averages, all items[a]					42	51	64

[a]Excludes girdles (no ads), but includes career shirts because of ads for dress shirts, a related item.

EXHIBIT B.2
Summary of Television Recall

Item	Budget	Adult Audience (000)	Got Idea	Learned of Special	Direct Recall
Career shirts	$2,998	1,373.4	15%	16%	27%
Draperies	2,714	776.5	11	15	37
Pant suits	2,494	885.4	8	9	39
Playtex girdles	2,364	752.1	25	34	32
Dress shirts	2,028	824.8	16	16	29
Handbags	1,922	649.2	10	10	34
Shoes	1,909	724.7	11	14	41
Vacuum cleaners	1,867	627.4	19	36	42
Carpeting	1,790	624.5	8	12	29
Mattresses	1,627	691.9	40	48	49
Color televisions			0	0	5
Averages, all items[a]			16	21	36

[a]Excludes color televisions (no commercials).

EXHIBIT B.3

Summary of Radio Recall

Item	Budget	Adult Audience (000)	Got Idea	Learned of Special	Direct Recall
Career shirts	$903	489.1	2%	6%	17%
Draperies	560	654.3	1	2	8
Shoes	544	566.8	5	6	14
Pant suits	539	633.9	1	2	12
Carpeting	513	590.9	8	7	24
Dress Shirts	498	496.4	4	5	12
Girdles	482	553.0	6	9	11
Mattresses	477	527.6	11	23	29
Handbags	476	475.1	2	3	20
Vacuum Cleaners	453	482.1	7	8	10
Color televisions		374.2		1	2
Averages, all items[a]			5	7	16

[a]Excludes color televisions (no commercials).

aided). Nonmedia answers to this question, such as "needed" item, "wanted" item, or "had past experience" with item were accepted.

2. *Learned of special.* Those customers who were aware of the store having a special on the specific item purchased were asked *where they learned about it.* In this question, answers involving media also came from top-of-mind recall and nonmedia responses such as "saw on display" or "friend told me" were accepted.

3. *Direct recall.* Customers were also asked if they recalled seeing or hearing any advertising that may have reminded them or helped them decide to buy the specific item. If they answered in the affirmative, they were then asked *where they saw or heard it.* If radio, newspaper, television, or mail circular were not mentioned by the respondent, they were also asked if they happened to hear a radio commercial, see a newspaper ad, and so on (aided recall). For purposes of analyzing the results, the unaided and aided answers to direct recall have been combined in this question.

Effect of Confusion and "Conditioning"

First, we would like to emphasize three points that should be taken into consideration when evaluating each advertising medium's performance based on the recall results of the study.

1. Because of the heavy amount of Rich's advertising activity in all media during the three-day period of interviewing, there was a certain amount of

confusion that occurred among the customer/respondents regarding where they saw or heard advertising. This fact will be documented in the pages to follow.
2. Because Rich's traditionally had done the vast majority of its *item* advertising in newspaper, customers are "conditioned" to this particular medium; that is, more inclined to think of Rich's merchandise being advertised in a newspaper.
3. During the three-day period of the study, *other department stores* were also running *newspaper* ads for items similar to Rich's items being tested. Some newspaper ad recall in this study could have been due to confusion with other stores' ads.

These points can all be substantiated by the following results.

Only Slight Confusion for Radio Commercials

There were *no* radio commercials for color television sets, since the spots were canceled before they were scheduled to run on Tuesday afternoon.

- 0% Claimed they got the idea to buy a color television set from radio commercials.
- 1% Thought they learned of color television sets being on sale from radio commercials.
- 2% Said they recalled hearing radio commercials for color television sets.

Only Slight Confusion for Television Commercials

There were *no* television commercials for color television sets, since the spots were canceled before they were scheduled to run on Tuesday afternoon.

- 0% Claimed that they got the idea to buy a color television set from television commercials.
- 0% Thought they learned of color television sets on sale from television commercials.
- 5% Said they recalled seeing television commercials for color television sets.

Some Confusion and "Conditioning" for Mail Circular

In the mail circular that Rich's distributed to its customers the week prior to the survey, there were *no* ads for any specific items, yet among the total sample of customer/respondents purchasing any of the 11 items tested:

- 3% Claimed that they got the idea to buy the specific item from a mail circular.
- 5% Thought they learned of the specific item being on sale from a mail circular.
- 18% Said they recalled seeing a mail circular for the specific item.

Greater Confusion and "Conditioning" for Newspaper Ads

There were *no* Rich's newspaper ads for Playtex girdles, yet:

12%	Claimed they got the idea to buy girdles from newspaper ads.
15%	Thought they learned of girdles being on sale from newspaper ads.
16%	Said they recalled seeing newspaper ads for girdles.

There were *no* Rich's newspaper ads for mattresses on either Sunday or Monday of the survey, yet among customers interviewed on Monday:

27%	Claimed they got the idea to buy a mattress from newspaper ads.
30%	Thought they learned of the mattress being on sale from newspaper ads.
49%	Said they recalled seeing newspaper ads for mattresses.

Caution in Comparing Media by Recall

As you can see, the extent of erroneous recall of newspaper advertising ranged from a low of 12 percent to a high of 49 percent. For this important reason, it is impossible to derive any accurate yardstick for measuring the separate value of each medium, dollar for dollar. In addition, these results cannot be converted to any type of advertising-to-sales ratio.

Radio May Have Been Higher with More WSB Spots

Due to the problem created by trying to find enough availabilities on WSB only in morning and evening drive time (because of the agency's buying criteria) to handle commercials for 11 different times in three days, Atlanta's dominant radio station was not able to contribute as much weight as it should have to most of the media schedules. As a result, a higher proportion of spots ran on WQXI (primarily teens), WAOK (primarily ethnic), WRNG (primarily 50 + listeners), and WPLO (lower socioeconomic level). A brief analysis of the number of radio commercials that ran for each item, showing the light proportion of WSB spots, is shown in the following table.

	Total Spots	WSB Spots	WSB morning Drive Spots[a]
Career shirts	48	10	0
Carpeting	23	6	3
Color televisions	—	—	—
Draperies	26	7	2

[a] Monday or Tuesday.

	Total Spots	WSB Spots	WSB morning Drive Spots[a]
Dress shirts	15	6	2
Girdles	27	5	1
Handbags	27	5	1
Mattresses	19	6	2
Pant suits	26	8	2
Shoes	27	6	2
Vacuum cleaners	22	5	2
Total	260	64	17

Television versus Newspaper

While television budgets were fairly even, newspaper budgets ranged from $260 for mattresses up to $4,412 for draperies. Television versus newspaper performance in all types of recall showed a good relationship to the amount of money spent in newspaper. The smaller the newspaper budget versus television, the better television performed versus newspaper in recall, and vice versa:

1. Television did *best* in all types of recall *compared to newspaper* for mattresses, career shirts, and vacuum cleaners. These items had the smallest amount of advertising space in the newspaper compared to the others.
2. Television did *poorest* in all types of recall *compared to newspaper* for draperies, pant suits, shoes, and carpeting. These items had the greater amount of advertising space in the newspaper.

Radio versus Newspaper

Again, radio budgets were fairly even compared to the wide range in newspaper budgets. Radio versus newspaper performance in all types of recall also showed a fairly strong relationship to the amount of money spent in newspaper. The smaller the newspaper budget versus radio, the better radio performed versus newspaper in recall, and vice versa:

1. Radio did *best* in all types of recall *compared to newspaper* for mattresses, vacuum cleaners, and career shirts. These items generally had the least newspaper space.
2. Radio did *poorest* in all types of recall *compared to newspaper* for draperies, pant suits, and handbags. These items generally had the greatest newspaper space.

Less Newspaper Space—No Harm to Sales Volume

We have just indicated that, as newspaper space was reduced, both radio and television did better in recall.

How about Rich's Sales Volume?

There appeared to be little, if any, correlation between the amount of newspaper space and sales volume as measured by department sales increases. If anything, the reverse occurred:

	Monday	Tuesday
Television and radio did best (least newspaper space)		
Girdles	+7%	+92%
Career shirts	+151	+349
Mattresses	+43	+76
Vacuum cleaners	+98	+222
Television and radio did poorest (most newspaper space)		
Draperies	0	+9
Pant suits	+17	+46
Shoes	−19	+14
Carpeting	−9	+526

Idea to Buy versus Direct Recall

One probable indication of the "conditioning" of Rich's customers to newspaper advertising comes from comparing initial "idea to buy" recall, where media responses came purely from top of mind, to the direct recall that came later in the interview, concentrating on each medium. All three media gained in regard to the proportion of customers recalling (from idea to buy to direct recall), but newspaper, having been recalled more from top of mind, gained the least, while television and especially radio, in the background during top of mind "idea to buy," came to the surface more in the direct recall.

	Average Recall, All Items[a]		
	Idea to Buy	Direct Recall	Percentage Increase
Newspaper	42%	64%	+52%
Television	16	36	+125
Radio	5	16	+220

[a] Girdles were eliminated for newspaper, and color television sets were eliminated for radio and television because of no advertising.

First-Day versus Second-Day Recall

Analysis of the direct-recall results by day of interview produced an interesting fact. The impact of newspaper was initial, while both radio and TV performed significantly better on the second day. This is probably due to the nature of the broadcast media, which gain impact and effectiveness with *increased frequency* (as listeners and viewers are exposed to more commercials). In addition, sales results for all items were generally better on Tuesday than on Monday, compared to a year ago. This also indicates that, if spots had been spread more evenly over Sunday, Monday, and Tuesday (rather than concentrated on Sunday and Monday in most cases), and if interviewing had been extended through Wednesday, both radio and television would have performed better in recall, at no increase in budget for either medium.

	Average Recall, All Items[a]		
	Monday	Tuesday	Tuesday Percentage Difference
Newspaper	66%	62%	−6%
Television	33	38	+15
Radio	13	18	+38

[a] Mattresses were eliminated for newspaper as an invalid comparison, since there were no ads on Sunday or Monday. However, even though there were no radio or television commercials for career shirts on Sunday or Monday, and no newspaper ads at all, this item was included in this comparison because there was advertising for dress shirts, a related item. Also, girdles were eliminated for newspaper and color televisions for radio and television because of no advertising.

High-Priced versus Low-Priced Items

In order to analyze media performance by item *price range*, the items were divided into either a high-price (carpeting, color television, draperies, mattresses, and vacuum cleaners), or a low-price (career shirts, dress shirts, girdles, handbags, pant suits, and shoes) group. All three media performed better among high-priced items compared to low-priced merchandise, especially radio and television. However, the differences were greater regarding "idea to buy" recall and "learned of special" recall than with the direct recall. Customers who had made up their minds to buy a large-ticket item were apparently more persuaded by advertising than those coming to Rich's for lower-priced merchandise. However, whether in the market for high- or low-priced items, both type customers were exposed to advertising, as indicated in the direct recall.

	High-Priced Items	Low-Priced Items	High-Priced Percentage Difference
Idea to buy			
Newspaper	47%	37%	+27%
Television	20	14	+43
Radio	7	3	+133
Learned of special			
Newspaper	60	42	+43
Television	28	16	+75
Radio	10	5	+100
Direct recall			
Newspaper	69	59	+17
Television	39	34	+15
Radio	18	14	+29

"Had in Mind" versus "Decided in Store"

In order to analyze media performance by the extent to which customers had in mind to buy the item before coming to the store, the items were divided into two groups: "had in mind" and "decided in store," based on results to the question covering this aspect of purchasing. The four items where roughly half of the customers indicated deciding in the store (pant suits, dress shirts, career shirts, and handbags) were placed in the "decided in store" group. The other seven items, where significantly less customers indicated deciding in store, were placed in the "had in mind" group. All three media performed significantly better among items in the "had in mind" group, that is, for items where a greater proportion of customers made their decision in advance. The differences were greater regarding "idea to buy" and "learned of special" recall than with the direct recall.

	"Had in Mind" Items	"Decided in Store" Items	"Had in Mind" Percentage Difference
Idea to buy			
Newspaper	48%	35%	+37%
Television	19	12	+58
Radio	6	2	+200
Learned of special			
Newspaper	59	38	+55
Television	26	13	+100
Radio	9	4	+125
Direct recall			
Newspaper	70	56	+25
Television	38	32	+19
Radio	16	15	+7

Broadcast Media Recall Reflected Younger Adults

By analyzing media recall by age of customer, it was determined that radio and television balanced newspaper quite well by reaching younger adults. In all three types of recall, the under-35 age group was proportionately higher for broadcast, especially radio, than for newspaper. These figures are based on all items combined.

Age	Radio	Television	Newspaper
Got idea			
Under 35	56%[a]	44%	36%
35–49	31	38	44
50 and over	13	18	20
Learned of special			
Under 35	50	43	36
35–49	34	41	41
50 and over	16	16	23

[a]Of those customers indicating that they "got the idea" to buy an item from radio commercials, 56 percent were in the under-35 age group.

Age	Radio	Television	Newspaper
Direct recall			
Under 35	49	44	41
35–49	33	38	41
50 and over	18	18	18

Rich's Dominant Position in Atlanta

In concluding this presentation, we would like to announce the results of separate research that we have just completed that indicates the extent to which Rich's dominates the department store market in Atlanta, a domination that we feel is due to:

- Outstanding management.
- Quality of merchandise.
- Attention to customer service and satisfaction.
- Efficient use of advertising and promotion, especially the *use of a media mix*.

Presentation Summary

1. With the use of a media mix for item selling, the pre–Harvest Sale was a success. All departments participating in the test were up in sales volume.
2. Because of confusion and conditioning factors, recall results are not completely comparable between media.
3. In general, as the amount of newspaper space was reduced, the proportion of recall for both television and radio was increased, and sales results were generally more favorable.
4. Sales volume was up significantly on Tuesday versus Monday in all departments, indicating a relationship with broadcast media recall, also up significantly on Tuesday as frequency increased.
5. All media had higher recall for higher-priced items and items where customer generally decided in advance.
6. Separate research confirms Rich's dominance of the Atlanta market, especially versus Davison's. Rich's uses radio and television effectively, Davison's uses very little broadcast media.

GLOSSARY

A

accessibility a market segmentation requirement that specifies the degree to which the resulting segments can be effectively reached and served.

acid-test ratio a financial ratio used to evaluate a firm's liquidity which measures cash and its equivalent divided by current liabilities.

accounts and notes receivable money that customers owe retailers for goods and services.

accounts payable money that retailers owe vendors for goods and services.

accumulation a sorting process that involves building up larger homogeneous supplies.

achieved markup see *maintained markup*.

active information gathering the collection and evaluation of information that will eventually lead to a decision either to purchase or not to purchase or which item to purchase and where. Active information gathering involves three stages: developing an initial consideration set, narrowing down the consideration set to a more manageable number of possibilities, and comparing the key attributes of the alternatives remaining on the shortened consideration set.

adjacencies plan a store layout plan that determines which categories of merchandise will be placed adjacent to each other.

administered vertical marketing systems marketing channels in which one of the channel members takes the initiative to lead the channel by applying the principles of effective interorganizational management.

advertising paid, nonpersonal communication through various media by business firms, nonprofit organizations, and individuals who are in some way identified in the advertising message and who hope to inform and/or persuade members of a particular audience.

advertising effectiveness the extent to which advertising has produced the desired result.

advertising efficiency the extent to which the advertising result was achieved with minimal effort.

Glossary

affordable method a method to determine the amount to be spent on advertising whereby the retailer allocates all the money it can afford for advertising in any given budget period.

allocation a sorting process that involves breaking down homogeneous supplies into smaller lots.

ambiance the overall feeling or mood projected by a store through its aesthetic appeal to human senses.

arbitration a form of conflict resolution in which parties voluntarily submit their dispute to a third party whose decision is considered final and binding.

asset anything of value that is owned by the retail firm.

assorting a sorting process that involves building up assortments of products for use in association with each other.

assortment see *breadth*.

automatic checkout machines (ACMs) a system whereby customers have the opportunity to check themselves out of a store by scanning their purchases with the POS system, entering their customer identification card, and receiving clearance to exit the store.

automatic merchandising machine operators establishments primarily engaged in the retail sale of products by means of automatic merchandising units, also referred to as vending machines.

award a form of procedural resolution in which a settlement is reached because both parties agree to accept the verdict of an outside person or agency rather than continue the conflict. An award is typically the result of a legal trial or arbitration.

B

bait-and-switch advertising promoting a product at an unrealistically low price to serve as "bait" and then trying to "switch" the customer to a higher-priced product.

bait pricing the practice of pricing a certain model of a shopping good at a low price to lure shoppers into a store and then once they are in the store trying to persuade them to purchase a higher-priced model.

balance sheet an accounting statement that shows the financial condition of a retailer's business at a particular point in time.

basic stock method (BSM) a method of inventory control that requires that the retailer always have a base level of inventory regardless of the predicted sales volume.

behavioral characteristics descriptions of actual shopping behaviors such as recognizing a need for merchandise, selecting a store, comparing prices, and purchasing.

block plan a store layout plan that delineates the actual sizes, shapes, and locations of all store components.

bona fide occupational qualification (BFOQ) an exception to discrimination laws where religion, sex, or national origin may be a reasonable requirement to perform the narrow operation of a particular enterprise.

book inventory an inventory accounting system that depends on bookkeeping entries.

breadth the number of merchandise brands that are found in the merchandise line.

bubble plan a store layout plan that shows the rough placement and adjacency of key elements of the proposed store.

buying power index (BPI) a single-weighted measure combining effective buying income (personal income less all tax and nontax payments), retail sales, and population into an overall indicator of a market's potential.

buy trigger event the point at which the consumer has decided to purchase a good or service and often where to buy it.

C

cash discount a discount earned by retailers for prompt payment of bills.

category killers a type of destination store that is usually large and that concentrates on one category, thus making it possible to carry both a broad assortment and deep selection of merchandise, coupled with low price and moderate service.

category signage signage that is used to call out and locate specific merchandise categories.

category specialists retailers that offer a narrow variety but deep assortment of merchandise.

central business district (CBD) an unplanned shopping area around the geographic point at which all public transportation systems converge.

central place theory a model that ranks communities according to the assortment of goods available in each. At the bottom of the hierarchy are communities that represent the smallest central places (centers of commerce). They provide the basic necessities of life. Further up the hierarchy are the larger central places, which carry all goods and services found in lower-order central places plus more specialized ones that are not necessary.

coercive power B's belief that A has a capacity to punish or harm B if B doesn't conform to A's desire.

community center a shopping center that provides convenience goods and personal services as well as a wider range of facilities for the sale of soft lines (apparel for men, women, and children) and hard lines (hardware and appliances).

compensation direct dollar payments (wages, commissions, and bonuses) and indirect payments (insurance, vacation time, and retirement plans) to employees.

competitive assortment a merchandise assortment characterized by both low gross margin return on inventory and low inventory intensity which results in poor space productivity.

compromise a form of procedural resolution in which each party is willing to settle for something less than his or her ideal position rather than continue the conflict.

confidential vendor analysis a list of the same companies as in the profitability analysis statement which provides a three-year financial summary as well as the names, titles, and negotiating points of all the vendor's sales staff.

consignment a selling arrangement in which the vendor retains ownership of the goods, usually establishes the selling price, and is paid only when the goods are sold.

content theories theories of motivation that attempt to explain what motivates individuals to behave.

contractual vertical marketing systems marketing channels that include wholesaler-sponsored voluntary groups, retailer-owned cooperatives, and franchised retail programs.

contribution margin net sales less cost of goods sold and any expenses that are directly traceable to specific product lines.

conventional marketing channel a marketing channel in which each member is loosely aligned with the other members.

corporate vertical marketing systems marketing channels that consist of either a manufacturer that has integrated vertically to reach the consumer, or a retailer that has integrated vertically to create a self-supply network.

cost complement the average relationship of cost to retail price for all merchandise available for sale during a given time period. The cost complement is equal to the total cost valuation divided by the total retail valuation.

cost method an inventory accounting system based on the cost of each item as recorded in the accounting records or as coded on the price tag.

cost of goods sold the cost of merchandise that has been sold during a given time period.

cost per thousand (CPM) method a form of media evaluation in which the cost for an ad or series of ads in a medium is divided by the reach or cumulative reach.

coverage the theoretical maximum percentage of a retailer's target market that can be reached by a medium—not the percentage actually reached.

cultural control an informal control wherein a wider set of norms guide employee actions in the entire organization.

cumulative quantity discount a price discount based on the total amount purchased over a period of time.

cumulative reach the actual number of target customers who come into contact with an advertising message over a given time period.

current assets cash and all other items that the retailer can easily convert into cash within a relatively short period of time.

current liabilities short-term indebtedness payable within one year.

current ratio a financial ratio used to evaluate liquidity which measures current assets to current liabilities.

customary pricing a pricing strategy in which a retailer sets prices for goods and services and seeks to maintain those prices over an extended period of time.

Customer Service and Sales Enhancement Audit a detailed analysis of current sales activity by location and by selling area.

customer spottings a technique to determine and evaluate trade areas by interviewing randomly selected customers.

D

deceitful diversion of patronage when a retailer publishes or verbalizes falsehoods about a competitor in an attempt to divert patrons from that competitor.

deceptive advertising false or misleading advertising claims about the physical makeup of a product, the benefits to be gained by its use, or the appropriate uses for it.

delivery terms terms that specify where title to the merchandise passes to the retailer, whether the vendor or buyer will pay the freight charges, and who is obligated to file any damage claims.

demand density the extent to which potential demand for the retailer's goods and services is concentrated in certain census tracts, ZIP codes, or parts of the community.

demand elasticity of price the percentage change in quantity demanded divided by the percentage change in price.

demographic characteristics defining characteristics that describe the population of the market (age, ethnic group, income, education, geography, family life cycle, and social class).

density of supply the extent to which retailers are already concentrated in different geographic areas of a given market.

depth the average number of stock-keeping units within each brand of the merchandise line.

destination merchandise merchandise that motivates or triggers a trip to a specific store.

destination stores stores to which consumers generally make a special trip with the intent of shopping.

dialectic process theory a theory of retail evolution wherein a retail innovation stimulates another innovation of the opposite type, and eventually the two are synthesized into a new form of retailing.

directional and departmental signage signage that helps guide the shopper through the shopping trip and locate specific departments of interest.

direct product profit (DPP) an individual item's gross margin dollars, plus discounts and allowances earned, less direct handling, selling, and inventory holding costs.

direct-selling establishments establishments primarily engaged in the retail sale of merchandise by telephone or house-to-house canvass or in the workplace.

diverters unauthorized, but legal, members of a marketing channel.

divertive competition a type of competition that occurs when a retailer intercepts a customer to purchase merchandise that normally would have been purchased at another retail store.

domain consensus when the members of the marketing channel agree on who should make decisions.

domain dissensus a source of latent conflict that occurs when there is disagreement among members of the marketing channel about who should make decisions.

drive time the period of driving to and from work.

dual distribution the manufacturer's practice of selling to independent retailers and also through its own retail outlets.

dwell time the amount of time customers spend waiting in line.

E

earnings per share total earnings available to common stockholders divided by shares of common stock outstanding.

electronic data interchange (EDI) a system that allows a retailer's computer to "talk" directly to a supplier's computer to transmit intercompany transactions.

electronic funds transfer (EFT) a system that allows banks to be electronically linked with their customers in order to make and receive payments.

employee theft employee removal of merchandise without paying for it. Often these losses occur when employees believe that free merchandise is part of their pay.

Engel's laws generalizations about a household's response to an increase in income. Spending increases for all categories of products as a result of an income increase, but the percentage of spending for some categories increases more than others.

expertise power B's perception that A has some special knowledge.

expert systems computer software systems that make important recurring retail decisions without human interference by modeling the decision rules of retail experts.

expressed warranties written or verbal warranties that cover all characteristics or attributes of the merchandise or only one attribute.

extra dating when the vendor allows the retailer some extra time before paying for the goods.

F

facilitating institutions the marketing institutions that do not actually take title but facilitate the marketing process by specializing in the performance of certain functions.

factory outlet centers shopping centers that specialize in manufacturer's outlets that dispose of excess merchandise and factory seconds.

fair trade see *vertical price fixing*.

family life cycle changes in family composition that, over time, substantially alter family needs, decision making, and market behavior.

felt conflict the affective dimension of conflict consisting of stress, tension, or hostility.

FIFO (first in, first out) a method for valuing inventory that assumes that the oldest merchandise is sold before the more recently purchased merchandise.

financial leverage total assets divided by net worth or owner's equity.

financial performance objectives objectives that can be stated in monetary or economic terms.

fixed component a component of a compensation plan that is typically composed of some base wage per hour, week, month, or year.

fixed costs the costs the retailer incurs regardless of the quantity of goods or services sold.

flexible pricing a pricing strategy in which a retailer offers the same products and quantities to different customers at different prices.

formal organization structure an arrangement of human resources that represents the way employees should behave in terms of lines of authority and responsibility.

franchising a form of licensing by which the owner of a product, service, or method—the franchisor—obtains distribution through affiliated dealers—franchisees.

free-flow layout the simplest type of store layout in which fixtures and merchandise are grouped into free-flowing patterns on the sales floor.

free-lance broker a facilitating institution that has no permanent ties with any manufacturer and may negotiate sales for a large number of manufacturers over time. No limit is placed on the territory in which sales may occur, but the free-lance broker is strictly bound by the manufacturer regarding prices, terms, and conditions of sale.

free merchandise a discount whereby merchandise is offered in lieu of price concessions.

freestanding retailer a retailer that locates along major traffic arteries, without any adjacent retailers to share traffic.

frequency the average number of times each person who is reached is exposed to an advertisement during a given time period.

fringe benefit package a component of a compensation plan that may include such things as health insurance, disability benefits, life insurance, and retirement plans.

full-line policy when a large national manufacturer with several very strongly demanded lines of merchandise forces the retailer to handle its entire merchandise assortment as a condition for being able to handle the most popular lines.

functional discount see *trade discount*.

G

goal incompatibility a source of latent conflict in which achieving the goals of either the supplier or the retailer would hamper the performance of the other.

golden assortment a merchandise assortment characterized by both high gross margin return on inventory and high inventory intensity which results in high space productivity.

goodwill an intangible asset, usually based on customer loyalty, that a retailer pays for when buying an existing business.

grid layout a type of store layout in which the counters and fixtures are placed in long rows or "runs," usually at right angles, throughout the store.

gross domestic product the total value of all the goods and services produced in a country during one year.

gross margin net sales less cost of goods sold.

gross margin return on inventory (GMROI) gross margin divided by average inventory investment.

gross margin return on sales gross margin divided by net sales.

gross sales the retailer's total sales before returns and allowances.

H

hierarchy of merchandising information strategically placed in-store messages that lead the customer through the shopping and buying process beginning with the customers entering the store and ending with them looking at specific merchandise.

horizontal cooperative advertising advertising in which several retailers share the cost.

horizontal price fixing when a group of competing retailers establishes a fixed price at which to sell their merchandise.

I

image engineering the ability to create and change market position image.

impact how strong an impression an advertisement

makes and how effectively it ultimately leads to a purchase.

implied warranty of fitness a warranty made by a retailer that implies that the product the retailer has selected or has assisted the customer in selecting will serve a particular purpose.

implied warranty of merchantability a warranty made by every retailer selling goods. By offering the goods for sale, the retailer implies that they are fit for the ordinary purpose for which such goods are typically used.

impulse-intercept merchandise merchandise purchased purely on impulse, when the customer happens to see it in the store, prior to which the customer had no perceived need.

income statement an accounting statement that provides a summary of the sales and expenses for a given time period.

index of retail saturation (IRS) an indicator of understored versus overstored markets.

informal organization structure an arrangement of human resources that depicts how the employees within a retail organization actually behave.

initial consideration set the set of possibilities that a consumer considers as well as the key attributes on which the purchase decision will be based.

initial markup the markup placed on the merchandise when the store receives it.

institutional signage signage that describes the merchandising mission, customer service policies, and other messages on behalf of the retail institution.

in-store marketing marketing dollars spent inside the store in the form of store design, merchandising, visual displays, or in-store promotions.

integrated information management system (IIMS) an information system that integrates all aspects of a retailer's operations and as a result will lessen the need for middle managers.

interbrand competition competition between retailers selling different brands of the same product class.

intercept merchandise merchandise that customers do not specifically go to a store to buy, but buy because the retailer "intercepts" them in the course of their lives.

intercept stores stores that intercept consumers passing by them.

interest rate the price paid for the use of money.

interorganizational management the management of relationships between organizational entities.

interstate commerce business that takes place among different states.

intertype competition a form of competition that exists each time retailers in different lines of retail trade sell the same lines and merchandise and compete for the same limited consumer dollars.

intrabrand competition competition between retailers selling the same brand.

intratype competition a form of competition that exists when two or more retailers of the same type (as defined in the Census of Retail Trade) compete with each other for the same households.

inventory-effective assortment a merchandise assortment characterized by a high gross margin return on inventory and low inventory intensity which results in reasonable space productivity.

inventory turnover the number of times per year the retailer sells its average inventory.

J

job enrichment the process of enhancing the core job characteristics for the purpose of increasing worker motivation, productivity, and satisfaction.

L

labor productivity net sales divided by the number of full-time-equivalent employees.

latent conflict an underlying situation that, if left unattended, could eventually result in a conflict.

leader pricing a pricing strategy in which a high-demand item is priced low and advertised heavily in an effort to attract consumers into a store.

legitimate power A's right to influence B, or B's belief that B should accept A's influence.

liability any legitimate claim against the retailer's assets.

LIFO (last in, first out) a method of inventory valuation that assumes that the most recently purchased merchandise is sold before the older merchandise.

liquidity a firm's ability to meet its current payment obligations.

long-term liabilities notes payable, mortgages, and other debt not due within the year.

loop layout a type of store layout that provides a major customer aisle which begins at the entrance, "loops" through the store, usually in the shape of a circle, square, or rectangle, and then returns the customer to the front of the store.

loss leader an item that is sold below a retailer's cost in an attempt to attract customers.

M

mail-order houses establishments primarily engaged in the retail sale of products by catalog and mail order.

maintained markup the actual selling price less the cost.

manifest conflict the behavioral dimension of conflict characterized by verbal or written threats or other actions by the supplier or retailer to block the actions of the other.

manufacturer's agent a facilitating institution that acts as the sales force for several manufacturers at the same time within a prescribed market area. The manufacturer's agent has a rather loose arrangement with the manufacturer that is seldom permanent beyond a year, and is strictly bound by the manufacturer for the prices, terms, and conditions of sale, as well as the geographic territory.

marketing channel a set of institutions necessary to move goods from the point of production to the point of consumption and, as such, it consists of all the institutions and all the marketing activities in the marketing process.

marketing system the set of institutions performing marketing functions, the relationships among these institutions, and the functions that are necessary to create transactions with target populations.

market performance objectives objectives that compare the retailer's dominance in the marketplace to that of the competition.

market position the segment of the market that the retailer hopes to attract with its strategy.

market positioning the process of identifying niches, determining which niches a retailer should occupy, and coordinating the various marketing variables to occupy these niches.

market position image the intangible perceptions of consumers that determine their image of a retailer's market position.

market saturation the extent to which a particular trading area is populated with retailers in a particular line of trade.

market segmentation the process of dividing a heterogeneous group of consumers into smaller, homogeneous groups.

market share the proportion of total sales in a particular market that the retailer has been able to capture.

markup the difference between the cost of the merchandise and the selling price.

maximum demand price the highest price (inclusive of all transportation costs) that a consumer would be willing to pay for one unit of a product.

measurability a market segmentation requirement that specifies the degree to which the size and purchasing power of the resulting segments can be measured.

merchandise budget a plan of projected sales for an upcoming season, when and how much merchandise is to be purchased, and what markups and reductions will likely occur.

merchandise line a group of products that are closely related because they are intended for the same end use, are sold to the same customer group, or fall within a given price range.

merchandise management the analysis, planning, acquisition, handling, and control of the merchandise investments of a retail operation.

merchandise productivity net sales divided by the average dollar investment in inventory.

merchandise productivity analysis a mathematical analysis of the productivity of various merchandise categories.

metropolitan statistical areas (MSAs) a Census Bureau term that describes metropolitan areas with populations greater than 50,000.

mission the retailer's overall justification for existing.

model stock plan a plan to determine what merchandise lines and items to stock. The model stock plan gives the precise items and quantities that should be on hand for each merchandise line.

monopolistic competition a type of competitive market structure in which there is a large number of sellers and some product differentiation exists.

motivation the drive within a person to excel, either individually or as a member of a firm.

multiple-unit pricing a pricing strategy in which the price of each unit in a multiple-unit package is less than the price it would carry if it were sold singly.

N

need recognition often called problem recognition, it is the consumer's recognition of a need or desire for an item or service.

neighborhood business district (NBD) a shopping area that evolves to satisfy the convenience-oriented shopping needs of a neighborhood.

neighborhood center a shopping center that provides for the sale of convenience foods (foods, drugs, and sundries) and personal services (laundry and dry cleaning, barbering, shoe repairing, etc.) for the day-to-day living needs of the immediate neighborhood.

net profit operating profit plus or minus other income and expenses not directly relating to the firm's retailing activities.

net sales gross sales less returns and allowances.

net worth the difference between the firm's total assets and total liabilities.

noncumulative quantity discount a discount based on a single purchase.

noncurrent assets assets that cannot be converted into cash in a short period of time in the normal course of business (e.g., buildings, parking lots, fixtures, and equipment).

O

100 percent location the location that is the best possible site for every store within a given shopping district.

odd pricing the practice of setting retail prices that end in the digits 5,7, and 9.

oligopolistic competition a type of competitive market structure in which the industry is controlled by a few larger sellers that establish entry barriers and do not take competitive actions without strong consideration of how competitors will react.

one-price policy a pricing strategy that involves charging all customers the same price for an item.

one-way exclusive dealing an arrangement in which the supplier agrees to give the retailer the exclusive right to merchandise the supplier's product in a particular trade area. The retailer, however, does not agree to do anything for the supplier.

open-to-buy the dollar amount that a buyer can currently spend on merchandise without exceeding the planned dollar stocks.

operating expenses the expenses that a retailer incurs in the operation of the business other than the cost of the merchandise (e.g., payroll, rent, utilities, advertising, depreciation, supplies, taxes, interest paid, repairs, and insurance).

operating profit net sales less cost of goods sold and operating expenses the retailer incurs.

operating profit margin the retailer's operating profit divided by net sales.

order getters retail employees who are involved in conversation with prospective purchasers for the purpose of making a sale. Order getters inform, guide, and persuade the customer in order to culminate a transaction either immediately or in the future.

order takers retail employees who sell only regular in-stock merchandise. Order takers might show the customer where the merchandise is located or may go to the storeroom to get an item, but they seldom, if ever, attempt to sell the merchandise or demonstrate its use.

other income or expenses income or expense items that the firm incurs, though not in the course of its normal retail operations.

outshopping the practice of residents of smaller communities traveling to larger communities to shop when prices become too high in the smaller communities.

overall review an analysis of the overall performance of the retailer to determine whether the objectives are reasonable and the strategy workable.

overstored a market condition that exists when a market has too many stores to yield a fair return on investment.

owner's equity the difference between the firm's total assets and total liabilities.

P

palming off when a retailer represents merchandise as being made by a firm other than the true manufacturer.

passive information gathering the ongoing receipt and processing of information regarding the existence and quality of merchandise, stores, shopping convenience, pricing, and other factors.

patent a legal right to market exclusively a product or process for a period of 17 years.

penetration price a pricing objective that seeks to establish a loyal customer base by entering the market with a low price.

perceived conflict the cognitive dimension of conflict representing the point at which either the supplier or the retailer becomes aware of one or more of the sources of latent conflict.

percentage-of-sales method a method to determine the amount to be spent on advertising whereby the retailer targets a specific percentage of sales to be used for advertising.

percentage variation method (PVM) a method of inventory control that assumes that the monthly percentage fluctuations from average stock should be half as great as the percentage fluctuations in monthly sales from average sales.

perceptual incongruity a source of latent conflict that occurs when the retailer and supplier have different perceptions of reality.

performance appraisal and review the formal, systematic assessment of how well employees are performing their jobs in relation to established standards, and the communication of that assessment to employees.

personal objectives objectives that relate to helping people employed in retailing fulfill some of their needs.

personal selling selling that involves a face-to-face interaction with the consumer.

physical inventory an inventory accounting system that involves an actual count of the merchandise.

planned urban development (PUD) a totally conceived and supervised community including housing, retail, and business activity.

planning the anticipation and organization of what needs to be done to reach an objective.

point of indifference the point at which shoppers would be equally willing to shop at either of two cities.

point-of-sale signage signage that is intended to give details about specific merchandise items and is usually affixed directly to fixtures.

post-purchase resentment a condition that emerges when a consumer is dissatisfied with a purchase and this dissatisfaction results in resentment toward the retailer.

power the ability of A to affect the decision variables of B.

power format a type of destination store that carries a wider variety of merchandise, but offers a narrower assortment within each category, enabling it to buy in large quantities and offer very low prices.

prepaid expenses items for which the retailer has already paid but the service has not been completed.

price discrimination when two retailers buy identical merchandise from the same supplier but pay different prices.

price lining a pricing strategy that involves establishing a specified number of price lines for each merchandise line and then purchasing goods that fit into each line.

price zone a range of price points for a particular merchandise line that appeals to customers in a certain demographic group.

pricing policies rules of action, or guidelines, that ensure uniformity of pricing decisions within a retail operation.

primary marketing institutions the marketing institutions in the marketing channel that take title to the goods.

principle of compatibility two compatible businesses located in close proximity will show an increase in business volume directly proportionate to the incidence of total customer interchange between them, inversely proportionate to the ratio of the business volume of the larger store to that of the smaller store, and directly proportionate to the sum of the ratios of purposeful purchasing to total purchasing in each of the two stores.

private-brand pricing a pricing practice wherein a private-brand item can have a higher markup percentage and still be priced lower than a comparable national brand.

process theories theories of motivation that attempt to explain how to motivate individuals.

profit maximization objective a pricing objective that seeks to obtain as much profit as possible.

programmed merchandise agreements joint ventures in which specific retailers and suppliers develop a comprehensive merchandising plan to market the suppliers' product lines.

promotional discount a discount given when the retailer performs an advertising or promotional service for the manufacturer.

prototype a store format that is developed and then repeated in all stores, with minor adaptations to local merchandising or market conditions.

psychographics the examination of the attitudes, interests, and opinions of the population or of a meaningful segment of the population.

publicity non-paid-for communications of information about a company or product, generally in some media form.

public warehouse a facilitating institution that stores goods for safekeeping in return for a fee.

purchasing agent a facilitating institution that seeks out sources of supply for some members of the channel. Purchasing agents operate on a contractual basis for a limited number of customers and receive a commission.

pure competition a type of competitive market structure in which there are no or few entry barriers to competition. Pure competition is characterized by many sellers, homogeneous products, and prices that cannot be controlled by individual buyers or sellers.

pure monopoly a type of competitive market structure in which there is only one producer or seller of the product.

Q

quantity discount a price reduction offered as an inducement to purchase large quantities of merchandise.

quick ratio a financial ratio used to evaluate liquidity which measures current assets, less inventory, divided by current liabilities.

R

range the maximum distance a consumer is willing to travel for a good or service; as such it determines the outer limit of a store's market area.

reach the actual total number of target customers who come into contact with an advertising message.

reconciliation a form of procedural conflict resolution in which the value systems of the parties so change that they now have common objectives and conflict is eliminated.

reductions markdowns, employee discounts, and stock shortages that reduce the retailer's inventory values.

referent power the identification of B with A. B wants to be associated or identified with A.

regional center the second-largest type of shopping center (typically 400,000 square feet of gross leasable space) that provides for the sale of general merchandise, apparel, furniture, and home furnishings, as well as a range of services and recreational facilities.

Reilly's law of retail gravitation two cities attract trade from an intermediate place approximately in direct proportion to the population of the two cities and in inverse proportion to the square of the distance from these two cities to the intermediate place.

resale price maintenance see *vertical price fixing*.

resident buyers purchasing agents who usually operate in the central market headquarters for a particular type of product. Resident buyers are specialists on the availability of products; the reliability of suppliers; present and future market trends; and special deals, prices, shipping, and other considerations.

resident buying offices (RBOs) retailer-owned and operated or independent organizations that are usually located in important merchandise centers and enable the participating retailers to have better contacts with vendors.

retail accordion theory retail institutions evolve from outlets that offer wide assortments to specialized stores that offer narrow assortments, and then return to the wide-assortment stores to continue through the pattern once more.

retail information system (RIS) a blueprint for the continual and periodic systematic collection, analysis, and reporting of relevant data about any past, present, or future developments that could influence or have influenced the retailer's performance.

retail inventories merchandise that the retailer has in the store or in storage and is available for sale.

retail life cycle a theory of retail competition that states that retailing institutions, like the products they distribute, pass through an identifiable cycle. This cycle can be partitioned into four distinct stages: (1) innovation, (2) accelerated development, (3) maturity, and (4) decline.

retail method an inventory accounting system based on the retail value of the merchandise.

retail mix the set of major retail decisions consisting of pricing, merchandise, selling environment (location and store building), promotion, and selling.

retail patronage model a comprehensive model that describes, and to some degree predicts, how the various socioeconomic, demographic, psychographic, and behavioral characteristics come together to affect consumer buying patterns.

retroactive (or retraction) advertising when a new advertisement is made in which false and deceptive statements made in former advertisements are contradicted and the truth is stated.

return on assets net profit divided by total assets.

return on net worth net profit divided by owner's or stockholder's equity.

returns and allowances reductions from gross sales realized by allowing customers to return merchandise or receive a price reduction to satisfy a complaint.

reward power the ability of A to reward B.

S

sales agent a facilitating institution that has long-term arrangements with one or a very few manufacturers. The sales agent sells the entire output for the manufacturer and has no limitation on the territory, prices, terms, or conditions of sale.

sales displacement a reduction in sales of a promoted brand during subsequent nonpromotional periods.

sales promotions the use of media and nonmedia marketing pressure applied for a predetermined, limited period of time at the level of consumer, retailer, or wholesaler in order to stimulate trial, increase consumer demand, or improve product availability.

scrambled merchandising carrying any merchandise line that can be sold profitably.

seasonal discount a discount given when retailers purchase and take delivery of merchandise in the off season.

secondary business district (SBD) a shopping area that is smaller than the CBD and evolves around at least one department or variety store at a major street intersection.

segmental review an in-depth analysis of only one area of performance in a retail organization or store.

self-control an informal control wherein the employee sets personal objectives, monitors attainment, and appropriately adjusts behavior if off course.

selling environment the place where interaction with the customer occurs and is typically comprised of a physical facility at a geographic location.

semifixed costs the costs that are constant over a range of sales volume, but past a crucial point they increase and then again remain constant at another, higher, sales volume range.

service quality an area of study that has developed to define and describe how services can be delivered in such a manner as to satisfy the recipient. High-quality service is defined as delivery of service that meets or exceeds customers' expectations.

shopping center a centrally owned or managed shopping district that is planned, has balanced tenancy (the stores complement each other in merchandise offerings), and is surrounded by parking facilities.

shop trigger event the point at which a consumer's perceived degree of need is high relative to the barriers to resolving it, and the consumer decides to shop actively.

shrinkage the loss of merchandise through theft, loss, and damage.

skimming a pricing objective that seeks to sell at the highest price possible in order to recover the initial investment faster before settling on a more competitive level.

social class relatively permanent and homogeneous divisions in a society, in which individuals or families share similar values, lifestyles, interests, and behavior.

social control an informal control wherein the work unit sets standards or norms, monitors conformity, and takes actions when behavior is inconsistent with norms.

societal objectives objectives that can be phrased in terms of helping society fulfill some of its needs.

sorting out a sorting process that involves breaking down heterogeneous supplies into more homogeneous groups.

sought-intercept merchandise merchandise for which consumers recognize a need, but do not see it as important enough to trigger a special trip to a store.

space-effective assortment a merchandise assortment characterized by a low gross margin return on inventory and high inventory intensity which results in reasonable space productivity.

space productivity net sales divided by the total square feet of retail floor space.

space productivity index a comparison of the gross margin of a particular category to its percentage of space utilized.

spine layout a type of store layout that combines the advantages of the free-flow, grid, and loop layouts.

statement of cash flow an accounting statement that explains the changes in cash and cash equivalents from one accounting period to the next by showing all cash inflows and all cash outflows from the operating, investing, and financing activities of the company for a given time period.

status quo objectives pricing objectives that seek to maintain current prices.

Steering Marketing Control Model (STEMCOM) an analytical model for performance control that predicts a final outcome and then monitors progress toward that outcome. STEMCOM alerts managers to deviations from some specified level of performance.

stock-keeping unit (SKU) the lowest level of identification of merchandise.

stock-to-sales method (SSM) a method of inventory control that uses a ratio of stock to estimated sales to determine the inventory level for a given time period.

stock-to-sales ratio the ratio that depicts the amount of stock to have on hand at the beginning of a given time period to support the forecasted sales for that time period.

store saturation a market condition that exists when store facilities are utilized efficiently and meet consumer demand. Saturation occurs when a market has just enough stores of a given type to serve the population of the market satisfactorily and yield a fair return on investment to the owners without raising prices to the customer.

strategic planning a type of planning that involves adapting the firm to the opportunities and constraints of an ever-changing marketplace.

substantiality a market segmentation requirement that specifies the degree to which the resulting segments are large and/or profitable enough to be worth considering for separate marketing attention.

substitution effect a reduction in current and future demand for competitive brands following a sales promotion.

super-regional center the largest type of shopping center (typically between 600,000 and 1,400,000 square feet of gross leasable area) that provides extensive variety in general merchandise, apparel, furniture, and home furnishings, as well as a variety of services and recreational facilities.

T

target return objective a pricing objective that sets a specific level of profit as an objective. This amount is often stated as a percentage of sales or a percentage of the retailer's capital investment.

task analysis identifying of all the tasks the retailer needs to perform and breaking those tasks down into jobs.

task-and-objective method a method to determine the amount to be spent on advertising whereby the retailer establishes its advertising objectives and then determines the advertising tasks that need to be performed to achieve those objectives.

territorial restrictions attempts by a supplier, usually a manufacturer, to limit the geographical area in which a retailer may resell its merchandise.

theme centers shopping centers located in places of historical interest and where a lot of tourist traffic is generated.

three-dimensional demand function a model that depicts consumer demand for a retailer's products. The three dimensions are: (1) quantity demanded per household, (2) price at the retail store, and (3) distance from the household's place of residence or work to the store. The quantity demanded by a household is inversely related to the prices charged and the distance to the store.

threshold the minimum amount of consumer demand that must exist in an area for a store to be economically viable.

total assets current assets plus noncurrent assets plus goodwill.

total liabilities current liabilities plus long-term liabilities.

trade discount a form of compensation the buyer may receive for performing certain services for the manufacturer.

trading area geographically delineated area that surrounds a community, within which households would generally be willing to travel to purchase goods and services.

two-way exclusive dealing an arrangement that occurs when the supplier offers the retailer the exclusive distribution of a merchandise line or product if in return the retailer will agree to do something for the supplier, such as agree not to handle competing brands.

tying agreement when a seller with a strong product or service forces a retailer to buy a weak product or service as a condition for buying the strong one.

U

understored a market condition that exists when a market has too few stores to provide satisfactorily for the needs of the consumer.

V

Values and Lifestyle (VALS) a systematic classification of American adults. It consists of four comprehensive groups, divided into nine lifestyles, each defined by distinct values, drives, beliefs, needs, dreams, and special points of view.

variable component a component of a compensation plan that is often composed of some bonus that is received if performance warrants it.

variable costs the costs that increase proportionately with sales volume.

variable pricing a pricing strategy that is used when differences in demand and cost force the retailer to change prices in a fairly predictable manner.

variety the number of different lines the retailer stocks in the store.

vendor collusion losses that occur when the merchandise is delivered. Such losses typically involve the delivery of less merchandise than is charged for, the removal of good merchandise disguised as old merchandise, and the theft of other merchandise from the stockroom or selling floor while making delivery. Vendor collusion often involves both the delivery people and the retail employee who signs for the delivery with the two splitting the profit.

vendor profitability analysis statement a record that lists all purchases made in given time period, the discount granted by the vendor, the transportation charges paid, the original markup, markdowns, and finally the season-ending gross margin on that vendor's merchandise.

vertical cooperative advertising advertising in which the retailer and other channel members share the cost.

vertical marketing systems rationalized, capital-intensive networks of several levels that are professionally managed and centrally programmed to realize technological, managerial, and promotional economies.

vertical price fixing a situation that occurs when a retailer collaborates with the manufacturer or wholesaler to resell an item at an agreed-on price. Vertical price fixing is often referred to as resale price maintenance or fair trade.

visual communications in-store signage and graphics.

visual merchandising the artistic display of merchandise and theatrical props used as scene-setting decoration in the store.

W

weeks' supply method (WSM) a method of inventory control in which the inventory level is set equal to a predetermined number of weeks' supply.

wheel of retailing hypothesis new types of retailers enter the market as low-status, low-margin, low-price operators. However, as they meet with success, these new retailers gradually acquire more sophisticated and elaborate facilities. These retailers must then raise prices and margins, thus becoming vulnerable to new types of low-margin retail competitors that progress through the same pattern.

within-market opportunity analysis evaluation of the demand and supply within each market, identification of the most attractive sites currently available within each market, and selection of the best possible site.

SUBJECT INDEX

Above-market pricing, 301, 325–326
Accessibility, 51, 836
Accounting rules, for international retailers, 244
Accounting statements, 235–247
Accounts receivable, 40, 240, 836
Accounts payable, 242, 836
Accumulation, 148, 836
Achieved markup. *See* Maintained markup
Acid-test ratio, 616, 836
Acquisitions, 206–208, 253, 719
Active information gathering, 103–104, 836
Actual costs, 121, 306–307
Adjacencies plan, 417, 836
Administered vertical marketing systems, 164–166, 836
Administrative management problems, 625–627
Advertising, 127, 481–482, 489–490, 500–508, 555, 811–836
Advertising agencies, 152–153
Affordable method, 496, 836–837
Age Discrimination in Employment Act of 1967 (ADEA), 554
Age distribution, 79–80
Allocation, 148, 837
Allowances, 236, 845
Ambiance, 433, 837
Americans with Disabilities Act, 209, 554
Anchor stores, 377
Anticipation discounts, 284
Antimerger Act (1950), 183
Arbitration, 174–175, 837
Assets, 240, 614–620, 627, 837
Assorting, 148, 837
Assortment. *See* Breadth
Assortment planning matrix, 291
Attitude data, uses of, 96–98
Attribute ratings, 97–99
Auditing assets, monitoring, 619–620

Automatic checkout machines (ACMs), 629, 837
Automatic merchandising machine operators, 118, 837
Automobile Information Disclosure Act, 183

Baby boom era, 78, 80
Bait-and-switch advertising, 194–195, 837
Bait pricing, 332, 837
Balance sheet, 236, 240–243, 837
Basic return on investment model, 38–40
Basic service, 541
Basic stock method (BSM), 257–258, 837
Beginning-of-the-month (BOM) inventories, planned, 224–225
Behavior, vs. attitude, 90
Behavioral characteristics, 75, 89–99, 837
Behavioral trends, 600–608
Below-market pricing, 301, 326
Benefactor objective, 44
Benefits, supplemental, 571–572
Better Business Bureau, 210
Black enterprise neighborhoods, 388
Block plan, 417–419, 837
Blue laws, 181, 210
Bona fide occupational qualification (BFOQ), 556, 837
Bonuses, year end, 283
Book inventory, 228–229, 837
Branch banking, case history, 693–699
Branch store organizations, 581–584
Breadth, 264–266, 837
Break-even, 125–126, 134
Brokerages, synthetic, 190
Brood hen and chick organizations, 581–582
Bubble plan, 417–418, 837

Building codes, 210
Bulk or capacity fixture, 425
Buyers
 behavior characteristics, 356–357
 planned gross margin, 227
 resident, 152
Buyer/vendor relationship, effectiveness of, 278
Buying, 90–106, 145–146, 262, 281, 319, 585
Buying power index (BPI), 364, 837
Buy trigger event, 105, 837

CACI Marketing Systems, 356, 360, 387
Careers in retailing, 19–20
Cash and other current assets, 40
Cash discount, 283–284, 837
Cash rebates, 283
Catalog houses, 8, 118
Category killers, 95, 114, 837
Category signage, 439, 837
Category specialists, 114, 837
Celler-Kefauver Act, 207–208
Census of Population and Housing, 1990, 355–356, 359
Census tracts, 379
Central business district (CBD), 370–372, 837
Central place theory, 348–351, 837–838
Chain stores, 5, 9–10, 584–585, 678–682
Channel behavior, 52
Channel constraints, 201–206
Channel partners, financial performance of, 604–605
Children of employees, before- and after-school programs for, 681
Choice criteria, 530–531
Circulation, 418–422
 pattern, 418
Civil Rights Act of 1964, Title VII, 554

849

Clayton Act, 183, 186, 204–208
Closing sale, 533–534
Closing signals, 534–535
Coercive power, 169, 838
Commodities, 187
Community center, 373, 838
Community characteristics, 354, 358–359, 362
Community life cycle, 358
Compensation plans, 562, 567, 568–571, 573, 838
Compensatory model, 97
Competition, 110–141, 361, 495, 520
Competitive assortment, 292, 838
Competitive market, 120–121
Competitors, 52, 145, 555, 606–608
Complementary products, 305
Compromise, 174, 838
Computer manufacturers, strategies to prevent diverters, 282–283
Computer superstores, 114
Conceptual model, 100
Confidential vendor analysis, 273–274, 276, 838
Conflict, 169–175, 530–531
Consignment, 266, 838
Consumer behavior, 52, 100, 145
Consumer costs, 121, 306–308
Consumer patronage process, 105
Consumer Product Safety Commission, 198
Consumers
  attitudes, 601
  choice objective, 44
  decision making, 104–105
  expectations, 460–463
  monitoring, 600–603
Content theories, 564–566, 838
Contractual vertical marketing systems, 157–164, 838
Contribution margin, 287, 838
Control, 253–254, 584–585
Control system(s), 59–62
Convenience store chains, case history, 756–772
Convenience stores, 95, 233, 464–465, 757–759
Convenience store sales, by product category, 761
Conventional marketing channel, 154–155, 838
Converse law of retail gravity, 344–346
Conversion rate, 539
Cooperative advertising, 493
Cooperatives (co-ops), 158–159, 798
Corporate image, 454–455
Corporate vertical marketing systems, 155–157, 838
Cost complement, 231–232, 838
Cost curves, 310–311

Cost functions, 124
Cost justification defense, 188
Cost method, 227–230, 838
Cost of goods sold, 40, 236–238, 838
Cost per thousand (CPM) method, 505, 838
Coupons, 184, 509
Coverage, 504, 838
Creativity, 20, 484–486
Credit, effect on price, 303–304, 617
Credit disclosure rules, 195–196
Critical mass, 500
Cultural control, 60, 838
Cumulative quantity discount, 280, 283, 838
Cumulative reach, 505, 838
Current assets, 240, 838
Current liability, 242, 838
Current ratio, 616–617, 838
Customary pricing, 327, 838
Customer contact, 541
Customers, 69–109, 488–489
  acknowledgement of, 541
  choice criteria, 530
  expectations, using selling environment to help form, 468–469
  types, 527–528
Customer satisfaction, 106, 601–603
Customer service, 53, 304
Customer Service and Sales Enhancement Audit, 543, 838

Debt, paying off, 236
Deceitful diversion of patronage, 192–193, 838
Deceptive advertising, 193–194, 838–839
Deceptive pricing, 190–192
Deceptive sales practices, 194–196
Decisions, 575
  major types, 14
  variables, 129
Decisiveness, requirements for, 20–21
Deferred payment price, 195
Delivery terms, 284, 839
Demand, 379–392
Demand density, 386–390, 839
Demand elasticity of price, 309–310, 839
Demand factors, 354–360, 387
Demand manager (DM), 631
Demand-oriented pricing, 305–310
Demand side of retailing, 121–124
Demand variables, 308–310
Demographic characteristics, 49–51, 75, 78–86, 89, 525–526, 839
Density of supply, 391, 839
Departmental signage, 439, 839

Department stores, 5, 113–116, 132, 149, 257, 289, 618
Depth, 264, 266, 839
Deregulation, of banks, 471
Destination merchandise, 93–94, 839
Destination stores, 93–96, 839
Dialectic process theory, 115–116, 839
Differential advantage, merchandising, 470–472
Directional signage, 439, 839
Direct mail, 504
Direct marketing, 118. See also Nonstore retailing
Direct product profit (DPP), 293–294, 839
Direct retailing, 118. See also Nonstore retailing
Direct-selling establishments, 8, 119, 839
Disclaimers, 199
Discount department stores, 11, 118, 131–132, 292
Discounts, 232
Discount stores, 5, 116, 170, 417
Distribution, 203–204, 683–688
Distributive Education Clubs of America (DECA), 555
Distributor training, 282
Diverters, 146, 204, 281–283, 839
Divertive competition, 133, 839
Dollar constraints, 266
Dollar merchandise control, 261–262
Dollar merchandise planning, 254–261
Domain consensus, 172, 839
Dual distribution, 203–204, 839
Dumping, 427
Dwell time, 473–474, 839

Early markdown policy, 321
Earnings per share, 38, 839
Economic trends, 85–86
Economic turbulence, 76–77
Education level, 49, 83
Electronic data interchange (EDI), 156, 591, 629–630, 839
Electronic funds transfer (EFT), 629–630, 839
Electronic retailing, 136
Employee discounts, 225, 571–572
Employees, 554–559, 575–576
  motivation for, 564–567
Employee seminars, 681
Employee theft, 285, 839
Ending book value at retail, sample, 232
End-of-the-month (EOM) dating, 283–284
End-of-the-month (EOM) inventories, planned, 224–225
Engel's laws, 357, 839

Subject Index

Entry barriers, 13–14
Environmental demand variables, 308–309
Environmental trends, 608, 613–614
Equal Credit Opportunity Act, 184
Equal stores, 583–584
Equity objective, 44
ESRI, 608
Ethics, 371, 484
Everyday low pricing strategy, 782
Exclusive dealing, 204–205
Expansion, case history, 651–656, 772–782
Expectancy theory, 566
Expenses, problems related to, 627–628
Expertise power, 168, 839
Expert systems, 630–632, 839
Expressed warranties, 198–199, 839
Extra dating, 266, 284, 839

Facilitating agencies, 603–604
Facilitating institutions, 150–151, 839
Factory outlet centers, 375, 839
Fair Debt Collection Practice Act, 184
Fair Labor Standards Act, 753
Fair Packaging and Labelling Act, 183
Fair trade. *See* Vertical price fixing
Fair trade laws, 186, 301
Family leave, 681
Family life cycle, 50, 840
Fast-food restaurants, 11, 95
Feature fixture, 425
Federal legislation, 183–184, 208–209
Federal Trade Commission (FTC), 183, 190–191, 196, 200–201, 208, 332
Felt conflict, 173, 840
FIFO (first in, first out), 230, 238–240, 840
Figure forms, 432
Financial Accounting Standards Board (FASB), 613
Financial leverage, 37–38, 40, 840
Financial marketplace, 471
Financial performance objectives, 36–42, 840
Financial records, 235
Financial resources, problems with, 626
Financial statements, 236
Financing, 145, 148
Fixed assets, 40
Fixed component, 568, 840
Fixed costs, 40, 124, 310, 840
Fixtures, 423–426, 429–431
Flexible pricing, 328, 840
Flexible time, 681
Floor merchandise space, 414
Folding, 426–427

Food Marketing Institute, 88
Food retailing, 138
Foreseeability doctrine, 198
Formal organization structure, 574, 840
Franchise(s), 159–164, 174, 205–206, 840
Franchise contract, 163–164
Free-flow layout, 419–420, 840
Free-lance broker, 152, 840
Free merchandise, 280, 840
Free on board (FOB), 284
Freestanding locations, 377–379, 840
Frequency, 505, 840
Fringe benefit package, 568, 840
FTC Rule, 753
Full-line policy, 205, 840
Functional discount. *See* Trade discount
Functional spaces, 413–414
Funeral homes, 446–447
Furniture market, 773–774
Future-dating negotiation, 283–284

Gas stations, 8, 116, 185, 465
Generally accepted accounting principles (GAAP), 613
General merchandise manager, case study, 688–693
General merchandise retailing, 56, 115–116, 134
General merchandise stores, 8, 413, 579
Geographic information system (GIS), 607–608
Geographic mobility, 17
Geographic shifts, 80–83
Ghetto retailing, 371
GLAD TO selling system, 536–538
GM/HBA, 712
Goal setting, for motivation, 566–567
Golden assortment, 291, 840
Gondola, 424
Good-faith defense, 188
Goodwill, 242, 244, 840
Government regulation, 753–754
Graying of America, 79
Green River ordinances, 210
Grid (maze) layout, 419–420, 840
Grocery retailing, 23, 56, 113, 285
Gross domestic product (GDP), 75–76, 108–109, 840
Gross margin, 10–11, 40, 227, 239, 287–289, 499, 840. *See also* Maintained markup
Gross margin return on inventory (GMROI), 42, 287–293, 321–322, 840

Gross margin return on labor (GMROL), 42
Gross margin return on sales (GMROS), 37, 41–42, 840
Gross margin return on selling space (GMROS), 289–290, 293
Gross profit, 11
Gross sales, 236, 840
Guarantees, 198, 283

Handling, 253
Hardlines fixtures, 423–424
Hardware stores, 7, 11, 703–706
Herzberg's two-factor theory, 565–566
Hierarchy of merchandising information, 472–473, 840
High-margin/high-turnover retailers, 11–12
High-margin/low-turnover retailers, 11
High performance, 216, 255, 289
High-quality services, 458–460, 462
High turnover (employee), actions to overcome, 680–681
Home shopping, 14, 88
Horizontal cooperative advertising, 490, 492, 840
Horizontal market allocation, 203
Horizontal price fixing, 184, 840
Horizontal territorial restrictions, 203
Households, 83–85, 358, 386
  age profile, 357–358
  characteristics, 354, 357–358
  demand variables, 309
  income, 357
Huff model of trading areas, 381–385, 402
Human resource manager (HRM), 632
Human resources, 15, 26, 60, 550–554, 557, 559–561, 574–586, 626
  compensation, 567–573
  management, 549–550
Hypermarkets, 350

Image engineering, 406–408, 841
IMPACT model, 134–135
Implied warranty of fitness, 199–200, 841
Implied warranty of merchantability, 199, 841
Impulse-intercept merchandise, 93, 841
Impulse purchasing, 402, 542
Income and education ratios, 701
Income growth, 85
Income statement, 229, 234–238, 620–621, 841
Independent Grocers Alliance (IGA), 158
Index of retail saturation (IRS), 353–354, 606, 841

Informal organization structure, 574, 841
Information, 593-594, 596-598
  gathering, 145, 149
  resources, 15-16, 26, 60, 104
  sources, 363-364, 594-598, 603
Information technology, developments that lead retail technology, 631
Initial consideration set, 103, 841
Initial markup, 315-317, 841
Inner-directedness, 89
Institutional confidence, deterioration of, 87
Institutional signage, 438-439, 841
In-store marketing, 408, 841
Intangible services, 455-456
Integrated information management system (IIMS), 629-630, 841
Interactive pricing, 302-305
Interbrand competition, 213, 841
Intercept competition, 133-134
Intercept merchandise, 93-94, 841
Interdependence, 168-172, 489
Interest rate, 76, 841
International Accounting Standards Committee (IASC), 244
International expansion, in franchising, 161
International Franchise Association, 160
International Franchise Association Educational Foundation, Inc., 159
International Mass Retail Association (IMRA), 94
International promotion, 508
International retailing, trends in, 6, 135-136, 244
Interorganizational management, 166, 841
Interstate commerce, 184, 841
Intertype competition, 132, 841
Intrabrand competition, 213, 841
Intratype competition, 131, 841
Inventory accounting systems, 227-228
Inventory-effective assortment, 291-292, 841
Inventory intensity, 289
Inventory profits, 230
Inventory stockturn, 255
Inventory turnover, 11, 254-257, 260, 289, 841
Inventory valuation, 227-235
Investors Management Service, 605

Job applicants, screening and selection of, 554-559
Job descriptions, development of, 552-553
Job enrichment, 573-574, 841
Job sharing, 681

Job specifications, development of, 552-553
Junk bonds, 246-247
Just-in-time inventory systems, 156

Labor, 125, 551
Labor force, 86, 524-525
Labor productivity, 38, 841
Lanham Act, 193
Late markdown policy, 321
Latent conflict, 170, 841
Leader pricing, 331, 841
Lease terms, 396
Lease versus buy decision, 395-396
Legal constraints, 305, 484
Legal environment, 145, 181, 610-613
Legislation, 174, 183-184, 208-210. See also specific law
Liability, 198, 240, 242-243, 841
Lifestyle graphics, 439-440
LIFO (last in, first out), 230, 238-240, 841
Lighting design, 434-435
Liquidity, 616, 841
Location, 26, 303, 326, 340-342, 369-379. See also Site selection
  resources, problems with, 626-627
Long-range analysis, 553
Long-term debt, exchanging for short-term, 236
Long-term liabilities, 243, 842
Loop (race-track) layout, 421, 842
Loss leader, 331, 842
Low-margin/high-turnover retailers, 11, 284
Low-margin/low-turnover retailers, 11-12

Magnuson-Moss Warranty Federal Trade Commission Act, 184, 200
Mail-order houses, 5, 8, 118, 181, 842
Maintained markup, 317-318, 842. See also Gross margin
Management, interorganizational, 166
Managerial demand variables, 309-310
Manifest conflict, 173, 842
Manufacturer's agent, 152, 842
Markdown, 225, 232, 311, 318-323
Market and Performance Assessment Project, 797, 799-808
Market area size, 495
Market constraints, 267
Market dominance, case history, 714-728
Market identification, 343-354, 364-365
Marketing
  functions, 145-149, 550-551
  goal of, 71
  management, 14-16
  strategies, 54-59

Marketing channel, 144, 154, 603-605, 842. See also Marketing system
Marketing institutions, 150-154
Marketing perspective, on retailing, 71-72
Marketing system, 143-154, 842
Market performance objectives, 36-37, 842
Marketplace, 14, 51-54, 56-57, 120
Market position, 47, 71-74, 842
Market position image, 73-74, 405-406, 409-410, 842
Market potential, 354-357
Market research studies, 598, 797-811
Market saturation, 606, 842
Market segmentation, 48-51, 74-75, 842
Market share, 37, 134-135, 607, 842
Market share dominance, 499-500
Markup, 311-315, 317, 842
Maslow's hierarchy of needs, 564-565
Maximum demand price, 122, 308-310, 842
Media exposure, 702-703
Media strategy, case history, 811-835
Melting-pot theory, 115-116
Menswear Retailers Association, 260
Merchandise agreements, programmed, 164-166
Merchandise assortment, 289
Merchandise budget, 216-220, 663-665, 842
Merchandise capacity calculations, 431
Merchandise handling, 253, 285-286
Merchandise intensity, 289
Merchandise management, 252-254, 269-270, 842
Merchandise mix, 127, 266-268, 606
Merchandise performance, evaluating, 286-294
Merchandise presentation, 423, 426-429
Merchandise productivity, 38, 842, 415-416, 842
Merchandise report, fine-line, 622-623
Merchandise stockturn, 255
Merchandising, 25, 216, 253, 263-264, 340, 406, 429-431
  decisions, 216-217
  errors, 319-320
  sources, selection of, 273-278
Mergers, 206-208
Metropolitan statistical areas (MSAs), 82, 842
Middle-of-the-month (MOM) dating, 284
Mission statement, 32-36
Mobility, 82-83, 359
Model stock plan, 268-272, 842
Mom-and-pop store, case history, 703-706

Subject Index

Monopolistic competition, 120, 122, 842
Motivation, 564, 842
Multi-attribute decision model, 96–98
Multiple-unit pricing, 330–331, 842

National Commission on Consumer Finance, 183
National debt, 77
National Planning Data Corporation, 51, 356, 360, 387, 608
National Retail Federation, 13, 210, 260
National Retail Trade Federation, 596
Natural selection, 114–115
Need recognition, 101–103, 843
Needs, 542, 564–565
Neighborhood business district (NBD), 372, 843
Neighborhood center, 373, 843
Neighborhood types, 388–389
Net profit, 227, 239, 397–398, 843
Net profit margin, 40
Net sales, 236, 843
Net worth, 40, 240, 243, 843
Nielsen Retail Index, 596
Noncumulative quantity discount, 280, 843
Noncurrent assets, 240–242, 843
Nonprice decisions, 127–129
Nonprice strategies, impact of, 128
Nonprice variables, 127, 132
Nonstore retailers, 8, 118–119

Objectives, 34–37, 45–47, 624
Occupations, Aristotle's ranking of, 4–5
Odd pricing, 329–331, 843
Off-price retailers, 327
Oligopolistic competition, 120, 843
100 percent location, 392, 843
One-price policy, 328, 843
One-way exclusive dealing, 204, 843
On-shelf merchandising, 423
Open-to-buy (OTB), 261–262, 843
Operating expenses, 239, 843
Operating margin percentage, 287
Operating performance trends, 614–623
Operating profit, 40, 227, 239, 287, 843
Operations management problems, 627–628
Opportunity costs, 121, 307
Optimal merchandise mix, 263–266
Optional stock list approach, 10
Order getters, 523–524, 843
Order takers, 523, 843
Organization structure(s), 576–583, 656–659
Organizing modes, 574–576

Other income or expenses, 239, 843
Outshopping, 121, 843
Overages, 233
Overstored, 130, 843
Owner's equity, 240, 843
Ownership groups, 585–586

Palming off, 843
Passive information gathering, 100–101, 843
Patents, 196–197, 213, 843
Payroll summary, 595
Pegging, 426
Penetration price, 324, 843–844
Penney idea, 716
People approach, 562
People greeters, 561, 570
Perceived conflict, 173, 844
Percentage-of-sales method, 496, 844
Percentage variation method (PVM), 258–259, 844
Perceptual incongruity, 170, 844
Performance appraisal, 399, 561–564, 844
Performance profiles, 622
Performance standards, 539, 616–619
Perpetual inventory system, 228, 230
Personal interview, 556–558
Personal objectives, 37, 44–45, 844
Personal selling, 127, 481–482, 844
Personal service, 466–467
Physical inventory, 228, 233, 844
Planned BOM and EOM inventories, 224–225
Planned purchases at cost, 226–227
Planned retail reductions, 225–226
Planned sales, 220–224
Planned urban development (PUD), 378, 844
Planning, 24, 31–32, 253–254, 262, 412–423, 592, 844. *See also* Strategic planning
Planograms, 632
Point of indifference, 344, 844
Point-of-Purchase Advertising Institute (POPAI), 103
Point-of-sale (POS) scanners, 605, 629
Point-of-sale (POS) signage, 439, 844
Point-of-sale (POS) terminals, 156
Population characteristics, 355–359
Population trends, 78–80, 700
Post-purchase resentment, 105–106, 844
Power, 168–169, 844
Predatory pricing, 192
Prepaid expenses, 240, 844
Price discrimination, 186–190, 844
Price effects, 304–305
Price elastic demand, 310
Price image, 521
Price inelastic demand, 310

Price lining, 328–329, 844
Price points, range of, 303
Price zone, 325, 844
Pricing, 25, 301–302, 305, 325, 340, 467–468, 606, 659–663
  constraints, 182–192
  errors, 319
  policies, 324–326, 844
  strategies, 216, 327–332
Primary marketing institutions, 150–151, 844
Principle of compatibility, 394, 844
Private-brand pricing, 332, 844
PRIZM neighborhood types, 383, 386
Problem identification subsystem, 598, 600–623
Problem recognition, 101–103
Problem solution subsystem, 624–628
Process theories, 564, 566–567, 844
Product constraints, 196–201
Productivity objectives, 38–40
Product liability, 198
Profit(s), 286–287, 311, 371
Profitability objectives, 37–38, 323, 844
Profit-maximizing price, 125–127
Profit-oriented objectives, 323–324
Pro forma return on investment model, 396–399
Programmed merchandise agreements, 164–167, 844
Projected sales, 224
Promotion(s), 132, 303, 479–484, 606–607, 707–713
Promotional discount, 281–282, 844
Promotion constraints, 192–196
Promotion mix, 481–482
Promotion strategy, 486–487
Protected niche, developing, 135
Prototype, 410, 844
Psychic costs, 121, 307
Psychographics, 75, 86–89, 844
Publicity, 481–482, 510–512, 844
Public Law 101-336. *See* Americans with Disabilities Act
Public service promotion, 488
Pull strategy, 156
Purchase probabilities, 600–601
Purchases at cost, planned, 226–227
Purchases at retail, planned, 226–227
Purchasing agent, 152, 844
Pure competition, 120, 844
Pure monopoly, 120, 844
Push strategy, 156

Quantity discount, 280–281, 845
Quick ratio, 616, 845
Quick response inventory control, 156, 413

Range, 349, 845
Rate of asset turnover, 40

Rate-shoppers' guide, 616
Ratio analysis, 236
Reach, 505, 845
Rebates, 184, 509
Receipt-of-goods (ROG) dating, 284
Receivables, borrowing against, 236
Reconciliation, 174, 845
Reductions, 225–226, 232–233, 845
Reference prices, 304
Referent power, 169, 845
Regional center, 56, 373–374, 845
Reilly's law of retail gravitation, 343, 345–348, 845
Repayment schedules, 236
Replenishment manager (RM), 631
Resale price maintenance, 184–186, 301, 845
Resident buying offices (RBOs), 277–278, 845
Restaurant chains, case history, 736–756
Restrictions, territorial, 201–203
Retail accordion theory, 113–114, 845
Retail career, 16–22
Retailer(s), 7–13, 150–151, 278
Retailer-owned cooperatives, 158–159
Retailer/supplier relations, 166–175
Retailer/vendor partnerships, 430
Retail gravity theory, 343–348
Retail identity, 437–438
Retail information system (RIS), 591–592, 598–599, 602, 628–632, 845
Retailing, 5–7, 9, 71, 216
 checks on, 121
 perspectives on, 1–29
 role of, 5
 as service, 450
Retailing trade associations, 210
Retail life cycle, 116–118, 845
Retail-Link program, 16
Retail method, 231–235, 845
Retail patronage model, 100–107, 845
Retail reporting calendar, 221–223
Retroactive (or retraction) advertising, 196, 845
Return clause, 174
Return on assets, 37, 40, 398–399, 845
Return on investment (ROI) goal, 288
Return on net worth, 38, 40, 845
Return policy, 521
Returns and allowances, 236, 845
Reward power, 168, 846
Risk taking, 21, 145, 149
Robinson-Patman Act, 183, 186–187, 189–190, 192, 212, 280

Salary commission, 570–571
Sale(s), 40, 320, 533–534
 displacement, 500, 846
 enhancement, 542
 forecasting, 218, 220

Sales agent, 152, 846
Sales and Marketing Management, 608
Sales-below-cost laws, 209–210
Sales-oriented objectives, 324
Sales per dollar invested, 617
Sales per hour, 539–540
Salesperson-initiated contact, 541
Sales personnel, 517–522, 525–531, 539–540
Sales per square feet of selling space, 617
Sales productivity, 405–406, 408–410
Sales promotions, 481–482, 509–510, 666–669, 846
Sales response curves, 492
Satellite communication systems, 633
Saturation theory, 352–354
Scrambled merchandising, 131, 133, 846
Seasonal discount, 282–283, 846
Secondary business district (SBD), 372, 846
Secondary markets, 82
Securities and Exchange Commission, 613
Segmental review, 61, 846
Self-gratification objective, 45
Selling, 145–147, 522–554
Selling laws, 209
Selling process, 531–536, 552
Selling program, 536–538
Selling time, 540
Semifixed costs, 124, 846
Service(s), 326, 446–453, 456–457, 463–470. *See also* Customer service
 costs, 522
 delivery, 457
 discrimination, 188–190
 offering, 466
 process, 463–464
Service quality, 457–468, 846
Service sector, selling in, 538–539
Services retailing, 378–379, 445–450, 453–457, 468–474
Shelving, 426–427
Sherman Antitrust Act, 183–184, 201–203, 205
Shipping terms, 284
Shopping, 6, 90–91, 98–99, 669–672
Shopping centers, 5, 372–377, 494, 731–736, 846
Shop trigger event, 102, 846
Shortages (overages), 233
Short-range analysis, 553
Shrinkage, 408–410, 422–423, 846
Sign ordinances, 181
Single-unit retailers, 9
Site selection, 387, 392–399, 402, 646–649
Skimming, 324, 846
Slotting fees, 267

Smells, 435–436
Social trends, 83–85
Societal objectives, 37, 42–44, 846
Socioeconomic environment, 75–78, 145, 608
Softlines fixtures, 424–426
Sorting, 145, 148
Sought-intercept merchandise, 93, 846
Space allocation, 412–415
Space-effective assortment, 291, 846
Space management, GMROI and, 289–293
Space productivity, 38, 290, 415, 846
Special promotions, 127
Specialty stores, 113, 115, 217, 672–678
Spine layout, 421–422, 846
Sponsorship, 490–492
Square feet per employee, 361
Standard industrial classification (SIC) codes, 7–9
Standard stock list approach, 9
State and local laws, 209–210
Statement of cash flow, 243–247, 846
Statement of market position, 47–51
Statement of mission, 32–36
Statement of objectives, 34–47
Status quo objectives, 324, 846
Steering Marketing Control Model (STEMCOM), 617–619, 846
Stock keeping units (SKUs), 263
Stock overage, 232–233
Stock-to-sales method (SSM), 260–261, 846–847
Stock-to-sales ratio, 224, 260–261, 847
Store(s), 6, 56, 96, 361, 495
 characteristics, 520
 choice, 96
 design, 433–436
 environment, 127, 405–412
 image, 304–305, 487–488
 layout, 415–418, 710
 location, 495
 name, 437–438
 policies, 529–530
Store density map, 391
Store saturation, 352–353, 847
Strategic planning, 30–67, 624–625, 847
Strategic profit model, 38–40
Strategic resource management model, 40–43
Substantiality, 51, 847
Substitution effect, 500, 847
Suggestion selling, 534–536, 542
Supermarket(s), 5, 11, 55, 88, 118, 131, 134–135, 149, 235, 267, 688–693
Supermarket industry, 82, 268
Super-regional center, 374, 847
Supplier support, 495–496
Supply, evaluation of, 379–392

Subject Index

Supply factors, 360–363
Supply-oriented pricing, 310–311
Supply side of retailing, 124–125
Synthetic brokerages, 190

10K report, 604–605
Target market, 47–48, 575
Target market income, 521–522
Task analysis, 550–553, 847
Task-and-objective method, 497–498, 847
Technological environment, 145, 613–614
Telemarketing, case history, 649–651, 682–683
Territorial restrictions, 201–203, 847
Theft, 285
Theme centers, 374–375, 847
Theory X, 566
Theory Y, 566
Three concentric circle model, 14–15
Three-dimensional demand model, 121, 123, 306
Threshold, 349, 847
TIGER (Topologically Integrated Geographic Encoding and Referencing system), 356
Time management crisis, 87–89
Topologically Integrated Geographic Encoding and Referencing system (TIGER), 356
Total assets, 40, 242, 397, 847
Total costs, 40, 124
Total liabilities, 243, 847
Total Quality Management (TQM), 726
Total reductions, 315

Total sales, 224, 396–397
Total sensory marketing, 435–436
Towne-Oller Index, 271
Trade associations, 260
Trade centers, arrangement according to Christaller's model of central place, 352
Trade discount, 279–280, 847
Trade Regulation Rule on Franchising (FTC Rule), 753
Trade shows, 225
Trading area, 345–347, 352, 380, 382–385, 607–608, 847
Traffic characteristics, 393–394
Training, 559–561
Transporting, 145, 147–148
Travel costs, 306–308
Truth-in-Lending Act (1968), 183
Turnover, 255, 267
Two-way exclusive dealing, 204–205, 847
Tying agreement, 205, 847

Unauthorized retailer(s), 204
Understored, 129–130, 847
Unemployment, 77–78
Unfair trade practices laws, 210
Unit stock planning, 263–273
Universal product code (UPC), 156, 629

Values and Lifestyle (VALS), 89, 847
Variable component, 568, 847
Variable costs, 40, 124, 310–311, 847
Variable pricing, 328, 848

Vendor, 170, 225, 274
Vendor classification, 274
Vendor collusion, 285, 848
Vendor negotiations, 278–284
Vendor profitability analysis statement, 273, 275, 848
Vertical color blocking, 428–429
Vertical cooperative advertising, 490–492, 848
Vertical marketing systems, 155–166, 848
Vertical price fixing, 184–186, 848
Vertical territorial restraints, 201–203
Visual communications, 436–440, 848
Voluntary groups, wholesaler-sponsored, 157–158

Wall merchandise space, 414
Warehouse clubs, 5, 14, 117, 132, 284, 413
Warranties, 198–201, 283
Weeks' supply method (WSM), 259, 848
Wheeler-Lea Act, 183, 190, 192–193
Wheel of retailing hypothesis, 112–113, 848
Wholesaler-sponsored voluntary groups, 157–158
WISDOM system, 598
Within-market opportunity analysis, 369, 848
Working capital manager (WCM), 632
Working parent exchange groups, 681

Zoning laws, 209

NAME INDEX

Aaker, David A., 53
Abend, Jules, 729
Achabal, Dale D., 514, 545, 618–619, 635
Akhter, Humayun, 67
Akhter, Syed H., 336
Albaum, Gerald, 336
Albrecht, Karl, 476
Alderson, Wroe, 177
Aldhizer, George, 244
Allaway, Arthur W., 67
Allford, Suzanne, 15, 726
Allison, Bob, 797, 803, 808–809
Alpert, Mark, 371
Alsop, Ronald, 297
Ambash, Joseph, 588
Anderson, Jim, 736
Anderson, Patricia M., 401
Andres, William A., 62, 67, 250
Angelmar, Reinhard, 24
Applebaum, William, 352, 367, 380, 401
Arbose, J., 782
Aristotle, 4–5
Arnold, Stephen J., 96, 109, 336
Austin, Nancy, 730
Avalon, Frankie, 748
Avila, Ramon A., 588
Avilova, Liza, 6
Avilova, Olga, 6
Axelrod, Joel, 401

Balazs, Anne L., 109
Baldo, Anthony, 178
Baliga, Rajaram, 335
Bard, Ray, 729
Barnes, Henry, 689
Barrier, Michael, 729
Bartlett, Richard C., 29
Bass, Stephen J., 29, 140
Bates, Albert D., 29, 66, 140, 336
Batogowski, Joseph, 784–785, 788
Bavishi, Vinod B., 250
Bawa, Kapil, 297, 336

Beamer, Wayne, 729
Bearden, William O., 336, 514
Beckman, Martin, 402
Bell, Martin J., 67
Bellizzi, Joseph A., 545
Bergman, Joan, 729
Bergschneider, Marc C., 754, 756
Berman, Barry, 719
Bernhardt, Kenneth L., 811
Bernstein, Peter W., 109
Berry, Leonard L., 109, 336, 458, 476–477
Bessom, R. M., 477
Bing, Louis, 484
Bitner, Mary Jo, 476–477, 544
Bitta, Albert J. Della, 297
Black, Jack, 654–655
Blackwell, Roger D., 67, 109
Blattberg, Robert C., 336, 514
Blumenthal, Karen, 729
Boatwright, Earl W., 545
Bolfing, Claire P., 635
Booms, Bernard H., 544
Borin, Norm, 298
Boulding, Kenneth E., 179
Boyle, Bjorn, 772
Boyt, Tom, 177
Bozic, Michael, 792
Bradford, Michael, 729
Bragg, Arthur, 729
Brauer, Molly, 729
Brennan, Bernard, 247
Brennan, Edward A., 782, 785, 795
Britney, Robert, 283, 297
Britt, Stewart Henderson, 336
Brookman, Faye, 729
Brooks, John R., Jr., 140
Brown, Daniel J., 297
Brown, Gene, 544
Brown, James K., 514
Brown, James R., 178
Brown, Julia A. N., 401
Brown, Russell A., 514
Brown, Stephen W., 476

Bruner, Gordon C., II, 109, 443
Bruner, Robert F., 28
Buchanan, Robert, 715
Bucklin, Louis P., 28
Burnside, Frank, 297
Bush, Alan J., 545, 563
Bush, Robert P., 545, 563
Butler, Tiffany, 703

Camerius, James W., 714
Caminiti, Susan, 67, 635, 729
Campeau, Robert, 58–59, 718
Carlson, Phillip G., 336
Carn, Neil, 367
Carney, Mick, 177
Carson, David J., 477
Carter, Paul R., 715
Castillo, Henry, 2–3
Chang, Kyu Yeol, 514
Chanil, Debra, 170
Choi, Frederick D. S., 250
Chonko, Lawrence B., 545
Christaller, Walter, 348–352, 365, 367, 380
Clapp, John M., 367
Clark, Dennis H., 738, 754–755
Clark, L., 109
Clow, Kenneth E., 335, 477
Cochran, Thomas N., 729
Cohen, Saul B., 352, 367
Coleman, Lyon G., 588
Combs, Linda J., 477
Converse, Paul D., 344, 346, 367
Coors, Adolph, 202
Coppett, John I., 649–651
Corwin, Pat, 729
Coulter, Ronald, 544
Cowles, Deborah, 545
Cox, Anthony, 304, 336, 515
Cox, Dena, 304, 336, 515
Craig, C. Samuel, 367, 401
Crask, Melvin R., 298
Crosby, Lawrence A., 545
Cunningham, Harry B., 55, 57

856

Name Index

Dabah, Haim, 724
Dalrymple, Douglas J., 476
d'Amico, Michael, 140
Dant, Rajiv P., 178
Dapiran, G. Peter, 772
Darden, William R., 108, 545, 588
Darian, Jean C., 109
Darwin, Charles, 114
Davidson, William R., 29, 116, 140, 177
Davis, Bob, 477
Dearth, Robert, 772
Deiderick, E. Terry, 66
DeKluyer, Cornelius, 297
Desmarais, Helen, 688–693
Deutsch, Morton, 178
Diaconis, Pam, 512
di Benedetto, C. Anthony, 66
Dickinson, Roger, 23, 29, 297
Dickson, Peter R., 335
Dickson, Warren L., 336
Dodge, H. Robert, 66
Dolittle, 108
Doody, Alton F., 177
Dora, P., 777
Dubinsky, Alan J., 545
Duhan, Dale F., 213
Duncan, Delbert J., 29, 140, 581, 588
Dunfee, T. W., 213
Dunne, Patrick M., 212, 250, 298, 335, 588

Eachus, H. T., 179
Eades, Kenneth M., 28
Edgerton, Jerry, 729
Edwards, Charles M., Jr., 514
Edwardson, B., 476
El-Ansary, Adel I., 178–179
Elias, Edwin A., 212
Eller, Karl, 758–759, 762–772
Elliott, Susan K., 729
Ellis, Larry, 694–695
Endicott, R. Craig, 729
Eng, Robert J., 67
Engel, James F., 109
Eroglu, Sevgin, 401, 443
Ettenson, Richard, 274, 297
Evans, Joel R., 719
Evans, Kenneth R., 545

Fabricant, Ross A., 335
Fain, Raymond N., 754–755
Falk, Susan, 19
Falvey, Jack, 132, 545
Fancher, Lynne A., 635
Farris, Paul, 297–298
Fedus, Cynthia, 19
Fein, Esther B., 6
Fern, Edward F., 588

Field, Marshall, 331
Finn, Adam, 401
Fischer, S., 777
Fishbein, Martin, 96, 109
Fisher, Christy, 729
Fitzgerald, Kate, 477
Flack, Robert P., 738, 754–755
Ford, Fredrick, 588
Forman, Andrew M., 544
Foster, E. E., 29
Foti, Sharon, 711
Fram, Eugene Ho, 401
Francis, Sally K., 297
Frayer, David J., 782
Freeman, Laurie, 141
French, J.R.P., 178
French, Warren A., 298
Frey, Stephen, 651–656
Fry, Joseph N., 336
Futrell, Charles M., 545, 588

Gable, Myron, 17, 29, 67, 514, 669
Gaeth, Gary J., 109, 274, 297
Gallagher, John, 514, 635
Gardner, Meryl P., 514
Garland, Susan, 514
Garrett, Dennis E., 635
Garry, Michael, 635
Gaski, John, 177
Gassenheimer, Jule, 178
Gawronski, F. J., 109
Gebhardt, Randall E., 443
Gedajlovic, Eric, 177
Gelb, Betsy, 545
Ghosh, Avijit, 351, 367, 401
Gifford, John B., 40, 66, 636
Gifford, Pat, 636
Gillespie, Karen R., 17, 29
Gilliam, Margaret A., 729
Gist, Ronald R., 115, 140
Glass, David, 726
Goldsby, Rachel, 703
Goodman, Jordon E., 729
Gordon, Harris, 635
Graham, Judith, 729
Green, Howard L., 401
Green, Jefferson, 757
Greene, Geoffrey, 66
Greenland, Steven J., 177
Grewal, Dhruv, 588
Grizzle, Jerry W., 754–755
Grottle, Robert L., 250
Gruber, Christina, 729
Guiltinan, Joseph P., 177–178
Gumbel, Peter, 6
Gummersson, Evert, 476
Gustavsson, Bengtove, 476

Hackman, J. Richard, 588
Hair, Joseph F., Jr., 545, 563

Hampton, Ronald D., 545, 588
Hanka, Carolyn J., 731
Harrell, Gilbert D., 401, 443
Hartley, Robert F., 545
Hartman, Sandra McCurley, 67
Hartnett, Michael, 729
Haverson, James T., 179
Hayes, Rodney, 663–665
Heald, G. I., 402
Hegel, 115
Heineke, John, 545
Helliker, Kevin, 443, 729
Hervey, Fred, 758
Herzberg, 565
Heskett, James L., 179, 476
Higby, Harold, 703
Higgins, Kevin T., 729
Higham, Paul, 303
Hirschman, Elizabeth C., 28, 297
Hite, Robert E., 545
Hollander, Stanley C., 29, 112–113, 140, 581, 588
Holman, Rebecca H., 336
Holmberg, Dave, 711
Hong, Sung-Tai, 274
Hood, Wayne, 795
Hoover, Jane, 656–659
House, Robert G., 178
Houston, Michael J., 402, 514
Hoving, Walter, 29
Howard, Craig, 712
Howell, Roy D., 29, 283, 297, 588
Hower, Ralph, 113, 140
Hoyer, Wayne D., 515
Hubbard, Burton, 23
Huber, Peter W., 212
Hudson, J. Clifford, 754–755
Huey, John, 729
Huff, David L., 380, 384, 402, 736
Hughes, James W., 401
Huizengo, H. Wayne, 139
Hunt, Shelby D., 177, 179, 213
Hurwood, David L., 514
Hyde, Linda, 29

Ingene, Charles A., 140, 367, 402, 545
Inman, J. Jeffrey, 515
Iyer, Easwar S., 336, 443

Jackson, D. W., 477
Jacober, Steve, 729
Jacobs, Lawrence, 515
Jacoby, Jacob, 443
Jaeb, Lorena, 764
Jaeb, Robert, 764
James, Michael, 646–649
James, Morton, 646
James, William L., 514

Jan-Benedict, E. M., 108
Jarratt, Denise G., 367
Jaworski, Bernard J., 67
Jessey, Joe, 711
Johnson, Brenda, 649–650, 682–683
Johnson, Gerry, 66
Johnson, Jay L., 156, 729–730
Johnson, Ron, 712
Johnston, Von, 562
Joseph, Ellis, 66

Kacker, Madhau, 28, 137, 141
Kahn, Robert, 508
Kalish, David, 109
Kamprad, Ingvar, 773
Kasaks, Sally Frame, 19
Kaufman, Patrick J., 177
Keith, Bill, 730
Kelley, J. Patrick, 514
Kelly, Kevin, 730
Kenney, William F., 717
Kerin, Roger A., 212, 683
Kernan, Jerome B., 213
Kerr, Dick, 730
King, Alfred Bailey, 659
King, Suzanne, 694–696
Kirshnan, R., 297
Klapper, Marvin, 730
Kochon, Thomas A., 179
Koopmans, Tjalin C., 402
Kopp, Robert J., 67
Kotler, Philip, 44, 51, 67
Krapfel, Robert E., Jr., 544
Krishna, Aradhna, 297, 336
Krmenec, A., 212
Kroc, Ray, 6
Kronquist, Stacy L., 250
Kumar, W., 212
Kurtz, Dave L., 477
Kuzdrall, Paul, 283, 297

LaLonde, Bernard, 367, 635
Lambert, Douglas M., 178
Lambert, Lauren, 782
Lambert, Zarrel V., 336–337
Landon, Jim, 812–813
Landwehr, Jane T., 297, 336
Langer, Judith, 66
Larson, James R., 250
Larson, Paul, 635
Leigh, James H., 336
Lettich, Jill, 108
Levering, Robert, 730
Levin, Alan, 588
Levine, Joshua, 447
Levitt, Mortimer, 44
Levitt, Theodore, 545
Lewis, M. Christine, 178
Lichtenstein, Donald R., 336, 514

Lieberman, Leonard, 754, 756
Liew, Chung, 689
Liles, Alan, 443
Lincoln, Douglas J., 109
Lindner, Carl, 758, 762, 766, 772
Link, Shirley, 44
Litterer, Joseph A., 178
Little, Michael W., 646
Little, Taylor E., Jr., 179
Lloyd, Bruce A., 730
Lodish, Leonard, 635
Logan, J. E., 66
Loomis, Carol J., 67
Losch, A., 351, 367
Loubier, J. M., 777
Louviere, Jordan J., 109
Lubove, Seth, 447, 477
Luchsinger, L. Louise, 212, 335
Lumpkin, James R., 545
Lusch, Robert F., 67, 108, 140, 178, 290–291, 298, 336, 367, 402, 635, 651, 656, 659, 663, 666, 688, 691, 736
Lusch, Virginia Newell, 672, 678, 693, 699, 703
Lynn, C. Stephen, 737–738, 754–755

Macaulay, Stuart, 179
Mader, Fred H., 298
Marcus, Bernard, 58
Marcus, Stanley, 29, 263, 297
Markin, Rom J., Jr., 367, 402
Maronick, Thomas J., 115, 140
Marshall, John Urquhart, 367
Martin, Christopher, 588
Martin, Greg, 28
Marvin, Rothenberg, 140
Maslow, Abraham, 564, 573
Mason, Joseph Barry, 67, 108, 212, 736
Mason, Todd, 730
Mathis, Kathy, 669, 671
Matthias, Rebecca, 376
Mattson, Bruce E., 514
Maursky, David, 443
May, Eleanor G., 48, 67
Mayer, Morris, 178, 736
Mazumdar, Tridib, 335
Mazur, Paul M., 579
McAlister, Leigh, 515
McCammon, Bert C., Jr., 165, 167, 177–178, 514
McCann, John M., 514, 635
McCarthy, E. Jerome, 177
McClain, Toni, 663–664
McDougall, Gordon H., 336
McGary, Edmund D., 177
McGoldrick, Peter J., 177
McIntyre, Shelby, 514, 545
McLafferty, Sara, 367
McLeod, Douglas, 730

McNair, Malcolm P., 112, 115, 140
McNeal, James V., 108
Meloche, Martin S., 66
Mendelovitz, Joe, 213
Mentzer, John T., 297
Merriam, John E., 66
Messner, Stephen D., 367
Milbank, Dana, 477
Miller, N. M., 777
Miller, William C., 29
Milliman, Ronald E., 443
Mills, Dick, 811–813
Mills, Kenneth H., 529
Miracle, Gordon, 514
Mitchell, Arnold, 109
Mittelstaedt, Robert, 336
Moin, David,, 20
Moinpour, Reza, 96, 109
Monroe, Kent B., 297, 335
Moore, Herff, 562
Moore, S. D., 782
Morgan, Fred W., 139, 213
Moriarty, Mark M., 514
Mosel, J. N., 545
Moutinho, Luiz, 401–402
Mowen, John C., 336
Muehling, Darrel D., 178
Mueller, Willard F., 213
Murphy, Patrick E., 67
Murray, Keith B., 477
Muser, Martin, 138

Nagao, Dennis, 588
Nalbone, Joanne, 711
Neill, Thomas P., 140
Nelson, Richard, 402
Neslin, Scott A., 336, 514
Nevin, John R., 179, 213, 402
Newman-Limata, Nancy, 250
Nichols, Grace, 20
Nielsen, A. C., 507
Nordstrom, James, 521
Nystrom, Paul H., 29

Oldham, Greg R., 588
Oliver, James, 297
Oliver, Richard L., 544
Omura, Glenn S., 29
Ortinau, David J., 545, 563
Orza, Vince, 2
O'Shaughnessy, John, 545
Oum, Tac H., 96, 109
Owens, Jan P., 443
Oxenfeldt, Alfred R., 335
Ozment, John, 28, 335, 477

Padgett, Tim, 730
Parasuraman, A., 458, 476–477, 545
Park, C. Whan, 336
Parrish, Jean, 274, 297
Parsons, Leonard J., 476

Name Index

Paterson, Thomas W., 213
Paul, Judith E., 529
Peach, E. Brian, 545, 588
Penney, James Cash, 606
Pennington, Allan L., 63, 67
Pereira, Arun, 212
Perreault, William D., 177
Peters, Tom, 28, 730
Peterson, Robert A., 29, 336
Petreycik, Richard M., 67, 707
Piech, Anton, 687
Piech, Ferdinand, 688
Pinson, Christian R. A., 24
Pinto, David, 108
Polonsky, Michael Jay, 367
Pomazal, Richard J., 109
Pondy, Louis R., 178
Porsche, Ferdinand, 684, 687
Porsche, Ferry, 687
Powell, Lonnie, 336
Prescott, Tom, 666–669
Price, Retha, 178
Pride, William M., 179

Rabianski, Joseph, 367
Ramirez, Art, 672–678
Rangan, V. Kasturi, 177
Rao, Akshay R., 335
Rao, Ashok, 297
Rasp, John, 67
Ratliff, Ron, 669, 671
Raven, Bertram H., 178–179
Rawn, Cynthia Dunn, 730
Ray, Nina M., 177
Read, B. J., 29
Reade, Robert, 764–765
Reed, Susan, 730
Regan, William J., 29
Reier, Sharon, 730
Reilly, William J., 343, 346, 348, 351, 365, 367, 380
Reiter, Tom, 735
Reynolds, J., 782
Rhodes, Tina, 672–678
Riche, Martha Farnsworth, 401
Ridgway, Nancy M., 336
Rieder, George A., 297
Robbins, John, 178
Robicheaus, Robert A., 178
Robinson, John P., 108–109, 477
Robinson, R. B., Jr., 66
Rocater, Ronald, 367
Roebuck, Alvah C., 782–783
Rogers, Alice, 140
Rood, Ferguson, 813
Rose, Matthew A., 401
Rosenberg, Milton J., 96, 109
Rosenbloom, Bert, 63, 67, 178–179, 614, 635
Rosenwald, Julius, 783

Rothenberg, Marvin J., 115, 518, 544–545
Rubel, Thomas, 141
Rudnitsky, Howard, 141, 730
Rushton, Angela, 477
Rushton, Gerald, 367
Russell, Cheryl, 732, 736
Rust, Roland T., 401, 736
Ryan, Charles, 3
Ryan, Franklin W., 177
Ryan, Matthews, 297

Sack, Steven Mitchell, 199
Sager, Jeffrey K., 588
Salem, M. Y., 66
Samli, A. Coskun, 109
Samuelson, Robert J., 477
Saporito, Bill, 730
Savitt, Ronald, 581, 588
Sawyer, Alan, 335
Scarborough, Norman M., 66
Schachner, Michael, 730
Schewe, Charles D., 109
Schindler, Robert, 336
Schlossberg, J., 775
Schmidt, Sandra L., 213, 635
Schmidt, Stuart M., 179
Schoell, William F., 177
Schor, Julet, 477
Schul, Patrick L., 178–179
Schultz, Peter, 683–688
Schwadel, Francine, 402, 730
Schwartz, Joe, 28, 66
Schwartzkopf, Albert B., 545, 588
Scitovsky, Tibor, 335
Sears, Richard W., 782–783
Seiders, Kathleen, 336
Seklemaian, M., 515
Selbert, Roger, 29, 66
Seldin, Maury, 367
Serpkenci, Ray R., 797
Sewell, Murphy A., 402
Sharma, Subhash, 618–619, 635
Sheets, Kenneth R., 730
Sheffet, Mary Jane, 213
Sheth, Jagdish, 140
Shunroku, Nishimura, 140
Siegel, Joseph B., 140
Sikora, Martin, 212
Simms, Kenneth, 703
Singley, Rodger R., 29
Skinner, Steven J., 178, 545
Smith, Daniel C., 336
Smith, Fred, 688–693
Smith, Richard, 771–772
Smith, Sarah, 730
Smith, Stephen, 514
Smith, Steve, 711–712
Smith, Troy, Sr., 737

Snyder, Glenn, 141
Soley, Lawrence C., 514
Spear, Joe, 736
Speh, Thomas, 178
Sprout, Alison L., 730
Sriram, Ven, 544
Stanley, Thomas J., 402
Staples, William A., 67, 649, 682
Stassen, Robert, 336
Stearns, James M., 40, 66
Steidtmann, Carl E., 29
Stephenson, Ronald, 178
Sterling, Jay U., 178
Stern, John, 660
Stern, Louis W., 178–179, 213
Stern, Scott, 653, 656
Sternlieb, George, 401
Stevens, Robert, 635
Stewart, Allan, 788
Stone, Donald, 140
Strand, Patricia, 729
Sturt, Charles, 367
Sutterfield, K. Keith, 754–755
Swan, John E., 477, 544
Sweeney, Daniel J., 29, 298
Sweeney, Randy, 707–709, 712
Swineyard, William R., 28

Tadlaqui, Ali, 514
Tadlavui, Ali, 635
Talarzyk, W. Wayne, 67, 96, 109
Taraba, Tibor, 514
Taub, Stephen, 730
Tauber, Edward M., 99, 108–109, 443
Taylor, Benny, 666
Taylor, Charles R., 514
Taylor, Marianne, 730–731
Teas, R. Kenneth, 545
Teel, Jessee E., 514
Tetreault, Mary Stanfield, 544
Thomas, Frank, 682–683
Thurik, Roy, 545
Thurmond, Shannon, 731
Tiedeman, Sally, 652
Tigert, Douglas J., 67, 96, 109, 336
Tinsley, Dillard B., 140
Topol, Martin T., 17, 29, 67, 514
Trimble, Vance H., 443, 716, 731
Tripuraneni, Ravi V., 63, 67, 614, 635
Turchiano, Francesca, 401
Turpin, Cheryl Nido, 20
Twomey, David P., 212, 588

Valery, Paul, 633
van der Wijst, Nico, 545
Van Sciver, Warner L., 754–755
Varadarajan, P. Rajan, 140, 336, 588
Virnich, Georg, 138

Wade, R. R., 545
Wagner, Janet, 274, 297
Walker, Bruce J., 115, 140, 162, 178
Walkup, Lewis E., 24
Walters, Rockney G., 297
Walton, Bud, 57
Walton, Nancy, 715
Walton, Sam, 57, 252, 345, 434, 562, 606, 714–717, 725–726
Walton, Thomas, 715
Wanamaker, John, 328
Wasson, Hilda C., 179
Wedel, Michel, 108
Weigand, Robert F., 179
Weinberg, Robert, 67
Weiner, Joshua, 336
Weiner, Steven B., 109, 731
Weinstein, Steve, 178–179
Weiss, Leonard W., 121, 140
Weitzel, William, 545, 588
Werner, Ray O., 213
Widing, Robert E., II, 544
Wijnholds, Heiko de B., 646
Wilcox, James B., 283, 297, 514, 588
Wilkes, Robert E., 514
Williams, Sharon, 2–3
Williamson, James, Jr., 763
Wilson, R. Dale, 336
Wold, Margorie, 29
Wold, Richard, 797, 808–809
Wolk, Harry I., 250, 298
Womach, Vance, 659–663
Wood, Robert E., 783
Wood, Van R., 177
Wotruba, Thomas R., 588
Wright, Stephen, 460
Wyer, Robert S., Jr., 274

Yokawa, Masaru, 140
Young, Clifford, 336
Young, Robert F., 477
Yudelson, Julian E., 66

Zaltman, Gerald, 24
Zeithaml, Valerie A., 458, 476–477
Zelek, E. F., Jr., 213
Zemke, Ron, 476
Zimmerer, Thomas W., 66
Zimmerman, Robert, 635
Zinn, Laura, 443
Zizzo, Deborah, 756
Zweig, Jason, 731

COMPANY INDEX

A. B. King's, 659–663
Abraham & Straus, 779
Ace Hardware, 158
Aetna, 145
Ahold, 776
Alamo Car Rental, 485
Albertsons, 131
Allied Department Stores, 58–59, 246, 324, 718–719
Allstate Insurance Company, 783–785, 790–791
Allstate Insurance Group, 722
Alphagraphics, 161
Alterman Foods, 719
American Airlines, 485
American Express, 304
American Fare, 720
American Financial Corporation, 762, 766
American Home Products, 196
American Stores, 82, 208
Ames Department Stores, 247, 719–720, 780
AMWAY, 8
Ann Taylor, 135, 417
A&P, 82, 362–363
Arlans, 720
Art Van, 779
Asko, 776
Associated Dry Goods, 11
Associated Grocers, 158
Athlete's Foot, 113, 664
Atlanta Newspapers, Inc., 812–824
Atlantic Mills, 720
Austin Reed, 776
Avis, Inc., 155
Avis Rent-A-Car, 190, 616
Avon, 308

B. Altman, 246, 719
B. Dalton, 559
The Banana Republic, 721
Bank One, 471
Baskin-Robbins, 13

Bass Shoes, 720
B.A.T. Industries PLC, 246, 719, 776
Bell Canada, 473
Benetton, 114, 137, 156, 341, 776
Ben Franklin, 158, 716–717, 723
Benjamin Books, 376
Bergdorf Goodman, 51
Bergner Department Stores, 719
Best, 780
Best Western International, 554
Big 5 Sporting Goods, 631
Blockbuster Video, 770
Bloomingdale's, 130, 361, 375–377, 395, 558, 586, 779
Bob Evans Restaurants, 469
Bombay Company, 780
Bonwit Teller, 246, 719
Bretts Department Store, 732–734
Breuners, 779
The Broadway, 779
Brooks Brothers, 719
Budget Rent A Car Corp., 155
Builders Square, 394
Bullock's, 719
Burdines, 779
Burger King, 13, 112, 324, 376
Burlington Coat Factory Warehouse, 720
Business Systems Centers, 722
Butler Brothers, 717
Builders Square, 722

Caldor, 631, 720
Campbell Soup, 603
Campeau Corporation, 58–59, 246, 586, 719
Carson, Pirie, Scott & Company, 719
Casual Corner, 83, 114
Central City Savings Bank, 693–699
Central Savings Bank, 693
Century 21 Real Estate, 162
Certified Grocers, 158
Chadwick's of Boston, 327
Charming Shoppes, 113–114

Charter Co., 766
Charter Marketing, 766–767
Chevrolet, 162
Chick-Fil-A, 373
Christian Dior, 326
Chrysler Corp., 155
Circle K Corporation, 7, 247, 265–266, 464–465, 756–772
Circle K Food Stores, 759
Circuit City, 95, 114
CitiBank, 474
City Bank, 693
City Drugstores, 646–649
Claire's Stores, 10, 369
Clothestime, 720
Coast-to-Coast, 723
Coca-Cola, 331, 551, 760
Coldwell Banker Real Estate Group, 722, 784–785, 790–791
Columbia Pictures, 760
Combined Communications Corporation, 759
Competitech, 649–651, 682–683
Comp USA, 114
Computer Land, 114
Conran's, 137, 779–781
Continental TV, 202
Coors, 603
CoreStates Bank, 474
Costco Wholesale Club, 10, 14, 129
County Seat Jeans, 342
Cox Broadcasting Corporation, 812–835
CPI photo finish, 88
Crest, 331
Cub Super Warehouse Stores, 171, 461
The Custom Shop Shirtmakers, 44
CUTCO, 119

Dairy Queen, 356
Dart Drug, 160
Davison's, 835

861

Dayton Hudson Corporation, 10, 62–63, 585, 611, 621–622, 625, 719, 779, 788
Dayton's, 625
Dean Witter Capital, 791
Dean Witter Financial Services Group, 722, 784–785, 790–791
Dee Corp., 719
Delhaie-Le Leon, 719
Delta, 485
Deluxe Store, 192
Denny's, 131
Dillard's Department Stores, 11, 156, 377, 592, 779
Discover Card, 791
Dixons, 776
Dollar General, 49, 326, 385, 522
Dollar Rent A Car Systems, Inc., 155
Domino's Pizza, 88, 495
Dot Discount Drugstores, 714
Drug Emporium, 160
Duckwall-ALCO, 723
Dunhill, 776
Dunkin' Donuts, 13, 162, 376, 767

East Towne Mall, 669–672
Economost, 158
Eddie Bauer, 8
E.J. Korvette, 720
Eller Outdoor Advertising, 759
Encyclopedia Brittanica, 119
Esprit, 155
Ethan Allen, 247
Eye Care Centers of America, 722, 794

Fallon Company, 230
Falls City Brewery, 188
Family Dollar Stores, Inc., 49, 82
Famolare, 155
Famous-Barr, 377
Farris Fashion, Inc., 724
Fastframe, 776
Federal Express, 464
Federals, 720
Federated Department Stores, 59, 246, 324, 585–586, 718–719
50%-Off, 522
Firestone, 131, 144
The First Boston Corporation, 736
First National Supermarkets, 371
Flanders Industries, Inc., 724
Fleet Farm, 721
Fleming Companies, 157
Foley's, 586
Folger Coffee, 188
Food Emporium, 82
Food Giant, 11, 131
Food4Less Stores, Inc., 797–811
Foot Locker, 265
Ford Motor Company, 106, 155, 605
47th Street Photo, 204

Franklin's, 659–660
Frey's Floorcovering, 651–656
Fuller O'Brien Paints, 470–471
Furniture Liquidator, 511
F.W. Woolworth Co., 720. *See also* Woolworth's

Gannett Company, 759–760
Gantos, 135
The Gap, 10, 467, 481
General Electric, 166
General Growth Company, 731, 734–735
General Host Corporation, 763
General Motors Corp., 145, 155, 190, 535
GIB Group, 776
Gitano Group, Inc., 724
Goldblatt's Department Stores, 721
Golden Corral, 131
Goodyear, 131, 144
The Great Atlantic & Pacific Tea Company, 362, 719
Greyhound, 13
GTE Sylvania, 202
Gucci, 326, 467
Guess, 155

Hallmark, 94
Handy Andy, 192
Hardee's Food Systems, 572
Harrod's, 135
Hart, Schaffner and Marx, 155
Haverty's, 779
H.E. Butt Grocery Company, 192
Health-More Pharmacies, Inc., 656–659
Hecht's, 395
Heck's, 720
Helig-Meyers, 779–780
Heller Financial Inc., 148
Herberger's, 734–735
Herman's, 114, 719
Hertz Corp., 155
Hickory Farms, 113
Higby's Hardware, 703–706
Hills, 795
Hit or Miss, 327
Holiday Inns, 155
Homart Development Co., 791
Home Depot, 10, 37, 58–59, 247, 366, 394, 437, 720
Home Interiors and Gifts, 119
Hooker Corporation, 246, 719
Hook-Super Rx, 631
Howard's, 723
H&R Block, 162, 454
Hudson's, 511
Hypermarket*USA, 714, 723
Hypermart USA, 722
Hy-Vee Supermarket, 733

I. Magnin, 130, 719
IBM, 281
IKEA, 58, 114, 131–132, 137, 484, 511–512, 772–782
Independent Grocers Alliance (IGA), 158, 192, 493
International House of Pancakes, 719

JCPenney Company, 10, 18, 73, 203, 268, 373, 377, 606, 611, 624, 631, 716, 719, 722, 725, 732–735, 779–781, 788
JCP Realty, 734
Jordan's, 779
Jusco Ltd., 719

Karl Eller Company Financial Consultants, 760
Kays Drive-In Grocery, 759
Keepsake, 166
Kellogg's, 103
Kelly Girl, 162
Kentucky Fried Chicken (KFC), 162
Kids Mart, 720
Kids "R" Us, 793
Kinder Care Learning Center, 387
Kinder Care of LaPetite, 355
King Bing Furniture Sales, 616–617
Kings Department Stores, 717
King Stores, 615
Kmart Corporation, 11, 50, 57, 59, 73, 116, 129, 131, 144, 169, 196, 200, 204, 216, 293, 325, 332, 345–346, 378, 502, 523, 536–538, 659, 717–719, 721–722, 780, 784–785, 788, 795
Knot Shop, 436
Korvette's, 201
Kresge, 788
Kroger Company, 11, 83, 131, 166, 192, 342, 438, 461

Lands End, 8
Levitz, 779–780
The Limited, 10, 19–20, 37, 49, 113, 115, 144, 247, 332, 432, 436, 467, 481, 721, 784–785
Little General Stores, 763–764, 767
Little Piggie, Ltd., 720
Liz Claiborne, 155
L.J. Hooker Corporation, 719
Loehmann's, 720
London Fog, 155
Lord & Taylor, 130
Lucky Stores, 82, 208

Macy's, 12, 53–54, 85, 148, 324, 481, 779–780
Madison East Mall, 732
Magic Chef, 724

Company Index

Manhattan's Brand Name Fashion Outlet, 720
Mankato Mall, 732–734
Manpower, 162
Mark Shale, 130
Marks & Spencer, 719
Marriott Hotels, 558
Marshall Field's, 130, 246, 325, 332, 395, 622, 779
Marshall's, 720
Mary Kay Cosmetics, 8, 119, 308
Maxwell House, 331
May Company, 585–586
May Department Stores Company, 720
May D & F Department Stores, 191
Mazzio's Pizza, 495
McDonald's, 5, 7, 11, 13, 22–23, 48, 60, 112, 131, 161–162, 324, 341, 346, 354, 356, 370, 387, 451, 453, 511, 611
McKids, 720
McLane Company, Inc., 724
Medco, 145
Medicine Shoppe International (MSI), 160
Meijer, 780
Melville Corporation, 10
Menard's, 721
Mercantile Stores Company, 585
Merry-Go-Round, 37
Mervyn's, 332, 502, 625, 664
Metropolitan Museum of Art, 467
Midas Mufflers, 162, 758
Milwaukee Boston Store, 719
Mission Viejo Company, 378
Mitchum, 331
Mitsukoshi Ltd., 135
Montgomery Ward, 196, 201, 247, 267, 373, 377, 719, 779–780, 788
Mothers Work, 376

National Car Rental, 155, 190
National Convenience Stores, Inc., 765, 767
Nebraska Furniture Mart, 779
Neiman-Marcus, 51, 85, 130, 307, 326, 330, 385, 488
N.K. Winston Corporation, 187
Nordstrom, 85, 130, 325–326, 330, 361, 395, 467, 488, 521
Norwalk, 166
Nucorp Energy, Inc., 759

Oakland Department Store, 663–665
Office Club, 720
Office Depot, 780
Open Country, 664
OshKosh B'Gosh, 203
Oshmans, 720
Outlets Ltd., 375

P. A. Bergner & Company, 719
PACE Membership Warehouse Club, 14, 129, 722
Pamida, 723
Pants West, 114
Paramount Pharmacy, 646–647
Pathmark, 801
Payless Drug Stores, 722
Pay 'n' Save, 194
Pergament, 780
Perkins, 131
Phar-Mor, 95
Physician's Weight Loss Centers, 469
Pier 1 Imports, 52, 720, 779–781
Pinstripes Petites, 722, 794
Pizza Hut, 5, 131, 161, 376, 495
Playboy, 603
Plum Tree, Inc., 187
Porsche AG, 683–688
Porter & Dietsch, 194
Price Chopper Supermarkets, 631
Price Club, 306, 780
Price Company, 14
Princess House, 119
Printemps, 776
Procter & Gamble, 277, 284
PS Associates, 719

Quality Markets, 707–713

Radio Shack, 155, 370, 780
Raley's, 157
Ralph Lauren, 203, 623
Red Lobster, 346
Resorts International, 247
R.H. Macy Company, 719
Rhodes, 779
Rich's Department Store, 718, 811
River Hills Mall, 734–735
RJR Nabisco, 785
Roadmaster Corporation, 724
Robinson's, 377
Roses, 723
R. W. Sears Watch Company, 782

Safeway, 11, 169
Sakowitz, 719
Saks Fifth Avenue, 130, 148, 246, 325, 332
Sam's Wholesale Club, 14, 58, 117, 129, 284, 306, 714, 722–723, 728
Scandinavian Design, 779
Schwegmann's Supermarkets, 306
Schwinn, 202
Scott, 166
Scotty's, 394
Sealy, 166
Seaman's, 779
Sears, Roebuck and Company, 35–36, 73, 118, 155, 166, 191, 196–197, 200, 203, 267–268, 326, 341, 373, 377, 409–410, 468, 578, 611, 621, 719–720, 722, 734, 758, 779–780, 782–796
Sears Business System Centers, 794
Sears Financial Network, 784, 789–791
Sears Ltd., 794
Sears Merchandise Group, 785, 791–794
Sears Mortgage Company, 791
Sears Retail Network, 789, 791–792, 794
Sears Savings Bank, 784
Second Baptist Church, 128
Service Merchandise, 780
7-Eleven, 247, 265, 387, 407–408, 464–465, 481, 511, 765
Sharper Image, 342
Sherwin Williams, 155
Shop & Go, Inc., 764–765, 767
Shopko Stores, 720
Shoprite, 801
Shopwell, 82
Silk Greenhouse, 720
Singer, 155
Smith Food & Drug, 157
Smith's IGA, 688–693
Snappy Rental, Inc., 155
Sock Appeal, 720
Sock Market, 720
Sonic Corp., 736–756
Sonic Restaurants, 737–738, 744–756
Sony, 370
Southland Corporation, 464, 765–767
Southland Ice Dock, 757
Spengel's Sporting Goods, 231–234
The Sports Authority, 722
Sportsmart, 265
S.S. Kresge, 55–57
Stanley, 166
Steak and Ale, 48
Stephens, Inc., 736
Steve's Homemade Ice Cream, Inc., 771
Stiffel Co., 197
Stix, Baer, & Fuller, 11
STOR, 780
Super Kmart, 720
Super Value, 171, 461

Taco Bell, 11, 131
Talbots, 135, 719
Target Greatland, 12
Target Stores, 11, 83, 116, 131, 144, 156, 325, 346, 523, 625, 720–721, 734–735, 780, 795
Taylor's Furniture, 666–669
Tengelmann, 719
T.G. & Y., 723
Thom McAn, 664
Thrift Drug, 722
Thrifty Rent-A-Car Systems, Inc., 155

Tie Rack, 776
T.J.Maxx, 327, 720
TJX Companies, 10, 326–327
Tom Thumb-Page, 23
Toyota, 104
Toys "R" Us, 95, 114, 341, 437, 699–703, 720, 785
Treasury Drug, 722
Tres Mariposas, 540
Tuesday Morning, 145–146
Tupperware, 308
Turner's Outdoorsman, 45

United Dairy Farmers, 465
U.P.S., 464
U.S. Post Service, 470
U.S. Shoe, 631
UtoteM Corp., 762–763, 767

Value City, 779
Van Heusen, 155
Vendex International, 776
Venture, 720, 780

Victoria's Secret, 49–50, 436, 721
Volkswagen of America (VWoA), 683, 686
Volkswagenwerk AG, 687
Von's Supermarkets, 54, 60

Wakefern Food Corp., 159
Waldbaums Supermarkets, 82
Waldenbooks, 114, 722
Walgreen Drugs, 160, 196, 656
Wal-Mart Discount City, 717
Wal-Mart Stores, 5, 10, 15–16, 37, 57–59, 73, 82, 113, 131, 135, 144, 152, 156, 166, 169, 216, 247, 252, 277, 293, 303, 323, 325–326, 342, 345–347, 350, 361, 378, 400, 409, 467, 481, 502, 523, 560–562, 570, 606, 714–728, 780, 784–785, 788, 795
Wal-Mart Super Centers, 714, 723
Walt Disney Company, 453
Walton's, 435
Walton's 5 & 10, 716
Wanamaker's Department Store, 328

Wendy's, 48, 112, 131, 453
West Bend, 119
Western Auto Supply, 158, 722, 794
White Motor Company, 202
Wickes, 779
Wienerwald, 719
Williams-Sonoma, 220
Winners Apparel Ltd., 327
Woolco, 720
Woolworth's, 13, 201, 341, 371, 585, 734, 788
World Book, 119
W.S. Badcock, 779
W.T. Grant, 720

Xerox, 155

Zale, 719
Zayre Corporation, 462–463, 466, 720, 780
Zig Zag, 672–678